Turn the page ...

We'll help you not only understand, but master the key concepts presented in *Understanding Business*, 6/e, with...

...the Concept Mastery
Toolkit CD-ROM

With each new copy of the text, you will receive (for FREE!) this new CD. Use it to:

- Prepare for exams by taking the chapter quizzes—true/false and multiple-choice questions related to the learning objectives and organized by chapter help your understanding of key concepts in the text.

- Get help with key terms in two languages with our digital Spanish-English glossary of terms.

- Find out if you are an auditory or visual learner by taking a learning style assessment in the Making the Grade section— and you might make better use of your time as you study.

- Learn the basics of starting your own e-business, with this BIG bonus on the CD—an entire e-text called *Building an E-Business From the Ground Up*, by Elizabeth Reding. Here you'll learn the basics of planning, designing, and implementing your e-business.

Achieve success in the course, in your education, and in your career—this CD will make it your business!

EDITION 6

UNDERSTANDING BUSINESS

WILLIAM G. NICKELS
University of Maryland

JAMES M. McHUGH
St. Louis Community College at Forest Park

SUSAN M. McHUGH
Applied Learning Systems

McGraw-Hill Irwin

Boston   Burr Ridge, IL   Dubuque, IA   Madison, WI   New York   San Francisco   St. Louis
Bangkok   Bogotá   Caracas   Kuala Lumpur   Lisbon   London   Madrid   Mexico City
Milan   Montreal   New Delhi   Santiago   Seoul   Singapore   Sydney   Taipei   Toronto

McGraw-Hill Higher Education ⟨⟩

A Division of The **McGraw-Hill** *Companies*

UNDERSTANDING BUSINESS

Published by McGraw-Hill, an imprint of The McGraw-Hill Companies, Inc. 1221 Avenue of the Americas, New York, NY, 10020. Copyright © 2002, 1999, 1996, 1993, 1990, 1987 by The McGraw-Hill Companies, Inc. All rights reserved. No part of this publication may be reproduced or distributed in any form or by any means, or stored in a database or retrieval system, without the prior written consent of The McGraw-Hill Companies, Inc., including, but not limited to, in any network or other electronic storage or transmission, or broadcast for distance learning. Some ancillaries, including electronic and print components, may not be available to customers outside the United States.

This book is printed on acid-free paper.

domestic   2 3 4 5 6 7 8 9 0 WCK/WCK 0 9 8 7 6 5 4 3 2 1
international 1 2 3 4 5 6 7 8 9 0 WCK/WCK 0 9 8 7 6 5 4 3 2 1

ISBN 0-07-232054-0
ISBN 0-07-245578-0 (annotated instructor's edition)

Publisher: *John E. Biernat*
Senior sponsoring editor: *Andy Winston*
Developmental editor: *Sarah Reed*
Marketing manager: *Ellen Cleary*
Senior project manager: *Mary Conzachi*
Lead production supervisor: *Heather D. Burbridge*
Freelance design coordinator: *Laurie J. Entringer*
Photo research coordinator: *Judy Kausal*
Photo researcher: *Burrston House, Ltd.*
Supplement producer: *Susan Lombardi*
Media producer: *Jennifer Becka*
Cover design: *Asylum Studios*
Interior design: *Diane Beasley*
Compositor: *Carlisle Communications, Ltd.*
Typeface: *10/12 New Aster*
Printer: *World Color Versailles*

Library of Congress Cataloging-in-Publication Data
Nickels, William G.
    Understanding business / William G. Nickels, James M. McHugh, Susan M. McHugh.—
6th ed.
      p. cm.
    Includes bibliographical references and index.
    ISBN 0-07-2320-54-0 (alk. paper)
    1. Industrial management. 2. Business. 3. Business-Vocational guidance. I. McHugh,
James M. II. McHugh, Susan M. III. Title.
    HD31 .N4897 2002
650—dc21

                                       2001031267

INTERNATIONAL EDITION ISBN 0-07-112348-2

Copyright © 2002. Exclusive rights by The McGraw-Hill Companies, Inc. for manufacture and export.
This book cannot be re-exported from the country to which it is sold by McGraw-Hill.
The International Edition is not available in North America.

www.mhhe.com

Dedication

Give a man a fish and you will feed him for a day,

Teach a man to fish and you will feed him for a lifetime.

Teach a person to start a fish farm and you will feed a

community for a lifetime.

We dedicate this text to all of you who want to make a

difference in the world by teaching people to start business

and nonprofit organizations that will feed, clothe, and

provide for all the needs of people throughout the world.

Brief Contents

Contents

Choosing the right course of study does matter. The study of business is not only interesting, it's practical.

The pace of change in business today is exhilarating. The trick in meeting the challenges and taking advantage of the opportunities it presents is to be well-prepared and adaptable.

CHAPTER 3
Competing in Global Markets 62

CHAPTER 4
Demonstrating Ethical Behavior and Social Responsibility 94

International trade is certainly on the rise, but not without opposition. Here a demonstrator in London protests the refusal of the French to import British beef due to concerns over mad cow disease, despite a mandate from the European Union for France to do so.

CHAPTER 6
Entrepreneurship and Starting a Small Business 164

PART ②
Business Ownership: Starting a Small Business

CHAPTER 5
Forms of Business Ownership 132

PART 3

Business Management: Empowering Employees to Satisfy Customers

CHAPTER 7

Management, Leadership, and Employee Empowerment   202

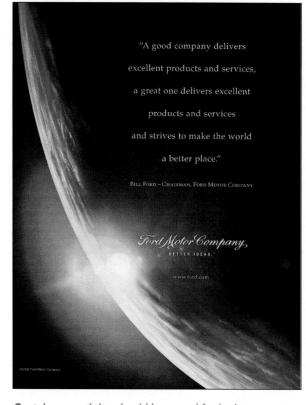

"A good company delivers
excellent products and services,
a great one delivers excellent
products and services
and strives to make the world
a better place."

BILL FORD – CHAIRMAN, FORD MOTOR COMPANY

Ford Motor Company
BETTER IDEAS.

www.ford.com

Social responsibility should be a goal for both companies and consumers. Bill Ford, Chairman of Ford Motor Company, recognizes its importance and has pledged that his company's policies and practices will as well.

CHAPTER 8

Managing the Move toward Customer-Driven Business Organizations   232

Are entrepreneurs different? If you judge Ann Beiler, founder of Auntie Anne's Pretzels, by her unusual pastime you might think so. But the truth is, successful entrepreneurs come in all shapes, sizes and backgrounds.

PART 4

**Management of Human Resources:
Motivating Employees to Produce
Quality Goods and Services**

CHAPTER 10

**Motivating Employees and Building Self-
Managed Teams   294**

The internet is a dynamic business tool which continues to impact and change the way business is conducted. Among its key advantages are speed and efficiency. Internet companies such as KillerBiz provide software and services to enable traditional businesses to access suppliers and resources that a few years ago were beyond their reach.

CHAPTER 11

Human Resource Management: Finding and Keeping the Best Employees   326

CHAPTER 12

Dealing with Employee – Management Issues and Relationships   360

PART 5

Marketing: Developing and Implementing Customer-Oriented Marketing Plans

CHAPTER 13

Marketing: Customer and Stakeholder Relationship Marketing   394

Was it a stampede? The shift of businesses to the Web seemed that way in the '90's, but with the dot com crash of 2000-2001 it's now closer to a crawl. Will this trend reverse itself? Stay tuned.

CHAPTER 14

Developing and Pricing Products and Services   426

CHAPTER 15

Distributing Products Efficiently and Competitively: Supply Chain Management   458

Is sound advice available about the securities market and investments? A good place to start is MotleyFool at Fool.com.

CHAPTER 16

Promoting Products Using Interactive and Integrated Marketing Communication   488

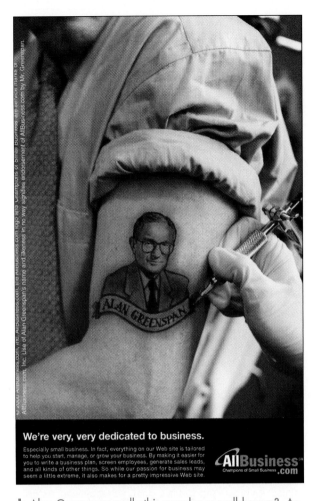

We're very, very dedicated to business.

Especially small business. In fact, everything on our Web site is tailored to help you start, manage, or grow your business. By making it easier for you to write a business plan, screen employees, generate sales leads, and all kinds of other things. So while our passion for business may seem a little extreme, it also makes for a pretty impressive Web site.

AllBusiness℠ *Champions of Small Business* **.com**

Is Alan Greenspan really this popular or well-known? As the long time director of the Federal Reserve Bank it seems so. The reason? He has great influence over financial institutions, interest rates, and U.S. monetary policy.

PART 6

Decision Making: Managing Information

CHAPTER 17

Using Technology to Manage Information 520

PART 7

Managing Financial Resources

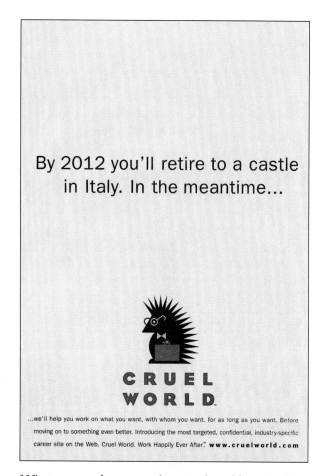

By 2012 you'll retire to a castle in Italy. In the meantime...

CRUEL WORLD.

...we'll help you work on what you want, with whom you want, for as long as you want. Before moving on to something even better. Introducing the most targeted, confidential, industry-specific career site on the Web. Cruel World. Work Happily Ever After. **www.cruelworld.com**

What message for success does Cruel World send with its name? If early retirement is a goal, you may want to take advantage of some serious, professional career planning.

About the Authors

The *Understanding Business (UB)* author team possesses a unique blend of university, community college, industry, public service, small business, and curriculum development experience that helps them breathe life into the dynamic business concepts presented in the text. As instructors who use the *UB* text and supplements in their own classrooms, Bill Nickels and Jim McHugh have a personal stake in the quality of the entire project. As a curriculum specialist, Susan McHugh is committed to making certain that Bill and Jim (and all of the other *UB* users) have the best materials possible for creating interesting and useful classes that make learning business an exciting experience.

BILL NICKELS is an associate professor of business at The University of Maryland, College Park. With over 30 years of teaching experience, he teaches introduction to business in large sections (250 students) every semester. He teaches smaller sections in the summer. He also teaches the marketing principles course to large sections (500 students). Bill has won the Outstanding Teacher on Campus Award four times. He received his M.B.A. degree from Western Reserve University and his Ph.D. from The Ohio State University. He has written a marketing communications text and two marketing principles texts in addition to many articles in business publications. He believes in living a balanced life and wrote a book called *Win the Happiness Game* to share his secrets with others. Bill gives marketing and general business lectures to a variety of business and nonprofit organizations. Bill and his wife, Marsha, proudly anticipate the impending graduation of their son, Joel, who will become the third Dr. Nickels in the family.

JIM McHUGH is an associate professor of business at St. Louis Community College/Forest Park. He holds an M.B.A. degree from Lindenwood University and had broad experience in education, business, and government. In addition to teaching several sections of introduction to business each semester for 20 years, Jim maintains an adjunct professorship at Lindenwood University, teaching in the marketing and management areas at both the undergraduate and graduate levels. Jim has conducted numerous seminars in business, and maintains several consulting positions with small and large business enterprises. He is also actively involved in the public service sector.

SUSAN McHUGH is a learning specialist with extensive training and experience in adult learning and curriculum development. She holds a M.Ed. degree from the University of Missouri and has completed her course work for a Ph.D. in education administration with a specialty in adult learning theory. As a professional curriculum developer, she has directed numerous curriculum projects and educator training programs. She has worked in the public and private sector as a consultant in training and employee development. While Jim and Susan treasure their participation in the *UB* project, their greatest accomplishment is their collaboration on their three children, Casey, Molly, and Michael, who have all grown up regarding *UB* as a fourth sibling. Casey was a fervent user of the 4th edition, Molly eagerly anticipates using this edition, and Michael will have to wait for the next edition.

Preface

We are grateful that over 500 colleges and universities in the United States and around the world adopted the fifth edition of *Understanding Business*. This again makes it the most widely used text available for the introduction to business course. This is truly a customer-driven text and one that is continuously tested by the authors in our own introduction to business classes. When you teach a course yourself, you have a personal interest in making the text and materials the best possible.

The Preface is the part of the text in which the authors normally brag about how great the book is and how lucky you are that it is available for your course. As authors, it is very difficult to write this section without sounding like we're about to break our arms patting ourselves on the back for doing such splendid work. However, the joy of performing this task for us is that, while we did play a significant role in the development of this text, there are so many other people who deserve credit for the evolution of this remarkable project.

Over 200 faculty who teach the course and hundreds of students who have used the book and its supplements were formally involved in various stages of our research and writing of this edition. We continue to hear informally from students and faculty throughout the country who call and e-mail us with comments and suggestions. We encourage you to do the same. We enjoy the interaction.

Prior to writing this edition, we held 12 close-to-the-customer focus groups in 11 cities around the country. Discussions with over 100 instructors and dozens of students in these sessions helped us define, clarify, and test the needs of the diverse group who teach and take this course.

Additionally, more than 20 instructors provided us with in-depth evaluations of the fifth edition, providing insights for the improvements that you will encounter on every page of this edition. Once the first draft was written, another group of instructors critiqued our initial effort, which led to many more important refinements.

Many consider this process the most extensive product development process ever implemented for a text of this type. While that's probably true, we consider this talking and sharing of ideas with our colleagues and students across the country as one of the greatest perks of our jobs.

Below are a few of the changes and improvements made in response to the recommendations from these dedicated educators (who themselves have now become part of the overall development team).

NEW GETTING READY FOR PRIME TIME

Our focus groups told us that many students do not have the skills they need to succeed in college. The new *Getting Ready for Prime Time* minibooklet at the front of this text is a fresh and friendly summary of the skills it takes to be a success in college and in business. Coverage includes a unique and popular business etiquette discussion, study skills and time management guidance, a primer to surfing the Internet, and advice about how to get a rewarding job that will lead to a successful career. *Getting Ready for Prime Time* combines the fifth edition's very popular "Driver's Ed for the Information Superhighway" and

"Getting the Job You Want" appendices and "Secrets to Your Success" prologue in one engaging resource.

THE LATEST IN TECHNOLOGY AND E-COMMERCE

Everyone agrees that we are in an era of rapid and constant change. Perhaps the fastest-changing and most dynamic element of business today is the use of the Internet. Many new e-businesses have already come and gone, but even in failure they have left in their wake a new way of doing business: clicks and bricks. That is, companies have learned to reach consumers using their traditional stores and the Internet as well. Although the whole business-to-business (B2B) market is in a state of flux, use of the Internet as a dynamic new business tool has resulted in the rethinking and restructuring of traditional business relationships, redesign of supply chains, and many other new ways of conducting and facilitating customer interaction. We cover them all in this edition.

Our focus groups told us that these changes are so important and pervasive that they should be woven into each chapter rather than segregated in a single chapter. In this way, students can see how these new developments are impacting every aspect of business. Therefore, every chapter contains sections that describe e-commerce related issues.

Every chapter also has new Taking It to the Net exercises that get students involved in using the Internet to find information and to make decisions. In addition to the new Taking It to the Net exercises, reviewers asked us to retain many of the exercises from the fifth edition that their students particularly enjoyed. We did so and labeled these "award-winning" exercises with a Blue Ribbon icon.

Beyond integrating technology and use of the Internet in all chapters, we devote all of Chapter 17 to the latest in information technology. In addition, we provide in-depth coverage of how the new economy affects areas such as human resource management, marketing, production, finance, etc., including new ethical problems with privacy and security.

Finally, with each copy of the book you will receive a Concept Mastery Toolkit CD-ROM, which includes an e-text entitled: *Building an E-Business from the Ground Up*, by Elizabeth Reding. This exciting new text is an "e-commerce" book that moves beyond a survey atmosphere to provide hands-on experience. It is designed specifically for those who want to develop Web skills and business plans for use in starting an e-business.

KEEPING UP WITH WHAT'S NEW

Users of *Understanding Business* have always appreciated the currency of the material and the large number of examples from companies of *all* sizes and industries (e.g., service, manufacturing, profit, and nonprofit) in the United States and around the world. A glance at the endnotes will show you that few of them are older than the year 2000. Accordingly, this edition features the latest developments and practices in business including:

- The rise, and sometimes fall, of B2C and B2B firms
- E-commerce's impact on the role of intermediaries
- E-tailing
- Customer relationship management (CRM)
- Application service providers (ASPs)
- Internet 2
- Knowledge management

- Broadband technology
- Virtual private networks
- Firestone's problems with faulty tires
- Viral marketing
- Online banking and smart cards
- Alan Greenspan's latest moves
- Issues surrounding Napster (P2P)

KEEPING IN TOUCH VIA THE WEB

Instructors across the country have emphasized repeatedly to us how important it is that we teach introduction to business courses ourselves. We, too, must read the latest business journals and keep up to date with the latest developments in business, government, and politics. Then we must find ways of incorporating all of this new information in our courses. Finding the time to read and assimilate information across so many disciplines can be difficult. Therefore, we know firsthand the value of the Web for sharing information. We offer four ways to use the Web to gather and use information:

NEW! PowerWeb   PowerWeb for *Understanding Business* is the first book-specific version of this dynamic Web tool. PowerWeb harnesses the vast world of Internet resources for you and your students. Our dedicated staff of professionals scour the Web to find the most relevant and interesting resources related to the materials presented in your course. Since this a book-specific site, the material will not just tie into the course, but it will actually correlate with the specific chapters of the text. All of these links are collected in one central area, not only enhancing the course material but also saving time for you along the way. Every user of this text will receive a password for the *Understanding Business*, 6/e, PowerWeb, which can be accessed from the book website.

NEW! UB6E Online Learning Center (www.mhhe.com/ub6e)   The popular and robust *Understanding Business* website has been incorporated into a larger tool, the *Understanding Business* Online Learning Center. This interactive site includes such features as links to professional resources and other exciting instructor support tools as well as Web-based projects. All information on the Online Learning Center is formatted for use with such standard course management systems as WebCT and Blackboard.

   Also *NEW* for the sixth edition is special e-commerce material for instructors who might prefer a compact presentation of e-commerce concepts. Here students can examine the latest e-commerce information in a concentrated area, while the far-reaching implications are integrated throughout the text's lessons. In addition, website addresses for all companies referenced in the text are located in one central area.

NEW! e-Learning Sessions   The e-Learning Sessions put the course content in context for your students with a self-quizzing function, a multilingual glossary, Internet exercises, concept checks, sample PowerPoint slides, and even crossword puzzles to help students master the course content in an engaging fashion. These resources are organized into chapter-specific outlines to help students review the material more effectively.

PageOut   With PageOut even the most inexperienced computer user can quickly and easily create a professional-looking course website. Simply fill in our templates with your information and with excellent content provided by McGraw-Hill, choose a design, and you've got a bang-up website specifically designed for your course! Best of all, it's FREE! Visit www.pageout.net to find out more.

MAINTAINING CURRENCY: THE *BUSINESS WEEK* CONNECTION

One way that many instructors expect their students to stay current is to read *Business Week* and other such business periodicals. Many instructors tell us that they would like to assign and use selected articles in their classes. In many schools, however, the typical cost of a subscription is too much to make such readings a requirement. In response, you can order a *Business Week* edition of the text, so that students and professors receive *Business Week* for 16 weeks at a special price—substantially less than the lowest subscription rate. Professors will also receive a weekly professor's guide with this option. Additionally, we continue to include a unique box titled "From the Pages of *Business Week*" to emphasize the importance of reading and staying current through business periodicals.

INTEGRATION OF IMPORTANT CONCEPTS THROUGHOUT TEXT

Based on our research and the preferences expressed by both users and nonusers of our text, we have incorporated the following *key* topics as themes throughout the text:

- E-commerce
- Small business and entrepreneurship
- Global business
- Technology and constant change
- Pleasing customers
- Ethics and social responsibility
- Teams
- Quality
- Cultural diversity

These themes reflect a strong consensus among introduction to business instructors that certain topics deserve and need special emphasis. Among these, they encouraged us to add particular focus in the areas of small business/ entrepreneurship, international business, and e-commerce (the positive as well as the negative). In response, we have added even more small business, international, and Internet examples throughout. And we continue to feature boxes titled "Spotlight on Small Business," "Making Ethical Decisions," and "Reaching Beyond Our Borders" in every chapter.

Our emphasis on entrepreneurship is maintained with an Entrepreneurship Readiness Questionnaire and a whole chapter on Entrepreneurship and the Challenge of Starting a Business. We are confident that no other introduction to business text offers as much coverage of small business and entrepreneurship as does *Understanding Business,* and since the great majority of students taking this course currently work or will work in small companies, reviewers agree that this emphasis is well placed.

EMPHASIS ON CAREERS

Many students who take this course are uncertain about their career choice or are in the process of changing careers. To accommodate their needs, we discuss careers in each of the topic areas and provide profiles of people who have followed those careers, including income and job descriptions. We provide sample cover letters and résumés so that students can prepare a résumé now and determine where the strengths and weaknesses are in their own résumés. They can then bolster what they've already accomplished with courses and outside studies to build their résumés into strong job-capturing documents. We also give students hints on how to do well at job interviews and how to conduct themselves personally to make the best impression. Sadly, many students today aren't being taught these essential behaviors anywhere else.

THE TEXT ON AUDIOTAPES

This feature, unique to *Understanding Business,* was another suggestion made by one of our focus groups conducted in connection with the fifth edition. These tapes contain the full text of each chapter minus the endmatter. These cassettes were designed for commuters and other students who are pressed for time and who wish to enhance their learning by *listening* to the text. These tapes have also proven to be invaluable to students who are visually impaired or who have other disabilities that make reading difficult or impossible. And finally, many instructors tell us that their non-native English-speaking students use the tapes to aid them in learning the language.

LEARNING BUSINESS SKILLS THAT WILL LAST A LIFETIME

The Secretary of Labor appointed a commission, the Secretary's Commission on Achieving Necessary Skills (SCANS), to identify the skills people need to succeed in the workplace. SCANS' fundamental purpose is to encourage a high-performance economy characterized by high-skill, high-wage employment. The commission's message to educators is this: Help your students connect what they learn in class to the world outside. To help educators prepare their students for the workplace, SCANS identified five workplace competencies that should be taught: (1) Resource skills (the ability to allocate time, money, materials, space, and staff); (2) Interpersonal skills (the ability to work on teams, teach others, serve customers, lead, negotiate, and work well with people from culturally diverse backgrounds); (3) Information ability (the ability to acquire and evaluate data, organize and maintain files, interpret and communicate, and use computers to process information); (4) Systems understanding (the ability to operate within various social, organizational, and technological systems and to monitor and correct performance in order to design or improve systems); and (5) Technology ability (the ability to select equipment and tools, apply technology to specific tasks, and maintain and troubleshoot equipment). The pedagogical tools in the text and package are designed to facilitate these SCANS competencies.

Here are the major pedagogical devices used in the text.

- *Learning Goals.* Tied directly to the summaries at the end of the chapter and to the test questions, these learning goals help students preview what they are supposed to know after reading the chapter, and then test that knowledge by answering the questions in the summary. The study guide is also closely linked to the learning goals as part of the total integrated teaching, learning, and testing system.

- *Getting to Know Business Professionals.* Each chapter begins with a story about a person whose career illustrates an important point covered in the chapter. Not all the personalities are famous since many of them work in small businesses and nonprofit organizations. These profiles provide a transition between chapters and a good introduction to the text material.

- *Progress Assessments.* Throughout the chapters there are Progress Assessments that ask students to assess their understanding of what they have just read. If students are not understanding and retaining the material, the Progress Assessments will stop them and show them that they need to review before proceeding. We have all experienced times when we were studying and our minds wandered. Progress Assessments are a great tool to prevent that from happening for more than a few pages.

- *Critical Thinking Questions.* These unique inserts, found throughout each chapter, ask students to pause and think about how the material they are reading applies to their own lives. This device is an excellent tool for linking the text material to the student's past experience to enhance retention. It greatly increases student involvement in the text and course as recommended by SCANS.

- *Informative Boxes.* Each chapter includes boxed inserts that apply the chapter concepts to particular themes, including small business, legal issues, making ethical decisions, and global business. Although examples of such topics are integrated throughout the text, these boxes highlight the application in a particular area. The *Business Week* boxes were developed in cooperation with *Business Week* magazine. The ethics boxes, entitled "Making Ethical Decisions," pose questions that require students to evaluate their own ethical behavior as recommended by SCANS.

- *Key Terms.* Key terms are developed and reinforced through a three-tiered system. They are introduced in boldface, repeated and defined in the margin, listed at the end of each chapter with page references, and defined in a glossary at the end of the text. *The glossary also contains American slang expressions used in the text.* Students from other countries enjoy learning American slang, but often need some help in translating since the expressions are not found in most dictionaries.

- *Cross-Reference System.* This system, unique to this text, refers students back to the **primary discussion** and examples of all **key** concepts. A specific page reference appears each time a key concept occurs in a chapter subsequent to its original discussion. This feature allows students to quickly review or study that concept (if necessary) in context in order to improve their comprehension of the material. It also eliminates the need to continuously revisit and restate key concepts, thus reducing overall text length.

- *Photo and Illustration Essays.* We sincerely believe that every photo in this edition is pedagogically relevant and we have attempted to treat the illustrative content with as much care as the narrative. As more and more students tell us in our research and classes that they are visually oriented learners, this increased emphasis on the pedagogical value of the illustration program is essential. Please note that each photo and illustration in the text is accompanied by a short paragraph that shows the relevance of the visual to the material in the text. The accompanying descriptions help the student understand what is being shown in the graphic and how it applies to concepts presented in the narrative. In order to enhance their pedagogical value, many of these photos were commissioned specifically for use in this edition.

- *Interactive Summaries.* The end-of-chapter summaries are directly tied with the learning goals and are written in a unique question and answer format. Answering the questions and getting immediate feedback helps prepare students for quizzes and exams. Students are extremely positive about this format.

- *Taking It to the Net Exercises.* Optional exercises at the end of every chapter allow students to research topics and issues on the Web.

- *Developing Workplace Skills.* The Developing Workplace Skills section has activities designed to increase student involvement in the learning process. Some of these miniprojects require library or Internet searches, but many of them involve talking with people to obtain their reactions and advice on certain subjects. Students then come to class better prepared to discuss the topics at hand. These assignments can be divided among groups of students so they can learn a great deal from outside sources and about teamwork without any one student having to do too much work. These are the type of learning experiences that facilitate the SCANS competencies.

- *Practice Cases.* Each chapter concludes with a short case to allow students to practice managerial decision making. They are intentionally brief and meant to be discussion starters rather than take up the entire class period. The answers to the cases are in the instructor's manual. Again these examples of real-world problem solving will help students achieve the SCANS competencies.

- *Video Cases.* Video cases are provided for *each* chapter—and many of them are new to this edition. These are placed at the end of the chapter and are optional as assignments. They feature companies, processes, practices, and managers that highlight and bring to life the key concepts, *and especially the themes of the sixth edition.*

Understanding Business is now the *text* that others benchmark for quality, readability, usability, and currency. But no competitor offers the variety and adaptability of the various packages (combinations of text and supplements) that are available to give your students the most value for their money. In addition to the *Business Week* package, where students get *Business Week* for the lowest price anywhere, faculty can order a package that includes a CD-ROM containing other business books worth hundreds of dollars. Talk to your McGraw-Hill/Irwin representative about the package that best suits your students' wants and needs.

THE BEST INSTRUCTIONAL MATERIALS

Because we use these materials in our own classrooms, we are meticulous with the preparation of the various instructional materials. Jim teaches traditional-size classes of 30-50 students in an urban community college, and Bill teaches large classes of 250 in lecture halls in a four-year institution. As a result, everything in this edition is designed to help instructors be more effective and make this course more practical and interesting for students. Users say that no introductory business text package is as market responsive, easy to use, and *fully integrated* as this one. To accomplish this integration, we designed the entire package of supplements and contributed to the content of the instructor's manual, test bank, and acetate package. The remaining supplements were prepared by outstanding practitioners who used the materials in their own classes.

KEY SUPPLEMENTS FOR INSTRUCTORS

Instructor's Manual   All material in the Instructor's Manual is easy to use and has been widely praised by new instructors, adjunct instructors, and experienced educators alike. Many instructors tell us that the IM is a valuable time-saver that makes them look good in class. The Instructor's Manual is unique in its thorough integration with both the text and package. Each chapter opens with a description of the differences between the fifth and sixth editions in order to facilitate the conversion of your own teaching notes to the new edition.

After a short topic outline of the chapter and listing of the chapter objectives and key terms, you will find a resource checklist with all of the supplements that correspond to each chapter. Consequently, there is no need to flip through half a dozen sources to find which supplementary materials are available for each chapter.

To make the system even easier to use, the detailed lecture outline contains marginal notes recommending where to use acetates, supplementary cases, lecture enhancers, and critical thinking exercises. Space is also available to add personal notes of your own so that they too may be integrated into the system.

Each chapter contains several lecture enhancers—short article summaries that provide additional examples for classroom use—allowing you to implement the latest business and social issues. Supplementary cases, similar to those in the text, are provided for each chapter for use as outside assignments and/or classroom discussions. The critical thinking exercises require students to analyze and apply chapter concepts, a tremendous aid in getting students more involved in the learning process. The Instructor's Manual has been revised and reformatted by Gayle Ross, a respected professional and expert in preparing such guides.

Annotated Instructor's Edition   The AIE is a reproduction of the student edition of the text with the addition of marginal notes that suggest where to use various instructional tools such as the overhead transparencies, supplementary cases, and lecture enhancers. It also identifies the activities that facilitate the SCANS competencies.

Test Bank   This part of our Integrated Teaching and Testing System always receives more attention than the rest. We're keenly aware that the success of your course depends on tests that are comprehensive and fair, and we have provided questions that measure recall and require students to apply the material to real-world situations.

The Nickels/McHugh/McHugh Test Bank is like no other on the market. It is designed to test three levels of learning.

1. **Knowledge** of key terms.
2. **Understanding** of concepts and principles.
3. **Application** of principles.

A rationale for the correct answer and the corresponding text page add to the uniqueness of our 4,000+-question Test Bank. Another helpful tool is our unique "Test Table." This chart helps you develop balanced tests by quickly identifying items according to objective and level of learning.

For the ultimate in ease, each chapter concludes with a Quick Quiz. These 10-item tests are ready for reproduction and distribution for testing or for outside assignments. The Test Bank was revised by the very capable team of Dennis Shannon and Jim McGowen of Southwestern Illinois College.

Diploma for Windows/Exam IV for Macintosh The Test Bank also comes in a computerized version. This enhanced test-generation software allows users to add and edit questions; save and reload multiple test versions; select questions based on type, difficulty, or key word; and utilize password protection. It supports over 250 printers; links graphics, tables, and text to a series of questions; supports numerous graphics including special characters, complex equations, subscripts, superscripts, bolds, underlines, and italics; and can run on a network.

Teletest For those who prefer not to use the computerized test-generator, McGraw-Hill/Irwin provides a Teletest Service. Using a toll-free phone number (800-338-3987, prompt 3), the instructor can order an exam prepared from the *Understanding Business* Test Bank. A master copy of the exam, with answer key, is sent first class mail the same day it is requested. Fax is also available within 30 minutes of the request.

Overhead Transparency Acetates with Lecture Notes Over 200 acetates augment the concepts and examples presented in the text. These acetates enable you to illustrate your lectures with colorful visual aids. Detailed lecture notes regarding content and suggested uses for each acetate are found on the acetate divider sheets and in the Instructor's Manual. In addition to being available in traditional transparency acetate form, these images are also reproduced for your convenience as PowerPoint slides (see below).

PowerPoint Presentation CD-ROM Over 400 electronic "slides" keyed to the text are available. These slide shows include the transparency acetate images as well many additional slides that support and expand the text discussion. These slides can be modified with PowerPoint. The talented Chuck Bowles from Pikes Peak Community College created the PowerPoint and transparency acetate packages.

Instructor's Presentation CD-ROM The instructor's manual, the PowerPoint slides, video clips, all figures from the text (formatted as transparency masters), lecture outlines, business forms, and more are compiled in electronic format on a CD for your convenience in customizing multimedia lectures.

New Videos for Selected Chapters In their report, SCANS stated that video and multimedia materials are essential to creating the realistic contexts in which the competencies are used. Most segments are 8 to 15 minutes in length and are suitable for classroom, home, or lab viewing. Detailed notes regarding content, running time, suggestions for use, and answers are included in the multimedia resource guide.

Media Resource Guide Puzzled about incorporating media in the classroom? Let this guide be your answer by providing helpful instruction on how to use all media components. In addition, this manual contains teaching notes and test questions for each of the videos.

Distance Learning Guide Do you teach Introduction to Business in a telecourse? Now you can use the Distance Learning Guide to make your job easier. This guide gives you step-by-step instructions and hints to tie the sixth edition in with telecourse material. (A student telecourse study guide is also available.)

Instructor's Orientation CD-ROM We offer you so much support, it's difficult to absorb it all at once. So we've put together this simple instructional CD that walks you through each supplement—a perfect tool for part-time faculty or as an orientation to effective use of classroom supplements for anyone.

KEY SUPPLEMENTS FOR STUDENTS

Text on Audio Tape A 16-cassette version of the text allows you to brush up on business concepts while commuting in your car, jogging, or wherever and whenever you like! Sight-impaired students and non-native English speakers will also find these tapes extremely useful in exploring the content of *Understanding Business.*

Student Assessment and Learning Guide Written by Barbara Barrett of St. Louis Community College/Meramec, the Student Assessment and Learning Guide contains various forms of open-ended questions that require the student to write out his or her personal summary of the material. The guide gives students the opportunity not only to prepare for tests, but also to develop and practice their business knowledge and skills. The following materials are provided for every chapter: learning goals, chapter outline, key terms and definitions, retention questions, critical thinking questions, and a practice test.

New! Concept Mastery Toolkit CD-ROM Free with each new copy of the text, this student CD contains a Spanish-English glossary of the terms in the text, chapter specific quizzes and their answers (formerly provided on the exam prep disk with the fifth edition), and the e-text of *Building an E-Business* that was mentioned earlier. This CD is an excellent resource for review and research for students.

Stock Market Experience This manual provides coverage using electronic spreadsheets and the Internet to manage a stock portfolio.

Mind-Q Internet CD-ROM This interactive software helps students learn to use the Internet at their own pace.

Essentials of Business CD-ROM This CD-ROM provides access to eight bestselling business textbooks, including *Understanding Business.* All texts are hyperlinked across disciplines, allowing students to retrieve information in a cross-functional format. Also included on this CD are a variety of business forms and templates. In addition, students will find a dynamic tutorial on New Venture creation.

We firmly believe that no course in college is more important than the introduction to business course. That's why we enjoy teaching it so much and why we are willing to spend so much time helping others make this the best course on campus. We are proud of the text and the integrated teaching and testing system that you have helped us develop over the years. We thank the many text and supplements users who have supported us through the years and welcome new instructors to the team. We look forward to a continuing relationship with all of you and to sharing what we consider the most exciting classroom experience possible: teaching introduction to business.

Bill Nickels
Jim McHugh
Susan McHugh

Acknowledgments

As we said at the outset, the authors are but members of a much larger team dedicated to making this sixth edition and package a success. We have been blessed to work with a remarkable group of talented people. At McGraw-Hill/Irwin, Andy Winston served as our executive editor. He put together and led the exceptional team that made this edition possible.

Serving as the developmental editors as they have so skillfully done since the fourth edition, Glenn Turner and Meg Turner of Burrston House continued to shepherd all aspects of the project. Their persistence in gathering market research and their diligence in keeping us focused on priorities were indispensable in assuring that the text and package is responsive to market needs. They again conducted the focus groups and managed the text reviews that have proven so helpful in revising the text and the supplements.

Burrston House also conducted and managed a comprehensive photo search that included commissioning over 40 custom-made photos to illustrate key points. Rosemary Hedger and Cherie Anderer of Burrston House carried out the extensive research for photos that was necessary to effectively reflect the concepts presented in the text.

The attractive cover was designed by Asylum Studios. The exceptionally inviting interior design was done by Diane Beasley. Mary Conzachi did a splendid job of keeping the production of the text on schedule. Manufacturing was kept on time under the watchful eye of Heather Burbridge.

Many thanks to Sue Lombardi and Betty Hadala for all their efforts in producing the finest supplemental materials. We want to thank Janet Renard for her excellent copyediting. Of course, we must thank Molly McHugh for surfing the Web to find the addresses for all of the organizations included in the text.

Many dedicated educators made extraordinary contributions to the quality and utility of this text and package. Dennis Shannon and Jim McGowen of Southwestern Illinois College again did an exceptional job in revising the Test Bank and creating the quizzes for the Online Learning Center and Concept Mastery Toolkit CD. Gayle Ross of Ross Publishing continued to achieve miracles for us with her contributions to and management of the various resources that eventually come together to form the Instructor's Manual and AIE. Mary Gorman did the handy media resource guide. Chuck Bowles of Pikes Peak Community College did a wonderful job crafting the transparency acetates and PowerPoint presentation slides. Many students would not be happy without the audio tapes prepared by Digital Excellence.

Barbara Barrett of St. Louis Community College/Meramec designed the features and authored the Study Guide—the most widely used one ever published for this course. John Knappenberger wrote the Stock Market Experience. Tom Filmyer produced the new videos, which add greatly to the classroom experience. Sarah Reed was an invaluable aid in bringing things together when we were facing a deadline. And many more people than we can ever acknowledge worked behind the scenes to translate our manuscript into the text you see; we thank them all.

Having a great text and package doesn't mean a thing if we don't find a way to get it to you. Our exceptional marketing manager, Ellen Cleary, is our liaison with the McGraw-Hill/Irwin sales staff. We appreciate the renowned service and commitment of these dedicated sales reps as much as you do. As he always has, Kurt Strand, Vice President of Marketing, continues to champion and enthusiastically support this project.

We want to thank the many instructors who contributed to the development of *Understanding Business.* An exceptional group of reviewers dedicated many long hours to critiquing the previous edition and subsequent drafts of this edition, and attending our focus groups. As we have stated previously in this Preface, their recommendations and contributions were invaluable in making this edition a stronger instructional tool. Our sincere thanks to the following reviewers:

REVIEWERS AND FOCUS GROUP PARTICIPANTS FOR THE SIXTH EDITION

Larry Aaronson, *Catonsville Community College*

Dennis G. Allen, *Grand Rapids Community College*

Kenneth Anderson, *Charles S. Mott Community College*

Kenneth F. Anderson, *CUNY-Borough of Manhattan Community College*

Lydia E. Anderson, *Fresno City College*

Maria Zak Aria, *Camden County College*

Xenia Balabkins, *Middlesex County College*

Fran Ballard, *Florida Community College*

Robert Bennett, *Delaware County Community College*

Ellen Benowitz, *Mercer County Community College*

Patricia Bernson, *County College of Morris*

Jane Bloom, *Palm Beach Community College*

James H. Boeger, *Rock Valley College*

Robert Bouck, *Lansing Community College*

Barbara Ann Boyington, *Brookdale Community College*

Sonya Brett, *Macomb Community College*

Harvey Bronstein, *Oakland Community College*

Richard Brooke, *Florida Community College at Jacksonville*

Deborah M. Brown, *Santa Fe Community College*

Howard Budner, *CUNY-Borough of Manhattan Community College*

William F. Burtis, *DeAnza College*

Nathaniel Calloway, *Univ. of Maryland University College*

Lesley Casula, *Lord Fairfax Community College*

Barbara Ching, *Los Angeles City College*

Nancy Christenson, *Brevard Community College*

Peter D. Churchill, *Diablo Valley College*

Gary Ciampa, *Wayne County Community College*

Paul Coakley, *The Community College of Baltimore County*

Jerry Cohen, *Raritan Valley Community College*

Ron Cooley, *South Suburban College*

William Crandall, *College of San Mateo*

Susan Cremins, *Westchester Community College*

Rex Cutshall, *Vincennes University*

Lawrence Danks, *Camden County College*

Cindy Del Medico, *Oakton Community College*

Evelyn Delaney, *Daytona Beach Community College*

Peter DelPiano, *Florida Metropolitan University*

Steve Dolvin, *Pensacola Christian College*

Frank Dumas, *Baker College/Flint*

Dana Dye, *Gulf Coast Community College*

Warren Enos, *Ohlone College*

David Erickson, *College of Lake County*

James Fatina, *College of Lake Cnty/Harper College*

Kevin Feldt, *University of Akron*

Ivan Figueroa, *Miami-Dade Community College*

Robert Fineran, *East-West University*

Joseph L. Flack, *Washtenaw Community College*

Ronald E. Foshee, *North Harris College*

Barry Freeman, *Bergen Community College*

Edward Friese, *Okaloosa Walton Community College*

John Frith, *Central Texas College*

J. Pat Fuller, *Brevard Community College*

Arlen Gastineau, *Valencia Community College*

Michael Geary, *Pensacola Christian College*

Eileen Baker Glassman, *Montgomery College*

Don Gordon, *Illinois Central College*

Mary E. Gorman, *Bellevue Community College*

Kay Gough, *Bellevue Community College*

Gary Greene, *Manatee Community College*

Bill Hafer, *South Suburban College*

Maurice Hamington, *Lane Community College*

Dennis L. Hansen, *Des Moines Area Community College*

Jean Harlan, *Glendale College*

Karen Harris, *Montgomery College*

Lewis Jerome Healy, *Chesapeake College*

Linda Hefferin, *Elgin Community College*

Charles P. Hiatt, *Central Florida Community College*

Dave Hickman, *Frederick Community College*

Nathan Himmelstein, *Essex County College*

Kevin Hofert, *Elgin Community College*

Stacey Hofert, *Elgin Community College*

Merrily Hoffman, *San Jacinto College-Central*

William Leigh Holt, *Mercer County Community College*

Gary Izumo, *Moorpark College*

Ralph Jagodka, *Mt. San Antonio College*

Velma Jesser, *Lane Community College*

Constance Johnson, *Tampa College*

Herbert J. Johnson, *Blinn College*

M. Gwen Johnson, *Black Hawk College*

Valerie Jones, *Kalamazoo Valley Community College*

Janice Karlen, *LaGuardia Community College*

Roland Kelley, *Tarrant County Junior College–NE Campus*

Scott Key, *Pensacola Junior College*

James H. King, *McLennan Community College*

Jerry Kinskey, *Sinclair Community College*

Betty Ann Kirk, *Tallahassee Community College*

Gregory Kishel, *Fullerton College*

Patricia Kishel, *Cypress College*

Karl Kleiner, *Ocean County College*

Micheale LaFalce, *Tampa College*

Fay Lamphear, *San Antonio College*

Keith Lane, *Fresno City College*

Bruce Leppien, *Delta College*

Dawn Lerman, *CUNY-Bernard Baruch College*

Richard Lewis, *Lansing Community College*

Ellen Ligons, *Pasadena City College*

Stephen Lindsey, *Citrus College*

Telissa K. Lindsey, *Peirce College*

Paul Londrigan, *Charles S. Mott Community College*

Barbara Luck, *Jackson Community College*

Carmelo Luna, *DeVry/DuPage*

Richard Lyons, *Indian River Community College*

James W. Marco, *Wake Technical Community College*

Leon E. Markowicz, *Lebanon Valley College*

Travaul Martin, *East-West University*

Jane Mattes, *Community College of Baltimore College-Dundalk Campus*

Stacy McAfee, *College of Southern Maryland*

Tom McFarland, *Mt. San Antonio College*

Noel McKeon, *Florida Community College*

Michael McNutt, *Orlando College South/FL Metropolitan Univ.*

Athena Miklos, *The College of Southern Maryland*

Kimberly Montney, *Kellogg Community College*

Ed Mosher, *Laramie County Community College*

Linda Newell, *Saddleback College*

Joe Newton, *Bakersfield College*

Janet Nichols, *Northeastern University*

Ron O'Neal, *Peirce College*

Susan Ockert, *Charles County Community College*

David Oliver, *Edison Community College*

Kenneth Olson, *County College of Morris*

Richard Packard, *City College/Richard J. Daley*

Jack Partlow, *Northern Virginia Comm. College*

Don Paxton, *Pasadena City College*

Melinda Philabaum, *Indiana University–Kelley School of Business*

Warren Pitcher, *Des Moines Area Community College*

Marie Pietak, *Bucks County Community College*

Robert Pollero, *Anne Arundel Community College*

Fred Pragasam, *University of North Florida*

Marva Pryor, *Valencia Community College*

Robert A. Redick, *Lincoln Land Community College*

Robert O. Reichl, *Morton College*

James Reinemann, *College of Lake County*

Dominic Rella, *Polk Community College*

Al Rieger, *Burlington County College*

Kathryn Roberts, *Chipola Junior College*

Pollis Robertson, *Kellogg Community College*

Paul Rompala, *Triton College*

Ali Roodsari, *Baltimore City Community College*

Barbara Rosenthal, *Miami-Dade Community College*

Bonnie S. Rucks, *DeVry Institute-DuPage*

Maurice M. Sampson, *Community College of Philadelphia*

Roy Sanchez, *San Jacinto College*

Joseph C. Santora, *Essex County College*

Jim (Wallace) Satchell, *St. Philips College*

Robert R. Schaller, *Charles County Community College*

Kurt Schindler, *City College/Wilbur Wright*

Linda Schmitigal, *Lake Superior State University*

Phyllis T. Shafer, *Brookdale Community College*

Charles Shatzer, *Solano Community College*

Lynette Shishido, *Santa Monica College*

James A. Smalley, *DeVry/DuPage*

Russell W. Southall, *Laney College*

Sandra Spencer, *DeAnza College*

Richard Stewart, *Gulf Coast Community College*

David Stringer, *DeAnza College*

William Syvertsen, *Fresno City College*

Robert Tansky, *St. Clair County Community College*

Gary W. Thomas, *Anne Arundel Community College*

Bill Thompson, *Foothill Community College*

Susan Thompson, *Palm Beach Community College*

Tom Thompson, *Univ. of Maryland University College*

Linda Tibbetts, *Sinclair Community College*

Darlene Tickle, *Southern Arkansas University-Magnolia*

Patricia Torpey, *National American University*

Jane A. Treptow, *Broward Community College*

Stephen Tsih, *San Jose City College*

Chuck Tychsen, *Northern Virginia Community College*

J. Robert Ulbrich, *Parkland College*

Michael Vijuk, *William Ranier/Harper College*

Douglas S. Viska, *William Rainey Harper College*

Steve Walker, *Midwestern State University*

Connie Wedemeyer, *McLennan Community College*

Ron Weidenfeller, *Grand Rapids Community College*

Richard Westfall, *Cabrillo College*

Frederick D. White, *Indian River Community College*

John Whitlock, *Community College of Baltimore County–Cantonsville*

Jean Wicks, *Bowie State University*

Stanley Williams, *Pensacola Christian College*

Amy Wojciechowski, *West Shore Community College*

Charles D. Zarubba, *Florida Metropolitan Univ-Tampa College*

John Ziegler, *Hagerstown Community College*

Milton Alderfer, *Miami-Dade Community College*

REVIEWERS AND OTHER PARTICIPANTS IN THE DEVELOPMENT OF PREVIOUS EDITIONS

Dan Anderson, *Sullivan Jr. College*

John Anstey, *University of Nebraska—Omaha*

Maria Aria, *Camden County College*

Glenann Arnold, *Pueblo Community College*

Ed Aronson, *Golden West College*

Larry Arp, *University of Southern Indiana*

Doug Ashby, *Lewis & Clark*

Harold Babson, *Columbus State Community College*

Herm Baine, *Broward Community College*

Russell Baker, *Florida Metropolitan University*

Michael Baldigo, *Sonoma State University*

John Balek, *Morton College*

Barbara Barrett, *St. Louis Community College*

Richard Bartlett, *Muskigan Area Technical College*

Lorraine Bassette, *Prince George's Community College*

Alec Beudoin, *Triton College*

Jade Beavers, *Jeferson State Community College*

Charles Beavin, *Miami Dade—North*

John Beem, *College of DuPage*

Michael Bejtlich, *Cape Cod Community College*

Larry Benke, *Sacramento City College*

Marcel Berard, *Community College of Rhode Island*

Pat Bernson, *County College of Morris*

John Berry, *Antelope Valley College*

Carol Bibly, *Triton College*

Dean Bittick, *East Central College*

John Blackburn, *The Ohio State University*

Jim Boeger, *Rock Valley College*

Mary Jo Boehms, *Jackson State Community College*

John Bowdidge, *Southwest Missouri State University*

Barbara Boyington, *Brookdale Community College*

Steven E. Bradley, *Austin Community College—Riverside*

Stephen Branz, *Triton College*

Robert Brechner, *Miami-Dade Community College*

Harvey Bronstein, *Oakland Community College*

Debie Brown, *Santa Fe Community College*

Joseph Brum, *Fayetteville Technical Community College*

Thomas Buchl, *Northern Michigan University*

Albert Bundons, *Johnson County Community College*

Barrett R. Burns, *Houston Community College*

Dennis Butler, *Orange Coast Community College,*

Ron Bytnar, *South Suburban College*

Willie Caldwell, *Houston Community College*

J. Callahan, *Florida Institute of Technology*

Nathaniel R. Calloway, *University of Maryland–University College*

B. J. Campsey, *San Jose State University*

Mary Margaret Cavera, *Davenport College*

Sandra Cece, *Triton College*

Sam Chapman, *Diablo Valley College*

Bruce Charnov, *Hofstra University*

Bonnie Chavez, *Santa Barbara City College*

William Chittenden, *Texas Tech University*

Larry Chonko, *Baylor University*

Jill Chown, *Mankato State University*

Michael Cicero, *Highline Community College*

J. Cicheberger, *Hillsborough Community College*

Monico Cisneros, *Austin Community College*

Robert Clobes, *St. Charles County Community College*

James Cocke, *Pima County Community College*

Jeffrey Conte, *Westchester Community College*

Allen Coon, *Robert Morris College*

Doug Copeland, *Johnson County Community College*

John Coppage, *Saginaw Valley State University*

Bobbie Corbett, *Northern Virginia Community College—Annandale*

John Courtney, *University of Maryland, University College*

James Cox, *Jefferson Community College*

Bill Crandall, *College of San Mateo*

Bruce Cudney, *Middlesex Community College*

C. Culbreth, *Brevard Community College*

Larry Danks, *Camden County College*

Clifford Davis, *SUNY—Cobleskill*

R. K. Davis, *University of Akron*

Burton V. Dean, *San Jose State University*

Vincent Deni, *Oakland Community College*

Kathleen Denisco, *SUNY—Buffalo*

S. Desai, *Cedar Valley College*

Jack Dilbeck, *Ivy Tech State College*

Katherine Dillon, *Ocean County College*

Samuel DiRoberto, *Penn State University—Ogontz*

Ronald Eggers, *Barton College*

Pat Ellsberg, *Lower Columbia College*

Frank Emory, *Northern Virginia Community College—Woodbridge*

Ted Erickson, *Normandale Community College*

Alton Evans, *Tarrant County Community College*

John Evans, *New Hampshire College*

C. S. Everett, *Des Moines Area Community College*

Shad Ewart, *Anne Arundel Community College*

Al Fabian, *IVY Tech*

Karen Fager, *Umpqua Community College*

Frank Falcetta, *Middlesex Community College*

S. Fante, *Central Florida Community College*

Bob Farris, *Mt. San Antonio College*

Edward Fay, *Canton College of Technology*

Janice Feldbauer, *Austin Community College*

David Felt, *Northern Virginia Community College—Manassas*

Bob Ferrentino, *Lansing Community College*

Robert Fishco, *Middlesex County Community College*

Charles FitzPatrick, *Central Michigan University*

Jane Flagello, *DeVry Institute of Technology—Lombard*

H. Steven Floyd, *Manatee Community College*

John Foster, *Montgomery College*

Barry Freeman, *Bergen Community College*

Leatrice Freer, *Pitt Community College*

Roger Fremier, *Monterey Peninsula College*

Michael Fritz, *Portland Community College*

Thomas Frizzel, *Massasoit Community College*

Alan Gbur, *Richard J. Daley College*

Lucille S. Genduso, *Nova Southeastern University*

James George, Jr., *Seminole Community College*

Tom Gilbertson, *Baker College*

Julie Giles, *DeVry Institute of Technology DuPage Campus*

Peter Giuliani, *Franklin University*

Eileen Glassman, *Montgomery College*

Bernette Glover, *Olive Harvey College*

Ron Gordon, *Florida Metropolitan University*

Patricia Graber, *Middlesex County College*

Mike Graves, *Portland Community College*

Joe Gray, *Nassau Community College*

Gary Greene, *Manatee Community College—South*

Roberta Greene, *Central Piedmont Community College*

Stephen Griffin, *Tarrant County Junior College*

Donald Gordon, *Illinois Central College*

John Gubbay, *Moraine Valley Community College*

Jonathan Gueverra, *Newbury College*

Paula Gulbicki, *Middlesex Community College*

James Hagel, *Davenport College*

Jim Hagen, *Cornell University*

Dan Hall, *East Central College*

Daniel Hallock, *St. Edward's University*

Clark Hallpike, *Ekgin Community College*

Ron Halsac, *Community College Allegheny North*

E. Hamm, *Tidewater Community College*

Paula W. Hansen, *Des Moines Area Community College*

Bob Harmel, *Midwestern State University*

Gene Hastings, *Portland Community College*

Frederic Hawkins, *Westchester Business Institute*

Joseph Hecht, *Montclair State College*

Douglas Heeter, *Ferris State University*

Michael Heim, *Lakewood Community College*

Sanford B. Helman, *Middlesex County College*

Tim Helton, *Juliet Junior College*

Edward Henn, *Broward Community College*

Chuck Hiatt, *Central Florida Community College*

David Hickman, *Frederick Community College*

George Hicks, *Muskigan Area Technical College*

Nathan Himelstein, *Essex County College*

B. Hoover, *Brevard Community College*

Vince Howe, *University of North Carolina—Wilmington*

Joseph Hrebenak, *Community College Allegheny County*

Tom Humphrey, *Palomar College*

Howard Hunnius, *John Tyler Community College*

Robert Ironside, *North Lake College*

Jim Isherwood, *Community College of Rhode Island*

Gloria Jackson, *San Antonio College*

Henry Jackson, *Delaware County Community College*

Paloma Jalife, *SUNY—Oswego*

William Jedlicka, *William Rainey Harper College*

Paul Jenner, *Southwest Missouri State University*

Gene Johnson, *Clarke College*

M. E. "Micki" Johnson, *Nova Southeastern University*

Michael Johnson, *Delaware County Community College*

Wallace Johnston, *Virginia Commonwealth University*

John Kalaras, *DeVry Institute of Technology*

Alan Kardoff, *Northern Illinois University*

Norman Karl, *Johnson County Community College*

Allen Kartchner, *Utah State University*

Bob Kegel, *Cypress College*

Warren Keller, *Grossmont College*

Roland Kelley, *Tarrant County Junior College-NE Campus*

Jim Kennedy, *Angelina College*

Daniel Kent, *Northern Kentucky University*

Robert Kersten, *St. Louis Community College—Florissant Valley*

Emogene King, *Tyler Junior College*

Jimmy King, *McLennan Community College*

Charles C. Kitzmiller, *Indian River Community College*

John A. Knarr, *University of Maryland—European Division*

Anna Kostorizos, *Middlesex Community College*

Pat Laidler, *Massasoit Community College*

Barbara G. Kreichbaum, *Hagerstown Business College*

Patrick C. Kumpf, *University of Cincinnati*

Kenneth Lacho, *University of New Orleans*

Jay LeGregs, *Tyler Junior College*

Roger Lattanza, *University of New Mexico*

Donna Lees, *Butte College*

Jim Lentz, *Moraine Valley Community College*

George Leonard, *St. Petersburg Junior College*

Thomas Lerra, *Quinsigamond Community College*

Murray Levy, *Glendale Community College*

Rich Lewis, *Lansing Community College*

Joseph Liebreich, *Reading Area Community College*

Tom Lifvendahl, *Cardinal Stritch College*

Ellen Reynolds Ligons, *Pasadena City College*

Yet Mee Lim, *Alabama State University*

Donald Linner, *Esex County College*

Corinne B. Linton, *Valencia Community College*

John Lloyd, *Monroe Community College*

Thomas Lloyd, *Westmoreland County Community College*

Paul James Londrigan, *Charles S. Mott Community College*

Patricia Long, *Tarrant Junior College*

Anthony Lucas, *Allegheny Community College*

Joyce Luckman, *Jackson Community College*

Judith Lyles, *Illinois State University*

Jerry Lunch, *Purdue University*

Rippy Madan, *Frostburg State University*

Richard Maringer, *University of Akron—Wayne College*

Alan Marks, *DeVry Institute of Technology*

Larry Martin, *Community College of Southern Nevada*

Randolph L. Martin, *Germanna Community College*

Thomas Mason, *Brookdale Community College*

Bob Mathews, *Oakton Community College*

Christine McCallum, *University of Akron—Wayne College*

Diana McCann, *Kentucky College of Business*

Mark M. McCarthy, *Davenport College*

Paul McClure, *Mt. San Antonio College*

Jimmy McKenzie, *Tarrant County Junior College*

Noel McKeon, *Florida Community College*

Pat McMahon, *Palm Beach Community College—Glades*

Carl Meskimen, *Sinclair Community College*

Duane Miller, *SUNY—Cobleskill*

Herbert Miller, *Indiana University—Kokomo*

Terrance Mitchell, *South Suburban College*

Joyce Mooneyhan, *Pasadena City College*

Willy Morris, *Northwestern Business College*

Richard Morrison, *Northeastern University*

William Morrison, *San Jose State University*

William Motz, *Lansing Community College*

Carolyn Mueller, *Ball State University*

Micah Mukabi, *Essex County College*

Gary R. Murray, *Rose State College*

Winford C. Naylor, *Santa Barbara City College*

Herschel Nelson, *Polk Community College*

Sharon J. Nickels, *St. Petersburg Junior College*

Carolyn Nickeson, *Del Mar College*

Elaine Novak, *San Jacinto College*

Phil Nufrio, *Essex County College*

Edward O'Brien, *Scotsdale Community College*

Eugene O'Connor, *California Polytechnical University—San Luis Obispo*

Cletus O'Drobinak, *South Suburban College*

Susan Oleson, *Central Piedmont Community College*

Dave Oliver, *Edison Community College*

Katherine Olson, *Northern Virginia Community College*

Kenneth A. Olson, *County College of Morris*

J. Ashton Oravetz, *Tyler Junior College*

George Otto, *Truman College*

Nikki Paahana, *DeVry Institute of Technology*

Robert A. Pacheco, *Massasoit Community College*

Mike Padbury, *Arapahoe Community College*

Teresa Palmer, *Illinois State University*

Dennis Pappas, *Columbus State Community College*

Dennis Pappas, *Columbus Technical Institute*

Knowles Parker, *Wake Technical Community College*

Patricia Parker, *Maryville University*

Janis Pasquali, *University of California—Riverside*

Darlene Raney Perry, *Columbus State*

Stephen Peters, *Walla Walla Community College*

John P. Phillips, *Northern Virginia Community College—Manassas*

Alison Adderley-Pittman, *Brevard Community College—Melbourne*

Joseph Platts, *Miami-Dade Community College*

Wayne Podgorski, *University of Memphis*

Raymond Pokhon, *MATC*

Geraldine Powers, *Northern Essex Community College*

Roderick Powers, *Iowa State University*

Renee Prim, *Central Piedmont Community College*

Brokke Quigg, *Pierce College*

Charles C. Quinn, *Austin Community College—rthridge*

Donald Radtke, *Richard J. Daley College*

Anne Ranczuch, *Monroe Community College*

Richard Randall, *Nassau Community College*

Richard J. Randolph, *Johnson County Community College*

Mary E. Ray, *Indiana Business College*

Scott Reedy, *Brookes College*

Jim Reinemann, *College of Lake County*

Carla Rich, *Pensacola Junior College*

John Rich, *Illinois State University*

Doug Richardson, *Eastfield College*

Karen Richardson, *Tarrant County Junior College*

Bob Roswell, *Jackson Community College*

Linda Roy, *Evergreen Valley College*

Jeri Rubin, *University of Alaska*

Jill Russell, *Camden County College*

Karl Rutkowski, *Peirce Jr. College*

Tom Rutkowski, *SUNY—Cobleskill*

Maurice Sampson, *Community College of Philadelphia*

Cathy Sanders, *San Antonio College*

Nicholas Sarantakes, *Austin Community College*

Billie Sargent, *National College*

Wallace J. Satchell, *St. Philips College*

Gordon Saul, *National Business College*

Larry Saville, *Des Moines Area Community College*

Kurt Schindler, *Wilbur Wright College*

Dennis Schmitt, *Emporia State University*

Marilyn Schwartz, *College of Marin*

Jim Seeck, *Harper College*

Daniel C. Segebath, *South Suburban College*

Patricia A. Serraro, *Clark College*

Greg Service, *Broward Community CollegeNorth*

Guy Sessions, *Spokane Falls Community College*

Dennis Shannon, *Belleville Area College*

Richard Shapiro, *Cuyahoga Community College*

Mark Sheehan, *Bunker Hill Community College*

Nora Jo Sherman, *Houston Community College*

Donald Shifter, *Fontbonne College*

Leon Singleton, *Santa Monica College*

Jerry Sitek, *Southern Illinois University*

Michelle Slagle, *The George Washington University*

Noel Smith, *Palm Beach Community College*

Bill Snider, *Cuesta College*

Paul Solomon, *San Jose State University*

Sol A. Solomon, *Community College of Rhode Island*

Carl Sonntag, *Pikes Peak Community College*

Rieann Spence-Gale, *Northern Virginia Community College*

Richard Stanish, *Tulsa Junior College*

Lynda St. Clair, *Bryant College*

Emanual Stein, *Queensborough Community College*

Scott Steinkamp, *Northwestern Business College*

Kenneth Steinkruger, *DeVry Institute of Technology—Chicago*

Carl Stem, *Texas Tech University*

Robert Stivender, *Wake Technical Community College*

Charles I. Stubbart, *Southern Illinois University*

Jacinto Suarez, *Bronx Community College*

Paul Sunko, *Olive Harvey College*

George Sutcliffe, *Central Piedmont Community College*

Lorraine Suzuki, *University of Maryland—Asian Division*

Carl Swartz, *Three Rivers Community College*

Bill Syversten, *Fresno City College*

James Taggart, *University of Akron*

Daryl Taylor, *Pasadena City College*

Merle E. Taylor, *Santa Barbara City College*

Verna Teasdale, *Prince George's Community College*

Ray Tewell, *American River College*

Darrell Thompson, *Mountain View College*

Linda Thompson, *Massasoit Community College*

Susan Thompson, *Palm Beach Community College—Central*

Vern Timmer, *SUNY—Alfred*

Amy Toth, *Northampton County Area Community College*

Robert Ulbrich, *Parkland College*

Pablo Ulloa, *El Paso Community College*

Robert Vandellen, *Baker College—Cadillac*

Richard Van Ness, *Schenectady County Community College*

Sal Veas, *Santa Monica College*

Heidi Vernon-Wortzel, *Northeastern University*

Janna P. Vice, *Eastern Kentucky University*

Mike Vijuk, *William Ranier/Harper College*

Martha Villarreal, *San Joaquin Delta College*

William Vincent, *Santa Barbara City College*

Cortez Walker, *Baltimore City Community College*

W. J. Waters, *Central Piedmont Community College*

Philip Weatherford, *Embry-Riddle Aeronautical University*

Pete Weiksner, *Lehigh County Community College*

Henry Weiman, *Bronx Community College*

Bernard Weinrich, *St. Louis Community College—Forest Park*

Bill Weisgerber, *Saddleback College*

Martin Welc, *Saddleback College*

William A. Weller, *Modesto Junior College*

James H. Wells, *Daytona Beach Community College*

Sally Wells, *Columbia College*

Aimee Wheaton, *Regis University*

Donald White, *Prince Georges Community College*

Walter Wilfong, *Florida Technical College*

Dick Williams, *Laramie County Community College*

Mary E. Williams, *University of Central Oklahoma*

Paul Williams, *Mott Community College*

Gayla Jo Wilson, *Mesa State College*

Wallace Wirth, *South Suburban Community College*

Judy Eng Woo, *Bellevue Community College*

Joyce Wood, *Northern Virginia Community College*

Bennie Woods, *Burlington County College*

Greg Worosz, *Schoolcraft College*

William Wright, *Mt. Hood Community College*

Merv Yeagle, *Hagerstown Junior College*

C. Yin, *DeVry Institute of Technology*

Ned Young, *Sinclair Community College*

Ron Young, *Kalamazoo Valley Community College*

C. Zarycki, *Hillsborough Community College*

Richard Zollinger, *Central Piedmont College*

In the sixth edition, it was our honor to receive direct input from a very special group of users—students. These introduction to business students provided us with an in-depth chapter-by-chapter review of the fifth edition. Their honest feedback enabled us to make significant improvements in the sixth edition, which we believe will better meet the needs of students that will follow them. We thank the following for sharing their ideas and course experiences:

Chani Badrian, *CUNY—Baruch College*

Morris Baird, *The Community College of Baltimore County*

Lee R. Baldwin, *Mt. San Antonio College*

Janet L. Bernard, *Tampa College*

Jessee Bolton, *Charles County Community College*

Nichole Burnes, *FMU–Tampa College*

Michele Lynn Carver, *The Community College of Baltimore County*

Shannon M. Ebersol, *Hagerstown Community College*

Robin Frazee, *Anne Arundel Community College*

Crystal Hance, *Charles County Community College*

Leslie Hickman, *Frederick Community College*

George M. Hihn, III, *University of Akron*

Trinh Hong Hoang, *Mt. San Antonio College*

Cheryl Lynn Holliday, *Calvert County Community College*

Curtis W. Hwang, *Mt. San Antonio College*

Lauren Jeweler, *Frederick Community College*

Jennifer Landig, *Saddleback Valley Community College*

Amy J. Lee, *Parkland College*

Hanh Long, *DeAnza College*

Marie D. O'Dell, *Anne Arundel Community College*

Charlotte A. Patterson, *Tampa College*

Quinn Sasaki, *Mt. San Antonio College*

Lance Schmeidler, *Northern Virginia Community College*

Justin Selden, *The University of Akron*

Melinda Soto, *Mt. San Antonio Community College*

Elizabeth Stanley, *Northern Virginia Community College*

Bonnie Luck-Yan Tsang, *DeAnza College*

Julie C. Verrati, *Montgomery College*

Christopher Walsh, *Hagerstown Community College*

Michael David Wentz, *Hagerstown Community College*

Cammie White, *Santa Monica College*

The *Understanding Business* product is more than just a textbook. It includes a treasure trove of supplementary materials that play a major role in our instructional programs. Two key supplements, the test bank and the study guide, were reviewed in order to ensure the highest quality UB instructors have grown to depend upon. Every test bank question was reviewed by the text authors along with Tom McFarland, Mt. San Antonio College, and Fred Pragasam, University of North Florida. The study guide was comprehensively reviewed by the text authors, Barbara Boyington, Brookdale Community College, Velma Jesser, Lane Community College, Warren Pitcher, Des Moines Area Community College, and Phyllis Shafer, Brookdale Community College. We thank these reviewers for making certain that the UB supplements are appropriate and accurate.

The sixth edition is all the stronger due to involvement of these committed instructors and students. We thank them all for their help, support, and friendship.

Bill Nickels
Jim McHugh
Susan McHugh

PROLOGUE

Getting Ready for Prime Time

TOP 10 REASONS TO READ THIS INTRODUCTION

(EVEN IF IT ISN'T ASSIGNED)

10 You don't want the only time you get a raise to be when the government increases the minimum wage.

9 What the heck—you already bought the book, you might as well get your money's worth.

8 You can learn what professional behavior is all about so you don't suddenly find yourself in a section of the classroom all alone.

7 You need to know that "Point and Click" is not a new music group.

6 You need to know that a time management course is not a class on clock repair.

5 Not many job-producing résumés and interviews start with "Like, you know, this is, like, what I want to, like, do you know."

4 Getting off to a good start in the course can improve your chances of getting a higher grade, and your Uncle Ernie will send you a quarter for every A you get.

3 It must be important because the authors spent so much time writing it.

2 You want to run with the big dogs someday.

And the number one reason for reading this introductory section is . . .

1 It could be on a test.

LEARNING THE SKILLS NEEDED TO SUCCEED TODAY AND TOMORROW

Your life is full. You're starting a new semester, probably even beginning your college career, and you're feeling pulled in many directions. Why take time to read this introductory section? We lightheartedly offer our top 10 reasons to read it on page GR-1, but the real importance of this section to your success is no joking matter. The purpose of this introduction and of the entire text is to help you learn principles, strategies, and skills for success that will help you not only in this course but also in your career and entire life. Whether or not you learn these skills is up to you. Learning them won't guarantee success, but *not* learning them—well, you get the picture.

We hope you invest the time to read the entire Getting Ready for Prime Time section. However, we realize that some parts of the material may be more relevant to your individual needs than others. To help you focus on the most important information for your needs, we've divided the material into three major categories:

1. *Succeeding in This Course*—an overview of the skills you'll need to succeed in this course and throughout college as well as the skills needed to succeed in your career after you earn your diploma. READ THIS SECTION BEFORE YOUR FIRST CLASS and make a great first impression!

2. *Surfing the Internet*—a quick and easy overview of how to surf the Internet.

3. *Getting the Job You Want*—guidelines to finding and getting the job you want with emphasis on job search, résumé writing, and interviewing skills.

This is an exciting and challenging time. Never before have there been more opportunities to become successful. And never before have there been more challenges. Success in any venture comes from understanding basic principles and having the skills to apply those principles effectively. What you learn now could help you be a success—for the rest of your life.

Begin applying these skills now to gain an edge on the competition. Good luck. We wish you the best.

Bill Nickels   **Jim McHugh**   **Susan McHugh**

SUCCEEDING IN THIS COURSE

Since you've signed up for this course, we're guessing you already know the value of a college education. But just to give you some numerical backup, you should know that the gap between the earnings of high school graduates and college graduates, which is growing every year, now ranges from 60 to 70 percent. According to the U.S. Census Bureau, the holders of bachelor's degrees will make an average of $40,478 per year as opposed to just $22,895 for high school graduates.[1] That's a whopping additional $17,583 a year. Thus, what you invest in a college education is likely to pay you back many times. See Figure G.1 to get an idea of how much salary difference a college degree makes by the end of a 30-year career. That doesn't mean there aren't good careers available to non–college graduates. It just means that those with an education are more likely to have higher earnings over their lifetime.

The value of a college education is more than just a larger paycheck. Other benefits include increasing your ability to think critically and communicate your ideas to others, improving your ability to use technology, and preparing yourself to live in a diverse world. Knowing you've met your goals and earned a college degree also gives you the self-confidence to continue to strive to meet your future goals.

Experts say it is likely that today's college graduates will hold seven or eight different jobs (often in several different careers) in their lifetime. There are many returning students in college today who are changing their careers and their plans for life. In fact, 41 percent of the people enrolled in college today are 25 or older. More than 1.6 million students are over 40.[2] Talk to them and learn from their successes and mistakes. You too may want to change careers some day. Often that is the path to long-term happiness and success. That means you will have to be flexible and adjust your strengths and talents to new opportunities. Many of the best jobs of the future don't even exist today. Learning has become a lifelong job. You will have to constantly update your skills if you want to achieve and remain competitive.

If you're typical of many college students, you may not have any idea what career you'd like to pursue. That isn't necessarily a big disadvantage in today's fast-changing job market. There are no perfect or certain ways to prepare for the most interesting and challenging jobs of tomorrow. Rather, you should continue your college education, develop strong computer skills, improve your verbal and written communication skills, and remain flexible while you explore the job market.

College students in general make 60 to 70 percent more money in their lifetimes than high school graduates. College not only prepares you for the jobs of the future, it also gives you the chance to network with other college graduates who may help you find jobs in the future. What can you do while in college to optimize the networking benefits it provides?

USING THIS COURSE TO PREPARE FOR YOUR CAREER

One of the objectives of this class is to help you choose an area in which you might enjoy working and in which you might succeed. This book and this course together may be one of your most important learning experiences ever. They're meant to help you understand business so that you can use business principles throughout your life. You'll learn about production, marketing, finance, accounting, management, economics, and more. At the end of the course, you should have a much better idea about what careers would be best for you and what careers you would *not* enjoy.

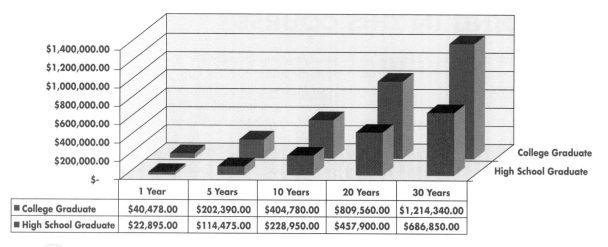

	1 Year	5 Years	10 Years	20 Years	30 Years
■ College Graduate	$40,478.00	$202,390.00	$404,780.00	$809,560.00	$1,214,340.00
■ High School Graduate	$22,895.00	$114,475.00	$228,950.00	$457,900.00	$686,850.00

FIGURE G.1

SALARY COMPARISON OF HIGH SCHOOL VERSUS COLLEGE GRADUATES

But you don't have to be in business to use business principles. You can use marketing principles to get a job and to sell your ideas to others. You can use your knowledge of investments to make money in the stock market. Similarly, you'll be able to use management skills and general business knowledge wherever you go and in whatever career you pursue—including government agencies, charities, and social causes.

ASSESSING YOUR SKILLS AND PERSONALITY

Many people return to college to improve their skills in areas such as computers and writing. Others return because they realize, once they enter the marketplace, how important a college education is. Can you see the advantage of going back to school periodically over your career to keep your skills current?

The earlier you can do a personal assessment of your interests, skills, and values, the better it will be for you in finding some career direction. In recognition of this need, many colleges offer self-assessment programs. Hundreds of schools use a software exercise called the System for Interactive Guidance and Information (SIGI). A different version, called DISCOVER, is used at hundreds of other schools. Both SIGI and DISCOVER feature self-assessment exercises, create personalized lists of occupations based on your interests and skills, and provide information about different careers and the preparation each requires. Visit your college's placement center, career lab, or library and learn what programs are available for you.

It would be helpful to use one or more self-assessment programs early in this course so you can determine, while you're learning about the different business fields, which ones most closely fit your interests and skills. Self-assessment will help you determine the kind of work environment you'd prefer (e.g., technical, social service, or business); what values you seek to fulfill in a career (e.g., security, variety, or independence); what abilities you have (e.g., creative/artistic, numerical, or sales); and what important job characteristics you stress most (e.g., income, travel, or amount of job pressure).

Even if you're one of the college students over 30 years old, an assessment of your skills will help you choose the right courses and career path to follow next. Many returning students have taken such tests

because they are not satisfied with what they're doing and are seeking a more rewarding occupation. Armed with the results of your self-assessment, you are more likely to make a career choice that will be personally fulfilling.

LEARNING PROFESSIONAL BUSINESS STRATEGIES

Business professionals have learned the importance of networking and of keeping files on subjects that are important to them. These are two secrets to success that students should begin practicing now. One thing that links students in all colleges is the need to retain what they learn. You need a strategy to help you meet this need. It's also extremely important to keep the names of contact people at various organizations. In addition, you may want to keep facts and figures of all kinds about the economy and business-related subjects. These are all reasons why you should develop resource files.

An effective way to become an expert on almost any business subject is to set up your own information system. Eventually you may want to store data on computer disks for retrieval on your personal computer and to access professional databases as businesspeople do. Meanwhile, it's effective to establish a comprehensive filing system on paper.

If you start now, you'll soon have at your fingertips information that will prove invaluable for use in term papers and throughout your career. Few college students do this filing; those who don't lose much of the information they read in college or thereafter. *Developing this habit is one of the most effective ways of educating yourself and having the information available when you need it.* The only space you'll need to start is a 12-inch by 12-inch corner of your room to hold a portable file box. The box should hold hanging folders in which you can place a number of tabbed file folders. To start filling these files you might put your course notes in them, with the names of your professors and the books you used. You may need this information later for employment references. Also, be sure to keep all the notes you make when talking with people about careers, including salary information, courses needed, and contacts.

> **A** simple file system can provide you with some useful advantages over students who do not keep such files. You will have at your fingertips articles that will be valuable in completing class assignments, the names of people you can use to network, the names of the best professors on campus so you can schedule them, and other resource information you deem worthwhile. What additional benefits do you see from keeping interesting information from newspapers, magazines, and similar sources?

Each time you read a story about a firm that interests you, either cut it out of the publication or photocopy it and then place it in an appropriate file. You might begin with files labeled Careers, Small Business, Economics, Management, and Resource People. You might summarize the article on a Post-it note and stick this summary on the front for later reference. Today, it is possible to find the latest data on almost any subject on the Internet. Good students know, or quickly learn, how to find such information efficiently. The best students know the importance of keeping such information in files so that it is readily accessible. Those files may be in their computers or on their desktops, ready for easy access.

You definitely want to have a personal data file titled Credentials for My Résumé or something similar. In that file, you'll place all reference letters and other information about jobs you may have held. Soon you'll have a tremendous amount of information available to you. You can add to these initial files until you have your own comprehensive information system.

Businesspeople are constantly seeking ways to increase their knowledge of the business world and to increase their investment returns. One way they do so is by watching television shows such as *Wall $treet Week* and *Nightly Business Report*. Watching such programs is like getting a free graduate education in business. Try viewing some of these shows or listening to similar shows on the radio, and see which ones you like best. Take notes and put them in your files. Another way, one of the best, to increase your business knowledge is to read your local newspaper. Keep up with the business news in your local area so you know what jobs are available and where. You may also want to join local business groups to begin networking with people and learning the secrets of the local business scene. Many business groups and professional societies accept student members.

LEARNING TO BEHAVE LIKE A PROFESSIONAL

Good manners are back, and for a good reason. As the world becomes increasingly competitive, the gold goes to the individuals and the teams that have an extra bit of polish. The person who makes a good impression will be the one who gets the job, wins the promotion, or clinches the deal. Manners and professionalism must become second nature to anyone who wants to achieve and maintain a competitive edge.

Often, students focus on becoming experts in their particular field and neglect other concerns, including proper attire and etiquette. Their résumés look great and they may get through the interview process, but then they get in the workplace and may not succeed. Their behavior, including their verbal behavior, is so unacceptable that they are rejected by their peers.

The lesson is this: You can have good credentials, but a good presentation is everything. You can't neglect etiquette, or somewhere in your career you will be at a competitive disadvantage because of your inability to use good manners or to maintain your composure in tense situations. You must constantly practice the basics until they become second nature to you. Such basics include saying "Please" and "Thank you" when you ask for something. They also include opening doors for others, standing when an older person enters the room, and using a polite tone of voice. You may want to take a class in etiquette to learn the proper way to eat in a nice restaurant and handle the various utensils, the proper way to act at a formal party, and so on. Of course, it is critical that you are honest, reliable, dependable, and ethical at all times.

You can probably think of sports stars who have earned a bad reputation by not acting professionally (e.g., spitting, swearing, criticizing teammates in front of others). People in professional sports are fined if they are late to meetings or refuse to follow the rules established by the team and coach. Business professionals also must follow set rules. Many of these rules are not formally written anywhere, but every successful businessperson learns them through experience.

You can begin the habits *now* while you are in college so that you will have the skills needed for success when you start your career. Those habits include the following:

1. *Making a good first impression.* An old saying goes, "You never get a second chance to make a good first impression." You have just a few seconds to make an impression. Therefore, how you dress and look is important.[3] Take a clue as to what is appropriate at any specific company by studying the people there who are most successful. What do they wear? How do they act?

2. *Focusing on good grooming.* Be aware of your appearance and its impact on those around you. Consistency is essential. You can't project a good image by dressing up a few times a week and then show up looking like you're getting ready to mow a lawn. Wear appropriate, clean clothing and accessories. For example, revealing shirts, nose rings, and such may not be appropriate in a work setting. It is not appropriate for men to wear hats inside buildings. It is also not appropriate, usually, to wear wrinkled clothing or to have shirttails hanging out of your pants. More businesses are adopting "business casual" policies, so knowing the proper clothes to buy is critical. What is business casual to some may not be acceptable to others, but there are a few guidelines most organizations accept. First of all, casual doesn't mean sloppy or shabby. For women, casual attire includes simple skirts and slacks (no jeans), cotton shirts, sweaters (not too tight), blazers, low-heeled shoes or boots (always with socks or stockings). For men, acceptable casual attire includes khaki trousers, sport shirts with collars, sweaters or sport jackets, casual loafers or lace-up shoes (no athletic shoes).[4]

3. *Being on time.* When you don't come to class or to work on time, you're sending a message to your teacher or boss. You're saying, "My time is more important than your time. I have more important things to do than be here." In addition to the lack of respect tardiness shows to your teacher or boss, it rudely disrupts the work of your colleagues. Promptness may not be a priority in some circles, but in the workplace promptness is essential. But being punctual doesn't always mean just being on time. You have to pay attention to the corporate culture. Sometimes you have to come earlier than others and leave later to get that promotion you desire. To develop good work habits and get good grades, it is important to get to class on time and not leave early.

4. *Practicing considerate behavior.* Considerate behavior includes listening when others are talking—for example, not reading the newspaper or eating in class. Don't interrupt others when they are speaking. Wait for your turn to present your views in classroom or workplace discussions. Of course, eliminate all words of profanity from your vocabulary. Use appropriate body language by sitting up attentively and not slouching. Sitting up has the added bonus of helping you stay awake! Professors and managers get a favorable impression from those who look and act alert. That may help your grades in school and your advancement at work.

5. *Practicing good "netiquette."* Computer technology, particularly e-mail, can be a great productivity tool. The basic courtesy rules of face-to-face communication also apply to e-mail exchanges. As in writing a letter, you should introduce yourself at the beginning of your first e-mail message. Next, you should let your recipients know how you got their names and e-mail addresses. Then you can proceed with your clear but succinct message, and finally close the e-mail with a signature.[5] Do not send an attachment (files of text or graphics attached to an e-mail

"Time is money" the saying goes. Actually many think that time is more valuable than money. If your bank account balance falls, often you can build it back up by finding a better paying job, taking on a second job, or even selling something you own. But you only have a limited amount of time and there is no way to make more. Don't be guilty of stealing someone else's valuable time by being late for appointments. If you are, what message are you sending the other person?

message) with your e-mail unless your correspondent has indicated that he or she will accept it. Ask first!

You can find much more information about proper Internet etiquette (netiquette) on the Internet. For example, the website PlanetClick rates and reviews netiquette websites (www.planetclick.com/cgi-bin/category.cgi?T=netiquette).

6. *Practicing good cell phone manners.* Cellular phones are a vital part of today's world, but it is important to be polite when using the phone. Turn off the phone when you are in class or a business meeting unless you are expecting a critical call. Your Introduction to Business class is not the place to be arranging a date for tonight. If you are expecting a critical call, turn off the audible phone ring and use the vibrating ring if your phone has that feature. If you do have to have your cellular phone turned on, sit by the aisle and near the door to leave if the phone rings. Leave the room before answering the call. Apologize to the professor after class and explain the nature of the emergency. Most professors are more sympathetic when you explain why you left the room abruptly.

7. *Being prepared.* A businessperson would never show up for a meeting without reading the materials assigned for that meeting and being prepared to discuss the topics of the day. *To become a professional, you must practice acting like a professional.* For students, that means reading assigned materials before class, asking questions and responding to questions in class, and discussing the material with fellow students.

It is crucial that business people learn business etiquette appropriate for the countries in which they do business. Behavior taken for granted in the United States can be insulting in other cultures. For example, in some cultures shaking hands when you first meet another person is considered rude. Is there a country in which you might like to do business? What are some of the cultural difference that might affect your business behavior in that country?

From the minute you enter your first job interview until the day you retire, people will notice whether you follow the proper business etiquette. Just as traffic laws enable people to drive more safely, business etiquette allows people to conduct business with the appropriate amount of dignity. How you talk, how you eat, and how you dress all create an impression on others. We encourage you to add a course or seminar on etiquette to your college curriculum. Many businesses today require their employees to complete such a course. Taking the initiative to do so on your own will help sharpen your competitive edge.

Business etiquette may encompass different rules in different countries. It is important, therefore, to learn the proper business etiquette for each country you visit. Areas that require proper etiquette include greeting people (shaking hands is not always appropriate); eating (Europeans, for example, often hold their knives and forks while eating); giving gifts; presenting and receiving business cards; and conducting business in general. Honesty, high ethical standards, and good character (e.g., reliability and trustworthiness) are important ingredients to success in any country. Having a reputation for integrity will enable you to be proud of who you are and will contribute a great deal to your business success. Unethical behavior can ruin your reputation, so think carefully before you act. When in doubt, don't! Ethics is so important to success that we will include ethics discussions throughout the text.

DOING YOUR BEST IN SCHOOL

The skills you need to succeed in college are the same skills you need to succeed in life after college. Career, family, and hobbies all involve the same organizational and time management skills. Applying these skills during your college years will ensure that you will have the life skills you need for a successful career. We will try to help you hone your skills by offering hints for improving your study habits, taking tests, and managing your time.

Study Hints

Studying is your business now. When you fill out a form you write "Student" in the occupation box, right? So until you get out of school and into a full-time job, studying is your business. Like any good businessperson, you aim for success. Let us suggest some strategies for success:

1. *Go to class.* It is often tempting to cut a class on a nice day or when there are other things to do. But nothing is more important to doing well in school than going to class every time. If possible, sit in the front near the instructor. This will help you focus more on what is being said and less on distractions in the room.

2. *Listen well.* It's not enough to show up for class if you use the time for a siesta. Make eye contact with the instructor. In your mind, form a picture of what is discussed. Try to include past experiences in your picture. This ties new knowledge to what you already know.

3. *Take careful notes.* Make two columns in your notebook and use one side to write down the important concepts and the other side to write examples or more detailed explanations. Use abbreviations and symbols whenever possible. Use wide spacing to make the notes easier to read. Rewrite the notes after class because hastily written notes are often difficult to decipher much later. Rereading and rewriting notes also helps store the information in your long-term memory. You learn the concepts in the course the same way you learn the words to your favorite song: through repetition and review.

Some students prefer to enter class notes directly into their computers during class. Others prefer to write notes by hand, using their own form of abbreviations and codes. What are the advantages of each of these methods? Which method do you use? How effective is it for you? If you take notes by hand, would it help you understand and retain the information if you rewrote your notes or copied them into your computer later? Why?

4. *Find a good place to study.* Find a place with good lighting and a quiet atmosphere. Some students do well with classical music or other music without lyrics playing in the background. Keep your study place equipped with extra supplies such as pens, pencils, calculator, folders, and paper so that you don't have to interrupt study time to hunt for what you need.

5. *Read the text using a strategy such as "survey, question, read, recite, review" (SQ3R).*

   • *Survey* or scan the chapter first to see what it is all about. This means looking over the table of contents, Learning Goals, headings, photo captions, and charts so you get a broad idea of the content. Scanning will provide an introduction and help get your mind in a learning mode.

   • Write *questions,* first by changing the headings into questions. For example, you could change the heading of this section to: "What hints can I use to study better?" Read the questions that appear throughout each chapter in the Progress Assessment and Critical Thinking sections. The Progress Assessment questions give you a chance to recall what you've read. The Critical Thinking questions help you relate the material to your own experiences. Research has shown that it is easier to retain information and concepts if you can relate to them personally.

   • *Read* the chapter to find the answers to your questions. Be sure to read the boxes throughout the text as well. They offer extended examples or discussions of the concepts in the text. You've probably asked, "Will the stuff in the boxes be on the tests?" Even if your instructor chooses not to test over them directly, they are often the most interesting parts and will help you retain the concepts.

   • *Recite* your answers to yourself or to others in a study group. Make sure you say the answers in your own words so that you clearly understand the concepts. Research has shown that saying things is a more effective way to learn them than seeing, hearing, or reading about them. Used in study groups, recitation is also good practice for working in teams in the work world.

   • *Review* by rereading and recapping the information. The chapter summaries are written in a question-and-answer form, much like a classroom dialogue. Cover the written answers and see if you can answer the questions yourself first. The summaries are directly tied to the learning goals so you can see whether you've accomplished the chapter's objectives.

6. *Use the study guide.* The Student Assessment Learning Guide gives you the chance to practice thinking through answers and writing them down. It also includes practice multiple-choice tests.

7. *Use flash cards.* Much of the material in this course consists of terminology. The key terms in the book are highlighted in boldface type, and their definitions appear in the margins. Page references to these terms are provided at the end of each chapter. Write the terms you don't know on index cards and go through them between classes and when you have other free time.

8. *Use the Concept Mastery Toolkit CD-ROM.* Using the computer software in the pocket on the inside back cover of the book is a great way to practice your test-taking skills. The software contains sample test questions. It will analyze your achievement and then provide page references to concepts you have trouble understanding.

9. *Go over old exams, if possible.* Sometimes a professor will make old exams available so that you can see the style of the exam. If such exams are not available, ask your professor exactly how the exam will be given. That is, ask how many multiple-choice questions and how many true-false and essay questions there will be. It is not unethical to ask your professor's former students what kind of questions are given and what material is usually emphasized. It is unethical, though, to go over illegally obtained exams.

10. *Use as many of your senses in learning as possible.* If you're an auditory learner—that is, if you learn best by hearing—record yourself reading your notes and answering the questions you've written. Listen to the tape while you're dressing in the morning. You can also benefit from reading or studying aloud. Use the text on tape (a set of audiotapes) that is available with this book. If you're a visual learner, you should use pictures, charts, colors, and graphs. Your professor has a set of videotapes that illustrate the concepts in this text. If you're a kinesthetic learner, you remember best by doing, touching, and experiencing. You can benefit from doing some of the Developing Workplace Skills and Taking It to the Net exercises at the end of each chapter.

Test-Taking Hints

Often students will say, "I know this stuff, but I'm just no good at taking multiple-choice (or essay) tests." Other students find test-taking relatively easy. A survey of such students reveals the following test-taking hints:

1. *Get plenty of sleep and a good meal.* It is better to be alert and awake during an exam than to study all night and be groggy. If you keep up with your reading and your reviews, there is no need to pull an all-nighter just before the exam. Proper nutrition plays an important part in your brain's ability to function.

2. *Bring all you need for the exam.* Sometimes you will need number 2 pencils, erasers, and a calculator. Ask beforehand what you'll need.

3. *Relax.* Begin at home before the test. Take deep, slow breaths. Picture yourself in the testing session, relaxed and confident. Get to class early to settle down. If you start to get nervous during the test, stop and take deep breaths. Turn the test over and write down information you remember. Sometimes this helps you connect the information you know to the questions on the test.

4. *Read the directions on the exam carefully.* You don't want to miss anything or do something you are not supposed to do.

5. *Read all the answers in multiple-choice questions.* Often there is more than one correct-sounding answer to a multiple-choice question, but one is clearly better. Be sure to read them all to be sure that the one you pick is best. A technique that may help you is to cover up the choices while reading the question. If the answer you think of is one of the choices, it is probably the correct answer. If you are still unsure of the answer, start eliminating options you know are wrong. Narrowing the choices to two or three improves your odds.

6. *Answer all the questions.* Unless your instructor takes off more for an incorrect answer than no answer at all, you have nothing to lose by guessing. Also, skipping a question can lead to inadvertently misaligning your answers on a scan sheet. You could end up with all of your subsequent answers scored wrong!

FRANK & ERNEST® by Bob Thaves

Because life really is mostly essay questions, this text includes a couple of critical thinking exercises in every chapter to encourage you to generate your own thoughts about the issues raised in the chapter. Can you see the benefit of pausing to answer such questions as your read? In the first place, it will put the material into your own context. Secondly, it will keep your aware of the issues and force you to think about your own perspectives.

7. *Read true–false questions carefully.* All parts of the statement must be true or the entire statement is false. Watch out for absolutes such as *never, always,* or *none.* These most likely make a statement false.

8. *Organize your thoughts before answering essay questions.* Think of the sequence you intend to use to present what you want to say. Use complete sentences with correct grammar and punctuation. Explain or defend your answers.

9. *Go over the test at the end.* Make sure you have answered all the questions and that you have put your name on the exam and followed all the other directions.

Time Management Hints

Throughout your life, the most important management skill you will learn is to manage your time. Now is as good a time to learn as any. Here are some hints that other students have learned—often the hard way:

1. *Write weekly goals for yourself.* Make certain your goals are realistic and attainable. Write the steps you will use to achieve each goal. Reward yourself when you reach a goal.

2. *Keep a "to do" list.* It is easy to forget things unless you have them written down. Jot tasks down the first time you think of them so that you don't "rediscover" chores when you think of them again. Writing them down gives you one less thing to do: remembering what you have to do.

3. *Prepare a daily schedule.* Use a commercial daily planner or create your own. Write the days of the week across the top of the page. Write the hours of the day from the time you get up until the time you go to bed down the left side. Draw lines to form columns and rows and fill in all the activities you have planned in each hour. Hopefully, you will be surprised to see how many slots of time you have available for studying.

4. *Prepare for the next day the night before.* Having everything ready to go will help you make a quick, unfrenzied start in the morning.

5. *Prepare weekly and monthly schedules.* Use a calendar to fill in activities and upcoming assignments. Include both academic and social activities so you can balance your work and fun.

6. *Space out your work.* Don't wait until the last week of the course to write all your papers and study for your exams. If you do a few pages a

day, you can do a 20-page paper in a couple of weeks with little effort. It is really difficult to push out 20 pages in a day or two.

7. *Defend your study time.* Fraternities and sororities often set aside time for everyone to study. It is important to study some every day. Use the time between classes to go over your flash cards and read the next day's assignments. Make it a habit to defend your study time so you don't slip.

8. *Take time for fun.* If you have some fun every day, life will be full. But if you don't have fun, life can be a real drag. Schedule your fun times along with your study schedule so that you have balance.

MAKING THE MOST OF THE RESOURCES FOR THIS COURSE

College courses are best at teaching you concepts and ways of thinking about business. However, to learn firsthand about real-world applications, you will need to explore and interact with actual businesses. Textbooks are like comprehensive tour guides in that they tell you what to look for and where to look, but they can never replace experience.

This text, then, isn't meant to be the only resource for this class. In fact, it's not even the primary resource. Your professor will be much better than the text at responding to your specific questions and needs. This book is just one of the resources he or she can use with you to satisfy your desire to understand what the business world is all about. There are seven basic resources for the class in addition to the text and study guide:

1. *The professor.* One of the most valuable facets of college is the chance to study with experienced professors. Your instructor is more than a teacher of facts and concepts. As mentioned above, he or she is a resource who's there to answer questions and guide you to the answers for others. It's important for you to develop a friendly relationship with all of your professors. One reason for doing so is that many professors get job leads they can pass on to you. Professors are also excellent references for future jobs. By following the rules of dress and etiquette outlined above, you can create a good impression, which will be valuable should you ask a professor to write a good letter of recommendation for you. Finally, your professor is one more experienced person who can help you find and access resource materials, both at your college and in the business world.

2. *The supplements that come with this text: the Concept Mastery Toolkit software, the Student Assessment Learning Guide, and the audiotapes.* The exam prep disk and study guide will help you review and interpret key material and give you practice answering test questions. Even if your professor does not assign the study guide and exam prep disk, you may want to use them anyhow. Doing so will improve your test scores and help you compete successfully with the other students. If you are an auditory learner (you learn best by listening) or if you have a long commute to class, you'll find the audiotaped version of this text to be a great resource.

3. *Outside readings.* We recommend that you review the following magazines and newspapers as well as other resources during the course and throughout your career: *The Wall Street Journal, Forbes, Inc., Business Week, Fortune, Harvard Business Review, Black Enterprise,* and *Entrepreneur.* You may also want to read your local newspaper's

business section and national news magazines such as *Time* and *Newsweek* to keep up with current issues. If you're not familiar with these sources, it's time to get to know them. You don't necessarily have to become a regular subscriber, but you should learn what information is available in these sources over time. All of these sources are probably available free of charge in your school's learning resource center or the local public library. One secret to success in business is staying current, and these magazines will help you do so.

4. *Your own experience and that of your classmates.* Many college students have had experience working in business or nonprofit organizations. Talking together about those experiences exposes you to many real-life examples that are invaluable for understanding business. Don't rely totally on the professor for answers to the cases and other exercises in this book. Often there is no single "right" answer, and your classmates may open up new ways of looking at things for you. Part of being a successful businessperson is knowing how to work with others. College classrooms are excellent places to practice this skill. Some professors provide opportunities for their students to work together in small groups. Such exercises build teamwork as well as presentation and analytical skills. If you have students from other countries in your class, working with them can help you learn about different cultures and different approaches to handling business problems. There is strength in diversity, so seek out people different from yourself to work with on teams.

5. *Outside contacts.* One of the best ways to learn about different businesses is to visit them in person. Who can tell you more about what it's like to start a career in accounting than someone who's doing it now? The same is true of other jobs. The world can be your classroom if you let it. When you go shopping, for example, think about whether you would enjoy working in and managing a store. Talk with the clerks and the manager to see how they feel about the job. Think about the possibilities of owning or managing a restaurant, an auto body shop, a health club, a print shop, or any other establishment you visit. If something looks interesting, talk to the employees and learn more about their jobs and the industry. Soon you may discover fascinating careers in places such as the zoo or a health club or in industries such as travel or computer sales. In short, be constantly on the alert to find career possibilities, and don't hesitate to talk with people about their careers. Typically, they'll be pleased to give you their time.

6. *The Internet.* Never before have students had access to information as easily as they do today. What makes information gathering so easy now is the Internet. Once you've learned to surf the Internet, you will find more material than you could use in a lifetime. On the Internet you can search through library catalogs all over the world, find articles from leading business journals, view paintings from leading museums, and more—much more. Throughout this text we will present information and exercises that will help you gain experience using the Internet. But don't rely on the text for all your knowledge. Talk with your friends and acquaintances and learn as much as you can about how to use the Internet. This resource will become even more important in the future. Information changes rapidly, and it is up to you to stay current. If you don't already know how to use the Internet, learn to do so now!

You are likely to want to learn more about specific topics in this text. You have a wealth of resources at your fingertips to do so. No time to run to the library to find the latest issues of the journals shown here? No problem. Just log on the Internet and visit one of the many journals that provide access to present and past articles. To find links to many of these publishing sites as well as direct links to some of our favorite articles, visit our website at www.mhhe.com/ub6e.

Reading the Surfing the Internet skills section beginning on p. GR-17 will get you started.

7. *The library or learning resource center.* The library is a great complement to the Internet as a valuable resource. Work with your librarian to learn how to best access the information you need.

Getting the Most from This Text

Many learning aids appear throughout this text to help you understand the concepts:

1. *List of Learning Goals at the beginning of each chapter.* Reading through these goals will help you set the framework and focus for the chapter material. Since every student at one time or other has found it difficult to get into studying, the Learning Goals are there to provide an introduction and to get your mind into a learning mode.

2. *Self-test questions.* Periodically, within each chapter, you'll encounter set-off lists of questions called Progress Assessment or Critical Thinking. These questions give you a chance to pause, think carefully about, and recall what you've just read.

3. *Key terms.* Developing a strong business vocabulary is one of the most important and useful aspects of this course. To assist you, all key terms in the book are highlighted in boldface type. Key terms are also defined in the margins, and page references to these terms are given at the end of each chapter. A full glossary is located in the back of the book. You should rely heavily on these learning aids in adding these terms to your vocabulary.

4. *Boxes.* Each chapter contains a number of boxes that offer extended examples or discussions of concepts in the text. This material is designed to highlight key concepts and to make the book more interesting to read. The boxes cover major themes of the book: (1) ethics (Making Ethical Decisions); (2) entrepreneurship (From the Pages of *Business Week*); (3) small business (Spotlight on Small Business); (4) legal environment of business (Legal Briefcase); and (5) global business (Reaching Beyond Our Borders).

5. *End-of-chapter summaries.* The summaries are directly tied to the Learning Goals so you can see whether you've accomplished the chapter's objectives.

6. *Developing Workplace Skills exercises.* Regardless of how hard we try to make learning easier, the truth is that students tend to forget most of what they read and hear. To really remember something, it's best to do it. That's why there are Developing Workplace Skills sections at the end of each chapter. The purpose of Developing Workplace Skills questions is to suggest small projects that reinforce what you've read and help you develop the skills you need to succeed in the workplace. These activities will help you develop skill in using resources, interpersonal skills, skills in managing information, skills in understanding systems, and computer skills.

7. *Taking It to the Net exercises.* These exercises not only give you practice surfing the Internet but, more important, they direct you to dynamic outside resources that reinforce the concepts introduced in the text.

8. *Practicing Management Decisions cases.* These end-of-chapter cases give you another chance to think about the material and apply it in

678   PART 7 • Managing Financial Resources

tives the government provides and the conditions you must meet to get them. Many people use their education to find successful careers and to improve their earning potential, but at retirement they have little to show for their efforts. Making money is one thing; saving, investing, and spending it wisely is something else. Less than 10 percent of the U.S. population has accumulated enough money by retirement age to live comfortably. Following the six steps listed in the next section will help you become one of those with enough to retire in comfort.

Six Steps in Learning to Control Your Assets

The only way to save enough money to do all of the things you want to do later in life is to make more than you spend! We know you may find it hard to save today, but saving money isn't only possible, it's imperative if you want to accumulate enough to be financially secure. The following are six steps you can take today to get control of your finances.

Step 1: Take an Inventory of Your Financial Assets To take inventory, you need to develop a balance sheet ▸ P.556 ◂ for yourself. Remember, a balance sheet starts with the fundamental accounting equation: Assets = Liabilities + Owners' equity. You can develop your own balance sheet by listing your assets (e.g., TV, VCR, DVD, computer, bicycle, car, jewelry, and clothes) on one side and liabilities (e.g., mortgage, credit card debt, and auto loans) on the other. Assets include anything you own. For our purpose, evaluate your assets based on their current value, not purchase price as required in formal accounting statements.

If the value of your liabilities exceeds the value of your assets, you aren't on the path to financial security. In fact, you may be one of those who find the Making Ethical Decisions box about bankruptcy particularly interesting. You need some discipline in your life.

Since we're talking about accounting, let's talk again about an income statement ▸ P.560 ◂. At the top of the statement is revenue (everything you take in from your job, investments, etc.). You subtract all your costs and expenses to get net income or profit. Software programs such as Quicken and websites such as www.dinky.town have a variety of tools that can easily help you with these calculations.

This may also be an excellent time to think about how much money you will need to accomplish all your goals. The more you visualize your goals, the easier it is to begin saving for them.

Step 2: Keep Track of All Your Expenses You may often find yourself running out of cash (a cash flow ▸ P.562 ◂ problem). In such circumstances, the only way to trace where the money is going is to keep track of every cent you spend. Keeping records of your expenses can be a rather tedious but necessary chore if you want to learn discipline. Actually, it could turn out to be an enjoyable task because it gives you such a feeling of control. Here's what to do: Carry a notepad with you wherever you go and record what you spend as you go through the day. That notepad is your journal. At the end of the week, record your journal entries into a record book or computerized accounting program.

Develop certain categories (accounts) to make the task easier and more informative. For example, you can have a category called "food" for all food you

Here's a halfway goal for you: a half million. Save that much and you can get personal financial advice from Neuberger/Berman. Are you ready to get started?

THE FIRST HALF MILLION
IS THE HARDEST.

Once you have $500,000 to invest, you qualify for convenient asset management. Now you can let your money work for you.

Atlanta • Boston • Chicago • Dallas • Houston • Los Angeles • Miami • New York
Philadelphia • San Francisco • West Palm Beach
Private Asset Management | Trust Company Services

1-877-237-0052   NEUBERGER BERMAN   www.nb.com

The cross-referencing system refers students back to the page of the primary discussion and examples of all key concepts.

real-life situations. Don't skip the cases even if they're not reviewed in class. They're an integral part of the learning process because they enable you to think about and apply what you've studied.

9. *Cross-reference system.* Cross-reference citations refer you back to the primary discussion and examples of all key concepts. Specific page references are given each time key concepts appear after their original discussions. Going back to the pages referenced allows you to quickly review or study a concept in context in order to improve your comprehension of the material.

If you use the suggestions we've presented here, you will not simply "take a course in business." Instead, you will actively participate in a learning experience that will help you greatly in your chosen career. The most important secret to success may be to enjoy what you are doing and to do your best in everything. You can't do your best without taking advantage of all the learning aids that are available to you.

SURFING THE INTERNET

Never surfed the World Wide Web? Want to learn some basic tips? The purpose of this section is to help ease novices toward the on-ramp to the information superhighway. If you are an experienced Internet user, you may just want to skim this material for features you haven't used yet. The material is arranged in a question-and-answer format so that you can easily jump to a topic you would like to know more about. Don't worry if you have never so much as pressed an Enter key—we won't get too technical for you. You don't have to understand the technical complexities of the Internet to travel on the information superhighway. But, as in learning to drive, it's usually a good idea to learn where the gas goes.

Technology changes so quickly that writing about how to use the Internet is like washing the windows of the Empire State Building—as soon as you're finished it's time to start over again. For this reason we've tried to keep the discussion as general as possible and not give too many specific steps that may be out of date by the time you read this. The important thing to remember is that you can't break anything on the information superhighway, so just jump right in, explore the online world, and have fun!

WHAT IS THE INTERNET?

The **Internet** is a network of networks. It involves tens of thousands of interconnected computer networks that include millions of host computers. The Internet is certainly not new. The Pentagon began the network in 1969 when the world feared that a nuclear war would paralyze communications. The computer network was developed to reach far-flung terminals even if some connections were broken. The system took on a life of its own, however, and grew as scientists and other academics used it to share data and electronic mail. No one owns the Internet. There is no central computer; each message you send from your computer has an address code that lets any other computer on the Internet forward it to its destination. There is no Internet manager. The closest thing to a governing body is the Internet Society in Reston, Virginia. This is a volunteer organization of individuals and corporate members who promote Internet use and oversee development of new communication software. See Figure G.2 for a description of how the Internet works.

WHAT IS THE WORLD WIDE WEB, AND HOW IS IT DIFFERENT FROM THE INTERNET?

The World Wide Web (WWW, or the Web) is a means of accessing, organizing, and moving through the information in the Internet. Therefore, the Web is part

If even the idea of learning how to use the Internet is enough to make your head spin, relax. We'll show you how easy it is to use this powerful business tool. How can the Internet help you simplify many of our everyday tasks; such as, communicating with instructors and colleagues, gathering information, and shopping for supplies?

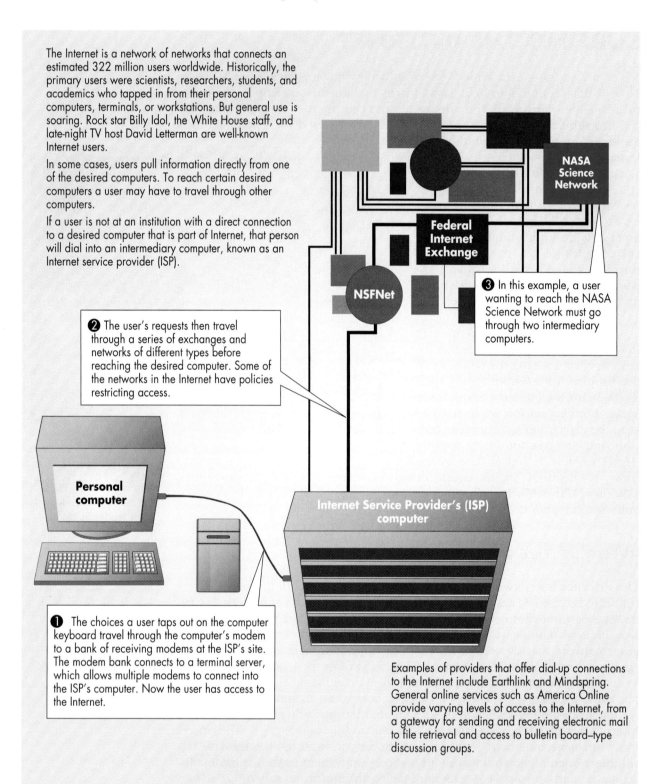

The Internet is a network of networks that connects an estimated 322 million users worldwide. Historically, the primary users were scientists, researchers, students, and academics who tapped in from their personal computers, terminals, or workstations. But general use is soaring. Rock star Billy Idol, the White House staff, and late-night TV host David Letterman are well-known Internet users.

In some cases, users pull information directly from one of the desired computers. To reach certain desired computers a user may have to travel through other computers.

If a user is not at an institution with a direct connection to a desired computer that is part of Internet, that person will dial into an intermediary computer, known as an Internet service provider (ISP).

NASA Science Network

Federal Internet Exchange

NSFNet

❸ In this example, a user wanting to reach the NASA Science Network must go through two intermediary computers.

❷ The user's requests then travel through a series of exchanges and networks of different types before reaching the desired computer. Some of the networks in the Internet have policies restricting access.

Personal computer

Internet Service Provider's (ISP) computer

❶ The choices a user taps out on the computer keyboard travel through the computer's modem to a bank of receiving modems at the ISP's site. The modem bank connects to a terminal server, which allows multiple modems to connect into the ISP's computer. Now the user has access to the Internet.

Examples of providers that offer dial-up connections to the Internet include Earthlink and Mindspring. General online services such as America Online provide varying levels of access to the Internet, from a gateway for sending and receiving electronic mail to file retrieval and access to bulletin board–type discussion groups.

FIGURE G.2

HOW THE INTERNET WORKS

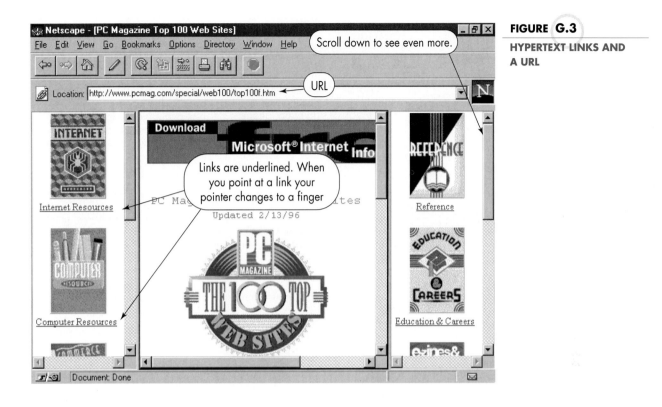

FIGURE G.3

HYPERTEXT LINKS AND
A URL

of the Internet. Think of the Internet as a gigantic library and the Web as the Dewey Decimal System. Until the creation of the World Wide Web in 1993, it was as though that gigantic library simply threw all of its books and other materials into mountainous piles. If you wanted to find something on the Internet, you needed to type in a complex code representing the exact address of the site you wanted.

The basic difficulty of navigating the Internet without the Web is twofold: (1) the traffic signs on the Internet are written in Unix, and (2) there is no defined structure for organizing information. Unix is an operating system that was designed long before anyone thought of the term *user-friendly*. And, since the Internet does not require a prescribed structure for entering information, even experienced users have difficulty retrieving information without a tool like the Web.

When the Web evolved, the game changed. Not only did the Web add graphics and sound, which breathed life into the dreary text-only Internet, but it also made navigating parts of the Internet easy even for beginners. Now Web cruisers don't need to know Unix in order to travel the Net. You can go from place to place on the Web simply by clicking on a word or a picture in a format called hypertext. Hypertext allows any part of any document to be linked to any other document, no matter where it is, allowing you to jump around from place to place with a click of the mouse. Hypertext links are usually shown in a contrasting color on the computer screen (see Figure G.3). *Cruising* or *surfing* means following hypertext links from page to page on the Web.

WHAT DO I NEED TO BE ABLE TO GET ON THE WEB?

The first thing you need in order to cruise the information superhighway is a computer with a modem (a device that connects your computer with other

	ADVANTAGES	DISADVANTAGES
Cable	• Theoretically, cable has the most bandwidth and therefore the fastest speed—as much as 100Mbps, compared to the mere 56k of traditional phone modems. • Uses same cable lines used to deliver TV. • Not limited by distance from a central office.	• Speed will decrease as more users sign up since all users on the network share the available bandwidth. • Not available in older, high-density areas (like cities), since it is expensive to dig up concrete to bury cables.
Digital subscriber line (DSL)	• Downloading speed can be as high as 7Mbps (most of the bandwidth is used for incoming data, with only a small amount used for outgoing). • Uses telephone lines already in place. • Can use the same phone line for voice even while you're online so there's no need for a separate phone line for computer connection.	• Limited to locations within 20,000 feet of telephone central office. • Good for downloading, but not for two-way communication like videoconferencing or Web hosting that requires the same bandwidth for incoming and outgoing data.
Satellite	• Download speed can be 400Kbps. Not nearly as fast as cable or DSL, but much better than the traditional 56Kbps.	• Most satellite services can only push data to you. Two-way services may be available by 2002. • Since data are beamed from a satellite in space, you need to place an 18-inch dish in the line of sight to the satellite. Weather conditions can affect reception.

computers via phone lines) and a Web browser. There are other ways to connect to the Internet (through special telephone lines, cable lines, or satellites), but until they become more widely available, many of us will use modems and standard phone lines to access the Net.

If cable Internet or digital subscriber line (DSL) service is available in your area, you may be interested in the comparison of these services that appears in Figure G.4. Keep in mind that your Internet connection is the pipeline used to move data to your computer. The bigger the pipe, the faster the flow. Whether your connection is by cable modem, telephone lines, DSL, satellite, or fixed wireless, the impact is much the same. Data can reach you more than 50 times as fast as with traditional 56k modems and normal phone lines (the kind that came with most computers in the late 1990s and early 2000s).[6]

Many schools offer students Internet service, so check out what is available at your school. You may have already paid computer-service fees that include Internet connection, so get your money's worth and get online now. If you can't connect through your school, you can connect to the Net by signing up with an Internet service provider (ISP). Your ISP will give you the phone number and a set of directions for connecting your computer to the Net. At this time, most ISPs provide unlimited access to the Internet for a flat monthly fee. Some ISPs offer "free" Internet access, but you must be willing to share private information about yourself and to give up a great deal of screen space to advertising messages.

What Is a Web Browser?

A Web browser is a program or application that provides you with a way to access the World Wide Web. The first graphical Web browser that allowed pointing and clicking was Mosaic, developed by Eric Bina and Marc Andreessen at the National Center for Supercomputing Applications. Andreessen, an undergraduate at the time, later went on to fame and fortune as the developer of Netscape Navigator. Mosaic was based on a code written by Tim Berners-Lee of CERN, the European laboratory for particle physics.

Which Is the Best Browser?

Currently, the two most popular Web browsers are Netscape Navigator and Microsoft Internet Explorer. At the time of this writing, the best browser is the one you have access to—in other words, neither one has a clear advantage over the other. The case may be different by the time you read this. If we had to predict the future, we would have to say that both Netscape and Microsoft will continue to improve their browsers to compete with each other and that Web users will benefit from the competition as the browsers become more powerful and easier to use.

WHERE DO I GO WHEN I CLICK ON SOMETHING?

When you're navigating the Net, you can go from a Web page in Paris to one in Peru. What happens? When you click on a link, your computer sends out a request for information to another server. That server, which may be next door or across the planet, interprets your request, finds the information (text, graphics, or entire Web pages), and then breaks it up into packets. The server sends the packets to your computer, where your browser puts them back together and you see the Web page, all in the blink of an eye (or an eternity—they don't call it the World Wide Wait for nothing).

Why Does It Take So Long to Move from One Place to Another on the Web?

The speed with which you reach other Internet sites depends not only on the speed and size of your phone line and computer but also on the speed and size of phone lines and computers at the other site. You won't get to class any faster in a Ferrari than in a bus if you're locked in a traffic jam. The same is true on the information superhighway. Sometimes your computer will seem to take forever to get to a site or to open an image. If this happens, you can click the Stop button on your menu bar and try again later when the Internet may be less busy.

WHY WOULD I WANT TO SURF THE INTERNET?

You can use the Internet to:

- *Communicate online.* You can communicate with others through the following:
    Newsgroups. These are special-interest groups in which you can get advice or just share thoughts with people.

    Electronic mail (e-mail). E-mail lets you stay in touch with friends, trade files, and do business, all from the comfort of your computer desktop.

Internet relay chat (IRC). IRCs allow you to chat with other people all over the world in real time (that is, talk with someone else while you are both on the line rather than send messages that are read later). Live and uncensored, IRC can sometimes sound like a junior high school boys' locker room, so choose your chats wisely.

Each of these is discussed in more detail in the pages that follow.

- *Gather information.* Internet users can tap into such diverse institutions as the Federal Reserve and the Library of Congress. Some websites offer news headlines, stock market information, access to encyclopedias, and other databases. Search engines can help you find the sites that have the information you need. There are special websites that offer push technology that makes gathering information automatic: After you tell it what you are interested in, the program searches the Web periodically and then pushes the information to you without your having to ask for it.

- *Shop.* Forgot your mom's birthday? No problem. Get online and order roses to be delivered to her door before she disinherits you. Or, if things get too bad, book a flight out of town with a few mouse clicks and a credit card number. Note, however, that credit card security is a concern that is getting lots of attention as more and more businesses open their doors to customers on the Internet.

- *Play games (after you finish studying, of course).* You can play games against another person or against the computer while you're online.

Do I Have to Be a Computer Major to Surf the Web?

There are only four simple things you need to know about to navigate the Web: (1) Web addresses, (2) directories and search engines, (3) links, and (4) the Back Page button.

What Are Web Addresses?

Every website has an address called a uniform resource locator (URL). Go back to Figure G.3 and look at the top of the browser window. See the line that starts with http://? That's the URL for the page. To get to any website, you just type its address in the space for the URL entry in your Web browser. This means, of course, that you know the exact URL. It is important to know that the Web is constantly evolving and therefore URLs often change as new sites are added and old ones dropped. Sometimes a new URL is supplied when you visit an old site, but often it is not, in which case you reach a dead end.

What If I Don't Know Which Site I Need, Much Less Its URL?

To find topics that interest you, you can use one of several Web directories or search engines. Once you are at the search engine's home page, all you have to do is to enter the key words for the topic you want and you will quickly receive a list of links to sites related to your request. Some of the most popular directories and search engines are Yahoo!, Infoseek, Lycos, Alta Vista, Excite, Dogpile, Google, and WebCrawler.

You'll always get better results from a search engine if you define what you're searching for as specifically as possible. The two easiest ways to narrow your search are by adding and subtracting terms from your search string. Let's say you want to buy a new stereo and you aren't sure which brands have the best sound. If you search Yahoo! for "stereo," you may get back 654 (or more) site matches. However, you can focus the search a little more by adding another search word. Just typing in the word itself isn't good enough, though. In order to receive only sites that contain both stereo and the other word, you have to use the word *and* to link them. If you search for "and review" you get eight matches—all sites that review stereo equipment.

If adding search items doesn't narrow the field enough, try subtracting them—tell the search engine what *not* to look for. Say you're looking for business opportunities. You search for "business and opportunity" and get overwhelmed by more than 2,500 site matches, most of which are Amway-type, multilevel marketing operations (commonly known as MLMs). You can narrow your search by asking for these items to be excluded. For example, use the word *not* instead of *and*. This time you search for "business and opportunity not mlm" and get just seven items back.

A third way to define your search more closely is to put your search term in quotes. That tells the search engine that you're looking for exactly those words in exactly that order.

Don't worry about remembering all these surfing tips. Most search engines have an Advanced Options menu that lists ways to search using a form. Also, many search engines offer specific instructions on how to make the most of your search on their site.

If you try different search engines to look for the same topic, you'll get different results. That's because the search engines are different. Each search engine uses its own program (called a bot or crawler) to search the Web. Not only do these programs use different methods of searching and indexing, but they start from different points on the Web. You probably will also get different results if you search on a directory rather than a search engine, again because of the different approach to indexing sites. You can search on multiple search engines all at once by using a metasearch engine such as WebCrawler or Dogpile. MetaCrawler returns answers to queries from nine popular search engines, 10 search channels, forums, and links to major e-commerce sites. Dogpile returns query results from other Web search engines, Usenet, and file transfer protocol (ftp) sites. It also supplies stock quotes and news from wire services.

America Online (AOL) is one of the United States most popular Internet Service Providers (ISP). One reason for this is that AOL provides a simple point-and-click method of finding information that has been organized in specific channels. Why do you think AOL is particularly attractive to new Internet users?

What Do I Need to Know about Links?

Once you're at a site, the two main ways to cruise around are by clicking on an icon button link or on a text link. One way to tell if something is a link is to place your cursor over the graphic icon or text. If it changes into a hand, then you know it is a live link. When you click on a link, you will be sent to another website or to another page on the current website.

What If I Want to Get Back to Someplace I've Been?

If you want to go back to a site you have left recently, you can just click on the Back Page button in your browser. This will lead you back through the exact same page route you traveled before. Or you can enter the desired site's URL. If you are on the same website, you can choose the home page link or one of the section icons to take you back to the home page or another section.

How Can I Communicate with Others Online?

You can reach out and touch your fellow Internet surfers via newsgroups, e-mail, or an IRC.

What Are Newsgroups?

The Usenet is a global network of discussion groups known as newsgroups. Newsgroups are collections of messages from people all over the world on any subject you can imagine (and some you'd rather not imagine). Newsgroups are divided into categories indicated by the first letters of their name. There are many different category prefixes, but the main ones you will see are comp (computer), sci (science), rec (recreation), soc (society), and alt (alternative). Under these headings are thousands of subcategories from alt.alien.visitors to za.humour.

How Do I Join a Newsgroup?

Web browsers have built-in newsreading capabilities. You first need to go to the Mail and News options menu and enter your server information, which is usually something like "news.myserver.com" (contact your Internet service provider to find out exactly what it is). There are also options for organizing how you read your messages. Some people like their messages "threaded" (meaning all postings on a particular topic are grouped together), while others prefer to sort their messages by date.

When you find a group you like, don't jump into the conversation right away. Take time to read the frequently asked questions (FAQ) list for that group first. The FAQ list includes the questions that most newcomers ask. After you

Web browsers, like the one for AOL shown here, offer advice to newsgroup newbies (new users). Notice that AOL suggests that you begin by reading netiquette hints so that you mind your online manners and don't jump into newsgroups on the wrong foot.

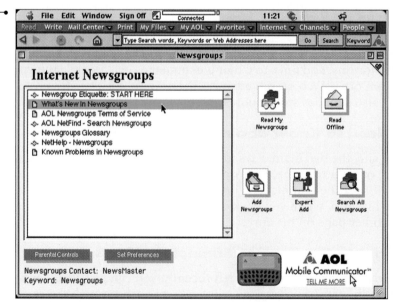

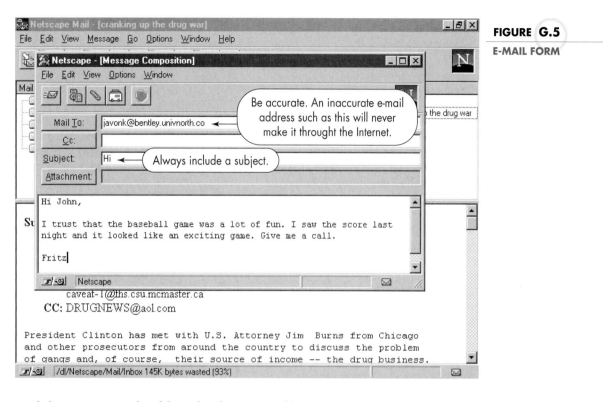

read the FAQs, you should read at least a week's worth of postings to get a feel for the group and what kinds of discussions its members have. Remember, you may be joining discussions that have been going on for a year or more, so you may feel like the new kid on the block for a while. But most newsgroups are quite friendly if you use basic netiquette.

How Do I Send E-Mail?

As with "snail mail," or letters delivered by the U.S. postal system, e-mail is delivered to its recipient by an address. An Internet e-mail address has two parts: the user name and the name of the computer on which that user has an account. For example, Professor Ulysses R. Smart's e-mail address at Ignatius Quinius University may be ursmart@iqu.edu. The symbol "@" is pronounced "at." The suffix ".edu" indicates that the address is one of an educational institution.

There are several e-mail software packages available. Netscape and Internet Explorer include e-mail capabilities. To compose a message, click on the Mail button (see Figure G.5). Enter the e-mail address of the person to whom you are writing in the *To:* field. Enter the subject of your message in the *Subject:* field. If you want others to receive the message, enter their e-mail addresses in the *CC:* field and separate each e-mail address with a comma. Next, enter the body of the message in the large space. When you have completed your message, click on the Send button. To check for new messages received, simply click on the Get Mail button. If you have received new mail, the subject and sender will be displayed in a window. Click on a message to display its contents.

You can also send files with your e-mail. To send files from a graphics program or word processor, simply choose *attach file* and navigate your hard drive to find the file you want to send. Before you send an attached file, make sure that the person you are sending it to can receive it. Some people have slow connections that come to a near halt if their system receives a large attachment. Others have mailboxes that fill too quickly if they receive a number of large files. So always ask before the first time you send someone attachments.

One of the more interesting ways to take advantage of e-mail is to join one or more mailing lists (or listservs, to use the technical term).

What Are Listservs?

Listservs, or mailing lists, are similar to Usenet newsgroups. Unlike newsgroups, though, listserv discussions are delivered to your in-box as e-mail, and responding is as easy as punching your Reply button (which sends the message to everyone on the mailing list). To find a mailing list that piques your interest, try the mailing list directory Listz at www.listz.com. Be careful, though; mailing lists can quickly jam your in-box.

What Is IRC?

Internet relay chat (IRC) is an Internet protocol that allows you to have real-time conversations with other people around the world. As with newsgroups, it's best at first to observe, or "lurk," and see how the others on the IRC channel interact. To use an IRC channel you must have a chat "client" or program. The two most popular freeware chat clients are PIRCH for Windows and Ircle for the Mac. DalNet is one of the largest IRC networks. DalNet offers extensive information on IRC and how to use it.

The first step is to connect to a server. Then choose a nickname, join a room (or "channel"), and start lurking away. All IRC channels start with the number sign (#), and most servers have a channel called #newbie where you can ease into the swing of things.

Not all IRC is idle chat. Many people have discovered ways to use IRC to help one another by developing virtual support groups online. Talk City is one example of an online community that uses IRC as a vehicle for people to draw support in a safe and friendly environment.

Although IRC is one of the most popular uses for the Internet, it could easily be replaced by Internet phones, or more advanced Web chat, like America Online's Virtual Places (VP). VP's attraction is that you create an on-screen avatar, or 3-D representation of yourself. Then you can go to designated Web pages and chat with other people who have VP.

Visit our website at www.mhhe.com/ub6e and look for online help in understanding the concepts you'll be reading about in this text. If you like, send us an e-mail message letting us know what you like about the book and the website. If there is something you think we should change, let us know that too!

WHERE CAN I GO TO LEARN MORE ABOUT THE WEB?

The best way to learn how to do something is by doing it, so the best place to learn about the Web is on the Web. It's time for you to put the pedal to the metal and get yourself onto the information superhighway. The following websites can help you learn more about the Web:

Learn the Net: *www.learnthenet.com*

Learning to Use the Internet: *www.webliminal.com/lrn-net.html*

Oprah Goes Online: *www.oprah-goesonline.com/learn/index.html*

GETTING THE JOB YOU WANT

One of the more important objectives of this text is to help you get the job that you want. First, you have to decide what you want to do. We'll help you explore this decision by explaining what people do in the various business functions: accounting, marketing, human resource management, finance, and so on. There are many good books about finding the job you want, so we can only introduce the subject here to get you thinking about careers as you read the various chapters.

If you are a returning student, you have blessings and handicaps that younger students do not have. First of all, you may have had a full-time job already. You are more likely to know what kind of job you *don't* want. That is a real advantage. By exploring the various business careers in depth, you should be able to choose a career path that will meet your objectives. If you have a full-time job right now, you've already discovered that working while going to school is exhausting. Many older students must juggle family responsibilities in addition to the responsibilities of school and work. But take heart. You have also acquired many skills from these experiences. Even if they were acquired in unrelated fields, these skills will be invaluable as you enter your new career. You should have no trouble competing with younger students because you have more focus and experience. We enjoy having both kinds of students in class because of the different perspectives they have.

So, whether you're beginning your first career or your latest career, it's time to develop a strategy for finding and obtaining a personally satisfying job.

In addition to all of the resources shown here, you can find help with your career search online by clicking to websites such as www.monster.com and www.careerpath.com. Such sites list companies currently looking for workers, offer help in creating a résumé, and provide many additional kinds of advice on conducting a job search.

JOB SEARCH STRATEGY

It is never too early to begin thinking about a future career or careers. The following strategies will give you some guidance in that pursuit:

1. *Begin with self-analysis.* You might begin your career quest by completing a self-analysis inventory. You can refer to Figure G.6 for a sample of a simple assessment.

2. *Search for jobs you would enjoy.* Begin at your college's career planning office or placement office, if your school has one. Keep interviewing people in various careers, even after you've found a job. Career progress demands continuous research.

3. *Begin the networking process.* You can start with your fellow students, family, relatives, neighbors, friends, professors, and local businesspeople. Be sure to keep a file with the names, addresses, and phone numbers of contacts—where they work, the person who recommended them to you, and the relationship between the source person and the contact. A great way to make contacts and a good impression on employers is to do part-time work and summer internships at those firms you find interesting.

Interests

1. How do I like to spend my time?
2. Do I enjoy being with people?
3. Do I like working with mechanical things?
4. Do I enjoy working with numbers?
5. Am I a member of many organizations?
6. Do I enjoy physical activities?
7. Do I like to read?

Abilities

1. Am I adept at working with numbers?
2. Am I adept at working with mechanical things?
3. Do I have good verbal and written communication skills?
4. What special talents do I have?
5. In which abilities do I wish I were more adept?

Education

1. Have I taken certain courses that have prepared me for a particular job?
2. In which subjects did I perform the best? The worst?
3. Which subjects did I enjoy the most? The least?
4. How have my extracurricular activities prepared me for a particular job?
5. Is my GPA an accurate picture of my academic ability? Why?
6. Do I want a graduate degree? Do I want to earn it before beginning my job?
7. Why did I choose my major?

Experience

1. What previous jobs have I held? What were my responsibilities in each?
2. Were any of my jobs applicable to positions I may be seeking? How?
3. What did I like the most about my previous jobs? Like the least?
4. Why did I work in the jobs I did?

5. If I had it to do over again, would I work in these jobs? Why?

Personality

1. What are my good and bad traits?
2. Am I competitive?
3. Do I work well with others?
4. Am I outspoken?
5. Am I a leader or a follower?
6. Do I work well under pressure?
7. Do I work quickly, or am I methodical?
8. Do I get along well with others?
9. Am I ambitious?
10. Do I work well independently of others?

Desired job enviornment

1. Am I willing to relocate? Why?
2. Do I have a geographic preference? Why?
3. Would I mind traveling in my job?
4. Do I have to work for a large, nationally known firm to be satisfied?
5. Must I have a job that initially offers a high salary?
6. Must the job I assume offer rapid promotion opportunities?
7. In what kind of job environment would I feel most comfortable?
8. If I could design my own job, what characteristics would it have?

Personal goals

1. What are my short- and long-term goals? Why?
2. Am I career-oriented, or do I have broader interests?
3. What are my career goals?
4. What jobs are likely to help me achieve my goals?
5. What do I hope to be doing in 5 years? In 10 years?
6. What do I want out of life?

FIGURE G.6

A PERSONAL ASSESSMENT

4. *Go to the Internet for help.* You will find details about finding jobs on a variety of websites. Many of these sites can help you write your résumé as well as help you search for jobs that meet your interests and skills. Later we'll list a number of these sites.

5. *Prepare a good cover letter and résumé.* Once you know what you want to do and where you would like to work, you need to develop a good résumé and cover letter. Your résumé lists your education, work

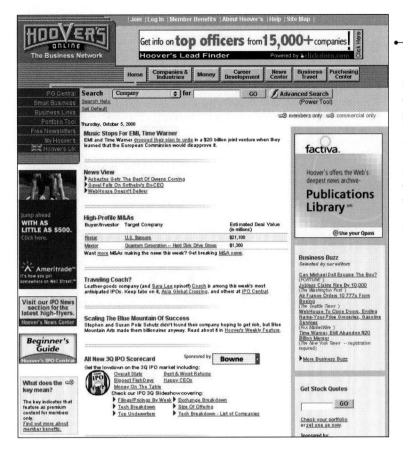

experience, and activities. We'll talk about these key job search tools in more detail.

6. *Develop interviewing skills.* Interviewers will be checking your appearance (clothes, haircut, fingernails, shoes); your attitude (friendliness is desired); your verbal ability (speak loud enough to be heard clearly); and your motivation (be enthusiastic). Note also that interviewers want you to have been active in clubs and activities and to have set goals. Have someone evaluate you on these scales now to see if you have any weak points. You can then work on those points before you have any actual job interviews. We'll give you some clues as to how to do this later.

7. *Follow up.* Write a thank-you note after interviews, even if you think they didn't go well. You have a chance to make a lasting impression with a follow-up note.[7] Keep in touch with companies in which you have an interest. Show your interest by calling periodically or sending e-mail and letting the company know you are still interested. Indicate your willingness to travel to various parts of the country or the world to be interviewed. Get to know people in the company and learn from them whom to contact and what qualifications to emphasize.

MORE HINTS ON THE JOB SEARCH

The placement bureau at your school is a good place to begin reading about potential employers. On-campus interviewing is by far the number one source of jobs (see Figure G.7). Another good source of jobs involves writing to compa-

WHERE COLLEGE STUDENTS FIND JOBS

SOURCE OF JOB	PERCENTAGE OF NEW EMPLOYEES
On-campus interviewing	49.3%
Write-ins	9.8
Current employee referrals	7.2
Job listings with placement office	6.5
Responses from want ads	5.6
Walk-ins	5.5
Cooperative education programs	4.8
Summer employment	4.7
College faculty/staff referrals	4.5
Internship programs	4.5
High-demand major programs	4.4
Minority career programs	2.9
Part-time employment	2.4
Unsolicited referrals from placement	2.1
Women's career programs	2.1
Job listings with employment agencies	1.9
Referrals from campus organizations	1.8

nies and sending a good cover letter and résumé. You can identify companies to contact in your library or on the Internet. Check such sources as the *Million Dollar Directory* or the *Standard Directory of Advertisers*. Your library and the Internet may also have annual reports that will give you even more information about your selected companies.

A very important source of jobs is networking, that is, finding someone in a firm to recommend you. You find those people by asking friends, neighbors, family members, and others if they know anyone who knows someone, and then you track those people down, talk with them, and seek their recommendation.

Other good sources of jobs include the want ads, job fairs, summer and other internship programs, placement bureaus, and sometimes walking into firms that appeal to you and asking for an interview. The *Occupational Outlook Quarterly*, produced by the U.S. Department of Labor, says this about job hunting:

> *The skills that make a person employable are not so much the ones needed on the job as the ones needed to get the job, skills like the ability to find a job opening, complete an application, prepare the résumé, and survive an interview.*

Here are a few printed sources you can use for finding out about jobs and other career choices:

Les Krantz, *Jobs Rated Almanac 2001* (New York: St. Martin's Press, 2001).

America's Top Jobs for College Graduates (Indianapolis, IN: JIST Publishing, 2001).

The Big Book of Jobs, 2000–2001 Edition, (Lincolnwood, IL: VGM Career Books, 2000).

Steven Graber and Mark Lipsman, *The Everything Get-A-Job Book: From Resume Writing to Interviewing to Finding Tons of Job Openings* (Holbrook, MA: Adams Media Corporation, 2000).

John W. Wright, *The American Almanac of Jobs and Salaries* (New York: Avon Books, 2000–2001 edition).

Travel services and tourism represent the largest nongovernmental industry in the United States. As the population of the United States ages and more and more people are retired, there will be greater demand for recreation, travel, and tourism services. Have you given any thought to working in such a diverse field? What types of career preparation would be desirable or necessary?

Richard Nelson Bolles, *What Color Is Your Parachute?* (Berkeley, CA: Ten Speed Press, 2001 edition).

Eric Schlesinger and Susan Musich, *E-Job Hunting*, Indianapolis, IN: SAMS, 2001.)

Ronald A. Reis, *The Everything Hot Careers Book* (Holbrook, MA: Adams Media Corporation, 2001).

Martin Gate, *Knock 'Em Dead 2001* (Holbrook, MA: Adams Media Corporation, 2001).

Mary B. Nemnich and Fred E. Jandt, *Cyberspace Job Search Kit, 2001–2002 Edition* (Indianapolis, IN: JIST Publishing, 2001).

Jean Erickson Walker, *The Age Advantage: Making the Most of Your Midlife Career Transition* (New York, The Berkeley Publishing Group, 2000).

Wendy S. Enelow and Louise Kursmark, *Cover Letter Magic* (Indianapolis, IN: JIST Publishing, 2001).

David F. Noble, *Gallery of Best Resumes* (Indianapolis, IN: JIST Publishing, 2001).

Ron Fry, *101 Great Answers to the Toughest Interview Questions* (Franklin Lakes, N.J.: Career Press, 2000).

The latest figures for Internet recruiting are not yet available, but the Net is becoming a great place to find jobs. To find information about careers or internships try these sites (though keep in mind that addresses on the Internet are subject to sudden and frequent change):

JobDirect: www.jobdirect.com

Jobtrak: www.jobtrak.com

CareerPath: www.careerpath.com

Hoovers: www.hoovers.com

Monster: www.monster.com

CareerMosaic: www.careermosaic.com

America's Job Bank: www.ajb.dni.us

Yahoo! Classifieds: www.classifieds.yahoo.com

Student Advantage: www.studentadvantage.com

Self-Directed Search: www.self-directed-search.com.

National Assembly of Voluntary Health and Social Welfare Organizations: www.nassembly.org

It's never too early in your career to begin designing a résumé and thinking of cover letters. Preparing such documents reveals your strengths and weaknesses more clearly than most other techniques. By preparing a résumé now, you may discover that you haven't been involved in enough outside activities to impress an employer. That information may prompt you to join some student groups, to become a volunteer, or to otherwise enhance your social skills.

You may also discover that you're weak on experience, and seek an internship or part-time job to fill in that gap. In any event, it's not too soon to prepare a résumé. It will certainly help you decide what you'd like to see in the area marked Education and, if you haven't already done so, help you choose a major and other coursework. Given that background, let's discuss how to prepare these materials.

WRITING YOUR RÉSUMÉ

A résumé is a document that lists information an employer would need to evaluate you and your background. It explains your immediate goals and career objectives. This information is followed by an explanation of your educational background, experience, interests, and other relevant data. Be sure to use industry buzzwords in your résumé (see Figure G.8) because companies use key words to scan such résumés. Having experience working in teams, for example, is important to many companies. For online résumé help, go to http://members.xoom.com/worksearch/reswri.htm.

If you have exceptional abilities but your résumé doesn't communicate them to the employer, those abilities aren't part of the person he or she will

Managed	Wrote	Budgeted	Improved
Planned	Produced	Designed	Increased
Organized	Scheduled	Directed	Investigated
Coordinated	Operated	Developed	Teamed
Supervised	Conducted	Established	Served
Trained	Administered	Implemented	Handled

FIGURE G.8

SAMPLE ACTION WORDS

evaluate. You must be comprehensive and clear in your résumé if you are to communicate all your attributes.

Your résumé is an advertisement for yourself. If your ad is better than the other person's ad, you're more likely to get the interview. In this case, "better" means that your ad highlights your attributes attractively. In discussing your education, for example, be sure to highlight your extracurricular activities such as part-time jobs, sports, clubs, and other such activities. If you did well in school, include your grades. The idea is to make yourself look as good on paper as you are in reality.

The same is true for your job experience. Be sure to describe what you did, any special projects in which you participated, and any responsibilities you had. For the interests section, if you include one, don't just list your interests but describe how deeply you were involved. If you organized the club, volunteered your time, or participated more often than usual in an organization, make sure to say so in the résumé. See Figure G.9 for a sample résumé. Most companies prefer that you keep your résumé to one page unless you have many years of experience.

PUTTING YOUR RÉSUMÉ ON THE INTERNET

You will probably want to post your résumé on the Internet because many larger firms are seeking candidates on the Net. An Internet résumé is different from a standard one because the elimination process is done by computer. Thus, you must understand what the computer is programmed to look for. It wants nouns, not verbs. Whereas the traditional résumé is built on verbs like *managed* and *supervised*, résumés on the Internet are built around nouns like *program management* and *teams*. They also emphasize software programs you have mastered like Microsoft Word. Listing jobs chronologically is no longer the best thing to do. Instead, emphasize knowledge, skills, and abilities. At the beginning of your résumé or after "Experience," you may write a new section called "Key Skills" or "Functional Expertise" and list all the nouns that fit your experience. For example, a salesperson might put terms that apply to selling such as *prospect, approach, presentations, close sale, follow up, focus groups, service.*

Zalee Harris lost her job just before Christmas but didn't bother going to the company's outplacement service or to the Help Wanted section of the newspaper. Instead, she built her own Web page on the Internet, complete with résumé and statement of purpose. She registered the address in search engines such as Yahoo and WebCrawler. In all, she posted her résumé on some 30 Internet job boards. In just over a month, she received 50 inquiries and found the job she wanted.[8] Harris represents the job candidate of the future, one who is Internet savvy and knows what she wants. One of the experts in this area says

Yann Ng
345 Big Bend Boulevard
Kirkwood, Missouri, 63122
314-555-5385
YNG@AOL.COM

Job objective: Sales representative in business-to-business marketing

Education:

St. Louis Community College at Meramec
A.A. in Business (3.6 grade point average)
Served on Student Representative Board

University of Missouri, St. Louis
B.S. in Business: Marketing major (3.2 grade point average, 3.5 in major)
Earned 100 percent of college expenses working 35 hours a week.
Member of Student American Marketing Association
Vice President of Student Government Association
Dean's List for two semesters

Work experience:
Schnuck's Supermarket: Worked checkout evenings and weekends for four years while in school. Learned to respond to customer requests quickly, and communicate with customers in a friendly and helpful manner.

Mary Tuttle's Flowers: For two summers, made flower arrangements, managed sales transactions, and acted as assistant to the manager. Also trained and supervised three employees. Often handled customer inquiries and complaints.

Special skills:
Fluent in Vietnamese, French, and English. Proficient at using WordPerfect and Word. Developed my own website (www.yan@stilnet.com) and use the Internet often to do research for papers and for personal interests.

Other interests:
Cooking: often prepare meals for my family and friends. Reading, especially the classics. Piano playing and aerobics. Traveling: Asia, Europe, and America. Doing research on the Internet.

that the best search engine is www.metacrawler.com because it sends queries to a number of search engines simultaneously.

From a company perspective, finding people on the Internet is a lot less expensive than hiring professional recruiters. Because more and more companies are using the Internet to find employees, it would be prudent for you to learn how to use this modern way to find jobs. Here are some hints on preparing your résumé for the Internet:

- Keep it simple. Use text only. Put a summary of your skills and your objective at the top so that the reader can capture as much as possible in the first 30 seconds.

- If you e-mail your résumé, send it in the text of the message: Don't put it as an attachment. It takes too long for the receiver to open an attachment.

Yann Ng
345 Big Bend Boulevard
Kirkwood, Missouri, 63122
314-555-5385
YNG@AOL.COM

Job objective: Sales representative in business-to-business marketing

Education:
St. Louis Community College at Meramec
A.A. in Business (3.6 grade point average)
Service on Student Representative Board
Courses included introduction to business, accounting, and marketing.

University of Missouri, St. Louis
B.S. in Business: Marketing major (3.2. grade point average, 3.5 in major)
Earned 100 percent of college expenses working 35 hours a week.
Member of Student American Marketing Association
Vice President of Student Government Association
Dean's List for two semesters

Work experience:
Schnuck's Supermarket: Worked checkout evenings and weekends for four
years while in school. Learned to respond to customer requests quickly, and
communicate with customers in a friendly and helpful manner.

Mary Tuttle's Flowers: For two summers, made flower arrangements, managed
sales transactions, and acted as assistant to the manager. Also trained and
supervised three employees. Often handled customer inquiries and complaints.

Special skills: Fluent in Vietnamese, French, and English. Proficient at using
MS Word 2000, MS Excel 2000, and MS PowerPoint 2000. Developed my own
website (www.yan@stilnet.com) and use the Internet often to do research for
papers and for personal interests. Sales skills include conducting focus groups,
prospecting, making presentations, and customer service.

Other interests: Cooking: often prepare meals for my family and friends.
Reading, especially the classics. Piano playing and aerobics. Traveling: Asia,
Europe, and America. Doing research on the Internet.

- Customize each mailing to that specific company. You may use a standard résumé, but add data to customize it and to introduce it.
- Put your cover letter and résumé in one file.
- Use any advertised job title as the subject of your e-mail message, citing any relevant job numbers. (Note that some companies don't want you to e-mail them your résumé and cover letter, preferring letters or faxes instead.)

You can find more details about applying for jobs on the Internet in Margaret Riley Dikel and Frances E. Roehm's 2000–2001 edition of *The Guide to Internet Job Searching* from VGM Career Horizons. See Figure G.10 for a sample Internet résumé.

WRITING A COVER LETTER

A cover letter is used to announce your availability and to introduce the résumé. The cover letter is probably one of the most important advertisements anyone will write in a lifetime—so it should be done right.

First, the cover letter should indicate that you've researched the organization in question and are interested in a job there. Let the organization know what sources you used and what you know about it in the first paragraph to get the attention of the reader and show your interest.

You may have heard people say, "It's not what you know, but whom you know that counts." This is only partly true—because both knowledge and personal contacts are necessary—but it's important nonetheless. If you don't know someone, you can get to know someone. You do this by calling the organization (or better yet, visiting its offices) and talking to people who already have the kind of job you're hoping to get. Ask about training, salary, and other relevant issues. Then, in your cover letter, mention that you've talked with some of the firm's employees and that this discussion increased your interest. You thereby show the letter reader that you "know someone," if only casually, and that you're interested enough to actively pursue the organization. This is all part of networking.

Second, in the description of yourself, be sure to say how your attributes will benefit the organization. For example, don't just say, "I will be graduating with a degree in marketing." Say, "You will find that my college training in marketing and marketing research has prepared me to learn your marketing system quickly and begin making a contribution right away." The sample cover letter in Figure G.11 will give you a better feel for how this looks.

Third, be sure to "ask for the order." That is, say in your final paragraph that you're available for an interview at a time and place convenient for the interviewer. Again, see the sample cover letter in Figure G.11 for guidance. Notice in this letter how Yann subtly showed that she read business publications and drew attention to her résumé.

Principles to follow in writing a cover letter and preparing your résumé include the following:

- Be self-confident. List all your good qualities and attributes.
- Don't be apologetic or negative. Write as one professional to another, not as a humble student begging for a job.
- Describe how your experience and education can add value to the organization.
- Research every prospective employer thoroughly before writing anything. Use a rifle approach rather than a shotgun approach. That is, write effective marketing-oriented letters to a few select companies rather than to a general list.
- Have your materials prepared by an experienced keyboarder if you are not highly skilled yourself. If you have access to a word processing system with a letter-quality laser printer, you can produce individualized letters efficiently.
- Have someone edit your materials for spelling, grammar, and style. Don't be like the student who sent out a second résumé to correct "some mixtakes." Or another who said, "I am acurite with numbers."
- Don't send the names of references until asked.

345 Big Bend Blvd.
Kirkwood, MO 63122
October 10, 2001

Mr. Carl Karlinski
Premier Designs
45 Apple Court
Chicago, Illinois 60536

Dear Mr. Karlinski: [Note that it's best to know whom to write by name.]
  Recent articles in *Inc.* and *Success* have praised your company for its innovative products and strong customer orientation. I'm familiar with your creative display materials. In fact, we've used them at Mary Tuttle's Flower Shop—my employer for the last two summers. Christie Bouchard, your local sales representative told me all about your products and your training program at Premier Designs.
  Christie mentioned the kind of salespeople you are seeking. Here's what she said and my qualifications.
  Requirement: Men and women with proven sales ability.
  Qualifications: Success making and selling flower arrangements at Mary Tuttle's and practicing customer relations at Schnuck's Supermarket. As you know, Schnuck's has one of the best customer-oriented training programs in the food industry.
  Requirement: Self-motivated people with leadership ability.
  Qualifications: Paid my way through college working nights and summers. Selected to be on the Student Representative Board at St. Louis Community College at Meramec and active in student government at the University of Missouri. Paid my own way to Asia, Europe, and the Americas.
  Could you use such a successful salesperson at Premier Designs? I will be in the Chicago area the week of January 4–9. What time and date would be most convenient for us to discuss career opportunities at Premier? I'll phone your secretary to set up an appointment.

Sincerely,

Yann Ng

PREPARING FOR JOB INTERVIEWS

Companies usually don't conduct job interviews unless they're somewhat certain that the candidate has the requirements for the job. The interview, therefore, is pretty much a make-or-break situation. If it goes well, you have a greater chance of being hired. That's why you must be prepared for your interviews. There are five stages of interview preparation:

1. *Do research about the prospective employers.* Learn what industry the firm is in, its competitors, the products or services it produces and their acceptance in the market, and the title of your desired position. You can

- How would you describe yourself?
- What are your greatest strengths and weaknesses?
- How did you choose this company?
- What do you know about the company?
- What are your long-range career goals?
- What courses did you like best? Least?
- What are your hobbies?
- Do you prefer a specific geographic location?

- Are you willing to travel (or move)?
- Which accomplishments have given you the most satisfaction?
- What things are most important to you in a job?
- Why should I hire you?
- What experience have you had in this type of work?
- How much do you expect to earn?

FIGURE G.12

FREQUENTLY ASKED QUESTIONS

find such information in the firm's annual reports, in Standard & Poor's, Moody's manuals, and various business publications such as *Fortune, Business Week,* and *Forbes.* Ask your librarian for help or search the Internet. You can look in the *Reader's Guide to Business Literature* to locate the company name and to look for articles about it. This important first step shows you have initiative and interest in the firm.

2. *Practice the interview.* Figure G.12 lists some of the more frequently asked questions in an interview. Practice answering these questions and more at the placement office and with your roommate, parents, or friends. Don't memorize your answers, but be prepared—know what you're going to say. Also, develop a series of questions to ask the interviewer. Figure G.13 shows sample questions you might ask. Be sure you know whom to contact, and write down the names of everyone you meet. Review the action words in Figure G.8 and try to fit them into your answers.

3. *Be professional during the interview.* You should look and sound professional throughout the interview. Do your homework and find out how managers dress at the firm. Make sure you wear an appropriate outfit. When you meet the interviewers, greet them by name, smile, and maintain good eye contact. Sit up straight in your chair and be alert and enthusiastic. If you have practiced, you should be able to relax and be confident. Other than that, be yourself, answer questions, and be friendly and responsive. When you leave, thank the interviewers and, if you're still interested in the job, tell them so. If they don't tell you, ask

FIGURE G.13

SAMPLE QUESTIONS TO ASK THE INTERVIEWER

- Who are your major competitors, and how would you rate their products and marketing relative to yours?
- How long does the training program last, and what is included?
- How soon after school would I be expected to start?
- What are the advantages of working for this firm?
- How much travel is normally expected?
- What managerial style should I expect in my area?
- How would you describe the working environment in my area?

- How would I be evaluated?
- What is the company's promotion policy?
- What is the corporate culture?
- What is the next step in the selection procedures?
- How soon should I expect to hear from you?
- What other information would you like about my background, experience, or education?
- What is your highest priority in the next six months and how could someone like me help?

1. **Ability to communicate.** Do yo have the ability to organize your thoughts and ideas effectively? Can you express them clearly when speaking or writing? Can you present your ideas to others in a persuasive way?

2. **Intelligence.** Do you have the ability to understand the job assignment? Learn the details of operation? Contribute original ideas to your work?

3. **Self-confidence.** Do you demonstrate a sense of maturity that enables you to deal positively and effectively with situations and people?

4. **Willingness to accept responsibility.** Are you someone who recognizes what needs to be done and is willing to do it?

5. **Initiative.** Do you have the ability to identify the purpose for work and to take action?

6. **Leadership.** Can you guide and direct others to obtain the recognized objectives?

7. **Energy level.** Do you demonstrate a forcefulness and capacity to make things move ahead? Can you maintain your work effort at an above-average rate?

8. **Imagination.** Can you confront and deal with problems that may not have standard solutions?

9. **Flexibility.** Are you capable of changing and being receptive to new situations and ideas?

10. **Interpersonal skills.** Can you bring out the best efforts of individuals so they become effective, enthusiastic members of a team?

11. **Self-knowledge.** Can you realistically assess your own capabilities? See yourself as others see you? Clearly recognize your strengths and weaknesses?

12. **Ability to handle conflict.** Can you successfully contend with stress situations and antagonism?

13. **Competitiveness.** Do you have the capacity to compete with others and the willingness to be measured by your performance in relation to that of others?

14. **Goal achievement.** Do you have the ability to identify and work toward specific goals? Do such goals challenge your abilities?

15. **Vocational skills.** Do you possess the positive combination of education and skills required for the position you are seeking?

16. **Direction.** Have you defined your basic personal needs? Have you determined what type of position will satisfy your knowledge, skills, and goals?

Source: "So You're Looking for a Job?" The College Placement Council.

them what the next step is. Maintain a positive attitude. Figures G.14 and G.15 outline what the interviewers will be evaluating.

4. *Follow up on the interview.* First, write down what you can remember from the interview: names of the interviewers and their titles, any salary figures mentioned, dates for training, and so on. Put the information in your career file. You can send a follow-up letter thanking each interviewer for his or her time. You can also send a letter of recommendation or some other piece of added information to keep their interest. "The squeaky wheel gets the grease" is the operating slogan. Your enthusiasm for working for the company could be a major factor in hiring you.

5. *Be prepared to act.* Know what you want to say if you do get a job offer. You may not want the job once you know all the information. Don't expect to receive a job offer from everyone you meet, but do expect to learn something from every interview. With some practice and persistence, you should find a rewarding and challenging job.

Candidate: "For each characteristic listed below there is a rating scale of 1 through 7, where '1' is generally the most unfavorable rating of the characteristic and '7' the most favorable. Rate each characteristic by *circling* just *one* number to represent the impression you gave in the interview that you have just completed."

Name of Candidate _____

1. **Appearance**

   Sloppy   1   2   3   4   5   6   7   Neat

2. **Attitude**

   Unfriendly 1   2   3   4   5   6   7   Friendly

3. **Assertiveness/Verbal Ability**

   a. Responded completely to questions asked

   Poor   1   2   3   4   5   6   7   Excellent

   b. Clarified personal background and related it to job opening and description

   Poor   1   2   3   4   5   6   7   Excellent

   c. Able to explain and sell job abilities

   Poor   1   2   3   4   5   6   7   Excellent

   d. Initiated questions regarding position and firm

   Poor   1   2   3   4   5   6   7   Excellent

   e. Expressed thorough knowledge of personal goals and abilities

   Poor   1   2   3   4   5   6   7   Excellent

4. **Motivation**

   Poor   1   2   3   4   5   6   7   High

5. **Subject/Academic Knowledge**

   Poor   1   2   3   4   5   6   7   Good

6. **Stability**

   Poor   1   2   3   4   5   6   7   Good

7. **Composure**

   Ill at ease 1   2   3   4   5   6   7   Relaxed

8. **Personal Involvement/Activities, Clubs, Etc.**

   Low   1   2   3   4   5   6   7   Very high

9. **Mental Impression**

   Dull   1   2   3   4   5   6   7   Alert

10. **Adaptability**

    Poor   1   2   3   4   5   6   7   Good

11. **Speech Pronunciation**

    Poor   1   2   3   4   5   6   7   Good

12. **Overall Impression**

    Unsatisfactory 1 2   3   4   5   6   7   Highly
                                                   satisfactory

13. **Would you hire this individual if you were permitted to make a decision right now?**

    Yes   No

BE PREPARED TO CHANGE CAREERS

If you're like most people, you'll find that you'll follow several different career paths over your lifetime. This is a good thing in that it enables you to try different jobs and stay fresh and enthusiastic. The key to moving forward in your career is a willingness to change jobs, always searching for the career that will bring the most personal satisfaction and growth. This means that you'll have to write many cover letters and résumés and go through many interviews. Each time you change jobs, go through the steps in this appendix to be sure you're fully prepared. Good luck.

Meeting the Challenges of Today's Dynamic Business Environment

LEARNING GOALS

AFTER YOU HAVE READ AND STUDIED THIS CHAPTER, YOU SHOULD BE ABLE TO

1 Describe how businesses and nonprofit organizations add to a country's standard of living and quality of life.

2 Explain the importance of entrepreneurship to the wealth of an economy and show the relationship of profit to risk assumption.

3 Examine how the economic environment and taxes affect businesses.

4 Illustrate how the technological environment has affected businesses.

5 Identify various ways in which businesses can meet and beat competition.

6 Demonstrate how the social environment has changed and what the reaction of the business community has been.

7 Analyze what businesses must do to meet the global challenge.

8 Review how trends from the past are being repeated in the present and what such trends will mean for the service sector.

Getting to Know Jenny Ming from Old Navy

As president of Old Navy, a part of San Francisco–based clothing retailer Gap Inc., Jenny J. Ming oversees everything from store operations to marketing and advertising. Ming's passion for fashion has helped drive record growth at Old Navy. Thanks to strong sales of fleece tops and vests, Old Navy is now the biggest contributor to the overall growth of its parent company. That's not bad for a chain that didn't even exist until 1994.

Jenny Ming came from humble beginnings. She was born in Macao, a Portuguese colony near Hong Kong. Her father was a printer, and her mother stayed home to take care of Jenny and her four siblings. The Ming family moved to San Francisco's North Beach area when Jenny was nine. When she became old enough to work, she found jobs first as a bank teller and then as a sales clerk at a Macy's department store. She also worked as a seamstress at home, finding clients through ads in the local paper.

Following her interest in fashion, Ming supplemented her economics major at San Jose State University with lots of courses in textiles. This education won her a job at Dayton Hudson's Mervyn's unit as a management trainee. Later she became a buyer in linens and junior wear. Her reputation as a buyer spread among other firms, and she was soon recruited to become a buyer for Gap's Old Navy stores.

Ming immediately began to make an impression on top management. For example, she increased the sale of T-shirts dramatically by adding colors and by promoting the shirts all year instead of just during the summer. She still enjoys selling T-shirts. Her favorite kind are girls' T-shirts bearing the Chinese characters for love and long life. Based on her excellent performance, Ming was promoted to a vice-presidential position after just three years. She was promoted to president in 1999.

Ming has always been in the vanguard of fashion and understands trends. She knows that teen fashions change quickly and that only those stores that keep up with the latest trends will prosper. She also knows that the way teens shop for clothes is changing. Young people are increasingly turning to the Internet to find and buy the items they want. For example, shopper Diane Young wanted to buy a three-quarter-sleeve black shirt from Old Navy. But the shirt was nowhere to be found in her local store. So Young went to her computer, logged on to Old Navy's website and bought it there instead. With just a few clicks, Young was assured the shirt she wanted was on its way. Ever since, shopping online has become a habit for her. Twice a month, she receives personalized e-mails from Old Navy promoting its latest specials. And thanks to the site's sharp graphics and easy-to-use format, Young figures she now spends 10 to 15 percent more at Old Navy than she did before using the Internet. She isn't alone. In fact, Old Navy's online sales tripled in 1999.

There are many risks associated with the fashion industry. Buying the wrong merchandise or using the wrong promotions can quickly ruin a business. Yet Jenny Ming has made the most of the opportunities available to those who understand business and prepare themselves for a successful career. The whole purpose of this text is to introduce you to people like Ming and to teach you the concepts and principles that enabled them to become successful businesspeople. You will also learn how the people who take the risks of starting and managing businesses benefit themselves, their employees, and society.

Sources: Louise Lee, "Trend Spotters: A Savvy Captain for Old Navy," *Business Week*, November 8, 1999; "Clicks and Mortar and Gap.com" and "The Top 25 Managers," *Business Week*, January 10, 2000.

WHAT IS A BUSINESS?

business
Any activity that seeks profit by providing goods and services to others.

profit
The amount a business earns above and beyond what it spends for salaries and other expenses.

One of the ways to become a huge success in the United States, or almost anywhere in the world, is to start a business. A **business** is any activity that seeks profit by providing goods and services to others. **Profit** is the amount a business earns above and beyond what it spends for salaries and other expenses. Businesses provide us with necessities such as food, clothing, housing, medical care, and transportation, as well as other goods and services that make our lives easier and better.

Businesses also provide people with the opportunity to become wealthy. Sam Walton of Wal-Mart began by opening one store in Arkansas and, over time, became the richest person in America; his heirs now have billions of dollars. Bill Gates started Microsoft and is now the richest person in the world. He is said to be worth about $65 billion (that's billion with a *b*, not million with an *m*). In fact, before Microsoft got into legal problems with the government, Gates was worth about $100 billion.

There are about 270 billionaires in the United States today. That number is expected to increase to 700 by the year 2025. Furthermore, there are about 11 million millionaires, and that number is expected to be about 30 million in 2025.[1] Could you be one of them? Learning about business is a great start, as you'll see next.

Businesses Can Provide Wealth and a High Quality of Life for Almost Everyone

entrepreneur
A person who risks time and money to start and manage a business.

A person who assumes the risk of starting a business is known as an **entrepreneur**. Many of the wealthiest people in the world began as entrepreneurs, and their businesses grew to become major corporations. Entrepreneurs such as Sam Walton and Bill Gates not only became wealthy themselves but also provided employment for other people. Wal-Mart is currently the nation's largest private employer. Employees pay taxes that the federal government and local communities use to build hospitals, schools, playgrounds, and other facilities. Taxes are also used to keep the environment clean and to support people in need. Businesses, too, pay taxes to the federal government and local communities. Thus, the wealth businesses generate helps everyone in their communities. The nation's businesses are part of an economic system that contributes to the standard of living and quality of life for everyone in the country.

standard of living
The amount of goods and services people can buy with the money they have.

The term **standard of living** refers to the amount of goods and services people can buy with the money they have. For example, the United States has one of the highest standards of living in the world, even though workers in some other countries, such as Germany and Japan, make more money per hour. How can that be? Prices for goods and services in Germany and Japan are higher, so what a person can buy in those countries is less than a person in the United States can buy with the same amount of money. The United States has such a high standard of living largely because of the wealth created by its businesses.

quality of life
The general well-being of a society.

The term **quality of life** refers to the general well-being of a society in terms of political freedom, a clean natural environment, education, health care, safety, free time, and everything else that leads to satisfaction and joy. Maintaining a high quality of life requires the combined efforts of businesses, nonprofit organizations, and government agencies. The more money businesses create, the more is available to improve the quality of life for everyone.

ByeByeNOW.com™ showed me the true meaning of life. VACATION.

Rega

"Come see me at ByeByeNOW.com™! They have everything you need to plan the perfect vacation! Thousands of choices! Great prices! You can even see your destination on video before you go. And get this - click a button...a live travel expert pops up on your computer to help you! Log on now. You're gonna love it!"

Each ByeByeNOW.com™ Travel Store is independently owned and operated.

The wealth created by businesspeople has led to a high standard of living in the United States and many other countries. Financial success allows people to enjoy *things* like homes, cars, computers, etc. Financial security also means more freedom for leisure activities such as travel, and companies like ByByeNOW.com have arisen to encourage and assist Americans in their pursuit of the right vacation experience. Fortunately, you don't have to be a 'millionaire' to use their services.

CRITICAL **THINKING**

Presently, some people in the United States are sacrificing a higher standard of living (having more things) for a higher quality of life (having more time). They are starting to buy smaller homes and smaller cars, and are taking more vacations and spending more time with their families.[2] As you approach your career, how can you balance having a high standard of living with maintaining a high quality of life?

Nonprofit Organizations Use Business Principles

Not everything that makes life easier and better is provided by businesses. Nonprofit organizations—such as public schools, civic associations, charities, and groups devoted to social causes—help make our country and the world more responsive to the needs of citizens. A **nonprofit organization** is an organization whose goals don't include making a personal profit for its owners. Nonprofit organizations often do strive for financial gains, but such gains are used to meet the stated social or educational goals of the organization, not to enrich the owners.

If you want to start or work in a nonprofit organization, you'll need to learn business skills such as information management, leadership, marketing, and financial management. Therefore, the knowledge and skills you acquire

nonprofit organization
An organization whose goals do not include making a personal profit for its owners.

in this and other business courses will be useful for careers in any organization, including a nonprofit one.

Because such crossover is possible, many businesspeople volunteer their expertise in nonprofit organizations. Others change careers to run non-profit organizations that require the same skills they had been using in the business world. Melissa Bradley, for example, started a profitable consulting firm her first year out of college. When she was 23, revenues reached $1 million. Seeing the opportunity that entrepreneurship offers, Melissa sold her consulting firm to launch The Entrepreneurial Development Institute (TEDI), an organization in Washington, D.C., that teaches entrepreneurship to at-risk young people.

Businesses, nonprofit organizations, and volunteer groups often strive to accomplish the same objectives. All such groups can help feed people, provide them with clothing and housing, clean up the environment and keep it clean, and improve the standard of living and quality of life for all. To accomplish such objectives, however, businesses in the United States must remain competitive with the best businesses in the rest of the world by offering quality goods and services.[3]

ENTREPRENEURSHIP VERSUS WORKING FOR OTHERS

There are two ways to succeed in business. One way, the way chosen by Jenny Ming, is to rise up through the ranks of a large company like the Gap. The other, more risky path, is to start your own business. The national anthem, "The Star Spangled Banner," says that the United States is the "land of the free and the home of the brave." Part of being free is being able to own your own business and to reap the profits from that business. But freedom to succeed also means freedom to fail, and many small businesses fail each year. Thus, it takes a brave person to start a small business.

Very few entrepreneurs have had more successes in the United States than Wu-Fu Chen, who has begun 11 start-up companies and is a multimillionaire as a result. Chen is the 10th child of Taiwanese farmers. Like Jenny Ming, he rose above his humble background by going to school and working hard. After earning a bachelor's degree in engineering, Chen began working for a producer of computerized financial systems. While on the job, he saw the income potential that comes from being an owner/entrepreneur rather than an employee. He worked for several different firms to learn different technologies and took business courses at night. Finally, he felt it was time to start his own business.

The first business Chen started, with four colleagues, was Communications Equipment Corporation. The owners sold the company after four years for $7 million. Chen and three others then started a company called Cascade in Westford, Massachusetts. Chen left that company five years later to start Arris Networks Inc., also in Westford. Arris was sold nine months later for $145 million. Chen then moved to California's Silicon Valley, where he started Ardent Communications Corp. In less than a year, computer networking giant Cisco Systems bought Ardent for $156 million.

You can learn a lot from studying the careers of entrepreneurs like Chen. First of all, *you start by getting a good education.* Then you get a job working for a firm where you can learn all about a certain business. Eventually, however, if you want to become a huge success, you might want to start your own business.[4]

Opportunities for Entrepreneurs

Millions of people from all over the world have taken the entrepreneurial risk and succeeded. You may know the name Hakeem Olajuwon from his basketball fame, but you may not know about his younger brother, Akinola, who is also a big success in his own way. Akinola Olajuwon's company was listed as one of *Black Enterprise* magazine's top 100 black-owned businesses for 2000. The Olajuwon Group of Companies owns 73 Denny's restaurants across 13 states. Other top African American business leaders include David L. Steward of World Wide Technology, Inc.; J. Bruce Llewellyn of the Philadelphia Coca-Cola Bottling Company; and John H. Johnson of Johnson Publishing.[5]

In the early 1990s the number of Hispanic-owned businesses in the United States grew by 76 percent—a faster rate than that of any other category of business. The next highest level of minority-business growth was for businesses owned by Asians, Pacific Islanders, American Indians, and Alaskan Natives; together, these businesses grew by 61 percent. Some 30 percent of Koreans who have immigrated to the United States own their own businesses. Other Asians are also prospering in business. In short, tremendous opportunities exist for all men and women willing to take the risk of starting a business.

The number of women business owners has dramatically increased in the last 20 years. In 1980, there were about 3 million women business owners; by 2000, there were over 8 million. Women now own over a third of all businesses. Names you may be familiar with include Martha Stewart, Oprah Winfrey, Donna Karan, and Lillian Vernon.

Matching Risk with Profit

You read earlier that profit is the amount of money a business earns above and beyond what it pays out for salaries and other expenses. For example, if you were to rent a vending cart and sell hot dogs this summer, you would have to pay for the cart, for the hot dogs and other materials, and for someone to run the cart while you were away. After you paid your employee and yourself, paid for the food and materials you used, paid the rent on the cart, and paid your taxes, any money left over would be profit. Keep in mind that profit is over and above the money you pay yourself in salary. You could use any profit you make to rent a second cart and hire another employee. After a few summers, you might have a dozen carts employing dozens of workers.

Not all businesses make a profit. Profit is revenue *minus* expenses. **Revenue** is the total amount of money a business earns in a given period by selling goods and services. A **loss** occurs when a business's expenses are more than its revenues. If a business loses money over time, it will likely have to close, putting its employees out of work. In fact, approximately 80,000 businesses in the United States fail each year. Most fail because of poor management or problems associated with cash flow (which we discuss later in this book).

The failure rate given above is actually overstated, because some people close down one business to start another one.[6] Even though such closings are not failures, they are reported as such in the statistics. Yet clearly, starting a business involves risk. **Risk** is the chance an entrepreneur takes

No occupation in the world is more diverse than entrepreneurship. Opportunities exist for virtually everyone to start and manage a small business, from a lawn care service to software training. With success, you may eventually own a number of businesses like Akinola Olajuwon, who now owns 73 Denny's restaurants. Almost all countries offer some form of entrepreneurial opportunity, but some are much more open than others. Why do you suppose so many people come to the United States to become entrepreneurs?

revenue
The total amount of money a business earns in a given period by selling goods and services.

loss
When a business's costs and expenses are more than its revenues.

risk
The chance an entrepreneur takes of losing time and money on a business that may not prove profitable.

SPOTLIGHT ON SMALL BUSINESS

www.emkf.org

The Environment for Small Businesses

A study by the Kauffman Center for Entrepreneurial Leadership in Kansas City, Missouri, revealed that, of 10 industrialized countries, the United States had the most people trying to start a business. About 1 in 12 U.S. citizens per year tries to start a business; that means that about 900,000 new businesses are being created annually, and that total doesn't count self-employed consultants and other sole proprietorships. Since this is a chapter on the environment of business, we list here some of what is happening in the United States that promotes such interest in starting small businesses:

• The strong economy creates opportunities for new business.

• Compared to other countries, there are more public and private groups teaching entrepreneurs how to build a business, so more try and fewer fail.

• Fabulous rags-to-riches success stories are luring others to try.

• Technology enables growth and opens a host of its own business opportunities—such as Internet-related companies.

• As corporations cut the number of managers through programs designed to empower employees, skilled managers are available to start their own businesses.

• There is a strong cultural need for independence.

• There is more risk in starting a business than there is in opening a new outlet of a successful franchise, but the rewards may be greater as well.

• The challenge of the New Economy (that is, economic growth spurred by the growth of Internet commerce) endows business with an irresistible calling, and an air of romance and bravado.

Sources: Margaret Webb Pressler, "So You Want to Start Your Own Business?" *The Washington Post*, June 27, 1999, pp. H1, H8; and Paulette Thomas, "Rewriting the Rules," *The Wall Street Journal*, May 22, 2000, p. R4.

of losing time and money on a business that may not prove profitable. Even among companies that do make a profit, not all make the same amount. Those companies that take the most risk may make the most profit. There is a lot of risk involved, for example, in building high-tech firms. Similarly, it may involve some risk to open a fast-food franchise in the inner city because insurance and land costs there are usually higher than in suburban areas. On the other hand, the chance of making substantial profits in the inner city is also good because there's less competition there than in other areas. For more about entrepreneurial risk taking, see the box called Spotlight on Small Business.

As a potential business owner, you want to invest your money in a company that's likely to make a large profit but that isn't too risky. You need to do research (e.g., talk to other businesspeople, read business publications) to find the right balance between risk and profit. You can choose whether to put your money in a bank, in the stock market, in real estate, or in some other investments—and the latter includes owning your own business. To decide which is the best choice, you have to calculate the risks each decision entails and the potential rewards from each. The more risks you take, the higher the rewards may be. In Chapter 6, you will learn more about the risks and the rewards that come with starting a business.

PROGRESS ASSESSMENT

• What is the difference between standard of living and quality of life?

• What is the difference between revenue and profit?

• What is risk, and how is it related to profit?

The Factors Needed to Create Wealth

It is easier to see how important entrepreneurship is to the success of a country when you examine all the factors needed for prosperity. The **factors of production** are the resources businesses use to create wealth. As Figure 1.1 shows, businesses use five major factors of production:

1. Land (and other natural resources).
2. Labor (workers).
3. Capital (e.g., machines, tools, and buildings).
4. Entrepreneurship.
5. Knowledge.

Traditionally, business texts have emphasized only four factors of production: land, labor, capital, and entrepreneurship, but management expert and business consultant Peter Drucker says that the most important factor of production in our economy is and will be knowledge. The young workers in the high-tech industries in the Silicon Valley area of California are sometimes called knowledge workers. Many have become millionaires while still in their 20s. Such results should motivate today's college students to get as much education as possible to prepare themselves for knowledge-oriented jobs. To become as rich as Bill Gates and other billionaires, however, they will have to become entrepreneurs as well.

If you were to analyze rich countries versus poor countries to see what causes the differences in the levels of wealth, you'd have to look at the factors of production in each country. Such analyses have revealed that some relatively poor countries often have plenty of land and natural resources. Russia and China, for example, both have vast areas of land with many resources, but they are not rich countries. In contrast, Japan is a relatively rich country but is poor in land and other natural resources. Therefore, land isn't the critical element for wealth creation.

Most poor countries have many laborers, so it's not labor that's the primary source of wealth today. Laborers need to find work to make a contribution; that is, they need entrepreneurs to provide jobs for them. Furthermore, capital—money for machinery and tools—is now becoming available in world markets, so capital isn't the missing ingredient. Capital is not productive without entrepreneurs to put it to use.

Clearly, then, what makes rich countries rich today is a combination of entrepreneurship and the effective use of knowledge. Together, lack of entrepreneurship and the absence of knowledge among workers, along with the lack

factors of production
The resources used to create wealth: land, labor, capital, entrepreneurship, and knowledge.

FIGURE 1.1

THE FIVE FACTORS OF PRODUCTION

Land:	Land and other natural resources are used to make homes, cars, and other products.
Labor:	People have always been an important resource in producing goods and services, but many people are now being replaced by technology.
Capital:	Capital includes machines, tools, buildings, and other means of manufacturing.
Entrepreneurship:	All the resources in the world have little value unless entrepreneurs are willing to take the risk of starting businesses to *use* those resources.
Knowledge:	Information technology has revolutionized business, making it possible to quickly determine wants and needs and to respond with desired goods and services.

of freedom, contribute to keeping poor countries poor. The box called Legal Briefcase discusses the importance of freedom to economic development.

Entrepreneurship also makes some states and cities in the United States rich while others remain relatively poor. The business environment either encourages or discourages entrepreneurship. In the following section, we'll explore what makes up the business environment and how to build an environment that encourages growth and job creation.

THE BUSINESS ENVIRONMENT

Today's dynamic business environment has a tremendous effect on the success or failure of entrepreneurs. Figure 1.2 identifies five elements that are key to business growth and job creation—and that together make up the business environment:

1. The economic environment, including taxes and regulation.
2. The technological environment.
3. The competitive environment.
4. The social environment.
5. The global business environment.

FIGURE 1.2

TODAY'S DYNAMIC BUSINESS ENVIRONMENT

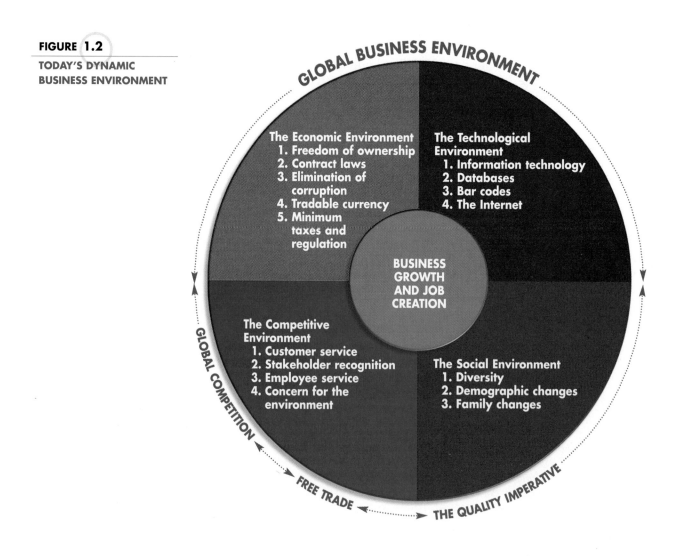

www.cipe.org

LEGAL BRIEFCASE
Freedom Equals Prosperity

A recent study found that the freer a country is, the wealthier its citizens are. Freedom includes freedom from excess taxation, government regulations, and restrictions on trade. The average per capita gross domestic product for the 23 freest countries in the mid-1990s was $14,829. For the least free, it was $2,541. As a country introduces more freedom, its economy also begins to grow. The per capita income in the United States was over $31,000 in 1999.

The legal environment of a country therefore has much to do with its economic prosperity. More freedom equals more prosperity for all. Recently, for example, the Heritage Foundation (a conservative think tank) prepared an index that measures the impact of laws, regulations, and government policies on the economy. This index classifies the governments of Singapore and the United States as among the least restrictive and those of Russia and Cuba as the most restrictive. It may not be a coincidence, then, that Singapore and the United States are relatively wealthy countries and Russia and Cuba are not. Such figures show why businesses must work closely with government to minimize taxes and maximize economic freedom.

The legal environment of business is a critical part of any economic growth plan. That is why this text focuses on legal issues throughout. By reading about such issues in the context of various business functions, you will see how important the legal system is to business.

Sources: Vivian Woo, "Comparing Countries," *Forbes*, July 26, 1999, pp. 164–68; Ted Bunker, "Freedom at Root of Prosperity," *The Boston Herald*, January 3, 2000; and Meg Richards, "Freedom on the Rise in Global Population," *The Washington Times*, December 21, 2000, p. A 17.

Businesses grow and prosper in a healthy environment. The result is job growth and the wealth that makes it possible to have both a high standard of living and a high quality of life. The wrong environmental conditions, in contrast, lead to business failure, loss of jobs, and a low standard of living and quality of life. In short, creating the right business environment is the foundation for social progress of all kinds, including good schools, clean air and water, good health care, and low rates of crime.

THE ECONOMIC ENVIRONMENT

People are willing to start new businesses if they feel that the risk of losing their money isn't too great. Part of that risk involves the economic system and how government works with or against businesses. Government can do a lot to lessen the risk of starting businesses and thus increase entrepreneurship and wealth. For example, a government can keep taxes and regulations to a minimum.

Entrepreneurs are looking for a high **return on investment (ROI),** including the investment of their time. If the government takes away much of what a business earns through high taxes, the ROI may no longer be worth the risk. This is true even within rich countries. States and cities that have high taxes and restrictive regulations tend to drive entrepreneurs out, while states and cities with low taxes attract entrepreneurs. This is happening all across the United States and the world. Some of the tax laws that help small businesses include the provisions for deducting home office expenses, business travel and meals, and other business expenses.

One way for government to actively promote entrepreneurship is to allow private ownership of businesses. In some countries, such as Cuba, the government owns most businesses and thus there's little incentive for people to work hard or create profit. All around the world today, however, various countries in which the government formerly owned all businesses are selling

Return on investment (ROI)
The return a businessperson gets on the money he and other owners invest in the firm; for example, a business that earned $100 on a thousand dollar investment would have a ROI of 10 percent: 100 divided by 1000.

When there are few incentives for entrepreneurs, countries such as Cuba often suffer from a lack or scarcity of needed goods and services, even food. As shown here, when Cubans go to a store, the shelves are mostly empty and they often cannot find what they want or need. What could the government do to make entrepreneurship more attractive in such countries?

those businesses to private individuals to create more wealth. Let's explore what else the government can do to foster entrepreneurial growth.

The government can lessen the risks of entrepreneurship by passing laws that enable businesspeople to write contracts that are enforceable in court. The Universal Commercial Code, for example, covers things like contracts and warranties. You will read more about such laws later. In countries that don't yet have such laws, the risks of starting a business are that much greater.

The government can establish a currency that's tradable in world markets. One element preventing Russia from joining world markets and gaining economic strength is its lack of a tradable currency.

The government can focus on eliminating corruption in business and in its own ranks. It's hard to do business in many poor countries because the governments are so corrupt. It's very difficult in such countries to get permission to build a factory or open a store without a government permit, which is obtained largely through bribery of public officials.[7] Among businesses themselves, leaders can threaten competitors and minimize competition. There are many laws in the United States to minimize corruption, and businesses can flourish as a result. You will read about such laws in the appendix titled "Working within the Legal Environment of Business" at the end of Chapter 4.

The economic environment is so important to businesses that we'll devote all of Chapter 2 to that subject. There you'll learn more about the influence of government on business success and failure.

PROGRESS ASSESSMENT

- What are the five factors of production?
- What are the five elements that constitute the business environment?
- What are three ways the government can reduce the risk of going into business?

THE TECHNOLOGICAL ENVIRONMENT

Since prehistoric times, humans have felt the need to create tools that make their jobs easier. We've come a long way from clicking stones together to make a spark; now we click a mouse to make a business transaction. Various tools and machines developed throughout history have changed the business environment tremendously, but few technological changes have had a more comprehensive and lasting impact on businesses than the emergence of information technology (computers, modems, cellular phones, etc.) and, most recently, the Internet.

The Internet is such a major force in business today that we discuss its impact on the business concepts in each chapter throughout the text. In addition, we provide Internet exercises at the end of each chapter to give you some hands-on experience with various companies and Internet uses. If you are new to the Net, the section called Surfing the Internet at the beginning of the text can guide you on your journey.

How the Internet Is Changing Everything

The Internet is more than just a massive network of computers. It is a revolution in communication. In 2000, nearly 100 million people were online (up from just 36 million in 1996).[8] Twenty-nine percent of all Americans were online in 2000, and by 2002 that number is expected to increase to 43 percent.[9] Why all the interest in the Internet? The Internet is a powerful communications medium that allows its users instant access and allows businesses to operate without borders:

- The Internet is a combination of software, print, video, audio, and telephone systems that offers maximum potential to communicate with a worldwide audience.

- Since the Internet can be accessed any time day or night, users can find information and/or place orders whenever it is convenient for them.

- There are no geographical limits in cyberspace. Before the Internet, most business transactions were restricted to some degree by location. Today, business can be conducted anywhere.

The E-Commerce Explosion

E-commerce is the buying and selling of products and services over the Internet. A business that sells goods and services exclusively over the Internet is called a **dot-com company**, since its Web address ends with .com. Businesses are lured to e-commerce by a number of factors:

- *Low transaction costs.* The automation of customer service lowers costs, which may make it possible for a company to offer products at a lower price. Also, there are no sales taxes (yet) on the Internet, so everything is a little less expensive than in stores.

- *Large purchases per transaction.* For example, online bookseller Amazon.com makes personalized recommendations to customers and, along with every title offered, lists related titles ("Customers who bought this book also bought…"). Another click or two will add one or more titles to an order. These features lead people to buy more books than they might in a traditional bookstore.

- *Integration of business processes.* The Internet offers companies the ability to make more information available to customers than ever before. For example, a computer company that tracks each unit through the manufacturing and shipping process can allow customers to see exactly where the order is at any time. This is what overnight package delivery company Federal Express did when it introduced online package tracking.

- *Flexibility.* Successful websites are not just glorified mail-order catalogs. The Internet offers companies the ability to configure products and build custom orders, to compare prices between multiple vendors easily, and to search large catalogs quickly.

- *Large catalogs.* Amazon.com offers a catalog of 3 million books on the Internet. Imagine fitting a paper catalog that size in your mailbox!

- *Improved customer interactions.* Online tools allow businesses to interact with customers in ways unheard of before, and at almost instant speeds. For example, customers can receive automatic e-mails to confirm orders and to notify them when orders are shipped.

There are two major types of e-commerce transactions: business-to-consumer (also known as B2C) and business-to-business (also known as B2B).

e-commerce
Electronic commerce; the buying and selling of products and services over the Internet.

dot-com company
An Internet company whose Web address ends with .com.

Big firms like Barnes & Noble have been driving smaller bookstores out of business for years. Now, the newest firms, such as Amazon.com, are offering books for less on the Internet, and by doing so they have forced Barnes & Noble onto the Internet to compete. Meanwhile, the small mom-and-pop bookstores such as the Mt. Kisco Book Company are finding it harder to compete. What can or should these smaller bookstores do to stay competitive with the larger brick-and-mortar firms and new Internet firms?

Business-to-consumer (B2C) e-commerce consists of selling retail items on the Internet—a process sometimes called e-tailing. U.S. e-tailers generated $20 billion in 1999. Yet since that figure accounts for only 0.8 percent of the overall $2.6 trillion retail industry in the United States, it has plenty of room to grow.[10] And it *is* growing! Amazon.com is one of the pioneers in B2C e-commerce. Its annual sales topped $150 million in its third year of running a website and a warehouse. It took Wal-Mart 12 years and 78 stores to reach that milestone.[11] At the time of this writing, the problem with many B2C companies, including Amazon.com, is that they are not yet making profits.[12] Even though their revenues are high, their costs are even higher. Many have gone out of business entirely. It would be interesting for you to see how Amazon is doing now by checking its latest earnings report.

Most profitable brick-and-mortar businesses (traditional stores) are growing by expanding onto the Internet and are thus giving rise to the term *click-and-mortar business* (a traditional retailer that also has a presence online). For example, the traditional brokerage firm Charles Schwab & Co. does more than half its business online. We will offer tips for starting a Web business in Chapter 6 and discuss e-tailing further in Chapter 15.

As revolutionary as the Internet has been in the consumer market, it has been even more revolutionary in the business-to-business (B2B) market, which consists of selling goods and services from one business to another, such as IBM selling consulting services to a local bank. B2B e-commerce is already at least five times as big as B2C e-commerce. According to Forrester Research (an independent firm that studies business and technology), U.S. B2B e-commerce revenue is expected to be $2.8 trillion by 2004.[13] Others project that by that year, B2B e-commerce will reach $7.29 trillion, or 40 percent of all B2B revenue.[14] The point is that while the potential of the B2C e-commerce market is measured in billions, B2B e-commerce is measured in *trillions*. (See the *Business Week* box for more examples of Internet businesses.)

The rise of Internet marketing came so fast and furious that it drew hundreds of competitors into the fray. As a result, many Internet companies are not proving as successful as people hoped, and their stocks have dropped in price tremendously. Companies such as CDnow, Peapod, eToys, and Drkoop.com have failed or seen their stock drop dramatically.[15] Many B2B stocks experienced similar failures. There is no question that some Internet businesses will grow and prosper, but along the way there are sure to be lots of failures, just as

FROM THE PAGES OF **BusinessWeek**   www.furniturefind.com

What's New in E-Commerce?

A few years ago, analysts believed that there were many products that simply could not be sold on the Internet—products like furniture. But time has proved them wrong. Katy Bremer bought her dining-room furniture from FurnitureFind.com. She was comfortable with the brand name and very happy with the price. "Who would buy car parts on the Internet?" some people said. Well, check out CarParts.com and you will see that it is quite possible to sell car parts on the Internet. "Certainly food products are not designed to be sold on the Net," people thought. But there are food companies selling groceries and specialty products of all kinds on the Internet.

People are now banking on the Internet, buying computers and hardware supplies on the Internet, and making investments on the Internet. The problem with many start-up Internet companies is that most of them are not very profitable, if they are making any profits at all. But investors seem confident that e-commerce vendors will make big bucks in the future. Are you willing to bet against them?

Source: Jim Kerstetter, "Meg Whitman of eBay," *Business Week Online*, May 15, 2000; and Rochelle Sharpe, Ann T. Palmer, Joann Muller, Elizabeth Hayes, and Deborah Rubin, "Teen Moguls," *Business Week*, May 29, 2000, pp. 108–18.

there have been in traditional businesses. There once were dozens of automobile companies; almost all of them failed and only a few large companies now dominate the auto industry. Success will come to those who offer quality products at good prices *and* offer great service. As noted earlier, many of those companies will be a combination of old brick-and-mortar companies, such as Sears and General Electric, with new Internet sites that make them more competitive. We'll explore such companies throughout the text.

How E-Commerce Is Changing the Roles of Intermediaries

Intermediaries are companies (such as wholesalers and retailers) that help move goods and services between producers and consumers. There are companies that make things and then sell those things to wholesalers, which then resell them to retailers, which sell them to consumers. Today, in addition to dot-com e-tailers, there are increasing numbers of companies that make things and sell those things directly to consumers through the Internet, eliminating the intermediary companies that once shipped and stored the goods. Someday we might see the elimination of many car dealers, insurance salespeople, video stores, bookstores, and so on. You and I would buy much of what we want and need on the Internet, directly from the manufacturers. Think of how such changes would affect local shopping malls, downtown malls, and retailing in general. For sure, such changes will have a profound effect on businesspeople and how they plan for the future. We will discuss how e-commerce is changing the roles of intermediaries in Chapter 15.

Using Technology to Be Responsive to Customers

One way traditional retailers can respond to the Internet revolution is to use technology to become much more responsive to customers.[16] For example, businesses mark goods with bar codes—those series of lines that you see on most consumer packaged goods. Bar codes tell retailers what size product you bought, in what color, and at what price. A scanner at the checkout counter reads that information and puts it into a database. A **database** is an electronic storage file where information is kept. One use of databases is to store vast amounts of information about consumers. For example, a retailer may ask for

database
Electronic storage file where information is kept.

On a balmy day last April, Craig A. Winn, a onetime housewares salesman, momentarily became a dot-com billionaire. As the stock in his e-tailing startup, Value America Inc., ascended from its initial public offering price of $23 a share to a giddy high of $74.25 on Apr. 8, 1999, it became clear that the charismatic entrepreneur had tapped into the mind-set of the New Economy. Investors flocked to his idea of a "Wal-Mart of the Internet" where shoppers could order jars of caviar along with their gas barbecues or desktop computers. And why not? Winn had already signed up some big-time investors, including Microsoft co-founder Paul Allen, financier Sam Belzberg, and FedEx Chairman Fred Smith, whose names added cachet to the venture.

When the stock settled down that day at $55 a share, the three-year-old, profitless company was valued at $2.4 billion. Yet the 45-year-old Winn maintains that he was overcome with melancholy as he watched shares trade that first day. "I

THE fall OF A DOT-COM

Blinded by Net fever, big-name investors poured millions into Craig Winn's chaotic Value America BY JOHN A. BYRNE

Value America was a promising Internet company whose stock soared when it was first available. The idea was to be a Cyber Wal-Mart. The reality was that orders were processed too slowly, discounting cut deeply into profits, and the company spent money, especially on advertising, too freely. The bottom line is that Internet businesses, like all companies, face intense competition and cannot succeed without a well-conceived strategy that focuses on profit. Can you name other Internet companies that have performed poorly or failed?

your name, address, and telephone number so that it can put you on its mailing list. The information you give the retailer is added to the database. Because companies routinely trade database information, soon many retailers know what you buy and for whom you buy it. Using that information, companies can send you catalogs and other direct mail advertising that offers the kind of products you might want, as indicated by your past purchases. Databases enable stores to carry only the merchandise that the local population wants. They also enable stores to carry less inventory, saving them money. We will talk more about how technology helps identify and meet the needs of target markets in Chapters 13 and 15.

Using Technology to Manage Information

Information management is becoming a critical part of most businesses. Many companies now have a chief information officer (CIO) or chief knowledge officer (CKO). That is the person responsible for giving workers and managers the information they need to turn their company into a world-class competitor. Ralph Pool is the director of Ernst & Young's Center for Business Knowledge. He helps his fellow employees by pulling together key pieces of knowledge such as interview guides, work schedules, benchmark data, and market segmentation analyses and storing them in the electronic depository for people to use. Because information technology has become such a central part of business success, we'll devote Chapter 17 to that subject.

THE COMPETITIVE ENVIRONMENT

Competition among businesses has never been greater than it is today. Some companies have found a competitive edge by focusing on making high-quality products.[17] The goal for many companies is zero defects—no mistakes in making the product. Some companies, such as Motorola in the United States and Toyota in Japan, have come close to meeting that standard. However, simply making a quality product isn't enough to allow a company to stay competitive in world markets. Companies now have to offer both quality products and outstanding service at competitive prices. That is why General Motors (GM) is building automobile plants in Argentina, Poland, China, and Thailand. Combining excellence with low-cost labor and minimizing distribution costs have resulted in larger markets and long-term growth for GM. Figure 1.3 shows the differences between yesterday's traditional businesses and today's world-class businesses.

Competing by Pleasing the Customer

Manufacturers and service organizations throughout the world have learned that today's customers are very demanding. Not only do they want good quality at low prices, but they want great service as well. In fact, products in the 21st century will be designed to "fascinate, bewitch, and delight" customers, exceeding their expectations. Every manufacturing and service organization in the world should have a sign over its door telling its workers that the customer is king. Business is becoming customer-driven, not management-driven as in the past. This means that customers' wants and needs must come first.

FIGURE 1.3

HOW COMPETITION HAS CHANGED BUSINESS

TRADITIONAL BUSINESSES	WORLD-CLASS BUSINESSES
Customer satisfaction	Delighting the customer[1]
Customer orientation	Customer and stakeholder orientation[2]
Profit orientation	Profit and social orientation[3]
Reactive ethics	Proactive ethics[4]
Product orientation	Quality and service orientation
Managerial focus	Customer focus

1. *Delight* is a term from total quality management. *Bewitch* and *fascinate* are alternative terms.

2. Stakeholders include employees, stockholders, suppliers, dealers, and the community; the goal is to please *all* stakeholders.

3. A social orientation goes beyond profit to do what is right and good for others.

4. *Proactive* means doing the right thing before anyone tells you to do it. *Reactive* means reacting to criticism after it happens.

Customer-driven organizations include Nordstrom department stores and Disney amusement parks. Moto Photo does its best to delight customers with fast, friendly service. Such companies can successfully compete against Internet firms such as Priceline.com if they continue to offer better and friendlier service. Many dot-com companies lost favor with customers during recent Christmas seasons because they simply could not keep up with demand. And many still have no clear policy regarding unwanted goods, which makes returns a real hassle. We'll discuss the battle between online firms and traditional retailers throughout the text.

Successful organizations must now listen more closely to customers to determine their wants and needs, then adjust the firm's products, policies, and practices to meet those demands.[18] It is important to consider the moral and ethical practices of the firm as well. The Making Ethical Decisions box discusses the trend toward creating ethics codes in businesses.

Competing with Speed

Have you noticed how everyone seems to be in a hurry today? Well, the truth is that most people are in a hurry, and businesses need to respond or risk losing their business. For example, companies used to say, "Allow six weeks for delivery." Today, customers want things delivered in two days or less. That's why FedEx and other high-speed delivery firms are doing so well. Today's consumers want fast food, fast delivery, fast responses to Internet searches, and so on. The companies that provide speedy service are those that are winning.

Businesses are demanding the same fast service from other businesses. The old saying "Time is money" has taken on new importance. The *Harvard Business Review* reports: "Not since the Industrial Revolution have the stakes of dealing with change been so high."[19] In a marketplace that wants things to happen faster every day, the battle more often than not is going to the swiftest competitor, not necessarily the biggest, strongest, or even the shrewdest. Some small companies have made speedy response the core of their business. For example, Pirtek USA LLC, based in Rockledge, Florida, provides mobile repair service for hydraulic hoses. When a jet airliner is out of service because of a broken hose, the airline doesn't want to wait days or

MAKING ETHICAL DECISIONS
Ethics Begin with You

www.depaul.edu/ethics/bentmba.html

Television, movies, and the print media all paint a dismal picture of ethics among businesspeople, government officials, and citizens in general. It is easy to criticize the ethics of these people. It is more difficult to see the moral and ethical misbehavior of your own social group. Do you find some of the behaviors of your friends morally or ethically questionable?

One of the major trends in business today is that many companies are creating ethics codes to guide their employees' behavior. We feel this trend toward improving ethical behavior is so important that we've made it a major theme of this book. Throughout the text you'll see boxes like this one, called Making Ethical Decisions. The boxes contain short descriptions of situations that pose ethical dilemmas and ask what you would do to resolve them. The idea is for you to think about the moral and ethical dimensions of every decision you make.

Here is your first ethical dilemma: Soon you will be taking exams in this course. Suppose you didn't prepare for one of the tests as thoroughly as you should have. As luck would have it, on exam day you are sitting in the desk right in front of the instructor, who has just happened to leave the answer key sticking out of her book. The instructor is called out of the room and everyone else is concentrating intently on his or her own work. No one will know if your eyes wander toward the answer key. A good grade on this test will certainly help your grade point average. What is the problem in this situation? What are your alternatives? What are the consequences of each alternative? Which alternative will you choose? Is your choice ethical?

FIGURE 1.4

A BUSINESS AND ITS STAKEHOLDERS

Often the needs of a firm's various stakeholders will conflict. For example, paying employees more may cut into stockholders' profits. Balancing such demands is a major role of business managers.

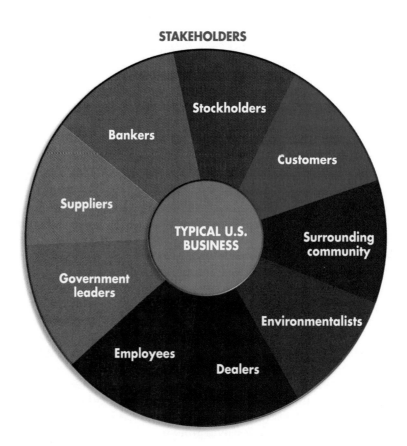

STAKEHOLDERS

Stockholders

Bankers

Customers

Suppliers

TYPICAL U.S. BUSINESS

Surrounding community

Government leaders

Environmentalists

Employees

Dealers

weeks to have it repaired. That's why Pirtek's Chicago franchise has a truck stationed right at O'Hare Airport.

Everything in the business world is changing very rapidly today. To keep up in such a dynamic business environment, people have to return to school periodically over their lifetime to learn the latest concepts, strategies, and tools. In response, schools have made it easier to take courses at night and on weekends. Masters of business administration (MBA) programs have been shortened and businesspeople are being given credit for on-the-job experience so that completion of the program goes faster. Community colleges have been very responsive to the needs of students at all stages of their careers, offering courses and schedules that fit the lifestyle of today's busy workers. That includes courses on the Internet and distance learning courses students can take from remote sites.

Competing by Meeting Community Needs

It is possible for businesses today to please their customers and still not meet some needs of the community in which they operate. For example, in their efforts to please employees and customers, firms may take actions that pollute the environment. Such an outcome is highly undesirable in today's business environment. World-class organizations in the future must attempt to meet the needs of all their stakeholders. **Stakeholders** are all the people who stand to gain or lose by the policies and activities of an organization. Stakeholders include customers, employees, stockholders, suppliers, dealers, bankers, people in the local community (e.g., community interest groups), environmentalists, and elected government leaders. (See Figure 1.4.) All of these groups are affected by the products, policies, and practices of the firm, and their concerns need to be addressed.

The challenge of the 21st century will be for organizations to work together to ensure that all stakeholders' needs are considered and satisfied as much as possible. Such an ambitious goal calls for both world-class employees and world-class organizational leaders.

To learn management skills, some employees go to a seminar. Ours go to the Lower East Side.

Companies need to meet the needs of all their stakeholders, including people in the local community. UPS, for example, sends their managers out to work in the community for a month at a time. They visit the home-bound elderly, mentor children, and build homes for those in need. Such a program enables their employees to become an intimate part of the community and makes them better listeners and managers. Would you prefer to work in a firm that has such an outreach program? If so, you can see how policies such as this help companies recruit.

stakeholders
Those people who stand to gain or lose by the policies and activities of an organization.

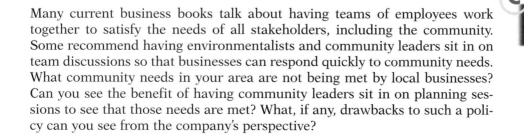

Many current business books talk about having teams of employees work together to satisfy the needs of all stakeholders, including the community. Some recommend having environmentalists and community leaders sit in on team discussions so that businesses can respond quickly to community needs. What community needs in your area are not being met by local businesses? Can you see the benefit of having community leaders sit in on planning sessions to see that those needs are met? What, if any, drawbacks to such a policy can you see from the company's perspective?

Competing by Restructuring and Meeting the Needs of Employees

empowerment
Giving frontline workers the responsibility and freedom to respond quickly to customer requests.

To meet the needs of customers, firms must give their frontline workers (office clerks, front-desk people at hotels, salespeople, etc.) the responsibility, freedom, training, and equipment they need to respond quickly to customer requests and to make other decisions essential to producing quality goods and providing good service. This is called **empowerment**, and we'll be talking about that process throughout this book. To implement a policy of empowerment, managers must train front-line people to make decisions without the need to consult managers. The new role of supervisors, then, is to support front-line people with training and the technology to do their jobs well, including handling customer complaints quickly and satisfactorily.

In this chapter, we simply want to acknowledge that many businesses must reorganize to make their employees more effective than they are now. Many firms have done so by forming cross-functional teams—that is, teams made up of people from various departments, such as design, production, and marketing. These teams have learned to work without close supervision; thus, they are often called *self-managed cross-functional teams.*

One aspect of empowerment has been the elimination of managers. Companies that have implemented self-managed teams expect a lot more from their lower-level workers than they did in the past and can therefore do without various levels of managers. Because they have less management oversight, such workers need more education. Furthermore, empowered employees need to be treated more as partners in the firm. Increasingly, managers' jobs will be to train, support, coach, and motivate lower-level employees. As many companies have discovered, it sometimes takes years to restructure an organization so that managers are willing to give up some of their authority and employees are willing to assume more responsibility.

Employees with increased responsibility are likely to demand increased compensation based on performance. Often, in larger firms, that will mean giving employees not only higher pay but partial ownership of the firm as well. It will also mean developing entirely new organizational structures to meet the changing needs of customers and employees. We'll discuss such organizational changes and models in Chapter 8.

MPG 52/45   F:⎯⎯E 566mi   CO₂ ½   NOₓ ¹/₁₀
TOYOTA HYBRID SYSTEM   all figures based on EPA estimates -- City/hwy mileage -- actual results may vary -- compared to conventional gasoline engines

Eat my voltage.

Introducing a work of pure genius. Prius, the world's first production car to combine a super-efficient gasoline engine with an advanced electric motor that never needs to be plugged in. No recharging stations. No plugs. No compromises. Prius is powered by the revolutionary Toyota Hybrid System, which stores the energy produced during deceleration and converts it back into electric power. It's fast, fun to drive and produces up to 90%* fewer harmful emissions. Prius. This changes everything.

The electric motor in Prius enhances performance while drastically reducing emissions.

The new Prius. Starting at $19,995. Destination Charge $485. Total MSRP $20,480.**
Visit www.toyota.com/prius or call 800-GO-TOYOTA.

TOYOTA PRIUS | genius

*Based on EPA estimates. Actual results may vary. **Based on manufacturer's suggested retail price. Excludes taxes, title and other optional or regionally required equipment. Actual dealer price may vary. ©2000 Toyota Motor Sales, U.S.A., Inc.

Today, more and more companies compete by better meeting the environmental needs of the community. The new Toyota Prius combines a super efficient gasoline engine with an advanced electric motor to power a car using less natural resources and creating less pollution. Have you bought any products because they were more environmentally friendly than competing alternatives?

Competing by Concern for the Natural Environment

In their rush to give consumers what they want and need, managers must be careful that they cause minimal damage to the natural environment. Business and government leaders throughout the coming years will be discussing issues such as the potential benefits and hazards of nuclear power, recycling, the management of forests, the ethical treatment of animals, and the protection of the air we breathe and the water we drink. Environmentalism must not be a social cause of a few; it must be a major focus of everyone, and it's becoming increasingly so.

THE SOCIAL ENVIRONMENT

Demography is the statistical study of the human population with regard to its size, density, and other characteristics such as age, race, gender, and income. In this book, we're particularly interested in the demographic trends that most affect businesses and career choices. The U.S. population is going through major changes that are dramatically affecting how people live, where they live, what they buy, and how they spend their time. Furthermore, tremendous population shifts are leading to new opportunities for some firms and to declining opportunities for others.

Diversity and Its Advantages for Business

The Bureau of the Census predicts that the U.S. population in 2050 will be very different from what it is today. The total population is expected to increase by approximately 35 percent: 383 million versus just over 280 million today. To put that in perspective, the world population is just over 6 billion people. As the population grows, today's students will find an increased demand for a wide variety of goods and services.

You bring flavor to the world. Why not bring it to work?

PEPSI-COLA COMPANY

The U.S. population's demographic makeup in the year 2050 will also be very different from what it is today. It is estimated that the Hispanic population will increase from 9 percent of the total to 25 percent, and the Asian population will rise from 3 to 8 percent.[20] African Americans, the largest minority group now, are expected to increase their numbers by 62 percent over the next 50 years.[21]

Think of the business opportunities and challenges such shifts will create. In a business context, the words **diversity** and **multiculturalism** are used almost interchangeably to refer to the process of optimizing (in the workplace) the contributions of people from different cultures. Having a multicultural population provides an opportunity for all U.S. citizens to learn to work with people of all nations. That should give Americans an advantage when it comes to negotiating and working with people in global markets.[22]

Moreover, a diverse population can provide ideas, concepts, and cultural norms to enrich the business culture. A diverse population is a strong population. Just as a healthy forest is made up of different kinds of trees and other plants, a thriving business population is made up of people of all different ages, creeds, experiences, and national origins. All in all, one of the reasons the United States is prosperous is because of its diversity and openness to people from all countries.

The Increase in the Number of Older Americans

The baby-boom generation consists of the 76 million people born between 1946 and 1964 who make up more than a quarter of the current U.S. population. By 2030, the baby boomers will be senior citizens. Americans aged 45 to 54 are currently the richest group in U.S. society. They spend more than others on everything except health care and thus represent a lucrative market for restaurants, transportation, entertainment, education, and so on. What do such demographics mean for you and for businesses in the future? Think of

The products Pepsi makes and sells appeal to a wide variety of people. It makes sense, therefore, for the company to hire a diverse workforce and to use their skills to create products that better meet the needs of multiple cultures. Can you see how such a diverse workforce could come up with new products that would appeal to consumers not yet reached by the company, including international markets?

demography
The statistical study of human population to learn its size, density, and other characteristics.

diversity, multiculturalism
Words used almost interchangeably to refer to the process of optimizing (in the workplace) the contributions of people from different cultures.

the products and services the middle-aged and elderly will need—medicine, nursing homes, assisted-living facilities, adult day care, home health care, recreation, and the like—and you'll see opportunities for successful businesses of the 21st century. Businesses that cater to the aging baby boomers will have the opportunity for exceptional growth in the near future. For example, there are lots of computer games for young people, but senior citizens may enjoy playing games and doing other things on the computer as well. The market would be huge.

Two-Income Families

Several factors have led to a dramatic growth in two-income families in the United States. The high costs of housing and of maintaining a comfortable lifestyle have made it difficult if not impossible for many households to live on just one income. Furthermore, many women today simply want a career outside the home.

One result of this trend is a host of programs that companies have implemented in response to the demands of two-income families. IBM and Procter & Gamble, for example, each offer employees pregnancy benefits, parental leave, flexible work schedules, and elder care programs. Some companies offer referral services that provide counseling to parents in search of child care or elder care. Such trends are creating many new opportunities for graduates in human resource management.

Many employers provide child care benefits of some type; some of these programs, such as the one at Johnson Wax, are on-site. Corporate day care centers are expensive to operate and often cause resentment from employees who don't use the benefits. The resentment has led companies to offer what are called cafeteria-style benefits packages, which enable families to choose from a "menu" of benefits. A couple may choose day care instead of a dental plan, for instance.

Many companies are increasing the number of part-time workers. This enables mothers and fathers to stay home with children and still earn income. On the other hand, many companies are hiring part-time workers so that they don't have to pay full benefits, and many workers have to take on two or more jobs to maintain their families. Some companies allow workers to **telecommute**, which means they work from home and keep in touch with the company through telecommunications (telephone, fax, e-mail, etc.). This lowers the company's cost for office space and also makes it possible for parents to meet the demands of both job and family.

Workplace changes due to the rise of two-income families create many job opportunities in day care, counseling, and other related fields. You'll learn more about what's happening in human resource management in Chapter 11.

Single Parents

The rapid growth of single-parent households has had a major effect on businesses as well. It is a tremendous task to work full-time and raise a family. New welfare rules force single parents to work after a certain period. Single parents have encouraged businesses to implement programs such as family leave (where workers can take time off to attend to a sick child) and flextime (where workers can come in or leave at selected times). Again, you will be able to read about such programs in more detail in Chapter 11.

THE GLOBAL ENVIRONMENT

The global environment of business is so important that we show it as surrounding all other environmental influences. (See again Figure 1.2.) Perhaps the number one global environmental change in recent years has been the

telecommute
To work at home and keep in touch with the company through telecommunications.

growth of international competition and the increase of free trade among nations. Japanese manufacturers like Honda, Mitsubishi, and Sony won much of the market for automobiles, videocassette recorders, TV sets, and other products by offering global consumers better-quality products than those of U.S. manufacturers. This competition hurt many U.S. industries, and many jobs were lost.

Today manufacturers in countries such as China, India, South Korea, and Mexico can produce high-quality goods at low prices because their workers are paid less money than U.S. workers and because they've learned quality concepts from Japanese, German, and U.S. producers. Late in the 1990s, however, Thailand, Malaysia, Hong Kong, Japan, South Korea, and other Asian countries had banking problems that caused a major upheaval in global markets. These problems affected all nations, showing the interdependence of countries around the world today.

U.S. manufacturers have been analyzing the best practices from throughout the world, and many have implemented the most advanced quality methods. In fact, U.S. workers in many industries are now more productive than workers in Japan and other competitive countries. **Productivity** is the total output of goods and services in a given period of time divided by work hours (output per work hour).

Better technology, machinery, tools, education, and training enable each worker to be more productive. U.S. companies such as Disney, FedEx, Intel, and Microsoft, as well as many smaller companies, are as good or better than competing organizations anywhere in the world. But some businesses have gone beyond simply competing with organizations in other countries by learning to cooperate with international firms. Cooperation among businesses has the potential to create rapidly growing world markets that can generate prosperity beyond most people's expectations. The challenge is tremendous, but so is the will to achieve. You'll read much more about the importance of global business in Chapter 3.

Competition today is global. That means that companies from all over the world can compete in the United States, just as U.S. firms seek new markets beyond our borders. This McDonald's restaurant, for example, is in Moscow. McDonald's actually sells more hamburgers and fries in other countries than it does in the United States, and their expansion internationally is also faster. How many products do you own that were produced by firms headquartered in other countries?

How Global Changes Affect You

As businesses expand to serve global markets, new jobs will be created in both manufacturing and service industries. U.S. exports are expected to continue to increase under new trade agreements, like the one with China, which will lead to expansion of the job market both in the United States and globally. To see how small businesses are going global by using the Internet, see the box called Reaching Beyond Our Borders.

Global trade also means global competition. The students who will prosper are those who are prepared for the markets of tomorrow. That means that you must prepare yourself now to compete in a rapidly changing environment. Rapid changes create a need for continuous learning. In other words, be prepared to continue your education throughout your career. Colleges will offer updated courses in computer technology, telecommunications, language skills, and other subjects you'll need to stay competitive. Students have every reason to be optimistic about job opportunities in the future if they prepare themselves well.

productivity
The total output of goods and services in a given period of time divided by work hours (output per work hour).

REACHING BEYOND OUR BORDERS

Global Yard Sales

www.ebay.com

Wayne and Shanna Bumbaca tried to run a variety store in Sheridan, Wyoming, but just couldn't survive in the area. The store was stuck with inventory like 144 red Santa figurines with tiny helicopter blades attached to their heads. The Bumbacas couldn't even give them away. Then they put the Santas up for sale on the Internet. The first offer came from a military base in Italy. Now the couple sells approximately 800 such items a week to people throughout the world. You can sell almost anything almost anywhere in the world on the Internet auction sites. Some 2.1 million people around the world visit online auctions at the eBay Inc. website, and Amazon.com has similar auctions. The biggest rival to eBay in Europe is called QXL.com. It operates in 12 different languages and deals with 12 different currencies.

The Internet has made it possible for even relatively small firms to compete in the global marketplace. E-commerce has torn down the invisible barriers between nations so that companies can sell products around the world with much greater ease than in the past. Keep in mind that, by 2003, almost half of the world's online spending is expected to take place beyond U.S. borders. By that year, e-commerce spending in Western Europe, which stood at $5.6 billion in 1998, is expected to balloon to $430 billion. In the Asia-Pacific region, it is expected to leap to $72 billion from $2.7 billion.

Businesses that sell on the Web will face many challenges as they develop a global Internet strategy. Such challenges include finding ways to ship goods cheaply from country to country, dealing with different languages, and converting different currencies. Oddly, another challenge in creating a successful global strategy involves thinking *locally* in each of the individual markets. Online shoppers may be more likely to trust a website that appears to be based in their own country rather than abroad.

Sources: George Anders, "Yard Sales in Cyberspace," *The Wall Street Journal*, April 1, 1999, p. B1; "E-Commerce Burgeons beyond U.S.," *Reuters*, August 25, 1999; and Thomas E. Weber, "E-Bays European Rival Expands Methodically, Country by Country," *The Wall Street Journal*, June 26, 2000, p. B1.

THE EVOLUTION OF AMERICAN BUSINESS

Many managers and workers are losing their jobs in major manufacturing firms. Businesses in the United States have become so productive that, compared to the past, fewer workers are needed in industries that produce goods. **Goods** are tangible products such as computers, food, clothing, cars, and appliances.

goods
Tangible products such as computers, food, clothing, cars, and appliances.

Due to the increasing impact of technology and global competition, shouldn't we be concerned about the prospect of high unemployment rates and low incomes? Where will the jobs be when you graduate? These important questions force us all to look carefully at the U.S. economy and its future.

Progress in the Agricultural and Manufacturing Industries

The United States has seen strong economic development since the beginning of the 1900s. The agricultural industry led the way, providing food for the United States and much of the world. That industry has become so efficient through the use of technology that the number of farmers has dropped from about 33 percent of the population to less than 2 percent. The number of farms in the United States declined from some 5.7 million at the turn of the twentieth century to under 2 million today. However, average farm *size* is now about 455 acres versus 160 acres in the past. In other words, agriculture is still a major industry in the United States. What has changed is that the millions of small farms that existed previously have been replaced by some huge farms, some merely large farms, and some small but highly specialized farms. The loss of farm workers over the past century is not a negative sign. It is instead an indication that U.S. agricultural workers are the most productive in the world, and they still are even though there are fewer of them.

Many farmers who lost their jobs went to work in factories. The manufacturing industry, much like agriculture, used technology to become more productive. The consequence, as in farming, was the elimination of many jobs. Again, the loss to society is minimal if the wealth created by increased productivity and efficiency creates new jobs elsewhere—and that's exactly what has happened over the past 50 years. Many workers in the industrial sector found jobs in the service sector. In fact, the unemployment rate in the United States dropped to 3.9 percent in 2000, the lowest in 30 years.[23] Those who can't find jobs today are largely people who need retraining and education to become qualified for jobs that now exist. We'll discuss the manufacturing sector and production in more detail in Chapter 9.

Agriculture is one of the largest and most important industries in the United States. The entire process of growing food and getting it to our tables is so smooth that it's easy to take for granted. But behind those well-stocked supermarkets is an army of farmers and distributors who supply our needs. Use of technology has led to increased productivity and made farmers more efficient, resulting in larger farms. This trend has meant less expensive food for us, but a continual reduction in the number of small, family-run farms. Is it still possible for small farms to be successful, and if so, how?

Progress in Service Industries

As noted above, many workers who could no longer find employment in manufacturing were able to find jobs in the service industry. **Services** are intangible products (i.e., products that can't be held in your hand) such as education, health care, insurance, recreation, and travel and tourism. In the past, the dominant industries in the United States produced goods (steel, railroads, machine tools, etc.). Today, the leading firms are in services (legal, telecommunications, entertainment, financial, etc.). Together, services make up about half of the American economy. Travel and tourism is now the nation's number two employer and a leading export. Tourism accounts for about 10 percent of all jobs in the United States.

Since the mid-1980s, the service industry has generated almost all of the U.S. economy's increases in employment. Although service-sector growth has slowed, it remains the largest area of growth. Chances are very high that you'll work in a service job at some point in your career. Figure 1.5 lists many service-sector jobs; look it over to see where the careers of the future are likely to be. Retailers like Gap are part of the service sector. Each new retail store creates many managerial jobs for college graduates.

Another bit of good news is that there are more high-paying jobs in the service sector than in the goods-producing sector. High-paying service-sector jobs can be found in health care, accounting, finance, telecommunications, architecture, law, and software engineering. Projections are that some areas of the service sector, such as telecommunications, will grow rapidly, while others, such as advertising, may have much slower growth. The strategy for college graduates is to remain flexible, to find out where the jobs are being created, and to move when appropriate.

services
Intangible products such as education, health care, and insurance.

Your Future in the Global Economy

Despite the growth in the service sector described above, the service era now seems to be losing out to a new era. We're now in the midst of an information-based global revolution that will alter all sectors of the economy: agricultural, industrial, and service. It's exciting to think about the role you'll play in that revolution. You may be a leader; that is, you may be one of the people who will implement the changes and accept the challenges of world

There's much talk about the service sector, but few discussions actually list what it includes. Here's a representative list of services as classified by the government:

Lodging Services

Hotels, rooming houses, and other lodging places
Sporting and recreation camps
Trailering parks and camp sites for transients

Personal Services

Laundries	Child care
Linen supply	Shoe repair
Diaper service	Funeral homes
Carpet cleaning	Tax preparation
Photographic studios	Beauty shops
Health clubs	

Business Services

Accounting	Exterminating
Ad agencies	Employment agencies
Collection agencies	Computer programming
Commercial photography	Research and development labs
Commercial art	Management services
Stenographic services	Public relations
Window cleaning	Detective agencies
Consulting	Interior design
Equipment rental	

Automotive Repair Services and Garages

Auto rental	Tire retreading
Truck rental	Exhaust system shops
Parking lots	Car washes
Paint shops	Transmission repair

Miscellaneous Repair Services

Radio and television	Welding
Watch	Sharpening
Reupholstery	Septic tank cleaning

Motion Picture Industry

Production	Theaters
Distribution	Drive-ins

Amusement and Recreation Services

Dance halls	Racetracks
Symphony orchestras	Golf courses
Pool halls	Amusement parks
Bowling alleys	Carnivals
Fairs	Ice skating rinks
Botanical gardens	Circuses
Video rentals	

Health Services

Physicians	Nursery care
Dentists	Medical labs
Chiropractors	Dental labs

Legal Services

Educational Services

Libraries	Correspondence schools
Schools	Data processing schools

Social Services

Child care	Family services
Job training	

Noncommercial Museums, Art Galleries, and Botanical and Zoological Gardens

Selected Membership Organizations

Business associations	Civic associations

Financial Services

Banking	Real estate agencies
Insurance	Investment firms (brokers)

Miscellaneous Services

Architectural	Surveying
Engineering	Utilities

FIGURE 1.5

WHAT IS THE SERVICE SECTOR?

competition based on world quality standards. This book will introduce you to some of the concepts that will make such leadership possible.

Remember that most of the concepts and principles that make businesses more effective and efficient are applicable in government agencies and nonprofit organizations as well. This is an introductory business text, so we'll tend to focus on business. Nonetheless, we'll remind you periodically that you can apply these concepts in other areas. Business can't prosper in the future without the cooperation of government and social leaders throughout the world.

- What is productivity and how does it affect workers?
- What led to the decline in the number of workers in farming and manufacturing?
- What are some of the high-paying jobs in the service sector?

SUMMARY

1. A business is any activity that seeks profit by providing goods and services to others.
   - *Where does the money come from that people use to buy goods and services?*
   Businesses and their employees create the wealth that people use to buy goods and services. Businesses also are the source of funds for government agencies and nonprofit organizations that improve the quality of life of society. The quality of life of a country refers to the general well-being of its people in terms of political freedom, a clean natural environment, safety, education, health care, free time, and other things that lead to satisfaction and joy. Thus, business adds to both quality of life and standard of living by creating the wealth needed to fund progress in these areas.

   1. Describe how businesses and nonprofit organizations add to a country's standard of living and quality of life.

2. People are willing to take the risk of starting businesses if they feel that the risk isn't too great.
   - *What is the importance of profit, loss, and risk to a business?*
   Profit is money a business earns above and beyond the money that it spends for salaries and other expenses. Businesspeople make profits by taking risks. *Risk* is the chance an entrepreneur takes of losing time and money on a business that may not prove profitable. A *loss* occurs when a business's costs and expenses are more than its revenues. If a business loses money over an extended period of time, it will likely have to close, putting its employees out of work.
   - *What factors of production do businesses use to create wealth?*
   Businesses use five factors of production: land, labor (workers), capital, entrepreneurship, and knowledge. Of these, the most important are entrepreneurship and knowledge.

   2. Explain the importance of entrepreneurship to the wealth of an economy and show the relationship of profit to risk assumption.

3. Economic factors affect business by increasing or decreasing the risks of starting a business.
   - *What are some things that government can do to lessen the risk of starting businesses?*
   Part of the risk of starting a business involves the way that government treats businesses. There's much a government can do to lessen the risk of starting businesses: allow private ownership of businesses, pass laws that enable businesspeople to write contracts that are enforceable in court, establish a currency that's tradable in world markets, focus on the elimination of corruption in business and government, and keep taxes and regulations to a minimum. From a business perspective, lower taxes mean lower risks, more growth, and more money for workers and the government.

   3. Examine how the economic environment and taxes affect businesses.

4. Illustrate how the technological environment has affected businesses.

4. The most successful college graduates of tomorrow will be those who can find their way on the Internet.
    - *How has technology benefited businesses and consumers?*
    Information technology (computers, modems, cellular phones, etc.) is used by business to monitor the business environment so that firms can quickly adapt to changing conditions. In fact, the Internet and e-commerce are, in short, changing everything. Technology has also made it possible for businesses to become much more responsive to consumers. Bar codes tell retailers what size product you bought, in what color, and at what price. Using that information, the retailers can send you catalogs and direct mail pieces offering you exactly what you want, as indicated by your past purchases.

5. Identify various ways in which businesses can meet and beat competition.

5. Competition among businesses has never been greater than it is today.
    - *What are some ways in which businesses meet and beat competition?*
    Some companies found a competitive edge in the 1980s by focusing on making quality products. By the early 1990s, meeting the challenge of making a quality product was not enough to stay competitive in world markets. Companies had to offer quality products and outstanding service at competitive prices. World-class organizations meet the needs of all their stakeholders. Modern businesses have teams of employees who work together to satisfy the needs of all stakeholders, including customers, employees, stockholders, suppliers, dealers, government officials, the community, and people concerned about the natural environment.

6. Demonstrate how the social environment has changed and what the reaction of the business community has been.

6. The United States is going through a social revolution that's having a dramatic impact on how people live, where they live, what they buy, and how they spend their time.
    - *How have such social changes affected businesses?*
    Changes in society are resulting in new opportunities for some firms and declining opportunities for others. As the world population grows, there will be many new opportunities for businesses to sell more products and services. Moreover, a diverse population provides businesses with ideas, concepts, and cultural norms that enrich the business culture. Because many more women have entered the labor force, companies have implemented a variety of programs to assist two-income and single-parent families. Many employers provide child care benefits of some type to keep their valued employees.

7. Analyze what businesses must do to meet the global challenge.

7. The number one global environmental change is growth of international competition and the opening of free trade among nations.
    - *How can businesses meet the global challenge?*
    Many businesses in the United States have met the challenge of quality. Now they're moving to form alliances with businesses all over the globe to take advantage of the best business practices in the world. New trade agreements are expected to expand the job market both in the United States and around the world. Rapid changes create a need for continuous learning among employees.

8. Review how trends from the past are being repeated in the present and what such trends will mean for the service sector.

8. The United States has seen strong economic development since the beginning of the 1900s.
    - *What is the history of our economic development and what does it tell us about the future?*
    What has sustained the United States as the world's economic leader is the development and use of technology to improve productivity. The agricultural sector, for example, has been able to produce more food with fewer workers. Displaced agricultural workers eventually went to work in factories producing more industrial goods. Improved productivity resulting from technology and increased competition from foreign firms combined to reduce the

need for factory workers and contributed to the development of a service economy in the United States. The service era is now giving way to an information-based global revolution that will affect all sectors of the economy.

KEY TERMS

business 4	**factors of production** 9	**revenue** 7
database 15	**goods** 24	**return on investment (ROI)** 11
diversity, multiculturalism 21	**loss** 7	**risk** 7
demography 21	**nonprofit organization** 5	**services** 25
dot-com company 13	**productivity** 23	**stakeholders** 19
e-commerce 13	**profit** 4	**standard of living** 4
empowerment 20	**quality of life** 4	**telecommute** 22
entrepreneur 4		

DEVELOPING WORKPLACE SKILLS

1. This text describes the growth trend in the numbers of businesses in the service sector. Look through your local yellow pages and list five businesses that provide services in your area. This text also describes how certain demographic and social changes affect businesses. Look at your list of local service businesses and consider how social trends might affect them. Distinguish the businesses that are negatively affected from those that are positively affected. Be prepared to explain your answers.

2. Using current business publications, identify which countries around the world have the fastest-growing economies. Choose one of the countries and describe its standard of living and quality of life. If you chose to find a job there, what language would you need to speak? What customs in that country might affect your ability to succeed in business there? Compose a list of other skills you'll need to prosper in that country.

3. Make a list of nonprofit organizations in your community that might offer you a chance to learn some of the skills you'll need in the job you hope to have when you graduate. How could you make time in your schedule to volunteer or work at one or more of those organizations? Write a letter to a nonprofit organization that inquires about such opportunities.

4. Use a computer word processing program to write a one-page report on how technology will change society in the next 10 years. Use a computer graphics program to create a chart (or draw a chart by hand) that illustrates the increased use of personal computers in American homes since 1980.

5. Form into teams of four or five and discuss the e-commerce revolution. How many students now shop for goods and services online? What have been their experiences? What do they see as the future for such purchases? Prepare a two-minute summary for the class.

TAKING IT TO THE NET

This exercise requires using the Internet. If you do not know how to navigate the powerful computer network, you need to read "Surfing the Internet," in the *Getting Ready for Prime Time* section.

Purpose of this exercise: To gather data about the size of global corporations and the level of profitability of the various global industries.

Exercise: Businesses seek to earn profits by providing goods and services to others. Ever wonder just how much profit the largest companies earn and which companies earn the highest profits? Try to answer the first two questions below *before* you search for the answers on the Web. Go to the *Fortune Magazine* website at www.fortune.com. Enter the Global 500 section. You may be surprised with what you find.

1. List the top 10 *revenue*-producing global corporations. How many small businesses with average revenues of $100,000/year would it take to match the revenue of the largest global corporation?

2. List the top 10 *profit*-producing global corporations. How many companies are on both of your lists?

3. How much *revenue per employee* does the trading industry generate? The tobacco industry? The airline industry? And, the mail, package, freight delivery industry?

4. ***KNOW YOUR BUSINESS***: Mitsui is one of the highest revenue-producing companies in the world. What industry is the Mitsui company a part of? Where is its home office? What are Mitsui's primary products?

PRACTICING MANAGEMENT DECISIONS

CASE

HERMAN CAIN'S PATH TO SUCCESS

Luther and Lenora Cain left farm life to find more opportunity in the business world. Luther found a job as a porter and Lenora as a maid. In fact, to earn enough to rear a family, Luther took on three jobs, including one as a chauffeur at Coca-Cola. Soon he became the chauffeur and personal valet to the president of Coca-Cola.

Herman Cain is Luther and Lenora's son. He learned from his parents that hard work and dedication pay off in the long run. He finished high school second in his class and attended Morehouse College, working after school and summers to help pay his tuition. His father had saved enough money to buy a grocery store, and Herman worked in that store for a while. Inspired by Dr. Martin Luther King, Herman Cain went on to get a master's degree at Purdue University and landed a job at Coca-Cola as an analyst. Four years later, he and his supervisor moved to Pillsbury, where in another five years Cain was vice president for corporate systems and services. His goal was to become president of a firm.

The president of Pillsbury told Cain that he would most likely reach his goal by rising up through the ranks at Burger King, a division of the company. But that meant starting from the bottom, flipping hamburgers and giving up his company car and nice office! Cain hoped it was the right thing to do and, as it turned out, it was. He completed the usual two-year training program in nine months and was named Burger King's vice president of the Philadelphia region, in charge of 450 units. His region had been a slow-growing one, but Cain turned it into the company's best region for growth, sales, and profit.

Cain was so successful at Burger King that he was chosen to become president of Pillsbury's Godfather's Pizza. Having reached his goal, Cain began his work as president of Godfather's by streamlining operations. Unprofitable units were closed, and others were made more efficient. Eventually Cain and a partner bought Godfather's from Pillsbury for $50 million. Since then, the value of the company has doubled.

Cain says that service is the driving force behind his business and that his number one rule is "The customer is always right."

He also says that if you love what you are doing, you will be successful. Following that philosophy, Cain became the first black president of the National Restaurant Association.

Now Cain is working hard to support his community. He supports an outreach program for troubled teens and gives speeches about what it takes to be a success. Many young people think the fast-food industry offers only dead-end jobs. Herman Cain doesn't see it that way. He sees such jobs as a chance to eventually run something—to own something. He sees opportunity.

Discussion Questions

1. Why do many youths resist working for fast-food restaurants when such jobs can provide a path to long-term success as a manager and potential owner?

2. What are the risks and opportunities involved in changing your job to seek faster advancement as Herman Cain did?

3. What obligations do small-businessowners have to give back to the community that made them a success?

4. Which career path has the most appeal to you: working your way up through a large corporation or working for yourself? Why?

VIDEO CASE

LEROY WRIGHT, YOUNG ENTREPRENEUR OF THE YEAR

Raised by blind grandparents in rough North St. Louis, Leroy Wright learned a great many things at a very young age. He learned to work hard and to be independent. He also learned to play hard—his years playing football at Mathews-Dickey Boys Club, a recreation club for inner-city kids, helped Wright earn a sports scholarship to Southern Illinois University-Carbondale.

After college, Wright continued on the road to success by landing a job at Southwestern Bell. He was top sales person by the end of his first year and maintained that position in his second and third year. After his third year at SW Bell, he thought he could sell more SW Bell products outside the company than in it. He put together a solid business plan, raised capital from private investors, used his personal savings and started his own cellular phone company, TLC Next Generation International Holdings. (TLC stands for "The Leroy Company.") Three years later, TLC was the number one wireless company in the Midwest and a fast-growing contender in California. Wright was named Young Entrepreneur of the Year in St. Louis in 1998 and went on to become one of 10 national finalists in the prestigious Ernst & Young annual competition.

Wright looked for the right business opportunity and believes wireless communication is one the fastest growing markets. People use their mobile phones for paging, voice mail, text messaging, e-mail and as a personal organizer. Wright thinks that soon people will use mobile phones as personal computers for total integrated communication.

Wright always has his primary mission firmly in mind. "I want to be extremely wealthy. I believe taking the company public [selling stock to private investors] and doing the right things with it is the way to go, not just for myself and my family, but to benefit others and help them find success as well." In addition to building a successful company that benefits himself, his employees, and his other stakeholders, Wright finds other ways to help others find success. He now serves on the board of the Mathews-Dickey Boys' Club and presents himself as an example of what such clubs can do for kids on the streets. He also shares his story with children in the St. Louis Public Schools through the Role Model Experience program. He's given about 200 speeches throughout the urban school district because he wants to motivate young people, to tell them success is attainable.

Discussion Questions

1. How do entrepreneurs like Wright help others succeed? What effect does their success have on their stakeholders?

2. Why do you think Wright identified wireless communications as the business opportunity that would help him reach his goals? Do you agree with him that this is a growth area? What risks might threaten Wright's success?

3. How might the five environmental factors that affect business growth and job creation discussed in the chapter affect Wright's continued success? (The five factors are: economic, technological, competitive, social, and global business environments.)

CHAPTER 2

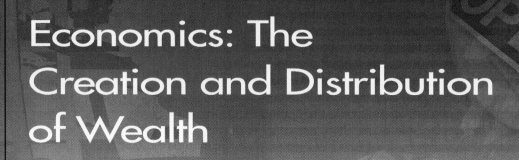

Economics: The Creation and Distribution of Wealth

LEARNING GOALS

AFTER YOU HAVE READ AND STUDIED THIS CHAPTER, YOU SHOULD BE ABLE TO

1. Compare and contrast the economics of despair with the economics of growth.

2. Explain the nature of capitalism and how free markets work.

3. Discuss the major differences between socialism and communism.

4. Explain the trend toward mixed economies.

5. Use key terms (e.g., GDP, CPI, PPI, productivity, inflation, recession, monetary policy, fiscal policy, and national debt) to explain the U.S. economic condition.

Getting to Know Greg Slyngstad and Steve Murch of VacationSpot.com

The chances for success when starting a business vary from country to country depending on the social and economic conditions. Few stories illustrate this concept better than the following one about competition between a team of entrepreneurs in Europe and a team in the United States.

The European entrepreneurs are friends Peter Ingelbrecht and Laurent Coppieters from Belgium. When they had trouble finding a house for a vacation on Spain's Costa del Sol, Ingelbrecht and Coppieters decided to start an online vacation-home booking agency called Rent-a-Holiday. The pair began seeking financial help from venture capitalists (people who lend money to new businesses for a share of the ownership). At first, Belgian financiers refused to help them. More cautious than many U.S. financiers, the Belgian venture capitalists wanted to see evidence of Rent-a-Holiday's success. Ingelbrecht and Coppieters were frustrated. How could they prove their business was successful before they even started it? Yet, determined to succeed, they were able to gather $400,000 from their families and eventually they found a venture capitalist firm willing to loan them $850,000.

In addition to the difficulty of finding the money to start their business, Ingelbrecht and Coppieters had difficulty finding people in Europe who were eager to work for a start-up Internet company. While there is a shortage of qualified computer workers across the globe, the shortage is even greater in Europe than in the United States. Potential employees considered the risks of working for a start-up company too great compared with working for established firms. Rent-a-Holiday tried to attract workers in the same way many U.S. start-ups do—that is, with the promise of stock options (you'll read about these in Chapter 12). However, unlike in the United States, the stock options in Europe are taxable, so the offer didn't help attract workers.

In the United States, Greg Slyngstad and Steve Murch had a similar idea about starting their own online vacation business, which they eventually called VacationSpot.com. They had been working for Microsoft Corporation and wanted to create something on their own. They too sought financing, but had much better success than the Belgian entrepreneurs. In fact, several companies wanted to finance the venture. The team accepted venture capitalist Technology Crossover's offer of $5 million and an additional $4 million from a variety of other investors. "It's heaven for entrepreneurs now in America," Slyngstad says. Furthermore, people with master of business administration (MBA) degrees were eager to join the new venture. They were more willing than their European counterparts to take a risk in working for a new business.

The American venture was also more successful in finding customers for its Internet site. The European entrepreneurs used real estate agents to complete transactions by phone or fax. The Americans did the same, but they also built a full-service website where people could book a holiday villa online. The site also supplied reviews of the vacation homes written by previous guests.

The end of the story is this: The American firm eventually bought the European firm and gave the European entrepreneurs a little over 20 percent ownership of the new combined firm, which retained the name VacationSpot.com. Then in 2000, Microsoft bought the company for nearly $71 million.

Chapter 2 is about economics and the creation of wealth. You will learn about different economic systems and how they either encourage or discourage entrepreneurship. You will also learn about the U.S. economy and how it works. At the end, you will have a better understanding of how economic conditions in the United States made it possible for two young entrepreneurs to succeed in starting a new Internet company while such a venture was harder to start in Europe.

Sources: William Echikson, "Home Field Advantage," *Business Week, E.BIZ*, December 13, 1999, pp. 72–74; Kate Pocock, "Send Your Mouse Shopping in Paris," *Toronto Sun*, May 25, 2000; and Craig Stoltz, "Internet Travel: Shakeout Time," *The Washington Post*, May 14, 2000.

THE IMPORTANCE OF THE STUDY OF ECONOMICS

Why is South Korea comparatively wealthy and North Korea suffering economically? Why is China's per capita (per person) annual income $500, while Taiwan's is closing in on $20,000? Such disparity in incomes may be one of the reasons why China continually threatens Taiwan.[1] How can China become as prosperous as Taiwan and lessen the tensions between the two countries? Such questions are part of the subject of economics. In this chapter, we explore the various economic systems of the world and how they either promote or hinder business growth, the creation of wealth, and a higher quality of life for all.

A major part of America's business success is due to an economic and social climate that allows businesses to operate freely. Any change in the U.S. economic or political system has a major influence on the success of the business system. World economics and politics also have a major influence on businesses in the United States. Therefore, to understand business, you must also understand basic economics and politics.

Greg Slyngstad, Steve Murch, Peter Ingelbrecht, and Laurent Coppieters are just four of millions of men and women who can create wealth for their families and their countries if given the chance. That chance comes when a free-market system (one not controlled by government) is introduced and people are provided with a little money to get started. The Reaching Beyond Our Borders box about Pablo Tesak will give you an idea of how a small business can grow and help whole communities prosper.

The three basic objectives of this chapter are to teach you (1) how the free-market system (capitalism) works to create wealth and prosperity, (2) how free-markets differ from government-controlled markets in the distribution of wealth, and (3) some basic terms and concepts from economics so that you'll understand what they mean when you encounter them in business periodicals.

What Is Economics?

Economics is the study of how society chooses to employ resources to produce goods and services and distribute them for consumption among various competing groups and individuals. Remember from Chapter 1 that these resources (land, labor, capital, entrepreneurship, and knowledge) are called factors of production. Economists usually work from one of two perspectives: **macroeconomics** looks at the operation of a nation's economy as a whole, and **microeconomics** looks at the behavior of people and organizations in particular markets. For example, while macroeconomics looks at

REACHING BEYOND OUR BORDERS

www.infomanage.com

Pablo Tesak, Entrepreneur in El Salvador

When Pablo Tesak came to El Salvador, he noticed that the majority of consumer products there were imported from the United States and Europe. Tesak decided to develop a line of snack products that would be produced in El Salvador and be made available to the poor people there. By setting up a factory to make simple and cheap snack items, Tesak prospered. Later, a civil war in the country caused dissent among his workers. In order to stabilize his workforce Tesak raised salaries, but he discovered that his employees needed still more compensation.

To keep his workers and increase their productivity, Tesak opened a "price club." He arranged to buy local products from nearby factories and make them available to employees at cost, with interest-free monthly payments. The club now sells beds, refrigerators, and other household goods to Tesak's employees and provides them with services such as medical care, English courses, and a summer camp for children. Tesak also set up a $500,000 home credit line so that his employees could borrow money to buy homes. As a result of these new benefits, employee morale and productivity increased substantially. Tesak learned that even when hunger, war, poverty, and disease are constant threats, entrepreneurship can flourish and can improve conditions for everyone involved.

how many jobs exist in the whole economy, microeconomics examines how many people will be hired in a particular industry or a particular region of the country.

There's no way to create peace and prosperity in the world by merely dividing the resources we have today among the existing nations. There aren't enough known resources available to do that. **Resource development** is the study of how to increase resources and to create the conditions that will make better use of those resources. Businesses may contribute to an economic system by inventing products that greatly increase available resources. For example, businesses may discover new energy sources, new ways of growing food, and new ways of creating needed goods and services.

resource development
The study of how to increase resources and to create the conditions that will make better use of those resources.

The Economics of Despair

Imagine the world when kings and other landowners had most of the wealth and the majority of the people were peasants. The peasants had many children, and it may have seemed to be a natural conclusion that there would soon be too many people and not enough food and other resources. English economist Thomas Malthus made this argument in the late 1700s and early 1800s. In response to such views, Scottish writer and thinker Thomas Carlyle called economics "the dismal science." Followers of Malthus today (they are called neo-Malthusians) still believe that there are too many people in the world and that the solution to poverty is birth control, which includes such measures as forced abortion (which is practiced in China) and forced sterilization (practiced in India).[2]

Others believe that a large population can be a valuable resource, especially if people are educated. They believe that one of the keys to economic growth throughout the world is to educate people better. You've probably heard or read the saying "Give a man a fish and you feed him for a day, but teach a man to fish and you feed him for a lifetime." You can add to that: "Teach a person to start a fish farm and he or she will be able to feed a village for a lifetime." *The secret to economic development is contained in this statement.* Business owners provide jobs and economic growth for their employees and communities as well as for themselves.

If there were no way to increase resources faster than population growth, we would all be in big trouble. But, thankfully, technological advances in many countries have provided the means to increase production of food and other resources so that people in many areas of the world are much better off than in Malthus's time. You have only to compare the world today with the world in the 18th and 19th centuries to see the differences. Countries such as the United States, Canada, and most of Europe are much richer now, and most people live much better lives.[3]

The challenge for economists is to determine what makes some countries relatively rich and other countries relatively poor, and then to implement policies and programs that lead to increased prosperity for everyone in all countries. One way to begin understanding this challenge is to consider the theories of Adam Smith.

Growth Economics and Adam Smith

The Scottish economist Adam Smith was one of the first people to imagine a system for creating wealth and improving the lives of everyone. Rather than simply believing that fixed resources had to be divided among competing groups and individuals, Smith envisioned creating *more* resources so that everyone could become wealthier. The year was 1776. Adam Smith's book *An Inquiry into the Nature and Causes of the Wealth of Nations* often is called simply *The Wealth of Nations.*

Adam Smith believed that freedom was vital to the survival of any economy, especially the freedom to own land or property and the freedom to keep the profits from working the land or running a business. He believed that people will work hard if they have incentives for doing so—that is, if they know they will be rewarded.

He made the desire for improving one's condition in life the basis of his theory. According to Smith, as long as farmers, laborers, and businesspeople (entrepreneurs) could see economic reward for their efforts (i.e., receive more money in the form of profits), they would work long hours. As a result of those efforts, the economy would prosper—with plenty of food and all kinds of products available to everyone. His ideas were later challenged by Malthus and others who believed that economic conditions would only get worse, but it is Smith, not Malthus, who is considered by some to be the father of modern economics.

The Invisible Hand

Under Adam Smith's theory, businesspeople don't necessarily deliberately set out to help others. They work primarily for their own prosperity and growth. Yet as people try to improve their own situation in life, Smith said, their efforts serve as an "invisible hand" that helps the economy grow and prosper through the production of needed goods, services, and ideas. Thus, the **invisible hand** turns self-directed gain into social and economic benefits for all.

How is it that people working in their own self-interest produce goods, services, and wealth for others? The only way farmers in a given area can become wealthy is to sell some of their crops to others. To become even wealthier, farmers would have to hire workers to produce more food. As a consequence, people in that area would have plenty of food available and some would have jobs

Adam Smith developed a theory of wealth creation more than 200 years ago. His theory relied on entrepreneurs working to improve their lives. To make money, they would provide goods and services, as well as jobs, for others.

invisible hand
A phrase coined by Adam Smith to describe the process that turns self-directed gain into social and economic benefits for all.

on the farms. So the farmers' self-centered efforts to become wealthy lead to jobs for some and food for almost all. Stop and envision that process for a minute because it is critical to your understanding of economic growth in the United States and other free countries.

The same principles apply to other products as well—everything from clothing to houses to cellular phones. To increase wealth for their families, manufacturers would work hard and hire others. As a consequence, nearly everyone in the area would have access to clothes, homes, phones, and so on, and almost everyone who was willing and able to work would have a job. That is how Adam Smith felt wealth would be created. Experience has shown that he was right in some countries.

Smith assumed that as people became wealthier, they would naturally reach out to help the less fortunate in the community, as Pablo Tesak did (review the Reaching Beyond Our Borders box on page 35). That has not always happened in the past. Today, however, many U.S. businesspeople are becoming concerned about social issues and their obligation to return to society some of what they've earned.[4]

Farmers try to maximize their income by providing food when and where people most desire it. Many cities have farmers' markets where restaurants and individuals can buy fresh produce directly from the growers. The produce is grown on small farms and often tastes better than genetically engineered, mass-produced products. For small farmers to prosper, they have to provide a better product and this incentive results in more food and choices for consumers. How could small farmers increase their output and still maintain the quality of their products?

UNDERSTANDING FREE-MARKET CAPITALISM

Following the ideas of Adam Smith, businesspeople in the United States, Europe, Japan, Canada, and other countries began to create more wealth than had ever been created before. They hired others to work on their farms and in their factories, and their nations began to prosper as a result. Businesspeople soon became the wealthiest people in society.

Great disparities in wealth remained or even increased. Businesspeople owned large homes and fancy carriages, while workers lived in humble surroundings. Nonetheless, there was always the promise of better times. One way to be really wealthy was to start a successful business of your own. Of course, it wasn't that easy—it never has been. Then and now, you have to accumulate some money to buy or start a business, and you have to work long hours to make it grow. But the opportunities are there.

The economic system that has led to wealth creation in much of the world is known as capitalism. **Capitalism** is an economic system in which all or most of the factors of production and distribution (e.g., land, factories, railroads, and stores) are privately owned (not owned by the government) and are operated for profit. In capitalist countries, businesspeople decide what to produce; how much to pay workers; how much to charge for goods and services; whether to produce certain goods in their own countries, import those goods, or have them made in other countries; and so on. No country is purely capitalist, however. Often the government gets involved in issues such as determining minimum wages and setting farm prices, as it does in the United States. But the *foundation* of the U.S. economic system is capitalism.

capitalism
An economic system in which all or most of the factors of production and distribution are privately owned and operated for profit.

The Foundation of Capitalism

Some people don't understand how the free-market system works or what rights it confers. As a result, they can't determine what the best economic system is. You should learn how the U.S. economy works and what mechanisms exist to promote economic growth. People under free-market capitalism have four basic rights:

- *The right to private property.* This is the most fundamental of all rights under capitalism. It means that individuals can buy, sell, and use land, buildings, machinery, inventions, and other forms of property. They can also pass property on to their children.

- *The right to own a business and to keep all of that business's profits.* Recall from Chapter 1 that profits equal revenues minus expenses (salaries, materials, taxes). Profits act as important incentives for business owners.

- *The right to freedom of competition.* Within certain guidelines established by the government, individuals are free to compete with other individuals or businesses by offering new products and promotions. To survive and grow, businesses need laws and regulations, such as the laws of contracts, which ensure that people will do what they say they'll do.

- *The right to freedom of choice.* People are free to choose where they want to work and what career they want to follow. Other freedoms of choice include where to live and what to buy or sell.

One benefit of such rights and freedoms is that people are willing to take more risks than they would otherwise. That is one of the reasons why Greg Slyngstad and Steve Murch were able to get funding for their business and why people were eager to join their new online firm. Now that you know those rights, let's explore how the free-market system works. What role do consumers play in the process? How do businesses learn what consumers need and want? These questions and more are answered next.

A free market system provides certain basic rights, such as the right to choose what kind of work you want to do. You also have the rights to own land, have your own business and keep the profits from that business. But entrepreneurs also need information and know-how. TechnoServe is one organization that teaches people in developing countries how best to start, improve and manage a business. How could retired farmers and other business people help developing countries increase their wealth?

Developing countries need know-how more than money.

Given a chance, farmers in Africa and Latin America will earn enough money. By bringing technical and marketing skills from our country to theirs, a non-profit group called TechnoServe gives them that chance. We show them how to pool resources, how to plan and how to sell.

Based on twenty-five years of success, the TechnoServe way not only creates more wealth in developing regions. It also builds self-esteem. And that doesn't carry a price tag. Please learn how you can help TechnoServe improve the quality of life in the world's poorer regions.

TechnoServe
A working solution to world hunger.

49 DAY ST., NORWALK C.T. 06854. 1-800-99-WORKS

How Free Markets Work

The free-market system is one in which decisions about what to produce and in what quantities are made by the market—that is, by buyers and sellers negotiating prices for goods and services. You and I and other consumers in the United States and in other free-market countries send signals to tell producers what to make, how many, in what color, and so on. We do that by choosing to buy (or not to buy) certain products and services.

For example, if all of us decided we wanted T-shirts from our favorite sports teams, the clothing industry would respond in certain ways. Manufacturers and retailers would increase the price of T-shirts, because they know people are willing to pay more than before. People in the clothing industry would also realize they could make more money by making more T-shirts. Thus, they would have incentive to start work earlier and end later. Furthermore, the number of clothing companies that make T-shirts would increase. How many T-shirts they make depends on how many we request in the stores. The prices and quantities would continue to change as the amount of T-shirts we buy changes.

The same process occurs with most other products. The price tells producers how much to produce. As a consequence, there's rarely a long-term shortage of goods in the United States. If something is wanted but isn't available, the price tends to go up until someone begins making more of that product, sells the ones already on hand, or makes a substitute.

How Prices Are Determined

How free markets work is an important part of economics. The main point is that, in a free market, prices are not determined by sellers; they are determined by buyers and sellers negotiating in the marketplace. A seller may want to receive $50 for a T-shirt, but the quantity demanded at that price may be quite low. If the seller lowers the price, the quantity demanded is likely to increase. How is a price determined that is acceptable to both buyers and sellers? The answer is found in the economic concepts of supply and demand.

The Economic Concept of Supply

Supply refers to the quantity of products that manufacturers or owners are willing to sell at different prices at a specific time. Generally speaking, the amount supplied will increase as the price increases because sellers can make more money with a higher price.

Economists show this relationship between quantity supplied and price on a graph. Figure 2.1 shows a simple supply curve for T-shirts. The price of the shirts in dollars is shown vertically on the left of the graph. The quantity of shirts sellers are willing to supply is shown horizontally at the bottom of the graph. The various points on the graph indicate how many T-shirts sellers would provide at different prices. For example, at a price of $5 a shirt, a T-shirt vendor would provide only 5 T-shirts, but at $50 a shirt a vendor would supply 50 shirts. The line connecting the dots is called a supply curve. The supply curve indicates the relationship between the price and the quantity supplied. All things being equal, the higher the price, the more the vendor will be willing to supply.

The Economic Concept of Demand

Demand refers to the quantity of products that people are willing to buy at different prices at a specific time. Generally speaking, the quantity demanded will increase as the price decreases. Again, the relationship between price and quantity demanded can be shown in a graph. Figure 2.2 shows a simple demand curve for T-shirts. The various points on the graph indicate the quantity demanded at various prices. For example, at a price of $50, the quantity demanded is just 1 shirt; but if the price were $5, the quantity demanded would increase to 35 shirts. The line connecting the dots is called a demand curve. It shows the relationship between quantity demanded and price.

This photo shows free enterprise at work in Russia as a customer negotiates a price with a street vendor. Market prices are determined by millions of such transactions each day. To attract more goods to the market, prices need to be high. But to get more consumers to buy goods, prices have to be lower. In the long run prices tend to seek a level where supply equals demand. At that price, there should be no surplus or shortage. Why, then, are there shortages of food and other products in some countries?

supply
The quantity of products that manufacturers or owners are willing to sell at different prices at a specific time.

demand
The quantity of products that people are willing to buy at different prices at a specific time.

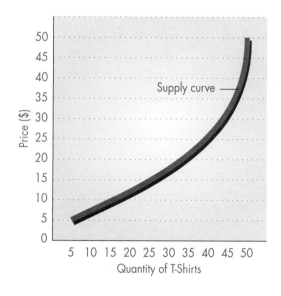

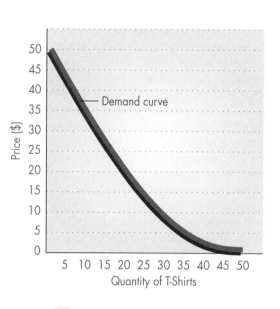

FIGURE 2.1

THE SUPPLY CURVE AT VARIOUS PRICES

The supply curve rises from left to right. Think it through. The higher the price of T-shirts goes (the left margin), the more sellers will be willing to supply.

FIGURE 2.2

THE DEMAND CURVE AT VARIOUS PRICES

This is a simple demand curve showing the quantity of T-shirts demanded at different prices. The demand curve falls from left to right. It is easy to understand why. The lower the price of T-shirts, the higher the quantity demanded.

FIGURE 2.3

THE EQUILIBRIUM POINT

The interaction of quantity demanded and supplied is the equilibrium point. When we put both the supply and demand curves on the same graph, we find that they intersect at a price where the quantity supplied and the quantity demanded are equal. In the long run, the market price will tend toward the equilibrium point.

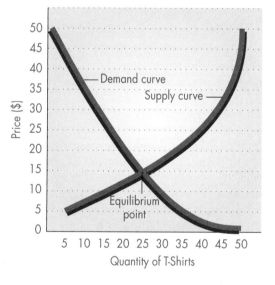

The Equilibrium Point, or Market Price

It should be clear to you after reviewing Figures 2.1 and 2.2 that the key factor in determining the quantity supplied and the quantity demanded is *price*. Sellers prefer a high price, and buyers prefer a low price. If you were to lay one of the two graphs on top of the other, the supply curve and the demand curve would cross. At that crossing point, the quantity demanded and the quantity supplied would be equal. Figure 2.3 illustrates that point. At a price of $15, the quantity of T-shirts demanded and the quantity supplied are equal (25 shirts).

That crossing point is known as the equilibrium point or the equilibrium price. In the long run, that price would become the market price. **Market price,** then, is determined by supply and demand.

Proponents of a free market would argue that, because supply and demand interactions determine prices, there is no need for government involvement or government planning. If surpluses develop (i.e., if quantity supplied exceeds quantity demanded), a signal is sent to sellers to lower the price. If shortages develop (i.e., if quantity supplied is less than quantity demanded), a signal is sent to sellers to increase the price. Eventually, supply will again equal demand if nothing interferes with market forces.

In countries without a free-market system, there is no such mechanism to tell businesses what to produce and in what amounts, so there are often shortages (not enough products) or surpluses (too many products). Furthermore, when the government interferes in otherwise free markets, such as when it subsidizes farm goods, surpluses and shortages may also develop.

One benefit of the free-market system is that it allows open competition among companies. Businesses must provide customers with quality products at fair prices with good service; otherwise, they will lose customers to those businesses that do provide good products, good prices, and good service. We'll discuss the nature of competition next.

market price
The price determined by supply and demand.

PROGRESS ASSESSMENT

- What did Adam Smith mean by the "invisible hand," and how does it create wealth for a country?
- What are the four basic rights under free-market capitalism?
- How do businesspeople know what to produce and in what quantity?
- How are prices determined?

Competition within Free Markets

Economists generally agree that four different degrees of competition exist: (1) perfect competition, (2) monopolistic competition, (3) oligopoly, and (4) monopoly.

Perfect competition exists when there are many sellers in a market and no seller is large enough to dictate the price of a product. Under perfect competition, sellers produce products that appear to be identical. Agricultural products (e.g., apples, corn, potatoes) are often considered to be the closest examples of such products. You should know, however, that there are no true examples of perfect competition. Today, government price supports and drastic reductions in the number of farms make it hard to argue that even farming is an example of perfect competition.

Monopolistic competition exists when a large number of sellers produce products that are very similar but are perceived by buyers as different (e.g., hot dogs, personal computers, T-shirts). Under monopolistic competition, product differentiation (the attempt to make buyers think similar products are different in some way) is a key to success. Think about what that means for just a moment. Through tactics such as advertising, branding, and packaging, sellers try to convince buyers that their products are *different* from those of competitors. Actually, the competing products may be similar or even interchangeable. The fast-food industry, in which there are often pricing battles between hamburger places, offers a good example of monopolistic competition.

An **oligopoly** is a form of competition in which just a few sellers dominate a market. Oligopolies exist in industries that produce products such as break-

perfect competition
The market situation in which there are many sellers of nearly identical products and no seller is large enough to dictate the price of the product.

monopolistic competition
The market situation in which there are a large number of sellers that produce similar products, but the products are perceived by buyers as different.

oligopoly
A form of competition in which the market is dominated by just a few sellers.

fast cereal, beer, automobiles, soft drinks, aluminum, and aircraft. One reason some industries remain in the hands of a few sellers is that the initial investment required to enter the business is tremendous.

In an oligopoly, prices for products from the different companies tend to be close to the same. The reason for this is simple. Intense price competition would lower profits for all the competitors, since a price cut on the part of one producer would most likely be matched by the others. As in monopolistic competition, product differentiation, rather than price, is usually the major factor in market success in a situation of oligopoly. Note, for example, that most cereals are priced about the same, as are soft drinks. Thus, advertising plays a major factor in which of the few available brands consumers buy because often it is advertising that creates the perceived differences.

A **monopoly** occurs when there is only one seller for a product or service ➤ P.25 ◄. That one seller controls the total supply of a product and the price. In the United States, laws prohibit the creation of monopolies. That is one reason Microsoft got into trouble with the law: it appeared to have monopoly power in the market for computer operating systems. We will discuss that case later in the text.

The U.S. legal system does permit monopolies in the markets for public utilities that sell gas, water, and electric power. These utility companies' prices and profits are usually monitored and controlled by public service commissions that are supposed to protect the interest of buyers. For example, the Florida Public Service Commission is the administering agency over the Florida Power and Light utility company. New legislation has ended the monopoly status of some utilities, and consumers are able to choose among utility providers. This is likely to result in fewer, larger utilities and lower prices, although that hasn't happened in California where the electric utilities are deregulated.

Monopolistic competition means that there are many similar products competing for the same market, as in the market for hamburgers in the United States. What are some of the techniques being used by U.S. fast-food marketers like McDonald's and Burger King to differentiate their products from the competition? Is price one of those competitive tools?

monopoly
A market in which there is only one seller.

Limitations of the Free-Market System

The free-market system—with its competition, freedom, and incentives—was a major factor in creating the wealth that people in developed countries now enjoy.[5] Some people even talk of the free-market system as an economic miracle. Free-market capitalism, more than any other system, provides opportunities for the poor to work their way out of poverty. For example, one study that tracked more than 50,000 American workers found that the lifetime income gains of those who began in the bottom 20 percent of income brackets to be four times the gains of those in the top 20 percent.[6] Capitalism also encourages businesses to be more efficient so that they can successfully compete on price and quality.

Yet even as free-market capitalism has brought prosperity to the United States and to much of the rest of the world, it has brought inequality as well. Business owners and managers will make more money and have more wealth than workers will. Similarly, people who are old, disabled, or sick may not be able to start and manage a business. Others may not have the talent or the drive to start and manage a business or farm. What does society do about such inequality? Not all business owners are as generous to their employees as Pablo Tesak has been in El Salvador. In fact, the desire to produce as much as possible and to create as much wealth as possible has led some businesspeople (throughout history and even in some places still today) to use such practices as slavery and child labor. Living conditions for workers throughout the world were modest at best in the 1700s and 1800s, and they remain so in certain areas even now.

Furthermore, free-market capitalism may lead to environmental damage as businesses pollute water and air, and cause other environmental problems. Clearly, some government rules and regulations are necessary to make sure that the environment is protected and that people who are unable to work get the basic care they need.[7] To overcome the limitations of capitalism, some countries have adopted an economic system called socialism. It, too, has its good and bad points. We explore the advantages and disadvantages of socialism next.

CRITICAL THINKING

Adam Smith anticipated that businesspeople would be like Pablo Tesak (see the Reaching Beyond Our Borders box, p. 35) and would voluntarily support their employees and the community at large. In the past, churches, temples, and other nonprofit organizations took a leadership position in supporting those in need. If the government were to stop supporting the needy, would private and nonprofit organizations fill in the gaps? What are the advantages and disadvantages of the government being the major source of support for those in need?

UNDERSTANDING SOCIALISM

Socialism is an economic system based on the premise that most basic businesses—such as steel mills, coal mines, and utilities—should be owned by the government so that profits can be evenly distributed among the people. For example, France owns 75 percent of the communications company France Telecom and over 44 percent of the automaker Renault. Furthermore, private businesses and individuals are taxed relatively steeply to pay for social programs.[8] Socialists acknowledge the major benefit of capitalism—wealth creation—but believe that wealth should be more evenly distributed than occurs in free-market capitalism. They believe that the government should be the agency that carries out the distribution.

Socialism has become the guiding economic platform for many countries in Europe, Africa, and much of the rest of the world. In some countries, such as Canada, businesses are expected to prosper, but businesses and workers also are required to pay very high taxes. The top personal income tax rate in the United States, for example, is 39.6 percent, but in Denmark and the Netherlands, the top rate is 60 percent, in Finland 57 percent and in Belgium (remember our entrepreneurs from the profile at the beginning of the chapter?) 55 percent.[9] In other socialist countries, many, if not most, major businesses are run by the government. Socialist nations tend to rely heavily on the government to provide education, health care, retirement benefits, unemployment benefits, and other social services.

socialism
An ecomonic system based on the premise that most basic businesses should be owned by the government so that profits can be evenly distributed among the people.

The Benefits of Socialism

The major benefit of socialism is social equality. There is more equality of outcome because income is taken from the richer people, in the form of taxes, and redistributed to the poorer members of the population through various government programs. Free education (even through the college level), free health care, and free child care are some of the benefits socialist governments give to their people. Workers in socialist countries usually get longer vacations than workers in capitalist countries. They also tend to work fewer hours per week and have more employee benefits, such as generous sick leave.

The Negative Consequences of Socialism

Socialism may create more equality than capitalism, but it takes away some of businesspeople's incentives to start work early and leave work late. In addition to the income tax rates listed above, marginal tax rates in some nations once reached 85 percent. (The marginal tax rate is the rate you pay on the additional money you earn after a certain income level.) Thus, professional athletes, doctors, lawyers, business owners, and others who earn a lot of money are taxed very highly. As a consequence, many of them leave socialist countries for more capitalistic countries with lower taxes, such as the United States and Monaco.

Imagine an experiment in socialism in your own class: Say that after the first exam, those with grades of 90 and above have to give some of their points to those who make 70 and below so that everyone ends up with grades in the 80s. What would happen to the incentive of those who got As on the first exam? Would they study as hard for the second exam, knowing that they would have to give away any points above 90? What about those who got 70s? Would they work hard if they know that they will get extra points if they don't do well? Can you see why workers may not work as hard or as well if they all get the same salary regardless of how hard they work? Capitalism results in the freedom of opportunity, which is the freedom to keep whatever you earn. That creates incentives to work hard, but it also results in an unequal distribution of outcomes.

Socialism strives for equality of outcomes. Socialist systems, therefore, tend to discourage the best from working as hard as they can. In the business world, socialism also results in fewer inventions and less innovation because those who come up with new ideas usually don't receive as much reward as they would in a capitalist system. Over the past decade or so, most socialist countries have simply not kept up with the United States in job creation or wealth creation.

It is important, however, not to confuse socialism with communism. We shall explore that system next.

UNDERSTANDING COMMUNISM

communism
An economic and political system in which the state makes all economic decisions and owns all the major forms of production.

The 19th-century German political philosopher Karl Marx saw the wealth created by capitalism, but he also noted the poor working and living conditions of laborers in the 1800s. He decided that workers should take over ownership of businesses and share in the wealth. In 1848 he wrote *The Communist Manifesto*, outlining the process. Marx thus became the father of communism. **Communism** is an economic and political system in which the state (the government) makes almost all economic decisions and owns all the major factors of production. It is more intrusive into the lives of people than socialism. For example, some communist countries do not allow their citizens to practice certain religions or move to the town of their choice.

One problem with communism is that the government has no way of knowing what to produce because prices don't reflect supply and demand as they do in free-market systems. As a result, shortages of many items may develop, including shortages of food and basic clothing. Another problem with communism is that it doesn't inspire businesspeople to work hard because the government takes most of their earnings. Therefore, although communists once held power in many nations around the world, communism is slowly disappearing as an economic form.

Most communist countries today are now suffering severe economic depression, and some people are starving (for example, in North Korea). The people in Cuba are suffering from the lack of goods and services readily available in most other countries. Some parts of the former Soviet Union remain communist, but the movement there is toward free markets.[10] The photo on page 46 shows the production of vouchers the government in Russia is using to privatize the economy. The same trend toward privitization is true in parts of China. China's government remains communist, but it has seen the success of neighboring Taiwan and Hong Kong and their free markets, and has experimented with economic freedom in certain regions.[11] Those regions have prospered greatly while the rest of China has grown only slowly.

Although China is still basically a communist country, there are many experiments being made in free markets, at least in some parts of the country. This unemployed twenty-something is using a kiosk to search for job possibilities. In a country with over a billion people, there simply are not enough jobs for everyone. How would the creation of more free markets lead to an increase in jobs and more wealth in China and other countries with high unemployment rates?

THE TREND TOWARD MIXED ECONOMIES

The nations of the world have largely been divided between those that followed the concepts of capitalism and those that adopted the concepts of communism or socialism. Thus, to sum up the preceding discussion, the two major economic systems vying for dominance in the world today can be defined as follows:

1. **Free-market economies** exist when the marketplace largely determines what goods and services get produced, who gets them, and how the economy grows. *Capitalism* ≻ **P.37** ≺ is the popular term used to describe this economic system.

2. **Command economies** exist when the government largely decides what goods and services will be produced, who will get them, and how the economy will grow. *Socialism* ≻ **P.43** ≺ and *communism* ≻ **P.44** ≺ are the popular terms used to describe variations of this economic system.

The experience of the world has been that neither free-market nor command economies have resulted in optimum economic conditions. Free-market mechanisms haven't been responsive enough to the needs of the poor, the old, or the disabled, nor have they sufficiently protected the environment. Therefore, over time, voters in free-market countries, such as the United States, elected officials who adopted many social and environmental programs such as Social Security, welfare, unemployment compensation, and various clean air and water acts.

Socialism and communism, on the other hand, haven't always created enough jobs or wealth to keep economies growing fast enough. As a consequence, communist governments are disappearing and socialist governments have been cutting back on social programs and lowering taxes on businesses and workers. The idea is to generate more business growth and thus generate more revenue.

The trend, then, has been for so-called capitalist countries to move toward more socialism and for so-called socialist countries to move toward more capitalism.[12] We say "so-called" because no country in the world is purely capitalist

free-market economies
Economic systems in which decisions about what to produce and in what quantities are decided by the market, that is, by buyers and sellers negotiating prices for goods and services.

command economies
Economic systems in which the government largely decides what goods and services will be produced, who will get them, and how the economy will grow.

Russia is in economic transition, away from communism and toward capitalism. This remarkable photo shows a stack of vouchers which will be distributed to employees as a first step toward privatizing formerly government-owned businesses. About 150 million people will use these vouchers to buy shares in private firms. What factors may hinder the development of private businesses in Russia?

mixed economies
Economic systems in which some allocation of resources is made by the market and some is made by the government.

or purely socialist. All countries have some mix of the two systems. The trend toward capitalism in socialist countries has slowed recently as countries such as France have selected socialist leaders. But the long-term global trend is toward a blend of capitalism and socialism. This trend likely will increase with the opening of global markets caused by the Internet.

The net effect of capitalist systems moving toward socialism and socialist systems moving toward capitalism is the emergence throughout the world of mixed economies. **Mixed economies** exist where some allocation of resources is made by the market and some by the government. Most countries don't have a name for such a system. If the dominant way of allocating resources is by free-market mechanisms, then the leaders of such countries still call their system capitalism. If the dominant way of allocating resources is by the government, then the leaders call their system socialism. Figure 2.4 compares the various economic systems.

Like most other nations of the world, the United States has a mixed economy. The degree of government involvement in the economy today is a matter of some debate, as it has been at various times in the past. The government has now become the largest employer in the United States, which means that the number of workers in the public sector is more than the number in the entire manufacturing sector. There's much debate about the role of government in health care, education, business regulation, and other parts of the economy. The government's perceived goal is to grow the economy while maintaining some measure of social equality. That goal is very hard to attain. Nonetheless, the basic principles of freedom and opportunity should lead to economic growth that is sustainable.

Governments have a great effect on businesses in the United States and throughout the world. Later in the chapter, we'll explore several issues having to do with the U.S. government and the economy. Keep in mind as you read this material that the foundation of the U.S. economy is capitalism. The government serves as a means to *supplement* that basic system as it tries to promote both economic growth and social equality.

This is an interesting time to monitor the relationship between business and government in the United States. This is also an interesting time to watch how the Internet affects other such relationships worldwide. The Internet is expected to unite businesses around the world in one electronic mall in which the economic systems of the individual countries involved will be less critical to business success than they ever have been before. We explore that notion in the Spotlight on Small Business box.

PROGRESS ASSESSMENT

- What led to the emergence of socialism?
- What are the benefits and drawbacks of socialism?
- What countries still practice communism?
- What is a mixed economy?

	CAPITALISM	SOCIALISM	COMMUNISM	MIXED ECONOMY
Social and economic goals	Private ownership of land and business. Liberty and the pursuit of happiness. Free trade. Emphasis on freedom and the profit motive for economic growth.	Public ownership of major businesses. Some private ownership of smaller businesses and shops. Government control of education, health care, utilities, mining, transportation, and media. Very high taxation. Emphasis on equality.	Public ownership of all businesses. Government-run education and health care. Emphasis on equality. Many limitations on freedom, including freedom to own businesses, change jobs, buy and sell homes, and to assemble to protest government actions.	Private ownership of land and business with government regulation. Government control of some institutions (e.g., mail). High taxation for defense and the common welfare. Emphasis on a balance between freedom and equality.
Motivation of workers	Much incentive to work efficiently and hard because profits are retained by owners. Workers are rewarded for high productivity.	Capitalist incentives exist in private businesses. Government control of wages in public institutions limits incentives.	Very little incentive to work hard or to produce quality goods or services.	Incentives are similar to capitalism except in government-owned enterprises, which have few incentives. High marginal taxes can discourage overtime work.
Control over markets	Complete freedom of trade within and among nations. No government control of markets.	Some markets are controlled by the government and some are free. Trade restrictions among nations vary and include some free-trade agreements.	Total government control over markets except for illegal transactions.	Some government control of trade within and among nations (trade protectionism). Government regulation to ensure fair trade within the country.
Choices in the market	A wide variety of goods and services is available. Almost no scarcity or oversupply exists for long because supply and demand control the market.	Variety in the marketplace varies considerably from country to country. Choice is directly related to government involvement in markets.	Very little choice among competing goods.	Similar to capitalism, but scarcity and oversupply may be caused by government involvement in the market (e.g., subsidies for farms).
Social freedoms	Freedom of speech, press, assembly, religion, job choice, movement, and elections.	Similar to mixed economy. Governments may restrict job choice, movement among countries, and who may attend upper-level schools (i.e., college).	Very limited freedom to protest the government, practice religion, or change houses or jobs.	Some restrictions on freedoms of assembly and speech. Separation of church and state may limit religious practices in schools.

FIGURE 2.4

COMPARISONS OF KEY ECONOMIC SYSTEMS

SPOTLIGHT ON SMALL BUSINESS

www.woodcam.com

The Internet Integrates World Markets

In the past, a small business was fairly confined in its market reach. It couldn't afford to advertise nationally, much less globally. Given such constraints, it was possible for the government to regulate businesses closely and for a country to stay isolated from other countries. Today, however, even small businesses have established websites that allow them to reach global markets quickly and easily.

Woodmere Camera in Lynbrook, New York, for example, sells rare cameras. The market for such cameras is global, but in the past Woodmere had no way to reach beyond its local clientele. Today, however, Woodmere has established a website (www.woodcam.com) that provides customers an online catalog and allows them to request information by e-mail and place orders by filling out an electronic order form. ArtSelect LLC (www.artselect.com) sells reproductions of paintings by great artists like Monet and Picasso out of its offices in Fairfield, Iowa. CDnow (www.cdnow.com) sells about 20 percent of its music outside the United States; its biggest customer is Japan.

Think of what such developments mean to the economies of various countries. Whether the country itself is capitalist or socialist makes little difference to World Wide Web entrepreneurs. They can establish their own businesses quickly and easily on the Internet. People in one country can also work for people in another country—over the Internet. For example, a software developer in India can work for a California company and send his or her programs to the company over the Internet as quickly and efficiently as someone from, say, Oklahoma could.

Where people live, therefore, no longer always determines where they work. What has developed because of the Internet is a global market with global workers making global products. To whom shall the small-business worker in India pay income taxes: India or the United States? Or both? Who pays worker benefits? When someone is unemployed in India, should he or she be counted in the unemployment figures in the United States? Such questions will be important in an era when workers can live anywhere in the world. The World Wide Web will have a profound effect on all the economies of the world and will likely force all countries to adopt a similar economic system or risk becoming social isolates in the world economy. What will that world economic system be? What will the rights of workers be? What union and environmental rules will apply? As you can see, the next few years will present tremendous challenges and opportunities to those who understand economics and business, especially small businesses that have whole new worlds to conquer.

Sources: Bill Spindle, "The Route to Asia," *The Wall Street Journal*, July 12, 1999, p. R22, Fred Sandsmark, "High Hurdles for Small Business," *Red Herring*, March 2000, pp. 198–204, and N. Venkatraman, "Five Steps to a Dot-Com Strategy: How to Find Your Footing on the Web," *Sloan Management Review*, Spring 2000, pp. 15–28.

UNDERSTANDING THE ECONOMIC SYSTEM OF THE UNITED STATES

Over the past few years, while many countries around the world have moved toward free-market economic systems, the United States has been moving toward having more social programs. Recently, for example, new programs were proposed to help fund students' first years of college and to provide day care for the children of workers in industries across the country. Furthermore, there has been much conflict between business leaders and government leaders. Some business leaders believe that taxes are too high and there are too many government regulations. Government leaders have been divided as to the direction the government should take. Some believe that the government should become more involved than it has been in health care, education, and environmental issues. Others believe there should be less involvement. Those subjects have dominated political debate throughout the latter half of the 20th century and are likely to continue into the 21st century.

Because of such uncertainty, the U.S. economic system is in a state of flux and keeping up with issues and events can be a challenge. The following sections will introduce the terms and concepts you'll need to understand the issues facing government and business leaders today. As an informed citizen, you can then become a leader in helping to create a world economy that is best for all.

Key Economic Indicators

Three major indicators of economic conditions are (1) the gross domestic product (GDP), (2) the unemployment rate, and (3) the price indexes. When you read business literature, you'll see these terms used again and again. It will greatly increase your understanding if you learn the terms now.

Gross Domestic Product   **Gross domestic product (GDP)** is the total value of goods and services produced in a country in a given year. Either a domestic company or a foreign-owned company may produce the goods and services included in the GDP as long as the companies are located within the country's boundaries. For example, production values from Japanese automaker Honda's factory in Ohio would be included in the U.S. GDP. Likewise, revenue generated by the Ford car factory in Mexico would be included in Mexico's GDP, even though Ford is a U.S. company. If GDP growth slows or declines, there are often many negative effects on businesses. A major influence on the growth of GDP is how productive the workforce is, that is, how much output workers create with a given amount of input.

Almost every discussion about a nation's economy is based on GDP. The total U.S. GDP in 1999 was over $6 trillion. The level of U.S. economic activity is actually larger than the GDP figures show because the figures don't take into account illegal activities (e.g., sales of illegal drugs). The high GDP in the United States is what enables Americans to enjoy such a high standard of living.

The Unemployment Rate   The **unemployment rate** refers to the number of civilians at least 16 years old who are unemployed and tried to find a job within the prior four weeks. Any rate below 5 percent is considered very good. The U.S. unemployment rate in 2000 was the lowest in over 30 years, reaching as low as 3.9 percent (see Figure 2.5).[13] Figure 2.6 describes the four types of unemployment: frictional, structural, cyclical, and seasonal. The United States tries to protect those who are unemployed because of recessions, industry shifts, and other cyclical factors. Nonetheless, for a variety of reasons, many of these individuals do not receive unemployment benefits.

This area of Los Angeles is called Fashion Alley. There you can buy counterfeit copies of famous brand names for less. The deals are often made in cash and the vendors may or may not pay their full share of income taxes. It is impossible to measure the full economic activity of the United States because illegal activities, such as the sale of drugs, are not recorded. Nonetheless, you can get a good feel for the economic growth of a nation by measuring its GDP.

gross domestic product (GDP)
The total value of goods and services produced in a country in a given year.

unemployment rate
The number of civilians at least 16 years old who are unemployed and tried to find a job within the prior four weeks.

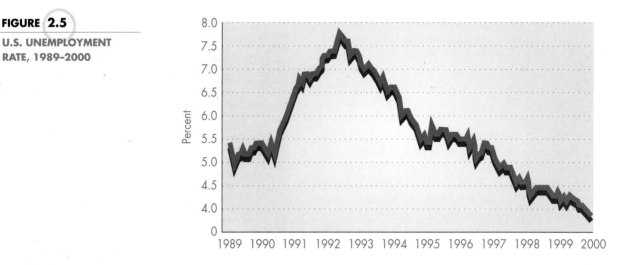

FIGURE 2.6

**FORMS OF
UNEMPLOYMENT**

Even with the unemployment rate around 4 percent, the U.S. economy is actually better off than the figures show because there will always be some unemployment. You'll see what we mean when you read about the following types of unemployment:

• *Frictional unemployment* refers to those people who have quit work because they didn't like the job, the boss, the working conditions and who haven't yet found a new job. It also refers to those people who are entering the labor force for the first time (e.g., new graduates) or are returning to the labor force after significant time away (e.g., parents who reared children). There will always be some frictional unemployment because it takes some time to find a first job or a new job.

• *Structural unemployment* refers to unemployment caused by the restructuring of firms or by a mismatch between the skills (or location) of job seekers and the requirements (or location) of available jobs (e.g., coal miners in an area where mines have been closed).

• *Cyclical unemployment* occurs because of a recession or a similar downturn in the business cycle (the ups and downs of business growth and decline over time). This type of unemployment is the most serious.

• *Seasonal unemployment* occurs where demand for labor varies over the year, as with the harvesting of crops.

**CRITICAL
THINKING**

Would the United States be better off today if the agricultural industry hadn't introduced modern farm machinery? Without mechanization, there would be more people employed on the farm. Would the world be better off in the future if we didn't introduce new computers, robots, and other such machinery in factories? They do take away jobs in the short run. What happened to the farmers who were displaced by machines? What will happen to today's workers who are being replaced by machines?

**consumer price index
(CPI)**
Monthly statistics that measure changes in the prices of about 400 goods and services that consumers buy.

The Price Indexes   The **consumer price index (CPI)** consists of monthly statistics that measure the pace of inflation (consumer prices going up) or deflation (consumer prices going down). Costs of about 400 goods and services—including housing, food, apparel, and medical care—are computed to see if they are going up or down. The CPI is an important figure because some wages and salaries, rents and leases, tax brackets, government benefits, and interest rates are based on it.

MAKING ETHICAL DECISIONS
Exploring the Tax Laws

Imagine that you've been out of school for a while and you and your spouse together are now earning $80,000 a year. To get to that point, you both paid your way through college. You look forward to buying a home, cars, and other goods and services that you postponed to get your education.

You decide to buy a nice home. The federal government allows you to deduct from your taxable income both the mortgage interest charges on that home and the local property taxes. That makes the payments much easier at first. In fact, almost all the money you're paying into the home the first few years is tax deductible.

You also feel that you should give some money to your religious group and other charities. The money you give these nonprofit organizations is also tax deductible if you itemize such deductions. You read in the paper that you and other people who buy homes and give money to charity are receiving unfair tax breaks. After all, poor people can't get deductions for the rent they pay and they can't afford to give to charity. Some people feel that you shouldn't receive a "government subsidy" to buy your home. You, on the other hand, feel that you're paying enough in taxes, but you want to give your fair share. You also know that some people can buy tax-free bonds and others get tax breaks to rent out a second home. Businesspeople can write off some entertainment and travel expenses, and more.

Should the tax laws of the United States be changed to eliminate certain deductions? What percentage of a person's income should go to the government? Should everyone pay equally, or should the rich pay more? What are the moral and ethical reasons for your position?

The **producer price index (PPI)** measures prices at the wholesale level. Other indicators of the economy's condition include housing starts, retail sales, and changes in personal income. You can learn more about such indicators by reading business periodicals and listening to business broadcasts on radio and television.

The government plays a major role in trying to maintain growth in the economy without causing prices to increase too much. How the government does that and how much of the GDP the government should have to work with are two critical issues.

producer price index (PPI)

An index that measures prices at the wholesale level.

Distribution of GDP

The income businesses earn from producing goods and services goes to the people who own the businesses (such as stockholders) in the form of dividends and to the government in the form of taxes. In some countries, taxes take a much larger percentage of GDP than in other countries. The question in the United States each year is, How much of GDP should go to the government and how much should go to businesses and their owners?

In 1959, the percentage of U.S. GDP taken by the government at all levels (federal, state, and local) was about 28 percent. By 1999, that rate had risen to about 35.7 percent.[14] When you count all fees, sales taxes, and more, income taxes on the highest-earning citizens can exceed 50 percent. Is that figure too high or not high enough? That is the question. The Making Ethical Decisions box explores some current tax issues.

After many years of running a budget deficit, the U.S. government is now taking in more money than it is paying out, resulting in a budget surplus. Should that surplus be used to pay off the national debt, increase social programs, or go back to the people in the form of tax cuts?[15] This question is the subject of debate among economists and politicians in the United States. The answer will have a great effect on businesses and you. It is important, therefore, to understand the basic terms and concepts so you can vote intelligently and help the country to continue prospering.

Productivity in the United States

As we noted in Chapter 1, productivity **> P.23 <** is the total output of goods and services in a given period of time divided by work hours (output per work hour). An increase in productivity means that a worker can produce more goods and services than before. Productivity in the United States has gone up in recent years because computers and other technology has made the process of production faster and easier for many workers. The higher productivity is, the lower costs are in producing goods and services, and the lower prices can be. Therefore, businesspeople are eager to increase productivity.

At the beginning of the 20th century in the United States, more than 30 out of 100 workers were needed to produce enough food to feed everyone and create some surplus for world use. Today it takes fewer than 2 out of 100 workers to produce far greater quantities of food that contribute a much larger share to world production. What made the difference? The answer is that the use of tractors, chemical fertilizers, combines, silos, and other machines and resources (capital) raised farmers' productivity.

Now that the U.S. economy is a service **> P.25 <** economy, productivity is an issue, because service firms are so labor intensive. Spurred by foreign competition, productivity in the manufacturing sector is rising rapidly. But manufacturing provides just over 20 percent of output in the United States. In the service sector, productivity is growing more slowly because there are fewer new technologies available to assist workers (e.g., teachers, clerks, lawyers, and personal service providers like barbers) than there are for factory workers.

Productivity in the Service Sector

In the service sector, computers, word processors, and other technology are beginning to make service workers more productive. The United States is ahead of much of the world in service productivity. However, one problem with the service industry is that an influx of machinery may add to the *quality* of the service provided but not to the *output per worker* (productivity).

For example, you've probably noticed how many computers are being installed on college campuses. They add to the quality of education but don't necessarily boost professors' productivity. The same is true of some new equipment in hospitals, such as CAT scanners. They improve patient care but don't necessarily increase the number of patients that can be seen. In other words, today's productivity measures fail to capture the increase in quality caused by new technology.

The United States and other countries need to develop new measures of productivity for the service

Time is money and the world of business is shrinking. Therefore, business people often buy or lease their own airplanes to reduce the time it takes to fly from one location to another to conduct business. This ad for private jets points out the productivity increases possible with such investments. How much time could business people save by not traveling to other cities and countries, and instead use videoconferencing and the Internet to conduct business? What are some disadvantages of not doing business face-to-face?

economy, measures that include quality as well as quantity of output. Otherwise, it will appear that the United States isn't making much progress toward improving the quality of life when, in fact, it's likely that the quality of life is continuing to improve.[16] New measures would prove the case one way or the other.

Inflation and the Consumer Price Index

One measure of the strength of an economy is its ability to control inflation. **Inflation** is a general rise in the prices of goods and services over time. It is sometimes described as too many dollars chasing too few goods. In economic terms, when the quantity demanded goes up, prices go up as well.

As explained earlier, the consumer price index (CPI) measures changes in the prices of about 400 goods and services that consumers buy. The CPI measures the price of an average market basket of goods for an average family over time. Among the items included in the basket of goods are food, automobiles, clothing, homes, furniture, medicine, and medical and legal fees. The consumer price index is closely followed because so many companies and government programs base their salary and payment increases on it.

Disinflation describes a condition where the increase in prices is slowing (the inflation rate is declining). That was the situation in the United States throughout the early 1990s. **Deflation** means that prices are actually declining. It occurs when countries produce so many goods that people cannot afford to buy them all (too few dollars chasing too many goods).

Recession versus Inflation

A **recession** is two or more consecutive quarters (three-month periods) of decline in the GDP. When a recession occurs, prices fall, people purchase fewer products, and businesses fail. A recession has many negative consequences for an economy: high unemployment, increased business failures, and an overall drop in living standards. A **depression** is a severe recession. It is usually accompanied by deflation. For years (since the Great Depression of the 1930s) the government has put much of its effort into preventing another recession or depression. Whenever business has slowed or unemployment has increased, the U.S. Federal Reserve System has pumped money into the economy to revive it. We'll explain that process in the next section.

There's much debate about the future of the U.S. economy as the government tries to keep employment high, inflation low, and businesses growing. To fight inflation and recession, the government and the Federal Reserve System try to manage the economy. To understand the economic situation in the United States and the world today with regard to inflation, recession, unemployment, and other economic matters, you must understand the government's and the Federal Reserve System's roles. Two terms that are crucial to your understanding are *monetary policy* and *fiscal policy*.

Monetary Policy

Monetary policy is the management of the money supply and interest rates. In learning about monetary policy, the first thing one must understand is the role of the Federal Reserve System (the Fed). The Fed is one of the sources of money in the economy; it can add or subtract money from the economy as it sees fit. For example, the Fed can increase the interest rate on money it lends to banks if it thinks such action is warranted. Banks would pass this increase on to borrowers, thus slowing the economy as businesses and households borrow less. For example, small businesses will not borrow the money they need to grow if they can't afford to pay the higher interest rates.

---

inflation
A general rise in the prices of goods and services over time.

disinflation
A condition where price increases are slowing (the inflation rate is declining).

deflation
A situation where prices are actually declining.

recession
Two or more consecutive quarters of decline in the GDP.

depression
A severe recession.

monetary policy
The management of the money supply and interest rates.

FROM THE PAGES OF **BusinessWeek**   *www.brillig.com/debt_clock*

What Do We Do with the Surplus?

For two decades the national debt grew higher and higher. Then, in 1999, there was a surplus (that is, the government was going to take in more than it spent in one year). Much of the surplus consisted of Social Security funds that weren't available for other use, although some politicians talked about taking this money away from the Social Security Administration and using it for other purposes. Even so, about $1 trillion in surplus funds were supposed to be generated over the next 15 years. That's assuming, of course, that the economy keeps growing and there is no major slowdown—a fairly large assumption.

Alan Greenspan, the head of the Federal Reserve, said that it would be best to use surplus funds to pay down the $5.6 trillion national debt. That would lead to lower interest rates and would be good for future generations because they wouldn't have to pay off such a huge debt. On the other hand, President Bush felt that taxpayers were paying in more money than was needed by the government and that money should be returned in the form of tax cuts. It was agreed that part of the surplus money should go to tax cuts and other parts used to reduce the debt and shore up Medicare.

The real danger, some people felt, was that Congress would see surplus money and find ways of spending it. That had happened in the past. In any case, though, it's a good thing that the economy is doing so well that government revenues exceed expenditures, if only for a short time.

Source: Robert Kuttner, "What's Wrong with Paying Off the National Debt," *Business Week*, May 15, 2000, and Gerald F. Seib and Dennis Farney, "Burden of Plenty," *The Wall Street Journal*, October 5, 2000, pp. A1 and A14.

The Federal Reserve System is a private organization that operates independently of the president and Congress and has the goal of keeping the economy growing without causing inflation. It does that by trying to manage the money supply and interest rates. (Chapter 21 discusses the Fed in more detail.)

Fiscal Policy

fiscal policy
Government efforts to keep the economy stable by increasing or decreasing taxes or government spending.

Fiscal policy refers to the federal government's efforts to keep the economy stable by increasing or decreasing taxes and/or government spending. For many years, the government tended to raise taxes to fund more and more programs. For example, between 1993 and 2000, federal spending on education went up by 59 percent, child services spending went up by 129 percent, and environmental spending went up by 23 percent.[17] Figure 2.7 illustrates the U.S. government's income and expenses for 2001.

When the government spends more than it raises in taxes, it creates a budget deficit. The government borrows money to pay this deficit. The result over a number of years is called the **national debt.** In 2000, the national debt was $5.6 trillion dollars. That's over $20,000 for every man, woman, and child in the United States. Figure 2.8 shows how the national debt is growing. (See the *Business Week* box for more on this issue.) Economists and politicians debated whether to lower the debt through more taxes, less spending, or both. In the late 1990s, the economy grew faster than anyone expected, and for the first time in years, the government now has a surplus (more money coming in than being spent by the government). Think of the surplus as similar to the money left over after you pay all of your bills.

national debt
The result of a series of government deficits (when the government spends more money than it collects in taxes) over time.

The debate now is how to handle the surplus. Should some money be given back to the people in the form of tax cuts?[18] Higher tax rates often discourage small-business owners because they decrease profits and therefore make entrepreneurship less rewarding than it would be otherwise. Or should the sur-

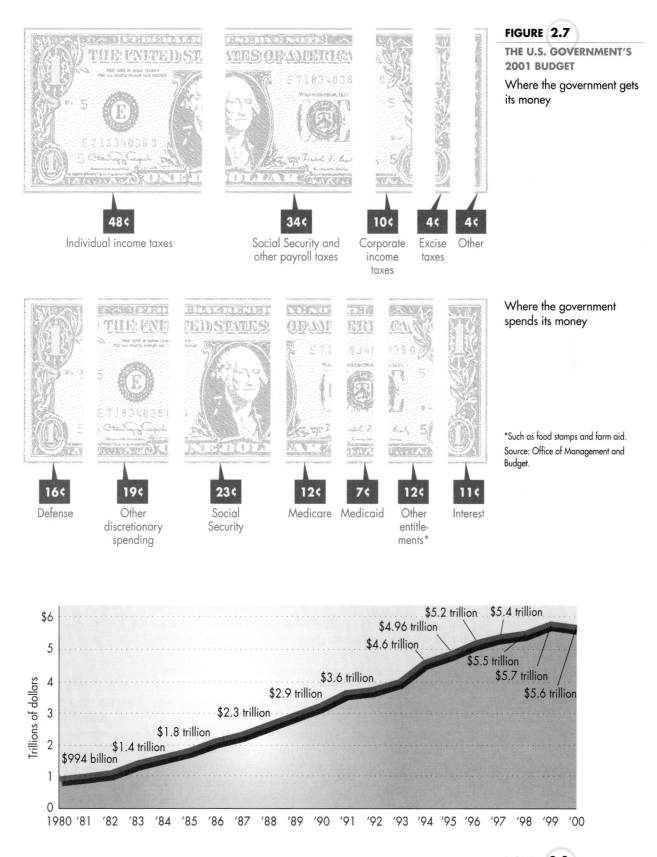

FIGURE **2.7**

THE U.S. GOVERNMENT'S 2001 BUDGET

Where the government gets its money

48¢
Individual income taxes

34¢
Social Security and other payroll taxes

10¢
Corporate income taxes

4¢
Excise taxes

4¢
Other

Where the government spends its money

16¢
Defense

19¢
Other discretionary spending

23¢
Social Security

12¢
Medicare

7¢
Medicaid

12¢
Other entitlements*

11¢
Interest

*Such as food stamps and farm aid.
Source: Office of Management and Budget.

$6
5
4
3
2
1
0

Trillions of dollars

$994 billion
$1.4 trillion
$1.8 trillion
$2.3 trillion
$2.9 trillion
$3.6 trillion
$4.6 trillion
$4.96 trillion
$5.2 trillion
$5.4 trillion
$5.5 trillion
$5.7 trillion
$5.6 trillion

1980 '81 '82 '83 '84 '85 '86 '87 '88 '89 '90 '91 '92 '93 '94 '95 '96 '97 '98 '99 '00

FIGURE **2.8**

THE NATIONAL DEBT

Source: Government data.

plus go to paying off the national debt and/or creating more social programs? This is like asking whether you should use the money left after paying your bills to repay your student loans or go on to graduate school. You can follow the news media to see what the politicians ultimately decide. Probably, it will be a little of everything. The economic goal in the future is to keep the economy growing so that more and more people can rise up the economic ladder and enjoy a satisfying quality of life.

PROGRESS ASSESSMENT

- Name the three economic indicators and describe how well the United States is doing using each one.
- What's the difference between a recession and a depression?
- What does *monetary policy* mean? What organization is responsible for it?
- How does the government manage the economy using fiscal policy?

SUMMARY

1. Compare and contrast the economics of despair with the economics of growth.

1. Economics is the study of how society chooses to employ resources to produce various goods and services and to distribute them for consumption among various competing groups and individuals.
   - ***What are the economics of despair?***
   In the late 1700s and early 1800s, Thomas Malthus theorized that the human population would grow so fast that resources could not keep up. Some countries today have placed severe restrictions on population, including forced sterilization and forced abortions.
   - ***How can wealth be created in a society so that more money, goods, and services are available for distribution?***
   In 1776, Adam Smith called the mechanism for creating wealth and jobs an invisible hand. Under his system (capitalism), businesspeople don't deliberately set out to help others. In fact, they work mostly for their own prosperity and growth. Yet people's efforts to improve their own situation in life act like an invisible hand to help the economy grow and prosper through the production of needed goods, services, and ideas.

2. Explain the nature of capitalism and how free markets work.

2. Capitalism is an economic system in which all or most of the means of production and distribution (e.g., land, factories, railroads, and stores) are privately owned and operated for profit.
   - ***Who decides what to produce under capitalism?***
   In capitalist countries, businesspeople decide what to produce; how much to pay workers; how much to charge for goods and services; whether to produce certain goods in their own countries, import those goods, or have them made in other countries; and so on.
   - ***What are the basic rights people have under capitalism?***
   The four basic rights under capitalism are (1) the right to private property, (2) the right to own a business and to keep all of that business's profits after taxes, (3) the right to freedom of competition, and (4) the right to freedom of choice.
   - ***How does the free market work?***
   The free-market system is one in which decisions about what to produce and in what quantities are made by the market—that is, by buyers and sellers negotiating prices for goods and services. Buyers' decisions in the mar-

ketplace tell sellers what to produce and in what quantity. When buyers demand more goods, the price goes up, signaling suppliers to produce more. The higher the price, the more goods and services suppliers are willing to produce. Price, then, is the mechanism that allows free markets to work.

3. Socialism is an economic system based on the premise that some businesses should be owned by the government.
   • *What are the advantages and disadvantages of socialism?*
   Socialism creates more social equity. Compared to workers in capitalist countries, workers in socialist countries not only receive more education and health care benefits but also work fewer hours, have longer vacations, and receive more benefits in general, such as child care. The major disadvantage of socialism is that it lowers the profits of owners and managers, thus cutting the incentive to start a business or to work hard. Socialist economies tend to have a higher unemployment rate and a slower growth rate than capitalist economies.
   • *How does socialism differ from communism?*
   Under communism, the government owns all production facilities and dictates what gets produced and by whom. Communism is also more restrictive when it comes to personal freedoms, such as religious freedom. While there are many countries practicing socialism, there are only a few (e.g., China, North Korea, Cuba) still practicing communism.

3. Discuss the major differences between socialism and communism.

4. A mixed economy is one that is part capitalist and part socialist. That is, some businesses are privately owned, but taxes tend to be high to distribute income more evenly among the population.
   • *What countries have mixed economies?*
   The United States has a mixed economy, as do most other countries of the world.
   • *What are the benefits of mixed economies?*
   A mixed economy has most of the benefits of wealth creation that free markets bring plus the benefits of greater social equality and concern for the environment that socialism offers.

4. Explain the trend toward mixed economies.

5. Three major indicators of economic conditions are (1) the gross domestic product (GDP), (2) the unemployment rate, and (3) the price indexes.
   • *What are the key terms used to describe the U.S. economic system?*
   Gross domestic product (GDP) is the total value of a country's output of goods and services in a given year. The *unemployment rate* refers to the number of civilians at least 16 years old who are unemployed and who tried to find a job within the most recent four weeks; an unemployment rate below 5 percent is considered good. The *consumer price index (CPI)* measures changes in the prices of about 400 goods and services that consumers buy. It contains monthly statistics that measure the pace of *inflation* (consumer prices going up) or *deflation* (consumer prices going down). *Productivity* is the total volume of goods and services one worker can produce in a given period. Productivity in the United States has increased due to the use of computers and other technology.
   • *What is the importance of monetary policy to the economy?*
   Monetary policy is the management of the money supply and interest rates. Fiscal policy refers to government efforts to keep the economy stable by increasing or decreasing taxes and/or government spending. When unemployment gets too high, the Federal Reserve System may put more money into the economy and lower interest rates.

5. Use key terms (e.g., GDP, CPI, PPI, productivity, inflation, recession, monetary policy, fiscal policy, and national debt) to explain the U.S. economic condition.

• *Why is fiscal policy important to the economy?*
The search is for a good balance between taxes and spending so that the
economy can grow and the government can fund its various programs.
• *How well is the U.S. economy doing?*
During 2000, the unemployment rate reached as low as 3.9 percent—very
good. Furthermore, there is now a reported government surplus for the
first time in many years.

KEY TERMS

capitalism 37	**gross domestic product (GDP)** 49	**oligopoly** 41
command economies 45	**inflation** 53	**perfect competition** 41
communism 44	**invisible hand** 36	**producer price index (PPI)** 51
consumer price index (CPI) 50	**macroeconomics** 34	**recession** 53
demand 39	**market price** 41	**resource development** 35
deflation 53	**microeconomics** 34	**socialism** 43
depression 53	**mixed economies** 46	**supply** 39
disinflation 53	**monetary policy** 53	**unemployment rate** 49
economics 34	**monopolistic competition** 41	
fiscal policy 54	**monopoly** 42	
free-market economies 45	**national debt** 54	

DEVELOPING WORKPLACE SKILLS

1. In a small group, develop a list of the advantages of living in a capitalist society. Then develop lists headed "What are the disadvantages?" and "How
   could such disadvantages be minimized?" Describe why a poor person in a
   socialist country might reject capitalism and prefer a socialist state. How
   could the United States overcome this situation to broaden the base of the
   free-market system?

2. Show your understanding of the principles of supply and demand by looking at the employment market today. Explain, for example, the high salaries
   that computer scientists are getting in Silicon Valley. Also explain why English professors with Ph.D.s aren't getting better pay than computer scientists who only have undergraduate degrees. Why do some teachers make
   less than some garbage collectors, even though the teachers may have a better education? Write a two-page paper explaining the principles.

3. This role-playing exercise will help you understand socialism from different perspectives. Form four groups. Each group should adopt a different
   role in a socialist economy: one group will be the business owners, another
   group will be workers, another will be unemployed citizens, and another
   will be government leaders. Within your group discuss and list the advantages and disadvantages to you of lowering taxes on businesses. Then have
   each group choose a representative to go to the front of the class and debate the tax issue with the representatives from the other groups.

4. Most of the world's nations are moving toward some variation of a mixed
   economy. What do you see as the primary differences between the emergence of mixed economies and pure capitalism? Which would you favor
   and recommend? Why?

5. Since some welfare programs in the United States have been moved from the federal level to the state level, do you expect religious organizations, local businesses, and other groups to provide support to those who can no longer receive welfare benefits? What are the advantages and disadvantages of having the government care for people versus the local citizens through charitable organizations?

Purpose

To compare the value of the dollar based on variances in the consumer price index.

Exercise

Do your parents ever tire of telling you how much things cost back in their day? Sure, things were cheaper then, but the value of a dollar was different too. Think about something you bought today (shoes, soda, candy bar, haircut—whatever). How much did the good or service you bought today cost your parents when they were your age? Find out by using the handy tool on the Federal Reserve Bank of Minneapolis's Woodrow website (http://woodrow.mpls.frb.fed.us/economy/calc/cpihome.html). The calculator uses the consumer price index to compare the value of the dollar in different years. Enter the cost of the item you bought today, the year you would like to compare it with, and—presto—you'll find out how Mom and Pop could get along on such a small paycheck. (For an even bigger shock, compare the current dollar to the dollar in your grandparents' day!)

1. How much would a $50 pair of jeans bought today have cost the year you were born?

2. How much would a job paying $6 an hour today have paid in 1970?

3. How much would a new car costing $18,000 today have cost the year you got your first driver's license?

4. Ask someone from another country how prices for products in the United States have compared with prices in their country over time. Search the Internet to see if you can find such comparisons.

Purpose

To familiarize students with the sources of economic information that are important to business decision makers.

Exercise

Imagine your boss asked you to help her in preparing the sales forecast for the next two years. In the past she felt that the trend in the nation's GDP, the employment trends in U.S. manufacturing, and in manufacturing in Illinois were especially helpful in forecasting sales. She would like for you to do the following:

1. Go to the website www.bea.doc.gov and locate the gross domestic product data. Compute an annual figure for the last four years by averaging the quarterly data. Plot this on graph paper or a spreadsheet. Leave enough space for six years so that you can draw a projection line for the next two years.

2. On the website www.bls.gov go to the page with the information about the manufacturing industry. What is the employment trend in that industry over the last four years?

3. On the same website, find the manufacturing employment for the state of Illinois. Using the data from July, plot the trend in manufacturing employment in Illinois over the last four years.

4. If sales in your company tend to increase as the GDP increases and as the employment in manufacturing in the United States and Illinois remains stable or increases, what do you think is going to happen to your company's sales?

PRACTICING MANAGEMENT DECISIONS

CASE

THE RULE OF 72

No formula is more useful for understanding inflation than the rule of 72. Basically, the rule allows you to quickly compute how long it takes the cost of goods and services to double at various compounded rates of growth. For example, if houses were increasing in cost at 9 percent a year, how long would it take for the price of a home to double? The answer is easy to calculate. Simply divide 72 by the annual increase (9 percent) and you get the approximate number of years it takes to double the price (eight years). Of course, the same calculation can be used to predict how high food prices or auto prices will be 10 years from now.

Here's an example of how you can use the rule of 72. If the cost of going to college goes up by 6 percent a year, how much might you have to pay to send your child to college in 24 years if college costs are now $10,000 a year? To find the answer, you divide 72 by

6, which shows that the cost of an education would double in 12 years. Therefore, it would double twice in 24 years. Your son or daughter can expect to pay $40,000 per year to attend college.

Discussion Questions

1. If the cost of a private college education is about $20,000 per year now, what will it cost your children per year if costs go up 9 percent a year and your children go to college 16 years from now?

2. If the value of a home doubles in 12 years, what is the annual rate of return? (Hint: Use the rule of 72 in reverse.)

3. If you put $1,000 into a savings account and earned 6 percent per year, how much money would you have in the account after 48 years?

4. If interest on the national debt is 6 percent a year, how long would it take for the debt to double? How long would it take if the interest rate went up to 8 percent?

VIDEO CASE

BREAKING DOWN THE GREAT WALL

China, with its 1.2 billion people and staggering abundance of natural resources, is expected to become the world's largest economy in the new millennium. This transition to global economic power will not be easy for the communist giant, since China has not historically embraced an open-door policy to world traders. For a 50-year period, China chose a self-imposed isolation, with its goal to become economically self-sufficient. The shift from communist to free-market trade policies seems like a mountain too steep to climb, but China enjoyed an enormous boost in its climb in the summer of 1997. After 150 years of British control, Hong Kong, the capitalist mecca of the Far East, returned to China's rule. This much-publicized shift in political control could be the best thing to ever happen economically to China.

Hong Kong has been a powerful engine in driving capitalism into high gear in many Asian markets. During the past 15 years, Hong Kong has grown from the 23rd to the 8th largest trade entity in the world. It has become a global center for finance, distribution, and trade and has established a complex and functioning business structure to compete in world markets. This efficient infrastructure caused many of the world's leading corporations to set up shop in Hong Kong. The Hong Kong business community also developed vast knowledge in governmental trade strategies and policies for economic growth. By gaining the trade facilities of Hong Kong, China can open its previously closed doors much wider and make effective use of the important theory of comparative advantage.

Still, the economic shift to unrestricted free-trade policies from a closed society is bound to cause some concern and fear in China. It's essential that the government establish specific trade strategies to confront and deal with these concerns. Trade policies involving tariffs, subsidies, import quotas, local content requirements, and administrative trade policies will need to be adapted for both political and economic reasons. By forging close ties with Hong Kong business leaders, China can take a giant step in bridging gaps and removing wedges that have separated the nation from global markets in the past.

Discussion Questions

1. Hong Kong's reentry into China should help the Chinese economy because it is so much further along in adopting free-market (capitalist) concepts. What are some of the changes China would have to make to become a free market economy?

2. What adjustments will China need to make to conform to the cultural, economic, and social practices of other countries?

3. If the Chinese impose stiff trade policies, what might be the reaction of their global trading partners?

CHAPTER 3

Competing in Global Markets

LEARNING GOALS

AFTER YOU HAVE READ AND STUDIED THIS CHAPTER, YOU SHOULD BE ABLE TO

1. Discuss the growing importance of the global market and the roles of comparative advantage and absolute advantage in international trade.

2. Explain the importance of importing and exporting, and understand key terms used in international business.

3. Describe the current status of the United States in global business.

4. Illustrate the strategies used in reaching global markets.

5. Evaluate the forces that affect trading in world markets.

6. Debate the advantages and disadvantages of trade protectionism.

7. Explain the role of multinational corporations in global markets.

8. Explain how technology affects global e-commerce.

Getting to Know Mary Lou Wilson of Enrich International

Mary Lou Wilson doesn't take getting laughed at lightly. When the chairman of her company, Enrich International (a division of the Dutch company Royal Numico, makers of a wide variety of nutritional and personal care products), asked his top distributors to choose a foreign country to target for opening up new business, Wilson picked Japan. Some of her colleagues burst out laughing at her choice. Others, trying to be diplomatic, explained that Japan's business fabric is a male-dominated network that would most likely be unreceptive to a woman, especially an older American woman. Today, 64-year-old Wilson has the last laugh: her network of 150,000 individual distributors in Japan sells more than $13 million worth of herbal and beauty products every month.

Like many successful businesspeople, Wilson had personal zeal for her company's products and felt they were a perfect fit for a global market like Japan. Her enthusiasm prompted her to ask several Japanese American distributors in her North American network for advice. To her delight she learned that Far Eastern medicine embraces the use of herbs and natural healing principles and that Japanese women found American beauty products enticing. These two trends fit Enrich products precisely. Wilson forged into high gear, enlisting the aid of two Japanese-speaking business contacts. She asked them to identify friends and relatives in Japan who might be interested in buying or selling Enrich products. These colleagues found 379 Japanese contacts interested in Enrich.

Still, Wilson knew that she needed to understand the Japanese culture. She began an intensive study of the country and its history. She taught herself to eat with chopsticks by picking up

paper clips at her desk. She learned that colors had a deep meaning for the Japanese people. Red, for example, is the color of success in Japan. The more she learned, the more she was convinced that to succeed in Japan you need to think and act Japanese.

With the company still skeptical, Wilson invited Enrich's chief executive officer to a company meeting she called in Yokohama. She borrowed money from her husband and rented a convention hall. By now her 379 interested customers and distributors had grown to over 3,000. Dressed in a red suit, red blouse, and red shoes, Wilson beamed when it was announced the company would go forward with the expansion into Japan. A short time later, the company agreed to schedule a Japanese-speaking phone operator for the all-night shift at its Orem, Utah, headquarters to take orders during a convenient time for Japanese customers. Customers in Japan can now order products over the Internet as well.

Mary Lou Wilson represents a growing number of forward-thinking U.S. businesspeople who have identified the vast opportunities that exist in global markets. The future of U.S. economic growth is tied to global markets. Read this chapter carefully and you may also one day turn laughter into global market success.

Source: Hilary Stout, "The Front Lines," *The Wall Street Journal,* July 16, 1999, p. B1; Gracie Bonds Staples, "A Woman's Place Is in the Boardroom," *Brownsville Herald,* December 19, 1999; Geoffrey A. Campbell, "Would-Be Retiree Oversees Japanese Distribution Network That Produces about $10 Million Monthly in Herbal Products Sales," *Tarrant Business,* December 26, 1999; and Claudia Rosett, "Think Locally, Dress Globally," *The Wall Street Journal,* May 11, 2000, p. A2.

THE DYNAMIC GLOBAL MARKET

exporting
Selling products to another country.

importing
Buying products from another country.

Over six billion human beings call planet Earth home. Twenty percent (1.2 billion) of them live in one country, China. It's little wonder why the United States and other industrialized nations see this far-east giant as the emerging market of the 21st century. American companies such as General Motors, Caterpillar, and Levi-Strauss have already invested heavily in its future despite concerns about its political system, human-rights policies, and financial markets. Do you see both advantages and disadvantages in free trade with nations such as China?

Do you dream of traveling to exotic cities like Paris, Tokyo, Rio de Janeiro, or Cairo? In times past, the closest most Americans would ever get to working in such cities was in their dreams. However, the situation has changed. Today it's hard to find a major U.S. company that does not cite international expansion as a link to future growth. A recent study noted that 91 percent of the companies doing business globally believe it's important to send employees on assignments in other countries.

Have you thought about the possibilities of a career in international business? Maybe a few facts will make such a career more interesting: The United States is a market of about 280 million people, but there are over 6 billion potential customers in the 193 countries that make up the global market.[1] (See Figure 3.1 for a map of what the world would look like based on population.) Perhaps more interesting is that approximately 75 percent of the world's population lives in developing areas where technology, education, and per capita income still lag behind those of developed nations.

Today Americans buy billions of dollars worth of goods from China and Japan. American Express credit card usage is on the rise in Germany, Saudi Arabia, and other markets. Major league baseball teams, the National Basketball Association, and the National Football League play games in Mexico, Italy, Japan, and elsewhere.[2] Mel Gibson, Will Smith, and Bruce Willis continuously draw crowds to movie theaters around the globe as American movies take center stage in the global entertainment market.[3]

The United States is the largest exporting nation in the world.[4] It is the largest importing nation as well. **Exporting** is selling products to another country. **Importing** is buying products from another country. Competition in exporting is very intense. The United States must compete against aggressive exporters such as Germany, Japan, and China.

These facts show that global trade is big business today and will grow even more important throughout the 21st century. Therefore, you must prepare yourself for the global challenge. Stop for just a moment and ask yourself the following questions: Are you studying a foreign language in school? Have you talked with anyone about the excitement and rewards of traveling to and trading with other countries? Do you recognize the many challenges the United States faces in the 21st century? Does your college offer students the opportunity to study abroad? To find out more about how your school can help you with any of these questions, talk with a guidance counselor, instructor, or faculty adviser.

The purpose of this chapter is to familiarize you with global business, including its potential and its problems. The demand for students with training in international business is almost certain to grow as the number of businesses competing in the global market increases. You might even decide that a career in international business is your long-term goal.

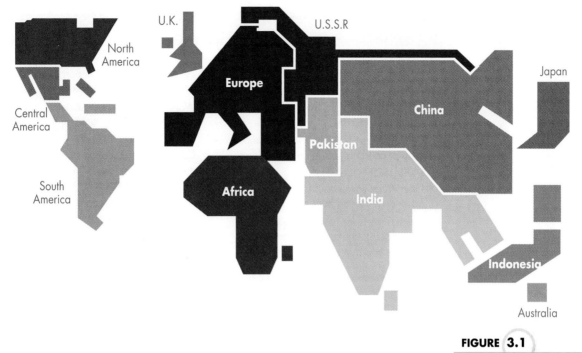

FIGURE 3.1

WHAT THE WORLD WOULD LOOK LIKE BASED ON POPULATION

Why Trade with Other Nations?

There are several reasons why countries trade with other countries. First, no nation, not even a technologically advanced one, can produce all of the products that its people want and need. Second, even if a country did become self-sufficient, other nations would seek trade with that country in order to meet the needs of their own people. Third, some nations like China and Russia have an abundance of natural resources and a lack of technological know-how while other countries (for example, Japan, Taiwan, and Switzerland) have sophisticated technology but few natural resources. Trade relations enable each nation to produce what it is most capable of producing and to buy what it needs in a mutually beneficial exchange relationship. This happens through the process of free trade. **Free trade** is the movement of goods and services among nations without political or economic trade barriers. Figure 3.2 offers some of the pros and cons of free trade.

free trade
The movement of goods and services among nations without political or economic obstruction.

The Theories of Comparative and Absolute Advantage

International trade is the exchange of goods and services across national borders. Exchanges between and among countries involve more than goods and services, however. Countries also exchange art, sports, cultural events, medical advances, space exploration, and labor. **Comparative advantage theory,** suggested in the early 19th century by English economist David Ricardo, was the guiding principle that supported this idea of free economic exchange.[5] Comparative advantage theory states that a country should sell to other countries those products that it produces most effectively and efficiently, and buy from other countries those products it cannot produce as effectively or efficiently.

The United States has a comparative advantage in producing many goods and services, such as computer chips, software, and engineering services. In contrast, the United States does not have a comparative advantage in growing coffee or making shoes. These products and many others are imported.

comparative advantage theory
Theory which asserts that a country should sell to other countries those products that it produces most efficiently.

FIGURE 3.2

THE PROS AND CONS OF FREE TRADE

PROS	CONS
• The global market contains over 6 billion potential customers for goods and services.	• Domestic workers in manufacturing lose jobs due to increased imports or production shifts to global markets.
• Productivity grows when countries produce goods and services in which they have a comparative advantage.	• Workers can face pay-cut demands from employers, who can threaten them with the possibility of sending jobs abroad.
• Global competition and lower-cost imports keep prices down, so inflation should not curtail economic growth.	• Competitive pressure often makes service and white-collar jobs vulnerable to operations moving overseas.
• Open trade encourages innovation, with fresh ideas coming from foreign markets.	• Domestic companies can lose their comparative advantage when competitors build advanced production operations in low-wage countries.
• Uninterrupted flow of capital gives countries access to foreign investments, which keeps interest rates low.	

Source: Aaron Bernstein, "Backlash: Behind the Anxiety over Globalization," *Business Week*, April 24, 2000, pp. 39–44; and Gail Nakada, "Bargains from America," *Business 2.0,* May 2000, pp. 202–5.

absolute advantage
When a country has a monopoly on producing a product or is able to produce it more efficiently than all other countries.

Through specialization and trade, the United States and its trading partners can realize mutually beneficial exchanges.

A country has an **absolute advantage** if it has a monopoly on the production of a specific product or is able to produce it more efficiently than all other nations. For instance, South Africa once dominated diamond production. Today there are very few instances of absolute advantage in the global economy.

CRITICAL THINKING

Many countries in the world are now called *developing countries* (former terms were *underdeveloped* or *less developed countries*). Why are they not fully industrialized? Is it because they lack natural resources? Then how do you explain the success of economies like Japan and Singapore, which have few natural resources?

GETTING INVOLVED IN GLOBAL TRADE

People interested in finding a job in international business often think of firms like Boeing, Ford, IBM, and Du Pont that have large multinational accounts. But the real job potential in global markets may be with small businesses. Today in the U.S. economy, small businesses generate about half of the private-sector commerce but account for only 20 percent of exports. These numbers are increasing, however, with the help of the U.S. Department of Commerce.

Getting started is often a matter of observation, determination, and risk. What does that mean? First of all, it is important to observe and study global markets. The college library, the Internet, and your fellow classmates are good starting points for doing your research. If you have the opportunity, travel to different countries is a great way to get some feel for the culture and lifestyles there and to see if doing business globally appeals to you.

For example, several years ago an American traveler in an African country noticed that there was no ice available for drinks, for keeping foods fresh, and so on. Further research showed that, in fact, there was no ice factory for hundreds of miles, yet the market seemed huge. The man returned to the United States, found some willing investors, and returned to Africa to build an ice-making plant. Much negotiation was necessary with the authorities (negotiation best done by locals who know the system), and the plant was built. This forward-thinking entrepreneur gained a considerable return on his investment and the people in that country can now buy a needed product.

Importing Goods and Services

Foreign students attending U.S. colleges and universities often notice that some products widely available in their countries are not available in the United States, or are more expensive here than at home. By working with foreign producers and finding some working capital, some students have become major importers while still in school.

Take Howard Schultz, for example. While traveling in Italy, Schultz became enthralled with the neighborhood coffee and espresso bars he frequented there. He loved the ambiance, the aroma, and especially the sense of community he saw and wondered why we lacked such great gathering places in the United States. Schultz saw an opportunity and, in 1987, bought the original Starbucks coffee shop in Seattle and built it into a national phenomenon.[6] Because the Italian coffee bars caught the attention of Howard Schultz, people across America now know what a "grande latte" is.

Importing products from other countries creates great opportunities for entrepreneurs. Take Marjorie Filmyer, owner of Tullycross Fine Irish Imports of Philadelphia for example. Here she is meeting with a representative of Belleek China Company at the Dublin, Ireland Showcase— an international trade show for buyers and sellers of Irish handcrafts. Does importing or exporting goods and services sound appealing to you as a potential career?

Travel is a way to learn about cultures and lifestyles in other countries. It also can be source of business inspiration. Take Howard Schultz for example. While traveling in Italy he came to appreciate the special sense of community the neighborhood coffee and espresso bars enjoyed in Italian communities. When he returned home to the United States, he purchased the Starbucks coffee shop in Seattle and proceeded to build it into an international phenomenon. Here Schultz cuts a ribbon at a new Starbucks opening in Tokyo. Can you think of goods or services currently not available in our economy that might appeal to U.S consumers?

Exporting Goods and Services

You may be surprised at what you can sell overseas. Who would think, for example, that U.S. firms could sell beer in Germany, where so many good beers come from? Yet right around the corner from a famous beer hall in Munich you can buy Samuel Adams Boston Lager. Thousands of cases have been sold, and a local licensing agreement (licensing will be discussed later in the chapter) assures more sales to come. American brewing giant Anheuser-Busch took the hint. It purchased the largest brewing company in central China and sells its flagship Budweiser product in major Chinese cities. If these company moves surprise you, well, you haven't heard anything yet. Can you imagine selling sand to countries in the Middle East? Meridan Group exports a special kind of sand used in swimming pool filters that sells well.

So what can you sell to other countries? Just about any good or service ➤ P.25 ◄ that is used in the United States can be used in other countries as well, and the competition abroad is often not nearly as intense for most providers of these products as it is at home. You can, for example, sell snowplows to the Saudi Arabians. They use them to plow sand off their driveways. Tropical Blossom Honey Company in Edgewater, Florida, was pleasantly surprised to find Saudis were significant consumers of honey. Why? Because the Koran (the Muslim holy book) suggests that honey has healing properties.[7] GlobalSight Corporation, a small global consulting and software company in San Jose, California, found expanded opportunities for its clients in e-commerce by adapting websites to the cultural and linguistic needs of a particular country or region.[8]

It's important for businesses to be aware of these great opportunities. It's also important to note that exporting is a terrific boost to the U.S. economy. The U.S. Department of Commerce estimates that every $1 billion in U.S. exports generates 25,000 jobs at home. But don't be misled: selling in global markets is not necessarily easy. We shall discuss a number of forces that affect trading later in this chapter. Adapting products to specific global markets is potentially profitable but difficult. A good example of how McDonald's attempts to do this is in the Reaching Beyond Our Borders box.

If you are interested in exporting, write for "The Basic Guide to Exporting," available from the U.S. Government Printing Office; Superintendent of Documents; Washington, D.C. 20402. More advice can be found at the U.S Department of Commerce's website at www.doc.gov or in *Business America,* a trade magazine published by the Department of Commerce's International Trade Administration. The magazine can be ordered from the U.S. Government Printing Office as well. Also, call the Small Business Administration at (800) 827-5722 and ask for a copy of the booklet *Exportise,* or visit the U.S. Department of Commerce website at www.commerce.gov. The Bureau of Export Administration offers key exporting advice at this site.

Measuring Global Trade

In measuring the effectiveness of global trade, nations carefully follow two key indicators: balance of trade and balance of payments. The **balance of trade** is a nation's relationship of exports to imports. A *favorable* balance of trade, or trade surplus, occurs when the value of the country's exports exceeds that of its imports. An *unfavorable* balance of trade, or **trade deficit,** occurs when the value of the country's imports exceeds that of its exports. It is easy to understand why countries prefer to export more than they import. If I sell you $200 worth of goods and buy only $100 worth, I have an extra $100 available to buy

---

balance of trade
A nation's relationship of exports to imports.

trade deficit
An unfavorable balance of trade; occurs when the value of a country's imports exceeds that of its exports.

Countries measure the effectiveness of global trade by statistics such as the balance of trade (the relationship of a nation's exports to imports.) The July 2000 numbers pictured here for the U.S. balance of trade present an unfavorable balance of trade or trade deficit for the nation's economy for that month. Could you explain why countries prefer to have a favorable balance of trade rather than a trade deficit?

Trade deficit hits record $31.9 billion

Oil prices, euro's woes push figure up 7% in July

By Gary Strauss and Adam Shell
USA TODAY

Soaring crude oil prices and a sagging euro pushed the U.S. trade deficit to a record level in July.

Given continued pressure from both, the trade deficit — and fallout on Wall Street — is likely to continue growing, experts s

The nation's m   tr le deficit   th   ad

REACHING BEYOND OUR BORDERS
The Sun Never Sets on the Golden Arches

The tremendous expansion of franchising led, by U.S. companies, has changed the landscape of the global market. Today small, midsize, and large franchises cover the globe, offering business opportunities in areas from exercise to education. Still, when the word *franchise* comes to mind, one name dominates all others: "McDonaldization" symbolizes the spread of franchising and the weaving of American pop culture into the world fabric. Whether in South Africa, Mexico, Germany, or Hong Kong, no one adapts better and blends the franchise values into the local culture better than McDonald's.

For example, after setting up its first franchises in Hong Kong in 1975, McDonald's altered the breakfast menu after realizing that customers there liked burgers for breakfast, then preferred chicken or fish for the rest of the day. The company also found that it was advisable to keep napkin dispensers away from the customers. It seems that older people in Hong Kong who went through hard times after World War II took huge wads of napkins from the holders and stuffed them in their pockets. Now it's one napkin per customer. McDonald's even spruced up the notoriously dirty toilet facilities that were a negative trademark of Hong Kong restaurants.

In Hong Kong, as in all markets in which it operates, the company continuously listens to customers and adapts to their preferences. For example, McDonald's quickly responded to Hong Kong customers' anxious appetite for promotions. Recently, to the delight of Hong Kong customers, McDonald's offered popular Japanese cat figures called Hello Kitty dolls as a follow-up to a very popular Snoopy-doll promotion. Even executives at high-tech companies and leading financiers gladly waited in line for the Hello Kitty dolls coveted by their children. Hong Kong children also cannot wait to visit "Suk-Suk" McDonald (Uncle Ronald McDonald) on their birthdays, since the company began to tout such events on local television. The company also encourages college students in Hong Kong to use the local McDonald's as a place to socialize and study.

By using such adaptive strategies in global markets, McDonald's reaps a large payoff. The company today derives more than half of its $72 billion in sales from abroad. Hong Kong actually boasts two of the world's busiest McDonald's, and about half of the city's 6.8 million people eat at a McDonald's restaurant every week. James L. Watson, a Harvard University anthropologist, perhaps said it best: "McDonald's has become a very important part of global culture. The company's efforts involving hygiene in its restrooms is just one example. Their efforts caused other restaurants to follow the lead. That's not bad diplomacy."

Source: Tom Philpott, "Can McDonald's Still Cook Up a Happy Meal for Investors?" *Ticker*, March 2000, pp. 50–52; Michael Flagg, "Cantonese Macs: Hong Kong Success Illustrates McDonald's Adaptability," *The Wall Street Journal*, July 7, 1999, pp. A1; James Cox and Paul Wiseman, "More U.S. Firms Expected to Fly Solo in China," *USA Today*, April 10, 2000, p. 1; Carla Power, Barbie Nadeau, Stefan, Juliette Terzieff, Kitty Gluckenberger and Toula Vlahou, "McParadox," *Newsweek International*, July 10, 2000, pp. 12.

---

other things. However, I'm in an unfavorable position if I buy $200 worth of goods from you and sell you only $100.

The **balance of payments** is the difference between money coming into a country (from exports) and money leaving the country (for imports) plus money flows coming into or leaving a country from other factors such as tourism, foreign aid, military expenditures, and foreign investment. The goal is always to have more money flowing into the country than flowing out of the country. A *favorable* balance of payments means more money is flowing into a country than flowing out. Conversely, an *unfavorable* balance of payments is when more money is flowing out of a country than coming in.

To make certain trade is conducted fairly on a global basis, different countries enforce laws to prohibit unfair practices such as dumping.[9] **Dumping** is the practice of selling products in a foreign country at lower prices than those

balance of payments
The difference between money coming into a country (from exports) and money leaving the country (for imports) plus money flows from other factors such as tourism, foreign aid, military expenditures, and foreign investment.

dumping
Selling products in a foreign country at lower prices than those charged in the producing country.

charged in the producing country. Companies sometimes use this tactic to reduce surplus products in foreign markets or to gain a foothold in a new market by offering products for lower prices than domestic competitors do. Japan and Brazil, for example, have been accused of dumping steel in the United States; China of dumping bicycles. U.S. laws against dumping are specific and require that foreign firms must price their products to include 10 percent overhead costs plus 8 percent profit margin. It can take time to prove accusations of dumping, however. There's also evidence that some governments offer financial incentives to certain industries to sell goods in global markets for less than they sell them at home.

Now that you understand some of the basic terms, we can begin discussing global business more deeply. We'll begin by looking at the U.S. experience in world trade. Before doing so, however, let's assess your progress so far.

PROGRESS ASSESSMENT

- How do world population and market statistics support the expansion of U.S. businesses into global markets?

- What is comparative advantage, and what are some examples of this concept in actual global markets?

- How are a nation's balance of trade and balance of payments determined?

TRADING IN GLOBAL MARKETS: THE U.S. EXPERIENCE

Fully 95 percent of the world's population lies outside the United States (see again Figure 3.1). However, the United States historically has never focused on exporting. How can this be true, you may ask, when we said earlier that the United States is the world's largest exporting nation? Even though the United States exports the largest *volume* of goods globally, it exports a much lower *percentage* of its products than other countries do. (Figure 3.3 lists the major trading economies in the world.) In the early 1980s for example, no more than 10 percent of American businesses exported products. However, slow economic growth in the United States and other economic factors lured more businesses to global markets beginning in the late 1980s. As we begin the 21st century, most large businesses are involved in global trade, and growing numbers of small and medium-sized businesses are going global as well.

For many years, the United States exported more goods and services ➤ **P.25** ◄ to other countries than it imported. Every year since 1985, however, the United States has bought more goods from other nations than it has sold to other nations. Remember that this is called a trade deficit or unfavorable balance of trade. In the 1990s, the United States ran its highest trade deficits with Japan and China.

Economists measure a nation's economic activity by comparing the amount of money it owes to foreign creditors and the value of what foreign investors own in the country with the money foreigners owe to it and the value of what it owns in foreign markets. During the 1980s, it was widely reported that the United States had become a debtor nation, that is, a country that owes more money to other nations than other nations owe it. This information caused quite a stir in the United States when it was first reported. Some even predicted that the United States was on the road to economic ruin. However, contrary to those gloomy interpretations, foreign investment in a country is not

FIGURE 3.3

THE MAJOR TRADING ECONOMIES OF THE WORLD

European Union
United States
Japan
China (includes Hong Kong)
Canada
Republic of Korea
Singapore
Taiwan
Switzerland

necessarily a bad sign. It means the country is perceived as a strong economic leader. What actually emerged in the United States is a trend toward more foreign direct investment. You will read more about foreign direct investment later in the chapter.

You have read that some 95 percent of the world's population lives outside the United States but that many U.S. companies, especially small businesses, still do not engage in global trade. Why is that? What does this indicate about the potential for increasing U.S. exports? What does it say about career opportunities in international business?

STRATEGIES FOR REACHING GLOBAL MARKETS

An organization may participate in global trade in many ways, including licensing, exporting, franchising, contract manufacturing, international joint ventures and strategic alliances, foreign subsidiaries, and foreign direct investment. Each of these strategies provides opportunities for becoming involved in global markets along with specific commitments and risks. Figure 3.4 places the strategies discussed in the following sections on a continuum showing the amount of commitment, control, risk, and profit potential associated with each one.

Licensing

A firm (the licensor) may decide to compete in a growing global market by **licensing** the right to manufacture its product or use its trademark to a foreign company (the licensee) for a fee (a royalty). A company with an interest in licensing generally needs to send company representatives to the foreign producer to help set up the production process. The licensor may also assist or work with a licensee in such areas as distribution and promotion.

    A licensing agreement can be beneficial to a firm in several different ways. Through licensing, an organization can gain additional revenues from a product that it normally would not have generated domestically. In addition, foreign licensees often must purchase start-up supplies, component materials,

licensing
An act by which a producer (the licensor) allows a foreign company (the licensee) to produce its product in exchange for a fee (a royalty).

FIGURE 3.4

MODES OF ENTRY INTO GLOBAL MARKETS

| Licensing | Exporting | Franchising | Contract manufacturing | International joint ventures and strategic alliances | Creating subsidiaries | Foreign direct investment |

LEAST   Amount of commitment, control, risk, and profit potential   MOST

Do things really go better with Coke? At long last, North Koreans will get the chance to answer that question. Since the United States eased trade sanctions against the Communist nation, North Koreans now join billions of customers around the globe who can enjoy the great taste of Coke and a smile. Coke in fact generates about 80 percent of its business from global markets mostly through licensing agreements between Coke and local bottling companies. What advantages do you see to licensing agreements? Any disadvantages?

and consulting services from the licensing firm. Such agreements have been very beneficial to companies like McDonald's. Coca-Cola and PepsiCo. These firms often enter foreign markets through licensing agreements that typically extend into long-term service contracts. Oriental Land Company and the Royal Canadian Mounted Police have licensing agreements with Walt Disney Company. Oriental Land Company owns and operates Tokyo Disneyland under a licensing agreement, and the Royal Canadian Mounted Police have an agreement with Disney to market products bearing the Mounties images.[10] A final advantage of licensing worth noting is that licensors spend little or no money to produce and market their products. These costs come from the licensee's pocket. Therefore, licensees generally work very hard to see that the product they license succeeds in their market.

However, as you may suspect, licensing agreements may provide some disadvantages to a company. One major problem is that often a firm must grant licensing rights to its product for an extended period, maybe as long as 20 years.[11] If a product experiences remarkable growth and success in the foreign market, the bulk of the revenues earned belongs to the licensee. Perhaps even more threatening is that a licensing firm is actually selling its expertise in a product area. If a foreign licensee learns the company's technology, it may break the agreement and begin to produce a similar product on its own. If legal remedies are not available, the licensing firm may lose its trade secrets, not to mention the agreed-on royalties.

Exporting

As global competition has intensified, the U.S. government has created Export Assistance Centers (EACs) to provide hands-on exporting assistance and trade-finance support for small and medium-sized businesses that choose to directly export goods and services. A nationwide network of EACs now exists in 17 U.S. cities, with further expansion planned. In 1998, over 35,000 small and medium-sized businesses were helped by EACs. This activity led to 9,000 export transactions worth a total of $2.28 billion.[12] EACs represent the future of federal export promotion efforts.

Still, even with the help of EACs available, many U.S. firms are reluctant to go through the trouble of establishing trading relationships. Therefore, it makes sense that a specialized organization would step in to negotiate such exchanges for them. These specialists are called export-trading companies. An export-trading company serves the role of matching buyers and sellers from different countries and providing services (such as dealing with customs offices, documentation, even weights and measures) to ease the process of entering foreign markets. Companies that work with export-trading companies are involved in indirect exporting. If you are considering opportunities in global business, you should know that export-trading companies often provide internships or part-time opportunities for students. Learning a foreign language in school and taking courses related to international trade are good ways to attract the attention of an export-trading firm.

Franchising

Franchising ➤ **P.150** ◄ is popular both domestically and internationally. We will discuss franchising in depth in Chapter 5. Firms such as McDonald's, 7-Eleven, and Dunkin' Donuts have many global units operated by foreign franchisees.

Franchisors have to be careful to adapt in the countries they serve. For example, KFC's first 11 Hong Kong outlets failed within two years. Apparently the chicken was too greasy and eating with fingers was too messy for the fastidious people of Hong Kong. McDonald's made a similar mistake when entering the Netherlands market. It originally set up operations in the suburbs, as it does in the United States, but soon learned that the Dutch mostly live in the cities. Therefore, McDonald's began to open outlets in downtown Amsterdam. Domino's Pizza originally approached the global market with a one-pie-fits-all approach. The company found out the hard way that Germans like small individual pizzas, not large pies, and Japanese customers enjoy squid and sweet mayonnaise pizza.

Contract Manufacturing

Contract manufacturing involves a foreign country's production of private-label goods to which a domestic company then attaches its own brand name or trademark. This process is also referred to as *outsourcing*. Many well-known U.S. firms such as Levi-Strauss and Nike practice contract manufacturing. The consumer electronics industry also makes extensive use of this practice. Cisco Systems, the world leader in Internet-routing gear, depends heavily on contract manufacturers.[13] Contract manufacturing often enables a company to experiment in a new market without incurring heavy start-up costs. If the brand name becomes a success, the company has penetrated a new market with relatively low risk. A firm can also use contract manufacturing temporarily to meet an unexpected increase in orders

International Joint Ventures and Strategic Alliances

A **joint venture** is a partnership ➤ **P.137** ◄ in which two or more companies (often from different countries) join to undertake a major project. According to Coopers & Lybrand, a New York–based international professional services firm, companies that participate in such partnerships grow much faster than their counterpart companies that are not participating. Joint ventures can even be mandated by governments as a condition of doing business in their country. It is often hard to gain entry into a country like China, whose economy is centrally planned, but agreeing to a joint venture can help a firm gain such entry. Joint ventures are developed for different business reasons as well. Campbell Soup Company formed joint ventures with Japan's Nakano Vinegar Company and Malaysia's

contract manufacturing
A foreign country's production of private-label goods to which a domestic company then attaches its brand name or trademark; also called *outsourcing*.

joint venture
A partnership in which two or more companies (often from different countries) join to undertake a major project.

Tired of studying? Maybe a pizza break will help. How about a Domino's pizza with squid and sweet mayonnaise or a pizza topped with duck gizzards to perk you up? As the photo illustrates, Domino's serves pizza according to tastes throughout the world. Franchises like Domino's have to be aware that the world's a big place and preferences, even in pizza, can vary considerably. What can franchises do to ensure that the products they offer are appropriate for the global markets they hope to reach?

strategic alliance
A long-term partnership between two or more companies established to help each company build competitive market advantages.

foreign subsidiary
A company owned in a foreign country by another company (called the *parent company*).

Cheong Chan Company to expand its rather low share of the market in both countries.

While most joint ventures are usually limited to a specific time frame, some extend many years beyond what the participating companies originally anticipated. Xerox and Fuji Photo Film Company of Japan entered into their joint venture 37 years ago to improve the film processing industry, and the relationship shows no signs of deteriorating. Joint ventures can also bring together unique partners. For example, the University of Pittsburgh and the Italian government have entered a joint venture to bring a new medical transplant center to Sicily.[14]

The benefits of international joint ventures are clear:

1. Shared technology.
2. Shared marketing and management expertise.
3. Entry into markets where foreign companies are not allowed unless their goods are produced locally.
4. Shared risk.

The drawbacks are not so obvious. An important one, however, is that one partner can learn the other's technology and practices, and then go off on its own as a competitor. Also, over time, a shared technology may become obsolete or the joint venture may become too large to be as flexible as needed.

Global market potential is also fueling the growth of strategic alliances. A **strategic alliance** is a long-term partnership between two or more companies established to help each company build competitive market advantages. Such alliances can provide access to markets, capital, and technical expertise. Unlike joint ventures, however, they do not typically involve sharing costs, risks, management, or even profits. Many executives and management consultants predict that few companies in the 21st century will succeed in the global market by going it alone; most will need strategic alliances. Strategic alliances can be flexible, and they can be effective between firms of vastly different sizes. The communications equipment manufacturer Motorola has a strategic alliance with a small Canadian firm that has only six employees. Oracle Corporation, a leader in computer software, has alliances with 15,000 different partners that range from giant companies like Ford Motor Company and Chevron to emerging firms like Nantucket Nectars (a maker of juice-based beverages).[15]

Foreign Subsidiaries

As the size of a foreign market expands, many firms establish a foreign subsidiary. A **foreign subsidiary** is a company that is owned in a foreign country by another company (called the *parent company*). Such a subsidiary would operate much like a domestic firm, with production, distribution, promotion, pricing, and other business functions under the control of the foreign subsidiary's management. Of course, the legal requirements of both the home and host countries would have to be observed. The primary advantage of a subsidiary is that the company main-

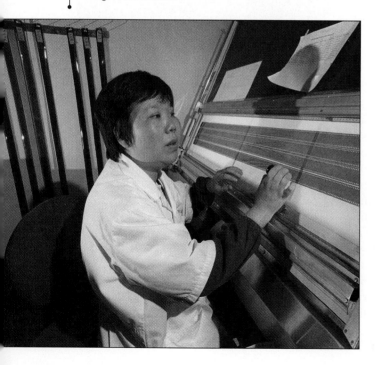

Many large global firms like Kodak and Nestlé spend billions to establish foreign subsidiaries. Unfortunately, sometimes the exporting of jobs naturally follows the purchase of a foreign subsidiary. Here a Chinese worker is being trained in a Kodak plant in China. Should workers in the United States be compensated for the loss of their jobs due to companies moving jobs to foreign subsidiaries?

tains complete control over any technology or expertise it may possess. Food giant Nestlé is an example of a major firm with many foreign subsidiaries.[16] The Swiss company spent billions of dollars acquiring foreign subsidiaries such as Carnation in the United States and Perrier in France, and it continues to look for opportunities around the globe.[17]

The major shortcoming associated with creating a subsidiary is that the parent company is committing a large amount of funds and technology within foreign boundaries. Should relations with the host country falter, the firm's assets could be taken over by the foreign government. Such a takeover is called an *expropriation.*

Foreign Direct Investment

Foreign direct investment is the buying of permanent property and businesses in foreign nations. In the 1980s, the surge in foreign direct investment by countries such as Japan caused much concern in the United States. When the Japanese obtained American landmarks such as Rockefeller Center, Pebble Beach Golf Course, and Columbia Pictures, many Americans felt they were losing the "soul of our nation."[18] The simple fact was that U.S. property, buildings, and company stock were all more attractive than comparable alternatives in other countries. In the late 1990s, Americans barely raised an eyebrow when foreign investors purchased companies such as Chrysler (automobiles), Amoco (oil), and Random House (publishing). Foreign direct investment can be viewed as a sign of strength in a nation's economy. The time to worry is when investors no longer find a country attractive. Figure 3.5 lists the five nations with the largest direct foreign investment in the United States.

Becoming involved in global trade requires selecting a strategy to enter a global market that best fits the goals of the business. As you can see, the different strategies discussed reflect different levels of ownership, financial commitment, and risk that a company can assume. However, this is just the beginning. It's important to be aware of forces that affect a business's ability to trade in global markets. Let's discuss these forces next.

FORCES AFFECTING TRADING IN GLOBAL MARKETS

Succeeding in any business takes work and effort, due to the many challenges that exist in all markets. Unfortunately, the hurdles get higher and more complex in global markets. This is particularly true in dealing with differences in sociocultural forces, economic and financial forces, legal and regulatory forces, and physical and environmental forces. Let's take a look at each of these challenges and see how they affect even the most established global businesses.

Sociocultural Forces

We are all aware that the United States is a multicultural nation, yet understanding cultural diversity in America remains one of the true business challenges of the 21st century. Furthermore, if you hope to get involved in global trade, it's critical to be aware of the cultural differences among nations. Different nations have very different ways of conducting business, and unfortunately American businesspeople are notoriously bad at adapting. In fact, American businesspeople have consistently been accused of *ethnocentricity,* which is an attitude that one's own culture is superior to all others. In contrast, foreign businesspeople are very good at adapting to U.S. culture. Think of how effectively German and Japanese carmakers have adapted to Americans' wants and

---

foreign direct investment
The buying of permanent property and businesses in foreign nations.

FIGURE 3.5

TOP FIVE COUNTRIES WITH THE LARGEST DIRECT FOREIGN INVESTMENT IN THE UNITED STATES ($ BILLIONS)

United Kingdom	$183
Japan	149
Netherlands	130
Germany	111
Canada	79

Source: U.S. Department of Commerce, Bureau of Economic Analysis www.bea.doc.gov/bea/di/fdipos.

Can you think of anything more appetizing than a tasty fish head? No? Well, the cheeseburgers and "finger-lickin good chicken" we gulp down in the United States can get a similar reaction in other cultures. Understanding different sociocultural perspectives related to time, change, natural resources, even diet can be important to success in global markets. Companies today understand this and often provide training for managers and their families on how to adapt to different cultures and avoid culture shock.

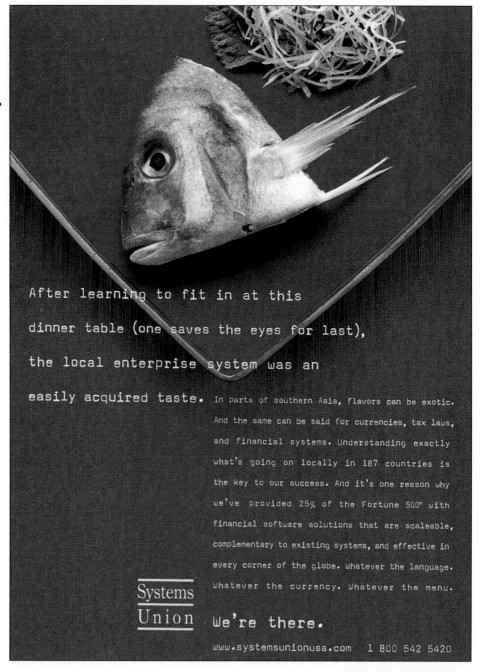

After learning to fit in at this dinner table (one saves the eyes for last), the local enterprise system was an easily acquired taste. In parts of southern Asia, flavors can be exotic. And the same can be said for currencies, tax laws, and financial systems. Understanding exactly what's going on locally in 187 countries is the key to our success. And it's one reason why we've provided 25% of the Fortune 500® with financial software solutions that are scaleable, complementary to existing systems, and effective in every corner of the globe. Whatever the language. Whatever the currency. Whatever the menu.

Systems Union We're there.

www.systemsunionusa.com   1 800 542 5420

needs in the auto industry. Let's look at some examples of how American businesses have had difficulty in adapting to important sociocultural differences.

Religion is an important part of any society's culture and can have a significant impact on business operations. Consider the violent clashes between religious communities in Bosnia, Kosovo, Northern Ireland, and the Middle East, all of which have crippled these economies. Companies at times do not consider the religious implications of business decisions. Both McDonald's and Coca-Cola offended Muslims in Saudi Arabia by putting the Saudi Arabian flag on their packaging. The flag's design contains a passage from the Koran, and Muslims feel their Holy Writ should never be wadded up and thrown away. In another example, an American manager in Islamic Pakistan toured a new plant under his control. While the plant was in full operation, he went to his office to make some preliminary forecasts of production. As he was working, sud-

- PepsiCo attempted a Chinese translation of "Come Alive, You're in the Pepsi Generation" that read to Chinese customers as "Pepsi Brings Your Ancestors Back from the Dead."
- Coor's Brewing Company put its slogan "Turn It Loose" into Spanish and found it translated as "Suffer from Diarrhea."
- Perdue Chicken used the slogan "It Takes a Strong Man to Make a Chicken Tender," which was interpreted in Spanish as "It Takes an Aroused Man to Make a Chicken Affectionate."
- KFC's patented slogan "finger-lickin' good" was understood in Japanese as "Bite Your Fingers Off."
- On the other side of the translation glitch, Electrolux, a Scandinavian vacuum manufacturer, tried to sell its products in the U.S. market with the slogan "Nothing Sucks Like an Electrolux."

FIGURE 3.6

OOPS, DID WE SAY THAT?
A global marketing strategy can be very difficult to implement. Look at the problems these well-known companies encountered in global markets.

denly all the machinery in the plant stopped. He rushed out suspecting a possible power failure and instead found his production workers on their prayer rugs. Upon learning that Muslims are required to pray five times a day, the manager returned to his office and proceeded to lower his production estimates. Whirlpool Company has experienced similar challenges at its Nashville, Tennessee, appliance factory, where it employs approximately 200 Muslims during peak production periods from January to June.[19]

Sociocultural differences can also affect important business decisions involving human resource management. In Latin American countries, workers believe that managers are placed in positions of authority in order to make decisions and be responsible for the well-being of the workers under their control. Consider what happened to one American manager in Peru who was unaware of this important cultural characteristic and believed workers should participate in managerial functions. This manager was convinced he could motivate his workers to higher levels of productivity by instituting a more democratic decision-making style than the style already in place. Soon workers began quitting their jobs in droves. When asked why, the Peruvian workers said the new production manager and supervisors did not know their jobs and were asking the workers what to do. All stated they wanted to find new jobs, since obviously this company was doomed because of incompetent managers.

Learning about important cultural perspectives related to time factors, change, competition, natural resources, achievement, and even work itself can be of great assistance in global markets. Today, firms often provide classes and training for managers and their families on how to adapt to different cultures and avoid culture shock. Taking courses in cultural variations and anthropology can help you gain a better understanding of foreign cultures.

Sociocultural differences affect not only management behaviors but also global marketing strategies. *Global marketing* is the term used to describe selling the same product in essentially the same way everywhere in the world. Some companies have developed brand names—such as Intel, Nike, IBM, Ford, and Toyota—with widespread global appeal and recognition. However, even these successful global marketers often face difficulties. For example, translating an advertising theme into a different language can be disastrous. To get an idea of the problems companies have faced with translations, take a look at Figure 3.6.

A sound philosophy to adopt in global markets is this: *Never assume that what works in one country will work in another.* Take for example Kids "R" Us, the clothing subsidiary of Toys "R" Us. The company missed the profit mark in Puerto Rico by banking heavily on back-to-school sales. Toys "R" Us planners failed to understand that Puerto Rican kids wear uniforms to school. They wrongly assumed that Puerto Rico's being a territory of the United States made the Puerto Rican market almost identical to the U.S. market. Thousands of similar stories could be told. The truth is that many U.S. companies often fail to think globally. For another example, in times past U.S. auto producers didn't adapt automobiles to drive on the left side of the road, as is done in many countries, and they printed owner's manuals only in English. Also, the United States is one of only five nations in the world that still refuse to conform to the metric system.

Since global marketing works only in limited cases, it's critical that U.S. exporters thoroughly research their objectives before attempting to penetrate global markets. "Think global, act local" is a valuable motto to follow.

Economic and Financial Forces

Economic differences can also muddy the water in global markets. Surely it's hard for us to imagine buying chewing gum by the stick instead of by the package. Yet this buying behavior is commonplace in economically depressed nations like Haiti, because customers there have only enough money to buy small quantities. You might suspect that, with over 1 billion people, India would be a dream market for companies like Coca-Cola and Pepsi-Cola.[20] However, Indians annually consume an average of only three soft drinks per person; compare this to the 50-plus *gallons* per person Americans consume each year. While some of this uneven consumption may be somewhat due to cultural differences, it's also clearly related to the low per capita income level of Indian consumers. Thus, what might seem like the global opportunity of a lifetime may not be a viable opportunity at all due to economic conditions.[21]

Global financial markets unfortunately do not have a universal currency. Mexicans shop with pesos, South Koreans with won, Japanese with yen, and Americans with dollars. Globally, the U.S. dollar is considered the world's dominant and most stable form of currency. This doesn't mean, however, that the dollar always retains the same value or that currencies such as the euro (discussed later this chapter) may not someday displace or challenge the U.S. dollar.[22]

For example, in an international transaction today, one dollar may be exchanged for 3 euros; tomorrow, however, you may only get 2.5 euros for the same dollar. The **exchange rate** is the value of one nation's currency relative to the currencies of other countries. Changes in a nation's exchange rates can have important implications in global markets. A *high value of the dollar* means that a dollar would be traded for more foreign currency than normal. The products of foreign producers would be cheaper because it takes fewer dollars to buy them, but the cost of U.S.-produced goods would become more expensive to foreign purchasers because of the dollar's high value. Conversely, a *low value of the dollar* means that a dollar is traded for less foreign currency than normal. Therefore, foreign goods become more expensive because it takes more dollars to buy them, but American goods become cheaper to foreign buyers because it takes less foreign currency to buy American goods.

Global financial markets operate under a system called *floating exchange rates*, in which currencies "float" according to the supply and demand in the market for the currency. This supply and demand for currencies is created by global currency traders, who create a market for a nation's currency based on the perceived trade and investment potential of the country. At certain times, however, a country itself will intervene and adjust the value of its currency, often to increase the export potential of its products. Both Mexico and Japan devalued their currencies in the 1990s.[23] **Devaluation** is lowering the value of a nation's currency relative to other currencies.

---

exchange rate
The value of one currency relative to the currencies of other countries.

devaluation
Lowering the value of a nation's currency relative to other currencies.

Such changes in currency values cause many problems globally. Consider a company like Nestlé, which has factories in 74 countries and employs over 200,000 workers around the world.[24] Labor costs can vary considerably as currency values shift. Or consider a medium-sized company like the H. B. Fuller Company, which has 43 plants in 27 countries making paints, adhesives, and coatings. Company President Albert Stroucken feels that the most dramatic problem his business faces is in dealing with currency fluctuations. The company has learned to use currency fluctuations to its advantage by buying raw materials from sources with currencies lowered in value.

Currency valuation problems can be especially harsh on developing economies. The only possibility of trade in many developing nations is through one of the oldest forms of trade: *bartering*, which is the exchange of merchandise for merchandise or service for service with no money involved.[25] **Countertrading** is a complex form of bartering in which several countries may be involved, each trading goods for goods or services for services.[26] It has been estimated that countertrading accounts for 25 percent of all international exchanges. For example, let's say that a developing country such as Jamaica wants to buy vehicles from Ford Motor Company in exchange for Jamaican bauxite. Ford, however, does not have a need for Jamaican bauxite but does have a need for computer monitors. In a countertrade agreement, Ford may trade vehicles to Jamaica, which then trades bauxite to another country, say India, which then exchanges computer monitors with Ford. This countertrade is thus beneficial to all three parties. With many countries still in the developing stage, there is no question that countertrading will continue in global markets through much of the 21st century. Trading products for products helps businesses avoid some of the financial problems and constraints that exist in global markets.

Understanding economic conditions, currency fluctuations, and countertrade opportunities is vital to a company's success in the global market. In financing export operations in the United States, banks have traditionally been the best source of the capital needed for global investment. However, when U.S. banks are not willing to provide export financing, U.S. exporters often turn to foreign banks and other sources for financing. This is especially true for small and medium-sized businesses. These companies must be creative in scouring the globe for financing. Fortunately, a growing number of U.S. government, multilateral, and interregional agencies now provide financing to all companies, large or small. (A partial list of these organizations is included in Figure 3.7.) Make

countertrading
Bartering among several countries.

Export-Import Bank   This bank makes loans to exporters that can't secure financing through private sources and to foreign countries that use the funds to buy American goods.

International Finance Corporation (IFC)   This organization makes loans to private businesses when they can't obtain loans from more conventional sources. It's affiliated with the World Bank.

International Development Association (IDA)   This organization makes loans to private businesses and to member countries of the World Bank.

Inter-American Investment Corporation (IIC)   This organization operates as an autonomous merchant banking corporation that will give preference to small and midsized companies that wish to expand.

European Bank for Reconstruction and Development   Based in London, this bank has a mandate to devote 60 percent of its investment activity to private-sector loans.

Overseas Private Investment Corporation   This organization sells insurance to U.S. firms that operate overseas. It covers damages caused by war, revolution, or insurrection; inability to convert local currencies to U.S. dollars; and expropriation (takeover by foreign governments).

FIGURE 3.7

U.S. GOVERNMENT, MULTILATERAL, AND INTERREGIONAL SOURCES OF GLOBAL FINANCING

Technology to the Rescue

As you read through this chapter, one point is obvious: It's not easy to do business in global markets. Sociocultural, economic, legal, regulatory, physical, and environmental forces all challenge and strain even the strongest of market competitors. In addition to these forces, there's the constant concern about currency fluctuations, which can change the price of a company's goods or services daily. International money transactions can be an absolute nightmare and are a major reason why small and medium-sized businesses have consistently avoided global involvement. The high costs of exchanging currency through bank wires and personal checks, not to mention delays, are frequently too much for the small-business owner to bear. But help is on the way.

According to Steve Flett, senior vice president of American Express Foreign Exchange Services in New York, the Internet can solve a large number of the problems small businesses face when dealing with international payments. His company has launched a website to help small businesses initiate payments to suppliers or distributors in more than 41 foreign currencies. All the small-business owner needs to do after establishing an account is to simply log on, type in the name and account number of the firm, and enter payment and currency information.

With one click, American Express receives the transaction and makes the payment. Western Union also provides services that enable small businesses to send payments overseas or receive payments from international customers. Small businesses can elect to have funds directly deposited into company bank accounts or have checks printed from Western Union.

Internet assistance can be especially useful to small companies such as Garmont U.S.A., a ski-equipment company in Virginia, or Reeves Floral Products in Georgia. Both companies distribute or buy products in global markets and heretofore have had to spend a great deal of time and resources dealing with currency fluctuations. Not having to worry about currency fluctuations lowers trade costs and adds a sense of stability to market transactions. Since about 80 percent of small-business transactions globally are conducted only in dollars, such services as those provided by American Express and Western Union open up new and uncomplicated opportunities. Score another point for technology.

Source: Allison Stern Wellner, "Riding the Greenback," *Business Week*, April 24, 2000, p. F10; "Let the Good Times Roll," *The Economist* 355 (April 15, 2000); and David Fairlamb, "Tame the Currency Markets? Think Again," *Business Week*, April 24, 2000, p. 86.

sure to read the Spotlight on Small Business box to see how small businesses are finding needed assistance to deal with this challenging part of global business.

Legal and Regulatory Forces

In any economy, both the conduct and direction of business are firmly tied to the legal and regulatory environment. In the United States, for example, federal, state, and local laws and regulations heavily impact business practices. In global markets, no central system of law exists, so several groups of laws and regulations may apply. (See the Making Ethical Decisions box for a hypothetical example.) This makes the task of conducting global business extremely difficult. What businesspeople find in global markets is a myriad of laws and regulations that are often inconsistent. Important legal questions related to antitrust rules, labor relations, patents, copyrights, trade practices, taxes, product liability, child labor, prison labor, and other issues are written and interpreted differently country by country.[27]

American businesspeople are required to follow U.S. laws and regulations in conducting business globally. U.S. legislation such as the Foreign Corrupt Practices Act of 1978 often creates competitive disadvantages for American

Deciding the Fate of Nightie Nite's Nightgowns

As a top manager of Nightie Nite, a maker of children's sleepwear, you must be aware of all the U.S. government regulations that affect your industry. A recently passed safety regulation prohibits the use of the fabric that you have been using for young girls' nightgowns for the past 15 years. Apparently the fabric does not have sufficient flame-retardant capabilities to meet U.S. government standards. In fact, last week Nightie Nite lost a lawsuit brought against it by the parents of a young child severely burned because the nightgown she was wearing burst into flames when she ventured too close to a gas stove. Not only did you lose the lawsuit, but you may also lose your nightshirt if you don't find another market for the warehouse full of nightgowns you have in inventory. You realize that some countries do not have such restrictive laws concerning products sold within their borders. You are considering exporting your inventory of products barred in the United States to these countries. What are your alternatives? What are the consequences of each alternative? What will you do?

businesspeople in competing with foreign competitors. This law specifically prohibits "questionable" or "dubious" payments to foreign officials to secure business contracts. The problem is this law runs contrary to beliefs and practices in many countries, where corporate or government bribery is not only acceptable but also perhaps the only way to secure a lucrative contract.[28] Fortunately for U.S. companies, the Organization for Economic Cooperation and Development (OECD) is leading a global effort to fight corruption and bribery in foreign markets. We will discuss these efforts more in Chapter 4.

To be successful in global markets, it's often important to contact local businesspeople in the host countries and gain their cooperation and sponsorship. Such local contacts can help a company penetrate the market and deal with what can be imposing bureaucratic barriers. Local businesspeople are also familiar with laws and regulations that could have an important impact on a foreign firm's business in their country.

Physical and Environmental Forces

Certain physical and environmental forces can also have an important impact on your ability to conduct business in global markets. In fact, technological constraints may make it difficult or perhaps impossible to build a large global market. For example, some developing countries have such primitive transportation and storage systems that international distribution is ineffective, if not impossible. This is especially true with regard to food, which is often spoiled by the time it reaches the market in certain countries. Compound this fact with unclean water and the lack of effective sewer systems, and you can sense the intensity of the problem.

American exporters > **P.64** ◄ must also be aware that certain technological differences affect the nature of exportable products. For example, houses in most developing countries do not have electrical systems that match those of U.S. homes, in kind or capacity. How would the differences in electricity available (110 versus 220 volts) affect an American appliance manufacturer wishing to export? It's also not uncommon in certain areas of developing countries for there to be only one telephone per 100 or more people. You can see how this would make for a difficult business environment in general and would make e-commerce nearly impossible.

TRADE PROTECTIONISM

trade protectionism
The use of government regulations to limit the import of goods and services; advocates believe that it allows domestic producers to survive and grow, producing more jobs.

tariff
A tax imposed on imported products.

import quota
A limit on the number of products in certain categories that can be imported.

embargo
A complete ban on the import or export of a certain product.

As we discussed in the previous section, sociocultural, economic and financial, legal and regulatory, and physical and environmental forces are all challenges to trading globally. What is often a much greater barrier to global trade, however, is the overall political atmosphere between nations. **Trade protectionism** is the use of government regulations to limit the import of goods and services. Advocates of trade protectionism believe it allows domestic producers to survive and grow, producing more jobs. Countries often use protectionist measures to guard against such practices as dumping; many are wary of foreign competition in general. To understand how this political climate affects global business, let's review some economic history of world trade.

Business, economics, and politics have always been closely linked. In fact, what we now call economics was once referred to as "political economy," indicating the close ties between politics (government) and economics. For centuries, businesspeople have tried to influence economists and government officials. Back in the 16th, 17th, and 18th centuries, nations were trading goods (mostly farm products) with one another. Businesspeople at that time advocated an economic principle called *mercantilism.* Basically, the overriding idea of mercantilism was for a nation to sell more goods to other nations than it bought from them, that is, to have a favorable balance of trade.[29] This condition was expected to result in a flow of money to the country that sold the most globally. Governments assisted in this process by charging a **tariff,** basically a tax on imports, thus making imported goods more expensive.

Generally, there are two different kinds of tariffs: protective and revenue. *Protective tariffs* (import taxes) are designed to raise the retail price of imported products so that domestic goods will be more competitive. These tariffs are meant to save jobs for domestic workers and to keep industries (especially infant industries, which consist of new companies in the early stages of growth), from closing down entirely because of foreign competition. *Revenue tariffs* are designed to raise money for the government. Revenue tariffs are also commonly used by developing countries to help infant industries compete in global markets. Today there is still considerable debate about the degree of protectionism a government should practice.

An **import quota** limits the number of products in certain categories that a nation can import > **P.64**<. The United States has import quotas on a number of products, such as beef and sugar. Again, the goal is to protect U.S. companies in order to preserve jobs. An **embargo** is a complete ban on the import or export > **P.64**< of a certain product.[30] Political hostilities provoked embargoes on Cuban cigars and Iraqi oil imports.[31] The United States also prohibits the export of some products globally. The Export Administration Act prohibits the exporting of goods that would endanger national security. Political considerations have caused many countries to establish embargoes.

Nontariff barriers are not as specific as tariffs and embargoes but can be as detrimental to free trade. It's common for countries to set restrictive standards that detail exactly how a product must be sold in a country. For example, Denmark requires companies to sell butter in cubes, not tubs. J. W. Kisling of Multiplex Company—a medium-sized U.S. maker of beverage-dispensing equipment with offices in Germany, France, Taiwan, England, and Canada—feels

In Japan, the price charged by rice farmers is protected by the government through strict import quotas that limit the amount of foreign-grown rice that can be imported into the country. Such trade protectionism has generated much protest from American businesses that feel the Japanese market is still ridden with tariff and nontariff barriers that hinder imports into the country. Can you think of any U.S. products that are protected by import quotas?

that a good deal of trade is stifled by nontariff barriers. James Thwaits, president of international operations of the 3M Company, agrees. He believes that one-half of all global trade is limited by nontariff barriers.

Japan, for instance, has steadfastly argued that it has some of the lowest tariffs in the world and welcomes foreign exporters, yet for many years American businesses found it difficult to establish trade relationships with the Japanese.[32] Observers believe that a Japanese tradition in which major companies forge semipermanent ties with suppliers, customers, and distributors was the root of the problem.[33] Often these relationships were forged through *keiretsu* (pronounced "care-yet-sue"), which are close-knit groups of Japanese companies within an industry.[34] The Japanese believed that these huge corporate alliances would provide economic payoffs by nurturing long-term strategic thinking and mutually beneficial cooperation. Today, however, noted keiretsu such as the automaker Nissan (now partly owned by Renault) have moved their business focus away from the traditional keiretsu model.[35] The major problems keiretsu experienced in the 1990s and 2000 ironically relate to factors touted as innovative in the 1980s. Consensus-driven management, lifetime employment, and intricate supplier webs did not fit the fast pace and changing market demands of the Internet economy.[36] Today, U.S. businesses are finding that as the Japanese businesses become more active in e-commerce, they are becoming quite a bit more import friendly.[37]

Would-be exporters could view the trade barriers discussed above as good reasons to avoid global trade. The Legal Briefcase box offers particular pros and cons concerning tariffs. But irrespective of where you stand on the tariff issue, you are likely to view overcoming trade constraints as a tremendous business opportunity. In the next sections, we look at organizations and agreements created to facilitate trade among nations.

The General Agreement on Tariffs and Trade, and the World Trade Organization

In 1948, government leaders from nations throughout the world established the General Agreement on Tariffs and Trade (GATT).[38] This agreement among 23 countries provided a forum for negotiating mutual reductions in trade restrictions. In short, the countries agreed to negotiate to create monetary and trade agreements that might facilitate the exchange of goods, services, ideas, and cultural programs. In 1986, the Uruguay Round of GATT talks was convened to specifically deal with the renegotiation of trade agreements. After eight years of meetings, 124 nations at the Uruguay Round voted to modify the GATT. The U.S. House of Representatives and Senate approved the new agreement in 1994. Under the new GATT, tariffs were lowered an average of 38 percent worldwide. The agreement also extended GATT rules to new areas such as agriculture, services, and the protection of patents.

On January 1, 1995, the **World Trade Organization (WTO),** headquartered in Geneva, Switzerland, was created by the GATT and assumed the primary task of mediating future trade disputes.[39] With 134 member nations, the WTO acts as an independent entity that oversees key cross-border trade issues and global business practices.[40] It's the world's first attempt at establishing a global mediation center. Trade issues are expected to be re-

World Trade Organization (WTO)
The international organization that replaced the General Agreement on Tariffs and Trade, and was assigned the duty to mediate trade disputes among nations.

The World Trade Organization (WTO) found itself at the center of a major dispute with protest groups at the WTO's summit meeting in Seattle, Washington. More than 1,200 labor, environmental, consumer, religious, human rights, and animal rights groups from ninety nations called on governments to halt the expansion of the WTO. These groups argued that the needs of people, not simply the world's corporations should be the focus of economic globalization. What do you feel is the key role an organization like the WTO should play in dealing with global business?

To Tariff or Not to Tariff

Advocates of trade protectionism feel that tariffs are necessary to protect national markets from foreign competition. Some of the arguments they use are as follows:

- Tariffs save jobs. Tariffs should be used to keep cheap foreign labor from displacing American workers.
- Tariffs are imposed on the United States by its competitors. To make competition fair, we have to take mutual measures.
- Tariffs protect industries vital to a nation's security (automobiles, aerospace, and shipbuilding) and are needed for defense.
- Tariffs protect new domestic industries (also called infant industries) from established foreign competition.

Critics of tariff policies have other ideas. Their principal arguments are as follows:

- Tariffs reduce competition and restrain international trade.
- Tariffs increase inflationary pressure and thus raise consumer prices.
- Tariffs benefit special-interest groups such as local manufacturers at the expense of the public at large.
- Tariffs lead to foreign retaliation and subsequent trade wars.

Debates over tariffs and trade restrictions are a major part of international politics. Help yourself by staying current on the issues, because the future of global trade may very well depend on the outcome of the debates.

solved within 12 to 15 months instead of languishing for years. In its first four years of operations, the WTO handled 163 cases.[41]

Before you get the impression that all's well in global trade, it's important to note the GATT did not totally eliminate the internal national laws that impede trade expansion. For example, it did not fully address critical areas such as intellectual property rights (trademarks and copyrights) and financial services. While the efforts of the WTO are admirable, many tough decisions lay ahead. For example, the admission of China to the WTO promises to stir differing emotions within the organization.[42]

Common Markets

common market
A regional group of countries that have a common external tariff, no internal tariffs, and a coordination of laws to facilitate exchange; also called a *trading bloc;* an example is the European Union.

One of the issues not resolved by the GATT is whether common markets will create regional alliances at the expense of global expansion. A **common market** (also called a *trading bloc*) is a regional group of countries that have a common external tariff, no internal tariffs, and the coordination of laws to facilitate exchange among member countries. Let's take a brief look at two such common markets, the European Union (EU) and the South American Common Market, called the Mercosur (see Figure 3.8).

FIGURE 3.8

MEMBERS OF THE EUROPEAN UNION AND MERCOSUR

EUROPEAN UNION MEMBERS			MERCOSUR MEMBERS
France	Germany	Italy	Argentina
Belgium	Netherlands	Luxembourg	Brazil
Great Britian	Denmark	Greece	Uruguay
Ireland	Portugal	Spain	Paraguay
Austria	Finland	Sweden	

The European Union began as an alliance of six trading partners (then known as the Common Market or European Economic Community) in the late 1950s. Today the European Union is a group of 15 nations that united economically in the early 1990s. The objective was to make Europe, the world's second largest economy (behind the U.S.)—with almost 20 percent of the world's GDP and representing some 360 million people—an even stronger competitor in global commerce. Europeans see economic integration as the major way to compete, particularly with the United States, for global business. It's possible the European Union could grow to 25 nations in the next 10 years as many Eastern European nations seek membership.

The path to European unification, however, has been slow and sometimes difficult. A significant step was taken on January 1, 1999, when the European Union officially launched its joint currency. At the end of this rather awesome financial effort, which won't be complete until July 2002, the separate currencies of the EU nations will be transformed into a single monetary unit: the euro. European businesses expect to save approximately $12.8 billion a year on currency conversions that had to be made prior to the introduction of the euro.

The European Union clearly hopes that having a unified currency will bring its member nations more economic clout, as well as more buying power and greater economic and political stability. C. Fred Bergsten, director of the Washington-based Institute for International Economics, suggests that, over time, the euro will become a worthy challenger to the U.S. dollar in global markets due to the economic strength and size of the European Union.

Mercosur is a common market that groups Brazil, Argentina, Paraguay, Uruguay, and associate members Chile and Bolivia.[43] With $20 billion in internal trade among its member nations, Mercosur is gaining attention from other major trading blocs in the world.[44] Like the European Union, Mercosur has ambitious economic goals that include a single currency.[45] An agreement combining Mercosur and the Andean Pact (which includes Venezuela, Colombia, Peru, and Ecuador) paves the way for an economic free-trade zone that will span South America.

The launching of the euro as the official currency of the European Union (EU) was expected to be a great milestone in the history of the continent. To date, the euro has not lived up to its expectations. It has been very weak against the U.S. dollar and two members of the European Union, Denmark and the United Kingdom, have yet to accept it as their currency. Economists agree it's too soon to write-off the euro, but most acknowledge the euro caused more problems than expected. What do you see as the key advantage of having one currency in the European market rather than the many different currencies traded with in the past?

The North American Free Trade Agreement (NAFTA)

One of the most debated issues of the early 1990s was the North American Free Trade Agreement (NAFTA). Opponents, led primarily by organized labor and billionaire businessman and presidential candidate Ross Perot, promised nothing short of economic disaster if the U.S. Congress passed this treaty. The primary questions focused on the issues of U.S. employment, exports, and the environment. Both labor leaders and Perot predicted a "giant sucking sound" of jobs and capital leaving the United States. In contrast, proponents predicted that NAFTA would open a vast new market for exports that would create jobs and opportunities in the long term. In 1994, Congress approved the NAFTA treaty and President Bill Clinton signed it into law, linking the United States, Canada, and Mexico in a free-trade area of over 370 million people with a gross domestic product of over $7 trillion.

The NAFTA countries can lower trade barriers with each other while maintaining independent trade agreements with nonmember countries.

Since its approval, NAFTA has experienced both success and difficulties. The devaluation of the Mexican peso in 1995 forced the United States to commit $30 billion in aid to Mexico. Concerns continue to persist today regarding issues such as job loss and creation, child-labor laws and sweatshop violations, illegal immigration, environmental concerns, and the long-term strength of the peso. On the positive side, U.S. exports to the NAFTA partners increased approximately 66 percent during the agreement's first five years. Mexico has in fact replaced Japan as America's number two trading partner (behind Canada).[46]

Like other economic trading blocs, NAFTA has changed the landscape of global trade. Possible expansion of NAFTA into a Free Trade Area of the Americas (FTAA) would create a free-trade area of 800 million people and range in scope from Patagonia to Alaska.[47] Some advocates say that it could be operational by the year 2005. Other free-trade advocates suggest that a Transatlantic Free Trade Area in union with the European Union is possible. Such suggestions draw resounding praise from some economists while eliciting concern from those who fear that, as the world divides itself into certain major trading blocs, poorer countries that don't fit in to any of the common markets will suffer. The issues surrounding common markets and free-trade areas will extend far into the 21st century.

PROGRESS ASSESSMENT

- What are the major hurdles to successful global trade?
- What does the word *ethnocentricity* mean?
- Which cultural and societal differences are likely to affect global trade efforts? (Name at least two.)
- What are the advantages and disadvantages of trade protectionism? Of tariffs?

MULTINATIONAL CORPORATIONS

There has been much discussion in the media about the economic power of multinational corporations such as General Motors, Siemens, and Royal Dutch Shell. It may be hard to imagine, but the annual sales of just one multinational company can be larger than the gross domestic product of a nation such as Pakistan, Venezuela, or Turkey. If you are thinking about a career in international business, you will need an understanding of what multinational corporations are and what they mean for global business.

multinational corporation (MNC)
An organization that manufactures and markets products in many different countries and has multinational stock ownership and multinational management.

A **multinational corporation (MNC)** is an organization that manufactures and markets products in many different countries; it has multinational stock ownership and multinational management. The more nations in which a company operates, the more it attempts to avoid restrictions from various governments.[48] Multinational corporations are typically extremely large corporations, but not all large firms involved in global business are multinationals. A business could literally be exporting everything it produces, thus deriving 100 percent of its sales and profits globally, and still not be a multinational corporation. Only firms that have *manufacturing capacity* or some other physical presence in different nations can truly be called multinational.

THE FUTURE OF GLOBAL TRADE: GLOBAL E-COMMERCE

Global trade opportunities grow more interesting each day. New and expanding markets present great potential for trade and development. Changes in technology also have changed the landscape of global trade, as businesses find that many foreign markets are often no farther than a mouse click away. Let's look briefly at issues certain to influence global markets in the 21st century.

Advanced communication has made distant global markets instantly accessible. Also the lure of 6 billion customers (as noted at the beginning of this chapter) is hard to pass up. Nowhere is the lure keener than in the developing countries in Asia, and particularly in the world's most populous country, the People's Republic of China. With more than 1.2 billion people, China is a fast-growing economy that currently appears to be shifting its economic philosophy from central planning to free markets **➤ P.37➤**.[49]

Multinational companies such as General Motors, Caterpillar, and Levi-Strauss have invested heavily in China's future. Not long ago, such investments in China were considered too risky and not worth the effort; today, however, U.S. companies are flocking to China and are eager to trade with the Chinese. Economists suggest that soon U.S. foreign direct investment could surpass exports as the primary means by which U.S. companies deliver goods to China.[50] Concerns remain about China's one-party political system, its human rights policies, the growing trade imbalance, and difficulties in China's financial markets.[51] Yet in 2000 the U.S. Congress granted the nation permanent normal trading rights, which should pave the way for China's entry into the World Trade Organization (WTO) and to an economic acceptance by other trading nations around the world. Still, many analysts warn that profits will take a long time to materialize for companies doing business with China.[52]

Russia is also a prize coveted by global traders. Like China, Russia presents enormous opportunities. Philip Morris, Bristol-Myers, and Gillette are multinational firms with manufacturing facilities in Russia. However, severe political and social problems still persist in the formerly communist nation, and many firms do not expect their profit potential to be realized until far into the 21st century. Even so, Russia's 150 million potential customers, craving American goods, represent an opportunity too good to pass up.

While China, Russia, and Japan attract most of the attention in Asia, U.S. businesses are not forgetting the rest of the continent. Add India, Taiwan, Indonesia, Thailand, Singapore, the Philippines, Korea, and Malaysia to the growing list of developing countries in Asia, and it's easy to see the great potential the Asian market holds for U.S. business, and possibly for you.

As technology continues its unprecedented growth, markets not only in Asia but also in the rest of the world are instantly accessible. The growth of the Internet and advances in e-commerce **➤ P.13➤** enable companies worldwide to bypass normally required distribution channels to reach a large market. Take New England Pottery Company, for example. Adopting Internet technology helped the company become the largest global vendor in the garden pottery industry. By speeding up the flow of information between buyers and its manufacturing partners in Europe, South America, and Asia, the company increased its sales by 20 percent per year. Autobytel.com, an Irvine, California, company, took its e-commerce system into Scandinavia and the United Kingdom. The company lets consumers buy, lease, and insure new cars and trucks online. Such attention to global potential and the ability to react quickly often gives start-up companies like Autobytel.com an advantage over their larger counterparts in penetrating global markets.

It's important, though, to remember that obstacles and problems with technology still exist in global trade. For example, American Express Foreign Exchange Services and International Strategies Inc. report that 43 percent of the small businesses they polled could not find information on the Web that could help them do business globally. Many also stated that communication with companies in Asia still needed to be carried out by faxing hard copies of documents—a process now seen as almost old-fashioned in comparison to Internet communication. In addition, some developing nations fear e-commerce will lead to the erosion of their local and national languages and cultures. Overcoming such technological and social obstacles is one of the key challenges facing business in the 21st century. Yet despite these hurdles, technology has the potential to radically change industries and create opportunities for all businesses in global trade regardless of size.

Globalization and You

Whether you aspire to be an entrepreneur ➤ **P.4**◂, a manager, or some other type of business leader, you must now think globally as you plan your career. As this chapter points out, global markets are overflowing with opportunity, yet they are laced with many challenges and complexities. By studying foreign languages, learning about foreign cultures through courses in anthropology and world literature, and taking business courses, you can develop a global perspective on your future. As we have emphasized, the potential of global markets does not belong only to the multinational corporations. Small and medium-sized businesses are often better prepared to take the leap into global markets than are large, cumbersome corporations saddled with bureaucracies. It's the ability of small and medium-sized businesses to react quickly to opportunities that give them an advantage. Also don't forget the potential of franchising, which we will examine in more detail in Chapter 5.

PROGRESS
ASSESSMENT

- What is a multinational corporation (MNC)? Can you name at least three multinational corporations?

- What are the major risks of doing business in countries like the People's Republic of China or Russia?

- What might be some important factors that will have an impact on global trading?

SUMMARY

1. Discuss the growing importance of the global market and the roles of comparative advantage and absolute advantage in international trade.

1. The world market for trade is huge. Some 95 percent of the people in the world live outside the United States.
   - *Why should nations trade with other nations?*
   (1) No country is self-sufficient, (2) other countries need products that prosperous countries produce, and (3) natural resources and technological skills are not distributed evenly around the world.
   - *What is the theory of comparative advantage?*
   The theory of comparative advantage contends that a country should make and then sell those products it produces most efficiently but buy those it cannot produce as efficiently.
   What is absolute advantage?
   Absolute advantage means that a country has a monopoly on a certain product or can produce the product more efficiently than any other country can. There are few examples of absolute advantage.

2. Explain the importance of importing and exporting, and understand key terms used in international business.

2. Students can get involved in world trade through importing and exporting. They do not have to work for big multinational corporations.
   - *What kinds of products can be imported and exported?*
   Just about any kind of product can be imported and exported. Companies can sometimes find surprising ways to succeed in either activity. Selling in global markets is not necessarily easy, though.

• *What terms are important in understanding world trade?*
Exporting is selling products to other countries. *Importing* is buying products from other countries. The *balance of trade* is the relationship of exports to imports. The *balance of payments* is the balance of trade plus other money flows such as tourism and foreign aid. *Dumping* is selling products for less in a foreign country than in your own country. *Trade protectionism* is the use of government regulations to limit the importation of products. See the Key Terms list at the end of this chapter to be sure you know the other important terms.

3. It was widely reported during the late 1980s and early 1990s that the United States was a "debtor nation." In fact, it was called the largest debtor nation in the world. However, the United States was attracting a good deal of foreign direct investment. The United States was never in the gloomy position many claimed. Its market was perceived by other nations as being more lucrative and attractive for investment.

3. Describe the current status of the United States in global business.

• *What's the best way to look at debt figures in global markets?*
The best way to determine whether or not a nation is a net debtor is to look at income flows among nations. When income from foreign investments exceeds outgo, a nation is not likely a debtor. Also, if direct foreign investment is growing, the nation may show a debt position but the market is perceived as viable for foreign investment.

4. A company can participate in world trade in a number of ways.

4. Illustrate the strategies used in reaching global markets.

• *What are some ways in which a company can get involved in international business?*
Ways of entering world trade include licensing, exporting, franchising, contract manufacturing, joint ventures and strategic alliances, foreign subsidiaries, and direct foreign investment.

5. There are many restrictions on foreign trade.

5. Evaluate the forces that affect trading in world markets.

• *What are some of the forces that can discourage participation in international business?*
Potential stumbling blocks to world trade include sociocultural forces, economic and financial forces, legal and regulatory forces, and physical and environmental forces.

6. Political differences are often the most difficult hurdles to international trade.

6. Debate the advantages and disadvantages of trade protectionism.

• *What is trade protectionism?*
Trade protectionism is the use of government regulations to limit the import of goods and services; advocates believe that it allows domestic producers to survive and grow, producing more jobs. The key tools of protectionism are tariffs, import quotas, and embargoes.
• *What are tariffs?*
Tariffs are taxes on foreign products. There are two kinds of tariffs: (1) protective tariffs, which are used to raise the price of foreign products, and (2) revenue tariffs, which are used to raise money for the government.
• *What is an embargo?*
An embargo prohibits the importing or exporting of certain products.
• *Is trade protectionism good for domestic producers?*
That is debatable. Trade protectionism offers pluses and minuses. Check the Legal Briefcase box to see the pros and cons of tariffs.
• *Why do governments continue such practices?*
The theory of mercantilism started the practice of trade protectionism and it has persisted, though in a lesser form, ever since.

7. Explain the role of multinational corporations in global markets.

7. Multinational corporations have a huge impact on world trade.
   • ***How do multinational corporations differ from other companies that participate in international business?***
   Unlike other companies that are involved in exporting or importing, multinational corporations also have manufacturing facilities or some other type of physical presence in different nations.

8. Explain how technology affects global e-commerce.

8. Technology is changing the way businesses communicate around the globe.
   • ***How is technology affecting global e-commerce?***
   The Internet has made distant global markets instantly accessible. E-commerce enables companies to bypass normal distribution channels to reach large global markets quickly.

KEY TERMS

absolute
  advantage   66
balance of
  payments   69
balance of trade   68
common market   84
comparative
  advantage
  theory   65
contract
  manufacturing   73
countertrading   79
devaluation   78

dumping   69
embargo   82
exchange rate   78
exporting   64
foreign direct
  investment   75
foreign subsidiary
  74
free trade   65
import quota   82
importing   64
joint venture   73

licensing   71
multinational
  corporation
  (MNC)   86
strategic alliance   74
tariff   82
trade deficit   68
trade protectionism
  82
World Trade
  Organization
  (WTO)   83

DEVELOPING WORKPLACE SKILLS

1. Call or visit a business such as a rug dealer or some other importer of foreign goods. Talk with the owner or manager about the problems and joys of being involved in international trade. Compile a list of advantages and disadvantages. Then get together with others in the class and compare notes.

2. Using a computer word-processing program, write a short essay describing the advantages and disadvantages of trade protectionism. Share your ideas with others in the class and debate the following statement: The United States should increase trade protection to save American jobs and American companies.

3. Many U.S. firms have made embarrassing mistakes when trying to sell products overseas. Sometimes the product is not adapted to the needs of the country, sometimes the advertising makes no sense, sometimes the color or packaging is wrong, and so forth. Find an example of such a marketing mistake and suggest how the company could have been more responsive to the needs of foreign markets. If possible, use a graphics program to illustrate a more appropriate advertisement or packaging option.

4. I. M. Windy is a candidate for the U.S. House of Representatives from your district. He just delivered an excellent speech at your college. He spoke at great length on the topic of tariffs. His major arguments were that we need tariffs to
   a. Provide revenues.
   b. Protect our young industries.

   c. Encourage Americans to buy U.S.-made products because doing so is patriotic.

   d. Keep our militarily strong.

   e. Protect American workers and wages.

   f. Help us maintain a favorable balance of trade.

   g. Create a favorable balance of payments.

   Do you agree with Mr. Windy? Evaluate each of the candidate's major points by indicating whether you consider it valid or invalid. Justify your position.

5. Choose a good, service, or idea that you would like to market to a specific country. Identify the benefits of supplying the product to this market. Identify the sociocultural, economic and financial, legal and regulatory, and physical and environmental forces you might encounter. Provide alternatives you can use to address these forces. Form your own joint venture with three classmates to deal with this exercise. Have each member make a list of the strengths and weaknesses he or she would bring to such an assignment. Decide among yourselves whether a joint venture would be worthwhile to achieve your market objectives or whether you each would be better choosing another strategy in entering this market. Explain why your group decided to organize the way it did.

Purpose

To compare the shifting exchange rates of various countries and to predict the effects of such exchange shifts on international trade.

Questions

One of the difficulties of engaging in international trade is the constant shift in exchange rates. How much do exchange rates change over a 30-day period? Research this by choosing five countries and recording the exchange rate for each country's currency (the Euro, British Pound, Japan's yen, Mexico's peso, etc.) for 30 days. The rates are available on the Internet at www.washingtonpost.com/wp-srv/business/longterm/stocks/currency.htm. Chart the amount of foreign currency per dollar. What effect would these currency shifts have on your company's trade with each of these countries?

Purpose:

To identify those nations with high export potential and those that have low export potential (except for basic goods, such as food).

Exercise:

Imagine your company is ready to expand its products to foreign countries. Which countries are most likely to buy your products? The potential to export to a specific country is based on a number factors including the size of its population and the strength of its GDP.

1. From the population data given on the website www.undp.org/popin, prepare a list of the 20 countries with the largest population.

2. Go to the InfoNation section of the website www.un.org/Pubs/CyberSchoolBus/ and find the GDP per person for each of the nations on your population list. Rate each of the nations in your population list for its

export potential. Using the GDP per capita and the population size, place each of those nations into the following categories:

a. High export potential (those nations whose population is one of the 10 largest and whose GDP per capita is greater than $20,000).

b. Medium-high export potential (those nations whose population is ranked 11 to 21 and whose GDP per capita is greater than $20,000).

c. Medium export potential (those nations whose population is one of the ten largest and whose GDP per capita is between $3,000 and $20,000).

d. Low export potential (those nations whose population is ranked 11 to 21 and whose GDP per capita is less than $3,000).

PRACTICING MANAGEMENT DECISIONS

CASE

WHAT IS A LIVING WAGE?

In the late 1800s and early 1900s, labor conditions in the United States were certainly less than ideal. The average workweek was 60 hours, but it was not unusual for workers to spend 80 hours on the job every week; children toiled in unsafe conditions sometimes 10 hours a day, six days a week; wages were low and fears of unemployment high; and job benefits such as sick leave and medical care were nonexistent. Labor unions, religious groups, and social reformers were active, attempting to ignite efforts to reform the workplace and end the existence of "sweatshops," where workers often spent their entire lives in atrocious conditions. These efforts, plus publication of Upton Sinclair's novel *The Jungle*, heightened public awareness of the abuses existing in the workplace. Sinclair portrayed the dark side of Chicago's meat-packing industry, whose inhuman conditions destroyed the lives and spirit of workers.

A real-life tragedy at the Triangle Shirtwaist Company on March 25, 1911 also intensified the efforts aimed at eliminating sweatshops. Triangle employed young women in the garment industry. A fire at the company's factory led to the death of 126 young women, who could not exit the building due to locked doors and the lack of a fire escape. News reports faulted the company and brought to light the harsh conditions in which these women worked. The fallout from Sinclair's book and the Triangle Shirtwaist Company fire generated an impassioned public outcry and eventually led to strong federal legislation that improved working conditions throughout the United States.

The issue of sweatshops has surfaced again in the media. However, today's issue does not deal directly with U.S. shops and is championed not just by unions and other such organizations but also by college students. At college campuses across the country, students are demanding assurances that clothing bearing their universities' names and logos are produced under humane conditions in global markets. United Students Against Sweatshops (USAS) represents students at some 100 colleges across the nation. The organization demands that universities employ a vigorous monitoring campaign that forces companies to publicly disclose the location of foreign factories so human rights groups can independently monitor their actions. They also demand that employers pay a so-called living wage that meets the basic needs of workers in various global markets.

Apparel industry leaders Nike, Reebok, Liz Claiborne, and Phillips–Van Heusen have responded by agreeing to join the Fair Labor Association (FLA), a sweatshop-monitoring group established by a presidential task force of apparel makers and human rights groups. Students counter that this group is nothing more than a publicity stunt, with a weak code of conduct and very little accountability. They also contend the FLA and others in the industry have resisted the efforts of the Council on Economic Priorities (CEP) to establish a living-wage standard in global markets. The CEP has devised a formula that it says ensures a wage structure that meets the basic needs of workers in different countries.

Apparel companies contend that their businesses involve thousands of factories operating in very diverse economies. The idea of establishing a formal living-wage structure is impossible and could in fact place significant burdens on the industry and workers in the global economies they seek to help. Malaysia's prime minister Mahathir Mohammed and other leaders of countries in which wages for workers are quite low agree; they fear that such standards could price them out of global markets. Their countries depend on foreign investment money, the loss of which could shatter local economies. Dani Rodrik, a Harvard University economist, and Elizabeth Bogan, a lecturer in economics at Princeton, both fear that the concept of a living wage will cost many workers their jobs. They also agree that it is difficult to define a living wage down to the penny and say that the term *living wage* is an emotional term rather than a definable economic term. The debate will certainly continue.

Decision Questions

1. An argument can be offered that all developed countries in the world experienced poor working conditions as their economies matured. Therefore, over time, workers in devel-

oping countries will gain the same benefits as their counterparts in countries such as the United States, Germany, and Japan. What's your opinion?

2. What role should the U.S. government take in this issue of a living wage?

3. Would you buy an apparel item with your college name or logo if you knew it was produced in a country where workers are toiling in sweatshops? Why or why not?

Sources: Andrew T. Dawson, "Protesters Rally to End University of Iowa 'Sweatshop Connection,' " *University Wire*, March 3, 2000; Mary Deibel, "Students Protest Colleges' Profiting Off Sweatshop Garb," *Washington Times*, September 13, 1999, p. A2; Travis Reed and Max Rust, "Universities Consideration of FLA Concerns Students," *University Wire*, February 15, 2000; and Louise Lee and Aaron Bernstein, "Who Says Student Protests Don't Matter?" *Business Week*, June 12, 2000, p. 94.

VIDEO CASE

SELLING COCA-COLA IN JAPAN

Coca-Cola and Pepsi are major competitors throughout the world as well as in the United States. When it comes to Japan, however, Coke is the clear winner. Why? The sale of soft drinks in Japan began on military bases after WWII. However, the rapid growth stage didn't begin until 1957 when a Japanese businessperson bought a license to manufacture Coke in Japan.

What made Coke a success in Japan over time was its willingness to partner with local businesspeople. Rather than simply being a multinational firm, Coke was successful in becoming a multilocal firm. That is, it found partners in various cities and worked closely with them to develop sales in those areas.

As many U.S. firms have found, it wasn't easy to break into the Japanese market. For one thing, Coke wanted to sell directly to retailers. That simply was not—and *is* not—the tradition in Japan. The tradition is to sell through a whole series of middlemen that control the distribution.

When trying to sell in a different country, it is fundamentally important to adapt as much as possible to the local culture. Coca-Cola did that by setting up in-house social clubs like those in other Japanese firms. It also helped employees buy homes with low-interest loans. Every effort was made to adjust to the tastes of the local people, including the creation of a 50 percent juice drink.

Relationship marketing is especially important in Japan, where negotiations take time, and patience is truly a virtue. Consensus building is the norm, and that requires more time than U.S. firms are used to investing. Nonetheless, the payoff can be extraordinary. For example, Coke has approximately 1,000,000 dealers and 700,000 vending machines in Japan as a result of its patience and care in establishing local relationships.

Pepsi, on the other hand, remains a minor competitor due to its failure to invest the time necessary to establish local partners and relationships. Consequently, Pepsi's market penetration in Japan continues to be hindered and shallow.

Discussion Questions

1. What evidence can you cite showing that foreign firms have been very careful to adapt to U.S. culture when marketing their products here?

2. Many U.S. firms have had difficulty establishing relationships in Japan. Do you think that they could learn from Coke's experience and try again? Would a similar approach work for U.S. automakers?

3. Talk with a local storeowner or manager who sells products from various parts of the world. Ask him or her what foreign manufacturers do to establish and maintain good relationships with that store and its suppliers.

CHAPTER 4

Demonstrating Ethical Behavior and Social Responsibility

LEARNING GOALS

AFTER YOU HAVE READ AND STUDIED THIS CHAPTER, YOU SHOULD BE ABLE TO

1 Explain why legality is only the first step in behaving ethically.

2 Ask the three questions one should answer when faced with a potentially unethical action.

3 Describe management's role in setting ethical standards.

4 Distinguish between compliance-based and integrity-based ethics codes, and list the six steps in setting up a corporate ethics code.

5 Define social responsibility and examine corporate responsibility to various stakeholders.

6 Analyze the role of American businesses in influencing ethical behavior and social responsibility in global markets.

Getting to Know Judy and Chuck Ruggeri, Fantastic Sams Franchisees

For Judy and Chuck Ruggeri, success for their six Fantastic Sams hair salons in Pennsylvania means more than contributing to their bottom line. It also means contributing to the communities they serve. With the help of Fuzzy (a big orange stuffed bear), the shops' hair stylists visit hospitals and preschools. The stylists cut the kids' hair and teach them grooming techniques while Fuzzy entertains them. "If we teach them while they're young, they'll learn to respect themselves," say the Ruggeris.

The Ruggeris serve the older members of their community as well. Their stylists donate their time and skills by giving free in-home haircuts to the elderly. The company's other charitable efforts include fund-raisers for the Make-A-Wish Foundation, the Muscular Dystrophy Association, and cancer research organizations. What's their latest community-support effort? Wigs. Fantastic Sams recruits volunteers who let the stylists snip off ponytails and send the hair to a charity that makes wigs for cancer patients. The effort is called Locks of Love.

"These events allow us to get along with the community," notes Chuck Ruggeri. "They inspire our employees to do more, which inspires us to do more, too. It's a rewarding experience for everyone." The rewards come in many ways. Certainly there is the sense of satisfaction people gain by doing something for someone else, but businesses obviously seek financial rewards as well. According to research by John Kay, director of the Said Business School in Oxford, England, exceptional focus on profitability is not among the common features of exceptionally successful companies. The companies in the study, Kay notes, "were particularly profitable, but not particularly profit oriented, and that is an important distinction . . . Successful businesses serve the needs of their customers, provide a rewarding environment for their workers, satisfy the needs of those who finance them, and support the development of their communities." Andrew Wilson, director of the Ashridge Centre for Business and Society, agrees: "To sustain long-term development, businesses need to be managed for all their stakeholders. People want to do business with people they trust."

In this chapter, we explore the responsibility of businesses to all of their stakeholders: customers, investors, employees, and society. We look at the responsibilities of individuals as well. After all, responsible business behavior depends on responsible behavior of each individual in the business.

Sources: Karen E. Spaeder, "For Good Cause," *Entrepreneur*, July 1999, pp. 130–32; Philip Schoefield, "Good Ethics Lead to Healthy Profits," *Independent on Sunday*, May 2, 1999, p. 1; and Melany Miller, "Utah County Residents Get a Haircut for a Good Cause," *University Wire*, May 11, 2000.

MANAGING BUSINESSES ETHICALLY AND RESPONSIBLY

Ethical behavior involves both knowing what is right and wrong and behaving accordingly. Behaving ethically can contribute to your success in business. In fact, a recent survey of chief financial officers ranked it the most important personal attribute of college graduates.

Beyond personal ethics, **social responsibility** is a business's concern for the welfare of society as a whole. In this chapter we will look at ethics from both an individual and an organizational perspective, and then we will look at how organizations show social responsibility.

social responsibility
A business's concern for the welfare of society as a whole.

ethics
Standards of moral behavior, that is, behavior that is accepted by society as right versus wrong.

Legality Is Only the First Ethical Standard

Some people wonder if being ethical these days simply means not getting caught doing something illegal. The only question seems to have become "Is it legal?" A society gets in trouble when it considers ethics and legality to be the same. Ethics and legality are two very different things. Although following the law is an important first step, ethical behavior requires more than that. Ethics reflects people's proper relations with one another: How should people treat others? What responsibility should they feel for others? Legality is more limiting. It refers to laws we have written to protect ourselves from fraud, theft, and violence. Many immoral and unethical acts fall well within our laws. (See the Making Ethical Decisions box.)

We define **ethics** as the standards of moral behavior, that is, behavior that is accepted by society as right versus wrong. Many Americans today have few moral

absolutes. Many decide situationally whether it's alright to steal, lie, or drink and drive. They seem to think that what is right is whatever works best for the individual, that each person has to work out for himself or herself the difference between right and wrong. This isn't the way it always was. When Thomas Jefferson wrote that all men have the right to life, liberty, and the pursuit of happiness, he didn't add, "At least that's my opinion." He declared it to be the truth. Going back even further in time, the Ten Commandments were not called the "The Ten Highly Tentative Suggestions."

In a country blessed with so many diverse cultures, you might think it is impossible to identify common standards of ethical behavior. However, among sources from many different times and places such as the Bible, Aristotle's *Ethics*, William Shakespeare's *King Lear*, the Koran, and the *Analects* of Confucius, you'll find the following basic moral values: integrity, respect for human life, self-control, honesty, courage, and self-sacrifice are right; cheating, cowardice, and cruelty are wrong. All of the world's major religions support a version of the Golden Rule, even if it is only the negative form: Do not do unto others as you would not have them do unto you.[1]

Superstar cyclist Richard Virenque and his teammates were expelled from the 1998 Tour de France when performance-enchancing drugs were discovered in the team's belongings. Virenque and others were charged with conspiracy to sell drugs to three other teams in the race. Athletes who use performance-enchancing drugs don't win trophies; they steal them. What messages do such actions send to young people watching star athletes?

Personal Ethics Begin at Home

It is easy to criticize business and political leaders for their moral and ethical shortcomings, but we must be careful in our criticism to note that Americans in general are not too socially minded. A recent study revealed that two-thirds of the American population reported never giving any time to the community in which they live. Nearly one-third said they never contributed to a charity. Both managers and workers cited low managerial ethics as a major cause of American business's competitive woes. Employees reported that they often violate safety standards and goof off as much as seven hours a week. Young people learn from such behavior: in one recent study, 50 percent of college students, 70 percent of high school students, and 54 percent of middle school students said they had cheated on an exam in the past 12 months.[2]

When someone tipped off a San Diego State University instructor that one of his classes was getting the answer keys to his quizzes from classes held earlier in the day, he tested the students' honestly by scrambling the questions. A full third

MAKING ETHICAL DECISIONS

www.napster.com

Did Napster Catch the Music Industry Napping?

When 19-year-old Shawn Fanning began writing a new software program, his goal was to create a tool for helping people search for music files on the Internet and to talk to each other about the types of music they liked. When he finished the project and got Napster up on the Web in 1999, it attracted thousands of college kids looking for an easy way to find tunes. The number of users doubled every five to six weeks. Soon Fanning had the attention of most college students—and just about all of the record companies.

What was the attraction? Napster enabled users to trade music over the Internet—for free. For years, people have been able use tape recorders to copy music. But until Napster such copying was usually limited to making one copy at a time, usually shared between friends. Napster, however, allowed an unlimited number of copies to be made and shared with millions of "friends."

As of this writing, the court has ordered Napster to close down. Napster has appealed the ruling, claiming that it has done nothing illegal. Much of the music industry feels otherwise. People were reproducing compact discs and other products for free. To record companies, that's like walking into music stores and stealing CDs. But Napster argued that since no one was *selling* the music, it wasn't illegal. (Don't get the idea that Napster didn't make money simply because it didn't actually sell music. Venture capitalists didn't invest $15 million in Napster just so cash-poor students could get free music.)

Some Napster supporters said that it was a way of sampling music risk-free and that when they found an artist's work they liked, they actually bought more CDs than they would have bought otherwise. But a recent study indicated that CD purchases have plummeted at stores near college campuses (Napster country). A small-business owner in Syracuse, New York, said his business dropped 80 percent in the first six months Napster was out. He said kids would check out his bins for new CDs and then go home and download them instead of buying them. He had to close his business.

Members of the music group Metallica sued Napster for distributing their work without their permission; the band members also appeared before the Senate to debate what action should be taken to protect their work from unauthorized distribution. Napster supporters, however, pointed out that there are many musicians who *like* having their music available to so many users on sites such as Napster. This is one way that unknown musicians can distribute their work easily. That's fine with Metallica members, who agreed that groups have the right to choose to share their work on Napster, but also said that groups should have the right to choose *not* to give their work away.

The debate about Napster is really a concern about intellectual property ownership. With Napster, we're talking about music. But the issue includes almost anything in the creative realm: movies, books, art, and so on. Should musicians work without getting paid? Movie producers? Authors? Engineers? If they don't get paid adequately, will people continue to work to produce high-quality music, software, books? Would you work if you didn't get paid fairly?

Technology changes so rapidly that by the time you read this it is possible that other music-download tools have evolved to take Napster's place. Remember, too, that just because something is legal doesn't mean it is ethical. How will you respond to these new ethical challenges? If such technology is available today, are you willing to pass up the opportunity to get free music if you think it is the ethical thing to do?

Source: Amy Kover, "Napster: The Hot Idea of the Year," *Fortune*, June 26, 2000, pp. 128–36; Steve Levy, "The Noisy War over Napster," *Newsweek*, June 5, 2000, pp. 46–54; Walter S. Mossberg, "Behind the Lawsuit: Napster Offers Model for Music Distribution," *The Wall Street Journal*, May 11, 2000, p. B1; Lars Ulrich, "It's Our Property," *Newsweek*, June 5, 2000, p. 54; and Dave Bartiromo, "Fight Napster with Price Cuts," *Business 2.0*, January 23, 2001.

Salt Lake Olympic Committee (SLOC) Chairman Robert Garff and Utah Governor Mike Leavitt discuss the Board of Ethics report that confirmed local officials gave Olympic officials Super Bowl trips, kitchen appliances, college tuition, a violin, cash and other payments in order to persuade them to bring the 2002 Winter Games to Utah. Two SLOC executives were indicted on fraud and conspiracy charges. What affect do the actions of SLOC and the Olympic officials who accepted the bribes have on other stakeholders (e.g. local, national, and international communities, the athletes, the sponsors)?

of the students simply wrote the answers from the pirated test key. Some of the dishonest students, who subsequently flunked the course, said the instructor should share the blame because giving the same test to different classes was "negligent and stupid." Apparently they thought they didn't have a choice but to cheat since the teacher didn't make it impossible for them to do so. What course was it? Business Ethics.[3]

It is always healthy when discussing moral and ethical issues to remind ourselves that ethical behavior begins with you and me. We cannot expect society to become more moral and ethical unless we as individuals commit to becoming more moral and ethical ourselves.

The purpose of the Making Ethical Decisions boxes you see throughout the text is to demonstrate to you that it is important to keep ethics in mind whenever you are making a business decision. The choices are not always easy. Sometimes the obvious solution from an ethical point of view has drawbacks from a personal or professional point of view. For example, imagine that your supervisor has asked you to do something you feel is unethical. You have just taken out a mortgage on a new house to make room for your first baby, due in two months. Not carrying out your supervisor's request may get you fired. What would you do? Sometimes there is no desirable alternative. Such situations are called *ethical dilemmas* because you must choose between equally unsatisfactory alternatives. It can be very difficult to maintain a balance between ethics and other factors such as pleasing stakeholders or advancing in your career.

It is helpful to ask yourself the following questions when faced with an ethical dilemma:[4]

1. *Is it legal?* Am I violating any law or company policy? Whether you are gathering marketing intelligence, designing a product, hiring or firing employees, planning on how to get rid of waste, or using a questionable nickname for an employee, it is necessary to think about the legal implications of what you do. This question is the most basic one in behaving ethically in business, but it is only the first.

2. *Is it balanced?* Am I acting fairly? Would I want to be treated this way? Will I win everything at the expense of another party? Win-lose situations often end up as lose-lose situations. There is nothing like a major loss to generate retaliation from the loser. Within a company, imbalances can eventually lead you to use your limited resources to combat the competition in the "back room" rather than to compete in the marketplace. Not every situation can be completely balanced, but it is important to the health of our relationships that we avoid major imbalances over time. An ethical businessperson has a win-win attitude. In other words, such a person tries to make decisions that benefit all parties involved.

3. *How will it make me feel about myself?* Would I feel proud if my family learned of my decision? Would I be able to discuss the proposed situation or action with my immediate supervisor? The company's clients? How would I feel if my decision were announced on the evening news?

Will I have to hide my actions or keep them secret? Has someone warned me not to disclose my actions? Am I feeling unusually nervous? Decisions that go against our sense of right and wrong make us feel bad—they corrode our self-esteem. That is why an ethical businessperson does what is proper as well as what is profitable.

There are no easy solutions to ethical problems. Individuals and companies that develop a strong ethics code and use the three ethics-check questions presented above have a better chance than most of behaving ethically. If you would like to know which style of recognizing and resolving ethical dilemmas you favor, fill out the ethical orientation questionnaire in Figure 4.1.

Think of a situation you were involved in recently that tested your ethical behavior. For example, maybe your best friend forgot about a term paper due the next day and asked you if he could copy and hand in a paper you wrote for another instructor last semester. What are your alternatives, and what are the consequences of each one? Would it have been easier to resolve this dilemma if you had asked yourself the three questions listed above? Try answering them now and see if you would have made a different choice.

Ethics Is More Than an Individual Concern

Some managers think that ethics is a personal matter—that either individuals have ethical principles or they don't. These managers feel that they are not responsible for an individual's misdeeds and that ethics has nothing to do with management. But a growing number of people think that ethics has *everything* to do with management. Individuals do not usually act alone; they need the implied, if not the direct, cooperation of others to behave unethically in a corporation.

For example, when Sears, Roebuck & Company was besieged with complaints about its automotive services, Sears management introduced new goals and incentives for its auto center employees. The increased pressure on the Sears employees to meet service quotas caused them to become careless and to exaggerate to customers the need for repairs. Did the managers say directly, "Deceive the customers"? No, but the message was clear anyway. The goals and incentives created an environment in which mistakes did occur and managers did not make efforts to correct the mistakes. Sears settled pending lawsuits by offering coupons to customers who had paid for unnecessary repairs. The estimated cost to Sears was $60 million.[5] Such misbehavior does not reflect a management philosophy that intends to deceive. It does, however, show an insensitivity or indifference to ethical considerations. In an effort to remedy this insensitivity, Sears replaced 23,000 pages of policies and procedures with a simple booklet called "Freedoms & Obligations," which discusses the company's code of business conduct from a commonsense approach.[6]

Organizational Ethics Begins at the Top

Ethics is caught more than it is taught. That is, people learn their standards and values from observing what others do, not from hearing what they say. This is as true in business as it is at home. The leadership and example of strong top managers instill corporate values in employees.

IBM, Xerox, McDonald's, Marriott, and dozens of other companies are known to have strong, effective, and ethical leadership. Within these firms, a high value system has become pervasive, and employees feel they are part of a

Please answer the following questions.

1. Which is worse?
   A. Hurting someone's feelings by telling the truth.
   B. Telling a lie and protecting someone's feelings.

2. Which is the worse mistake?
   A. To make exceptions too freely.
   B. To apply rules too rigidly.

3. Which is it worse to be?
   A. Unmerciful.
   B. Unfair.

4. Which is worse?
   A. Stealing something valuable from someone for no good reason.
   B. Breaking a promise to a friend for no good reason.

5. Which is it better to be?
   A. Just and fair.
   B. Sympathetic and feeling.

6. Which is worse?
   A. Not helping someone in trouble.
   B. Being unfair to someone by playing favorites.

7. In making a decision you rely more on
   A. Hard facts.
   B. Personal feelings and intuition.

8. Your boss orders you to do something that will hurt someone. If you carry out the order, have you actually done anything wrong?
   A. Yes.
   B. No.

9. Which is more important in determining whether an action is right or wrong?
   A. Whether anyone actually gets hurt.
   B. Whether a rule, law, commandment, or moral principle is broken.

To score: The answers fall in one of two categories, J or C. Count your number of J and C answers using this key:
1. A = J, B = C; 2. A = C, B = J; 3. A = J, B = C; 4. A = C, B = J; 5. A = C, B = J; 6. A = J, B = C; 7. A = C, B = J; 8. A = J, B = C; 9. A = J, B = C

What your score means: The higher your J score, the more you rely on an ethic of *justice*. The higher your C score, the more you prefer an ethic of *care*. Neither style is better than the other, but they are different. Because they appear so different they may seem opposed to one another, but they're actually complementary. In fact, your score probably shows you rely on each style to a greater or lesser degree. (Few people end up with a score of 9 to 0.) The more you can appreciate both approaches, the better you'll be able to resolve ethical dilemmas and to understand and communicate with people who prefer the other style.

An ethic of justice is based on principles like justice, fairness, equality, or authority. People who prefer this style see ethical dilemmas as conflicts of rights that can be solved by the impartial application of some general principle. The advantage of this approach is that it looks at a problem logically and impartially. People with this style try to be objective and fair, hoping to make a decision according to some standard that's higher than any specific individual's interests. The disadvantage of this approach is that people who rely on it might lose sight of the immediate interests of particular individuals. They may unintentionally ride roughshod over the people around them in favor of some abstract ideal or policy. This style is more common of men than women.

An ethic of care is based on a sense of responsibility to reduce actual harm or suffering. People who prefer this style see moral dilemmas as conflicts of duties or responsibilities. They believe that solutions must be tailored to the special details of individual circumstances. They tend to feel constrained by policies that are supposed to be enforced without exception. The advantage of this approach is that it is responsive to immediate suffering and harm. The disadvantage is that, when carried to an extreme, this style can produce decisions that seem not simply subjective, but arbitrary. This style is more common of women than men.

To learn more about these styles and how they might relate to gender, go to www.ethicsandbusiness.org/index3.htm.

Source: Center for Ethics and Business, ,www.ethicsandbusiness.org.

FIGURE 4.1

**ETHICAL ORIENTATION
QUESTIONNAIRE**

corporate mission that is socially beneficial. On the other hand, corporate standards can work the other way, too, as you learned from the Sears example. Even managers with strong personal values may place their concern for the corporation's profits ahead of those values.

Any trust and cooperation between workers and managers must be based on fairness, honesty, openness, and moral integrity. The same can be said about relationships among businesses and among nations. A business should be managed ethically for many reasons: to maintain a good reputation; to keep existing customers; to attract new customers; to avoid lawsuits; to reduce employee turnover; to avoid government intervention (the passage of new laws and regulations controlling business activities); to please customers, employees, and society; and simply to do the right thing.

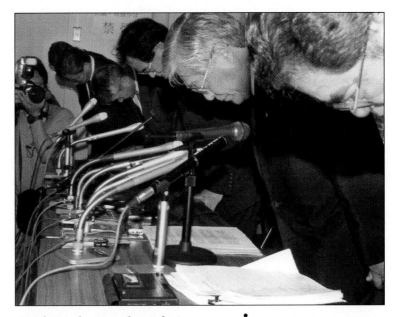

Contradicting what they had said the month before, Mitsubishi Motor Corp. executives finally admitted that the company concealed safety documents and motorists' complaints from the government. Mitsubishi's recall of over 600,000 vehicles in August 2000 cost the company over $79 million. In addition to the cost of the recalled vehicles, do you think the scandal will cost the company even more in future sales as consumer confidence in the company and its products plummet?

SETTING CORPORATE ETHICAL STANDARDS

Formal corporate ethics codes are popular these days. Eighty percent of the organizations surveyed recently by the Ethics Resource Center have written codes of ethics. Whether or not a business has a written ethics code seems to be determined by the size of the company. Ninety percent of the organizations with more than 500 employees have written standards.[7] Figure 4.2 offers a sample from one company's code of ethics.

Although ethics codes vary greatly, they can be classified into two major categories: compliance-based and integrity-based. **Compliance-based ethics codes** emphasize preventing unlawful behavior by increasing control and by penalizing wrongdoers. Whereas compliance-based ethics codes are based on avoiding legal punishment, **integrity-based ethics codes** define the organization's guiding values, create an environment that supports ethically sound behavior, and stress a shared accountability among employees. See Figure 4.3 for a comparison of compliance-based and integrity-based ethics codes.

The following six-step process can help improve America's business ethics:

1. Top management must adopt and unconditionally support an explicit corporate code of conduct.
2. Employees must understand that expectations for ethical behavior begin at the top and that senior management expects all employees to act accordingly.
3. Managers and others must be trained to consider the ethical implications of all business decisions.
4. An ethics office must be set up. Phone lines to the office should be established so that employees who don't necessarily want to be seen with an ethics officer can inquire about ethical matters anonymously.

compliance-based ethics codes
Ethical standards that emphasize preventing unlawful behavior by increasing control and by penalizing wrongdoers.

integrity-based ethics codes
Ethical standards that define the organization's guiding values, create an environment that supports ethically sound behavior, and stress a shared accountability among employees.

FIGURE 4.2

OVERVIEW OF LOCKHEED
MARTIN'S CODE OF ETHICS

**TREAT IN AN ETHICAL MANNER THOSE TO
WHOM LOCKHEED MARTIN HAS AN OBLIGATION**

We are committed to the ethical treatment of those to whom we have an obligation.

For our employees we are committed to honesty, just management, and fairness, providing a safe and healthy environment, and respecting the dignity due everyone.

For our customers we are committed to produce reliable products and services, delivered on time, at a fair price.

For the communities in which we live and work we are committed to acting as concerned and responsible neighbors, reflecting all aspects of good citizenship.

For our shareholders we are committed to pursuing sound growth and earnings objectives and to exercising prudence in the use of our assets and resources.

For our suppliers we are committed to fair competition and the sense of responsibility required of a good customer.

This excerpt from Lockheed Martin's Web page is an overview of the stakeholders to whom Lockheed Martin has an obligation to treat in an ethical manner. To see the company's complete code of ethics go to its Setting the Standard Web page at www.lmco.com/exeth/ethset.html.

FIGURE 4.3

STRATEGIES FOR ETHICS
MANAGEMENT

As you can see from the following chart, integrity-based ethics codes are similar to compliance-based ethics codes in that both have a concern for the law and use penalties as enforcement. Integrity-based ethics codes move beyond legal compliance to create a "do-it-right" climate that emphasizes core values such as honesty, fair play, good service to customers, a commitment to diversity, and involvement in the community. These values are ethically desirable, but not necessarily legally mandatory.

FEATURES OF COMPLIANCE-BASED ETHICS CODES		**FEATURES OF INTEGRITY-BASED ETHICS CODES**	
Ideal:	Conform to outside standards (laws and regulations)	Ideal:	Conform to outside standards (laws and regulations) and chosen internal standards
Objective:	Avoid criminal misconduct	Objective:	Enable responsible employee conduct
Leaders:	Lawyers	Leaders:	Managers with aid of lawyers and others
Methods:	Education, reduced employee discretion, controls, penalties	Methods:	Education, leadership, accountability, decision processes, controls, and penalties

5. Outsiders such as suppliers, subcontractors, distributors, and customers must be told about the ethics program. Pressure to put aside ethical considerations often comes from the outside, and it helps employees resist such pressure when everyone knows what the ethical standards are.

6. The ethics code must be enforced. It is important to back any ethics program with timely action if any rules are broken. That is the best way to communicate to all employees that the code is serious.[8]

An important factor to the success of enforcing an ethics code is the selection of the ethics officer. The most effective ethics officers set a positive tone, communicate effectively, and relate well with employees at every level of the company. They are equally comfortable serving as counselors or as investigators. An ethics director's background or functional area seems to be unimportant. For example, the head of Texas Instrument's ethics office came from operations, whereas another of the company's ethics officers has a background in public relations.

PROGRESS ASSESSMENT

* When faced with ethical dilemmas, what questions can you ask yourself that might help you make ethical decisions?
* What are the six steps to follow in establishing an effective ethics program in a business?

CORPORATE SOCIAL RESPONSIBILITY

As we said at the beginning of the chapter, corporate social responsibility is the concern businesses have for the welfare of society. The social performance of a company has several dimensions:

* **Corporate philanthropy** includes charitable donations to nonprofit groups of all kinds. Strategic philanthropy involves companies making long-term commitments to one cause, such as McDonald's founding and support of Ronald McDonald Houses, which house families whose critically ill children require treatment away from home. Philanthropy isn't limited to large corporations. The Spotlight on Small Business box describes how small businesses can become involved.

* **Corporate responsibility** includes everything from hiring minority workers to making safe products, minimizing pollution, using energy wisely, and providing a safe work environment—that is, everything that has to do with acting responsibly with society.

* **Corporate policy** refers to the position a firm takes on social and political issues.

So much news coverage is devoted to the social problems caused by corporations that people tend to get a negative view of the impact that companies

corporate philanthropy
Dimension of social responsibility that includes charitable donations.

corporate responsibility
Dimension of social responsibility that includes everything from hiring minority workers to making safe products.

corporate policy
Dimension of social responsibility that refers to the position a firm takes on social and political issues.

Xerox employee Susan Goldberg is proud of the results of her work on the renovation of these apartment houses. Xerox is one of many companies that offer their employees paid leave to work for nonprofit organizations. How do such policies benefit the companies, employees, and communities in which they work?

Myths about Small-Business Philanthropy

Many entrepreneurs have a hard time determining how to start a charitable-giving program in their businesses. Often, this is because of misconceptions.

Myth 1: Charities need cash, so struggling small businesses can't help them without jeopardizing their own cash flow.

Reality: Sure, charities need money. But they also need equipment (such as used computers), food, clothing, and volunteers. Pat Heffron, a franchisee of Chem-Dry (which specializes in carpet and upholstery cleaning), found a way to train his employees and help the community at the same time. New Chem-Dry employees learn how to do their jobs by cleaning discarded furniture, which Heffron then donates to local battered women and homeless shelters. Another way a small business can contribute to charities without taking a penny out of the cash register is to shop for business supplies through Internet charity sites such as Greatergood.com. Companies listed on such sites donate between 2 and 20 percent of their revenues to the buyer's charity of choice. One extra click—no extra money.

Myth 2: If your business is small, you can't make a significant difference.

Reality: If you target your involvement to small programs within your community, you'll be able to have a notable impact. For instance, one Chicago manufacturer invested just $1,500 in a new local early-childhood literacy program that rewarded inner-city parents with grocery money when they read to their children.

Myth 3: Charity organizers will pay attention only to large contributors with well-known names.

Reality: Nonprofits look for ways to form partnerships with both large and small companies. For example, Dine Across America, a fund-raising effort for a national antihunger organization, received funding for administrative expenses from American Express. But more important, it was small businesses—restaurants and food wholesalers—that donated the food and labor.

Business owners who don't know how to locate nonprofit organizations that need donations can call Gifts in Kind International (703-836-2121), which serves as an intermediary by collecting clothing, office equipment, and other useful materials and distributing them to more than 50,000 nonprofit organizations and schools across the nation.

Source: Karen E. Spaeder, "For Good Cause," *Entrepreneur*, July 1999, pp. 130–32; Louis Lavelle, "Americans Were in a Generous Mood Last Year," *(Bergen County, NJ) Record*, May 25, 2000, p. B1; Sam Howe Verhovek, "From Web Fortunes Innovative Philanthropy," *Minneapolis Star Tribune*, April 9, 2000, p. 4E; and Jonathan Alter, "Charity Begins with a Click," *Newsweek*, June 5, 2000.

have on society. Few people know, for example, that Xerox has a program called Social Service Leave, which allows employees to leave for up to a year and work for a nonprofit organization. While on Social Leave, the employee gets full salary and benefits, including job security. IBM and Wells-Fargo Bank have similar programs. In fact, many companies are jumping on the volunteerism bandwagon by allowing employees to give part-time help to social agencies of all kinds.[9] One of the goals of the 1997 President's Summit for America's Future, led by General Colin Powell, was to increase the numbers of corporate volunteers. VolunteerAmerica is a Web-based program that matches nonprofit organizations that need volunteers with people looking for volunteer opportunities (see www.volunteeramerica.net).

Two-thirds of the MBA students surveyed by a group called Students for Responsible Business said they would take a lower salary to work for a socially responsible company. But when the same students were asked to define a socially responsible company, things got complicated. It appears that even those who want to be socially responsible can't agree on what it involves. Maybe it would be easier to understand social responsibility if we looked at the concept through the eyes of the stakeholders ➤ **P.19**◄ to whom businesses are responsible: customers, investors, employees, and society in general.

Responsibility to Customers

One responsibility of business is to satisfy customers by offering them goods and services ➤ **P.25** ◄ of real value. A recurring theme of this book is the importance of pleasing customers. This responsibility is not as easy to meet as it seems. Keep in mind that three out of five new businesses fail—perhaps because their owners failed to please their customers. One of the surest ways of failing to please customers is not being totally honest with them. For example, in 1988 a consumer magazine reported that the Suzuki Samurai was likely to roll over if a driver swerved violently in an emergency. When Suzuki executives denied there was a problem, sales plummeted.

In contrast, Daimler Benz suffered a similar problem in 1997 during a test simulating a swerve around a wayward elk, when its new A-class "Baby Benz" rolled over. The company quickly admitted a problem, came up with a solution, and committed the money necessary to put that solution into action. In addition, company representatives continued to answer questions in spite of aggressive press coverage. Daimler admitted that it had made a mistake in full-page ads: "We should like to thank our customers most warmly for their loyalty. You have given us the chance to remedy a mistake." Since the test flip, only 2 percent of the orders for the vehicle were canceled. The solution cost the company $59 million in 1997 and $118 million each year thereafter. Analysts say those costs probably eliminate any profit on the vehicle. However, the quick resolution of the problem protected the company's reputation, thus allowing its other models to become such hits that Daimler's net earnings remained the same.[10]

The payoff for socially conscious behavior could result in new business as customers switch from rival companies simply because they admire the company's social efforts—a powerful competitive edge. Consumer behavior studies show that, all else being equal, a socially conscious company is likely to be viewed more favorably than less socially responsible companies. The important point to remember is that customers prefer to do business with companies they trust and, even more important, do not want to do businesses with companies they don't trust.

Responsibility to Investors

American economist Milton Friedman made a classic statement when he said that corporate social responsibility means making money for stockholders. Ethical behavior is good for

Hip-Hop trio L.N.E. donated the proceeds from their CD, "Stop the Violence" to the families of the students killed in the Columbine High School shooting in Littleton, CO and to the Easter Seals Circle of Friends Program. The song calls for an end to violence and a return to social responsibility. The Easter Seals program strives to prevent youth violence by boosting children's social skills and self-esteem through a variety of structured activities.

shareholder wealth. It doesn't subtract from the bottom line; it adds to it. Those cheated by financial wrongdoing are the shareholders themselves.

Some people believe that *before* you can do good you must do well; others believe that *by* doing good, you can also do well.[11] For example, Bagel Works, a New England–based chain of bagel stores, has a dual-bottom-line approach that focuses on the well-being of the planet as well as profits. Bagel Works received national recognition for social responsibility. Its mission involves commitments to the environment and to community service. In addition to employing environmentally protective practices such as promoting in-store recycling, composting, using organically grown ingredients, and using nontoxic cleaners, each store includes donations for community causes in its budget. The company donates 10 percent of its pretax profits to charities each year.

Many people believe that it makes financial as well as moral sense to invest in companies that are planning ahead to create a better environment. By choosing to put their money into companies whose goods and services benefit the community and the environment, investors can improve their own financial health while improving society's health.

insider trading
A form of investment in which insiders use private company information to further their own fortunes or those of their family and friends.

A few investors, known as inside traders, have chosen unethical means to improve their own financial health. **Insider trading** involves insiders using private company information to further their own fortunes or those of their family and friends. For example, before it was publicly known that IBM was going to take over Lotus Development, an IBM secretary told her husband, who told two co-workers, who told friends, relatives, business associates, even a pizza delivery man. A total of 25 people received the information and traded illegally on the insider tip within a six-hour period. When the deal was announced publicly, the stock soared 89 percent. One of the inside traders, a stockbroker who passed the information to a few of his customers, made $468,000 in profits. The Securities and Exchange Commission filed charges against the secretary, her husband, and 23 others. Four of the defendants settled out of court by paying penalties that equaled twice their profit. Prosecutors are placing increased emphasis on the prosecution of insider trading cases in order to ensure that the public is able to conduct business in a securities market that is fair and equally accessible to all.[12]

Companies can misuse information for their own benefit at investors' expense as well. In the case of McKesson HBO & Co., an Atlanta-based maker of health care software, the company reported revenues in its financial statements that hadn't actually been completed yet. Many investors use such statements to evaluate a company they are considering investing in. When an audit revealed the $44 million discrepancy, McKesson's stock price dropped immediately by nearly half and lawsuits weren't far behind. In time, McKesson will probably make up the shortfall in revenue. However regaining shareholders' trust won't be a swift process.[13]

Responsibility to Employees

Businesses have several responsibilities to employees. First, they have a responsibility to create jobs. It's been said that the best social program in the world is a job. Once a company creates jobs, it has an obligation to see to it that hard work and talent are fairly rewarded. Employees need realistic hope of a better future, which comes only through a chance for upward mobility. People need to see that integrity, hard work, goodwill, ingenuity, and talent pay off. Studies have shown that the factor that most influences a company's effectiveness and financial performance is human resource management.[14] We will discuss human resource management in Chapter 11.

If a company treats employees with respect, they will respect the company as well. For example, Fel-Pro, an Illinois manufacturer of gaskets and other engine parts, established a summer camp for children of employees. Those who used this company benefit were more productive than they had been before because they felt their children were safe. Employees who made the most of Fel-Pro's corporate social responsibility programs were its highest performers. In addition, the increased benefits reduced employee turnover. Given that the U.S. Department of Labor estimates that replacing employees costs approximately 150 percent of their annual salaries, retaining workers is good for business as well as for morale.

When employees feel they've been treated unfairly, they strike back. Getting even is one of the most powerful incentives for good people to do bad things. Not many disgruntled workers are desperate enough to resort to the violence in the workplace, but a great number do relieve their frustrations in more subtle ways, such as blaming mistakes on others, not accepting responsibility for decision making, manipulating budgets and expenses, making commitments they intend to ignore, hoarding resources, doing the minimum needed to get by, and making results look better than they are. The loss of employee commitment, confidence, and trust in the company and its management can be very costly indeed. You will read more about issues that affect employee–management relations in Chapter 12.

Responsibility to Society

One of business's major responsibilities to society is to create new wealth. If businesses don't do it, who will? More than a third of working Americans receive their salaries from nonprofit organizations that in turn receive their funding from others, who in turn receive their money from business. Foundations, universities, and other nonprofit organizations own billions of shares in publicly held companies. As those stock prices increase, more funds are available to benefit society.

Businesses are also responsible for promoting social justice. Business is perhaps the most crucial institution of civil society. For its own well-being, business depends on its employees being active in politics, law, churches and temples, arts, charities, and so on. Rhino Entertainment, a vintage music and video distributor, has a simple mission: "To put out some great stuff, have some fun, make some money, learn from each other, and make a difference wherever we can." Individual staff members are assigned to oversee community and environmental activities. The company has bins for can and paper recycling and for clothing donations spread throughout its offices. Employees receive extra vacation days each year in exchange for 16 hours of community service. They regularly participate in monthly activities at a local youth center. The company budgets a percentage of its revenues to go to charities that empower groups to help themselves.[15]

Many companies believe that business has a role in building a community that goes well beyond giving back. To them, charity is not enough. Their social contributions include cleaning

Senator Sam Brownback of Kansas shows a video game and an action figure during a Senate Commerce Committee hearing on marketing violence to children. Many believe that we need to pass laws against deceptive ads and to punish entertainment companies that target children with movies, games and music that are not age-appropriate. What do you think? The tobacco industry got into trouble for using Joe Camel to target kids. Should the entertainment industry be responsible for what it markets to children?

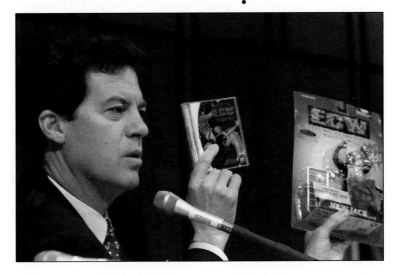

up the environment, building community toilets, providing computer lessons, and supporting the elderly and children from low-income families. Samsung, a Korean electronics conglomerate, emphasizes volunteer involvement. For example, a busload of Samsung employees and managers are transported each month to a city park, where they spread out to pick up garbage, pull weeds, and plant saplings. Managers even volunteer to help spruce up employee homes. Local employees feel such loyalty to the company that in the height of the 1999 unrest that destroyed many businesses in Indonesia, local employees and their neighbors pulled together to protect Samsung's refrigerator factory there and shield foreign managers from violence. With the help of relatives in the countryside, the local employees set up a food supply network that helped protect their colleagues from skyrocketing prices for food staples such as rice and palm oil.[16]

Businesses are clearly responsible for helping to make their own environment a better place. Environmental efforts may increase the company's cost, but they also may allow the company to charge higher prices, to increase market share, or both. For example, Ciba Specialty Chemicals, a Swiss textile-dye manufacturer, developed dyes that require less salt than traditional dyes. Since used dye solutions must be treated before they are released into rivers or streams, having less salt and unfixed dye in the solution means lower water-treatment costs. Patents protect Ciba's low-salt dyes, so the company can charge more for its dyes than other companies can charge for theirs. Ciba's experience illustrates that lowering environmental costs can add value to a business, just as a new machine enhances labor productivity.

Not all environmental strategies prove to be as financially beneficial to the company as Ciba's, however. For instance, in the early 1990s StarKist responded to consumer concerns about dolphins dying in the process of tuna fishing because the nets meant to capture tuna also caught dolphins swimming over the yellowfin tuna schools in the eastern Pacific. The company announced that it would sell only tuna from the western Pacific, where the skipjack tuna do not swim underneath dolphins. Unfortunately, the company found that customers were unwilling to pay a premium for the dolphin-safe tuna and that they considered the taste of the skipjack inferior to that of yellowfin tuna. In addition, it turned out that there was no clear environmental gain: in exchange for every dolphin saved by not fishing in the eastern Pacific, thousands of immature tuna and dozens of sharks, turtles, and other marine animals died in the western Pacific fishing process.

Environmental quality is a public good; that is, everyone gets to enjoy it regardless of who pays for it. The trick for companies is to find the right public good that will appeal to their target market.[17] Many corporations are publishing reports that document their net social contribution. To do that, a company must measure its positive social contributions and subtract its negative social impacts. We shall discuss that process next.

Social Auditing

It is nice to talk about having organizations become more socially responsible. It is also encouraging to see some efforts made toward creating safer products, cleaning up the environment, designing more honest advertising, and treating women and minorities fairly. But is there any way to measure whether organizations are making social responsibility an integral part of top management's decision making? The answer is yes, and the term that represents that measurement is *social auditing*.

A **social audit** is a systematic evaluation of an organization's progress toward implementing programs that are socially responsible and responsive. One of the major problems of conducting a social audit is establishing proce-

social audit
A systematic evaluation of an organization's progress toward implementing programs that are socially responsible and responsive.

FIGURE 4.4

SOCIALLY RESPONSIBLE BUSINESS ACTIVITIES

- Community-related activities such as participating in local fund-raising campaigns, donating executive time to various nonprofit organizations (including local government), and participating in urban planning and development.
- Employee-related activities such as establishing equal opportunity programs, offering flextime and other benefits, promoting job enrichment, ensuring job safety, and conducting employee development programs. (You'll learn more about these activities in Chapters 11 and 12.)
- Political activities such as taking a position on nuclear safety, gun control, pollution control, consumer protection, and other social issues; and working more closely with local, state, and federal government officials.
- Support for higher education, the arts, and other nonprofit social agencies.
- Consumer activities such as ensuring product safety, creating truthful advertising, handling complaints promptly, setting fair prices, and conducting extensive consumer education programs.

dures for measuring a firm's activities and their effects on society.[18] What should be measured? See Figure 4.4 for an outline of business activities that could be considered socially responsible.

There is some question as to whether positive actions should be added (e.g., charitable donations, pollution control efforts) and then negative effects subtracted (e.g., layoffs, overall pollution levels) to get a net social contribution. Or should just positive actions be recorded? In general, social responsibility is becoming one of the aspects of corporate success that business evaluates, measures, and develops.

In addition to the social audits conducted by the companies themselves, there are four types of groups that serve as watchdogs regarding how well companies enforce their ethical and social responsibility policies:

1. *Socially conscious investors* who insist that a company extend its own high standards to all its suppliers.

2. *Environmentalists* who apply pressure by naming names of companies that don't abide by the environmentalists' standards.

Water pollution is one of the major environmental concerns in the United States today. Here you see pollution in the Ohio River in Cincinnati. What responsibility should local businesses assume in cleaning up the river?

3. *Union officials* who hunt down violations and force companies to comply to avoid negative publicity.

4. *Customers* who take their business elsewhere if a company demonstrates unethical or socially irresponsible practices.

One important thing to remember is that it isn't enough for a company to be right when it comes to ethics and social responsibility. It also has to convince its customers and society that it's right.

INTERNATIONAL ETHICS AND SOCIAL RESPONSIBILITY

Ethical problems and issues of social responsibility are not unique to the United States. Top business and government leaders in Japan were caught in a major "influence peddling" (read bribery) scheme in Japan. Similar charges have been brought against top officials in South Korea, the People's Republic of China, Italy, Brazil, Pakistan, and Zaire.[19] What is new about the moral and ethical standards by which government leaders are being judged? They are much stricter than in previous years. Top leaders are now being held to a higher standard.

Government leaders are not the only ones being held to higher standards. Many American businesses are demanding socially responsible behavior from their international suppliers by making sure their suppliers do not violate U.S. human rights and environmental standards. For example, Sears will not import

▶ P.25 ◀ products made by Chinese prison labor. The clothing manufacturer Phillips–Van Heusen said it would cancel orders from suppliers that violate its ethical, environmental, and human rights code. Dow Chemical expects its suppliers to conform to tough American pollution and safety laws rather than just to local laws of their respective countries. McDonald's denied rumors that one of its suppliers grazes cattle on cleared rain forest land but wrote a ban on the practice anyway.[20]

In contrast to companies that demand that their suppliers demonstrate socially responsible behavior are those that have been criticized for exploiting workers in less developed countries. Nike, the world's largest athletic shoe company, has been accused by human rights and labor groups of treating its workers poorly while lavishing millions of dollars on star athletes to endorse its products. Cartoonist Gary Trudeau featured an anti-Nike campaign in his popular Doonesbury syndicated series.

An Ernst & Young report on Nike's operations in Asia indicated that thousands of young women labored over 10 hours a day, six days a week, in excessive heat, noise, and foul air, for slightly more than $10 a week. The report also found that workers with skin or breathing problems caused by the factory conditions had not been transferred to departments free of chemicals. More than half the workers who dealt with dangerous chemicals did not wear protective masks or gloves. Haryanto, a native of Jakarta, travels the globe speaking on college campuses to advocate workers' rights. He describes how he lost two fingers of his right hand making soles for Nike sneakers and how seven of his friends also lost fingers in the same machine. Nike refused to fix the machine's broken switches.

Former United Nations Ambassador Andrew Young discusses his report on the conditions at Nike's Asian Factories. While Young said he did not see widespread abuse, he did recommend improvements. Many human rights advocates would have liked for him to make a stronger case regarding Nike's need to change its working conditions. Go to www.nike.com to learn more about what Nike says it is doing to address these concerns.

REACHING BEYOND OUR BORDERS   *www.pathfinder.com*
Ethical Culture Clash

Communications and electronics giant Motorola describes itself as dedicated to "uncompromising integrity." Robert W. Galvin, Motorola's board chairman, says that the company's ethical values and standards are an "indispensable foundation" for the company's work, relationships, and business success. Almost half of Motorola's employees are non-American, and more than half of its revenues come from non-American markets. Is it difficult for Motorola employees to adhere to the company's ethical values while at the same time respecting the values of the host countries in which Motorola manufactures and markets its products?

Here's an example of how corporate ethics can clash with cultural ethics. Joe, the oldest son of a poor South American cloth peddler, managed to move to the United States, earn an engineering degree, and get a job with Motorola. After five years, Joe seemed to have bought into the Motorola culture and was happy to have been granted a transfer back to his home country. Joe was told that the company expected him to live there in a safe and presentable home of his choice. To help him afford such a residence, Motorola agreed to reimburse him a maximum of $2,000 a month for the cost of his rent and servants. Each month Joe submitted rental receipts for exactly $2,000. The company later found out that Joe was living in what was, by Western standards, a shack in a dangerous slum area of town. Such a humble home could not have cost more than a couple hundred dollars a month. The company was concerned for Joe's safety as well as for the effect the employee's unseemly residence would have on Motorola's image. The human resource manager was ultimately concerned about Joe's lack of integrity, given that he had submitted false receipts for reimbursement.

Joe was upset with what he considered the company's invasion of his privacy. He argued that he should receive the full $2,000 monthly reimbursement that all of the other Motorola employees received. He explained his choice of housing by saying that he was making sacrifices so he could send the extra money to his family and put his younger siblings through school. This was especially important since his father had died and his family had no one else to depend on but Joe. "Look, my family is poor," Joe said, so poor that most Westerners wouldn't believe our poverty even if they saw it. This money means the difference between hope and despair for all of us. For me to do anything less for my family would be to defile the honor of my late father. Can't you understand?"

Often it is difficult to understand what others perceive as being ethical. Different situations often turn the clear waters of "rightness" downright muddy. In Joe's case, one could see that Joe was trying to do the honorable thing for his family. One could also argue that Motorola's wish to have its higher-level people live in safe housing is not unreasonable, given the dangerous conditions of the city in which Joe lived. The policy of housing reimbursement supports Motorola's intent to make its employees' stay in the country reasonably comfortable and safe, not to increase their salaries. If Joe worked in the United States, where he would not receive a housing supplement, it would clearly be unethical for him to falsify expense reports in order to receive more money to send to his family. In South America, though, the issue is not so clear.

Source: R. S. Moorthy, Robert C. Solomon, William J. Ellos, and Richard T. De George, "Friendship or Bribery?" Across the Board, January 1999, pp. 43–47; and "Motorola Emphasizes 'People Development in the Information Age' at the Asia Society/Dow Jones Conference in Shanghai, China," news release, May 10, 2000.

Nike officials say they are working to improve conditions, but their critics say they are not doing enough quickly enough.[21] While customers still seem to favor brand, price, and quality over their perception of a company's humane treatment and social responsibility, surveys show that the vast majority of respondents would pay an extra few dollars for a garment that had been made in a worker-friendly environment.

The justness of requiring international suppliers to adhere to American ethical standards is not as clear-cut as you might think. Is it always ethical for companies to demand compliance with the moral standards of their own countries? What about countries where child labor is an accepted part of the society, where families depend on the children's salaries for survival? What about foreign companies doing business in the United States? Should they expect American companies to comply with their ethical standards? What about multinational corporations? Since they span different societies, do they not have to conform to any one society's standards? Why is Sears applauded for not importing goods made in Chinese prisons when there are many prison-based enterprises in the United States? None of these questions are easy to answer, but they give you some idea of the complexity of social responsibility issues in international markets.[22] (See the Reaching Beyond Our Borders box for an example of an ethical culture clash.)

In an effort to identify some form of common global ethic and to fight corruption in global markets, the partners in the Organization of American States signed the Inter-American Convention Against Corruption. A similar anticorruption convention was signed by 29 member states of the Organization for Economic Cooperation and Development (OECD) and five other states that are home to nearly all of the major multinational corporations. The OECD convention covers only those companies and governments that offer bribes and not the individuals who accept them. However, such loopholes are expected to be eliminated in the years ahead. In many places, "Fight corruption" remains a slogan. But even a slogan is a start.[23]

PROGRESS ASSESSMENT

- What is corporate social responsibility, and how does it relate to each of business's major stakeholders?
- What is a social audit, and what kinds of activities does it monitor?

SUMMARY

1. Explain why legality is only the first step in behaving ethically.

1. Ethics goes beyond obeying laws. It also involves abiding by the moral standards accepted by society.
   - *How is legality different from ethics?*
   Ethics reflects people's proper relation with one another. Legality is more limiting; it refers only to laws written to protect people from fraud, theft, and violence.

2. Ask the three questions one should answer when faced with a potentially unethical action.

2. It is often difficult to know when a decision is ethical.
   - *How can we tell if our business decisions are ethical?*
   Our business decisions can be put through an ethics check by asking three questions: (1) Is it legal? (2) Is it balanced? and (3) How will it make me feel?

3. Describe management's role in setting ethical standards.

3. Some managers think ethics is an individual issue that has nothing to do with management, while others believe ethics has *everything* to do with management.
   - *What is management's role in setting ethical standards?*
   Managers often set formal ethical standards, but more important are the messages they send through their actions. Management's tolerance or intolerance of ethical misconduct influences employees more than any written ethics codes do.

4. Distinguish between compliance-based and integrity-based ethics codes, and list the six steps in setting up a corporate ethics code.

4. Ethics codes can be classified as compliance-based or integrity-based.
   - *What's the difference between compliance-based and integrity-based ethics codes?*
   Whereas compliance-based ethics codes are concerned with avoiding legal punishment, integrity-based ethics codes define the organization's guiding

values, create an environment that supports ethically sound behavior, and stress a shared accountability among employees.

5. Social responsibility is the concern businesses have for society.
    • ***How do businesses demonstrate corporate responsibility toward stakeholders?***
    Business is responsible to four types of stakeholders: (1) business's responsibility to *customers* is to satisfy them with goods and services of real value; (2) business is responsible for making money for its *investors;* (3) business has several responsibilities to *employees:* to create jobs, to maintain job security, and to see that hard work and talent are fairly rewarded; and (4) business has several responsibilities to *society:* to create new wealth, to promote social justice, and to contribute to making its own environment a better place.
    • ***How are a company's social responsibility efforts measured?***
    A corporate social audit measures an organization's progress toward social responsibility. Some people believe that the audit should add together the organization's positive actions and then subtract the negative effects of business to get a net social benefit.

    5. Define social responsibility and examine corporate responsibility to various stakeholders.

6. Many customers are demanding that companies deal only with other companies that share a commitment to environmental and human rights issues.
    • ***How can American companies influence ethical behavior and social responsibility in global markets?***
    Companies like Sears, Phillips–Van Heusen, and Dow Chemical will not import products from companies that do not meet their ethical and social responsibility standards.

    6. Analyze the role of American businesses in influencing ethical behavior and social responsibility in global markets.

KEY TERMS

compliance-based ethics codes 101

corporate philanthropy 103

corporate policy 103

corporate responsibility 103

ethics 96

insider trading 106

integrity-based ethics codes 101

social audit 108

social responsibility 95

DEVELOPING WORKPLACE SKILLS

1. What sources have helped shape your personal code of ethics and morality? What influences, if any, have pressured you to compromise those standards in recent years? Think of an experience you had at work or school that tested your ethical standards. What did you decide to do to resolve your dilemma? Now that time has passed, are you comfortable with the decision you made? If not, what would you do differently?

2. Newspapers and magazines are full of stories about individuals and businesses that are *not* socially responsible. What about those individuals and organizations that *do* take social responsibility seriously? We don't normally read or hear about them. Do a little investigative reporting of your own. Identify a public interest group in your community and identify its officers, objectives, sources and amount of financial support, and size and characteristics of membership. List some examples of its recent actions and/or accomplishments. You should be able to choose from environmental groups, animal protection groups, political action committees, and so on. Call the local chamber of commerce, the Better Business Bureau, or local government agencies for help. Try using one of the Internet search engines to help you find more information.

3. You are manager of a coffeehouse called the Morning Cup. One of your best employees desires to be promoted to a managerial position; however, the

owner is grooming his slow-thinking son for the promotion your employee seeks. The owner's act of nepotism may hurt a valuable employee's chances for advancement, but complaining may hurt your own chances for promotion. What do you do?

4. Contact a local corporation and ask for a copy of its written ethics code. Would you classify its code as compliance-based or integrity-based? Explain.

5. Where do you see leadership emerging to improve the moral standards of the United States? What could you do to support such leadership?

TAKING IT TO THE NET

Purpose

To demonstrate the level of commitment one business has to social responsibility.

Exercise

Richard Foos of Rhino Records built a multimillion-dollar entertainment experience out of a pile of dusty old records, and did it by sticking to his ideals. Foos fosters ethical practices in Rhino's day-to-day business, supporting numerous charitable groups, and promoting community service by Rhino employees. See for yourself how Foos responds to social and environmental issues by going to the Rhino's website at www.rhino.com/about.

1. What is the social mission of Rhino Records?

2. What does the SERT team do to implement this mission?

3. How does Rhino Records encourage its employees to get involved in community service?

4. How do they communicate their social mission to their customers?

PRACTICING MANAGEMENT DECISIONS

CASE

GOT A DEADLINE? CLICK HERE

Have a term paper due soon? Dreading the thought of all the work involved? With the advent of the World Wide Web, plagiarism has become as easy as point and click. Some websites list thousands of term papers on hundreds of topics—and the papers are there to be downloaded 24 hours a day. Boston University developed a plan in which a law student posed as a student wanting to buy a term paper to see how easily it could be done. The student secured papers from eight companies in seven states and paid fees ranging from $45 to $175. The university charged the companies in federal court with wire fraud, mail fraud, racketeering, and violating a Massachusetts law that bans the sale of term papers.

Some websites are not affected by current laws because they offer the papers for free. The sites are funded by advertisers who buy space on the sites. The owner of one such websites says that the papers on his site are posted there not so that students can plagiarize them but rather to show the substandard writing skills of many college students. You get the idea from the papers on the site that students get rewarded for length. The papers consist of pages and pages of junk, yet many instructors accept them. The owner notes that this says something about the mediocre assignments some professors give year after year. He thinks it is absurd that class assignments can be so vague that a student can go to the Internet, find a generic essay, and receive credit for it. He believes he is doing education a favor by forcing professors to give more specific writing assignments and to require extensive footnotes.

If recycling term papers is now so easy, why do professors continue to assign them? While the writing style used for term papers is different from that used in the workplace, writing develops critical thinking skills and the ability to express thoughts and ideas. Tom Rocklin, director of the Center for Teaching at the University of Iowa, puts it this way: "I have sat down with a group of businesspeople, and they say what they are looking for in new hires are skills developed by a traditional liberal arts education. Discussion, reading, and extended writing are a crucial part of that." Yet simply downloading a paper from a website does nothing to help a student develop these skills.

Decision Questions

1. Would you consider purchasing a paper from a website and submitting it as your own? Why or why not? Consider that there is now a website that helps professors check for plagiarism by comparing student papers with millions of online pages using the top 20 search engines. The system even identifies papers composed of bits and pieces of online text. Does knowing this change your answer to the questions above?

2. Do you agree with the website owner who said he is improving education by posting certain term papers as the mediocre results of mediocre assignments? Justify your answer.

3. View this issue through the eyes of your professor. The websites are out there, and your students have access to them. What would you do to discourage your students from committing plagiarism?

VIDEO CASE

ETHICS IN THE WORKPLACE

In college, you learn how to do many things the right way. For example, in accounting and math classes, you learn how to prepare financial statements and solve quadratic equations. With time and study, you learn how to do these things in a technically proficient manner. You face a much tougher challenge, however, in learning *how to do the right thing* when faced with ethical dilemmas. Imagine working as an accountant for a manufacturing firm that looks like it's going to miss its budget projections for the first time in three years. Missing projections frustrates everyone, but the situation becomes even more intolerable when a major customer places a large order for delivery the next quarter. If the order had only been four weeks prior, it could have been filled this quarter and would have put the company's sales over the top of the projections. A foreman suggests you record the order for the present quarter rather than the next. He advises, "If we don't get the order delivered this quarter, who's going to know anyway?"

Ethical questions abound in all business departments and disciplines. For example, how far should you go to promote a product? Suppose you are urged to design a blatantly sexist campaign just because it will please the client. Should you go along with such a suggestion even if it violates what you consider to be good taste and respect? When is the proper time to follow your own beliefs as opposed to following orders?

Decisions involving finance are not much easier. Consider the challenge of investing funds for clients. Is it important that you invest your client's money in a high-yield company even if that company has a reputation for questionable behavior with regard to the environment? Or should you consider a socially responsible firm that offers a bit lower yield but over the long term offers more value to the environment?

What do you do if you see someone else violating what you believe to be ethical standards? Should you report such infractions to others? What could be the consequences of your behavior?

Discussion Questions

1. What are other difficult ethical issues you may face on the job?

2. What do you think happens to people who follow their ethical standards completely, even when such standards go against the wishes of their supervisors? Would you advise such people to compromise?

3. How would you personally handle all the situations presented above? Why would you behave in the manner you chose?

APPENDIX

Working within the Legal Environment of Business

THE NEED FOR LAWS

Imagine a society without laws. Just think, no speed limits to control how fast we drive, no age restrictions on the consumption of alcoholic beverages, no limitations on who can practice medicine—a society in which people are free to do whatever they choose, with no interference. Obviously, the more we consider this possibility, the more unrealistic we realize it is. Laws are an essential part of a civilized nation. Over time, though, the depth and scope of the body of laws must change to reflect the needs and changes in society. The **judiciary** is the branch of government chosen to oversee the legal system through the court system.

The court system in the United States is organized at the federal, state, and local levels. At both the federal and state levels, *trial courts* hear cases involving criminal and civil law. *Criminal law* defines crimes, establishes punishments, and regulates the investigation and prosecution of people accused of committing crimes. *Civil law* involves legal proceedings that do not involve criminal acts; it includes laws regulating marriage, payment for personal injury, and so on. Both federal and state systems have *appellate courts*. Such courts hear appeals of decisions made at the trial-court level brought by the losing party in the case. Appellate courts can review and overturn decisions made at the trial-court level.

The judiciary also governs the activities and operations of business. In fact, businesspeople often complain that the government is stepping in more and more to govern the behavior of business. Thus, you see laws and regulations regarding sexual harassment on the job, hiring and firing practices, unpaid leave for family emergencies, environmental protection, safety, and more. As you may suspect, businesspeople prefer to set their own standards of behavior. However, the U.S. business community has not been perceived as implementing acceptable practices fast enough. To hasten the process, the federal government has expanded its control and enforcement procedures. In this appendix we will look at some of the laws and regulations now in place and how they affect business.

Business law refers to rules, statutes, codes, and regulations that are established to provide a legal framework within which business may be conducted and that are enforceable by court action. A businessperson should be familiar with laws regarding product liability, sales, contracts, fair competition, consumer protection, taxes, and bankruptcy. Let's start at the beginning and discuss the foundations of the law. It's hard to understand the law unless you know what the law is.

judiciary
The branch of government chosen to oversee the legal system through the court system.

business law
Rules, statutes, codes, and regulations that are established to provide a legal framework within which business may be conducted and that are enforceable by court action.

Statutory and Common Law

There are two major kinds of law: statutory law and common law. Both are important for businesspeople.

Statutory law includes state and federal constitutions, legislative enactments, treaties of the federal government, and ordinances—in short, written law. You can read the statutes that make up this body of law, but they are often written in language whose meaning must be determined in court. That's one reason why there are 900,000 lawyers in the United States.

Common law is the body of law that comes from decisions handed down by judges. Common law is often referred to as *unwritten law* because it does not appear in any legislative enactment, treaty, and so forth. Under common law principles, what judges have decided in previous cases is very important to today's cases. Such decisions are called **precedent,** and they guide judges in the handling of new cases. Common law evolves through decisions made in trial courts, appellate courts, and special courts. Lower courts (trial courts) must abide by the precedents set by higher courts (appellate courts) such as the U.S. Supreme Court. In law classes, therefore, students study case after case to learn about common law as well as statutory law.

Executives from the Firestone/Bridgestone Tire Company testified before Congress regarding the safety of their products. The company recalled and replaced 6.5 million of its tires, due to complaints about the tires coming apart at high speeds. Most of the defective tires were installed on Ford Explorer vehicles. Does the company have additional liabilities to consumers for producing the defective tires?

Administrative Agencies

Different organizations within the government issue many rules, regulations, and orders. **Administrative agencies** are federal or state institutions and other government organizations created by Congress or state legislative bodies with powers to pass rules and regulations within a specific area of authority. Legislative bodies can not only create administrative agencies but also terminate them. Some administrative agencies hold quasi-legislative, quasi-executive, and quasi-judicial powers. This means an agency is allowed to pass rules and regulations within its area of authority, conduct investigations in cases of suspected rules violations, and hold hearings when it feels the rules and regulations have been violated. Administrative agencies actually issue more rulings affecting business and settle more disputes than courts do. Figure A.1 lists and describes the powers and functions of several administrative agencies at the federal, state, and local levels of government. How many of these agencies have you heard about?

TORT LAW

The tort system is an example of common law at work. A **tort** is a wrongful act that causes injury to another person's body, property, or reputation. Although

statutory law
State and federal constitutions, legislative enactments, treaties, and ordinances—in other words, *written laws.*

common law
The body of law that comes from judges' decisions; also referred to as *unwritten law.*

precedent
Decisions judges have made in earlier cases that guide the handling of new cases.

administrative agencies
Institutions created by Congress or state legislatures with delegated power to pass rules and regulations within their mandated area of authority.

tort
A wrongful act that causes injury to another person's body, property, or reputation.

FIGURE A.1

EXAMPLES OF FEDERAL, STATE, AND LOCAL ADMINISTRATIVE AGENCIES

EXAMPLES	POWERS AND FUNCTIONS
FEDERAL AGENCIES	
Federal Trade Commission	Enforces laws and guidelines regarding unfair business practices and acts to stop false and deceptive advertising and labeling
Food and Drug Administration	Enforces laws and regulations to prevent distribution of adulterated or misbranded foods, drugs, medical devices, cosmetics, and veterinary products, as well as any hazardous consumer products
STATE AGENCIES	
Public utility commissions	Set rates that can be charged by various public utilities to prevent unfair pricing by regulated monopolies (e.g., natural gas, electric power companies)
State licensing boards	Licenses various trades and professions within a state (e.g., state cosmetology board, state real estate commission)
LOCAL AGENCIES	
Maricopa County Planning Commission	Oversees land-use proposals, long-term development objectives, and other long-range issues in Maricopa County, Arizona
City of Chesterfield Zoning Board	Sets policy regarding zoning of commercial and residential property in the city of Chesterfield, Missouri

torts often are noncriminal acts, victims can be awarded compensation. This is especially true if the conduct that caused harm is considered intentional. An intentional tort is a willful act that results in injury. The question of intent has been a major factor in the recent tobacco industry lawsuits. Courts are investigating whether cigarette makers willfully withheld from the public information about the harmful effects of their products.[1] **Negligence,** in tort law, is behavior that causes unintentional harm or injury. In the 1990s, decisions involving negligence often led to huge judgments against businesses. McDonald's, for example, lost a lawsuit to a person burned by its hot coffee while driving in a car. The jury felt the company failed to provide an adequate warning on the cup. Product liability is another example of tort law that's often very controversial. This is especially true regarding torts related to business actions. Let's look briefly at this issue.

negligence
Behavior that causes unintentional harm or injury.

Product Liability

product liability
Part of tort law that holds businesses liable for harm that results from the production, design, sale, or use of products they market.

strict product liability
Legal responsibility for harm or injury caused by a product regardless of fault.

Few issues in business law raise as much debate as product liability. **Product liability,** covered under tort law, holds businesses liable for harm that results from the production, design, sale, or use of products they market. At one time the legal standard for measuring product liability was whether a producer *knowingly* placed a hazardous product on the market. Today, many states have extended product liability to the level of **strict product liability.** Legally, this means *without regard to fault.* Thus, a company could be held liable for damages caused by placing a defective product on the market even if the company did not know of the defect at the time of sale. In such cases, the company is required to compensate the injured party financially.

The rule of strict liability has caused serious problems for businesses. The manufacturers of chemicals and drugs, for example, are often susceptible to lawsuits under strict product liability. A producer may place a drug or chemical on the market that everyone agrees is safe. Years later, a side effect or other

COMPANY	YEAR	SETTLEMENT
Ford Motor Company	1978	$125 million in punitive damages awarded in the case of a 13-year-old boy severely burned in a rear-end collision involving a Ford Pinto
A. H. Robins	1987	Dalkon Shield intrauterine birth-control devices recalled after eight separate punitive-damage awards
Playtex Company	1988	Considered liable and suffered a $10 million damage award in the case of a toxic shock syndrome fatality in Kansas; removed certain types of tampons from the market
Jack in the Box	1993	Assessed large damages after a two-year-old child who ate at Jack in the Box died of *E. coli* poisoning and others became ill
Sara Lee Corporation	1998	Costly company recall necessitated when tainted hot dogs caused food-poisoning death of 15 people
General Motors	1999	Suffered $4.8 billion punitive award in faulty fuel-tank case
Major Tobacco Firms	2000	$145 billion punitive judgment in Florida case (on appeal)

Sources: U.S. Department of Justice, American Trial Lawyers Association.

health problem could emerge. Under the doctrine of strict liability, the manufacturer can be held liable.

The gun industry has been accused of damages under the rules of strict product liability. Cities such as Philadelphia, Chicago, New Orleans, Miami, and Atlanta have filed lawsuits against gun manufacturers seeking financial payments to cover the costs of police work and medical care necessitated by gun violence.[2] Lawsuits have also been filed on behalf of private individuals affected by gun violence.[3] Critics contend the industry is liable because it does nothing to enhance the safety of its products or prevent the criminal misuse of its products.[4] The gun industry has strongly refuted such charges and denied liability.

Businesses and insurance companies have called for legal relief from huge losses that are often awarded in strict product liability suits. They have lobbied Congress to set limits on the amounts of damages for which they are liable should their products harm consumers. Figure A.2 highlights some major product liability awards that cost companies dearly.

Businesses are held to standards of strict liability; that is, they can be assessed damages caused by defective products even if they did not know of the defects. After successful lawsuits against tobacco companies, several cities filed similar lawsuits against gun manufacturers seeking damages to cover costs of police work and medical care due to gun violence. In this photo, gun protestors from the Million-Mom March show their support for such actions taken against the gun industry. Do you think producers of alcoholic beverages should also be liable for the health problems and deaths caused by their products?

LAWS PROTECTING IDEAS: PATENTS, COPYRIGHTS, AND TRADEMARKS

patent
A document that gives inventors exclusive rights to their inventions for 20 years.

From the Arch in St. Louis to the Pyramids in Egypt, Coca-Cola is one of the most recognized words in the world. It's not surprising then that this world famous word is a registered trademark of the Coca-Cola Company. As such, Coca-Cola has the exclusive legal protection to use this name and symbols associated with it. Look closely at the small circle with the "R" inside at the end of the word Cola on a bottle. This signifies the brand is a registered trademark.

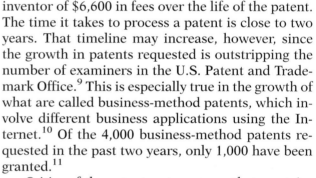

Many people, including you perhaps, have invented products that are assumed to have commercial value. The question that obviously surfaces is what to do next. One step may be to apply for a patent. A **patent** is a document that gives inventors exclusive rights to their inventions for 20 years from the date they file the patent applications.[5] The U.S. Patent Office issues approximately 170,000 patents a year.[6] In addition to filing forms, the inventor must make sure the product is truly unique. Since patent applicants are usually recommended to seek the advice of a lawyer, less than 2 percent of product inventors file on their own.[7]

Patent owners have the right to sell or license the use of a patent to others. Foreign companies are also eligible to file for U.S. patents and account for nearly half the U.S. patents issued. The penalties for violating a patent can be very severe.[8] The U.S. Patent and Trademark Office, however, cannot take action on behalf of patent holders if infringement of a patent occurs. The defense of patent rights is solely the job of the patent holder. In a rather famous case, the camera and film company Polaroid was able to force Kodak to recall all of its instant cameras because Polaroid had several patents that Kodak violated. Kodak lost millions of dollars, and Polaroid maintained market leadership in instant cameras. In another case inventor Robert Kearns won millions of dollars from Ford and Chrysler by proving that both companies violated his patent on intermittent windshield wipers.

How good are your chances of receiving a patent if you file for one? Over 60 percent of patent applications are approved, each at a minimum cost to the inventor of $6,600 in fees over the life of the patent. The time it takes to process a patent is close to two years. That timeline may increase, however, since the growth in patents requested is outstripping the number of examiners in the U.S. Patent and Trademark Office.[9] This is especially true in the growth of what are called business-method patents, which involve different business applications using the Internet.[10] Of the 4,000 business-method patents requested in the past two years, only 1,000 have been granted.[11]

Critics of the patent system argue that some inventors intentionally delay or drag out a patent application because they expect others to develop similar products or technology. When someone else does file for a similar patent, these inventors surface to claim the patent—referred to as a submarine patent—and demand large fees.[12] The late engineer Jerome Lemelson, for example, reportedly collected millions of dollars in patent royalties for a series of long-delayed patents, including one that was the forerunner of the bar-code scanner.[13] The U.S. Congress in 1999 passed changes to current patent law through the American Inventor's Protection Act, which requires patent applications to be made public after 18 months regardless of whether a patent has been granted.

Just as a patent protects an inventor's right to a product or process, a **copyright** protects a creator's rights to materials such as books, articles, photos, paintings, and cartoons. Copyrights are filed with the Library of Congress and involve a minimum of paperwork. They last for the lifetime of the author or artist plus 70 years, and can be passed on to the creator's heirs. The Copyright Act of 1978, however, gives a special term of 75 years from publication to works published before January 1, 1978, whose copyrights had not expired by that date. The holder of an exclusive copyright may charge a fee to anyone who wishes to use the copyrighted material. If a work is created by an employee in the normal course of a job, the copyright belongs to the employer and lasts 95 years from publication or 120 years from creation, whichever comes first.[14]

copyright
Exclusive rights to materials such as books, articles, photos, and cartoons.

A **trademark** is a legally protected name, symbol, or design (or combination of them) that identifies the goods or services of one seller and distinguishes them from those of competitors. Trademarks generally belong to the owner forever, as long as they are properly registered and renewed every 20 years. Some well-known trademarks include the Pillsbury Doughboy, the Disney Company's Mickey Mouse, and the Golden Arches of McDonald's. We will discuss trademarks in more detail in Chapter 14.

trademark
A legally protected name, symbol, or design (or combination of these) that identifies the goods or services of one seller and distinguishes them from those of competitors.

SALES LAW: THE UNIFORM COMMERCIAL CODE

At one time, laws involving businesses varied from state to state, making interstate trade extremely complicated. Today, all states have adopted the same commercial law. The **Uniform Commercial Code (UCC)** is a comprehensive commercial law that covers sales laws and other commercial laws. Since all states have adopted the law, the UCC simplifies trading across state lines.

Uniform Commercial Code (UCC)
A comprehensive commercial law adopted by every state in the United States; it covers sales laws and other commercial laws.

The UCC has 11 articles, which contain laws covering sales; commercial paper such as promissory notes and checks; bank deposits and collections; letters of credit; bulk transfers; warehouse receipts, bills of lading, and other documents of title; investment securities; and secured transactions. We do not have space to discuss all 11 articles, but we would like to discuss two of them: Article 2, which contains laws regarding warranties, and Article 3, which covers negotiable instruments.

Warranties

A warranty guarantees that the product sold will be acceptable for the purpose for which the buyer intends to use it. **Express warranties** are specific representations by the seller that are relied on by the buyer regarding the goods.[15] The warranty you receive in the box with a clock, toaster, or VCR is the express warranty. It spells out the seller's warranty agreement. **Implied warranties** are legally imposed on the seller. It is implied, for example, that the product will conform to the customary standards of the trade or industry in which it competes.

express warranties
Specific representations by the seller regarding the goods.

implied warranties
Guarantees legally imposed on the seller.

Warranties offered by sellers can be either full or limited. A *full warranty* requires a seller to replace or repair a product at no charge if the product is defective, whereas a *limited warranty* typically limits the defects or mechanical problems that are covered. Many of the rights of buyers, including the acceptance and rejection of goods, are spelled out in Article 2 of the UCC. Both buyers and sellers should become familiar with the UCC. You can read more about it on the Internet or in business law books in the library.

Negotiable Instruments

Negotiable instruments are forms of commercial paper (such as checks) that are transferable among businesses and individuals and represent a promise to

negotiable instruments
Forms of commercial paper (such as checks) that are transferable among businesses and individuals and represent a promise to pay a specified amount.

pay a specified amount. Article 3 of the Uniform Commercial Code states that negotiable instruments must follow four conditions. They must (1) be written and signed by the maker or drawer, (2) be made payable on demand or at a certain time, (3) be made payable to the bearer (the person holding the instrument) or to specific order, and (4) contain an unconditional promise to pay a specified amount of money. Checks or other forms of negotiable instruments are transferred (negotiated for payment) when the payee signs the back. The payee's signature is referred to as an endorsement.

CONTRACT LAW

If I offer to sell you my bike for $35 and later change my mind, can you force me to sell the bike, saying we had a contract? If I lose $120 to you in a poker game, can you sue in court to get your money? If I agree to sing at your wedding for free and back out at the last minute, can you claim I violated a contract? These are the kinds of questions that contract law answers.

A **contract** is a legally enforceable agreement between two or more parties. **Contract law** specifies what a legally enforceable agreement is. Basically, a contract is legally binding if the following conditions are met:

1. *An offer is made.* An offer to do something or sell something can be oral or written. If I agree to sell you my bike for $35, I have made an offer. That offer is not legally binding, however, until other conditions are met.

2. *There is a voluntary acceptance of the offer.* The principle of mutual acceptance means that both parties to a contract must agree on the terms. If I use duress in getting you to agree to buy my bike, the contract would not be legal. Duress occurs if there is coercion through force or threat of force. You couldn't use duress to get me to sell my bike, either. Even if we both agree, though, the contract is still not legally binding without the following.

3. *Both parties give consideration.* **Consideration** means something of value. If I agree to sell you my bike for $35, the bike and the $35 are consideration, and we have a legally binding contract. If I agree to sing at your wedding and you do not give me anything in return (consideration), we have no contract.

4. *Both parties are competent.* A person under the influence of alcohol or drugs, or a person of unsound mind (one who has been legally declared incompetent), cannot be held to a contract. In many cases, a minor may not be held to a contract, either. For example, if a 15-year-old agrees to pay $10,000 for a car, the seller will not be able to enforce the contract due to the buyer's lack of competence.

5. *The contract must be legal.* A contract covering the sale of illegal drugs or stolen merchandise would be unenforceable since both types of sales are violations of criminal law.

6. *The contract is in proper form.* An agreement for the sale of goods worth $500 or more must be in writing. Contracts that cannot be fulfilled within one year also must be put in writing. Contracts regarding real property (land and everything attached to it) must be in writing.

Breach of Contract

Breach of contract occurs when one party fails to follow the terms of a contract. Both parties may voluntarily agree to end a contract; but if one person violates the contract, the following may occur:

---

contract
A legally enforceable agreement between two or more parties.

contract law
Set of laws that specify what constitutes a legally enforceable agreement.

consideration
Something of value; consideration is one of the requirements of a legal contract.

breach of contract
When one party fails to follow the terms of a contract.

1. *Specific performance.* The person who violated the contract may be required to live up to the agreement if money damages would not be adequate. For example, if I legally offered to sell you a rare painting, I would have to sell you that painting.

2. *Payment of damages.* The term **damages** refers to the monetary settlement awarded to a person who is injured by a breach of contract. If I fail to live up to a contract, you can sue me for damages, usually the amount you would lose from my nonperformance. If we had a legally binding contract for me to sing at your wedding, for example, and I failed to come, you could sue me for the cost of hiring a new singer.

3. *Discharge of obligation.* If I fail to live up to my end of a contract, you could agree to drop the matter. Generally you would not have to live up to your end of the agreement either.

damages
The monetary settlement awarded to a person who is injured by a breach of contract.

Lawyers would not be paid so handsomely if the law were as simple as implied in these rules of contracts. In fact, it is always best to have a contract in writing even if not required under law. The offer and consideration in a contract should be clearly specified, and the contract should be signed and dated. A contract does not have to be complicated as long as it has these elements: (1) it's in writing, (2) mutual consideration is specified, and (3) there is a clear offer and agreement.

LAWS TO PROMOTE
FAIR AND COMPETITIVE PRACTICES

One objective of legislators is to pass laws that the judiciary will enforce to ensure a competitive atmosphere among businesses and promote fair business practices. Chapter 2 explained how competition is a cornerstone of the free-market system ➤ **P.37** ◄. In the United States, the Justice Department's antitrust division and other government agencies serve as watchdogs to ensure that competition among sellers flows freely and that new competitors have open access to the market.[16] The scope of the government is broad and extensive. The Justice Department's antitrust division has tackled the competitive practices of market giants such as Microsoft, Visa, and MasterCard.[17] Figure A.3 highlights key high-profile antitrust cases.

There was, however, a time when big businesses were able to drive smaller competitors out of business with little resistance. The following discussion shows how government responded to these troubling situations in the past and how business must deal with new challenges facing them today.

The History of Antitrust Legislation

In the late 19th century, big oil companies, railroads, steel companies, and other industrial firms dominated the U.S. economy. The fear was that such large and powerful companies would be able to crush any competitors and then charge high prices. It was in that atmosphere that Congress passed the Sherman Antitrust Act in 1890.[18] The Sherman Act was designed to prevent large organizations from stifling the competition of smaller or newer firms. The Sherman Act forbids the following: (1) contracts, combinations, or conspiracies in restraint of trade, and (2) actual monopolies ➤ **P.41** ◄ or attempts to monopolize any part of trade or commerce.

FIGURE A.3

HISTORY OF HIGH-PROFILE ANTITRUST CASES

CASE	OUTCOME
United States v. Standard Oil 1911	Standard Oil broken up into 34 companies; Amoco, Chevron, and Exxon-Mobil are results of the breakup
United States v. American Tobacco 1911	American Tobacco split into 16 companies; British Tobacco and R. J. Reynolds are results of the breakup
United States v. E. I. du Pont de Nemours 1961	Dupont ordered to divest its 23 percent ownership stake in General Motors
United States v. AT&T 1982	Settled after Ma Bell agreed to spin off its local telephone operations into seven regional operating companies
United States v. Microsoft 2000	Undecided to date

Source: U.S. Department of Justice.

Because of the act's vague language, there was some doubt about just what practices it prohibited. The following laws were passed later to clarify some of the legal concepts in the Sherman Act:

- *The Clayton Act of 1914.* The Clayton Act prohibits exclusive dealing, tying contracts, interlocking directorates, and buying large amounts of stock in competing corporations. *Exclusive dealing* is selling goods with the condition that the buyer will not buy goods from a competitor (when the effect lessens competition). A *tying contract* requires a buyer to purchase unwanted items in order to purchase desired items. For example, let's say I wanted to purchase 20 cases of Pepsi Cola per week to sell in my restaurant. Pepsi, however, says it will sell me the 20 cases only if I also agree to buy 10 cases each of its Mountain Dew and Diet Pepsi products. My purchase of Pepsi Cola would be *tied* to the purchase of the other two products. An *interlocking directorate* occurs when a board of directors includes members of the board of competing corporations.

- *The Federal Trade Commission Act of 1914.* The Federal Trade Commission Act prohibits unfair methods of competition in commerce. This legislation set up the five-member Federal Trade Commission (FTC) to enforce compliance with this act. The FTC deals with wide-ranging competitive issues—everything from preventing companies from making misleading "Made in the USA" claims to insisting that funeral providers give consumers accurate, itemized price information about funeral goods and services.[19] The involvement and activity of the FTC typically depends on the members serving on the board at the time. For example, the FTC conducted three times as many investigations and brought twice as many cases of unfair competition in the 1990s as it did during the 1980s. The Wheeler-Lea Amendment of 1938 gave the FTC additional jurisdiction over false or misleading advertising. It also gave the FTC power to increase fines if its requirements aren't met within 60 days.

- *The Robinson-Patman Act of 1936.* The Robinson-Patman Act prohibits price discrimination. One interesting aspect of the Robinson-Patman Act is that it applies to both sellers and buyers who "knowingly" induce or receive an unlawful discrimination in price. It also stipulates that certain types of price-cutting are criminal offenses punishable by fine and imprisonment. This act applies to business-to-business transactions and does not apply to consumers in business transactions.

The changing nature of business from manufacturing to knowledge technology has called for new levels of regulation on the part of federal agencies. For example, in recent years Microsoft's competitive practices have been the focus of intense investigation.[20] One of the major accusations against the computer software giant was that it hindered competition by refusing to sell the Windows operating system to computer manufacturers who did not agree to sell Window-based computers exclusively.[21] Computer manufacturers had a choice of buying only Windows or no Windows at all.[22] Given that many consumers wanted Windows, the computer companies had little choice but to agree. Read the description of the Clayton Act again. Do you think Microsoft violated the law?

Competition is the cornerstone of the free-market system. In the United States, the antitrust division of the Justice Department is charged with enforcing laws that keep markets open and competitive. Charges questioning the competitive practices of Microsoft, MasterCard, and Visa show the intensity and scope of the department's mission. Here attorneys, along with former Attorney General Janet Reno, conduct a post trial news conference related to the Microsoft case. Why is competition so important to a free-market system?

Laws to Protect Consumers

Consumerism is a social movement that seeks to increase and strengthen the rights and powers of buyers in relation to sellers. Although consumerism is not a new movement, it took on new vigor and direction throughout the 1990s. Consumerism is the people's way of getting a fair share in marketing exchanges. It's vital that businesses recognize consumer needs and interests in making important decisions. In the 1960s, President John F. Kennedy proposed four basic rights of consumers: (1) the right to safety, (2) the right to be informed, (3) the right to choose, and (4) the right to be heard. These rights will not be maintained if consumers passively wait for organizations to recognize them; they will come partially from consumer action in the marketplace. Figure A.4 lists several major consumer protection laws.

Tax Laws

Mention the word *taxes* and most people frown. That's because taxes affect almost every individual and business in the United States. **Taxes** are how the government (federal, state, and local) raises money. Traditionally, taxes have been used primarily as a source of funding for government operations and programs. They have also been used as a method of encouraging or discouraging taxpayers from doing something. For example, if the government wishes to reduce the use of certain classes of products (cigarettes, liquor, etc.), it passes what are referred to as *sin taxes*. The additional cost of the product from increased taxes *perhaps* discourages additional consumption. In other situations, the government may encourage businesses to hire new employees or purchase

consumerism
A social movement that seeks to increase and strengthen the rights and powers of buyers in relation to sellers.

taxes
How the government (federal, state, and local) raises money.

LEGISLATION	PURPOSE
Pure Food and Drug Act (1906)	Protects against the adulteration and misbranding of foods and drugs sold in interstate commerce.
Food, Drug, and Cosmetic Act (1938)	Protects against the adulteration and sale of foods, drugs, cosmetics, or therapeutic devices and allows the Food and Drug Administration to set minimum standards and guidelines for food products.
Wool Products Labeling Act (1940)	Protects manufacturers, distributors, and consumers from undisclosed substitutes and mixtures in manufactured wool products.
Fur Products Labeling Act (1951)	Protects consumers from misbranding, false advertising, and false invoicing of furs and fur products.
Flammable Fabrics Act (1953)	Prohibits the interstate transportation of dangerously flammable wearing apparel and fabrics.
Automobile Information Disclosure Act (1958)	Requires auto manufacturers to put suggested retail prices on all new passenger vehicles.
Textile Fiber Products Identification Act (1958)	Protects producers and consumers against misbranding and false advertising of fiber content of textile fiber products.
Cigarette Labeling Act (1965)	Requires cigarette manufacturers to label cigarettes as hazardous to health.
Fair Packaging and Labeling Act (1966)	Makes unfair or deceptive packaging or labeling of certain consumer commodities illegal.
Child Protection Act (1966)	Removes from sale potentially harmful toys and allows the FDA to pull dangerous products from the market.
Truth-in-Lending Act (1968)	Requires full disclosure of all finance charges on consumer credit agreements and in advertisements of credit plans.
Child Protection and Toy Safety Act (1969)	Protects children from toys and other products that contain thermal, electrical, or mechanical hazards.
Fair Credit Reporting Act (1970)	Requires that consumer credit reports contain only accurate, relevant, and recent information and are confidential unless a proper party requests them for an appropriate reason.
Consumer Product Safety Act (1972)	Created an independent agency to protect consumers from unreasonable risk of injury arising from consumer products and to set safety standards.
Magnuson–Moss Warranty–Federal Trade Commission Improvement Act (1975)	Provides for minimum disclosure standards for written consumer products warranties and allows the FTC to prescribe interpretive rules and policy statements regarding unfair or deceptive practices.
Alcohol Labeling Legislation (1988)	Provides for warning labels on liquor saying that women shouldn't drink when pregnant and that alcohol impairs a person's abilities.
Nutrition Labeling and Education Act (1990)	Requires truthful and uniform nutritional labeling on every food the FDA regulates.

FIGURE A.4

CONSUMER PROTECTION LAWS

new equipment by offering a tax credit. A tax credit is an amount that can be deducted from a tax bill.

Taxes are levied from a variety of sources. Income (personal and business), sales, and property are the major bases of tax revenue. The federal government receives its largest share of taxes from income. States and local communities often make extensive use of sales taxes. School districts are generally dependent on property taxes. The tax policies of states and cities are taken into consideration when businesses seek to locate operations. Tax policies also affect personal decisions such as retirement. A key tax issue sure to dominate the early years of the 21st century involves Internet taxation, especially Internet transactions (e-commerce ➤ **P.13** ◄).[23] Expect this issue to be debated fiercely

TYPE	PURPOSE
Income taxes	Taxes paid on the income received by businesses and individuals. Income taxes are the largest source of tax income received by the federal government.
Property taxes	Taxes paid on real and personal property. *Real property* is real estate owned by individuals and businesses. *Personal property* is a broader category that includes any movable property such as tangible items (wedding rings, equipment, etc.) or intangible items (stocks, checks, mortgages, etc.). Taxes are based on their assessed value.
Sales taxes	Taxes paid on merchandise when it's sold at the retail level.
Excise taxes	Taxes paid on selected items such as tobacco, alcoholic beverages, airline travel, gasoline, and firearms. These are often referred to as *sin taxes.* Income generated from the tax goes toward a specifically designated purpose. For example, gasoline taxes often help the federal government and state governments pay for highway construction or improvements.

in the years ahead. Figure A.5 highlights the primary types of taxes levied on individuals and businesses.

BANKRUPTCY LAWS

Bankruptcy is the legal process by which a person, business, or government entity unable to meet financial obligations is relieved of those debts by a court. The court divides any assets among creditors, allowing creditors to get at least part of their money and freeing the debtor to begin anew.[24] The U.S. Constitution gives Congress the power to establish bankruptcy laws, and there has been bankruptcy legislation since the 1890s. Two major amendments to the bankruptcy code include the Bankruptcy Amendments and Federal Judgeships Act of 1984 and the Bankruptcy Reform Act of 1994. The 1984 legislation allows a person who is bankrupt to keep part of the equity (ownership) in a house, $1,200 in a car, and some other personal property. The Bankruptcy Reform Act of 1994 amends more than 45 sections of the bankruptcy code and creates reforms that speed up and simplify the process.

In 1998 a record 1.44 million Americans filed for bankruptcy; in 1999 the number dropped a bit, to 1.3 million.[25] By contrast, only 172,000 Americans filed for bankruptcy in 1978. The number of bankruptcies began to increase in the late 1980s and grew tremendously in the 1990s. While high-profile bankruptcies such as the Planet Hollywood restaurants and the city of Camden, New Jersey, sometimes dominate the news, over 90 percent of bankruptcy filings each year are by individuals. Bankruptcy attorneys say the increase in filings is due to a lessening of the stigma of bankruptcy, the changing economy, an increase in understanding of bankruptcy law and the protection it offers, increased advertising by bankruptcy attorneys, and the ease with which some consumers can get credit.[26]

Bankruptcy can be either voluntary or involuntary. In **voluntary bankruptcy** cases the debtor applies for bankruptcy, whereas in **involuntary bankruptcy** cases the creditors start legal procedures against the debtor. Most bankruptcies today are voluntary because creditors usually want to wait in hopes that they will be paid all of the money due them rather than settle for only part of it.

bankruptcy
The legal process by which a person, business, or government entity unable to meet financial obligations, is relieved of those obligations by having the court divide any assets among creditors, freeing the debtor to begin anew.

voluntary bankruptcy
Legal procedures initiated by a debtor.

involuntary bankruptcy
Bankruptcy procedures filed by a debtor's creditors.

"That's all folks!" Pull down the curtains, the show may be over at the United Artists Theatres chain. The company filed for bankruptcy under Chapter 11 and plans to close 70 locations throughout the nation. Under Chapter 11 bankruptcy laws, a company can continue to operate while it tries to devise a plan to pay off its debts. Unfortunately, the track record for companies filing Chapter 11 and returning successfully to the market is not encouraging. What do you think of bankruptcy laws that permit a company to continue operating while devising a reorganization plan?

Bankruptcy procedures begin when a petition is filed with the court under one of the following sections of the Bankruptcy Code:

Chapter 7—"straight bankruptcy" or liquidation (used by businesses and individuals).

Chapter 11—reorganization (used by businesses and some individuals).

Chapter 13—repayment (used by individuals).

Chapter 7 calls for straight bankruptcy, which requires the sale of nonexempt assets of debtors. Under federal exemption statutes, a debtor may be able to retain up to $7,500 of equity in a home ($15,000 in a joint case); up to $1,200 of equity in an automobile; up to $4,000 in household furnishings, apparel, and musical instruments; and up to $500 in jewelry. States may have different exemption statutes.[27] When the sale of assets is over, the resulting cash is divided among creditors, including the government. Almost 70 percent of bankruptcies follow Chapter 7 procedures. Chapter 7 stipulates the order in which the assets are to be distributed among the creditors. First, creditors with *secured* claims receive the collateral for their claims or repossess the claimed asset. Then *unsecured* claims are paid in this order:

1. Costs involved in the bankruptcy case.
2. Any business costs incurred after bankruptcy was filed.
3. Wages, salaries, or commissions (limited to $2,000 per person).
4. Employee benefit plan contributions.
5. Refunds to consumers who paid for products that weren't delivered (limited to $900 per claimant).
6. Federal and state taxes.

The remainder (if any) is divided among unsecured creditors in proportion to their claims. See Figure A.6 for the steps used in liquidating assets under Chapter 7.

Chapter 11 bankruptcy allows a company to reorganize and continue operations while paying only a limited proportion of its debts. The company does not have to be insolvent in order to file for relief under Chapter 11. The Bankruptcy Reform Act of 1994 extends a "fast-track" procedure for small businesses filing under Chapter 11. Under certain conditions, the company can sell assets, borrow money, and change officers to strengthen its market position. A trustee appointed by the court to protect the interests of creditors usually supervises all such matters. Chapter 11 is designed to help both debtors and creditors find the best solution.

Under Chapter 11, a company continues to operate but has court protection against creditors' lawsuits while it tries to work out a plan for paying off its debts. In theory, Chapter 11 is a way for sick companies to recover. In reality, less than 25 percent of Chapter 11 companies emerge healthy—usually only the big ones with lots of cash available. In 1991, the U.S. Supreme Court gave individuals the right to file bankruptcy under Chapter 11.

Chapter 13 bankruptcy permits individuals, including small-business owners, to pay back creditors over a period of three to five years. Chapter 13 pro-

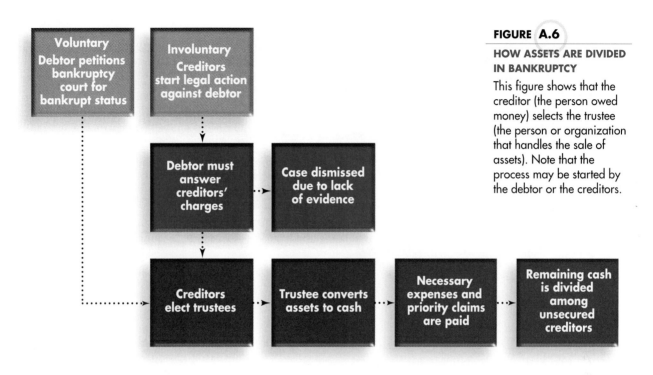

FIGURE A.6

HOW ASSETS ARE DIVIDED IN BANKRUPTCY

This figure shows that the creditor (the person owed money) selects the trustee (the person or organization that handles the sale of assets). Note that the process may be started by the debtor or the creditors.

ceedings are less complicated and less expensive than Chapter 7 proceedings. The debtor files a proposed plan for paying off debts to the court. If the plan is approved, the debtor pays a court-appointed trustee in monthly installments as agreed on in the repayment plan. The trustee then pays each creditor. In legislation proposed by the U.S. Congress in 2000, more debtors would be required to file bankruptcy under Chapter 13.[28]

deregulation
Government withdrawal of certain laws and regulations that seem to hinder competition.

DEREGULATION

By 1980, the United States had developed laws and regulations covering almost every aspect of business. There was concern that there were too many laws and regulations, and that these laws and regulations were costing the public money (see Figure A.7). Thus began the movement toward deregulation. **Deregulation** means that the government withdraws certain laws and regulations that seem to hinder competition.

Perhaps the most publicized examples of deregulation are those in the airlines and the telecommunications industry. At one time, the government restricted airlines as to where they could land and fly. When such restrictions were lifted, the airlines began

In 1996, the Telecommunications Reform Act ended local telephone companies monopolies encouraging companies like Teligent (pictured here) to compete for business in markets where they were previously restricted. Can you think of business situations where government restrictions related to competition are necessary?

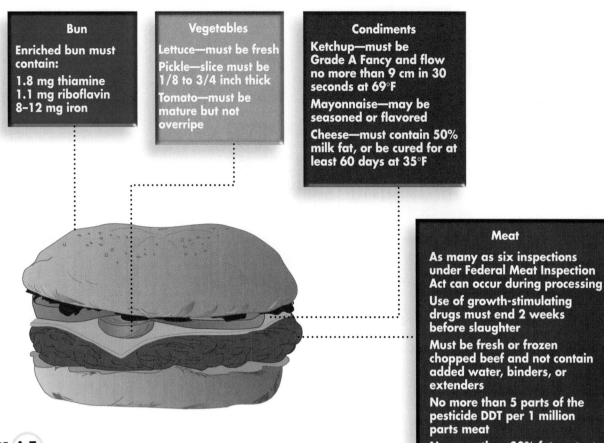

Bun

Enriched bun must contain:

1.8 mg thiamine
1.1 mg riboflavin
8–12 mg iron

Vegetables

Lettuce—must be fresh
Pickle—slice must be 1/8 to 3/4 inch thick
Tomato—must be mature but not overripe

Condiments

Ketchup—must be Grade A Fancy and flow no more than 9 cm in 30 seconds at 69°F
Mayonnaise—may be seasoned or flavored
Cheese—must contain 50% milk fat, or be cured for at least 60 days at 35°F

Meat

As many as six inspections under Federal Meat Inspection Act can occur during processing
Use of growth-stimulating drugs must end 2 weeks before slaughter
Must be fresh or frozen chopped beef and not contain added water, binders, or extenders
No more than 5 parts of the pesticide DDT per 1 million parts meat
No more than 30% fat content

FIGURE A.7

HAMBURGER REGULATIONS

Does this amount of regulation seem just right, too little, or too much for you?

competing for different routes and charging lower prices. This was a clear benefit to consumers, but it put tremendous pressure on the airlines to be more competitive. New airlines such as Southwest Airlines were born to take advantage of the opportunities. Similar deregulation in telecommunications gave consumers a flood of options in the telephone service market.

Deregulation also made the trucking industry more competitive as well. Today the electric power industry and other utilities are the targets of deregulation.[29] In 1999, California became the first state to deregulate the electric power industry. Since then, 25 other states have instituted or approved free-market control of the price of electricity.[30] Such shifts in utility services could affect virtually every region and citizen in the United States as the cost of power and the number of service providers grow. There is also a call for new regulations in the banking and investments industries that would change the nature of financial markets and make them more competitive.

It seems some regulation of business is necessary to ensure fair and honest dealings with the public. But there now appears to be more dialogue and more cooperation between business and government than in the past. Businesses have adapted to the laws and regulations, and have done much toward producing safer, more effective products. Competition, though, is often fierce, as many small and innovative firms have started to capture selected markets. Global competition is also increasing. Business and government need to continue to work together to create a competitive environment that is fair and open. If businesses do not want additional regulation, they must accept their responsibilities to society.

KEY TERMS

administrative
  agencies 117

bankruptcy 127

breach of
  contract 122

business law 116

common law 117

consideration 122

consumerism 125

contract 122

contract law 122

copyright 121

damages 123

deregulation 129

express
  warranties 121

implied
  warranties 121

involuntary
  bankruptcy 127

judiciary 116

negligence 118

negotiable
  instruments 121

patent 120

precedent 117

product liability 118

statutory law 117

strict product
  liability 118

taxes 125

tort 117

trademark 121

Uniform Commercial
  Code (UCC) 121

voluntary
  bankruptcy 127

Forms of Business Ownership

AFTER YOU HAVE READ AND STUDIED THIS CHAPTER, YOU SHOULD BE ABLE TO

1 Compare the advantages and disadvantages of sole proprietorships.

2 Describe the differences between general and limited partners, and compare the advantages and disadvantages of partnerships.

3 Compare the advantages and disadvantages of corporations, and summarize the differences between C corporations, S corporations, and limited liability companies.

4 Define and give examples of three types of corporate mergers and explain the role of leveraged buyouts and taking a firm private.

5 Outline the advantages and disadvantages of franchises and discuss the opportunities for diversity in franchising and the challenges of international franchising.

6 Explain the role of cooperatives.

Getting to Know Rachel Bell and Sara Sutton of JobDirect.com

There's an old adage in business that says, "Never go into business with a good friend. It's a sure way to end the friendship." Well, don't tell that to Rachel Bell and Sara Sutton, best friends since the fifth grade. In 1995, at age 21, the two best friends were getting ready for their senior year in college. They shared their concerns about their future and the prospect of finding good jobs. Sutton complained that her Internet search for an internship got her nowhere. Then it clicked: "Let's start our own Internet job service for entry-level positions. We could reach out to students like us, and we could help our friends."

Bell and Sutton were aware that the Internet was becoming increasingly popular as a communications tool for students and business professionals alike. After reading just about every business publication they could find and raising $60,000 from family members and acquaintances, the two friends became business partners and started JobDirect.com in August 1995.

JobDirect.com links entry-level job seekers and prospective employers. Instead of just listing jobs at the site, employers can search for qualified candidates in the database. The companies pay monthly fees, but the service is free to job seekers.

Unfortunately, as in many new companies, the first year in business was challenging and revenue was scarce. Bell and Sutton found that their website was not attracting the number of hits they had forecast. They knew that with such low numbers, it was unlikely that they could attract the corporate clients they needed. The friends knew it was time to come up with a solution. They also knew that their solution would probably require more money than they had, so they incorporated their business and issued shares to those willing to invest in their company.

The team knew they had to find a way to get their message to the students. Since the high-tech approach wasn't working, they decided to try something more low tech. They bought an old school bus, hired several graffiti artists to custom-paint it to look like their company website, and equipped the bus with 15 laptop computers on which students could type in their résumés. They set out on a promotional tour of college campuses to sign up prospective job seekers. Forty-three campus visits later, JobDirect.com had 5,000 résumés in its database. Bell and Sutton soon had three tour buses and 100,000 résumés. Their employer client base included IBM, Intel, and Sears. By 1999, the company had 24 employees, over $3 million in client contact bookings and 60 stockholders. Bell and Sutton also paid more than 250 student representatives to talk up the service at schools around the country.

In order to achieve this success, Bell and Sutton realized that they needed to hire experts to execute their vision. They hired a university professor to serve as president and chief operating officer and a former bank executive to serve as chief executive officer.

As the business grew more successful, it caught the attention of Korn/Ferry International, one of the world's largest recruiting companies. To expand its service, JobDirect.com agreed to be acquired by Korn/Ferry in July 2000.

Rachel Bell and Sara Sutton were friends, business partners, two major shareholders in a growing corporation, and now are part of one of the biggest corporations in its field. As the partners learned, a business may start with one form of ownership, but it can later change to another form as business conditions require. Whether you dream of going into business for yourself, starting a business with a friend, or someday leading a major corporation, it's important to know that each form of ownership has its advantages and disadvantages. You will learn about them all in this chapter.

Sources: Geoff Williams, "Buddies in Business," *Business Start-Ups*, April 1999, pp. 52–57; Yuki Noguchi, "Making Connections; Job Fair Uses Internet, Face-to-Face Meetings to Create Opportunities," *Washington Post*, April 6, 2000; and "Korn/Ferry International Signs Agreement to Acquire JobDirect.Com," press release, July 5, 2000.

Basic Forms of Business Ownership

Like Rachel Bell and Sara Sutton, hundreds of thousands of people start new businesses in the United States every year. Chances are, you have thought of owning your own business or know someone who has. One key to success in starting a new business is understanding how to get the resources you need. You may have to take on partners or find other ways of obtaining money. To stay in business, you may need help from someone with more expertise than you have in certain areas, or you may need to raise more money to expand. How you form your business can make a tremendous difference in your long-term success. You can form a business in one of several ways. The three major forms of business ownership are (1) sole proprietorships, (2) partnerships, and (3) corporations.

It can be easy to get started in your own business. You can begin a word processing service out of your home, open a car repair center, start a restaurant, develop a website, or go about meeting other wants and needs of your community. An organization that is owned, and usually managed, by one person is called a **sole proprietorship.** That is the most common form of business ownership.

Many people do not have the money, time, or desire to run a business on their own. They prefer to have someone else or some group of people get together to form the business. When two or more people legally agree to become co-owners of a business, the organization is called a **partnership.**

There are advantages to creating a business that is separate and distinct from the owners. A legal entity with authority to act and have liability separate from its owners is called a **corporation.** The almost 3.9 million corporations in the United States comprise only 19 percent of all businesses, but they earn 89 percent of the total receipts (see Figure 5.1).

As you will learn in this chapter, each form of business ownership has its advantages—and disadvantages. It is important to understand these advantages and disadvantages before attempting to start a business. Keep in mind that just because a business starts in one form of ownership, it doesn't always

sole proprietorship
A business that is owned, and usually managed, by one person.

partnership
A legal form of business with two or more owners.

corporation
A legal entity with authority to act and have liability separate from its owners.

FIGURE 5.1

FORMS OF BUSINESS OWNERSHIP

Although corporations make up only 19 percent of the total number of businesses, they make 89 percent of the total receipts. Sole proprietorships are the most common form (74 percent), but they only earn 6 percent of the receipts.

Source: U.S. Internal Revenue Service.

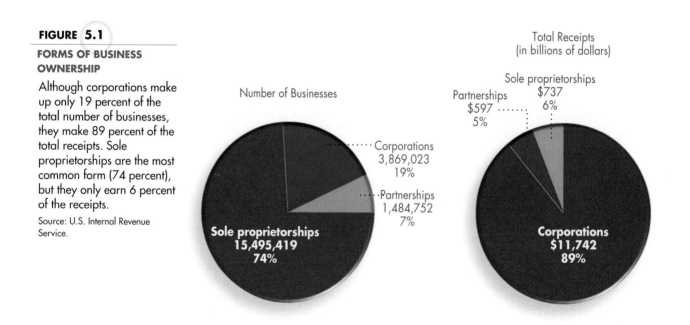

Number of Businesses

Corporations
3,869,023
19%

Partnerships
1,484,752
7%

Sole proprietorships
15,495,419
74%

Total Receipts
(in billions of dollars)

Sole proprietorships
$737
6%

Partnerships
$597
5%

Corporations
$11,742
89%

stay in that form. Many companies start out in one form, then add (or drop) a partner or two, and eventually become corporations, limited liability companies, or franchisors. Let's begin our discussion by looking at the most basic form of ownership—the sole proprietorship.

SOLE PROPRIETORSHIPS

Advantages of Sole Proprietorships

Sole proprietorships are the easiest kind of businesses for you to explore in your quest for an interesting career. Every town has sole proprietors you can visit. Talk with some of these businesspeople about the joys and frustrations of being on their own. Most will mention the benefits of being their own boss and setting their own hours. Other advantages they mention may include the following:

1. *Ease of starting and ending the business.* All you have to do to start a sole proprietorship is buy or lease the needed equipment (e.g., a saw, a word processor, a tractor, a lawn mower) and put up some announcements saying you are in business. It is just as easy to get out of business; you simply stop. There is no one to consult or to disagree with about such decisions. You may have to get a permit or license from the local government, but often that is no problem.

2. *Being your own boss.* Working for others simply does not have the same excitement as working for yourself—at least, that's the way sole proprietors feel. You may make mistakes, but they are your mistakes—and so are the many small victories each day.

3. *Pride of ownership.* People who own and manage their own businesses are rightfully proud of their work. They deserve all the credit for taking the risks and providing needed goods or services.

4. *Leaving a legacy.* Business owners have something to leave behind for future generations to build on.

5. *Retention of company profit.* Other than the joy of being your own boss, there is nothing like the pleasure of knowing that you can earn as much as possible and not have to share that money with anyone else (except the government, in taxes).

6. *No special taxes.* All the profits of a sole proprietorship are taxed as the personal income of the owner, and the owner pays the normal income tax on that money. (However, owners do have to estimate their taxes and make quarterly payments to the government.)

Due in part to the services provided by firms such as Kelloggs, minority and woman-owned businesses have many opportunities for success in today's markets if they can provide quality goods and services at competitive prices.

Disadvantages of Sole Proprietorships

Not everyone is equipped to own and manage a business. Often it is difficult to save enough money to start a business and keep it going. The costs of inventory, supplies, insurance, advertising, rent, computers, utilities, and so on may be too much to cover alone. There are other disadvantages of owning your own business:

Collette Renfro owns and has developed a very successful business, The Blackberry Harvest Dollhouse Museum Shoppe in Homewood, IL. As a sole proprietor she has the freedom to make all her own business decisions that she would not necessarily have if she had a partner. But this increased freedom also includes increased risks. Just as Collette gets to keep all the profits, she must also pay for any mistakes she makes. What are some of the key decisions she has to make on a frequent basis?

unlimited liability
The responsibility of business owners for all of the debts of the business

1. *Unlimited liability—the risk of personal losses.* When you work for others, it is their problem if the business is not profitable. When you own your own business, you and the business are considered one. You have **unlimited liability;** that is, any debts or damages incurred by the business are your debts and you must pay them, even if it means selling your home, your car, or whatever else you own. This is a serious risk ➤ **P.7** ◄, and one that requires not only thought but also discussion with a lawyer, an insurance agent, an accountant, and others.

2. *Limited financial resources.* Funds available to the business are limited to the funds that the one (sole) owner can gather. Since there are serious limits to how much money one person can raise, partnerships and corporations have a greater probability of obtaining the needed financial backing to start a business and keep it going.

3. *Management difficulties.* All businesses need management; that is, someone must keep inventory records, accounting records, tax records, and so forth. Many people who are skilled at selling things or providing a service are not so skilled in keeping records. Sole proprietors may have no one to help. It is often difficult to find good, qualified people to help run the business. A common complaint among sole proprietors is that good employees are hard to find.

4. *Overwhelming time commitment.* Though sole proprietors may say they set their own hours, it's hard to own a business, manage it, train people, and have time for anything else in life. This is true of any business, but a sole proprietor has no one with whom to share the burden. The owner often must spend long hours working. The owner of a store, for example, may put in 12 hours a day, at least six days a week—almost twice the hours worked by a nonsupervisory employee in a large company. Imagine how this time commitment affects the sole proprietor's family life. Tim DeMello, founder of the successful company Wall Street Games Inc., echoes countless other sole proprietors when he says, "It's not a job, it's not a career, it's a way of life."

5. *Few fringe benefits.* If you are your own boss, you lose the fringe benefits that often come from working for others. You have no paid health insurance, no paid disability insurance, no sick leave, and no vacation pay. These and other benefits may add up to 30 percent or more of a worker's income.

6. *Limited growth.* Expansion is often slow since a sole proprietorship relies on its owner for most of its creativity, business know-how, and funding.

7. *Limited life span.* If the sole proprietor dies, is incapacitated, or retires, the business no longer exists (unless it is sold or taken over by the sole proprietor's heirs).

Don't forget to talk with a few local sole proprietors about the problems they have faced in being on their own. They are likely to have many interesting stories to tell, such as problems getting loans from the bank, problems with theft, and problems simply keeping up with the business. These problems are also reasons why many sole proprietors choose to find partners to share the load.

Have you ever dreamed of opening your own business? If you did, what would it be? What talents or skills do you have that you could use? Could you start a business in your own home? How much would it cost to start? Could you begin part-time while you worked elsewhere? What satisfaction and profit could you get from owning your own business? What could you lose?

PARTNERSHIPS

A partnership is a legal form of business with two or more owners. There are several types of partnerships: (1) general partnerships, (2) limited partnerships, and (3) master limited partnerships. A **general partnership** is a partnership in which all owners share in operating the business and in assuming liability for the business's debts. A **limited partnership** is a partnership with one or more general partners and one or more limited partners. A **general partner** is an owner (partner) who has unlimited liability and is active in managing the firm. Every partnership must have at least one general partner. A **limited partner** risks an investment in the firm but enjoys limited liability and cannot legally help manage the company. **Limited liability** means that limited partners are not responsible for the debts of the business beyond the amount of their investment—their liability is *limited* to the amount they put into the company; their personal assets are not at risk.

A new form of partnership, the **master limited partnership (MLP),** looks much like a corporation (which we discuss next) in that it acts like a corporation and is traded on the stock exchanges like a corporation, but it is taxed like a partnership and thus avoids the corporate income tax. Two well-known MLPs are Burger King and Perkins Family Restaurants.

All states except Louisiana have adopted the Uniform Partnership Act (UPA) to replace laws relating to partnerships. The UPA defines the three key elements of any general partnership as (1) common ownership, (2) shared profits and losses, and (3) the right to participate in managing the operations of the business.

Advantages of Partnerships

There are many advantages to having one or more partners in a business. Often, it is much easier to own and manage a business with one or more partners. Your partner can cover for you when you are sick or go on vacation. Your partner may be skilled at inventory control and accounting, while you do the selling or servicing. A partner can also provide additional money, support, and expertise. Some of the people who are enjoying the advantages of partnerships today are doctors, lawyers, dentists, accountants, and other professionals. Partnerships usually have the following advantages:

1. *More financial resources.* When two or more people pool their money and credit, it is easier to pay the rent, utilities, and other bills incurred by a business. A limited partnership is specially designed to help raise capital (money). As mentioned earlier, a limited partner invests money in the business but cannot legally have any management responsibility and has limited liability.

2. *Shared management and pooled knowledge.* It is simply much easier to manage the day-to-day activities of a business with carefully chosen partners. Partners give each other free time from the business and provide different skills and perspectives. Some people find that the best

general partnership
A partnership in which all owners share in operating the business and in assuming liability for the business's debts.

limited partnership
A partnership with one or more general partners and one or more limited partners.

general partner
An owner (partner) who has unlimited liability and is active in managing the firm.

limited partner
An owner who invests money in the business but does not have any management responsibility or liability for losses beyond the investment.

limited liability
The responsibility of a business's owners for losses only up to the amount they invest; limited partners and shareholders have limited liability.

master limited partnership (MLP)
A partnership that looks much like a corporation in that it acts like a corporation and is traded on the stock exchanges like a corporation, but is taxed like a partnership and thus avoids the corporate income tax.

partner is a spouse. That is why you see so many husband-and-wife teams managing restaurants, service shops, and other businesses.

3. *Longer survival.* One study reported that of 2,000 businesses started since 1960, partnerships were four times as likely to succeed as sole proprietorships. Having a partner watching over him or her can help a businessperson become more disciplined.

Disadvantages of Partnerships

Anytime two people must agree on anything, there is the possibility of conflict and tension. Partnerships have caused splits among families, friends, and marriages. Let's explore the disadvantages of partnerships:

Many of the disadvantages of owning your own business are reduced when you find a business partner. Finding funding for partnerships is easier than for sole proprietorships. When Mike Roth and Frank Capan formed a partnership to start their business they borrowed $30,000 from Capan's father. Today Access Cash International is the largest nonbank ATM deployer in the United States with annual sales of over $45 million.

limited liability partnership (LLP)
A partnership that limits partners' risk of losing their personal assets to only their own acts and omissions and to the acts and omissions of people under their supervision.

1. *Unlimited liability.* Each *general* partner is liable for the debts of the firm, no matter who was responsible for causing those debts. You are liable for your partners' mistakes as well as your own. Like sole proprietors, general partners can lose their homes, cars, and everything else they own if the business loses a lawsuit or goes bankrupt. Many states are now allowing partners to form what is called a **limited liability partnership (LLP)** to limit this disadvantage. LLPs limit partners' risk of losing their personal assets to only their own acts and omissions and to the acts and omissions of people under their supervision.

2. *Division of profits.* Sharing risk means sharing profits and that can cause conflicts. There is no set system for dividing profits in a partnership, so profits are not always divided evenly. For example, two people form a partnership in which one puts in more money and the other puts in more hours working the business. Each may feel justified in asking for a bigger share of the profits. Imagine the resulting conflicts.

3. *Disagreements among partners.* Disagreements over money are just one example of potential conflict in a partnership. Who has final authority over employees? Who hires and fires employees? Who works what hours? What if one partner wants to buy expensive equipment for the firm and the other partner disagrees? Potential conflicts are many. Because of such problems, all terms of partnership should be spelled out in writing to protect all parties and to minimize misunderstandings. The Spotlight on Small Business box offers a few tips about choosing a partner.

4. *Difficult to terminate.* Once you have committed yourself to a partnership, it is not easy to get out of it. Sure, you can end a partnership just by quitting. However, questions about who gets what and what happens next are often very difficult to solve when the partnership ends. Surprisingly, law firms often have faulty partnership agreements and find that breaking up is hard to do. How do you get rid of a partner you don't like? It is best to decide such questions up front in the partnership agreement.[1] Figure 5.2 gives you more ideas about what should be included in partnership agreements.

FIGURE 5.2

HOW TO FORM A PARTNERSHIP

It's not hard to form a partnership, but it's wise for each prospective partner to get the counsel of a lawyer experienced with such agreements. Lawyers' services are usually expensive, so would-be partners should read all about partnerships and reach some basic agreements before calling a lawyer.

For your protection, be sure to put your partnership agreement in writing. The Model Business Corporation Act recommends including the following in a written partnership agreement:

1. The name of the business. Many states require the firm's name to be registered with state and/or county officials if the firm's name is different from the name of any of the partners.

2. The names and addresses of all partners.

3. The purpose and nature of the business, the location of the principal offices, and any other locations where the business will be conducted.

4. The date the partnership will start and how long it will last. Will it exist for a specific length of time, or will it stop when one of the partners dies or when the partners agree to discontinue?

5. The contributions made by each partner. Will some partners contribute money, while others provide real estate, personal property, expertise, or labor? When are the contributions due?

6. The management responsibilities. Will all partners have equal voices in management, or will there be senior and junior partners?

7. The duties of each partner.

8. The salaries and drawing accounts of each partner.

9. Provision for sharing of profits or losses.

10. Provision for accounting procedures. Who'll keep the accounts? What bookkeeping and accounting methods will be used? Where will the books be kept?

11. The requirements for taking in new partners.

12. Any special restrictions, rights, or duties of any partner.

13. Provision for a retiring partner.

14. Provision for the purchase of a deceased or retiring partner's share of the business.

15. Provision for how grievances will be handled.

16. Provision for how to dissolve the partnership and distribute the assets to the partners.

The best way to learn about the advantages and disadvantages of partnerships is to interview several people who have experience with such agreements. They will give you insights and hints on how to avoid problems.[2] (See the Making Ethical Decisions box for a problem with a partner's ethics.)

One common fear of owning your own business or having a partner is the fear of losing everything you own if the business loses a lot of money or someone sues the business. Many businesspeople try to avoid this and the other disadvantages of sole proprietorships and partnerships by forming corporations. We discuss this basic form of business ownership in the following section.

PROGRESS ASSESSMENT

- Most people who start businesses in the United States are sole proprietors. What are the advantages and disadvantages of sole proprietorships?

- What are some of the advantages of partnerships over sole proprietorships?

- Why would unlimited liability be considered a major drawback to sole proprietorships and general partnerships?

- What is the difference between a limited partner and a general partner?

Choose Your Partner

Suppose you need money and want help running your business, and you decide to take on a partner. You know that partnerships are like marriages and that you won't really know the other person until after you live together. How do you choose the right partner? Before you plunge into a partnership, do three things:

1. Talk to people who have been in successful—and unsuccessful—partnerships. Find out what worked and what didn't. Ask them how conflicts were resolved and how decisions were made.

2. Interview your prospective partner very carefully. What skills does the person have? Are they the same as yours, or do they complement your skills? What contacts, resources, or special attributes will the person bring to the business? Do you both feel the same about family members working for the business? Do you share the same vision for the company's future?

3. Evaluate your prospective partner as a decision maker. Ask yourself, "Is this someone with whom I could happily share authority for all major business decisions?"

Just like most good marriages, the best way to avoid major conflicts is to begin with an honest communication of what each partner expects to give and get from the partnership.

CORPORATIONS

Although the word *corporation* makes people think of big businesses like General Motors, IBM, Ford, Exxon, General Electric, Microsoft, and Wal-Mart, it is not necessary to be big in order to incorporate. Obviously, many corporations are big and contribute substantially to the U.S. economy. However, incorporating may be beneficial for small businesses as well.

A **conventional (C) corporation** is a state-chartered legal entity with authority to act and have liability separate from its owners (the corporation's stockholders are its owners). What this means for the owners is that they are not liable for the debts or any other problems of the corporation beyond the money they invest. Owners no longer have to worry about losing personal belongings such as their house, car, or other property because of some business

conventional (C) corporation
A state-chartered legal entity with authority to act and have liability separate from its owners.

Are You Your Brother's Keeper?

Imagine that you and your partner own a construction company. You both feel it's time for the company to grow, so your bid on a major shopping center project will be the biggest and riskiest project in the company's history. Part of the project will demand the use of subcontractors hired by your firm. You receive a bid from a subcontractor who has worked with you before and has always provided quality workman-

ship. You know the bid is at least 20 percent too low. Such a loss to the subcontractor could put him out of business. Accepting the bid will certainly improve your chances of winning the lucrative contract for the shopping center project. Your partner wants to take the bid and let the subcontractor suffer the consequences of his bad estimate. What do you think you should do? What will be the consequences of your decision?

FIGURE 5.3

CORPORATE TYPES

You may find some confusing types of corporations when reading about them. Here are a few of the more widely used terms:

An *alien corporation* does business in the United States but is chartered (incorporated) in another country.

A *domestic corporation* does business in the state in which it's chartered (incorporated).

A *foreign corporation* does business in one state but is chartered in another. About one-third of all corporations are chartered in Delaware because of its relatively attractive rules for incorporation. A foreign corporation must register in states where it operates.

A *closed (private) corporation* is one whose stock is held by a few people and isn't available to the general public.

An *open (public) corporation* sells stock to the general public. General Motors and Exxon are examples of public corporations.

A *quasi-public corporation* is a corporation chartered by the government as an approved monopoly to perform services to the general public. Public utilities are examples of quasi-public corporations.

A *professional corporation* is one whose owners offer professional services (doctors, lawyers, etc.). Shares in professional corporations aren't publicly traded.

A *nonprofit corporation* is one that doesn't seek personal profit for its owners.

A *multinational corporation* is a firm that operates in several countries.

problem—a significant benefit. A corporation not only limits the liability of owners but often enables many people to share in the ownership (and profits) of a business without working there or having other commitments to it. Corporations can choose whether to offer such ownership to outside investors or whether to remain privately held. (We will discuss stock ownership in Chapter 20.) Figure 5.3 describes various types of corporations.

Advantages of Corporations

Most people are not willing to risk everything to go into business. Yet for a business to grow and prosper and create economic opportunity, many people would have to be willing to invest their money in it. One way to solve this problem is to create an artificial being, an entity that exists only in the eyes of the law—a corporation. Let's explore some of the advantages of corporations:

1. *More money for investment.* To raise money, a corporation can sell ownership (stock) to anyone who is interested. This means that

When neighbors got a whiff of the all natural treats Dan Dye and Mark Beckloff baked for their dogs, they came to their door begging for biscuits. Thinking they could take a bite out of the specialized pet food market, the pair decided to open a bakery just for dogs. Nine years later they had 29 stores around the country. Sniff out more about the corporation at their Web site www.threedog.com. We hear the SnickerPoodles are really something to bark about!

millions of people can own part of major companies like IBM, Xerox, and General Motors and smaller companies as well, such as JobDirect.com. If a company sold 10 million shares for $50 each, it would have $500 million available to build plants, buy materials, hire people, manufacture products, and so on. Such a large amount of money would be difficult to raise any other way. Corporations may also find it easier to obtain loans since lenders find it easier to place a value on the company when they can review how the stock is trading. Many small or individually owned corporations that do not trade actively may not have such opportunities, however.

2. *Limited liability.* A major advantage of corporations is the limited liability of owners. Corporations in England and Canada have the letters *Ltd.* after their name, as in British Motors, Ltd. The *Ltd.* stands for "limited liability," probably the most significant advantage of corporations. Remember, limited liability means that the owners of a business are responsible for losses only up to the amount they invest.

3. *Size.* That one word summarizes many of the advantages of some corporations. Because they have the ability to raise large amounts of money to work with, corporations can build modern factories or software development firms with the latest equipment. They can also hire experts or specialists in all areas of operation. Furthermore, they can buy other corporations in other fields to diversify their risk. (What this means is that a corporation can be involved in many businesses at once so that if one fails, the effect on the total corporation is lessened.) In short, a major advantage of corporations is that they have the size and resources to take advantage of opportunities anywhere in the world. Corporations, remember, do not have to be large to enjoy the benefits of incorporating. Many doctors, lawyers, and individuals, as well as partners in a variety of businesses, have incorporated. The vast majority of corporations in the United States are small businesses.

4. *Perpetual life.* Because corporations are separate from those who own them, the death of one or more owners does not terminate the corporation.

5. *Ease of ownership change.* It is easy to change the owners of a corporation. All that is necessary is to sell the stock to someone else.

6. *Ease of drawing talented employees.* Corporations can attract skilled employees by offering such benefits as stock options (the right to purchase shares of the corporation for a fixed price).

7. *Separation of ownership from management.* Corporations are able to raise money from many different investors without getting them involved in management. The corporate hierarchy looks like Figure 5.4.

The pyramid in Figure 5.4 shows that the owners/stockholders are separate from the managers and employees. The owners/stockholders elect a board of directors. The directors hire the officers of the corporation and oversee major policy issues. They also hire managers and employees. The owners/stockholders thus have some say in who runs the corporation, but they have no control over the daily operations.

Disadvantages of Corporations

There are so many sole proprietorships and partnerships in the United States that clearly there must be some disadvantages to incorporating. Otherwise,

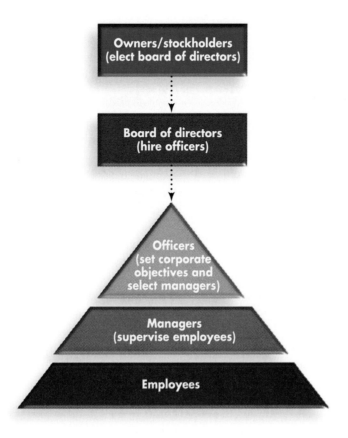

FIGURE 5.4

HOW OWNERS AFFECT MANAGEMENT
Owners have an influence on how business is managed by electing a board of directors. The board hires the top managers (or fires them). It also sets the pay for top managers. Top managers then select other managers and employees with the help of the human resources department.

more people would incorporate their businesses. The following are a few of the disadvantages:

1. *Initial cost.* Incorporation may cost thousands of dollars and involve expensive lawyers and accountants. There are less expensive ways of incorporating in certain states (see the subsection called Individuals Can Incorporate later in this chapter), but many people do not have the time or confidence to go through this procedure without the help of a lawyer.

2. *Extensive paperwork.* The paperwork filed to start a corporation is just the beginning. Tax laws demand that a corporation prove that all its expenses and deductions are legitimate. Corporations must therefore process many forms. A sole proprietor or a partnership may keep rather broad accounting records; a corporation, on the other hand, must keep detailed financial records, the minutes of meetings, and more.

3. *Two tax returns.* If an individual incorporates, he or she must file both a corporate tax return and an individual tax return. Depending on the size of the corporation, a corporate return can be quite complex and require the assistance of a certified public accountant (CPA).

4. *Size.* Size may be one advantage of corporations, but it can be a disadvantage as well. Large corporations sometimes become too inflexible and too tied down in red tape to respond quickly to market changes.

5. *Difficulty of termination.* Once a corporation is started, it's relatively hard to end.

6. *Double taxation.* Corporate income is taxed twice. First the corporation pays tax on income before it can distribute any to stockholders. Then the stockholders pay tax on the income (dividends) they receive from

FROM THE PAGES OF BusinessWeek   *www.nikebiz.com*

Target Practice in Cyberspace

Few companies, large or small, would argue that the Internet is bad for business or has jeopardized potential profits. Companies are using the marketing potential of the Internet to both attract new buyers and obtain customer information that would otherwise cost considerable amounts of promotion or research dollars. It appears that things are glowing in cyberspace and will only get better for business, right? Nice thought, but unfortunately all is not well in the world of websites.

Hundreds of U.S. companies such as Wal-Mart and United Airlines have become the targets of "hate sites" on the Web. Critics, whether individuals or organizations, use their First Amendment rights to set up sites that attack a particular company and cite its shortcomings. While many companies have tried to unarm these "cybercritics," few have succeeded. The only real legal remedy is filing a lawsuit, an act that could focus additional unwanted attention on the company.

While the negative websites are often just a nuisance to large companies such as Chase Manhattan Bank, they can be devastating to smaller companies. Express Success, a multilevel marketing company that sells car products, saw its revenues fall from $60,000 per month to nearly zero after a billing dispute with two Internet site designers. The designers created a website on which they described the company as a scam. This case is currently in litigation.

Several companies have reacted to the negative sites with Internet counteroffensives. Nike, for example, responded to several negative sites that questioned its treatment of workers in less developed countries. The company created a site that featured pictures of its manufacturing facilities overseas and described the benefits it gave to employees. Other companies have taken another strategy: they have offered to buy the negative sites from the creators. However they respond, companies have to get used to the good and bad sides of technology in the 21st century.

Source: Mike France and Joann Muller, "A Site for Soreheads," *Business Week*, April 12, 1999, pp. 86–90 and Timothy J. Mullaney, "Gone but not Forgotten," *Business Week*, January 22, 2001.

the corporation. States often tax corporations more harshly than other enterprises. Sometimes they levy special taxes that apply to corporations but not to other forms of business.

7. *Possible conflict with board of directors.* Some conflict may brew if the stockholders elect a board of directors that disagrees with the present management. Since the board of directors chooses the company's officers, entrepreneurs could find themselves forced out of the very company they founded. This is what happened to Rod Canion, one of the founders of Compaq Computer.

Many people are discouraged by the costs, paperwork, and special taxes corporations must pay. The *Business Week* box highlights a new problem spawned by the growth of technology and the Internet. Many businesspeople feel the hassles of incorporation outweigh the advantages.

Individuals Can Incorporate

Not all corporations are large organizations with hundreds of employees or thousands of stockholders. Individuals (e.g., doctors, lawyers, plumbers, athletes, and movie stars) can also incorporate. Normally they do not issue stock to outsiders; therefore, small corporations do not share all of the same advantages and disadvantages of large corporations (such as more money for investment and size). Their major advantage is limited liability and possible tax benefits.[3] As noted in Figure 5.3, many firms incorporate in Delaware because it is relatively easy to do so. Although you are not required to file for incorporation through a

FIGURE 5.5

HOW TO INCORPORATE

The process of forming a corporation varies somewhat from state to state. The articles of incorporation are usually filed with the secretary of state's office in the state in which the company incorporates. The articles contain

- The corporation's name.
- The names of the people who incorporated it.
- Its purposes.
- Its duration (usually perpetual).
- The number of shares that can be issued, their voting rights, and any other rights the shareholders have.
- The corporation's minimum capital.
- The address of the corporation's office.
- The name and address of the person responsible for the corporation's legal service.
- The names and addresses of the first directors.
- Any other public information the incorporators wish to include.

Before a business can so much as open a bank account or hire employees, it needs a federal tax identification number. To apply for one, get an SS-4 form from the IRS.

In addition to the articles of incorporation listed, a corporation also has bylaws. These describe how the firm is to be operated from both legal and managerial points of view. The bylaws include

- How, when, and where shareholders' and directors' meetings are held, and how long directors are to serve.
- Directors' authority.
- Duties and responsibilities of officers, and the length of their service.
- How stock is issued.
- Other matters, including employment contracts.

lawyer, it is usually wise to consult one. In addition to lawyer fees, the secretary of state's office charges a fee for incorporating a business. Such fees vary widely by state, from a low of $40 in Maryland and South Dakota to a high of $300 in Texas. Like the fee, the length of time it will take to actually have your business incorporated will vary widely by state. The average time is approximately 30 days from the date of application.[4] Figure 5.5 outlines how to incorporate.

S Corporations

One issue that has received much attention in recent years is the formation of S corporations. An **S corporation** is a unique government creation that looks like a corporation but is taxed like sole proprietorships and partnerships. The paperwork and details of S corporations are similar to those of conventional (C) corporations. S corporations have shareholders, directors, and employees and have the benefit of limited liability, but their profits are taxed as the personal income of the shareholders—thus avoiding the double taxation of C corporations.

Avoiding double taxation was reason enough for more than 2 million U.S. companies to operate as S corporations. Yet not all businesses can become S corporations. In order to qualify, a company must:

1. Have no more than 75 (or 150, including spouses) shareholders.
2. Have shareholders that are individuals or estates and are citizens or permanent residents of the United States.
3. Have only one class of outstanding stock.
4. Not have more than 25 percent of income derived from passive sources (rents, royalties, interest, etc.).

The tax structure of S corporations isn't attractive to all businesses. Since the top tax rate for S corporations (39.6 percent) is almost five points higher

S corporation
A unique government creation that looks like a corporation but is taxed like sole proprietorships and partnerships.

than the highest corporate rate (35 percent), fast-growing small businesses such as those in technology often choose C corporation status to avoid the higher taxes. These companies don't intend to pay dividends to owners for a long time because they need the money for new investment in the business. Thus, they are not subject to double taxation. Many slower-growing businesses, in contrast, have selected the S corporation form of ownership. It's important to note that the benefits of S corporations change every time the tax rules change. The best way to learn all the benefits or shortcomings for a specific business is to go over the tax advantages and liability differences with a lawyer, an accountant, or both.[5]

Limited Liability Companies

limited liability company (LLC)
A company similar to an S corporation but without the special eligibility requirements.

Many businesses are being attracted to the newest form of business ownership: the limited liability company (LLC). Billed as the "business entity of the future," a **limited liability company (LLC)** is similar to an S corporation but without the special eligibility requirements. LLCs were introduced in Wyoming in 1977 and were recognized by the Internal Revenue Service as a partnership for federal income tax purposes in 1988. In 1995 the National Conference of Commissioners on Uniform State Laws approved the final version of the Uniform Limited Liability Company Act. By 1996, all 50 states and the District of Columbia recognized LLCs. The number of LLCs has risen dramatically since 1988, when there were less than 100 filings. By 1996, nearly one in every six new business registrations in the country was an LLC.[6] LLCs are particularly attractive to professionals such as doctors, accountants, attorneys and contractors.

Why the drive toward forming LLCs? LLCs offer businesses the best of all corporate worlds: personal-asset protection (normally available only to shareholders of C corporations), choice to be taxed as partnership or as corporation (partnership-level taxation was previously a benefit normally reserved for partners or S corporation owners), and flexible ownership rules (which S corporations lack).[7] The start-up cost for an LLC is approximately $2,500, with annual charges of $1,500 for tax-return preparation and legal fees. Information about LLCs is available from the Association of Limited Liability Companies in Washington, D.C. The Commerce Clearinghouse also has a user-friendly introduction called *A Guide to Limited Liability Companies;* call 800-835-5224 for information. Another recommended guidebook on LLCs is *The Essential Limited Liability Company Handbook* (Oasis Press, 800-228-2275). You can review answers to frequently asked questions about LLCs on the Web at www.hia.com/llcweb/ll-faq.html.

Figure 5.6 lists the advantages and disadvantages of the major forms of business ownership.

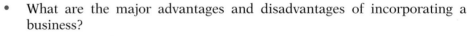

- What are the major advantages and disadvantages of incorporating a business?
- What is the role of owners (stockholders) in the corporate hierarchy?
- If you buy stock in a corporation and someone gets injured by one of the corporation's products, can you be sued? Why or why not? Could you be sued if you were a general partner in a partnership?

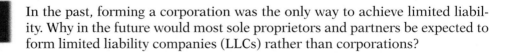

In the past, forming a corporation was the only way to achieve limited liability. Why in the future would most sole proprietors and partners be expected to form limited liability companies (LLCs) rather than corporations?

	SOLE PROPRIETORSHIP	PARTNERSHIPS		CORPORATIONS		
		GENERAL PARTNERSHIP	LIMITED PARTNERSHIP	CONVENTIONAL CORPORATION	S CORPORATION	LIMITED LIABILITY COMPANY
Documents needed to start business	None, may need permit or license	Partnership agreement (oral or written)	Written agreement; must file certificate of limited partnership	Articles of incorporation, bylaws	Articles of incorporation, bylaws, must meet criteria	Articles of organization and operating agreement; no eligibility requirements
Ease of termination	Easy to terminate: just pay debts and quit	May be hard to terminate, depending on the partnership agreement	Same as general partnership	Hard and expensive to terminate	Same as conventional corporation	May be difficult, depending upon operating agreement
Length of life	Terminates on the death of owner	Terminates on the death or withdrawal of partner	Same as general partnership	Perpetual life	Same as conventional corporation	Same as partnership
Transfer of ownership	Business can be sold to qualified buyer	Must have other partner(s)' agreement	Same as general partnership	Easy to change owners; just sell stock	Can sell stock, but with restrictions	Can't sell stock
Financial resources	Limited to owner's capital and loans	Limited to partners' capital and loans	Same as general partnership	More money to start and operate; may sell stocks and bonds	Same as conventional corporation	Same as partnership
Risk of losses	Unlimited liability	Unlimited liability	Limited liability	Limited Liability	Limited liability	Limited liability
Taxes	Taxed as personal income	Taxed as personal income	Same as general partnership	Corporate, double taxation	Taxed as personal income	Taxed as personal income
Management responsibilities	Owner manages *all* areas of the business	Partners share management	Can't participate in management	Separate management from ownership	Same as conventional corporation	Varies
Employee benefits	Usually fewer benefits and lower wages	Often fewer benefits and lower wages; promising employee could become a partner	Same as general partnership	Usually better benefits and wages, advancement opportunities	Same as conventional corporation	Varies

FIGURE 5.6

COMPARISON OF FORMS OF BUSINESS OWNERSHIP

CORPORATE EXPANSION: MERGERS AND ACQUISITIONS

In the 1990s, merger mania in the U.S continued rolling at a fever pitch. Nine of the 10 largest merger transactions of all time occurred in 1998. The $77 billion merger of Exxon and Mobil ranked as the largest ever until the start of the new millennium greeted a new round of megamergers. In January 2000, America Online and Time Warner announced that they would merge to form a company with a combined net worth of a staggering $270 billion.[8] Mergers involving financial institutions and telecommunications companies led the corporate consolidation parade. Most of the new deals involved companies trying to expand within their own fields to save costs, enter new markets, position for international competition, or adapt to changing technologies or regulations.

What's the difference between mergers and acquisitions? A **merger** is the result of two firms forming one company. Sounds like a marriage, doesn't it? An **acquisition** is one company buying the property and obligations of another company. It is more like buying a house than entering a marriage.

There are three major types of corporate mergers: vertical, horizontal, and conglomerate. A **vertical merger** is the joining of two firms involved in different stages of related businesses. Think of a merger between a bicycle company and a company that produces bike wheels. Such a merger would ensure a constant supply of wheels needed by the bicycle manufacturer. It could also help ensure quality control of the bicycle company's products. A **horizontal merger** joins two firms in the same industry and allows them to diversify or expand their products. An example of a horizontal merger is the merger of a bicycle company and a tricycle company. The business can now supply a variety of cycling products. A **conglomerate merger** unites firms in completely unrelated industries. The primary purpose of a conglomerate merger is to diversify business operations and investments. The acquisition of a restaurant chain by a tricycle company would be an example of a conglomerate merger. Figure 5.7 illustrates the differences in the three types of mergers.

merger
The result of two firms forming one company.

acquisition
A company's purchase of the property and obligations of another company.

vertical merger
The joining of two companies involved in different stages of related businesses.

horizontal merger
The joining of two firms in the same industry.

conglomerate merger
The joining of firms in completely unrelated industries.

FIGURE 5.7

TYPES OF MERGERS

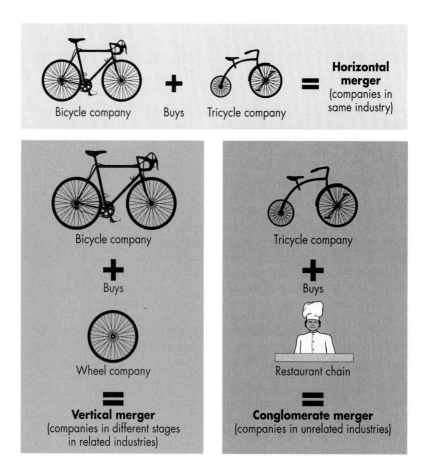

REACHING BEYOND OUR BORDERS

www.bp.com

The Invasion of Corporate America—Merger Attack

The offers are fast and furious and certainly not for the weak of heart: $62.8 billion for AirTouch Communications, $55 billion for Amoco Oil. Sounds like the Wall Street money machine is at it again. Well, not exactly. Merger mania is no longer a superbucks phenomenon strictly intended to combine U.S. businesses. The megabillion-dollar offers cited above involved British firms Vodaphone Group Plc. and British Petroleum (BP). In fact, British firms acquired 152 U.S. firms in 1998 and more in 1999. The British, however, are not alone in this merger activity. Canadian firms acquired 149 U.S. firms in 1998. French, German, and Dutch companies obtained an additional 136 U.S. businesses. Why all the interest in U.S. firms?

Eugenia Shepard, vice president of the Los Angeles–based, merger-tracking firm Mergerstat contends, "The U.S. is attractive for merger activity because Americans are more receptive to foreign companies than are citizens in many other countries." The Chrysler merger with Daimler-Benz of Germany (which formed DaimlerChrysler) is such an example. Americans didn't seem to bat an eye. Shepard also notes that a common language also helps limit cultural differences in global business. She predicts that soon mergers involving foreign businesses and U.S. firms could top $715 billion.

Still, it's important not to forget that the cultural hurdle should not be taken lightly. Successful global mergers depend on a thorough evaluation of corporate cultures and national values, not just a sharp-eyed reading of a firm's financial condition.

Can you think of any mergers involving foreign firms with local companies in your geographic area in the past few years? What's the opinion of the community?

Source: Megan Santosus, "Arranged Marriage," CIO Enterprise, July 15, 1999, p. 20; and "The British Are Coming (Canadians, Too!)," CFO, August 1999, p. 21; Robert J. Samuelson, "The Mysterious Merger Frenzy," Newsweek, October 16, 2000, p. 55 and Joann Muller and Jeff Green, "Chrysler's Rescue Team," Business Week, January 15, 2001.

Rather than merge or sell to another company, some corporations decide to maintain control, or in some cases regain control, of a firm internally. For example, Steve Stavro, the majority owner and head of a group that invested in the Maple Leaf Gardens Ltd. (owners of the Toronto Maple Leafs hockey team) decided to take the firm private. *Taking a firm private* involves the efforts of a group of stockholders or management to obtain all the firm's stock for themselves. In the Maple Leaf Gardens situation, Stavro's investors group successfully gained total control of the company by buying all of the company's stock. For the first time in 65 years, investors in the open market could no longer purchase stock in the Maple Leafs.

Suppose the employees in an organization feel there is a good possibility they may lose their jobs. Or what if the managers believe that corporate performance could be enhanced if they owned the company? Do either of these groups have an opportunity of taking ownership of the company? Yes—they might attempt a

Old media joins new media as the world's largest media and entertainment company, Time Warner, merged with the world's largest Internet provider, AOL. What type of merger was this (vertical, horizontal or conglomerate)?

leveraged buyout. A **leveraged buyout (LBO)** is an attempt by employees, management, or a group of investors to purchase an organization primarily through borrowing. The funds borrowed are used to buy out the stockholders in the company. The employees, managers, or investors now become the owners of the firm. LBOs have ranged in size from $50 million to $6 billion and have involved everything from small family businesses to giant corporations like R. J. Reynolds and Northwest Airlines.

Today, merger mania isn't restricted to American companies. Foreign companies are gobbling up U.S. companies. The 1998 $41 billion merger of Stuttgart, Germany–based Daimler-Benz and Chrysler created a global automotive giant, DaimlerChrysler.[9] Foreign companies have found that often the quickest way to grow is to buy an established operation and bring the brands and technology back to Europe. The Reaching Beyond our Borders box gives some reasons why this trend in merger activity is likely to continue.

SPECIAL FORMS OF BUSINESS OWNERSHIP

In addition to the three basic forms of business ownership, we shall discuss two special forms of ownership: franchises and cooperatives. Let's look at franchises first.

FRANCHISES

Basically, a **franchise agreement** is an arrangement whereby someone with a good idea for a business (the **franchisor**) sells the rights to use the business name and to sell a product or service (the **franchise**) to others (the **franchisee**) in a given territory.

Some people are more comfortable not starting their own business from scratch. They would rather join a business with a proven track record through a franchise agreement. A franchise can be formed as a sole proprietorship, partnership, or corporation. Some of the best-known franchises are McDonald's, Jiffy Lube, 7-Eleven, Weight Watchers, and Holiday Inn.[10]

Over 8 million people in the United States work in a franchise. Franchised businesses now take in $1 of every $3 spent by Americans for goods or services ➤ P.25 ◄, or 40 percent of all national retail sales (about $1 trillion). In fact, 1 out of 12 American businesses are franchises, and a new franchise opens every six and a half minutes of each business day. The most popular businesses for franchising are restaurants (more than 80 percent of all franchises), retail stores, hotels and motels, and automotive parts and service centers.

When you think of franchising, however, don't confine your thoughts to the United States. Small, midsized, and large U.S. franchisors have expanded overseas, often with great success. For example, McDonald's has over 25,000 restaurants in 117 countries serving 40 million customers.[11] Ranked as the world's greatest brand by the Interbrand Group, an independent branding consultant, McDonald's plans to accelerate its global business by adding as many restaurants outside the United States in the next 4 years as it did in the last 30 years. Foreign franchises such as Faces (a Canadian-based cosmetics store) and V-KOOL (a window-glass-coating franchise from Hong Kong) have expanded to the United States and are eager to grow in the world's largest market.

Advantages of Franchises

Franchising has penetrated every aspect of American and global business life by offering products and services that are reliable, convenient, and competi-

This may look like the set of Camelot, but it is actually the Holiday Inn in downtown Edinburgh, Scotland. Holiday Inn franchises try to complement the environment of the areas they serve. What are the payoffs for such efforts? What do you think the local reaction would have been if the franchise tried to build the typical American-style hotel in this area?

tively priced. The growth experienced in franchising throughout the world could not have been accomplished by accident. Franchising clearly has some advantages:

1. *Management and marketing assistance.* A franchisee (the person who buys a franchise) has a much greater chance of succeeding in business because he or she has an established product (e.g., Wendy's hamburgers, Domino's pizza); help with choosing a location and promotion; and assistance in all phases of operation. It is like having your own store with full-time consultants available when you need them. Some franchisors are helping their franchisees succeed by helping with local marketing efforts rather than having them depend solely on national advertising. Furthermore, you have a whole network of fellow franchisees who are facing similar problems and can share their experiences with you. For example, Mail Boxes Etc. provides its 3,600 franchisees with a software program that helps them build data banks of customer names and addresses. The company also provides one-on-one phone support and quick e-mail access through its help desk. The help desk focuses on personalizing contact with the company's franchisees by immediately addressing their questions and concerns.

2. *Personal ownership.* A franchise operation is still your store, and you enjoy much of the incentives and profit of any sole proprietor. You are still your own boss, although you must follow more rules, regulations, and procedures than you would with your own privately owned store.

3. *Nationally recognized name.* It is one thing to open a gift shop or ice cream store. It is quite another to open a new Hallmark store or Baskin-Robbins. With an established franchise, you get instant recognition and support from a product group with established customers from around the world.

4. *Financial advice and assistance.* A major problem with small businesses is arranging financing and learning to keep good records. Franchisees get valuable assistance and periodic advice from people with expertise

in these areas. In fact, some franchisors will even provide financing to potential franchisees they feel will be valuable parts of the franchise system. For example, SRA International Inc., an executive-recruiting franchise, eases entry for selected new franchisees by allowing $20,000 of the $35,000 initiation fee to be paid from revenue over a period of two years or more.

5. *Lower failure rate.* Historically, the failure rate for franchises has been lower than that of other business ventures. According to the International Franchise Association, a Washington, D.C.-based trade group, franchises have a 66 percent higher success rate than independent businesses.[12] However, franchising has grown so rapidly that many weak franchises have entered the field, so you need to be careful and invest wisely.

Disadvantages of Franchises

It almost sounds like the potential of franchising is too good to be true. However, you should carefully research any franchise before buying. You must be sure to check out any such arrangement with present franchisees and possibly discuss the idea with an attorney and an accountant. Disadvantages of franchises include the following:

1. *Large start-up costs.* Most franchises will demand a fee just for the rights to the franchise. Fees for franchises can vary considerably. Start-up costs for a Jazzercise franchise, for example, range from $2,000 to $3,000, compared to over $4 million needed to start a Holiday Inn franchise.[13]

2. *Shared profit.* The franchisor often demands a large share of the profits in addition to the start-up fees, or a percentage commission based on sales, not profit. This share demanded by the franchisor is generally referred to as a *royalty.* For example, if a franchisor demands a 10 percent royalty on a franchise's net sales, 10 cents of every dollar collected at the franchise (before taxes and other expenses) must be paid to the franchisor.

3. *Management regulation.* Management "assistance" has a way of becoming managerial orders, directives, and limitations. Franchisees may feel burdened by the company's rules and regulations, and lose the spirit and incentive of being their own boss with their own business. One of the biggest changes in franchising in recent years is the banding together of franchisees to resolve their grievances with franchisors rather than each fighting their battles alone.[14] For example, franchisees joined forces to sue franchisor Meineke Discount Muffler Shops, Inc., for fraudulently pocketing money they gave the company for advertising. The franchisees won an initial judgment of $390 million against the company, but the award was overturned on appeal.

When we think of franchises, we often think of mammoth corporations such as McDonalds or KFC. But not all franchise chains are large. Ebenezer's Café has only four stores including its headquarters in Marlton, New Jersey. The trendy restaurants specialize in gourmet foods, sandwiches, and coffees.

www.ftc.gov/bcp/conline/
pubs/invest/homewrk.htm

LEGAL BRIEFCASE

Franchising Follies—The Dark Side of Franchising

It's a story we've all heard before. Uncle Dick, Aunt Jane, or some enterprising person down the street dips into his or her life savings, retirement accounts, or other personal funds to invest in a new franchise opportunity. The next thing we hear is that the franchisee is basking on a beach on the French Riviera. Sounds like we better get to the bank pronto and then make a quick stop to pick up some sun tan lotion.

Actually, you better not move too fast. It's true that a franchise is often a fast and efficient way for people who lack experience or detailed business training to grow a business. The lure of some franchises can almost be seductive. It's important to remember, though, that not all franchises have fairytale endings. In fact, investors lose hundreds of millions of dollars a year to franchise scams and ill-conceived franchises.

Many fraudulent franchise schemes are offered at business opportunity and franchise shows. Sleazy salespersons peddle franchise opportunities to wide-eyed, would-be millionaires, yet the businesses are clearly destined to flop. Fatty Arburgers might sound like the next McDonald's and Kelly's Coffee & Fudge Factory the next Starbucks, but be sure the franchise has stores up and operating before putting your money on the table. The important thing to remember is, beware of business opportunities that sound too good to be true—they probably are. To protect yourself against franchise fraud, do your homework and don't be afraid to ask questions.

Source: Boris Worrall, "Victims Lured by a Bright Idea," *Evening Mail*, January 12, 2001 and Andrew A. Caffey, "Presidential Secrets," *Entrepreneur*, January 2001.

4. *Coattail effects.* What happens to your franchise if fellow franchisees fail? Quite possibly you could be forced out of business even if your particular franchise has been profitable. This is often referred to as a *coattail effect.* The actions of other franchisees clearly have an impact on your future growth and level of profitability.[15] Franchisees must also look out for competition from fellow franchisees. For example, TCBY franchisees' love for frozen yogurt melted as the market became flooded with new TCBY stores. McDonald's franchisees complain that due to the McDonald's Corporation's relentless growth formula, some of the new stores have cannibalized business at existing locations, squeezing franchisees' profits per outlet.[16]

5. *Restrictions on selling.* Unlike owners of private businesses, who can sell their companies to whomever they choose on their own terms, many franchisees face restrictions in the reselling of their franchises. In order to control the quality of their franchisees, franchisors often insist on approving the new owner, who must meet their standards.

6. *Fraudulent franchisors.* Contrary to common belief, most franchisors are not large systems like McDonald's. Many are small, rather obscure franchises that prospective franchisees may know little about. Most franchisors are honest, but there has been an increase in complaints to the Federal Trade Commission ➤ **P.124** ◄ about franchisors that delivered little or nothing of what they promised. See the Legal Briefcase box for advice about avoiding fraudulent practices.

Figure 5.8 also gives you some tips on becoming a franchisee.

Since buying a franchise is a major investment, be sure to check out a company's financial strength before you get involved. Watch out for scams, too. Scams called *bust-outs* usually involve people coming to town, renting nice offices, taking out ads, and persuading people to invest. Then they disappear with the investors' money. For example, in San Francisco a company called T.B.S. Inc. sold distributorships for in-home AIDS tests. It promised an enormous market and potential profits of $3,000 for an investment of less than $200. The test turned out to be nothing more than a mail-order questionnaire about lifestyle.

A good source of information about franchise possibilities is available from Franchise Watchdog in Burlington, Vermont. It compares what franchisors have to offer, including fees and support services, and also rates franchisors by sampling franchisees. Another good resource for evaluating a franchise deal is the handbook *Investigate before Investing*, available from International Franchise Association Publications.

CHECKLIST FOR EVALUATING A FRANCHISE

The franchise

Did your lawyer approve the franchise contract you're considering after he or she studied it paragraph by paragraph?

Does the franchise give you an exclusive territory for the length of the franchise?

Under what circumstances can you terminate the franchise contract and at what cost to you?

If you sell your franchise, will you be compensated for your goodwill (the value of your business's reputation and other intangibles)?

If the franchisor sells the company, will your investment be protected?

The franchisor

How many years has the firm offering you a franchise been in operation?

Does it have a reputation for honesty and fair dealing among the local firms holding its franchise?

Has the franchisor shown you any certified figures indicating exact net profits of one or more going firms that you personally checked yourself with the franchisee? Ask for the company's disclosure statement.

Will the firm assist you with

A management training program?

An employee training program?

A public relations program?

Capital?

Credit?

Merchandising ideas?

Will the firm help you find a good location for your new business?

Has the franchisor investigated you carefully enough to assure itself that you can successfully operate one of its franchises at a profit both to itself and to you?

You, the franchisee

How much equity capital will you need to purchase the franchise and operate it until your income equals your expenses?

Does the franchisor offer financing for a portion of the franchising fees? On what terms?

Are you prepared to give up some independence of action to secure the advantages offered by the franchise? Do you have your family's support?

Does the industry appeal to you? Are you ready to spend much or all of the remainder of your business life with this franchisor, offering its product or service to the public?

Your market

Have you made any study to determine whether the product or service that you propose to sell under the franchise has a market in your territory at the prices you'll have to charge?

Will the population in the territory given to you increase, remain static, or decrease over the next five years?

Will demand for the product or service you're considering be greater, about the same, or less five years from now than it is today?

What competition already exists in your territory for the product or service you contemplate selling?

Sources: U.S. Department of Commerce, *Franchise Opportunities Handbook;* Andrew A. Caffey, "Analyze This," *Entrepreneur,* January 2000, pp. 163–67; and Todd D. Maddocks, "Write the Wrongs," *Entrepreneur,* January 2001.

FIGURE 5.8

BUYING A FRANCHISE

Diversity in Franchising

Today there is a gap between female business owners (80 percent of all new businesses in 2000) and the number of female franchise owners (only 24 percent of the U.S. franchises). In an effort to promote diversity in business, some franchisors actively recruit women to be owners. For example, Church's Chicken coordinated a year-long community-based effort entitled Church's Professional Mentoring Program (Church's PMP). The support program, led by the company's president Hala Moddelmog, provided tools for success in franchising, maintained ongoing online chats by franchise experts, and partnered each new franchisee with a successful franchisee. "We've found that almost half of all successful women business owners have relied on a female mentor, especially in the beginning stages," said Moddelmog. By sponsoring the program, Church's hopes to demonstrate that franchising can be a profitable and rewarding choice for women.[17]

A growing number of women are getting the message. In fact, women aren't just franchisees anymore either; they are becoming franchisors as well. The top-rated franchise companies Decorating Den and Jazzercise, for example, are owned by women.

When women have difficulty obtaining financing for expanding their businesses, they often turn to finding franchisees to sidestep expansion costs. For example, Marilyn Ounijan, founder and CEO of Careers USA, claims that having franchisees pay for inventory and other costs of growing a business allowed the company to grow from her office in her home to 22 locations throughout the country. Franchising provided Careers USA a cost-effective way to enter new markets.

Black Enterprise magazine publisher Earl Graves encourages African Americans to look for opportunities in franchising in his book *How to Succeed in Business without Being White*. Franchising opportunities seem perfectly attuned to the needs of aspiring minority businesspeople. The U.S. Commerce Department's Federal Minority Business Development Agency provides minorities with training in how to run franchises.

Home-Based Franchises

Home-based businesses offer many obvious advantages, including relief from the stress of commuting, extra time for family activities, and low overhead expenses. But one of the disadvantages of owning a business based at home is the feeling of isolation. Unlike home-based entrepreneurs, home-based franchisees feel less isolated. Experienced franchisors share their knowledge of building a profitable enterprise with franchisees. For example, when Henry and Paula Feldman decided to quit sales jobs that kept them on the road for weeks, they wanted to find a business to run at home together.

The Feldmans started their home-based franchise, Money Mailer, Inc., with nothing more than a table and a telephone. Five years later, they owned 15 territories, which they ran from an office full of state-of-the-art equipment. They grossed more than $600,000 during their fifth year. Henry says that the real value of being in a franchise is that the systems are in place: "You don't have to develop them yourself. Just be willing to work hard, listen, and learn. There's no greater magic than that." See the Taking it to the Net exercise at the end of the chapter for a website that will help you explore home-based franchise opportunities.

E-Commerce in Franchising

We've already talked about how e-commerce ➤ **P.13** ◄ is revolutionizing the way we do business. Online business is not limited to those with technical knowledge and the risk tolerance to start their own businesses from scratch. Today, Internet users all over the world are able to obtain franchises to open online retail stores fully stocked with merchandise made in all parts of the world. For example, a Hong Kong–based e-commerce site called Asia4Sale.com creates virtual stores and provides franchisors with products made in Asia. The company provides the technical expertise as well as the store's products. How much does a franchise cost? It's free. Before you jump online and sign up, however, make certain you check out the facts fully. The saying "You get what you pay for" may be old, but it's not old-fashioned.

Many franchisees with existing brick-and-mortar stores are expanding their businesses online. These franchisees that started with a limited territory are now branching out to customers throughout the world. For example, Carole Shutts owns a Rocky Mountain Chocolate Factory franchise in Galena, Illinois. Her website generates 15 percent of her sales. Other Rocky Mountain franchisees have competing websites. Right now, Shutts isn't concerned about the competition from her colleagues because she thinks multiple sites will build brand awareness.[18]

Many franchisors prohibit franchisee-sponsored websites. Conflicts between franchisors and franchisees can erupt if the franchisor then creates its own website. The franchisees may be concerned that the site will pull sales from their brick-and-mortar locations. Sometimes the franchisors send "reverse royalties" to outlet owners who feel their sales were hurt by the franchisor's Internet sales, but that doesn't always bring about peace. Before buying a franchise, you would be wise to read the small print regarding online sales.

Buying a franchise takes research. Harness the power of the Internet to find information about specific franchises. A good place to start is www. betheboss.com (see the Taking It to the Net exercise at the end of this chapter).

Using Technology in Franchising

Franchisors are speeding onto the information superhighway in an effort to meet the needs of both their customers and their franchisees. For example, U.S. Web Corp. set up its website to streamline processes of effective communication for its employees, customers, and vendors. It built an intranet to allow communication among its 50 franchisees, almost eliminating paperwork. Using the website, every franchisee has immediate access to every subject that involves the franchise operation, even the forms to fill out. There is a chat room where franchisees can leave messages and comments for each other. All franchisees are kept up-to-date on company news via e-mail. The company has found that the Internet is a great way of disseminating information and is revolutionizing franchisor support and franchisee communications.[19]

Franchising In International Markets

The attraction of global markets has carried over into franchising. Today, American franchisors are counting their profits in pesos, won, euros, krona, baht, yen, and many other global currencies. More than 450 of America's 3,000 franchisors have outlets overseas. Canada is by far the most popular target because of proximity and language. Many franchisors are finding it surprisingly easy to move into South Africa and the Philippines. Even though franchisors find the costs of franchising high in these markets, the costs are counterbalanced by less competition and a rapidly expanding consumer base.

Newer, smaller franchises are going international as well. Smaller franchises such as SpeeDee Oil Change & Tune-Up, Rug Doctor Pro, and Merry

Maids have all ventured into the international market. Long Island–based Nathan's Famous Inc. sells hot dogs in the Caribbean and Middle East. Auntie Anne sells hand-rolled pretzels in Indonesia, Malaysia, the Philippines, Singapore, Japan, Venezuela, and Thailand.

What makes franchising successful in international markets is what makes it successful in the United States: convenience and a predictable level of service and quality. Franchisors, though, must be careful to adapt to the region. In France, people thought a furniture-stripping place called Dip 'N' Strip was a bar that featured strippers. In general, however, U.S. franchises are doing well all over the world and are adapting to the local customs and desires of consumers.

COOPERATIVES

Some people dislike the notion of having owners, managers, workers, and buyers as separate individuals with separate goals. These people have formed a different kind of organization to meet their needs for things such as electricity, child care, housing, health care, food, and financial services. Such an organization, called a **cooperative,** is owned and controlled by the people who use it—producers, consumers, or workers with similar needs who pool their resources for mutual gain. In many rural parts of the country, for example, electrical power is sold through cooperatives. The government sells wholesale power to electric cooperatives at average rates that are from 40 to 50 percent below the rates nonfederal utilities charge.

cooperative
A business owned and controlled by the people who use it—producers, consumers, or workers with similar needs who pool their resources for mutual gain.

There are 47,000 cooperatives in the United States today. Some co-ops ask members/customers to work at the cooperative for a number of hours a month as part of their duties. Members democratically control these businesses by electing a board of directors that hires professional management. You may have one of the country's 4,000 food cooperatives near you. If so, stop by and chat with the people and learn more about this growing aspect of the U.S. economy. If you are interested in knowing more about cooperatives, contact the National Cooperative Business Association (800-636-6222).

There is another kind of cooperative in the United States, set up for different reasons. These cooperatives are formed to give members more economic power as a group than they would have as individuals. The best example of such cooperatives is a farm cooperative. The idea at first was for farmers to join together to get better prices for their food products. Eventually, however, the organization expanded so that farm cooperatives now buy and sell fertilizer, farm equipment, seed, and other products needed on the farm. This has become a multibillion-dollar industry. The cooperatives now own many manufacturing facilities. Farm cooperatives do not pay the same kind of taxes that corporations do, and thus have an advantage in the marketplace.

In spite of debt and mergers, cooperatives are still a major force in agriculture today. Some top co-ops have familiar names such as Land O Lakes, Sunkist, Ocean Spray, Blue Diamond, Associated Press, Ace Hardware, True Value Hardware, Riceland Foods, and Welch's.

WHICH FORM OF OWNERSHIP IS FOR YOU?

As you can see, you may participate in the business world in a variety of ways. You can start your own sole proprietorship, partnership, corporation, or cooperative—or you can buy a franchise and be part of a larger corporation. There are advantages and disadvantages to each. However, there are risks no matter which form you choose. Before you decide which form is for you, you need to evaluate all the alternatives carefully.

The miracle of free enterprise is that the freedom and incentives of capitalism make risks acceptable to many people, who go on to create the great corporations of America. You know many of their names: J. C. Penney, Malcolm Forbes, Richard Warren Sears and Alvah C. Roebuck, Levi Strauss, Henry Ford, Thomas Edison, and so on. They started small, accumulated capital, grew, and became industrial leaders. Could you do the same?

PROGRESS ASSESSMENT

• What are some of the factors to consider before buying a franchise?

• What opportunities are available for starting a global franchise?

• What is a cooperative?

SUMMARY

1. Compare the advantages and disadvantages of sole proprietorships.

1. The major forms of business ownership are sole proprietorships, partnerships, and corporations.
   • *What are the advantages and disadvantages of sole proprietorships?*
   The advantages of sole proprietorships include ease of starting and ending, being your own boss, pride of ownership, retention of profit, and no special taxes. The disadvantages include unlimited liability, limited financial resources, difficulty in management, overwhelming time commitment, few fringe benefits, limited growth, and limited life span.

2. Describe the differences between general and limited partners, and compare the advantages and disadvantages of partnerships.

2. The three key elements of a general partnership are common ownership, shared profits and losses, and the right to participate in managing the operations of the business.
   • *What are the main differences between general and limited partners?*
   General partners are owners (partners) who have unlimited liability and are active in managing the company. Limited partners are owners (partners) who have limited liability and are not active in the company.
   • *What does unlimited liability mean?*
   Unlimited liability means that sole proprietors and general partners must pay all debts and damages caused by their business. They may have to sell their houses, cars, or other personal possessions to pay business debts.
   • *What does limited liability mean?*
   Limited liability means that corporate owners (stockholders) and limited partners are responsible for losses only up to the amount they invest. Their other personal property is not at risk.
   • *What is a master limited partnership?*
   A master limited partnership is a partnership that acts like a corporation but is taxed like a partnership. Burger King is a well-known master limited partnership.
   • *What are the advantages and disadvantages of partnerships?*
   The advantages include more financial resources, shared management and pooled knowledge, and longer survival. The disadvantages include unlimited liability, division of profits, disagreements among partners, and difficulty of termination.

3. A corporation is a state-chartered legal entity with authority to act and have liability separate from its owners.
   • *What are the advantages and disadvantages of corporations?*
   The advantages include more money for investment, limited liability, size, perpetual life, ease of ownership change, ease of drawing talented employees, and separation of ownership from management. The disadvantages include initial cost, paperwork, size, difficulty of termination, double taxation, and possible conflict with a board of directors.
   • *Why do people incorporate?*
   Two important reasons for incorporating are special tax advantages and limited liability.
   • *What are the advantages of S corporations?*
   S corporations have the advantages of limited liability (like a corporation) and simpler taxes (like a partnership). In order to qualify for S corporation status, a company must have fewer than 75 stockholders; its stockholders must be individuals or estates and U.S. citizens or permanent residents; and the company cannot have more than 25 percent of its income derived from passive sources.
   • *What are the advantages of limited liability companies?*
   Limited liability companies have the advantage of limited liability without the hassles of forming a corporation or the limitations imposed by S corporations. LLCs may choose whether to be taxed as partnerships or corporations.

   3. Compare the advantages and disadvantages of corporations, and summarize the differences between C corporations, S corporations, and limited liability companies.

4. The number of mergers increased at the start of the new millennium.
   • *What is a merger?*
   A merger is the result of two firms forming one company. The three major types of mergers are vertical mergers, horizontal mergers, and conglomerate mergers.
   • *What are leveraged buyouts, and what does it mean to take a company private?*
   Leveraged buyouts are attempts by managers and employees to borrow money and purchase the company. Individuals who, together or alone, buy all of the stock for themselves are said to take the company private.

   4. Define and give examples of three types of corporate mergers and explain the role of leveraged buyouts and taking a firm private.

5. A person can participate in the entrepreneurial age by buying the rights to market a new product innovation in his or her area.
   • *What is this arrangement called?*
   An arrangement to buy the rights to use the business name and sell its products or services in a given territory is called a franchise.
   • *What is a franchisee?*
   A franchisee is a person who buys a franchise.
   • *What are the benefits and drawbacks of being a franchisee?*
   The benefits include a nationally recognized name and reputation, a proven management system, promotional assistance, and the pride of ownership. Drawbacks include high franchise fees, managerial regulation, shared profits, and transfer of adverse effects if other franchisees fail.
   • *What are the opportunities for women and minorities in franchising?*
   Women now own 24 percent of the nation's franchises. Minority franchise ownership is not growing as quickly as franchise ownership in general, largely because of the large start-up capital needed to purchase a franchise.
   • *What is the major challenge to international franchises?*

   5. Outline the advantages and disadvantages of franchises and discuss the opportunities for diversity in franchising and the challenges of international franchising.

It is often difficult to transfer an idea or product that worked well in the United States to another culture. It is essential to adapt to the region.

6. Explain the role of cooperatives

6. People who dislike organizations in which owners, managers, workers, and buyers have separate goals often form cooperatives.
   • *What is the role of a cooperative?*
   Cooperatives are organizations that are owned by members/customers. Some people form cooperatives (Farmland, for example) to give members more economic power than they would have as individuals. Small businesses often form cooperatives to give them more purchasing, marketing, or product development strength.

KEY TERMS

acquisition 148
conglomerate
  merger 148
conventional (C)
  corporation 140
cooperative 157
corporation 134
franchise 150
franchise
  agreement 150
franchisee 150
franchisor 150

general partner 137
general
  partnership 137
horizontal
  merger 148
leveraged
  buyout 150
limited liability 137
limited liability
  company (LLC) 146
limited liability
  partnership
  (LLP) 138

limited partner 137
limited
  partnership 137
master limited
  partnership 137
merger 148
partnership 134
S corporation 145
sole
  proprietorship 134
unlimited
  liability 136
vertical merger 148

DEVELOPING WORKPLACE SKILLS

1. Research businesses in your area and identify companies that use each of the following forms of ownership: sole proprietorship, partnership, corporation, and franchise. Arrange interviews with managers from each form of ownership and get their impressions, hints, and warnings. (If you are able to work with a team of fellow students, divide the interviews among team members.) How much does it cost to start? How many hours do they work? What are the specific benefits? Share the results with your class.

2. Have you thought about starting your own business? What opportunities seem attractive? Think of a friend or friends whom you might want for a partner or partners in the business. List all the financial resources and personal skills you will need to launch the business. Then make separate lists of the personal skills and the financial resources that you and your friend(s) might bring to your new venture. How much capital and what personal skills do you need but neither of you have? Develop an action plan to obtain them.

3. Let's assume you want to open one of the following new businesses. What form of business ownership would you choose for each business? Why?
   a. Video game rental store.
   b. Wedding planning service.
   c. Software development firm.
   d. Computer hardware manufacturing company.
   e. Online bookstore.

4. Successful businesses continually change. Methods of change discussed in this chapter include mergers, acquisitions, taking a firm private, and lever-

aged buyouts. Find an article in the library or on the Internet that illustrates how one of these methods changed an organization. What led to the change? How will this change affect the company's stakeholders? What benefits does the change provide? What new challenges does it create?

5. Go on the Internet and find information about a business cooperative. Find out how it was formed, who may belong to it, and how it operates.

Purpose

To explore current franchising opportunities and to evaluate the strengths and weaknesses of a selected franchise.

Exercise

Go to Be The Boss: The Ultimate Franchising And Business Opportunity Web Site (www.betheboss.com).

1. Take the interactive self-test in the website's Basics section to see if franchising is a good personal choice for you.

2. Use the search tool on this website to find a franchise that has the potential of fulfilling your entrepreneurial dreams. Navigate to the profile of the franchise you selected. Explore the franchise's website if such a link is available. Refer to the questions listed in Figure 5.8 on p. 154 in this chapter and assess the strengths and weaknesses of your selected franchise. (Hint: The website also contains tips for evaluating a franchise listing.)

3. Do the franchise profile and website give you enough information to answer most of the questions in Figure 5.8? If not, what other information do you need, and where can you obtain it?

Purpose

To explore the advantages of LLC's and to compare the cost of incorporating with the cost of registering an LLC.

Exercise

You and your partner own a small home-based business and are uncomfortable with the unlimited liability of this form of ownership. Using the information found on the website, www.iaas.com, consider the following questions:

1. What is an LLC? What are the major advantages of forming an LLC? The major disadvantages?

2. Which state has the largest fee for forming an LLC? Which state has the lowest fee for forming an LLC?

3. What is the range of prices for incorporating in the various states? Which is the most expensive state in which to incorporate? The least expensive state?

4. The website describes five types of corporate structures in addition to LLCs. If you and your partner were going to change the structure of your small home-based business, which of the six structures would you prefer? Why?

CASE

KEEPING THE AIR IN BLIMPIE

In 1964 Tony Conza borrowed $2,000 to open his first sandwich shop with two of his old schoolmates in Hoboken, New Jersey. Three years later they had 10 stores. What they didn't have was enough experience to manage the business. The growing losses pushed the partners out, but Conza's self-confidence told him to stick with it. He hired an operations expert to help him learn management skills. As the business grew stronger, Tony decided that franchising might be a boost to the struggling company. He hired a lawyer to prepare franchise arrangements. By 1983, there were 150 franchises and revenues approaching $1 million a year. Conza went public (sold stock to the general public) that year, putting Blimpie stock on the open market.

Blimpie added only 50 new franchises in the next five years. This made Tony grow restless. He felt that he let the details of managing his business deflate his entrepreneurial passion. He vowed to change from a manager drowning in day-to-day details into a leader who could create a vision and inspire his employees and franchisees to maximize their talents. Conza chose a team of his senior managers to revise goals for the company and then delegated the new responsibilities of meeting those goals to his managers. Since then, Blimpie has more than tripled in size, with more than 700 stores. Now Blimpie sandwiches are served in such diverse places as on campus at the University of Texas at Austin; in a bowling alley in Collinsville, Illinois; on some Delta airline flights; and in a hospital in Atlanta, Georgia. Conza adds a personal touch to Blimpie advertising by appearing in national radio and regional television ads.

In 1997, Conza hired a consultant to help find another food brand to franchise in combination with Blimpie. In 1999, some 100 Blimpie outlets installed Pasta Central franchises in their shops. The stores now offer lasagna, macaroni and cheese, and other pasta products on their menus. Conza feels that the combination will build dinner traffic and help the company compete for better retail locations. In the past, the company had to pass up some choice retail sites because they were too large for Blimpie outlets by themselves. With the two brands sharing space, more sites become feasible. Blimpie is not the first company to move to co-branding of franchises. Co-branding of franchise outlets has helped several franchises stand out in especially competitive and crowded fields. On a busy road in Columbus, Ohio, for example, an all-in-one Shell Oil/Charley's Steakery/TCBY caters to shoppers who want to fill their cars and their stomachs in one stop.

Conza's business started as a partnership, changed to a sole proprietorship, changed again to a strict franchise operation, and finally changed to a franchise corporation. Each form of ownership has its advantages and disadvantages.

Decision Questions

1. What are the major advantages of franchising for a firm such as Blimpie?
2. What are some of the advantages and disadvantages for a company such as Blimpie changing from private ownership to a corporate form of ownership?
3. What opportunities are created for firms such as Blimpie by entering into co-branding agreements with other franchises? What are the disadvantages of such a franchise union?

VIDEO CASE

YO QUIERO FISH

You have read all about the advantages and disadvantages of the various forms of organization: sole proprietorships, partnerships, corporations, and so forth. It's very exciting to contemplate starting your own business, but there is always the fear of failure. Isn't there some way to start a business that is more likely to have success? Yes, there is. The answer is to buy into an established and growing franchise. You have to look around to find out what is new and exciting. Then you have to do your homework and talk to managers and employees of various franchise organizations to learn all you can. With luck, you will find one that has the excitement and growth potential of Rubio's Baha Grill.

This franchise is based in San Diego. It sells Mexican-style seafood from 128 company-owned restaurants in five western states. Their most popular item is the fish taco. If you are from some other part of the country, a fish taco may not sound too wonderful to you, but in Rubio country, you're talking good-tasting food. People who try them like them. Ralph Rubio is now beginning to offer this successful operation to franchisees. He needed to do that to grow as fast as he would like. He hopes to have a national chain some day.

Rubio's began as a family-owned business. It was a sole proprietorship. A couple of years later, the family decided to incorporate so that ownership could be widely shared and easily transferred. Now that Rubio's is expanding into franchising, it wants to maintain its professional image. Thus it wants franchisees with lots of experience and with the capital and marketing experience to succeed. Rubio's will provide any needed training and marketing support.

To maintain the same culture in all franchise outlets, training is held in San Diego to capture the Mission Bay feeling. Managers, cooks, and others will travel to the various outlets to see that the processes implemented maintain the same cultural look and feel. It is important, when trying to maintain a quality image, to have only the best workers. To keep workers, Rubio's pays competitive wages and offers flexible scheduling.

Rubio understands the need to have a careful balance between company-owned outlets and franchised outlets. At company stores, you can maintain more control, but it is difficult to grow without franchising, so the managerial challenge is to make the best of both worlds.

Rubio recommends that people have relevant experience before trying to start a franchise of their own. You need to know how to manage the cash register, empty the garbage bins, clean the bathrooms, handle the money, and do everything that a manager has to do. And that means everything! There's risk involved in starting any kind of business. But, with some experience under your belt, and the backing of an established franchisor, your chances of succeeding are much better.

Discussion Questions

1. What do you see as the main impediment to raising money when you start a business using the sole proprietorship or partnership form of business?

2. What disadvantages do you see of buying a franchise rather than starting your own fast-food business? Why do you suppose most people choose franchising?

3. What are some of the bigger franchise organizations in your town? Do they have independent competitors? Which would you rather own and why?

4. As you drive down the road, it seems that there are more and more of the typical fast-food restaurants opening: McDonald's, Burger King, KFC, and the like. What do you see as the advantages and disadvantages of having so many competitors from the same company within such close distances?

CHAPTER 6

Entrepreneurship and Starting a Small Business

LEARNING GOALS

AFTER YOU HAVE READ AND STUDIED THIS CHAPTER, YOU SHOULD BE ABLE TO

1. Explain why people are willing to take the risks of entrepreneurship, list the attributes of successful entrepreneurs, describe the benefits of entrepreneurial teams and intrapreneurs, and explain the growth of home-based and Web-based businesses.

2. Discuss the importance of small business to the American economy and summarize the major causes of small-business failure.

3. Summarize ways to learn about how small businesses operate.

4. Analyze what it takes to start and run a small business.

5. Outline the advantages and disadvantages small businesses have in entering global markets.

Getting to Know Andy Wilson of Boston Duck Tours

In 1992, Andy Wilson's friends began to question his sanity. Equipped with a lucrative job in corporate finance and a promising corporate future, Andy represented what living the good life was all about. However, Wilson did not see things quite as brightly. He knew he wanted to navigate his life in a different direction—and navigate is what he did.

While on a cross-country trip, Wilson took a tour on a Duck in Memphis. A Duck is a World War II amphibious vehicle that's part bus, part truck, part boat. After this inspirational Memphis tour ride and later a non-inspirational trolley tour through Boston, Wilson was convinced the best way to experience Boston's great and vivid history was on a Duck that crossed both land and water.

skippers such as Vincent van Duck, Salty Magoo, and Guido Gondolier. You can find a full list of the captains and their vessels, and a description of what's called the most historically accurate tour of Boston, at www.bostonducktours.com. The Ducks today are such a fixture in the Boston landscape that Bostonians on the street react to the Duckmobiles by flapping their arms, à la the chicken dance, prompting riders to quack-quack as they go by. The passengers, of course, expect a quack back. Every year Wilson sponsors a contest in which local schoolchildren can name the new Ducks headed to the Charles River. He also gives free tours to veterans during the week around Veteran's Day in honor of his father, a World War II veteran.

Unfortunately, like many aspiring entrepreneurs, Andy Wilson found that the road to success was often rather "fowl." In his first two years in business, Wilson found little support from either investors or the more than 100 government agencies involved with getting the proper permits to get his Ducks moving. After finally obtaining all the needed permits in 1994, he had spent all his personal funds and the business was $250,000 in debt. It looked like Wilson's dream was a dead duck.

Yet with the spirit of a true entrepreneur, Wilson dug down and played his last card by calling associates from his old corporate job. Through his former accounting and finance contacts, he found a firm that helped him raise the $1.25 million he needed to get his Ducks in a row and on the streets of Boston. In 1999, the company celebrated its 1 millionth customer to take the plunge on one of Wilson's 16 candy-colored Ducks.

Every day the Ducks, with appropriate names like Beantown Betty and Fenway Fannie, navigate through historic Boston with

Andy Wilson's persistence and confidence paid off. Yet he still refuses to take personal credit for his success. Instead, he credits the city of Boston: "I realized all along that if this was going to succeed, it was because Boston existed. It's a wonderful city and I've done everything I can to be a responsible citizen." The city evidently agrees: in 1997 Andy Wilson was named Small Business Person of the Year for the Commonwealth of Massachusetts from the Massachusetts Small Business Association and the Greater Boston Convention and Visitors Bureau.

Stories about people who take risks, like Andy Wilson, are commonplace in this age of the entrepreneur. As you read about such risk takers in this chapter, maybe you'll be inspired not to duck the opportunity and to become an entrepreneur yourself.

Source: Laura Tiffany, "Making Waves," *Entrepreneur*, June 1999, pp. 97–99; and Jerry Ward, "Unique Tour All It's Quacked Up to Be," *Edmonton Sun*, April 17, 1999, p. 48.

The Age of the Entrepreneur

A poll of college seniors showed that 51 percent of the men and 31 percent of the women were more attracted to starting their own businesses than to joining the corporate ranks. Generation X people (now in their 20s and early 30s) seem to share the pragmatic view that in this time of post-downsized America it doesn't make sense to work in a company where your reward can just as easily be a pink slip as a promotion or bonus. Why not get a piece of the action by working in your own company? Of the 5.6 million Americans going into business for themselves in 1996, almost a third were 30 or younger.[1] Colleges around the country are responding to this trend by offering more courses on the subject of entrepreneurship.[2] **Entrepreneurship** is accepting the risk of starting and running a business. Explore this chapter and think about the possibility of entrepreneurship in your future.

entrepreneurship
Accepting the risk of starting and running a business.

The Job-Creating Power of Entrepreneurs in the United States

One of the major issues in the United States today is the need to create more jobs. You can get some idea about the job-creating power of entrepreneurs ➤ **P.4** ◄ when you look at some of the great American entrepreneurs from the past and the present. The history of the United States is the history of its entrepreneurs. Consider just a few of the many entrepreneurs who have helped shape the American economy:

- Du Pont, which manufactures thousands of products under such brand names as Teflon and Lycra, was started in 1802 by French immigrant Éleuthère Irénée du Pont de Nemours. Some 18 shareholders provided $36,000 in start-up money.

- Avon started in 1886 on $500 David McConnell borrowed from a friend.

Generation Xer's (people in their 20s and 30s) like Chris Spencer, a senior at North Carolina State University, don't waste their time just hanging around. When he isn't practicing his rock climbing hobby, Chris is climbing to the top of his career by building his own business. He is the founder and chief technology officer of Sentrissystems.com, a company that protects Web-based transactions. Chris found many business resources to help start his business right at the University. If you were considering becoming an entrepreneur, would you know where to look for start-up assistance?

- George Eastman launched Kodak in 1880 with a $3,000 investment.
- Procter & Gamble was formed in 1837 by William Procter and James Gamble with a total of $7,000 in capital.
- Ford Motor Company began with an investment of $28,000 by Henry Ford and 11 associates.

The stories are all about the same. One entrepreneur or a couple of entrepreneurs had a good idea, borrowed a few dollars from friends and family, and started a business. That business now employs thousands of people and helps the country prosper.

The United States still has plenty of entrepreneurial talent. Names such as Steve Jobs (Apple Computer), Ross Perot (Electronic Data Systems), Michael Dell (Dell Computer), Bill Gates (Microsoft), Howard Schultz (Starbucks), Mary Kay Ash (Mary Kay Cosmetics), Scott Cook (Intuit), and Ted Turner (Cable News Network) have become as familiar as those of the great entrepreneurs of the past.

WHY PEOPLE TAKE THE ENTREPRENEURIAL CHALLENGE

Taking the risks of starting a business can be scary and thrilling at the same time. One entrepreneur described it as almost like bungee-jumping. You might be scared, but if you watch six other people do it and they survive, you're then able to do it yourself. Some of the many reasons people are willing to take the risks of starting a business are the following:

- *Opportunity.* The opportunity to share in the American dream is a tremendous lure. Many people, including those new to this country, may not have the necessary skills for working in today's complex organizations. However, they may have the initiative and drive to work the long hours demanded by entrepreneurship. The same is true of many corporate managers who left the security of the corporate life (either by choice or as a result of corporate downsizing) to run businesses of their own.

- *Profit.* Profit is another important reason to become an entrepreneur. At one time the richest person in America was Sam Walton, the entrepreneur who started Wal-Mart. Now the richest person in America is William Henry Gates III, the entrepreneur who founded Microsoft Corporation.

- *Independence.* Many entrepreneurs simply do not enjoy working for someone else. Many lawyers, for example, do not like the stress and demands of big law firms. Some have found more enjoyment and self-satisfaction in starting their own businesses.

- *Challenge.* Some people believe that entrepreneurs are excitement junkies who flourish on taking risks. Nancy Flexman and Thomas Scanlan, however, in their book *Running Your Own Business*, contend that entrepreneurs take moderate, calculated risks; they are not just gambling. In general, though, entrepreneurs seek achievement more than power.

What Does It Take to Be an Entrepreneur?

Would you succeed as an entrepreneur? You can learn about the managerial and leadership skills needed to run a firm. However, you may not have the personality to assume the risks, take the initiative, create the vision, and rally others to follow your lead. Those traits are harder to learn or acquire. A list of entrepreneurial attributes you would look for in yourself includes the following:

1. *Self-directed.* You should be thoroughly comfortable and thoroughly self-disciplined even though you are your own boss. You will be responsible for your success or possible failure.[3]

2. *Self-nurturing.* You must believe in your idea even when no one else does, and be able to replenish your own enthusiasm. When Walt Disney suggested the possibility of a full-length animated feature film, *Snow White,* the industry laughed. His personal commitment and enthusiasm caused the Bank of America to back his venture. The rest is history.

3. *Action-oriented.* Great business ideas are not enough. The most important thing is a burning desire to realize, actualize, and build your dream into reality.

4. *Highly energetic.* It's your business, and you must be emotionally, mentally, and physically able to work long and hard. John Schnatter, founder of Papa John's Pizza, says he devotes 17 hours a day to the business.[4]

5. *Tolerant of uncertainty.* Successful entrepreneurs take only calculated risks (if they can help it). Still, they must be able to take some risks. Remember, entrepreneurship is not for anyone who is squeamish or bent on security.[5]

It is important to know that most entrepreneurs don't get the ideas for their products and services from some flash of inspiration. Rather than a flash, the source of innovation is more like a flash*light.* Imagine a search party, walking around in the dark, shining lights, looking around, asking questions, and looking some more. The late Sam Walton used such a flashlight approach. He visited his stores and those of competitors and took notes. He'd see a good idea on Monday, and by Tuesday every Wal-Mart manager in the country knew about it. He expected his managers to use flashlighting too. Every time they traveled on business, they were expected to come back with at least one idea worth more than the cost of their trip. "That's how most creativity happens," says business author Dale Dauten. "Calling around, asking questions, saying 'What if?' till you get blisters on your tongue."

Keep in mind that necessity isn't always the mother of invention. Entrepreneurs don't always look for what customers need—they look for what they *don't* need as well. Aaron Lapin thought we didn't need the hassles of the touchy process of whipping heavy cream to top our pies. He made millions selling his invention: Reddi Wip. Although we'd rather reach for a can in the refrigerator than whip our own cream, Reddi Wip isn't a necessity. If you think you may have the entrepreneurial spirit in your blood, take the entrepreneurial test on page 196. There is also some advice for would-be entrepreneurs in Figure 6.1.

CRITICAL **THINKING**

entrepreneurial team
A group of experienced people from different areas of business who join together to form a managerial team with the skills needed to develop, make, and market a new product.

Do you know anyone who seems to have the entrepreneurial spirit? What about him or her makes you say that? Are there any similarities between the characteristics demanded of an entrepreneur and those of a professional athlete? Would an athlete be a good prospect for entrepreneurship? Why or why not? Could teamwork be important in an entrepreneurial effort?

Entrepreneurial Teams

An **entrepreneurial team** is a group of experienced people from different areas of business who join together to form a managerial team with the skills needed to develop, make, and market a new product. A team may be better than

FIGURE 6.1

ADVICE FOR POTENTIAL ENTREPRENEURS

- Work for other people first and learn on their money.
- Research your market, but don't take too long to act.
- Start your business when you have a customer. Maybe try your venture as a sideline at first.
- Set specific objectives, but don't set your goals too high. Remember, there's no easy money.
- Plan your objectives within specific time frames.
- Surround yourself with people who are smarter than you—including an accountant and an outside board of directors who are interested in your well-being and who'll give you straight answers.
- Don't be afraid to fail. Former football coach Vince Lombardi summarized the entrepreneurial philosophy when he said, "We didn't lose any games this season, we just ran out of time twice." New entrepreneurs must be ready to run out of time a few times before they succeed.

Sources: Mark Binder, "Stay the Course," *Home Office Computing,* February 2000, pp. 96–98; Julie Carrick Dalton, "Startup's Epitaph: One Product Beats Three," *Inc.,* February 2000, p. 28; and Amy Wilson Sheldon, "Slow Down You Move Too Fast," *Fast Company,* February 1, 2001.

an individual entrepreneur because team members can combine creative skills with production and marketing skills right from the start. Having a team also can ensure more cooperation and coordination among functions.

One of the exciting companies begun in the 1980s was Compaq Computer. It was started by three senior managers at Texas Instruments: Bill Murto, Jim Harris, and Rod Canion. All three were bitten by the entrepreneurial bug and decided to go out on their own. They debated what industry to enter but finally decided to build a portable personal computer that was compatible with the IBM PC.

The key to Compaq's early success was that the company was built around this "smart team" of experienced managers. The team wanted to combine the discipline of a big company with an environment where people could feel they were participating in a successful venture. The trio of corporate entrepreneurs recruited seasoned managers with similar desires. All the managers worked as a team. For example, the company's treasurer and top engineer contributed to production and marketing decisions. Everyone worked together to conceive, develop, and market products.

Today, Compaq is one of the most successful of all PC makers in building powerful systems while keeping costs down to ensure healthy profit margins. Entrepreneurs such as the three from Compaq often turn their companies over to professional managers once the companies reach a certain size. Often such a change is good for the firm because the professionals introduce new ideas and instill new entrepreneurial spirit.

Micropreneurs and Home-Based Businesses

Not every person who starts a business has the goal of growing it into a mammoth corporation. Some are interested in simply enjoying a balanced lifestyle while doing the kind of work they want to do. Business writer Michael LeBoeuf calls such a business owner a **micropreneur.** While other entrepreneurs are committed to the quest for growth, micropreneurs know they can be happy even if their companies never appear on a list of topranked businesses.

Many micropreneurs are home-based business owners. Nearly half of the small businesses in the United States are run out of the owner's home. Nearly half of those home-based businesses are in service industries. Micropreneurs

micropreneur
An entrepreneur willing to accept the risk of starting and managing the type of business that remains small, lets them do the kind of work they want to do, and offers them a balanced lifestyle.

include writers, consultants, video producers, architects, bookkeepers, and such. In fact, the development of this textbook involved many home-based business owners. The authors, the developmental editors, the copy editor, and even the text designer operate home-based businesses.

Many home-based businesses are owned by people who are trying to combine career and family. Don't misunderstand and picture home-based workers as female child-care givers; nearly 60 percent are men.[6] In addition to helping business owners balance work and family, other reasons for the growth of home-based businesses include:

- Computer technology has leveled the competitive playing field, allowing home-based businesses to look and act as big as their corporate competitors. High-speed Internet connections, fax machines, and other technologies are so affordable that setting up a business takes a much smaller initial investment than it used to.
- Corporate downsizing has made workers aware that there is no such thing as job security, leading many to venture out on their own. Meanwhile, the work of the downsized employees still needs to be done and corporations are outsourcing much of the work to smaller companies; that is, they are contracting with small companies to temporarily fill their needs. (We'll talk more about outsourcing in Chapter 8.)
- Social attitudes have changed. Whereas home-based entrepreneurs used to be asked when they were going to get a "real" job, they are now likely to be asked instead for how-to-do-it advice.
- New tax laws have loosened the restrictions regarding deductions for home offices.

Working at home has its challenges, of course. In setting up a home-based business, you could expect the following major challenges:

- *Getting new customers.* Getting the word out can be difficult because you don't have signs or a storefront.

Home is where the heart is — and more and more often these days — where business is. What are some of the advantages and disadvantages of operating a home-based business?

- *Managing time.* Of course, you save time by not commuting, but it takes self-discipline to use that time wisely.

- *Keeping work and family tasks separate.* Often it is difficult to separate work and family tasks. It's great to be able to throw a load of laundry in the washer in the middle of the workday if you need to, but you have to keep such distractions to a minimum. It is also difficult to leave your work at the office if the office is at home. Again, it takes self-discipline to keep work from trickling out of the home office and into the family room.

- *Abiding by city ordinances.* Government ordinances restrict such things as the types of businesses that are allowed in certain parts of the community and how much traffic a home-based business can attract to the neighborhood.

- *Managing risk.* Home-based entrepreneurs should review their home-owner's insurance policy since not all policies cover business-related claims. Some even void the coverage if there is a business in the home.

Those who wish to get out of an office building and into a home office should focus on finding opportunity instead of accepting security, getting results instead of following routines, earning a profit instead of earning a paycheck, trying new ideas instead of avoiding mistakes, and creating a long-term vision instead of seeking a short-term payoff. Figure 6.2 lists 10 ideas for potentially successful home-based businesses, and Figure 6.3 highlights clues to avoiding home-based business scams. You can find a wealth of online information about starting a home-based business at Small and Home-Based Business Links (www.bizoffice.com).

Web-Based Businesses

The Web has sprouted a world of small home-based businesses that sell everything from staplers to refrigerator magnets to wedding dresses. In 2000, approximately 64 percent of small businesses took orders over the Web.[7] That is a tremendous increase from the 10 percent total just two years earlier.[8] By

FIGURE 6.2

POTENTIAL HOME-BASED BUSINESSES

Many businesses can be started at home. Listed below are 10 businesses that have low start-up costs, don't require an abundance of administrative tasks, and are in relatively high demand and easy to sell:

1. Cleaning service.
2. Gift-basket business.
3. Web merchant.
4. Mailing list service.
5. Microfarming (small plots of land for such high-value crops as mushrooms, edible flowers, or sprouts).
6. Tutoring.
7. Résumé service.
8. Web design.
9. Medical claims assistance.
10. Personal coaching.

If one of these businesses doesn't fit you, you can find suggestions for 400 more on *Entrepreneur* magazine's website (www.entrepreneurmag.com/bizopp500/home400.hts). Look for one that meets these important criteria: (1) the job is something you truly enjoy doing; (2) you know enough to do the job well or you are willing to spend time learning it while you have another job; and (3) you can identify a market for your product or service.

Source: "Hundreds of Home-Based Business Ideas," YourHomeBiz.com, January 2001.

You've probably read many ads selling home-based businesses in newspapers and magazines. You may have even received unsolicited e-mail messages touting the glory of particular work-at-home opportunities. Beware of work-at-home scams! Here are a few clues that tell you a home business opportunity is a scam:

1. The ad promises that you can earn hundreds or even thousands of dollars a week working at home.
2. No experience is needed.
3. You only need to work a few hours a week.
4. There are loads of CAPITAL LETTERS and exclamation points!!!!!
5. You need to call a 900 number for more information.
6. You're asked to send in some money to receive a list of home-based business opportunities.
7. You're pressured to make a decision NOW!!!!

Do your homework before investing in a business opportunity. Call and ask for references. Contact the Better Business Bureau (www.bbb.org), county and state departments of consumer affairs, and the state attorney general's office. Conduct an Internet search and ask people in chat rooms, Usenet discussion groups, or bulletin boards if they've dealt with the company. Visit websites such as www.friendsinbusiness.com and www.home-business-mall.com to find advice on specific online scams. Most important, don't pay a great deal of money for a business opportunity until you've talked to an attorney.

2003, the number of small businesses using the Internet is expected to mushroom to over 4 million.[9]

Wendy Gem Davis, a 30-year-old mother of 5-year-old quadruplets, logged onto eBay a couple of years ago to see if she could buy porcelain figurines for her collection. When she saw all of the trading going on, she thought of a way to make extra money without leaving her kids. She has since moved from trading figurines to selling clothes her kids outgrew to buying cut-rate goods from a nearby Walt Disney discount outlet store. She doubles the price of the Disney items and sells them to people as far away as Australia and Kuwait. Her profit of between $1,000 and $5,000 a month has allowed her family to move to a bigger house.

The Internet community has numerous sites that lend entrepreneurs a helping hand in setting up their online stores:[10]

- Hypermart.com offers full e-commerce ▸ **P.13** ◂ capability that allows small businesses to build their own security or electronic shopping carts.

Jon Roska is a true believer that business is going to the dogs. In fact, his Internet start-up company PetFoodDirect.com does just that. PetFoodDirect.com carries premium pet-food brands at prices comparable to other e-tailers and traditional pet stores. His company promises to ship a customer's order within 24 hours or the order is free. The growth of e-commerce has led many entrepreneurs like Jon to start their own online stores. What do you think is the future of e-tailing? Continued growth or just a fad?

FIGURE 6.4

TIPS FOR OPENING A WEB-BASED BUSINESS

Web-based businesses are still in their infancy. Much of their early success could be due to the novelty of shopping online. In order to stand out in the crowd of e-commerce businesses and still be around when the novelty fades, you need to build a loyal and ever-growing customer base by providing first-class customer care.

Here are some tips for attracting and retaining online customers:

1. *Keep it simple.* Avoid unnecessary graphics and special effects. If your site requires a specific browser add-on, your customers may move on to another site rather than stop to upgrade their browsers.

2. *Provide added value.* The more information you provide about your products or services, the more likely customers will buy. Examples of well-designed sites are those of Garden.com and Homepoint.com.

3. *Make buying easy.* Make it easy for customers to drop items into a cart while browsing. For good examples of this feature, see Amazon.com and REI.com.

4. *Display certification.* You will gain credibility if you display a seal of approval from an organization such as VeriSign (www.verisign.com) that identifies your site as secure for online credit card purchases.

5. *Post a privacy policy.* Assure customers that you will not pass personal information on to others.

6. *Deliver low prices.* Online shoppers expect good value.

7. *Be accessible.* Provide a phone number, an e-mail address, a fax number, and a physical address.

8. *Add a toll-free number.* If customers become frustrated, they want to speak to a live person.

9. *Get it right the first time.* Customers who receive their entire order on time are more likely to buy from you again.

10. *Respond quickly.* Immediate response gives the customer a sense of support and service.

11. *Use an autoresponder.* Sending out automatic e-mail responses to specific types of e-mail questions helps to reduce your online support load and costs.

12. *Provide inexpensive shipping.* Break even on shipping.

13. *Guarantee satisfaction.* If customers aren't happy with a product, assure them they can return it at no cost.

14. *Keep track of what's selling.* You learn a little bit more about your business every time a customer buys something. E-commerce products gather sales statistics that let you analyze buying trends and customer habits that help you plan your inventory.

15. *Build a support network.* You can build relationships with other Web-based entrepreneurs by participating in business chat rooms and by subscribing to different professional associations' websites.

Sources: Eric Hellweg and Sean Donahue, "The Smart Way to Start an Internet Company," *Business 2.0*, March 2000; and "No Bandwidth, No Problems," *Business 2.0*, January 23, 2001.

- Shownow.com offers a variety of services to help you build your own online store.
- Microsoft's LinkExchange can get your advertising banners on key sites.
- Electronic Commerce Guide (www.ecommerce.internet.com) offers information for both beginners and experts.
- The E-Commerce Research Room (www.webcommercetoday.com/research) offers more than 1,500 reports and resources about e-commerce.
- Builder.com (www.builder.com) offers one-stop shopping for advice and tools for creating websites.

Figure 6.4 offers tips on setting up a Web-based business.

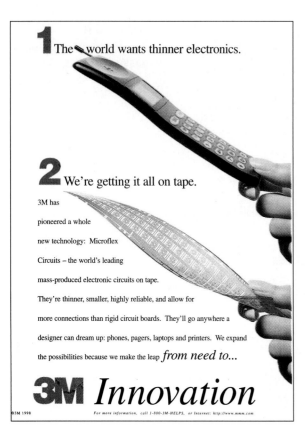

1 The world wants thinner electronics.

2 We're getting it all on tape.

3M has pioneered a whole new technology: Microflex Circuits – the world's leading mass-produced electronic circuits on tape. They're thinner, smaller, highly reliable, and allow for more connections than rigid circuit boards. They'll go anywhere a designer can dream up: phones, pagers, laptops and printers. We expand the possibilities because we make the leap *from need to...*

3M *Innovation*

©3M 1998   For more information, call 1-800-3M-HELPS, or Internet: http://www.mmm.com

When you come up with a winning idea, stick with it. That's certainly been the motto of the 3M company. 3M encourages intrapreneurship among its employees by requiring them to devote at least 15 percent of their time to thinking about new products. Does a career as an intrapreneur interest you?

intrapreneurs
Creative people who work as entrepreneurs within corporations.

Don't get the idea that a Web-based business is always a fast road to success. It can also be a shortcut to failure. Hundreds of high-flying dot-coms have crashed after promising to revolutionize the way we shop. For example, flashy fashion site Boo.com lost millions in its six months of existence.[11] Tracking such Internet failures has become a sort of sport for some sadistic souls. Websites such as dotcomfailures.com posts the bankruptcy filings, layoffs, lawsuits, and sinking sales of e-tailers. Other sites have taken a more positive perspective. Startupfailures.com bills itself as "The place for bouncing back!" It offers job listings, a feature called "Ask the Coach," and a story reminding site visitors that failing doesn't make you a failure, only failing to learn from your mistakes does. Learning from others' mistakes is less painful. If you would like to learn more about the pitfalls of Web-based businesses, the "Lessons Learned from a Startup Failure" tab on the Startupfailures.com site provides an archive of stories by Internet hopefuls who have been there, done that.[12]

Entrepreneurship within Firms

Entrepreneurship in a large organization is often reflected in the efforts and achievements of intrapreneurs. **Intrapreneurs** are creative people who work as entrepreneurs within corporations. The idea is to use a company's existing resources—human, financial, and physical—to launch new products and generate new profits. At 3M, which produces a wide array of products from adhesives (Scotch tape) to nonwoven materials for industrial use, managers are expected to devote 15 percent of their time to thinking up new products or services.[13] You know those bright-colored Post-it® Notes people use to write messages on just about everything? That product was developed by Art Fry, a 3M employee. He needed to mark the pages of a hymnal in a way that wouldn't damage the book or fall out. He came up with the idea of the self-stick, repositionable paper. The 3M labs soon produced a sample, but distributors thought the product wasn't important, and market surveys were inconclusive. Nonetheless, 3M kept sending samples to secretaries of top executives. Eventually, after launching a major sales and marketing program, the orders began pouring in, and Post-it® Notes became a big winner. The company continues to update the product; making the notes from recycled paper is just one of the many innovations. Post-it® Notes have gone international as well—the notepads sent to Japan are long and narrow to accommodate vertical writing. Now you can even use Post-it® Notes electronically—the software program, Post-it® Software Notes, allows you to type messages onto brightly colored notes and store them on memo boards, embed them in documents, or send them through e-mail.

Hewlett-Packard calls its intrapreneurial approach the Triad Development Process. The idea is to link the design engineer, the manufacturer, and the marketer (the Triad) in a cross-functional team from the design phase on. Everything, even the assembly line, shuts down if the Triad team wants to test an innovation.

The classic intrapreneurial venture is the Skunkworks of Lockheed Martin Corporation. The Skunkworks is a top-secret research and development center that turned out such monumental products as America's first fighter jet in 1943 and the Stealth fighter in 1991.

ENCOURAGING ENTREPRENEURSHIP— WHAT GOVERNMENT CAN DO

Part of the Immigration Act passed by Congress in 1990 was intended to encourage more entrepreneurs to come to the United States. The act created a category of "investor visas" that allows 10,000 people to come to the United States each year if they invest $1 million in an enterprise that creates or preserves 10 jobs. Some people are promoting the idea of increasing the number of such immigrants. They believe the more entrepreneurs that can be lured to the United States, the more jobs will be created and the more the economy will grow.

One way to encourage entrepreneurship is through enterprise zones that feature low taxes and government support. The government could have a significant effect on entrepreneurship by offering investment tax credits that would give tax breaks to businesses that make the kind of investments that would create jobs. The government could also institute a plan of public investment to rebuild the nation's infrastructure (bridges, roads, etc.). Such money would go to businesses that would then hire people whose spending would stimulate economic growth.

States are becoming stronger supporters of entrepreneurs as they create programs that invest directly in new businesses. Often, state commerce departments serve as clearinghouses for such investment programs. States are also creating incubators and technology centers to reduce start-up capital needs. **Incubators** are centers that offer new businesses low-cost offices with basic business services such as accounting, legal advice, and secretarial help. The number of incubators in the United States now exceeds 800. Over the last 20 years, business incubators have created nearly 19,000 companies that are still in business and, more important, about 245,000 jobs. Incubators help companies survive because they provide assistance in the critical stage of early development.[14] One incubator graduate, Visual Networks, grew so rapidly that it displaced the incubator that housed it, forcing the Maryland Technology Development Center to move elsewhere.[15]

Incubators have helped create 19,000 companies and almost 250,000 jobs in the U.S. over the past twenty years. Tony Hsieh and Alfred Lin hope to add to that number. Their incubator for Internet start-up companies offers low cost offices and needed business services to aspiring new companies. Ever the entrepreneurs, Tony and Alfred also run a restaurant next door to their incubator, where hungry high-tech wannabees can chow down on eBay Eggplant and Microsoft Minced Chicken. Is there an incubator in or near your community for high-tech start-ups?

- Why are people willing to take the risks of entrepreneurship?
- What are the advantages of entrepreneurial teams?
- How do micropreneurs differ from other entrepreneurs?
- What are some of the opportunities and risks of Web-based businesses?

PROGRESS ASSESSMENT

GETTING STARTED IN SMALL BUSINESS

Let's suppose you have a great idea for a new business, you have the attributes of an entrepreneur, and you are ready to take the leap into business for yourself. How do you start a business? How much paperwork is involved? That is what the rest of this chapter is about. We will explore small businesses, their role in

incubators
Centers that offer new businesses low-cost offices with basic business services.

A hard worker with a firm business plan, former model B. Smith challenged the stereotype of models being airheads by opening up B. Smith's restaurant in New York. Success there led to additional restaurants, a series of books on entertaining, and her TV show *B Smith with Style*. Now B. plans to invade the publishing business with a lifestyle magazine. Minority-owned businesses are becoming a major part of the U.S. economy. Can you name a fast-growing minority business operating in your community?

small business
A business that is independently owned and operated, is not dominant in its field of operation, and meets certain standards of size (set by the Small Business Administration) in terms of employees or annual receipts.

the economy, and small-business management. It may be easier to identify with a small neighborhood business than with a giant global firm, yet the principles of management are similar. The management of charities, government agencies, churches, schools, and unions is much the same as the management of small and large businesses. So, as you learn about small-business management, you will make a giant step toward understanding management in general. All organizations demand capital, good ideas, planning, information management, budgets (and financial management in general), accounting, marketing, good employee relations, and good overall managerial know-how. We shall explore these areas as they relate to small businesses and then, later in the book, apply the concepts to large firms, even global organizations.

Small versus Big Business

The Small Business Administration (SBA) defines a **small business** as one that is independently owned and operated, is not dominant in its field of operation, and meets certain standards of size in terms of employees or annual receipts (e.g., less than $2 million a year for service businesses). A small business is considered "small" only in relation to other businesses in its industry. A wholesaler may sell up to $22 million and still be considered a small business by the SBA. In manufacturing, a plant can have 1,500 employees and still be considered small. For example, before its merger with Chrysler, American Motors was considered small because it was tiny compared to Ford, General Motors, and Chrysler. Let's look at some interesting statistics about small businesses:[16]

- There are about 24.5 million full- and part-time home-based businesses in the United States.
- Nearly 750,000 tax-paying, employee-hiring businesses are started every year.
- Small businesses create 75 percent of the new jobs in the United States.
- Of all nonfarm businesses in the United States, almost 97 percent are considered small by SBA standards.
- Small businesses account for over 40 percent of the gross domestic product (GDP).
- The total number of U.S. employees who work in small business is greater than the populations of Australia and Canada combined.
- About 80 percent of Americans find their first jobs in small businesses.
- The number of women owning small businesses has increased rapidly. Women now own nearly 6 million small businesses. That's more than one-third of all small businesses and a 43 percent increase from 4.1 million in 1987.
- Minority-owned businesses are one of the fastest-growing segments of the U.S. economy. In the last decade, the number of small businesses owned by Asians has grown 463 percent, Hispanics 417 percent, and African Americans 108 percent.

As you can see, small business is really a big part of the U.S. economy. How big a part? We'll explore that question next.

Importance of Small Businesses

Since 75 percent of the nation's new jobs are in small businesses, there is a very good chance that you will either work in a small business someday or start one. A quarter of the small businesses list "lack of qualified workers" as one of their biggest obstacles to growth.

In addition to providing employment opportunities, small firms believe they offer other advantages that larger companies do not. Owners of small companies report that their greatest advantages over big companies are their more personal customer service and their ability to respond quickly to opportunities.

Bigger is not always better. Picture a hole in the ground. If you fill it with big boulders there are many empty spaces between them. However, if you fill it with sand, there is no space between the grains. That's how it is in business. Big businesses don't serve all the needs of the market. There is plenty of room for small companies to make a profit filling those niches.

Small-Business Success and Failure

You can't be naive about business practices, or you'll go broke. There is some debate about how many new small businesses fail each year. Conventional wisdom says that four out of five businesses (80 percent) fail in their first five years, and the SBA reports a 62 percent death rate within six years. Yet a study by economist Bruce Kirchhoff shows that the failure rate is only 18 percent over the first eight years. Kirchhoff contends that the other failure rates were the result of misinterpretations of Dun & Bradstreet statistics. When small-business owners went out of business to start new and different businesses, they were included in the "business failure" category when obviously that was not the case. Similarly, when a business changed its form of ownership from partnership to corporation, it was counted as a failure. Retirements of sole

---

Small businesses are more likely to fail when

- Plunging in without first testing the waters on a small scale.
- Underpricing or overpricing goods or services.
- Underestimating how much time it will take to build a market.
- Starting with too little capital.
- Starting with too much capital and being careless in its use.
- Going into business with little or no experience and without first learning something about the industry or market.
- Borrowing money without planning just how and when to pay it back.
- Attempting to do too much business with too little capital.

- Not allowing for setbacks and unexpected expenses.
- Buying too much on credit.
- Extending credit too freely.
- Expanding credit too rapidly.
- Failing to keep complete, accurate records, so that the owners drift into trouble without realizing it.
- Carrying habits of personal extravagance into the business.
- Not understanding business cycles.
- Forgetting about taxes, insurance, and other costs of doing business.
- Mistaking the freedom of being in business for oneself for the liberty to work or not, according to whim.

FIGURE 6.5

CAUSES OF SMALL-BUSINESS FAILURE

Small businesses are more likely to succeed when

- The customer requires a lot of personal attention, as in a beauty parlor.
- The product is not easily made by mass-production techniques (e.g., custom-tailored clothes or custom auto-body work).
- Sales are not large enough to appeal to a large firm (e.g., a novelty shop).
- The neighborhood is not attractive because of crime or poverty. This provides a unique opportunity for small grocery stores, and laundries.
- A large business sells a franchise operation to local buyers. (Don't forget franchising as an excellent way to enter the world of small business.)
- The owner pays attention to new competitors.
- The business is in a growth industry (e.g., computer services or Web design).

owners were also included as business failures. All in all, the good news for entrepreneurs is that business failures are much lower than has traditionally been reported.

Although the chances of business survival may be greater than some used to think, keep in mind that even the most optimistic interpretation of the statistics shows that nearly one out of five businesses that cease operations is left owing money to creditors. Figure 6.5 lists reasons for small-business failures, among which are managerial incompetence and inadequate financial planning.

Choosing the right type of business is critical. Many of the businesses with the lowest failure rates require advanced training to start—veterinary services, dentist practices, medical practices, and so on. While training and degrees may buy security, they do not tend to produce much growth. If you want to be both independent and rich, you need to go after growth. The businesses with the highest odds of significant growth are in manufacturing. But these are not easy businesses to start and are even more difficult to keep going.

In general it seems that the easiest businesses to start are the ones that tend to have the least growth and the greatest failure rate (e.g., restaurants). The easiest businesses to keep alive are difficult ones to get started (e.g., manufacturing). And the ones that can make you rich are the ones that are both hard to start and hard to keep going (e.g., automobile assembly). See Figure 6.6 to get an idea of the business situations that are most likely to lead to success.

When you decide to start your own business, you must think carefully about what kind of business you want. You are not likely to find everything you want in one business—easy entry, security, and reward. Choose those characteristics that matter the most to you; accept the absence of the others; plan, plan, plan; and then go for it!

Imagine yourself starting a small business. What kind of business would it be? How much competition is there? What could you do to make your business more attractive than those of competitors? Would you be willing to work 60 to 70 hours per week?

LEARNING ABOUT SMALL-BUSINESS OPERATIONS

Hundreds of would-be entrepreneurs of all ages have asked the same question: "How can I learn to run my own business?" Many of these people had no idea what kind of business they wanted to start; they simply wanted to be in busi-

What do Bill Gates, Michael Dell, and Steven Jobs all have in common? They all started their companies (Microsoft, Dell Computer, and Apple) while still in college. Today, various programs challenge you to do the same thing. For the North American Collegiate Entrepreneur Awards, budding entrepreneurs are encouraged to submit their business ideas for evaluation. State winners are selected and go on to a national competition, where they are judged by an international panel of experts. The first-place prizewinner receives $5,000.

Sharon Bower, creator and administrator of the North American Awards, brags outwardly about the abilities of the student entrepreneurs who compete. She proudly boasts, "One winner is in the process of taking his computer company public. (selling stock in the company.) Another won a scholarship to Oxford University as a Rhodes Scholar." The 1999 winner was Maisie Jane Bertagna, a sophomore business major at Butte College in Oroville, California. She won with Maisie Jane's California Sunshine Products, a line of 12 different food products, including dry-roasted flavored almonds, caramel corn and almonds, and almond butter. Her business has increased in profits almost 100 percent a year for the past three years. Maisie actually started her business while she was still in high school.

It's never too early to think about making that business opportunity of your dreams a reality. Tahira Abdur-Rahim, 16, earns $400 a month selling homemade lollipops, and Cristina Smith, 13, makes personalized accessories for dogs. Aron Leifer started MultiMedia Audiotext, a company that designs computer software, when he was 16. Now, at 19, he has his own office, seven full-time employees, 87 part-time international freelancers, and a client list that includes Bell Atlantic. Oh yes—he brings in an impressive $50,000 a month. Not bad for a teenager who still lives with his parents.

For information concerning the North American Collegiate Entrepreneur Awards, contact the Jefferson Smurfit Center for Entrepreneurial Studies at www.slu.edu. To learn more online about starting your own business, check out the lessons in the SBA Classroom at www.sba.gov or Quicken's small business advice site at www.quicken.com/small_business. Who knows, someday your name may be on the great entrepreneurs list along with Gates, Dell, and Jobs.

Sources: Sharon Nash, "Teenage Entrepreneurs," *PC Magazine*, May 9, 2000, p. 81; Meridith Levinson, "And a Child Shall Lead Them," *CIO*, February 15, 2000, p. 38; Hilary Rosenberg, "Student Power," *Business Week Online*, June 19, 2000; and Rochelle Sharpe, "Teen Moguls," *Business Week*, May 29, 2000.

ness for themselves. That seems to be a major trend among students today. Therefore, here are some hints for learning about small business.

Learn from Others

Your search for small-business knowledge might begin by investigating your local community college for classes on the subject. There are more than 1,400 entrepreneurship programs in postsecondary schools throughout the United States.[17] One of the best things about such courses is that they bring together entrepreneurs from diverse backgrounds. (Many entrepreneurs have started businesses as students—see the Spotlight on Small Business box.) An excellent way to learn how to run a small business is to talk to others who have already done it. They will tell you that location is critical. They will caution you not to be undercapitalized, that is, not to start without enough money. They will warn you about the problems of finding and retaining good workers. And, most of all, they will tell you to keep good records and hire a good accountant and lawyer before you start. Free advice like this is invaluable.

MAKING ETHICAL DECISIONS ———————— *www.ethicscenter.com/home.htm*

Going Down with the Ship

Suppose you have worked for two years in a company and you see signs that the business is beginning to falter. You and a co-worker have some ideas about how to make a company like your boss's succeed. You are considering quitting your job and starting your own company with your friend. Should you approach other co-workers about working for your new venture? Will you try to lure your old boss's customers to your own business? What are your alternatives? What are the consequences of each alternative? What is the most ethical choice?

Get Some Experience

There is no better way to learn small-business management than by becoming an apprentice or working for a successful entrepreneur. In fact, 42 percent of small-business owners got the idea for their businesses from their prior jobs. The rule of thumb is: Have three years' experience in a comparable business.

Many new entrepreneurs come from corporate management. They are tired of the big-business life or are being laid off because of corporate downsizing. Such managers bring their managerial expertise and enthusiasm with them.

Getting experience before you start your own business isn't a new concept.[18] In fact, way back in 1818, Cornelius Vanderbilt sold his own sailing vessels and went to work for a steamboat company so he could learn the rules of the new game of steam. After learning what he needed to know, he quit, started his own steamship company, and became the first American to accumulate $100 million.

By running a small business part-time, during your off hours or on weekends, you can experience the rewards of working for yourself while still enjoying a regular paycheck. Learning a business while working for someone else may also save you money because you are less likely to make "rookie mistakes" when you start your own business. (See the Making Ethical Decisions box, though, for a scenario that raises a number of questions.)

Take Over a Successful Firm

Small-business management takes time, dedication, and determination. Owners work long hours and rarely take vacations. After many years, they may feel stuck in their business. They may think they can't get out because they have too much time and effort invested. Consequently, there are millions of small-business owners out there eager to get away, at least for a long vacation.

This is where you come in. Find a successful businessperson who owns a small business. Tell him or her that you are eager to learn the business and would like to serve an apprenticeship, that is, a training period. Say that at the end of the training period (one year or so), you would like to help the owner or manager by becoming assistant manager. As assistant manager, you would free the owner to take off weekends and holidays, and to take a long vacation—a good deal for him or her. For another year or so, work very hard to learn all about the business—suppliers, inventory, bookkeeping, customers, promotion, and so on. At the end of two years, make the owner this offer: He or she can retire or work only part-time, and you will take over the business. You can establish a profit-sharing plan for yourself plus a salary. Be generous with yourself; you will earn it if you manage the business. You can even ask for 40 percent or more of the profits.

The owner benefits by keeping ownership in the business and making 60 percent of what he or she earned before—without having to work. You benefit by making 40 percent of the profits of a successful firm. This is an excellent deal for an owner about to retire who is able to keep his or her firm and a healthy profit flow. It is also a clever and successful way to share in the profits of a successful small business without any personal money investment.

If profit sharing doesn't appeal to the owner, you may want to buy the business outright. How do you determine a fair price for a business? Value is based on (1) what the business owns, (2) what it earns, and (3) what makes it unique. Naturally, your accountant will need to help you determine the business's value.

If your efforts to take over the business through either profit sharing or buying fail, you can quit and start your own business fully trained.

MANAGING A SMALL BUSINESS

The Small Business Administration has reported that 90 percent of all small-business failures are a result of poor management. Keep in mind, though, that the term *poor management* covers a number of faults. It could mean poor planning, poor record keeping, poor inventory control, poor promotion, or poor employee relations. Most likely it would include poor capitalization. In the following sections we explore the functions of business in a small-business setting so you can become one of the successful owners:

- Planning your business.
- Financing your business.
- Knowing your customers (marketing).
- Managing your employees (human resource development).
- Keeping records (accounting).

Although all of the functions are important in both the start-up phase and the management phase of the business, the first two functions—planning and financing—are the primary concerns when you start your business. The remaining functions are the heart of the actual running of the business, once it is started.

Begin with Planning

It is amazing how many people are eager to start a small business but have only a vague notion of what they want to do. Eventually they come up with an idea for a business and begin discussing the idea with professors, friends, and other businesspeople. It is at this stage that the entrepreneur needs a business plan. A **business plan** is a detailed written statement that describes the nature of the business, the target market, the advantages the business will have in relation to competition, and the resources and qualifications of the owner(s). A business plan forces potential owners of small businesses to be quite specific about the products or services they intend to offer. They must analyze the competition, calculate how much money they need to start, and cover other details of operation. A business plan is also mandatory for talking with bankers or other investors.

Michael Celello, president of the People's Commercial Bank, says that fewer than 10 percent of prospective borrowers come to a bank adequately prepared. He offers several tips to small-business owners, including picking a bank that serves businesses the size of yours, having a good accountant

business plan
A detailed written statement that describes the nature of the business, the target market, the advantages the business will have in relation to competition, and the resources and qualifications of the owner(s).

The dot.com express was riding high in the late 1990s. Entrepreneurs felt confident that the clear path to success was adding .com to their company's name. Well as this cartoon implies, things have changed. It's not enough for a company to "sound" innovative; experience, knowledge, and a solid business plan are still the hallmarks of building a start-up company into a long-lasting business success. Can you name three .com companies that have failed within the past year?

prepare a complete set of financial statements and a personal balance sheet, making an appointment before going to the bank, going to the bank with an accountant and all the necessary financial information, and demonstrating to the banker that you're a person of good character: civic minded and respected in business and community circles. Finally, he says to ask for all the money you need, be specific, and be prepared to personally guarantee the loan.

Writing a Business Plan

A good business plan takes a long time to write, but you've got to convince your readers in five minutes not to throw the plan away. While there is no such thing as a perfect business plan, prospective entrepreneurs do think out the smallest details. Jerrold Carrington of Inroads Capital Partners advises that one of the most important parts of the business plan is the executive summary. The summary has to catch the reader's interest. Bankers receive many business plans every day. "You better grab me up front," says Carrington. The box on p. 183 gives you an outline of a comprehensive business plan.

Sometimes one of the most difficult tasks in undertaking complex projects such as writing a business plan is knowing where to start. There are many computer software programs on the market now to help you get organized. One highly rated business-plan program is Plan Write by Business Resource Software. You can find online help with the MiniPlan (www.miniplan.com), a free interactive Web tool that guides you through the business-plan writing process.

Getting the completed business plan into the right hands is almost as important as getting the right information in the plan. Finding the funding requires research. Next we will discuss some of the many sources of money available to new business ventures. All of them call for a comprehensive business plan. The time and effort you invest before starting a business will pay off many times later. With small businesses, the big payoff is survival.

Getting Money to Fund a Small Business

An entrepreneur has several potential sources of capital: personal savings, relatives, former employers, banks, finance companies, venture capitalists, government agencies such as the Small Business Administration (SBA), the Farmers Home Administration, and the Economic Development Authority.[19] You may even want to consider borrowing from a potential supplier to your future business. Helping you get started may be in the supplier's interest if there is a chance you will be a big customer later. It's usually not a good idea to ask such an investor for money at the outset. Begin by asking for advice; if the supplier likes your plan, he or she may be willing to help you with funding.

Technology-minded entrepreneurs often have the best shot at attracting start-up capital. Not only are such potential businesses more attractive to venture capitalists and state governments, but also the federal government has several grant programs that provide funds for computer-related ventures.

OUTLINE OF A COMPREHENSIVE BUSINESS PLAN

A good business plan is between 25 and 50 pages long and takes at least six months to write.

Cover letter

Only one thing is certain when you go hunting for money to start a business: You won't be the only hunter out there. You need to make potential funders want to read *your* business plan instead of the hundreds of others on their desks. Your cover letter should summarize the most attractive points of your project in as few words as possible. Be sure to address the letter to the potential investor by name. "To whom it may concern" or "Dear Sir" is not the best way to win an investor's support.

Section 1—Executive Summary

Begin with a two-page or three-page management summary of the proposed venture. Include a short description of the business, and discuss major goals and objectives.

Section 2—Company Background

Describe company operations to date (if any), potential legal considerations, and areas of risk and opportunity. Summarize the firm's financial condition, and include past and current balance sheets, income and cash-flow statements, and other relevant financial records (you will read about these financial statements in Chapter 18). It is also wise to include a description of insurance coverage. Investors want to be assured that death or other mishaps do not pose major threats to the company.

Section 3—Management Team

Include an organization chart, job descriptions of listed positions, and detailed résumés of the current and proposed executives. A mediocre idea with a proven management team is funded more often than a great idea with an inexperienced team. Managers should have expertise in all disciplines necessary to start and run a business. If not, mention outside consultants who will serve in these roles and describe their qualifications.

Section 4—Financial Plan

Provide five-year projections for income, expenses, and funding sources. Don't assume the business will grow in a straight line. Adjust your planning to allow for funding at various stages of the company's growth. Explain the rationale and assumptions used to determine the estimates. Assumptions should be reasonable and based on industry/historical trends. Make sure all totals add up and are consistent throughout the plan. If necessary, hire a professional accountant or financial analyst to prepare these statements.

Stay clear of excessively ambitious sales projections; rather, offer best-case, expected, and worst-case scenarios. These not only reveal how sensitive the bottom line is to sales fluctuations but also serve as good management guides.

Section 5—Capital Required

Indicate the amount of capital needed to commence or continue operations, and describe how these funds are to be used. Make sure the totals are the same as the ones on the cash-flow statement. This area will receive a great deal of review from potential investors, so it must be clear and concise.

Section 6—Marketing Plan

Don't underestimate the competition. Review industry size, trends, and the target market segment. Sources like *American Demographics* magazine and the *Rand McNally Commercial Atlas and Marketing Guide* can help you put a plan together. Discuss strengths and weaknesses of the product or service. The most important things investors want to know are what makes the product more desirable than what's already available and whether the product can be patented. Compare pricing to the competition's. Forecast sales in dollars and units. Outline sales, advertising, promotion, and public relations programs. Make sure the costs agree with those projected in the financial statements.

Section 7—Location Analysis

In retailing and certain other industries, the location of the business is one of the most important factors. Provide a comprehensive demographic analysis of consumers in the area of the proposed store as well as a traffic-pattern analysis and vehicular and pedestrian counts.

Section 8—Manufacturing Plan

Describe minimum plant size, machinery required, production capacity, inventory and inventory-control methods, quality control, plant personnel requirements, and so on. Estimates of product costs should be based on primary research.

Section 9—Appendix

Include all marketing research on the product or service (off-the-shelf reports, article reprints, etc.) and other information about the product concept or market size. Provide a bibliography of all the reference materials you consulted. This section should demonstrate that the proposed company won't be entering a declining industry or market segment.

If you would like to see sample business plans that successfully secured funding, go to the sample business plan resource center at www.bplans.com/samples. You can also learn more about writing business plans on the SBA website at www.sba.gov/starting.

FROM THE PAGES OF — BusinessWeek   *www.ecompanies.com*

Creating Businesses at Internet Speed

Imagine walking into a sparsely furnished, dimly lit office with gaping holes in the ceiling that expose concrete beams and dirty air-conditioning ducts. Your first reaction might be to turn around and walk right out. That would be a big mistake. This eighth-floor hovel in Santa Monica, California, holds the temporary offices of eCompanies, one of the hottest Internet incubator companies in the United States.

The brainchild of Internet heavyweights Jake Winebaum (former head of Internet business for Walt Disney) and Sky Dayton (founder of Internet service provider Earthlink Network Inc.), eCompanies is housed in these rather austere quarters until its new offices are ready for occupancy. Yet eCompanies' lack of regal setting has not slowed down the enthusiasm of mouse-clicking entrepreneurs hoping to win a spot in this richly funded incubator, which hopes to have eight companies leave the incubator each year. Since eCompanies opened its website in mid-1999, it has received as many as 300 proposals a day.

Typically, start-up entrepreneurs can spend up to 90 percent of their time raising money, securing partners, finding talent, and performing countless other activities associated with starting a company. That leaves them with very little time to devote to the two activities that will make the company win in the market: product develop-ment and marketing. Incubators such as eCompanies provide start-up entrepreneurs with all the services they need so they can concentrate on getting to market quickly with the right product. The 22 employees of eCompanies include experts in finance, marketing, strat-egy, and Web design. Entrepreneurs can tap a whole team of Internet veterans who've done it before.

The incubator strives to take Web wannabes from business plan to economic reality in six months. To ac-complish this ambitious task, eCompanies has estab-lished a $130 million venture fund to finance the new Internet companies once they are ready to go out on their own. Investors in the fund include heavy hitters such as Disney, Times Mirror, SunAmerica, and Goldman Sachs.

Although the owners are successful Internet entre-preneurs themselves, they are unknowns in the venture capital business. Frank Creer, managing director of Zone Ventures, a Los Angeles venture capital affiliate, agrees: "They haven't proven they can pick and choose." Winebaum and Dayton admit they are novices to venture capital, but they are confident that they can pick as well as click. It will be interesting to see what they hatch!

Source: Larry Armstrong and Ron Grover, "Where Net Startups Go to Be Born," *Business Week*, September 13, 1999, pp. 46–48; and Arlene Weintraub, "Can Icebox Heat Up Online Animation?" *Business Week*, April 11, 2000.

Other than personal savings, individual investors are the primary source of capital for most entrepreneurs. Such investors provide 6 of every 10 dollars for firms with fewer than four employees and sales of under $150,000 a year. About $56 billion in risk capital comes from these angel investors each year.[20] *Angel investors* are private individuals who invest their own money in poten-tially hot new companies before they go public. Internet sites, such as www. financehub.com and www.garage.com, are now available that link entrepre-neurs with potential investors. (See the *Business Week* box for a description of an Internet incubator.)

venture capitalists
Individuals or companies that invest in new businesses in exchange for partial ownership of those businesses.

Investors known as **venture capitalists** may finance your project—for a price. Venture capitalists may ask for a hefty stake (as much as 60 percent) in your company in exchange for the cash to start your business. If the ven-ture capitalist demands too large a stake, you could lose control of the busi-ness. According to the SBA, venture capitalists invest approximately $10 bil-lion a year, but they fund fewer than 2,000 ventures per year, each needing $5 million or more.[21] Therefore, if you're a very small company, you don't have a very good chance getting venture capital. You'd have a better chance finding an angel investor. If your proposed venture does require millions of dollars to start, experts recommend that you talk with at least five investment firms and their clients in order to find the right venture capitalist. You can get a list of venture capitalists from the Small Business Administration. Ask for the brochure called "Directory of Operating Small Business Investment Companies." Or visit the National Venture Capital Association at www.nvca.org. You can also follow the ups and downs of venture capital availability in *Inc.* magazine.

The Small Business Administration (SBA)

The Small Business Administration (SBA) is a valuable source of expertise on starting a new business (see Figure 6.7). The SBA started the microloan demonstration program in 1992. The program is administered by 101 nonprofit organizations chosen by the SBA in all states except Wyoming. Rather than base the awarding of loans on collateral, credit history, or previous business success, these programs decide worthiness on the basis of belief in the borrowers' integrity and the soundness of their business ideas. The SBA microloan program helps people like Karla Brown start their own businesses. Newly divorced and facing a mountain of debt, Brown needed to find a way to support her daughter. She bought two buckets of flowers and headed to the subway to sell them. Continuing the process, she made enough money to keep a steady inventory, but she needed help from her friends to pay her bills. She thought she could make a living if she could take her flowers out of the subway and into a store. She obtained a $19,000 SBA microloan and rented a store in the heart of Boston, soon after, Brown's flower shop brought in $100,000 in sales.

You may also want to consider requesting funds from the **Small Business Investment Company** (SBIC) **Program.** SBICs are private investment companies licensed by the Small Business Administration to lend money to small businesses. An SBIC must have a minimum of $1 million in capital and can borrow up to four dollars from the SBA for each dollar of capital it has. It lends to or invests in small businesses that meet its criteria. Often SBICs are able to keep defaults to a minimum by identifying a business's trouble spots early; giving entrepreneurs advice; and, in some cases, rescheduling payments.[22]

Perhaps the best place for young entrepreneurs to start shopping for an SBA loan is a Small Business Development Center (SBDC). SBDCs are funded jointly by the federal government and individual states and are usually associated with state universities. SBDCs can help you evaluate the feasibility of your idea, develop your business plan, and complete your funding application—all for free.

If you want to know what loan officers look for when reviewing SBA guaranteed loan applications, invest $69 for the book *SBA Lending Made Easy,* put out by the American Bankers Association (800-338-0626) to help out loan officers.

Government can do a great deal to promote entrepreneurship and it in fact does. For instance, a major obstacle to starting a new business is a lack of financing. Most entrepreneurs must use their own financial resources or borrow from friends and family. Some however, like Nita and Pravin Patel are fortunate enough to get financial support from the Small Business Administration (SBA). The Patels were able to purchase a pharmacy in Philadelphia using a Small Business Administration backed loan.

Small Business Investment Company (SBIC) Program
A program through which private investment companies licensed by the Small Business Administration lend money to small businesses.

FIGURE 6.7

TYPES OF SBA FINANCIAL
ASSISTANCE

The SBA may provide the following types of financial assistance:

- Direct loans—loans made directly to selected small-business owners who have difficulty securing conventional loans (e.g., disabled owners, veterans, and other special cases).
- Guaranteed loans—loans made by a financial institution that the government will repay if the borrower stops making payments. The maximum individual loan guarantee is capped at $750,000.
- Participation loans—combination direct and guaranteed loans. The SBA will guarantee part of the loan and will lend the balance directly.
- Loans from minority enterprise small business investment companies (MESBICs)—finance companies that make loans to minority-owned businesses.
- Loans from the Women's Financing Section—guaranteed loans to qualified women for less than $50,000, created by the Women's Business Ownership Act of 1988.
- Loans from the Women's Prequalification Pilot Loan Program—loans to businesses that are at least 51 percent owned and operated by women; loan size is limited to $250,000.
- Microloans—amounts ranging from $100 to $25,000 (average $10,000) to people such as single mothers and public housing tenants.

The SBA recently reduced the size of its application from 150 pages to 1 page for loans under $50,000.

You may want to write or call the SBA in Washington, D.C., for the latest information about SBA programs. The SBA's address is 1441 L Street NW, Washington, D.C. 20005. The telephone number of the Small Business Administration Answer Desk is 800-U-ASK-SBA. The SBA home page (www.sba.gov) gives detailed information on the agency and other business services.

Obtaining money from banks, venture capitalists, and government sources is very difficult for most small businesses. (You will learn more about financing in Chapter 19.) Those who do survive the planning and financing of their new ventures are eager to get their businesses up and running. Your success in running a business depends on many factors. Three important factors for success are knowing your customers, managing your employees, and keeping efficient records.

PROGRESS
ASSESSMENT

- A business plan is probably the most important document a small-business owner will ever create. There are nine sections in the business plan outline on p. 183. Can you describe at least five of those sections now?
- What are three of the reasons given by the Small Business Administration for why small businesses fail financially?

Knowing Your Customers

market
People with unsatisfied wants and needs who have both the resources and the willingness to buy.

One of the most important elements of small-business success is knowing the market. In business, a **market** consists of people with unsatisfied wants and needs who have both the resources and the willingness to buy. For example, we can confidently state that most of our students have the willingness to take a Caribbean cruise during their spring break. However, few of them have the resources necessary to satisfy this want. Would they be considered a good market for the local travel agency to pursue?

Once you have identified your market and its needs, you must set out to fill those needs. The way to meet your customers' needs is to offer top quality at a fair price with great service. Remember it isn't enough to get customers—you have to keep them. As Victoria Jackson, founder of the $50 million Victoria Jackson Cosmetics Company, says of the stars who push her products on television infomercials, "All the glamorous faces in the world wouldn't mean a thing if my customers weren't happy with the product and didn't come back for more." Everything must be geared to bring the customers the satisfaction they deserve.

You will gain more insights about markets in Chapters 13 and 14. Now let's consider the importance of effectively managing the employees who help you serve your market.

Managing Employees

As a business grows, it becomes impossible for an entrepreneur to oversee every detail, even if he or she is putting in 60 hours per week. This means that hiring, training, and motivating employees is critical.

It is not easy to find good, qualified help when you offer less money, skimpier benefits, and less room for advancement than larger firms do. That is one reason employee relations is such an important part of small-business management. Employees of small companies are often more satisfied with their jobs than are their counterparts in big business. Why? Quite often they find their jobs more challenging, their ideas more accepted, and their bosses more respectful. Over 90 percent of the top growth companies listed by *Inc.* magazine share ownership and profits with their employees.

Often entrepreneurs reluctantly face the reality that to keep growing, they must delegate authority to others. Nagging questions such as "Who should be delegated authority?" and "How much control should they have?" create perplexing problems.

This can be a particularly touchy issue in small businesses with long-term employees, and in family businesses. As you might expect, entrepreneurs who have built their companies from scratch often feel compelled to promote employees who have been with them from the start—even when those employees aren't qualified to serve as managers. Common sense probably tells you this could be detrimental to the business.

The same can be true of family-run businesses that are expanding. Attitudes such as "You can't fire family" or you must promote certain workers because "they're family" can hinder growth. Entrepreneurs can best serve themselves and the business if they gradually recruit and groom employees for management positions. By doing this, entrepreneurs can enhance trust and support of the manager among other employees and themselves.

When Heida Thurlow of Chantal Cookware suffered an extended illness, she let her employees handle the work she once had insisted on doing herself. The experience transformed her company from an entrepreneurial company into a managerial one. She says, "Over the long run that makes us stronger than we were." You'll learn more about managing employees in Chapters 7 through 12.

Keeping Records

Small-business owners often say that the most important assistance they received in starting and managing the business involved accounting. A businessperson who sets up an effective accounting system early will save much grief later. Computers make record keeping much easier and enable a small-business owner to follow the progress of the business (sales, expenses, profits) on a daily basis. An inexpensive computer system can also help owners with other record-keeping chores, such as inventory control, customer records, and payroll.

A good accountant is invaluable in setting up such systems and showing you how to keep the system operating smoothly. Many business failures are caused by poor accounting practices. A good accountant can help make decisions such as whether to buy or lease equipment and whether to own or rent the building. Help may also be provided for tax planning, financial forecasting, choosing sources of financing, and writing up requests for funds.

Other small-business owners may tell you where to find an accountant experienced in small business. It pays to shop around for advice. You'll learn more about accounting in Chapter 18.

Looking for Help

Small-business owners have learned, sometimes the hard way, that they need outside consulting advice early in the process. This is especially true of legal, tax, and accounting advice but may also be true of marketing, finance, and other areas. Most small and medium-size firms cannot afford to hire such experts as employees, so they must turn to outside assistance.[23]

A necessary and invaluable aide is a competent, experienced lawyer—one who knows and understands small businesses. Partners have a way of forgetting agreements unless the contract is written by a lawyer and signed. Lawyers can help with a variety of matters, including leases, contracts, and protection against liabilities. Lawyers don't have to be expensive. In fact, there are several prepaid legal plans that offer services (such as drafting legal documents) for an annual rate of $150 to $350. Lenders that offer legal plans for small businesses include Prodigy (800-284-5933), AT&T Home Office Network (800-446-6311 extension 1000), and Caldwell Legal (800-222-3035). Of course, you can find plenty of legal services online. For example Parsons Technology (www.parsonstech.com) and E-Z Legal Forms Inc. (www.e-zlegal.com) offer prepared legal documents such as agreements and contracts.

Marketing decisions should be made long before a product is produced or a store opened. An inexpensive marketing research study may help you determine where to locate, whom to select as your target market, and what would

"Listen and learn" is advice that entrepreneurs should heed. Jim Blasingame of the Talk America Radio Network considers his 2-year-old radio talk show the "talking partner of small business." Each show features three experts and includes topics such as credit-card fraud, demographics, and financing techniques. Listeners can either call in or e-mail their questions. What are some other sources of advice for entrepreneurs?

be an effective strategy for reaching those people. Thus, a marketing consultant with small-business experience can be of great help to you.

Given the marketing power of the Internet, your business will benefit from a presence on the Internet even if you do not sell products or services directly from the Web. In fact, 64 percent of the small businesses surveyed in 1999 said that they used the Web to establish a business presence.[24] For example, Brandt's, a small restaurant in St. Louis, has a website that features the day's menu and specials, highlights the credentials of the head chef, and displays photos of the restaurant. It also includes an interactive calendar that lists the scheduled live entertainment. Click on the names of the entertainers to learn what kind of music they play. Some entertainers even include audio samples of their work for you to preview. Websites such as workz.com (www.workz.com) gives you access to tools to build your own website, including sources for Web graphic design and search engine submission tactics.

Two other invaluable experts are a commercial loan officer and an insurance agent. The commercial loan officer can help you design an acceptable business plan and give you valuable financial advice as well as lend you money when you need it. An insurance agent will explain all the risks associated with a small business and how to cover them most efficiently with insurance and other means (e.g., safety devices and sprinkler systems).

An important source of information for small businesses is the **Service Corps of Retired Executives (SCORE).** This SBA office has 13,000 volunteers who provide consulting services for small businesses at no cost (except for expenses). You can find a SCORE counselor by calling your local SBA office or SCORE's Washington, D.C., number, (202) 205-6762. The SBA also sponsors volunteers from industry, trade associations, and education who counsel small businesses. They are called the **Active Corps of Executives (ACE).**

Often a local college has business professors who will advise small-business owners for a small fee or for free. Some universities have clubs or programs that provide consulting services by MBA candidates for a nominal fee. For example, Columbia University's Small Business Consulting Group charges only $15 an hour for the consulting services of a team of three MBA students with complementary skills in marketing, finance, and management.

It also is wise to seek the counsel of other small-business owners. Other sources of counsel include local chambers of commerce, the Better Business Bureau, national and local trade associations, the business reference section of your library, and many small-business-related sites on the Internet. There are websites that can help you find the help you need by matching your consulting needs with the proper consultant. Such sites include the Consultants' Bureau (www.kts-cb.com) and National Consultant Referrals Inc. (www.referrals.com).

Service Corps of Retired Executives (SCORE)
An SBA service with 13,000 volunteers who provide consulting services for small businesses free (except for expenses).

Active Corps of Executives (ACE)
SBA volunteers from industry, trade associations, and education who counsel small businesses.

GOING INTERNATIONAL: SMALL-BUSINESS PROSPECTS

As we noted in Chapter 3, there are only about 280 million people in the United States, but nearly 6 billion people in the world. Obviously, the world market is potentially a much larger, much more lucrative market for small businesses than the United States alone. In spite of that potential, most small businesses still do not think internationally. Only 20 percent of small-business executives say they export ► **P.64** ◄. By Commerce Department estimates, there are 18,000 manufacturers (most of them small) that could export their products but don't. Only 2,000 U.S. firms are responsible for 80 percent of the nation's exports. Figure 6.8 lists the industries with the highest potential in global markets.

FIGURE 6.8

U.S. INDUSTRIES WITH THE HIGHEST POTENTIAL IN INTERNATIONAL MARKETS

1. Computers and peripherals (hardware).
2. Telecommunications equipment and systems.
3. Computer software and services.
4. Medical instruments, equipment, and supplies.
5. Electronic parts.
6. Analytical and scientific laboratory instruments.
7. Industrial process control instruments.
8. Aircraft and parts, and avionics and ground support equipment.
9. Automotive parts and service equipment and accessories.
10. Electronic production and test equipment.
11. Electronic power generation and distribution systems and transmission equipment.
12. Food processing and packaging equipment and machinery.
13. Safety and security equipment.
14. Printing and graphic arts equipment.
15. Water resources equipment.

Global markets offer tremendous growth potential for small businesses. Mindy and David Goldenberg increased their family-owned business's sales by 10 percent by exporting their Chew-ets candies to countries in South America. Working with the State of Pennsylvania's Agriculture Department, the two entrepreneurs were able to locate global distribution for their sweets. They acted fast and built a growing market. What products do you feel have the greatest potential for penetrating global markets?

Why are these companies missing the boat to the huge global markets? Primarily because the voyage involves a few major hurdles: (1) Financing is often difficult to find, (2) many would-be exporters don't know how to get started, (3) potential global businesspeople do not understand the cultural differences of prospective markets, and (4) the bureaucratic paperwork can bury a small business.[25]

Besides the fact that most of the world's market lies outside the United States, there are other good reasons for going international. For instance, exporting products can absorb excess inventory, soften downturns in the domestic market, and extend product lives. It can also spice up dull routines.

Small businesses have several advantages over large businesses in international trade:

- Overseas buyers enjoy dealing with individuals rather than with large corporate bureaucracies.
- Small companies can usually begin shipping much faster.
- Small companies provide a wide variety of suppliers.
- Small companies can give more personal service and more undivided attention, because each overseas account is a major source of business to them.

The growth potential of small businesses overseas is phenomenal. For example, John Stollenwerk found customers for his Wisconsin-made shoes in Italy, and Ohio's Andrew Bohnengel opened his tape company to the rest of the world by adopting the metric standard. Web-based business applications are helping small businesses cross boundaries like never before. CPI Process Systems Inc., a six-employee import/export oil-field equipment company in Houston, Texas, won a contract away from Swiss giant ABB to build a power station in China. CPI won the

REACHING BEYOND OUR BORDERS

www.ashoka.org

Building Global Communities through Entrepreneurship

When he was five years old, Bill Drayton exhibited his entrepreneurial passion by selling small items he made to his parents' dinner guests. Later, as a student at Harvard University and then Yale Law School, he broadened his mission and launched initiatives that involved fellow students in cultural and social issues. Today, almost 50 years after his first entrepreneurial venture, Drayton has blended his entrepreneurial passion and commitment to social change into a new concept he calls "social entrepreneurship." Drayton is the founder of Ashoka, an international organization with a worldwide staff of 89 based in Arlington, Virginia, that has supported 937 "social entrepreneurs" in 33 countries.

According to Drayton, "Social entrepreneurs are very rare. They see their role in life is to change society for the better. Our purpose is to find those individuals that can have a giant impact." Ashoka offers stipends that range from $2,500 to $20,000 a year to entrepreneurs who demonstrate both business skills and social sensitivities. For example, Magdaleno Rose-Avila, a youth worker in El Salvador, used his entrepreneurial talent to establish Homeboys United, an antigang effort that encourages finding solutions from within gangs that lead youngsters away from violent lifestyles. Marilena Lazzarini and Josue

Rios founded the Institute for Consumer Defense in Brazil after the Brazilian government froze bank accounts and eliminated nearly $14 billion in people's savings. The organization sued on behalf of the citizens for restoration of their savings—and won. According to Drayton, "What's the point to all these efforts? Change the world."

Success didn't come easy. Like many entrepreneurs, Drayton found his entrepreneurial dream had trouble igniting financial interest at first. He refused to give up. Drayton personally knocked on the doors of countless foundations and corporations asking for support. He received little. Finally, persistence paid off when the John D. and Catherine T. MacArthur Foundation awarded Drayton $200,000 over five years. The grant helped pay the bills and also gave the company credibility. Today, Ashoka operates with close to a $7 million budget. It's also been the leader in promulgating the concept that social entrepreneurship can be a rewarding career.

Source: "Entrepreneur Establishes Internet Global Organization of Friends," *Business Wire*, May 5, 1999; Scott Kirsner, "Social Entrepreneurs," FastCompany, November 2000, pp. 314-24; and Albert R Hunt, "Social Entrepreneurs: Compassionate and Tough-Minded," *The Wall Street Journal*, July 13, 2000, p. A27.

---

deal thanks to a strong relationship with small overseas suppliers—a relationship facilitated by frequent e-mail. Dave Hammond, inventor and founder of Wizard Vending, began to push his gum-ball machines into the international market via a website. In the site's first year, Hammond sold machines in Austria, Belgium, and Germany, and the Internet sales accounted for 10 percent of the company's revenues. (See the Reaching Beyond Our Borders box for a description of international "social entrepreneurship.")

There is an abundance of information about exporting on the Internet. A good place to start is with the Department of Commerce's Bureau of Export Administration (www.bxa.doc.gov). Other sources of information include the SBA's list of international business resources (www.sba.gov/hotlist/internat.html).

PROGRESS ASSESSMENT

- Why do many small businesses avoid doing business overseas?
- What are some of the advantages small businesses have over large businesses in selling in global markets?

SUMMARY

1. Explain why people are willing to take the risks of entrepreneurship, list the attributes of successful entrepreneurs, describe the benefits of entrepreneurial teams and intrapreneurs, and explain the growth of home-based and Web-based businesses.

1. There are many reasons people are willing to take the risks of entrepreneurship.
   - *What are a few of the reasons people start their own businesses?*
   Reasons include profit, independence, opportunity, and challenge.
   - *What are the attributes of successful entrepreneurs?*
   Successful entrepreneurs are self-directed, self-nurturing, action-oriented, highly energetic, and tolerant of uncertainty.
   - *What have modern entrepreneurs done to ensure longer terms of management?*
   They have formed entrepreneurial teams that have expertise in the many different skills needed to start and manage a business.
   - *What is a micropreneur?*
   Micropreneurs are people willing to accept the risk of starting and managing the type of business that remains small, lets them do the kind of work they want to do, and offers them a balanced lifestyle.
   - *What is intrapreneuring?*
   Intrapreneuring is the establishment of entrepreneurial centers within a larger firm where people can innovate and develop new product ideas internally.
   - *Why has there been such an increase in the number of home-based and Web-based businesses in the last few years?*
   The increase in power and decrease in price of computer technology has leveled the field and made it possible for small businesses to compete against larger companies—regardless of location.

2. Discuss the importance of small business to the American economy and summarize the major causes of small-business failure.

2. Of all the nonfarm businesses in the United States, almost 97 percent are considered small by the Small Business Administration.
   - *Why are small businesses important to the U.S. economy?*
   Small business accounts for over 40 percent of GDP. Perhaps more important to tomorrow's graduates, 80 percent of American workers' first jobs are in small businesses.
   - *What does the **small** in small business mean?*
   The Small Business Administration defines a small business as one that is independently owned and operated, not dominant in its field of operation, and meets certain standards of size in terms of employees or sales (depends on the size of others in the industry).
   - *Why do many small businesses fail?*
   Many small businesses fail because of managerial incompetence and inadequate financial planning. See Figure 6.5 (p. 177) for a list of causes of business failure.

3. Summarize ways to learn about how small businesses operate.

3. Most people have no idea how to go about starting a small business.
   - *What hints would you give someone who wants to learn about starting a small business?*
   First, learn from others. Take courses and talk with some small-business owners. Second, get some experience working for others. Third, take over a successful firm. Finally, study the latest in small-business management techniques, including the use of computers for things like payroll, inventory control, and mailing lists.

4. Analyze what it takes to start and run a small business.

4. Writing a business plan is the first step in organizing a business.
   - *What goes into a business plan?*
   See the box on p. 183.

- *What sources of funds should someone wanting to start a new business consider investigating?*

A new entrepreneur has several sources of capital: personal savings, relatives, former employers, banks, finance companies, venture capital organizations, government agencies, and more.

- *What are some of the special problems that small-business owners have in dealing with employees?*

Small-business owners often have difficulty finding competent employees and grooming employees for management responsibilities.

- *Where can budding entrepreneurs find help in starting their businesses?*

Help can be found from many sources: accountants, lawyers, marketing researchers, loan officers, insurance agents, the SBA, SBDCs, SBICs, and even college professors.

5. The future growth of some small businesses is in foreign markets.

- *What are some advantages small businesses have over large businesses in global markets?*

Foreign buyers enjoy dealing with individuals rather than large corporations because (1) small companies provide a wider variety of suppliers and can ship products more quickly and (2) small companies give more personal service.

- *Why don't more small businesses start trading internationally?*

There are several reasons: (1) financing is often difficult to find, (2) many people don't know how to get started, (3) many do not understand the cultural differences of foreign markets, and (4) the bureaucratic red tape is often overwhelming.

5. Outline the advantages and disadvantages small businesses have in entering global markets.

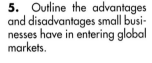

Active Corps of Executives (ACE) 189
business plan 181
entrepreneurial team 168
entrepreneurship 166

incubators 175
intrapreneurs 174
market 186
micropreneurs 169
Service Corps of Retired Executives (SCORE) 189

small business 176
Small-business investment company (SBIC) 185
venture capitalists 184

---

1. Find issues of *Entrepreneur, Success,* and *Inc.* magazines in the library or on the Internet. Read about the entrepreneurs who are heading today's dynamic new businesses. Write a profile about one entrepreneur.

2. Select a small business that looks attractive as a career possibility for you. Talk to at least one person who manages such a business. Ask how he or she started the business. Ask about financing; personnel problems (hiring, firing, training, scheduling); accounting problems; and other managerial matters. Prepare a summary of your findings, including whether the job was rewarding, interesting, and challenging—and why or why not.

3. Contact your local Small Business Administration office by visiting a local office or by going to the organization's website at www.sbaonline.sba.gov. Learn as much as possible about the programs and sources of information offered there.

4. Select a small business in your area that has gone out of business. List the factors you think led to its failure. Recommend actions the business owners' might have taken to prevent the failure.

5. Choose a partner from among your classmates and put together a list of factors that might mean the difference between success and failure of a new company entering the business software industry. Can small start-ups realistically hope to compete with companies such as Microsoft and Intel? Discuss the list and your conclusions in class.

TAKING IT TO THE NET

Purpose

To assess your potential to succeed as an entrepreneur and to evaluate a sample business plan.

Exercise

1. Go to www.bizmove.com/other/quiz.htm and take the interactive entrepreneurial quiz to find out if you have the qualities to be a successful entrepreneur.

2. If you have entrepreneurial traits and decide you would like to start your own business, you will need to develop a business plan. Go to www.quicken.com/small_business/cch/tools/retailer.rtf and review the business plan for Joe's Redhots. Although Joe's plan does not follow the same format as the business plan outline on p. xxx, does it contain all of the necessary information listed in the outline? If not, what is missing?

PRACTICING MANAGEMENT DECISIONS

CASE

BMOC: STARTING A SMALL BUSINESS AT SCHOOL

Many students do not wait until they complete school before they try to get their feet wet in small-business management. Quite a few go beyond the planning stage and actually run their businesses while still in school. For example, high school senior Jason Bernard runs his drawing firm, called Architectural Rendering, from his bedroom. Other young people look around, see thousands of students, and try to develop small businesses that would appeal to students. For example, some students assemble and sell "home emergency kits" for students returning in the fall. The kits contain items like pens, chocolate chip cookies, aspirin, and other college "necessities." The kits are sold to the parents and distributed to students the first week of class as a start-the-year-right gift from home.

Some students produce and sell calendars with pictures of beautiful women or male "hunks" on campus. Others sell desk mats with advertising messages on the sides. Some students become salespeople for beer companies, cosmetic companies, and other traditional firms. They, too, feel as if they are in their own business on campus, because they have exclusive sales rights but don't have to assume as many risks.

One student earns more than his professors by selling ice cream from a truck. Others try to learn the retail business by delivering pizza or other fast foods. Some students have started moving services, moving students' goods from home to school and back.

Dick Gilbertson considered a number of options when he was a student at Indiana University. He felt students might enjoy having food other than pizza and subs delivered to the dorms. His research showed that students preferred McDonald's hamburgers and Taco Bell burritos. Students said they were willing to pay $1.00 more for delivery of a Big Mac, fries, and a Coke rather than ride the mile or so to McDonald's. Gilbertson's company, Fast Breaks, now serves 13,000 students. Guess who his partner is? A professor of entrepreneurship at the university.

Jimmy Enriquez was busy getting a degree in accounting at the University of Texas when he started two companies. One is a construction-site cleaning business run by his sister. It has 15 employees, grosses about $4,000 a week, and has expanded to Dallas and Houston. The other business is a vending company that leases Foosball games. Foosball was dead when Jimmy and his brother Rocky set out. But they started Foosball leagues, let beginners play for free, and built a prosperous business. Jimmy's advice to potential entrepreneurs: "If you wait until you're out of school and working for somebody else, you're going to get used to that big car—and you're not going to want to gamble with that stuff. It's better to start a company when you're a student, while you're still used to driving a junker and living like a dog." Jimmy started a University of Texas entrepreneur club that now has 260 members. It is one of more than 350 entrepreneurship clubs on college campuses across the United States. The Association of Collegiate Entrepreneurs published a list of the top 100 businesses started by people under 30. All are worth over $1 million.

College campuses aren't the only places to find guidance in entrepreneurship. The National Foundation for Teaching Entrepreneurship to Handicapped and Disadvantaged Youth in Newark, New Jersey, trains former drug dealers, street toughs, and special-education students to sell goods and services. Their businesses range from sneakers and lingerie sales to manicures and car repair. Maybe you should consider getting started now, too.

Decision Questions

1. What are the advantages and potential problems of starting a business while in school?
2. What kinds of entrepreneurs are operating around your school? Talk to them and learn from their experiences.
3. What opportunities exist for satisfying student needs at your school? Pick one idea, write a business plan, and discuss it in class (unless it is so good you don't want to share it; in that case, good luck).

VIDEO CASE

JAY GOLTZ, ARTISTS' FRAME SERVICE

Starting with $5,000 he saved from summer jobs and a determination to succeed, Jay Goltz built his business the hard way—from the ground up. Goltz was fresh out of college with an accounting degree when he started Artists' Frame Service in 1978. Artists' Frame Service is now a $9 million business employing 120 people at its main location, a 35,000-square-foot showroom and production facility in Chicago. The custom picture-framing facility is 30 times the size of the industry average, making it the world's largest.

People are willing to take the risks of starting a business for many reasons, including profit, independence, challenge, and opportunity. Goltz recognized the opportunities in picture framing since most frame shops at that time did not focus on modern management principles. Goltz maintains that most successful businesses aren't based on new concepts, but rather are great executions of old businesses. He uses Nike as an example. People have been making gym shoes for 75 years; Nike just executed it better. Picture framing was not a new concept, but Goltz started Artists' Frame Service with the theory that pleasing customers was the key to business success. He believed that good service and high-quality framing were the keys to pleasing customers. He offered his customers low prices through aggressive purchasing and increased volume of framing materials. He decided to give his customers a one-week turnaround, whereas other shops took six to eight weeks.

Goltz actively shares his business acumen with other entrepreneurs through his Boss School seminars. Since he was out on his own from the beginning of his career, Goltz can explain the emotional and intellectual transition from a seat-of-the-pants start-up to the building of a well-run organization.

Goltz believes that customer service and execution require a fundamental understanding of business principles, such as leveraging your assets and having the appropriate skills in marketing, management, and finance. These skills can be acquired through classes and experience. It is much more difficult to develop the personality traits needed to be a successful entrepreneur: tolerance of uncertainty, self-direction, self-nurturance, high energy, and action orientation.

Success has not gone unnoticed for Jay Goltz. He has received numerous awards: the Minority Advocate of the Year Award in 1989; named one of the top 100 young entrepreneurs in the United States by the Association of Collegiate Entrepreneurs (ACE) in 1988; finalist in the Arthur Anderson Entrepreneur Awards in 1989; and Arthur Anderson's Entrepreneur Hall of Fame in 1992. Goltz attributes his success to taking care of customers: "Service is the cheapest commodity you can provide, yet it's the surest way to success. Take care of customers and the rest will take care of itself."

Discussion Questions

1. Why do you think entrepreneurs like Jay Goltz succeed when so many others fail?
2. Can a person develop the personality traits necessary to be a successful entrepreneur? How?
3. How important is a business plan in getting started in a business such as Artist's Frame Service? Explain.

APPENDIX

Entrepreneur Readiness Questionnaire

Not everyone is cut out to be an entrepreneur. The fact is, though, that all kinds of people with all kinds of personalities have succeeded in starting small and large businesses. There are certain traits, however, that seem to separate those who'll be successful as entrepreneurs from those who may not be. The following questionnaire will help you determine in which category you fit. Take a couple of minutes to answer the questions and then score yourself at the end. Making a low score doesn't mean you won't succeed as an entrepreneur. It does indicate, however, that you may be happier working for someone else.

Each of the following items describes something that you may or may not feel represents your personality or other characteristics about you. Read each item and then circle the response (1, 2, 3, 4, or 5) that most nearly reflects the extent to which you agree or disagree that the item seems to fit you.

Scoring: Give yourself one point for each 1 or 2 response you circled for questions 1, 2, 6, 8, 10, 11, 16, 17, 21, 22, 23.

Give yourself one point for each 4 or 5 response you circled for questions 3, 4, 5, 7, 9, 12, 13, 14, 15, 18, 19, 20, 24, 25.

RESPONSE

Looking at my overall philosophy of life and typical behavior, I would say that . . .	Agree Completely (1)	Mostly Agree (2)	Partially Agree (3)	Mostly Disagree (4)	Disagree Completely (5)
1. I am generally optimistic.	1	2	3	4	5
2. I enjoy competing and doing things better than someone else.	1	2	3	4	5
3. When solving a problem, I try to arrive at the best solution first without worrying about other possibilities.	1	2	3	4	5
4. I enjoy associating with co-workers after working hours.	1	2	3	4	5
5. If betting on a horse race I would prefer to take a chance on a high-payoff "long shot."	1	2	3	4	5
6. I like setting my own goals and working hard to achieve them.	1	2	3	4	5
7. I am generally casual and easy-going with others.	1	2	3	4	5
8. I like to know what is going on and take action to find out.	1	2	3	4	5
9. I work best when someone else is guiding me along the way.	1	2	3	4	5
10. When I am right I can convince others.	1	2	3	4	5
11. I find that other people frequently waste my valuable time.	1	2	3	4	5
12. I enjoy watching football, baseball, and similar sports events.	1	2	3	4	5
13. I tend to communicate about myself very openly with other people.	1	2	3	4	5
14. I don't mind following orders from superiors who have legitimate authority.	1	2	3	4	5
15. I enjoy planning things more than actually carrying out the plans.	1	2	3	4	5
16. I don't think it's much fun to bet on a "sure thing."	1	2	3	4	5
17. If faced with failure, I would shift quickly to something else rather than sticking to my guns.	1	2	3	4	5
18. Part of being successful in business is reserving adequate time for family.	1	2	3	4	5
19. Once I have earned something, I feel that keeping it secure is important.	1	2	3	4	5
20. Making a lot of money is largely a matter of getting the right breaks.	1	2	3	4	5
21. Problem solving is usually more effective when a number of alternatives are considered.	1	2	3	4	5
22. I enjoy impressing others with the things I can do.	1	2	3	4	5
23. I enjoy playing games like tennis and handball with someone who is slightly better than I am.	1	2	3	4	5
24. Sometimes moral ethics must be bent a little in business dealings.	1	2	3	4	5
25. I think that good friends would make the best subordinates in an organization.	1	2	3	4	5

Source: Kenneth R. Van Voorhis, *Entrepreneurship and Small Business Management* (New York: Allyn & Bacon, 1980).

Add your points and see how you rate in the following categories:

21–25	Your entrepreneurial potential looks great if you have a suitable opportunity to use it. What are you waiting for?
16–20	This is close to the high entrepreneurial range. You could be quite successful if your other talents and resources are right.
11–15	Your score is in the transitional range. With some serious work you can probably develop the outlook you need for running your own business.
6–10	Things look pretty doubtful for you as an entrepreneur. It would take considerable rearranging of your life philosophy and behavior to make it.
0–5	Let's face it. Entrepreneurship isn't really for you. Still, learning what it's all about won't hurt anything.

PART 2

BUSINESS FORMATION

When you drive through any town or city, you see dozens, often hundreds and thousands, of small businesses. The kinds of businesses are as varied as the people who own and operate them. If you were to interview the owners, you would also find a great variety of reasons for choosing a specific business, for settling in a certain location, and for choosing business ownership as a way of life.

Many people become entrepreneurs ➤ **P.4** ◄ today because they see the risks as similar to working for someone else—but the rewards much greater. The workplace as a whole is becoming increasingly risk-intensive. Many jobs are riskier propositions than they would have been 10 years ago. Downsizing and restructuring are just two reasons that job security assumptions are changing. The incentive for some risk-taking with a payoff of independence, high job satisfaction, and possible high profits just might be more enticing to you in the future than it already is now.

One of the first objections people often have when encouraged to start their own business is that "Everything has already been tried." That simply isn't true. You have probably seen ideas of your own that were put into practice by someone else—someone else who made all the profits. Although the number of possibilities seem smaller than, say, 50 years ago, the opportunities for new, creative business ideas are still lurking in a veiled reality somewhere, awaiting discovery by an innovative entrepreneur—maybe you.

SKILLS

You will need certain qualities to succeed, no matter what type of business you choose to start.

1. You must be willing to take risks ➤ **P.7** ◄. This doesn't mean being reckless; it means being comfortable with trying things that could possibly fail. It means feeling that you control your own fate—that you affect circumstances at least as much as they affect you.

2. You must be able to see the possibilities in new ways of doing things. You need to be able to "see the big picture" with both creativity and practicality. An entrepreneur cannot be too set in the old ways of doing things—or of perceiving reality.

3. You need to be a self-starter—someone who doesn't need to have others tell you what to do and when. An entrepreneur should be motivated. Getting up in the morning should be exciting and challenging rather than threatening or depressing.

4. You need to be ambitious and competitive. Entrepreneurs often have to work hard and long hours, especially in the first few years in business. A successful entrepreneur sees himself or herself as a winner and *expects* to win. You also need the health and physical stamina to work long hours day after day.

5. You need to be someone who is not easily discouraged. Many successful businesspeople have experienced setback after setback, but they refuse to see setbacks as "failures." An entrepreneur should see setbacks as lessons that won't have to be learned again.

CAREER PATHS

Entrepreneurs get started in many ways. One way is to purchase an existing business. Another is to get involved with a franchise operation. Still another is to create an original idea and develop it on your own. Whatever starting point you choose, remember that entrepreneurship usually offers rewards that are commensurate with the energy you are willing to put into the enterprise. Beyond that, the career path is up to you, the entrepreneur.

SOME POSSIBLE POSITIONS FOR WOULD-BE ENTREPRENEURS

OPPORTUNITY	EARNINGS	INVESTMENT	TASKS AND RESPONSIBILITIES/ CAREER PATH	GROWTH POSSIBILITIES
Home-based, owner-run businesses	Low at first, but great potential.	Will vary; usually very low compared with other entrepreneurial ventures.	Bookkeeping, marketing, customer relations, organization of business. Must be self-motivated and able to see opportunities.	Home-based businesses promise to be a fast-growing trend.
Franchising	Considerably higher than nonfranchise operations from the first month of operation.	Varies roughly from $10,000–several million, depending on size and scope of franchise.	Most franchisors provide considerable training and support for the beginning of operations. Owner must accept less freedom, but trades that for a greater chance of success. Opportunities in fast foods, office backup, auto repair, and many others.	Franchising will continue to be popular. One of 12 businesses is a franchise.
Small business consultant	Earnings vary greatly, based on number of contacts and ability to market the service.	Can work for large consulting firms and thus not actually be in business. Operating on one's own, very little investment necessary.	Act as adviser to businesses in various stages of success or failure. A degree in business will help your credibility greatly. Should have a background of both experience and education. Eventually should have master's degree in business (MBA).	The demands for consultants will continue to grow, especially in the areas of international business and high technology.
Franchise director	Usually depends on the number of franchises in the territory and the size and scope of the overall operation.	Once on its feet, your business can grow using mostly the investment of others (franchisees).	Provide direction for the franchisee, provide training, and help the franchisee become successful. Many franchisors start by working first for another franchise to learn the strategies necessary for success.	Franchising will continue to be popular.

KAREN'S KLOSET

Name: Karen Boudreau

Age: 45 years old

Position/title: Owner

Time in this position: 10 years

Company name: Karen's Kloset, Quality Women's Clothing on Consignment

Company description: Karen's Kloset is an upscale resale clothing store. We sell quality women's, maternity, and men's clothing on consignment.

Major factors in the decision to open my own business:
I first thought about opening a consignment store because I was somewhat of a "shopaholic." Although I shopped in every kind of store from Marshall Fields, Saks, Burdines, Neiman Marcus, and boutiques, my favorite shopping was resale. As a responsible single parent I knew I was headed for trouble financially if I didn't stop shopping. I love people and I love resale shopping but I don't like thrift stores, dirty, dingy places or "cheap" clothes. I felt there was a real market out there in educating the professional working women on consignment/resale shopping. During the 90s resale shopping 'came out of the closet' and was no longer just for low income people, but for anyone who wanted a good value for their money. I started with a 750 sq. ft. store with $50,000 in sales and in 10 years have expanded my business to a 5,000 sq. ft. store with $500,000 in sales.

Job description: Owning a consignment store is a lot of hard work involving long hours. For example, we receive 200-400 items daily so one of my many jobs as the owner is to process these items before they can be sold. We use a computer software program designed specifically for the consignment industry to help us run the business.

Best part of your job: The best part of my profession is the people. I have made wonderful friends who are customers and consignors. I also belong to NARTS (National Association of Resale and Thrift Shops) and have met some lifelong friends by attending regional and national meetings. Also, since I love to travel I make it a point to visit stores wherever I go. You can pick up great ideas in every store that you visit!

Worst part of your job: Turning down clothes that don't meet our standards.

Educational background: I'm a lifelong learner with over 100 credit hours having attended Illinois State University and Parkland College. I am always taking courses that will help me with my business or just interest me.

Favorite course: Business 101 at Parkland College was my favorite because of the variety of information I learned.

Best course for your career: I have benefited greatly from the management and computer courses.

Recommended by Bob Ulbrich, Parkland College

Management, Leadership, and Employee Empowerment

LEARNING GOALS

AFTER YOU HAVE READ AND STUDIED THIS CHAPTER, YOU SHOULD BE ABLE TO

1. Explain how the changes that are occurring in the business environment are affecting the management function.

2. Enumerate the four functions of management.

3. Relate the planning process and decision making to the accomplishment of company goals.

4. Describe the organizing function of management, including staffing and diversity management.

5. Explain the differences between leaders and managers, and describe the various leadership styles.

6. Summarize the five steps of the control function of management.

7. Differentiate the skills needed at each level of management.

Getting to Know John Chambers of Cisco Systems

Many people consider John Chambers to be the number one business leader in the United States today. He has been the chief executive officer (CEO) of Cisco Systems since 1995. If you had invested $1,000 in Cisco Systems when Chambers first came on the job, by 2001 you would have had approximately $75,000—a 7,500 percent increase in six years! That's one reason why there are over 3 million stockholders in the company.

What does Cisco do? Cisco changes so quickly that one cannot easily define everything that it does. Put simply, it is involved in computer networking—providing the equipment that ties computers together into complex, integrated systems. It is a leading company of the Internet age. More than 75 percent of all Net traffic travels over products from Cisco.

One way Chambers ensures that Cisco remains an Internet leader is by acquiring other companies that develop new and better technology. Cisco has bought not just dozens of companies but dozens of companies *per year*. Altogether, it has bought 55 companies, for a combined total of over $20 billion. And it intends to buy 20 more.

Acquiring businesses is a good way of acquiring better technology. It is also a clever way to acquire top engineering talent. Competition for Internet engineers is very intense; buying another company and retaining its top engineers is one way Chambers succeeds in building a superior staff.

Getting talented people through an acquisition is one thing; keeping them is another. Chambers is an excellent manager in that respect as well. Howard Charney, a Cisco senior vice president, could be a CEO in some other company, but he stays at Cisco, he says, because of Chambers: "John treats us like peers . . . He asks our advice. He gives us power and resources, then sets the sales targets incredibly high, which keeps us challenged." A true leader, Chambers has a participative managerial style that brings out the best in people.

Chambers takes good care of Cisco employees. All are given stock options (the right to buy company stock in the future at today's prices) and are given bonuses based on customer satisfaction. Cisco is now building a day care center that will accommodate some 450 children of employees.

Chambers learned his leadership and management skills in college and on the job. He got a business degree and a law degree at West Virginia University and an MBA at Indiana University. He worked at IBM in sales right out of college and then went to work for Wang Computers, heading up Asian sales. It was at these companies that Chambers learned to focus on customers. "John Chambers is the most customer-focused human being you will ever meet," says venture capitalist John Doerr. "When it comes to customers, we will do whatever it takes to win them," Chambers says.

So the keys to Chambers's success are providing the best products by acquiring the best companies, retaining the best employees by motivating and compensating them well, and focusing relentlessly on customer needs. Chambers says of Cisco, "Everything we do here is based on four principles: our customers' success, the quality of our team, our own aggressive use of information technology, and all of that applied to our overall strategy."

John Chambers is a brilliant manager and an inspirational leader for his company and for any company that wants to compete in the new Internet age. This chapter will introduce you to the principles of management, leadership, and employee empowerment that made Chambers so effective. You will learn the functions of management and the various leadership styles. In the end, you will know what it takes to be a manager and a leader in today's fast-paced business and social environment.

Sources: Andy Serwer, "There's Something about Cisco," *Fortune,* May 15, 2000, pp. 114–38; Robert X. Cringely, "The Best CEOs," *Worth,* May 2000, pp. 126–30; and "The Top 25 Managers to Watch," *Business Week,* January 8, 2001, p. 77.

THE NEW BUSINESS ENVIRONMENT

The emergence of the Internet over the last several years has radically changed the nature of modern management. Change is now happening faster than ever, and global competition is just a click away. Managing change is an important element of success, particularly in light of today's emphasis on speed in the global marketplace. Thomas Middelhoff, chief executive officer of Bertelsmann AG, the international publishing company, says, "We have nothing less than an industrial revolution . . . That means speed is king."[1]

National borders mean much less now than ever before, and cooperation and integration among companies has greatly increased. For example, Celarix, a Massachusetts-based company founded in 1998, provides services so that shippers worldwide can collaborate with their factories, transportation providers, customers, and brokers, all via the Internet.[2] The *Business Week* box discusses how the new Internet culture can have a major effect on giants like Wal-Mart.

As we noted in Chapter 1, the acceleration of technological change has increased the need for a new breed of worker, one who is more educated and more skilled than workers in the past. These new workers (sometimes called knowledge workers) demand more freedom of operation and different managerial styles. The increasing diversity of the workforce is creating additional challenges. Because the workforce is becoming much more educated and self-directed than ever before, many managerial and nonmanagerial jobs are being eliminated. The corporate term for this is *downsizing* or *rightsizing*, but for the managers and others, a better term would be *shocking loss of jobs and income*.

The Internet has increased the power of consumers in the buyer–seller relationship. Consumers now have vast amounts of information at their fingertips and can demand not only the best-quality goods at the best prices but also the best delivery times. Businesses, for their part, now have vast amounts of information about consumers' wants and needs, and thus can respond quickly to the market.[3] In short, the whole business environment has changed, and managers need to change as well. John Chambers, featured at the beginning of this chapter, is a good example of a manager who has learned to adapt quickly to technological change.

In the *new* economy the fastest way to link companies is on the Internet, and few companies have done more to implement those connections than Sun Microsystems. This ad promotes the "superfantastic net economy," but as they say, "You ain't seen nothing yet." Business to business growth on the Internet is projected to increase faster than any business change in history. What evidence have you seen of changes brought about by the new economy? How does it differ from the "old" economy?

Managers Are No Longer Bosses

Managers must practice the art of getting things done through organizational resources (e.g., workers, financial resources, information, and equipment). At one time, managers were called bosses, and their job was to tell people what to do and watch over them to be sure they did it. Bosses tended to reprimand those who didn't do things correctly and generally acted stern. Many managers still behave that way. Perhaps you've witnessed such behavior.

Today, progressive management is changing. Managers are being educated to guide, train, support, motivate, and coach employees rather than to tell them what to do. Managers like John Chambers realize that workers often know much more about technology than they do. Thus, most modern managers emphasize teamwork and cooperation rather

Wal-Mart Organizes Online Business to Stay Competitive

Many successful businesses have watched in amazement as new Internet companies have come in and stolen a part of their market. Borders and other bookstores have seen their customers turn to Amazon.com, and music stores face competition from a plethora of online music sellers. Almost any successful retailer, if not careful, can lose business to online sellers. Even service organizations, such as stockbrokers, have lost market share to online brokers and to brokers that have pursued click-and-mortar strategies, such as Charles Schwab. Real estate brokers, insurance companies, and others in the service industry are also facing such challenges.

Wal-Mart managers do not intend to have the retailing superstore be among the losers. Wal-Mart had a website for several years, but the company was not nearly as serious as some other firms in pushing that aspect of the business. For example, Wal-Mart had some 800,000 people visit its site, but Amazon.com had 10 million visitors. Now Wal-Mart has a new site, which has products from 25 different categories of goods (the same as a Wal-Mart store). That is more than double the selection that was on the old site. And it offers some 700,000 book titles. Watch out Amazon! Also, customers can return products bought on the Internet to any of Wal-Mart's 2,451 stores—a real advantage to shoppers.

Will Wal-Mart shoppers be loyal to the company and follow it online? Management at Wal-Mart is not about to give in to Internet newcomers. The question is: Can the company adapt to this new environment and create a cybermart that is as efficient and effective as its stores? That depends on the product assortment (which will be good), prices (which can be lower than those of other companies given Wal-Mart's profits), and service. Clearly, the service component will be a critical one.

Just as Wal-Mart management studies ways to speed up checkout lines in its traditional stores, it will have to find ways to speed up deliveries from online sales. Wal-Mart has to spend as much time on that aspect of its online business as any other to keep from losing out in the world of e-commerce.

Sources: Joann Muller, "A Blue-Light Specialist," *Business Week Online*, June 19, 2000; Arlene Weintraub, "I-Way Bumps," *Business Week E.Biz*, May 15, 2000, pp. EB 110–14; and Wendy Zellner, "Will Wal-Mart Get it Right This Time," *Business Week*, November 6, 2000.

---

than discipline and order giving. Managers in some high-tech firms and in progressive firms of all kinds are more friendly and generally treat employees as partners rather than unruly workers; many even dress more casually than before. For example, John Rieber is vice president of programming at E! Entertainment television. When he gathers together the 20 staffers of a show called *Wild On*, he doesn't use the old bossy mode of motivating but rather praise and gentle suggestion. "Scripts are fine," he says to his employees, "but if you see something better, do it." Rieber fosters camaraderie and gives lots of freedom.[4]

In the past, a worker would expect to work for the same company for many years, maybe even a lifetime. Similarly, companies would hire people and keep them for a long time. Today, many companies don't hesitate to layoff employees, and employees don't hesitate to leave if their needs are not being met. Traditional long-term contracts between management and employees—and the accompanying trust—are often no longer there. This makes the management task more difficult because managers must earn the trust of their employees, which includes rewarding them and finding other ways to encourage them to stay in the firm.

In general, management is experiencing a revolution. Managers in the future are likely to be working in teams, to be evaluated by those below them as well as those above, and to be assuming completely new roles in the firm. We'll discuss these roles and the differences between managers and leaders in detail later in the chapter.

What this means for you and other graduates of tomorrow is that management will demand a new kind of person: a skilled communicator and team player as well as a planner, coordinator, organizer, and supervisor. These trends will be addressed in the next few chapters to help you decide whether management is the kind of career you would like.

Functions of Management

Well-known management consultant Peter Drucker says managers give direction to their organizations, provide leadership, and decide how to use organizational resources to accomplish goals. Such descriptions give you some idea of what managers do. In addition to those tasks, managers today must deal with conflict resolution, create trust in an atmosphere where trust has been badly shaken, and help create balance between work lives and family lives. Managers must also effectively and efficiently use organizational resources such as buildings, equipment, and supplies. Managers look at the "big picture," and their decisions make a major difference in organizations. The following definition of management provides the outline of this chapter: **management** is the process used to accomplish organizational goals through (1) planning, (2) organizing, (3) leading, and (4) controlling people and other organizational resources (see Figure 7.1).

Planning includes anticipating trends and determining the best strategies and tactics to achieve organizational goals and objectives. One of those objectives is to please customers. The trend today is to have planning teams to help monitor the environment, find business opportunities, and watch for challenges. Planning is a key management function because the other functions often depend on having a good plan.

Organizing includes designing the structure of the organization and creating conditions and systems in which everyone and everything work together to achieve the organization's goals and objectives. Many of today's organizations are being designed around the customer. The idea is to design the firm so that everyone is working to please the customer at a profit. Thus, organizations

management
The process used to accomplish organizational goals through planning, organizing, leading, and controlling people and other organizational resources.

planning
A management function that involves anticipating trends and determining the best strategies and tactics to achieve organizational goals and objectives.

organizing
A management function that includes designing the structure of the organization and creating conditions and systems in which everyone and everything work together to achieve the organization's goals and objectives.

FIGURE 7.1

WHAT MANAGERS DO

Some modern managers perform all of these tasks with the full cooperation and participation of workers. Empowering employees means allowing them to participate more fully in decision making.

PLANNING

- Setting organizational goals.
- Developing strategies to reach those goals.
- Determining resources needed.
- Setting standards.

ORGANIZING

- Allocating resources, assigning tasks, and establishing procedures for accomplishing goals.
- Preparing a structure (organization chart) showing lines of authority and responsibility.
- Recruiting, selecting, training, and developing employees.
- Placing employees where they'll be most effective.

LEADING

- Guiding and motivating employees to work effectively to accomplish organizational goals and objectives.
- Giving assignments.
- Explaining routines.
- Clarifying policies.
- Providing feedback on performance.

CONTROLLING

- Measuring results against corporate objectives.
- Monitoring performance relative to standards.
- Rewarding outstanding performance.
- Taking corrective action.

Many managers today are working in teams and many more will in the future. These teams are likely to be ethnically diverse and include people of varied ages and backgrounds. Since managers will function primarily as trainers, coaches, and motivators of teams, it is expected that members of the team will do year-end evaluations of the manager and vice versa. How do you think most managers will react to having lower level employees evaluate *their* effectiveness?

must remain flexible and adaptable because customer needs change, and organizations must either change along with them or risk losing their business. For example, traditional bookstores had to go on the Internet to keep from losing business to Amazon.com and other Internet booksellers.

Leading means creating a vision for the organization and communicating, guiding, training, coaching, and motivating others to work effectively to achieve the organization's goals and objectives. The trend is to empower ➤ **P.20** ◄ employees, giving them as much freedom as possible to become self-directed and self-motivated.

leading
Creating a vision for the organization and guiding, training, coaching, and motivating others to work effectively to achieve the organization's goals and objectives.

Controlling involves establishing clear standards to determine whether an organization is progressing toward its goals and objectives, rewarding people for doing a good job, and taking corrective action if they are not. Basically, it means measuring whether what actually occurs meets the organization's goals.

The four functions just addressed—planning, organizing, leading, and controlling—are the heart of management, so let's explore them in more detail. The process begins with planning; we'll look at that right after the Progress Assessment.

controlling
A management function that involves determining whether or not an organization is progressing toward its goals and objectives, and taking corrective action if it is not.

PROGRESS **ASSESSMENT**

- What were some of the environmental factors that have forced managers to change their organizations and managerial styles?

- What's the definition of management used in this chapter, and what is involved in performing the four functions in that definition?

PLANNING: CREATING A VISION BASED ON VALUES

Planning, the first managerial function, involves setting the organizational vision, goals, and objectives. Leaders are expected to create a vision for the firm. A **vision** is more than a goal; it's the larger explanation of why the organization exists and where it's trying to head. A vision gives the organization a sense of purpose and a set of values that, together, unite workers in a common destiny. A vision always precedes a creation. Thomas Edison had to envision what a

vision
An explanation of why the organization exists and where it's trying to head.

light bulb would be like and how it might work best before he created one. Managing an organization without first establishing a vision can be counterproductive. It's like motivating everyone in a rowboat to get really excited about going somewhere, but not giving them any direction. As a result, the boat will just keep changing directions rather than speeding toward an agreed-on goal.

A vision is simply a picture of what the company would like to become. For example, Aurora Foods Inc. (a company that has acquired such brands as Mrs. Butterworth's, Log Cabin, Duncan Hines, and Chef's Choice) has developed the following vision: "We aspire to be the leader in restoring and revitalizing well-known packaged food brands which have become non-core businesses to their previous owners."

Usually employees work with managers to design a mission statement that reflects the organization's vision and values. A **mission statement** outlines the fundamental purposes of the organization. For example, Aurora's mission statement reads as follows:

> *We aim to:*
>
> - *Build long-term shareholder value.* We seek to maximize shareholder returns.
>
> - *Develop and energize our employees.* We are committed to having our employees develop their potential to the fullest extent. In so doing, they will infuse the Company with creativity and energy while attaining professional and personal fulfillment.
>
> - *Form partnerships with our suppliers and customers.* The growth of our brands will enable our suppliers and customers to prosper along with us. Our mutual success forms the basis of long-lasting partnerships and relationships.
>
> - *Exceed consumer expectations.* We will win in the marketplace by not only satisfying consumers' needs but exceeding their expectations.

The mission statement becomes the foundation for setting goals and selecting and motivating employees. **Goals** are the broad, long-term accomplishments an organization wishes to attain. Goals need to be mutually agreed on by workers and management. Thus, goal setting is often a team process.

Objectives are specific, short-term statements detailing how to achieve the goals. One of your goals for reading this chapter, for example, may be to learn basic concepts of management. An objective you could use to achieve this goal is to answer correctly the chapter's Progress Assessment questions. Objectives must be measurable. For example, you can measure your progress in answering questions by determining what percentage you answer correctly over time.

Planning is a continuous process. It's unlikely that a plan that worked yesterday would be successful in today's market. Most planning follows a pattern. The procedure you would follow in planning your life and career is basically the same as that used by businesses for their plans. Planning answers several fundamental questions for businesses:

1. What is the situation now? What is the state of the economy and other environments? What opportunities exist for meeting people's needs? What products and customers are most profitable? Why do people buy (or not buy) our products? Who are our major competitors? What threats are they to our business? These questions are part of what is called **SWOT analysis,** which is an analysis of the organization's *s*trengths, *w*eaknesses, *o*pportunities, and *t*hreats. The company begins such a process with an analysis of the business environment in general.

mission statement
An outline of the fundamental purposes of an organization.

goals
The broad, long-term accomplishments an organization wishes to attain.

objectives
Specific, short-term statements detailing how to achieve the goals.

SWOT analysis
An analysis of an organization's strengths, weaknesses, opportunities, and threats.

Taking a SWOT at the Competition

David Dayton is the CEO of AlumiPlate, a small metal-coating company in Minneapolis. As part of the company's annual strategic planning process, Dayton did a SWOT analysis. SWOT, remember, stands for strengths, weaknesses, opportunities, and threats. The analysis gave him a few areas to focus on for the next year. For example, Dayton found that one strength of the company was the high barrier to competition; that is, it is not easy to get into the metal-coating business. Dayton also found that the company's proprietary aluminum coating technology was its best opportunity. A weakness was the company's lack of high-volume production, and a threat was the set of heavy demands on key personnel.

Some other strengths that Dayton and other CEOs might look for include special skills, motivations, technology, or financial capacities. Weaknesses may include lack of capital, shortages of skilled workers, or unproved products. Opportunities are positive circumstances that, if exploited, may boost the company's success. They include things like untapped markets, promising customer relationships, and weak competitors. Threats include both clearly visible threats (such as pending regulations) and potential threats (such as new competitors or changes in consumer tastes). Certainly, the emergence of the Internet has proved to be a threat to almost all businesses, from those selling automobiles to those selling zoo equipment. But the chance to go on the Internet and sell products almost anywhere is a real opportunity.

Sources: Mark Henricks, "Analyze This," *Entrepreneur*, June 1999, pp 72–75, and Madhavi Acharya, "Cost of Doing Online Business," *The Toronto Star*, September 13, 2000.

Then it identifies internal strengths and weaknesses. Finally, as a result of the environmental analysis, it identifies opportunities and threats. The Spotlight on Small Business box gives you an example of SWOT analysis in action.

2. Where do we want to go? How much growth do we want? What is our profit goal? What are our social objectives? What are our personal development objectives?

3. How can we get there from here? This is the most important part of planning. It takes four forms: strategic, tactical, operational, and contingency (see Figure 7.2).

Strategic planning determines the major goals of the organization. It provides the foundation for the policies, procedures, and strategies for obtaining and using resources to achieve those goals.[5] In this definition, policies are broad guides to action, and strategies determine the best way to use resources. At the strategic planning stage, the company decides which customers to serve, what products or services to sell, and the geographic areas in which the firm will compete. Every firm faces unique challenges that influence what the strategic plans must be. Some firms, for example, need to cut costs, while others need to improve performance, and still others, like many of the new B2B dot-coms, need to increase their profits.

In today's rapidly changing environment, strategic planning is becoming more difficult because changes are occurring so fast that plans—even those set for just months into the future—may soon be obsolete. Therefore, some companies are making shorter-term plans that allow for quick responses to customer needs and requests. The goal is to be flexible and responsive to the market. For example, Akamai, an Intenet company, considers 90 days to be the long

strategic planning
The process of determining the major goals of the organization and the policies and strategies for obtaining and using resources to achieve those goals.

FIGURE 7.2

FIGURE 7.2

PLANNING FUNCTIONS

Very few firms bother to make contingency plans. If something changes the market, such companies may be slow to respond. Most organizations do strategic, tactical, and operational planning.

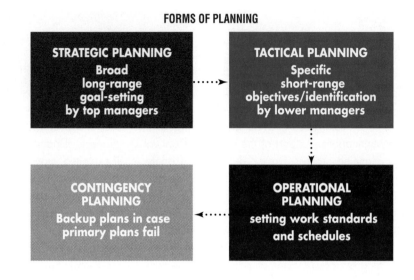

FORMS OF PLANNING

STRATEGIC PLANNING
Broad
long-range
goal-setting
by top managers

TACTICAL PLANNING
Specific
short-range
objectives/identification
by lower managers

CONTINGENCY PLANNING
Backup plans in case
primary plans fail

OPERATIONAL PLANNING
setting work standards
and schedules

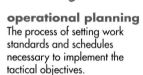

tactical planning
The process of developing detailed, short-term decisions about what is to be done, who is to do it, and how it is to be done.

operational planning
The process of setting work standards and schedules necessary to implement the tactical objectives.

contingency planning
The process of preparing alternative courses of action that may be used if the primary plans do not achieve the objectives of the organization.

term. At weekly meetings, the managers revisit their commitments to see how they are doing.[6]

Tactical planning is the process of developing detailed, short-term statements about what is to be done, who is to do it, and how it is to be done. Tactical planning is normally done by managers or teams of managers at lower levels of the organization, whereas strategic planning is done by the top managers of the firm (e.g., the president and vice presidents of the organization). Tactical planning, for example, involves setting annual budgets and deciding on other details and activities necessary to meet the strategic objectives. If the strategic plan, for example, is to sell more trucks in the South, the tactical plan might be to fund more research of southern truck drivers' wants and needs, and to plan advertising to reach those people.

Operational planning is the process of setting work standards and schedules necessary to implement the tactical objectives. Whereas strategic planning looks at the organization as a whole, operational planning focuses on specific supervisors, department managers, and individual employees. The operational plan is the department manager's tool for daily and weekly operations. An operational plan may include, say, the specific dates for certain truck parts to be completed and the quality specifications those parts must meet. You will read about operations management in detail in Chapter 9.

Contingency planning is the process of preparing alternative courses of action that may be used if the primary plans don't achieve the organization's objectives. The economic and competitive environments change so rapidly that it's wise to have alternative plans of action ready in anticipation of such changes. For example, if an organization doesn't meet its sales goals by a certain date, the contingency plan may call for more advertising or a cut in prices at that time. *Crisis planning* is a part of contingency planning that involves reacting to sudden changes in the environment. For example, trucking and airline firms had to do some crisis planning when gas prices soared in 2000.

Planning is a key management function because the other management functions depend on having good plans. The leaders of market-based companies (companies that respond quickly to changes in competition or to other environmental changes) set direction, not detailed strategic plans. The idea is to stay flexible, listen to customers, and seize opportunities when they come, whether they were planned or not. The opportunities, however, must fit into the company's overall goals and objectives or the company could lose its focus. Clearly, then, much of management and planning involves decision making.

Decision Making: Finding the Best Alternative

All management functions involve decision making. **Decision making** is choosing among two or more alternatives. It sounds easier here than it is in practice. In fact, decision making is the heart of all the management functions. The rational decision-making model is a series of steps managers should follow to make logical, intelligent, and well-founded decisions. These steps can be thought of as the seven Ds of decision making:

1. Define the situation.
2. Describe and collect needed information.
3. Develop alternatives.
4. Develop agreement among those involved.
5. Decide which alternative is best.
6. Do what is indicated (begin implementation).
7. Determine whether the decision was a good one and follow up.

Change is happening so rapidly that successful businesses must be flexible enough to change their plans as conditions evolve. The goal is to be responsive to the market by being strong enough to stand out, but flexible enough to adapt to new environments.

The best decisions are based on sound information. Managers often have computer terminals at their desks so they can easily retrieve internal records and look up external data of all kinds. But all the data in the world can't replace a creative manager who makes brilliant decisions. Decision making is more an art than a science. It's the one skill most needed by managers and leaders in that all the other functions depend on it.

decision making
Choosing among two or more alternatives.

PROGRESS
ASSESSMENT

• What's the difference between goals and objectives?
• What does a company analyze when it does a SWOT analysis?
• What's the difference between strategic, tactical, and operational planning?
• What are the seven Ds in decision making?

ORGANIZING: CREATING A UNIFIED SYSTEM

After managers have planned a course of action, they must organize the firm to accomplish their goals. Operationally, organizing means allocating resources (such as funds for various departments), assigning tasks, and establishing procedures for accomplishing the organizational objectives. An **organization chart** is a visual device that shows relationships among people and divides the organization's work: it shows who is accountable for the

organization chart
A visual device which shows the relationship and divides the organization's work: it shows who is accountable for the completion of specific work and who reports to whom.

Published Image is just one of many small companies that have formed self-managed teams to get work done quickly and efficiently. Not all companies give employees the freedom to set their own work schedules and do their own budgets, however. What are the advantages and disadvantages you see to giving employees such freedom?

top management
Highest level of management, consisting of the president and other key company executives who develop strategic plans.

middle management
The level of management that includes general managers, division managers, and branch and plant managers who are responsible for tactical planning and controlling.

supervisory management
Managers who are directly responsible for supervising workers and evaluating their daily performance.

completion of specific work and who reports to whom. The problems involved in developing an organization structure will be discussed in more detail in Chapter 8. For now, it's important to know that the corporate hierarchy may include top, middle, and first-line managers.

Top management (the highest level of management) consists of the president and other key company executives who develop strategic plans. Terms you're likely to see often are chief executive officer (CEO), chief operating officer (COO), chief financial officer (CFO), and chief information officer (CIO), or (in some companies) chief knowledge officer (CKO). The CEO is often the president of the firm and is responsible for all top-level decisions in the firm. CEOs are responsible for introducing change into an organization. The COO is responsible for putting those changes into effect. His or her tasks include structuring work, controlling operations, and rewarding people to ensure that everyone strives to carry out the leader's vision. The CFO is responsible for obtaining funds, planning budgets, collecting funds, and so on. The CIO or CKO is responsible for getting the right information to other managers so they can make correct decisions.

Middle management includes general managers, division managers, and branch and plant managers (in colleges, deans and department heads) who are responsible for tactical planning and controlling. Many firms have eliminated some middle managers through downsizing because fewer are needed when employees work in self-managed teams.

Supervisory management includes those who are directly responsible for supervising workers and evaluating their daily performance; they're often known as *first-line managers* because they're the first level above workers (see Figure 7.3).

The Trend toward Self-Managed Teams

One trend in the United States is toward placing more workers on cross-functional teams composed of people from various departments of the firm, such as marketing, finance, and distribution. Many of these teams are self-managed. That means that more planning, organizing, and controlling are

FIGURE 7.3

LEVELS OF MANAGEMENT
This figure shows the three levels of management. In many firms, there are several levels of middle management. Recently, however, firms have been eliminating middle-level managers in a cost-cutting attempt.

being delegated to lower-level managers.[7] What will this trend mean for managers and leaders in the 21st century? It means developing and training employees to assume greater responsibility in planning, teamwork, and problem solving.

Teamwork usually aids communication, improves cooperation, reduces internal competition, and maximizes the talents of all employees on a project. Companies such as BellSouth, Qwest Communications, and Ryder Systems use cross-functional teams to explore ways to make their companies operate faster and become more responsive to customers and other stakeholders, such as suppliers and the community. You'll read more about such teams in Chapter 8.

The Stakeholder-Oriented Organization

A dominating question of the past 20 years or so has been how to best organize a firm to respond to the needs of customers and other stakeholders. Remember, *stakeholders* ➤ **P.19** ◄ include anyone who's affected by the organization and its policies and products. That includes employees, customers, suppliers, dealers, environmental groups, and the surrounding communities. The consensus seems to be that smaller organizations are more responsive than larger organizations. Therefore, many large firms are being restructured into smaller, more customer-focused units.

The point is that companies are no longer organizing to make it easy for *managers* to have control. Instead, they're organizing so that *customers* have the greatest influence. The change to a customer orientation is being aided by technology. For example, establishing a dialogue with customers on the Internet enables some firms to work closely with customers and respond quickly to their wants and needs.[8]

There's no way an organization can provide high-quality goods and services ➤ **P.25** ◄ to customers unless suppliers provide world-class parts and materials with which to work.[9] Thus, managers have to establish close relationships with suppliers. To make the entire system work, similar relationships have to be established with those organizations that sell directly to consumers—retailers.

In the past, the goal of the organization function in the firm was to clearly specify who does what *within the firm.* Today, the organizational task is much more complex because firms are forming partnerships, joint ventures, and other arrangements that make it necessary to organize the *whole system,* that is, several firms working together, often across national boundaries.[10] One organization working alone is often not as effective as many organizations working together. Creating a unified system out of multiple organizations will be one of the greatest management challenges of the 21st century. We'll discuss this issue in more depth in Chapter 8.

Staffing: Getting and Keeping the Right People

staffing
A management function that includes hiring, motivating, and retaining the best people available to accomplish the companies objectives.

Staffing involves recruiting, hiring, motivating, and retaining the best people available to accomplish the company's objectives. Recruiting good employees has always been an important part of organizational success. Today, however, it is critical, especially in the Internet and high-tech areas. At companies like Cisco, Yahoo, Intuit, Amazon, and eBay, the primary capital equipment is brainpower. One day the company may be selling books (Amazon) and suddenly an employee comes up with the idea of selling music or having auctions online or whatever. Any of these opportunities may prove profitable in the long run. The opportunities seem almost limitless. Thus the firms with the most innovative and creative workers can go from start-up to major competitor with leading companies in just a year or two.[11]

John Featherstone, U.S. employment director at Sun Microsystems, says that his company hires about 6,000 people a year, and competition among companies for the best new hires is incredibly intense. To win, Sun has developed an online recruiting program. The company pays bonuses of $1,500 to current employees who provide good leads for new workers. Sun's home page is easy to use and has an employment button that puts employment data a mouse click away.

Once they are hired, good people must be retained. With a low national unemployment rate, people are no longer willing to work at companies unless they are treated well and get fair pay. Employees may leave to find companies that offer them a better balance between work and home. Staffing is becoming a greater part of each manager's assignment, and all managers need to cooperate with human resource management to win and keep good workers.

Staffing is such an important subject that we cannot cover it fully in this chapter. It is enough for now to understand that staffing is becoming more and more important as companies search for skilled and talented workers.[12] All of Chapter 11 will be devoted to human resource issues, including staffing. All managers must also become more aware of diversity, another human resource area, because of today's diverse workforce. We'll explore that important topic next.

One of the most critical resources in firms today is knowledgeable workers. Although increasingly these workers come from diverse backgrounds, they have one thing in common—they are all talented. And competition among companies to recruit them is very spirited. Therefore, every effort must be made to find, attract, and keep these workers.

Managing Diversity

Managing diversity means building systems and a climate that unite different people in a common pursuit without undermining their individual strengths. Diversity includes but also goes beyond differences in race, gender, ethnicity, sexual orientation, abilities, and religious affiliation. At least a third of Silicon Valley's scientists and engineers are immigrants. The mixing of people is central to the success of businesses in that area.[13]

If people are to work on teams, they have to learn to work together with people who have different personalities, different priorities, and different lifestyles. In the past, firms tended to look for people much like those who were already working at the firm. Today, such recruiting would probably be illegal, and it certainly would be less than optimal.

Research has shown that heterogeneous (mixed) groups are more productive than homogeneous (similar) groups in the workplace. Men and women, young and old, and all other mixes of people can not only learn to work together but also can do so successfully. Furthermore, it is often quite profitable to have employees who match the diversity of customers so that the company as a whole can understand cultural differences and match them effectively. Managers must learn how to work with people from many different cultures, and many will also be asked to work in foreign countries. The more you can do now to learn other languages and work with diverse cultural groups, the better off you'll be when you become a manager.

Managing diversity also means working with minority business enterprises (MBEs) to maintain a strong and diverse supplier network. Companies such as the Chase Manhattan Bank, Ford Motor Company, J. C. Penney, and Pitney Bowes have built strong relationships with minority suppliers. American Airlines has demonstrated its awareness of the need to manage diversity by running ads that say, "At American, we believe our success comes from diversity. If you are a diversified supplier and would like to explore opportunities with us, we'd like to hear from you." Likewise, aircraft manufacturer Boeing says in one of its ads, "Working with women- and minority-owned companies, we have been able to build business with superior products."

managing diversity
Building systems and a climate that unite different people in a common pursuit without undermining their individual strengths.

LEADING: PROVIDING CONTINUOUS VISION AND VALUES

In business literature there's a trend toward separating the notion of management from that of leadership. A person could be a good manager and not a good leader. Another could be a good leader without being a good manager. One difference between managers and leaders is that managers strive to produce order and stability while leaders embrace and manage change. *Leadership* is creating a vision for others to follow, establishing corporate values and ethics, and transforming the way the organization does business in order to improve its effectiveness and efficiency. Good leaders motivate workers and create the environment for workers to motivate themselves. *Management* is the carrying out of the leadership's vision.

Now and in the future, all organizations will need leaders who can supply the vision as well as the moral and ethical foundation for growth. You don't have to be a manager to be a leader. All employees can lead. That is, any employee can contribute to producing order and stability and can motivate others to work well.

Organizations will need workers and managers who share a vision and know how to get things done cooperatively. The workplace is changing from a place where a few dictate the rules to others to a place where all employees work together to accomplish common goals. Furthermore, managers must lead by doing, not just by saying.

In summary, leaders must

- *Communicate a vision and rally others around that vision.* In doing so, the leader should be openly sensitive to the concerns of followers, give them responsibility, and win their trust.
- *Establish corporate values.* These values include a concern for employees, for customers, and for the quality of the company's products. When companies set their business goals today, they're defining the values of the company as well.
- *Promote corporate ethics.* Ethics ➤ **P.96** ◄ include an unfailing demand for honesty and an insistence that everyone in the company gets treated fairly. That's why we stress ethical decision making throughout this text. Many businesspeople are now making the news by giving away huge amounts to charity, thus setting a model of social concern for their employees and others. The Making Ethical Decisions box shows how some corporate leaders are walking the walk when it comes to charitable giving as opposed to just talking the talk.
- *Embrace change.* A leader's most important job may be to transform the way the company does business so that it's more effective and efficient.

As you think about leadership, keep in mind, too, that it is now a global issue. The Reaching Beyond Our Borders box will give you some idea about how international leadership is being approached today.

Leadership Styles

Nothing has challenged researchers in the area of management more than the search for the "best" leadership traits, behaviors, or styles. Thousands of studies have been made just to find leadership traits, that is, characteristics that make leaders different from other people. Intuitively, you would conclude about the same thing that researchers have found: leadership traits are

www.pgdc.net/TCFI

MAKING ETHICAL DECISIONS
Leading by Example

The popular press does not report it much, but many business leaders are quite generous when it comes to giving away the money they earn. Robert Krieble, for example, made millions of dollars. He was the founder of Loctite, a company that makes metal-locking adhesives. When people asked Krieble why he drove a Ford Festiva instead of a more expensive car, he replied, "The less money I spend on myself, the more I have to give away."

Bill Gates of Microsoft has said that he will give about $10 million to each of his children, but will give most of the rest of his billions (he has about $65 billion now) to charity. He has already placed some $21 billion into the Bill and Melinda Gates Foundation.

Home Depot chairman Bernard Marcus intends to leave $850 million in stock to the Marcus Foundation, which supports education and the handicapped. Pierre Omidyar of the online auction company eBay has given away millions of dollars and is planning to give away much more. Alfred Mann of MiniMed has vowed to give $500 million to leading universities. George Soros gave $540 million to support education and drug policy initiatives. The Triangle Community Foundation enlisted 43 entrepreneurs who were willing to commit $10,000 or more in stock to the cause of addressing community needs.

Fortune magazine reported on the 40 most generous Americans in 1999. In that year, they gave a combined total of $3.5 billion. Remember, that's just one year's gifts. These modern-day managers follow in the footsteps of other business leaders who have given generously to charity. That includes Andrew Carnegie, who gave away the equivalent (in today's figures) of $3.5 billion to libraries and other causes. In other words, some business leaders make a lot of money, but they give much of it to charities and communities. By being so generous with their money, such business leaders set an example for their employees and for all of us.

Are you willing to make a commitment now to donate 5 to 10 percent of your after-tax income to charitable causes? What would be the consequences of such a decision?

Sources: Quentin Hardy, "The Radical Philanthropist," *Forbes*, May 1, 2000, pp. 114–21, "The Promise of the New Economy Is at Risk," *Fast Company*, March 2000, pp. 166–67, and Steven Wright, "Boss Family Donates $10 Million More to Duke," *University Wire*, January 26, 2001.

---

hard to pin down. In fact, results of most studies on leadership have been neither statistically significant nor reliable. Some leaders are well groomed and tactful, while others are unkempt and abrasive—yet the latter may be just as effective as the former.

Just as there's no one set of traits that can describe a leader, there's also no one style of leadership that works best in all situations. Even so, we can look at a few of the most commonly recognized leadership styles and see how they may be effective:

1. **Autocratic leadership** involves making managerial decisions without consulting others. Such a style is effective in emergencies and when absolute followership is needed—for example, when fighting fires. Autocratic leadership is also effective sometimes with new, relatively unskilled workers who need clear direction and guidance.

   Coach Phil Jackson used an autocratic leadership style to take the Los Angeles Lakers to a National Basketball Association championship in 2000. By following his leadership, a group of highly skilled *individuals* became a winning *team*.

2. **Participative (democratic) leadership** consists of managers and employees working together to make decisions. Research has found that

autocratic leadership
Leadership style that involves making managerial decisions without consulting others.

participative (democratic) leadership
Leadership style that consists of managers and employees working together to make decisions.

REACHING BEYOND OUR BORDERS

Teaching Global Management

www.jibs.net

Managers work within organizational boundaries. Leaders set those boundaries and constantly change the organization to meet new challenges. Today's excellent corporations are, more often than not, reflections of their leaders. The leaders of successful corporations have had a vision of excellence and have led others to share that vision. Business schools are seeing a mood change these days. As students read about countries that made up the former Soviet Union going toward a market economy and Eastern European countries opening their doors to Western businesses, they're demanding to know more about global business management. Because of the growth of the Internet, many young people know they'll be involved in international business even if they never leave the United States. They also know that American companies are looking to business schools for managers who know how to work in the new global context, especially e-commerce.

How are business schools responding to this student demand? Many are revamping their existing curriculum by integrating international examples into basic courses. This reduces the need for specific international courses. The idea is to bring international dimensions into the mainstream.

Still, some students demand more. They feel that global enterprise is too important to be mixed in with other courses, and they want courses that are entirely international. Many business schools now offer exchange programs with business schools in other countries. Professors are encouraged to participate in international research and to gain teaching experience overseas. Students are encouraged—and in some cases required—to study foreign languages. Students have caught the international fever and have passed the sense of urgency on to colleges.

employee participation in decisions may not always increase effectiveness, but it usually increases job satisfaction. Many new, progressive organizations are highly successful at using a democratic style of leadership that values traits such as flexibility, good listening skills, and empathy. At the beginning of this chapter, we highlighted John Chambers of Cisco as one such leader.

Organizations that have successfully used this style include Wal-Mart, Fed Ex, IBM, Xerox, AT&T, and most smaller firms. At meetings in such firms, employees discuss management issues and resolve those issues together in a democratic manner. That

One of the more successful autocratic leaders in business today is Tom Siebel, founder and head of Siebel Systems. He is described as very demanding and someone who is unwilling to take "No" for an answer. As you might expect, he is not the most beloved manager, but few executives are as effective when measured by company performance. Have you had experience with a similar leader? What was your reaction?

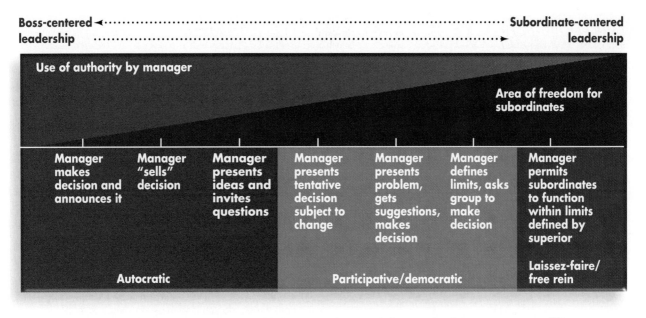

Boss-centered ◀┈┈ **Subordinate-centered**
leadership ┈┈▶ **leadership**

Use of authority by manager	
	Area of freedom for subordinates

Manager makes decision and announces it	Manager "sells" decision	Manager presents ideas and invites questions	Manager presents tentative decision subject to change	Manager presents problem, gets suggestions, makes decision	Manager defines limits, asks group to make decision	Manager permits subordinates to function within limits defined by superior
	Autocratic			**Participative/democratic**		**Laissez-faire/ free rein**

Source: Reprinted by permission of the *Harvard Business Review*. An exhibit from "How to Choose a Leadership Pattern" by Robert Tannenbaum and Warren Schmidt (May/June 1973). Copyright © 1973 by the President and Fellows of Harvard College, all rights reserved.

FIGURE 7.4

VARIOUS LEADERSHIP STYLES

is, everyone has an equal say. Many firms have placed meeting rooms throughout the company and allow all employees the right to request a meeting.

3. **Laissez-faire (free-rein) leadership** involves managers setting objectives and employees being relatively free to do whatever it takes to accomplish those objectives. In certain organizations, where managers deal with doctors, engineers, or other professionals, often the most successful leadership style is laissez-faire. The traits needed by managers in such organizations include warmth, friendliness, and understanding. More and more firms are adopting this style of leadership with at least some of their employees.

laissez-faire (free-rein) leadership
Leadership style that involves managers setting objectives and employees being relatively free to do whatever it takes to accomplish those objectives.

Individual leaders rarely fit neatly into just one of these categories. Researchers illustrate leadership as a continuum with varying amounts of employee participation, ranging from purely boss-centered leadership to subordinate-centered leadership (see Figure 7.4).

Which leadership style is best? Research tells us that successful leadership depends largely on who's being led and in what situations. It also supports the notion that any leadership style, ranging from autocratic to laissez-faire, may be successful depending on the people and the situation. In fact, a manager may use a variety of leadership styles depending on a given situation.[14] A manager may be autocratic but friendly with a new trainee; democratic with an experienced employee who has many good ideas that can only be fostered by a flexible manager who's a good listener; and laissez-faire with a trusted, long-term supervisor who probably knows more about operations than the manager does.

There's no such thing as a leadership trait that is effective in all situations, or a leadership style that always works best. A truly successful leader has the ability to use the leadership style most appropriate to the situation and the employees involved (see Figure 7.5).

THE 12 GOLDEN RULES OF LEADERSHIP

1. *Set a good example.* Your subordinates will take their cue from you. If your work habits are good, theirs are likely to be too.

2. *Give your people a set of objectives and a sense of direction.* Good people seldom like to work aimlessly from day to day. They want to know not only what they're doing but why.

3. *Keep your people informed of new developments of the company and how they'll affect them.* Let people know where they stand with you. Let your close assistants in on your plans at an early stage. Let people know as early as possible of any changes that will affect them. Let them know of changes that won't affect them but about which they may be worrying.

4. *Ask your people for advice.* Let them know that they have a say in your decisions whenever possible. Make them feel a problem is their problem too. Encourage individual thinking.

5. *Let your people know that you support them.* There's no greater morale killer than a boss who resents a subordinate's ambition.

6. *Don't give orders.* Suggest, direct, and request.

7. *Emphasize skills, not rules.* Judge results, not methods. Give a person a job to do and let him or her do it. Let an employee improve his or her own job methods.

8. *Give credit where credit is due.* Appreciation for a job well done is the most appreciated of "fringe benefits."

9. *Praise in public.* This is where it will do the most good.

10. *Criticize in private.*

11. *Criticize constructively.* Concentrate on correction, not blame. Allow a person to retain his or her dignity. Suggest specific steps to prevent recurrence of the mistake. Forgive and encourage desired results.

12. *Make it known that you welcome new ideas.* No idea is too small for a hearing or too wild for consideration. Make it easy for them to communicate their ideas to you. Follow through on their ideas.

THE SEVEN SINS OF LEADERSHIP

On the other hand, these items can cancel any constructive image you might try to establish.

1. *Trying to be liked rather than respected.* Don't accept favors from your subordinates. Don't do special favors in trying to be liked. Don't try for popular decisions. Don't be soft about discipline. Have a sense of humor. Don't give up.

2. *Failing to ask subordinates for their advice and help.*

3. *Failing to develop a sense of responsibility in subordinates.* Allow freedom of expression. Give each person a chance to learn his or her superior's job. When you give responsibility, give authority too. Hold subordinates accountable for results.

4. *Emphasizing rules rather than skill.*

5. *Failing to keep criticism constructive.* When something goes wrong, do you tend to assume who's at fault? Do you do your best to get all the facts first? Do you control your temper? Do you praise before you criticize? Do you listen to the other side of the story?

6. *Not paying attention to employee gripes and complaints.* Make it easy for them to come to you. Get rid of red tape. Explain the grievance machinery. Help a person voice his or her complaint. Always grant a hearing. Practice patience. Ask a complainant what he or she wants to do . Don't render a hasty or biased judgment. Get all the facts. Let the complainant know what your decision is. Double-check your results. Be concerned.

7. *Failing to keep people informed.*

Source: "To Become an "Effective Executive: Develop Leadership and Other Skills," *Marketing News*, April 1984, p. 1 and Brian Biro, *Beyond Success*, (New York: Berkley, 2001).

FIGURE 7.5

RULES OF LEADERSHIP

Empowering Workers

Traditional leaders give explicit instructions to workers, telling them what to do to meet the goals and objectives of the organization. The term for such a process is *directing.* In traditional organizations, directing involves giving assignments, explaining routines, clarifying policies, and providing feedback on performance.

Progressive leaders, such as those in many high-tech firms and Internet companies, are less likely than traditional leaders to give specific instructions to employees. Rather, they're more likely to empower employees to make decisions on their own. **Empowerment** ‣ **P.20** ‹ means giving employees the authority (the right to make a decision without consulting the manager) and responsibility (the requirement to accept the consequences of one's actions) to respond quickly to customer requests. In cooperation with employees, managers will set up teams that will work together to accomplish objectives and goals.[15] The manager's role is becoming less that of a boss and director and more that of a coach, assistant, counselor, or team member. **Enabling** is the term used to describe giving workers the education and tools they need to assume their new decision-making powers.

empowerment
Giving employees the authority and responsibility to respond quickly to customer requests.

enabling
Giving workers the education and tools they need to assume their new decision-making powers.

Managing Knowledge

There's an old saying that still holds true today: "Knowledge is power." Empowering employees means giving them knowledge, that is, getting them the information they need to do the best job they can. Finding the right information, keeping the information in a readily accessible place, and making the information known to everyone in the firm is known as **knowledge management.**[16] The first step to developing a knowledge management system is determining what knowledge is most important. Do you want to know more about your customers? Do you want to know more about competitors? What kind of information would make the company more effective or more efficient or more responsive to the marketplace? Once you have decided what you need to know, you set out to find answers to those questions.

knowledge management
Finding the right information, keeping the information in a readily accessible place, and making the information known to everyone in the firm.

Knowledge management tries to keep people from "reinventing the wheel"—that is, duplicating the work of gathering information—every time a decision needs to be made. A company really progresses when each person in the firm asks continually, "What do I still not know?" and "Whom should I be asking?" It's as important to know what's not working as what is working. Employees and managers now have e-mail, fax machines, intranets, and other means of keeping in touch with each other, with customers, and with other stakeholders. The key to success is learning how to process that information effectively and turn it into knowledge that everyone can use to improve processes and procedures. That is one way to enable workers to be more effective. We'll discuss information technology and knowledge management in much more detail in Chapter 17.

CRITICAL THINKING

Do you see any problems with a democratic managerial style? Can you see a manager getting frustrated when he or she can't control others? Can someone who's trained to give orders (e.g., a military sergeant) be retrained to be a democratic manager? What problems may emerge? What kind of manager would you be? Do you have evidence to show that?

Controlling: Making Sure It Works

The control function involves measuring performance relative to the planned objectives and standards, rewarding people for work well done, and then taking corrective action when necessary. Thus, the control process (see Figure 7.6) is the heart of the management system because it provides the feedback that enables managers and workers to adjust to any deviations from plans and to changes in the environment that have affected performance. Controlling consists of five steps:

1. Setting clear performance standards.
2. Monitoring and recording actual performance (results).
3. Comparing results against plans and standards.
4. Communicating results and deviations to the employees involved.
5. Providing positive feedback for work well done and taking corrective action when needed.

The control system's weakest link tends to be the setting of standards. To measure results against standards, the standards must be specific, attainable, and measurable. Vague goals and standards such as "better quality," "more efficiency," and "improved performance" aren't sufficient because they don't describe in enough detail what you're trying to achieve. For example, let's say you're a runner and you have made the following statement: "My goal is to improve my distance." When you started your improvement plan last year, you ran 2 miles a day; now you run 2.1 miles a day. Did you meet your goal? Well, you did increase your distance, but certainly not by very much. A more appropriate statement would be "My goal is to increase my running distance from two miles a day to four miles a day by January 1." It's important to have a time period established when goals are to be met. The following examples of goals and standards meet these criteria:

- Cutting the number of finished product rejects from 10 per 1,000 to 5 per 1,000 by March 31.

FIGURE 7.6

THE CONTROL PROCESS

The whole control process is based on clear standards. Without such standards, the other steps are difficult, if not impossible. With clear standards, performance measurement is relatively easy and the proper action can be taken.

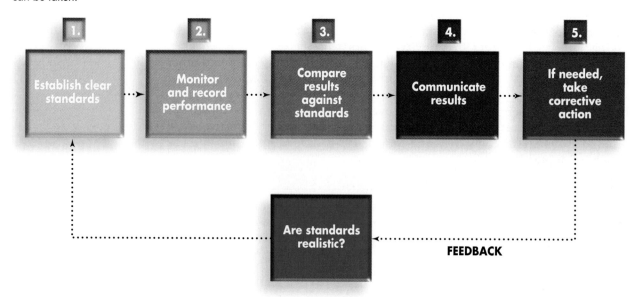

- Increasing the number of times managers praise employees from 3 per week to 12 per week by the end of the quarter.
- Increasing sales of product X from 10,000 per month to 12,000 per month by July.

One way to make control systems work is to establish clear procedures for monitoring performance. Accounting and finance are often the foundations for control systems because they often provide the numbers management needs to evaluate progress. We shall explore both accounting and finance in detail later in the text.

A New Criterion for Measurement: Customer Satisfaction

The criterion for measuring success in a customer-oriented firm is customer satisfaction. This includes satisfaction of both external and internal customers. **External customers** include dealers, who buy products to sell to others, and ultimate customers (also known as end users) such as you and me, who buy products for their own personal use. **Internal customers** are individuals and units within the firm that receive services from other individuals or units. For example, the field salespeople are the internal customers of the marketing research people who prepare research reports for them. One goal today is to go beyond simply satisfying customers by "delighting" them with unexpectedly good products and services.

Other criteria of organizational effectiveness may include the firm's contribution to society and its environmental responsibility in the area surrounding the business.[17] The traditional measures of success are usually financial, defined in terms of profits or return on investment. Certainly these measures are still important, but they're not the whole purpose of the firm. The purpose of the firm today is to please employees, customers, and other stakeholders. Thus, measurements of success must take all these groups into account. Firms have to ask questions such as these: Do we have good relations with our employees, our suppliers, our dealers, our community leaders, the local media, our stockholders, and our bankers? What more could we do to please these groups? Are the corporate needs (such as making a profit) being met as well?

The Corporate Scorecard

A broad measurement tool that has grown in popularity in the last few years is the *corporate scorecard*. In addition to measuring customer satisfaction, the corporate scorecard measures financial progress, return on investment, and all else that needs to be managed for the firm to reach its final destination—profits. One scorecard, for example, might follow both customer service (Is it getting better or worse?) and, at the same time, product defects. Some companies use software that enables everyone in the firm to see the results of the corporate scorecard and work together to improve them. Some companies, like Shell Oil, use strictly financial measures of success. Others, like Motorola, use a more balanced approach. That is, they measure both financial progress and other, softer issues, such as employee and customer satisfaction. Most companies would do better by having a balanced approach that measures both financial growth and employee and customer satisfaction.

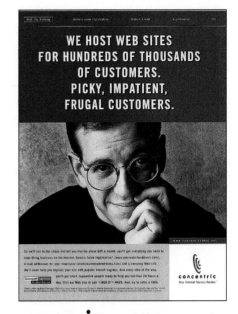

Successful businesses today are focused on customer satisfaction. As this ad says, customers can be picky, impatient, and frugal. The challenge is to listen closely to such customers and then reward them with service or products that exceed their expectations.

external customers
Dealers, who buy products to sell to others, and ultimate customers (or end users), who buy products for their own personal use.

internal customers
Individuals and units within the firm that receive services from other individuals or units.

FIGURE 7.7

SKILLS NEEDED AT VARIOUS LEVELS OF MANAGEMENT

All managers need human relation skills. At the top, managers need strong conceptual skills and rely less on technical skills. First-line managers need strong technical skills and rely less on conceptual skills. Middle managers need to have a balance between technical and conceptual skills.

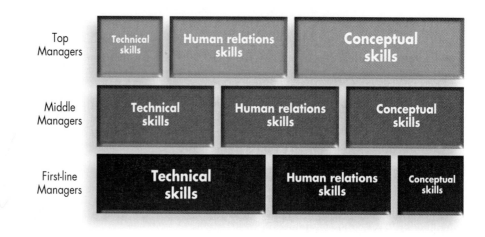

technical skills
Skills that involve the ability to perform tasks in a specific discipline or department.

human relations skills
Skills that involve communication and motivation; they enable managers to work through and with people.

conceptual skills
Skills that involve the ability to picture the organization as a whole and the relationship among its various parts.

TASKS AND SKILLS AT DIFFERENT LEVELS OF MANAGEMENT

Few people are trained to be good managers. Usually a person learns how to be a skilled accountant or sales representative or production-line worker, and then—because of his or her skill—is selected to be a manager. The tendency is for such managers to become deeply involved in showing others how to do things, helping them, supervising them, and generally being very active in the operating task.

The further up the managerial ladder a person moves, the less important his or her original job skills become. At the top of the ladder, the need is for people who are visionaries, planners, organizers, coordinators, communicators, morale builders, and motivators. Figure 7.7 shows that a manager must have three categories of skills:

1. **Technical skills** involve the ability to perform tasks in a specific discipline (such as selling a product or developing software) or department (such as marketing or information systems).

2. **Human relations skills** involve communication and motivation; they enable managers to work through and with people. Such skills also include those associated with leadership, coaching, morale building, delegating, training and development, and help and supportiveness.

3. **Conceptual skills** involve the ability to picture the organization as a whole and the relationships among its various parts. Conceptual skills are needed in planning, organizing, controlling, systems development, problem analysis, decision making, coordinating, and delegating.

Looking at Figure 7.7, you'll notice that first-line managers need to be skilled in all three areas. Most of their time is spent on technical and human relations tasks (assisting operating personnel, giving directions, and so forth). First-line managers spend little time on conceptual tasks. Top managers, in contrast, need to use few technical skills. Instead, almost all of their time is devoted to human relations and conceptual tasks. A person who is competent at a low level of management may not be competent at higher levels and vice versa. The skills needed are different at different levels.

One of the most important decisions you will make while in college is your choice of a career path. Who can help? You might want to use the Internet to check out sites like thingamajob.com. As you narrow your choices and begin thinking about long-range goals, Internet counselors can be of great assistance in providing insights regarding what's available, what companies are looking for, and so forth.

Management Skills Are Transferable

One exciting thing about the study of management and leadership is that it prepares people for careers in all sorts of organizations. Managers and leaders are needed not only in business organizations but also in schools, churches, charities, government organizations, unions, associations, and clubs.

When selecting a career in management, you will have several decisions to make:

- What kind of organization is most desirable? That is, do you want to work for a business, government, or nonprofit organization?

- What type of managerial position seems most interesting? You may become a production manager, a sales manager, a human resource manager, an accounting manager, a traffic (distribution) manager, a credit manager, or some other type of manager. There are dozens of managerial positions from which to choose. In the future, graduates are likely to move among several different functions, so it pays to have a broad education in business.

- What type of industry is most appealing to you: sporting goods, computers, automobiles, tourism, aircraft, or what? Would it be more interesting to work for a relatively new firm or an established one? What courses and training are needed to prepare for various managerial careers? Only careful research will help you answer these questions.

Management will be discussed in more detail in the next few chapters. Let's pause now, review, and do some exercises. Management is doing, not just reading.

What kind of management are you best suited for: human resource, marketing, finance, accounting, production, credit, or what? Why do you feel this area is most appropriate? Would you like to work for a large firm or a small business? Private or public? In an office or out in the field? Would you like being a manager? If you aren't sure, read the following chapters and see what's involved.

- How does enabling help empowerment?
- What are the five steps in the control process?
- What's the difference between internal and external customers?
- What kinds of decisions must you make when choosing a career?

SUMMARY

1. Explain how the changes that are occurring in the business environment are affecting the management function.

1. Many managers are changing their approach to corporate management.
   • *What reasons can you give to account for these changes in management?*
   Some of the reasons given in this text for management changes are the emergence of the Internet, global competition, rapid technological change, a new kind of worker, and consumers with more power.
   • *What has replaced the old "boss" style of management?*
   Managers are being educated to guide, train, support, and teach employees rather than tell them what to do.

2. Enumerate the four functions of management.

2. Managers perform a variety of functions.
   • *What are the four primary functions of management?*
   The four primary functions are (1) planning, (2) organizing, (3) leading, and (4) controlling.

3. Relate the planning process and decision making to the accomplishment of company goals.

3. The planning function involves the process of setting objectives to meet the organizational goals.
   • *What's the difference between goals and objectives?*
   Goals are broad, long-term achievements that organizations aim to accomplish, whereas objectives are specific, short-term plans made to help reach the goals.
   • *What is a SWOT analysis?*
   Managers look at the strengths, weaknesses, opportunities, and threats facing the firm.
   • *What are the four types of planning, and how are they related to the organization's goals and objectives?*
   Strategic planning is broad, long-range planning that outlines the goals of the organization. *Tactical planning* is specific, short-term planning that lists organizational objectives. *Operational planning* is part of tactical planning and involves setting specific timetables and standards. *Contingency planning* involves developing an alternative set of plans in case the first set doesn't work out.
   • *What are the steps involved in decision making?*
   The seven Ds of decision making are (1) define the situation, (2) describe and collect needed information, (3) develop alternatives, (4) develop agreement among those involved, (5) decide which alternative is best, (6) do what is indicated (begin implementation), and (7) determine whether or not the decision was a good one and follow up.

4. Describe the organizing function of management, including staffing and diversity management.

4. Organizing means allocating resources (such as funds for various departments), assigning tasks, and establishing procedures for accomplishing the organizational objectives.
   • *What are some of the latest trends in organizational management?*
   Many firms are creating self-managed teams. In those firms, managers tend to do more coaching and training than telling people what to do. Another trend is toward stakeholder-oriented management. In those cases, management tries to satisfy the needs of all stakeholders, including employees, customers, suppliers, dealers, environmental groups, and the surrounding communities.
   • *What changes in the marketplace have made staffing more important?*
   E-commerce CEOs must spend a lot of time recruiting because their companies grow so fast and run on the knowledge of mostly young workers.

Keeping people is also critical because there are lots of companies seeking new talent and people feel free today to go where the action is fastest (and pays the most in dollars or stock options). Also, the labor force is much more diverse today than in the past and managers must learn to make the most of the talents of each person.

5. Executives today must be more than just managers; they must be leaders as well.
   • *What's the difference between a manager and a leader?*
   A manager plans, organizes, and controls functions within an organization. A leader has vision and inspires others to grasp that vision, establishes corporate values, emphasizes corporate ethics, and doesn't fear change.
   • *Describe the various leadership styles.*
   Figure 7.4 (on p. 219) shows a continuum of leadership styles ranging from boss-centered to subordinate-centered leadership.
   • *Which leadership style is best?*
   The best (most effective) leadership style depends on the people being led and the situation. The challenge of the future will be to empower self-managed teams to manage themselves. This is a move away from autocratic leadership.
   • *What does empowerment mean?*
   Empowerment means giving employees the authority and responsibility to respond quickly to customer requests. *Enabling* is the term used to describe giving workers the education and tools they need to assume their new decision-making powers. Knowledge management involves finding the right information, keeping the information in a readily accessible place, and making the information known to everyone in the firm. Knowledge management is another way of enabling workers to do the best job they can.

5. Explain the differences between leaders and managers, and describe the various leadership styles.

6. The control function of management involves measuring employee performance against objectives and standards, rewarding people for a job well done, and taking corrective action if necessary.
   • *What are the five steps of the control function?*
   Controlling incorporates (1) setting clear standards, (2) monitoring and recording performance, (3) comparing performance with plans and standards, (4) communicating results and deviations to employees, and (5) providing positive feedback for a job well done and taking corrective action if necessary.
   • *What qualities must standards possess to be used to measure performance results?*
   Standards must be specific, attainable, and measurable.
   • *What are the latest performance standards?*
   Modern companies consider customer satisfaction to be a key measure of success. A corporate scorecard enables a company to measure customer satisfaction as well as traditional standards of success, such as profit and return on investment.

6. Summarize the five steps of the control function of management.

7. Managers must be good planners, organizers, coordinators, communicators, morale builders, and motivators.
   • *What skills do managers need to be all of these things?*
   Managers must have three categories of skills: (1) technical skills (ability to perform specific tasks such as selling products or developing software), (2) human relations skills (ability to communicate and motivate), and (3) conceptual skills (ability to see organizations as a whole and how all the parts fit together.

7. Differentiate the skills needed at each level of management.

• Are these skills equally important at all management levels?
Managers at different levels need different skills. Top managers rely heavily on human relations and conceptual skills and rarely use technical skills, while first-line supervisors need strong technical and human relations skills but use conceptual skills less often. Middle managers need to have a balance of all of three skills (see Figure 7.7).

KEY TERMS

autocratic leadership 217

conceptual skills 224

contingency planning 210

controlling 207

decision making 211

empowerment 221

enabling 221

external customers 223

goals 208

human relations skills 224

internal customers 223

knowledge management 221

laissez-faire (free-rein) leadership 219

leading 207

management 206

managing diversity 215

middle management 212

mission statement 208

objectives 208

operational planning 210

organization chart 211

organizing 206

participative (democratic) leadership 217

planning 206

staffing 214

strategic planning 209

supervisory management 212

SWOT analysis 208

tactical planning 210

technical skills 224

top management 212

vision 207

democratic leadership

DEVELOPING WORKPLACE SKILLS

1. Do some career planning by doing a SWOT analysis of your present situation. What does the marketplace for your chosen career(s) look like today? What skills do you have that will make you a winner in that type of career? What weaknesses might you target to improve? What are the threats to that career choice? What are the opportunites? Prepare a two-minute presentation to the class.

2. Bring several decks of cards to class and have the class break up into teams of six or so members. Each team should then elect a leader. Each leader should be assigned a leadership style: autocratic, participative (democratic), or laissez-faire. Have each team try to build a house of cards by stacking them side by side and on top of each other. Each team member should then report his or her experience under that style of leadership.

3. In small groups, debate the advantages and disadvantages of becoming a manager. Does the size of the business make a difference? What are the advantages of a career in business versus a career in a nonprofit organization?

4. On the Internet or in the library, review several issues of *Business Week, Forbes, Inc.,* and other business journals for information about key executives and managers. How much do they make? (See *Business Week*'s annual survey.) Do you believe top managers earn their pay? Be prepared to give a two-minute presentation to the class about your findings and beliefs.

5. Review Figure 7.4 and discuss managers you have known, worked for, or read about who have practiced each style. Which did you like best? Why? Which were most effective? Why?

Purpose

To test your ability to make appropriate supervisory decisions.

Exercise

Go to the Leadership Challenge part of the Positive Employee Relations Council Web site (www.perc.net/Background.html). This simulation, the site claims, "will involve you in fictional but realistic situations. It is broken down into moves or steps and the objective is to finish with the least number of steps and a high score. You will discover that this simulation is a maze of related decisions and interacting problems. You will find that effective supervisory decisions bring you closer to the end of the challenge, and weaker decisions inhibit your efforts, require additional steps, and get you further involved."
Print the scorecard to record your results.

1. How did you score?

2. Improve your score by taking the challenge again using what you learned on the first round to make wiser decisions.

3. What did you learn from this exercise?

Purpose:

To perform a simple SWOT analysis.

Exercise:

Go to www.marketingteacher.com/Lessons/lesson_swot.htm and complete the SWOT analysis for Highly Brill Leisure Center.

1. What are Brill's strengths, weakness, opportunities, and threats?

2. Analyze Brill's weaknesses. How do you think the company's strengths might be used to overcome some of its weaknesses?

3. Analyze Brill's opportunities and threats. What additional opportunities can you suggest for Brill? What additional threats can you identify?

PRACTICING MANAGEMENT DECISIONS

CASE

LEADING IN A LEADERLESS COMPANY

Business Week magazine devoted a recent issue to the future of business. Writer John Byrne speculated about the future of leadership. He said that the 21st century would be unfriendly to leaders who try to run their companies by the sheer force of will. He said that success would come, instead, to companies that are "leaderless"—or companies whose leadership is so widely shared that they resemble ant colonies or beehives. In a world that is becoming more dependent on brainpower, having teams at the top will make more sense than having a single top manager. The Internet enables companies to act more like beehives because information can be shared horizontally rather than sent up to the top manager's office and then back down again. Decisions can be made instantly by the best people equipped to make them.

In the past, uniform thinking from the top could cripple an organization. Today, however, team leadership is ideally suited for the new reality of fast-changing markets. Urgent projects often require the coordinated contribution of many talented people working together. Such thinking does not happen at the top of the organization; it takes place down among the workers.

In the future, therefore, managers are more likely to be chosen for their team experience and their ability to delegate rather than make all key decisions themselves. Companies in the future, it is said, will be 'led' by people who understand that in business, as in nature, no one person can be really in control.

Discussion Questions

1. What would you look for on a résumé that would indicate that a candidate for work was a self-motivated team player? Are you that type? How do you know?
2. Given your experience with managers in the past, what problems do you see some managers having with letting employees decide for themselves the best way to do things and giving them the power to obtain needed equipment?
3. What would happen if all the businesses in your area had their employees mix with customers to hear their comments and complaints? Would that be a good or bad thing? Why?
4. What are the various ways you can think of for companies to pay bonuses to team members? One way is to divide the money equally. What are other ways? Which would you prefer as a team member?

Sources: John A. Byrne, "The Global Corporation Becomes the Leaderless Corporation," *Business Week*, August 30, 1999, pp. 88–90, and Etienne C. Wenger and William M. Synder, "Communities of Practice: The Organizational Frontier," *Harvard Business Review*, January–February 2000, pp. 139–45.

VIDEO CASE

THE CISCO KID

Leaders are expected to create a vision for their firms. It gives the organization a sense of purpose and a set of values. For Cisco Systems, that vision is set by John Chambers. You can read all about Chambers in the profile at the beginning of this chapter. This video is an opportunity for you to see Chambers in action and hear what he has to say.

His vision for the future is based on the Internet. This is no surprise since he provides the switches and routers that provide the intersections and direct the traffic on the information highway. You will see that his vision extends into the telecom business where he expects to have a dominant position in the future.

What makes Cisco an outstanding company is its leader's devotion to two groups: employees and customers. You need great employees to put out a great product. To motivate his employees, Chambers is very generous with stock options for everyone, including those below the management ranks. Any employee can come in on his or her birthday and talk with Chambers about whatever is on his or her mind. Chambers talks to key customers daily and responds to their wants and needs as quickly as he can.

Worth magazine conducted a poll to see who the most admired leaders in business are today. Chambers was number one. Steve Jobs of Apple Computer was second. He too was able to create a vision for his employees. That vision led to computers that were easier to use. When Jobs left Apple, the company began to falter. When he came back, he had a vision of a more attractive computer. His leadership brought the company back.

Third was Michael Dell of Dell Computer. His vision was to deliver custom-made computers to people in a few days. His vision became a reality and Dell became a leader in the industry.

Fourth was Larry Ellison of Oracle. He, like the others, is a visionary and has led his company to rapid growth. It is no accident that all of these leaders are in high-tech firms because high tech dominated the market in the 1990s. The stock market downturn of 2000–2001 has been a test of the leadership abilities of these men. They must now create a new vision and convince investors that they still have what it takes to be market leaders. The Internet is not dead: It is merely resting. Telecom is not dead either. It too will have its day. The stock market goes up and down, but great companies always seem to find the resources to stay in front. The most important resource is a leader like John Chambers.

Discussion Questions

1. What is the difference between a brilliant manager and a great leader?

2. What kind of leader seems to prosper in today's economic environment: autocratic, democratic, or bureaucratic? Why?

3. How important is staffing to today's high-tech firms? Is it more or less important than in other firms?

4. Why is knowledge management so important in today's firms and how does Cisco and other companies assist in that process?

8

Managing the Move Toward Customer-Driven Business Organizations

LEARNING GOALS

AFTER YOU HAVE READ AND STUDIED THIS CHAPTER, YOU SHOULD BE ABLE TO

1 Explain the organizational theories of Fayol and Weber.

2 Discuss the various issues involved in structuring and restructuring organizations.

3 Describe traditional organizations and their limitations.

4 Show how matrix-style organizations and cross-functional teams help companies become more customer oriented.

5 Defend the use of various organizational tools and techniques such as networking, reengineering, and outsourcing.

6 Give examples to show how organizational culture and the informal organization can hinder or assist organizational change.

Getting to Know Carly Fiorina of Hewlett-Packard

Carleton (Carly) Fiorina got her MBA in marketing from the University of Maryland in 1980. She started her career in AT&T's government sales office and then moved into network systems, where she saw more opportunity for her creativity. When Lucent Technologies split off from AT&T to focus on wireless products, Fiorina followed. Using her organizational skills, she was instrumental in making the firm a leading Internet company. She became president of Lucent's global service-provider business in 1998.

When Hewlett-Packard (HP) began searching for a new CEO, it was looking for someone who could restructure the firm to make it a leader in e-commerce. Fiorina was selected from some 300 candidates. One of her competitors for the position was another woman: Ann Livermore, the CEO of Enterprise Computing, one of the four main "product companies" at HP. Livermore had developed HP's e-service strategy and was the top *internal* candidate. She is still at HP, and she and Fiorina together are working to make HP a leading Internet company.

At her first major presentation to Wall Street analysts, Fiorina announced a major reorganization of HP's business structure. Specifically, she planned to merge HP's four product companies into two and put much more focus on customer relations. The idea was to make HP a more flexible, faster-moving, and customer-oriented firm than it had been. In short, she wanted to "reinvent" the firm. Here is how she described the task: "Reinvention to me is about four things. It's about culture, it's about strategy, it's about what you measure and how you reward those measurements, and it's about business process." In another interview she said,

"We're going to preserve the best, and we've got to reinvent the rest—but we've got to get on with it in a hurry . . . We'll startle the world with our speed. We'll startle the world with our aggressiveness. And we'll startle the world delivering on inventions." In the first quarter of Fiorina's leadership, HP saw revenues rise by 14 percent and its stock price by 36 percent.

Fiorina slashed bloated operating costs, reorganized divisions, and changed the sales compensation plan. To increase brand recognition, Fiorina cut the number of different brand names used by the company from 100 to 1. The hiring of Fiorina at HP has been compared to the hiring of Lou Gerstner at IBM. Both companies brought in an outsider to turn a stodgy Fortune 500 technology concern into a more responsive, customer-oriented industry leader.

Many top companies are restructuring their operations in order to focus on pleasing customers. This chapter will teach you the foundational principles behind organizational design and then lead you to discover the latest concepts. When Carly Fiorina was selected to be the new CEO at Hewlett-Packard, she made a break in the "glass ceiling," the invisible barrier that long seemed to keep women from becoming top managers at leading corporations. Other talented men and women will find such exciting new opportunities in those firms that are dynamic enough to reorganize to meet the demands of the information age.

Sources: "Wake-Up Call for HP," *Technology Review,* May–June 2000, pp. 94–100; "She Can Turn Anything into Gold," *Success,* December / January 2001, p. 30; and "Are Women Better Leaders," *U.S. News and World Report,* January 29, 2001.

THE CHANGING ORGANIZATION

Never before in the history of business has so much change been introduced so quickly, sometimes too quickly.[1] As you learned in earlier chapters, much of that change is due to the changing business environment—that is, more global competition and faster technological change, especially new challenges from Internet commerce. Equally important to many businesses is the change in consumer expectations. Consumers today expect high-quality products and fast, friendly service—at a reasonable cost. Managing change, then, has become a critical managerial function. That sometimes includes changing the whole organizational structure, as Carly Fiorina did at Hewlett-Packard.

Organizations in the past were designed more to facilitate management than to please the customer. Companies designed many rules and regulations to give managers control over employees. To supplement the work of the line managers, who were responsible for making products and distributing them to customers, companies hired specialists in areas such as law and human resource management. We shall explore in some detail the history of organizational design so that you can see what the foundations are. Then we shall explore the newest forms of organization, forms that are being designed to better serve the customer. Though often dramatic and disruptive, the changes keep companies competitive in today's dynamic business environment. One way to introduce such changes is to bring in new managers from *outside* the firm, managers who have experience with the Internet and with flexible ways of organizing. That's what IBM did when it brought in Lou Gerstner and what Hewlett-Packard did when it brought in Carly Fiorina.

The Historical Development of Organizational Design

To understand what is happening in organizations today, it is best to begin with a firm foundation of organizational principles. Many principles of traditional organizational design are still important today. However, some have lost importance and others may no longer apply at all, and organizational leaders need to understand which principles are still important and which are not. So let's begin by exploring the history of organizations.

Until the 20th century, most businesses were rather small, the processes for producing goods were rather simple, and organizing workers was fairly easy. Not until the 1900s and the introduction of mass production (efficiently producing large quantities of goods) did businesses become complex in terms of production processes and economics. The bigger the plant, the more efficient production became. Business growth led to what was called **economy of scale.** This term refers to the fact that companies can produce goods more inexpensively if they can purchase raw materials in bulk; the average cost of goods goes down as production levels increase.

During this era of mass production, organization theorists emerged. In France, Henri Fayol published his book *Administration industrielle et générale* in 1919. It was popularized in the United States in 1949 under the title *General and Industrial Management.* Sociologist Max Weber (pronounced "Vay-ber") was writing about organization theory in Germany about the same time Fayol was writing his books in France. Note that it was only a little more than 50 years ago that organization theory became popular in the United States.

Fayol's Principles of Organization

Fayol introduced such principles as the following:[2]

- *Unity of command.* Each worker is to report to one, and only one, boss. The benefits of this principle are obvious. What happens if two different

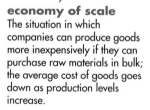

economy of scale
The situation in which companies can produce goods more inexpensively if they can purchase raw materials in bulk; the average cost of goods goes down as production levels increase.

bosses give you two different assignments? Which one should you follow? To prevent such confusion, each person is to report to only one manager.

- *Hierarchy of authority.* All workers should know to whom they should report. Managers should have the right to give orders and expect others to follow.

- *Division of labor.* Functions are to be divided into areas of specialization such as production, marketing, and finance.

- *Subordination of individual interests to the general interest.* Workers are to think of themselves as a coordinated team. The goals of the team are more important than the goals of individual workers.

- *Authority.* Managers have the right to give orders and the power to exact obedience. Authority and responsibility are related: Whenever authority is exercised, responsibility arises.

- *Degree of centralization.* The amount of decision-making power vested in top management should vary by circumstances. In a small organization, it's possible to centralize all decision-making power in the top manager. In a larger organization, however, some decision-making power should be delegated to lower-level managers and employees on both major and minor issues.

- *Clear communication channels.* All workers should be able to reach others in the firm quickly and easily.

- *Order.* Materials and people should be placed and maintained in the proper location.

- *Equity.* A manager should treat employees and peers with respect and justice.

- *Esprit de corps.* A spirit of pride and loyalty should be created among people in the firm.

Management courses in colleges throughout the world taught these principles for years, and they became synonymous with the concept of management. Organizations were designed so that no person had more than one boss, lines of authority were clear, and everyone knew to whom they were to report. Naturally, these principles tended to be written down as rules, policies, and regulations as organizations grew larger. That process of rule making often led to rather rigid organizations that didn't respond quickly to consumer requests. For example, the Department of Motor Vehicles (DMV) in various cities and auto repair facilities have often been cited as relatively slow to adapt to the needs of their customers. For example, many customers expect to wait in long lines at the DMV, only to speak to employees who are not empowered to be flexible when responding to their unique needs. Some DMVs are still organized that way, but others have reorganized; some even allow customers to conduct their business over the Internet.

Max Weber and Organizational Theory

Max Weber's book *The Theory of Social and Economic Organizations,* like Fayol's, also appeared in the United States in the late 1940s. It was Weber who promoted the pyramid-shaped organization structure that became so popular in large firms. Weber put great trust in managers and felt that the firm would do well if employees simply did what they were told. The less decision making employees had to do, the better. Clearly, this is a reasonable way to operate if you're dealing with relatively uneducated and untrained workers. Often, such workers were the only ones available at the time Weber was writing; most

When you go to a store and the clerk says, "I'm sorry I can't do that, it's against company policy," you can blame Max Weber and his theories. At one time less-educated workers were best managed, it was believed, by having them follow many strict rules and regulations monitored by managers or supervisors. Are there industries or businesses today where you think it would be desirable or necessary to continue to use such controls?

employees did not have the kind of educational background and technical skills that most of today's workers have.

Weber's principles of organization were similar to Fayol's. In addition, Weber emphasized

- Job descriptions.
- Written rules, decision guidelines, and detailed records.
- Consistent procedures, regulations, and policies.
- Staffing and promotion based on qualifications.

Weber believed that large organizations demanded clearly established rules and guidelines that were to be followed precisely. Although his principles seemed to make a great deal of sense at the time, the practice of establishing rules and procedures became so rigid in some companies that it became counterproductive.

Today, many organizations are attempting to rid themselves of the pyramid structure because it slows the process of change. In the past, when several layers of management had to be included in a decision, that decision could take weeks to make. In today's companies, decisions often have to be made within days or minutes. Thus, many firms are eliminating many managerial and nonmanagerial positions and giving more authority and responsibility to those employees who deal directly with consumers. As you learned in Chapter 7, the process of eliminating these positions is called **downsizing** because it allows the organization to operate with fewer managers and workers. Sometimes the process is called *rightsizing* because the idea is to make the organization just the right size to adapt quickly to consumer wants and needs. Many managers who have been downsized have started their own businesses, in which they have more control and are able to adapt more quickly to the marketplace than they could in a large corporation.

downsizing
The process of eliminating managerial and non-managerial positions.

Turning Managerial Concepts into Organizational Design

Following the concepts of theorists like Fayol and Weber, managers in the mid-1900s began designing organizations that could implement those concepts. **Organizational design** is the structuring of workers so that they can best accomplish the firm's goals. In the past, many organizations were designed so that managers could control workers, and most organizations are still organized that way, with everything set up in a hierarchy. A **hierarchy** is a system in which one person is at the top of the organization and there is a ranked or sequential ordering from the top down of managers who are responsible to that person. Since one person can't keep track of thousands of workers, the top manager needs many lower-level managers to help. Figure 8.1 shows a typical hierarchical organization structure.

Some organizations have had as many as 10 to 14 layers of management between the chief executive officer (CEO) and the lowest-level employees. If employees wanted to introduce work changes, they would ask a supervisor, who would ask a manager, who would ask a manager at the next level up, and so on. Eventually a decision would be made and passed down from manager to manager until it reached the employee. Such decisions could often take weeks or months to be made.

Max Weber used the word *bureaucrat* to describe a middle manager whose function was to implement top management's orders. Thus, **bureaucracy**

organizational design
The structuring of workers so that they can best accomplish the firm's goals.

hierarchy
A system in which one person is at the top of the organization and there is a ranked or sequential ordering from the top down of managers who are responsible to that person.

bureaucracy
An organization with many layers of managers who set rules and regulations and oversee all decisions

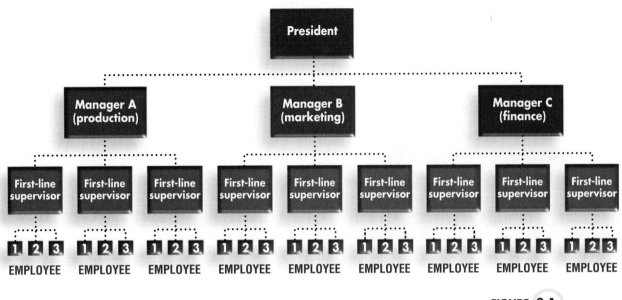

```
                              ┌─────────────┐
                              │  President  │
                              └─────────────┘
```

| Manager A (production) | Manager B (marketing) | Manager C (finance) |

First-line supervisor (×9)

1 2 3 EMPLOYEE (×9)

FIGURE 8.1

TYPICAL ORGANIZATION CHART

This is a rather standard chart with managers for major functions and supervisors reporting to the managers. Each supervisor manages three employees.

came to be the term used for an organization with many layers of managers who set rules and regulations and oversee all decisions (see Figure 8.2). It is such bureaucracy that forces employees to say to customers, "I'm sorry, but I can't do what you want. I have to follow the rules." If police officers operated that way, they would *have* to give a ticket to everyone driving over 55 miles per hour on a highway where that was the speed limit. Many people would be upset by such a rigid following of the rules. Similarly, many customers are upset by employees who insist on following the rules to the letter and don't go a little out of their way to make customers happy.

When employees have to ask their managers for permission to make a change, the process may take so long that customers become annoyed. This is as true in a small organization such as a flower shop as it is in a major organization like Ford Motor Company. The employee has to find the manager, get permission, come back to the customer, and so on. Since many customers want efficient service—and they want it *now*—slow service due to bureaucracy is not acceptable in today's competitive environment.

To make customers happy, organizations are giving employees more power to make decisions on their own. Rather than having to follow strict rules and regulations, they are encouraged to please the customer no matter what. For example, at Nordstrom, a chain of upscale department stores, an employee can accept a return from a customer without seeking managerial approval, even if the garment

What can an auto manufacturer do to assure customers of the finest service through its dealers? The answer for Chrysler is to use annual audits and customer satisfaction surveys to establish standards for quality service and to monitor dealer performance and achievement. If you were a dealer what would your perspective be on this initiative by Chrysler?

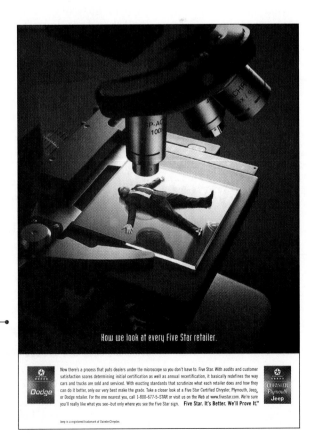

How we look at every Five Star retailer.

FIGURE 8.2

BUREAUCRATIC
ORGANIZATION
STRUCTURE

was not originally sold at that store. As you read earlier, giving employees such authority and responsibility to make decisions and please customers is called *empowerment* ▶P.20◀. Since an individual employee may not have all the skills and knowledge needed to please customers, employees have been encouraged to form small groups or teams so that someone in the group can be responsive to customer requests. After we have explored the major issues involved in organizational design, we will discuss such teams in depth.

Bureaucratic Organizations Emphasize Functional Separation In a bureaucratic organization, a chain of command goes from the top down. To make the process easier, organizations are set up by function. That is, there are separate departments for design, engineering, production, marketing, finance, human resource management, accounting, legal issues, and so on.

Bureaucracies encourage people to specialize in one function, for which they prepare by specializing in school. Communication among departments in traditional businesses is minimal. Career advancement for the typical employee means moving up within a function. For example, an employee in a traditional company might move up from salesperson to sales trainer to sales manager to regional manager to marketing manager to marketing vice president.

In the past, such an organization structure worked well because employees could specialize in one area and learn it well. The problem today is that such organizations aren't very responsive to customer wants and needs. Such a career progression doesn't regularly expose people to other functions in the firm and therefore doesn't create much interfunctional cooperation. As you shall see later in the chapter, one answer is to develop cross-functional teams.

PROGRESS ASSESSMENT

• How many of Fayol's principles can you name?

• What principles did Weber add?

• What is a hierarchy?

CRITICAL THINKING

Start noticing how many clerks and other customer-contact people say things like "That's not our policy" or "We don't do things that way" when you request some unusual service. Such answers are the result of bureaucratic rules and regulations that employees are forced to follow. Imagine a day when employees are free to adjust to the wants and needs of customers. What organizational changes would have to be made? Would the results be worth the effort?

ISSUES INVOLVED IN STRUCTURING AND RESTRUCTURING ORGANIZATIONS

restructuring
Redesigning an organization so that it can more effectively and efficiently serve its customers.

Restructuring is redesigning an organization so that it can more effectively and efficiently serve its customers. In designing or redesigning more responsive organizations, firms have had to deal with the following organizational issues:

(1) tall versus flat organization structures, (2) span of control, (3) departmentalization, and (4) centralization versus decentralization.

Tall versus Flat Organization Structures

In the early 20th century, organizations grew bigger and bigger, adding layer after layer of management until they came to have what are called *tall organization structures*. This means, simply, that the pyramidal organization chart would be quite tall because of the various levels of management. Some organizations, such as General Motors, had as many as 14 levels. You can imagine how a message would be distorted as it moved up the organization from manager to manager and then back down. When viewing such a tall organization, you saw a huge complex of managers, management assistants, secretaries, assistant secretaries, supervisors, trainers, and so on. The cost of keeping all these managers and support people was quite high. The paperwork they generated was enormous, and the inefficiencies in communication and decision making became intolerable.

General Motors.

"If the people who make the car don't fit together, the car won't either."

Welcome to the Excel training course. Before it's over, Saturn's Dennis Bowman will take these General Motors employees on a real adventure. They'll scale walls. Walk across high wires. Plunge backwards into the waiting arms of their coworkers. And take away some valuable lessons about trust, cooperation and seeing things from the other person's point of view. Developed by Saturn, Excel is now used throughout General Motors. It's turning out graduates who know the power of teamwork. Who go a little further to build quality automobiles. And who believe that the right way to treat a customer is the way you'd want to be treated yourself.

The result was the development of flat organizations. A *flat organization structure* is one where there are few layers of management (see Figure 8.3). Such structures are usually much more responsive to customer demands because power to make decisions may be given to lower-level employees, and managers don't have to make so many decisions. In a bookstore that has such a structure, employees may have the authority to arrange shelves by category, process special orders for customers, and so on. In many ways, larger organizations were trying to match the friendliness of smaller firms where the workers often knew the customers by name. One question that came up in larger firms trying to become flatter was "How many people can effectively report to one manager?" We'll explore that question next.

One of the most important goals of organizations today is teamwork. Teamwork builds trust, cooperation, and joint commitments to achieve the firm's objectives. Are you working in teams while in school in order to develop the team-building skills that companies will need in the future?

Choosing the Appropriate Span of Control

Span of control refers to the optimum number of subordinates a manager supervises or should supervise. There are many factors to consider when determining span of control. At lower levels, where work is standardized, it's possible to implement a wide span of control (15 to 40 workers). For example, one supervisor can be responsible for 20 or more workers who are assembling computers or cleaning up movie theaters. However, the number gradually narrows at higher levels of the organization because work is less standardized and there's more need for face-to-face communication. Variables in span of control include the following:

1. *Capabilities of the manager.* The more experienced and capable a manager is, the broader the span of control can be. (More workers can report to that manager.)

2. *Capabilities of the subordinates.* The more the subordinates need supervision, the narrower the span of control should be. (Fewer workers report to one manager.)

span of control
The optimum number of subordinates a manager supervises or should supervise.

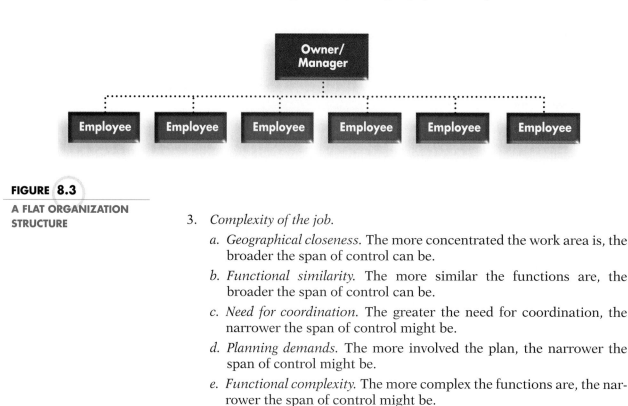

FIGURE 8.3

A FLAT ORGANIZATION STRUCTURE

3. *Complexity of the job.*

   a. *Geographical closeness.* The more concentrated the work area is, the broader the span of control can be.

   b. *Functional similarity.* The more similar the functions are, the broader the span of control can be.

   c. *Need for coordination.* The greater the need for coordination, the narrower the span of control might be.

   d. *Planning demands.* The more involved the plan, the narrower the span of control might be.

   e. *Functional complexity.* The more complex the functions are, the narrower the span of control might be.

Other factors to consider include the professionalism of superiors and subordinates and the number of new problems that occur in a day.

In business, the span of control varies widely. The number of people reporting to the president may range from 1 to 80 or more. The trend is to expand the span of control as organizations get rid of middle managers and hire more educated and talented lower-level employees. It's possible to increase the span of control as employees become more professional, as information technology makes it possible for managers to handle more information, and as employees take on more responsibility for self-management. At Rowe Furniture in Salem, Virginia, for example, the manufacturing chief dismantled the assembly line

This is Dell Computer's Metic 12 facility in Austin, Texas. Employees work in teams of two, like this one, to assemble computers. One supervisor can be responsible for many such teams because the work is standardized. What advantages does Dell's system provide the company? What advantages does working in small teams afford Dell's employees?

and gave the people who had previously performed limited functions (sewing, gluing, stapling) the freedom to make sofas as they saw fit. Productivity and quality soared because the people were so talented. More companies could expand the span of control if they trained their employees better and were willing to trust them more.[3]

Advantages and Disadvantages of Departmentalization

Departmentalization is the dividing of organizational functions into separate units. The traditional way to departmentalize organizations is by function. Functional structure is the grouping of workers into departments based on similar skills, expertise, or resource use. There might be, for example, a production department, a transportation department, a finance department, an accounting department, a marketing department, a data processing department, and so on. Departmentalization enables employees to specialize and work together more efficiently. Other advantages include the following:

departmentalization
The dividing of organizational functions into separate units.

1. Employees can develop skills in depth and can progress within a department as they master those skills.

2. The company can achieve economies of scale in that it can centralize all the resources it needs and locate various experts in that area.

3. There's good coordination within the function, and top management can easily direct and control various departments' activities.

As for disadvantages of departmentalization,

1. There may be a lack of communication among the different departments. For example, production may be isolated from marketing so that the people making the product do not get the proper feedback from customers.

2. Individual employees may begin to identify with their department and its goals rather than with the goals of the organization as a whole.

3. The company's response to external changes may be slow.

Some furniture manufacturers still rely on assembly lines, as shown here. Rowe Furniture dismantled the assembly line and let workers make the furniture in the way they preferred. As workers become more self-managed, fewer supervisors are needed. Can you see how workers would become more motivated if they are allowed to design their own workplace and use their own processes?

4. People may not be trained to take different managerial responsibilities; rather, they tend to become narrow specialists.

5. People in the same department tend to think alike (engage in group think) and may need input from outside the department to become more creative.

CRITICAL THINKING

Given the limitations of departmentalization, businesses are now trying to re-design their structures to optimize skill development while increasing communication among employees in different departments. The goal, remember, is to better serve customers and to win their loyalty. What kind of skills and attributes might you need to prepare yourself to work in such an organization?

Different Ways to Departmentalize

Companies have tried various ways to departmentalize to better serve customers. Figure 8.4 shows five ways a firm can departmentalize. One form of departmentalization is by product. A book publisher might have a trade book department (books sold to the general public), a textbook department, and a technical book department. Customers for each type of book are different, so separate development and marketing processes are created for each type.

The most basic way to departmentalize, as we discussed above, is by function. This text is divided by business functions because such groupings are most common. Production, marketing, finance, human resource management, and accounting are all distinct functions calling for separate skills. Companies are now discovering, however, that functional separation isn't always the most responsive form of organization.

It makes more sense in some organizations to departmentalize by customer group. A pharmaceutical company, for example, might have one department that focuses on the consumer market, another that calls on hospitals (the institutional market), and another that targets doctors.

Some firms group their units by geographic location because customers vary so greatly by region. The United States is usually considered one market area. Japan, Europe, and Korea may involve separate departments.

The decision about which way to departmentalize depends greatly on the nature of the product and the customers served. A few firms find that it's more efficient to separate activities by process. For example, a firm that makes leather coats may have one department cut the leather, another dye it, and a third sew the coat together.

Some firms use a combination of departmentalization techniques. For example, they could departmentalize simultaneously among the different layers by function, by geography, and by customers.

The development of the Internet has created whole new opportunities for reaching customers. Not only can you sell to customers directly over the Internet, but you can interact with them, ask them questions, and provide them with any information they may want. Companies must now learn to coordinate the efforts made by their traditional departments and their Internet people to create a friendly, easy-to-use process for accessing information and buying goods and services. Not many firms have implemented such coordinated systems for meeting customer needs, but those that have are winning market share.[4]

Centralization versus Decentralization of Authority

Imagine for a minute that you're a top manager for a retail company such as J. C. Penney. Your temptation may be to preserve control over all your stores in

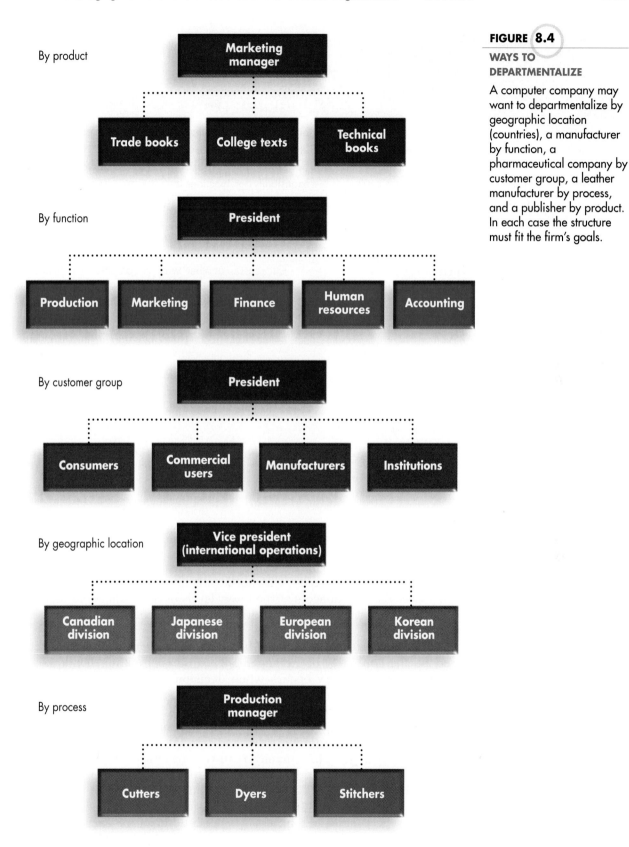

By product

Marketing manager

Trade books   College texts   Technical books

By function

President

Production   Marketing   Finance   Human resources   Accounting

By customer group

President

Consumers   Commercial users   Manufacturers   Institutions

By geographic location

Vice president (international operations)

Canadian division   Japanese division   European division   Korean division

By process

Production manager

Cutters   Dyers   Stitchers

FIGURE 8.4

WAYS TO DEPARTMENTALIZE

A computer company may want to departmentalize by geographic location (countries), a manufacturer by function, a pharmaceutical company by customer group, a leather manufacturer by process, and a publisher by product. In each case the structure must fit the firm's goals.

REACHING BEYOND OUR BORDERS
www.ford.com

Ford Decentralizes to Meet the New Competition

Nothing has done more to unite organizations throughout the world than the emergence of the Internet. The Internet is a ready-made marketplace that consists of a $1 trillion worth of computer power, network connections, and databases stuffed with information about individual consumers and groups. What's more amazing is that it's available free to anyone with a phone line, a personal computer, a modem, and an Internet connector—and it's open 24 hours a day, seven days a week. This may sound wonderful to you, but it is a tremendous challenge to traditional organizations organized in traditional ways. They simply cannot respond quickly enough to marketplace changes or reach global markets as quickly and efficiently as new companies can—companies designed to take advantage of the Internet. But what are they to do? How do they reorganize to match such competition?

The CEO of Ford Motor Company says that traditional companies have to become more nimble and more closely attuned to consumers. One source at Ford says, "You've got to break down the business into the smallest possible units to give the employees in them authority and accountability." (Throughout this text, we call that empowerment.) In the past, Ford centralized worldwide responsibility for functions such as product development, purchasing, design, and manufacturing. The new model decentralizes such decisions so that managers in Europe and South America can more readily adapt to consumers in those markets.

Of course, another way to compete with Internet firms is to start an Internet firm of your own or join one of the established firms. Even smaller firms can reach global markets by joining Amazon.com and selling their products online. Automobile companies can get in touch with consumers throughout the world and learn their preferences. Design and production can be placed anywhere as long as the input of the consumer is readily available. And it is on the Internet.

Sources: Kathleen Kerwin and Jack Ewing, "Nasser: Ford Be Nimble," *Business Week*, September 27, 1999, pp. 42–43; and "Ambitious Ford Aims High as It Sets Targets," *Birmingham Post*, January 12, 2001, p. 22.

---

order to maintain a uniform image and merchandise. You've noticed such control works well for McDonald's; why not J. C. Penney? The degree to which an organization allows managers at the lower levels of the managerial hierarchy to make decisions determines the degree of decentralization that an organization practices.

centralized authority
An organization structure in which decision-making authority is maintained at the top level of management at the company's headquarters.

decentralized authority
An organization structure in which decision-making authority is delegated to lower-level managers more familiar with local conditions than headquarters management could be.

Centralized authority occurs when decision-making authority is maintained at the top level of management at the company's headquarters. **Decentralized authority** occurs when decision-making authority is delegated to lower-level managers and employees who are more familiar with local conditions than headquarters management could be.

J. C. Penney customers in California, for example, are likely to demand clothing styles different from those demanded in Minnesota or Maine. It makes sense, therefore, to give store managers in various cities the authority to buy, price, and promote merchandise appropriate for each area. Such a delegation of authority is an example of decentralized management.

In contrast, McDonald's feels that purchasing, promotion, and other such decisions are best handled centrally. There's little need for each McDonald's restaurant to carry different food products. McDonald's would therefore lean toward centralized authority. Today's rapidly changing markets, added to global differences in consumer tastes, tend to favor more decentralization and thus more delegation of authority. Even McDonald's has learned that its restaurants in England should offer tea, those in Germany should offer beer, those in Japan should offer rice, and so on. Rosenbluth International is a service organization in the travel industry. It too has decentralized so that its separate units can offer the kinds of services demanded in each region while still getting needed resources from corporate headquarters. The Reaching Beyond Our Borders box describes how Ford Motor Company used the Internet to decentralize decision making.

ORGANIZATION MODELS

Now that we've explored the basic principles of organizational design, we can explore in depth the various ways to structure an organization. We'll look at four models: (1) line organizations, (2) line-and-staff organizations, (3) matrix-style organizations, and (4) cross-functional self-managed teams.

Line Organizations

A **line organization** has direct two-way lines of responsibility, authority, and communication running from the top to the bottom of the organization, with all people reporting to only one supervisor. Many small businesses are organized this way. For example, a pizza parlor may have a general manager and a shift manager. All the general employees report to the shift manager, and he or she reports to the general manager or owner.

In larger businesses, a line organization may have the disadvantages of being too inflexible, of having few specialists or experts to advise people along the line, of having lines of communication that are too long, and of being unable to handle the complex decisions involved in an organization with thousands of sometimes unrelated products and literally tons of paperwork.

line organization
An organization that has direct two-way lines of responsibility, authority, and communication running from the top to the bottom of the organization, with all people reporting to only one supervisor.

Line-and-Staff Organizations

To minimize the disadvantages of simple line organizations, many organizations today have both line and staff personnel. A couple of definitions will help. **Line personnel** perform functions that contribute directly to the primary goals of the

line personnel
Employees who perform functions that contribute directly to the primary goals of the organization.

In high-tech industries, technology and competition changes so rapidly that often traditional forms of organization simply won't work. They are being replaced with project management teams and other arrangements that bring together employees from many different areas of the firm. What do you see as the benefits and drawbacks of constant change for employees in high-tech industries?

FIGURE 8.5

**LINE-AND-STAFF
ORGANIZATIONS**

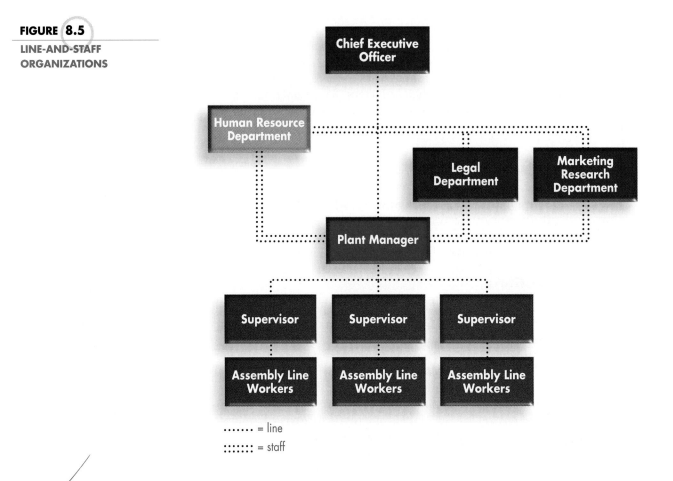

FIGURE 8.5

**LINE-AND-STAFF
ORGANIZATIONS**

······ = line

∷∷∷∷ = staff

staff personnel
Employees who perform functions that assist line personnel in achieving their goals.

organization (e.g., making the product, distributing it, and selling it). **Staff personnel** perform functions that advise and assist line personnel in performing their goals (e.g., marketing research, legal advising, and human resource management). (See Figure 8.5 for a diagram of a line-and-staff organization.)

Many organizations have benefited from the expert advice of staff assistants in areas such as safety, quality control, computer technology, human resource management, and investing. Staff positions strengthen the line positions and are by no means inferior or lower-paid. Having people in staff positions is like having well-paid consultants on the organization's payroll.

Matrix-Style Organizations

Both line and line-and-staff organization structures suffer from a certain inflexibility. Both allow for established lines of authority and communication, and both work well in organizations with a relatively unchanging environment and slow product development, such as firms selling consumer products like toasters and refrigerators. In such firms, clear lines of authority and relatively fixed organization structures are assets that ensure efficient operations.

Today's economic scene, however, is dominated by high-growth industries (e.g., telecommunications, computers, robotics, biotechnology, and aerospace) unlike anything seen in the past. In such industries, competition is stiff and the life cycle of new ideas is short. Emphasis is on new-product development, creativity, special projects, rapid communication, and interdepartmental teamwork. The economic, technological, and competitive environments are rapidly changing.

From those changes grew the popularity of the matrix organization. In a **matrix organization,** specialists from different parts of the organization are

matrix organization
An organization in which specialists from different parts of the organization are brought together to work on specific projects but still remain part of a traditional line-and-staff structure.

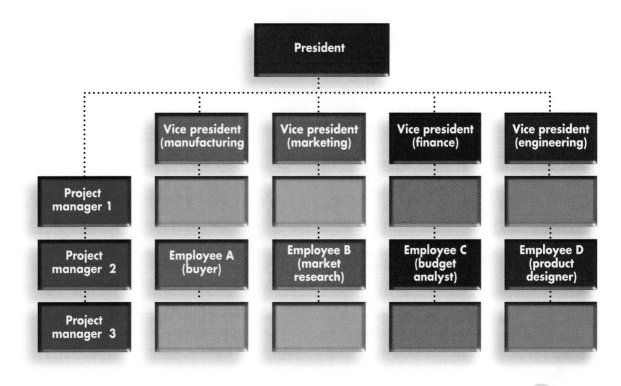

FIGURE 8.6

A MATRIX ORGANIZATION

In a matrix organization, project managers are in charge of teams made up of members of several departments. In this case, project manager 2 supervises employees A, B, C, and D. These employees are accountable not only to project manager 2, but also to the head of their individual departments. For example, employee B, a market researcher, reports to project manager 2 *and* to the vice president of marketing.

brought together to work on specific projects, while still remaining part of a line-and-staff structure. (See Figure 8.6 for a diagram of a matrix organization.) In other words, a project manager can borrow people from different departments to help design and market new product ideas.

Matrix organization structures were first developed in the aerospace industry at firms such as Boeing and Lockheed. The structure is now used in banking, management consulting firms, accounting firms, ad agencies, and school systems. Advantages of a matrix organization structure include the following:

- It gives flexibility to managers in assigning people to projects.
- It encourages interorganizational cooperation and teamwork.
- It can result in creative solutions to problems such as those associated with new-product development.
- It provides for more efficient use of organizational resources.

Although it works well in some organizations, the matrix style doesn't work well in others. As for disadvantages,

- It's costly and complex.
- It can cause confusion among employees as to where their loyalty belongs—to the project manager or to their functional unit.
- It requires good interpersonal skills and cooperative employees and managers.
- It can be only a temporary solution to a long-term problem.

If it seems to you that matrix organizations violate some traditional managerial principles, you're right. Normally a person can't work effectively for two bosses. (Who has the real authority? Which directive has the first priority: the one from the project manager or the one from the employee's immediate supervisor?) In reality, however, the system functions more effectively than you might imagine. To develop a new product, a project manager may be given temporary authority to "borrow" line personnel from engineering, production, marketing, and other line functions. Together, they work to complete the project and then return to their regular positions. Thus, no one really reports to more than one manager at a time. The effectiveness of matrix organizations in high-tech firms has led to the adoption of similar concepts in many firms, including such traditional firms as Rubbermaid. During most of the 1990s, Rubbermaid turned out an average of one new product every day using the team concept from matrix management.

A potential problem with matrix management, however, is that the project teams are *not permanent*. They are formed to solve a problem or develop a new product, and then they break up. There is little chance for cross-functional learning because experts from each function are together for such little time.

The newest trend, therefore, is to develop *permanent* teams and to empower them to work closely with suppliers, customers, and others to quickly and efficiently bring out new, high-quality products while giving great service.[5] The teams are often self-managed. That means that the members of the team don't have to ask a manager whether or not they can do what they want to do to please the customer. They automatically have the freedom and authority to do so.

For empowerment ➤ **P.20** ◄ and/or self-managed teams to work effectively, the organization has to be changed to support that new orientation. Moving from a manager-driven to an employee-driven or team-driven company isn't easy. Managers often resist giving up their authority over workers, while workers often resist the responsibility that comes with self-management. Nonetheless, many of the world's leading organizations are moving in that direction. They're trying to develop an organizational design that best serves the needs of all stakeholders ➤ **P.19** ◄—employees, customers, stockholders, and the community.

Cross-Functional Self-Managed Teams

cross-functional teams
Groups of employees from different departments who work together on a semipermanent basis.

Cross-functional teams are groups of employees from different departments who work together on a semipermanent basis (as opposed to the temporary teams established in matrix-style organizations). As we've said, usually the teams are empowered to make decisions on their own without having to seek the approval of management. That's why the teams are called self-managed.

The barriers between design, engineering, marketing, distribution, and other functions fall when interdepartmental teams are created.

Mei-Lin Cheng and Julie Anderson are managers at Hewlett-Packard's North American distribution organization, which manages the flow of billions of dollars' worth of products, from personal computers to toner cartridges, from order to delivery. Cheng and Anderson had a problem: HP was tak-

Hewlett-Packard (H-P) has to have the best fulfillment system possible. That is, computers and other products have to be shipped within a few days after an order is received. Mei-Lin Cheng and Julie Anderson, shown here, were able to design such a system only when they threw out all the old procedures and began from scratch. What should H-P do to ensure that its fulfillment system remains competitive?

ing 26 days to ship products to customers, while competitors were shipping out PCs within a couple of days.

Since customer responsiveness is one of the most important competitive advantages, HP had to do something to improve its response time. Cheng and Anderson assembled a team of 35 people from HP and two other companies, and gave them total freedom to do what was needed to improve the process. A pilot program was able to cut delivery time from 26 to 8 days for one of HP's bigger customers. The customer, in turn, was able to cut inventories by 20 percent and increase its service level to its own customers.

Cheng and Anderson were able to accomplish their objective by changing all the rules. There was no longer any hierarchy, no titles, no job descriptions, no plans, no step-by-step measures of progress. Instead, team members were encouraged to do whatever it took to make the system work better and faster. The two managers encouraged diversity of views and systems thinking. As a consequence of this change process, everyone in the organization learned to learn. The firm is now capable of responding quickly to other challenges. Employees have learned to work and think in teams. In short, the HP's distribution organization is now a learning system where operations get better over time and people are more content and productive.[6] This example suggests that cross-functional teams result in a greater commitment from employees who take more ownership for their work.

GOING BEYOND ORGANIZATIONAL BOUNDARIES

Cross-functional teams work best when the voice of the customer is brought into organizations. Customer input is especially valuable to product development teams. Suppliers and distributors should be included on the team as well. A cross-functional team that includes customers, suppliers, and distributors goes beyond organizational boundaries.

Some firms' suppliers and distributors are in other countries. Thus, cross-functional teams may share market information across national boundaries. The government may encourage the networking of teams, and government coordinators may assist such projects. In that case, cross-functional teams break the barriers between government and business.

Networking and Virtual Corporations

Whether it involves customers, suppliers and distributors, or the government, **networking** is using communications technology and other means to link organizations and allow them to work together on common objectives. Organizations are so closely linked by the Internet that each organization can find out what the others are doing in real time. **Real time** simply means the present moment or the actual time in which something takes place. Internet data are available in real time because they are sent instantly to various organizational partners as they are developed or collected. The net effect is a rather new concept called transparency. **Transparency** occurs when a company is so open to other companies working with it that the once-solid barriers between them become "see-through" and electronic information is shared (often on extranets, which we define in the next section) as if the companies were one.[7] Because of this integration, two companies can now work as closely together as two departments once did in traditional firms.

Can you see the implications for organizational design? Most organizations are no longer self-sufficient or self-contained. Rather, many modern organizations are part of a vast network of global businesses that work closely to-

networking
Using communications technology and other means to link organizations and allow them to work together on common objectives.

real time
The present moment or the actual time in which something takes place; data sent over the Internet to various organizational partners as they are developed or collected are said to be available in real time.

transparency
A concept that describes a company being so open to other companies working with it that the once-solid barriers between them become "see-through" and electronic information is shared (often on extranets) as if the companies were one.

gether. An organization chart showing what people do within any one organization is simply not complete because the organization is part of a much larger *system* of firms. A modern organization chart would show people in different organizations and how they are networked together. This is a relatively new concept, so few such charts are yet available.

The organization structures tend to be flexible and changing. That is, a company may work with a design expert from a different company in Italy for a year and then not need that person anymore. Another expert from another company in another country may be hired next time for another project. Such a temporary, networked organization, made up of replaceable firms that join the network and leave it as needed is called a **virtual corporation** (see Figure 8.7). This may sound confusing because it is so new and so different from traditional organization structure. In fact, traditional managers often have trouble adapting to the speed of change and the impermanence of relationships that have come about in the age of networking.

FIGURE 8.7

A VIRTUAL CORPORATION

A virtual corporation has no permanent ties to the firms that do its production, distribution, legal, and other work. Such firms are very flexible and can adapt to changes in the market quickly.

virtual corporation
A temporary, networked organization made up of replaceable firms that join the network and leave it as needed.

extranet
An extension of the Internet that connects suppliers, customers, and other organizations via secure websites.

intranet
A set of communications links within one company that travel over the Internet but are closed to public access.

Extranets and Intranets

One of the latest organizational trends is to link firms on an extranet. An **extranet** is an extension of the Internet that connects suppliers, customers, and other organizations via secure Web sites. For example, Wal-Mart is connected to its suppliers via an extranet. It is made up of linked intranets. An **intranet** is a set of communication links within one company that travel over the Internet but are closed to public access.[8] Service organizations like Wells Fargo Bank and manufacturing firms like Silicon Graphics both use intranets.

Although intranets are used mostly at larger firms, smaller firms are using them as well. The idea is to link everyone in the firm electronically so they can communicate freely and work together on projects. For example, workers at Hallmark Cards once pasted creative ideas on a bulletin board for others to comment on. Because of limited space on the physical board, old cards were simply not available for easy comparison. Today, old and new cards are available on the intranet; anyone in the company can make comments about the cards and can adapt them at any time. Any information a Hallmark employee wants others in the firm to see can be placed on the intranet. A company can also make such information available to employees at suppliers and dealers if they are part of an extranet. We shall explore intranets and extranets more fully in Chapter 17. Meanwhile, the Business Week box discusses in detail how Weyerhaeuser used its intranet to save its door business.

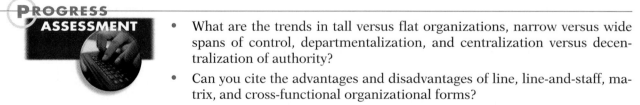

PROGRESS ASSESSMENT

• What are the trends in tall versus flat organizations, narrow versus wide spans of control, departmentalization, and centralization versus decentralization of authority?

• Can you cite the advantages and disadvantages of line, line-and-staff, matrix, and cross-functional organizational forms?

• What is the difference between a matrix form of organization and cross-functional teams?

• What are extranets and intranets?

FROM THE PAGES OF BusinessWeek www.weyerhaeuser.com

Opening the Door to Intranets

Just a few years ago, the Weyerhaeuser plant in Marshfield, Wisconsin, which manufactures custom-made doors for homes and other buildings, was faltering because of high costs, declining sales, and bad morale. The plant's organization structure and processes were dramatically changed by the introduction of a state-of-the-art communications network that used the Internet to compare prices almost instantly, to boost on-time deliveries, and to track orders as they moved through the plant. The new technology has doubled Weyerhaeuser's production, and the company's share of the market has gone from 12 percent to 26 percent.

The process of reorganizing Weyerhaeuser began internally, but recently the company has taken its new technology out to distributors. That link enables the company to speed up the ordering process for customers while eliminating costly errors, waste, and delivery problems. As a consequence, distributors have been forced to reorganize themselves so they can more effectively and efficiently link up with Weyerhaeuser.

The heart of Weyerhaeuser's communication network is an intranet. The intranet links all the workers in the company while plugging into vast databases of information, factory-floor operations, supplier inventory, price lists, and order taking. More than half the compa-

nies in the United States with annual revenues over $1 billion have intranets or are considering installing them. While an organization chart can visually show the links between departments in a firm, it takes an intranet to make those links real. What is really exciting is that intranets can also link suppliers and customers to the network (in which case they become extranets) so that the whole system works like clockwork. Today at Weyerhaeuser customers can assemble their own customized door configurations through a website on the Net or through a direct extranet link that allows them to tap into suppliers' lists and get instant packages and pricing.

When designing corporate structure, therefore, you have to develop the central nervous system of the company at the same time. That central nervous system is called an intranet, and it links all the employees together. Furthermore, extranets link intranets so that companies can work together as one unified system that is more efficient than that of competitors. That is why Ford, 3M, and other companies are turning to such systems.

Source: Marcia Stepanek, "How an Intranet Opened the Door to Profits," *Business Week*, July 26, 1999, pp. EB 33–38, and Darnell Little, "3M-Glued to the Web," *Business Week E BIZ*, November 20, 2000, pp. 63–70.

THE RESTRUCTURING PROCESS AND TOTAL QUALITY

It's not easy to move from an organization dominated by managers to one that relies heavily on self-managed teams. How you restructure an organization depends on the status of the present system. If the system already has a customer focus but isn't working well, a total quality management approach may work.

Total quality management (TQM) is the practice of striving for customer satisfaction by ensuring quality from all departments in an organization. Total quality management calls for continuous improvement of present processes. *Processes* are sets of activities strung together for a reason, such as the process for handling a customer's order. The process may consist of getting the order in the mail, opening it, sending it to someone to fill, putting the order into a package, and sending it out. **Continuous improvement** means constantly improving the way the organization does things so that customer needs can be better satisfied.

In an organization with few layers of management and a customer focus, it's possible that new computer software and employee training could lead to a team-oriented approach with few problems. In bureaucratic organizations with

total quality management (TQM)
The practice of striving for customer satisfaction by ensuring quality from all departments in an organization.

continuous improvement
Constantly improving the way the organization does things so that customer needs can be better satisfied.

Square D of Palatine, Illinois, is a supplier of electrical industrial controls and automation systems. The company holds its leadership position in the market by maintaining the highest quality standards. Quality can only be maintained by *constant* monitoring of manufacturing processes (or services), measuring customer satisfaction, and keeping the firm's employees focused on improving and delivering quality products and/or services.

reengineering
The fundamental rethinking and radical redesign of organizational processes to achieve dramatic improvements in critical measures of performance.

inverted organization
An organization that has contact people at the top and the chief executive officer at the bottom of the organization chart.

many layers of management, however, TQM is not suitable. And, when the whole process is being done incorrectly, continuous improvement doesn't work. When an organization needs dramatic changes, only reengineering will do. **Reengineering** is the fundamental rethinking and radical redesign of organizational processes to achieve dramatic improvements in critical measures of performance. Note the words *radical redesign* and *dramatic improvements.*

At IBM's credit organization, for example, the process for handling a customer's request for credit once went through a five-step process that took an average of six days. By completely reengineering the customer-request process, IBM cut its credit request processing time from six days to four hours! In reengineering, narrow, task-oriented jobs become multidimensional. Employees who once did as they were told now make decisions on their own. Functional departments lose their reason for being. Managers stop acting like supervisors and instead behave like coaches. Workers focus more on the customers' needs and less on their bosses' needs. Attitudes and values change in response to new incentives. Practically every aspect of the organization is transformed, often beyond recognition.

Can you see how reengineering is often necessary to change a firm from a managerial orientation to one based on cross-functional self-managed teams?[9] Reengineering may also be necessary to adapt an organization to fit into a virtual network. Remember, reengineering involves radical redesign and dramatic improvements. Not all organizations need such dramatic change. In fact, because of the complexity of the process, many reengineering efforts fail. In firms where reengineering is not feasible, *restructuring* may do. Restructuring (which we defined earlier in this chapter) involves making relatively minor changes to an organization in response to a changing environment. For example, a firm might add an Internet marketing component to the marketing department. That is a restructuring move, but it is not drastic enough to be called reengineering.

How Restructuring Affects Organizational Design

We have already noted that many firms are discovering that the key to long-term success in a competitive market is to empower front-line people (often in teams) to respond quickly to customer wants and needs. That means restructuring the firm to make front-line workers the most important people in the organization. For example, doctors have long been treated as the most important people in hospitals, pilots are the focus of airlines, and professors are the central focus of universities—yet front-desk people in hotels, clerks in department stores, and tellers in banks haven't been considered *the* key personnel. Instead, managers have been considered the key people, and they have been responsible for "managing" the front-line people. The organization chart in a typical firm looked something like the organization pyramid shown earlier in Figure 8.2.

The most advanced service organizations have turned the traditional organization structure upside down. An **inverted organization** has contact people at the top and the chief executive officer at the bottom. There are few layers of management, and the manager's job is to assist and support front-line people, not boss them around. Figure 8.8 illustrates the difference between an inverted and a traditional organizational structure.

A good example of an inverted organization is NovaCare, a provider of rehabilitation care. At its top are some 5,000 physical, occupational, and speech

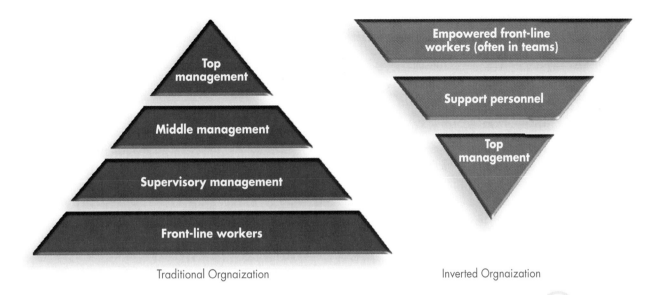

Traditional Orgnaization   Inverted Orgnaization

therapists. The rest of the organization is structured to serve those therapists. Managers consider the therapists to be their bosses, and the manager's job is to support the therapists by arranging contacts with nursing homes, handling accounting and credit activities, and providing training.

Companies based on this organization structure support front-line personnel with internal and external databases, advanced communication systems, and professional assistance. Naturally, this means that front-line people have to be better educated, better trained, and better paid than in the past. It takes a lot of trust for top managers to implement such a system—but when they do, the payoff in customer satisfaction and in profits is often well worth the effort. In the past, managers controlled information—and that gave them power. In more progressive organizations, everyone shares information and that gives everyone power.

The Movement toward Outsourcing

Traditionally, organizations have tried to do all functions themselves. That is, each organization had a separate department for accounting, finance, marketing, production, and so on. Today's organizations are looking to other organizations to help them in areas where they are not able to generate world-class quality.[10] Total quality management demands that organizations compare each function against the best in the world. For example, K2 is a company that makes skis, snowboards, in-line skates, and related products. It studied the compact-disc industry and learned to use ultraviolet inks to print graphics on skis. It went to the aerospace industry to get Piezo technology to reduce vibration in its snowboards (the aerospace industry uses the technology for wings on planes). And, finally, it learned from the cable-TV industry how to braid layers of fiberglass and carbon to make skis.

FIGURE 8.8

COMPARISON OF AN INVERTED ORGANIZATION STRUCTURE AND A TRADITIONAL ORGANIZATION STRUCTURE

Knowledge is increasing and technology is developing so fast that companies can only maintain a leading edge by benchmarking everything they do against the best in all industries. That's how K-2 was able to find the best materials and processes for making its skis. Think of how you could apply this concept in your own life. Who might you study to learn the best way to prepare for classes and exams?

MAKING ETHICAL DECISIONS

When Does Benchmarking Become Unethical?

www.benchnet.com

There is nothing illegal or unethical about studying your competitors and other companies to learn their best practices and then using those best practices in your own firm. In fact, that is one of the key strategies for staying competitive in today's rapidly changing marketplace. But when does such research become unethical? For example, is it ethical to hire away a company's best employees to get the secrets they have learned on the job? Most companies would say no. Is it

ethical to spy—that is, to place an employee in another firm so he or she can learn as much as possible about that firm's operations? Again, most firms would say no.

So how far can you go in learning about another organization? Suppose that your firm offers to pay you to work temporarily for a competitor to find out as many secrets as you can. If you take the assignment, you will get a good promotion when you return to your own company. What will you do? What might the consequences be?

competitive benchmarking
Rating an organization's practices, processes, and products against the world's best.

outsourcing
Assigning various functions, such as accounting and legal work, to outside organizations.

core competencies
Those functions that the organization can do as well or better than any other organization in the world.

organizational (or corporate) culture
Widely shared values within an organization that provide coherence and cooperation to achieve common goals.

Competitive benchmarking is rating an organization's practices, processes, and products against the world's best.[11] For example, Kmart may compare itself to Wal-Mart to see what, if anything, Wal-Mart does better. Kmart would then try to improve its practices or processes to become even better than Wal-Mart. If an organization can't do as well as the best in any particular area, such as shipping, it will try to outsource the function to an organization that is the best (e.g., UPS or FedEx). **Outsourcing** is assigning various functions, such as accounting, production, security, maintenance, and legal work, to outside organizations.[12] Some functions, such as information management and marketing, may be too important to assign to outside firms. In that case, the organization should benchmark on the best firms and restructure their departments to try to be equally good. It is important to monitor benchmarking efforts so that they don't overreach the bounds of ➤ **P.96** ◄ ethical behavior. The Making Ethical Decisions box explores that issue.

When a firm has completed its outsourcing process, the remaining functions are the firm's core competencies. **Core competencies** are those functions that the organization can do as well as or better than any other organization in the world. For example, Nike is great at designing and marketing athletic shoes. Those are its core competencies. It outsources the manufacturing of those shoes, however, to other companies that can make shoes better and less expensively than Nike itself can.

ESTABLISHING A CUSTOMER-ORIENTED CULTURE

Figure 8.9 summarizes the differences between bureaucratic and customer-focused organizational structures. Any organizational change is bound to cause some stress and resistance among members of the firm. Therefore, a shift from bureaucracy ➤ **P.236** ◄ to a customer focus should be accompanied by the establishment of an organizational culture that facilitates such change. **Organizational (or corporate) culture** may be defined as widely shared values within an organization that provide coherence and cooperation to achieve common goals. Recall from the chapter opening profile that establishing the right culture was the first of four things that Carly Fiorina focused on at Hewlett-Packard. Usually the culture of an organization is reflected in stories, traditions, and myths.

It's obvious from visiting any McDonald's restaurant that every effort has been made to maintain a culture that emphasizes quality, service, cleanliness, and value. Each restaurant has the same feel, the same look, the same atmosphere. In short, each has a similar organizational culture.

An organizational culture can also be negative. Have you ever been in an organization where you feel that no one cares about service or quality? The clerks may seem uniformly glum, indifferent, and testy. The mood often seems to pervade the atmosphere so that patrons become moody and upset. It may be hard to believe that an organization, especially a profit-making one, can be run so badly and still survive. Are there examples in your area?

The very best organizations have cultures that emphasize service to others, especially customers. The atmosphere is one of friendly, concerned, caring people who enjoy working together to provide a good product at a reasonable price. Those companies that have such cultures have less need for close supervision of employees, not to mention policy manuals; organization charts; and formal rules, procedures, and controls. The key to productive culture is mutual trust. You get such trust by giving it. The very best companies stress high moral and ethical values such as honesty, reliability, fairness, environmental protection, and social involvement. The Spotlight on Small Business box looks at how one small organization successfully implemented a customer-oriented culture.

Thus far, we've been talking as if organizational matters were mostly controllable by management. The fact is that the formal organization structure is just one element of the total organizational system. In the creation of organizational culture, the informal organization is of equal or greater importance. Let's explore this notion next.

The Informal Organization

All organizations have two organizational systems. One is the **formal organization,** which is the structure that details lines of responsibility, authority, and position. It's the structure shown on organization charts. The other is the **informal organization,** which is the system of relationships that develop spontaneously as employees meet and form power centers. It consists of the various cliques, relationships, and lines of authority that develop outside the formal organization. It's the human side of the organization that doesn't show on any organization chart.

No organization can operate effectively without both types of organization. The formal system is often too slow and bureaucratic to enable the organization to adapt quickly. However, the formal organization does provide helpful guidelines and lines of authority to follow in routine situations.

The informal organization is often too unstructured and emotional to allow careful, reasoned decision making on critical matters. It's extremely effective, however, in generating creative solutions to short-term problems and providing a feeling of camaraderie and teamwork among employees.

In any organization, it's wise to learn quickly who the important people are in the informal organization. Typically, there are formal rules and procedures

formal organization
The structure that details lines of responsibility, authority, and position; that is, the structure shown on organization charts.

informal organization
The system of relationships and lines of authority that develops spontaneously as employees meet and form power centers; that is, the human side of the organization that does not appear on any organization chart.

BUREAUCRATIC	CUSTOMER-FOCUSD
Coordination from the top	Self-management
Top-down chain of command	Bottom-up power relationships
Many rules and regulations	Employees free to make decisions
Departmentalization by function	Cross-functional teams
Specialization	Integration and cooperation
One firm does it all	Outsourcing
Management controls information	Information goes to all
Largely domestic orientation	Global orientation
Focus on external customers	Focus on both internal and external customers

FIGURE 8.9

BUREAUCRATIC VERSUS CUSTOMER-FOCUSED ORGANIZATIONAL STRUCTURES

Fun Night at the Ice Cream Parlor

Amy's ice cream parlors in Austin and Houston, Texas, attract a lot of customers because of their offbeat corporate culture. On any given night, you might see the servers juggling with their serving spades, tossing scoops of ice cream to each other, or break-dancing on the freezer top. If there is a long line, they pass out samples or give a free cone to any customer who will sing, dance, recite a poem, or otherwise entertain those in line. Employees might be wearing pajamas (Sleepover Night) or masks (*Star Wars* Night). Lighting may be provided by candles (Romance Night) or strobe lights (Disco Night). You get the idea. It's fun at Amy's—for the employees and for the customers. Corporate culture can go a long way toward making a small company a success or a failure.

to follow for getting certain supplies or equipment, but those procedures may take days. Who in the organization knows how to obtain supplies immediately without following the normal procedures? Which administrative assistants should you see if you want your work given first priority? These are the questions to answer to work effectively in many organizations.

The informal organization's nerve center is the *grapevine* (the system through which unofficial information flows between and among managers and employees). The key people in the grapevine usually have considerable influence in the organization.

In the old "us-versus-them" system of organizations, where managers and employees were often at odds, the informal system often hindered effective management. In the new, more open organizations, where managers and employees work together to set objectives and design procedures, the informal organization can be an invaluable managerial asset that often promotes harmony among workers and establishes the corporate culture.[13] That's a major advantage, for example, of self-managed teams.

As effective as the informal organization may be in creating group cooperation, it can still be equally powerful in resisting management directives. Employees may form unions, go on strike together, and generally disrupt operations. Learning to create the right corporate culture and to work within the informal organization is a key to managerial success.

At Amy's ice cream parlors the corporate culture of "fun" leads to good publicity, friendly relations with the community, willing workers, and more (read profit). Have you ever experienced or are you aware of an organization where the corporate culture made everyone feel good about the company and the work experience?

• What's the difference between restructuring and reengineering?
• What is the significance of inverted organizations?
• Why do organizations outsource functions?
• What is organizational culture?

PROGRESS
ASSESSMENT

SUMMARY

1. The 20th century saw the introduction of the concept of economies of scale. *Economies of scale* exist when companies can produce goods more inexpensively by purchasing raw materials in bulk; the average cost of each item goes down as production levels increase.
   • ***What concepts did Fayol and Weber contribute?***
   Fayol introduced principles such as unity of command, hierarchy of authority, division of labor, subordination of individual interests to the general interest, authority, clear communication channels, order, and equity. Weber added principles of bureaucracy such as job descriptions, written rules and decision guidelines, consistent procedures, and staffing and promotions based on qualifications.

   1. Explain the organizational theories of Fayol and Weber.

2. Issues involved in structuring and restructuring organizations include (1) tall versus flat organization structures, (2) span of control, (3) departmentalization, and (4) centralization versus decentralization.
   • ***What are the basics of each?***
   The problem with tall organizations is that they slow communications. The trend is to eliminate managers and flatten organizations. The span of control becomes larger as employees become self-directed. Departments are often being replaced or supplemented by matrix organizations and cross-functional teams. Use of cross-functional teams results in decentralization of authority.

   2. Discuss the various issues involved in structuring and restructuring organizations.

3. Organizational design is the coordinating of workers so that they can best accomplish the firm's goals.
   • ***What are the traditional forms of organization and their advantages?***
   The two traditional forms of organization explored in the text are (1) line organizations and (2) line-and-staff organizations. A line organization has the advantages of having clearly defined responsibility and authority, being easy to understand, and providing one supervisor for each person. Most organizations have benefited from the expert advice of staff assistants in areas such as safety, quality control, computer technology, human resource management, and investing.

   3. Describe traditional organizations and their limitations.

4. New forms of organization are emerging that enable firms to be more responsive to customers.
   • ***What are the new forms of organization?***
   Matrix organizations and cross-functional self-managed teams.
   • ***How do they differ?***
   Matrix organizations involve temporary assignments (projects) that give flexibility to managers in assigning people to projects and encourage interorganizational cooperation and teamwork. Cross-functional self-managed teams are more permanent and have all the benefits of the matrix style.

   4. Show how matrix-style organizations and cross-functional teams help companies become more customer oriented.

5. Defend the use of various organizational tools and techniques such as networking, reengineering, and outsourcing.

5. Networking is using communications technology and other means to link organizations and allow them to work together on common objectives.

• **What is a virtual corporation?**

A virtual corporation is a networked organization made up of replaceable firms that join the network and leave it as needed.

• **How are networked firms linked?**

An intranet links all the employees of one firm to a central database so that everyone in the firm knows what everyone else is doing. An extranet ties two or more firms together so that all the employees in all the firms know what the others are doing.

• **What's the difference between restructuring and reengineering?**

It's basically a matter of degree. Restructuring is making needed changes in the firm so that it can more effectively and efficiently serve its customers. For example, a firm may add more computers or change how they process orders. Reengineering is the fundamental rethinking and radical redesign of organizational processes to achieve dramatic improvements in critical measures of performance.

• **How do inverted organizations fit into these concepts?**

An inverted organization usually results from a major reengineering effort because the changes are dramatic in that employees are placed at the top of the hierarchy and are given much training and support while managers are at the bottom and are there to train and assist employees.

• **Why do firms outsource some of their functions?**

Some firms are very good at one function: for example, marketing. Competitive benchmarking tells them that they are not as good as some companies at production or distribution. The company may then outsource those functions to companies that can perform those functions more effectively and efficiently.

6. Give examples to show how organizational culture and the informal organization can hinder or assist organizational change.

6. Organizational culture may be defined as widely shared values within an organization that provide coherence and cooperation to achieve common goals.

• **How can organizational culture and the informal organization hinder or assist organizational change?**

The very best organizations have cultures that emphasize service to others, especially customers. The atmosphere is one of friendly, concerned, caring people who enjoy working together to provide a good product at a reasonable price. Companies with such cultures have less need than other companies for close supervision of employees; policy manuals; organization charts; and formal rules, procedures, and controls. This opens the way for self-managed teams.

KEY TERMS

bureaucracy 236
centralized
   authority 244
competitive
   benchmarking 254
continuous
   improvement 251
core
   competencies 254
cross-functional
   teams 248
decentralized
   authority 244

departmentalization
   241
downsizing 236
economy of
   scale 234
extranet 250
formal
   organization 255
hierarchy 236
informal
   organization 255
intranet 250
inverted
   organization 252

line organization
   245
line personnel 245
matrix
   organization 246
networking 249
organizational
   (or corporate)
   culture 254
organizational
   design 236
outsourcing 254
real time 249
reengineering 252

DEVELOPING WORKPLACE SKILLS

1. There is no way to better understand the effects of having many layers of management on communication accuracy than to play the game of Message Relay. Choose seven or more members of the class and have them leave the classroom. Then choose one person to read the following paragraph and another student to listen. Then call in one of the students from outside and have the "listener" tell him or her what information was in the paragraph. Then bring in another student and have the new listener repeat the information to him or her. Continue the process with all those who left the room. Do not allow anyone in the class to offer corrections as each listener becomes the storyteller in turn. In this way, all the students can hear how the facts become distorted over time. The distortions and mistakes are often quite humorous, but they are not so funny in organizations such as Ford, which once had 22 layers of management.

    Here's the paragraph:

    Dealers in the Midwest region have received over 130 complaints about steering on the new Commander and Roadhandler models of our minivans. Apparently, the front suspension system is weak and the ball joints are wearing too fast. This causes slippage in the linkage and results in oversteering. Mr. Berenstein has been notified, but so far only 213 out of 4,300 dealers have received repair kits.

2. Describe some informal groups within an organization with which you are familiar (at school, at work, etc.). What have you noticed about how those groups help or hinder progress in the organization?

3. Imagine you are working for Kitchen Magic, an appliance manufacturer that produces, among other things, dishwashers for the home. Imagine further that a competitor introduces a new dishwasher that uses sound waves to clean dishes. The result is a dishwasher that cleans even the worst burnt-on food and sterilizes the dishes and silverware as well. You need to develop a similar offering fast, or your company will lose the market. Write an e-mail to management outlining the problem and explaining your rationale for recommending use of a cross-functional team to respond quickly.

4. Divide the class into teams of five. This is the assignment: Imagine that your firm has been asked to join a virtual network. You are a producer of athletic shoes. What might you do to minimize the potential problems of being involved with a virtual corporation? Begin by defining a virtual corporation and listing the potential problems. Also, list the benefits of being part of such a system.

5. As discussed in this chapter, many of the work groups of the future, including management, will be cross-functional and self-managed. To practice working in such an organization, break your class up into groups of five or so students. (Try to find students with different backgrounds and interests.) Each group must work together to prepare a report on the advantages and disadvantages of working in teams. Many of the problems and advantages should emerge in your group as you try to complete this assignment.

Purpose:

To explore the nature of teams and to emphasize that good teams use the strengths of all team members.

Exercise:

Imagine that you are a member of a space crew originally scheduled to rendezvous with a mother ship on the lighted side of the moon. Due to mechanical difficulties, however, your ship was forced to land 200 miles away from the rendezvous point. Much of the equipment aboard was damaged during landing and since survival depends on reaching the mother ship, the most critical items available must be chosen for the 200 mile trip. Go to http://engr111.tamu.edu/space_survival.htm to find a list of the 15 items left intact and undamaged after landing.

1. Rank each item in order of importance to your crew in allowing them to reach the rendezvous point. Print the grid provided to record your answers. Place the number 1 by the most important item, the number 2 by the second most important item, and so on, through number 15, the least important item.

2. Ask three or four of your classmates to form a team with you. As a team, rank the items again. Discuss your individual choices and decide on a ranking as a group. Record your team choices in the appropriate column in your printed grid.

3. Now go to www.ivcfne.org/missions/172 and scroll down to the answers compiled by a team of scientists and engineers at NASA. Compare your individual and group answers with the NASA answers. Calculate your score as directed on the grid.

4. Was your team score better than your individual score? Why or why not?

PRACTICING MANAGEMENT DECISIONS

CASE

IBM IS BOTH AN OUTSOURCER AND A MAJOR OUTSOURCE FOR OTHERS

Few companies are better known for their manufacturing expertise than IBM. Nonetheless, even IBM has to adapt to the dynamic marketplace of today. In the area of personal computers, for example, IBM was unable to match the prices or speed of delivery of mail-order firms such as Dell Computer. Dell built machines after receiving orders for them and then rushed the computers to customers. IBM, in contrast, made machines ahead of time and hoped that the orders would match its inventory.

To compete against firms like Dell, IBM had to custom-make computers for its business customers, but IBM was not particularly suited to do such work. However, IBM did work with several distributors that were also having problems. The distributors were trying to custom-make IBM machines but were forced to carry a heavy inventory of parts and materials to do so. Distributors were also tearing IBM computers apart and putting them back together with other computer companies' parts to produce custom-made computers.

IBM decided to allow its distributors to store parts and materials and then custom-make computers to customer demand. In other words, IBM outsourced about 60 percent of its commercial PC business. Distributors such as Inacom Corporation became profitable and IBM was able to offer custom-made PCs competitive in price with those of Dell and other direct-mail companies.

More recently, IBM has begun selling its technology—tiny disc drives, speedy new chips, and more—to its former competitors! For some of these new partners, IBM will design their new products and let them explore its labs. In short, IBM is doing a bit of reverse outsourcing in that it is offering itself as a research and product development company ready to work with others. Thus, IBM will sell networking chips to Cisco Systems and not compete with that company anymore. And it will likewise sell disk drives to EMC. IBM benchmarked its final products against these companies and saw that it was not winning. The winning strategy, it decided, was to join them and become an even better team.

Discussion Questions

1. What does it say about today's competitive environment when leading companies, such as IBM, give up competing and decide to work with competitors instead?
2. What effects will outsourcing have on trade relationships among countries?

3. If more U.S. companies unite their technologies, what will that do to competitors in other countries? Should foreign companies do more uniting with U.S. companies themselves? What about U.S. companies uniting with foreign companies?
4. How much influence will the Internet have on world trade and outsourcing among countries? What does the Internet provide that wasn't available before?

Sources: Daniel Lyons, "IBM's Giant Gamble," *Forbes*, October 4, 1999, pp. 90–95; and Michael Useem and Joseph Harder, "Leading Laterally in Company Outsourcing," *Sloan Management Review*, Winter 2000, pp. 25–36.

VIDEO CASE

FLIPPING OVER AT MCDONALD'S

In today's rapidly changing business environment, you can't stand still or the competition will rapidly pass you by. That's just as true for an established firm such as McDonald's as it is for one of the newest dot-coms.

McDonald's was the king of fast food since its beginnings. The company made an art of pushing large volumes of food through the preparation process quickly. By building up quantities of menu items in advance for the two peak periods of the day (lunch and dinner), McDonald's was ready for anything. Anything, that is, except changing customer demands. Customers grew intolerant of standard sandwiches prepared in advance, and more intolerant of waiting for "special" orders like "hold the onions."

With Burger King promising customers they could "have it their way," McDonald's had to change. Launching a concept called *Made for You Operating System*, the company replaced kitchen equipment and communication technology to improve the way orders flow through the kitchen. The new technology helped the crews do their work, but it required them to do things differently. So in addition to renovating over 12,000 stores, the company needed to retrain employees to the new Made for You System.

To renovate 12,000 stores, the company reorganized by retaining research and development in the main office and decentralizing the staff support functions by moving them into five regional offices. This way the R&D would be centralized, but the implementation would be the responsibility of the local regions.

It didn't take McDonald's long to learn that this form of organization didn't work. With only two or so suppliers servicing five regions and no one to prioritize which orders were most important, the regions were often at odds with each other as they tried to make their own transition to Made for You. The solution was to put together a cross-functional team to oversee the nationwide transition. The team was made up of members of each of the regions and of various departments from the main office as well as representatives of the franchisees and suppliers. The task of the Made for You team was to share successful practices and align resources. The team created a Made for You database that tracked the progress of the transitions in all of the regions. The team also created a document library that contained all of the communication among the team as well as press releases.

The Made for You cross-functional team successfully completed the transition of 12,300 stores—on time! By using organizational concepts such as teamwork, technology, and planning, McDonald's improved product quality, customer service, and efficiency.

Discussion Questions

1. What special organizational issues may arise in the overseas restaurants of McDonald's?
2. Does McDonald's seem to be following most of the traditional principles of management as set out by Fayol? Explain.
3. Has McDonald's been able to establish a service-oriented culture?

9

Managing Production and Operations

LEARNING GOALS

AFTER YOU HAVE READ AND STUDIED THIS CHAPTER, YOU SHOULD BE ABLE TO

1 Define *operations management*.

2 Describe the operations management functions that are involved in both the manufacturing and service sectors.

3 Discuss the problem of measuring productivity in the service sector, and tell how new technology is leading to productivity gains in service companies.

4 Explain process planning and the various manufacturing processes being used today.

5 Describe the seven new manufacturing techniques that have made U.S. companies more productive: just-in-time inventory control, Internet purchasing, flexible manufacturing, lean manufacturing, mass customization, competing in time, and computer-aided design and manufacturing.

6 Explain the use of PERT and Gantt charts.

Getting To Know Demetria Giannisis, Business Doctor

Demetria Giannisis earned a B.S. in political science from Northwestern University and an M.S. in public policy from the University of Chicago. While working at the Chicago High Tech Association, she learned of the Manufacturing Extension Partnership, a network of private not-for-profit consulting organizations funded in part by the U.S. Department of Commerce. Giannisis spearheaded the effort to bring productivity and technology services to manufacturers in the Chicago region. In 1994 she established the Chicago Manufacturing Center.

CMC has enjoyed many successes since then. The organization started at ground zero and over the years, has built a customer base of more than 1,000 clients.

One of CMC's clients is Hi-Tech Manufacturing in Schiller Park, Illinois. A small job shop, Hi-Tech has enjoyed a 15 percent annual revenue growth. Ironically, this growth masked the company's problems. Orders were processed carelessly, 1 percent of materials were left over as scrap, there were no procedures for handling customer complaints, and machines went for months without maintenance.

CMC assembled a team of experts to help the company address its problems and help get it back on track. The team found one machine that cut materials inaccurately and suggested that it be replaced. Maintenance checks were scheduled monthly and product sampling was introduced to catch other mistakes. Machinists now work off to-do lists, rather than blueprints. The to-do lists guide the product through the entire production cycle—from measuring and sawing raw material—to final inspection. As a result of these changes, scrap went down to .1 percent, and revenues are expected to grow from $5.6 million to $6.5 million.

At Allied Tube & Conduit in Harvey, Illinois, it once took more than five hours for employees to shift from making one sized tube to another. CMC productivity experts helped the company streamline its processes.

A worker team videotaped a typical mill changeover. The workers then watched the tape and saw themselves wasting time looking for tools, goofing off, asking questions, performing activities out of sequence, and operating in poor lighting. It turned out that there were four hours and 45 minutes of wasted time in each six-hour changeover. Following CMC's advice, activities were resequenced, tools were stocked closer, parts were given correct labels, and jobs were re-assigned. There was also a period of training so that each team member understood his job better. As a result of these basic changes, the company can save some 2,000 hours—or $2.5 million—in labor costs.

These case studies demonstrate that basic changes in operations can have a significant effect on profits. This is true for both manufacturing plants and service companies, for large and small organizations alike.

"Inefficient companies are going to be left behind unless they utilize the tools of the New Economy," said Giannisis.

Everyone in business should be familiar with the terms and concepts involved in operations management. That is what you will learn in this chapter.

Source: Joanne Gordon, "Calling Dr. Demetria," *Forbes,* June 12, 2000, pp. 212-214, and Richard Karpinski, "E-Hub Essentials," *B to B,* July 3, 2000, pp. 1 and 30-32.

AMERICA'S EVOLVING MANUFACTURING AND SERVICES BASE

During the 1970s and 1980s, foreign manufacturers captured huge chunks of the U.S. market for basic products such as steel, cement, machinery, and farm equipment using the latest in production techniques. That competition forced U.S. companies to greatly alter their production techniques and managerial styles. You'll read about the managerial changes in Chapter 8. Many U.S. firms are now as good or better than competitors anywhere in the world. What have American manufacturers done to regain a competitive edge? They've implemented the following:

1.   A customer focus.

2.   Cost savings through site selection.

3.   Total quality management ➤ **P.251** ◄ using ISO 9000 and ISO 14000 standards

4.   New manufacturing techniques such as enterprise resource planning, computer-integrated manufacturing, flexible manufacturing, and lean manufacturing.

5.   Reliance on the Internet to unite companies.

We'll discuss these developments in detail in this chapter. You'll see that operations management has become a challenging and vital element of American business. The rebuilding of America's manufacturing base will likely remain a major business issue in the near future. There will be debates about the merits of moving production facilities to foreign countries. Serious questions will be raised about replacing workers with robots and other machinery. Major political decisions will be made regarding protection of American manufacturers through quotas and other restrictions on free trade. Regardless of how these issues are decided, however, tomorrow's college graduates will face tremendous challenges (and career opportunities) in redesigning and rebuilding America's manufacturing base.

The service sector of the economy will also be getting more attention as it becomes a larger and larger part of the overall economy. Service productivity is a real issue, as is the blending of service and manufacturing through the Internet. This chapter will devote major attention to operations management in both the service and the manufacturing sectors. Since the majority of tomorrow's graduates will likely find jobs in the service sector, it is important to understand the latest operations management concepts for this sector.

Each year companies discover new ways of automating that eliminate the need for human labor. This photo shows a new, automated apparatus known as a Flipper. It can pour a dozen pancakes and flip them when needed on one griddle while, at the same time, flipping burgers on another grill. Are McDonald's or any other restaurants in your area already using equipment like this?

From Production to Operations Management

production
The creation of finished goods and services using the factors of production: land, labor, capital, entrepreneurship, and knowledge.

Production is the creation of goods and services ➤ **P.25** ◄ using the factors of production, which, you should recall, are the inputs land, labor, capital, entrepreneurship ➤ **P.4** ◄, and knowledge. Thus, *production management* has been the term used to describe all the activities managers do to help their firms create goods. In Chapter 1, we defined *goods* as tangible products such as computers, food, clothing, cars, and appliances. And we defined *services* as intangible products such as education, health care, and insurance. Services also include those provided by manufacturers, including credit, delivery, and installation. Production has historically been associated with manufacturing. But the nature of business has changed significantly in the last 20 years or so. The service sector, including Internet services, has grown dramatically, and the manufacturing sector has not grown much at all. The United States now has what is called a *service economy*—that is, one dominated by the service sector. This can be a benefit to future college graduates because many of the top-paying jobs are in legal services; medical services; and business services such as accounting, finance, and management consulting.

To reflect the change of importance from manufacturing to services, the term *production* often has been replaced by *operations* to reflect both goods and services production. **Operations management,** then, is a specialized area in management that converts or transforms resources (including human resources) into goods and services. It includes inventory management, quality control, production scheduling, and more. It is what Demetria Giannisis, as described in the chapter opening story, helps small businesses do more efficiently. In an automobile plant, operations management transforms raw materials, human resources, parts, supplies, paints, tools, and other resources into automobiles. It does this through the processes of fabrication and assembly. In a college, operations management takes inputs—such as information, professors, supplies, buildings, offices, computer systems—and creates services that transform students into educated people. It does this through a process called education.

Some organizations—such as factories, farms, and mines—produce mostly goods. Others—such as hospitals, schools, and government agencies—produce mostly services. Still others produce a combination of goods and services. For example, an automobile manufacturer not only makes cars but also provides services such as repairs, financing, and insurance. And at McDonald's you get goods such as hamburgers and fries, but you also get services such as order taking, order filling, and cleanup.

Carol Higgins is CEO of Binky Computers for Kids in Alexandria, Virginia. She is an information systems specialist, but recognized that developing the effective website she needed and envisioned for her company was too specialized for her to do on her own. She, like many other smaller firms, turned to a professional website developer, Vista.com, for help. Using their software, Higgins had an Internet store designed and open for business in just a few hours. Sales tripled!

Manufacturers Turn to Services and a Customer Orientation for Profit

Most traditional large manufacturers in the United States have had slow profit growth for the last decade despite spending an enormous amount of money on productivity and quality initiatives. Companies that have prospered and grown—IBM, General Electric, and Dell, just to name a few—have all taken a similar road to success. They've expanded operations management out of the factory and moved it closer to the customer, providing services such as custom manufacturing, fast delivery, credit, installation, and repair.

Take the automobile industry, for example. While new-car sales have been rather flat in recent years, at some 17 million a year, the number of used-car

operations management
A specialized area in management that converts or transforms resources (including human resources) into goods and services.

sales has grown to about 200 million a year. Thus, car companies can potentially increase their revenues by providing parts for and servicing used cars rather than selling new ones.

Another example of the growing importance of services is in the area of corporate computing. The average company spends only one-fifth of its annual personal computer budget on purchasing the hardware. The rest (80 percent) goes to technical support, administration, and other maintenance activities. Because of this, IBM has shifted from its dependence on selling computer hardware to becoming a major supplier of computer services, software, and technology components. General Electric is doing the same; it generates more than $5 billion a year in worldwide revenues from Internet transactions.[1]

Application service providers (ASPs) are companies that provide software services online so that companies do not have to buy their own software, but can have instant access to the latest programs for a fee. Companies such as Boeing and Ford have outsourced much of their production processes and are focusing more on building customer relationships and building brand images.[2] As you can see, operations management has become much more focused on services because that's where the growth and profits are.

OPERATIONS MANAGEMENT FUNCTIONS

Operations management in the service sector involves many of the same functions as operations management in the manufacturing sector. Overlapping functions include facility location, facility layout, and quality control. The resources used may be different, but the management functions are similar.

Facility Location

facility location
The process of selecting a geographic location for a company's operations.

Facility location is the process of selecting a geographic location for a company's operations. One strategy is to make it easy for consumers to access your service. Thus flower shops and banks are putting facilities in supermarkets so that their products and services are more accessible than they are in freestanding facilities. And you can find a McDonald's inside some Wal-Mart stores. The ultimate in convenience is never having to leave home at all to get services. That's why there is so much interest in Internet banking, Internet car shopping, Internet education, and so on. For brick-and-mortar businesses (e.g., retail stores) to beat such competition, they have to choose good locations and offer outstanding service to those who do come. Study the location of service-sector businesses—such as hotels, banks, athletic clubs, and supermarkets—and you will see that the most successful are conveniently located.

Facility Location for Manufacturers A major issue of the recent past has been the shift of manufacturing organizations from one city or state to another in the United States or to foreign sites. Such shifts sometimes result in pockets of unemployment in some geographic areas and lead to tremendous economic growth in others.

Why would entrepreneurs ➤ **P.4** ◄ spend millions of dollars to move their facilities from one location to another? One major reason some businesses move is the availability of inexpensive labor or the right kind of skilled labor. Even though labor cost is becoming a smaller percentage of total cost in some highly automated industries, the low cost of labor remains a key reason many less technologically advanced producers move their plants. For example, low-cost labor is one reason why some firms are moving to Malaysia, Mexico, and other countries with low wage rates. Some of these firms have been charged with providing substandard working conditions and/or exploiting children in the countries where they have set up factories. Others, such as Grupo Moraira (Grupo M), a real estate construction and sales company in the Dominican Republic, are being used as role models for global manufacturing. Grupo M provides its employees with higher pay than local businesses, transportation to and from work, day care centers, discounted food, and health clinics. Its *operations* are so efficient that it can compete in world markets and provide world-class services to its employees.[3]

Inexpensive resources are another major reason for moving production facilities. Companies usually need water, electricity, wood, coal, and other basic resources. By moving to areas where natural resources are inexpensive and plentiful, firms can significantly lower costs— not only the cost of buying such resources but also the cost of shipping finished products. Often the most important resource is people, so companies tend to cluster where smart and talented people are. Witness Silicon Valley in California and similar areas in Colorado, Massachusetts, and Virginia.

Reducing time-to-market is another decision-making factor. As manufacturers attempt to compete globally, they need sites that allow products to move through the system quickly, at the lowest costs, so that they can be delivered rapidly to customers. Access to various modes of transportation (i.e., highways, rail lines, airports, and the like) is thus critical. Information technology (IT) is also important to quick response, so many firms are seeking countries with the most advanced information systems.

Locating Close to Markets Many businesses are building factories in foreign countries to get closer to their international customers. That's a major reason why the Japanese automaker Honda builds cars in Ohio and the German company Mercedes builds them in Alabama. When U.S. firms select foreign sites, they consider whether they are near airports, waterways, and highways so that raw materials and finished goods can be moved quickly and easily. Businesses also study the quality of life for workers and managers. Quality-of-life questions include these: Are there good schools nearby? Is the weather nice? Is the crime rate low? Does the local community welcome new businesses? Do the chief executive and other key managers want to live there? In short, facility location has become a critical issue in operations management. The Making Ethical Decisions box on p. 269 explores one of the major ethical issues involved.

Fresh flowers from a vending machine— anytime, anywhere? Since making products and services available to consumers when and where they want them is an important key to success, facility location is a critical decision for many companies. The solution for 24-Hour Flowers was to place flower vending machines where people are most likely to buy them, such as the exits for commuter trains or in airports and shopping malls. What other kinds of products or services would you purchase more often if they were more convenient?

Facility Location in the Future New developments in information technology (computers, modems, e-mail, voice mail, teleconferencing, etc.) are giving firms and employees more flexibility than ever before in choosing locations while staying in the competitive mainstream.[4] As we noted in Chapter 1, telecommuting ➤ **P.22** ◄ (working from home via computer and modem) is a major trend in business. Companies that no longer need to locate near sources of labor will be able to move to areas where land is less expensive and the quality of life may be nicer.

One big incentive to locate or relocate in a particular city or state is the tax situation and degree of government support. Some states and local governments have higher taxes than others, yet many engage in fierce competition by

•Few developments will have a greater impact on the future of business than wireless technology. And few companies will have a greater influence in that realm than Qualcomm. In this photo David Clapp, the company's chief engineer, and his assistant, Stan Helm, are testing new wireless equipment that gives them remote access to the Internet at speeds we are only now beginning to appreciate. What types of businesses will benefit the most from the freedom wireless technology offers?

facility layout
The physical arrangement of resources (including people) in the production process.

giving tax reductions and other support, such as zoning changes and financial aid, so that businesses will locate there. Recently, for example, there has been a major revival of neighborhoods in downtown Los Angeles, in part because the city government, is giving companies tax breaks and helping them find new market opportunities.[5]

Facility Layout

Facility layout is the physical arrangement of resources (including people) in the production process. The idea is to have offices, machines, storage areas, and other items in the best possible position to enable workers to produce goods and provide services to their customers. Facility layout depends greatly on the processes that are to be performed. For *services*, the layout is usually designed to help the consumer find and buy things. More and more, that means helping consumers to find and buy things on the Internet. Some stores have added kiosks that enable customers to search for goods on the Internet and then place orders in the store. The store also handles returns and other customer-contact functions. In short, services are becoming more and more customer oriented in how they design their stores and their Internet services.[6] Some services use layouts that make the production process more efficient, just like other producers. For example, a hospital may be designed that way.

For manufacturing plants, facilities layout has become critical because the possible cost savings are enormous. The Delphi Automotive Systems plant in Oak Creek, Wisconsin, is huge—a walk around the outside would be more than a mile. Delphi makes catalytic converters for 40 different automobile manufacturers. Catalytic converters are those stainless-steel pollution strainers in automobile exhaust systems. Delphi has a history that goes back almost 100 years. Its facility layout was typical of older plants—an assembly line that made all of the converters. The plant floor is now organized around customer-focused work cells that are modular and portable. Delivery once took 21 days, but with today's more modern layout, delivery takes less than a week. The plant was redesigned to reduce cost, to increase productivity ➤ **P.23** ◄, to simplify the process, and to speed things up. Compared to the old plant, the new plant uses only half of the space, 2 percent of its powered conveyor system, and 230 fewer processes. Productivity increased by over 25 percent, and the plant is now more profitable.[7]

Many companies like Delphi are moving from an assembly-line layout, where workers do only a few tasks at a time, to a modular layout, where teams of workers combine to produce more complex units of the final product. For example, where there may have been a dozen or more work stations on an assembly line to complete an automobile engine in the past, all of that work may be done in one module today. When working on a major project, such as a bridge or an airplane, companies use a fixed-position layout that allows workers to congregate around the product to be completed.

Taking Operations Management to the Internet Many of today's rapidly growing companies do very little production themselves. Instead, they outsource ► **P.254** ◄ engineering, design, manufacturing, and other tasks to outside companies, such as Solectron, Flextronics, and SCI Systems, that can perform those functions better.[8] Furthermore, companies are creating whole new relationships with suppliers over the Internet such that operations management is becoming an *interfirm* process where companies work together to design, produce, and ship products to customers. Coordination among companies is nearly as close as coordination among departments in a single firm.

To facilitate such transactions, companies called electronic hubs (e-hubs) have emerged to make the flow of goods among firms faster and smoother. For example, e-hubs Ariba, MRO.com, and BizBuyer.com help companies develop long-term relationships with suppliers. Some e-hubs are industry-specific. For example, Chemdex facilitates exchanges in the chemical industry and PlasticsNet.com does the same in the plastics industry. Much of the attention of investors these days is

Delphi Automotive Systems is a dynamic company that recognizes constant change and global competition as central factors in today's business environment. It is essential to employ the latest in operations management techniques and to maintain state of the art production facilities that are efficient and more productive. What other implications does the constantly evolving field of technology have for Delphi's managers?

focused on business-to-business (B2B) transactions and the companies that make them possible.[9] It's no wonder, since the B2B market, which stood at $177 billion in the year 2000, is expected to reach nearly $2.5 trillion by 2003.[10]

Most of the major manufacturing companies are developing whole new Internet-focused strategies that will enable them to compete more effectively in the future. Such changes are having a dramatic effect on operations managers as they adjust from a one-firm system to an interfirm environment and from a relatively stable environment to one that is constantly changing and evolving. The ultimate linkage of firms is called *supply chain management* and is too complex to be discussed here. However, you will learn all about it in Chapter 15.

Quality Control

quality control
The measurement of products and services against set standards.

Quality control is the measurement of products and services against set standards. Earlier in America, quality control was often done at the end of the production line. It was done by a quality control department. Today things have changed. *Quality* now means satisfying customers by building in and ensuring quality from product planning to production, purchasing, sales, and service. Emphasis is placed on customer satisfaction, so quality is everyone's concern, not just the concern of the quality control people at the end of the assembly line. In total quality management (TQM) ➤ **P.251** ◄, which we discussed in Chapter 8, everybody is permitted and expected to contribute to the production of a product or service that meets customer standards every time. Providing such service is expected to lead to more business and more profits.

A major purpose of quality control is to make the consumer happy. Therefore, a TQM program begins by analyzing the market to see what quality standards need to be established. Quality is then designed into products, and every product must meet those standards every step of the way in the production process. The following are examples of how quality is being introduced into service and manufacturing firms:

- Holiday Inn authorized its hotel staff to do almost anything to satisfy an unhappy customer, from handing out gift certificates to eliminating charges for certain services. Empowered ➤ **P.20** ◄ managers and employees were given the authority to waive charges for the night's stay if the customer was still unhappy.

- Motorola set a goal of attaining "six sigma" quality—just 3.4 defects per million products. The Spotlight on Small Business box discusses how small businesses are also using this standard.

- In the past, Xerox found 97 defects for every 100 copiers coming off the assembly line. Now it finds only 12.

Dozens of other manufacturers and service organizations could be discussed here, but you get the idea: The customer is ultimately the one who determines what the standard for quality should be. American businesses are getting serious about providing top customer service, and many are already doing it. Service organizations are finding it difficult to provide outstanding service every time because the process is so labor intensive. Physical goods (e.g., a gold ring) can be designed and manufactured to near perfection. However, it is hard to reach such perfection when designing and providing a service experience such as a dance on a cruise ship or a cab drive through New York City.

Meeting the Six Sigma Standard

"Six sigma" is a quality measure that allows only 3.4 defects per million units. It is one thing for Motorola or General Electric to reach for such standards, but what about a small company like Dolan Industries? Dolan is a 41-person manufacturer of fasteners. It spent a few years trying to meet ISO 9000 standards, which are comparable to six sigma.

Once the company was able to achieve six sigma quality itself, it turned to its suppliers and demanded six sigma quality from them as well. It had to do that because its customers were demanding that level of quality. Companies such as General Electric, Allied-Signal, and Motorola are all seeking six sigma quality. The benefits include better performing products and, more important, happier customers—and higher profits.

Here is how six sigma works: If you can make it to the level of one sigma, two out of three products will meet specifications. If you can reach the two sigma level, then more than 95 percent of products will qualify. But when you meet six sigma quality, as we've said, you have only 3.4 defects in a million products (which means that 99.99966 percent will qualify). The bottom line is that small businesses are being held to a higher standard, one that reaches near perfection.

Sources: Mark Henricks, "Is It Greek to You?" *Entrepreneur*, July 1999, pp. 65–67; and Thomas Pyzdek, "Six Sigma: Needs Standardization," *Quality Digest*, March 2001, p. 20.

Quality Standards: The Baldrige Awards In the United States in 1987, a standard was set for overall company quality with the introduction of the Malcolm Baldrige National Quality Awards, named in honor of the U.S. secretary of commerce. To qualify for one of these awards, a company has to show quality in seven key areas: leadership, strategic planning, customer and market focus, information and analysis, human resources focus, process management, and business results. Major criteria for earning the award include whether customer wants and needs are being met and whether customer satisfaction ratings are better than those of competitors. As you can see, the focus is shifting away from just making quality goods and services to providing top-quality customer service in all respects.

One of the recent award winners was Sunny Fresh Foods, a small company that makes about 200 different egg products. Sunny Fresh was the first food company to win the award, and one of few small companies. The company used the Baldrige criteria to drive business systems development and business systems redesign.[11] Another recent small-business winner was Texas Nameplate. The company, which makes metal nameplates, etching many of them with chemicals, is a quality company not only when it comes to production but also when it comes to the environment. It has cut its waste dispersal to almost zero.

ISO 9000 and ISO 14000 Standards The International Organization for Standardization (known by the acronym *ISO*) sets the global measures for the quality of individual products. **ISO 9000** is the common name given to quality management and assurance standards. The latest standards, called ISO 9001:2000, were published in November of 2000.[12] They are a revised version of 1994 standards. The new standards require, for example, that a company must determine what customer needs are, including regulatory and legal requirements. The company must also make communication arrangements to

ISO 9000

The common name given to quality management and assurance standards.

Can small companies meet the high standards necessary to qualify for the Baldrige Award? Sunny Fresh Foods, a division of Cargill, Inc., did. Shown here accepting the award and standing next to former President Clinton is the chief executive officer of Cargill Inc., Warren R. Staley. What are the advantages for a small business in establishing the procedures and quality practices necessary to qualify for such a prestigious award?

ISO 14000
A collection of the best practices for managing an organization's impact on the environment.

handle issues such as complaints. Other standards involve process control, product testing, storage, and delivery.[13]

Prior to the establishment of the ISO standards, there were no international standards of quality against which to measure companies. Now the ISO, based in Europe, provides a common denominator of business quality accepted around the world.

What makes ISO 9000 so important is that the European Union (EU), the group of European countries that have established free-trade agreements, is demanding that companies that want to do business with the EU be certified by ISO standards. There are several accreditation agencies in Europe and in the United States whose function is to certify that a company meets the standards for all phases of its operations, from product development through production and testing to installation.

ISO 14000 is a collection of the best practices for managing an organization's impact on the environment. It does not prescribe a performance level. ISO 14000 is an environmental management system (EMS). The requirements for certification include having an environmental policy, having specific improvement targets, conducting audits of environmental programs, and maintaining top management review of the processes. Certification in both ISO 9000 and ISO 14000 would show that a firm has a world-class management system in both quality and environmental standards. In the past, firms assigned employees separately to meet both standards. Today, ISO 9000 and 14000 standards have been blended so that an organization can work on both at once.

OPERATIONS MANAGEMENT IN THE SERVICE SECTOR

Let's look at the life of an operations manager to see how he got to that position and what it entails. At the age of 17, Horst Schulze started work as a busboy at a spa in Cologne, Germany. He then worked his way around Europe as a waiter in Switzerland, France, and England. Eventually, he headed for the United States and visited the Waldorf-Astoria in New York City to see for himself how a well-run hotel operates. Schulze was impressed by the grandeur of the Waldorf and set that as his model for how operations management should be done.

He took a restaurant job in Houston, Texas, to learn more operations procedures and then left for a more upscale restaurant in San Francisco where he could improve on those skills. He then worked at the University Club in Chicago and moved on to management jobs with Hilton and Hyatt. With all of that experience behind him, Schulze went to work for Marriott as operations manager. With Marriott's backing, he created a chain of luxury hotels from one single Ritz-Carlton property in Boston. Today, Horst Schulze is its top executive. The chain has hotels in Australia, Bali, Canada, Hong Kong, and other countries around the globe.

Operations management in the service industry is all about creating a good experience for those who use the service. In a Ritz-Carlton hotel, operations management includes restaurants that offer the finest in service, elevators that run smoothly, and a front desk that processes people quickly. It also includes placing fresh-cut flowers in the lobbies and dishes of fruit in every room. More important, it means spending $4,500 for every new employee to provide training in quality management.

Operations management in luxury hotels is changing with today's new executives. As customers in hotels, executives are likely to want in-room Internet access and a help center with toll-free telephone service. Also, when an executive has to give a speech or presentation, he or she needs video equipment and a whole host of computer hardware and other aids. Foreign visitors would like multilingual customer-support services. Hotel shops need to carry more than souvenirs, newspapers, and some drugstore and food items to serve today's high-tech travelers. The shops may also carry laptop computer supplies, electrical adapters, and the like. Operations management is responsible for locating and providing such amenities to make customers happy.

In short, delighting customers by anticipating their needs has become the quality standard for luxury hotels, as it has for most other service businesses. But knowing customer needs and satisfying them are two different things. That's why operations management is so important: It is the implementation phase of management.[14] Like manufacturers, hotels are turning to the Internet to purchase production inputs inexpensively. GoCo-Op, Inc., for example, helps hotels reach the 15,000 suppliers who provide them with food, beverages, soap, linens, and other such products.[15]

Measuring Quality in the Service Sector

The greatest productivity ➤ **P.23** ◄ problems in the United States are reported to be in service organizations. While productivity growth was relatively good for manufacturers during the 1980s and 1990s (following the changes in the 1970s and 1980s noted at the start of this chapter), it was reported to be next to nothing for service organizations. More than 70 percent of U.S. jobs are now in the service sector, with more to come. A truly strong America must therefore be progressive in introducing the latest technology to services ➤ **P.25** ◄ as well as to manufacturing.

Despite the negative reports mentioned above, there's strong evidence that productivity in the service sector is rising, but the government simply doesn't have the means to measure it.[16] One problem is that productivity measures don't capture improvements in quality. In an example from health care, positron emission tomography (PET) scans are much better than X rays, but that quality improvement is not reported in productivity figures.[17] The traditional way to measure productivity involves tracking inputs (worker-hours) compared to outputs (dollars). Notice that there is no measure for quality improvement. When new information systems are developed to measure the quality improvement of goods and services—including the speed of their delivery and customer satisfaction—productivity in the service sector will go up dramatically.

Using computers is one way the service sector is improving productivity,

The Bridgestone Firestone plant in Decatur, Illinois, had been certified as meeting both ISO 9000 and ISO 14000 qualifications. Nonetheless, federal regulators have linked over 100 fatalities in car accidents to tire separation in Firestone tires, the majority of which were made at the Decatur plant. This tragic outcome shows clearly that quality standards are *only* meaningful if rigorously applied by management and workers. Do you think Bridgestone Firestone will win back public confidence?

but not the only way. Think about labor-intensive businesses like McDonald's and Burger King, where automation plays a big role in controlling costs and improving service. Today at Burger King, customers fill their own drink cups from soda machines, which allows workers to concentrate on preparing the food. And, because the people working at the drive-up window now wear headsets instead of using stationary mikes, they aren't glued to one spot anymore and can do four or five tasks while taking an order.

Most of us have been exposed to similar productivity gains in banking. For example, people in most towns no longer have to wait in long lines for tellers to help them deposit and withdraw money. Instead, they use automated teller machines (ATMs), which usually involve little or no waiting and are available 24 hours a day. Internet banking makes certain other processes in banking even easier.

Another service that was once annoyingly slow was grocery store checkout. The system of marking goods with universal product codes enables computerized checkout and allows cashiers to be much more productive than before. Now many stores are enabling customers to go through the checkout process on their own.[18] Some grocery chains and smaller, independent companies are implementing Internet services that allow customers to place orders online and receive home delivery; the potential for productivity gains in this area are enormous.

Airlines are another service industry experiencing tremendous productivity increases through the use of computers for everything from processing reservations, to serving prepackaged meals on board, to standardizing the movements of luggage, passengers, and so on. On the one hand, you may have enjoyed using an automated ticketing machine or ticketless boarding to avoid the congestion at airline ticket counters. On the other hand, you probably have also noticed the need for much more improvement in operations management for the airlines. Long lines, lost bags, and delayed flights annoy customers tremendously.[19]

In short, operations management has led to tremendous productivity increases in the service sector but still has a long way to go. Also, service workers are losing jobs to machines just as manufacturing workers did. Again, the secret to obtaining and holding a good job is to acquire appropriate education and training. Such education and training must go on for a lifetime to keep up with the rapid changes that are happening in all areas of business. That message can't be repeated too frequently.

Services Go Interactive

The service industry has always taken advantage of new technology to increase customer satisfaction. Jet travel enabled FedEx to deliver goods overnight. Computer databases enabled AT&T to provide individualized customer service. Cable TV led to pay-per-view services. And now interactive computer networks are revolutionizing services. Interactive services are already available from banks, stockbrokers, travel agents, and information providers of all kinds. Individuals may soon be able to participate directly in community and national decision making via telephone, cable, and computer networks.

You can now buy a greater variety of books and CDs on the Internet than you can in most retail stores. You can also search for and buy new and used automobiles and new and used computers. As computers and modems get faster, the Internet may take over much of traditional retailing. Regardless of what is being sold, however, the success of service organizations in the future will depend greatly on establishing a dialogue with consumers so that the operations managers can help their organizations adapt to consumer demands faster and more efficiently. Such information systems have been developed and should prove highly useful.

- Can you name and define three functions that are common to operations management in both the service and manufacturing sectors?
- What are the major criteria for facility location?
- What are ISO 9000 and ISO 14000 standards?

OPERATIONS MANAGEMENT IN THE MANUFACTURING SECTOR

Common sense and some experience have already taught you much of what you need to know about production processes. You know what it takes to write a term paper or prepare a dinner. You need money to buy the materials, you need a place to work, and you need to be organized to get the task done. The same is true of the production process in industry. It uses basic inputs to produce outputs (see Figure 9.1). Production adds value, or utility, to materials or processes. **Form utility** is the value added by the creation of finished goods and services, such as the value added by taking silicon and making computer chips or putting services together to create a vacation package. Form utility can exist at the retail level as well. For example, a butcher can produce a specific cut of beef from a whole cow or a baker can make a specific type of cake out of basic ingredients.

To be competitive, manufacturers must keep the costs of inputs down. That is, the costs of workers, machinery, and so on must be kept as low as possible. Similarly, the amount of output must be relatively high. The question today is: How does a producer keep costs low and still increase output? This question will dominate thinking in the manufacturing and service sectors for years to come. In the next few sections, we explore process planning and the latest technology being used to cut costs.

Process Planning

Process planning is choosing the best means for turning resources into useful goods and services. There are several different processes manufacturers use to produce goods. Andrew S. Grove, chairman of computer chip manufacturer Intel, uses a great analogy to explain production:

> *To understand the principles of production, imagine that you're a chef . . . and that your task is to serve a breakfast consisting of a three-minute soft-boiled egg, buttered toast, and coffee. Your job is to prepare and deliver the three items simultaneously, each of them fresh and hot.*

form utility
The value added by the creation of finished goods and services, such as the value added by taking silicon and making computer chips or putting services together to create a vacation package.

process planning
Choosing the best means for turning resources into useful goods and services.

FIGURE **9.1**

THE PRODUCTION PROCESS

The production process consists of taking the factors of production (land, etc.) and using those inputs to produce goods, services, and ideas. Planning, routing, scheduling, and the other activities are the means to accomplish the objective—output.

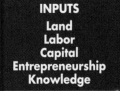

INPUTS	PRODUCTION CONTROL	OUTPUTS
Land	Planning	Goods
Labor	Routing	Services
Capital	Scheduling	Ideas
Entrepreneurship	Dispatching	
Knowledge	Follow-up	

Grove goes on to say that the task here encompasses the three basic requirements of production: (1) to build and deliver products in response to the demands of the customer at a scheduled delivery time, (2) to provide an acceptable quality level, and (3) to provide everything at the lowest possible cost.

Using the breakfast example, it's easy to understand two manufacturing terms: process and assembly. **Process manufacturing** physically or chemically changes materials. For example, boiling physically changes the egg. (Similarly, process manufacturing turns sand into glass or computer chips.) The **assembly process** puts together components (eggs, toast, and coffee) to make a product (breakfast). (Cars are made through an assembly process that puts together the frame, engine, and other parts.)

In addition, production processes are either continuous or intermittent. A **continuous process** is one in which long production runs turn out finished goods over time. As the chef in our diner, for example, you could have a conveyor belt that lowers eggs into boiling water for three minutes and then lifts them out on a continuous basis. A three-minute egg would be available whenever you wanted one. (A chemical plant, for example, is run on a continuous process.)

It usually makes more sense when responding to specific customer orders to use an **intermittent process.** This is an operation where the production run is short (one or two eggs) and the machines are changed frequently to make different products (like the oven in a bakery or the toaster in the diner). (Manufacturers of custom-designed furniture would use an intermittent process.)

Today most new manufacturers use intermittent processes. Computers, robots, and flexible manufacturing processes allow firms to turn out custom-made goods almost as fast as mass-produced goods were once turned out. We'll discuss how they do that in detail later in the chapter. For now, let's look at some of the newer techniques being used to make the production process more efficient.

Materials Requirement Planning

Materials requirement planning (MRP) is a computer-based operations management system that uses sales forecasts to make sure that needed parts and materials are available at the right time and place. In our diner, for example, we could feed the sales forecast into the computer, which would specify how many eggs or how much coffee to order and then print out the proper scheduling and routing sequence. The same can be done with the seats and other parts of an automobile.

MRP is now considered old; it was most popular with companies that made products with a lot of different parts. MRP quickly led to MRP II, an advanced version of MRP that allowed plants to include all the resources involved in the efficient making of a product, including projected sales, personnel, plant capacity, and distribution limitations. MRP II was called *manufacturing resource* (not *materials requirement*) planning because the planning involved more than just material requirements.

The newest version of MRP is **enterprise resource planning (ERP).** ERP is a computer-based production and operations system that links multiple firms into one integrated production unit. The software enables the monitoring of quality and customer satisfaction as it's happening. ERP is much more sophisticated than either MRP or MRP II because it monitors processes in multiple firms at the same time.[20] For example, it monitors inventory at the supplier as well as at the manufacturing plant. ERP systems are going

process manufacturing
That part of the production process that physically or chemically changes materials.

assembly process
That part of the production process that puts together components.

continuous process
A production process in which long production runs turn out finished goods over time.

intermittent process
A production process in which the production run is short and the machines are changed frequently to make different products.

materials requirement planning (MRP)
A computer-based production management system that uses sales forecasts to make sure that needed parts and materials are available at the right time and place.

enterprise resource planning (ERP)
Computer-based production and operations system that links multiple firms into one integrated production unit.

global now that the Internet is powerful enough to handle the data flows. At the plant level, dynamic performance monitoring (DNP) enables plant operators to monitor the use of power, chemicals, and other resources and to make needed adjustments. In short, flows to, through, and from plants have become automated.

Some firms are providing a service called *sequential delivery.* These firms are suppliers that provide components in an order sequenced to their customers' production process. For example, Ford's seat supplier would load seats onto a truck so that, when off-loaded, the seats would be in perfect sequence for the type of vehicle coming down the assembly line.

Eventually, such programs will link more suppliers, manufacturers, and retailers in a completely integrated manufacturing and distribution system that will be constantly monitored for the smooth flow of goods from the time they're ordered to the time they reach the ultimate consumer. Companies now using sequential delivery systems include Coors Ceramics (structural products); Phoenix Designs (office systems and furniture); and Red Devil (sealants, caulks, and hand tools).

PROGRESS ASSESSMENT

- Can you define form utility and process planning?
- Can you explain the differences among the following: process manufacturing, assembly process, continuous process, and intermittent process?
- What is the difference between materials resource planning (MRP) and enterprise resource planning (ERP)?

MODERN PRODUCTION TECHNIQUES

The ultimate goal of manufacturing and process management is to provide high-quality goods and services instantaneously in response to customer demand. As we have stressed throughout this book, traditional organizations were simply not designed to be so responsive to the customer. Rather, they were

REACHING BEYOND OUR BORDERS
www.apqc.org
Benchmarking the Best

Today's trend toward globalization means that the world's best manufacturers can enter almost any market at almost any time. In other words, if you aren't one of the world's best manufacturers, you're likely to go out of business. In fact, you can be one of the world's best producers and still lose the bulk of your business if you aren't also one of the most innovative and cost-efficient producers. Mercedes and BMW, for example, were long known as two of the best car manufacturers in the world. Then along came Lexus and Infiniti not only to challenge their technological lead but to offer similar quality at a much lower price. Consequently, Mercedes was forced to produce less expensive car models. If Mercedes hadn't responded, it would have continued to lose its market share.

Even being an industry leader doesn't ensure world dominance for long. Japanese companies, for example, introduced high-definition television (HDTV) in 1988 at the Olympics in Seoul, Korea. U.S. manufacturers considered this a challenge much like the old challenge from the Soviet Union to be the first country to get to the moon. Working together, U.S. manufacturers developed a better television technology that leapfrogged Japanese products. European companies are now doing the same. Similarly, IBM once led the world in computer technology but is now just one of many competitors, no longer the dominant industry leader.

Staying on top means meeting the world's standard. The term, *benchmarking* refers to a process by which a company compares its own products and processes to those of the best companies in the world. A company must compare each one of its processes to that same process as practiced by the best. It must then bring its processes up to the world-class standard or outsource the process to a firm that can. But the company can't rest there; it must empower its workers to become the best in the world and to continuously improve processes and products to maintain a leadership position. Often that means the company must develop products that will make its own products obsolete. So be it. If it doesn't do so, someone else will. The American Productivity and Quality Center has an International Benchmarking Clearinghouse, through which companies can learn about best practices throughout the world. The center's phone number is 800-776-4020.

---

mass production
The process of making a large number of a limited variety of products at very low cost.

designed to make goods efficiently. The whole idea of **mass production** was to make a large number of a limited variety of products at very low cost.

Over the years, low cost often came at the expense of quality and flexibility. Furthermore, suppliers didn't always deliver when they said they would, so manufacturers had to carry large inventories of raw materials and components. Such inefficiencies made U.S. companies subject to foreign competitors who were using more advanced production techniques. The Reaching Beyond Our Borders box above discusses how companies use benchmarking to compare themselves with the world's leading companies and to find the best practices possible.

As a result of global competition, largely from Japan and Germany, companies today must make a wide variety of high-quality custom-designed products at very low cost. Clearly, something had to change on the production floor to make that possible. Seven major developments have radically changed the production process in the United States: (1) just-in-time inventory control, (2) Internet purchasing, (3) flexible manufacturing, (4) lean manufacturing, (5) mass customization, (6) competing in time, and (7) computer-aided design and manufacturing.

Just-in-Time Inventory Control

One major cost of production is holding parts, motors, and other items in storage for later use. Storage not only subjects such items to obsolescence, pilferage, and damage but also requires construction and maintenance of costly warehouses. To cut such costs, the Japanese implemented a concept called **just-in-time (JIT) inventory control.** JIT systems keep a minimum of inventory on the premises; parts, supplies, and other needs are delivered just in time to go on the assembly line. There is a scarcity of land in Japan, so minimizing the area needed for storage is a major issue. There is much more land available in the United States. Nonetheless, some U.S. manufacturers have adopted JIT and are quite happy with the results. To work effectively, however, the process requires excellent coordination with carefully selected suppliers. Sometimes the supplier builds new facilities close to the main producer to minimize distribution time.

Here's how it works: A manufacturer sets a production schedule using ERP or one of the other systems just described, and then determines what parts and supplies will be needed. It informs suppliers electronically of what it will need. The supplier must deliver the goods just in time to go on the assembly line. Naturally, this calls for more effort (and more costs) on the supplier's part. The company maintains efficiency by having the supplier linked electronically to the producer so that the supplier becomes more like another department in the firm than a separate business.

You can imagine how the system would work in Andrew Grove's breakfast example. Rather than ordering enough eggs, butter, bread, and coffee for a whole week and storing them, the chef would have his suppliers deliver a certain amount every morning. That way the food would be fresh and deliveries could be varied depending on customer demand. An employee from the supplier could be on hand at all times to ensure freshness.

ERP and JIT systems make sure the right materials are at the right place at the right time at the cheapest cost to meet both customer and production needs. That's the first step in modern production innovation. Part of that process is rethinking the purchasing process. We shall explore that issue next.

Internet Purchasing

Purchasing is the function in a firm that searches for quality material resources, finds the best suppliers, and negotiates the best price for quality goods and services. In the past, manufacturers tended to deal with many different suppliers with the idea that, if one supplier or another couldn't deliver, materials would be available from someone. Today, however, manufacturers are relying more heavily on one or two suppliers because the firms share so much information that they don't want to have too many suppliers knowing their business. The relationship between suppliers and manufacturers is thus much closer than ever before.

The Internet has transformed the purchasing function in recent years. For example, a business looking for supplies can contact any one of dozens of Internet-based purchasing services and

just-in-time (JIT) inventory control
A production process in which a minimum of inventory is kept on the premises and parts, supplies, and other needs are delivered just in time to go on the assembly line.

purchasing
The function in a firm that searches for quality material resources, finds the best suppliers, and negotiates the best price for goods and services.

Ted Farnsworth started farmbid.com, a website that allows farmers to buy and sell seed, chemicals, machinery, and other agricultural products. Farmbid.com is only one of more than a dozen such sites available to farmers, illustrating that the B2B cybermarket is huge. Just as many of the B2C Internet companies have failed, not all of the B2B firms will survive either. What are some of the factors that separate the winners from the losers?

find the best supplies at the best price. Similarly, a company wishing to sell supplies can use the Internet to find all the companies looking for such supplies.[21] The cost of purchasing items has thus been reduced tremendously.

Net marketplaces come in three different forms: (1) *trading exchange platforms*, like VerticalNet and i2 Technologies, which assist companies in multiple markets, (2) *industry-sponsored exchanges*, like the one provided by the Big Three automakers, and (3) *Net market makers*, like e-STEEL and BuildPoint which host electronic marketplaces. Farmers have their own Internet markets, with names like DirectAg.com, XSAg.com, and Farmbid.com.[22] You will be reading more and more about these business-to-business (B2B) exchange companies as hundreds emerge to help link companies together efficiently. An example of the savings possible is provided by General Electric, which has estimated that if all of its B2B transactions went to the Web, costs would drop from the current $50–$100 per transaction to just $5 per transaction.[23]

Flexible Manufacturing

flexible manufacturing
Designing machines to do multiple tasks so that they can produce a variety of products.

Flexible manufacturing involves designing machines to do multiple tasks so that they can produce a variety of products. Ford Motor Company, for example, uses flexible manufacturing at its Romeo, Michigan, plant. As many as six variations of V-8 and V-6 engines can be built from the same machinery.

Allen-Bradley Company, Inc., a maker of industrial automation controls, uses flexible manufacturing to build motor starters. Orders come in daily, and within 24 hours the company's 26 machines and robots manufacture, test, and package the starters—which are untouched by human hands. Allen-Bradley's machines are so flexible that a special order, even a single item, can be included in the assembly without slowing down the process.

CRITICAL THINKING

Earlier we talked about continuous processes versus intermittent processes. Can you see how flexible manufacturing makes it possible for intermittent processes to become as fast as continuous processes? What are the implications for saving time on the assembly line, saving money, and cutting back on labor?

Lean Manufacturing

lean manufacturing
The production of goods using less of everything compared to mass production.

Lean manufacturing is the production of goods using less of everything compared to mass production: less human effort, less manufacturing space, less investment in tools, and less engineering time to develop a new product. A company becomes lean by continuously increasing its capacity to produce high-quality goods while decreasing its need for resources.

To make the Saturn automobile, for example, General Motors abandoned its assembly-line production process. The fundamental purpose of restructuring was to dramatically cut the number of worker-hours needed to build a car. GM made numerous changes, the most dramatic of which was to switch to modular construction. GM suppliers preassemble most of the auto parts into a few large components called modules. Workers are no longer positioned along miles of assembly line. Instead, they're grouped at various workstations, where they put the modules together. Rather than do a few set tasks, workers perform a whole cluster of tasks. Trolleys carry the partly completed car from station to station. Compared to the assembly line, modular assembly takes up less space and calls for fewer workers—both money-saving steps.

robot
A computer-controlled machine capable of performing many tasks requiring the use of materials and tools.

Finally, GM greatly expanded its use of robots in the manufacturing process. A **robot** is a computer-controlled machine capable of performing many tasks requiring the use of materials and tools. Robots, for example, spray-paint cars and do welding. Robots usually are fast, efficient, and accurate. Robots and machinery perform routine, repetitive jobs quickly, efficiently, and accurately. This provides opportunities for workers to be more creative.

Mass Customization

To *customize* means to make a unique product or provide a specific service to an individual. Although it once may have seemed impossible, **mass customization,** which means tailoring products to meet the needs of a large number of individual customers, is now practiced widely. The National Bicycle Industrial Company in Japan, for example, makes 18 bicycle models in more than 2 million combinations, with each combination designed to fit the needs of a specific customer. The customer chooses the model, size, color, and design. The retailer takes various measurements from the buyer and faxes the data to the factory, where robots handle the bulk of the assembly. Thus, flexible manufacturing, as described above, is one of the factors that makes mass customization possible. Given the exact needs of a customer, flexible machines can produce a customized good as fast as mass-produced goods were once made.

mass customization
Tailoring products to meet the needs of individual customers.

competing in time
Being as fast or faster than competition in responding to consumer wants and needs and getting goods and services to them.

More and more manufacturers are learning to customize their products. For example, some General Nutrition Center (GNC) stores feature machines that enable shoppers to custom-design their own vitamins, shampoo, and lotions. Other companies produce custom-made books with a child's name inserted in key places, and custom-made greeting cards have appeared on the market. The Custom Foot stores use infrared scanners to precisely measure each foot so shoes can be crafted to fit perfectly. InterActive Custom Clothes (www.ic3d.com) offers a wide variety of options in custom-made jeans, including four different rivet colors. You can also buy custom-made Levi jeans. Motorola's Pager Division has 30 million possible permutations of pagers.

Mass customization is coming to services as well. Capital Protective Insurance (CPI), for example, sells customized risk-management plans to companies. The latest in computer software and hardware makes it possible for CPI to develop such custom-made policies. Health clubs now offer unique fitness programs for individuals, travel agencies provide vacation packages that vary according to individual choices, and some colleges allow students to design their own majors. Actually, it is much easier to custom-design service programs than it is to custom-make products, because there is no fixed tangible good that has to be adapted. Each customer can specify what he or she wants, within the limits of the service organization—limits that seem to be ever widening.

The Sunrise Medical Mobility Products Division in Fresno, California is one of those organizations that practices mass customization. That is, they can design products that exactly meet your requirements and get them to you quickly. What advantages do you see to having customized products rather than mass-produced goods?

Competing in Time

Competing in time means being as fast or faster than competition in responding to consumer wants and needs and getting goods and services to them. Speedy response is essential to competing at all in a global marketplace. Ford Motor Company estimates that, to match the best, it must be 25 percent faster than it is now in creating new products. Using the latest in technology, Ford should have no problem meeting that goal. The following section explores dramatic changes that are mak-

ing the production process much faster and are maintaining American competitive strength in manufacturing. Such changes as computer-aided design and computer-aided manufacturing enable firms to compete in time and in efficiency.

Computer-Aided Design and Manufacturing

The one development in the recent past that appears to have changed production techniques and strategies more than any other has been the integration of computers into the design and manufacturing of products. The first thing computers did was help in the design of products; this is called **computer-aided design (CAD).** The latest CAD systems allow designers to work in three dimensions. The next step was to involve computers directly in the production process; this is called **computer-aided manufacturing (CAM).**

CAD/CAM (the use of both computer-aided design and computer-aided manufacturing) made it possible to custom-design products to meet the needs of small markets with very little increase in cost. A manufacturer programs the computer to make a simple design change, and that change can be incorporated directly into the production line.

Computer-aided design and manufacturing are invading the clothing industry. A computer program establishes a pattern and cuts the cloth automatically. Today, a person's dimensions can be programmed into the machines to create custom-cut clothing at little additional cost. In food service, computer-aided manufacturing is used to make cookies in fresh-baked cookie shops. On-site, small-scale, semiautomated, sensor-controlled baking makes consistent quality easy to achieve.

Computer-aided design has doubled productivity ➤ **P.23** ◄ in many firms. But it's one thing to design a product and quite another to set the specifications to make a machine do the work. The problem in the past was that computer-aided design machines couldn't talk to computer-aided manufacturing machines directly. Recently, however, software programs have been designed to unite CAD with CAM: the result is **computer-integrated manufacturing (CIM).** The new software is expensive, but it cuts as much as 80 percent of the time needed to program machines to make parts, and it eliminates many errors.

computer-aided design (CAD)
The use of computers in the design of products.

computer-aided manufacturing (CAM)
The use of computers in the manufacturing of products.

computer-integrated manufacturing (CIM)
The uniting of computer-aided design with computer-aided manufacturing.

CRITICAL THINKING

Computer-integrated manufacturing (CIM) has begun to revolutionize the production process. Now, everything from cookies to cars can be designed and manufactured much more cheaply than before. Furthermore, customized changes can be made with very little increase in cost. What will such changes mean for the clothing industry, the shoe industry, and other fashion-related industries? What will they mean for other consumer and industrial goods industries? How will you benefit as a consumer?

CONTROL PROCEDURES: PERT AND GANTT CHARTS

program evaluation and review technique (PERT)
A method for analyzing the tasks involved in completing a given project, estimating the time needed to complete each task, and identifying the minimum time needed to complete the total project.

An important function of an operations manager is to be sure that products are manufactured and delivered on time, on budget, and to specifications. The question is, How can one be sure that all of the assembly processes will go smoothly and end up completed by the required time? One popular technique for maintaining some feel for the progress of production was developed in the 1950s for constructing nuclear submarines: the **program evaluation and review technique (PERT).** PERT users analyze the tasks involved in completing

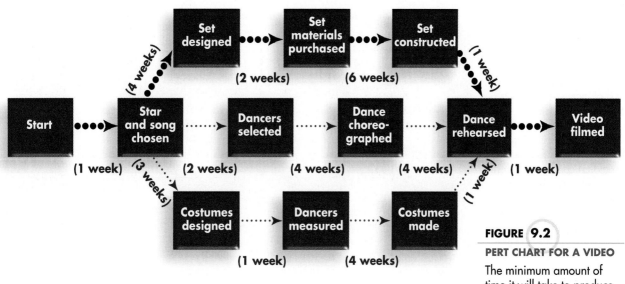

FIGURE 9.2

PERT CHART FOR A VIDEO

The minimum amount of time it will take to produce this video is 15 weeks. To get that number, you add the week it takes to pick a star and a song to the four weeks to design a set, the two weeks to purchase set materials, the six weeks to construct the set, the week before rehearsals, and the final week when the video is made. That's the critical path. Any delay in that process will delay the final video.

a given project, estimate the time needed to complete each task, and identify the minimum time needed to complete the total project.

Formally, the steps involved in using PERT are (1) analyzing and sequencing tasks that need to be done, (2) estimating the time needed to complete each task, (3) drawing a PERT network illustrating the information from steps 1 and 2, and (4) identifying the critical path. The **critical path** is the sequence of tasks that takes the longest time to complete. This word *critical* is used in this term because a delay in the time needed to complete this path would cause the project or production run to be late.

Figure 9.2 illustrates a PERT chart for producing a music video. Note that the squares on the chart indicate completed tasks and the arrows leading to the squares indicate the time needed to complete each task. The path from one completed task to another illustrates the relationships among tasks. For example, the arrow from "set designed" to "set materials purchased" shows that designing the set must be completed before the materials can be purchased. The critical path (indicated by the bold black arrows) reflects that producing the set takes more time than auditioning dancers and choreographing dances as well as designing and making costumes. The project manager now knows that it's critical that set construction remain on schedule if the project is to be completed on time, but short delays in the dance and costume preparation shouldn't affect completing the total project on time.

A PERT network can be made up of thousands of events over many months. Today, this complex procedure is done by computer. Another, more basic, strategy used by manufacturers for measuring production progress is a Gantt chart. A **Gantt chart** (named for its developer, Henry L. Gantt) is a bar graph that clearly shows what projects are being worked on and how much has been completed at any given time. Figure 9.3 shows a Gantt chart for a doll manufacturer. The chart shows that the dolls' heads and bodies should be completed before the clothing is sewn. It also shows that at the end of week 3, the dolls' bodies are ready, but the heads are about half a week behind. All of this calculation was once done by hand. Now the computer has taken over. Using a Gantt-like computer program, a manager can trace the production process minute by minute to determine which tasks are on time and which are behind so that adjustments can be made to allow the company to stay on schedule.

critical path
The sequence of tasks that takes the longest time to complete.

Gantt chart
Bar graph showing production managers what projects are being worked on and what stage they are in at any given time.

FIGURE 9.3

A GANTT CHART FOR A DOLL MANUFACTURER

A Gantt chart enables a production manager to see at a glance when projects are scheduled to be completed and what the status now is. For example, the dolls' heads and bodies should be completed before the clothing is sewn, but they could be a little late as long as everything is ready for assembly in week 6. This chart shows that at the end of week 3, the dolls' bodies are ready, but the heads are about half a week behind.

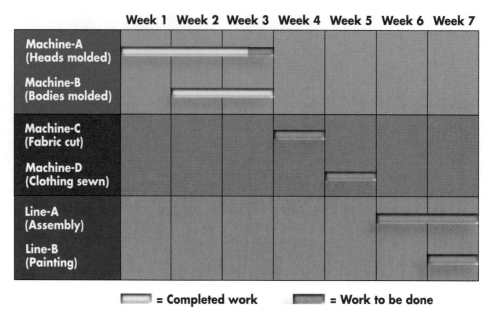

= Completed work   = Work to be done

PREPARING FOR THE FUTURE

The United States remains a major industrial country and is likely to become even stronger. This means that there are tremendous opportunities for careers in operations management. Today relatively few college students major in production and operations management, inventory management, and other careers involving manufacturing and operations management in the service sector. That means more opportunities for those students who can see the future trends and have the skills to own or work in tomorrow's highly automated, efficient factories, mines, service facilities, and other production locations.

What does technological innovation mean to you? It means that, as a college student, you will have marvelous new learning opportunities. It means new career choices and a higher standard of living and quality of life. But it also means preparing for such changes. Clearly, the workplace will be dominated by computers, robots, and other advanced machinery. Even the service sector will require the widespread use of computers, whether desktop, laptop, or handheld.

If all this sounds terribly cold and impersonal, then you recognize one of the needs of the future. People will need much more contact than before with others outside the work environment. There will be new demands for recreation, social clubs, travel, and other diversions. The America of the next century will be radically different from the America at the turn of the millennium. It will take both technically trained people and people skilled in human relationships to guide us through the transition.

Carnegie-Mellon University now requires a course in manufacturing management for its master of business administration degree. Courses in robotics and manufacturing strategy are optional. Some Carnegie-Mellon students act as consultants to manufacturers in the Pittsburgh area. Stanford University has its Institute for Manufacturing and Automation. Georgia Tech has a program in computer-integrated manufacturing. Such programs have become commonplace nationwide at both the undergraduate and graduate levels. Check your local schools for such programs.

Some schools are training students to *manage* the new high-tech workforce. Emphasis is on participative management and the design of attractive work environments. All this will come together in the next decade to bring a new era in both the manufacturing and the service sectors. You have every reason to be optimistic about the future for both U.S. and world economic growth because of these changes. You can also expect to find many exciting new careers in America's new industrial boom.

- What is just-in-time inventory control?
- How does flexible manufacturing differ from lean manufacturing?
- What is meant by the phrase *competing in time?*
- Draw a PERT chart for making a breakfast of three-minute eggs, buttered toast, and coffee. Define the critical path. How could you use a Gantt chart to keep track of production?

SUMMARY

1. Operations management is a specialized area in management that converts or transforms resources (including human resources) into goods and services.

   1. Define *operations management.*

   • *What kind of firms use operations managers?*
   Firms in both the manufacturing and service sectors use operations managers.

2. Functions involved in both the manufacturing and service sectors include facility location, facility layout, and quality control.

   2. Describe the operations management functions that are involved in both the manufacturing and service sectors.

   • *What is facility location and how does it differ from facility layout?*
   Facility location is the process of selecting a geographic location for a company's operations. *Facility layout* is the physical arrangement of resources (including people) to produce goods and services effectively and efficiently. *Quality control* is the measurement of products and services against set standards.

   • *Why is facility location so important, and what criteria are used to evaluate different sites?*
   The very survival of U.S. manufacturing depends on its ability to remain competitive, and that means either making inputs less costly, (reducing costs of labor and land) or increasing outputs from present inputs (increasing productivity). Labor costs and land costs are two major criteria for selecting the right sites. Other criteria include whether (1) resources are plentiful and inexpensive, (2) skilled workers are available or are trainable, (3) taxes are low and the local government offers support, (4) energy and water are available, (5) transportation costs are low, and (6) the quality of life and quality of education are high.

3. There's strong evidence that productivity in the service sector is rising, but the government simply doesn't have the means to measure it.

   3. Discuss the problem of measuring productivity in the service sector, and tell how new technology is leading to productivity gains in service companies.

   • *Why is productivity so hard to measure?*
   The traditional way to measure productivity involves tracking inputs (worker-hours) compared to outputs (dollars). Quality improvements are not weighed. New information systems must be developed to measure the *quality* of goods and services, the speed of their delivery, and customer satisfaction.

   • *How is technology creating productivity gains in service organizations?*
   Computers have been a great help to service employees, allowing them to perform their tasks faster and more accurately. ATM machines make bank-

ing faster and easier, automated checking machines enable grocery clerks (and customers) to process items faster. And automated ticketing machines make airlines more efficient, although they have a long way to go before they truly delight customers.

4. Explain process planning and the various manufacturing processes being used today.

4. Process planning is choosing the best means for turning resources into useful goods and services.
   • *What is process manufacturing and how does it differ from assembly processes?*
   Process manufacturing physically or chemically changes materials. Assembly processes put together components.
   • *Are there other production processes?*
   Production processes are either continuous or intermittent. A continuous process is one in which long production runs turn out finished goods over time. An intermittent process is an operation where the production run is short and the machines are changed frequently to produce different products.
   • *What relationship does enterprise resource planning (ERP) have with the production process?*
   A manufacturer sets a production schedule. Its suppliers are automatically informed electronically of what will be needed. The supplier must deliver the goods just in time for the production or assembly process, making the supplier part of the process.

5. Describe the seven new manufacturing techniques that have made U.S. companies more productive: just-in-time inventory control, Internet purchasing, flexible manufacturing, lean manufacturing, mass customization, competing in time, and computer-aided design and manufacturing.

5. Companies are using seven new production techniques to become more profitable: (1) just-in-time inventory control, (2) Internet purchasing, (3) flexible manufacturing, (4) lean manufacturing, (5) mass customization, (6) competing in time, and (7) computer-aided design and manufacturing.
   • *What is just-in-time inventory control?*
   JIT involves having suppliers deliver parts and materials just in time to go on the assembly line so they don't have to be stored in warehouses.
   • *How have purchasing agreements changed?*
   Purchasing agreements now involve fewer suppliers who supply quality goods and services at better prices in return for getting the business. Many new Internet companies have emerged to help both buyers and sellers complete the exchange process more efficiently.
   • *What is flexible manufacturing?*
   Flexible manufacturing involves designing machines to produce a variety of products.
   • *What is lean manufacturing?*
   Lean manufacturing is the production of goods using less of everything compared to mass production: less human effort, less manufacturing space, less investment in tools, and less engineering time to develop a new product.
   • *What is mass customization?*
   Mass customization means making custom-designed goods and services for a large number of individual customers. Flexible manufacturing makes mass customization possible. Given the exact needs of a customer, flexible machines can produce a customized good as fast as mass-produced goods were once made. Mass customization is also important in service industries.
   • *How does competing in time fit into the process?*
   Getting your product to market before your competitors is essential today, particularly in the electronics industry. Thus, competing in time is critical. JIT inventory control allows for less inventory and fewer machines to move goods. This allows for more flexibility and faster response times.

• *How do CAD/CAM systems work?*
Design changes made in computer-aided design (CAD) are instantly incorporated into the computer-aided manufacture (CAM) production process. The linking of the two systems—CAD and CAM—is called computer-integrated manufacturing (CIM).

6. The program evaluation and review technique (PERT) is a method for analyzing the tasks involved in completing a given project, estimating the time needed to complete each task, and identifying the minimum time needed to complete the total project. A Gantt chart is a bar graph that clearly shows what projects are being worked on and how much has been completed at any given time.

6 Explain the use of PERT and Gantt charts.

• *Is there any relationship between a PERT chart and a Gantt chart?*
Figure 9.2 (p. 283) shows a PERT chart. Figure 9.3 (p. 284) shows a Gantt chart. Whereas PERT is a tool used for planning, a Gantt chart is a tool used to measure progress.

KEY TERMS

assembly
  process 276
competing in
  time 281
computer-aided
  design (CAD) 282
computer-aided
  manufacturing
  (CAM) 282
computer-integrated
  manufacturing
  (CIM) 282
continuous
  process 276
critical path 283
enterprise resource
  planning (ERP) 276
facility location 266

facility layout 268
flexible
  manufacturing 280
form utility 275
Gantt chart 283
intermittent
  process 276
ISO 9000 271
ISO 14000 272
just-in-time (JIT)
  inventory
  control 279
lean manufacturing
  280
mass customization
  281
mass production 278

materials
  requirement
  planning (MRP) 276
operations
  management 265
process
  planning 275
process
  manufacturing 276
production 264
program evaluation
  and review
  technique (PERT)
  282
purchasing 279
robot 280
quality control 270

DEVELOPING WORKPLACE SKILLS

1. Choosing the right location for a manufacturing plant or a service organization is often critical to its success. Have each member of a small group pick one manufacturing plant or one service organization in town and list at least three reasons why its location helps or hinders its success. If its location is not ideal, where would be a better one?

2. In teams of four or five, discuss the need for better operations management at airports and with the airlines in general. Have the team develop a three-page report listing (*a*) problems students have encountered in traveling by air and (*b*) suggestions for improving operations so such problems won't occur in the future.

3. Find two resources in the library or on the Internet that discuss some of the advantages and disadvantages of producing goods overseas using inexpensive labor. Summarize the moral and ethical issues of this practice.

4. Find any production facility (e.g., sandwich shop or woodworking facility) or service center at your school (e.g., library, copy room) and redesign the

layout (make a pencil drawing placing people and materials) so it could more effectively serve its customers and so that the workers would be more effective and efficient.

5. Think about some of the experiences you have had with service organizations recently (e.g., the admissions office at your school), and select one incident where you had to wait for an unreasonable length of time to get what you wanted. Tell what happens when customers are inconvenienced, and explain how management could make the operation more efficient and customer-oriented.

TAKING IT TO THE NET

1

Purpose

To illustrate production processes, using the production of M&Ms as an example.

Exercise

Take a tour of the M&Ms factory and visit the company store at www.m-ms.com/factory/index.html.

1. Is the production of M&Ms an example of an intermittent or continuous production process? Justify your answer.

2. Is mass customization used in M&M production? If so, how?

3. What location factors might go into the selection of a manufacturing site for M&Ms?

TAKING IT TO THE NET

2

Purpose:

To evaluate the benefits of lean manufacturing

Exercise:

To see how lean manufacturing improved the production performance of several companies go to Duggan and Associates' website at http://dugganinc.com.

1. What is lean manufacturing?

2. What are the five principles of lean manufacturing?

3. Watch the four slide shows that illustrate how lean manufacturing changed the layout and processes in different companies. What were the results of the new lean manufacturing techniques?

PRACTICING MANAGEMENT DECISIONS

CASE

GRIFFIN HOSPITAL

Imagine that you are pregnant and are going to the hospital to have your baby. You walk into the hospital parking lot and are met by an attendant who smiles and walks you to the reception room. You enter a lobby with tasteful wood decor and a friendly receptionist who assigns someone to take you to your room. You notice soft piano music as you walk down the hallway.

When you get to your room, you see not only big windows and skylights but also a double bed so that your husband can stay over if that's what you and he would like. Nearby is a big, comfortable lounge where your family can gather and visit. There is also a home-style kitchen, open 24 hours a day, where you or your family members can prepare meals. There are flowers in the room, and a notice explaining that a Jacuzzi is available.

After the baby is born, a nurse offers to come to your home in three days to see how you are doing and answer any questions you may have.

This is not a make-believe hospital. Griffin Hospital really exists, in Derby, Connecticut. And it isn't expensive, like the well-known Memorial Sloan-Kettering, with its marble walls and antique armoires. The Griffin Hospital operations manager and project architects used computer-aided design to create the layout of the maternity ward described above. They then played around with cardboard models and finally built a mock-up room in a warehouse. They invited patients to come see the new room and make comments. They used patient input throughout the process and made the whole hospital customer-friendly.

It would probably not surprise you to learn that turnover among nurses at Griffin Hospital is low and that obstetrics admissions have doubled in the last few years.

Discussion Questions

1. Hospitals are not the only organizations that could make their facilities more customer-friendly. If you were the operations manager in a hotel, how would you redesign the rooms so that your visit would be more pleasant?

2. What could operations managers at other service organizations—like schools, churches, and concert halls—do to make their customers more satisfied with the experience?

3. What experiences have you had when staying or visiting at a hospital? What could an operations manager have done to make that experience better?

4. What kinds of goods does a hospital provide along with its services?

Sources: David H. Freedman, "Intensive Care," *Inc.*, February 1999, pp. 72–80; and Ann Japenga, "Is a Luxury Hospital in Your Future?" *USA Weekend*, October 27–29, 2000, p. 10.

THE PRODUCTION PROCESS AT WASHBURN GUITARS

When you think of manufacturing firms, names like GM and IBM come to mind. But there are thousands of smaller manufacturers in the marketplace that provide us with many of the products that make life more enjoyable. Certainly guitars are one of those products. Washburn Guitars in Chicago, Illinois, is a manufacturing company that uses an intermittent process of production called small-batch manufacturing. That is, Washburn makes a few of one model of guitar and then shifts production to a different model.

Even though Washburn makes only a few products each day (about 15 guitars), the company still needs to use the latest in production techniques to stay competitive. For example, it uses flexible manufacturing. The Washburn production facility has a machine that is capable of doing many different tasks: building guitar necks, drilling holes for the fretboard, and so on.

Washburn also follows the total quality concepts that other, larger firms follow. When planning the production process, the company keeps in mind the need for profits. Therefore, the popular, more expensive guitars take precedence over less expensive items. Today, all of Washburn's acoustic guitars are made overseas, but the company is planning to build a new facility for producing acoustic guitars in Nashville, Tennessee. Total quality management and modern production techniques now make it possible to manufacture acoustic guitars in the United States and still stay competitive on price.

When making career plans, you may want to include smaller firms like Washburn Guitars in your thoughts. It is often exciting to work in a small, relatively intimate environment, especially if the firm practices participative management and other modern techniques.

Discussion Questions

1. What small manufacturing facilities are located in or near your city or town? Visit them and see for yourself what it's like to work for a small manufacturer.
2. Do you think that a guitar is the kind of item that lends itself well to continuous process manufacturing? Why?
3. One of the more important aspects of small-batch manufacturing is scheduling. What kinds of scheduling techniques have you learned in this chapter that you could use in a business similar to Washburn?
4. Does a career in production management seem attractive to you? Why or why not?

PART 3

MANAGEMENT

Management is the people part of business. Although managers are also responsible for managing finance, information, and various processes, their main responsibility is to the people who work for them. The managers are the people who run the organization. Without managers, there would be no business.

As everything else in the human realm is constantly changing, so is management and our attitudes toward it. Management careers have always been among the most challenging and fulfilling in the field of business. They still are. And the role of managers is changing rapidly as we approach the end of the century.

SKILLS

Managers today need different skills from those they needed a generation ago. Today's managers must know how to be both team players and team leaders. They cannot get away with the "jump when I say jump" mentality of the past. More than ever, managers need to be effective communicators. They especially need to know how to listen, to hear, and to understand the needs of both their subordinates and their own managers. They also need the ability to organize and to keep others organized and to possess the know-how to motivate workers.

CAREER PATHS

Today's management opportunities often start out as management training positions that later develop into full-blown management opportunities. Both government and larger companies have management training programs. Some of these organizations will hire workers through campus recruiters. Others look for skills that can be acquired outside the classroom. Another common way to become a manager is to start as an employee and work your way up the management ladder. College courses and other forms of management training are often available tuition-free to the ambitious employee.

Once a manager is hired, the progress into middle and top management is far from automatic. As one gets closer to the top, there are fewer and fewer opportunities. Getting to the top, then, means learning to be competitive and good at what you do. Understanding office politics is also certainly a plus, though some companies are more political than others.

As a manager moves up in an organization, his or her responsibilities and authority increase. Becoming an integral part of planning and running an organization brings excitement as well as rewards.

SOME POSSIBLE POSITIONS IN MANAGEMENT

JOB TITLE	SALARY	JOB DUTIES	CAREER PATH	PROSPECTS
General manager; CEO; executive vice president	Amount varies widely. Top companies: $5.7 million average; median $800,000	Establish the organization's general goals and policies. Act as liaison with other companies; direct the individual department or division; direct supervisor in motivation and control of workers.	Most general managers and top CEOs have college degrees, but some do not. Qualifications vary widely. Most vacancies are filled by promoting lower-level managers up through the ranks.	Average growth in opportunities through year 2008, but competition is keen.
Management trainee	Mid $20,000 (to start).	Learn basic responsibilities of a manager, training for the specific industry. Work in closely supervised situations in departments such as production, sales, research and development, finance. Training period is usually specified and is treated as probationary.	Usually, a two-year associate degree is the minimum. Four-year degrees are preferred. Previous management experience can be helpful, though some companies want applicants to have none, so they can be trained the company way.	Outlook through 2008 is good.
Supervisor, blue collar	Median is $37,180	Manage and train employees; keep track of time and scheduling, oversee use of equipment and materials. Work with union when union is present.	Knowledge of the technical part of the workers' task is the most important knowledge area. A two- or four-year degree is usually an aid in obtaining promotion.	Outlook through 2008 is slower than the average. Moderate growth is expected due to developments in technology.
Management Consultant	Varies greatly, based on experience, education, & employer.	Act as an adviser and analyst of management concerns in host organizations.	Degree and work experience help market credibility of the consultant. However, knowledge of the industry and self-confidence are most important qualities.	Demand will increase through 2008, especially in firms doing business internationally.

Source: *Occupational Outlook Handbook, 2000–2001 Edition: Bureau of Labor Statistics.*

HILTON WASHINGTON EMBASSY ROW

Name: Dixie L. Eng

Age: 41

Position/title: General Manager

Salary range: $45,000–$125,000

Time in this position: 10 years as Hotel General Manager, 22 years in hospitality.

Company name: Hilton Washington Embassy Row
Doral International, Inc.

Major factors in the decision to take this position: Entrepreneural spirit and the opportunity to oversee an operation that truly offers a diverse and exciting work environment.

Job description: I oversee the operation of a hotel with revenues in excess of $10 million. Rooms—Front Office, Housekeeping, Maintenance; Food and Beverage; Sales and Catering; Accounting and Human Resources.

Career path: I started as a hotel concierge, which taught me the essence of true hospitality. As the front-line make-it-happen person, I realized that I truly enjoyed the hospitality business. When a General Manager recognized my managerial talents and offered me a senior manager role, I wasn't so sure I wanted to leave the position I felt so satisfied doing. Reluctantly, I accepted and I have enjoyed creating the same growth opportunities for others.

Ideal next job: I enjoy the independent unit operation. I work with team members and guests. Many would suggest a corporate position, but I am most effective in the field and enjoy reaping the immediate satisfaction of seeing the cause and effect of changes.

Best part of your job: Creating a great guest experience and a productive work environment with opportunities for advancement for our team members.

Worst part of your job: The hours are long. Hospitality is a way of life for those who truly love this industry. So, the worst part might be, leaving work for the day.

Educational background: I have associate's degrees in Business Management and Merchandising. I majored in marketing and have a bachelor's degree in Business Administration.

Favorite course: I thought marketing was the easiest of the business disciplines only to find out it can be so subjective. I actually enjoyed business law.

Best course for your career: All the financial accounting classes. Basic math is something I find many managers need to improve on. Business success depends on being able to evaluate and critique profitability and business performance. English and public speaking—communication skills—both written and verbal will set you apart from the others.

Recommended by Jack Partlow, Northern Virginia Community College.
Photographer: Kevin Mattingly.

10

Motivating Employees and Building Self-Managed Teams

LEARNING GOALS

AFTER YOU HAVE READ AND STUDIED THIS CHAPTER, YOU SHOULD BE ABLE TO

1. Explain Taylor's scientific management.

2. Describe the Hawthorne studies and relate their significance to human-based management.

3. Identify the levels of Maslow's hierarchy of needs and relate their importance to employee motivation.

4. Differentiate among Theory X, Theory Y, and Theory Z.

5. Distinguish between the motivators and hygiene factors identified by Herzberg.

6. Explain how job enrichment affects employee motivation and performance.

7. Identify the steps involved in implementing a management by objectives (MBO) program.

8. Explain the key factors involved in expectancy theory.

9. Examine the key principles of equity theory.

10. Explain how open communication builds teamwork, and describe how managers are likely to motivate teams in the future.

Getting to Know Herb Kelleher of Southwest Airlines

The skies are not always friendly, but they do seem to smile for one airline. Southwest Airlines has continued flying high while other airlines have struggled to stay aloft. It's the only U.S. airline that has remained profitable every year since 1973, and it now ranks as the fourth largest in the nation. Analysts credit much of this achievement to the engaging management style of the company's unconventional chairman, Herb Kelleher. In fact, Kelleher was named the 1999 CEO of the Year by *Chief Executive* magazine. Known to show up at company events dressed as Elvis or the Easter bunny, Kelleher is the jokemeister of the airline industry. He is usually at the center of Southwest's employee activities. Asked once to speak to a group about the accomplishments he's most proud of, Kelleher took the podium and said, "Well, I'm here to tell you that I *am* proud of a couple of things. First, I'm very good at projectile vomiting." Such unorthodox statements rarely fail to capture his audience's attention.

But it's his employees' attention that Kelleher has most of the time. Under his coaching, Southwest has been a consistent winner of the service triple crown—highest customer satisfaction, most on-time flights, and best baggage handling. Kelleher's employees are far more productive than employees of competing airlines. Per worker, Southwest flies more planes and serves more passengers than any other airline. Southwest employees also pitch in wherever needed. Pilots might work the boarding gate if things back up; ticket agents might haul luggage to get the plane out on time. When fuel prices accelerated during the Gulf War, employees even began a voluntary payroll deduction program to defray costs. Southwest workers (approximately 90 percent of whom are union members) are paid competitively.

How does Kelleher do it? For starters, he actively avoids hierarchy. He has managers spend time in the trenches once a month, he de-emphasizes the importance of rules relative to good judgment, and he promotes the company as a "family." The result is the promotion of creativity and employee empowerment, which ultimately leads to greater productivity and job satisfaction.

The major role fun plays in motivating Southwest employees shows that it can be more than just having a good time—fun can develop employees who are happy, productive, and intensely loyal. A company can promote fun either by organizing events such as a weekly barbecue or by simply making it known that a sense of humor is a highly valued trait. Kelleher believes that humor reduces stress. When he was diagnosed with prostate cancer in 1999, some investors were worried about what would happen to the airline if Kelleher had to leave the company. Kelleher handled the concern in his usual flamboyant style: "At this point, I must tell you in all sincerity that my principal concern about all this is the possibility that my tan line [from the radiation treatments] will show in my bathing suits."

His employees say Kelleher motivates them because his actions support his belief that people are the company's most important resource. Kelleher says, "You have to work harder than anybody else to show them you are devoted to the business. It's also important to be with your employees through all their difficulties, and show that you are interested in them personally. They may be disappointed in their country. Even their family might not be working out the way they wish it would. But I want them to know that Southwest will always be there for them."

Many analysts believe that the corporate culture is so finely ingrained at Southwest that the airline will continue its success. According to Kelleher, that culture "is the hardest thing for competitors to imitate. You can get an airplane. You can get ticket-counter space, you can get baggage conveyors. But it is our espirit de corps—the culture, the spirit—that is truly our most valuable competitive asset."

Sources: Katrina Booker, "Can Anyone Replace Herb?" *Fortune,* April 17, 2000; Katherine Young, "A Long Wild Ride: Southwest's CEO Makes No Plans to Slow Down," *Dallas Morning News,* May 14, 2000; and Dan Weil and Stephen Pounds, "The Airline Everyone Seems to Like," *The Palm Beach Post,* January 20, 2001, p. 1A.

THE IMPORTANCE OF MOTIVATION

"If work is such fun, how come the rich don't do it?" quipped Groucho Marx.[1] Well, the rich do work—Bill Gates didn't make his billions playing computer games. And workers *can* have fun—if managers like Herb Kelleher make the effort to motivate them. As the chapter opening profile of Kelleher and Southwest Airlines shows, the importance of satisfaction among the workforce cannot be overstated. Happy workers lead to happy customers, and happy customers lead to successful businesses.[2] On the opposite side, unhappy workers are likely to leave the company, and when this happens, the company usually loses out. Losing an employee could cost more than $100,000 for such things as exit interviews, severance pay, the process of hiring a replacement worker, and lost productivity while the new employee is learning the job. The "soft" costs are even greater: loss of intellectual capital, decreased morale, increased employee stress, and a negative reputation.[3] Motivating the right people to join and remain with the organization is a key function of managers.

People are willing to work, and work hard, if they feel that their work makes a difference and is appreciated. People are motivated by a variety of things, such as recognition, accomplishment, and status.[4] **Intrinsic reward** is the personal satisfaction you feel when you perform well and complete goals. The belief that your work makes a significant contribution to the organization or society is a form of intrinsic reward. An **extrinsic reward** is something given to you by someone else as recognition for good work. Such things as pay increases, praise, and promotions are examples of extrinsic rewards. Although ultimately motivation—the drive to satisfy a need—comes from within an individual, there are ways to stimulate people that bring out their natural drive to do a good job.[5]

intrinsic reward
The good feeling you have when you have done a job well.

extrinsic reward
Something given to you by someone else as recognition for good work; extrinsic rewards include pay increases, praise, and promotions.

Corporate America can seem like an all boys' club. Only 12 percent of the corporate officers in the largest 500 U.S. companies are women. Southwest Airlines takes pride in bucking this trend. At Southwest Airlines, 33 percent of the corporate officers are women— double the level at their chief rivals. What do you think is the key reason why women rarely attain top corporate jobs?

The purpose of this chapter is to teach you the concepts, theories, and practice of motivation. The most important person to motivate, of course, is yourself. One way to do that is to find the right job in the right organization, one that enables you to reach your goals in life. The whole purpose of this book is to help you in that search and to teach you how to succeed once you get there. One secret of success is to recognize that everyone else is on a similar search. Naturally, some are more committed than others. The job of a manager is to find that commitment, encourage it, and focus it on some common goal.

This chapter will begin with a look at some of the traditional theories of motivation. You will learn about the Hawthorne studies because they created a whole new interest in worker satisfaction and motivation. Then you'll look at some assumptions about employees that come from the traditional theorists. You will see the names of these theorists over and over in business literature and courses: Taylor, Mayo, Maslow, McGregor, and Herzberg. Finally, you will look at the modern applications of motivation theories and the managerial procedures for implementing them.

Early Management Studies (Taylor)

Several books in the 19th century presented management principles, but not until the early 20th century did there appear any significant works with lasting implications. One of the most well-known, *The Principles of Scientific Management*, was written by American efficiency engineer Frederick Taylor and published in 1911. This book earned Taylor the title "father of scientific management." Taylor's goal was to increase worker productivity in order to benefit both the firm and the worker. The way to improve productivity ➤ **P.23** ◄, Taylor thought, was to scientifically study the most efficient ways to do things, determine the one "best way" to perform each task, and then teach people those methods; this became known as **scientific management.** Three elements were basic to Taylor's approach: time, methods, and rules of work. His most important tools were observation and the stopwatch. It's Taylor's ideas that are behind today's questions of how many burgers McDonald's expects its flippers to flip and how many callers the phone companies expect operators to assist.

scientific management
Studying workers to find the most efficient ways of doing things and then teaching people those techniques.

A classic Taylor story involves his study of men shoveling rice, coal, and iron ore with the same type of shovel. Taylor felt that different materials called for different shovels. He proceeded to invent a wide variety of sizes and shapes of shovels and, with stopwatch in hand, measured output over time in what were called **time-motion studies**—studies of the tasks performed to complete a job and the time needed to do each task. Sure enough, an average person could shovel more (in fact, from 25 to 35 tons more per day) using the most efficient motions and the proper shovel. This finding led to time-motion studies of virtually every factory job. As the most efficient ways of doing things were determined, efficiency became the standard for setting goals.

time-motion studies
Studies, begun by Frederick Taylor, of which tasks must be performed to complete a job and the time needed to do each task.

Taylor's scientific management became the dominant strategy for improving productivity in the early 1900s. Hundreds of time-motion specialists developed standards in plants throughout the country. One follower of Taylor was Henry L. Gantt, who developed charts by which managers plotted the work of employees a day in advance down to the smallest detail. (See Chapter 9 for a discussion of Gantt charts.) American engineers Frank and Lillian Gilbreth used Taylor's ideas in a three-year study of bricklaying. They developed the **principle of motion economy,** which showed that every job could be broken down into a series of elementary motions called a therblig (Gilbreth spelled

principle of motion economy
Theory developed by Frank and Lillian Gilbreth that every job can be broken down into a series of elementary motions.

backward with the *t* and *h* transposed). They then analyzed each motion to make it more efficient.

Scientific management viewed people largely as machines that needed to be properly programmed. There was little concern for the psychological or human aspects of work. Taylor felt simply that workers would perform at a high level of effectiveness (that is, be motivated) if they received high enough pay.

As mentioned earlier, some of Taylor's ideas are still being implemented. Referring to a set of papers supporting ratification of the U.S. Constitution, management guru Peter Drucker even calls Taylor's ideas "the most lasting contribution America has made to Western thought since *The Federalist Papers*."[6] Some companies still place more emphasis on conformity to work rules than on creativity, flexibility, and responsiveness. For example, United Parcel Service (UPS) tells drivers how fast to walk (three feet per second), how many packages to pick up and deliver a day (average of 400), and how to hold their keys (teeth up, third finger). Drivers even wear "ring scanners," electronic devices on their index fingers wired to a small computer on their wrists that shoot a pattern of photons at a bar code on a package to let a customer trolling the Internet know exactly where his or her package is at any given moment. See the Legal Briefcase box for more about scientific management at UPS.

The benefits of relying on workers to come up with creative solutions to productivity problems have long been recognized, as we shall discover next.

The Hawthorne Studies (Mayo)

One of the studies that grew out of Frederick Taylor's research was conducted at the Western Electric Company's Hawthorne plant in Cicero, Illinois. The study began in 1927 and ended six years later. Let's see why it was one of the major studies in management literature.

Elton Mayo and his colleagues from Harvard University came to the Hawthorne plant to test the degree of lighting associated with optimum productivity. In this respect, theirs was a traditional scientific management study; the idea was to keep records of the workers' productivity under different levels of illumination. But the initial experiments revealed what seemed to be a problem: The productivity of the experimental group compared to that of other workers doing the same job went up regardless of whether the lighting was bright or dim. This was true even when the lighting was reduced to about the level of moonlight. These results confused and frustrated the researchers, who had expected productivity to fall as the lighting was dimmed.

A second series of experiments was conducted. In these, a separate test room was set up where temperature, humidity, and other environmental factors could be manipulated. In the series of 13 experimental periods, productivity went up each time; in fact, it increased by 50 percent overall. When the experimenters repeated the original condition (expecting productivity to fall to original levels), productivity increased yet again. The experiments were considered a total failure at this point. No matter what the experimenters did, productivity went up. What was causing the increase?

In the end, Mayo guessed that some human or psychological factor was involved. He and his colleagues then interviewed the workers, asking them about their feelings and attitudes toward the experiment. The researchers' findings began a profound change in management thinking that has had repercussions up to the present. Here is what they concluded:

LEGAL BRIEFCASE

Scientific Management Is Alive and Well at UPS

United Parcel Service (UPS) is truly a powerhouse of a company. With over $27 billion in revenues and 327,000 employees, UPS is the world's largest package distribution company. *Fortune* magazine rates UPS as the most admired company in its industry. The company grew from a small bicycle-messenger service in 1907 to today's mammoth delivery service in part by dictating every task for its employees. Drivers are required to step out of their trucks with their right foot, fold their money faceup, and carry packages under their left arm. If they are considered slow, a supervisor rides with them, prodding them with stopwatches and clipboards. The need to improve productivity to meet increased competition from other delivery services recently prompted UPS to add 20 new services that require more skill. Drivers had to learn an assortment of new codes and billing systems and deliver an increasing number of time-sensitive packages that have special-handling requirements.

Drivers have long accepted such work requirements, taking comfort in good wages, generous benefits, and an attractive profit-sharing plan. All of this pressure, however, has taken its toll. Many UPS drivers suffer from anxiety, phobias, or back strain, and UPS has twice the injury rate of other delivery companies. In 1994, UPS settled a $3 million complaint from the Occupational Safety and Health Administration that it did not provide adequate safety for workers who handle hazardous wastes. UPS has spent nearly $1 billion since 1995 on improving health and safety programs. The total of days lost to disability has been on the decline, dropping by 7.5 percent in the first quarter of 1999 alone.

In August 1997, the Teamsters Union, which represents 200,000 of UPS's employees, called a nationwide strike against the company because workers and managers couldn't reach agreement on a new contract. The Teamsters said they wanted better wages and pensions, and a safer workplace. They also wanted the company to limit its use of part-time workers, who receive fewer benefits, and provide more full-time jobs. The 15-day strike ended when the union and UPS managers agreed on a five-year deal that created 10,000 new full-time jobs from existing part-time positions, increased full-time pay by $3.10 an hour, and retained the pension plan.

UPS's CEO James Kelly says the company is using new technologies and better planning to achieve greater productivity without overloading employees. Competition from services such as Federal Express (where workers earn 30 to 50 percent less than UPS workers) also requires greater efficiency. Nelson says that the variety of new services requires drivers to remember more things. Because the jobs require more thinking, the company has begun hiring a new breed of skilled, college-educated workers. Do you think the new breed of UPS workers will be more or less tolerant of the company's rules and demands?

Sources: Brian O'Reilly, "They've Got Mail! The Growth of Internet Commerce Has Raised the Stakes in the Boxing Match between UPS and FedEx," *Fortune*, February 7, 2000; "Most Admired: Where Companies Rank in Their Industries," *Fortune*, February 21, 2000; Jim Landers, "The Whole Package: Delivery Services Expanding to Bring All Things to All People," *Dallas Morning News*, May 28, 2000, p. 1H; and Kelly Barron, "UPS Company of the Year: Logistics in Brown," *Forbes*, January 10, 2000, pp. 78–83.

- The workers in the test room thought of themselves as a social group. The atmosphere was informal, they could talk freely, and they interacted regularly with their supervisors and the experimenters. They felt special and worked hard to stay in the group. This motivated them.

- The workers were involved in the planning of the experiments. For example, they rejected one kind of pay schedule and recommended another, which was used. The workers felt that their ideas were respected and that they were involved in managerial decision making. This, too, motivated them.

- No matter what the physical conditions were, the workers enjoyed the atmosphere of their special room and the additional pay they got for more productivity. Job satisfaction increased dramatically.

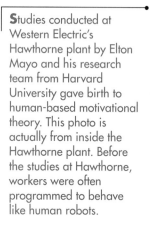

Studies conducted at Western Electric's Hawthorne plant by Elton Mayo and his research team from Harvard University gave birth to human-based motivational theory. This photo is actually from inside the Hawthorne plant. Before the studies at Hawthorne, workers were often programmed to behave like human robots.

Hawthorne effect
The tendency for people to behave differently when they know they are being studied.

Researchers now use the term **Hawthorne effect** to refer to the tendency for people to behave differently when they know they're being studied. The Hawthorne study's results encouraged researchers to study human motivation and the managerial styles that lead to more productivity. The emphasis of research shifted away from Taylor's scientific management and toward Mayo's new human-based management.

Mayo's findings led to completely new assumptions about employees. One of those assumptions, of course, was that pay was not the only motivator. In fact, money was found to be a relatively ineffective motivator. That change in assumptions led to many theories about the human side of motivation. One of the best-known motivation theorists was Abraham Maslow, whose work we discuss next.

MOTIVATION AND MASLOW'S HIERARCHY OF NEEDS

Psychologist Abraham Maslow believed that to understand motivation at work, one must understand human motivation in general. It seemed to him that motivation arises from need. That is, people are motivated to satisfy *unmet* needs; needs that have been satisfied no longer provide motivation. He thought that needs could be placed on a hierarchy of importance.

Figure 10.1 shows **Maslow's hierarchy of needs,** whose levels are as follows:

Maslow's hierarchy of needs
Theory of motivation that places different types of human needs in order of importance, from basic physiological needs to safety, social, and esteem needs to self-actualization needs.

Physiological needs: basic survival needs, such as the need for food, water, and shelter.

FIGURE 10.1

MASLOW'S HIERACHY OF NEEDS
Maslow's hierarchy of needs is based on the idea that motivation comes from need. If a need is met, it's no longer a motivator so a higher-level need becomes the motivator. Higher-level needs demand the support of lower-level needs. This chart shows the various levels of need.

Safety needs: the need to feel secure at work and at home.

Social needs: the need to feel loved, accepted, and part of the group.

Esteem needs: the need for recognition and acknowledgment from others, as well as self-respect and a sense of status or importance.

Self-actualization needs: the need to develop to one's fullest potential.

When one need is satisfied, another, higher-level need emerges and motivates the person to do something to satisfy it. The satisfied need is no longer a motivator. For example, if you just ate a full-course dinner, hunger would not (at least for several hours) be a motivator, and your attention may turn to your surroundings (safety needs) or family (social needs). Of course, lower-level needs (e.g., thirst) may emerge at any time they are not met, and take your attention away from higher-level needs such as the need for recognition or status.

Most of the world's workers struggle all day simply to meet the basic physiological and safety needs. In developed countries, such needs no longer dominate, and workers seek to satisfy growth needs (social, esteem, and self-actualization needs).

To compete successfully, U.S. firms must create a work environment that motivates the best and the brightest workers. That means establishing a work environment that includes goals such as social contribution, honesty, reliability, service, quality, dependability, and unity

CRITICAL THINKING

Your job right now is to finish reading this chapter. How strongly would you be motivated to do that if you were sweating in a 105-degree room? Imagine now that your roommate has turned on the air-conditioning. Now that you are more comfortable, are you more likely to read? Look at Maslow's hierarchy of needs to see what need would be motivating you at both times. Can you see how helpful Maslow's theory is in understanding motivation by applying it to your own life?

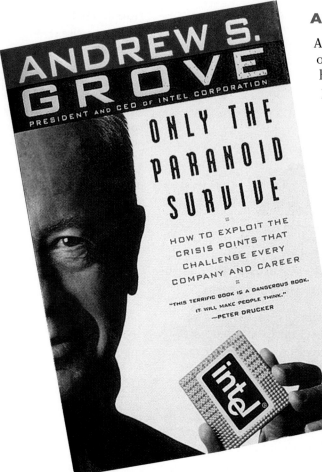

Andrew Grove, Intel's Board Chairman and former CEO, has long been respected as having one of the best business minds in America. He holds a Ph.D. and is a best-selling author. Grove is also a believer in Maslow's theory and contends that managers can use his concepts to improve worker's job performance. Can you see how managers can apply Maslow's theory in the workplace?

Applying Maslow's Theory

Andrew Grove, former CEO and current chairman of Intel, observed Maslow's concepts in action in his firm.[7] One woman, for example, took a low-paying job, which did little for her family's standard of living. Why? Because she needed the companionship her work offered (social/affiliation need). One of Grove's friends had a midlife crisis when he was made a vice president. This position had been a lifelong goal, and when the man reached it he felt unsettled because he had to find another way to motivate himself (self-actualization need). People at a research and development lab were motivated by the desire to know more about their field of interest, but they had little desire to produce marketable results, and thus little was achieved. Grove had to find new people who wanted to learn not just for the sake of learning but to achieve results.

Once one understands the need level of employees, it is easier to design programs that will trigger self-motivation. Grove believes that all motivation comes from within. He believes that self-actualized persons are achievers. Personally, Grove was motivated to earn a doctorate from the University of California at Berkeley and to write a best-selling book, *Only the Paranoid Survive*. He also proceeded at Intel to design a managerial program that emphasized achievement. Now Intel's managers are highly motivated to achieve their objectives because they feel rewarded for doing so.

PROGRESS **ASSESSMENT**

• What are the similarities and differences between Taylor's time-motion studies and Mayo's Hawthorne studies?

• How did Mayo's findings influence scientific management?

• Can you draw a diagram of Maslow's hierarchy of needs? Label and describe the parts.

• According to Andrew Grove, what is the ultimate source of all motivation?

MᴄGʀᴇɢᴏʀ's Tʜᴇᴏʀʏ X ᴀɴᴅ Tʜᴇᴏʀʏ Y

The way managers go about motivating people at work depends greatly on their attitudes toward workers. Management theorist Douglas McGregor observed that managers' attitudes generally fall into one of two entirely different sets of managerial assumptions, which he called Theory X and Theory Y.

Theory X

The assumptions of Theory X management are as follows:

- The average person dislikes work and will avoid it if possible.
- Because of this dislike, workers must be forced, controlled, directed, or threatened with punishment to make them put forth the effort to achieve the organization's goals.
- The average worker prefers to be directed, wishes to avoid responsibility, has relatively little ambition, and wants security.
- Primary motivators are fear and money.

The natural consequence of such attitudes, beliefs, and assumptions is a manager who is very "busy" and who hangs over people telling them what to do and how to do it. Motivation is more likely to take the form of punishment for bad work rather than rewards for good work. Theory X managers give workers little responsibility, authority, or flexibility. With his scientific management, Taylor and other theorists who preceded him would have agreed with Theory X. That is why management literature focused on time-motion studies that calculated the *one best* way to perform a task and the *optimum* time to be devoted to a task. It was assumed that workers needed to be trained and carefully watched to see that they conformed to the standards.

Theory X management still dominates some organizations. Many managers and entrepreneurs ➤ **P.4** ◄ still suspect that employees cannot be fully trusted and need to be closely supervised. No doubt you have seen such managers in action. How did this make you feel? Were these managers' assumptions accurate regarding the workers' attitudes?

Theory Y

Theory Y makes entirely different assumptions about people:

- Most people like work; it is as natural as play or rest.
- Most people naturally work toward goals to which they are committed.
- The depth of a person's commitment to goals depends on the perceived rewards for achieving them.
- Under certain conditions, most people not only accept, but also seek responsibility.
- People are capable of using a relatively high degree of imagination, creativity, and cleverness to solve problems.
- In industry, the average person's intellectual potential is only partially realized.
- People are motivated by a variety of rewards. Each worker is stimulated by a reward unique to that worker (time off, money, recognition, etc.).

Rather than emphasize authority, direction, and close supervision, Theory Y emphasizes a relaxed managerial atmosphere in which workers are free to set objectives, be creative, be flexible, and go beyond the goals set by management. A key technique in meeting these objectives is empowerment. Empowerment ➤ **P.20** ◄ gives employees the ability to make decisions and the tools to implement the decisions they make. For empowerment to be a real motivator, management should follow these three steps:

1. Find out what people think the problems in the organization are.
2. Let them design the solutions.
3. Get out of the way and let them put those solutions into action.

Often employees complain that they're asked to become involved in company decision making, but then their managers fail to actually empower them to make decisions. Have you ever worked in such an atmosphere? How did that make you feel?

The trend in many U.S. businesses is toward Theory Y management. One reason for this trend is that many service industries are finding Theory Y helpful in dealing with on-the-spot problems. Dan Kaplan of Hertz Rental Corporation would attest to this. He empowers his employees in the field to think and work as entrepreneurs. Leona Ackerly of Mini Maid, Inc., agrees: "If our employees look at our managers as partners, a real team effort is built."

Selina Lo of Alteon Websystems, Inc., may not fit the stereotype but she's as tough and exacting as any Theory X manager. Selina, a University of California at Berkeley graduate, has an in-your-face style that has earned her a reputation as one of the toughest managers in the industry. Would you like to work for a Theory X manager like Selina or a Theory Y manager?

OUCHI'S THEORY Z

In addition to the reasons given above for the trend toward Theory Y management, another reason for companies to adopt a more flexible managerial style is to meet competition from foreign firms such as those in Japan, China, and the European Union. Back in the 1980s, Japanese companies seemed to be outperforming American businesses. William Ouchi, a management professor at UCLA, wondered if the secret to Japanese success was the way Japanese companies managed their workers. The Japanese management approach (what Ouchi called *Type J*) involved lifetime employment, consensual decision making, collective responsibility for the outcomes of decisions, slow evaluation and promotion, implied control mechanisms, nonspecialized career paths, and holistic concern for employees. In contrast, the American management approach (what Ouchi called *Type A*) involved short-term employment, individual decision making, individual responsibility for the outcomes of decisions, rapid evaluation and promotion, explicit control mechanisms, specialized career paths, and segmented concern for employees.

Type J firms are based on the culture of Japan, which includes a focus on trust and intimacy within the group and family. Likewise, Type A firms are based on the culture of America, which includes a focus on individual rights and achievements. Ouchi wanted to help American firms adopt the successful Japanese strategies, but he realized that it wouldn't be practical to expect American managers to accept an approach based on the culture of another country. Judge for yourself. A job for life in a firm may sound good until you think of the implications: no chance to change jobs and no opportunity to move up quickly through the ranks. Therefore, Ouchi recommended a hybrid of the two approaches in what he called Theory Z (see Figure 10.2). Theory Z blends the characteristics of Type J and Type A into an approach that involves long-term employment, collective decision making, individual responsibility for the outcome of decisions, slow evaluation and promotion, moderately special-

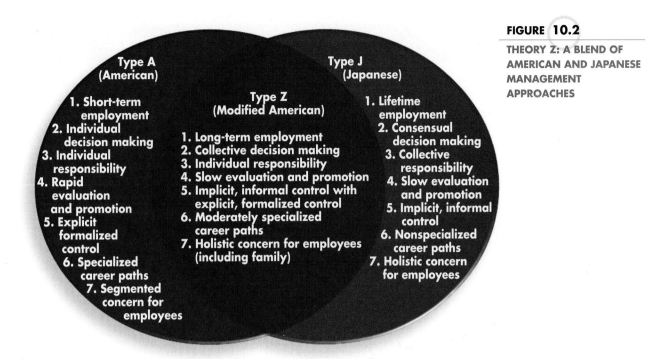

ized career path, and holistic concern for employees (including family). The theory views the organization as a family that fosters cooperation and organizational values.

Today, economic decline, demographic and social changes, and fierce global competition are forcing Japanese managers to reevaluate the way they conduct business. Whereas a decade ago the Japanese system was admired for its focus on building long-term business relationships, today there is a realization that Japanese firms need to become both more dynamic and more efficient in order to compete effectively in today's rapidly changing global economy. Feeling the pain of the worst recession in their country's history, some Japanese managers are changing the way they do business. For example, electronics giant Hitachi is the first major Japanese company to announce it would quit doing corporate calisthenics—exercises done in groups not only for health but also to foster cohesion among employees. "The idea of getting everyone in one place at the same time to do the same thing is outdated," said a Hitachi spokesperson.[8] Having everyone start the day with group exercises symbolized doing the same thing the same way. It reinforced the cultural belief that employees should not take risks or think for themselves. Many managers think that such conformity is what has hurt Japanese business.[9] Will the Japanese managers move toward the hybrid Theory Z in the future? We'll have to wait and see. The appropriate managerial style is one that matches the culture, the situation, and the specific needs of the organization and its employees. (See Figure 10.3 for a summary of Theories X, Y, and Z.)

HERZBERG'S MOTIVATING FACTORS

Theories X, Y, and Z are concerned with styles of management. Another direction in managerial theory is to explore what managers can do with the job itself to motivate employees (a modern-day look at Taylor's research). In

THEORY X	THEORY Y	THEORY Z
1. Employees dislike work and will try to avoid it.	1. Employees view work as a natural part of life.	1. Employee involvement is the key to increased productivity.
2. Employees prefer to be controlled and directed.	2. Employees prefer limited control and direction.	2. Employee control is implied and informal.
3. Employees seek security, not responsibility.	3. Employees will seek responsibility under proper work conditions.	3. Employees prefer to share responsibility and decision making.
4. Employees must be intimidated by managers to perform.	4. Employees perform better in work environments that are nonintimidating.	4. Employees perform better in environments that foster trust and cooperation.
5. Employees are motivated by financial rewards.	5. Employees are motivated by many different needs.	5. Employees need guaranteed employment and will accept slow evaluations and promotions.

FIGURE 10.3

A COMPARISON OF THEORIES X, Y, AND Z

other words, some theorists are more concerned with the content of work than with style of management. They ask: Of all the factors controllable by managers, which are most effective in generating an enthusiastic work effort?

The most discussed study in this area was conducted in the mid-1960s by psychologist Frederick Herzberg. He asked workers to rank various job-related factors in the order of importance relative to motivation. The question was, What creates enthusiasm for workers and makes them work to full potential? The results showed the most important factors that motivate workers to be the following:

1. Sense of achievement.
2. Earned recognition.
3. Interest in the work itself.
4. Opportunity for growth.
5. Opportunity for advancement.
6. Importance of responsibility.
7. Peer and group relationships.
8. Pay.
9. Supervisor's fairness.
10. Company policies and rules.
11. Status.
12. Job security.
13. Supervisor's friendliness.
14. Working conditions.

Herzberg noted that the factors receiving the most votes were all clustered around job content. Workers like to feel that they contribute to the company (sense of achievement was number one). They want to earn recognition (number two) and feel their jobs are important (number six). They want responsibility (which is why learning is so important) and want recognition for that responsibility by having a chance for growth and advancement. Of course, workers also want the job to be interesting.

Herzberg noted further that factors having to do with the job environment were not considered motivators by workers. It was interesting to find that one of those factors was pay. Workers felt that the absence of good pay, job security, friendly supervisors, and the like could cause dissatisfaction, but the presence of those factors did not motivate them to work harder; they just provided satisfaction and contentment in the work situation.

The conclusions of Herzberg's study were that certain factors, called **motivators,** did cause employees to be productive and gave them a great deal of satisfaction. These factors mostly had to do with job content. Herzberg called some other elements of the job **hygiene factors** (or maintenance factors). These had to do mostly with the job environment and could cause dissatisfaction if missing, but would not necessarily motivate employees if increased. See Figure 10.4 for a list of both motivators and hygiene factors.

Combining McGregor's Theory Y with Herzberg's motivating factors, we come up with the following conclusions:

- Employees work best when management believes they are competent and self-motivated (Theory Y). Theory Y calls for a participative style of management.
- The best way to motivate employees is to make the job interesting, help them to achieve their objectives, and recognize that achievement through advancement and added responsibility.

motivators
Job factors that cause employees to be productive and that give them satisfaction.

hygiene factors
Job factors that can cause dissatisfaction if missing but do not necessarily motivate employees if increased.

Applying Herzberg's Theories

Kingston Technology, a manufacturer of computer chips, was identified in 2000 by *Fortune* magazine as one of the 100 best companies to work for in America. Why? You might think that its employees would point to the special annual bonus (which averages $30,000 per worker). Or perhaps they would cite the free lunches once a month or the driving range behind the plant. No, the majority of Kingston employees say what matters most to them is the respect they're paid by the company's founders, John Tu and David Sun.[10]

Pat Blake, a Sunnen Products Co. employee, says that what makes her happy to work extra hours or learn new skills is less tangible than money or

MOTIVATORS	HYGIENE (MAINTENANCE) FACTORS
(These factors can be used to motivate workers.)	(These factors can cause dissatisfaction, but changing them will have little motivational effect.)
Work itself	Company policy and administration
Achievement	Supervision
Recognition	Working conditions
Responsibility	Interpersonal relations (co-workers)
Growth and advancement	Salary, status, and job security

FIGURE 10.4

HERZBERG'S MOTIVATORS AND HYGIENE FACTORS

There's some controversy over Herzberg's results. For example, sales managers often use money as a motivator. Recent studies have shown that money can be a motivator if used as part of a recognition program.

FIGURE 10.5

COMPARISON OF
MASLOW'S HIERARCHY OF
NEEDS AND HERZBERG'S
THEORY OF FACTORS

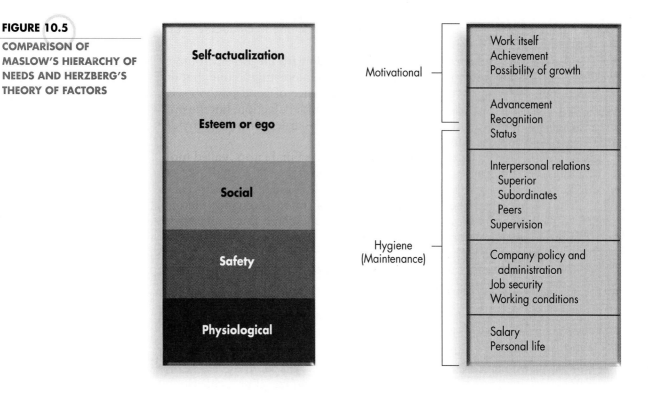

bonuses—it's a kind word from her boss: "When something good happens, like we have a shipping day with so many thousands of dollars going out the door, they let us know about that. It kind of makes you want to go for the gold." Improved working conditions (such as better wages or increased security) are taken for granted after workers get used to them. This is what Herzberg meant by hygiene (or maintenance) factors: their absence causes dissatisfaction, but their presence (maintenance) does not motivate. The best motivator for some employees is a simple and sincere "Thanks, I really appreciate what you're doing."

Many surveys conducted to test Herzberg's theories have supported his finding that the number one motivator is not money but a sense of achievement and recognition for a job well done. If you're skeptical about this, think about the limitations of money as a motivating force. Most organizations review an employee's performance only once a year and allocate raises at that time. To inspire and motivate employees to perform at their highest level of capability, managers must recognize their achievements and progress more than once a year. In the National Survey of the Changing Workforce conducted by the Families and Work Institute in New York, salary ranked 16th in a list of items considered very important in rating jobs. A study prepared by Robert Half International, a staffing and recruitment firm in Menlo Park, California, identified lack of enough praise and recognition as the primary reason employees leave their job.

Look back at Herzberg's list of motivating factors and identify the ones that tend to motivate you. Rank them in order of importance to you. Keep these factors in mind as you consider jobs and careers. What motivators do your job opportunities offer to you? Are they the ones you consider important? Evaluating your job offers in terms of what's really important to you will help you make a wise career choice.

A review of Figure 10.5 shows that there is a good deal of similarity in Maslow's hierarchy of needs and Herzberg's theory of factors.

JOB ENRICHMENT

Both Maslow's and Herzberg's theories have been extended by job enrichment theory. **Job enrichment** is a motivational strategy that emphasizes motivating the worker through the job itself. Work is assigned to individuals so that they have the opportunity to complete an identifiable task from beginning to end. They are held responsible for successful completion of the task. The motivational effect of job enrichment can come from the opportunities for personal achievement, challenge, and recognition. Go back and review Maslow's and Herzberg's work to see how job enrichment grew out of those theories.

Those who advocate job enrichment believe five characteristics of work to be important in affecting individual motivation and performance:

1. *Skill variety.* The extent to which a job demands different skills.

2. *Task identity.* The degree to which the job requires doing a task with a visible outcome from beginning to end.

3. *Task significance.* The degree to which the job has a substantial impact on the lives or work of others in the company.

4. *Autonomy.* The degree of freedom, independence, and discretion in scheduling work and determining procedures.

5. *Feedback.* The amount of direct and clear information that is received about job performance.

Many find it hard to believe that money doesn't motivate workers. NBA players like Kevin Garnett make huge salaries (his long-term contract pays him $120 million). However when he's on the court, is it the money that motivates him or the challenge of competition that makes him play harder? What other factors drive superstars like Kevin Garnett?

Variety, identity, and significance contribute to the meaningfulness of the job. Autonomy gives people a feeling of responsibility, and feedback contributes to a feeling of achievement and recognition.

Job enrichment is what makes work fun. Although it was stressed in the profile of Herb Kelleher and Southwest Airlines at the beginning of this chapter, the word *fun* can be misleading. We're not talking about having parties all the time. For example, Roger Sant, founder and chairman of AES, the global electricity company, says that what makes working at AES fun is that people are fully engaged: "They have total responsibility for decisions. They are accountable for results. What they do every day matters to the company, and it matters to the communities we operate in. We do celebrate a lot—because lots of great things are happening. We just did a billion-dollar deal, for instance, and that called for a party. But it's what happens before the celebrations that's really fun."[11]

As mentioned above, job enrichment is based on Herzberg's higher motivators such as responsibility, achievement, and recognition. It stands in contrast to **job simplification,** which produces task efficiency by breaking down a job into simple steps and assigning people to each of those steps. Job simplification is sometimes necessary, particularly with people learning new skills. In some cases, managers can assign tasks that cannot be enriched to developmentally disabled workers. For example, Red Lobster hires such employees to

job enrichment
A motivational strategy that emphasizes motivating the worker through the job itself.

job simplification
The process of producing task efficiency by breaking down a job into simple steps and assigning people to each of those steps.

www.pacebutler.com

SPOTLIGHT ON SMALL BUSINESS

Motivating Employees in a Small Business

When you run a small business, every dollar counts. When you waste the intelligence, energy, or skills of your employees, it's like throwing money out the window, according to Rhonda Abrams, author of *Wear Clean Underwear: Business Wisdom from Mom*. Abrams says the surest way to get the best value from your employees is to treat them with respect: "When you allow your employees to think about how to solve problems, not just carry out specific tasks, you can unleash an amazing amount of creativity and energy. To do so, however, they'll need information, patience, and a sense they won't be 'punished' if they make an honest mistake."

To help your employees be more productive, Abrams recommends that you:

• *Train* your employees to do a wide variety of tasks. In a small business, employees have to pitch in on many jobs, so instead of teaching them specific tasks, you need to teach them about the whole business and encourage problem solving.

• *Communicate* frequently. Tom Pace of Pace/Butler Corporation in Oklahoma City has 15-minute motivation sessions each morning. Employees compliment each other for recent behaviors, both minor and major. Then each person shares something they've done well. Pace says, "These meetings raise individual self-esteem and set the tone for the rest of the day."

• *Empower* your employees to make decisions. Let them use their brains, not just their backs.

• *Acknowledge* their contributions. The least productive thing you can say is "I don't need to thank employees; I pay them." We all need to be thanked and recognized.

It's difficult for a small company to match the financial benefits of large corporations, so it's even more important for small-business owners to make every employee feel valued, included, and respected. As your employees grow, your business is more likely to grow.

Sources: Rhonda Abrams, "When You Run a Small Company, You Can't Afford to . . . ," *Gannett News Service*, May 14, 1999, p. ARC; and Rhonda Abrams, "How Small Business has Grown and Changed," *The Arizona Republic*, January 30, 2001, p. D2.

---

job enlargement
A job enrichment strategy that involves combining a series of tasks into one challenging and interesting assignment.

job rotation
A job enrichment strategy that involves moving employees from one job to another.

goal-setting theory
The idea that setting ambitious but attainable goals can motivate workers and improve performance if the goals are accepted, are accompanied by feedback, and are facilitated by organizational conditions.

roll silverware into napkins. But on the whole there isn't much motivation in doing boring, repetitive work.

Another type of job enrichment used for motivation is **job enlargement,** which combines a series of tasks into one challenging and interesting assignment. For example, Maytag, the home appliance manufacturer, redesigned the production process of its washing machines so that employees could assemble an entire water pump instead of just one part. **Job rotation** also makes work more interesting and motivating by moving employees from one job to another. One problem with job rotation, of course, is having to train employees to do several different operations. However, the resulting increase in employee motivation and the value of having flexible, cross-trained employees offsets the additional costs.

Job enrichment is one way to ensure that workers enjoy responsibility and a sense of accomplishment. The Spotlight on Small Business box offers advice on using job enrichment strategies in small business.

GOAL-SETTING THEORY AND MANAGEMENT BY OBJECTIVES

Goal-setting theory is based on the notion that setting ambitious but attainable goals will lead to high levels of motivation and performance if the goals are accepted, accompanied by feedback, and facilitated by organizational conditions. All members of an organization should have some basic agreement about the overall goals of the organization and the specific objectives to be met by each department and individual. It follows, then, that there should be a system to involve everyone in the organization in goal setting and implementation.

Peter Drucker developed such a system in the 1960s. Drucker asserted, "Managers cannot motivate people; they can only thwart people's motivation because people motivate themselves." Managers, he believed, can only create the proper environment for the seed to grow. Thus, he designed his system to help employees motivate themselves. Called **management by objectives (MBO),** it is a system of goal setting and implementation that involves a cycle of discussion, review, and evaluation of objectives among top and middle-level managers, supervisors, and employees. Large corporations ➤ **P.140** ◄ such as the Ford Motor Company have used MBO, as has the U.S. Defense Department. MBO also spread to other companies and government agencies. When implemented properly, MBO meets the criteria of goal-setting theory and can be quite effective. MBO calls on managers to formulate goals in cooperation with everyone in the organization, to commit employees to those goals, and then to monitor results and reward accomplishment. There are six steps in the MBO process (see Figure 10.6). Can you tell how the model is intended to help workers motivate themselves?

MBO was widely used in the 1960s, and the management literature of the 1970s was packed with articles about MBO, but very little was written about it in the 1980s and 1990s. Some critics of MBO now see it as being outdated and inconsistent with contemporary management thought and practice. Does that mean that MBO isn't used any longer? Not according to one 1995 study, which found that 47 percent of the organizations surveyed use some form of MBO.

MBO is most effective in relatively stable situations where long-range plans can be made and implemented with little need for major changes. It is also important to MBO that managers understand the difference between helping and

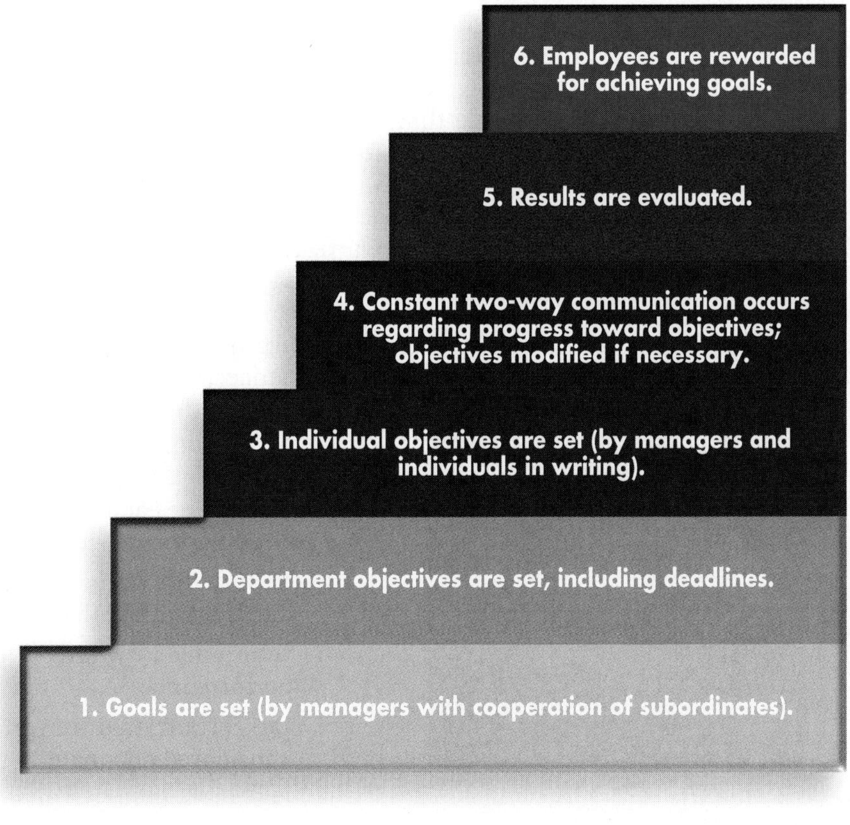

management by objectives (MBO)
A system of goal setting and implementation that involves a cycle of discussion, review, and evaluation of objectives among top and middle-level managers, supervisors, and employees.

6. Employees are rewarded for achieving goals.

5. Results are evaluated.

4. Constant two-way communication occurs regarding progress toward objectives; objectives modified if necessary.

3. Individual objectives are set (by managers and individuals in writing).

2. Department objectives are set, including deadlines.

1. Goals are set (by managers with cooperation of subordinates).

FIGURE 10.6

SIX STEPS OF MANAGEMENT BY OBJECTIVES

The critical step in the MBO process is sitting down with workers, discussing objectives, and getting the workers to commit to those objectives in writing. Commitment is the key.

coaching subordinates. *Helping* means working with the subordinate and doing part of the work if necessary. *Coaching* means acting as a resource—teaching, guiding, and recommending—but not helping (that is, not participating actively or doing the task). The central idea of MBO is that employees need to motivate themselves.

Problems can arise when management uses MBO as a strategy for *forcing* managers and workers to commit to goals that are not really mutually agreed on but are set by top management. Employee involvement and expectations are important.

Victor Vroom identified the importance of employee expectations and developed a process called expectancy theory. Let's examine this concept next.

MEETING EMPLOYEE EXPECTATIONS: EXPECTANCY THEORY

expectancy theory
Victor Vroom's theory that the amount of effort employees exert on a specific task depends on their expectations of the outcome.

According to Victor Vroom's **expectancy theory,** employee expectations can affect an individual's motivation. Therefore, the amount of effort employees exert on a specific task depends on their expectations of the outcome. Vroom contends that employees ask three questions before committing maximum effort to a task: (1) Can I accomplish the task? (2) If I do accomplish it, what's my reward? (3) Is the reward worth the effort?

Think of the effort you might exert in your class under the following conditions: Your instructor says that to earn an A in the course you must achieve an average of 90 percent on coursework plus jump 8 feet high. Would you exert maximum effort toward earning an A if you knew you could not possibly jump 8 feet high? Or what if your instructor said any student can earn an A in the course but you know that this instructor has not awarded an A in 25 years of teaching? If the reward of an A seems unattainable, would you exert significant effort in the course? Better yet, let's say that you read in the newspaper that businesses actually prefer hiring C-minus students to hiring A-plus students. Does the reward of an A seem worth it? Now think of the same type of situations that may occur on the job.

Expectancy theory does note that expectation varies from individual to individual. Employees therefore establish their own views in terms of task difficulty and the value of the reward. Researchers David Nadler and Edward Lawler modified Vroom's theory and suggested that managers follow five steps to improve employee performance:

The managers at Yoplait Yogurt grew a thriving business by setting goals for themselves that were actually higher than those set by the parent company, General Mills. When they surpassed their goals they were rewarded with bonuses that amounted to almost half their annual salaries. How does this example relate to Vroom's expectancy theory?

1. Determine what rewards are valued by employees.

2. Determine each employee's desired performance standard.

3. Ensure that performance standards are attainable.

4. Guarantee rewards tied to performance.

5. Be certain that rewards are considered adequate.[12]

TREATING EMPLOYEES FAIRLY: EQUITY THEORY

Equity theory deals with the questions "If I do a good job, will it be worth it?" and "What's fair?" It has to do with perceptions of fairness and how those perceptions affect employees' willingness to perform. The basic principle is that employees try to maintain equity between inputs and outputs compared to others in similar positions. Equity comparisons are made from the information that is available through personal relationships, professional organizations, and so on.

When workers do perceive inequity, they will try to reestablish equitable exchanges in a number of ways. For example, suppose you compare the grade you earned on a term paper with your classmates' grades. If you think you received a lower grade compared to the students who put out the same effort as you, you will probably react in one of two ways: (1) by reducing your effort on future class projects or (2) by rationalizing. The latter may include saying, "Grades are overvalued anyway!" If you think your paper received a higher grade than comparable papers, you will probably (1) increase your effort to justify the higher reward in the future or (2) rationalize by saying, "I'm worth it!" In the workplace, inequity may lead to lower productivity ➤ **P.23**◄, reduced quality, increased absenteeism, and voluntary resignation.

Remember that equity judgments are based on perceptions and are therefore subject to errors in perception. When workers overestimate their own contributions—as happens often—they are going to feel that any rewards given out for performance are inequitable. Sometimes organizations try to deal with this by keeping employee salaries secret, but secrecy may make things worse; employees are likely to overestimate the salaries of others in addition to overestimating their own contribution. In general, the best remedy is clear and frequent communication. Managers must communicate as clearly as possible the results they expect and what will follow when those results are achieved or when they are not.

equity theory
The idea that employees try to maintain equity between inputs and outputs compared to others in similar positions.

• Briefly describe the managerial attitudes behind Theories X, Y, and Z.
• Relate job enrichment to Herzberg's motivating factors.
• What are the six steps in management by objectives?
• Evaluate expectancy theory. Can you think of situations where expectancy theory could apply to your efforts or lack of effort?

PROGRESS
ASSESSMENT

BUILDING TEAMWORK THROUGH OPEN COMMUNICATION

Companies with highly motivated workforces usually have several things in common. Among the most important factors are open communication systems and self-managed teams. Open communication helps both top managers and team members understand the objectives and work together to achieve them. Communication must flow freely throughout the organization when teams are empowered to make decisions—they can't make these decisions in a vacuum. It is crucial for people to be able to access the knowledge they need when they need it.

Having teams creates an environment in which learning can happen because most learning happens at the peer level—peers who have an interest in helping each other along. Empowerment ➤ **P.20** ◄ works when people volunteer to share their knowledge with their colleagues. For example, when Flora Zhou, an AES business development manager, was putting together a bid to the Vietnam government, she sent a detailed e-mail about what she was planning to bid and why to about 300 people within AES. She asked for and received lots of advice and comments. Most people thought her proposal was fine, but Sarah Slusser, a group manager in Central America, sent Zhou a three-page response that contained a wealth of information about a similar situation she had with a plant in the Yucatan. Slusser told Zhou what technology issues she needed to pay attention to. A few days later, Zhou made the bid. It was the lowest bid by two-tenths of a percent. Did Slusser tell Zhou the exact dollar to bid? No, but she and many others, including plant leaders and board members, gave her the best information and judgments they had to help her make her decision. They shared everything they knew with her.[13]

Teamwork does not happen by itself. The whole organization must be structured to make it easy for managers and employees to talk to one another. Procedures for encouraging open communication include the following:

- *Create an organizational culture that rewards listening.* Top managers must create places to talk, and they must show employees that talking with superiors counts—by providing feedback, adopting employee suggestions, and rewarding upward communication—even if the discussion is negative. Employees must feel free to say anything they deem appropriate. Jerry Stead, chairman of technology provider Ingram Micro, has his own 24-hour toll-free phone line to take calls from employees. Yes, he really answers it. He says: "If we are doing something right, I love to hear about it. If there's something we should be doing differently, I want to know that too." Stead has also given his home number to all 13,000 Ingram Micro employees.[14]

- *Train supervisors and managers to listen.* Most people receive no such training in school or anywhere else, so organizations must do the training themselves or hire someone to do it.

- *Remove barriers to open communication.* Having separate offices, parking spaces, bathrooms, dining rooms, and so on only places barriers between managers and workers. Other barriers are different dress codes and different ways of addressing one another (e.g., calling workers by their first names and managers by their last). Removing such barriers may require imagination and willingness on the part of managers to give up their special privileges.

- *Actively undertake efforts to facilitate communication.* Large lunch tables where all organization members eat, conference rooms, organizational picnics, organizational athletic teams, and other such efforts all allow managers to mix with each other and with workers.[15]

Let's see how one organization addresses the challenge of open communication in teams.

Applying Open Communication in Self-Managed Teams

Kenneth Kohrs, vice president of car product development at Ford Motor Company, says that an inside group known as "Team Mustang" sets the guidelines for how production teams should be formed. Given the challenge to create a car that would make people dust off their old "Mustang Sally" records and dance into the showrooms, the 400-member team was also given the freedom to make decisions without waiting for approval from headquarters or other de-

Highly motivated work teams depend on open communications and self-management. Ford Motor Company provided such an atmosphere for its "Team Mustang" work group. The work team, suppliers, the company, and consumers worked together to make the Mustang convertible a winner in the competitive automobile market.

partments. The team moved everyone from various departments into cramped offices under one roof of an old warehouse. Draftsmen sat next to accountants, engineers next to stylists. Budgetary walls that divided departments were knocked down as department managers were persuaded to surrender some control over their subordinates.

When the resulting Mustang convertible displayed shaking problems, suppliers were called in, and the team worked around the clock to solve the problem. The engineers were so motivated to complete the program on schedule and under budget that they worked late into the night and slept on the floors of the warehouse when necessary. The senior Ford executives were tempted to overrule the program, but they stuck with their promise not to meddle. The team solved the shaking problem and still came in under budget and a couple of months early. The new car was a big hit in the marketplace, and sales soared.[16] In fact, the automotive pricing and review website Edmunds.com named it one of the top American muscle cars of today.

To implement such teams, managers at most companies must reinvent work. This means respecting workers, providing interesting work, rewarding good work, developing workers' skills, allowing autonomy, and decentralizing authority. In the process of reinventing work, it is essential that managers behave ethically toward all employees. The Making Ethical Decisions box illustrates a problem managers may face when filling temporary positions.

Changing Organizations Is Not Easy

We have come a long way from the time-motion studies of Frederick Taylor. The work of Maslow, Mayo, Herzberg, Vroom, and others has taught some managers to treat employees as associates and to get them more involved in decision making. This increases motivation and leads to greater productivity.

Other managers, however, have been brought up under a different system. Those from the military are used to telling people what to do rather than consulting with them, and those from the football-coach school of management tend to yell and direct rather than consult and discuss.

Furthermore, employees often are not used to participative management. The transition from Theory X to Theory Y management, from Taylor to Herzberg, is still going on. It is important, then, to have examples to follow when trying to implement the new approaches.

Miller Brewing Company and Mary Kay Cosmetics are glowing examples of companies that succeeded at taking a lead in employee motivation, customer service, and establishment of a general partnership with employees. Let's review the experience of these two companies to see what lessons we can learn.

A Model for the Future: Employee Empowerment

Miller Brewing Company is the second largest brewer in the United States. It opened its brewery of the future in Trenton, Ohio, with a mandate to develop a totally new workplace design that abandoned the rigidity of traditional brewery operations. The company decided to experiment by employing self-directed, cross-functional teams of 6 to 19 employees. It assigned the teams to handle brewing, packaging, and distribution.

To keep communications open, the company established an electronic mailbox for each employee and gave each team its own local area network terminal. In the daily operations at the brewery, employees rotated jobs, routinely backed each other up, and learned exactly how their actions affected the other employees. Workers enjoyed the freedom and flexibility offered at the plant, and the Trenton brewery enjoyed a 30 percent increase in productivity in comparison to Miller's other breweries. The top union official at the plant says, "We're partners in the business. We don't just make beer, we manage day-to-day operations. At this facility we have so many different tasks we don't check our brains at the door." According to company officials, "That's what teamwork is all about. Employees can't just say this is my job and my job only."

Mary Kay Ash started her $613 million cosmetics company in 1963 when the promotion she had been working toward was given to her male assistant, whom she had just spent nine months training. She vowed to run a company that would treat women right, not "ruin their self-esteem," she said, or limit how much money they could make. Developing women's leadership potential was a priority at Mary Kay Cosmetics from the start. Many Mary Kay consultants are refugees from corporate America. There are lawyers, a Harvard MBA, and even a pediatrician in the Mary Kay ranks.

But everyone starts off on the same foot. If you were a rocket scientist in your last job, great—but you still need to buy a beauty case and start calling your friends. Your earnings will increase as your sales do and as you recruit more Mary Kay employees, who are known as consultants. More important, though, is the emotional compensation the job provides.

Every summer, for example, more than 36,000 Mary Kay beauty consultants invade Dallas, Texas, to participate in a three-day sales rally called Seminar—at which there is plenty of emotion. Seminar is part convention, part *Hello Dolly*. Caught up in the Mary Kay enthusiasm, the women laugh, cry, and sing as the company doles out diamonds and pink Cadillacs under enough spotlights and sequins to rival any Broadway musical. Color-coded suits, badges, sashes, crowns, and other emblems show how far each person has come—like military insignia, they immediately indicate who's done what. Joan Watson, a former medical secretary now a Mary Kay executive senior director says, "A lot of people really don't understand what we are doing. I still have people say, 'Pink Cadillac?! They're so gaudy.' And I say, 'What color car does your boss give you?' "

Cars, vacations, and diamonds are awarded to Mary Kay's high performing consultants at the three-day sales rally called Seminar. All the company's consultants share in the emotional compensation the job provides. Do you have the motivation to work for a firm such as Mary Kay? Could you be one of those that drive away in a new Cadillac?

Despite the glitter of the diamonds and cars given out at Seminar, the most treasured rewards are the vacations, which often offer consultants special treatment. On one trip to London, Mary Kay got the famous Harrods department store to close for an hour so that only Mary Kay consultants could shop there. Mary Kay Ash herself goes on many of these trips. Her consultants consider her to be uniquely approachable. "Mary Kay calls you her daughter and looks you dead in the eye. She is so sincerely concerned about your welfare that you feel you can do anything," reports one consultant. Mary Kay consultants are trained to treat their customers with the same kind of interest. They remember their customers' birthdays, send them notes, and find other ways to show concern. Mary Kay is not just a job, it's a way of life.[17]

Learning from Miller Brewing's and Mary Kay's Experiences Understanding what motivates employees is the key to success in companies such as Miller Brewing Company and Mary Kay Cosmetics. Miller learned at its Trenton plant that teamwork promotes a self-starting philosophy among employees that encourages them to be superior. In fact, someone at the plant said the letters in *TEAM* stand for "Together, Everyone Achieves More."

Mary Kay Ash developed not just a business but a true American success story. She feels that success in business depends on believing in yourself and showing interest in your employees and your customers. The best way to lead is by example, and Mary Kay is a model for employees and for managers in all types of firms.

The lessons we can learn from the Miller and Mary Kay examples include the following:

- The growth of industry and business in general depends on a motivated, productive workforce.

- Motivation is largely internal, generated by workers themselves; giving employees the freedom to be creative and rewarding achievement when it occurs will release their energy.

- The first step in any motivational program is to establish open communication among workers and managers so that the feeling generated is one of cooperation and teamwork. A family-type atmosphere should prevail.

MOTIVATION IN THE FUTURE

Today's customers expect high-quality, customized goods and services ➤ **P.25** ◄. That means employees must provide extensive personal service and pay close attention to details. Employees will have to work smart as well as hard. No amount of supervision can force an employee to smile or to go the extra mile to help a customer. Managers need to know how to motivate their employees to meet customer needs.

Tomorrow's managers will not be able to use any one formula for all employees. Rather, they will have to get to know each worker personally and tailor the motivational effort to the individual. As you learned in this chapter, different employees respond to different managerial and motivational styles. This is further complicated by the increase in global business and the fact that managers now work with employees from a variety of cultural backgrounds. Different cultures experience motivational approaches differently; therefore, the manager of the future will have to study and understand these cultural factors in designing a reward system. The Reaching Beyond our Borders box describes how Digital Equipment Corporation dealt with these cultural issues within global teams.

Cultural differences are not restricted to groups of people from various countries. Such differences also exist between generations raised in the same country. Members of generations such as the baby boomers (born between 1946 and 1964) and Generation X (born between 1965 and 1980) are linked through shared life experiences in their formative years—usually the first 10 years of life. The beliefs you gather as a child affect how you view risk and challenge, authority, technology, relationships, and economics; and, if you are in a management position, they can affect even whom you hire, fire, or promote. While boomers were raised in families that experienced unprecedented economic prosperity, parents with secure jobs, and optimism about the future, "Gen Xers" were raised in dual-career families with parents who focused on work while they attended day care or became latchkey kids. Their parents' successive layoffs added to their insecurity about a lifelong job.

How do these generational differences affect motivation in the workplace? For the boomer managers, it means that they will need to be flexible with their Gen X employees or they will lose them. For Gen X employees, it means that they will need to use their enthusiasm for change and streamlining to their advantage. Although Gen Xers are unwilling to pay the same price for success that their parents and grandparents did, concern about undue stress and long work hours does not mean they have a lack of ambition. Gen Xers' desire for security equals that of older workers, but there is a big difference in their approach to achieving it. Rather than focusing on *job* security, Gen Xers focus on *career* security. As they look for opportunities to expand their skills and grow professionally, they are willing to change jobs to do it.[18]

The new global economy has altered the world landscape by bringing products and services to every corner of the earth and helping many people in less developed countries improve their quality of life. Business globalization has also resulted in the creation of global work teams, a rather formidable task.

Even though the concept of teamwork is nothing new, building a harmonious global work team is a new task and can be complicated. Global companies must recognize differing attitudes and competencies in the team's cultural mix and the technological capabilities among team members. For example, a global work team needs to determine whether the culture of its members is high-context or low-context. In a high-context team culture, members build personal relationships and develop group trust before focusing on tasks. In the low-context culture, members often view relationship building as a waste of time that diverts attention from the task. Koreans, Thais, and Saudis (high-context cultures), for example, often view American team members as insincere due to their need for data and quick decision making.

When Digital Equipment Corporation (now a part of Compaq Computers) decided to consolidate its operations at six manufacturing sites, the company recognized the need to form multicultural work teams. Realizing the challenge it faced, Digital hired an internal organization-development specialist to train the team in relationship building, foreign languages, and valuing differences. All team members from outside the United States were assigned American partners and invited to spend time with their families. Digital also flew the flags of each employee's native country at all its manufacturing sites. As communication within the teams increased, the company reduced the time of new-product handoffs from three years to just six months.

Understanding the motivational forces in global organizations and building effective global teams is still new territory for most companies. Developing group leaders who are culturally astute, flexible, and able to deal with ambiguity is a challenge businesses must face in the 21st century.

Many Gen Xers are now or soon will be managers themselves and responsible for motivating other employees. What type of management will this generation provide? In general, Gen X managers will be well equipped to motivate people. They understand that there is more to life than work, and they think a big part of motivating people is letting them know you recognize that fact. As a result, Gen X managers will tend to focus more on results than on hours in the workplace. They will be flexible and good at collaboration and consensus building. They tend to think in broader terms than their predecessors because, through the media, they have been exposed to a lot of problems around the world. They will tend to have a great impact on their team members because they will give the people working for them the goals and the parameters of the project and then leave them alone to do their work.

Perhaps their best asset will be their ability to give their employees feedback, especially positive feedback. One reason they will be better at providing feedback is that they expect more of it themselves. One new employee remarked that he was frustrated because he hadn't received feedback from his boss since he was hired—two weeks earlier. In short, managers will need to realize that younger workers demand performance reviews and other forms of feedback more than a once or twice a year.

In every generational shift, the old generation says the same thing about the new generation: They broke the rules. The generation that lived through the Great Depression and World War II said it of the baby boomers. Now boomers look at Gen Xers and say, "Why are they breaking the rules?" And you can be sure the Gen Xers will look at the next group and say, "What's wrong with these kids?"

One thing in business is likely to remain constant, though: Motivation will come from the job itself rather than from external punishments or rewards. Managers will need to give workers what they need to do a good job: the right tools, the right information, and the right amount of cooperation.

Motivation doesn't have to be difficult. It begins with acknowledging a job well done. You can simply tell those who do such a job that you appreciate them, especially in front of others. After all, as we said earlier in this chapter, the best motivator is frequently a sincere "Thanks, I really appreciate what you're doing."[19]

PROGRESS ASSESSMENT

- What are several steps firms can take to increase internal communications and thus motivation?

- What problems may emerge when trying to implement participative management?

- Why is it important today to adjust motivational styles to individual employees? Are there any general principles of motivation that today's managers should follow?

SUMMARY

1. Explain Taylor's scientific management.

1. Human efficiency engineer Frederick Taylor was one of the first people to study management.
   - ***What is Frederick Taylor known for?***
   Frederick Taylor has been called the father of scientific management. He did time-motion studies to learn the most efficient way of doing a job and then trained workers in those procedures. He published his book, *The Principles of Scientific Management*, in 1911. Henry L. Gantt and Frank and Lillian Gilbreth were followers of Taylor.

2. Describe the Hawthorne studies and relate their significance to human-based management.

2. Management theory moved away from Taylor's scientific management and toward theories that stress human factors of motivation.
   - ***What led to the more human managerial styles?***
   The greatest impact on motivation theory was generated by the Hawthorne studies in the late 1920s and early 1930s. In these studies, Elton Mayo found that human factors such as feelings of involvement and participation led to greater productivity gains than did physical changes in the workplace.

3. Identify the levels of Maslow's hierarchy of needs and relate their importance to employee motivation.

3. Abraham Maslow studied basic human motivation and found that motivation was based on needs; he said that a person with an unfilled need would be motivated to satisfy it and that a satisfied need no longer served as motivation.
   - ***What were the various levels of need identified by Maslow?***
   Starting at the bottom of Maslow's hierarchy of needs and going to the top, the levels of need are physiological, safety, social, esteem, and self-actualization.
   - ***Can managers use Maslow's theory?***
   Yes, they can recognize what unmet needs a person has and design work so that it satisfies those needs.

4. Douglas McGregor held that managers will have one of two opposing attitudes toward employees. They are called Theory X and Theory Y. William Ouchi introduced Theory Z.
   - ***What is Theory X?***
   Theory X assumes that the average person dislikes work and will avoid it if possible. Therefore, people must be forced, controlled, and threatened with punishment to accomplish organizational goals.
   - ***What is Theory Y?***
   Theory Y assumes that people like working and will accept responsibility for achieving goals if rewarded for doing so.
   - ***What is Theory Z?***
   Theory Z comes out of Japanese management and stresses long-term employment; collective decision making; individual responsibility; slow evaluation and promotion; implicit, informal control with explicit, formalized control; moderately specialized career paths; and a holistic concern for employees (including family).

   4. Differentiate among Theory X, Theory Y, and Theory Z.

5. Frederick Herzberg found that some factors are motivators and others are hygiene (or maintenance) factors; hygiene factors cause job dissatisfaction if missing but are not motivators if present.
   - ***What are the factors called motivators?***
   The work itself, achievement, recognition, responsibility, growth, and advancement.
   - ***What are hygiene (maintenance) factors?***
   Factors that do not motivate but must be present for employee satisfaction, such as company policies, supervision, working conditions, interpersonal relations, and salary.

   5. Distinguish between the motivators and hygiene factors identified by Herzberg.

6. Job enrichment describes efforts to make jobs more interesting.
   - ***What characteristics of work affect motivation and performance?***
   The job characteristics that influence motivation are skill variety, task identity, task significance, autonomy, and feedback.
   - ***Name two forms of job enrichment that increase motivation.***
   Job enrichment strategies include job enlargement and job rotation.

   6. Explain how job enrichment affects employee motivation and performance.

7. One procedure for establishing objectives and gaining employee commitment to those objectives is called management by objectives (MBO).
   - ***What are the steps in an MBO program?***
   (1) Managers set goals in cooperation with subordinates, (2) objectives are established for each department, (3) managers and workers together discuss the objectives and commit themselves in writing to meeting them, (4) two-way communication and review show workers how they're doing, (5) feedback is provided and corrections are made if necessary, and (6) employees are rewarded for achieving goals.

   7. Identify the steps involved in implementing a management by objectives (MBO) program.

8. According to Victor Vroom's expectancy theory, employee expectations can affect an individual's motivation.
   - ***What are the key elements involved in expectancy theory?***
   Expectancy theory centers on three questions employees often ask about performance on the job: (1) Can I accomplish the task? (2) If I do accomplish it, what's my reward? and (3) Is the reward worth the effort?

   8. Explain the key factors involved in expectancy theory.

9. According to equity theory, employees try to maintain equity between inputs and outputs compared to other employees in similar positions.
   - ***What happens when employees perceive that their rewards are not equitable?***

   9. Examine the key principles of equity theory.

If employees perceive that they are underrewarded they will either reduce their effort or rationalize that it isn't important. If they perceive that they are overrewarded, they will either increase their effort to justify the higher reward in the future or rationalize by saying "I'm worth it!" Inequity leads to lower productivity, reduced quality, increased absenteeism, and voluntary resignation.

10. Explain how open communication builds teamwork, and describe how managers are likely to motivate teams in the future.

10. Companies with highly motivated workforces often have open communication systems and self-managed teams.
- *Why is open communication so important in building effective self-managed teams?*

Open communication helps both top managers and team members understand the objectives and work together to achieve them. Teams establish an environment in which learning can happen because most learning happens at the peer level.

- *How are Generation X managers likely to be different from their baby-boomer predecessors?*

Baby boomers are willing to work long hours to build their careers and often expect their subordinates to do likewise. Gen Xers strive for a more balanced lifestyle and are likely to focus on results rather than on how many hours their teams work. Gen Xers are better than previous generations at working in teams and providing frequent feedback. They are not bound by traditions that may constrain those who have been with an organization for a long time and are willing to try new approaches to solving problems.

KEY TERMS

equity theory 313	**intrinsic reward** 296	**Maslow's hierarchy of**
extrinsic reward 296	**job enlargement** 310	**needs** 300
expectancy	**job enrichment** 309	**motivators** 307
theory 312	**job rotation** 310	**principle of motion**
goal-setting	**job**	**economy** 297
theory 310	**simplification** 309	**scientific**
Hawthorne effect 300	**management by**	**management** 297
hygiene factors 307	**objectives**	**time-motion**
	(MBO) 311	**studies** 297

DEVELOPING

WORKPLACE SKILLS

1. Talk with several of your friends about the subject of motivation. What motivates them to work hard or not work hard in school and on the job? How important is self-motivation to them?

2. Look over Maslow's hierarchy of needs and try to determine where you are right now on the hierarchy. What needs of yours are not being met? How could a company go about meeting those needs and thus motivate you to work better and harder?

3. One of the most recent managerial ideas is to let employees work in self-managed teams. There is no reason why such teams could not be formed in colleges as well as businesses. Discuss the benefits and drawbacks of dividing your class into self-managed teams for the purpose of studying, doing cases, and so forth.

4. Think of all the groups with which you have been associated over the years—sports groups, friendship groups, and so on—and try to recall how the leaders of those groups motivated the group to action. Did the lead-

ers assume a Theory X or a Theory Y attitude? How often was money used as a motivator? What other motivational tools were used and to what effect?

5. Herzberg concluded that pay was not a motivator. If you were paid to get better grades, would you be motivated to study harder? In your employment experiences, have you ever worked harder to obtain a raise or as a result of receiving a large raise? Do you agree with Herzberg?

Purpose

To assess your personality type using the Keirsey Character Sorter and to evaluate how well the description of your personality type fits you.

Exercise

Sometimes understanding differences in employees' personalities helps managers understand how to motivate them. Find out about your personality by going to the Keirsey Temperament Sorter website (http://keirsey.com) and answer the 36-item Keirsey Character Sorter questionnaire or the 70-item Keirsey Temperament Sorter questionnaire. Each test identifies four temperament types: Guardian, Artisan, Idealist, and Rational. (Disclaimer: The Keirsey tests, like all other personality tests, are only a preliminary and rough indicator of personality.)

1. After you identify your personality, read the corresponding personality portrait. How well or how poorly does the identified personality type fit?

2. Sometimes a personality test does not accurately identify your personality, but it may give you a place to start looking for a portrait that fits. After you have read the portraits on the Keirsey website, ask a good friend or relative which one best describes you.

Purpose

To analyze why employees of the Container Store agree with *Fortune* magazine that their employer is the best company to work for by going to their website at www.containerstore.com

Exercise

Employees at the Container Store sell boxes and garbage cans for a living. Find out why *Fortune* magazine rated it the best company to work for by going to their website at www.containerstore.com.

1. What are the Container Store's foundation principles?

2. Give an example of how the Container Store employees are empowered to please their customers.

3. The national average turnover rate for salespeople is 73.6 percent. The Container Store's turnover rate is a mere 28 percent. Many of its employees took pay cuts to join the company. Identify at least five ways the company motivates its employees and explain why they are one of the most motivated workforces in America.

CASE

MAKING TEAMS WORK IN A CHANGING MARKET

Winning the Malcolm Baldrige National Quality Award is no small feat. To be given the Baldrige award, a company must excel in three major measurements of quality: (1) customer satisfaction, (2) product and service quality, and (3) quality of internal operations. Previous winners have included such companies as Solectron and the General Motors Saturn Division.

Taking home the Baldrige award was the last thing on the minds of Judith Corson and her partner, Jeffrey Pope, when they evaluated the situation at their Minneapolis-based market research firm, Custom Research, in the early 1990s. The two partners faced a market full of client companies that had downsized and were asking more of Custom Research. The problem for Corson and Pope was that Custom Research was experiencing a flattening of growth and the firm had neither the resources it needed to expand its employee base nor the technological capacity it needed to meet the growing demands. The business partners were facing the hard reality that to survive in the market they would have to provide better management of clients' work with their current staff and resources. Corson and Pope realized they had to do something quickly.

The two partners decided to abandon the traditional departmentalized structure of the organization and group their 100 or so employees into account teams. Each account team would have an account and research team leader assigned to facilitate the direction of the team. In just a short time, communication and the tracking of work improved. Workers were more interested and involved, and clients were expressing satisfaction at a job well done. The business began to thrive.

But after the system had been in place for a couple of years, the partners saw a problem developing. Team members were becoming limited, learning only about the clients or the business categories handled by their group. Corson and Pope swung into action again. They decided that once or twice a year, employees would be reorganized into new teams with their size determined by the volume of work at hand.

Using the team approach at Custom Research has changed things quite a bit. The firm watched its billings go from $10 million in 1985 to $22 million in 1996. Revenue per full-time employee has risen by 70 percent. The firm meets or exceeds its client expectations on 97 percent of its projects and is rated by 92 percent of its clients as better than the competition. Such outstanding performance enabled Custom Research to become not only the smallest but also the first professional-services firm to receive the prestigious Malcolm Baldrige Award. Leonard Berry, a professor at Texas A&M University, identified Custom Research as one of the 14 best service companies in the world in his book *Discovering the Soul of Service*. Berry describes Custom Research as "a highly progressive marketing research company that has built a strong business with Fortune 500 clients through team service delivery, innovative practices, competence, and an emphasis on continuous improvement."

Corson says her company always did strategic planning, but in hindsight it wasn't very focused. The Baldrige contest emphasized the need to concentrate on just a few "key business drivers"—the very core of the business. So Custom changed its strategy to identify its key drivers and list goals each year that would enhance each one. Besides helping growth, the strong planning kept missteps to a minimum. "You don't have as many gaps or surprises," Judith Corson says of the company's concentration on its core competencies.

Decision Questions

1. Why do you think worker performance increased so significantly at Custom Research?
2. What principles of motivation seemed to work well for Corson and Pope in increasing employee productivity?
3. Would you like to work in a team-centered organization or in a more traditional organizational setting? Why?

VIDEO CASE

WORKPLACE TRENDS

Workers today face a host of challenges and obstacles in the workplace. Longer hours, less job security, and balancing career and family are just a few factors that can raise workers' stress levels to a boiling point. But workers are not alone. Managers also feel the pressure. Managers know that contented, happier workers tend to be more productive workers. The challenge is to provide employees with the resources that will result in a motivated, empowered workforce. Examples of companies that use a number of creative perks to motivate workers include:

- S.C. Johnson Company in Racine, Wisconsin, encourages its workers and supervisors in the customer service department to fight pressure and stress on the job by going to war with each other. It's not unusual for a supervisor and worker to arm themselves with full battle gear (water soakers) and fight it out to the drenching end.

- CIGNA Insurance Company employees who don't have the energy at the end of a 10-hour workday to face the challenge of preparing a meal for the family at home, can place take-home meal orders with the company chef. The company also offers an exercise physiologist to help employees suffering from stress.

- Salomon Smith Barney employees can visit a physician in their office building and have a prescription delivered to them right at the office.

- Wilton-Connor Packaging Company employees can bring their laundry to work with them and have it done for $1 per load (ironing is 25 cents extra). The company also provides the services of a handyman to perform jobs such as painting at employees' homes. The only cost to the employee is the cost of the paint.

- Andersen Consulting provides its employees a rather sophisticated perk. The company employs a concierge to run errands (such as shopping) for employees loaded down with other responsibilities.

- Coca-Cola and Home Depot offer wellness and exercise programs to reduce stress and enhance employee health at the same time. Management at Coca-Cola found that employees that participated in such activities used fewer sick days and tended to be more productive on their jobs. Home Depot found the same results and now provides exercise facilities and classes on-site for employees to help them stop smoking, learn to eat and exercise right, manage work and home, and so on. Such applications are highly recommended by officials at the Center for Disease Control in Atlanta.

The development of happier, more productive workers seems to support the investment and time in all of these innovative efforts.

Discussion Questions

1. What are the advantages and disadvantages of companies offering creative perks and special programs to workers in the workplace?
2. Do you think the number and variety of perks will continue to grow or do you think this is just a management fad that will fade in the future?
3. What other perks might companies consider to lower stress levels and increase employee productivity?

Human Resource Management: Finding and Keeping the Best Employees

LEARNING GOALS

AFTER YOU HAVE READ AND STUDIED THIS CHAPTER, YOU SHOULD BE ABLE TO

1 Explain the importance of human resource management and describe current issues in managing human resources.

2 Summarize the six steps in planning human resources.

3 Describe methods that companies use to recruit new employees and explain some of the issues that make recruitment challenging.

4 Outline the six steps in selecting employees.

5 Illustrate the use of various types of employee training and development methods.

6 Trace the six steps in appraising employee performance.

7 Summarize the objectives of employee compensation programs, and describe various pay systems and fringe benefits.

8 Explain scheduling plans managers use to adjust to workers' needs.

9 Describe the ways employees can move through a company: promotion, reassignment, termination, and retirement.

10 Illustrate the effects of legislation on human resource management.

Getting to Know Diane Charness of Flextime Staffing Inc.

Diane Charness, president of Flextime Staffing Inc. of Bethesda, Maryland, believes that organizations should offer a choice of the types of work arrangements that workers want. Job security is important to some, flexibility to others. As their staff needs rise and fall with the flow of the global marketplace, many companies say they require a flexible workforce made up of people who can come and go as they are needed. More and more workers, too, are demanding flexible schedules to help balance work and life. Such schedules include non-traditional work arrangements such as part-time and temporary jobs.

That's where Charness comes in. Her company helps place people in flexible work arrangements. Some of these people are students, others are full-time parents who need extra income, and still others are educated professionals who command high fees. Flextime Staffing employs the workers and sends them to work at companies on temporary assignments. Such temporary employees are now called *contingent workers*. For example, Kadah Stackhouse is a 42-year-old lawyer with two young sons. Working through Flextime Staffing, Stackhouse does part-time work in a Washington law firm. Now she has enough time to spend with her children during the day. Stackhouse is happy that her need for flexibility is matched by her employer's need for a flexible worker.

Today, fewer workers expect to work at one company their entire careers. Unlike their parents, who could build a career with one skill, today's workers must seek out ongoing education and diverse work experience. The specific job you take is becoming much less important today than the skills you build over time. Contingent workers view their temporary positions as opportunities to build their skills and gain the necessary experience. Many employers also view temporary agencies such as Flextime Staffing as excellent training grounds for workers to develop the skills the company needs.

Employers say that hiring people for temporary work is an efficient way to "test-drive" employees before committing to hire them full-time.

Although many contingent workers find such flexibility liberating because it gives them more time with their families, while giving them opportunities to build skills or switch careers, not everyone considers this flexibility so positively. Labor leaders fear that the new employer–employee relationship will make it harder for the employees to provide for their families. They fear that the flexibility will actually result in workers having less control of their lives, since part-time workers do not receive the insurance and pension benefits that full-time employees do. A growing number of workers who cannot count on a paycheck for 40 hours of work and benefits have to take multiple jobs in order to pay their bills.

As you can see, these new employer–employee relationships are partly good and partly bad. Contingent workers increase companies' flexibility and therefore their competitiveness. However, the drive for cost cutting and flexibility crashes head-on into another important aspect: the belief that competitive success is based on retaining a motivated, creative, empowered workforce. Can this goal be met by a largely disposable workforce? That is one of the issues that human resource managers face as they strive to recruit, hire, train, evaluate, and compensate the best people to accomplish the objectives of their organizations.

Sources: Timothy Burn, "Part-Time, Flexible Work Wave Has Yet to Crest," *Washington Times,* May 9, 1999, p. C1; John Kador, "The End of Work as We Know It," *InfoWorld,* August 21, 2000; and Jim Miller "Define Duties, Skills to Blend Full-Time, Other Employees," *The Arlington Morning News,* January 11, 2001.

WORKING WITH PEOPLE IS JUST THE BEGINNING

Students have been known to say they want to go into human resource management because they want to "work with people." It is true that human resource managers work with people, but they are also deeply involved in planning, record keeping, and other administrative duties. To begin a career in human resource management, you need to develop a better reason than "I want to work with people." This chapter will discuss various aspects of human resource management, which involves recruiting, hiring, training, evaluating, and compensating people. **Human resource management** is the process of evaluating human resource needs, finding people to fill those needs, and getting the best work from each employee by providing the right incentives and job environment, all with the goal of meeting the objectives of the organization (see Figure 11.1). Let's explore some of the trends.

human resource management
The process of evaluating human resource needs, finding people to fill those needs, and getting the best work from each employee by providing the right incentives and job environment, all with the goal of meeting the objectives of the organization.

Developing the Ultimate Resource

One reason human resource management is receiving increased attention now is that the U.S. economy has experienced a major shift from traditional manufacturing industries to service ➤ **P.26** ◄ and high-tech manufacturing industries that require more technical job skills. This shift means that many workers must be retrained for new, more challenging jobs. For example:

- Prudential Insurance Company instituted a $1 billion mandatory training program for its 4,500 information technology staff members. The idea is to retrain existing workers before going outside for skilled employees.[1]

- Levi-Strauss has such a commitment to retraining the workers that it laid off from its El Paso plant that it now has more former workers in its retraining and skill-development programs than it has employees there.[2]

- At Motorola, continuous learning is built into the culture. The company's training programs are run from Motorola University in Illinois, with regional campuses not only in Arizona and Texas but also abroad, in India. That the employees have learned to learn is evidenced by so

FIGURE 11.1

HUMAN RESOURCE MANAGEMENT

Note that human resource management includes motivation as discussed in Chapter 10 and union relations as discussed in Chapter 12. As this shows, human resource management is more than hiring and firing personnel.

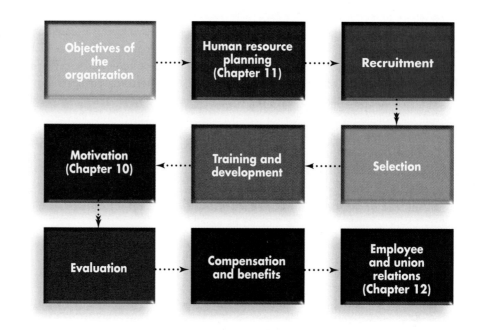

Advanced technology has increased the need to continuously update employee skills. At Motorola, training programs such as the one pictured here, are used to develop the people who will develop the products that change our lives. Do you believe that continuous learning will be part of your work life?

many employees volunteering to participate in the company's "total customer satisfaction" competition that the plant had to close during presentation week.[3]

Some people have called employees the ultimate resource, and when you think about it, nothing could be more true. People develop the ideas that eventually become the products that satisfy consumers' wants and needs. Take away their creative minds, and leading firms such as IBM, GE, Hewlett-Packard, and GM would be nothing. The problem is that human resources have always been relatively plentiful, so there was little need to nurture and develop them. If you needed qualified people, you simply went out and hired them. If they didn't work out, you fired them and found others. But *qualified* labor is scarcer today, and that makes recruiting more difficult.[4]

Historically, most firms assigned the job of recruiting, selecting, training, evaluating, compensating, motivating, and, yes, firing people to the various functional departments. For years, the personnel department was more or less responsible for clerical functions such as screening applications, keeping records, processing the payroll, and finding people when necessary.

Today the job of human resource management has taken on an entirely new role in the firm. In the future it may become the most critical function in that it will be responsible for dealing with all aspects of a business's most critical resource—people. In fact, the human resource function has become so important that it is no longer the function of just one department; it is a function of all managers. Most human resource functions are shared between the professional human resource manager and the other managers. What are some of the challenges in the human resource area that managers face?

The Human Resource Challenge

The changes in the American business system that have had the most dramatic impact on the workings of the free enterprise system are the changes in the labor force. The ability of the U.S. business system to compete in international markets depends on new ideas, new products, and new levels of productivity ➤ **P.23** ◄—in other words, on people with good ideas. The following are some of the challenges and opportunities being encountered in the human resource area:

- Shortages in people trained to work in the growth areas of the future, such as computers, biotechnology, robotics, and the sciences. It is estimated that 346,000 U.S. high-tech jobs went unfilled in 2000.[5]

- A huge population of skilled and unskilled workers from declining industries, such as steel, automobiles, and garment-making, who are unemployed or underemployed and who need retraining. Underemployed workers are those who have more skills or knowledge than their current jobs require.[6]

- A growing percentage of new workers who are undereducated and unprepared for jobs in the contemporary business environment.[7]

- A shift in the age composition of the workforce, including aging baby boomers, many of whom are deferring retirement.[8]

- A complex set of laws and regulations involving hiring, safety, unionization, and equal pay that require organizations to go beyond a profit orientation and be more fair and socially conscious.[9]

- An increasing number of both single-parent and two-income families, resulting in a demand for day care, job sharing, maternity leave, and special career advancement programs for women.[10]

- A shift in employee attitudes toward work. Leisure time has become a much higher priority, as have concepts such as flextime and a shorter workweek.[11]

- Continued downsizing that is taking a toll on employee morale as well as increasing the demand for temporary workers.[12]

- A challenge from overseas labor pools whose members are available for lower wages and subject to many fewer laws and regulations. This results in many jobs being shifted overseas. The Reaching Beyond Our Borders box discusses the new human resource challenges faced by global businesses.

- An increased demand for benefits tailored to the individual.[13]

- A growing concern over such issues as health care, elder care, child care (discussed in Chapter 12), equal opportunities for people with disabilities, and special attention given to affirmative-action programs.[14]

- A decreased sense of employee loyalty resulting in increased employee turnover and increased costs of replacing lost workers.[15]

Given all of these issues, and others that are sure to develop, you can see why human resource management has taken a more central position in management thinking than ever before. Let's see what is involved.

CRITICAL THINKING

Based on the complex situations you'd be addressing, does human resource management seem like a challenging career area? What have been your experiences in dealing with people who work in human resource management? Would you enjoy working in such an environment?

REACHING BEYOND OUR BORDERS   *www.shrm.org*
Managing a Global Workforce

Many U.S. companies send employees to different countries. How do human resource personnel manage employees in, say, an office in Spain, a service center in Brazil, or a new plant in Korea? How do they cope with hiring employees from other countries for a company's headquarters in the United States? Human resource people who manage a global workforce begin by understanding the customs, laws, and local business needs of every country in which the organization operates.

Varying cultural and legal standards can affect a variety of human resource functions:

- *Compensation.* Salaries must be converted to and from foreign currencies. Often employees with international assignments receive special allowances for relocation, children's education, housing, travel, or other business-related expenses.

- *Health and pension standards.* Human resource managers must consider the different social contexts for benefits in other countries. For example, in the Netherlands the government provides retirement income and health care.

- *Paid time off.* Cultural differences can be quite apparent when it comes to paid time off. Employees in other countries enjoy more vacation time than those in the United States. For example, four weeks of paid vacation is the standard of many European employers. But other countries do not have the short-term and long-term absence policies we have in the United States. They do not have sick leave, personal leave, or family and medical leave. Global companies need a standard definition of what time off is.

- *Taxation.* Different countries have varying taxation rules, and the payroll department is an important player in managing immigration information.

- *Communication.* When employees leave to work in another country they often feel a disconnection from their home country. Wise companies use their intranet and the Internet to help these faraway employees keep in direct contact. Several companies use these tools for posting both job vacancies and notices to help returning employees find positions back in the United States.

Human resource policies will be influenced more and more by conditions and practices in other countries and cultures. Human resource managers will need to move away from the assumed dominance and/or superiority of American business practices and sensitize themselves and their organizations to the cultural and business practices of other nations.

Sources: Fay Hansen, "Currents in Compensation and Benefits," *Compensation and Benefits Review,* September, 18, 1999; Michael A. Verespej, "Each Country Has Different Work/Life Issues to Balance," *Industry Week,* April 19, 1999; Reena Jana, "Preventing Culture Clashes," *InfoWorld,* April 24, 2000; and Claude Smadja, "Wake Up to Globalization," *Time International,* January 29, 2001.

DETERMINING YOUR HUMAN RESOURCE NEEDS

All management, including human resource management, begins with planning. Six steps are involved in the human resource planning process:

1. *Preparing forecasts of future human resource needs.*

2. *Preparing a human resource inventory of the organization's employees.* This inventory should include ages, names, education, capabilities, training, specialized skills, and other information pertinent to the specific organization (e.g., languages spoken). Such information reveals whether or not the labor force is technically up-to-date, thoroughly trained, and so forth.

job analysis
A study of what is done by employees who hold various job titles.

job description
A summary of the objectives of a job, the type of work to be done, the responsibilities and duties, the working conditions, and the relationship of the job to other functions.

job specifications
A written summary of the minimum qualifications required of workers to do a particular job.

3. *Preparing a job analysis.* A **job analysis** is a study of what is done by employees who hold various job titles. Such analyses are necessary in order to recruit and train employees with the necessary skills to do the job. The results of job analysis are two written statements: job descriptions and job specifications. A **job description** specifies the objectives of the job, the type of work to be done, the responsibilities and duties, the working conditions, and the relationship of the job to other functions. **Job specifications** are a written summary of the minimum qualifications (education, skills, etc.) required of a worker to fill specific jobs. In short, job descriptions are statements about the job, whereas job specifications are statements about the person who does the job. See Figure 11.2 for hypothetical examples of a job description and job specifications.

4. *Assessing future demand.* Because technology changes rapidly, training programs must be started long before the need is apparent. Human resource managers who are proactive—that is, who anticipate the organization's future needs identified in the strategic planning process—make sure that trained people are available when needed.

5. *Assessing future supply.* The labor force is constantly shifting: getting older, becoming more technically oriented, attracting more women, and so forth. There are likely to be increased shortages of some workers in the future (e.g., computer and robotic repair workers) and oversupply of others (e.g., assembly-line workers).

6. *Establishing a strategic plan.* The plan must address recruiting, selecting, training and developing, appraising, compensating, and scheduling the labor force. Because the previous five steps lead up to this one, this chapter will focus on these elements of the strategic human resource plan.

FIGURE 11.2

JOB ANALYSIS

A job analysis yields two important statements: job descriptions and job specifications. Here you have a job description and job specifications for a sales representative.

Job Analysis

Observe current sales representatives doing the job.
Discuss job with sales managers.
Have current sales reps keep a diary of their activities.

Job Description

Primary objective is to sell company's products to stores in Territory Z. Duties include servicing accounts and maintaining positive relationships with clients. Responsibilities include

• Introducing the new products to store managers in the area.
• Helping the store managers estimate the volume to order.
• Negotiating prime shelf space.
• Explaining sales promotion activities to store managers.
• Stocking and maintaining shelves in stores that wish such service.

Job Specifications

Characteristics of the person qualifying for this job include

• Two years' sales experience.
• Positive attitude.
• Well-groomed appearance.
• Good communication skills.
• High school diploma and two years of college credit.

RECRUITING EMPLOYEES FROM A DIVERSE POPULATION

Recruitment is the set of activities used to obtain a sufficient number of the right people at the right time; its purpose is to select those who best meet the needs of the organization. One would think that, with a continuous flow of new people into the workforce, recruiting would be easy. On the contrary, recruiting has become very difficult, for several reasons:

recruitment
The set of activities used to obtain a sufficient number of the right people at the right time; its purpose is to select those who best meet the needs of the organization.

- Sometimes people with the necessary skills are not available; in this case, workers must be hired and then trained internally.[16]

- The emphasis on corporate culture, teamwork, and participative management makes it important to hire people who not only are skilled but also fit in with the culture and leadership style of the organization.[17]

- Some organizations have policies that demand promotions from within, operate under union regulations, or offer low wages, which makes recruiting and keeping employees difficult or subject to outside influence and restrictions.

Because recruiting is a difficult chore that involves finding, hiring, and training people who are an appropriate technical and social fit, human resource managers turn to many sources for assistance (see Figure 11.3).[18] These sources are classified as either internal or external. Internal sources include employees who are already within the firm (and may be transferred or promoted) and employees who can recommend others to hire.[19] Using internal sources is less expensive than recruiting outside the company. The great-

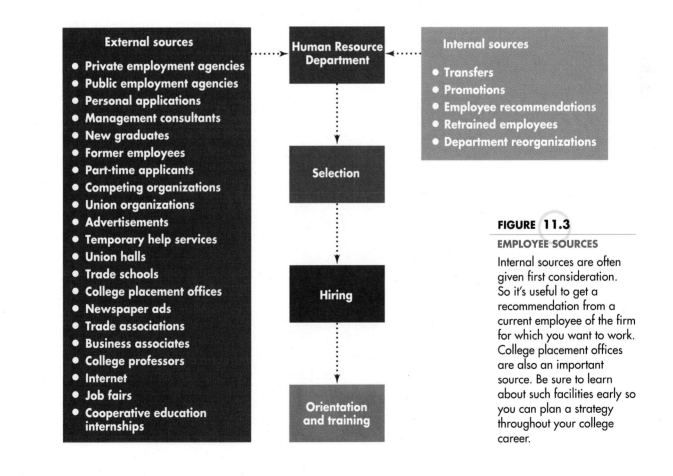

External sources

- Private employment agencies
- Public employment agencies
- Personal applications
- Management consultants
- New graduates
- Former employees
- Part-time applicants
- Competing organizations
- Union organizations
- Advertisements
- Temporary help services
- Union halls
- Trade schools
- College placement offices
- Newspaper ads
- Trade associations
- Business associates
- College professors
- Internet
- Job fairs
- Cooperative education internships

Human Resource Department

Selection

Hiring

Orientation and training

Internal sources

- Transfers
- Promotions
- Employee recommendations
- Retrained employees
- Department reorganizations

FIGURE 11.3

EMPLOYEE SOURCES

Internal sources are often given first consideration. So it's useful to get a recommendation from a current employee of the firm for which you want to work. College placement offices are also an important source. Be sure to learn about such facilities early so you can plan a strategy throughout your college career.

www.business-ethics.com

MAKING ETHICAL DECISIONS

Recruiting Employees from Competitors

As human resource manager for Technocrat, Inc., it is your job to recruit the best employees. Your most recent human resource inventory indicated that Technocrat currently has an abundance of qualified designers and that several lower-level workers will soon be eligible for promotions to designer positions as well. In spite of the surplus of qualified designers, you are considering offering a similar position to a designer who is now with a major competitor. Your thinking is that the new employee will be a source of information about the competition's new products. What are your ethical considerations in this case? Will you lure the employee away from the competition even though you have no need for a designer? What will be the consequences of your decision?

est advantage of hiring from within is that it helps maintain employee morale.[20] It isn't always possible to find qualified workers within the company, however, so human resource managers must use external recruitment sources such as advertisements, public and private employment agencies, college placement bureaus, management consultants, professional organizations, referrals, and walk-in applications.[21] While most external sources are straightforward, some may involve difficult decisions; the Making Ethical Decisions box presents questions about recruiting employees from competitors.

Recruiting qualified workers may be particularly difficult for small businesses ➤ P.176 ◄ that don't have enough staff members to serve as internal sources and may not be able to offer the sort of competitive compensation that attracts external sources. The Spotlight on Small Business box outlines some ways in which small businesses can address their recruiting needs. The newest tools for recruiting employees are Internet services such as CareerMosaic, the

Internet job search services such as Career Mosaic have changed the nature of recruiting employees and searching for jobs. Finding the right employee or the right job is often just a click away. Career Mosaic can offer you immediate results in the job search or can notify you by e-mail when the right job match becomes available. Check out its services at www.careermosiac.com.

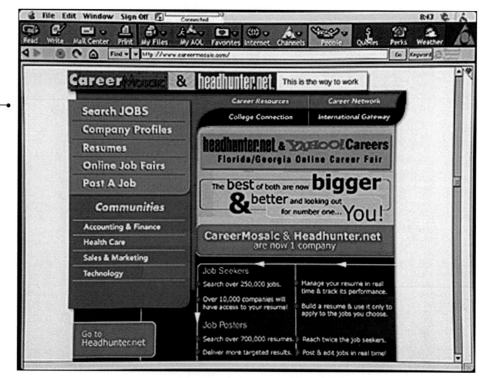

Small Businesses Must Compete to Attract Qualified Workers

It's harder now than ever before for businesses to find qualified employees, and it is becoming more expensive. Small-business owners across the country agree that competition for qualified employees is intensifying. Small businesses want top talent but often can't afford corporate-level benefits or expensive recruiters to hunt down the best people. Despite the hurdles, small-business management consultants say there are many ways to lure desirable workers:

- *Transform ads into promotional tools.* For example, Ecoprint, a small print shop in Maryland, brags in its advertisements about the benefits of working for this collegial company.

- *Post job openings on the Internet.* Running a 20-line ad on an online service like CareerMosaic or the Monster Board costs $100 to $150 for 30 days. A comparable ad in the *New York Times* can cost $1,728 for only a week.

- *Let your staff help select hires.* The more staff people involved in the interview process, the better chance you have to find out who has the personality and skills to fit in.

- *Create a dynamic workplace to attract local, energetic applicants.* Sometimes word of mouth is the most effective recruiting tool.

- *Test-drive an employee.* Hiring temporary workers can allow you to test candidates for a few months before deciding whether to make an offer or not.

- *Hire your customer.* Loyal customers sometimes make the smartest employees.

- *Check community groups and local government agencies.* Don't forget to check out state-run employment agencies. The new welfare-to-work programs may turn up excellent candidates you can train.

- *Lure candidates with a policy of promotions and raises.* Most employees want to know that they can move up in the company. Give employees an incentive for learning the business.

Sources: "Hire.com Helps Level the Recruiting Playing Field for Emerging Businesses," *Business Wire,* May 16, 2000; "Some Employers Can't Afford the Minimum Wage," *Business Week,* August 7, 2000, p. 15; and Susan T. Port, "Staff Leasing Firms Help Small Businesses Compete," *The Palm Beach Post,* January 27, 2001, p. 2D.

Monster Board, and Jobtrak (see the Taking It to the Net exercise at the end of this chapter).[22]

SELECTING EMPLOYEES WHO WILL BE PRODUCTIVE

Selection is the process of gathering information and deciding who should be hired, under legal guidelines, for the best interests of the individual and the organization. The cost of selecting and training employees has become prohibitively high in some firms. Think of what's involved: interview time, medical exams, training costs, unproductive time spent learning the job, moving expenses, and so on. It's easy to see how selection expenses can amount to over $130,000 for a manager. It can even cost one and a half times the employee's annual salary to recruit, process, and train an entry-level worker.[23] In the United States, the amount businesses spent on training alone skyrocketed from $30 billion in 1991 to $60.7 billion in 1998.[24] Thus, the selection process is an important element of any human resource program. A typical selection process would involve six steps:

1. *Obtaining complete application forms.* Once this was a simple procedure with few complications. Today, however, legal guidelines limit the

selection
The process of gathering information and deciding who should be hired, under legal guidelines, for the best interests of the individual and the organization.

kinds of questions that may appear on an application form. Nonetheless, such forms help the employer discover the applicant's educational background, past work experience, career objectives, and other qualifications directly related to the requirements of the job.

2. *Conducting initial and follow-up interviews.* A staff member from the human resource department often screens applicants in a first interview. If the interviewer considers the applicant a potential employee, the manager who will supervise the new employee interviews the applicant as well. It's important that managers prepare adequately for the interview to avoid selection decisions they may regret. Certain mistakes, such as asking an interviewee about his or her family, no matter how innocent the intention, could later be used as evidence if that applicant files discrimination charges. Southwest Airlines places so much importance on the interviewing process that it can take as long as six weeks before an applicant is hired.[25]

3. *Giving employment tests.* Employment tests have been severely criticized as potential sources of illegal discrimination. Nonetheless, organizations continue to use them to measure basic competencies in specific job skills (e.g., welding, word processing) and to help evaluate applicants' personalities and interests. In using employment tests, it's important that they be directly related to the job. Many companies test potential employees in assessment centers where applicants perform actual tasks of the real job. This will make the selection process more efficient and generally satisfy legal requirements.

4. *Conducting background investigations.* Most organizations now investigate a candidate's work record, school record, credit history, and references more carefully than they have in the past. It is simply too costly to hire, train, and motivate people only to lose them and have to start the process over. Background checks help an employer identify which candidates are most likely to succeed in a given position. Websites such as PeopleWise allow prospective employers not only to conduct speedy background checks of criminal records, driving records, and credit his-

Hiring the wrong person can cost a company significant time and money. Companies like PeopleWise.com help businesses learn more about prospective employees. The company conducts background checks that can help weed out job prospects that have little chance of success in a particular position. How important do you think background checks are in the recruitment process?

tories but also to verify work experience and professional and educational credentials.[26]

5. *Obtaining results from physical exams.* There are obvious benefits in hiring physically and mentally healthy people. However, medical tests cannot be given just to screen out individuals. (See the discussion of the Americans with Disabilities Act on p. 353.) In some states, physical exams can be given only after an offer of employment has been accepted. In states that allow preemployment physical exams, the exams must be given to everyone applying for the same position. There has been some controversy about preemployment testing to detect drug or alcohol abuse, as well as screening to detect carriers of the virus that causes AIDS. Eighty percent of U.S. companies now test both current and potential employees for drug use.[27]

6. *Establishing trial (probationary) periods.* Often an organization will hire an employee conditionally. This enables the person to prove his or her worth on the job. After a specified probationary period (perhaps six months or a year), the firm may either permanently hire or discharge that employee based on evaluations from supervisors. Although such systems make it easier to fire inefficient or problem employees, they do not eliminate the high cost of turnover.

The selection process is often long and difficult, but it is worth the effort to select new employees carefully because of the high costs of replacing workers. The process helps ensure that new employees meet the requirements in all relevant areas, including communication skills, education, technical skills, experience, personality, and health.

Hiring Contingent Workers

When more workers are needed in a company, human resource managers may want to consider finding creative staffing alternatives rather than simply hiring new permanent employees. A company with a varying need for employees, from hour to hour, day to day, week to week, and season to season may find it cost-effective to hire contingent workers. **Contingent workers** are defined as workers who do not have the expectation of regular, full-time employment. Such workers include part-time workers (anyone who works 1 to 34 hours per week), temporary workers (workers paid by temporary employment agencies), seasonal workers, independent contractors, interns, and co-op students.[28]

A varying need for employees is the most common reason for hiring contingent workers. Companies may also look to hire contingent workers when full-time employees are on some type of leave (such as maternity leave), when there is a peak demand for labor, or when quick service to customers is a priority.[29] Companies in areas where qualified contingent workers are available, and in which the jobs require minimum training, are most likely to consider alternative staffing options.

Temporary staffing has evolved into a $40 billion industry. According to the U.S. Bureau of Labor Statistics, about 12.6 million people in the United States (10 percent of workers) are employed in an alternative working arrangement. That's more than double the 1.15 million people who were employed in such arrangements in 1991.[30] At the beginning of the 1990s, half of those jobs were office-clerical positions and one-quarter were industrial (construction, trucking, plumbing, etc.). Now industrial jobs account for more than one-third of all temps. As you recall from the profile at the beginning of this chapter, an increasing number of contingent workers are educated professionals such as accountants, attorneys, and engineers.

contingent workers
Workers who do not have the expectation of regular, full-time employment.

Contingent workers receive few benefits; they are rarely offered health insurance, vacation time, or private pensions.[31] They also earn less than permanent workers do. On the positive side, about 40 percent of those on temporary assignments are eventually offered full-time positions. Managers see using temporary workers as a way of weeding out poor workers and finding good hires. Furthermore, in an era of downsizing and rapid change, some contingent workers have even found that "temping" can be less insecure than full-time employment.[32]

PROGRESS ASSESSMENT

• What is human resource management?

• What are the six steps in human resource planning?

• What factors make it difficult to recruit qualified employees?

• What are the six steps in the selection process?

• What are contingent workers? Why do companies hire such workers?

TRAINING AND DEVELOPING EMPLOYEES FOR OPTIMUM PERFORMANCE

training and development
All attempts to improve productivity by increasing an employee's ability to perform.

Because employees need to learn how to work with new equipment—such as word processors, computers, and robots—companies are finding that they must offer training programs that often are quite sophisticated.[33] **Training and development** include all attempts to improve productivity by increasing an employee's ability to perform. Training focuses on short-term skills, whereas development focuses on long-term abilities. But both training and development programs include three steps: (1) assessing the needs of the organization and the skills of the employees to determine training needs; (2) designing training activities to meet the identified needs; and (3) evaluating the effectiveness of the training. Some common training and development activities are employee orientation, on-the-job training, apprenticeship, off-the-job training, vestibule training, job simulation, and management training.

employee orientation
The activity that introduces new employees to the organization; to fellow employees; to their immediate supervisors; and to the policies, practices, and objectives of the firm.

• **Employee orientation** is the activity that initiates new employees to the organization; to fellow employees; to their immediate supervisors; and to the policies, practices, and objectives of the firm. Orientation programs include everything from informal talks to formal activities that last a day or more and include scheduled visits to various departments and required reading of handbooks.[34] For example, at British Airways new employees participate in meetings that provide an education in the company's values and in its brand integrity. Part history lesson, part rules-of-the-road orientation, the training covers everything from principles of customer service to the choice of colors on the aircraft.[35]

on-the-job training
Training program in which the employee immediately begins his or her tasks and learns by doing, or watches others for a while and then imitates them, all right at the workplace.

• **On-the-job training** is the most fundamental type of training. The employee being trained on the job immediately begins his or her tasks and learns by doing, or watches others for a while and then imitates them, right at the workplace. Salespeople, for example, are often trained by watching experienced salespeople perform. Naturally, this can be either quite effective or disastrous, depending on the skills and habits of the person being watched. On-the-job training is obviously the easiest kind of training to implement when the job is relatively simple (such as clerking in a store) or repetitive (such as collecting refuse, cleaning carpets, or mowing lawns). More demanding or intricate jobs require a more intense training effort. Intranets and other new forms of technology are

leading to cost-effective on-the-job training programs available 24 hours a day, all year long. Computer systems can monitor workers' input and give them instructions if they become confused about what to do next. MCI WorldCom's intranet training system saved the company nearly $3 million by reducing the training cost per employee by 22 percent.[36]

- **Apprentice programs** involve a period during which a learner works alongside an experienced employee to master the skills and procedures of a craft. Some apprenticeship programs also involve classroom training. Many skilled crafts, such as bricklaying and plumbing, require a new worker to serve as an apprentice for several years. Trade unions often require new workers to serve apprenticeships to ensure excellence among their members as well as to limit entry to the union. Workers who successfully complete an apprenticeship earn the classification of *journeyman*. In the future, there are likely to be more but shorter apprenticeship programs to prepare people for skilled jobs in changing industries. For example, auto repair will require more intense training as new automobile models include advanced computers and other electronic devices.

apprentice programs
Training programs involving a period during which a learner works alongside an experienced employee to master the skills and procedures of a craft.

- **Off-the-job training** occurs away from the workplace and consists of internal or external programs to develop any of a variety of skills or to foster personal development. Training is becoming more sophisticated as jobs become more sophisticated. Furthermore, training is expanding to include education (through the Ph.D.) and personal development—subjects may include time management, stress management, health and wellness, physical education, nutrition, and even art and languages.[37]

off-the-job training
Training that occurs away from the workplace and consists of internal or external programs to develop any of a variety of skills or to foster personal development.

- **Online training** offers an example of how technology is improving the efficiency of many off-the-job training programs. In such training, employees "attend" classes via the Internet.[38] For example, The Business Channel (TBC), at www.pbstbc.com, offers business education programs over the Internet. Such programs are sometimes called *distance learning* because the students are separated by distance from the instructor or content source.[39]

online training
Training programs in which employees "attend" classes via the Internet.

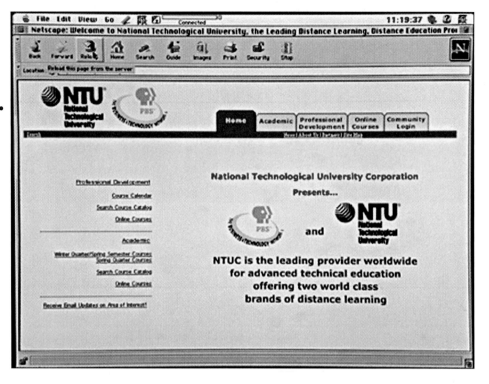

More and more learners are attending classes via the Internet instead of through traditional education channels. Services like the Business Channel (TBC) offer business education programs at www.pbstbc.com. What advantages do training services provide to students or employees?

vestibule training
Training done in schools where employees are taught on equipment similar to that used on the job.

job simulation
The use of equipment that duplicates job conditions and tasks so that trainees can learn skills before attempting them on the job.

- **Vestibule training** (near-the-job training) is done in classrooms where employees are taught on equipment similar to that used on the job. Such classrooms enable employees to learn proper methods and safety procedures before assuming a specific job assignment in an organization. Computer and robotics training is often completed in a vestibule classroom.

- **Job simulation** is the use of equipment that duplicates job conditions and tasks so that trainees can learn skills before attempting them on the job. Job simulation differs from vestibule training in that the simulation attempts to duplicate the *exact* combination of conditions that occur on the job. This is the kind of training given to astronauts, airline pilots, army tank operators, ship captains, and others who must learn difficult procedures off the job.

Management Development

Managers need special training. To be good communicators, they especially need to learn listening skills and empathy. They also need time management, planning, and human relations skills.

management development
The process of training and educating employees to become good managers and then monitoring the progress of their managerial skills over time.

Management development, then, is the process of training and educating employees to become good managers and then monitoring the progress of their managerial skills over time. Management development programs have sprung up everywhere, especially at colleges, universities, and private management development firms.[40] Managers participate in role-playing exercises, solve various management cases, attend films and lectures, and so on. In some organizations, managers are paid to take college-level courses through the doctoral level.

Management development is increasingly being used as a tool to accomplish business objectives. For example, Ford Motor Company is using education to teach executives how to be more responsive to customers. Most management training programs also include several of the following:

- *On-the-job coaching.* This means that a senior manager will assist a lower-level manager by teaching him or her needed skills and generally providing direction, advice, and helpful criticism.[41]

- *Understudy positions.* Job titles such as *undersecretary* and *assistant* are part of a relatively successful way of developing managers. Selected employees work as assistants to higher level managers and participate in planning and other managerial functions until they are ready to assume such positions themselves.

- *Job rotation.* So that they can learn about different functions of the organization, managers are often given assignments in a variety of departments. Through job rotation, top managers gain the broad picture of the organization necessary to their success.

- *Off-the-job courses and training.* Managers periodically go to schools or seminars for a week or more to hone their technical and human relations skills. Such courses expose them to the latest concepts and create a sense of camaraderie as the managers live, eat, and work together in a college-type atmosphere. Case studies and simulation exercises of all kinds are often part of such training. Many companies, such as Mobil Corporation, offer tuition reimbursement for such courses as a fringe benefit. Other companies, such as McDonald's Corporation, have their own "colleges" for managers. At McDonald's Hamburger University, managers and potential franchise owners attend six days of classes, a course of study equivalent to 36 hours of college business-school credit.[42]

Networking

Networking is the process of establishing and maintaining contacts with key managers in one's own organization and in other organizations and using those contacts to weave strong relationships that serve as informal development systems. Of equal or greater importance to potential managers is a **mentor,** a corporate manager who supervises, coaches, and guides selected lower-level employees by introducing them to the right people and generally being their organizational sponsor. In reality, an informal type of mentoring goes on in most organizations on a regular basis as older employees assist younger workers.[43] However, many organizations, such as Merrill Lynch and FedEx, use a formal system of assigning mentors to employees considered to have strong potential.[44]

It's also important to remember that networking and mentoring can go beyond the business environment. For example, college is a perfect place to begin networking. Associations you nurture with professors, with local businesspeople, and especially with your classmates might provide you with a valuable network you can turn to for the rest of your career.[45]

Diversity in Management Development

As women moved into management, they also learned the importance of networking and of having mentors. But since (even now) most older managers are male, women often have more difficulty than men do in finding mentors and entering the network. Women managers won a major victory when the U.S. Supreme Court ruled that it was illegal to bar women from certain clubs, long open to men only, where business activity and contact making flows. More and more, women are now entering established networking systems or, in some instances, creating their own.[46]

Similarly, African American managers are learning the value of networking. Working together, African Americans are forming pools of capital and new

networking
The process of establishing and maintaining contacts with key managers in one's own organization and other organizations and using those contacts to weave strong relationships that serve as informal development systems.

mentor
An experienced employee who supervises, coaches, and guides lower-level employees by introducing them to the right people and generally being their organizational sponsor.

opportunities that are helping many individuals overcome traditional barriers to success.[47] *Black Enterprise* magazine sponsors several networking forums each year for African American professionals.

Other ethnic groups are networking as well. For example, Mark Shir, a financial and computer specialist from Taiwan, felt that he would never get ahead in the U.S. companies he had worked in for 10 years. When he joined Monte Jade, an association that helps Taiwanese and Chinese assimilate in American business, he met people who helped him start his own successful hardware-packaging company.[48]

Companies that take the initiative to develop female and minority managers understand three crucial principles: (1) grooming women and minorities for management positions isn't about legality, morality, or even morale; it is about bringing more talent in the door—the key to long-term profitability; (2) the best women and minorities will become harder to attract and retain, so the companies that start now will have an edge later; and (3) having more women and minorities at all levels means that businesses can serve their increasingly female and minority customers better. If you don't have a diversity of people working in the back room, how are you going to satisfy the diversity of people coming in the front door?

APPRAISING EMPLOYEE PERFORMANCE TO GET OPTIMUM RESULTS

performance appraisal
An evaluation in which the performance level of employees is measured against established standards to make decisions about promotions, compensation, additional training, or firing.

Managers must be able to determine whether or not their workers are doing an effective and efficient job, with a minimum of errors and disruptions. They do so by using performance appraisals. A **performance appraisal** is an evaluation in which the performance level of employees is measured against established standards to make decisions about promotions, compensation, additional training, or firing. Performance appraisals consist of these six steps:

1. *Establishing performance standards.* This is a crucial step. Standards must be understandable, subject to measurement, and reasonable. They must be accepted by both the manager and the employees.

Performance appraisals are among the least preferred tasks that managers must perform. However, such appraisals can be helpful to both managers and workers if clear standards are established and communicated. Remember the objective of performance appraisals is to improve the employee's performance and productivity. Do you think performance appraisals can be effective if they are not conducted face-to-face?

FIGURE 11.4

MAKING APPRAISALS AND
REVIEWS MORE EFFECTIVE

1. **DON'T** attack the employee personally. Critically evaluate his or her work.
2. **DO** allow sufficient time, without distractions, for appraisal. (Take the phone off the hook or close the office door.)
3. **DON'T** make the employee feel uncomfortable or uneasy. *Never* conduct an appraisal where other employees are present (such as on the shop floor).
4. **DO** include the employee in the process as much as possible. (Let the employee prepare a self-improvement program.)
5. **DON'T** wait until the appraisal to address problems with the employee's work that have been developing for some time.
6. **DO** end the appraisal with positive suggestions for employee improvement.

2. *Communicating those standards.* Often managers assume that employees know what is expected of them, but such assumptions are dangerous at best. Employees must be told clearly and precisely what the standards and expectations are and how they are to be met.

3. *Evaluating performance.* If the first two steps are done correctly, performance evaluation is relatively easy. It is a matter of evaluating the employee's behavior to see if it matches standards.

4. *Discussing results with employees.* Most people will make mistakes and fail to meet expectations at first. It takes time to learn a new job and do it well. Discussing an employee's successes and areas that need improvement can provide managers with an opportunity to be understanding and helpful and to guide the employee to better performance. Additionally, the performance appraisal can be a good source of employee suggestions on how a particular task could be better performed.

5. *Taking corrective action.* As an appropriate part of the performance appraisal, a manager can take corrective action or provide corrective feedback to help the employee perform his or her job better. Remember, the key word is *performance*. The primary purpose of conducting this type of appraisal is to improve employee performance if possible.

6. *Using the results to make decisions.* Decisions about promotions, compensation, additional training, or firing are all based on performance evaluations. An effective performance appraisal system is a way of satisfying certain legal conditions concerning such decisions.

Effective management means getting results through top performance by employees. That is what performance appraisals are for—at all levels of the organization. Even top-level managers benefit from performance reviews made by their subordinates. The latest form of performance appraisal is called the 360-degree review because it calls for feedback from all directions in the organization: up, down, and all around. Figure 11.4 illustrates how managers can make performance appraisals more meaningful.

• Can you name and describe four training techniques?
• What is the primary purpose of a performance appraisal?
• What are the six steps in a performance appraisal?

PROGRESS ASSESSMENT

COMPENSATING EMPLOYEES: ATTRACTING AND KEEPING THE BEST

Companies don't just compete for customers; they also compete for employees. Compensation is one of the main marketing tools companies use to attract qualified employees, and it is one of the largest operating costs for many organizations. The long-term success of a firm—perhaps even its survival—may depend on how well it can control employee costs and optimize employee efficiency. For example, service organizations such as hospitals, airlines, and banks have recently struggled with managing high employee costs. This is not unusual since these firms are considered labor intensive. That is, their primary cost of operations is the cost of labor. Manufacturing firms in the auto and steel industries have asked employees to take reductions in wages to make the firm more competitive. Many employees have agreed, even union employees who have traditionally resisted such cuts. They know that not to do so is to risk going out of business and losing their jobs forever. In other words, the competitive environment is such that compensation and benefit packages are being given special attention. In fact, some experts believe that determining how best to pay people has replaced downsizing as today's greatest human resources challenge.[49]

A carefully managed compensation and benefit program can accomplish several objectives:

- Attracting the kinds of people needed by the organization, and in sufficient numbers.
- Providing employees with the incentive to work efficiently and productively.
- Keeping valued employees from leaving and going to competitors, or starting competing firms.
- Maintaining a competitive position in the marketplace by keeping costs low through high productivity from a satisfied workforce.
- Providing employees with some sense of financial security through insurance and retirement benefits.

Great Plains Software CEO Doug Burgum says lifestyle is his key recruitment tool. Based in rural Fargo, North Dakota, the company does not offer access to exotic restaurants or sprawling museums. It does offer good wages, family-friendly attitudes, flexible work rules, telecommuting, good schools and a low cost of living. Does a job with a company like Great Plains Software interest you? Why or why not?

Pay Systems

How an organization chooses to pay its employees can have a dramatic effect on efficiency and productivity. Managers want to find a system that compensates employees fairly. Figure 11.5 outlines some of the most common pay systems.

Many companies still use the pay system devised by Edward Hay for General Foods. Known as the Hay system, this compensation plan is based on job tiers, each of which has a strict pay range. In some firms, you're guaranteed a raise after 13 weeks if you're still breathing. Conflict can arise when an employee who is performing well earns less than an employee who is not performing well simply because the latter has worked for the company longer.

FIGURE 11.5

PAY SYSTEMS

Some of the different pay systems are as follows:

- **Salary:** fixed compensation computed on weekly, biweekly, or monthly pay periods (e.g., $1,500 per month or $400 per week). Salaried employees do not receive additional pay for any extra hours worked.

- **Hourly wage or daywork:** wage based on number of hours or days worked, used for most blue-collar and clerical workers. Often employees must punch a time clock when they arrive at work and when they leave. Hourly wages vary greatly. The federal minimum wage is $5.15, and top wages go as high as $20 to $30 per hour for skilled craftsmen. This does not include benefits such as retirement systems, which may add 30 percent or more to the total package.

- **Piecework system:** wage based on the number of items produced rather than by the hour or day. This type of system creates powerful incentives to work efficiently and productively.

- **Commission plans:** pay based on some percentage of sales. Often used to compensate salespeople, commission plans resemble piecework systems.

- **Bonus plans:** extra pay for accomplishing or surpassing certain objectives. There are two types of bonuses: monetary and cashless. Money is always a welcome bonus. Cashless rewards include written thank-you notes, appreciation notes sent to the employee's family, movie tickets, flowers, time off, gift certificates, shopping sprees, and other types of recognition.

- **Profit-sharing plans:** share of the company's profits over and above normal pay. Ninety-nine percent of the Fortune 500 companies use some sort of performance-based incentives. These companies set goals with the input from employees ahead of time. Bonuses are based on progress in meeting the goals.

- **Stock options:** right to purchase stock in the company at a specific price over a specific period of time. Often this gives employees the right to buy stock cheaply despite huge increases in the price of the stock in the marketplace. For example, Rob Gordon started out at Home Depot 10 years ago as an assistant manager. Today, at 39, he's a general manager—and a millionaire due to the growth of Home Depot's stock price. With his stock options, Gordon was able to buy stock worth $63.75 a share for as little as $15 a share. Once a perk given only to top-ranking executives, stock options in the past few years began being offered to lower-level employees. Such options plans are often offered by the high-tech, pharmaceutical, and financial services sectors to attract and retain skilled workers.

John Whitney, author of *The Trust Factor,* believes that companies should begin with some base pay and give all employees the same percentage merit raise. Doing so, he says, sends out the message that everyone in the company is important. Fairness remains the issue. What do you think is the fairest pay system?

Compensating Teams

Thus far we've talked about compensating individuals. What about teams? Since you want your teams to be more than simply a group of individuals, would you compensate them as you would individuals? If you can't answer that question immediately, you are not alone. A recent team-based pay survey found that most managers believed in using teams (87 percent), but fewer were sure about how to pay them (41 percent).[50] This suggests that team-based pay programs are not as effective or as fully developed as managers would hope. Measuring and rewarding individual performance on teams while at the same time rewarding team performance can be tricky.

Kellogg's employees can use the company's "Feeling Grrreat" Fitness Center to make sure the Frosted Flakes they eat don't expand their waistlines. Can you think of firms that offer other unique fringe benefits?

Nonetheless, it can be done. Football players are rewarded as a team when they go to the playoffs and to the Super Bowl, but they are paid individually as well. Companies are now experimenting with and developing similar incentive systems.

Jay Schuster, co-author of an ongoing study of team pay, found that when pay is based strictly on individual performance, it erodes team cohesiveness and makes it less likely that the team will meet its goals as a collaborative effort. Schuster recommends basing pay on team performance.[51] Skill-based pay and profit-sharing are the two most common compensation methods for teams.

Skill-based pay is related to the growth of both the individual and the team. Base pay is raised when team members learn and apply new skills. For example, Baldrige Award winner Eastman Chemical Co. rewards its teams' proficiency in technical, social, and business knowledge skills. A cross-functional compensation policy team defines the skills. The drawbacks of the skill-based pay system are twofold: the system is complex, and it is difficult to correlate skill acquisition and bottom-line gains.

In most gain-sharing systems, bonuses are based on improvements over a previous performance baseline. For example, Behlen Manufacturing, a diversified maker of agricultural and industrial products, calculates its bonuses by dividing quality pounds of product by worker-hours. *Quality* means no defects; any defects are subtracted from the total. Workers can receive a monthly gain-sharing bonus of up to $1 an hour when their teams meet productivity goals.

It is important to reward individual team players also. Outstanding team players—those who go beyond what is required and make an outstanding individual contribution to the firm—should be separately recognized for their additional contribution. Recognition can include cashless as well as cash rewards. A good way to avoid alienating recipients who feel team participation was uneven is to let the team decide which members get what type of individual award. After all, if you really support the team process, you need to give teams freedom to reward themselves.

Fringe Benefits

fringe benefits
Benefits such as sick-leave pay, vacation pay, pension plans, and health plans that represent additional compensation to employees beyond base wages.

Fringe benefits include sick-leave pay, vacation pay, pension plans, and health plans that provide additional compensation to employees beyond base wages. Fringe benefits in recent years grew faster than wages. In fact, employee benefits can't really be considered "fringe" anymore. While such benefits only accounted for less than 2 percent of payrolls in 1929, they account for approximately 30 percent of payrolls today. U.S. companies now spend an average of approximately $13,000 a year per employee for benefits. Many employees request more fringe benefits, instead of more salary, to avoid higher taxes. This has resulted in much debate and much government investigation.

Fringe benefits can include everything from paid vacations to health care programs, recreation facilities, company cars, country club memberships, day care services, and executive dining rooms. Employees want packages to include dental care, mental health care, elder care, legal counseling, eye care, and shorter workweeks.[52] Understanding that it takes many attractions to retain the best employees, dozens of companies on *Fortune* magazine's list of the 100 best companies to work for offer so-called soft benefits. Soft benefits help workers maintain the balance between work and family life that is as important to hard-working employees as the nature of the job itself. These perks include things such as on-site haircuts and shoe repair, concierge services, and free breakfasts. Freeing employees from spending time on errands and chores gives them more time for family—and work.[53]

To counter these growing demands, over half of all large firms offer **cafeteria-style fringe benefits** plans, in which employees can choose the benefits they want, up to a certain dollar amount.[54] Choice is the key to flexible, cafeteria-style benefits plans. At one time, most employees' needs were similar. Today, employees are more varied and more demanding. Some employees may need child care benefits, whereas others may need relatively large pension benefits. Rather than giving all employees identical benefits, managers can equitably and cost-effectively meet employees' individual needs by allowing employees some choice.[55]

Managing the benefit package will continue to be a major human resource issue in the future. The cost of administering benefits programs has become so great that a number of companies outsource ➤ **P.254** ◄ this function—that is, they are hiring outside companies to run their employee benefits plans. IBM, for example, decided to spin off its human resources and benefits operation into a separate company, Workforce Solutions, which provides customized services to each of IBM's independent units. The new company saves IBM $45 million each year. Workforce Solutions now handles benefits for other organizations such as the National Geographic Society. In addition to saving them money, outsourcing fringe benefits administration helps companies avoid the growing complexity and technical requirements of the plans.

To put it simply, benefits are as important to wage negotiations and recruitment now as salary. In the future, benefits may become even more important than salary.

Businesses can outsource fringe benefit administration tasks to firms such as the Principal Financial Group. Principal offers companies personalized services in areas such as managing employees 401 (k) plans (discussed in depth in chapter 22). How can outsourcing fringe benefits administration help businesses?

cafeteria-style fringe benefits
Fringe benefits plan that allows employees to choose the benefits they want up to a certain dollar amount.

SCHEDULING EMPLOYEES TO MEET ORGANIZATIONAL AND EMPLOYEE NEEDS

By now, you are quite familiar with the trends occurring in the workforce that result in managers and workers demanding more from jobs in the way of flexibility and responsiveness. From these trends have emerged several new or

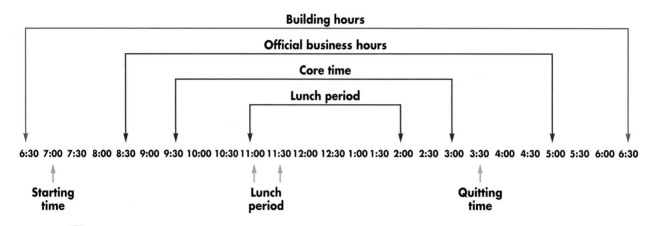

FIGURE 11.6

A FLEXTIME CHART

At this company, employees can start work anytime between 6:30 and 9:30 AM. They take a half hour for lunch anytime between 11:00 AM and 1:30 PM, and can leave between 3:00 and 6:30 PM. Everyone works an eight-hour day. The blue arrows show a typical flextime day.

flextime plan
Work schedule that gives employees some freedom to choose when to work, as long as they work the required number of hours.

core time
In a flextime plan, the period when all employees are expected to be at their job stations.

compressed workweek
Work schedule that allows an employee to work a full number of hours per week but in fewer days.

renewed ideas such as flextime, in-home employment, and job sharing.[56] Let's see how these innovations affect the management of human resources.

Flextime Plans

A **flextime plan** gives employees some freedom to choose when to work, as long as they work the required number of hours. Nearly 90 percent of large U.S. companies offer some version of flextime.[57] The most popular plans allow employees to come to work at 7:00, 8:00, or 9:00 AM and leave between 4:00 and 6:00 PM. Usually, flextime plans will incorporate what is called core time. **Core time** refers to the period when all employees are expected to be at their job stations. For example, an organization may designate core time as between 9:30 and 11:00 AM and between 2:00 and 3:00 PM. During these hours all employees are required to be at work (see Figure 11.6). Flextime plans, like job-sharing plans, are designed to allow employees to adjust to the demands of the times; two-income families find them especially helpful. The federal government has experimented extensively with flextime and found it to be a boost to employee productivity ► **P.23** ◄ and morale.[58]

There are some real disadvantages to flextime as well. Flextime is certainly not for all organizations. For example, it cannot be offered in assembly-line processes where everyone must be at work at the same time. It also is not effective for shift work.

Another disadvantage to flextime is that managers often have to work longer days in order to assist and supervise employees. Some organizations operate from 6:00 AM to 6:00 PM under flextime—a long day for supervisors. Flextime also makes communication more difficult; certain employees may not be there when others need to talk to them. Furthermore, if not carefully supervised, some employees could abuse the system, and that could cause resentment among others. You can imagine how you'd feel if half the workforce left at 3:00 PM on Friday and you had to work until 6:00 PM.

Another popular option used in approximately 24 percent of companies is a **compressed workweek.** That means that an employee works a full number of hours in fewer days. For example, an employee may work four 10-hour days and then enjoy a long weekend instead of working five 8-hour days with a traditional weekend. There are the obvious advantages of working only four days and having three days off, but some employees get tired working such long hours, and productivity could decline. Many employees find such a system of great benefit, however, and are quite enthusiastic about it.[59]

Although flexible schedules are offered by so many companies, few employees take advantage of them. Most workers report that they resist using the programs because they fear it will hurt their careers. Managers signal (directly

	BENEFITS	CHALLENGES
To Organization	• Increases productivity due to fewer sick days, fewer absences, higher job satisfaction, and higher work performance ratings • Broadens available talent pool • Reduces costs of providing on-site office space	• Makes it more difficult to appraise job performance • Can negatively affect the social network of the workplace and can make it difficult to promote team cohesiveness • Complicates distribution of tasks (Should office files, contact lists, and such be allowed to leave the office?)
To Individual	• Makes more time available for work and family by reducing or eliminating commute time • Reduces expenses of buying and maintaining office clothes. • Avoids office politics • Helps balance work and family • Expands employment opportunities for disabled individuals	• Can cause feeling of isolation from social network • Can raise concerns regarding promotions and other rewards due to being "out of sight, out of mind" • May diminish individual's influence within company due to limited opportunity to learn the corporate culture
To Society	• Decreases traffic congestion • Discourages community crime that might otherwise occur in bedroom communities • Increases time available to build community ties	• Increases need to resolve zoning regulations forbidding business deliveries in residential neighborhoods • May reduce ability to interact with other people in a personal, intimate manner

or indirectly) that employees who change their hours are not serious about their careers.

Home-Based and Other Mobile Work

As we noted in Chapter 1, telecommuting ➤ **P.22** ◄ has grown tremendously in recent years. Nearly 57 percent of U.S. workers now work at least several days per month at home.[60] Home-based workers can choose their own hours, interrupt work for child care and other tasks, and take time out for various personal reasons.[61] Working at home isn't for everyone, however. To be successful, a home-based worker must have the discipline to stay focused on the work and not be easily distracted.[62]

Telecommuting can be a cost saver for employers.[63] For example, IBM used to have a surplus of office space, maintaining more offices than there were employees. Now, the company has cut back on the number of offices, with employees telecommuting, "hoteling" (being assigned to a desk through a reservations system), and "hot-desking" (sharing a desk with other employees at different times).[64] About 10,000 IBM employees now share offices, typically with four people to an office, saving the company approximately $75 million per year in real estate expenses.[65] Figure 11.7 outlines the benefits and challenges of home-based work to organizations, individuals, and society.

Job-Sharing Plans

Job sharing is an arrangement whereby two part-time employees share one full-time job. The concept has received great attention as more and more women with small children have entered the labor force. Job sharing enables parents to work only during the hours their children are in school. It has also

FIGURE 11.7

BENEFITS AND CHALLENGES OF HOME-BASED WORK

Home-based work (also known as telecommuting) offers many benefits and challenges to organizations, individuals, and to society as a whole.

job sharing
An arrangement whereby two part-time employees share one full-time job.

proved beneficial to others with special needs, such as students and older people who want to work part-time before fully retiring. The benefits include:

- Employment opportunities to those who cannot or prefer not to work full-time.
- A high level of enthusiasm and productivity.
- Reduced absenteeism and tardiness.
- Ability to schedule people into peak demand periods (e.g., banks on payday) when part-time people are available.

However, as you might suspect, disadvantages include having to hire, train, motivate, and supervise twice as many people and to prorate some fringe benefits. Nonetheless, most firms that were at first reluctant to try job sharing are finding that the benefits outweigh the disadvantages.

CRITICAL THINKING

What effects have dual-career families had on the human resource function? What problems can arise when family members work together in the same firm? What is your reaction to employees who date one another?

PROGRESS ASSESSMENT

- Can you name and describe five alternative compensation techniques?
- What advantages do compensation plans such as profit sharing offer an organization?
- What are the benefits and challenges of flextime? Telecommuting? Job sharing?

MOVING EMPLOYEES UP, OVER, AND OUT

Employees don't always stay in the position they were initially hired to fill. They may excel and move up the corporate ladder or fail and move out the front door. In addition to being moved through promotion and termination, employees can be moved by reassignment and retirement. Of course, employees often choose to move themselves by quitting and going to another company.

Promoting and Reassigning Employees

Many companies find that promotion from within the company improves employee morale. Promotions are also cost-effective in that the promoted employees already familiar with the corporate culture and procedures do not need to spend valuable time on basic orientation.

Due to the prevalence of flatter corporate structures, there are fewer levels for employees to reach now as compared to the past. Therefore, it is more common today for workers to move *over* to a new position than to move *up* to one. Such transfers allow employees to develop and display new skills and to learn more about the company overall. This is one way of motivating experienced employees to remain in a company with few advancement opportunities.

Terminating Employees

As we discussed in previous chapters, downsizing and restructuring ➤ **P.238** ◄, increasing customer demands for greater value, and the relentless pressure of

Consultants offer this advice to minimize the chance of a lawsuit for wrongful discharge:

- Prepare before hiring by requiring recruits to sign a statement that retains management's freedom to terminate at will.
- Don't make unintentional promises by using such terms as *permanent employment.*
- Document reasons before firing and make sure you have an unquestionable business reason for the firing.
- Fire the worst first and be consistent in discipline.
- Buy out bad risk by offering severance pay in exchange for a signed release from any claims.
- Be sure to give employees the true reasons they are being fired. If you do not, you cannot reveal it to a recruiter asking for a reference without risking a defamation lawsuit.
- Disclose the reasons for an employee's dismissal to that person's potential new employers. For example, if you fired an employee for dangerous behavior and you withhold that information from your references, you can be sued if the employee commits a violent act at his or her next job.

Sources: "When Firing Can Backfire," *Washington Post,* March 2, 1997, p. H4; and "In Economics Old and New, Treatment of Workers is Paramount," *The Washington Post,* February 11, 2001, p. L1.

FIGURE 11.8

HOW TO AVOID WRONGFUL DISCHARGE LAWSUITS

global competition and shifts in technology have human resource managers struggling to manage layoffs and firings. Even companies that regain financial strength, however, are hesitant to rehire permanent employees. Why? One reason is that the cost of terminating employees is prohibitively high. The cost of firing comes from lost training costs as well as damages and legal fees paid in wrongful discharge suits. To save money, many companies are either using temporary employees or outsourcing > **P.254** < certain functions.[66]

At one time the prevailing employment doctrine was "employment at will." This meant that managers had as much freedom to fire workers as workers had to leave voluntarily. Most states now have written employment laws that limit the at-will doctrine to protect employees from wrongful firing; for example, an employer can no longer fire an employee simply because that person exposed the company's illegal actions, refused to violate a law, or was a member of a minority or other protected group. This well-meaning legislation restricted management's ability to terminate employees as it increased workers' rights to their jobs. In some cases, workers fired for using illegal drugs have sued on the ground that they have an illness (addiction) and are therefore protected by laws barring discrimination against the handicapped. See Figure 11.8 for advice about how to minimize the chance of wrongful-discharge lawsuits.

Retiring Employees

In addition to laying off employees, another tool used to downsize companies is to offer early retirement benefits to entice older (and more expensive) workers to retire. Such benefits usually involve financial incentives such as one-time cash payments, known in some companies as *golden handshakes.* The advantage of offering early retirement benefits over laying off employees is that early retirement offers increase the morale of the surviving employees. Retiring senior workers also increases promotion opportunities for younger employees.

Although you may have yet to begin your career, keep in mind for later that studies have shown that if you're offered early retirement, you should accept the first offer, when employers are more likely to feel guilty and, therefore, generous.

Losing Employees

In spite of a company's efforts to retain talented workers by offering flexible schedules, competitive salaries, and attractive fringe benefits, some employees will choose to pursue opportunities elsewhere. Learning about their reasons for leaving can be invaluable in preventing the loss of other good people in the future.[67] One way to learn the real reasons employees leave is to have a third party (not the employee's direct manager) conduct an exit interview. Harvard Pilgrim Health Care goes a step further—it offers a "knowledge bounty" of up to $5,000 for departing information left behind in a document or in a conversation with senior-level managers.[68]

LAWS AFFECTING HUMAN RESOURCE MANAGEMENT

Legislation has made hiring, promoting, firing, and managing employee relations in general very complex and subject to many legal complications and challenges. Let's see how changes in the law have expanded the role and the challenge of human resource management.

The U.S. government had little to do with human resource decisions until the 1930s. Since then, though, legislation and legal decisions have greatly affected all areas of human resource management, from hiring to training and working conditions (see the Legal Briefcase box). These laws were passed because many businesses would not exercise fair labor practices voluntarily.

One of the most important pieces of social legislation ever passed by Congress was the Civil Rights Act of 1964. This act generated much debate and was actually amended 97 times before final passage. Title VII of that act brought the government directly into the operations of human resource management. Title VII prohibits discrimination in hiring, firing, compensation, apprenticeships, training, terms, conditions, or privileges of employment based on race, religion, creed, sex, or national origin. Age was later added to the conditions of the act. The Civil Rights Act of 1964 was expected to stamp out discrimination in the workplace. However, specific language in the act often made its enforcement quite difficult. With this in mind, Congress took on the task of amending the law.

In 1972, the Equal Employment Opportunity Act (EEOA) was added as an amendment to Title VII. It strengthened the Equal Employment Opportunity Commission (EEOC), which was created by the Civil Rights Act of 1964. Congress gave rather broad powers to the EEOC. For example, it permitted the commission to issue guidelines for acceptable employer conduct in administering equal employment opportunity. The EEOC also set forth specific record-keeping procedures as mandatory. In addition, Congress vested the commission with the power of enforcement to ensure that these mandates were carried out. The EEOC became a formidable regulatory force in the administration of human resource management.[69]

affirmative action
Employment activities designed to "right past wrongs" by increasing opportunities for minorities and women.

Probably the most controversial program enforced by the EEOC concerns **affirmative action;** that is, activities designed to "right past wrongs" by increasing opportunities for minorities and women. Interpretation of the affirmative-action law eventually led employers to actively recruit and give preference to women and minority group members. As you might expect, interpretation of the law was often controversial, and enforcement difficult. Questions persisted about the legality of affirmative action and the effect the program could have in creating a sort of reverse discrimination in the workplace. **Reverse discrimination** has been defined as discrimination against whites or males. Charges of reverse discrimination have occurred when companies have been perceived as un-

reverse discrimination
Discrimination against whites or males in hiring or promoting.

LEGAL BRIEFCASE

Government Legislation

National Labor Relations Act of 1935. Established collective bargaining in labor–management relations and limited management interference in the right of employees to have a collective bargaining agent.

Fair Labor Standards Act of 1938. Established a minimum wage and overtime pay for employees working more than 40 hours a week.

Manpower Development and Training Act of 1962. Provided for the training and retraining of unemployed workers.

Equal Pay Act of 1963. Specified that men and women doing equal jobs must be paid the same wage.

The Civil Rights Act of 1964. Outlawed discrimination in employment based on sex, race, color, religion, or national origin.

Age Discrimination in Employment Act of 1967. Outlawed personnel practices that discriminate against people aged 40 to 69. An amendment outlaws company policies that require employees to retire before age 70.

Occupational Safety and Health Act of 1970. Regulated the degree to which employees can be exposed to hazardous substances and specified the safety equipment to be provided by the employer.

Equal Employment Opportunity Act of 1972. Strengthened the Equal Employment Opportunity Commission (EEOC) and authorized the EEOC to set guidelines for human resource management.

The Comprehensive Employment and Training Act of 1973. Provided funds for training unemployed workers. (Was known as the *CETA* program.)

Employee Retirement Income Security Act of 1974. Regulated company retirement programs and provided a federal insurance program for bankrupt retirement plans.

Immigration Reform and Control Act of 1986. Required employers to verify the eligibility for employment of *all* their new hires (including U.S. citizens).

Supreme Court ruling against set-aside programs (affirmative action), 1989. Declared that setting aside 30 percent of contracting jobs for minority businesses was reverse discrimination and therefore unconstitutional.

Older Workers Benefit Protection Act, 1990. Protects older people from signing away their rights to things like pensions or to fight against illegal age discrimination.

Civil Rights Act of 1991. Applies to firms with over 15 employees. It extends the right to a jury trial and punitive damages to victims of intentional job discrimination.

Americans with Disabilities Act (1992 implementation). Prohibits employers from discriminating against qualified disabled individuals in hiring, advancement, or compensation, and requires them to adapt the workplace if necessary.

Family and Medical Leave Act of 1993. Businesses with 50 or more employees must provide up to 12 weeks of unpaid leave per year upon birth or adoption of employee's child or upon serious illness of parent, spouse, or child.

---

fairly giving preference to women or minority group members in hiring and promoting. The term has generated much heated debate.

The Civil Rights Act of 1991 expanded the remedies available to victims of discrimination by amending Title VII of the Civil Rights Act of 1964. Now victims of discrimination have the right to a jury trial and punitive damages. One still-open question is whether or not companies would have to establish "quotas" in hiring. Human resource managers continue to follow court cases closely to see how the law is enforced. This issue is likely to persist for years to come.

Laws Protecting the Disabled and Older Employees

The courts have continued their activity in issues involving human resource management. As you read above, the courts look carefully into any improprieties concerning possible discrimination in hiring, firing, training, and so forth specifically related to race or sex. The Vocational Rehabilitation Act of

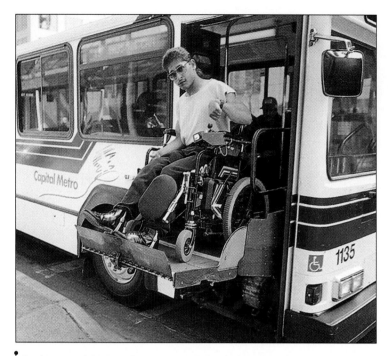

In the United States, everyone is guaranteed equal opportunity. In 1990, the U.S. Congress passed the Americans with Disabilities Act that required businesses, including public transportation systems, to make "reasonable accommodations" to persons with disabilities. How do such laws affect businesses?

1973 extended the same protection to people with disabilities. Today, businesses cannot discriminate against people on the basis of any physical or mental handicap.

The Americans with Disabilities Act (ADA) of 1990 requires employers to give disabled applicants the same consideration for employment as people without disabilities. It also requires that businesses make "reasonable accommodations" for people with disabilities. This means doing such things as modifying equipment or widening doorways. Reasonable accommodations are not always expensive. For about $6 a month, a company can rent a headset phone that allows someone with cerebral palsy to talk on the phone and write at the same time. The ADA also protects disabled individuals from discrimination in public accommodations, transportation, and telecommunications.

Equal opportunity for people with disabilities promises to be a continuing issue into the next decade. Most companies are not having trouble making structural changes to be accommodating; what they are finding difficult are the cultural changes. Employers used to think being fair meant treating everyone the same. Now a key concept is *accommodation*, which means treating different people differently. In 1997, the EEOC issued new ADA guidelines that tell employers how they are supposed to treat workers and applicants with mental disabilities. The accommodations include putting up barriers to isolate people readily distracted by noise, reassigning workers to new tasks, and making changes in supervisors' management styles.[70]

Older employees are also guaranteed protection against discrimination in the workplace. Courts have ruled against firms in unlawful-discharge suits where age appeared to be the major factor in the dismissal. Additionally, protection through the Age Discrimination in Employment Act outlawed mandatory retirement in most organizations before age 70. Many companies are voluntarily phasing out mandatory retirement after age 70 as well.

Effects of Legislation

Clearly, legislation affects all areas of human resource management. Such legislation ranges from the Social Security Act of 1935, to the Occupational Safety and Health Act of 1970, to the Employment Retirement Income Security Act of 1974.[71] Human resource managers must read *The Wall Street Journal, Business Week,* and other current publications to keep up with all human resource legislation and rulings.

We have devoted so much space to civil rights and related legislation because such decisions have greatly affected human resource programs and will continue to do so. It's apparent that a career in human resource management offers a challenge to anyone willing to put forth the effort. In summary:

• Employers must know and act in accordance with the legal rights of their employees or risk costly court cases.

- Legislation affects all areas of human resource management, from hiring and training to compensating employees.

- Court cases have made it clear that it is sometimes legal to go beyond providing equal rights for minorities and women to provide special employment (affirmative action) and training to correct discrimination in the past.

- New court cases and legislation change human resource management almost daily; the only way to keep current is to read the business literature and become familiar with the issues.

Can you explain what was covered by the following laws?

PROGRESS ASSESSMENT

- The Civil Rights Act of 1964.
- The Equal Employment Opportunity Act of 1972.
- The Americans with Disabilities Act of 1990.

SUMMARY

1. Human resource management is the process of evaluating human resource needs, finding people to fill those needs, and getting the best work from each employee by providing the right incentives and job environment, all with the goal of meeting organizational objectives.
   - *What are some of the current challenges and opportunities in the human resource area?*
   Many of the current challenges and opportunities revolve around the changing demographics of workers: more women, minorities, immigrants, and older workers. Other challenges concern a shortage of trained workers and an abundance of unskilled workers, skilled workers in declining industries requiring retraining, changing employee work attitudes, and complex laws and regulations.

   1. Explain the importance of human resource management and describe current issues in managing human resources.

2. Like all other types of management, human resource management begins with planning.
   - *What are the steps in human resource planning?*
   The six steps are (1) preparing forecasts of future human resource needs; (2) preparing a human resource inventory of the organization's employees; (3) preparing a job analysis; (4) assessing future demand; (5) assessing future supply; and (6) establishing a plan for recruiting, hiring, educating, appraising, compensating, and scheduling employees.

   2. Summarize the six steps in planning human resources.

3. Recruitment is the set of activities used to obtain a sufficient number of the right people at the right time to select those who best meet the needs of the organization.
   - *What methods do human resource managers use to recruit new employees?*
   Recruiting sources are classified as either internal or external. Internal sources include hiring from within the firm (transfers, promotions, etc.) and employees who recommend others to hire. External recruitment sources include advertisements, public and private employment agencies, college placement bureaus, management consultants, professional organizations, referrals, walk-in applications, and the Internet.

   3. Describe methods that companies use to recruit new employees and explain some of the issues that make recruitment challenging.

• *Why has recruitment become more difficult?*

Legal restrictions complicate hiring and firing practices. Finding suitable employees can also be made more difficult if companies are considered unattractive workplaces.

4. Outline the six steps in selecting employees.

4. Selection is the process of gathering and interpreting information to decide which applicants should be hired.

• *What are the six steps in the selection process?*

The steps are (1) obtaining complete application forms; (2) conducting initial and follow-up interviews; (3) giving employment tests; (4) conducting background investigations; (5) obtaining results from physical exams; and (6) establishing a trial period of employment.

5. Illustrate the use of various types of employee training and development methods.

5. Employee training and development include all attempts to improve employee performance by increasing an employee's ability to perform through learning.

• *What are some of the procedures used for training?*

Training procedures include employee orientation, on- and off-the-job training, apprentice programs, online training, vestibule training, and job simulation.

• *What methods are used to develop managerial skills?*

Management development methods include on-the-job coaching, understudy positions, job rotation, and off-the-job courses and training.

• *How does networking fit in this process?*

Networking is the process of establishing contacts with key managers within and outside the organization to get additional development assistance.

6. Trace the six steps in appraising employee performance.

6. A performance appraisal is an evaluation of the performance level of employees against established standards to make decisions about promotions, compensation, additional training, or firing.

• *How is performance evaluated?*

The steps are (1) establish performance standards; (2) communicate those standards; (3) evaluate performance; (4) discuss results; (5) take corrective action when needed; and (6) use the results for decisions about promotions, compensation, additional training, or firing.

7. Summarize the objectives of employee compensation programs, and describe various pay systems and fringe benefits.

7. Employee compensation is one of the largest operating costs for many organizations.

• *What kind of compensation systems are used?*

They include salary systems, hourly wages, piecework, commission plans, bonus plans, profit-sharing plans, and stock options.

• *What types of compensation systems are appropriate for teams?*

The most common are gains-sharing and skill-based compensation programs. It is also important to reward outstanding individual performance within teams.

• *What are fringe benefits?*

Fringe benefits include such items as sick leave, vacation pay, pension plans, and health plans that provide additional compensation to employees beyond base wages.

8. Explain scheduling plans managers use to adjust to workers' needs.

8. Workers' increasing need for flexibility has generated new innovations in scheduling.

• *What scheduling plans can be used to adjust to employees' need for flexibility?*

Such plans include job sharing, flextime, compressed workweeks, and working at home.

9. Employees often move from their original positions in a company.
   • *How can employees move within a company?*
   Employees can be moved up (promotion), over (reassignment), or out (termination or retirement) of a company. Employees can also choose to leave a company to pursue opportunities elsewhere.

9. Describe the ways employees can move through a company: promotion, reassignment, termination, and retirement.

10. There are many laws that affect human resource planning.
   • *What are those laws?*
   See the Legal Briefcase box on p. 353 and review the text section on laws. This is an important subject for future managers to study.

10. Illustrate the effects of legislation on human resource management.

KEY TERMS

affirmative action 352
apprentice programs 339
cafeteria-style fringe benefits 347
compressed workweek 348
contingent workers 337
core time 348
employee orientation 338
flextime plan 348
fringe benefits 346

human resource management 328
job analysis 332
job description 332
job sharing 349
job simulation 340
job specifications 332
management development 340
mentor 341
networking 341
off-the-job training 339

on-the-job training 338
online training 339
performance appraisal 342
recruitment 333
reverse discrimination 352
selection 335
training and development 338
vestibule training 340

DEVELOPING WORKPLACE SKILLS

1. Look in the classified ads in your local newspaper and find at least two positions that you might like to have when you graduate. List the qualifications specified in each of the ads. Identify methods the companies might use to determine how well applicants meet each of those qualifications.

2. Read several current business periodicals to find information on the latest court rulings involving fringe benefits, affirmative action, and other human resource issues. Compose a summary of your findings. What seems to be the trend? What will this mean for tomorrow's college graduates?

3. Recall the various training programs you have experienced. Think of both on-the-job and off-the-job training sessions. What is your evaluation of such programs? Write a brief critique of each. How would you improve them? Share your ideas with the class.

4. Consider these occupations: doctor, computer salesperson, computer software developer, teacher, and assembly worker. Identify the method of compensation you think is appropriate for determining the wages for each of these workers. Explain your answer.

5. Choose one of these positions: a human resource manager notifying employees of mandatory drug testing or an employee representative protesting such testing. Write a memorandum supporting your position.

TAKING IT TO THE NET

Purpose

To use job-search websites to identify employment options and to compare the services offered by several recruiting-related sites.

Exercise

1

There are many recruiting-related sites on the Internet. You can find links to such sites at Teleport Internet Services' Job Central website (www.teleport.com/destinations/job.phtml). Select three job-search websites (found in the list of National Employment Resources). Use the search feature in each site to try to identify a position for which you might qualify after graduation. Find the website for the companies offering the jobs.

1. Do some job search engines offer services that the others don't? Compare the strengths and weaknesses of each site from both the job seeker and employer perspectives. Include such criteria as variety of occupations in the database, volume of jobs, number of employers, geographical locations, ease of use, supplemental job hunting advice, and unique features.

2. What types of information did the individual companies' websites offer to attract potential employees?

TAKING IT TO THE NET

Purpose

The purpose of this exercise is two-fold. From a manager's perspective, the purpose is to illustrate the types of questions managers typically ask during interviews. From an applicant's perspective, the purpose is to practice answering such questions in a safe environment.

2

Exercise

Go to Monster Campus at http://campus.monster.com. Answer the sample interview questions in the Virtual Interview section. This interactive section gives you to the opportunity to test your answers so that when you do go on an actual interview you are less likely to fumble for an answer.

PRACTICING MANAGEMENT DECISIONS

CASE
DUAL-CAREER PLANNING

Carey Moler is a 32-year-old account executive for a communications company. She is married to Mitchell Moler, a lawyer. Carey and Mitchell did not make any definite plans about how to juggle their careers and family life until Carey reached age 30. Then they decided to have a baby, and career planning took on a whole new dimension. A company named Catalyst talked to 815 dual-career couples and found that most of them, like the Molers, had not made any long-range career decisions regarding family lifestyle.

From the business perspective, such dual-career families create real concerns. There are problems with relocation, with child care, and so on that affect recruiting, productivity, morale, and promotion policies.

For a couple such as the Molers, having both career and family responsibilities is exhausting. But that is just one problem. If Carey is moving up in her firm, what happens if Mitchell gets a terrific job offer a thousand miles away? What if Carey gets such an offer? Who is going to care for the baby? What happens if the baby becomes ill? How do they plan their vacations when there are three schedules to balance? Who will do the housework?

Dual careers require careful planning and discussion, and those plans need to be reviewed over time. A couple who decide at age 22 to do certain things may change their minds at 30. Whether or not to have children, where to locate, how to manage the household—all such issues and more can become major problems if not carefully planned.

The same is true for corporations. They, too, must plan for dual-career families. They must give attention to job sharing, flextime, paternity leave policies, transfer policies, nepotism rules (i.e., rules about hiring family members), and more.

Decision Questions

1. What are some of the issues you can see developing because of dual-career families? How is this affecting children in such families?
2. What kind of corporate policies need changing to adapt to these new realities?
3. What are the advantages of dual careers? Disadvantages? What can newlywed couples do to minimize the problems of dual careers? How can a couple achieve the advantages?

VIDEO CASE

NEED SOME HELP?

Rarely have times been more difficult for human resource managers. There is a tremendous demand for skilled workers and a scarcity of supply. Companies are doing everything they can to lure people to their firms. That includes stock options, health clubs, and more. But, when push comes to shove, there are times when a company needs someone and needs them NOW. That's where companies such as Creative Staffing Solutions come in. They provide part-time help for a variety of functions. Such jobs are a good deal for the employee because they may lead to full-time work. They are good for those who hire them because they get trained workers when they need them. And, of course, they are good for staffing firms because the demand is so great.

Creative Staffing Solutions is a minority-run firm. That means that they have a special relationship with larger firms who are seeking diversity in both employees and suppliers of those employees. The people that Creative Staffing places vary from those who answer phones to high-level executives and information technology specialists. The people Creative Staffing finds jobs for are carefully screened, and trained if necessary.

Finding the right people for the job begins with research. Creative Staffing personnel meet with the CEO or human resource manager of a company to learn exactly what the needs are. Then the task is to find people to fill those slots. One way to do that is to go on the Internet and search for people who are looking for a job. It's a two-way search really, and both staffing companies and job seekers benefit from finding each other. The staffing company can evaluate your skills, train you, and find you a job.

Human resource management is made easier by companies like Creative Staffing Solutions. Without their help, HRM departments would have to be much larger and the expense would be tremendous. Have you ever tried finding a job at such a firm?

Discussion Questions

1. What are the main advantages of finding part-time workers through a staffing agency?
2. What do you see are the disadvantages of finding part-time employees through staffing agencies like Creative Staffing Solutions?
3. What are the advantages of working with a minority firm when seeking new employees? Do you see any advantages?
4. How important do you think it is to have a diverse workforce at this time? What are some of the ways a company can create diversity other than through race and gender?

CHAPTER 12

Dealing with Employee–Management Issues and Relationships

LEARNING GOALS

AFTER YOU HAVE READ AND STUDIED THIS CHAPTER, YOU SHOULD BE ABLE TO

1. Trace the history of organized labor in the United States and discuss the major legislation affecting labor unions.

2. Outline the objectives of labor unions.

3. Describe the tactics used by labor and management during conflicts and discuss the role of unions in the future.

4. Explain some of the controversial employee–management issues such as executive compensation; comparable worth; child care and elder care; AIDS testing, drug testing, and violence in the workplace; and employee stock ownership plans (ESOPs).

Getting to Know Don Fehr, Executive Director of the Major League Baseball Players Association

Ever thought about the benefits of joining a labor union? Well, whether you have or have not, consider the conditions of one union's most recent negotiated labor–management agreement: Union members are paid a minimum wage of $200,000 for a maximum nine-month work year. The wages are paid irrespective of whether the employee works every day or not. Also, after just a few successful years on the job, the possibility of expanding employee wages well into the millions is almost guaranteed, again for the same time period of nine months.

Sound enticing? Wondering how to get an application for membership in this union? The man to write is Donald Fehr, the executive director and general counsel for the Major League Baseball Players Association (MLBPA). Fehr has been executive director of the MLBPA since 1988, when he replaced the union's legendary founder, Marvin Miller, who forged the first collective bargaining agreement in the sport's history. As the top executive in the players union, Fehr has been at the forefront of baseball's highs and lows over the past 15 years. It's no wonder that after such a long tenure in a difficult job, he elicits varying opinions of his efforts from different individuals. For example, under Fehr's leadership professional baseball players have seen their salaries escalate to levels equal to those of top corporate executives. Fehr continues to enjoy the players' enthusiastic support. However, longtime fans of the game complain that inflated salaries for players have made it impossible for younger fans and families to afford tickets to games.

Other critics blame Fehr for the union's work stoppage in 1994 that forced the cancellation of the World Series that season. Many of the game's historians and analysts insist that the strike badly tarnished baseball's reputation and that the national pastime is only slowly recovering from that black mark in its history.

Obviously, Don Fehr is a controversial figure who arouses conflicting emotions. While few would argue over the past two decades that the nature of professional sports and the stature of professional athletes have both changed, many question how far players' demands will go. Also, some fear that the wealthy teams in large markets will continue to dominate the game by paying ever-increasing salaries to the sport's best performers, since better performers mean better chances for championships.

Controversies such as these are the subject of this chapter. Labor–management relations, executive pay, and comparable worth will dominate the headlines and thoughts of businesspeople, workers, and consumers well into the new millennium. This chapter will familiarize you with all these topics.

Sources: Bill Chastain, "Baseball Can't Withstand Labor Dispute," *Tampa Tribune,* March 5, 2000, p. 14; Michael K. Ozanian and Kurt Badenhausen, "Baseball Going Broke? Don't Believe It," *The Wall Street Journal,* July 27, 2000, p. A23; "Selig's Contract Negotiations a Risky Business," *USA Today,* January 26, 2001, p. 3C; and Walter R. Mears, "Bush Says Baseball Must Find Solutions," *The Washington Times,* January 20, 2001, p. C1.

EMPLOYEE–MANAGEMENT ISSUES

The relationship between managers and employees has never been very smooth. Management has the responsibility to produce a profit through maximum productivity ➤ **P.23** ◄. Managers have to make hard decisions that often do not let them win popularity contests. Labor (the collective term for nonmanagement workers) is interested in fair and competent management, human dignity, and a reasonable share in the wealth its work generates. Many issues affect the relationship between managers and employees: executive compensation, comparable worth, child care and elder care, AIDS testing and drug testing, violence in the workplace, and employee stock ownership plans (ESOPs). This chapter discusses such issues.

Like other managerial challenges, employee–management issues must be worked out through open discussion, goodwill, and compromise. It is important to know both sides of an issue, however, in order to make reasoned decisions.

Any discussion of employee–management relations in the United States probably should begin with a discussion of labor unions. **Unions** are employee organizations that have the main goal of representing members in employee–management bargaining over job-related issues. Workers originally formed unions to protect themselves from intolerable work conditions and unfair treatment from owners and managers. They also united to secure some say in the operations of their jobs. As the number of union members grew, workers gained more negotiating power with managers and more political power as well.

Historically, employees turned to unions for assistance in gaining specific workplace rights and benefits. Labor unions were largely responsible for the establishment of minimum-wage laws, overtime rules, worker's compensation, severance pay, child-labor laws, job safety regulations, and more. Recently, however, union strength has waned. Throughout the 1990s, unions failed to regain the power they once had and membership continued to decline. Business observers suggest that global competition, shifts from manufacturing to service and high-tech industries, growth in part-time work, and changes in management philosophies are some of the reasons for labor's decline.

While many labor analysts forecast that unions may regain strength in the 21st century, others suggest that unions have seen their brightest days.[1] Still, there's no question that the role and position of unions in the workplace will continue to arouse emotions and opinions that contrast considerably. Let's briefly look at some different viewpoints concerning labor unions and then look at other key issues affecting employee–management relations.

unions
Employee organizations that have the main goal of representing members in employee–management bargaining over job-related issues.

LABOR UNIONS FROM DIFFERENT PERSPECTIVES

Are labor unions essential in the American economy today? This question is certain to evoke emotional responses from various participants in the workplace.[2] An electrician carrying a picket sign in New York might elaborate on the dangers to our free society if employers continue to try to "bust," or break apart, authorized unions. Small manufacturers would likely embrace a different perspective and complain about having to operate under union wage and benefit obligations in a growing global economy.

Most historians generally agree that today's unions are an outgrowth of the economic transition caused by the Industrial Revolution of the 19th and early

20th centuries. Workers who once toiled in the fields, dependent on the mercies of nature for survival, suddenly became dependent on the continuous roll of the factory presses and assembly lines for their living. Breaking away from an agricultural economy to form an industrial economy was quite difficult. Over time, workers learned that strength through unity (unions) could lead to improved job conditions, better wages, and job security.

Critics of organized labor maintain that few of the inhuman conditions that once dominated U.S. industry still exist in the workplace. They charge that organized labor has in fact become a large industrial entity in itself and that the real issue of protecting workers has become secondary. Critics also maintain that the current legal system and management attitudes minimize the chances that the sweatshops of the late 19th and early 20th centuries will reappear in the United States.[3] They do appear in other countries, however, and workers around the world are struggling to gain the right to join unions. A short discussion of the history of labor unions will cast a better light on the issues involved.

The Early History of Organized Labor

The presence of formal labor organizations in the United States dates back almost to the time of the American Revolution. As early as 1792, cordwainers (shoemakers) in Philadelphia met to discuss fundamental work issues of pay, hours, conditions, and job security—many of the same issues that dominate labor negotiations today. The cordwainers were a **craft union,** which is an organization of skilled specialists in a particular craft or trade. They were typical of the labor organizations formed before the Civil War in that they were local or regional in membership. Also, most were established to achieve some short-range goal such as curtailing the use of convict labor as an alternative to available free labor (this is still an issue in some states). Often, after attaining a specific objective, the labor group disbanded. This situation changed dramatically in the late 19th century with the expansion of the Industrial Revolution.

The Industrial Revolution changed the economic structure of the United States.[4] Enormous productivity increases gained through mass production and job specialization made the United States a true world economic power. This growth, however, brought problems for workers in terms of productivity expectations, hours of work, wages, and unemployment.

Workers were faced with the reality that production was vital. Anyone who failed to produce lost his or her job. People had to go to work even if they were ill or had family problems. Over time, the increased emphasis on production led firms to expand the hours of work. The length of the average workweek in 1900 was 60 hours, but an 80-hour week was not uncommon for some industries. Wages were low, and the use of child labor was widespread. Furthermore, periods of unemployment were hard on families who lived on subsistence wages. As you can sense, these were not short-term issues that would easily go away. The workplace was ripe for the emergence of national labor organizations.

STRIKE SYMPATHIZERS

Historically, workers formed unions to gain basic rights and benefits in the workplace. Unions succeeded in making some significant changes in wages and work conditions. Here two young union sympathizers encourage others to support the union and "Don't Be A Scab" (a worker that takes the job of a striking union member). Is it fair to take the job of a union worker during a strike?

craft union
An organization of skilled specialists in a particular craft or trade.

Knights of Labor
The first national labor union; formed in 1869.

American Federation of Labor (AFL)
An organization of craft unions that championed fundamental labor issues; founded in 1886.

industrial unions
Labor organizations of unskilled and semiskilled workers in mass-production industries such as automobiles and mining.

Congress of Industrial Organizations (CIO)
Union organization of unskilled workers; broke away from the AFL in 1935 and rejoined it in 1955.

The first truly national labor organization was the **Knights of Labor,** formed by Uriah Smith Stephens in 1869. By 1886, the Knights claimed a membership of 700,000. The organization offered membership to all working people, including employers, and promoted social causes as well as labor and economic issues. The intention of the Knights was to gain significant political power and eventually to restructure the entire U.S. economy. The organization fell from prominence after being blamed for a bomb that killed eight policemen during a labor rally at Haymarket Square in Chicago in 1886.[5]

A rival group, the **American Federation of Labor (AFL),** was formed that same year. By 1890, the AFL, under the dynamic leadership of Samuel Gompers, stood at the forefront of the labor movement.[6] The AFL was an organization of craft unions that championed fundamental labor issues. It intentionally limited membership to skilled workers (craftspeople), assuming they would have better bargaining power than unskilled workers in attaining concessions from employers. It's important to note that the AFL was never one big union. Rather, it functioned as a federation of many individual unions that could become members yet keep their separate union status. Over time, an unauthorized AFL group, called the Committee of Industrial Organization, began to organize workers in **industrial unions,** which consisted of unskilled and semiskilled workers in mass-production industries such as automobile manufacturing and mining. John L. Lewis, president of the United Mine Workers, led this committee.

Lewis's objective was to organize both craftspeople and unskilled workers. When the AFL rejected his proposal in 1935, Lewis broke away to form the **Congress of Industrial Organizations (CIO).** The CIO soon rivaled the AFL in membership, partly because of the passage of the National Labor Relations Act (also called the Wagner Act) that same year (see below). For 20 years, the two organizations struggled for power in the labor movement. It wasn't until passage of the Taft-Hartley Act in 1947 that the two organizations saw the benefits of a merger. In 1955, under the leadership of George Meany, 16 million labor members united to form the AFL–CIO. Today, the AFL–CIO includes affiliations with 68 national and international labor unions.[7]

Failing to reach a fair contract under collective bargaining can cause a strike or boycott by the union. Here actor Rob Schneider encourages the public to boycott Procter & Gamble products because the company used nonunion workers in its commercials in place of striking members of the Screen Actor's Guild. Why do management and labor unions work hard to prevent strikes?

LABOR LEGISLATION AND COLLECTIVE BARGAINING

The growth and influence of organized labor in the United States have primarily depended on two major factors: the law and public opinion. Figure 12.1 outlines five major federal laws that have had a significant impact on the rights and operations of labor unions. (Take a few moments to read the basics involved in each of these laws before going on.)

The National Labor Relations Act, or Wagner Act, provided labor with legal justification to pursue key issues that were strongly supported by Samuel

Norris–La Guardia Act, 1932	Prohibited courts from issuing injunctions against nonviolent union activities; outlawed contracts forbidding union activities; outlawed the use of yellow-dog contracts by employers. (Yellow-dog contracts were contractual agreements forced on workers by employers whereby the employee agreed not to join a union as a condition of employment.)
National Labor Relations Act (Wagner Act), 1935	Gave employees the right to form or join labor organizations (or to refuse to form or join); the right to collectively bargain with employers through elected union representatives; and the right to engage in labor activities such as strikes, picketing, and boycotts. Prohibited certain unfair labor practices by the employer and the union, and established the National Labor Relations Board to oversee union election campaigns and investigate labor practices. This act gave great impetus to the union movement.
Fair Labor Standards Act, 1938	Set a minimum wage and maximum basic hours for workers in interstate commerce industries. The first minimum wage set was 25 cents an hour, except for farm and retail workers.
Labor–Management Relations Act (Taft-Hartley Act), 1947	Amended the Wagner Act; permitted states to pass laws prohibiting compulsory union membership (right-to-work laws); set up methods to deal with strikes that affect national health and safety; prohibited secondary boycotts, closed-shop agreements, and featherbedding (the requiring of wage payments for work not performed) by unions. This act gave more power to management.
Labor–Management Reporting and Disclosure Act (Landrum-Griffin Act), 1959	Amended the Taft-Hartley Act and the Wagner Act; guaranteed individual rights of union members in dealing with their union, such as the right to nominate candidates for union office, vote in union elections, attend and participate in union meetings, vote on union business, and examine union records and accounts; required annual financial reports to be filed with the U.S. Department of Labor. One goal of this act was to clean up union corruption.

FIGURE 12.1

MAJOR LEGISLATION AFFECTING LABOR–MANAGEMENT RELATIONS

Gompers and the AFL. One of these issues, **collective bargaining,** is the process whereby union and management representatives put together a contract for workers. The Wagner Act expanded labor's right to collectively bargain, and legally obligated employers to meet at reasonable times and bargain in good faith with respect to wages, hours, and other terms and conditions of employment. Gompers believed collective bargaining was the key to attaining a fairer share of the economic pie for workers. He further believed that collective bargaining would enhance the well-being of workers by improving conditions on the job.

The Wagner Act also established an administrative agency, the National Labor Relations Board (NLRB), to oversee labor–management relations. The NLRB provides guidelines and offers legal protection to workers who seek to vote on organizing a union to represent them in the workplace. **Certification** is the formal process whereby a labor union is recognized by the NLRB as the authorized bargaining agent for a group of employees. Figure 12.2 describes the steps involved in a union-organizing campaign leading to certification. The Wagner Act also provided workers with a clear process to remove a union as the workers' representative. **Decertification,** also described in Figure 12.2, is the process by which workers take away a union's right to represent them.

collective bargaining
The process whereby union and management representatives form a labor–management agreement, or contract, for workers.

certification
Process of a union's becoming recognized by the National Labor Relations Board as the bargaining agent for a group of employees.

decertification
The process by which workers take away a union's right to represent them.

Objectives of Organized Labor

As you might suspect, the objectives of organized labor frequently change according to shifts in social and economic trends. For example, in the 1970s the primary objective of labor unions was to obtain additional pay and benefits for their members. Throughout the 1980s, objectives shifted toward issues related to job security and union recognition. In the 1990s, unions also

FIGURE 12.2

STEPS IN UNION-ORGANIZING AND DECERTIFICATION CAMPAIGNS

Note that the final vote in each case requires that the union receive over 50 percent of the *votes cast.* Note, too, that the election is secret.

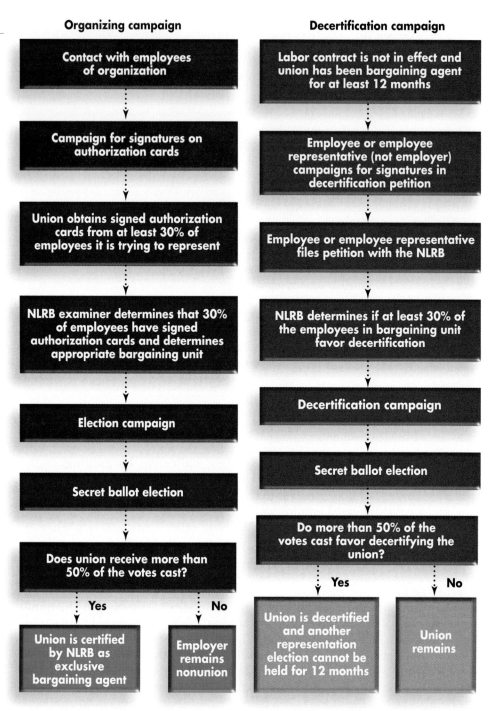

Organizing campaign

Contact with employees of organization

Campaign for signatures on authorization cards

Union obtains signed authorization cards from at least 30% of employees it is trying to represent

NLRB examiner determines that 30% of employees have signed authorization cards and determines appropriate bargaining unit

Election campaign

Secret ballot election

Does union receive more than 50% of the votes cast?

Yes   No

Union is certified by NLRB as exclusive bargaining agent

Employer remains nonunion

Decertification campaign

Labor contract is not in effect and union has been bargaining agent for at least 12 months

Employee or employee representative (not employer) campaigns for signatures in decertification petition

Employee or employee representative files petition with the NLRB

NLRB determines if at least 30% of the employees in bargaining unit favor decertification

Decertification campaign

Secret ballot election

Do more than 50% of the votes cast favor decertifying the union?

Yes   No

Union is decertified and another representation election cannot be held for 12 months

Union remains

focused on job security, but the issue of global competition and its effects often took center stage. The AFL–CIO, for example, was a major opponent of the North American Free Trade Agreement (NAFTA) passed by Congress in 1994; it also opposed Congress's decision to normalize trade relations with China in 2000.[8] The labor organization also was instrumental in encouraging Congress in 1997 to deny President Bill Clinton's request to speed up trade agreements through what is called fast-track legislation.

The **negotiated labor–management agreement,** more informally referred to as the *labor contract,* sets the tone and clarifies the terms and condi-

negotiated labor–management agreement (labor contract)
Agreement that sets the tone and clarifies the terms under which management and labor agree to function over a period of time.

1. Management rights
2. Union recognition
3. Union security clause
4. Strikes and lockouts
5. Union activities and responsibilities
   a. Dues checkoff
   b. Union bulletin boards
   c. Work slowdowns
6. Wages
   a. Wage structure
   b. Shift differentials
   c. Wage incentives
   d. Bonuses
   e. Piecework conditions
   f. Tiered wage structures
7. Hours of work and time-off policies
   a. Regular hours of work
   b. Holidays
   c. Vacation policies

    d. Overtime regulations
    e. Leaves of absence
    f. Break periods
    g. Flextime
    h. Meal time allotments
8. Job rights and seniority principles
    a. Seniority regulations
    b. Transfer policies and bumping
    c. Promotions
    d. Layoffs and recall procedures
    e. Job bidding and posting
9. Discharge and discipline
    a. Suspension
    b. Conditions for discharge
10. Grievance procedures
    a. Arbitration agreement
    b. Mediation procedures
11. Employee benefits, health, and welfare

FIGURE 12.3

ISSUES IN A NEGOTIATED LABOR–MANAGEMENT AGREEMENT

Labor and management often meet to discuss and clarify the terms that specify employees' functions within the company. The topics listed in this figure are typically discussed during these meetings.

tions under which management and organized labor will function over a specific period. Negotiations cover a wide range of topics and can often take a long time. Figure 12.3 provides a list of topics commonly negotiated by labor and management before reaching an agreement.

A **union security clause** stipulates that employees who reap benefits from a union must either officially join or at least pay dues to the union. After passage of the Wagner Act, organized labor sought strict security in the form of the

union security clause
Provision in a negotiated labor–management agreement that stipulates that employees who benefit from a union must either officially join or at least pay dues to the union.

NAFTA has been a thorn in organized labor's side since its approval in 1994. This photo illustrates labor's key opposition to NAFTA (NAFTA causes the loss of U.S. jobs). Since passage of NAFTA, the United States has seen a shift from a trade surplus to a growing deficit with Mexico. Do you feel trade agreements such as NAFTA cost the U.S. jobs?

FIGURE 12.4

**DIFFERENT FORMS OF
UNION AGREEMENTS**

TYPE OF AGREEMENT	DESCRIPTION
Closed shop	The Taft-Hartley act made this form of agreement illegal. Under this type of labor agreement, employers could hire only current union members for a job.
Union shop	The majority of labor agreements are of this type. In a union shop, the employer can hire anyone, but as a condition of employment, employees hired must join the union to keep their jobs.
Agency shop	Employers may hire anyone. Employees need not join the union, but are required to pay a union fee. A small percentage of labor agreements are of this type.
Open shop	Union membership is voluntary for new and existing employees. Those who don't join the union don't have to pay union dues. Few union contracts are of this type.

**closed shop
agreement**
Clause in a labor–management agreement that specified that workers had to be members of a union before being hired (outlawed in 1947).

**union shop
agreement**
Clause in a labor–management agreement that says workers do not have to be members of a union to be hired, but must agree to join the union within a prescribed period.

**agency shop
agreement**
Clause in a labor–management agreement that says employers may hire nonunion workers; employees are not required to join the union but must pay a union fee.

right-to-work laws
Legislation that gives workers the right, under an open shop, to join or not join a union if it is present.

open shop agreement
Agreement in right-to-work states that gives workers the option to join or not join a union, if one exists in their workplace.

closed-shop agreement. A **closed shop agreement** specified that workers had to be members of a union before being hired for a job. To labor's dismay, the Labor–Management Relations Act (Taft-Hartley Act) outlawed this practice in 1947 (see Figure 12.4). Today, labor clearly favors the union shop agreement as the most effective means of ensuring workers' security. Under the **union shop agreement,** workers do not have to be members of a union to be hired for a job, but must agree to join the union within a prescribed period (usually 30, 60, or 90 days). Under a contingency called an **agency shop agreement,** employers may hire nonunion workers; these workers are not required to join the union, but must pay a special union fee or pay regular union dues. Unions justify payment of a fee or dues under an agency shop agreement because they represent all workers in collective bargaining undertaken by the union, not just the union's members.

The Taft-Hartley Act recognized the legality of the union shop but granted individual states the power to outlaw such agreements through passage of **right-to-work laws.** To date, 21 states have passed such legislation (see Figure 12.5). In a right-to-work state, an **open shop agreement** gives workers the option to join or not join a union, if one is present in the workplace. Furthermore, if they choose not to join the union that is certified in their workplace, they cannot be forced to pay a fee or dues to the union.

In the future, the focus of union negotiations may continue to shift as issues such as child and elder care, worker retraining, two-tiered wage plans, employee empowerment ➤ **P.20** ◄, and even integrity and honesty testing further challenge union members' rights in the workplace. Unions also intend to carefully monitor global agreements such as NAFTA to see that U.S. jobs are not lost.[9]

Resolving Labor–Management Disagreements

The rights of labor and management are outlined in the negotiated labor–management agreement. Upon acceptance by both sides, the agreement becomes a guide to work relations between the firm's employees and managers. However, signing the agreement doesn't necessarily end the employee–management negotiations. As you might suspect, there are sometimes differences concerning interpretations of the labor–management agreement. For ex-

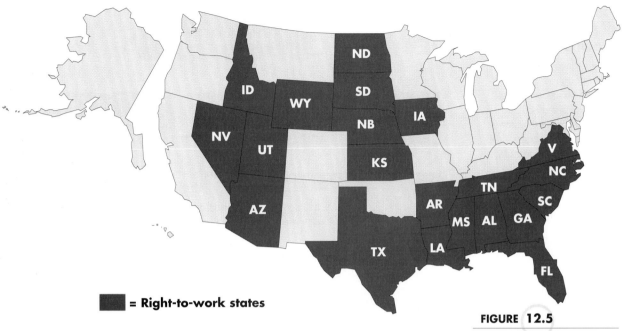

= **Right-to-work states**

FIGURE 12.5

STATES WITH RIGHT-TO-WORK LAWS

ample, managers may interpret a certain clause in the agreement to mean that they are free to select who works overtime. Union members may interpret the same clause to mean that managers must select employees for overtime based on employee seniority. If controversies such as this cannot be resolved between the two parties, employees may file a grievance.

A **grievance** is a charge by employees that management is not abiding by or fulfilling the terms of the negotiated labor–management agreement according to how they perceive it. Overtime rules, promotions, layoffs, transfers, job assignments, and so forth are generally sources of employee grievances. Handling such grievances demands a good deal of contact between union officials and managers. Grievances, however, do not imply that a company has broken the law or the labor agreement. In fact, the vast majority of grievances are negotiated and resolved by **shop stewards** (union officials who work permanently in an organization and represent employee interests on a daily basis) and supervisory-level managers. However, if a grievance is not settled at this level, formal grievance procedures will begin. Figure 12.6 illustrates the different steps the formal grievance procedure could follow.

Mediation and Arbitration

During the negotiation process, there is generally what's called a **bargaining zone,** which is a range of options between the initial and final offer that each party will consider before negotiations dissolve or reach an impasse. If labor–management negotiators aren't able to agree on alternatives within this bargaining zone, mediation may be necessary. **Mediation** is the use of a third party, called a mediator, who encourages both sides to continue negotiating and often makes suggestions for resolving a work dispute. However, it's important to remember that mediators make suggestions, not decisions. Elected officials (current and past), attorneys, and college professors are often called on to serve as mediators in a labor dispute.

Another option used to resolve labor–management conflicts is arbitration. **Arbitration** is an agreement to bring in an impartial third party (an arbitrator) to render a binding decision in a labor dispute.[10] Many of the negotiated labor–management agreements in the United States call for the use of an

grievance
A charge by employees that management is not abiding by the terms of the negotiated labor–management agreement.

shop stewards
Union officials who work permanently in an organization and represent employee interests on a daily basis.

bargaining zone
Range of options between the initial and final offer that each party will consider before negotiations dissolve or reach an impasse.

mediation
The use of a third party, called a mediator, who encourages both sides to continue negotiating and often makes suggestions for resolving the dispute.

arbitration
An agreement to bring in an impartial third party (an arbitrator) to render a binding decision in a labor dispute.

FIGURE 12.6

THE GRIEVANCE RESOLUTION PROCESS

The grievance process may move through several steps before the issue is resolved. At each step, the issue is negotiated between union officials and managers. If no resolution comes internally, an outside arbitrator may be mutually agreed on. If so, the decision by the arbitrator is binding (legally enforceable).

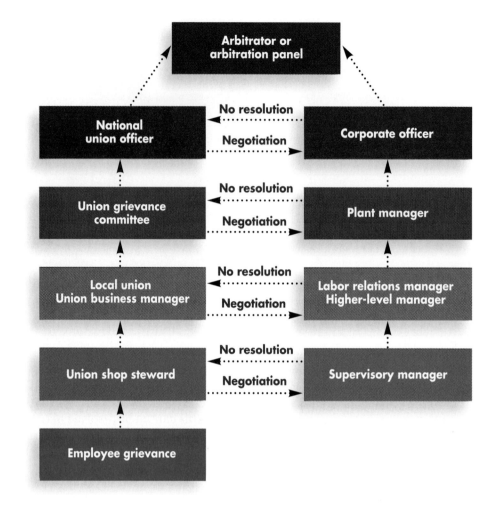

arbitrator to end labor disputes. The arbitrator must be acceptable to both labor and management. The non-profit American Arbitration Association is the dominant force in dispute resolution. You may have heard of baseball players filing for arbitration to resolve a contract dispute with their teams.

Labor unions play a key workplace role in countries other than the United States as well. In Europe organized labor is a major force throughout the continent. Unions in Europe have historically held a good deal more influence in the workplace than unions have in the United States. The Reaching Beyond Our Borders box discusses a formidable challenge the European Union faces with its unions as it works toward the goals of regional unity and a single currency, the euro.

At times, management and labor negotiators admit it's not possible to reach an agreement; an arbitrator may be the only way to resolve the impasse. An arbitrator must be acceptable to both sides and the decision is binding. The American Arbitration Association (AAA) boasts its reputation as a leader in dispute resolution for the past 75 years. What type of person would make a good arbitrator?

REACHING BEYOND OUR BORDERS
The Euro Versus the Unions

www.europa.eu.int

The European Union (EU) accomplished what many said were impossible dreams. For starters, the EU established a single market that abolished economic borders among its member nations. Then in January 1999, the European Union introduced a common currency, the euro. Supporters cheered the euro as an economic elixir that would improve European competitiveness and provide an economic edge in the global economy. Some of the cheering has since been silenced by wage tension. For the first time in European history, there are discussions of transnational collective bargaining to reach common salary and benefits. In the past, fluctuations in the various currencies made it difficult for businesses to compare labor costs in different countries. Now that there is a common currency, the comparison is much easier.

The problem is that the hourly wage rate varies greatly among the 15 member countries of the EU (Great Britain has not converted to the euro). Labor unions in high-wage countries such as Germany, the Netherlands, and Belgium view the presence of a single currency as a threat to their members. In Germany the average hourly labor cost in manufacturing is 28.68 euros. Compare this rate with other EU members such as Portugal, where the cost is only 7.51 euros per hour. Wages in France are about 24 per-cent below those in Germany but 31 percent above those in Spain. Ireland has labor costs double those of Portugal but one-third lower than those of the Netherlands. It's these wage differences that cause unions to fear that competitive pressures will encourage companies to go from country to country to test how far down they can get wages.

Hans de Vries, national negotiator for the metal and electrical workers in the Netherlands, is one of the leaders pressing for transnational collective bargaining in Europe. Yet he admits that common salary and benefit policies would be difficult to implement across national borders. Low-wage nations are less than eager for such talks because they hope that their low wages will help attract new businesses and new jobs. Still, the unions are firm in their resolve and promise to fight on toward common salaries that would protect current high-wage workers and press countries to compete for new businesses on the basis that their workers are productive rather than cheap.

Sources: Nicholas Kralev, "Blair Plans Economic Reforms as Cost of Strong Pound Revives," *Washington Times*, March 23, 2000, p. A17; Tomasz Janowski, "No Wage Boom Seen This Year for Euro-Zone Unions," Reuters, January 14, 2000; "EMU: Fall in Euro Worries ECB More Each Day," *European Report*, February 16, 2000; and Tony Emerson and Scott Johnson, "It's a Jungle Out There," *Newsweek International*, February 5, 2001, p. 36.

TACTICS USED IN LABOR–MANAGEMENT CONFLICTS

If labor and management reach an impasse in collective bargaining and negotiations break down, either side or both sides may use specific tactics to enhance their position and perhaps sway public opinion. The primary tactics used by organized labor are the strike and the boycott. Unions might also use pickets and work slowdowns to get desired changes. Management, for its part, may implement lockouts, injunctions, and even strikebreakers. The following sections look briefly at each of these contrasting tactics.

Union Tactics

The strike has historically been the most potent tactic unions use to achieve their objectives. A **strike** is when workers collectively refuse to go to work. Strikes can attract public attention to a labor dispute and at times cause operations in a company to slow down or totally cease. You may remember the delivery slowdowns caused by the United Parcel Service (UPS) strike in 1997; or perhaps you were affected by the Communications Workers of America

strike
A union strategy in which workers refuse to go to work; the purpose is to further workers' objectives after an impasse in collective bargaining.

strike against Verizon Communications in 2000.[11] Besides refusing to work, strikers may also picket, which means they walk around the outside of the organization carrying signs and talking with the public and the media about the issues in the labor dispute. Unions also use picketing as an informational tool. The purpose is to alert the public to an issue that is stirring labor unrest even though no strike has been voted. Strikes have often led to resolution of a labor dispute; however, they also have generated violence and extended bitterness when emotions on both sides reached a boiling point. The United Auto Workers' 17-month strike against Caterpillar, for example, caused a great deal of bitterness on both sides in the mid-1990s. When the strike was finally settled, both labor and management remained openly hostile toward each other and mutual complaints of violations of the negotiated labor–management agreement continued.

The public often realizes how important a worker is when he or she goes on strike. Imagine what an economic and social disaster it would be if doctors and nurses at a large hospital went on strike, or police officers in a town voted to strike. That's why many states prohibit such job actions. Nonetheless, police officers, firefighters, teachers, and others sometimes exert their frustrations by engaging in "sick-outs" or the "blue flu," where the members of the union don't strike, but refuse to come to work on the pretext of illness. Employees of the federal government, such as postal workers, can organize unions but are denied the right to strike. In fact, under the provisions of the Taft-Hartley Act, the president can ask for a cooling-off period to prevent a strike in what's considered a critical industry. During a **cooling-off period,** workers return to their jobs while the union's bargaining team and management continue negotiations. The cooling-off period can last up to 80 days. Bill Clinton was the first U.S. president to use this provision in 19 years when he halted an American Airlines pilots' strike in 1997.

cooling-off period
When workers in a critical industry return to their jobs while the union and management continue negotiations.

Both labor and management seek to avoid strikes if at all possible, and very few labor disputes lead to a strike. Social perceptions and attitudes can also affect the potential for strikes. For example, after former president Ronald Reagan fired striking air traffic controllers in 1981 and broke their union, other unions then hesitated to strike. The successful UPS strike in 1997, however, changed organized labor's aversion to strikes. Since then, strikes and other labor–management confrontations involving highly visible, high-profile businesses have become news. As technological change and the Internet economy continue to alter the traditional workplace, it's unlikely that labor disputes in the 21st century will disappear.[12] Strikes in air and ground transportation, publishing, telecommunications, aerospace and auto manufacturing, overnight delivery, and professional sports have illustrated

During a labor dispute, unions often encourage their members and the general public to boycott a particular company. Here a union member urges customers to support his union in a boycott of Safeway Foods. Have you ever been asked to support the boycott of a labor union or other group against a specific company?

that the strike is not yet dead as a labor tactic. Following their 2000 strike, for example, Verizon workers won a 12 percent raise over three years, provisions against layoffs, and strict limitations on shifting jobs to other parts of the company. Some workers got a cap on required overtime at eight hours a week.[13]

Unions also use boycotts in an attempt to obtain their objectives. Boycotts can be classified as primary or secondary. A

primary boycott is when organized labor encourages both its members and the general public not to buy the products of a firm involved in a labor dispute. A **secondary boycott** is an attempt by labor to convince others to stop doing business with a firm that is the subject of a primary boycott. For example, a union could initiate a secondary boycott against a supermarket chain because that chain carries goods produced by the target of a primary boycott. Labor unions can legally authorize primary boycotts, but the Taft-Hartley Act prohibits the use of secondary boycotts.

Management Tactics

Like labor, management also uses specific tactics to achieve its contract goals. Historically, to thwart a union management would use a **yellow-dog contract,** which required employees to agree as a condition of employment not to join a union. In 1932, the passage of the Norris–La Guardia Act made such contracts illegal. A **lockout** is an attempt by managers to put pressure on union workers by temporarily closing the business. If workers are not working, they are not paid. Today, management rarely uses lockouts as a tactic to achieve its contract objectives, though there was a lockout of National Basketball Association (NBA) players by the owners in 1998–99.[14] Management now most often uses injunctions and strikebreakers to defeat labor demands it sees as excessive.

An **injunction** is a court order directing someone to do something or to refrain from doing something. Management has sought injunctions to order striking workers back to work, limit the number of pickets that can be used during a strike, or otherwise deal with actions that could be detrimental to the public welfare. For a court to issue an injunction, management must show a "just cause," such as the possibility of violence or the destruction of property.

The use of strikebreakers has been a particular source of hostility and violence in labor relations. **Strikebreakers** (called scabs by unions) are workers who are hired to do the jobs of striking employees until the labor dispute is resolved. Employers have had the right to replace strikers since a 1938 Supreme Court ruling, but it wasn't until the 1980s that this tactic was frequently used.

The Future of Unions and Labor–Management Relations

Many new labor–management issues have emerged that affect labor unions.[15] Increased global competition, advanced technology and the changing nature of work have threatened or altered the jobs of many workers. To save jobs, many unions have granted concessions, or **givebacks,** to management. In such acts, union members give back previous gains from labor negotiations.[16] It's obvious that for unions to grow they will have to adapt to a workforce that is increasingly culturally diverse, white-collar, female, and foreign born. The AFL–CIO, for example, plans to specifically target membership campaigns to women in traditionally low-paying fields, such as health care and garment sewing. Other efforts are focused toward contingent workers like freelancers, temporary employees, telecommuters ➤ **P.22** ◂, and high-tech consultants.[17] Today, the largest labor organization in the United States is the National Education Association (NEA), which represents over 2.5 million members.[18] The Spotlight on Small Business box discusses the movement of doctors toward union membership.

Organized labor is at a crossroads. From 1970 to 2000, membership in the United Auto Workers fell by almost half, from 1.4 million to 762,439.[19] The unionized share of the private-sector workforce has declined from a peak

primary boycott
When a union encourages both its members and the general public not to buy the products of a firm involved in a labor dispute.

secondary boycott
An attempt by labor to convince others to stop doing business with a firm that is the subject of a primary boycott; prohibited by the Taft-Hartley Act.

yellow-dog contract
A type of contract that required employees to agree as a condition of employment not to join a union; prohibited by the Norris–La Guardia Act.

lockout
An attempt by management to put pressure on unions by temporarily closing the business.

injunction
A court order directing someone to do something or to refrain from doing something.

strikebreakers
Workers hired to do the jobs of striking workers until the labor dispute is resolved.

givebacks
Concessions made by union members to management; gains from labor negotiations are given back to management to help employers remain competitive and thereby save jobs.

FIGURE 12.7

UNION MEMBERSHIP AS A
PERCENTAGE OF THE
NONAGRICULTURAL
WORKFORCE, 1886–2000

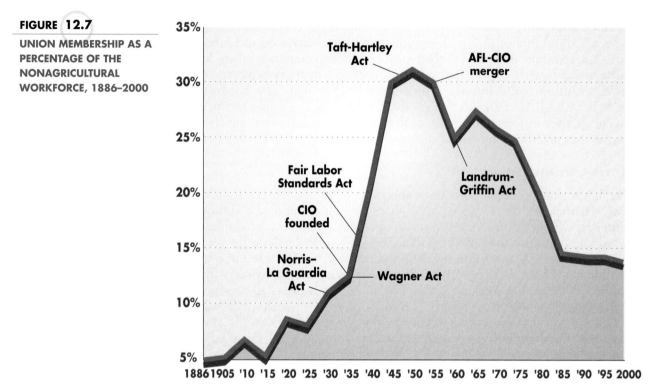

of 35.5 percent in 1945 to just 13.9 percent today (see Figure 12.7).[20] It's safe to assume that the role of unions in the 21st century is likely to be quite different from their role in the past. Union leaders and members know as well as anyone the necessity for U.S. firms to remain competitive with foreign firms. It's expected that organized labor will do its part in maintaining U.S. competitiveness.

In the future, unions may actually assist management in training workers, redesigning jobs, and assimilating the new workforce; that is, they will recruit and train foreign workers, unskilled workers, former welfare recipients, and others who may need special help in adapting to the job requirements of the 21st century. Workplace concepts such as continuous improvement ▸ **P.251** ◂, constant creative innovation, and worker involvement programs cannot be implemented without the cooperation of employees. Business has witnessed such cooperation already at companies like Saturn, where unions have taken a leadership role with management in making things happen.[21] The rewards unions can expect for cooperating with management include improved job security, profit sharing, and sometimes increased wages. How organized labor handles these major challenges may well define the future for unions.

**PROGRESS
ASSESSMENT**

- What are the major laws that affected union growth, and what is covered in each?
- Why do the objectives of unions change over time?
- What are the major tactics used by unions and by management to assert their power in contract negotiations?
- What kinds of workers are joining unions today, and why are they joining?

Take Two Aspirin and Call Me at the Union Hall

Can you imagine entering a doctor's office and not saying "Ahhhh" but instead asking to see the doctor's union card? This might seem a bit absurd, but it's not unrealistic. Many private-practice physicians are leaning closer toward unionizing to gain the right to collectively bargain with managed health care organizations such as health maintenance organizations (HMOs). The American Medical Association (AMA) launched a new physicians union in late 1999 called Physicians for Responsible Negotiations (PRN). The name was selected by the AMA with great care. While the PRN will not actively seek to solicit doctors into the union as other labor groups do, it will provide expertise that physicians need to form bargaining units. The PRN will also provide services such as petitioning the National Labor Relations Board on behalf of doctors' grievances and help in negotiations if asked or needed. To date, more than 40,000 U.S. doctors belong to a labor organization. These numbers could grow significantly in the years ahead even though federal antitrust provisions currently prohibit most doctors from unionizing. According to antitrust law, competitors in an industry are prohibited from joining together to set prices and working conditions.

Still, over 100,000 doctors employed by hospitals or municipalities are able to unionize and may lean toward organizing into collective bargaining units. The AMA has even suggested that it may lobby Congress to lift the antitrust ban for all doctors. If this effort materializes, potentially 500,000 doctors could bargain collectively.

The future of organized labor promises to be interesting, especially in areas such as health care. According to Dr. Edmund R. Donoghue, a Cook County, Illinois, medical examiner and strong labor supporter, "Doctors in the U.S. have become terribly unhappy and are in a position for someone to organize them." Dr. Donoghue even believes that doctors should have the right to strike, a proposal the AMA strongly opposes. Who knows—someday the president of the AFL–CIO may be called away from the annual Labor Day parade to perform an emergency appendectomy or deliver a baby.

Sources: Robert Reno, "Doctors Want to Stitch on a Union Label," *Newsday*, July 5, 2000, p. A40; Tedd Mitchell, "Why Doctors Are Thinking about Unionizing," *USA Weekend*, July 16, 2000, p. 4; "Doctors' Unions Are Part of American Tradition," *USA Today*, January 21, 2000, p. 16A; and Sewell Chan, "Bargaining Rights for Doctors Rejected," *The Washington Post*, January 18, 2001, p. B5.

CONTROVERSIAL EMPLOYEE–MANAGEMENT ISSUES

This is an interesting time in the history of employee–management relations. Organizations are involved in outsourcing ➤ **P.254** ◄, technology change, and global expansion. The government has eliminated some social benefits to workers and is taking a much more active role in mandating what benefits and assurances businesses must provide to workers. In other instances, employees are raising general questions of fairness. Let's look at several controversial issues, starting with that of executive compensation.

Executive Compensation

Tiger Woods putts his way to over $47 million a year, Tom Hanks acts his way to $72 million a year, and Oprah Winfrey talks her way to over $150 million a year.[22] Is it out of line, then, that Steve Case, the chief executive of America Online, should make $117 million a year? Or that Louis Gerstner of IBM should earn almost $103 million a year?[23] In Chapter 2 we explained that the U.S. free-market ➤ **P.37** ◄ system is built on incentives that allow top executives to make that much or more. Today, however, the government, boards of directors, stock-

LEGAL BRIEFCASE

www.benjerry.com

Getting the Most Out of Getting Canned

The loss of a job usually provokes immediate questions from workers such as "Where is my next paycheck coming from?" and "How can I pay the bills if I get sick?" It's true, losing a job is a financially traumatic, gut-wrenching experience for any employee to endure. Well, maybe not *any* employee.

Departing bosses often find that when they are forced out of a job, they are better off than if they had stayed—at least in monetary terms. Take Eckhard Pfeiffer, who was the chief pilot in Compaq Computer's crash in the late 1990s. He glided away after he was discharged from Compaq with a $150 million payout in salary and stock options. Due to generous employment agreements, Stephen Hilbert CEO of Conseco and Jill Barad CEO of Mattel exited their companies with more money than they would have received if they had fulfilled their employment contracts. When Doug Ivester was forced out as CEO at Coca-Cola, he walked away with a financial package worth about $166 million even though he lacked an employment agreement. Mike Ovitz at Disney and John Walter at AT&T fared similarly. Yale Tauber, a compensation consultant at William M. Mercer, Inc., found that chief executives working with or without a contract walked off with approximately 185 percent of their annual pay after losing their jobs.

Tauber's study included executives who lost their jobs for no other reason except overall poor performance.

A CEO's pay, however, is not the only goodie along the exit path. When Robert Holland left Ben & Jerry's Homemade after three years due to disagreements with the company founders, he collected an unusual perk—free ice cream for life. (Ben & Jerry's Homemade has been sold to Unilever Corporation, but the ice cream keeps flowing.) Increasing numbers of companies are agreeing to pay lifetime premiums for health and long-term care insurance for executives and often their spouses. Such "corporate benevolence" is causing stockholders and lower-level employees to question the disparity of treatment for top executives. Lawsuits are certainly not out of the question. The issue may land in the U.S. Congress, where senators and representatives can debate the merits and logic of companies bestowing bonus pay and perks to discharged executives that blundered their way to the unemployment line.

Sources: Suzanne Koudsi, "Why Are CEOs Paid So Much to Beat It?" *Fortune*, May 29, 2000, pp. 34–36; Lisa Bannon, "Mattel Proxy Says Jill Barad Received Severance Package of about $50 Million," *The Wall Street Journal*, May 1, 2000, p. B27; Michael K. Ozanian, "Upward Bias," *Forbes*, May 15, 2000, pp. 210–15; "Optical Illusions," *InfoWorld*, January 8, 2001.

holders, and unions have challenged this principle and argue that executive compensation is getting out of line. In 1999, the total compensation (salary and bonuses) of an average CEO of a major company was $1,688,088.[24] Even after adjustments for inflation, this represents a huge increase from the $160,000 average compensation in 1960. The CEOs running the 800 largest U.S. public companies were paid $5.8 billion in compensation in 1999.[25]

In the past, an executive's compensation and bonuses were generally determined by the firm's profitability or an increase in its stock price.[26] Many executives receive stock options (the ability to buy company stock at a set price at a later date) as part of their compensation. The assumption in using such options as part of executive compensation is that the CEO will improve the performance of the company and raise the price of the firm's stock. Today, however, executive pay often soars even if the performance of a company is weak compared to competitors. What's even more confusing is that the compensation paid to a CEO whose poor performance forced him or her to resign. For example, CEO Jill Barad of toymaker Mattel received close to $50 million upon her resignation.[27] Make sure to read the Legal Briefcase box for further discussion of this strange phenomenon.

Noted management consultant Peter Drucker has been criticizing executive pay levels since the mid-1980s, when he suggested that CEOs should not earn much more than 20 times the salary of the company's lowest-paid employee. Companies that have followed Drucker's advice include Herman Miller Inc., a Michigan producer of office furniture. At this company, pay for the chief executive is limited to 20 times the average worker's pay. Many companies, however, have turned a deaf ear to this suggestion, and today the average chief executive of a major corporation makes 475 times as much as a typical American factory worker. Back in 1980, the average CEO made only 42 times as much. At some companies the numbers can be staggering. For example, a hot dog or souvenir vendor making minimum wage at any of the Walt Disney theme parks would have to work 52,327 years to make what CEO Michael Eisner earned in 1998 ($575.6 million).[28]

As global competition intensifies, looking at what executives in other countries earn provides another point of view. American CEOs typically earn two to three times as much as executives in Europe and Canada. It's worth noting that some European companies often have workers who sit on the board of directors. Since boards set executive pay, this could be a reason why the imbalance between starting pay and top pay is less for European executives. In Japan, the CEO of a large corporation makes approximately 40 times what the average factory worker makes. Also, in Japan chief executives do not generally receive stock options.

It's important to recognize, however, that most U.S. executives are responsible for multibillion-dollar corporations and work 70-plus hours a week. Many can show their stockholders that their decisions turned potential problems into success. Disney's stock, for example, has increased by 2,400 percent since Michael Eisner became CEO. Clearly, there is no easy answer to the question of what is fair compensation for executives.

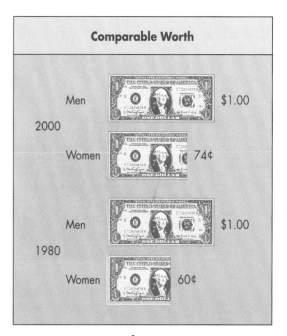

Comparable Worth

2000	Men	$1.00
	Women	74¢
1980	Men	$1.00
	Women	60¢

Close but still a distant second. Women have made some important strides in the fight for equal pay, but today earn only 74 percent of what men make in the workplace. Such statistics cause many to support the case for comparable worth. Since women comprise a growing percentage of workers, this issue promises to persist. What's your opinion about comparable worth?

Comparable Worth

Another controversial issue is that of pay equity, or comparable worth, for women versus men. **Comparable worth** is the concept that people in jobs that require similar levels of education, training, or skills should receive equal pay. This somewhat thorny issue has become more important as women have entered the labor force in increasing numbers.[29] In 1890, for example, women made up only 15 percent of the labor force; in 2000, the rate was 50 percent.

Comparable worth goes beyond the concept of equal pay for equal work. The Equal Pay Act of 1963 requires companies to give equal pay to men and women who do the same job.[30] It's against the law, for example, to pay a female nurse less than a male nurse. Rather, the issue of comparable worth centers on comparing the value of jobs such as nurse or librarian (traditionally women's jobs) with jobs such as truck driver or plumber (traditionally men's jobs). Such a comparison shows that "women's" jobs tend to pay less—sometimes much less.

In the United States today, women earn approximately 74 percent of what men earn, though the disparity varies considerably by profession, job experience and tenure, and level of education.[31] In the past, the primary explanation for this disparity was that women only worked 50 to 60 percent of their available years

comparable worth
The concept that people in jobs that require similar levels of education, training, or skills should receive equal pay.

Is Wall Street the place where all have an equal opportunity to grow their fortunes? No, according to Nancy Thomas, seen here protesting against Merrill Lynch. Nancy and others have led the fight against sexual discrimination regarding pay and executive job opportunities in Wall Street brokerage firms. Do you think sex discrimination is common in U.S. business?

once they left school (experience and tenure), whereas men, on the whole, worked all of those years. This explanation weakened in the 1990s as fewer women left the workforce for an extended period of time. Other explanations suggested that many women try to work as well as care for their families and therefore fall off the career track, while others voluntarily choose more flexible jobs that pay less, such as bookkeeping, nursing, or secretarial work.

The Clinton administration supported the principles of comparable worth to correct pay discrepancies and suggested wage increases in so-called women's jobs. Labor unions also voiced support and endorsed comparable worth legislation in 22 states. Evidence, however, shows that it's difficult to determine whether comparable worth would lead to better market equilibrium or just create more chaos. In today's knowledge-based economy, women appear poised to compete financially with men in growing fields such as health care, telecommunications, and knowledge technology. Two University of Michigan professors found, for example, that earnings of women college graduates were 94 percent of men's. Female engineers make 98 percent as much as male engineers.[32] Nonetheless, as women continue to comprise a large percentage of the labor force, comparable worth promises to be an intriguing issue in the 21st century.

CRITICAL THINKING

Should college football coaches be paid the same as college volleyball coaches? Should basketball players in the Women's National Basketball Association be paid the same as their counterparts in the National Basketball Association? That is, are their jobs of comparable worth? How would that affect the supply and demand for football coaches and NBA players? What role should the market and government play in determining wages?

Sexual Harassment

sexual harassment
Unwelcome sexual advances, requests for sexual favors, and other conduct (verbal or physical) of a sexual nature.

Sexual harassment refers to unwelcome sexual advances, requests for sexual favors, and other conduct (verbal or physical) of a sexual nature. It became a major issue in the workplace in the 1980s, but the sexual harassment furor intensified in 1991 during the televised confirmation hearing of Supreme Court Justice Clarence Thomas. At the hearing before the Senate Judiciary Committee, an attorney and college professor named Anita Hill accused Thomas of sexual impropriety.[33] Although it did not block Thomas's appointment to the Court, Hill's testimony clearly heightened the interest in this issue. During the 1990s, charges of sexual harassment were raised against President Bill Clinton, Senator Bob Packwood, and several high-ranking U.S. military officers.

Legally, both men and women are covered under the Civil Rights Act of 1991, which governs sexual harassment. This fact was reinforced in 1997, when the Supreme Court agreed that same-sex harassment also falls within the purview of sexual harassment law. Women, however, still file the majority of sexual harassment cases. The number of sexual harassment complaints filed annually with the Equal Employment Opportunity Commission (EEOC) grew from 6,000 in 1990 to over 16,000 in 2000.

In evaluating sexual harassment, a person's conduct on the job can be considered illegal under specific conditions:

- The employee's submission to such conduct is made either explicitly or implicitly a term or condition of employment, or an employee's submission to or rejection of such conduct is used as the basis for employment decisions affecting the worker's status. A threat such as "Go out with me or you are fired" or "Go out with me or you will never be promoted here" would constitute "quid pro quo" sexual harassment.

- The conduct unreasonably interferes with a worker's job performance or creates an intimidating, hostile, or offensive working environment.[34] This type of harassment is referred to as "hostile environment" harassment.

The Thomas hearings and subsequent disclosures involving companies such as the Mitsubishi Motor Manufacturing Company of America introduced managers to the concept of a *hostile workplace,* which is any workplace where behavior occurs that would offend a reasonable person. The Supreme Court in 1996 broadened the scope of what can be considered a hostile work environment. In evaluating charges of sexual harassment the key word seems to be *unwelcome,* a term the courts have hotly debated and will continue to debate.

There's no question that managers and workers are now much more sensitive to comments and behavior of a sexual nature. Still, EEOC statistics report that sexual harassment is the fastest growing area of employee complaint. A major problem is that workers and managers often know that a policy concerning sexual harassment exists but have no idea what it says. Former U.S. labor secretary Lynn Martin suggests that companies offer management training, require sexual harassment workshops for all employees, and revamp the human resource department if necessary to ensure compliance. Such efforts may save businesses millions of dollars in lawsuits and make the workplace more productive and harmonious. Nonetheless, it's safe to bet sexual harassment is likely to remain an important issue in the 21st century.

PROGRESS ASSESSMENT

- How does top-executive pay in the United States compare with that in other countries?
- What's the difference between comparable worth and equal pay for equal work?
- How is sexual harassment defined, and when does sexual behavior become illegal?

Child Care

Child care became an increasing important workplace issue in the 1990s and promises to remain a workplace concern in the 21st century. Questions involving responsibilities for child care subsidies, child care programs, and even parental leave are topics that promise to be debated in the private and public

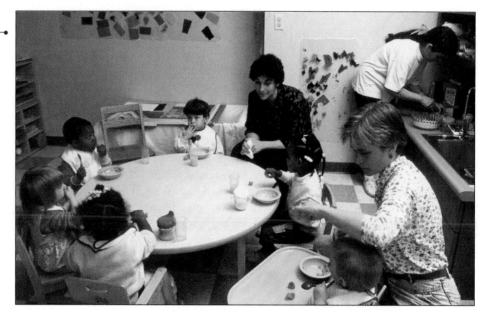

A corporate-sponsored daycare center is an enticing perk used to attract qualified workers and keep productive employees. Here children of workers at Lotus's daycare center are fed a snack while their parents are at their jobs. Such company-sponsored daycare centers offer a wide variety of services. Is it fair to workers without children to offer daycare services at company expense?

sectors of the economy. Many workers seriously question these workplace benefits and argue that single workers or single-income families should not subsidize dual-income families who must pay for child care. Additionally, federal child care assistance has risen significantly since the passage of the Welfare Reform Act of 1996.[35] Still, the issue of child care is an obvious concern to business.

According to the U.S. Census Bureau, a sizable number of today's 50 million working women are likely to become pregnant during their working years. Such statistics obviously raise the eyebrows and concerns of employers. Why? It's estimated that absences related to child care already cost American businesses billions of dollars annually. It's also apparent that child care issues will persist in the workplace, raising the ultimate question: Who should pay for child care services?

The number of companies that offer child care as an employee benefit is growing. Some of the more extensive child care programs are offered at large firms such as Johnson & Johnson, Stride Rite, and Campbell Soup. A few companies even provide emergency child care services for employees whose children are ill or whose regular child care arrangements are disrupted. NCR opened an 8,800-square-foot day care facility in Georgia that includes lessons for employees' children ranging from preschool instruction to a computer curriculum.[36]

Small companies also often implement creative child care programs that meet specific employee needs and help the company compete for qualified employees. For example, Haemonetics Corporation in Braintree, Massachusetts, has a state-of-the-art child care facility called the Kids' Space at Haemonetics. In the summer, the facility includes Camp Haemonetics—the kids come to work with their parents and then get bused off for swimming, hiking, and so forth at a nearby state park. At noon, they come back for lunch with Mom or Dad, and then return for more camp activities until about 5:00 PM.[37]

What's obvious to businesses of all sizes is that working parents have made it clear that safe, affordable child care is an issue on which they will not compromise. Companies have responded by providing:

- Discount arrangements with national child care chains.
- Vouchers that offer payments toward whatever type child care the employee selects.
- Referral services that help identify high-quality child care facilities to employees.
- On-site child care centers where parents can visit children at lunch or lag times during the workday.
- Sick-child centers to care for moderately ill children.

As single-parent and two-income households continue to grow, it will be interesting to follow this very important workplace issue. However, even as child care remains a hotly contested issue in some areas, a new workplace storm is brewing over the issue of elder care. Let's look at this next.

Elder Care

The workforce in the United States is aging. By 2005, 40 percent of all U.S. workers will be aged 40 to 58. Fortunately, many of these workers will not have to concern themselves with finding child care for children. However, they will confront another problem: how to care for older parents and other relatives. Statistically, the number of households with at least one adult providing elder care has tripled in the past 10 years. In 1940, only 13 percent of persons age 60 or over had an elderly parent still alive. Today 44 percent of persons 60 or over have an elderly parent living. James Hughes, dean of the School of Planning and Public Policy at Rutgers University, claims we are just seeing the tip of the iceberg.[38] Expectations persist that over the next five years 18 percent of the U.S. workforce will be involved in the time-consuming and stressful task of caring for an aging relative. Sally Coberly, director of public policy and a specialist on aging at the Washington Business Group, predicts that in coming years elder care will have a greater impact on the workplace than child care.

Some firms are already reacting to the effect of elder care on their workforce. At Boeing and AT&T, employees are offered elder care programs that include hot lines where workers can seek help or counseling for older relatives.[39] Unfortunately for workers though, a very small percentage of U.S. companies (large, medium-size, or small) now provide any type of elder care programs. The government also provides little relief with this issue. Both Medicare and Medicaid place very heavy financial burdens on family caregivers. Some companies are trying to help ease this burden for their employees. A 1999 survey of companies with more than 100 employees found that 23 percent offered elder care referral or resource services, 9 percent were underwriting long-term care insurance for their employees or relatives, and 5 percent had made contributions to elder care programs.

Andrew Scharlach, a professor of aging at the University of California at Berkeley, estimates that elder care costs employers billions of dollars in lost output and replacement costs. He expects these costs to rise even higher as more experienced and high-ranking employees become involved in caring for older parents and other relatives. His arguments make good sense. Since older workers are often more critical to the company than younger workers (who are most affected by child care problems), many businesses will see the cost of elder care skyrocket. Already some companies note that transfer and promotion decisions are especially difficult for employees whose elderly parents need ongoing care. Unfortunately, as the nation gets older, the situation will grow considerably worse. With an aging workforce, this issue promises to persist well into the 21st century.

Should You Keep the Tap Flowing?

You are the owner of a small regional brewery that serves a specialized market in three Midwestern states. In the past you have considered automating one of the brewery's operations, the racking room, by replacing the workers there with robots. However, the employees in the racking room have been loyal and hardworking. In the past they voted down union representation, feeling it could cause difficulties for your plant. They even agreed to freeze their pay a few years back when the brewery was in a cash crunch. To compound your problem, you are aware that the possibility of finding alternative employment for these workers is slim.

The other day, however, you heard that one of the employees in the racking room was diagnosed as having the HIV antibody. You realize that this person's medical bills could escalate to over $250,000 over the course of the illness, not to mention missed workdays, production slowdowns, co-worker concerns, and so forth. Without question, insurance premiums for your firm will also increase. You know that, legally, this employee cannot be dismissed because of this medical misfortune. But you do have the option of closing the racking room, pleading the necessity to automate. Of course, all of the employees in this department would lose their jobs. What would you do? Is your decision good for the business? Is your decision ethical?

AIDS Testing, Drug Testing, and Violence in the Workplace

The war against HIV has made remarkable gains. "Business Responds to AIDS" is an educational program developed by the Center for Disease Control in Atlanta. Business knows that until the final battle against this lethal illness is won, a uniform and humanitarian policy in the workplace must exist. Who should lead the fight against AIDS, the government or private industry?

The spread of acquired immune deficiency syndrome (AIDS), though declining, is still a top national concern. AIDS is a leading cause of death for Americans between the ages of 25 and 44—a group that represents almost half of the nation's workforce.[40] Such statistics have caused businesses to direct their attention to the issue of AIDS, since no one predicts a quick victory over this disease. The U.S. Centers for Disease Control launched a program called Business Responds to AIDS, which explains how companies can teach employees about the basics of AIDS and how to deal with it on the job. Certainly the development of clear-cut policies is needed to confront this critical issue.

One controversial employee–management issue concerns the mandatory testing for the human immunodeficiency virus (HIV), which is believed to be the virus that causes AIDS. Preemployment medical testing cannot be used selectively to screen out anyone who may be HIV-positive. If administered, the tests must be given to all potential employees across the board. More and more firms are insisting on mandatory HIV testing because an AIDS-afflicted employee can cost an employer an enormous amount in terms of insurance, losses in productivity ➤ **P.23** ◀, increased absenteeism, and turnover. Many firms have gone beyond preemployment testing and suggested that all existing employees should be tested for the HIV antibody. Managers argue that the information they would gain would allow for the development of a uniform and humanitarian AIDS policy at the workplace. Nevertheless, this issue, like others, has no easy answer. The Making Ethical Decisions box asks how you would deal with a worker who has AIDS.

Some companies feel that alcohol and drug abuse are more serious workplace issues than AIDS because substance abuse involves far more workers. An estimated 11 percent of employed adults in the United States are believed to be current illicit drug users, and 8 percent of full-time workers—or 6.3 million Americans—have used illegal drugs within the past month.[41] Individuals who use drugs are three and a half times more likely to be involved in workplace accidents and five times as likely to file a worker's compensation claim. Illegal drug use costs U.S. companies from $60 to $110 billion a year, according to the Institute for a Drug-Free Workplace in Washington, D.C. The National Institute of Health estimates that each drug abuser costs an employer approximately $7,000 annually. Such losses have caused drug testing at work to grow at a rapid pace. Over 70 percent of major companies now test workers and job applicants for substance abuse.[42]

Employers are also struggling with a growing trend toward violence in the workplace. The U.S. Department of Labor now cites homicide as the second leading cause of job-related fatalities.[43] In 1986, a postal service employee in Oklahoma killed 14 fellow workers before taking his own life. Since then, dozens of other postal employees have perished on the job at the hands of fellow employees. Still, many executives and managers don't take workplace violence seriously and believe that reports of it are primarily media hype. According to an American Management Association study, 69 percent of its member companies do not provide any formal training for dealing with prevention of violence in the workplace. However, other organizations, such as the U.S. Postal Service, have recognized the threat and have begun to hold focus groups for employee input and hire managers with strong interpersonal skills to deal with growing employee violence.

While issues such as AIDS testing, drug testing, and violence present a somewhat grim picture of issues in the workplace, many employees are assuming new roles within their companies. In fact, some are becoming owners. Let's see how this is happening.

Employee Stock Ownership Plans (ESOPs)

No matter how hard workers fight for better pay, they will never become as wealthy as the people who actually own the company. At least that is the theory behind **employee stock ownership plans (ESOPs).** An ESOP enables employees to buy part or total ownership of the firm. Louis O. Kelso, a San Francisco lawyer and economist, conceived the idea of ESOPs about 50 years ago. His plan was to turn workers into owners by selling them stock. Using this concept, he helped the employees of a newspaper buy their company. Since then, the idea of employees taking over all or some of the ownership of their companies has gained much favor—there are approximately 11,500 ESOPs today.[44] Employee participation in ownership has emerged as an important issue in many different industries and every type of company.

Small businesses **> P.176 <** are joining their larger counterparts and enjoying the growth ESOPs can provide in encouraging and increasing worker productivity. Giving employees a share in the profits of the firm motivates them to enhance their involvement in the firm and increases morale. For example, Marburn Curtain Warehouse started in 1956 as a single department in a Home Fair store and has grown to become a chain of 19 home furnishings outlets in New Jersey, New York, and Pennsylvania. Bernard Hinden, the founder and chief executive of Marburn, attributes the success to the other owners of the company—all 120 of them. Marburn adopted an employee stock ownership plan in 1990, transforming employees into employee-owners and increasing productivity. "I'm not just looked at as the boss," Hinden says. "I am a member of a team of bosses. We

employee stock ownership plans (ESOPs)
Programs that enable employees to buy part or total ownership of the firm.

EXPECTED BENEFITS OF ESOPs	POTENTIAL PROBLEMS WITH ESOPs
Increased employee motivation	Lack of employee stock voting rights within the firm
Shared profitability through shared ownership of the firm	Lack of communication between management and employees
Improved management–employee relations	
Higher employee pride in the organization	Little or no employee representation on the company board of directors
Better customer relations	
	Lack of job security assurances

FIGURE 12.8

BENEFITS AND PROBLEMS OF ESOPs

have no egos running around. Everybody is right on target for the bottom line." The ESOP has been a success, Hinden says: "It's the American way. What could be better than everybody having a piece of the action? We are masters of our own destinies."[45]

Many people consider ESOPs examples of capitalism ➤ **P.37** ◄ at its best. The facts are, however, that ESOPs have had mixed results. Not all ESOPs work as planned. They can be used to refinance a firm with employees' money without giving employees added participation or more job security. Weirton Steel's ESOP was once praised as an ideal model. Unfortunately, over time, the mood of Weirton employees has changed from cooperation to confrontation. Though workers agreed to several wage reductions and job cuts and sold 33 percent of their stock to finance a $550 million modernization, the company still lost money. Union leaders now say that the company executives no longer even talk with them. At Avis Rent-A-Car, employee-owners (as participants in ESOPs are called) complain of having no representation on the company's board and no voting rights. In fact, at 85 percent of the companies with ESOPs, employees do not have voting rights and rarely have a strong voice on the company's board of directors.

Figure 12.8 outlines the benefits and problems of ESOPs. When used correctly, ESOPs can be a powerful strategy for improving corporate profitability and increasing employee satisfaction, participation, and income.

Firms that have healthy employee–management relations have a better chance to prosper. As managers, taking a *proactive approach* is the best way to ensure workable employee–management environments. The proactive manager anticipates potential problems and works toward resolving those issues before they get out of hand—a good lesson to remember.

PROGRESS ASSESSMENT

- What are some of the issues related to child care and elder care, and how are companies addressing those issues?
- What are ESOPs, and what are the benefits and drawbacks of ESOPs?

SUMMARY

1. Trace the history of organized labor in the United States and discuss the major legislation affecting labor unions.

1. Organized labor in the United States dates back almost to the American Revolution.

   • *What was the first union?*

   The cordwainers (shoemakers) organized a craft union of skilled specialists in 1792. The Knights of Labor, which was formed in 1869, was the first national labor organization.

- *How did the AFL–CIO evolve?*

The American Federation of Labor (AFL), formed in 1886, was an organization of craft unions. The Congress of Industrial Organizations (CIO), a group of unskilled and semiskilled workers, broke off from the AFL in 1935. Over time, the two organizations saw the benefits of joining together and thus became the AFL–CIO in 1955.

- *What are the provisions of the major legislation affecting labor unions?*

See Figure 12.1 on p. 365.

2. The objectives of labor unions shift in response to changes in social and economic trends.

2. Outline the objectives of labor unions.

- *What topics typically appear in labor–management agreements?*

See Figure 12.3 on p. 367.

3. If negotiations between labor and management break down, either or both sides may use certain tactics to enhance their position or sway public opinion.

3. Describe the tactics used by labor and management during conflicts and discuss the role of unions in the future.

- *What are the tactics used by unions and management in conflicts?*

Unions can use strikes and boycotts. Management can use injunctions and lockouts.

- *What will unions have to do to cope with declining membership?*

In order to grow, unions will have to adapt to a workforce that is becoming more white-collar, female, and culturally diverse. To help keep American businesses competitive in international markets, unions must soften their historic "us-versus-them" attitude and build a new "we" attitude with management.

4. Some controversial employee–management issues are executive compensation, comparable worth, child care and elder care, AIDS testing, drug testing, violence in the workplace, and ESOPs.

4. Explain some of the controversial employee–management issues such as executive compensation; comparable worth; child care and elder care; AIDS testing, drug testing, and violence in the workplace; and employee stock ownership plans (ESOPs).

- *What is a fair wage for managers?*

The market and the businesses in it set managers' salaries. What is fair is open to debate. The top executives of the 800 largest public companies were paid $5.8 billion in 1999.

- *What is comparable worth?*

Comparable worth is the demand for equal pay for jobs requiring similar levels of education, training, and skills.

- *Isn't pay inequity caused by sexism?*

There is evidence on both sides of that question, but government or corporate actions indicate that some remedial action will be taken regardless of causes.

- *How are some companies addressing the child care issue?*

Responsive companies are providing day care on the premises, emergency care when scheduled care is interrupted, discounts with child care chains, vouchers to be used at the employee's chosen care center, and referral services.

- *What is elder care, and what problems do companies face with regard to this growing problem?*

Workers with older parents or other relatives often need to find some way to care for them. It's becoming a problem that will perhaps outpace the need for child care. Workers who need to care for dependent parents are generally more experienced and vital to the mission of the organization. The cost to business is very large and growing.

- *What are some concerns surrounding AIDS and mandatory HIV testing?*

An employee with AIDS can cost an employer an enormous amount in terms of insurance increases, losses in productivity, increased absenteeism, and employee turnover. Employees may question the accuracy of HIV tests and may see the tests as an infringement on their personal right to privacy.

• *Why are more and more companies now testing workers and job applicants for substance abuse?*

Estimates are that 11 percent of employed adults in the United States are believed to be current illicit drug users. Individuals who use drugs are three and a half times more likely to be involved in workplace accidents and five times more likely to file a worker's compensation claim.

• *How well are employee stock ownership plans (ESOPs) working?*

ESOPs have had mixed results, but the overall trend is favorable. Some 11,000 businesses now have ESOPs. Properly implemented, such plans can increase morale, motivation, commitment, and job satisfaction. The problem is that many firms have used ESOPs as a capital-raising scheme and have not given employees more participation in management. The issue of the administration of ESOPs will be a major one in the next decade.

KEY TERMS

agency shop agreement 368
American Federation of Labor (AFL) 364
arbitration 369
bargaining zone 369
certification 365
closed shop agreement 368
collective bargaining 365
comparable worth 377
Congress of Industrial Organizations (CIO) 364
cooling-off period 372

craft union 363
decertification 365
employee stock ownership plans (ESOPs) 383
givebacks 373
grievance 369
industrial unions 364
injunction 373
Knights of Labor 364
lockout 373
mediation 369
negotiated labor–management agreement (labor contract) 366
open shop agreement 368

primary boycott 373
right-to-work laws 368
secondary boycott 373
sexual harassment 378
shop stewards 369
strike 371
strikebreakers 373
unions 362
union security clause 367
union shop agreement 368
yellow-dog contract 373

DEVELOPING WORKPLACE SKILLS

1. Many health care professionals, especially doctors and nurses, do not belong to a union. Nurses' pay has fallen behind compensation in industry, and doctors feel they are losing a good deal of control over their patients because of strict rules enforced in many health maintenance organizations (HMOs). Talk with several health care professionals about their feelings of possible unionization in health care professions. List the pros and cons they offer concerning unions advancing in the medical profession.

2. Debate the following statement with several classmates: "Unions are dinosaurs that have outlived their usefulness in today's technological world." Consider such questions as these: Do unions serve a key purpose in some industries? Do unions make the United States less competitive in global markets? To get a better feeling for the other side's point of view, take the opposite side of this issue from the one you normally would. Include information from outside sources to substantiate your position.

3. Find the latest information on federal legislation and state legislation related to child care, parental leave, and elder care benefits for employees. In what direction are the trends pointing? What will be the cost to businesses for these new initiatives? Do you favor or reject such advancements in workplace legislation? Why?

4. Compile a list of two or three employee–management issues not covered in the chapter. Compare your list with those of several fellow classmates and see what issues you selected in common and ones unique to each individual. Collectively select one or two workplace issues you all agree will be important in the new millennium and discuss its likely effects and outcomes.

5. Do businesses and government agencies have a duty to provide additional benefits to employees beyond fair pay and good working conditions? Does providing benefits such as child care and elder care to some employees discriminate against those who do not require such assistance? Propose a fringe benefits system that you consider fair and workable for both employees and employers.

Purpose

To understand why workers choose to join unions and how unions have made differences in certain industries.

Exercise

Visit the AFL–CIO website at www.aflcio.com. Navigate through the site and find information regarding why workers join unions and what the benefits have been.

1. There have been many debates about right-to-work laws. Compare the average wages of workers in right-to-work states with those in states without right-to-work laws. Which states offer the higher wages? In addition to union pressure, what else could account for the wage differences?

2. What percentage of workers in your state belongs to a union? If the percentage of union workers is higher or lower than the national average, explain why unions do or do not have strength in your state.

3. Explain how union membership has affected minorities, women, younger and older workers, and part-time workers.

4. The AFL-CIO site presents the *union's* perspective on labor issues. Choose one of these issues and find other resources that support *management's* perspective of the issue.

PRACTICING MANAGEMENT DECISIONS

CASE

WALKING PAST THE PICKET LINES

As you learned in this chapter, the strike is a weapon used by unions to obtain their objectives in a contract dispute. During a strike, workers will generally set up picket lines to inform the general public about the contract impasse. In fact, in striking, organized labor's fundamental purpose often is to win public support for its position.

Until 1938 companies could not legally replace striking workers with strikebreakers (called scabs by the union). This tactic increased in frequency in the early 1980s. Many unions felt company mind-sets shifted when President Ronald Reagan replaced striking air traffic controllers with nonunion controllers in 1983. Businesses felt that Reagan's actions made the process of replacing striking workers legitimate. Furthermore, a loophole in the National Labor Relations Act made the process legal. Today it's not uncommon for firms to advertise for replacement workers if they believe a strike may be forthcoming. Caterpillar, for example, advertised for replacement workers during the 17-month strike by the United Auto Workers against the company. Companies also have made use of replacement workers in strikes that involve low-paying, less-skilled jobs. Aramark, for example, brought in strikebreakers to take the jobs of striking laundry workers whose average earnings were only about $8 per hour. Cleaning contractors who handle most of Los Angeles's commercial properties brought in outside workers to replace striking janitors, though the strikebreakers earned only about $7.00 per hour.

Needless to say, unions are very much opposed to firms hiring replacement workers during a strike. At some companies such as Coors Brewing, replacement workers have become permanent employees, taking the jobs of former union workers. Also, striking workers have at times been fired from their jobs and been replaced by workers who are paid higher wages than the striking union employees. For example, a medical clinic in Minnesota fired its striking nurses and replaced them with replacement workers at a higher rate of pay. Unions also cite the quality of work provided by replacement workers. Some people blamed the recall of millions of deficient tires produced by the Firestone Company in 2000 on replacement workers used in the bitter Firestone strike in 1995. Firestone replaced 2,300 of the company's 4,200 striking workers in the largest use of replacement workers in U.S. history.

President Bill Clinton strongly supported union rights during his presidency and promised to sign into law a bill prohibiting the use of permanent replacement workers if it reached his desk. Labor unions dug deep in their treasuries and spent over $75 million in the elections of 1996 and 1998 trying to regain control of the Congress from the Republicans. The unions felt a Democratic Congress would be more sympathetic to their cause. The Republicans, however, maintained a majority in both houses of Congress, dooming any possibility of legislation against replacement workers reaching President Clinton's desk. Still, the issue did not die. In 1998, President Clinton used his constitutional power and signed an executive order barring federal contractors from using replacement workers, a decision (applauded by organized labor) that affected some 26 million workers employed by federal contractors. The order was overturned, however, by the U.S. Court of Appeals and the right of federal contractors to replace striking workers was reaffirmed.

Still, unions have refused to roll over and play dead. When Johnson Controls, Inc., a producer of automobile seats, replaced striking members of the United Auto Workers with strikebreakers, the union asked Ford Motor Company to decline to accept the seats made by the replacement workers. Ford refused to accept the seats, and Johnson Controls settled with the union. Ford has said, however, that this was an isolated incident and will not become standard company practice. The question of replacement workers remains in the court of popular opinion.

Decision Questions

1. Should companies have the legal right to replace striking workers? If so, should replacement workers be permitted to keep their jobs after the labor dispute has ended?

2. What are some potentially negative effects of replacing striking workers?

3. Does either the company or the union really ever win during a strike? What are some of the negative effects of strikes for both the company and the union?

4. Would you cross a picket line and fill the job of a striking worker? Why or why not?

Sources: Kevin McDermott, "Firestone's Central Illinois Plant Grabs Suspicion, If Not Blame, for Blowouts," *St. Louis Post-Dispatch*, August 20, 2000, p. B1; James R. Healey and Sara Nathan, "Could $1 Worth of Nylon Have Saved People's Lives?" *USA Today*, August 9, 2000, p. 1B; and "Flaws Caused Failures Of Tires," *Newsday*, February 2, 2001, p. A23.

VIDEO CASE

CLASSIC CASE: SATURN

Labor and management working harmoniously together—sounds like an impossible dream. Well, the impossible dream is a reality at the Saturn plant in Spring Hill, Tennessee. At this facility workers and managers have joined together in a unique union-management partnership that's governed by a slender 18-page labor agreement that gives workers a voice in planning and operating decisions at the company. This new work culture at Saturn has both management and workers beaming.

What makes this accomplishment even more unique is that all the workers at the Saturn plant come from other General Motors plants around the country, including some locations that were a hotbed of hostility between the union and management. At the Saturn facility, workers feel they have a clearer voice in how their jobs are structured and more control over the final product that leaves the plant. Union workers also believe empowerment and the effective use of teams are key factors in managing quality and enhancing productivity.

Michael Bennett, president of the United Autoworkers Local 1853 at the plant, credits both management and the union for the change in the Saturn work environment. He concedes that his role and that of fellow union members has changed and admits that he represents not only the union members but also GM customers and stockholders. His management counterpart, Robert Boroff, vice president of production, admits to some problems adjusting his style from traditional management practices, but agrees the team approach is working at Saturn. Both men feel that the key to the plant's long-term growth is maintaining an aura of compromise where solutions are acceptable to all. Since its entry into the market in the 1980s, Saturn has maintained a set of key concepts as its base of operations. These concepts include:

- Everyone in the company has ownership and is responsible for its successes and failures.
- Equality is practiced not just preached.
- People are the company's most important asset.
- Barriers to doing a good job have been eliminated.
- Union and management are partners, sharing responsibility for ensuring the success of the company.
- People have authority to do their job.

How have operations at Saturn fared? Saturn turned a profit for General Motors just three years after the company began. However, in 1999 sales started falling and temporary factory shutdowns were inevitable. Employee hours were not cut by the new schedule though. Under Saturn's unique labor contract (separate from the master agreement in place at other GM Motors Corp. auto factories) workers remained on the clock during production halts, doing training, plant maintenance and other tasks. Ask any member of a work team at Saturn about their jobs and they agree resoundingly about two things: they will go out of their way to help a fellow team member and product quality is the goal. When asked about the competition in this intensely competitive industry, Saturn workers smile and ring out in a loud chorus. Bring 'em on.

Discussion Questions

1. What key elements are needed in a company such as Saturn to make such unique labor/management relations work?
2. Do you think the Saturn experiment is an example of a workplace fad or an indicator of how future labor/management agreements will function?
3. Which side has the toughest job adjusting to such a revolutionary type work arrangement such as Saturn?

MANAGEMENT OF HUMAN RESOURCES

Human resources are the people in an organization. How those people are hired, managed, and treated is the responsibility of human resource managers. These key people used to be called personnel managers or directors—and still are in some companies. They are personnel specialists who help to make management more effective in hiring and in overall job satisfaction. Many organizations are too large to allow close contact between top management and most subordinates. In such firms, human resource people provide this link.

Human resource specialists select, interview, and recommend prospective employees for job openings. They are involved in training for both employees and managers. Human resource personnel will often be directly involved in writing training guides, and they keep everyone in the organization informed about training opportunities. A director of human resources may manage several departments in larger companies, including equal employment opportunity specialists and recruitment specialists.

SKILLS

A human resource manager must have a thorough knowledge of current laws. Since the early 1960s, many new laws affecting employment have been passed, especially in the area of equal employment opportunity. Not knowing the law can damage a company and even cause it to lose credibility with the public.

Like other managers, human resource managers need the ability to organize themselves and to keep others organized. They also need good communications skills, both oral and written. Since human resource planning is an integral part of the job, they must also be good planners, able to project both long- and short-term needs. Good human resource managers should also like to persuade and influence the actions of others. Often they have to sell their ideas on such issues as creative training programs, changing company traditions, and staffing changes.

Other skills are more specific to the careers in the area. For example, training specialists need skills in teaching and developing training programs. Directors of labor relations need to have extensive training in labor union operations and law. Human resource planning specialists must be adept at forecasting future trends and planning for them.

CAREER PATHS

In today's workplace, most companies want to hire college graduates, even for entry-level human resource positions. An increasing number of colleges offer programs that lead to a human resources management degree. Graduate programs leading to master's and doctoral degrees are also numerous. Human resource management is also one field that hires many women and minorities.

Entry-level jobs include administrative assistant, human resource assistant, or office assistant. Even with the academic training that is required, experience in a human resource department is important for success as a human resource manager. Just as in other management positions, promotion to the top in a large organization is likely to be competitive—and even political.

SOME POSSIBLE POSITIONS IN HUMAN RESOURCE MANAGEMENT

JOB TITLE	SALARY	JOB DUTIES	CAREER PATH	PROSPECTS
Training specialist	Median: $37,710	Assess needs for training, plan and implement training programs. Conduct orientation and on-the-job training programs.	A background in teaching or psychology is helpful. Degree in human resource management can also help. Often will be promoted into management within human resource department.	Average growth through 2008.
Employment interviewer/ counselor	Median $29,800	Act as broker, brining job and applicant together.	College degree desirable. Jobs are available in state employment agencies and in private career placement companies.	Average growth through 2008.
Employee benefits specialist	Median: $38,300	Administer programs in health insurance, retirement plans, profit sharing, etc. Apply ever-changing federal laws to the process.	Begin by following orders of human resource manager; given more responsibility with experience.	Above average growth through 2008.
Labor relations specialist	Median: $37,710	Assist management in conducting negotiations with the union and help in labor–management disputes.	Entry-level specialists deal with minor grievances and other minor labor–management issues. After experience, they become involved in higher-level negotiations.	Average growth through 2008.

Source: *Occupational Outlook Handbook,* 2000–2001 Edition: Bureau of Labor Statistics.

CREATIVE STAFFING SOLUTIONS

Name: Joy A. Peace-Thomas

Age: 33

Position/title: Operations Manager

Salary range: $45,000–$70,000

Time in this position: 1 year

Company name: Creative Staffing Solutions

Company's Web address: CSSrecruiting.com

Company description: Creative Staffing Solutions (CSS) has successfully provided diverse staffing solutions to clients ranging from small to large businesses. Specializing in the fields of information technology, administrative support, and professional personnel, we have positioned ourselves to effectively offer staffing/recruiting services with competitive pricing.

Major factors in the decision to take this position: Creative Staffing Solutions has allowed me to work as a staffing consultant as well as a consultative partner to assist the company with grant writing, budgets, advertising, and strategic planning.

Job description: Responsible for the development of staff personnel, customer satisfaction, customer retention, branch profitability, credit procedures, and branch operational cost. This position involves training, workforce development, coordinating open houses, and on-site visits to clients.

Career path: I began working as a Assistant Job Placement Coordinator in 1990 for PSI Institute in Philadelphia. After three successful months of developing business relationships with clients, I was promoted to Director of Job Placement. I then began working at the Private Industry Council of Philadelphia as a Placement Specialist for PIC's subcontractors. After five years of contracted employment, I entered the staffing arena by joining "The Placers" in 1997. Placers led me into the direction of London Personnel Services where I secured my first Branch Managers/Assistant District Managers role. By 2000, with my newly attained skills, I was able to secure a position with Creative Staffing Solutions as Operations Manager.

Ideal next job: HR Generalist for the Company

Best part of your job: Training others on the fundamentals of developing consultative relationships with clients, staffing, team work, and recruiting. I enjoy sharing my knowledge and continuing to educate others about the staffing arena. Creative Staffing has positioned me as a change agent to work on behalf of my clients and workforce.

Worst part of your job: Lack of commitment from a candidate. Often times candidates are unsure of an assignment, so at the last second a candidate may decide to decline a position or not show up for an assignment.

Educational background: Master's Degree from Lincoln University, PA

Favorite course: Systems/Strategic Planning and Management and Ethics. The systems classes allowed me to successfully plan and manage staff within an organization.

Best course for your career: Self and others. This course allowed me to learn the fundamentals of others in relation to business and how to deal with mixed company. Dealing with real life situations and individuals on the job, this course allowed me to learn the personalities of others at the workplace and how to relate to them. I learned how to view others and accept their challenges, strengths, and weaknesses.

Recommended by Maurice Sampson, Community College of Philadelphia.

13

Marketing: Customer and Stakeholder Relationship Management

LEARNING GOALS

AFTER YOU HAVE READ AND STUDIED THIS CHAPTER, YOU SHOULD BE ABLE TO

1 Explain the marketing concept.

2 Give an example of how to use the four Ps of marketing.

3 Describe the marketing research process, and tell how marketers use environmental scanning to learn about the changing marketing environment.

4 Explain various ways of segmenting the consumer market.

5 List several ways in which the business-to-business market differs from the consumer market.

6 Show how the marketing concept has been adapted to fit today's modern markets.

7 Describe the latest marketing strategies, such as stakeholder marketing and customer relationship management.

Getting to Know Robert L. Johnson of BET Holdings Inc.

Robert L. Johnson is a dreamer, but one who works tirelessly to make his dreams come true. As the ninth of ten children of factory workers, Johnson dreamed of a better life and he knew he needed a good education to get it. He realized his dream when he earned a degree in international affairs from Princeton University. In 1979, when he was vice president of the National Cable TV Association, he had a dream of a cable channel targeted to an African American audience. Johnson developed a plan for such a channel, got funding, and bought two hours of weekly satellite time. At 11 PM on January 8, 1980, Johnson's dream reached 3.8 million subscribers. The first Black Entertainment Television (BET) signal carried the 1974 African safari movie *Visit to a Chief's Son.* BET now airs 24 hours a day and reaches about 67 million homes, including almost 100 percent of the 6.8 million African American households with cable.

BET Holdings has expanded into a billion-dollar enterprise with two movie channels, a jazz channel, BET Weekend (a weekend newspaper insert), a health and fitness magazine called *Heart and Soul,* a financial services company, a clothing line, an airline called DC Air, and more, including a planned chain of music-themed restaurants. Also in the plans are 10 TV movies, a late-night talk show, and a Las Vegas restaurant.

All of this success is due to an entrepreneur with a vision. Johnson noted that African Americans watched more TV than many groups, and that advertisers wanted to reach them. The market potential was so great that Johnson was able to get funding easily. That's the power of market segmentation—breaking the total market into smaller segments based on age or sex or income or some other category (such as ethnicity)—and then designing products and services to meet the specific needs of those segments.

Once you have found such a market niche, the next step is to develop a close relationship with those customers and de-velop a loyal following among them. Most of BET's nearly 600 employees are African American. Many of them are young and knowledgeable about their peers. They are able to talk with BET's customers and work with them to develop new products and services that they want. The African American market segment is made up of some 35 million people and their incomes are rising fast. Johnson recognizes the fact that there are other market segments that may prove equally profitable. He says, "We're moving toward more market fragmentation, so markets can become sustainable with smaller and smaller numbers, customized down to even one person. . . You can combine strong brand identification with niche marketing if you're nimble."

Media giant Viacom bought BET Holdings for $3 billion in 2000. Viacom has the money, TV movies, feature films, and other resources to greatly improve BET's offerings. Viacom already owned CBS, UPN, MTV, VH1, Nickelodeon, TNN, Showtime, Country Music Television, and TV Land—and some of these shows may soon be shown on BET.

There are marketing opportunities available in other market segments, including people over the age of 60, Asian Americans, and teens. You could be the next entrepreneur who develops TV shows, restaurants, and other products to meet the needs of these specialized market segments. In this chapter, we explore marketing in general and then look at marketing strategies, including market segmentation, targeting, and relationship building.

Sources: Scott S. Smith, "BETting on Success," *Entrepreneur,* August 1999, pp. 112–16; Peter Binzen, "Indian Food Maker Hopes to Fly Like Its Cuisine," *Philadelphia Inquirer,* March 13, 2000, pp. F1, F3; Brian Sharp, "BET Executive Robert Johnson, an Icon in the Making," *Gannett News Service,* June 16, 2000; and Neil Irwin, "Deal Means Potential Change for BET.com," *The Washington Post,* November 4, 2000. pp. E1, E2.

A BRIEF HISTORY OF MARKETING

marketing concept
A three-part business philosophy: (1) a customer orientation, (2) a service orientation, and (3) a profit orientation.

customer relationship management
Learning as much as possible about customers and doing everything you can to satisfy them or even delight them with goods and services over time.

marketing
The process of determining customer wants and needs and then providing customers with goods and services that meet or exceed their expectations.

When asked what marketing is, many people say "selling" or "advertising." Yes, there was a time when the emphasis in marketing was on selling and advertising, but that was in the 1930s and 1940s. During that time, most companies emphasized selling and advertising, and did not pay much attention to what consumers wanted or needed or how to best satisfy those wants and needs. Marketers often annoyed consumers with their constant promotions designed to persuade them to buy existing products, and did little to service them after the sale. As you are well aware, some companies today continue to annoy consumers and don't always provide good customer service.

Marketing slowly developed a more customer-oriented approach. After World War II ended in 1945, there was tremendous demand in the United States for goods and services among the returning veterans who were starting a new life with new families. Competition for consumers' dollars was fierce. Business owners recognized the need to be responsive to consumers if they wanted to get their business, and a philosophy emerged in the 1950s called the marketing concept.

The **marketing concept** had three parts:

1. *A customer orientation.* Find out what consumers want and provide it for them. (Note the emphasis on consumers rather than promotion.)

2. *A service orientation.* Make sure everyone in the organization has the same objective—*customer satisfaction.* This should be a total and integrated organizational effort.

3. *A profit orientation.* Market those goods and services that will earn the firm a profit and enable it to survive and expand to serve more consumer wants and needs.

You can summarize much of marketing with the slogan, "Find a need and fill it."

It took a while for businesses to implement the marketing concept. During the 1980s, businesses began to apply the marketing concept more aggressively than they had done over the preceding 30 years. That led to the focus on marketing management that we'll discuss shortly. In the 1990s, managers extended the marketing concept by adopting the concept of customer relationship management. **Customer relationship management (CRM)** is learning as much as possible about customers and doing everything you can to satisfy them or even delight them with goods and services > P.25 < over time.[1] The idea is to get very close to your present customers and to spend more time with them rather than to constantly seek new customers. We shall explore this concept in more depth later in the chapter.

Defining Marketing as Meeting Customer Needs

Marketing is the process of determining customer needs and wants and then providing customers with goods and services that meet or exceed their expectations. More simply, the goal of the marketing process is to

FIND A NEED AND FILL IT

Knowing what customers need and want is much easier today than ever before because purchases can be recorded in a database ➤ **P.15** ◄ (an electronic file).[2] For example, a grocery store that uses such a database knows what each customer has purchased over the last few months. Such purchases may include baby food, diapers, and dog food. From that information, the store knows that the customer likely has small children and a dog. Using that information, the store can send out coupons and advertisements specifically designed to be useful to families with small children and pets. You can see, then, how a store can establish a close relationship with its customers and provide them with a group of goods and services made specifically for their needs.[3]

Nonprofit Organizations Use Marketing Too

Even though the marketing concept emphasizes a profit orientation, marketing is a critical part of almost all organizations, whether profit or nonprofit.[4] Charities use marketing to raise funds or to obtain other resources. For example, the Red Cross might have a promotion to encourage people to donate blood when local or national supplies run low. Churches use marketing to attract new members and to raise funds. Politicians use marketing to get votes. States use marketing to attract new businesses and tourists. Many states, for example, have competed to get automobile plants from other countries to locate in their area. Schools use marketing to attract new students. Other organizations, such as unions and social groups, also use marketing. The Advertising Council, for example, uses marketing to create awareness and change attitudes on such issues as drunk driving and fire prevention.[5]

A great example of a person who has learned to "find a need and fill it" is Mary Ann Liebert. Her company publishes more than 60 medical journals, books and newsletters. Her secret is to find untapped niches and then bring out journals to meet the needs of researchers in those areas, areas such as gene therapy, cloning, and biotech.

Using the concept of "Find a need and fill it," which of your needs are not being met by businesses in your area? Are there enough people with similar needs to attract a business that would meet those needs? How would you find out?

CRITICAL THINKING

MARKETING MANAGEMENT AND THE MARKETING MIX

Implementing the marketing concept has led to more emphasis on marketing management so that pleasing the customer has become a priority for management. **Marketing management** is the process of planning and executing the conception, pricing, promotion, and distribution (place) of ideas, goods, and services (products) to create mutually beneficial exchanges. The idea is to please customers *and* make a profit doing so.

marketing management
The process of planning and executing the conception, pricing, promotion, and distribution of ideas, goods, and services (products) to create mutually beneficial exchanges.

FIGURE 13.1

**THE MARKETING MIX AND
THE MARKETING
MANAGER'S ROLE**

The marketing manager
chooses the proper price,
promotion, and place to
develop a comprehensive
marketing program. This
figure shows the mix for a
new cereal. Included would
be decisions about
packaging, couponing, and
more.

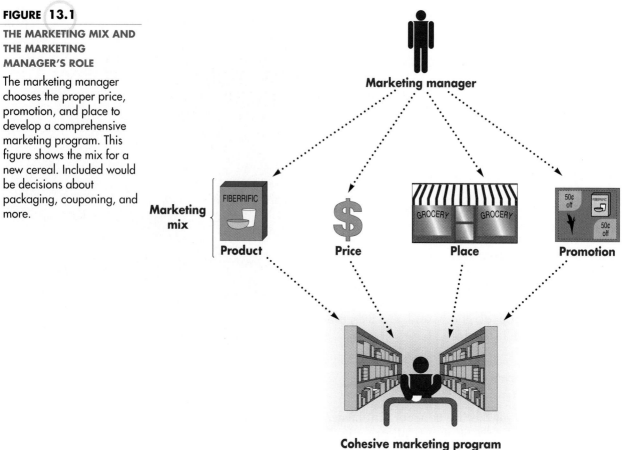

Much of what marketing managers do has been conveniently divided into
four factors, called the *four Ps*, to make them easy to remember and implement. They are:

1. Product
2. Price
3. Place
4. Promotion

marketing mix
The ingredients that go into a
marketing program: product,
price, place, and promotion.

Managing the controllable parts of the marketing process, then, involves:
(1) designing a want-satisfying *product*, (2) setting a *price* for the product,
(3) distributing the product to a *place* where people will buy it, and (4) *promoting* the product. These four factors are sometimes called the **marketing
mix** because they're the ingredients that go into a marketing program. A
marketing manager designs a marketing program that effectively combines
the ingredients of the marketing mix (see Figure 13.1). The *Business Week*
box discusses how the automobile industry is adjusting to the market using
the four Ps.

Applying the Marketing Process

One of the best ways for you to understand the marketing process is to take
a product and follow the process that led to the development and sale of that

FROM THE PAGES OF BusinessWeek
www.autobytel.com

Automakers Strategize Using the Four Ps

You can see the four Ps of marketing in action if you closely follow changes that are occurring in the automobile industry. New products are being designed to meet market niches. There are, for example, sports cars to compete with the Porsche Boxster to appeal to successful young executives, and sport utility vehicles (SUVs) for nearly every taste. Never before have there been more choices in cars—from small personal cars to large vans. And in those cars is every conceivable convenience from phones to CD players, cup holders to global positioning devices. Automobile companies truly seem to be listening to customers and trying to meet their needs. This is the *product* part of the four Ps.

When it comes to *pricing,* there is a whole new revolution going on in this industry. On the Web, sites such as Autobytel.com and AutoWeb.com provide product and price information and dealer referrals. Customers can thus determine the best price before going to a dealership. Some dealers are offering no-haggle pricing to eliminate one of the most annoying parts of buying a car.

Getting cars to a *place* that is convenient for customers is also being done by auto websites. Autobytel.com and AutoWeb.com help customers find the dealer closest to them that will offer the best price for the automobile they choose. Ford and General Motors are experimenting with websites and factory-owned stores. GM's service, called BuyPower, gives consumers access to every vehicle on participating dealers' lots as well as independent data about competing models. Meanwhile, chains such as AutoNation and CarMax are selling both new and used cars at convenient locations. Consumers can now order almost any car from anywhere in the world via the Internet. The car will be shipped to a nearby port, and all paperwork is handled with ease.

Promotion for new and used cars is also changing. Dealers are trying low-pressure salesmanship because they know that customers are now armed with much more information than in the past. More and more power is being shifted to consumers. They can go on the Internet; learn about various cars and their features, including safety features; pick which features they want; get the best price available; and order the car—without leaving their homes. In such an atmosphere the marketing task shifts from helping the seller sell to helping the buyer buy. Internet sellers make every effort to help buyers find the car that best meets their needs and minimize the hassle involved in getting that car.

In the future, the real difference among dealers may be in postpurchase (after-sales) service. Those dealers who treat customers best through relationship marketing (discussed later in this chapter) may develop loyalty that can't be matched in any other way. Such relationships are built through service contracts, guarantees, reminder cards telling customers when to come in for various services, parties with customers, and more. The model for such relationships is that set by Harley-Davidson with its motorcycles. No customers are more loyal and more united with each other than Harley buyers. Developing such loyalty will be the goal of most marketers, including automakers and auto dealers.

Sources: Joann Muller, Keith Naughton and Larry Armstrong, "Old Carmakers Learn New Tricks," *Business Week,* April 12, 1999, pp. 116–18, and Bob Thompson, "If Profit Is the Point, Loyalty Is the Key," *Business Week* (advertisement), July 3, 2000, pp. 67ff.

product (see Figure 13.2). Remember that the basis of marketing is finding a need and filling it. So your first step is to find a need. Imagine that you and your friends don't have time to eat big breakfasts. You want something for breakfast that's fast, nutritious, and good tasting. Some of your friends eat a cereal made with 100 percent natural oats and honey, but you and others are not happy with this product. In fact, you know that the Center for the Public Interest named this cereal number one on its list of "10 Foods You Should *Never* Eat!" because of its high sugar content. Furthermore, you've read in a magazine that the cereal industry has been slow to innovate.[6] You sense opportunity.

FIGURE 13.2

THE MARKETING PROCESS

Find a need

Conduct research

Design a product to meet the need based on research

Do product testing

Determine a brand name, design a package, and set a price

Select a distribution system

Design a promotional program

Build a relationship with customers

product
Any physical good, service, or idea that satisfies a want or need.

test marketing
The process of testing products among potential users.

brand name
A word, letter, or group of words or letters that differentiates one seller's goods and services from those of competitors.

You ask around among your acquaintances and find that a huge demand exists for a good-tasting breakfast cereal that's nutritious, high in fiber, and low in sugar. This fact leads you to conduct a more extensive marketing research study to determine whether there's a large enough market for such a cereal. Your research supports your assumption: there *is* a large market for a high-fiber cereal. By now it's becoming obvious that you have found a need. You have completed one of the first steps in marketing: researching consumer wants and needs and finding a need for a product that's not yet available.

Designing a Product to Meet Needs

Once you have researched consumer needs, the four Ps of marketing begin. You start by developing a product. A **product** is any physical good, service, or idea that satisfies a want or need. In this case, your proposed product is a multigrain cereal made with an artificial sweetener. It's a good idea at this point to do *concept testing*. That is, you develop an accurate description of your product and ask people, in person or online, whether the concept (the idea of the cereal) appeals to them.[7] If it does, you might go to a manufacturer that has the equipment and skills to design such a cereal, and begin making prototypes. *Prototypes* are samples of the product that you take to consumers to test their reactions. The process of testing products among potential users is called **test marketing.**

If consumers like the product and agree they would buy it, you may turn the production process over to an existing manufacturer or you may decide to produce the cereal yourself. *Outsourcing,* ➤ **P.254** ◄ remember, is the term used to describe the allocation of production and other functions to outside firms. The idea is to retain only those functions that you can do most efficiently and outsource the rest. The Reaching Beyond Our Borders box describes how outsourcing helps businesses reach global markets.

Once the product meets taste and quality expectations, you have to design a package and think of an appropriate brand name.[8] A **brand name** is a word, letter, or group of words or letters that differentiates one seller's goods and services from those of competitors. Cereal brand names, for example, include Cheerios, Frosted Flakes, and Raisin Bran. Let's say that you name your cereal Fiberrific to emphasize the high fiber content and terrific taste. We'll discuss the product development process, including packaging,

REACHING BEYOND OUR BORDERS
Help Is Available
www.eastwest-global.com

Marketing abroad is getting easier and easier as companies have emerged to provide third-party services to help other companies reach and serve foreign customers. Such services include marketing support, e-commerce development, and transportation.

At first, only large companies such as UPS World Wide Logistics provided third-party services to global marketers. But lately smaller companies have emerged to offer more specialized services, such as website development and follow-up services after the sale. Selling in China, for example, has never been easy for U.S. firms. But East-West Equipment and Technology, Inc., now operates as a development and trade management company with offices in Beijing and Wuhan. The company was originally set up to sell secondhand equipment to Chinese buyers. It turned out that Chinese buyers didn't have enough information as they tried to choose from thousands of pieces of used equipment. So East-West began providing guidance and detailed in-formation to Chinese buyers. It now does the same for U.S. buyers who need information about Chinese business practices.

U.S. firms once found it difficult to set up distribution networks in Mexico. Now GATX Corporation has a logistics subsidiary in Mexico that helps U.S. firms to reach Mexican consumers. The company also operates in Chile. Many more companies could be cited that provide services to firms wishing to sell internationally. The Internet may provide access to global markets, but there still is the problem of transporting goods. Transportation and logistics services in general (e.g., warehousing) are available in most countries to help finalize the sale.

Sources: Robert Selwitz, "The Logistics of Geography," *Global Business*, February 2000, pp. 48–56; Scott Thrum, "Getting the Goods," *The Wall Street Journal*, November 22, 1999, p. R39; and Cheryl D. Krivda, "E-Supply Chain," *Fortune* (advertisement), June 21, 2000, pp. 341ff.

branding, and pricing, in detail in Chapter 14. In other chapters, we will follow the Fiberrific case to show you how the concepts apply to one particular product. For now, we're simply sketching the whole process to give you an idea of what the overall marketing picture is all about. So far, we've only covered the first P of the marketing mix: product. Next comes price.

Setting an Appropriate Price

After you developed the product or designed the service you want to offer consumers, you have to set an appropriate *price*. That price depends on a number of factors. For example, in the cereal business, the price should probably be close to what other cereal makers charge since most cereals are priced competitively. You also have to consider the costs involved in producing, distributing, and promoting the product. We shall discuss all of these issues in more detail in Chapter 14.

Getting the Product to the Right Place

Once the product is manufactured, you have to choose how to get it to the consumer.[9] Remember, *place* is the third P in the marketing mix. You may want to sell the cereal directly to supermarkets or health food stores, or you may want to sell it through organizations that specialize in distributing food

Now Available On Earth

Introducing FedEx Ground. Finally, date-definite, door-to-door ground delivery to every business address in North America and Puerto Rico. Along with FedEx Express, one phone number and one website cover all your shipping needs. That's heaven on earth for your business. Call 1-800-Go-FedEx or visit fedex.com

Be absolutely sure: **FedEx** Ground

Place is the third P of the marketing mix, and few companies are better suited to perform that function than FedEx. For most companies, it is simply not possible to match the speed and reliability of a company like FedEx, so they outsource much of the distribution (place) function to FedEx or some other specialist. Do you see any disadvantages to giving up this key function to another company?

products. Such organizations, called *intermediaries,* are in the middle of a series of organizations that distribute goods from producers to consumers. (The more traditional word for such companies is *middlemen.*) Getting the product to consumers when and where they want it is critical to market success. We'll discuss the importance of marketing intermediaries and distribution in detail in Chapter 15.

Developing an Effective Promotional Strategy

The last of the four Ps of marketing is promotion. **Promotion** consists of all the techniques sellers use to motivate people to buy products or services. They include advertising; personal selling; public relations; publicity; word-of-mouth; and various sales promotion efforts, such as coupons, rebates, samples, and cents-off deals.[10] Promotion is discussed in detail in Chapter 16.

This last step in the marketing process often includes relationship building with customers. That includes responding to suggestions consumers may make to improve the product or its marketing. Postpurchase, or after-sale, service may include exchanging goods that weren't satisfactory and making other adjustments to ensure consumer satisfaction, including recycling. Marketing is an ongoing process. To remain competitive, companies must continually adapt to changes in the market and to changes in consumer wants and needs.

PROGRESS ASSESSMENT

• What are the three parts of the marketing concept?
• What are the four Ps of the marketing mix?

PROVIDING MARKETERS WITH INFORMATION

promotion
All the techniques sellers use to motivate people to buy products or services.

marketing research
The analysis of markets to determine opportunities and challenges, and to find the information needed to make good decisions.

Every step in the marketing process depends on information that is used to make the right decisions. **Marketing research** is the analysis of markets to determine opportunities and challenges, and to find the information needed to make good decisions. If you were to major in marketing, marketing research would be one of the courses you would likely take.

Marketing research helps determine what customers have purchased in the past, what situational changes have occurred to alter not only what consumers want now but also what they're likely to want in the future. In addition, marketers conduct research on business trends, the ecological impact of their decisions, international trends, and more (see Figure 13.3). Businesses need information in order to compete effectively, and marketing research is the activity that gathers that information. Note, too, that in addition to listening to customers, marketing researchers should pay attention to what employees, shareholders, dealers, consumer advocates, media representatives, and other stakeholders have to say.

The Marketing Research Process

The marketing research process consists of four key steps:

1. Defining the problem (or opportunity) and determining the present situation.
2. Collecting data.
3. Analyzing the research data.
4. Choosing the best solutions.

The following sections look at each of these steps.

FIGURE 13.3

MARKETING RESEARCH TOPICS

Many organizations do research to determine market potential, to evaluate market share, and to learn more about the people in various markets. Most also do short- and long-range sales forecasting and competitor analysis.

ADVERTISING RESEARCH

1. Motivation research
2. Copy research
3. Media research
4. Studies of ad effectiveness
5. Studies of competitive advertising

BUSINESS ECONOMICS AND CORPORATE RESEARCH

1. Short-range forecasting (up to 1 year)
2. Long-range forecasting (over 1 year)
3. Studies of business trends
4. Pricing studies
5. Plant and warehouse location studies
6. Acquisition studies
7. Export and international studies
8. Management information system (MIS)
9. Operations research
10. Internal company employees

CORPORATE RESPONSIBILITY RESEARCH

1. Consumers' "right-to-know" studies
2. Ecological impact studies
3. Studies of legal constraints on advertising and promotion
4. Social values and policies studies

PRODUCT RESEARCH

1. New product acceptance and potential
2. Competitive product studies
3. Testing of existing products
4. Packaging research

SALES AND MARKET RESEARCH

1. Measurement of market potential
2. Market share analysis
3. Determination of market characteristics
4. Sales analysis
5. Establishment of sales quotas and territories
6. Distribution channel studies
7. Test markets and store audits
8. Consumer panel operations
9. Sales compensation studies
10. Promotional studies

INTERNET RESEARCH

1. Impact of the Internet on business
2. Trends in usage
3. New competitors
4. New uses

One-way glass walls enable managers and employees to watch consumers as they discuss various aspects of a company and its products. From those discussions, companies learn exactly what consumers like and dislike about products and what they would like to see developed in the future. Can you imagine professors using such techniques to learn about various lectures and how they might be improved?

Defining the Problem and Determining the Present Situation It's important to know what an organization does well; it's also critical to know what it doesn't do so well. Marketing researchers should be given the freedom to help discover what the present situation is, what the problems are, what the alternatives are, what information is needed, and how to go about gathering and analyzing data.

Collecting Data Obtaining usable information is vital to the marketing research process. Research can become quite expensive, so some trade-off must often be made between the need for information and the cost of obtaining that information.

Normally it is less expensive to gather information that has already been compiled by others and published in journals and books or made available online. Such existing data are called *secondary data* since you aren't the first one to gather them. Figure 13.4 lists the principal sources of secondary marketing research information.

Often, secondary data don't provide all the information necessary for important business decisions. When additional, in-depth information is needed, marketers must do their own research. The results of such new studies are called *primary data*. One way to gather primary information is the *observation method*, in which trained people observe and record the actions of potential buyers. For example, companies have followed customers in supermarkets to record the behaviors involved in purchasing different products such as meat, bread, and vegetables. Do you think the observation method would be helpful in gathering information you need to promote Fiberrific?

A more formal way to gather primary data is to conduct a survey. Telephone surveys, online surveys, mail surveys, and personal interviews are the most common forms. Focus groups are another popular method of surveying individuals. A **focus group** is a small group of people (8 to 14 individu-

focus group
A small group of people who meet under the direction of a discussion leader to communicate their opinions about an organization, its products, or other given issues.

GOVERNMENT PUBLICATIONS

Statistical Abstract of the United States
Survey of Current Business
Census of Retail Trade
Census of Transportation
Annual Survey of Manufacturers

COMMERCIAL PUBLICATIONS

A. C. Nielsen Company studies on retailing and media
Marketing Research Corporation of America studies on consumer purchases
Selling Areas–Marketing, Inc., reports on food sales

MAGAZINES

Entrepreneur	*Journal of Marketing*	Trade magazines
Business Week	*Journal of Retailing*	appropriate to your industry
Fortune	*Journal of Consumer Research*	such as *Progressive Grocer*
Inc.	*Journal of Advertising*	Reports from various
Advertising Age	*Journal of Marketing Research*	chambers of commerce
Forbes	*Marketing News*	
Harvard Business Review	*Journal of Advertising Research*	

NEWSPAPERS

The Wall Street Journal
Barron's

INTERNAL SOURCES

Company records
Balance sheets
Income statements
Prior research reports

GENERAL SOURCES

Internet searches
Commercial databases

FIGURE 13.4

SELECTED SOURCES OF SECONDARY AND PRIMARY INFORMATION
You should spend a day or two at the library becoming familiar with these sources. You can read about primary research in any marketing research text from the library.

als, for example) who meet under the direction of a discussion leader to communicate their opinions about an organization, its products, or other given issues.

Marketers can now gather both secondary and primary data online.[11] Using that research, marketing managers are ready to do what it takes to please consumers.

Analyzing the Research Data The data collected in the research process must be turned into useful information. Careful, honest interpretation of the data collected can help a company find useful alternatives to specific marketing

MAKING ETHICAL DECISIONS   *www.kelloggs.com*

No Kidding

Marketers have long recognized that children can be an important influence on their parents' buying decisions. In fact, many direct appeals for products are focused on children. Let's say that at Fiberrific, you've experienced a great response to your new high-fiber, high-protein cereal among health-conscious consumers. The one important group you haven't been able to attract is children. Therefore, the product development team is considering introducing Fiberrific Jr. to expand the product line.

Fiberrific Jr. may have strong market potential if you follow two recommendations of the research department. First, coat the flakes generously with sugar (significantly changing the cereal's nutritional benefits). Second, promote the product exclusively on children's TV programs.

Such a promotional strategy should create a strong demand for the product, especially if you offer a premium (a toy or other "surprise") in each box. The consensus among the research department is that kids will love the new taste, plus parents will agree to buy Fiberrific Jr. because of their positive impression of your best-selling brand. The research director commented, "The chance of a parent actually reading our label and noting the addition of sugar is nil."

Would you introduce Fiberrific Jr. according to the recommendations of your research department? What are the benefits of doing so? What are the risks involved in following the recommendations? What would you do if you were the marketing manager for this product?

---

challenges. For example, Fresh Italy, a small Italian pizzeria, found in its research that its pizza's taste was rated superior compared to the larger pizza chains. However, the company's sales lagged behind the competition. Research pointed out that free delivery (which Fresh Italy did not offer) was more important to customers than taste. Fresh Italy now delivers and has increased its market share.

Choosing the Best Solution After collecting and analyzing data, market researchers determine alternative strategies and make recommendations as to which strategy may be best and why. This final step in a research effort involves following up on the actions taken to see if the results were as expected. If not, the company can take corrective action and conduct new studies in the ongoing attempt to provide consumer satisfaction at the lowest cost. You can see, then, that marketing research is a continuous process of responding to changes in the marketplace and changes in consumer preferences.

Company websites have vastly improved the marketing research process in both domestic and global markets. Businesses can now continuously interact with their customers as they strive to improve products and services.[12] The information exchanged can be very useful in determining what customers want. Keeping customer information in a database ➤ **P.15** ◄ enables a company to improve its product offerings over time and to design promotions that are geared exactly to meet the needs of specific groups of consumers. That is the idea behind continuous improvement ➤ **P.251** ◄.

In today's customer-driven market, ethics is also important in every aspect of marketing. Companies should therefore do what's right as well as what's profitable. This step could add greatly to the social benefits of marketing decisions. (See the Making Ethical Decisions box.)

FIGURE 13.5

**THE MARKETING
ENVIRONMENT**

The Marketing Environment

Marketing managers must be aware of the surrounding environment when making marketing mix decisions. **Environmental scanning** is the process of identifying the factors that can affect marketing success. As you can see in Figure 13.5, those factors include global, technological, social, competitive, and economic influences. We discussed these factors in some detail in Chapter 1, but it is helpful to review them from a strictly marketing perspective as well.

Global Factors The most dramatic global change is probably the growth of the Internet. Now businesses can reach many of the consumers in the world relatively easily and carry on a dialogue with them about the goods and services they want. (See the Legal Briefcase box, though, for some issues of concern.) This globalization of marketing puts more pressure on those whose responsibility it is to deliver products. Many marketers outsource that function to companies like FedEx, UPS, and DHL, which have a solid reputation for delivering goods quickly. Small, home-based businesses can contact www.smartship.com to find information about local shipping companies, including pickup or drop-off services.[13]

Technological Factors The most important technological changes also involve the Internet and the growth of consumer databases. Using consumer databases, companies can develop products and services that closely match the needs of consumers. As you read in Chapter 9, it is now possible to produce customized goods and services for about the same price as mass-produced goods. Thus, flexible manufacturing and mass customization are also major influences on marketers.

Social Factors There are a number of social trends that marketers must monitor to maintain their close relationship with customers. Population growth and changing demographics are examples of social trends that can have an ef-

**environmental
scanning**
The process of identifying the
factors that can affect
marketing success.

LEGAL BRIEFCASE

www.landsend.com

Guaranteed Problems

Now that Internet companies are selling globally, they have to abide by all the rules of all the countries they are in—and that is not easy. For example, Lands' End got into trouble in Germany by promoting its guarantee on goods purchased. Such guarantees are not legal in Germany. Germany's reasoning is that the cost of offering a guarantee is hidden in a higher sales price. Anyhow, small companies advertising on the Internet must be careful to not break any laws of the countries they reach. The cost of fighting such laws is too high for a small firm. Lands' End may have the money, but most small firms do not. Many companies are now having second thoughts about selling goods and services globally on the Internet.

The European Union is now considering a law that would require vendors to comply with 15 different sets of national rules. They include France's requirement that all contracts must be concluded in French. Which countries and which consumers are likely to suffer most from such restrictions—those from developed countries or those from poorer countries?

Sources: "Globalization: Lessons Learned," *Business Week*, November 6, 2000, p. 228; Robert Guy Matthews, "Tariffs Impede Trade via Web on Global Scale," *The Wall Street Journal*, April 17, 2000, pp. B1, B4 and "Globalization: Lessons Learned," *Business Week*, November 6, 2000, p. 228.

---

fect on sales. For example, one of the fastest growing segments of the U.S. population in the 21st century is older people. The increase in the number of older Americans creates growing demand for nursing homes, health care, prescription drugs, recreation, continuing education, and more. Other shifts in the American population are creating new challenges for marketers as they adjust their products to meet the tastes and preferences of Hispanic, Asian, and other growing ethnic groups.[14]

Competitive Factors   Of course, marketers must pay attention to the dynamic competitive environment.[15] Many brick-and-mortar companies must

Competition has forced smaller businesses to go on the Internet to be competitive with larger businesses. The problem is that building a website often takes a lot of money. That's why Chestnut Cheese Company turned to Freemerchant.com to build their website. The service is free. Can you see why a small company might turn to a local website developer who also provided follow-up services and charged a fee?

be aware of new competition from the Internet, including those that sell automobiles, insurance, music videos, clothes, and more.[16] In the book business, Barnes & Noble and Borders Books are still adjusting to the new reality of Amazon.com's huge selection of books at good prices. Now that consumers can literally search the world for the best buys through the Internet, marketers must adjust their pricing policies accordingly. Similarly, they have to adjust to competitors who can deliver products quickly or provide excellent service.

Economic Factors Marketers must pay close attention to the economic environment. As we began the new millennium, the United States was experiencing unparalleled growth and customers were eager to buy even the most expensive automobiles, watches, and vacations. But as the economy slowed, marketers had to adapt by offering products that were less expensive and more tailored to consumers with modest incomes.[17] Marketers in countries such as Indonesia had already gone through such an economic fall, and are now recovering. You can see, therefore, that environmental scanning is critical to a company's success during rapidly changing economic times.

What environmental changes are occurring in your community? What environmental changes in marketing are most likely to change your career prospects in the future? How can you learn more about those changes? What might you do to prepare for them?

Recognizing Different Markets: Consumer and Business-to-Business

Marketers must know as much as possible about the market they wish to serve. As we defined it in Chapter 6, a market consists of people with unsatisfied wants and needs who have both the resources and the willingness to buy. Thus, if there are people who want a high-fiber, low-sugar cereal, like Fiberrific, and if those people have the resources and willingness to buy it, then it is said that there's a market for Fiberrific.

There are two major markets in business: the consumer market and the business-to-business market. The **consumer market** consists of all the individuals or households that want goods and services for personal consumption or use and have the resources to buy them. The **business-to-business (B2B) market** consists of all the individuals and organizations that want goods and services to use in producing other goods and services or to sell, rent, or supply goods to others. Oil drilling bits, cash registers, display cases, office desks, public accounting audits, and corporate legal advice are examples of B2B goods and services. Traditionally, they have been known as *industrial goods and services* because they were used in industry.

The important thing to remember is that the buyer's reason for buying—that is, the end use of the product—determines whether a product is considered a consumer product or a B2B product. For example, a box of Fiberrific cereal bought for a family's breakfast is considered a consumer product. However, if the same box of Fiberrific were purchased by Dinnie's Diner to sell to its breakfast customers, it would be considered a B2B product. The following sections will outline in more detail consumer and B2B markets.

consumer market
All the individuals or households that want goods and services for personal consumption or use.

business-to-business (B2B) market
All the individuals and organizations that want goods and services to use in producing other goods and services or to sell, rent, or supply goods to others.

The business to business market is much like the consumer market in that companies must learn to find profitable segments. In fact, the B2B market is one huge segment of the total market that includes both business to consumer (B2C) and business to business markets (B2B). This ad shows that the B2B market involves multiple firms and you may miss out on some markets by targeting too narrowly. Can you see how this might happen?

- What are the four parts of the marketing research process?
- What is environmental scanning?
- Can you define the terms *consumer market* and *business-to-business market?*

THE CONSUMER MARKET

As we noted in Chapter 4, the total potential consumer market consists of the over 6 billion people in global markets. Because consumer groups differ greatly in age, education level, income, and taste, a business usually can't fill the needs of every group. Therefore, it must first decide which groups to serve and then develop products and services specially tailored to their needs.

Take Campbell soups, for example. You know Campbell for its traditional soups such as chicken noodle and tomato. You may also have noticed that Campbell has expanded its product line to appeal to a number of different tastes. Campbell noticed the population growth in the American South and in the Latino community in cities across the nation, so it introduced a Creole soup for the southern market and a red bean soup for the Latino market. In Texas and California, where people like their food with a bit of kick, Campbell makes its nacho cheese soup spicier than in other parts of the country. Campbell is just one company that has had some success studying the consumer market, breaking it down into categories, and then developing products for separate groups of consumers.

The process of dividing the total market into several groups whose members have similar characteristics is called **market segmentation.** Marketing

market segmentation
The process of dividing the total market into several groups whose members have similar characteristics.

MAIN DIMENSION	SAMPLE VARIABLES	TYPICAL SEGMENTS
Geographic segmentation	Region	Northeast, Midwest, South, West
	City or county size	Under 5,000; 5,000–10,999; 20,000–49,000; 50,000–99,999
	Density	Urban, suburban, rural
Demographic segmentation	Gender	Male, female
	Age	Under 5; 5–10; 11–18; 19–34; 35–49; 50–64; 65 and over
	Education	Some high school or less, high school graduate, some college, college graduate, postgraduate
	Race	Caucasian, African American, Indian, Asian, Hispanic
	Nationality	American, Asian, Eastern European, Japanese
	Life stage	Infant, preschool, child, teenager, collegiate, adult, senior
	Income	Under $15,000; $15,000–$24,999; $25,000–$44,999; $45,000–$74,999; $75,000 and over
	Household size	1; 2; 3–4; 5 or more
	Occupation	Professional, technical, clerical, sales supervisors, farmers, students, home-based business owners, retired, unemployed
Psychographic segmentation	Personality	Gregarious, compulsive, extroverted, aggressive, ambitious
	Values	Actualizers, fulfillers, achievers, experiencers, believers, strivers, makers, strugglers
	Lifestyle	Upscale, moderate
Benefit segmentation	Comfort	(Benefit segmentation divides an already established market into smaller, more homogeneous segments. Those people who desire economy in a car would be an example. The benefit desired varies by product.)
	Convenience	
	Durability	
	Economy	
	Health	
	Luxury	
	Safety	
	Status	
Volume segmentation	Usage	Heavy users, light users, nonusers
	Loyalty status	None, medium, strong

FIGURE 13.6

MARKET SEGMENTATION

This table shows some of the methods marketers use to divide the market. The aim of segmentation is to break the market into smaller units.

directed toward those groups (market segments) an organization decides it can serve profitably is called **target marketing.** For example, a shoe store may choose to sell only women's shoes, only children's shoes, or only athletic shoes. The issue is finding the right target market for the new venture.

Segmenting the Consumer Market

There are several ways a firm can segment, or divide, the consumer market (see Figure 13.6). For example, rather than trying to sell Fiberrific throughout the United States, you might try to focus on just one or two regions of the country where you might be successful. One option is to focus on people in southern states such as Florida and North Carolina. Dividing the market by geographic area is called **geographic segmentation.**

target marketing
Marketing directed toward those groups (market segments) an organization decides it can serve profitably.

geographic segmentation
Dividing the market by geographic area.

Sports Illustrated recognizes that it appels to different market segments. Thus, they have issues called Sports Illustrated for Kids, Sports Illustrated for Women, and so forth. Do you think there's a sufficient market for a college edition of Sports Illustrated—one that focuses primarily on college sports?

demographic segmentation
Dividing the market by age, income, and education level.

psychographic segmentation
Dividing the market using the group's values, attitudes, and interests.

benefit segmentation
Dividing the market by determining which benefits of the product to talk about.

volume segmentation
Dividing the market by usage (volume of use).

niche marketing
The process of finding small but profitable market segments and designing custom-made products for them.

one-to-one marketing
Developing a unique mix of goods and services for each individual customer.

Alternatively, you could aim Fiberrific's promotions toward people aged 25 to 45 who have some college training and have above-average incomes. Automobiles such as Lexus are often targeted to this audience. This segment is interested in health and fitness and might respond to a new, healthy cereal. Segmentation by age, income, and education level are ways of **demographic segmentation.** The Commerce Department's census data from 2000 provides much useful demographic information.

You may want Fiberrific ads to portray a group's lifestyle. To do that, you could study the group's values, attitudes, and interests. This segmentation strategy is called **pychographic segmentation.** For example, if you decide to target Generation Y (teenagers), you would do an in-depth study of their values and interests. Such research reveals which TV shows they watch and which actors they like the best. That information could then be used to develop advertisements for those TV shows using those stars. Pepsi Cola did such a segmentation study for its Mountain Dew brand. The resulting promotion dealt with Generation Y's living life to the limit.

What benefits of Fiberrific might you talk about? Should you emphasize high fiber, low sugar, price, health in general, or what? Determining which benefits are preferred and using those benefits to promote a product is called **benefit segmentation.**

You can also determine who are the big eaters of cereal. Children certainly eat a good deal of cereal, but so do adults. Separating the market by usage (volume of product use) is called **volume segmentation.** Most cereal companies seem to target children. Why not go for the adult segment, a less competitive area?

The best segmentation strategy is to use all the variables to come up with a consumer profile (a target market) that's sizable, reachable, and profitable. Remember, Robert Johnson (the man we got to know at the beginning of the chapter) found a hugely profitable niche in targeting African American consumers.

Reaching Smaller Market Segments

Niche marketing is the process of finding small but profitable market segments and designing or finding products for them. Just how small such a segment can be is illustrated by Fridgedoor.com. This company sells refrigerator magnets on the Internet. It keeps some 1,500 different magnets in stock and sells as many as 400 a week.[18]

One-to-one marketing means developing a unique mix of goods and services for each individual customer. Travel agencies often develop such packages, including airline reservations, hotel reservations, rental cars, restaurants, and admission to museums and other attractions for individual customers. This is relatively easy to do in B2B markets where each customer may buy in huge volume. But one-to-one marketing is now becoming possible in consumer markets as well.

Moving Away from Mass Marketing toward Relationship Marketing

In the world of mass production following the Industrial Revolution, marketers responded by practicing mass marketing. **Mass marketing** means developing products and promotions to please large groups of people. The mass marketer tries to sell products to as many people as possible. That means using mass media, such as TV, radio, and newspapers. Although mass marketing led many firms to success, marketing managers often got so caught up with their products and competition that they became less responsive to the market. Levi Strauss, for example, lost a good deal of its market share because it didn't respond quickly enough to new consumer tastes.

Relationship marketing tends to lead away from mass production and toward custom-made goods and services. The goal is to keep individual customers over time by offering them products that exactly meet their requirements. The latest in technology enables sellers to work with individual buyers to determine their wants and needs and to develop goods and services specifically designed for them (e.g., hand-tailored shirts and unique vacations). One-way messages in mass media give way to a personal dialogue among participants. The following are just a couple examples of relationship marketing:

- Airlines, rental car companies, and hotels have frequent user programs through which loyal customers can earn special services and awards. For example, a traveler can earn bonus miles good for free flights on an airline. He or she can also earn benefits at a car rental agency (that includes no stopping at the rental desk—just pick up a car and go), and special services at a hotel including faster check-in and check-out procedures, flowers in the room, free breakfasts, and free exercise rooms.
- A small express-delivery company established a long-term B2B relationship with a major manufacturer by offering a customized air and ground transportation system. The manufacturer, in turn, offered a guaranteed volume of business.

Relationship marketing is more concerned with retaining old customers than with creating new ones. Special deals, fantastic service, loyalty programs (e.g., frequent-flyer programs), and the like are just the beginning. By maintaining current databases, companies can custom-make products for individuals. Levi Strauss, for example, tried to recapture lost market share by permitting some stores to sell custom-made Levi's for about $10 more than mass-produced Levi's. Through an agreement with Levi's, once the store has your measurements, you can be assured of a perfect fit every time (as long as you don't gain or lose weight) at a reasonable price. The Spotlight on Small Business box shows how a small business can compete with larger firms by using relationship marketing.

One to one marketing means designing a separate product for each individual customer. An example is Kool Calendars. Using Xerox technology, the company can take pictures that you give them and make a customized calendar from those pictures. It is easier to customize services because you only have to find what a customer wants and then adapt the service accordingly. For example, it is relatively easy to customize a workout schedule at a health club. What other services could be customized to each individual?

mass marketing
Developing products and promotions to please large groups of people.

relationship marketing
Marketing whose goal is to keep individual customers over time by offering them products that exactly meet their requirements.

Relationship Marketing of Bicycles

Putting into practice old marketing techniques has enabled small retailers to compete with the giants such as Wal-Mart and Sears. Zane's Cycles in Branford, Connecticut, is a good example. Chris Zane, the owner, began the shop when he was still a teenager. Early on, he learned that to keep customers a store has to offer outstanding service and more. The principle behind such service is a concept now called *customer relationship management.* Long before such a concept emerged, however, small stores knew that the secret to long-term success against giant competitors is to give superior service.

Most large stores focus on making a sale, and give follow-up service little thought. The goal is to make the transaction, and that is the end of it; thus, such an approach is called *transactional marketing.*

With relationship marketing, on the other hand, the goal is to keep a customer for life. Zane's Cycles attracts customers by setting competitive prices (and providing free coffee). Zane keeps customers by giving them free lifetime service on their bicycles. He also sells helmets to young people at cost to encourage safety.

Zane keeps a database on customers so he knows what they need and when they will need it. For example, if he sells a bicycle with a child's seat, he knows that soon that customer may be buying a regular bicycle for the child and he can send out an appropriate brochure at just the right time. Zane encourages people to give him their names, addresses, and other such information by offering to make exchanges without receipts for those people whose transaction information is in the database.

Zane also establishes close community relationships by providing scholarships for local students. Because of Zane's competitive prices, great service, and community involvement, his customers recommend his shop to others. No large store can compete with Zane's in the areas of friendly service and personal attention to each customer. That is what the new style of marketing is all about.

Sources: Rekha Balu, "Listen Up," *Fast Company,* May 2000, pp. 304–14; Ross Atkin, "Getting Past the Schwinn Mentality," *The Christian Science Monitor,* August 8, 2000, p. 16, and Donna Fenn, "A Bigger Wheel," *Inc.,* November 2000, pp. 78–88.

Forming Communities of Buyers

Relationship marketing eventually leads to a dialogue with customers, often on the Internet (e.g., consumer chat rooms).[19] As we described earlier, a database is established so that every contact with consumers results in more information about them. For example, whenever a customer buys something, the color, the size, and other important data are recorded in the database. If the consumer sends a letter, that letter is also included. Over time, the seller learns more and more about its customers; the next step is to put that knowledge to use in establishing a community of buyers.

Fly & Field, for example, is a small store in Glen Ellyn, Illinois, that sells fly-fishing equipment. Fly fishers are a relatively small market locally, but a nice-sized market nationally. To reach the national audience, Fly & Field has established an interactive website (*www.flyfield.com*) where customers and prospects can chat with each other. Naturally, visitors to the site can also access fly-fishing materials and an online catalog where they can buy what they want.

Fly & Field is not alone. Many companies are using interactive websites as part of the move from relationship marketing to forming communities of buyers. Others are using a wide variety of activities. Harley-Davidson has a 220,000-member club that has its own newsletter, meetings, and rallies. The Wally Byam Caravan Club is made up of owners of Airstream trailers and motor homes; they have events for which the manufacturer sends merchandise, staff, information, giveaway items, and more. Community bonding leads to a strong commitment to the products and the company. Such loyalty is hard to match.

Relationship marketing depends greatly on understanding consumers and responding quickly to their wants and needs. Therefore, knowing how consumers make decisions is important to marketers. An understanding of the consumer decision-making process helps marketers adapt their strategies in reaching customers and developing lasting relationships.

The Consumer Decision-Making Process

A major part of the marketing discipline is called *consumer behavior*. Figure 13.7 shows the consumer decision-making ➤ **P.211** ◄ process and some of the outside factors that influence it. The five steps in the process are often studied in courses on consumer behavior. "Problem recognition" may occur, say, when your washing machine breaks down. This leads to an information search—you look for ads about washing machines and read brochures about them. You may even consult a secondary data source like *Consumer Reports* or other information sources. And, most likely, you will seek advice from other people who have purchased washing machines. After compiling all this information, you evaluate alternatives and make a purchase decision. But the process does not end here. After the purchase, you may first ask the people you

spoke to previously how their machines perform and then do other comparisons. Marketing researchers investigate consumer thought processes and behavior at each stage to determine the best way to facilitate marketing exchanges.

Consumer behavior researchers also study the various influences that impact on consumer behavior. Figure 13.7 shows several such influences that affect consumer buying: *marketing mix variables* (the four Ps); *psychological influences*, such as perception and attitudes; *situational influences*, such as the type of purchase and the physical surroundings; and *sociocultural influences*, such as reference groups and culture. Other factors important in the consumer decision process whose technical definitions may be unfamiliar to you include the following:

- *Learning* involves changes in an individual's behavior resulting from previous experiences and information. For example, if you've tried a particular brand of shampoo and you don't like it, you may not ever buy it again.

- *Reference group* is the group that an individual uses as a reference point in the formation of his or her beliefs, attitudes, values, or behavior. For example, a college student who carries a briefcase instead of a backpack may see businesspeople as his or her reference group.

- *Culture* is the set of values, attitudes, and ways of doing things that are transmitted from one generation to another in a given society. The American culture, for example, emphasizes education, freedom, and diversity.

- *Subculture* is the set of values, attitudes, and ways of doing things that result from belonging to a certain ethnic group, religious group, racial group, or other group with which one closely identifies (e.g., teenagers). This group is one small part of the larger culture. Your subculture may prefer rap and hip-hop music, while your parents' subculture may prefer light jazz.

Relationship marketing is especially important for lifetime services such as financial planning and insurance. The idea is to establish a relationship with the customer to learn all of his or her needs and then to develop a product that will serve their needs over a long period of time. Can you see how relationship marketing would help someone trying to sell computer consulting services?

FIGURE 13.7

THE CONSUMER DECISION-MAKING PROCESS AND OUTSIDE INFLUENCES

There are many influences on consumers as they decide which goods and services to buy. Marketers have some influence, but it's not usually as strong as sociocultural influences. Helping consumers in their information search and their evaluation of alternatives is a major function of marketing.

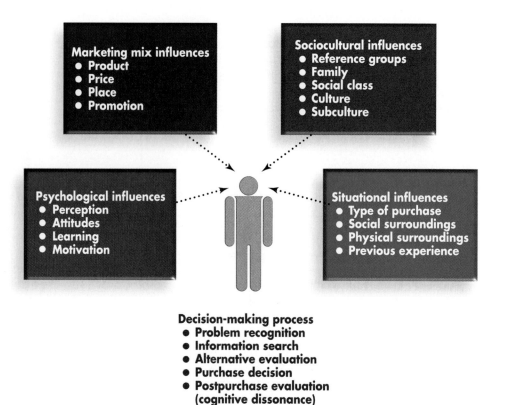

- *Cognitive dissonance* is a type of psychological conflict that can occur after a purchase. Consumers who make a major purchase like a car may have doubts about whether they got the best product at the best price. Marketers must therefore reassure such consumers after the sale that they made a good decision. An auto dealer, for example, may send positive press articles about the particular car a consumer purchased. The dealer may also offer product guarantees and provide certain free services to the customer. Remember, the primary objective of the marketer is to establish a long-term relationship.

Consumer behavior courses are a long-standing part of a marketing curriculum. Today, colleges are expanding their offerings in marketing to include courses in business-to-business marketing. The following section will give you some insight into that growing and important area.

THE BUSINESS-TO-BUSINESS MARKET

B2B marketers include manufacturers; intermediaries such as retailers; institutions (e.g., hospitals, schools, and charities); and the government. The basic principle of B2B marketing is still "Find a need and fill it," but the strategies differ from consumer marketing because the nature of the buyers is different. Several factors make B2B marketing different. Some of the more important are as follows:

1. The *number* of customers in the B2B market is relatively few; that is, there are just a few construction firms or mining operations compared to the 70 million or so households in the U.S. consumer market.

2. The *size* of business customers is relatively large; that is, a few large organizations account for most of the employment and production of various goods and services. Nonetheless, there are many small to medium-size firms in the United States that together make an attractive market.

3. B2B markets tend to be *geographically concentrated.* For example, oilfields tend to be concentrated in the Southwest and in Alaska. Consequently, marketing efforts may be concentrated on a particular geographic area and distribution problems can be minimized by locating warehouses near industrial centers.

4. Business buyers generally are more *rational* (as opposed to emotional) than ultimate consumers in their selection of goods and services; they use specifications and often more carefully weigh the "total product offer," including quality, price, and service.

5. B2B sales tend to be *direct.* Manufacturers sell products, such as tires, directly to auto manufacturers but tend to use intermediaries, such as wholesalers and retailers, to sell to ultimate consumers. One technology research firm estimates that the worldwide B2B market will grow from $145 billion in 1999 to $7.29 *trillion* in 2004.[20]

6. There is much more emphasis on *personal selling* in B2B markets than in consumer markets. Whereas consumer promotions are based more on advertising, B2B sales are based on selling. That is because there are fewer customers who demand more personal service.

Figure 13.8 shows some of the differences between buying behavior in the B2B market compared to the consumer market. You will learn all about the business-to-business market if you take advanced marketing courses.

UPDATING THE MARKETING CONCEPT

As we noted earlier in the chapter, the marketing concept was developed in the 1950s to meet the consumer needs of the time. Now that we're in the 21st century, marketers have to readjust their strategies to meet the needs of modern consumers. That means each of the elements of the marketing concept: a consumer orientation, a service orientation, and a profit orientation all have to be updated. Let's explore each of those changes next.

From a Consumer Orientation to Delighting Customers and Other Stakeholders

Marketing's goal in the past was to provide customer satisfaction. Today, the goal of some total quality firms is to please or even delight customers by providing goods and services that exactly meet their requirements or exceed their expectations. One objective of a company's marketing effort, therefore, is to make sure that the response to customer wants and needs is so fast and courteous that customers are truly surprised and pleased by the experience.

You don't have to look far to see that most organizations haven't yet reached the goal of delighting customers. Retail stores, government agencies, and other organizations may still irritate customers as often as they please them. Nonetheless, global competition is forcing organizations to adopt total quality concepts, which means, above all, adapting organizations to customers.

Businesses have learned that employees won't provide first-class goods and services to customers unless they receive first-class treatment themselves. Marketers must therefore work with others in the firm, such as human resource

	BUSINESS-TO-BUSINESS MARKET	**CONSUMER MARKET**
Market Structure	Relatively few potential customers	Many potential customers
	Larger purchases	Smaller purchases
	Geographically concentrated	Geographically dispersed
Products	Require technical, complex products	Require less technical products
	Frequently require customization	Sometimes require customization
	Frequently require technical advice, delivery, and after-sale service	Sometimes require technical advice, delivery, and after-sale service
Buying procedures	Buyers are trained	No special training
	Negotiate details of most purchases	Accept standard terms for most purchases
	Follow objective standards	Use personal judgment
	Formal process involving specific employees	Informal process involving household members
	Closer relationships between marketers and buyers	Impersonal relationships between marketers and consumers
	Often buy from multiple sources	Rarely buy from multiple sources

FIGURE 13.8

COMPARING BUSINESS-TO-BUSINESS AND CONSUMER BUYING BEHAVIOR

personnel, to help make sure that employees are pleased. In some firms, such as IBM, employees are called *internal customers* to show the need to treat them well—like customers.

From an Organizational Service Orientation to Uniting Organizations

As we explained in Chapter 8, determining whether organizations are providing first-class service and quality is done through *competitive benchmarking*. That means that companies compare their processes and products with those of the best companies in the world to learn how to improve them. Xerox Corporation, for example, has benchmarked its functions against corporate leaders such as American Express (for billing), Ford (for manufacturing floor layout), Mary Kay Cosmetics (for warehousing and distribution), and Florida Power & Light (for quality processes).

Manufacturers, unfortunately, cannot delight consumers on their own. They have to have the cooperation of suppliers to assure customers that they are getting the finest parts. They have to have close relationships with dealers to make sure that the dealers are providing fast, friendly service. We shall discuss the close relationships among marketing intermediaries in Chapter 15.

Maintaining a Profit Orientation

Marketing managers must make sure that everyone in the organization understands that the purpose behind pleasing customers and uniting organizations is to ensure a profit for the firm. Using that profit, the organization can then satisfy other stakeholders ➤ **P.19** ◄ of the firm such as stockholders, environmentalists, and the local community.

It has been estimated that reducing by 5 percent the number of customers who defect—that is, who switch from buying your products to buying another company's—can increase profit by as much as 85 percent (though this figure varies by industry). Some of that profit comes from increased purchases and some from referrals. Thus, customer relationship management is becoming an intimate part of any organization seeking to maximize profits.

Often the goal of marketing is to exceed customer expectations to the point where they are actually delighted with the outcome. This office building in Helsinki, Finland goes the extra step of displaying signs for all the tenants in the building. Such added value delights the tenants and draws them to this building rather than others just down the street. How many retailers delight you with their outstanding service?

ESTABLISHING RELATIONSHIPS WITH ALL STAKEHOLDERS

The traditional marketing concept emphasized giving *customers* what they want. Modern marketing goes further by recognizing the need to please other stakeholders as well. If you go too far in giving customers what they want, the organization may lose money and hurt other stakeholders. Likewise, you could please customers but harm the environment, thus harming relationships with the larger community. Balancing the wants and needs of all the firm's stakeholders—employees, customers, suppliers, dealers, stockholders, media representatives, and the community—is a much bigger challenge than marketing has attempted in the past.

Stakeholder marketing, then, is establishing and maintaining mutually beneficial exchange relationships over time with all the stakeholders of the organization. Organizations that adopt stakeholder marketing take the community's needs into mind when designing and marketing products. For example, many companies have responded to the environmental movement by introducing "green products" into the marketplace. A **green product** is one whose production, use, and disposal is not harmful to the environment. For example, Ventura, California-based Patagonia sells outdoor clothing that exclusively uses organically grown cotton; that means less use of fertilizers to pollute the soil. Patagonia also pledges 1 percent of sales or 10 percent of pretax profit, whichever is greater, to local preservation efforts.

stakeholder marketing
Establishing and maintaining mutually beneficial exchange relationships over time with all the stakeholders of the organization.

green product
A product whose production, use, and disposal don't damage the environment.

Customer Relationship Management

In marketing, the 80/20 rule says that 80 percent of your business is likely to come from just 20 percent of your customers. That's why some companies, like banks, have found it more profitable to discourage some unprofitable

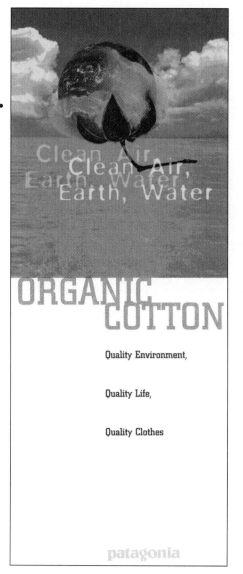

Marketing tries to please all stakeholders, including those concerned with the environment. This ad for Patagonia's outdoor clothing emphasizes the use of organic cotton. Growing such cotton protects people's health and at the same time preserves the air, water, and land.

customers and put more focus on profitable ones—giving them better, more personal service. It is far more expensive to get a new customer than to strengthen a relationship with an existing one. That is what customer relationship management (CRM) is all about.

What makes customer relationship management (CRM) so popular today is the number of companies competing to provide computer software to make the process more effective. These companies have made CRM an all-encompassing business strategy, and a "customer-centric" philosophy of doing business. Top-selling software include ACT! and Goldmine for small businesses ➤ **P.176** ◄ and SalesLogix and Pivotal for mid-range companies.[21] Siebel.com, for example, is a leading provider of e-business applications software, including CRM technology for larger companies. Nexgenix.com offers an integrated CRM program with database management, relationship marketing, and brand-loyalty programs. Epiphany.com and peoplesoft.com are other CRM vendors. We mention these companies because you will be hearing more and more about them as customer-relationship management becomes the most profitable way of doing business.[22]

Your Prospects in Marketing

There is a wider variety of careers in marketing than in most business disciplines. Therefore, if you were to major in marketing, a wide variety of career options would be available to you. You could become a manager in a retail store, like Sears. You could do marketing research or get involved in product management. You could go into selling, advertising, sales promotion, or public relations. You could get involved in transportation, storage, or international distribution. You could design interactive websites to implement customer relationship management. These are just a few of the possibilities. As you read through the following marketing chapters, consider whether a marketing career would interest you. We'll discuss marketing careers again later, after you have reviewed all the marketing chapters.

CRITICAL THINKING

When businesses buy goods and services from other businesses, they usually buy in very large volume. Salespeople in the business-to-business area usually are paid on a commission basis; that is, they earn a certain percentage of each sale they make. Can you see why B2B sales may be a more financially rewarding career area than consumer sales? Industrial companies sell goods such as steel, lumber, computers, engines, parts, and supplies. Where would you find the names of such companies?

PROGRESS ASSESSMENT

- Can you name and describe five ways to segment the consumer market?
- What are four key factors that make industrial markets different from consumer markets?
- What is niche marketing, and how does it differ from one-to-one marketing?
- What is stakeholder marketing?

SUMMARY

1. Marketing is the process of determining customer wants and needs and then providing customers with goods and services that meet or exceed their expectations.
    - *What are the three parts of the marketing concept?*
    The three parts of the marketing concept are (1) a customer orientation, (2) a service orientation and (3) a profit orientation (that is, market those goods and services that will earn the firm a profit and enable it to survive and expand to serve more customer wants and needs).
    - *What is the basic goal of marketing?*
    To find a need and fill it.
    - *What kinds of organizations are involved in marketing?*
    All kinds of organizations use marketing, both profit and nonprofit organizations (including charities, churches, and nonprofit schools).

1. Explain the marketing concept.

2. The marketing mix consists of the four Ps of marketing: product, price, place, and promotion.
    - *How do marketers implement the four Ps?*
    The idea is to design a product that people want, price it competitively, place it in a location where consumers can find it easily, and promote it so that consumers know it exists.

2. Give an example of how to use the four Ps of marketing.

3. Marketing research is the analysis of markets to determine opportunities and challenges and to find the information needed to make good decisions.
    - *What are the steps to follow when conducting research?*
    (1) Define the problem and determine the present situation, (2) collect data, (3) analyze the research data, and (4) choose the best solution.
    - *What is environmental scanning?*
    Environmental scanning is the process of identifying the factors that can affect marketing success. Marketers pay attention to all the environmental factors that create opportunities and threats.
    - *What are some of the more important environmental trends in marketing?*
    The most important global and technological change is probably the growth of the Internet. An important technological change is the growth of consumer databases. Using consumer databases, companies can develop products and services that closely match the needs of consumers. There are a number of social trends that marketers must monitor to maintain their

3. Describe the marketing research process, and tell how marketers use environmental scanning to learn about the changing marketing environment.

close relationship with customers—population growth and shifts, for example. Of course, marketers must also monitor the dynamic competitive environment and pay attention to the economic environment.

4. Explain various ways of segmenting the consumer market.

4. The process of dividing the total market into several groups whose members have similar characteristics is called market segmentation.
   • *What are some of the ways marketers segment the consumer market?*
   Geographic segmentation means dividing the market into different regions. For example, you could choose the Northeast as a market segment of the total United States. Segmentation by age, income, and education level are ways of demographic segmentation. We could study a group's values, attitudes, and interests; this segmentation strategy is called psychographic segmentation. Determining which benefits customers prefer and using those benefits to promote a product is called benefit segmentation. Separating the market by usage (volume of use) is called volume segmentation. The best segmentation strategy is to use all the variables to come up with a consumer profile (a target market) that's sizable, reachable, and profitable.

5. List several ways in which the business-to-business market differs from the consumer market.

5. The B2B market consists of manufacturers, intermediaries such as retailers, institutions (e.g., hospitals, schools, and charities), and the government.
   • *What makes the business-to-business market different from the consumer market?*
   The number of customers in the B2B market is relatively small and the size of business customers is relatively large. B2B markets tend to be geographically concentrated, and industrial buyers generally are more rational than ultimate consumers in their selection of goods and services. B2B sales tend to be direct, and there is much more emphasis on personal selling in B2B markets than in consumer markets. In the automobile industry, for example, there are only a few manufacturers; these few companies tend to buy directly from suppliers with no intermediaries. Companies that sell tires and other parts and supplies tend to use salespeople and little advertising.

6. Show how the marketing concept has been adapted to fit today's modern markets.

6. Now that we're in the 21st century, marketers have to readjust their strategies to meet the needs of modern consumers. That means each of the elements of the marketing concept—a consumer orientation, a service orientation, and a profit orientation—all have to be updated.
   • *How has the marketing concept been adapted to today's environment?*
   Marketing is becoming more customer-oriented than ever before. Originally, marketing's goal was simply to satisfy customers. Now marketing tries to please or "delight" customers. Rather than rely on their own resources to provide quality service, companies are counting on their suppliers, dealers, and others to help provide world-class service to customers. And profit is being maintained by focusing on present customers rather than finding new customers all the time.

7. Describe the latest marketing strategies, such as stakeholder marketing and customer relationship management.

7. Stakeholder marketing is establishing and maintaining mutually beneficial exchange relationships over time with all the stakeholders of the organization. Organizations that adopt stakeholder marketing take the community's needs into mind when designing and marketing products.
   • *What is customer relationship management?*
   Customer relationship management (CRM) is learning as much as possible about customers and doing everything you can to satisfy them or even delight them with goods and services over time.

KEY TERMS

**benefit
  segmentation** 412
brand name 400
**business-to-business
  (B2B) market** 409
consumer market 409
**customer relationship
  management** 396
**demographic
  segmentation** 412
**environmental
  scanning** 407
focus group 404
**geographic
  segmentation** 411

green product 419
**market
  segmentation** 410
marketing 396
**marketing
  concept** 396
**marketing
  management** 397
marketing mix 398
**marketing
  research** 402
mass marketing 413
niche marketing 412
**one-to-one
  marketing** 412

product 400
promotion 402
**psychographic
  segmentation** 412
**relationship
  marketing** 413
**stakeholder
  marketing** 419
target marketing 411
test marketing 400
**volume
  segmentation** 412

DEVELOPING
WORKPLACE
SKILLS

1. Develop what you would consider an effective marketing mix for one of the
   following goods and services: a new electric car, an easy-to-use digital camera, or a car wash for your neighborhood. Write a one-page description of
   that strategy.

2. Working in teams of five (or on your own if class size is a problem), think
   of a product or service that your friends want but cannot get on or near
   campus. You might ask your friends at other schools what's available there.
   Find a product or service to fill that need. Develop a promotional scheme
   and design a system to distribute it to students.

3. Relationship marketing efforts include frequent-flyer deals at airlines, special discounts for members at certain supermarkets (e.g., Safeway), and
   websites that remember your name and what you've purchased in the past
   and recommend new products that you may like (e.g., Amazon.com). Evaluate any one of these programs (look up such programs on the Internet).
   What might they do to increase your satisfaction and loyalty?

4. How would you segment the market for a new, nutritious cereal that contains no sugar and has all the vitamins required for a day? Describe a target market that you feel would be the most profitable.

5. Give an example of a company you know that seems to apply the marketing
   concept and one that apparently does not. How would the company that
   does not apply the concept benefit by doing so?

TAKING IT TO
THE NET

Purpose

To demonstrate how the Internet can be used to enhance relationship marketing.

Exercise

Nike wants to help its customers add soul to their soles and express their indi-
viduality by customizing their own shoes. See for yourself at www.nike.com.
Click on NIKEiD and build a shoe that fits your style.

1. What if you're in the middle of your shoe design and have questions about
   what to do next? Where can you go for help?

2. How does Nike's website help the company strengthen its relationships with its stakeholders? Give examples to support your answer.

3. How do the elements of the website reflect Nike's target market?

4. Does Nike invite comments from visitors to its website? If so, how does this affect its attempt to build positive relationships with its customers?

PRACTICING MANAGEMENT DECISIONS

CASE
CUSTOMER-ORIENTED MARKETING CONCEPTS AT THERMOS

Thermos is the company made famous by its Thermos bottles and lunch boxes. Thermos also manufactures cookout grills. Its competitors include Sunbeam and Weber. To become a world-class competitor, Thermos completely reinvented the way it conducted its marketing operations. By reviewing what Thermos did, you can see how new marketing concepts affect organizations.

First, Thermos modified its corporate culture. It had become a bureaucratic firm organized by function: design, engineering, manufacturing, marketing, and so on. That organizational structure was replaced by flexible, cross-functional, self-managed teams. The idea was to focus on a customer group—for example, buyers of outdoor grills—and build a product development team to create a product for that market.

The product development team for grills consisted of six middle managers from various disciplines, including engineering, manufacturing, finance, and marketing. They called themselves the Lifestyle Team because their job was to study grill users to see how they lived and what they were looking for in an outdoor grill. To get a fresh perspective, the company hired Fitch, Inc., an outside consulting firm, to help with design and marketing research. Team leadership was rotated based on needs of the moment. For example, the marketing person took the lead in doing field research, but the R&D person took over when technical developments became the issue.

The team's first step was to analyze the market. Together, they spent about a month on the road talking with people, videotaping barbecues, conducting focus groups, and learning what people wanted in an outdoor grill. The company found that people wanted a nice-looking grill that didn't pollute the air and was easy to use. It also had to be safe enough for apartment dwellers, which meant it had to be electric.

As the research results came in, engineering began playing with ways to improve electric grills. Manufacturing kept in touch to make sure that any new ideas could be produced economically. Design people were already building models of the new product. R&D people relied heavily on Thermos's strengths. Thermos's core strength was the vacuum technology it had developed to keep hot things hot and cold things cold in Thermos bottles. Drawing on that strength, the engineers developed a domed lid that contained the heat inside the grill.

Once a prototype was developed, the company showed the model to potential customers, who suggested several changes. Employees also took sample grills home and tried to find weaknesses. Using the input from potential customers and employees, the company used continuous improvement to manufacture what became a world-class outdoor grill.

No product can become a success without communicating with the market. The team took the grill on the road, showing it at trade shows and in retail stores. The product was such a success that Thermos is now using self-managed, customer-oriented teams to develop all its product lines.

Decision Questions

1. How could the growth of self-managed cross-functional teams affect marketing departments in other companies? Do you believe that would be a good change or not? Why?
2. How can Thermos now build a closer relationship with its customers using the Internet?
3. What other products might Thermos develop that would appeal to the same market segment that uses outdoor grills?
4. What do you think the Thermos team would have found if it had asked customers what they thought about having consumers put the grills together rather than buying them assembled? What other questions might Thermos place on its website to learn more about customer wants and needs?

VIDEO CASE

ALLIGATOR RECORDS HAS THE BLUES (FOR SALE)

In 1971, Bruce Iglauer, a 23-year-old blues fan, used a $2,500 inheritance to follow his heart and start a record company to record and promote his favorite band, Hound Dog Taylor and the HouseRockers. Today that company, Alligator Records, is home to some of the world's premiere blues performers and is regarded as a top label. Its recordings have won more awards than any other contemporary blues label, including a total of 30 Grammy nominations.

When Iglauer was a student at Lawrence University in Appleton, Wisconsin, he hosted the blues show on his college radio station. When the college activities committee was in need of a band, Iglauer convinced them to book blues legend Howlin' Wolf. Iglauer was disappointed with the promotional push given by the university. He knew he could do better, so he offered to guarantee the costs—out of his own pocket—of booking Luther Allison in exchange for full control over the promotion. The two shows were completely sold out. Not long after that, Iglauer started Alligator Records.

Alligator Records is a small business that competes with giants in the music industry. It does that through marketing. Selling the blues is more than a marketing task for Iglauer, however—it is his mission in life.

If marketing is a process of finding a need and filling it, Alligator Records strives to fill blues lovers' need to buy the recordings they like, particularly those made by musicians who are talented but not well known. Iglauer, therefore, became a bridge that linked the two groups (blues musicians and blues lovers). That is what marketing is all about.

Marketing management means managing the four Ps of product, price, place, and promotion. Marketing begins with understanding the wants and needs of customers. Iglauer has been around blues enthusiasts for so long that he instinctively knows what they will like. Nonetheless, he must still do some research to stay in tune with the market (pun intended).

Once the recordings are produced, Iglauer's job is to distribute the music, not only in the United States but around the world. Like most marketers, he relies on intermediaries like wholesalers and retailers to do that job. He also has to find overseas distributors.

Iglauer deals with both the consumer market and the B2B market. He has to convince wholesalers to push his products among retailers. He also has to encourage radio personalities to play the music. Ultimately, however, Iglauer sells his performers and his music to consumers in clubs and on CDs and cassettes. Blues lovers form what is called a niche market, or one small part of the overall music market.

The marketing concept calls for a customer orientation. That means providing value to customers. It also means establishing long-term relationships with a relatively small market segment—those who love the blues. This is known as relationship marketing. One way to maintain such relationships is to establish a website that allows visitors to hear the latest releases and order them directly from the recording company. Visit Alligator Records at www.alligator.com to sample the sounds or read more about the company and its artists.

Alligator Records is still fueled by the same principles that established the label in 1971. Although the staff has increased to 22 full-time employees, the focus hasn't changed. Iglauer is as driven as he ever was: "I just want to keep bringing the blues to new fans and getting them as excited about it as I am."

Discussion Questions

1. What role will the Internet play in music industry marketing in the future? Will most recordings be sold in stores or over the Internet? What might Iglauer do to prepare for that?

2. Does the marketing of musicians and music differ from the marketing of other products, such as clothes or automobiles? What are the similarities and differences?

3. What role does Iglauer play in creating value for customers? How are the four Ps used to accomplish that goal?

4. What growth prospects do you see in the international promotion of the blues? How would you go about popularizing the blues in other countries?

14

Developing and Pricing Products and Services

LEARNING GOALS

AFTER YOU HAVE READ AND STUDIED THIS CHAPTER, YOU SHOULD BE ABLE TO

1 Explain the concept of a value package.

2 Describe the various kinds of consumer and industrial goods.

3 List and describe the six functions of packaging.

4 Give examples of a brand, a brand name, and a trademark, and explain the concepts of brand equity and loyalty.

5 Explain the role of brand managers and the six steps of the new-product development process.

6 Identify and describe the stages of the product life cycle, and describe marketing strategies at each stage.

7 Give examples of various pricing objectives and strategies.

8 Explain why nonpricing strategies are growing in importance.

Getting to Know Jack Greenberg of McDonald's

Jack M. Greenberg was an accountant at Ernst & Young before he came to McDonald's to be its chief executive. His accounting background prepared him for the task of analyzing the McDonald's product mix (a combination of hamburgers, chicken sandwiches, salads, desserts, and the like). He found that same-store sales growth was only 1 percent versus the 4 percent average at competitors such as Burger King and Wendy's. He determined through consumer research that the McDonald's menu was stale. The last successful new product was Chicken McNuggets in 1983. Other new products, such as the McDLT, the McLean, and the Arch Deluxe, had failed to win customer acceptance. McDonald's had to focus on new-product development. That process begins with listening to consumers to determine exactly what they want.

What Greenberg decided, based on discussions with McDonald's customers, was to change from the old way McDonald's prepared food to a more modern custom-designed format called "Made for You." Instead of preparing a sandwich ahead of time, wrapping it, and placing it under a heat lamp to stay warm, McDonald's stores would put in machinery that would toast buns in 11 seconds and custom-make sandwiches in just one minute. Each store would have to spend some $100,000 on new equipment, but the change would increase sales and decrease the cost of having to throw out sandwiches that weren't sold after a given time.

The chicken sandwich product line was also increased to include a new McCrispy Chicken sandwich and a Chicken Mc-Grill—products of higher quality than the existing chicken offerings. Part of the overall product development strategy was to de-emphasize price and put more focus on quality. Another part of the strategy was to allow franchisees to come up with their own product innovations. In Wisconsin and Minnesota, for example, the franchisees had some success with the McBrat, a bratwurst sandwich with sauerkraut and onion. In Sacramento,

California, customers could order one of several baked-in flavors including pepper-enhanced Santa Fe, barbecue, and teriyaki. Similarly, you can find a McLobster Roll in New England and a hot-mustard-laden Homestyle Burger in Texas.

A tossed-salad line, Mc-Salad Shakers, and fruit-and-yogurt parfaits were also tested. Greenberg always has his eye on additional lines like pizza, cold sandwiches, and more. The latest offering is a new tastes menu with 40 items. He has to keep ahead of the competitors or risk losing market share. Already Burger King is planning to install equipment that will heat a bun in eight seconds—a three-second difference from McDonald's that will add up over time.

One way McDonald's hopes to stay ahead of the competition and keep responding to consumer interests is by opening nonhamburger eateries to appeal to new markets. The new outlets have names like Chipotle Mexican Grill, Donato's Pizza, and Aroma Café. Greenberg says that it's a good idea to look outside the arches for new concepts since the company is close to saturating the U.S. market with its burger restaurants.

The purpose of this chapter is to introduce you to the concepts of product development and pricing. Most firms are like McDonald's in that they must constantly add new products to their offering and decide what pricing strategy would be best, given the changes occurring in the market. Product decisions include packaging, branding, and all the other influences on consumer choices, such as color, size, feel, smell, and taste.

Source: Marilyn Much, "McDonald's Ventures from Arches, Asks, 'You Want Salsa with That?' " *Investor's Business Daily*, May 10, 2000, p. A1; and Kate MadArthur, "McDonald's Revisits Pizza with New Happy Meal Test," *Advertising Age*, February 28, 2000, p. 28; and Kate MacArthur, "McDonald's Varies Menu, Promos," *Advertising Age*, January 22, 2001, pp. 4 & 38

PRODUCT DEVELOPMENT AND THE VALUE PACKAGE

value

Good quality at a fair price; when consumers calculate the value of a product, they look at the benefits and then subtract the cost to see if the benefits exceed the costs.

International competition today is so strong that American businesses could lose some part of the market to foreign producers. The only way to prevent such losses is to design and promote better products—meaning products that are perceived to have the best **value**—good quality at a fair price. When consumers calculate the value of a product, they look at the benefits and then subtract the cost to see if the benefits exceed the costs. As we'll see in this chapter, whether a consumer perceives a product as the best value depends on many factors, including the benefits they seek and the service they receive.[1] To satisfy consumers, marketers must learn to listen better than they do now and to adapt constantly to changing market demands. Managers must also constantly adapt to price challenges from competitors.

Learning to manage change, especially new-product changes, is critical for tomorrow's managers.[2] An important part of the impression consumers get about products is the price. This chapter, therefore, will explore two key parts of the marketing mix: product and price.

McDonald's CEO Jack Greenberg and other marketers have learned that adapting products to new competition and new markets is an ongoing necessity. An organization can't do a one-time survey of consumer wants and needs, design a group of products to meet those needs, put them in the stores, and then just relax. It must constantly monitor changing consumer wants and needs, adapting products, policies, and services accordingly.

▶ Producers are constantly adapting products to meet the changing needs of consumers. For example, this photo shows a product that reads your fingerprint and then starts the engine of your car, adjusts the steering wheel and mirrors to your specifications, and tunes the radio to your favorite station. Soon such products will be used to open the car doors and give you access to buildings and more.

Fast-food organizations, for example, must constantly monitor all sources of information for new-product ideas. McDonald's isn't alone in that. KFC put in a new line of chicken sandwiches. Burger King added a new X-treme Double Cheeseburger and Pancake Minis.[3] Wendy's was able to greatly increase its product sales when it added stuffed pitas to its product mix. Offerings differ in various locations, based on the wants of the local community. In Iowa, pork tenderloin is big, but in Oklahoma City, it's tortilla scramblers. Overseas, companies must adapt to local tastes. At Bob's Big Boy in Thailand, for example, you can get Tropical Shrimp; at Carl's Junior in Mexico, you can order the Machaca Burrito; and at Shakey's Pizza in the Philippines, you can get Cali Shandy, a Filipino beer.[4]

Product development, then, is a key activity in any modern business. There's a lot more to new-product development than merely introducing goods and services, ▶ **P.25** ◀ however. What marketers do to create excitement for those products is as important as the products themselves.

Developing a Value Package

value package

Everything that consumers evaluate when deciding whether to buy something; also called the *total product offer.*

From a strategic marketing viewpoint, a value package is more than just the physical good or service. A **value package** (also called the *total product offer*) consists of everything that consumers evaluate when deciding whether to buy something. Thus, the basic product or service may be a washing machine, an insurance policy, or a beer, but the value package also consists of the following:

Price.

Package.

Store surroundings (atmospherics).

Image created by advertising.

Guarantee.

Reputation of the producer.

Brand name.

Service.

Buyer's past experience.

Speed of delivery.

Accessibility of marketer (e.g., on the Internet).

When people buy a product, ➤ **P.400** ◄ they may evaluate and compare value packages on all these dimensions. Note that some of the attributes are tangible (the product itself and its package) and others are intangible (the reputation of the producer and the image created by advertising). A successful marketer must begin to think like a consumer and evaluate the value package as a total collection of impressions created by all the factors listed above. It is wise to talk with consumers to see which features and benefits are most important to *them*.

Let's go back and look at the highly nutritious, high-fiber, low-sugar breakfast cereal Fiberrific, which we introduced in Chapter 13. The value package as perceived by the consumer is much more than the cereal itself. Anything that affects a consumer's perceptions about the cereal's benefits and value may determine whether he or she purchases the cereal. The price certainly is an important part of the perception of product value.

A high price may indicate exceptional quality. The store surroundings also are important. If the cereal is being sold in an exclusive health food store, it takes on many characteristics of the store (e.g., healthy and upscale). A guarantee of satisfaction can increase the product's value in the mind of consumers, as can a well-known brand name.[5] Advertising can create an attractive image, and word of mouth can enhance the reputation.[6] Thus, the Fiberrific value package is more than a cereal; it's an entire bundle of impressions.

Sometimes an organization can use low price to create an attractive value package. For example, outlet stores often offer brand-name goods for less than regular retail stores do. Shoppers must be careful, however, because outlet stores also carry lower-quality products with similar but not exactly the same features as those carried in regular stores. Consumers like shopping in outlet stores in any case because they believe they are getting quality goods at low prices.

What's the product of a library? One branch of the Chicago Public Library actually lends out expensive power tools and such accessories as fiberglass extension ladders. At the Carnegie Library in Pittsburgh, Pennsylvania, volunteer psychologists go to the library, listen to people's troubles, and refer them to appropriate help. The Broome High School Media Center in Spartanburg, South Carolina, lends out prom, wedding, and mother-of-the-bride dresses donated by members of the community. What do you think prompted libraries to become so creative in their product offers?

Product Lines and the Product Mix

product line
A group of products that are physically similar or are intended for a similar market.

product mix
The combination of product lines offered by a manufacturer.

product differentiation
The creation of real or perceived product differences.

Companies usually don't sell just one product. Rather, they sell several different but complementary products. Figure 14.1 shows product lines for Procter & Gamble (P&G). A **product line,** as the figure shows, is a group of products that are physically similar or are intended for a similar market. P&G's product lines include bar soaps, laundry detergents, and dishwashing detergents. In one product line, there may be several competing brands. Thus, P&G has many brands in its laundry detergent product line, including Bold, Cheer, Tide, and Ivory Snow. All of P&G's product lines make up its **product mix,** which is the combination of product lines offered by a manufacturer. As we see in Figure 14.1, P&G's product mix consists of product lines of soap, detergents, toothpastes, shampoos, and so forth.

Service providers have product lines and product mixes as well. For example, a bank or credit union may offer a variety of services from savings accounts, automated teller machines, and computer banking to money market funds. A bank's product mix may include safety deposit boxes, loans (home, car, etc.), traveler's checks, online banking, mutual funds, and insurance. AT&T combines services (telephone) with goods (computers, phones) in its product mix.

PRODUCT DIFFERENTIATION

Product differentiation is the creation of real or perceived product differences. Actual product differences are sometimes quite small, so marketers must use a clever mix of pricing, advertising, and packaging to create a unique, attractive image. Evian, for example, which sells bottled water, successfully attempted product differentiation. The company made its water so attractive through pricing and promotion that now restaurant customers often order it by brand name instead of a Coke or Pepsi.

There's no reason why you couldn't create an attractive image for your product, Fiberrific. With a high price and creative advertising, it could become the Evian of cereals. But different products call for different marketing strategies, as we'll see next.

Small businesses > P.176 < can often win market share with creative product differentiation. For example, yearbook photographer Charlie Clark competes with other yearbook photographers by offering multiple clothing changes, backgrounds, and poses along with special allowances, discounts, and guar-

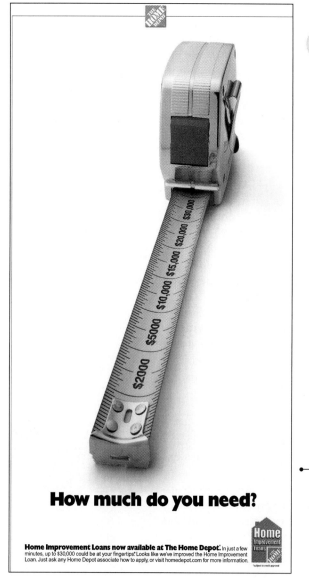

How much do you need?

Home Improvement Loans now available at The Home Depot. In just a few minutes, up to $30,000 could be at your fingertips.* Looks like we've improved the Home Improvement Loan. Just ask any Home Depot associate how to apply, or visit homedepot.com for more information.
*subject to credit approval

The product mix at Home Depot includes paints, plumbing supplies, electrical supplies and more. What may delight homeowners is to learn that the company also includes home improvement loans in the mix. That makes it possible for home owners to buy all the rest of the items they need. Do you think home delivery would prove to be a popular addition?

PRODUCT LINES	BRANDS
P Bar soaps	Camay, Coast, Ivory, Kirk's, Lava, Monchel, Safeguard, Zest
R	
O Laundry detergents	Bold, Cheer, Dash, Dreft, Era, Gain, Ivory Snow, Liquid Bold-3, Liquid Cheer, Liquid Tide, Oxydol, Solo, Tide
D	
U	
C Dishwashing detergents	Cascade, Dawn, Ivory Liquid, Joy, Liquid Cascade
T Cleaners and cleansers	Comet, Comet Liquid, Mr. Clean, Spic & Span, Spic & Span Pine Liquid, Top Job
Shampoos	Head & Shoulders, Ivory, Lilt, Pert-Plus, Prell
M Toothpastes	Crest, Denquel, Gleem
I Paper tissue products	Banner, Charmin, Puffs, White Cloud
X Disposable diapers	Luvs, Pampers
Shortening and cooking oils	Crisco, Crisco Oil, Crisco Corn Oil, Puritan

Most large companies make more than one product. Here we see various products and brands Procter & Gamble makes. Note how physically similar the products are. Why would one company sell so many laundry detergents?

antees. He has been so successful that companies use him as a speaker at photography conventions. This is just one more example of how small businesses may have the advantage of being more flexible than big businesses in adapting to customer wants and needs and giving them attractive product differences. The Making Ethical Decisions box explains how a product can be differentiated by making it environmentally sound and asks you to reflect on your own environmental choices.

Marketing Different Classes of Consumer Goods and Services

Several attempts have been made to classify consumer goods and services. One classification, based on consumer purchasing behavior, has four general categories—convenience, shopping, specialty, and unsought.

1. **Convenience goods and services** are products that the consumer wants to purchase frequently and with a minimum of effort (e.g., candy, gum, milk, snacks, gas, banking services). One store that sells mostly convenience goods is 7-Eleven. Location, brand awareness, and image are important for marketers of convenience goods and services. The Internet has taken convenience to a whole new level, especially for banks and other service companies. Companies that don't offer such services are likely to lose market share to those who do unless they offer *outstanding* service to customers who visit in person.

convenience goods and services
Products that the consumer wants to purchase frequently and with a minimum of effort.

Jyoti (JO-tee) Gupta makes specialty frozen vegetarian meals. She now sells them to British Airways and US Airways for their passengers. Do you think this is a good example of a company that would benefit from going on the Internet and finding wider exposure so that vegetarians could find them instead of vice versa?

MAKING ETHICAL DECISIONS

Taking Care of the Environment

Eighty-seven percent of adults in the United States say they are concerned about the condition of the nation's environment, and almost half of them say they are very concerned. These results come from a twice-a-year poll conducted by Environmental Research Associates. Air pollution was the major concern, followed by water pollution. Global warming is also being taken more seriously than in the past. Earth Day has been celebrated for some 30 years, and today's young people have been taught environmental values throughout their education. So now, more than ever, companies can take an environmental stance and create a win-win situation for all. Since about half of U.S. consumers look for environmental labeling on products, companies can profit from offering products that help preserve the environment.

Businesses are very involved in producing environmentally friendly products. Herman Miller, for example, uses recycled materials to make office furniture that is simple in design, durable, and in turn recyclable. Electrolux makes water-efficient washing machines, a solar-powered lawnmover, and a refrigerator free of ozone-depleting refrigerants. Outdoor-clothing manufacturer Patagonia has switched to organic cotton and donates 1 percent of sales or 10 percent of pretax profits (whichever is larger) to environmental causes. Toyota and others are making electric cars or gas/electric cars that use less fuel and are less polluting than gasoline-powered cars. Ford has promised to increase the mileage on its sport-utility vehicles by 25 percent to cut emissions.

Consumers must also do their part to protect the environment. Are you a green consumer? Do you look for and buy products that are recycled? Do you recycle paper products, cans, and other materials? Do you pick up trash when you see it? Do you walk the walk when it comes to the environment by doing all you can to prevent air and water pollution, including everything from driving a small, fuel-efficient car to putting gum wrappers in your recycling bin?

Sources: Lisa A. Phillips, "Green Attitude," *American Demographics*, April 1999, pp. 46–47; Justin Hyde, "Ford Cites Conflicts for SUVs," *Philadelphia Inquirer*, May 12, 2000, p. C1; and Kimberly O'Neill Packard and Forest Reinhardt, "What Every Executive Needs to Know about Global Warming," *Harvard Business Review*, July–August 2000, pp. 129–35.

---

shopping goods and services
Those products that the consumer buys only after comparing value, quality, and price from a variety of sellers.

2. **Shopping goods and services** are those products that the consumer buys only after comparing value, quality, style, and price from a variety of sellers. Shopping goods and services are sold largely through shopping centers where consumers can shop around. Sears is one store that sells mostly shopping goods. Because many consumers carefully compare such products, marketers can emphasize price differences, quality differences, or some combination of the two. Examples include clothes, shoes, appliances, and auto repair services. It is so easy to make price comparisons on the Internet today that companies will instead have to compete on service in the future.

specialty goods and services
Products that have a special attraction to consumers who are willing to go out of their way to obtain them.

3. **Specialty goods and services** are products that appeal to a relatively small market segment, but have a special attraction to consumers who are willing to go out of their way to obtain them. Examples are beekeeping equipment, fur coats, jewelry, fine chocolates, and expensive imported cigars, as well as services provided by medical specialists or business consultants. A Jaguar automobile dealer is an example of a specialty good retailer. These products are often marketed through specialty magazines. For example, specialty skis may be sold through sports magazines and specialty foods through gourmet magazines. By establishing interactive websites where customers can place orders, companies that sell specialty goods and services can make buying their goods as easy or easier than shopping at a local mall.

FROM THE PAGES OF BusinessWeek

E-Commerce Retailers Need Good Customer Service Also

One major advantage small businesses have over large ones is their ability to get closer to the customer and provide more personal and friendly service. That includes new companies trying to reach customers on the Internet. For example, QVC has an online division called iqvc. Harris Interactive's commercePlus survey of consumer satisfaction with e-stores found that iqvc had really high scores (as high as 9.5 on a scale of 10). It got such scores by filling orders quickly (90 percent within two days), answering e-mail promptly, and making customers feel comfortable buying goods without being able to touch them beforehand.

About 70 percent of iqvc's customers are women, so iqvc does everything it can to help women find the kind of products they want. That includes a feature called My Style Advisor that recommends clothes and makeup based on what women users tell iqvc about their coloring, weight, and style. Some 80,000 items are available on the website.

It may turn out, however, that many small Internet businesses, like iqvc, may not be able to compete with larger businesses on the Internet. The costs associated with setting up such a site, advertising it, and providing great service could be too great. So smaller Internet providers must learn to provide excellent service and build close relationships with customers in order to compete as iqvc has done.

Ultimately, sales on the Internet come from sales in stores. It is largely a zero-sum game; that is, sales on the Internet come mostly from retailers, as opposed to new sales being generated. Small Internet providers will have to win their market share by offering such good service that customers will be less inclined to get in their cars, drive to the store, find a parking place, and walk to the store.

Sources: Amy Barrett, "Just Another Medium," *Business Week e.biz*, September 27, 1999, p. 78; Robert D. Hof, "Is That E-Commerce Road Kill I See?" *Business Week e.biz*, September 27, 1999, p. 96; and Ellen Neuborne, "E-Tail: Gleaming Storefronts with Nothing Inside," *Business Week*, May 1, 2000, pp. 94–98.

4. **Unsought goods and services** are products that consumers are unaware of, haven't necessarily thought of buying, or find that they need to solve an unexpected problem. Some examples of unsought products are emergency car-towing services, burial services, and insurance.

unsought goods and services
Products that consumers are unaware of, haven't necessarily thought of buying, or find that they need to solve an unexpected problem.

The marketing task varies depending on the category of product; that is, convenience goods are marketed differently from specialty goods, and so forth. The best way to promote convenience goods is to make them readily available and to create the proper image. Price, quality, and service are the best appeals for shopping goods. Specialty goods rely on reaching special market segments through advertising. Unsought goods such as life insurance rely on personal selling; car towing relies on Yellow Pages advertising.

Whether a good or service falls into a particular class depends on the individual consumer. A shopping good for one consumer (e.g., coffee) could be a specialty good for another consumer (e.g., flavored gourmet coffee). Some people shop around to compare different dry cleaners, so dry cleaning is a shopping service for them. Others go to the closest store, making it a convenience service. Therefore, marketers must carefully monitor their customer base to determine how consumers perceive their products. Can you see how Fiberrific could be either a convenience good or a shopping good?

Furthermore, the Internet has made it possible for consumers to purchase shopping goods from home. That puts much greater pressure on retailers to offer such outstanding service that consumers will be willing to leave their homes to get it. The *Business Week* box discusses this trend in more detail.

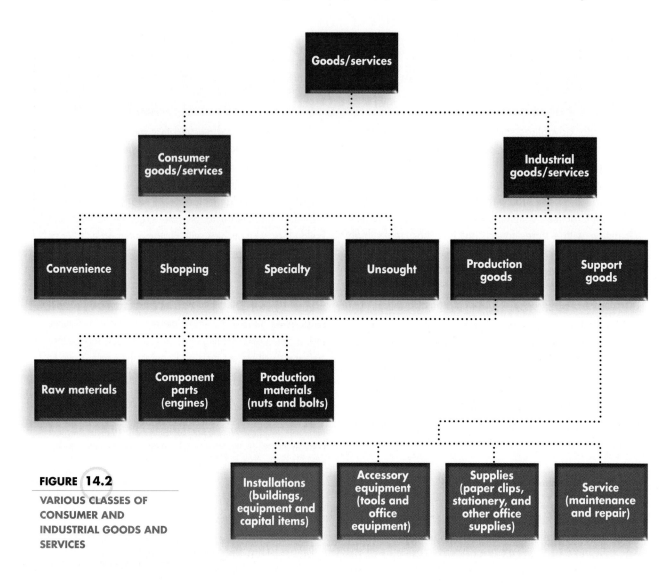

FIGURE 14.2

VARIOUS CLASSES OF CONSUMER AND INDUSTRIAL GOODS AND SERVICES

Marketing Industrial Goods and Services

industrial goods
Products used in the production of other products.

Industrial goods are products used in the production of other products. They are sold in the business-to-business (B2B) ➤ **P.409** ◄ market. Some products can be classified as both consumer goods and industrial goods. For example, personal computers could be sold to consumer markets or business-to-business markets. As a consumer good, the computer might be sold through computer stores like CompUSA or through computer magazines. Most of the promotional task would go to advertising. As an industrial good, personal computers are more likely to be sold by salespeople or on the Internet. Advertising would be less of a factor in the promotion strategy. You can see that classifying goods by user category helps determine the proper marketing mix strategy. Figure 14.2 shows some categories of both consumer and industrial goods and services.

Installations consist of major capital equipment such as new factories and heavy machinery. *Capital items* are products that last a long time and cost a lot of money. A new factory building where Fiberrific would be produced would be considered both a capital item and an installation. *Accessory equipment* consists of capital items that are not quite as long lasting or as expensive as installations. Examples include computers, photocopy machines, and various tools. Other industrial goods and examples are labeled in the chart.

- What attributes are included in a value package?
- What's the difference between a product line and a product mix?
- Name the four classes of consumer goods and services, and give examples of each.
- Describe three different types of industrial goods.

PACKAGING CHANGES THE PRODUCT

We've said that consumers evaluate many aspects of the value package, including the brand. It's surprising how important packaging can be in such evaluations. Many years ago people had problems with table salt because it would stick together and form lumps during humid or damp weather. The Morton Salt Company solved that problem by designing a package that kept salt dry in all kinds of weather, thus the slogan "When it rains, it pours." Packaging made Morton's salt more desirable than competing products, and even though other salt companies developed similar packaging, Morton's is still the best-known salt in the United States.

Other companies have also used packaging to change and improve their basic product. Thus, we've had squeezable ketchup bottles; plastic bottles for motor oil that eliminate the need for funnels; toothpaste pumps; plastic cans for tennis balls; packaged dinners and other foods, like popcorn, that can be cooked in a microwave oven; whipped cream in dispenser cans; and so forth. In each case, the package changed the product in the minds of consumers and opened large markets. Packaging can also help make a product more attractive to retailers. For example, the Universal Product Codes (UPCs) on many packages make it easier to control inventory; the UPC is the combination of a bar code (those familiar black and white lines) and a preset number that gives the retailer information about the product (price, size, color, etc.). In short, packaging changes the product by changing its visibility, usefulness, or attractiveness.

Recently there has been a glut of tuna on the market, making it difficult for tuna sellers to make much money. The price of a can of tuna was simply too low for much profit. Therefore, Sunkist turned to packaging for more profit. It developed resealable pouches that made sandwich making easier. There is no need to drain the tuna, the package is sandwich size, and there is a firmer texture to the product. Are there other packaging innovations that you have found helpful or convenient?

The Growing Importance of Packaging

Packaging has always been an important aspect of the product offer, but today it's carrying more of the promotional burden than in the past. Many products that were once sold by salespersons are now being sold in self-service outlets, and the package has been given more sales responsibility. The package must perform the following functions:

1. Protect the goods inside, stand up under handling and storage, be tamperproof, deter theft, and yet be easy to open and use.
2. Attract the buyer's attention.
3. Describe the contents and give information about the contents.
4. Explain the benefits of the good inside.
5. Provide information on warranties, warnings, and other consumer matters.
6. Give some indication of price, value, and uses.

Packaging of services has been getting more attention recently. For example, Virgin Airlines includes door-to-door limousine service and in-flight massages in its total package. When combining goods or services into one package, it's important not to include so much that the price gets too high. It's best to work with customers to develop offers that meet their individual needs.

BRANDING AND BRAND EQUITY

brand
A name, symbol, or design (or combination thereof) that identifies the goods or services of one seller or group of sellers and distinguishes them from the goods and services of competitors.

Closely related to packaging is branding. A **brand** is a name, symbol, or design (or combination thereof) that identifies the goods or services of one seller or group of sellers and distinguishes them from the goods and services of competitors. The term *brand* is sufficiently comprehensive to include practically all means of identification of a product. A *brand name* is that part of the brand consisting of a word, letter, or group of words or letters comprising a name that differentiates a seller's goods or services from those of competitors. Brand names you may be familiar with include QVC, Sony, Del Monte, Campbell, Levi's, Snackwell's, Borden, Michelob, and Macintosh. Such brand names give products a distinction that tends to make them attractive to consumers.

trademark
A brand that has been given exclusive legal protection for both the brand name and the pictorial design.

A **trademark** is a brand that has been given exclusive legal protection for both the brand name and the pictorial design. Trademarks such as McDonald's golden arches are widely recognized.

People are often impressed by certain brand names, even though they say they know there's no difference between brands in a given product category. For example, when people say that all aspirin is alike, put two bottles in front of them—one with the Anacin label and one labeled with an unknown brand. See which they choose. Most people choose the brand name, even when they say there's no difference.

manufacturers' brand names
The brand names of manufacturers that distribute products nationally.

knockoff brands
Illegal copies of national brand-name goods.

Brand Categories

Several categories of brands are familiar to you. **Manufacturers' brand names** are the brand names of manufacturers that distribute products nationally—Xerox, Polaroid, Kodak, Sony, and Chevrolet, for example. **Knockoff brands** are illegal copies of national brand-name goods. If you see an expensive brand-name item such as a Polo shirt or a Rolex watch for sale at a ridiculously low price, you can be pretty sure it's a knockoff.[7]

Dealer (private) brands are products that don't carry the manufacturer's name but carry a distributor or retailer's name instead. Kenmore and Diehard are dealer brands sold by Sears. These brands are also known as *house brands* or *distributor brands*.

Many manufacturers fear having their brand names become generic names. A **generic name** is the name for a product category. Did you know that aspirin and linoleum, which are now generic names for products, were once brand names? So were nylon, escalator, kerosene, and zipper. All those names became so popular, so identified with the product, that they lost their brand status and became generic. (Such issues are decided in the courts.) Their producers then had to come up with new names. The original Aspirin, for example, became Bayer aspirin. Companies that are working hard to protect their brand names today include Xerox (one ad reads, "Don't say 'Xerox it'; say 'Copy it' "), Styrofoam, and Rollerblade (in-line skates).

Generic goods are nonbranded products that usually sell at a sizable discount compared to national or private brands. They feature basic packaging and are backed with little or no advertising. Some are of poor quality, but many come close to having the same quality as the national brand-name goods they copy. There are generic tissues, generic cigarettes, generic peaches, and so forth. Consumers today are buying more generic products because their overall quality has improved so greatly in recent years that it approximates or equals that of more expensive brand names.

Generating Brand Equity and Loyalty

A major goal of marketers in the future will be to reestablish the notion of brand equity. **Brand equity** is the combination of factors, such as awareness, loyalty, perceived quality, images, and emotions, people associate with a given brand name. In the past companies tried to boost their short-term performance by offering coupons and price discounts to move goods quickly.[8] This eroded consumers' commitment to brand names. Now companies realize the value of brand equity and are trying to measure the earning power of strong brand names.[9]

The core of brand equity is brand loyalty. **Brand loyalty** is the degree to which customers are satisfied, like the brand, and are committed to further purchases. A loyal group of customers represents substantial value to a firm, and that value can be calculated.

dealer (private) brands
Products that don't carry the manufacturer's name but carry a distributor or retailer's name instead.

generic name
The name for a product category (versus a brand name).

generic goods
Nonbranded products that usually sell at a sizable discount compared to national or private brands.

brand equity
The combination of factors such as awareness, loyalty, perceived quality, images, and emotions people associate with a given brand name.

brand loyalty
The degree to which customers are satisfied, like the brand, and are committed to further purchase.

No figure in golf is more instantly recognizable than Tiger Woods. By using Tiger in their ads, Buick hopes to attract readers' attention and to have them associate Buick with a quality winner. Buick is trying to build its image among golfers because Tiger brings to mind many positive traits Buick hopes consumers will associate with their brand. What other products might benefit from having Tiger Woods as a spokesperson?

brand awareness
How quickly or easily a given brand name comes to mind when a product category is mentioned.

Brand awareness refers to how quickly or easily a given brand name comes to mind when a product category is mentioned. Advertising helps build strong brand awareness. Older brands, such as Coca-Cola and Pepsi, are usually the highest in brand awareness. Event sponsorship (e.g., the Winston-Salem auto races and Virginia Slims tennis tournament) helps improve brand awareness.

Perceived quality is an important part of brand equity. A product that's perceived as having better quality than its competitors can be priced accordingly. The key to creating a perception of quality is to identify what consumers look for in a high-quality product and then to use that information in every message the company sends out. Factors influencing the perception of quality include price, appearance, and reputation. Consumers often develop brand preference (that is, they prefer one brand over another) because of such cues.

It's now so easy to copy a product's benefits that off-brand products are being developed to draw consumers away from brand-name goods. Brand X disposable diapers, for example, has increased its market share from 7 to 20 percent. Paragon Trade Brands gives retailers higher-than-normal margins (the difference between purchasing cost and selling price) and quickly matches the product innovations of the major companies. Brand-name manufacturers, like Intel Corporation, have to develop new products and new markets faster and promote their names better than ever before to hold off the challenge of competitors.

Creating Brand Associations

brand association
The linking of a brand to other favorable images.

The name, symbol, and slogan a company uses can assist greatly in brand recognition for that company's products. **Brand association** is the linking of a brand to other favorable images. For example, you can link a brand to other product users, to a popular celebrity, to a particular geographic area, or to competitors. Note, for example, how ads for Mercedes-Benz and Buick associate those companies' cars with rich people who may spend their leisure time playing or watching golf or polo. Tiger Woods was chosen as a spokesperson for Buick because of his golf popularity. Note, too, the success of associating basketball shoes with stars such as Shaquille O'Neal. What person might we associate with Fiberrific to give the cereal more appeal?

The person responsible for building brands is known as a brand manager or product manager. We'll explore that position right after the Progress Assessment.

P**ROGRESS**
ASSESSMENT

- What six functions does packaging now perform?
- What's the difference between a brand name and a trademark?
- Can you explain the difference between a manufacturer's brand, a private brand, and a generic brand?
- What are the key components of brand equity?

BRAND MANAGEMENT

brand manager
A manager who has direct responsibility for one brand or one product line.

A **brand manager** (known as a *product manager* in some firms) has direct responsibility for one brand or one product line. This responsibility includes all the elements of the marketing mix: product, price, place, and promotion. Thus, the brand manager might be thought of as a president of a one-product firm. Imagine being the brand manager for Fiberrific. You'd be responsible for everything having to do with that one brand. One reason many large consumer-product companies created the position of brand manager is to have greater control over new-product development and product promotion.

For the buyer, a brand name assures quality, reduces search time, and adds prestige to purchases. For the seller, brand names facilitate new-product introductions, help promotional efforts, add to repeat purchases, and differentiate products so that prices can be set higher.

New-Product Success

Chances that a new product will fail are overwhelmingly high. About 86 percent of products introduced in one year failed to reach their business objectives. Not delivering what is promised is a leading cause of new-product failure. Other reasons for failure include poor positioning, not enough differences from competitors, and poor packaging. Smaller firms may experience a lower success rate unless they do proper product planning.

The New-Product Development Process

As Figure 14.3 shows, product development for producers consists of several stages:

1. Idea generation, based on consumer wants and needs.
2. Screening.
3. Product analysis.
4. Development, including building prototypes.
5. Testing.
6. Commercialization (bringing the product to the market).

Despite all their efforts to produce products that we like, companies fail more often than not. The New Products Showcase and Learning Center in Ithaca, New York, has thousands of such failed products on display. What products have you noticed disappearing from the grocery shelves?

New products continue to pour into the market every year, and the profit potential looks tremendous. Think, for example, of the potential of home video conferencing, interactive TV, large-screen high-definition TV sets, virtual reality games and products, Internet-connected phones, and other innovations. Where do these ideas come from? How are they tested? What's the life span for an innovation? The following material looks at these issues.

Generating New-Product Ideas

Figure 14.4 gives you a good idea of where new-product ideas come from. Note that 38 percent of the new-product ideas for consumer goods come from analyzing competitors (the source of 27 percent of ideas for new industrial products). Such copying of competitors slows the introduction of original ideas.

A strong point can be made for listening to employee suggestions for new products. The number one source of ideas for new industrial products has been company sources (e.g., employees) other than research and development. It was also a major source for new consumer goods.

Look through Figure 14.4 carefully and think about the implications. Notice that more than a third of all new-product ideas for industrial products came from users, user research, or supplier suggestions. This finding emphasizes the principle that a firm should listen to its suppliers and customers and give them what they want.

FIGURE 14.3

THE NEW-PRODUCT DEVELOPMENT PROCESS
Product development is a six-stage process. Which stage do you believe to be the most important?

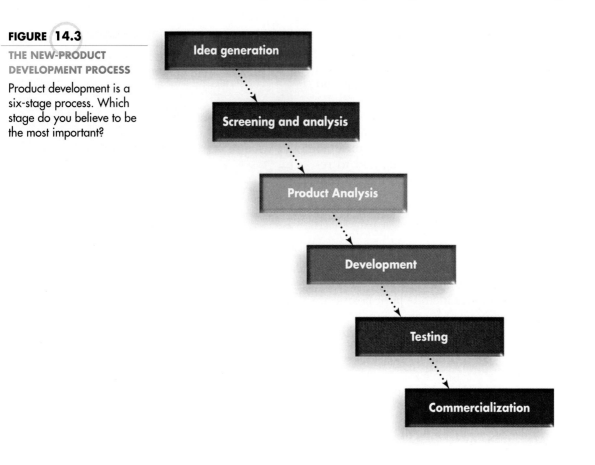

FIGURE 14.3

THE NEW-PRODUCT DEVELOPMENT PROCESS
Product development is a six-stage process. Which stage do you believe to be the most important?

Product Screening

product screening
A process designed to reduce the number of new-product ideas being worked on at any one time.

Product screening is designed to reduce the number of new-product ideas being worked on at any one time. Criteria needed for screening include whether the product fits in well with present products, profit potential, marketability, and personnel requirements. Each of these factors may be assigned a weight, and total scores are then computed. A software package called Quick Insight now helps companies analyze the potential of new goods and services. By answering about 60 questions and then reviewing the answers, the user can gain an understanding of the likely problems and potential strengths of the new offering. Nonetheless, it still takes about seven ideas to generate one commercial product.

Product Analysis

product analysis
Making cost estimates and sales forecasts to get a feeling for profitability of new product ideas.

Product analysis is done after product screening. It's largely a matter of making cost estimates and sales forecasts to get a feeling for profitability. Products that don't meet the established criteria are withdrawn from consideration.

Product Development and Testing

If a product passes the screening and analysis phase, the firm begins to develop it further. A product idea can be developed into many different *product concepts,* which are alternative product offerings based on the same product idea that have different meanings and values to consumers.[10] For example, a firm that makes packaged meat products may develop the concept of a chicken dog—a hot dog made of chicken that tastes like an all-beef hot dog. A *prototype,* or sample, may be developed so that consumers can actually try the taste.

CONSUMER PRODUCTS
(based on a survey of 79 new products)

Analysis of the competition	38.0%
Company sources other than research and development	31.6
Consumer research	17.7
Research and development	13.9
Consumer suggestions	12.7
Published information	11.4
Supplier suggestions	3.8

INDUSTRIAL PRODUCTS
(based on a survey of 152 new products)

Company sources other than research and development	36.2%
Analysis of the competition	27.0
Research and development	24.3
Product users	15.8
Supplier suggestions	12.5
Product user research	10.5
Published information	7.9

FIGURE 14.4

SOURCES OF NEW-PRODUCT IDEAS

This survey shows where ideas for new products originate. As you know, research plays an important role in the development of new products. Have you ever tried to sell a new product idea to a company?

PRODUCT DEVELOPMENT	COMMUNICATION DEVELOPMENT	STRATEGY DEVELOPMENT
Identify unfilled need	Select a name	Set marketing goals
Preliminary profit/payout plan for each concept	Design a package and test	Develop marketing mix (after communication developed)
Concept test	Create a copy theme and test	Estimate cost of marketing plan (after product development)
Determine whether the product can be made	Develop complete ads and test	
Test the concept and product (and revise as indicated)		
Develop the product		
Run extended product use tests		

FIGURE 14.5

STEPS TO TAKE BEFORE TEST MARKETING A PRODUCT

Product development, communication development, and strategy development all are used as a company develops a new product. Extensive testing is used to guarantee the new product's success. Have you ever participated in such a test?

Concept testing involves taking a product *idea* to consumers to test their reactions (see Figure 14.5). Do they see the benefits of this new product? How frequently would they buy it? At what price? What features do they like and dislike? What changes would they make? Different samples are tested using different packaging, branding, ingredients, and so forth until a product emerges that's desirable from both production and marketing perspectives. Can you see the importance of concept testing for Fiberrific?

concept testing
Taking a product idea to consumers to test their reactions.

Commercialization

Even if a product tests well, it may take quite a while before the product achieves success in the market. Take the zipper, for example, the result of one of the longest development efforts on record for a consumer product. After Whitcomb Judson received the first patents for his clothing fastener in the early 1890s, it took more than 15 years to perfect the product—and even then consumers weren't interested. Judson's company suffered numerous financial setbacks, name changes, and relocations before settling in Meadville, Pennsylvania. Finally, the U.S. Navy started using zippers during World War I. Today, Talon Inc. is the leading U.S. maker of zippers, producing some 500 million of them a year.

commercialization

Promoting a product to distributors and retailers to get wide distribution and developing strong advertising and sales campaigns to generate and maintain interest in the product among distributors and consumers.

This example shows that the marketing effort must include **commercialization.** This includes (1) promoting the product to distributors and retailers to get wide distribution and (2) developing strong advertising and sales campaigns to generate and maintain interest in the product among distributors and consumers. New products are now getting rapid exposure to global markets by being promoted on the Internet.[11] Interactive websites enable consumers to view new products, ask questions, and make purchases easily and quickly.

The International Challenge

U.S. marketers have learned through experience that the secret to success in today's rapidly changing environment is to bring out new products, high in quality, and to bring them out quickly. This is especially true in light of the rapid development process occurring in other countries.

The Big Three U.S. automakers (Ford, General Motors, Chrysler) all formed task forces to cut product development cycles that had swollen to nearly five years. The Japanese cycles were taking about three and a half years. The American firms are now down to less than two years. To stay competitive in world markets, U.S. businesses must develop an entirely new product development process. To keep products competitive requires continuous incremental improvements in function, cost, and quality. Cost-sensitive design and new process technologies are critical.

More attention in the United States must be given to the product development process; that is, developing products in cooperation with their users. To implement the new-product development process, managers must go out into the market and interact closely with their dealers and their ultimate customers. Successful new-product development is an interactive process whereby customers present their needs and new-product designs are prepared to meet those needs. Changes are made over time to make sure that the total product offer exactly meets the customer's needs. The focus shifts from internal product development processes to external customer responsiveness.

The Reaching Beyond Our Borders box explores how McDonald's has been so successful in global markets. The answer has been to adapt the product offering to the wants and need of consumers in each country.

THE PRODUCT LIFE CYCLE

product life cycle

A theoretical model of what happens to sales and profits for a product class over time.

Once a product has been developed and tested, it is placed on the market. Products often go through a life cycle consisting of four stages: introduction, growth, maturity, and decline. This is called the **product life cycle** (see Figure 14.6). The product life cycle is a theoretical model of what happens to sales and profits for a product class (e.g., all dishwasher soaps) over time. However, not all products follow the life cycle, and particular brands may act differently. For example, while frozen foods as a generic class may go through the entire cycle, one brand may never get beyond the introduction stage. Nonetheless, the product life cycle may provide some basis for anticipating future market developments and for planning marketing strategies. Some products, such as microwave ovens, stay in the introductory stage for years. Other products, such as fad clothing, may go through the entire cycle in a few months.

REACHING BEYOND OUR BORDERS
www.mcdonalds.com

The Globalization of McDonald's

You read in the chapter opening Profile how McDonald's has added new products to its U.S. franchises and changed the way it prepared them. But don't forget that McDonald's sells about half of its burgers in foreign markets, and it is rapidly gobbling up market share. In fact, 95 percent of all new McDonald's stores will be overseas, at least for the next five years. Since 1993, McDonald's has opened 415 stores in France alone. There are some 700 such stores in Brazil. Therefore, McDonald's has to use product development to keep its customer base in foreign markets as well.

Why is McDonald's so successful in global markets? Because it adapts its products to local tastes. In Taiwan and Singapore, the stores sell a bone-in chicken dish called Chicken McCrispy. In the United Kingdom, people love Indian food, so McDonald's offers a McChicken Tikka Naan dish to satisfy that desire. In Australia, there is the McOz burger, and in Japan the Chicken Tatsuta. In India, you can buy a Maharajah Mac.

McDonald's is also patient. It doesn't mind taking years to become established in a new foreign market. When McDonald's opened a store in Rome near the Spanish Steps, the outcry from Italian citizens was so loud that zoning laws were passed to keep the stores out of city centers. But McDonald's was able to buy an Italian burger chain called Burghy's and now has 220 stores in Italy and some 98 percent of the burger market there.

McDonald's is now in 117 countries and has some 40 million customers served daily, up from 30 million just five years ago. Some 11,300 new stores will go up outside of the United States by 2004.

Sources: Bruce Upbin, "Beyond Burgers," *Forbes*, November 1, 1999, pp. 218–23, Louise Kramer, "Fast-Feeders Play Game of Chicken," *Advertising Age*, November 8, 1999, p. 44; and Robert Frank, "Big Boy's Big Adventure in Thailand," *The Wall Street Journal*, April 12, 2000, pp. B1, B4.

Example of the Product Life Cycle

You can see how the theory works by looking at the product life cycle of instant coffee. When it was introduced, most people didn't like it as well as "regular" coffee, and it took several years for instant coffee to gain general acceptance (introduction stage). At one point, though, instant coffee grew rapidly in popularity, and many brands were introduced (growth stage). After a while, people became attached to one brand and sales leveled off (maturity stage). Sales then went into a slight decline when freeze-dried coffees were introduced (decline stage). At present, freeze-dried coffee is, in turn, at the maturity stage. It's extremely important to recognize what stage a product is in because such an analysis may lead to intelligent and efficient marketing decisions.

The Importance of the Product Life Cycle

The importance of the product life cycle to marketers is this: Different stages in the product life

Many movie houses are going out of business, indicating that they are in the decline phase of the product life cycle. To renew the life cycle, some theaters are offering a whole new experience to customers, including a full bar, meals, and luxury seating. Would you be willing to pay $12.50 to see a good movie and be able to order a fine meal at the same time?

FIGURE 14.6

SALES AND PROFITS DURING THE PRODUCT LIFE CYCLE

Note that profit levels start to fall *before* sales reach their peak. When profits and sales start to decline, it's time to come out with a new product or to remodel the old one to maintain interest and profits.

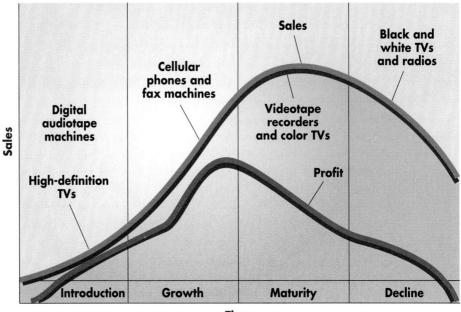

FIGURE 14.6

SALES AND PROFITS DURING THE PRODUCT LIFE CYCLE

	MARKETING MIX ELEMENTS			
LIFE CYCLE STAGE	**PRODUCT**	**PRICE**	**PLACE**	**PROMOTION**
Introduction	Offer market-tested product; keep mix small	Go after innovators with high introductory price (skimming strategy) or use penetration pricing	Use wholesalers, selective distribution	Dealer promotion and heavy investment in primary demand advertising and sales promotion to get stores to carry the product and consumers to try it
Growth	Improve product; keep product mix limited	Adjust price to meet competition	Increase distribution	Heavy competitive advertising
Maturity	Differentiate your product to satisfy different market segments	Further reduce price	Take over wholesaling function and intensify distribution	Emphasize brand name as well as product benefits and differences
Decline	Cut product mix; develop new-product ideas	Consider price increase	Consolidate distribution; drop some outlets	Reduce advertising to only loyal customers

FIGURE 14.7

SAMPLE STRATEGIES FOLLOWED DURING THE PRODUCT LIFE CYCLE

cycle call for different marketing strategies. Figure 14.7 outlines the marketing mix decisions that might be made. As you go through the table, you'll see that each stage calls for multiple marketing mix changes. Remember, these concepts are largely theoretical and should be used only as guidelines.

Figure 14.8 shows in table form the theory of what happens to sales volume, profits, and competition during the product life cycle. You can compare this table to the graph in Figure 14.6. For instance, both figures show that a product at the mature stage may reach the top in sales growth while profit is decreasing. At that stage, a marketing manager may decide to create a new image for the product to start a new growth cycle. You may have noticed, for example, how Arm & Hammer baking soda gets a new image every few years to

LIFE CYCLE STAGE	SALES	PROFITS	COMPETITORS
Introduction	Low sales	Losses may occur	Few
Growth	Rapidly rising sales	Very high profits	Growing number
Maturity	Peak sales	Declining profits	Stable number, then declining
Decline	Falling sales	Profits may fall to become losses	Declining number

FIGURE 14.8

HOW SALES, PROFITS, AND COMPETITION VARY OVER THE PRODUCT LIFE CYCLE

All products go through these stages at various times in their life cycle. What happens to sales as a product matures?

generate new sales. One year it's positioned as a deodorant for refrigerators and the next as a substitute for harsh chemicals in swimming pools. Knowing what stage in the cycle a product is in helps marketing managers decide when such strategic changes are needed.

CRITICAL THINKING

In what stage of the product life cycle are laptop computers? What does Figure 14.7 indicate firms should do at that stage? What will the next stage be? What might you do at that stage to optimize profits?

Peanut butter is in the maturity or decline stage of the product life cycle. Does that explain why Skippy recently introduced a reduced-fat version of its peanut butter? What other variations on older products have been introduced in the last few years?

PROGRESS ASSESSMENT

- What are the five steps in the new-product development process?
- Can you draw a product life cycle and label its parts?

COMPETITIVE PRICING

Pricing is so important to marketing and the development of value packages that it has been singled out as one of the four Ps in the marketing mix, along with product, place, and promotion. Price is also a critical ingredient in consumer evaluations of the product. In this section, we'll explore price both as an ingredient of the value package and as a strategic marketing tool.

Pricing Objectives

A firm may have several objectives in mind when setting a pricing strategy. When pricing Fiberrific, we may want to promote the product's image. If we price it high and use the right promotion, maybe we can make it the Evian of cereals, as we discussed earlier. We also might price it high to achieve a certain profit objective or return on investment. We could also price Fiberrific lower than its competitors because we want poor people and older people to be able to afford this nutritious cereal. That is, we could have some social or ethical goal in mind. Low pricing may also discourage competition because the profit potential is less in this case. A low price may also help us capture a larger share of the market. The point is that a firm may have several pricing objectives over time, and it must formulate these objectives clearly before developing an overall pricing strategy. Popular objectives include the following:

1. *Achieving a target return on investment or profit.* Ultimately, the goal of marketing is to make a profit by providing goods and services to others.

Naturally, one long-run pricing objective of almost all firms is to optimize profit.[12]

2. *Building traffic.* Supermarkets often advertise certain products at or below cost to attract people to the store. These products are called loss leaders. The long-run objective is to make profits by following the short-run objective of building a customer base. Yahoo is providing an auction service for free in competition with eBay. Why give such a service away free? Because it generates more advertising revenue on its site and it attracts more people to its other services.[13]

3. *Achieving greater market share.* The auto industry is in a fierce international battle to capture and hold market share. U.S. automakers lost market share to foreign producers in the 1980s and have used price incentives (and quality) to win it back.

4. *Increasing sales.* Sometimes a firm will lower prices to increase sales. Such a move could hurt profit margins in the short run but will enable the company to become more financially secure in the long run. Then prices could again be raised.

5. *Creating an image.* Certain watches, perfumes, and other socially visible products are priced high to give them an image of exclusivity and status.

6. *Furthering social objectives.* A firm may want to price a product low so that people with less money can afford the product. The government often gets involved in pricing farm products so that everyone can get basic needs such as milk and bread at a low price.

Note that a firm may have short-run objectives that differ greatly from its long-run objectives. Both should be understood at the beginning and put into the strategic marketing plan. Pricing objectives should be influenced by other marketing decisions regarding product design, packaging, branding, distribution, and promotion. All of these marketing decisions are interrelated.

People believe intuitively that the price charged for a product must bear some relation to the cost of producing the product. In fact, we'd generally agree that prices are usually set somewhere above cost. But as we'll see, prices and cost aren't always related.

Cost-Based Pricing

Producers often use cost as a primary basis for setting price. They develop elaborate cost accounting systems to measure production costs (including materials, labor, and overhead), add in some margin of profit, and come up with a price. The question is whether the price will be satisfactory to the market as well. In the long run, the market—not the producer—determines what the price will be. Pricing should take into account costs, but it should also include the expected costs of product updates, the objectives for each product, and competitor prices.

An opposing strategy to cost-based pricing is one called target costing. **Target costing** is designing a product so that it satisfies customers and meets the profit margins desired by the firm. Target costing makes cost an input to the product development process, not an outcome of it. You estimate the selling price people would be willing to pay for a product and subtract the desired profit margin. The result is the target cost of production. Japanese companies such as Isuzu Motors, Komatsu Limited, and Sony all use target costing.

Value Pricing

Value pricing is when marketers provide consumers with brand-name goods and services at fair prices. Manufacturers and service organizations, as you might expect, are finding it hard to maintain profits while offering value pricing

target costing
Designing a product so that it satisfies customers and meets the profit margins desired by the firm.

value pricing
When marketers provide consumers with brand-name goods and services at fair prices.

to consumers. The best way to offer value prices and not go broke is to redesign products from the bottom up and to cut costs wherever possible. Taco Bell, for example, cut its kitchen space to provide more seating and specifically designed its menu to increase the number of items that took little kitchen space to prepare. Now 70 percent of each Taco Bell restaurant is seating, compared with 30 percent in the past. Some companies are refurbishing old equipment and selling it at attractive prices. Again, the idea is to sell brand-name items at low prices.

Small businesses ➤ **P.176** ◂ can often capture a healthy share of the market by offering a great price right from the start. Emachines, for example, sold computers at prices between $399 and $599. The only lower prices are those computers that companies are offering for free! The catch is that you either have to pay for several years of high-priced Internet services or put up with lots of ads on your computer screen. Today it is getting easier and easier for consumers to find the best values in goods and services.[14] All they have to do is use a shopping site like mySimon.com to find good values.

Go figure.

What's Your Priority?™

Value Pricing in the Service Sector

Service ➤ **P.25** ◂ industries are adopting many of the same pricing tactics as goods-producing firms. They begin by cutting costs as much as possible. Then they determine what services are most important to customers; those that aren't important are cut. For example, some airlines have eliminated meals on their flights. Southwest doesn't incur the administrative costs of assigned seats. In return, customers get good value. Some of the bigger airlines are trying to cut costs but are stuck with high fixed costs. American Airlines often won't even try to match other airlines' prices. It must offer exceptional service to compete. United Airlines is creating an airline within the airline that will offer low fares on shorter routes. Midway Airlines out of Raleigh-Durham, North Carolina, offers low fares for short-haul flights.

With both goods and services, the idea is to give the consumer value. But trying to give the consumer value while maintaining profits is a challenge. Break-even analysis helps an organization relate sales, profit, and price.

> **W**ho says the government can't compete with private business? Not the United States Postal Service. It takes on private competition head to head with a comparative ad on prices. What's your priority? it asks. If your priority is price, $3 anywhere is a good deal. What non-price factors may lead someone to use UPS or Fed Ex instead?

Break-Even Analysis

Before you go into the business of producing Fiberrific cereal, it may be wise to determine how many boxes of cereal you'd have to sell before making a profit. You'd then determine whether you could reach such a sales goal. **Break-even analysis** is the process used to determine profitability at various levels of sales. The break-even point is the point where revenues from sales equal all costs. The formula for calculating the break-even point is as follows:

$$\text{Break-even point (BEP)} = \frac{\text{Total fixed cost (FC)}}{\text{Price of one unit (P)} - \text{Variable cost (VC) of one unit}}$$

Total fixed costs are costs that do not change in relationship to how many products are made or sold. Among the expenses that make up fixed costs are the amount paid to own or rent a factory or warehouse and the amount paid for business insurance. **Variable costs** change according to the level of production. Included are the expenses for the materials used in making products

break-even analysis
The process used to determine profitability at various levels of sales.

total fixed costs
All the expenses that remain the same no matter how many products are sold.

variable costs
Costs that change according to the level of production.

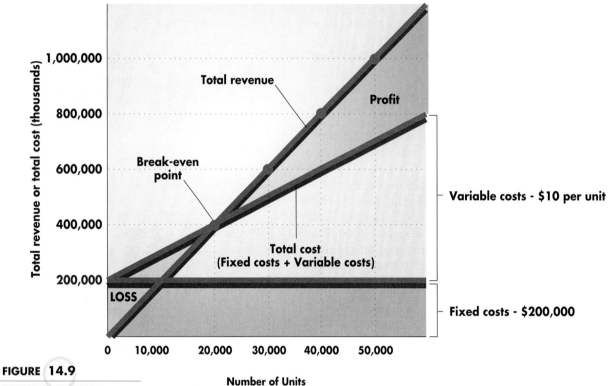

FIGURE 14.9

BREAK-EVEN CHART

At 20,000 units the company breaks even. Above 20,000 units, the firm earns a profit.

and the direct costs of labor used in making those goods. For example, imagine that you are a manufacturer selling a sweater for $20 and have a fixed cost of $200,000 (for mortgage interest, real estate taxes, equipment, and so on). Your variable cost (e.g., labor and materials) per sweater is $10. The break-even point would be 20,000 sweaters. In other words, you wouldn't make any money selling sweaters unless you sold more than 20,000 of them:

$$BEP = \frac{FC}{P - VC} = \frac{\$200,000}{\$20 - \$10} = \frac{\$200,000}{\$10} = 20,000 \text{ sweaters}$$

Figure 14.9 illustrates this break-even point in the form of a graph.

Pricing Strategies

Let's say a firm has just developed a new line of products, such as high-definition television (HDTV) sets. The firm has to decide how to price these sets at the introductory stage of the product life cycle. One strategy would be to price them high to recover the costs of developing the sets and to take advantage of the fact that there are few competitors. A **skimming price strategy** is one in which a new product is priced high to make optimum profit while there's little competition. Of course, those large profits will attract competitors. That happened when high-priced HDTVs were introduced in the 1990s.

A second strategy would be to price the new HDTVs low. This would attract more buyers and discourage other companies from making sets because the profit is so low. This strategy enables the firm to penetrate or capture a large share of the market quickly. A **penetration strategy,** therefore, is one in which a product is priced low to attract more customers and discourage competitors. The Japanese successfully used a penetration strategy with videocassette recorders. No U.S. firm could compete with the low prices the Japanese offered. Additional pricing strategies are listed in the accompanying chart (see Figure 14.10).

There are several pricing strategies used by retailers. One is called **everyday low pricing (EDLP).** That's the pricing strategy used by Home Depot and

skimming price strategy
Strategy in which a new product is priced high to make optimum profit while there's little competition.

penetration strategy
Strategy in which a product is priced low to attract many customers and discourage competition.

everyday low pricing (EDLP)
Setting prices lower than competitors and then not having any special sales.

It's impossible to cover all pricing tactics in detail in this book, but you should at least be familiar with the following terms:

1. *Adaptive pricing* allows an organization to vary its prices based on factors such as competition, market conditions, and resource costs. Rather than relying on one set price, the firm adjusts the price to fit different situations.

2. *Cost-oriented pricing* is the strategy of setting prices primarily on the basis of cost. For example, retailers often use cost plus a certain markup, while producers use a system of cost-plus pricing.

3. *Customary pricing* means that most sellers will adapt the product to some established, universally accepted price such as the price for gum or candy bars. Notice that when the price goes up, almost all producers adjust their price upward.

4. *Product-line pricing* is the procedure used to set prices for a group of products that are similar but aimed at different market segments. For example, a beer producer might have a low-priced beer, a popular-priced beer, and a premium-priced beer.

5. *Target pricing* means that an organization will set some goal such as a certain share of the market or a certain return on investment as a basis for setting a price. Usually, market conditions prevent a firm from establishing prices this way, but such goals do give some direction to pricing policies.

6. *Uniform pricing,* also known as *single-price policy,* means that all customers buying the product (given similar circumstances) pay the same price. Although it's the most common policy in the United States, uniform pricing is unusual in many foreign markets, especially among private sellers.

7. *Odd pricing* or *psychological pricing* means pricing an item a few cents under a round price ($9.98 instead of $10) to make the product appear less expensive.

8. *Price lining* is the practice of offering goods at a few set prices such as $30, $40, and $50. Such a tactic makes both pricing and checkout easier, and it appeals to a market segment interested in that level of pricing.

FIGURE 14.10

ADDITIONAL PRICING TACTICS

Wal-Mart. Such stores set prices lower than competitors and do not have any special sales. The idea is to have consumers come to those stores whenever they want a bargain, rather than wait until there is a sale, as they do for most department stores.

Department stores and other retailers most often use a **high–low pricing strategy.** The idea is to have regular prices that are higher than those at stores using everyday low pricing but also to have many special sales where the prices are lower than those of competitors. The problem with such pricing is that it teaches consumers to wait for sales, thus cutting into profits. As the Internet grows in popularity, you may see fewer stores with a high–low strategy because consumers will be able to find better prices on the Internet and begin buying more and more from online retailers.

Some retailers use price as a major determinant of the goods they carry. For example, there are stores that promote goods that sell for only $1 or only $10. Outlet stores supposedly sell

high–low pricing strategy
Set prices that are higher than EDLP stores, but have many special sales where the prices are lower than competitors

One way producers are able to keep prices low is to downsize the product. Usually customers can't tell the difference, and the producer is able to keep prices low and still make a good profit. What are the ethical implications of such practices?

This is DealTime's website. Such companies enable consumers to compare prices across a broad range of items. The list includes everything from appliances to wireless and telecom. You can also search for gift ideas and more. Do you know people who hesitate to use such online companies? What is holding them back?

price leadership
The procedure by which one or more dominant firms set the pricing practices that all competitors in an industry follow.

brand-name goods at discount prices, and sometimes they do. Other stores, sometimes called discount stores, sell "seconds," or damaged goods. Consumers must take care to carefully examine such goods to be sure the flaws are not too major.

How Market Forces Affect Pricing

Ultimately, price is determined by supply and demand > **P.39** < in the marketplace, as described in Chapter 2. For example, if you charge $3 for Fiber-rific and nobody buys your cereal at that price, you'll have to lower the price until you reach a point that's acceptable to customers and to you. The price that results from the interaction of buyers and sellers in the marketplace is called the *market price*.

Recognizing the fact that different consumers may be willing to pay different prices, marketers sometimes price on the basis of consumer demand rather than cost or some other calculation. That's called *demand-oriented pricing* and is reflected by movie theaters with low rates for children and by drugstores with discounts for senior citizens. The Washington Opera Company in Washington, D.C., for example, raised its prices on prime seating and lowered its pricing on less attractive seating; this strategy raised the company's revenues by 9 percent.

Besides supply and demand forces, another factor in the marketplace is competition. **Price leadership** is the procedure by which one or more dominant firms set the pricing practices that all competitors in an industry follow. You may have noticed that practice among oil and cigarette companies. Competition-oriented pricing is a strategy based on what all the other competitors are doing. The price can be at, above, or below competitors' prices. Pricing depends on customer loyalty, perceived differences, and the competitive climate.

Marketers will face a new pricing problem in the next few years. Customers can now compare prices of many goods and services on the Internet. For example, you may want to check out deals on sites such as DealTime.com, BrandsForLess.com, or ICanBuy.com. Priceline.com introduced us to a "demand collection system" where buyers post the prices they are willing to pay and invite sellers to either accept or decline the price. Consumers can get great prices on airlines, hotels, and other products by naming the price they are willing to pay. Furthermore, Mercata introduced us to group buying. Individuals can gather into buying blocks to leverage their combined purchasing power to get prices lower.[15] You can also buy used goods online. Have you or any of your friends bought or sold anything on eBay or Amazon.com? Clearly, price competition is going to heat up as consumers have more access to price information from all around the world.[16] In that case, nonprice competition is likely to increase.

NONPRICE COMPETITION

In spite of the emphasis placed on price in microeconomic theory, marketers often compete on product attributes other than price.[17] You may have noted that price differences are small with products such as gasoline, men's haircuts, candy bars, and even major products such as compact cars and private colleges. Typically, you will not see price used as a major promotional appeal on

Going from Low-End to Upscale Restaurants

Dave Thomas was a marketing major at George Washington University. Like many small-business owners, he was able to build a small fortune using his marketing skills to build, grow, and sell Subway sandwich shops. He built his first shop in 1994, just before graduating from college. He went on to build four more stores in the District of Columbia. Thomas learned a lot as a sandwich shop owner. For one thing, he learned how to offer a low-priced value meal. But Thomas always dreamed of owning an upscale restaurant where he could charge higher prices and make even more money.

There are many midpriced restaurants in and around Washington, D.C., that were started by small-business owners; Clyde's and the Capitol City Brewing Company are just two of the more popular ones. They attract customers with consistent service and fair prices. There are also many upscale restaurants that feature outstanding food and service at upscale pricing. It is this latter market that Thomas was after.

Thomas found a chef who had worked at such upscale restaurants as the Four Seasons, the Grand Hotel Café, and the Watergate Hotel's Aquarelle. The chef, Robert Wiedmaier, was eager to become a small-business owner himself and jumped at the idea when Thomas offered him the chance to open one in a premier Washington, D.C., location. Together, they opened a restaurant called Marcel's on Pennsylvania Avenue. Now Thomas was in a new marketing situation where a nonprice strategy was more important than value pricing. Customers in an upscale restaurant care less about pricing and more about great food, great service, and a pleasant ambiance. Thomas's favorite dish at Marcel's is quail stuffed with foie gras. You just can't buy something like that at Subway.

Sources: Brian Krebs, "A Restauranteur Moves Up the Food Chain," *Washington Business*, April 5, 1999, p. 15; Bill Kelley, "The Price Is Right?" *Entrepreneur*, October 1999, pp. 136–37; and Robert Shoffner, David Dorsen and Thomas Head, "Really Prime Beef," *Washingtonian*, April 2000, pp. 149–51.

television. Instead, marketers tend to stress product images and consumer benefits such as comfort, style, convenience, and durability.

Many smaller organizations promote the services that accompany basic products rather than price in order to compete with bigger firms. The idea is to make a relatively homogeneous product "better" by offering more service. Danny O'Neill, for example, is a small wholesaler who sells gourmet coffee to upscale restaurants. He has to watch competitor prices and see what services they offer so that he can charge the premium prices he wants. To charge high prices, he has to offer superior service. The Spotlight on Small Business box looks at upscale pricing at the retail level.

Larger companies often do the same thing. For example, some airlines stress friendliness, promptness, more flights, better meals, and other such services. High-priced hotels stress "no surprises," cable TV, business services, health clubs, and other extras.

Nonprice Strategies

Often marketers emphasize nonprice differences because prices are so easy to match. However, few competitors can match the image of a friendly, responsive, consumer-oriented company. The following are some other strategies for avoiding price wars:

1. *Add value.* Some drugstores with elderly customers add value by offering home delivery. Training videos add value to any product that's difficult to use. Lawn mower manufacturer Toro gives "lawn parties" during which it teaches customers lawn care strategies.

2. *Educate consumers.* Home Depot teaches its customers how to use the equipment it sells and how to build decks and other do-it-yourself projects. The Iowa Beef Processors educate their customers about the value of buying top-grade beef, which has less waste.

3. *Establish relationships.* Customers will pay more for products and services when they have a friendly relationship with the seller. Today some auto dealers, like Saturn, may send out cards reminding people when service is needed. They may also have picnics and other special events for customers. Airlines, supermarkets, hotels, and car rental agencies have frequent-buyer clubs that offer all kinds of fringe benefits to frequent users. The services aren't less expensive, but they offer more value.[18]

As you can see, this chapter begins and ends with one theme: Give customers value and they'll give you their loyalty.

PROGRESS ASSESSMENT

- Can you list two short-term and two long-term pricing objectives? Are the two compatible?
- What's wrong with using a cost-based pricing strategy?
- What's the purpose of break-even analysis?
- Can you calculate a product's break-even point if producing it costs $10,000 and revenue from the sale of one unit is $20?

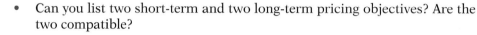

SUMMARY

1. Explain the concept of a value package.

1. A value package consists of everything that consumers evaluate when deciding whether to buy something.
   - ***What's included in a value package?***
   A value package includes price, brand name, satisfaction in use, and more.
   - ***What's the difference between a product line and a product mix?***
   A product line is a group of physically similar products. (A product line of gum may include bubble gum, sugarless gum, etc.) A product mix is a company's combination of product lines. (A manufacturer may offer lines of gum, candy bars, chewing tobacco, etc.)
   - ***How do marketers create product differentiation for their goods and services?***
   Marketers use a mix of pricing, advertising, and packaging to make their products seem unique and attractive.

2. Describe the various kinds of consumer and industrial goods.

2. Consumer goods are sold to ultimate consumers like you and me and not to businesses.
   - ***What are the four classifications of consumer goods and services, and how are they marketed?***
   There are convenience goods and services (requiring minimum shopping effort), shopping goods and services (for which people compare price and quality), specialty goods and services (which consumers go out of their way to get), and unsought goods and services (which consumers did not intend to buy when they entered the store). Convenience goods and services are best promoted by location, shopping goods and services by some price/quality appeal, and specialty goods and services by word of mouth. Unsought goods (impulse items) are often displayed at the checkout counter where consumers see them while waiting in line and are attracted to buy them.

    • *What are industrial goods and how are they marketed differently from consumer goods?*

Industrial goods are products sold in the business-to-business market (B2B), and are used in the production of other products. They're sold largely through salespeople and rely less on advertising. Installations are major capital equipment such as new factories and heavy machinery. Accessory equipment are capital items that are not quite as long lasting or as expensive as installations. Examples include computers, photocopy machines, and various tools.

3. Packaging changes the product and is becoming increasingly important, taking over much of the sales function for consumer goods.

    • *What are the six functions of packaging?*

The six functions are (1) to attract the buyer's attention; (2) to describe the contents; (3) to explain the benefits of the product inside; (4) to provide information on warranties, warnings, and other consumer matters; (5) to indicate price, value, and uses; and (6) to protect the goods inside, stand up under handling and storage, be tamperproof, deter theft and yet be easy to open and use.

3. List and describe the six functions of packaging.

4. Branding also changes a product.

    • *Can you give examples of a brand, a brand name, and a trademark?*

There are endless examples. One example of a brand name of crackers is Waverly by Nabisco. The brand consists of the name Waverly as well as the symbol (a red triangle in the corner with Nabisco circled in white). The brand name and the symbol are also trademarks, since Nabisco has been given legal protection for this brand.

    • *What is brand loyalty, and how do managers create brand awareness?*

Brand loyalty is the degree to which customers are satisfied, like the brand, and are committed to further purchases. Customer relationship management is designed to create brand loyalty. Advertising helps build strong brand awareness. Event sponsorship (e.g., the Winston-Salem auto races and Virginia Slims tennis tournament) helps improve brand awareness. Brand association is the linking of a brand to other favorable images. For example, you can link a brand to other product users, to a popular celebrity, to a particular geographic area, or to competitors.

4. Give examples of a brand, a brand name, and a trademark, and explain the concepts of brand equity and loyalty.

5. Brand managers coordinate product, price, place, and promotion decisions for a particular product.

    • *What are the six steps of the product development process?*

The steps are (1) generation of new-product ideas, (2) screening, (3) product analysis, (4) development, (5) testing, and (6) commercialization.

5. Explain the role of brand managers and the six steps of the new-product development process.

6. Once a product is placed on the market, marketing strategy varies as the product goes through various stages of acceptance called the product life cycle.

    • *How do marketing strategies theoretically change at the various stages?*

See Figures 14.6, 14.7, and 14.8.

    • *What are the stages of the product life cycle?*

They are introduction, growth, maturity, and decline.

6. Identify and describe the stages of the product life cycle, and describe marketing strategies at each stage.

7. Pricing is one of the four Ps of marketing.

    • *What are pricing objectives?*

Objectives include achieving a target profit, building traffic, increasing market share, increasing sales, creating an image, and meeting social goals.

7. Give examples of various pricing objectives and strategies.

• *What's the break-even point?*

At the break-even point, total cost equals total revenue. Sales beyond that point are profitable.

• *What strategies can marketers use to determine a product's price?*

A skimming price strategy is one in which the product is priced high to make optimum profit while there's little competition, whereas a penetration strategy is one in which a product is priced low to attract more customers and discourage competitors. Demand-oriented pricing is based on consumer demand rather than cost. Competition-oriented pricing is based on all competitors' prices. Price leadership occurs when all competitors follow the pricing practice of one or more dominant companies. Please review Figure 14.10 to be sure you understand all the terms used for other pricing strategies.

8. Explain why nonpricing strategies are growing in importance.

8. In spite of the emphasis placed on price in microeconomic theory, marketers often compete on product attributes other than price.

• *Why do companies use nonprice strategies?*

Pricing is one of the easiest marketing strategies to copy. Therefore, often it is not a good long-run competitive tool. Instead, marketers may compete using nonprice strategies that are less easy to copy, including offering great service, educating consumers, and establishing long-term relationships with customers.

KEY TERMS

brand 436
brand
  association 438
brand
  awareness 438
brand equity 437
brand loyalty 437
brand manager 438
break-even
  analysis 447
commercialization
  442
concept testing 441
convenience goods
  and services 431
dealer (private)
  brands 437
everyday low pricing
  (EDLP) 448

generic goods 437
generic name 437
high–low pricing
  strategy 449
industrial goods 434
knockoff brands 436
manufacturers'
  brand names 436
penetration
  strategy 448
price leadership 450
product analysis 440
product
  differentiation 430
product life
  cycle 442
product line 430
product mix 430

product
  screening 440
shopping goods and
  services 432
skimming price
  strategy 448
specialty goods and
  services 432
target costing 446
total fixed costs 447
trademark 436
unsought goods and
  services 433
value 428
value package 428
value pricing 446
variable costs 447

DEVELOPING WORKPLACE SKILLS

1. Look around your classroom and notice the different types of shoes that students are wearing. What product qualities were they looking for when they chose those shoes? What was the importance of price, style, brand name, and color? Describe the product offerings you would feature in a new shoe store designed to appeal to college students.

2. A value package consists of everything that consumers evaluate when choosing among products, including price, package, service, and reputation. Working in teams, compose a list of as many factors that consumers might consider when evaluating the following products: a vacation resort, a college, a new car.

3. Take some time when you are at your local grocery store and compare prices from different manufacturers on items such as cereal, peanut butter, and soup. What is the relationship of brand name to price, if any? Develop what you would consider the best value package of goods based on your research. Write a brief analysis of your findings.

4. Go to your medicine cabinet and take an inventory of all the branded and nonbranded items. Then discuss with your classmates the brand names they buy for the same goods. Do most students buy brand-name goods or generic goods? Why?

5. Determine where in the product life cycle you would place each of the following products and then prepare a marketing strategy for each product based on the recommendations in this chapter:
   a. Alka-Seltzer.
   b. Cellular phones.
   c. Electric automobiles.
   d. Campbell's chicken noodle soup.

TAKING IT TO THE NET

1

Purpose

To assess how the Internet can be used to shop for various goods.

Exercise

Shopbots are Internet sites that you can use to find the best prices on goods you need. No shopbot searches the entire Internet, so it's a good idea to use more than one to get the best deals. Furthermore, not all shopbots figure in shipping and handling. Here are some to try:

mySimon.com
Bottomdollar.com
ShopFind.com
PriceSCAN.com
Clickthebutton.com

Questions

1. Which of the shopbots seem most comprehensive—offering the most goods or the most information?

2. Which shopbot is the easiest to use? The hardest?

3. Write down some of the prices you find on the Internet and then go to a local discount store, such as Wal-Mart, and compare prices. Which are lowest, or does it depend on the product?

4. Evaluate shopping on the Internet versus shopping in stores. What are the advantages and disadvantages of each?

TAKING IT TO THE NET

Purpose

To determine the appropriate pricing strategy for specific products.

Exercise

2 Go to www.marketingteacher.com/Lessons/lesson_pricing.htm and review the various types of pricing strategies.

1. Click on the exercise button and place the products listed in the appropriate cells of the grid provided.

2. Click on the answer button to check your work. If you do not agree with the answers, scroll down the screen for an explanation.

PRACTICING MANAGEMENT DECISIONS

CASE

EVERYDAY LOW PRICING (EDLP)

Wal-Mart, Kmart, and wholesale clubs such as Costco have had great success with a concept they call everyday low pricing (EDLP). Rather than have relatively high prices and then barrage consumers with coupons and price discounts (a high–low pricing strategy), such stores promote the fact that they offer lower prices every day. Similarly, some manufacturers are offering everyday low purchase prices. Instead of having a relatively high price for products sold to retailers, manufacturers such as Procter & Gamble have everyday low purchase prices. It's the same concept as EDLP applied to industrial goods instead of consumer goods.

Many retailers have decided to follow the lead of Wal-Mart and others by cutting prices on all their goods. But recent research shows that this isn't always wise. Dominick's Finer Foods, with 28 percent of the Chicago-area food business, tried an EDLP policy and boosted sales by 3 percent—yet profits declined by 18 percent. It has been calculated, in fact, that supermarket volume would have to increase by 39 percent for supermarkets to avoid losing money after a 7 percent price drop. Consumers say location is usually their most important factor in choosing a supermarket. Thus, supermarkets shouldn't have to have the lowest prices to keep market share.

Usually sales volume falls after the introduction of everyday low prices, but it picks up later. That is true in Europe as well as in the United States.

In spite of the potential drawbacks of everyday low pricing, 7-Eleven implemented it in 250 stores in the Dallas–Fort Worth area. This pricing policy was just one part of an overall revamping of 7-Eleven's image, including updated interiors, fresh produce, and gourmet items. In fact, 7-Eleven no longer wants its former image of a high-priced convenience store, and is seeking to appear as a small yet viable alternative to supermarkets.

Decision Questions

1. As a consumer, would you prefer that your local supermarket offer everyday low prices, offer some products at major discounts (half off) periodically, or offer some combination of the two?

2. What could your local supermarket do other than offer low prices or price discounts to win your business (delight you) and still maintain a high profit margin?

3. What advantages and disadvantages do you see for manufacturers to offer everyday low purchase prices to retailers?

4. Are manufacturers and retailers pushing price so much that they're in danger of lowering profits? Is this especially true on the Internet? Why is price competition so common?

VIDEO CASE

ROLLERBLADE: PRICE AS PART OF THE FOUR Ps

The marketing mix, or four Ps of marketing, work together to create value for the consumer. It begins with a product. In the case of Rollerblade, the product is in-line skates. When the company began in 1986, it was the only manufacturer of in-line skates in the world. The company created a new sport based on a combination of two other popular sports: skating and skateboarding. Skateboards had been popular, but skates could be used in more places and could appeal to more diverse groups of people. But old-fashioned skates weren't flexible enough to allow users to do the moves skateboards did. The innovation of in-line skates proved so popular there are now 30 competing companies in the industry.

Rollerblade continues to be the market leader because of its constant product innovation. For example, it introduced ABT brakes, and RB Grind Shoes for the aggressive segment of the market. The Grind Shoe is a regular athletic shoe with twin roller bars on the instep of the sole that enables the wearer to slide across railings, curbs, or whatever, to "grind." The thinking was, "Kids do these tricks on rails with skateboards and in-line skates, why not do it with shoes?" Likewise, the company developed the Nature because students needed something they could skate to class in, and then be able to wear into class (shoes are easily detached from the blades). The price for these types of skates must be in a range that the teens and early 20-year-olds can afford.

Technology made it possible to create a whole line of in-line skates for different purposes: Coyote skates were made for downhill racers and Outback skates were made for rough roads. Rollerblade designed products for a broad range of market segments, from the large mass market stores to specialty in-line dealers. To attract as many customers as possible, the skates had to have different prices—from upscale to lower-priced. The company uses a different brand name, Bladerunner, for lower-priced skates. Giving the lower-priced skates a different brand name allows the Rollerblade name to retain its high-quality image while still giving beginners an opportunity to test the sport.

Competitors such as K-2, Solomon, and Nike make it necessary to price Rollerblade skates competitively. By developing unique skates for unique sports, Rollerblade is hoping to put more importance on the product and technology rather than price. The company promotes grass skating, downhill slalom skating, rough terrain skating, bump competition, and ramp competition. Each calls for a different (and often more expensive) upgraded skate.

To reach a diverse public, Rollerblade must have distribution in a variety of stores, everything from Target to specialized in-line dealers. Naturally, the company wants to reach overseas to young people in other countries. The Internet makes it possible to reach overseas without spending too much on stores and other facilities. Often the technological innovations and the new sports create so much free publicity that Rollerblade doesn't have to spend as much money on promotion. Word of mouth among skaters spreads quickly and TV broadcasts of skating competitions exposes the company to a wide audience. People are amazed to see what can be done on skates.

Ultimately, the success of Rollerblade depends on the same factors as most products. That is, does the company offer value for the money? In this case, the value is created by a whole new sport that is fun, healthy, and exciting. Very young people can begin to skate on local sidewalks. As they get more practice, they can upgrade to rough terrain skates and downhill skates. All of them are priced within a reasonable range for the markets being served.

This video captures the excitement of in-line skating. By giving permission to the authors of the text to use the video, Rollerblade is able to reach thousands of college students who are the target audience for many of its upscale products. This keeps the cost of promotion down and that makes it possible to keep prices competitive.

Discussion Questions

1. What problems may emerge when a company tries to keep prices low in order to reach beginners who are younger and not familiar with in-line skating?

2. What possibilities exist for the company to sell other equipment to go with in-line skating, such as helmets and knee pads? How should these products be priced—low to attract as many people as possible to the sport or high to add as much as possible to profits?

3. Has Rollerblade succeeded in putting the focus more on technology than price, such that you would buy this brand over some other brand because of the superior features?

4. The video discusses three Ps: promotion, price, and place (distribution). Does this mean that the company pays less attention to product design than other companies, or does it mean that the product is so important that it deserves more attention than the other Ps of the marketing mix?

CHAPTER 15

Distributing Products Efficiently and Competitively: Supply Chain Management

LEARNING GOALS

AFTER YOU HAVE READ AND STUDIED THIS CHAPTER, YOU SHOULD BE ABLE TO

1. Explain the concept of marketing channels and the value of marketing intermediaries.

2. Give examples of how intermediaries perform the six marketing utilities.

3. Describe the various wholesale organizations in the distribution system.

4. Explain the ways in which retailers compete and the distribution strategies they use.

5. Explain the various kinds of nonstore retailing.

6. Discuss how a manufacturer can get wholesalers and retailers in a channel system to cooperate by the formation of systems.

7. Describe some supply-chain management problems and how they are solved.

8. Review the various distribution modes and their benefits and how they tie in with the materials handling and storage functions.

Getting to Know Randall Larrimore of United Stationers

The Internet has created rapid change in the sale and distribution of most goods. Perhaps nowhere is such change more apparent than in the office supply market. By the early 1990s, half of the smaller stationers in the United States had gone out of business—about 6,000 stores. Staples, Office Depot, and other large retailers, many of them with online services, rapidly replaced them. So, what happened to companies like United Stationers, that supplied those small stationers with the products they sold?

In 1994 United Stationers wasn't doing too well. It was then that Randall Larrimore became the company's chief executive. Larrimore was determined to reverse United Stationers' fortunes. He modernized United Stationers by using the latest supply-chain concepts. We shall discuss those concepts in this chapter, but first let's see what the results have been.

Come with us to Ketchum, Idaho, to visit a stationer called Business as Usual. It's a small store; only 1,500 square feet. Despite its size, its prices are competitive with those of not only the office superstores in nearby Twin Falls but also online sellers. The reason Business as Usual remains competitive is that United Stationers can readily provide it with some 35,000 items from more than 500 manufacturers at prices lower than those it could get by ordering directly from the manufacturers. United Stationers can purchase the products from the manufacturers more cheaply than small stores because it orders in such large volumes. It can then pass part of the savings on to its customers.

If Business as Usual places an order to United Stationers by 4 PM, the store gets the supplies by the next day. Even better, Business as Usual can have United Stationers send the supplies directly to its customers. By providing a large inventory and speedy delivery at low prices, United Stationers has made it possible for small companies to survive. It was Randall Larrimore who helped make all this possible.

Staples and Office Depot also use the services of United Stationers. These superstores order in such large volumes that they buy most of their products directly from manufacturers. However, there are many products that are not very popular but that superstores must carry in order to become one-stop shopping centers for office supplies. Since ordering these products directly from the manufacturer is not efficient, the superstores turn to United Stationers. United Stationers also supplies many of the office products that get sold online by Dell Computer and 125 other such companies.

In the United States there are hundreds of thousands of suppliers like United Stationers, providing similar services to retailers of products ranging from automobile supplies to zoo shop souvenirs.

The whole system for distributing goods has changed over the last decade or so. The advent of online retailers has altered the way customers buy and the way manufacturers sell. More important for this chapter, the Internet has also changed the way goods are distributed. This chapter will explore these and other changes.

Sources: Ashlea Ebling, "Paper Tiger," *Forbes*, February 21, 2000, pp. 71–74; "ebuyxpress.com, Leading B2B MRO Procurement Web Site, Cuts Cost of Goods 20% by Eliminating Distribution Layer and Aggregating Millions in Buying Power," *Business Wire*, May 2, 2000; and Marshall L. Fisher, Ananth Raman, and Anna Sheen McClelland, "Rocket Science Retailing Is Almost Here: Are You Ready?" *Harvard Business Review*, July–August 2000, pp. 115–24.

THE IMPORTANCE OF CHANNELS OF DISTRIBUTION

Look around at your fellow students. Many of them are wearing shoes made by Timberland. Now, try to imagine the challenge of getting the raw materials together, making 12 million pairs of shoes, as Timberland does, and then distributing those shoes to stores throughout the world. That's what thousands of manufacturing firms—making everything from automobiles to toys—have to deal with every day. It is an important task and creates a vast number of career opportunities. There are hundreds of thousands of marketing intermediaries whose job it is to help move goods from the raw-material state to producers and then on to consumers. All of them need college-educated workers to manage their operations.

marketing intermediaries

Organizations that assist in moving goods and services from producers to industrial and consumer users.

Marketing intermediaries are organizations that assist in moving goods and services from producers to business and consumer users. They're called intermediaries because they're organizations in the middle of a whole series of organizations that join together to help distribute goods from producers to consumers. (Traditionally, such firms were called *middlemen* because they were in the middle of the distribution network, but that term has been rejected by many as being sexist.) A **channel of distribution** consists of a whole set of marketing intermediaries, such as wholesalers and retailers, who join together to transport and store goods in their path (or channel) from producers to consumers. A **wholesaler** is a marketing intermediary that sells to other organizations, such as retailers, manufacturers, and hospitals. They are part of the business-to-business (B2B) ▸ **P.409** ◂ system. A **retailer** is an organization that sells to ultimate consumers (that is, people like you and me). Figure 15.1 pictures channels of distribution for both consumer and industrial (or B2B) goods.

channel of distribution

A whole set of marketing intermediaries, such as wholesalers and retailers, who join together to transport and store goods in their path (or channel) from producers to consumers.

wholesaler

A marketing intermediary that sells to other organizations.

retailer

An organization that sells to ultimate consumers.

Channels of distribution ensure communication flows and the flow of money and title to goods. They also help ensure that the right quantity and assortment of goods will be available when and where needed. The latest trend in distribution channels is to try to eliminate wholesalers and the need for retail stores by selling over the Internet and shipping directly to customers. The *Business Week* box on p. 462 discusses the problems that such efforts have caused and the remedies that are needed.

This message from Business Express, a British trucking company, recognizes that companies can design the best products and price them attractively and still lose customers if they are unable to deliver the products when the buyer needs them. Most manufacturers don't have the facilities to deliver goods overnight or in a couple of days. Instead, they outsource the delivery function to someone else.

Channels for industrial goods

This is the common channel for industrial products such as glass, tires, and paint for automobiles.

This is the way that lower-cost items such as supplies are distributed. The wholesaler is called an industrial distributor.

This channel is used by craftspeople and small farmers.

This channel is used for cars, furniture, and clothing.

Channels for consumer goods

This channel is the most common channel for consumer goods such as groceries, drugs, and cosmetics.

This is a common channel for food items such as produce.

This is a common channel for consumer services such as real estate, stocks and bonds, insurance, and nonprofit theater groups.

This is a common channel for nonprofit organizations that want to raise funds. Included are museums, government services, and zoos.

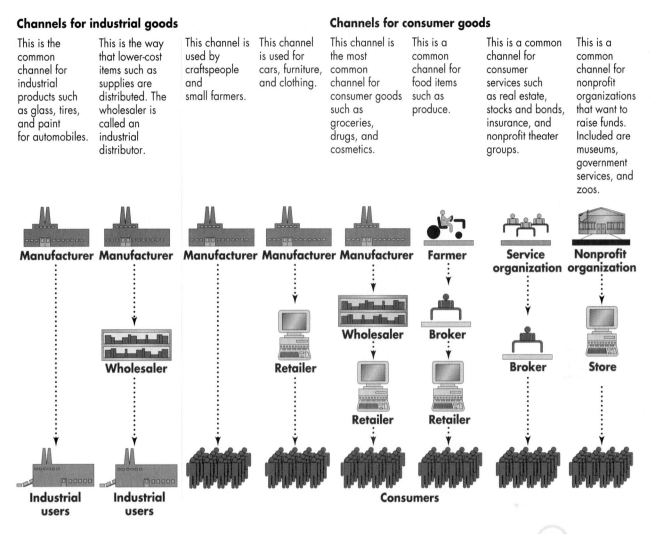

FIGURE 15.1

CHANNELS OF DISTRIBUTION FOR INDUSTRIAL AND CONSUMER GOODS AND SERVICES

Why Marketing Needs Intermediaries

Manufacturers don't always need marketing intermediaries to sell their goods to consumer and business buyers. Figure 15.1 shows that some manufacturers sell directly to buyers. You can sell directly to buyers on the Internet as well. So why have marketing intermediaries at all? The answer is that intermediaries perform certain marketing tasks such as transporting, storing, selling, advertising, and relationship building more effectively and efficiently than most manufacturers could. A simple analogy is this: You could deliver packages in person to people anywhere in the world, but usually you don't. Why not? Because it's usually cheaper and faster to have them delivered by the United States Postal Service or some private agency such as UPS or FedEx. Universal Parcel Shipping Software Systems provides software that helps larger companies compare prices and shipping methods (ground, next-day air, and so forth) to areas in the United States and Canada. Small companies can get similar help through SmartShip.com. Using such software, a small company can find a way to get goods to consumers quickly and at a reasonable cost. So companies, like you do, often outsource distribution to others.

Similarly, you could sell your home by yourself or buy stock directly from other people, but most people don't. Why? Again, because there are specialists (brokers) who make the process more efficient and easier. **Brokers** are marketing intermediaries who bring buyers and sellers together and assist in

brokers
Marketing intermediaries who bring buyers and sellers together and assist in negotiating an exchange but don't take title to the goods.

E-Commerce Calls for New Distribution Systems

E-businesses like Amazon.com and online grocer Webvan thought that they could sell products online and then have producers ship the goods directly to the consumer. By eliminating the wholesaler, the whole process would be more efficient. Such e-tailers learned quickly that it wouldn't be as easy as they thought. Manufacturers ran out of inventory and delivered late; also, multiple items from one order—shipped from multiple firms—arrived at different times, making product returns costly.

Amazon.com responded by spending $300 million to build 3 million square feet of warehouse space to store its books, CDs, and other products. Webvan is spending $1 billion to build a warehouse system including a fleet of delivery vans. In short, e-commerce companies cannot get rid of the wholesale function, although they may shun traditional wholesalers and do the job themselves. More often than not, however, traditional wholesalers remain in business because they have learned to perform their functions (storage and delivery and information processing) more efficiently than others.

Traditional retailers like Sears have also learned that selling on the Internet calls for a new kind of distribution system. Sears' warehouses are accustomed to delivering truckloads of goods to their retail outlets. But they are not prepared to make deliveries to individual consumers—except for large orders like furniture and appliances. It turns out, therefore, that both traditional retailers and new e-tailers have to develop new distribution systems to meet the demands of today's Internet-wise shoppers.

Sources: Robert D. Hof, "What's with All the Warehouses?" *Business Week e.biz,* November 1, 1999, p. EB88; and Bill Fahrenwald and Dean Wise, "E-Commerce Meets the Material World," *Business Week,* June 26, 2000, pp. 109ff.

negotiating an exchange, but don't take title to the goods—that is, at no point do they own the goods. Usually, they don't carry inventory, provide credit, or assume risk. Examples include insurance brokers, real estate brokers, and stockbrokers. In California, brokers help in the gathering and sale of produce, and in the airline industry brokers consolidate airline seats and sell them for a discount. Many students are finding challenging and lucrative jobs as stock, insurance, or real estate brokers.

How Intermediaries Create Exchange Efficiency

The benefits of using marketing intermediaries can be illustrated rather easily. Suppose that five manufacturers of various food products each tried to sell directly to five retailers. The number of exchange relationships that would have to be established is 5 × 5, or 25. But picture what happens when a wholesaler enters the system. The five manufacturers would contact one wholesaler to establish five exchange relationships. The wholesaler would have to establish contact with the five retailers. That would mean another five exchange relationships. Note that the number of exchanges is reduced from 25 to only 10 by the addition of a wholesaler. Figure 15.2 shows this process.

In the past, intermediaries conducted exchanges not only more efficiently than manufacturers but more effectively as well. This meant that intermediaries were often better at performing their functions than a manufacturer could be. Recently, however, technology has made it possible for manufacturers to reach consumers much more efficiently than in the past. For example, some manufacturers reach consumers directly on the Internet. Companies such as Dell Computer are famous for their direct-selling capability. They then outsource their delivery function to a distribution firm.

Retailers are now so closely linked with manufacturers that they can get delivery as often as once or twice a day. When this happens, there is usually no

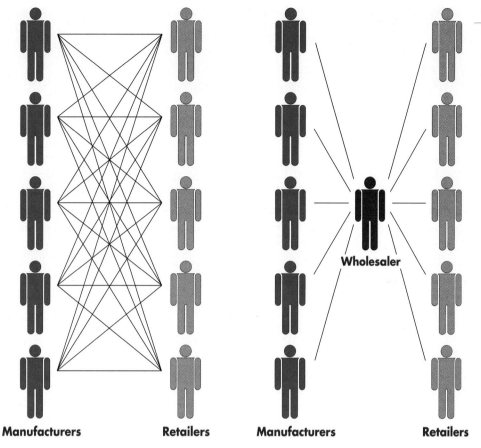

FIGURE 15.2

HOW INTERMEDIARIES CREATE EXCHANGE EFFICIENCY

This figure shows that adding a wholesaler to the channel of distribution cuts the number of contacts from 25 to 10. This makes distribution more efficient.

Wholesaler

Manufacturers   **Retailers**   **Manufacturers**   **Retailers**

need for a wholesaler to perform functions such as storage and delivery. Does that mean that wholesalers are obsolete? The answer is *not yet*, but wholesalers do need to change their methods to remain viable in today's rapidly changing distribution systems. In the next section, we shall explore the value that intermediaries can provide.

The Value versus the Cost of Intermediaries

Marketing intermediaries have always been viewed by the public with some suspicion. Some surveys have shown that about half the cost of the things we buy are marketing costs that go largely to pay for the work of intermediaries. People reason that if we could only get rid of intermediaries, we could greatly reduce the cost of everything we buy. Sounds good, but is the solution really that simple?

Let's take as an example a box of Fiberrific cereal (you were introduced to Fiberrific in Chapter 13) that sells for $4. How could we, as consumers, get the cereal for less? Well, we could all drive to Michigan where some of the cereal is produced and save some shipping costs. But would that be practical? Can you imagine millions of people getting in their cars and driving to Michigan just to buy some cereal? No, it doesn't make sense. It's much cheaper to have intermediaries bring the cereal to major cities. That might involve transportation and warehousing by wholesalers. These steps add cost, don't they? Yes, but they add value as well, the value of not having to drive to Michigan.

The cereal is now in a warehouse somewhere on the outskirts of the city. We could all drive down to the wholesaler and pick it up. But that still isn't the most economical way to buy cereal. If we figure in the cost of gas and time, the cereal would be too expensive. Instead, we prefer to have someone move the cereal from the warehouse to a truck, drive it to the corner supermarket, unload it, unpack it, stamp it with a price, put it on the shelf, and wait for us to come in to buy it. To make it even more convenient, the supermarket may stay open for 24 hours a day, seven days a week. Think of the costs. But think also of the value! For $4, we can get a box of cereal when we want it, with little effort on our part.

If we were to get rid of the retailer, we could buy a box of cereal for a little less, but we'd have to drive farther and spend time in the warehouse looking through rows of cereals. If we got rid of the wholesaler, we could save a little more money, not counting our drive to Michigan. But a few cents here and a few cents there add up—to the point where marketing may add up to 75 cents for every 25 cents in manufacturing costs. (See the Making Ethical Decisions box for another issue related to marketing costs.)

Figure 15.3 shows where your money goes in the distribution process. Notice that the largest percentage goes to people who drive trucks and work in wholesale and retail organizations. Don't think of these expenses as just money you need to spend; think of the jobs that must be available in trucking firms and wholesale and retail facilities. Note also that only 3.5 cents goes to profit. That's

You can buy and sell items online at eBay and other sites, but where do businesses go to buy, sell, and barter items? One site is iSolve.com. If a business gets stuck with too much inventory, it can go online and sell to other businesses. Outlet stores can find discount items at the same site. How will such sites affect traditional outlet stores and intermediaries (middlemen)?

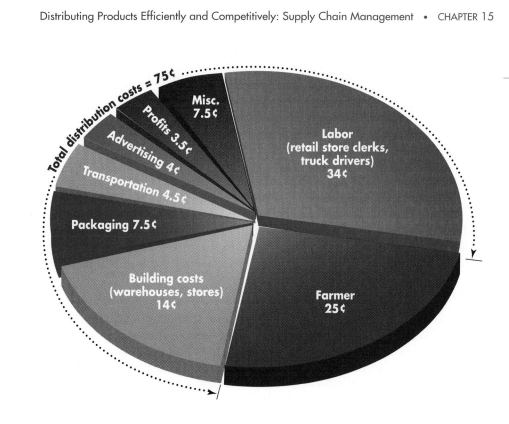

Total distribution costs = 75¢

Misc. 7.5¢

Profits 3.5¢

Advertising 4¢

Transportation 4.5¢

Packaging 7.5¢

Building costs (warehouses, stores) 14¢

Labor (retail store clerks, truck drivers) 34¢

Farmer 25¢

FIGURE 15.3

DISTRIBUTION'S EFFECT ON YOUR FOOD DOLLAR

Note that the farmer gets only 25 cents of your food dollar. The bulk of your money goes to intermediaries to pay distribution costs. Their biggest cost is labor (truck drivers, clerks), followed by warehouses and storage.

probably less than you imagined. Figure 15.4 shows the share of distribution costs that go to various intermediaries. Note that the percentages vary greatly among products. Here are three basic points about intermediaries:

- Marketing intermediaries can be eliminated, but their activities can't; that is, you can eliminate some wholesalers and retailers, but then consumers or someone else would have to perform the retailer's tasks, including transporting and storing goods, finding suppliers, and establishing communication with suppliers. Today, many of those functions are being performed on the Internet, and intermediaries *are* being eliminated.

- Intermediary organizations have survived in the past because they have performed marketing functions more effectively and efficiently than others could. To maintain their competitive position in the channel, intermediaries must adopt the latest in technology.[1]

- Intermediaries add costs to products, but these costs are usually more than offset by the values they create.

FIGURE 15.4

HOW INTERMEDIARIES SHARE YOUR FOOD DOLLAR

ITEM	FARMER	PROCESSOR	WHOLESALER	RETAILER
1 pound choice beef	66.3%	5.4%	7.4%	20.9%
1 dozen grade A large eggs	69.7	11.5	5.1	13.7
1 half-gallon milk	50.8	21.6	19.8	7.8

Imagine that we have eliminated intermediaries and you have to go shopping for groceries and shoes. How would you find out where the shoes and groceries were? How far would you have to travel to get them? How much money do you think you'd save for your time and effort? Which intermediary do you think is most important and why? How might the Internet change your shopping in the future?

THE UTILITIES CREATED BY INTERMEDIARIES

utility
An economic term that refers to the value or want-satisfying ability that's added to goods or services by organizations when the products are made more useful or accessible to consumers than before.

Utility is the value or want-satisfying ability that's added to goods or services > **P.25** < when the products are made more useful or accessible to consumers. Six utilities are added: form, time, place, possession, information, and service.

Form Utility

form utility
Taking raw materials and changing their form so that they become useful products.

Form utility is performed mostly by producers. It consists of taking raw materials and changing their form so that they become useful products > **P.400** <. Thus, a farmer who separates the wheat from the chaff and the processor who turns the wheat into flour are creating form utility. Retailers and other marketers sometimes perform form utility as well. For example, a retail butcher may cut pork chops from a larger piece of meat and trim off the fat. The server at Starbucks makes coffee just the way you want it. Normally, however, marketers concentrate on performing the other five utilities: time, place, possession, information, and service. The following are some examples of how they do that.

Time Utility

time utility
Adding value to products by making them available when they're needed.

Intermediaries, such as retailers, add **time utility** to products by making them available *when* they're needed. For example, Devar Tennent lives in Boston. One winter evening while watching TV with his brother, Tennent suddenly got the urge for a hot dog and Coke. The problem was that there were no hot dogs or Cokes in the house. Devar ran down to the corner delicatessen and bought some hot dogs, buns, Cokes, and potato chips. He also bought some frozen

You can sell almost anything to almost anyone on the Internet, but getting products to customers is not so easy. Sellers in Japan have found a clever answer. They send products to the local 7-Eleven where customers can pick them up, pay for them, and take them home. 7-Eleven stores in Japan act as gathering places for local neighborhoods and make an excellent pickup stop for customers. Would such a delivery system work in your neighborhood?

strawberries and ice cream. Devar was able to get these groceries at 10 PM because the local deli was open 24 hours a day. That's time utility.

Place Utility

Intermediaries add **place utility** to products by having them *where* people want them. For example, while traveling through the badlands of South Dakota, Juanita Ruiz grew hungry and thirsty. There are no stores for miles in this part of the country. Juanita saw one of many signs along the road saying that Wall Drug with fountain service was up ahead. Lured by the signs, she stopped at the store for refreshments. She also bought sunglasses and souvenir items there. The goods and services provided by Wall Drug are in a convenient place for vacationers. Throughout the United States, 7-Eleven stores remain popular because they are usually located in places where they are easy to reach. They provide place utility, as do vending machines.

Does *your* McDonald's deliver? This one in central London does! Of all the marketing utilities, possession utility is the least understood. It is a catch-all utility that means adding value by doing whatever the customer needs to complete the sale, including providing credit, delivery, or whatever. What other products or services might benefit by offering free delivery?

Possession Utility

Intermediaries add **possession utility** by doing whatever is necessary to transfer ownership from one party to another, including providing credit. Activities associated with possession utility include delivery, installation, guarantees, and follow-up service. For those consumers who don't want to own goods, possession utility makes it possible for them to use goods through renting or leasing.

For example, Larry Rosenberg wanted to buy a nice home in the suburbs. He found just what he wanted, but he didn't have the money he needed. So he went with the real estate broker to a local savings and loan and borrowed the money to buy the home. Both the real estate broker and the savings and loan are marketing intermediaries that provide possession utility.

Information Utility

Intermediaries add **information utility** by opening two-way flows of information between marketing participants. For example, Jerome Washington couldn't decide what kind of TV set to buy. He looked at various ads in the newspaper, talked to salespeople at several stores, and read material at the library. He also got some booklets from the government about radiation hazards and consumer buying tips. Newspapers, salespeople, libraries, and government publications are all information sources made available by intermediaries. They provide information utility. What websites have you used to get information about products and places? Can you see how the Internet will be taking over many of the functions that advertising and personal selling now do?

Service Utility

Intermediaries add **service utility** by providing fast, friendly service during and after the sale and by teaching customers how to best use products over time. For example, Sze Leung bought a personal computer for his office at home. Both the computer manufacturer and the retailer where he bought the computer continue to offer help whenever Leung needs it. He also gets software updates for a small fee to keep his computer up-to-date. What attracted Leung to the retailer in the first place was the helpful, friendly service he re-

place utility
Adding value to products by having them where people want them.

possession utility
Doing whatever is necessary to transfer ownership from one party to another, including providing credit, delivery, installation, guarantees, and follow-up service.

information utility
Adding value to products by opening two-way flows of information between marketing participants.

service utility
Providing fast, friendly service during and after the sale and by teaching customers how to best use products over time.

REACHING BEYOND OUR BORDERS *www.mktplc.com/cfnet/spmenu.html*
What Intermediaries to Use

It's one thing to decide to sell a product internationally; it's something else again to try to implement such a program. How are you going to reach the consumer? You could, of course, send sales representatives to contact people directly, but that would be costly and risky. How can you get your product into foreign markets at a minimum cost and still have wide distribution?

• *Use brokers.* As explained in the chapter text, a broker is an intermediary who keeps no inventory and takes no risk. A broker can find distributors for you. Brokers sell for you and make a commission on the sale. This is the least expensive way to enter foreign markets, but you still assume the risks of transportation.

• *Use importers and exporters.* Importers and exporters take all the risks of business and sell your products to international markets. Their commission is much higher than that of brokers, but they do much more for you. They may find you distributors or do the selling to ultimate consumers themselves.

• *Call on distributors directly.* You can bypass exporters and brokers and call on distributors yourself. In that case, you actually become your own exporter and deliver directly to distributors, but again you assume the risks of transportation.

• *Sell direct.* The most costly and risky way to sell internationally is to set up your own distribution system of wholesalers and retailers. On the other hand, this maximizes potential profits in the long run. Many firms start out selling through importers and exporters and end up setting up their own distribution system as sales increase.

• *Use third-party logistics (3PL) providers.* This new kind of company will distribute goods worldwide for you. The U.S. market leader is Ryder Integrated Logistics. Ryder designs, implements, and manages the whole system for delivering goods in the United States and overseas.

International distribution will be a major growth area in marketing, with many challenges and opportunities for tomorrow's college graduates. Does a career in this area sound interesting to you?

Sources: Christopher A. Bartlett and Sumantra Ghoshal, "Going Global," *Harvard Business Review*, March–April 2000, pp. 133–42; Amy Feldman, "Investing Coke: The Real Thing Coke Stock Finally Has Some Fizz Again," *Money*, October 1, 2000, p. 33.; and Courtney Fingar, "Are You World Ready?" *Global Business*, January 2001, pp. 28-30;

ceived from the salesperson in the store. Service utility is rapidly becoming the most important utility for many retailers because without it they could lose business to direct marketing (e.g., marketing by catalog or on the Internet).

For consumers to receive the maximum benefit from marketing intermediaries, the various organizations must work together to ensure a smooth flow of goods and services to the consumer. Historically, there hasn't always been total harmony in the channel of distribution. As a result, channel members have created certain systems that make the flows more efficient. We'll discuss those systems next. The Reaching Beyond Our Borders box tells how to reach global consumers; after reading it, you should better understand the need for carefully choosing distribution systems.

PROGRESS ASSESSMENT

• What is a channel of distribution, and what intermediaries are involved?

• Why do we need intermediaries? Can you illustrate how intermediaries create exchange efficiency? How would you defend intermediaries to someone who said that getting rid of them would save millions of dollars?

• Can you give examples of the six utilities and how intermediaries perform them?

WHOLESALE INTERMEDIARIES

There's often some confusion about the difference between wholesalers and retailers. It's helpful to distinguish wholesaling from retailing and to clearly define the functions performed so that more effective systems of distribution can be designed. Some producers won't sell directly to retailers but will deal only with wholesalers. Some producers give wholesalers a bigger discount than retailers. What confuses the issue is that some organizations sell much of their merchandise to other intermediaries (a wholesale sale) but also sell to ultimate consumers (a retail sale). The office superstore Staples is a good example. It sells office supplies to small businesses and to consumers as well. Warehouse clubs, such as Sam's Club, and Costco are also examples.

The issue is really rather simple: A **retail sale** is the sale of goods and services to consumers for their own use. A **wholesale sale** is the sale of goods and services to businesses and institutions (e.g., hospitals) for use in the business or to wholesalers or retailers for resale. Wholesalers sell business to business (B2B) **> P.469 <**.

Merchant Wholesalers

Merchant wholesalers are independently owned firms that take title to the goods they handle. About 80 percent of wholesalers fall in this category. There are two types of merchant wholesalers: full-service wholesalers and limited-function wholesalers. *Full-service wholesalers* perform all of the distribution functions: transportation, storage, risk bearing, credit, market information, standardization and grading, buying, and selling (see Figure 15.5). *Limited-function wholesalers* perform only selected functions, but try to do them especially well.

Rack jobbers furnish racks or shelves full of merchandise to retailers, display products, and sell on consignment. This means that they keep title to the goods until they're sold, and then they share the profits with the retailer. Merchandise such as toys, hosiery, and health and beauty aids are sold by rack jobbers. (A rack jobber that doesn't supply credit to customers is classified as a limited-function wholesaler.)

Cash-and-carry wholesalers serve mostly smaller retailers with a limited assortment of products. Traditionally, retailers went to such wholesalers, paid cash, and carried the goods back to their stores—thus the term *cash-and-carry*. Today, stores such as Office Depot and Staples allow retailers and others to use credit cards for wholesale purchases.

Drop shippers solicit orders from retailers and other wholesalers and have the merchandise shipped directly from a producer to a buyer. They own the

Freshnex.com is a limited function wholesaler who connects top chefs with suppliers from distant locations, and then ensures overnight delivery—all possible due to the Internet.

FIGURE 15.5

**A FULL-SERVICE
WHOLESALER**

A full service wholesaler will:

1. Provide a sales force to sell the goods to retailers and other buyers.
2. Communicate manufacturers' advertising deals and plans.
3. Maintain inventory, thus reducing the level of the inventory suppliers have to carry.
4. Arrange or undertake transportation.
5. Provide capital by paying cash or quick payments for goods.
6. Provide suppliers with market information they can't afford or can't obtain themselves.
7. Undertake credit risk by granting credit to customers and absorbing any bad debts, thus relieving the supplier of this burden.
8. Assume the risk for the product by taking title.

The wholesaler may perform the following services for customers:

1. Buy goods the end market will desire and make them available to customers.
2. Maintain inventory, thus reducing customers' costs.
3. Transport goods to customers quickly.
4. Provide market information and business consulting services.
5. Provide financing through granting credit, which is critical to small retailers especially.
6. Order goods in the types and quantities customers desire.

Source: Thomas C. Kinnear and Kenneth L. Bernhardt, *Principles of Marketing*, 2nd ed. (Glenview, IL: Scott, Foresman, 1986), p. 369

merchandise but don't handle, stock, or deliver it. That's done by the producer. Drop shippers tend to handle bulky products such as coal, lumber, and chemicals.

Smaller manufacturers or marketers that don't ship enough products to fill a railcar or truck can get good rates and service by using a freight forwarder. A **freight forwarder** puts many small shipments together to create a single large shipment that can be transported cost-effectively to the final destination. Some freight forwarders also offer warehousing, customs assistance, and other services along with pickup and delivery. You can see the benefits of such a company to a smaller shipper.

freight forwarder
An organization that puts many small shipments together to create a single large shipment that can be transported cost-effectively to the final destination.

Business-to-Business (B2B) Wholesaling

Leading companies in the consumer marketplace, such as America Online, eBay, and Yahoo, are building e-commerce ➤ **P.13** ◄ sites aimed at small and midsize businesses. They hope to sell PCs and other items to businesses just like they do to consumers.

The eBay site is called Business Exchange, and Yahoo's site is called Yahoo! Business-to-Business Marketplace. The business-to-business market is huge (bigger than the consumer market), and businesses that go to B2B wholesaling hope to capture some of that business.[2]

There are dozens of B2B sites offering everything from used machinery and equipment to lumber and other commodity goods.[3] Lee Iacocca, the former Chrysler Corporation president is now on the board of Online Asset Exchange, a company that sells used machinery and equipment. Companies such as Commerce One and Ariba sell everything from paper clips to personal computers on the Internet B2B. But business-to-business marketing is getting more sophisticated every day. Companies are selling not only software packages but also complex business solutions that involve all parts of the company—from production to accounting to shipping—on the Internet.[4]

RETAIL INTERMEDIARIES

Perhaps the most useful marketing intermediaries, as far as you're concerned, are retailers. They're the ones who bring goods and services to your neighborhood and make them available day and night. Next time you go to the supermarket to buy groceries, stop for a minute and look at the tremendous variety of products in the store. Think of how many marketing exchanges were involved to bring you the 18,000 or so items that you see. Some products (e.g., spices) may have been imported from halfway around the world. Other products have been processed and frozen so that you can eat them out of season (e.g., corn and green beans).

A supermarket is a retail store. A retailer, remember, is a marketing intermediary that sells to consumers. The United States boasts approximately 2.3 million retail stores. This does not include the retail websites on the Internet. Retail organizations employ more than 11 million people and are one of the major employers of marketing graduates. There are many careers available in retailing in all kinds of firms.

When you log-on at www.buyitnow.com you'll discover a whole new concept in shopping. You'll find a kitchen store for the chef, tools for the wood worker, toys for the kids, a pet store for the pet lover and almost everything else. All with the best customer service on the web through e-mail, live chat, or phone @ 1-888-55BUYIT. Shopping has never been this easy or fun. Shop today @ www.buyitnow.com.

How Retailers Compete

There are five major ways for retailers to compete for the consumer's dollar: price, service, location, selection, and entertainment. Since consumers are constantly comparing retailers on price, service, and variety, it is important for retailers to use benchmarking to compare themselves against the best in the field to make sure that their practices and procedures are the most advanced. The following sections describe the five major ways to compete.

Price Competition Discount stores such as Wal-Mart, Target, Kmart, and T.J. Maxx/Marshall's—not to mention all the various Internet discount sites—succeed by offering low prices. It's hard to compete with these price discounters over time, especially when they offer good service as well.

Service organizations also compete on price. Note, for example, Southwest Airlines' success with its low-price strategy. The same is true of H&R Block in income tax preparation services, Hyatt Legal Plans for legal services, and Motel 6 or Red Roof Inns for motel-room rentals.

Price competition is getting fiercer as Internet firms like mySimon.com help consumers find the best prices on a wide range of items. Look up BotSpot (www.botspot.com) for other companies that do price searches. As you learned earlier, prices are easy to match, so most retailers have to turn to other strategies—like service—to win and keep customers.

Service Competition A second competitive strategy for retailers is service.[5] Retail service involves putting the customer first. This requires all frontline people to be courteous and accommodating to customers. Retail service also means follow-up service such as on-time delivery, guarantees, and fast installation. Consumers are frequently willing to pay a little more for goods and services if the retailer offers outstanding service.

The benchmark companies in this regard include Dayton's, Lord & Taylor, Dillard's, and Nordstrom. These retailers show that if you hire good people,

It wasn't very long ago that companies like Buyitnow.com threatened leading companies like Sears and Wal-Mart. But the crash of dot.coms late in 2000 hit this company like many other business to consumer (B2C) companies. What factors led to their dramatic fall? Have you personally experienced any problems with online shopping?

train them well, and pay them fairly, you will be able to provide world-class service. Service organizations that have successfully competed using service include Scandinavian Airlines, Tokyo's Imperial Hotel, Metropolitan Life Insurance Company, and Florida Power & Light. Small service providers, such as The Hair Cuttery, Sam's Auto Repair, and Beautiful Nails, also compete by offering superior service.

Location Competition   Many services, especially convenience services like banks and dry cleaners, compete effectively by having good locations. That's why you find automated teller machines in convenient places such as supermarkets and train stations. Many fast-food stores, such as Burger King and Pizza Hut, now have locations on college campuses so that students can reach them quickly. Some dry cleaners pick up and deliver laundry at your home or business.

Often, nothing is more convenient than shopping online: You don't have to go outside at all and fight crowds or traffic. But online retailers have to learn to deliver goods faster and more reliably and handle returns better, or they will lose the advantage of convenience. Also, many consumers are nervous about giving their credit card numbers to online retailers for fear of having them stolen. Each of these problems will be solved someday, but meanwhile competition between brick-and-mortar retailers and online retailers will intensify.[6]

category killer stores
Large stores that offer wide selection at competitive prices.

Selection Competition   A fourth competitive strategy for retailers is selection. Selection is the offering of a wide variety of items in the same product category. **Category killer stores** offer wide selection at competitive prices. Toys "R" Us stores carry some 18,000 toys, and the company has over 500 stores around the world. Many small, independent toy stores went out of business because they simply couldn't compete with the low prices and selection found at Toys "R" Us. Tower Records carries over 75,000 titles. Borders Books carries some 150,000 different titles. Sportmart carries over 100,000 sporting goods items. PetsMart and other pet food superstores have some 10,000 items each.

Despite their initial success, many category killer stores are in turn being "killed" by discount department stores like Wal-Mart.[7] Wal-Mart has become a huge challenge to Toys "R" Us. Consumers are finding it more convenient to shop for multiple items at stores like Costco rather than go out of their way to find stores selling only sports equipment or only pet supplies. Thus, location may be more important than selection for consumer items.

Internet stores can offer products from dozens of suppliers and offer almost unlimited selection (e.g., Amazon.com). There may come a day when category killer online retailers drive brick-and-mortar category killers out of the market.

Small retailers sometimes compete with category killers by offering wide selection within one or a few categories of items. Thus, you have successful small stores that sell nothing but coffee beans or party products. Small retailers also compete with category killers by offering personalized service. Restoration Hardware, with stores in the Bay Area of California and around the country, is one store that has survived the competition against Home Depot and the other giant lumber and hardware stores. Restoration was able to succeed by offering consumers products that couldn't be found in the other stores.

Service organizations that compete successfully on selection include Blockbuster (wide selection of rental videos), most community colleges (wide selection of courses), and Schwab Mutual Funds (hundreds of funds).

Entertainment Competition   The Internet may be a convenient place to shop, but it can't possibly be as much fun as a brick-and-mortar store designed to provide entertainment as well as a place to buy things. When you approach a Jordan's furniture store in New England, for example, you notice that the design team has recreated French Quarter facades like those in New Orleans. As you walk in, you see a Louis Armstrong look-alike playing in a room that resembles Bourbon Street. There is even a replica of a riverboat that features live music every weekend. You can eat a free fresh-baked cookie and, if its raining, you can get an umbrella.[8]

One mall calls it "shoppertainment." In any case, it's getting more fun to shop at stores and malls as a result.[9] At Bass Pro Shops in Springfield, Missouri, you are treated to giant aquariums, waterfalls, trout ponds, rifle ranges, and classes in everything from ice fishing to conservation. In San Francisco, Sony's Metreon is a Sony Entertainment Center with a restaurant, an IMAX theater, and lots of exciting video games to play. You get to see and experience all the latest high-tech equipment and have fun at the same time. Vans, Inc., a sporting goods retailer, opened a 60,000 square-foot skate park and off-road bicycle track at Ontario Mills Mall near Los Angeles.

Retail Distribution Strategy

A major decision marketers must make is selecting the right retailers to sell their products. Different products call for different retail distribution strategies. There are three categories of retail distribution: intensive distribution, selective distribution, and exclusive distribution.

Intensive distribution puts products into as many retail outlets as possible, including vending machines. Products that need intensive distribution include convenience goods such as candy, cigarettes, gum, and popular magazines.

Selective distribution is the use of only a preferred group of the available retailers in an area. Such selection helps to assure producers of quality sales and service. Manufacturers of appliances, furniture, and clothing (shopping goods) usually use selective distribution.

Exclusive distribution is the use of only one retail outlet in a given geographic area. Because the retailer has exclusive rights to sell the product, he or she is more likely to carry more inventory, give better service, and pay more attention to this brand than to others. Auto manufacturers usually use exclusive distribution, as do producers of specialty goods such as sky diving equipment or fly-fishing products.

NONSTORE RETAILING

Nothing in retailing received more attention recently than e-tailing. This may be one more step in the evolution of retailing away from traditional stores to nonstore retailing. Other categories of nonstore retailing include telemarketing; vending machines, kiosks, and carts; direct selling; multilevel marketing; and direct marketing. Small business can use nonstore retailing to open up new channels of distribution for their products (see the Spotlight on Small Business box on p. 474).

E-tailing

E-tailing means selling goods and services to ultimate consumers (e.g., you and me) over the Internet. Many smaller companies think that selling over the Internet is a simple, low-overhead way to build a business. Often it isn't.

Online malls will have a hard time keeping up with malls that offer "shoppertainment" that attracts local shoppers. This skate park and off-road bicycle track at the Ontario Mills Mall near Los Angeles is an example of the kind of draw that no online site can match. Some malls have amusement rides, computer games, and all kinds of attractions for young people and old. Do you enjoy visiting malls with such attractions?

intensive distribution
Distribution that puts products into as many retail outlets as possible.

selective distribution
Distribution that sends products to only a preferred group of retailers in an area.

exclusive distribution
Distribution that sends products to only one retail outlet in a given geographic area.

e-tailing
Selling goods and services to ultimate customers (e.g., you and me) over the internet.

Opening New Channels for Consumers

Ouidad is a hair salon in New York City. The owners noticed that some customers who moved out of the area still wanted to buy the products that the owners had developed for the salon. The solution was to open a new channel of distribution for the salon: Ouidad Products Division. The new channel enabled customers to order hair care products by phone, fax, mail, or on the Internet.

Small businesses that already have facilities and established customers have an advantage over new firms trying to sell by catalog or over the Internet. They have an established customer list and they know what their customers want. Since they are familiar with the store and the people who work there, they feel comfortable calling by phone or fax to order things.

Ouidad has learned that it is important to make it easy for customers to order. That means offering 24-hour ordering. It also means contracting with an independent order-taking service and using a toll-free number. Small businesses know that it is important to listen to their customers. Ouidad was running monthly specials, and customers told them that such promotions were too closely spaced. They didn't need new products every month. So the company timed its promotions to the patterns its customers established.

It's also good to study what direct marketers have learned over time. That includes maintaining a history of customer transactions in a database, keeping a proper inventory level, and getting products to customers quickly.

Source: Pierre Passavant, "E-tailers Need DM Skills," *Advertising Age*, January 17, 2000, p. 28; Arlyn Tobias Gajlian, "Small Business: Wish I'd Thought of That! Aim Small to Make it Big? You Bet," *Fortune*, May 15, 2000, p. F372; and Scott Kirsner, "The New Lure of Internet Marketing," *Fast Company*, January 2001, pp. 44-46.

According to a recent study by Forrester Research, 47 percent of U.S. companies spend up to $5 million developing a website and 17 percent spend more than $20 million.[10] But getting customers is only half the battle, as we have been telling you throughout this chapter. The other half is delivering the goods, providing helpful service, and keeping your customers. When e-tailers fail to have sufficient inventory or fail to deliver goods on time (especially at Christmastime and other busy periods), customers give up and go back to brick-and-mortar stores. Thus, many e-tailers have failed.

Most e-tailers now offer e-mail confirmation. But sometimes e-tailers are not so good at handling complaints, taking back goods that customers don't like, and providing online personal help. Some sites are trying to improve customer service by adding help buttons that you can click on to get almost instant assistance from a real person. Rightstart.com, for example, is a seller of children's toys and products. It has a live chat function to its online retailing. If you have a problem, you click the live help icon and a customer-service representative answers within minutes.[11]

The latest trend in e-commerce > **P.13** < is for the traditional retailers like Wal-Mart and Kmart to go online. Wal-Mart got help from a venture capital firm called Accel Partners to set up its site. Softbank's venture arm helped Kmart set up its site.[12] Best Buy was late to the online game, but will carry its entire inventory online and will try to create a seamless marketplace for consumers where they can purchase products in the store or online with ease. They know that competition is only a click away and thus need to offer low prices and good service to keep customers coming.[13]

What is happening rapidly is that old brick-and-mortar stores are going online. The result, sometimes called a click-and-mortar store, allows customers to choose which shopping technique suits them best. They may shop online and then go to a store to get the merchandise, or go to a store to learn all they can about product choices and then go to the Internet to find the best deal. In any case, most companies that want to compete in the future will probably need both a real store presence and an online presence to provide consumers with all the options they want. Part of that strategy is to include the company's phone number in any promotions so that consumers can call in an order as well.

Telemarketing

Telemarketing is the sale of goods and services by telephone. Some 80,000 companies use telemarketing today to supplement or replace in-store selling and to complement online selling. Many send a catalog to consumers and let them order by calling a toll-free number. As we noted, others provide a help feature online that serves the same function.

telemarketing
The sale of goods and services by telephone.

Vending Machines, Kiosks, and Carts

A vending machine dispenses convenience goods when consumers deposit sufficient money in the machine. The benefit of vending machines is their location in airports, office buildings, schools, service stations, and other areas where people want convenience items. Vending machines in Japan sell everything from bandages and face cloths to salads and spiced seafood. Vending by machine will be an interesting area to watch as such innovations are introduced in the United States.

Carts and kiosks have lower overhead costs than stores do; therefore, they can offer lower prices on items such as T-shirts and umbrellas. You often see vending carts outside stores on the sidewalk or along walkways in malls; mall owners often love them because they're colorful and create a marketplace atmosphere. Kiosk workers dispense coupons and provide all kinds of helpful information to consumers, who tend to enjoy the interaction. Hot items in kiosks today include miniature aquariums, candles, diet supplements, aromatherapy, and calendars. Also, kiosks serve as gateways to the Internet, so consumers can shop at a store and still have access to all the products available on the Internet in one place.

Direct Selling

Direct selling involves selling to consumers in their homes or where they work. Major users of this category include cosmetics producers (Avon) and vacuum cleaner manufacturers (Electrolux). Trying to emulate the success of those products, other businesses are now using direct selling for lingerie, artwork, plants, and many other goods. Many of these sales are made at "house parties" sponsored by sellers.

Because so many women work now and aren't at home during the day, companies based on direct selling are sponsoring parties at workplaces or in the evenings and on weekends. Some companies, such as those selling encyclopedias, have dropped direct selling in favor of Internet selling.

There are literally thousands of vending machines all over Japan selling almost anything you need. In this photo, a woman is using a vending machine that provides photos of men as part of a dating service. Would you like such a machine on campus?

Multilevel Marketing

Over 1,000 U.S. companies have had great success using multilevel marketing (MLM). MLM salespeople work as independent contractors. They earn commissions on their own sales and they also create commissions for the "upliners" who recruited them. In turn, they receive commissions from any "downliners" they recruit to sell.

Shopping **online** beats standing **in line**.

www.landsend.com

From catalog to the web, the store is yours.™

www.landsend.com/1-800-478-8576

©1999 Lands' End, Inc.

When you think about it, a good retail website is much like an interactive catalog. It makes sense, therefore, that companies like Lands' End would have success on the Internet, and they do. Can you see a day when the Internet takes over from catalogs? What are the advantages and disadvantages of catalogs versus the Internet for searching for items and buying them?

When you have hundreds of downliners—that is, people who have been recruited by the people you recruit—the commissions can be quite sizable. Some people make tens of thousands of dollars a month this way.

Multilevel marketing has been successful around the world in selling a wide variety of products. One MLM firm is Rexall Sundown, which sells nutritional and health-related products. Salespeople not only earn commissions at Rexall but may also buy stock options.

The main attraction of multilevel marketing for employees, other than the huge potential for making money, is the low cost of entry. For a small investment, the average person can start up a business and begin recruiting others. The success of this form of marketing is revealed by the fact that MLM sales overall have reached $18 billion a year.

Be careful not to confuse multilevel marketing with "pyramid" schemes, which often aren't involved in the selling of legitimate products and are therefore illegal. They focus on recruiting new people, whose initial "investment" is used to compensate those who have already joined. Pyramid schemes usually involve substantial start-up costs, whereas multilevel marketing programs may cost less than $100 to join. The goal of a pyramid scheme is not to sell products, but to recruit more and more people who will pay to join. It is often hard to distinguish a legitimate MLM marketer from a pyramid scheme. Check with your local Better Business Bureau and ask a lot of questions before getting involved. The most important questions is: What is the product line and how many products does the typical first-year person sell? If the suggestion is made that you won't have to do any selling yourself and you can still make a lot of money, be careful. That is the pitch made by pyramid companies.

Direct Marketing

One of the fastest-growing aspects of retailing is direct marketing. Direct marketing includes any activity that directly links manufacturers or intermediaries with the ultimate consumer. Thus, direct retail marketing includes direct mail, catalog sales, and telemarketing as well as online marketing. Popular consumer catalog companies that use direct marketing include Coldwater Creek, L. L. Bean and Lands' End.[14] Direct marketing has created tremendous competition in some high-tech areas as well. For example, direct sales by Dell Computers, Gateway 2000, and other computer manufacturers has led IBM and Compaq to use price-cutting tactics to meet the competition. Compaq also decided to go online to compete more directly and to offer its own custom-designed computers.

Direct marketing has become popular because shopping from home or work is more convenient for consumers than going to stores. Instead of driving to a mall, people can "shop" in catalogs and free-standing advertising supplements in the newspaper and then buy by phone, by mail, or by computer. Interactive online selling is expected to provide even greater competition for retail stores in the near future.

Direct marketing took on a new dimension when consumers became involved with interactive video. Producers now provide all kinds of information on CD-ROMs or on websites that consumers access with their computers. The potential of such systems seems almost limitless. Consumers can ask questions, seek the best price, and order goods and services—all by computer. Companies that use interactive video and interactive websites have become major competitors for those who market by catalog.

CRITICAL **THINKING**

How important are intermediaries such as wholesalers, retailers, trucking firms, and warehouse operators to the progress of less developed countries? Is there a lack of intermediaries in less developed countries? How do intermediaries contribute to the development of a less developed country? How will the Internet provide third world consumers with access to worldwide markets? What intermediaries will be needed most to serve those customers?

BUILDING COOPERATION IN CHANNEL SYSTEMS

One way that traditional retailers can stay competitive with online retailers is to make the whole system so efficient that online retailers can't beat them out on cost—given the need to pay for delivery. That means that manufacturers and wholesalers and retailers (members of the channel of distribution) must work closely together to form a unified system. How can manufacturers get wholesalers and retailers to cooperate to form such an efficient distribution system? One way is to somehow link the firms together in a formal relationship. Four systems have emerged to tie firms together: corporate systems, contractual systems, administered systems, and supply chains.

Corporate Distribution Systems

A **corporate distribution system** is one in which all of the organizations in the channel of distribution are owned by one firm. If the manufacturer owns the retail firm, clearly it can influence much greater control over its operations. Sherwin-Williams, for example, owns its own retail stores and thus coordinates everything: display, pricing, promotion, inventory control, and so on. Other companies that have tried corporate systems include General Electric, Firestone, and Xerox.

corporate distribution system
A distribution system in which all of the organizations in the channel of distribution are owned by one firm.

Contractual Distribution Systems

If a manufacturer can't buy retail stores, it can try to get retailers to sign a contract to cooperate. A **contractual distribution system** is one in which members are bound to cooperate through contractual agreements. There are three forms of contractual systems:

1. *Franchise systems* such as McDonald's, KFC, Baskin-Robbins, and AAMCO. The franchisee ➤ **P.150** ◄ agrees to all of the rules, regulations, and procedures established by the franchisor. This results in the consistent quality and level of service you find in most franchised organizations.
2. *Wholesaler-sponsored chains* such as Ace Hardware and IGA food stores. Each store signs an agreement to use the same name, participate in chain promotions, and cooperate as a unified system of stores, even though each store is independently owned and managed.
3. *Retail cooperatives* such as Associated Grocers. This arrangement is much like a wholesaler-sponsored chain except that it is initiated by the retailers. The same cooperation is agreed to, however, and the stores remain independent. The normal way such a system is formed is for retailers to

contractual distribution system
A distribution system in which members are bound to cooperate through contractual agreements.

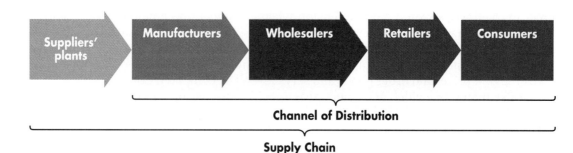

Channel of Distribution

Supply Chain

agree to focus their purchases on one wholesaler, but cooperative retailers could also purchase a wholesale organization to ensure better service.

Administered Distribution Systems

administered distribution system
A distribution system in which producers manage all of the marketing functions at the retail level.

If you were a producer, what would you do if you couldn't get retailers to sign an agreement to cooperate? One thing you could do is to manage all the marketing functions yourself, including display, inventory control, pricing, and promotion. A system in which producers manage all of the marketing functions at the retail level is called an **administered distribution system.** Kraft does that for its cheeses; Scott does it for its seed and other lawn care products. Retailers cooperate with producers in such systems because they get so much free help. All the retailer has to do is ring up the sale.

Supply Chains

supply chain
The sequence of linked activities that must be performed by various organizations to move goods from the sources of raw materials to ultimate consumers.

The latest in systems coordination involves the supply chain. The **supply chain** consists of all the organizations that move goods and services from the source of raw materials to the final customer. The supply chain is longer than a channel of distribution because it includes suppliers to manufacturers, whereas the channel of distribution begins with manufacturers. Channels of distribution are part of the overall supply chain (See Figure 15.6). Included in the supply chain, therefore, are farmers, miners, suppliers of all kinds (e.g., parts, equipment, supplies), manufacturers, wholesalers, and retailers.

Companies such as SAP, PeopleSoft, i2, and Manugistics have developed software that makes it possible to coordinate the movement of goods and information so that consumer wants can be translated into products with the least amount of materials, inventory, and time. The flows among firms are almost seamless. Naturally, the systems are quite complex and quite expensive, but they pay for themselves in the long run because of inventory savings, customer service improvement, and responsiveness to market changes.[15]

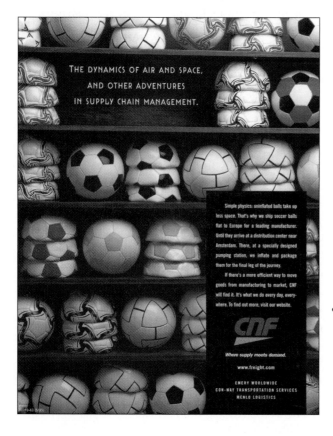

Getting products from the manufacturer to the consumer quickly and efficiently may be the most important challenge for marketers in the new millennium. Companies such as CNF have emerged to assist companies with this important function. What would be a major disadvantage of letting some other company take over your logistics functions?

- Can you briefly describe the activities of rack jobbers, drop shippers, and freight forwarders?
- Can you describe and give examples of the six ways that retailers compete?
- What kind of products would call for each of the different distribution strategies: intensive, selective, exclusive?
- What are the differences among direct selling, multilevel marketing, and telemarketing?
- Can you explain each of the four systems that have evolved to tie together members of the channel of distribution?

SUPPLY-CHAIN MANAGEMENT

Supply-chain management is the process of managing the movement of raw materials, parts, work in progress, finished goods, and related information through all the organizations involved in the supply chain; managing the return of such goods if necessary; and recycling materials when appropriate. It coordinates inbound logistics, factory processes, materials handling, and outbound logistics.

Inbound logistics brings raw materials, packaging, other goods and services, and information from suppliers to producers. *Factory processes* change raw materials and parts and other inputs into outputs, such as finished goods (e.g., shoes, cars, clothes). We described such processes in Chapter 9. *Outbound logistics* manages the flow of finished products and information to business buyers and consumers like you and me.[16]

supply-chain management
The process of managing the movement of raw materials, parts, work in progress, finished goods, and related information through all the organizations involved in the supply chain; managing the return of such goods, if necessary; and recycling materials when appropriate.

The New Challenges in Supply-Chain Management

Outbound logistics has been the biggest problem for the new online retailers. Peapod Inc., for example, is an online merchant that sells and delivers groceries directly to consumers. It outsourced the delivery process to other companies because this seemed like the least expensive way to do business. What happened was that 8 to 10 percent of the grocery items ordered online by its customers weren't being shipped because outside vendors were out of stock. This is a typical but deadly problem for online retailers.[17] Customers started dropping the service as a result. Peapod then built warehouses near Chicago, San Francisco, and New York City, and its out-of-stock rate fell to less than 2 percent. Despite all its efforts, however, Peapod is stilling struggling to survive.[18]

Other online vendors of groceries, such as 800.com and the Webvan Group, have also learned that they could not serve customers well enough without building their own facilities. But one of the main advantages of online dealers was that they avoided the need for costly stores and other facilities. They are losing that advantage as they spend more and more on warehouses and trucks and other distribution needs. As traditional retailers, such as Barnes & Noble and Sears go online, the competition becomes intense. And who will be the winners? The answer seems to be: Those who best manage the supply chain will have a real advantage.

CHOOSING THE RIGHT DISTRIBUTION MODE AND STORAGE UNITS

A primary concern of supply-chain managers is selecting a transportation mode that will minimize costs and ensure a certain level of service. The largest percentage of goods in the United States is shipped by rail. Railroad shipment

MODE	COST	PERCENTAGE OF DOMESTIC VOLUME	SPEED	ON-TIME DEPENDABILITY	FLEXIBILITY HANDLING PRODUCTS	FREQUENCY OF SHIPMENTS	REACH
Railroad	Medium	38%	Slow	Medium	High	Low	High
Trucks	High	25	Fast	High	Medium	High	Most
Pipeline	Low	21	Medium	Highest	Lowest	Highest	Lowest
Ships (water)	Lowest	15	Slowest	Lowest	Highest	Lowest	Low
Airplane	Highest	1	Fastest	Low	Low	Medium	Medium

FIGURE 15.7

COMPARING TRANSPORTATION MODES

Combining trucks with railroads lowers cost and increases the number of locations reached. The same is true when combining trucks with ships. Combining trucks with airlines speeds goods over long distances and gets them to almost any location.

is best for bulky items such as coal, wheat, automobiles, and heavy equipment. Figure 15.7 compares the various modes on several dimensions.

For the past 20 years or so, railroads have handled about 35 to 40 percent of the total volume of goods in the United States. As a result of practices such as piggyback shipments, railroads should continue to hold better than a 38 percent share of the market. (*Piggyback* means that a truck trailer is detached from the cab; loaded onto a railroad flatcar; and taken to a destination where it will be offloaded, attached to a truck, and driven to customers' plants.) Railroad shipment is a relatively energy-efficient way to move goods and could therefore experience significant gains if energy prices continue to climb.

The second largest surface transportation mode is motor vehicles (trucks, vans, and so forth). Such vehicles handle a little over 25 percent of the volume. As Figure 15.7 shows, trucks reach more locations than trains. Trucks can deliver almost any commodity door-to-door.

Railroads have joined with trucking firms to further the process of piggybacking. The difference lately is that the new, 20-foot-high railroad cars, called double-stacks, can carry two truck trailers, one on top of the other.

Water transportation moves a greater volume of goods than you might expect. Over the past 20 years, water transportation has carried 15 to 17 percent of the total. If you live near the Mississippi River, you've likely seen towboats hauling as many as 30 barges at a time, with a cargo of up to 35,000 tons. On smaller rivers, about eight barges can be hauled, carrying up to 20,000 tons—that's the equivalent of four 100-car railroad trains. Thus, you can see the importance of river traffic. Add to that Great Lakes shipping, shipping from coast to coast and along the coasts, and international shipments, and water transportation takes on a new dimension as a key transportation mode. When truck trailers are placed on ships to travel long distances at lower rates, the process is

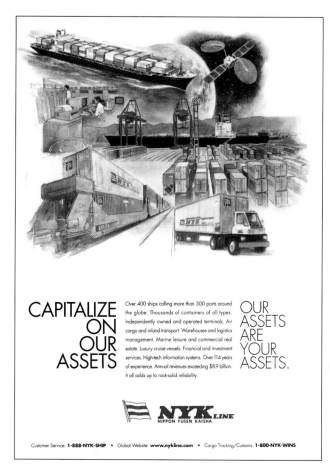

Moving goods from one country to another and then from the shipping dock to the interior of the country often takes a combination of ships, trucks, storage facilities, and more. How do you manage such a system? One way is to have one company, like NYK provide all of the services by themselves.

called *fishyback* (see the explanation of piggyback). (When they are placed in airplanes, by the way, the process is called *birdyback*.)

One transportation mode that's not visible to the average consumer is movement by pipeline. About 21 percent of the total volume of goods moves this way. Pipelines are used primarily for transporting petroleum and petroleum products, but a lot more products than you may imagine may be sent by pipeline. One company, for example, sent coal by pipeline by first crushing it and mixing it with water.

Today, only a small part of shipping is done by air. Nonetheless, air transportation is a critical factor in many industries. Airlines carry everything from small packages to luxury cars and elephants, and are expanding to be a competitive mode for other goods. The primary benefit of air transportation is *speed*. No firm knows this better than FedEx. As just one of several competitors vying for the fast-delivery market, FedEx has used air transport to expand into global markets.

The air freight industry is starting to focus on global distribution. Emery has been an industry pioneer in establishing specialized sales and operations teams aimed at serving the distribution needs of specific industries. KLM Royal Dutch Airlines has cargo/passenger planes that handle high-profit items such as diplomatic pouches and medical supplies. Specializing in such cargo has enabled KLM to compete with FedEx, TNT, and DHL, which carry bulk items.

Intermodal Shipping

Intermodal shipping uses multiple modes of transportation—highway, air, water, rail—to complete a single long-distance movement of freight. Services that specialize in intermodal shipping are known as intermodal marketing companies. While the United States has developed numerous intermodal shipping systems, Europe is catching up. Today railroads are merging with each other and with other transportation companies to offer intermodal distribution.

You can imagine such a system in action. Picture an automobile made in Japan for sale in the United States. It would be shipped by truck to a loading dock where it would be moved by ship to a port in the United States. It may be placed on another truck, taken to a railroad station for loading on a train that will take it across country to again be loaded on a truck for delivery to a local dealer. No doubt you have seen automobiles being hauled across country by train and by truck. Now imagine that all of that movement was handled by one integrated shipping firm. That's what intermodal shipping is all about.

The Storage Function

About 25 to 30 percent of the total cost of physical distribution is for storage. This includes the cost of the warehouse and its operation plus movement of goods within the warehouse. There are two major kinds of warehouses: storage and distribution. A *storage warehouse* stores products for a relatively long time. Seasonal goods such as lawn mowers would be kept in such a warehouse.

Distribution warehouses are facilities used to gather and redistribute products. You can picture a distribution warehouse for FedEx or United Parcel Service handling thousands of packages for a very short time. General Electric's combination storage and distribution facility in San Gabriel Valley, California, gives you a feel for how large such buildings can be. At nearly a half mile long and 465 feet wide, it's big enough to hold three Statues of Liberty, two *Queen Marys*, and one Empire State Building.

intermodal shipping
The use of multiple modes of transportation to complete a single long-distance movement of freight.

Don't underestimate the importance of materials handling to the whole supply-chain process. As you can see from this photo of Harry and David's packing facility, it is important to have a smooth flow of goods going to each packing module. Without a carefully designed system, goods can pile up and get lost and get ruined. Can you imagine the materials handling system necessary to bring all the parts together to assemble a car or an airplane?

Materials Handling

materials handling
The movement of goods within a warehouse, factory, or store.

Materials handling is the movement of goods within a warehouse, factory, or store. The increased use of just-in-time inventory control is cutting back on the significant costs associated with such movement. Many manufacturers have also installed robots and automated equipment to move goods efficiently within the firm. Nonetheless, materials handling can still be quite costly to some firms.

What All This Means to You

You now understand that the life or death of a firm often depends on its ability to take orders, process them, keep the customer informed as to the progress of the order, get the goods out to customers quickly, handle returns, and manage any recycling issues. Some of the most exciting firms in the stock market are those that assist in some aspect of supply-chain management. They include business-to-business firms that supply Web-based catalogs and supply chain solutions such as Commerce One. Ariba develops software for online purchasing and teams up with companies like SAP, Oracle, and PeopleSoft to manage the rest of the supply chain.

UPS and DHL both sold new stock offerings to the public and were eagerly received, since people were not sure which Internet companies would succeed—but they knew for sure that someone would have to deliver the goods—and UPS and DHL were among the best.

What all this means to you is that there are many new jobs becoming available in the exciting area of supply-chain management. These include jobs with the companies providing the various modes of distribution: trains, airplanes, trucks, ships, and pipelines. It also means new jobs handling information flows between and among companies (e.g., website development). But there are also jobs processing orders, keeping track of inventory, following the path of products as they move from seller to buyer and back, recycling goods and more—much more. [19]

PROGRESS ASSESSMENT

- How does supply chain management differ from managing the channel of distribution?
- Which transportation mode is fastest, which cheapest, and which most flexible?
- Which transportation modes can be combined?
- What percentage of the distribution cost comes from storage?

SUMMARY

1. Explain the concept of marketing channels and the value of marketing intermediaries.

1. A channel of distribution consists of marketing intermediaries, such as wholesalers and retailers, who join together to transport and store goods in their path (or channel) from producers to consumers.

• *What are marketing intermediaries?*
Marketing intermediaries are organizations that assist in moving goods and services from producers to industrial and consumer users.

• *Why do we need marketing intermediaries?*
We need intermediaries when they perform marketing functions more effectively and efficiently than others can. Marketing intermediaries can be eliminated, but their activities can't. Intermediaries add costs to products, but these costs are usually more than offset by the values they create.

2. *Utility* is an economic term that refers to the value or want-satisfying ability that's added to goods or services by organizations because the products are made more useful or accessible to consumers.

   • ***What different types of utilities do intermediaries add?***

   Normally, marketing intermediaries perform the following utilities: form, time, place, possession, information, and service.

   • ***How do intermediaries perform the six utilities?***

   A retail grocer may cut or trim meat, providing some form utility. But marketers are more often responsible for the five other utilities. Time utility is provided by having goods available when people want them. Place utility is provided by having goods where people want them. Possession utility is provided by making it possible for people to own things by providing them with credit, delivery, installation, guarantees, and anything else that will help complete the sale. Marketers also inform consumers of the availability of goods and services with advertising, publicity, and other means. That provides information utility. Finally, marketers provide fast, friendly, and efficient service during and after the sale (service utility).

2. Give examples of how intermediaries perform the six marketing utilities.

3. A wholesaler is a marketing intermediary that sells to organizations and individuals, but not to final consumers.

   • ***What are some wholesale organizations that assist in the movement of goods from manufacturers to consumers?***

   Merchant wholesalers are independently owned firms that take title to (own) goods that they handle. Rack jobbers furnish racks or shelves full of merchandise to retailers, display products, and sell on consignment. Cash-and-carry wholesalers serve mostly small retailers with a limited assortment of products. Drop shippers solicit orders from retailers and other wholesalers and have the merchandise shipped directly from a producer to a buyer. Freight forwarders consolidate small shipments into larger ones that can be shipped less expensively.

3. Describe the various wholesale organizations in the distribution system.

4. A retailer is an organization that sells to ultimate consumers.

   • ***How do retailers compete in today's market?***

   There are five major ways of competing for the consumer's dollar today: price, service, location, selection, and entertainment.

   • ***What are three distribution strategies retailers use?***

   Retailers use three basic distribution strategies: Intensive (putting products in as many places as possible, selective (choosing only a few stores in a chosen market), and exclusive (using only one store in each market area).

4. Explain the ways in which retailers compete and the distribution strategies they use.

5. Retailing is evolving away from traditional stores to nonstore retailing.

   • ***What is included in nonstore retailing?***

   Nonstore retailing includes e-tailing (online marketing); telemarketing (marketing by phone); vending machines, kiosks, and carts (marketing by putting products in convenient locations, such as in the halls of shopping centers); direct selling (marketing by approaching consumers in their homes or places of work); multilevel marketing (marketing by setting up a system of salespeople who recruit other salespeople and help them to sell directly to customers); and direct marketing (direct mail and catalog sales). Telemarketing and online marketing are also forms of direct marketing.

   • ***What's the difference between direct selling and direct marketing?***

   Direct selling means that a salesperson will come to your home or office to make the sale. Direct marketing uses catalogs, the Internet, phone marketing, and other means to sell directly to customers without being physically present.

5. Explain the various kinds of nonstore retailing.

6. Discuss how a manufacturer can get wholesalers and retailers in a channel system to cooperate by the formation of systems.

6. One way of getting manufacturers, wholesalers, and retailers to cooperate in distributing products is to form efficient distribution systems.
   • *What are the four types of distribution systems?*
   The four distribution systems that tie firms together are (1) corporate systems, in which all organizations in the channel are owned by one firm; (2) contractual systems, in which members are bound to cooperate through contractual agreements; (3) administered systems, in which all marketing functions at the retail level are managed by manufacturers; and (4) supply chains, in which the various firms in the supply chain are linked electronically to provide the most efficient movement of information and goods possible. Note that the supply chain system is longer because it includes organizations selling to manufacturers while the other systems only merge firms in the channel of distribution after a product is made.

7. Describe some supply-chain management problems and how they are solved.

7. Supply chain management is the process of managing the movement of raw materials, parts, work in progress, finished goods, and related information through all the organizations involved in the supply chain in a timely manner; managing the return of such goods if necessary; and the recycling of materials when appropriate.

8. Review the various distribution modes and their benefits and how they tie in with the materials handling and storage functions.

8. Distribution modes include ships (for slow, inexpensive movement of goods, often internationally), rail (for heavy shipments within the country or between bordering countries), trucks (for getting goods directly to consumers), airplanes (for shipping goods quickly), and pipelines (for moving water and oil and other such goods).
   • *How do these transportation modes fit in with materials handling and storage functions?*
   Often goods must be stored in warehouses until they are needed on the factory floor or are purchased by consumers. Materials handling moves the goods within the firm (e.g., from the warehouse to the factory floor or from the receiving dock into the warehouse).
   • *Why should college students be interested in channel and supply chain management?*
   Because there are many jobs available in these fields and because some of the fastest-growing firms (e.g., Internet firms) desperately need expertise in these areas if they want to compete in the long run with traditional brick-and-mortar stores that have years of experience in these fields.

KEY TERMS

1. The six utilities of marketing are form, time, place, possession, information, and service. Give examples of organizations in your area specifically designed to perform each of these functions.

2. In groups of five, search on the Internet for various types of companies in logistics, such as drop shippers, freight forwarders, wholesalers, and so on. As a marketer, what information would you desire in your decision to use each of these logistics providers? With the instructor's approval, carry out the research and present your findings to the class.

3. This text describes five kinds of retail competition: price, service, location, selection, and entertainment. Using local stores for examples, give a three-minute report on your experience as a consumer with at least two types of competition. Do you prefer one type of store over the others? Why?

4. Visit the stores in your community or use your experience having done so. Compare their prices, products, and services with companies on the Internet selling the same products (e.g., books, VCRs, automobiles). Write a one-page paper discussing the differences in price (be sure to add shipping costs).

5. Recall some of the experiences you have had with telemarketers (those people who tend to call at dinnertime trying to sell you things). How could they change their approach so you would be more responsive and positive about their calls?

1

Purpose

To examine how small businesses can learn to use the Internet to distribute their products directly to customers.

Exercise

Many small businesses have no idea how to begin selling goods over the Internet. Several free websites have been developed to help small businesses get started. Some have links to other sites that provide all kinds of help from setting up the site to doing marketing, handling credit purchases, and more. Many businesses will need help setting up websites of their own. You may be able to help if you learn now all that is involved. Begin by going to www.bigstep.com to learn the steps involved. Take the eight-step tour and learn as much as you can. Then go to www.workz.com and check out all the sites that are available to provide help.

Questions

1. What kind of information were you able to gather about starting a website?

2. What additional information would you like before getting started? Where might you turn for such help?

3. What other advice would you give a small company about trying to sell on the Internet? What would you say about credit cards, answering consumer questions, distribution, returns?

4. What other issues may come up for foreign visitors to the site?

Purpose

To analyze how products move from online retailers to end customers.

Exercise

2

Let's say that you've done your research and have found the perfect product for your needs at the lowest price available and you've ordered it online. Now what? How does the online merchant get the product to you? One of the most commonly used delivery services is United Parcel Service (UPS). To learn more about UPS, go to its website at www.ups.com.

1. UPS delivers approximately 13 million packages a day. Describe how UPS grew from a Seattle-based messenger service started by 19-year old Jim Casey with a borrowed $100 to a worldwide delivery service that invests $1 billion each year in information technology alone.

2. How does UPS work? That is, describe what happens from the moment a request is made to ship a product to the moment it arrives at the customer's doorstep.

3. In the mid-1980s, UPS shifted its emphasis from an operations focus to a customer needs focus. Today, UPS provides many tools that help its customers meet their shipping needs. Give an example of one such tool.

PRACTICING MANAGEMENT DECISIONS

CASE

MULTILEVEL MARKETING

Multilevel marketing often doesn't get the respect it deserves in marketing literature. When multilevel marketing companies succeed, their growth is often unbelievable. At least six multilevel marketing companies have reached the $500 million level in sales.

Multilevel marketing companies work like this: The founders begin by recruiting a few good people to go out and find managers to sell their products and to recruit other supervisors. These supervisors then recruit additional salespeople. That is, 20 people recruit 6 people each. That means 120 salespeople. Those people then recruit 6 people each, and you have 720 salespeople. If in turn those people all recruit 6 people, you then have almost 5,000 salespeople. All supervisors earn commissions on what they sell as well as on what everyone under them sells. When you get thousands of salespeople selling for you, commissions can be quite large. One company promotes the fact that 1 percent from 100 salespeople is as good as 100 percent from one successful salesperson. Companies often add new products or expand to other countries to keep a continuous growth pattern.

Distribution under multilevel marketing is relatively easy. Often the salespeople will carry inventory in their own homes and deliver products as ordered. Many companies also offer direct shipping to customers using UPS or other delivery firms.

Marketers cannot ignore the success of this sales and distribution strategy. Nu Skin (a seller of health and beauty products) alone will soon have $1 billion in sales. Looking for more growth, the company started a new division, Interior Design Nutrition, to make and sell vitamins and weight-control products. Amway, perhaps one of the most well-known multilevel marketers, has chosen the international route for growth; recently, its sales of home and personal care products *increased* by over $1 billion in one year.

Decision Questions

1. Amway and others have been successful in Japan. To what other countries could you lead such companies so that you could become a top earner?

2. What will happen as multilevel marketing distributors begin selling and recruiting others using the latest in technology such as the Internet?

3. Why do you suppose multilevel marketing hasn't received the same acceptance as other retail innovations such as catalog sales? What could the companies do to improve their image?

4. If multilevel marketing works so well for beauty and health care products, why not use the same concept to sell other products?

V IDEO CASE

BRICKS FOR AMAZON

One of the traditional principles of marketing is, "You can get rid of intermediaries (middlemen), but you can't get rid of their function." That is, you can eliminate wholesalers from the channel of distribution, but then someone else will have to do what wholesalers do. And that includes storing things until they are needed. Amazon.com was just one of many dot-coms that hoped that they could save money by not having warehouses. They would sell books to consumers and then have wholesalers distribute the books directly. Thus Amazon.com would save the cost of having expensive warehouses.

Well, it didn't work out as planned for most of the dot-coms. Their suppliers, whether of food or books or whatever, simply didn't have the inventory or couldn't ship fast enough to meet rapidly growing demand. The answer was for Amazon and other dot-coms to build their own warehouses. Mind you, these storage facilities were to process some $7 billion in orders. The cost of shipping is so high that most dot.coms couldn't make any money and most of them went out of business. Amazon.com managed to stay in business by building its own facilities, even though they were so expensive that by 2001 Amazon still wasn't making a profit, even though sales were rising rapidly.

The goal now is to become so efficient in warehouse management and distribution that the company will become profitable. The warehouse shown in this video is just part of the total system. It is a 600,000-square-foot facility in Reno, Nevada. It is one of seven such centers that process some 2.7 million items. The challenge is to make the clicks and computers economy more efficient than the old economy warehouses and distribution systems. But

Barnes & Noble and other competitors are not standing still. They are using computers and the Internet to develop their own competitive system.

The winners in the long run will be those companies that use technology—such as Amazon's use of bar codes and conveyor belts, and automated systems—to move goods quickly and inexpensively. For intermediaries to compete, they will have to develop even better systems.

This battle is being fought in the business to business (B2B) market as well. The Internet has proven to be so disruptive to traditional ways of doing things that businesses are still trying to adapt, many not very successfully. But the Internet is likely to rule in the future. Many analysts say that Amazon.com will be one of the winners. But only time will tell. The whole logistics field is being shaken to its roots by the Internet revolution and the competitive game is just beginning.

Discussion Questions

1. What do you see as the advantages and disadvantages of buying books, food, toys, and other items over the Internet as opposed to shopping for them in stores?
2. In Japan, manufacturers ship their goods to local stores, such as the local 7-Eleven where customers pick up items. Do you think such a system would work in the United States? It would save the cost of delivering to individual homes.
3. Are people more likely to buy more books browsing in a book store or browsing on the Internet? What does your answer say about the future of Amazon.com? What can Internet companies do to increase the volume of each order?
4. Do you see the Internet having a bigger effect in B2C or B2B markets? Why?

CHAPTER 16

Promoting Products Using Interactive and Integrated Marketing Communication

LEARNING GOALS

AFTER YOU HAVE READ AND STUDIED THIS CHAPTER, YOU SHOULD BE ABLE TO

1 Define promotion and list the four traditional tools that make up the promotion mix.

2 Define advertising and describe the advantages and disadvantages of various advertising media, including the Internet.

3 Illustrate the seven steps of the selling process and discuss the role of a consultative salesperson.

4 Describe the role of the public relations department and how publicity fits in that role.

5 Explain the importance of sales promotion and word of mouth as promotional tools.

6 Describe integrated marketing communication and the role of interactive communications within it.

Getting to Know Tina Damron of Coordinated Resources Inc.

Tina Damron's job as a sales representative for Coordinated Resources has changed dramatically since she started working for the San Jose, California, office furniture business. Just a couple of years ago, Damron had very little to do with computers or high technology in general. She was a traditional salesperson; that is, one who relied more on personality and service than on high-tech tools. For example, she would write orders using three sheets of carbon paper; if she made a mistake, she would have to recopy the whole thing.

Today, Coordinated Resources' high-tech tools help make Damron a better salesperson. Using her laptop computer, she can make dramatic three-dimensional presentations of desks, chairs, and cubicles. She can also chat with other salespeople

on the computer, obtain up-to-date information on furniture (e.g., the latest models and prices), and send orders. On one call, she knew that the customer was looking at a competitor's products, so she went on the Internet and found information about those products. She learned, for example, that you couldn't plug anything into the walls of the competitor's cubicles. That became a major selling point for Coordinated Resources' product. The website was provided by one of Coordinated's suppliers.

Damron also has access to a website called UpShot.com, which tracks new customer leads. When salespeople find leads, they put all the information into UpShot where all the other salespeople can access it. The salesperson who previously had Damron's job left all kinds of information in UpShot. For example, he wrote that one customer didn't like to joke around. Damron was able to use that information on all her calls to that account. Before UpShot, Damron made all of her notes in a folder, but folders can get lost and are not always

easy to share with others. Now all the information is available online, easily accessible to any colleagues who may need it.

Damron's customers place orders online and, as a result, receive faster delivery compared to those who place orders in person. Whereas an order used to take five *weeks* to be delivered, it can now be delivered within five *days*. What pleases Damron most about working online is that she can do more of her work at home. She's a single mother, and flexibility is important to her.

Damron is just one of thousands of salespeople whose jobs are changing because of the Internet. Buyers can now learn about product benefits online, so the salesperson's role is changing to one of an in-house consultant, helping customers solve problems. Although many questions can be handled online, there is still nothing like the personal attention and help a trained salesperson can provide.

Changes in technology have had a dramatic effect on all areas of promotion, not just selling. Advertising, for example, is changing because there are so many channels for a consumer to watch that advertising on any one of them simply is not effective as it was when there were just a few. Furthermore, advertising on the Internet is very different from traditional advertising. Consumers can now get coupons over the Internet, and companies are completely rethinking the whole promotional process. In this chapter, we shall explore such changes and introduce you to all the ways products and services are promoted and sold.

Sources: Andrea Peterson, "Making the Sale," *The Wall Street Journal,* November 15, 1999, p. R16; Philip B. Clark and Sean Callahan, "Sales Staffs: Adapt or Die," *BtoB,* April 10, 2000, pp. B1, B8, B55; and Rekha Balu, "Life of a (Digital) Salesman," *Fast Company,* May 2000, pp. 377–78.

CONSTANT CHANGE AND THE PROMOTION MIX

promotion
An attempt by marketers to inform people about products and to persuade them to participate in an exchange.

Promotion is an attempt by marketers to inform people about products and to persuade them to participate in an exchange. Marketers use many different tools to promote their products and services. Traditionally, as shown in Figure 16.1, those tools included advertising, personal selling, public relations, and sales promotion. The combination of promotional tools an organization uses is called its **promotion mix.** The value package is shown in the middle of the figure to illustrate the fact that the product itself can be a promotional tool (e.g., through giving away free samples). We'll discuss all of the promotional tools in this chapter.

promotion mix
The combination of promotional tools an organization uses.

integrated marketing communication (IMC)
A technique that combines all the promotional tools into one comprehensive and unified promotional strategy.

Integrated marketing communication (IMC) combines all the promotional tools into one comprehensive and unified promotional strategy. The idea is to use all the promotional tools and company resources to create a positive brand image.[1] Lately, companies have been including Internet promotions in that mix. Later, we'll take a special look at promotion on the Internet and the process for creating an integrated marketing communication system because they are two of the fastest-growing parts of promotion.

How Constant Change Is Affecting Promotion

The rapidly changing business environment has affected promotion as much as any other area in business. As you read in the chapter opening Profile, technology has dramatically changed the role and activities of salespeople. Similar changes have occurred in all the promotional areas. For example, the dramatic increase in the number of television channels available has lessened the number of viewers for any given program. This means that advertisers must be more creative in trying to reach large audiences, and competition for advertising on the Super Bowl and other popular shows has risen rapidly.

interactive promotion
Changing the promotion process from a monologue, where sellers tried to persuade buyers to buy things, to a *dialogue* in which buyers and sellers can work together to create mutually beneficial exchange relationships.

The Internet is changing the whole approach to working with customers. Note that we said "working with" rather than "promoting to."[2] The latest trend is to build relationships with customers over time. That means carefully listening to what consumers want, tracking their purchases, providing them with better service, and giving them access to more information.

Interactive promotion changes the promotion process from a monologue, where sellers tried to persuade buyers to buy things, to a *dialogue* in which buyers and sellers can work together to create mutually beneficial exchange relationships.[3] For example, Garden.com is an online retailer of garden products and services. Dionn Schaffner, vice president of marketing, says, "Gardening is an information-intensive activity. Customers obviously want to learn about gardening, but they also seek inspiration by communicating with fellow gardeners and experts."

The latest trend in advertising is "hybrid" campaigns that integrate traditional media with the Web, making consumers active participants. One of these campaigns is for Tommy Hilfiger. The ads feature finalists from an online talent search. Consumers are encouraged to go to Tommy.com to hear the various competitors and elect a winner, who will then record a demo. Have you become involved with such interactive ads? Do you like the idea?

FIGURE 16.1

THE TRADITIONAL PROMOTION MIX

Garden.com's answer is an interactive website through which customers can chat with each other and ask gardening questions. When customers come to the site, the company knows who they are and what they have asked in the past because it keeps track of them using *cookies* (little bits of data that are kept about customers on a database ➤ **P.15** ◂). Schaffner says, "By knowing about our customers, we can personalize the information content, as well as our product, for specific areas of the country."[4]

As we discuss each of the promotional tools, we shall explore the changes that are occurring in those areas. Then, at the end of the chapter, we shall examine the latest promotional strategies and how they can be combined to build better relationships with customers and other stakeholders ➤ **P.19** ◂.

ADVERTISING: PERSUASIVE COMMUNICATION

Advertising is paid, nonpersonal communication through various media by organizations and individuals who are in some way identified in the advertising message. Figure 16.2 lists various categories of advertising.

advertising
Paid, nonpersonal communication through various media by organizations and individuals who are in some way identified in the advertising message.

You may see ads just about anywhere these days, including on the car next to you on the freeway. Thanks to a practice known as "car wrapping," companies are turning ordinary cars into mobile billboards. People who are willing to have their cars wrapped get $400 a month. What is your reaction to having such mobile ads?

FIGURE 16.2

MAJOR CATEGORIES OF ADVERTISING

Different kinds of advertising are used by various organizations to reach different market targets. Major categories include the following:

- *Retail advertising*—advertising to consumers by various retail stores such as supermarkets and shoe stores.
- *Trade advertising*—advertising to wholesalers and retailers by manufacturers to encourage them to carry their products.
- *Business-to-business advertising*—advertising from manufacturers to other manufacturers. A firm selling motors to auto companies would use business-to-business advertising.
- *Institutional advertising*—advertising designed to create an attractive image for an organization rather than for a product. "We Care about You" at Giant Food is an example. "Virginia Is for Lovers" and "I ❤ New York" are two institutional campaigns by government agencies.
- *Product advertising*—advertising for a good or service to create interest among consumer, commercial, and industrial buyers.
- *Advocacy advertising*—advertising that supports a particular view of an issue (e.g., an ad in support of gun control or against nuclear power plants). Such advertising is also known as cause advertising.
- *Comparison advertising*—advertising that compares competitive products. For example, an ad that compares two different cold care products' speed and benefits is a comparative ad.
- *Interactive advertising*—customer-oriented communication that enables customers to choose the information they receive, such as interactive video catalogs that let customers select which items to view.
- *Online advertising*—advertising messages that appear on computers as people visit different websites.

FIGURE 16.3

ADVERTISING EXPENDITURE BY MEDIA (IN MILLIONS OF DOLLARS)

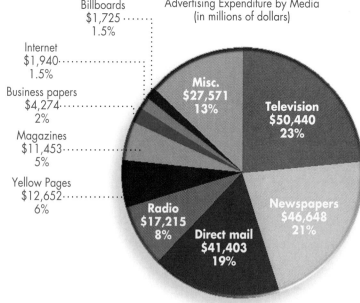

Advertising Expenditure by Media (in millions of dollars)

Billboards $1,725 1.5%
Internet $1,940 1.5%
Business papers $4,274 2%
Magazines $11,453 5%
Yellow Pages $12,652 6%
Radio $17,215 8%
Direct mail $41,403 19%
Misc. $27,571 13%
Television $50,440 23%
Newspapers $46,648 21%

The importance of advertising in the United States is easy to document; just look at the numbers in Figure 16.3. The total ad volume exceeds $215 billion yearly. Television in all its forms is the number one medium (about 23 percent of the total). Newspapers are number two, with about 21 percent of the total expenditures. Closely following is direct mail, at a little over 19 percent. Note that Internet advertising, while growing by about 85 percent a year, still only takes less than 2 percent of the total expenditure.

MEDIUM	ADVANTAGES	DISADVANTAGES
Newspapers	Good coverage of local markets; ads can be placed quickly; high consumer acceptance; ads can be clipped and saved.	Ads compete with other features in paper; poor color; ads get thrown away with paper (short life span).
Television	Uses sight, sound, and motion; reaches all audiences; high attention with no competition from other material.	High cost; short exposure time; takes time to prepare ads.
Radio	Low cost; can target specific audiences; very flexible; good for local marketing.	People may not listen to ad; depends on one sense (hearing); short exposure time; audience can't keep ad.
Magazines	Can target specific audiences; good use of color; long life of ad; ads can be clipped and saved.	Inflexible; ads often must be placed weeks before publication; cost is relatively high.
Outdoor	High visibility and repeat exposures; low cost; local market focus.	Limited message; low selectivity of audience.
Direct mail	Best for targeting specific markets; very flexible; ad can be saved.	High cost; consumers may reject ad as "junk mail"; must conform to post office regulations.
Yellow Pages advertising	Great coverage of local markets; widely used by consumers; available at point of purchase.	Competition with other ads; cost may be too high for very small businesses.
Internet	Inexpensive global coverage; available at any time; interactive.	Relatively low readership.

FIGURE 16.4

ADVANTAGES AND DISADVANTAGES OF VARIOUS ADVERTISING MEDIA

The most effective media are often very expensive. The inexpensive media may not reach your market. The goal is to use the most efficient medium that can reach your desired market.

The public benefits greatly from advertising expenditures. First, ads are informative. The number two medium, newspaper advertising, is full of information about products, prices, features, and more. So is direct mail advertising. Advertising not only informs us about products but also provides us with free TV and radio programs: The money advertisers spend for commercial time pays for the production costs. Advertising also covers the major costs of producing newspapers and magazines. Some companies have recently offered free goods—such as phone service or personal computers to anyone who agrees to listen to or watch enough ads. When we buy a magazine, we pay mostly for mailing or promotional costs. Figure 16.4 discusses the advantages and disadvantages of various advertising media to the advertiser. Newspapers, radio, and the Yellow Pages are especially attractive to local advertisers. Advertising in international markets is a little more difficult. Marketers must learn to adjust to the practices and culture of each country.

Television offers many advantages to national advertisers, but it's expensive. For example, the cost of 30 seconds of advertising during the Super Bowl telecast has risen to over $2 million.[5] How many bottles of beer or bags of dog food must a company sell to pay for such commercials? The answer may seem to be a lot, but, in the past, few other media besides television allowed advertisers to reach so many people with such impact. Marketers must now choose which media can best be used to reach the audience they desire.[6]

Radio advertising, for example, is less expensive than TV advertising and often reaches people when they have few other distractions, such as driving in their cars. Radio is especially good, therefore, for selling services that people don't usually read about in print media—services such as banking, mortgages, continuing education, brokerage services, and the like.

Brothers Robert and Jim Millican learned the benefit of radio advertising when they opened Smoothieville in Chapel Hill, North Carolina. It was 1996, and people in that area were not too familiar with fruit smoothies at that time. The brothers had decided to give out free smoothies the first day they were open, but though they used word-of-mouth and buy-one-get-one-free coupons, not much

Often government and nonprofit organizations use advertising to get their message out to the public. This message, for example, is part of an anti-smoking campaign from the Department of Health of Pennsylvania. How effective do you think such ads are in stopping smoking among teens and others?

happened—fewer than 100 customers enjoyed the free fruit shakes. Then the Millicans thought of radio. Putting a few thousand dollars into radio commercials got the business rolling. Profits became so good that Smoothieville now has two locations: one across from the University of North Carolina in Chapel Hill and another in Durham.[7]

The Growing Use of Infomercials

infomercial
A TV program devoted exclusively to promoting goods and services.

One growing form of advertising is the infomercial. An **infomercial** is a TV program devoted exclusively to promoting goods and services. Infomercials have been so successful because they show the product in great detail. A great product ► **P.400** ◄ can often sell itself if there's some means to show the public how it works. Infomercials provide that opportunity. People have said that a half-hour infomercial is the equivalent of sending your very best salespeople to a person's home where they can use everything in their power to make the sale: drama, demonstration, testimonials, graphics, and more. You may have seen infomercials for such products as the Thighmaster and other workout equipment, car wax, New Age ovens, silver cleaner, golf clubs, and more. RotoZip Tool Company thought that consumers would never buy its Spiral Saw line unless they saw the saws being used. So RotoZip spent $250,000 for an infomercial. Sales zoomed by 300 percent.[8]

Some products, such as personal development seminars or workout tapes, are hard to sell without showing people a sample of their contents (using infomercials) and using testimonials. The Spotlight on Small Business box discusses in more detail the benefit of testimonials in advertising.

Advertising and Promotion on the Internet

Advertising on the Internet is a relatively new phenomenon in marketing.[9] *Red Herring* magazine reports, "Most ads on the Internet today are like handbills

SPOTLIGHT ON SMALL BUSINESS ——————————— *www.jwrobel.com/test.html*

Using Testimonials to Build Business

Carol Boucher of Valley Forge, Pennsylvania, has a small company called Bridal Event that gives bridal shows. There is a lot of competition for such shows and Boucher wanted to stand out from the others. She went to an advertising consultant who recommended the following:

1. Top your ads with an attention-capturing headline like "I DO."

2. Put in a series of testimonials from attendees at previous shows (e.g., "I DO prefer the Bridal Event because . . ." and list the positive things people have said).

3. Remember that satisfied customers provide your best ad copy.

Some small companies pay their previous customers to recommend new customers. For example, they may give a previous customer $5 for every new customer who comes to the show because of their recommendation.

An important part of promotion for small businesses is getting stories printed about them in the local papers.

The way to get such free publicity is to take a picture of several brides and grooms and write an interesting story about how they met and why they went to a bridal show. Other stories could feature new wedding gowns, fun things to do at wedding receptions, or unusual flower arrangements. The latest thing is to fax the stories to the various papers or to make a short video and mail it to them. If the stories are interesting enough, they will get published free in the local paper.

According to *American Demographics*, "Eighty three percent of consumers ask for information from those they know already own the product." Gathering testimonials makes the whole process easier because people can see what others are saying without having to search them out themselves.

Source: Jerry Fisher, "Says Who?" *Entrepreneur*, October 1999, p. 134; and Rebecca Gardyn, "I'll Have What He's Having," *American Demographics*, July 2000, p. 22; and Anthony Tjan, "Challenge No. 9: Generating Buzz and Building a Brand," *Red Herring*, March 2000, pp. 82–83.

stapled on telephone poles: you walk by them, but don't pay too much attention to them."[10] Despite the fact that most people tend to ignore Internet ads, companies continue to use them because they hope to tap into the huge potential that online marketing offers. Ultimately, the goal is to send customers and potential customers over to a website where they can learn more about the company and vice versa. The benefits of the Internet become apparent once a customer visits the Web. Then the company has the opportunity to provide information and interact with the customer (that is, communicate with the customer). Internet advertising thus becomes a means to bring customers and companies together.

Because online promotion is so new, companies like Wal-Mart have turned to outside professionals to help them create world-class systems. Wal-Mart had been selling online since 1997, but rapid change in the environment forced the retailer to upgrade in 2000. It wanted to integrate its existing system for order fulfillment, credit card processing, and inventory keeping with BroadVision's One-to-One Retail Commerce software for customer relationship management. Wal-Mart also wanted its website to have the look and feel of its stores. Thus, you can click on tabs for the various departments—home, apparel, electronics—and the system takes you where you want to go.[11]

Customer relationship management > **P.396** < software, along with software such as Silknet Software Inc.'s Trusted Advisor, makes it possible to track customers' purchases and answer their questions online. Often the system can be so smooth and effective that people don't realize they are talking with a computer.

How do you attract people to online websites? One way is to offer them exotic prizes for clicking in. ePrize helps companies come up with creative prizes to attract customers. Have you ever been lured to a website by such an offer? If so, what was your reaction?

One subscriber to *Inc.* magazine, for example, wrote a letter to "Jill," *Inc.*'s online electronic help function, thanking her for her personal advice.[12]

New technology will greatly improve the speed and potential of Internet dialogues. Companies will be able to provide better online videos, online chat rooms, and other services that will take customers from a banner ad to a virtual store where they will be able to talk to other customers, talk to salespeople, examine goods and services ➤ **P.25** ◄ (including watching a video), and buy products. To create relationships, Internet advertising will be combined with Internet promotions (e.g., incentives to buy in volume) to give customers points for buying things that can be used to buy more goods and services in the future.

The fact that much of this information is available on palm-sized computers makes prospects for the future even more interesting. Consumers are able to *cybershop* at the same time they are shopping in a mall. They can get information, compare prices, and more. Thus, constant change will be affecting brick-and-mortar and online retailers for a long time to come. For one thing, more stores will have computer kiosks where customers can search for products and information and then pay in the store. In short, brick-and-mortar marketers will also be cybermarketers, and there will be complete integration between them. We noted in Chapter 15 that one term for this is *click-and-mortar retailing;* Wal-Mart calls it *surf and turf.*

Global Advertising

Harvard professor Theodore Levitt is a big proponent of global marketing and advertising. His idea is to develop a product and promotional strategy that can be implemented worldwide. Certainly that would save companies money in research and advertising design. In fact, that is the strategy being used by major companies such as Compaq, IBM, and Intel. However, other experts think that promotions targeted at specific countries or regions may be much more successful than global promotions since each country or region has its own culture, language, and buying habits.

The evidence supports the theory that promotional efforts specifically designed for individual countries often work best. For example, commercials for Camay soap that showed men complimenting women on their appearance were jarring in cultures where men don't express themselves that way. A different campaign is needed in such countries. (See the Reaching Beyond Our Borders box for a good example.)

In Chapter 3, we listed some problems that well-known companies encountered in global marketing. Others include the following: When a Japanese

REACHING BEYOND OUR BORDERS

www.dunkindonuts.com

Dunkin' Donuts Goes to Thailand

Dunkin' Donuts began operating outlets in Thailand in 1981. There are now some 127 shops in that country, serving more than 300,000 customers each week. Other U.S. franchisors in Thailand include KFC, McDonald's, Burger King, and Baskin-Robbins. The managers of these franchises have learned that the role fast-food establishments play in an Asian economy, economically and socially, is quite different from the role they play in the United States.

In Thailand, Dunkin' Donuts and other fast-food establishments are places where you meet your friends and family and you relax. Thus, most business is conducted in the afternoon and evening, much like a café. The Dunkin' Donuts in Thailand, therefore, promotes itself as a company that cares for society and believes in the importance of family. For example, one promotion was called the "Longest Love Message to Moms" for Mother's Day. All Thais were invited to come to a Dunkin' Donuts store and write a love note to their mother on a specially made vinyl banner, whether they bought something or not. Eventually the signed pieces were sewn together to form a mile-long banner with more than 50,000 love messages. During the promotion, the company offered special deals on donuts. For example, people could buy a "Millennium Moms" box of five donuts for $1.86. Those who bought the special boxes were eligible for prizes. There were more than 16,000 winners. The whole effort boosted sales by $375,000.

All in all, Dunkin' Donuts spent $14,000 on packaging, public relations, vinyl banners, and prizes to make the $375,000 increase in sales. This successful promotion shows the value of custom-designing promotions to match the social and economic conditions of each country where units are built. McDonald's and Burger King are using similar country-specific promotions to build their overseas success.

Sources: Paula Lyon Andruss, "Thais Sweet on Mom, 'Love' Campaign," *Marketing News*, September 11, 2000, pp. 6–7; Marilyn Much, "McDonald's Ventures from Arches, Asks, 'You Want Salsa with That?' " *Investor's Business Daily*, May 10, 2000, p. A1; and Aixa M. Pascual, "The Whopper Plays Catch-Up," *Business Week*, May 15, 2000, pp. 98–100.

company tried to use English words to name a popular drink, it called the product Pocari Sweat, not a good image for most English-speaking people. In England, the Ford Probe didn't go over too well because the image was of doctor's waiting rooms and medical examinations. People in the United States may have difficulty with Krapp toilet paper from Sweden. But perhaps not as bad as the translation of Coor's slogan "Turn it loose" where it became "Suffer from diarrhea." Clairol introduced its curling iron, the Mist Stick, to the German market. The problem is that *mist* in German can mean "manure." A T-shirt promoting a visit by the Pope in Miami read *la papa*, which means "the potato." The T-shirt should have said *el Papa*. As you can see, getting the words right in international advertising is tricky and critical. So is understanding the culture.

People in Brazil rarely eat breakfast, but they treat Kellogg's Corn Flakes as a dry snack like potato chips. Kellogg is trying a promotional strategy that shows people in Brazil how to eat cereal with cold milk in the morning. Many more situations could be cited to show that international advertising calls for researching the wants and needs of people in each specific country and then designing appropriate ads and testing them.

Even in the United States, selected groups are large enough and different enough to call for specially designed promotions. For example, Maybelline, which makes a wide array of cosmetics, is targeting special promotions to African American women. In short, much advertising today is moving from globalism (one ad for everyone in the world) to regionalism (specific ads for each country or for specific groups within a country). In the future, marketers

Many advertisers think it is a good idea to develop special ads for each country rather than use one campaign for all countries. This ad for VISA is in Italian. Could you see using the same visual for other countries, including the United States? What kind of appeal could VISA use to gain your business?

will prepare more custom-designed promotions to reach smaller audiences—audiences as small as one person.

PROGRESS ASSESSMENT

Now that there is a greater possibility of interactive communications between companies and potential customers, do you see the importance of traditional advertising growing or declining? What will be the effect on the price we consumers must pay for TV programs, newspapers, and magazines, if any?

PERSONAL SELLING: PROVIDING PERSONAL ATTENTION

personal selling
The face-to-face presentation and promotion of products and services.

Personal selling is the face-to-face presentation and promotion of products and services. It also involves the search for new prospects and follow-up service after the sale. Effective selling isn't simply a matter of persuading others to buy. In fact, it's more accurately described today as helping others to satisfy their wants and needs.

Given that perspective, you can see why salespeople are starting to use the Internet, portable computers, paging devices, fax machines, and other technology. They can use this technology to help customers search the Net, design custom-made products, look over prices, and generally do everything it takes to complete the order. The benefit of personal selling is that there is a person there to help you complete a transaction. The salesperson is there to listen to your needs, help reach a solution, and do all that is possible to make accomplishing that solution smoother and easier.

It is costly to provide customers with personal attention, especially since some companies are replacing salespeople with Internet services and information. Therefore, those companies that retain salespeople must train them to be especially effective, efficient, and helpful.

To illustrate personal selling's importance in our economy and the career opportunities it provides, let's look at some numbers. First, U.S. census data show that nearly 10 percent of the total labor force is employed in personal selling. When we add those who sell for nonprofit organizations, we find that over 7 million people are employed in sales.

The average cost of a single sales call to a potential B2B ➤ **P.409** ◄ buyer is about $400. Surely no firm would pay that much to send out anyone but a highly skilled, professional marketer and consultant. But how does one get to be that kind of sales representative? What are the steps along the way? Let's take a closer look at the process of selling.

Steps in the Selling Process

The best way to understand personal selling is to go through the selling process with a product and see what's involved. As we noted in Chapter 13, one product that is really hot these days, and one that is becoming critically important to establishing long-term relationships with customers, is customer relationship management ➤ **P.396** ◄ (CRM) software. Imagine that you are a software salesperson whose job is to show business users the advantages of using a particular program. Let's go through the selling process to see what you can do to make the sale. Although this is a business-to-business (B2B) example, the process is very much the same in consumer selling.

1. Prospect and Qualify The first step in the selling process is prospecting. **Prospecting** involves researching potential buyers and choosing those most likely to buy. That selection process is called *qualifying*. To **qualify** people means to make sure that they have a need for the product, the authority to buy, and the willingness to listen to a sales message. People who meet these criteria are called **prospects.** You often meet prospects at trade shows, where they come up to booths sponsored by manufacturers and ask questions. Other prospects may visit your website seeking information. But often the best prospects are people at companies who were recommended to you by others who use your product or know all about it.

2. Preapproach Before making a sales call, you must do further research. You must learn as much as possible about customers and their wants and needs. Before you try to sell the CRM software, you would want to know which people in the company are most likely to buy or use it. What kind of customers do they deal with? What kind of relationship strategies are they now using? All that information should be in a database, ➤ **P.15** ◄ such as UpShot, so that your company can carry information about customers from salesperson to salesperson, if one representative leaves the firm. Note that the selling process may take a long time and that gathering information before the sale takes place is critical.

There are lots of sales aids out there to help salespeople do a better job. This online service from sales.com offers help with sales forecasting, developing selling skills, and getting targeted leads. You can learn a lot about selling by checking out such websites for yourself.

prospecting
Researching potential buyers and choosing those most likely to buy.

qualify
In the selling process, to make sure that people have a need for the product, the authority to buy, and the willingness to listen to a sales message.

prospects
People with the means to buy a product, the authority to buy, and the willingness to listen to a sales message.

3. Approach An old saying goes "You don't have a second chance to make a good first impression." That's why the approach is so important. When you call on a customer for the first time, your opening comments are important. The idea is to give an impression of friendly professionalism, to create rapport, to build credibility, and to start a relationship. Often the decision of whether or not to use a software package depends on reliable service from the salesperson. You can help the prospect company train its employees to use the software and to upgrade the package when necessary, and it's important to make this known from the start.

4. Make Presentation In the actual presentation of the CRM software, the idea is to match the benefits of your value package to the client's needs. The presentation may involve audiovisual aids. Since you've done your homework and know the prospect's wants and needs, you can tailor the presentation accordingly. Using a portable computer, you can access the Internet to find any and all additional information you need. This is a great time to use testimonials (letters or statements from users praising the product) to show potential buyers that they are joining leaders in other firms in trying this new software.

5. Answer Objections You should anticipate any objections the prospect may raise and determine proper responses. Think of questions as opportunities for creating better relationships, not as a challenge to what you're saying. Customers have legitimate doubts, and you are there to resolve those doubts. Relationships are based on trust, and trust comes from successfully and honestly working with others. Often you can introduce the customer to others in the firm who can answer their questions and provide them with anything they need. Using a laptop computer, you may set up a virtual meeting where the customer can chat with other members of the firm and begin building a relationship.

6. Close Sale You have to "ask for the sale" to finalize the sales process. As a salesperson, you have limited time and can't spend forever with one potential customer answering questions and objections. **Closing techniques** include getting a series of small commitments and then asking for the order and showing the client where to sign. For example, the goal of the first close may be to get the client to agree to watch a demonstration. At the demonstration, the goal of the close may be to get the customer to try the product for a month to see its usefulness. Once a relationship is established, the goal of the sales call may be to get a testimonial from the company. As you can see, salespeople must learn to close many times before a long-term relationship is established.

closing techniques
Ways of concluding a sale including getting a series of small commitments and then asking for the order and showing the client where to sign.

7. Follow Up The selling process isn't over until the order is approved and the customer is happy. The sales relationship may continue for years as you respond to new requests for information. You can see why selling is often described as a process of establishing relationships, not just a matter of selling goods or services. The follow-up step includes handling customer complaints, making sure that the customer's questions are answered, and quickly supplying what the customer wants. *Often, customer service is as important to the sale as the product itself.* Most manufacturers have therefore established websites where information may be obtained and discussions may take place.

The selling process varies somewhat among different goods and services, but the general idea is the same. Your goals as a salesperson are to help the buyer buy and to make sure that the buyer is satisfied after the sale. *Sales force automation (SFA)*, in fact, includes over 400 software programs that help salespeople design products, close deals, tap into company intranets, and more. Some salespeople can even conduct virtual reality tours of the manufacturing plant for the customer.

Using Technology to Practice Consultative Selling

Salespeople now have at their fingertips data about the customer, about competitors, about where products are in the supply chain, ➤ **P.478** ◄ about pricing and special promotions, and more. You also are aware that B2B customers are buying more goods over the Internet. That means that B2B salespeople will have new roles to play in the future. Here is how Marc Miller, president and CEO of Change Master (a Cleveland-based sales-productivity improvement firm puts it: "If you're a salesperson who only communicates product value—'This is what we make, let me give you a presentation'—you're gone. But if you know how to *add value,* you're going to have a nice business as a consultative salesperson."[13]

What's a consultative salesperson? A **consultative salesperson** begins by analyzing customer needs and then comes up with solutions to those needs. At Dell Computer, for example, it's the sales team, not tech support, that builds and manages customers' extranet sites. They help determine what information should be available on such sites and they generally act as consultants on all matters having to do with computers, software, purchasing issues, and more.

Will selling to the consumer market change as dramatically as selling to the B2B market has? Probably so. Salespeople in retail stores will also see dramatic changes in the way they do things. Imagine an automobile salesperson, for example. A customer can go to a dealer and sit down with a salesperson at a computer and design a car custom-made to his or her specifications. Any product information the customer wants is available online, and the salesperson assists customers in finding that information. Often, customers will have searched the Internet to determine what car they want and will have explored most of the options. So what is the role of the salesperson? As in B2B selling, the role of the salesperson is to be a *consultant;* that is, to provide such helpful assistance that the customer feels it is worth while to go to the dealership to get help. That means that the salesperson will have to be computer proficient and be able to walk the customer through the whole exchange process quickly and easily, including not only getting financing, license plates, and insurance but also ensuring prompt delivery at the customer's convenience.

There will always be a need for the kind of salesperson who directs people to the proper place to find things, discusses product features, and helps buyers complete the sales process. But such salespeople will be fewer and will get paid much less than consultative salespeople who can use computers and other technology to help customers find and buy things quickly.

Tammy Chestnut wanted to spend more time with her child so she left the corporate world to start a résumé consulting business—via the Internet. Can you think of other consulting and marketing businesses made possible by advances in information technology?

consultative salesperson
A salesperson who begins by analyzing customer needs and then comes up with solutions to those needs.

CRITICAL THINKING

What kind of products do you think you would enjoy selling? Think of the customers for that product. Can you imagine yourself going through the seven-step selling process with them? Which steps would be hardest? Which would be easiest? Which step could you avoid by selling in a retail store? Can you picture yourself going through most of the sales process on the phone (telemarketing)?

- What are the four traditional elements of the promotion mix?
- What are the three most important advertising media in order of dollars spent?
- What are the seven steps in the selling process?
- What is a "consultative salesperson"?

PUBLIC RELATIONS: BUILDING RELATIONSHIPS WITH ALL PUBLICS

public relations (PR)
The management function that evaluates public attitudes, changes policies and procedures in response to the public's requests, and executes a program of action and information to earn public understanding and acceptance.

Public relations (PR) is defined as the function that evaluates public attitudes, changes policies and procedures in response to the public's requests, and executes a program of action and information to earn public understanding and acceptance. In other words, a good public relations program has three steps:

1. *Listen to the public.* Public relations starts with good marketing research ("evaluates public attitudes").

2. *Change policies and procedures.* Businesses don't earn understanding by bombarding the public with propaganda; they earn understanding by having programs and practices in the public interest. The best way to learn what the public wants is to listen to them often—in different forums, including on the Internet.

3. *Inform people that you're being responsive to their needs.* It's not enough to simply have programs in the public interest. You have to tell the public about those programs so that they know you're being responsive.

IT'S AMAZING WHAT CAN HAPPEN
WHEN YOU LISTEN TO YOUR CUSTOMERS.

Here's what you told us. You want a business partner with outstanding global resources and unmatched flexibility to solve your particular issues. With loss control engineering that can impact the bottom line. Streamlined communications, expanded capacity and responsive claim support. And here's how we responded. FM Global. The merged company of Allendale, Arkwright, Protection Mutual and Factory Mutual. Four organizations have converged to form one truly remarkable company. **Securing the future of your business.** FM Global

www.fmglobal.com or 800-343-7722.

Public relations demands a dialogue with customers so that information can be exchanged over time and trust can be developed through responsiveness. Customers today often complain that it is hard to find someone to talk to in a firm. They may spend literally hours on the phone going through choices, waiting, and not being satisfied. In desperation, they often call the PR department. In the past, the PR department sent them off to someone else in a long and futile chase for someone to handle the problem. Today, however, PR is taking a much more active role in listening to consumers and working with them to handle problems.[14] That means that PR must establish good relationships with production and service people so they can find answers to customer questions quickly.

This ad promotes the idea that "It's amazing what can happen when you listen to customers." To that, we can only say, "Amen." When companies think about promotion, too often they think about what to say to people through advertising, selling, and publicity. Not nearly enough time or money goes into the effort to listen to customers. Never forget that communication is a dialogue. Doesn't it annoy you when people don't listen to what you have to say?

PR is becoming so critical to a firm's success that many smaller companies cannot find a PR firm with which to work—they are too busy with larger firms. The U.S. Bureau of Labor Statistics reports that PR has become one of the three fastest-growing industries in the country. One firm that has had huge success because of PR is Yahoo. It began its PR campaign when the "new" Internet (one that was not just for academics) was just getting started in the early 1990s. The idea was to get stories in the media about the growing importance of the Internet. The second phase of the PR campaign came before the company sold any stock. The idea was to use the media to promote the head of the company, Tom Koogle, and his professionalism. If investors were not assured that the company had a good business model, it would not be able to sell much stock to first-time buyers. Once the company got started, the goal of PR was to show the company as a major Internet company, the equivalent of America Online. Then the goal was to show that Yahoo was as important to Internet commerce as it was in Internet communications. The success of Yahoo, then, is directly attributable to its long-term PR strategy.[15]

It is the responsibility of the public relations department to maintain close ties with the media, community leaders, government officials, and other corporate stakeholders ➤ **P.19** ◂. The idea is to establish and maintain a dialogue with all stakeholders so that the company can respond to inquiries, complaints, and suggestions quickly. The *Business Week* box illustrates the importance of public relations today.

What kinds of problems can emerge if a firm doesn't communicate with environmentalists, the news media, and the local community? In your area have you seen examples of firms that aren't responsive to the community? What have been the consequences?

Publicity: The Talking Arm of PR

Publicity is the talking arm of public relations. It is one of the major functions of almost all organizations. Here's how it works: Suppose that you want to introduce your new Fiberrific cereal to consumers but you have very little money to promote it. You need to get some initial sales to generate funds. One effective way to reach the public is through publicity. **Publicity** is any information about an individual, product, or organization that's distributed to the public through the media and that's not paid for, or controlled by, the seller. You might prepare a publicity release describing Fiberrific and the research findings supporting its benefits and send it to the various media. Much skill is involved in writing the story so that the media will want to publish it. You may need to write different stories for different media. If the stories are published, release of the news about Fiberrific will reach many potential consumers (and investors, distributors, and dealers), and you may be on your way to becoming a wealthy marketer.

The best thing about publicity is that the various media will publish stories *free* if the material seems interesting or newsworthy. The idea, then, is to write publicity that meets those criteria. Besides being free, publicity has several further advantages over other promotional tools, such as advertising. For example, publicity may reach people who wouldn't read an ad. Publicity may be placed on the front page of a newspaper or in some other prominent position, or given air time on a television news show. Perhaps the greatest advantage of publicity is its believability. When a newspaper or magazine publishes a story as news, the reader treats that story as news—and news is more believable than advertising. That's why Gardenburger and other companies that sell soybean

publicity
Any information about an individual, product, or organization that's distributed to the public through the media and that's not paid for or controlled by the seller.

Public Relations Key Promotional Tool

Asked to rank marketing tactics in the order of importance, only 10 percent of senior executives put advertising at the top. Number one for the group was product development, at nearly 30 percent. Clearly, a good product is the beginning of a successful promotional campaign. A poor product will only fail faster with good advertising. Of the promotional techniques listed, the top executives mentioned *public relations* first. Public relations sets the tone for a firm—creating an overall image both for the firm and its products. Then advertising can be used to further the image. Public relations is so effective that the U.S. mint has hired its own public relations firm to promote the new Sacagawea dollar.

Alvin Achenbaum is a consultant to advertising agencies. He notes that whereas companies 20 years ago devoted some 90 percent of their marketing budgets to advertising, today only a third of the budget goes to traditional advertising vehicles. Money is now being distributed to new promotional techniques such as licensing, sponsorships, public relations, and Internet marketing.

In spite of the new trends in promotion, the 155-year-old advertising agency J. Walter Thompson recently hired Charlotte Beers, a retired advertising executive, to be its CEO. Beers began as an account executive (read salesperson) at J. Walter Thompson in 1969. She eventually went to another agency, Ogilvy & Mather, became the CEO, and retired in 1997. She was drawn from retirement by today's exciting new challenges in promotion. She has the job of creating an integrated communication approach to her client's promotional problems. Her expertise is in building favorable brand images for products. Advertising has a critical role to play in creating ad imagery, but so do public relations and other promotional tools. What Beers adds to any campaign is her experience and her vision for integrating promotional efforts. You'll see the results in promotions for accounts like Ragu, Kimberly-Clark, Qwest, and Elizabeth Arden.

Sources: Ellen Neuborne, "Mad Ave: A Star Is Reborn," *Business Week*, July 26, 1999, pp. 54–64; and Ellen Neuborne and Richard S. Dunham, "$45 million for One Buck," *Business Week*, March 6, 2000, p. 146.

products have been so intent on sending out publicity releases about their health benefits.[16]

There are several disadvantages to publicity as well. For example, you have no control over how, when, or if the media will use the story. The media aren't obligated to use a publicity release, and most are thrown away. Furthermore, the story may be altered so that it's not so positive. There's good publicity (Compaq comes out with a new supercomputer) and bad publicity (Firestone tires cause accidents). Also, once a story has run, it's not likely to be repeated. Advertising, on the other hand, can be repeated as often as needed. One way to see that publicity is handled well by the media is to establish a friendly relationship with media representatives, cooperating with them when they seek information. Then, when you want their support, they're more likely to cooperate.

Publicity has the power to change public opinion about things. Therefore, certain ethical questions arise about the use of publicity. The box called Making Ethical Decisions explores one such decision.

PROGRESS ASSESSMENT

- What are the three steps involved in setting up a public relations program?
- What are the advantages and disadvantages of publicity over advertising?

SALES PROMOTION: GETTING A GOOD DEAL

Sales promotion is the promotional tool that stimulates consumer purchasing and dealer interest by means of short-term activities (such things as displays, trade shows and exhibitions, and contests). Figure 16.5 lists some *B2B* sales promotion techniques. Those free samples of products that you get in the mail, the cents-off coupons that you clip from newspapers, the contests that various retail stores sponsor, and the prizes in Cracker Jack boxes are examples of *consumer* sales promotion activities (see Figure 16.6). Sales promotion programs are designed to supplement personal selling, advertising, and public relations efforts by creating enthusiasm for the overall promotional program. There was a big increase in such promotions as the 21st century began, especially online. About 30 percent of online shoppers use online coupons.[17]

Sales promotion can take place both internally (within the company) and externally (outside the company). It's just as important to generate employee enthusiasm about a product as it is to attract potential customers. The most important internal sales promotion efforts are directed at salespeople and other customer-contact people, such as complaint handlers and clerks. Internal sales promotion efforts include (1) sales training; (2) the development of sales aids such as flip charts, portable audiovisual displays, and videotapes; and (3) participation in trade shows where salespeople can get leads. Other employees who deal with the public may also be given special training to make them more aware of the company's offerings and a more integral part of the total promotional effort.

After generating enthusiasm internally, it's important to get distributors and dealers involved so that they too are eager to help promote the product. Trade shows are an important sales promotion tool because marketing intermediaries are able to see products from many different sellers and make comparisons among them. Today, virtual trade shows—trade shows on the Internet—enable buyers to see many products without leaving the office. Furthermore, the information is available 24 hours a day, seven days a week.

After the company's employees and intermediaries have been motivated with sales promotion efforts, the next step is to promote to final consumers using samples, coupons, cents-off deals, displays, store demonstrations, premiums, contests, rebates, and so on. Sales promotion is an ongoing effort to maintain enthusiasm, so different strategies must be used over time to keep the ideas fresh.

Sampling Is a Powerful Sales Promotion Tool

One popular sales promotion tool is **sampling**—letting consumers have a small sample of the product for no charge. Because many consumers won't buy a new

sales promotion
The promotional tool that stimulates consumer purchasing and dealer interest by means of short-term activities.

sampling
A promotional tool in which a company lets consumers have a small sample of a product for no charge.

FIGURE 16.5

BUSINESS-TO-BUSINESS SALES PROMOTION TECHNIQUES

Trade shows
Portfolios for salespeople
Deals (price reductions)
Catalogs
Conventions

FIGURE 16.6

**CONSUMER SALES
PROMOTION TECHNIQUES**

Coupons	Bonuses (buy one, get one free)
Cents-off promotions	Catalogs
Sampling	Demonstrations
Premiums	Special events
Sweepstakes	Lotteries
Contests	In-store displays

If you have a great product, couponing and sampling are wonderful ways to get people to try it sooner than they might have as a result of any other kinds of promotion. What products do you now use regularly that you first bought because of a sample or a coupon?

product unless they've had a chance to see it or try it, grocery stores often have people standing in the aisles handing out small portions of food and beverage products. Sampling is a quick, effective way of demonstrating a product's superiority at the time when consumers are making a purchase decision.[18]

Recently, Pepsi introduced its Fruit Works product line with a combination of sampling, event marketing, and a new website. *Event marketing* means sponsoring events such as rock concerts or being at various events to promote your products. In the case of Fruit Works, Pepsi first sent samples to Panama City, Florida, and South Padre Island, Texas, for spring break. Students got free rides on the trucks and samples of the drinks. Similar sampling and event marketing efforts had been successful for SoBe (herbal-fortified drinks) and Snapple (fruit drinks and iced teas).[19]

Kiehl's is a small company that makes and sells hair and skin care products for women and men. Its packaging is dull and it does no advertising. So how does the company prosper? Sampling. People come from all over the world to visit Kiehl's East Village store in New York City. The company gives away $1.5 million annually in various samples and gift boxes. Store clerks have quotas on how many samples they pass out each day. If you request one, they are likely to give you many more to pass out to your friends. After all, if you have a great product, people will see that for themselves once they have tried it. Have you ever purchased a product because you sampled it once?

Word of Mouth

**word-of-mouth
promotion**
A promotional tool that involves people telling other people about products they've purchased.

Although word of mouth is not normally listed as one of the major promotional efforts, it is often one of the more effective tools, and is becoming recognized as such because so many people can be reached so easily on the Internet. **Word-of-mouth promotion** encourages people to tell other people about products that they've purchased and how much they like them. Anything that encourages people to talk favorably about an organization may be effective word of mouth. Notice, for example, how stores use clowns, banners, music, fairs, and other attention-getting devices to create word of mouth. Clever commercials can also generate much word of mouth. The whole idea is to get more and more people talking about your products and your brand name so they remember them when they go to buy things.

Viral Marketing and Other Word-of-Mouth Strategies

A number of companies have begun creating word of mouth by paying people to go into Internet chat rooms and hype (or talk enthusiastically and favorably about) bands, movies, video games, and sports teams. The success of the movie *The Blair Witch Project* was due largely to such promotion. People who agree to hype products in this way get free tickets, backstage passes, T-shirts, and other merchandise that the industry calls *swag*. What do you think of the ethics of paying ordinary people to promote goods and services?

Viral marketing is the term now used to describe everything from paying people to say positive things on the Internet to setting up multilevel selling schemes whereby consumers get commissions for directing friends to specific websites.[20] Here is how Barnes & Noble does it: You send your friends an e-mail and tell them how much you enjoyed reading a book and set up a link on your e-mail to the Barnes & Noble website. If they follow the link and buy a book, you get a 5 percent commission. An advanced version of this are websites like Mercata and its competitor Accompany, where potential buyers are urged to find other potential buyers. The more people you get to join you in buying something, the cheaper the product becomes.

One especially effective strategy for spreading positive word of mouth is to send testimonials (remember, these are letters or statements from customers praising a product) to current customers. Most companies use testimonials only in promoting to new customers, but testimonials are also effective in confirming customers' belief that they chose the right company. Positive word of mouth from other users further confirms their choice. Therefore, some companies make it a habit to ask customers for referrals.

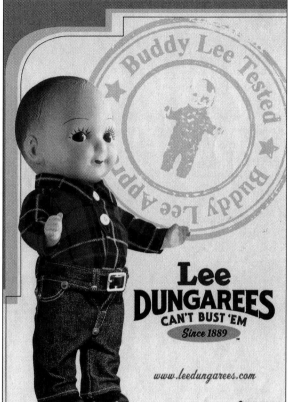

Word of mouth has always been an effective way to raise product awareness. Often called buzz or viral marketing, the idea is to get people talking about your product. Lee Dungarees, for example, used brand icon Buddy Lee to attract a youthful audience. Lee Dungarees' viral campaigns promoting Buddy Lee as a presidential hopeful and challenger of evil villans have helped the brand's popularity soar. The idea was to generate talk among Lee Dungarees' target audience, and it worked. Sales increased. What have you purchased lately because a friend recommended it?

It is important to note also that negative word of mouth can hurt a firm badly. Taking care of consumer complaints quickly and effectively is one of the best ways to reduce the effects of negative word of mouth. Today, negative word of mouth can spread faster than ever before. Online forums, chat rooms, bulletin boards, and websites can all be used as means to spread criticism about a product or company. For example, a company angered by insensitive customer service by a major express company triggered a chorus of agreements about the company that business managers worldwide read.

viral marketing
The term now used to describe everything from paying people to say positive things on the Internet to setting up multilevel selling schemes whereby consumers get commissions for directing friends to specific websites.

Other Ways That New Technologies Are Affecting Promotion

As we have explained in earlier chapters, as people purchase goods and services on the Internet, companies keep track of those purchases and gather other facts and figures about those consumers. Over time, companies learn who buys what, when, and how often. They can then use that information to design catalogs and brochures specifically designed to meet the wants and needs of individual consumers as demonstrated by their actual purchasing behavior. So, for example,

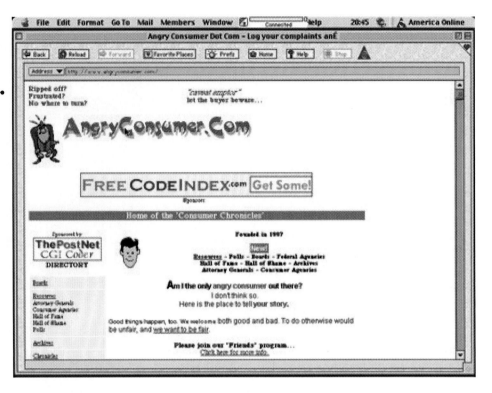

Companies today have to be really careful to treat their customers well. If not, unhappy customers can turn to websites like AngryConsumer.com to get even, and get even they do. They can tell their story on the site and reach thousands of people with their tale of woe. Are you so upset with the service you've received somewhere that you would write something to AngryConsumer.com?

a flower company may send you a postcard first reminding you that your spouse's birthday is coming up soon and that you bought a particular flower arrangement last time, and then recommending a new arrangement this time. Because so much information about consumers is now available, companies are tending to use the traditional promotional tools (e.g., advertising) less than before and are putting more money into direct mail and other forms of direct marketing, including catalogs and the Internet. Consumers are reacting favorably to such promotions, so you can expect the trend toward direct sales and Internet sales to accelerate. Promotional programs will change accordingly.

New technology offers consumers a continuous connection to the Internet and enables marketers to send video files and other data to them faster than ever before. Using such connections, marketers can interact with consumers in real time. As you have read in this chapter, that means that you can talk with a salesperson online and chat with other consumers about their experiences with products and services. You can also search the Net for the best price and find any product information you may want in almost any form you want—copy, sound, video, or whatever.

Such technology gives much more power to consumers like you. You no longer have to rely on advertising or other promotions to learn about products. You can search the Net on your own and find that information when you want it. If you cannot find the information you want, you can request it and get it immediately. Thus, promotion has become much more *interactive*. That is, you and the seller are able to participate in a dialogue over the Internet.

MANAGING THE PROMOTION MIX: PUTTING IT ALL TOGETHER

Each target group calls for a separate promotion mix. For example, large, homogeneous groups of consumers (that is, groups whose members share specific similar traits) are usually most efficiently reached through advertising.

Large organizations are best reached through personal selling. To motivate people to buy now rather than later, sales promotion efforts such as sampling, coupons, discounts, special displays, premiums, and so on may be used. Publicity adds support to the other efforts and can create a good impression among all consumers. Word of mouth is often the most powerful promotional tool and is generated effectively by listening, being responsive, and creating an impression worth passing on to others.

Promotional Strategies

There are two key ways to facilitate the movement of products from producers to consumers. The first is called a push strategy. In a **push strategy,** the producer uses advertising, personal selling, sales promotion, and all other promotional tools to convince wholesalers and retailers to stock and sell merchandise. If the push strategy works, consumers will then walk into a store, see the product, and buy it. The idea is to push the product through the distribution system to the stores (see Figure 16.7).

A second strategy is called a pull strategy. In a **pull strategy,** heavy advertising and sales promotion efforts are directed toward consumers so that they'll request the products from retailers. If the pull strategy works, consumers will go to the store and order the products. Seeing the demand for the products, the store owner will then order them from the wholesaler. The wholesaler, in turn, will order them from the producer. Products are thus pulled down through the distribution system (see Figure 16.8).

Dr Pepper has used TV advertising in a pull strategy to increase distribution. Tripledge, a maker of windshield wipers, also tried to get the interest of retail stores through a pull strategy. Of course, a company could use both push and pull strategies at the same time in a major promotional effort. The latest

push strategy
Promotional strategy in which the producer uses advertising, personal selling, sales promotion, and all other promotional tools to convince wholesalers and retailers to stock and sell merchandise.

pull strategy
Promotional strategy in which heavy advertising and sales promotion efforts are directed toward consumers so that they'll request the products from retailers.

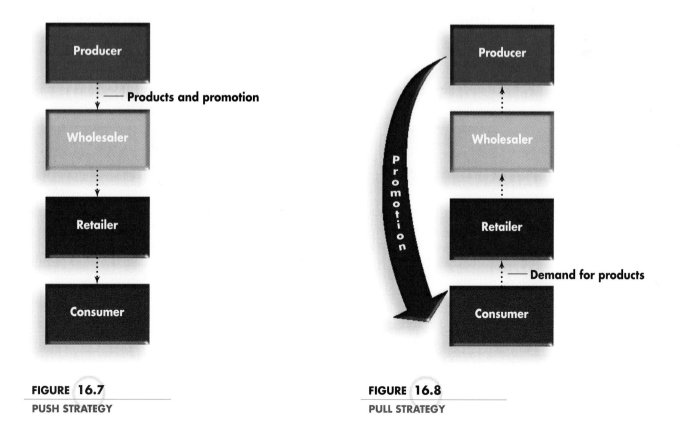

FIGURE 16.7

PUSH STRATEGY

FIGURE 16.8

PULL STRATEGY

in pull and push strategies are being conducted on the Internet, with companies sending messages to both consumers and businesses.

It is important to make promotion part of a total systems approach to marketing. That is, promotion should be part of supply-chain ➤ **P.478** ◄ management. In such cases, retailers would work with producers and distributors to make the supply chain as efficient as possible. Then a promotional plan would be developed for the whole system. The idea would be to develop a value package that would appeal to everyone: manufacturers, distributors, retailers, and consumers.

Creating an Integrated Marketing Communication (IMC) System

An integrated marketing communication (IMC) system is a formal mechanism for uniting all the promotional efforts in an organization to make them more consistent with each other and more responsive to that organization's customers and other stakeholders. That includes the latest in Internet communications and interactive tools.[21] The result is a unified image of the company in the public's mind. In the past, advertising was created by ad agencies, public relations was created by PR firms, and selling was done in-house. There was little coordination across promotional efforts. As a result, consumers often received conflicting messages about a company and its products. For example, TV advertising may have emphasized quality while the sales promotion people were pushing couponing and discounting. Such conflicting images aren't as effective as a unified image created by all promotional means.

Today, more and more companies are trying to create an integrated approach to promotion.[22] Ad agencies are buying direct marketing companies so that they can offer an integrated approach. To implement an IMC system, you start by gathering data about customers and stakeholders and their information needs. Gathering such data and making that information available to everyone in the value chain is a key to future marketing success. All messages reaching customers, potential customers, and other stakeholders would be consistent and coordinated (see Figure 16.9).

Building Interactive Marketing Programs

Earlier in this chapter, we described interactive promotion as an *exchange* between buyers and sellers. Thus, an **interactive marketing program** is one

interactive marketing program
A system in which consumers can access company information on their own and supply information about themselves in an ongoing dialogue.

FIGURE 16.9

INTEGRATED MARKETING COMMUNICATION

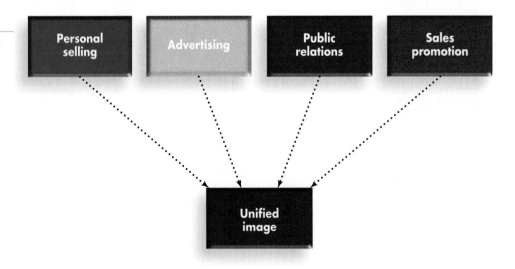

where consumers can access company information on their own and supply information about themselves in an ongoing dialogue. Here are the basic steps for implementing such a program:

1. *Constantly gather data about the groups affected by the organization (including customers, potential customers, and other stakeholders) and keep that information in a database.* Make the data available to everyone in the value chain. An up-to-date, easily accessible database ➤ **P.15** ◄ is critical to any successful program. Today, a company can gather data from sales transactions, letters, e-mail, and faxes. It may also turn to a company that specializes in gathering such data.

2. *Respond quickly to customer and other stakeholder information by adjusting company policies and practices and by designing wanted products and services for target markets.* A responsive firm adapts to changing wants and needs quickly and captures the market from other, less responsive firms. That's why information is so vital to organizations today and why so much money is spent on computers and information systems. You can also see how important it is for the marketing department to work closely with the information systems department and other departments in the firm to make the process of ordering and delivering goods fast and smooth.

3. *Make it possible for customers and potential customers to obtain the information they need to make a purchase.* Then make it easy for people to buy your products in stores or from the company directly by placing an order through e-mail, fax, phone, or other means.

The advantages of interactive marketing on the Internet include the fact that information is available 24 hours a day, seven days a week (24/7); that ads and catalogs can be updated continually; that buyers and sellers can engage in a dialogue over time; and that it can be used by small as well as large companies.

This is an exciting time to study promotion and marketing in general. Changes are happening daily, and you and your friends will find it easier and easier to purchase whatever you want. Soon you may read ads on your cellular phone or portable computer and order products immediately with just a push of a button.[23]

CRITICAL THINKING

Soon there may be as many Internet malls as there are regional malls. Shoppers will be able to request information from multiple firms, compare prices, and make purchases from their homes. What effect will this have on traditional retailers? What will promoters have to do to encourage customers to keep coming into their stores?

PROGRESS ASSESSMENT

- How many sales promotion techniques for reaching consumers can you remember? How many for reaching businesses?
- What is "viral marketing"?
- Could you describe how to implement a push strategy? A pull strategy?
- What are the three steps used in setting up an interactive marketing communication system?

SUMMARY

1. Define promotion and list the four traditional tools that make up the promotion mix.

1. Promotion is an attempt by marketers to inform people about products and to persuade them to participate in an exchange.
   - *What are the four traditional promotional tools that make up the promotion mix?*
   The four traditional promotional tools are advertising, personal selling, public relations, and sales promotion.

2. Define advertising and describe the advantages and disadvantages of various advertising media, including the Internet.

2. Advertising is limited to paid, nonpersonal (not face-to-face) communication through various media by organizations and individuals who are in some way identified in the advertising message.
   - *What are the advantages of using the various media?*
   You can review the advantages and disadvantages of the various advertising media in Figure 16.4.
   - *Why the growing use of infomercials?*
   Infomercials are growing in importance because they show products in use and present testimonials to help sell goods and services.

3. Illustrate the seven steps of the selling process and discuss the role of a consultative salesperson.

3. Personal selling is the face-to-face presentation and promotion of products and services. It also involves the search for new prospects and follow-up service after the sale.
   - *What are the seven steps of the selling process?*
   The steps of the selling process are (1) prospect and qualify, (2) preapproach, (3) approach, (4) make presentation, (5) answer objections, (6) close sale, and (7) follow up.
   - *What does a consultative salesperson do?*
   A consultative salesperson begins by analyzing customer needs and then comes up with solutions to those needs. He or she does much more than make sales presentations. Such salespeople are truly business consultants who do things like develop intranets for clients.

4. Describe the role of the public relations department and how publicity fits in that role.

4. Public relations (PR) is the function that evaluates public attitudes, changes policies and procedures in response to the public's requests, and executes a program of action and information to earn public understanding and acceptance.
   - *What are the three major steps in a good public relations program?*
   (1) Listen to the public—public relations starts with good marketing research; (2) develop policies and procedures in the public interest—one doesn't earn understanding by bombarding the public with propaganda, but rather one earns understanding by having programs and practices in the public interest; and (3) inform people that you're being responsive to their needs.
   - *What is publicity?*
   Publicity is the talking part of sales promotion; it is information distributed by the media that's not paid for, or controlled by, the seller. It's an effective way to reach the public. Publicity's greatest advantage is its believability.

5. Explain the importance of sales promotion and word of mouth as promotional tools.

5. Sales promotion motivates people to buy now instead of later, and word of mouth encourages people to talk about an organization and its products.
   - *How are sales promotion activities used both within and outside the organization?*
   Internal sales promotion efforts are directed at salespeople and other customer-contact people to keep them enthusiastic about the company.

Internal sales promotion activities include sales training, sales aids, audio-visual displays, and trade shows. External sales promotion (promotion to consumers) involves using samples, coupons, cents-off deals, displays, store demonstrators, premiums, and other such incentives.

• *How is word of mouth being used in promotions today?*

A number of companies have begun creating word of mouth by paying people to go into Internet chat rooms and hype (talk enthusiastically and favorably about) bands, movies, video games, and sports teams. People who agree to hype products in this way get free tickets, backstage passes, T-shirts, and other merchandise that the industry calls *swag*. Viral marketing is the term now used to describe everything from paying people to say positive things on the Internet to setting up multilevel selling schemes whereby consumers get commissions for directing friends to specific websites.

6. Marketers use various promotional strategies to move goods from producers to consumers.

• *What are the various promotional strategies?*

In a push strategy, the producer uses advertising, personal selling, sales promotion, and all other promotional tools to convince wholesalers and retailers to stock and sell merchandise. In a pull strategy, heavy advertising and sales promotion efforts are directed toward consumers so that they'll request the products from retailers.

• *How do you set up an integrated marketing communication system?*

An integrated marketing communication system consists of three ongoing parts: (1) Listen constantly to all groups affected by the organization, keep that information in a database, and make that information available to everyone in the organization; (2) respond quickly to customer and other stakeholder information by adjusting company policies and practices and by designing wanted products and services for target markets; and (3) use integrated marketing communication to let all customers and other stakeholders know that the firm is listening and responding to their needs.

• *How do you set up interactive marketing programs?*

There are three steps in setting up an interactive marketing program: (1) Gather data constantly about the groups affected by the organization, (2) respond quickly to customer and other stakeholder information by adjusting company policies and practices and by designing wanted products and services for target markets, and (3) make it possible for customers and potential customers to obtain the information they need to make a purchase. Then make it easy for people to buy your products in stores or from the company directly by placing an order through e-mail, fax, phone, or other means.

6. Describe integrated marketing communication and the role of interactive communications within it.

KEY TERMS

advertising   491
closing
 techniques   500
consultative
 salesperson   501
infomercial   494
integrated marketing
 communication
 (IMC)   490
interactive marketing
 program   510

interactive
 promotion   490
personal selling   498
promotion   490
promotion mix   490
prospects   499
prospecting   499
public
 relations (PR)   502

publicity   503
pull strategy   509
push strategy   509
qualify   499
sales promotion   505
sampling   505
viral marketing   507
word-of-mouth
 promotion   506

DEVELOPING WORKPLACE SKILLS

1. Choose four ads from a newspaper, magazine, or any other medium—two that you consider good and two that you don't consider good. Be prepared to discuss why you feel as you do about each ad. Select ads from at least two different media.

2. Scan your local newspaper for examples of publicity (stories about new products) and sales promotion (coupons, contests, sweepstakes). Share your examples and discuss the effectiveness of such promotional efforts with the class.

3. Check out FreeScholarships.com on the Internet. You may win a $50,000 scholarship. Then try iExchange.com to see how to win $20,000. Finally, look up ThinkLink.com to see how to win a new car. Write a paper of one to two pages describing your reaction to these promotional efforts to get college students on the Web and looking at ads. Did you look at the ads at each site? What might be done to make them more attractive to you and other students?

4. In small groups, discuss whether or not you are purchasing more goods using catalogs and/or the Internet and why. Do you look up information on the Internet before buying goods and services? How helpful are such searches? Present your findings to the class.

5. In small groups or individually, make a list of six products (goods and services) that most students own or use and then discuss which promotional techniques prompt you to buy these goods and services: advertising, personal selling, publicity, sales promotion, or word of mouth. Which tool seems to be most effective for your group? Why do you suppose that is?

TAKING IT TO THE NET

Purpose

To learn about online sales promotion efforts and save some money.

Exercise

1

Many marketers put coupons in magazines and newspapers. Others have coupons in supermarkets and other stores where you can tear them off from displays. The latest in couponing is to place them on the Internet. To find such sites, go to www.coupondepot.com and click on the Coupon Links button. Go to various sites and explore what is available. Sometimes the best deal is to pay nothing at all. To check out free offers on the Internet, go to www.yesfree.com and explore what is available there.

1. Are you willing to register at these various sites to get free coupons faxed to you? Why or why not?

2. What could these websites do to become more user friendly for you and your friends?

3. Have you become more price conscious now that websites give so much competitive information about price and coupons for so many products that are readily available? Is that a good thing or not for marketers?

4. Integrated marketing communication efforts are designed to create a good image for a firm, one that is consistent. Do sites like these fit into such a scheme? Why or why not?

TAKING IT TO THE NET

2

Purpose

To evaluate the promotional effectiveness of two websites.

Exercise

A promotional website is more like a product than an advertisement; that is, it is more like a constantly changing magazine than a brochure. It should be designed to pull consumers to the site and be action-oriented, set to move the consumer closer to a sale.

1. How well do the sites for Mountain Dew (www.mountaindew.com) and Rain Forest Café (www.rainforestcafe.com) use the Web to present their messages? Consider these criteria in evaluating the websites:
   a. Achieves marketing objectives (such as consumer awareness, image, trial, accelerating repurchase, attracting job candidates)
   b. Attracts target market
   c. Is useful to target market
   d. Is easy to navigate
   e. Is graphically pleasing
   f. Loads quickly.

2. Choose one of the websites and offer suggestions for improving the site.

PRACTICING MANAGEMENT DECISIONS

CASE

DEVELOPING A PROMOTIONAL STRATEGY FOR BILTMORE ESTATE

Travel and tourism is one of the top industries in the United States. Therefore, there are many jobs available for students who can market service organizations. This case will help you think through that process: Imagine that you are the marketing manager of a major tourist attraction, the Biltmore Estate. Part of your job is to manage the overall promotional effort and to be part of a marketing team that develops advertising, public relations, personal selling, word of mouth, publicity, and sales promotion.

Here is what you are working with: Biltmore is the largest private home in the United States. It was built in 1895 in Asheville, North Carolina, for George Vanderbilt. The estate includes the 250-room Biltmore House, acres of gardens and surrounding grounds, a winery, and restaurants. The whole estate is open to the public, and nearly a million people visit it each year. If you would like to see pictures of many of the estate's magnificent rooms and gardens, go to its website at www.biltmore.com. The website also contains information about the many motels that advertise their proximity to this great tourist attraction.

One goal of the promotional program at the estate is to increase the number of visitors who come annually. To do that, the estate maintains an internal database of customer names and searches external databases for the names of potential visitors. The total visitor market can be divided into three categories: passholders (who have one-year admission passes), general visitors (who come to visit for one day), and prospects (people who have never visited but may be interested). You are charged with developing separate promotional pieces for each of the market segments. Part of the overall plan should be to integrate all the promotional efforts to form one strong positive image about the estate.

Decision Questions

1. What could you do in cooperation with the other businesses in the area (e.g., motels, restaurants, taxi services) to promote the estate through them?
2. How would you promote to people who have never been to the estate before? How would that promotional program differ from the one you would develop for passholders?

3. Think about vacations that you have taken. What led you to go to those spots? How can you apply that knowledge to this case?

4. How important is website development to this promotional effort? List the following promotional tools by how effective they would be in this case: advertising (what media would you use?), personal selling, publicity, word of mouth, sales promotion.

VIDEO CASE

AIRWALK FOOTWEAR

Airwalk Footwear recently turned to Lambesis, a full-service promotional firm, to design a promotional strategy for its shoes. The goal was to create a brand image that would appeal to young people, which meant listening to that group more closely than most companies had done before. There was very little research available, so the company had to do its own. Lambesis went where teenagers ate, shopped, and hung out. Marketers observed, asked questions, and learned as much as possible about teens' lifestyle, especially among the trendsetters. At first the idea was to target the U.S. market, but Lambesis decided that a global appeal would be more effective. The company's research showed that a 17-year-old in Mexico City or Moscow had the same wants and needs as a 17-year-old in the United States. That may not be true of a different age group, but it was true of this one. Based on that research, Lambesis tried to design a universal message, perhaps one including romance, that would have appeal to teenagers in all countries.

Lambesis took an integrated marketing communication approach. To this company, that meant having all departments working together as a team to develop one unified message in all media and in all communications. Team members from product development, research, broadcast, and website development worked together to develop an overall strategy for Airwalk.

The strategy had three themes: (1) entertainment, (2) sports, and (3) style. Every message would try to combine these three elements—even the shoebox was designed in keeping with the themes. The integrated marketing communication effort included advertising, public relations, sales promotion, word of mouth, direct selling, and the Internet. Advertising vehicles included television programs, T-shirts, and posters all over town. A pull strategy was used for advertising. That is, advertising for leading-edge products was directed at teenagers, who then went into shoe stores and requested specific Airwalk shoes. The magazines chosen were mostly underground magazines, and the TV shows were ones that appealed to this group but few others. Sales promotion efforts included contests where the winners won trips to various places. Gifts were also sent to people who responded to direct marketing appeals.

Much effort also went into public relations and event sponsorship. That included events such as snowboard contests where the participants wore Airwalk snowboarding boots. Rock bands were given free shoes, and special promotions were built around those bands. Every communication tool conveyed the same clear message: these shoes are designed for you and your friends—and they are exciting. Word of mouth spread naturally among the targeted teens. The website was constantly updated to attract people back. It takes all the elements of entertainment, sports, and style to attract people to a website and have them spend some time there.

In short, the campaign was targeted precisely to the Airwalk teenage market. As a result of the integrated marketing communication effort, Airwalk sales doubled and then doubled again. Sales globally went from $20 million to $300 million in 14 different countries.

Discussion Questions

1. What are some of the challenges you would face if you were trying to develop a website for Airwalk Footwear that would have global appeal (multiple languages) and would allow teens to order by phone, fax, or mail?

2. Could Airwalk expand its market to other market segments? Which segments would offer the greatest opportunities?

3. Would you expand the Airwalk product mix to include clothing for skateboarders and snowboarders? Give reasons why or why not.

4. If you were in charge of developing a promotional strategy for the coming year, what would you do differently to maintain interest among this target audience? Would you emphasize advertising, public relations, sales promotion, word of mouth, direct marketing, or some combination? Justify your strategy.

FUNDAMENTALS OF MARKETING

Marketing is a challenging and dynamic area in which to choose a career. The field is so varied, it can attract people with a tremendous variety of talents, skills, and interest areas. For example, the "number crunching" person could choose marketing research; artistic individuals might be attracted to advertising or sales promotion; and entrepreneurial types might choose wholesaling or retailing. There are dozens of other combinations.

Marketing is based on the exchange of goods and services. Like every other area of business, it is dynamic and always changing, especially with the current emphasis on international markets. Anyone who wants to be involved in this exciting area must be flexible and able to change with the times as tastes for new products and services change and as new markets open and old ones close. Marketing is an area that remains wide open.

SKILLS

Although marketing draws on talents from a variety of personality types and skill areas, some realistic generalizations can be made about skills that most marketers have in common. Marketers need to be people oriented, even the number crunchers mentioned above. They also need to be tuned in to the culture of the country or region where they are marketing. They need to sense trends and changing habits of customers. Above all, they must be effective communicators, possessing an ability to be heard and noticed as well as to hear and notice the needs of others. The amount of education required varies widely from position to position, and even firm to firm.

CAREER PATHS

Many marketing careers start out as sales positions. Sales is a challenging area in which individuals can prove themselves, using that success as a means of moving up to sales manager or other positions of responsibility. Advertising is another avenue of interest, especially for those who are attracted to the tantalizing mixture of psychology, communications, and art that advertisers use. Retailing also offers a variety of opportunities, some more marketing-oriented than others.

Not all positions in marketing require a four-year degree, although one is usually a formally stated requisite. In many companies, your skill level is the important issue. Marketing skills can often be developed in two-year business programs and in real-world experience. On-campus clubs such as FBLA (Future Business Leaders of America) and DECA (Distributive Education Clubs of America) can help you learn to compete in the world of marketing while still in school.

SOME POSSIBLE POSITIONS IN MARKETING

JOB TITLE	SALARY	JOB DUTIES	CAREER PATH	PROSPECTS
Market researcher	$23,000–$34,000 (start) Market research director, as much as $140,000.	Design surveys, opinion polls, and questionnaires; collect data using various methods.	Bachelor's degree with marketing courses. Some positions require only talent and desire to learn.	Good prospects through 2006.
Sales representative	$23,000–$100,000+ (depends both on the company and initiative of the individual).	Call on customers; fulfill needs; provide follow-up; sometimes deal with credit issues; report regularly to home office.	Training programs usually provided by company. Successful representatives are usually promoted to sales manager.	Many new opportunities in the future, especially in high tech and international sales.
Purchasing agent (buyer)	$22,290–$86,740 (median $41,830).	Stay informed about buying opportunities; maintain good relations with company sales force. Maintain positive relations with suppliers.	Usually start out as buyer trainee, or assistant buyer. Can be promoted to purchasing manager or merchandising manager.	Growth through 2008 will be slower than average.
Advertising agent or manager	$27,000 to start; median $57,300.	Trainee positions are usually in copywriting, layout, or other less responsible positions. Copywriters must have a command of written English. Layout people need a talent for proportion and for predicting reader reaction.	Entry-level positions are usually in specific areas of advertising. A copywriter can be promoted to senior copywriter. The highest promotion will usually be to creative director.	Faster than average growth through 2008.
Public relations specialist	median $57,300; senior $84,950.	Build and maintain a good image for the company. Communicate the goals and purposes of the company to the public and stockholders, if any. Must be good writer and speaker and be comfortable in all areas of the mass media.	College degree with entry-level experience (as an unpaid student trainee, etc.). Many PR people started in some other career, such as journalism, but made this career move later. Can be promoted to management, often outside of public relations, sometimes into market research.	Faster than average growth through 2008.
Marketing consultant	Varies greatly, because a consultant is in business for himself or herself.	Begin like any service-based entrepreneur. Need especially to make contacts with firms needing your service.	Intensive training needed; essential to be correct in advice. Service as intern in consulting firm or start on your own with aggressive approach.	Growth good through 2006, especially in areas of international and high tech marketing.

Source: *Occupational Outlook Handbook,* 2000–2001 Edition: Bureau of Labor Statistics.

PALM BEACH COMMUNITY COLLEGE

Name: Louis "Rusty" Wallraff

Age: 43

Position/title: Coordinator, College Information Center

Salary range: $28,000–$43,000

Time in this position: 1 year

Company name: Palm Beach Community College

Company's Web address: www.pbcc.cc.fl.us

Company description: Community College

Major factors in the decision to take this position: I had worked at the college as a student and enjoyed it very much. To become an employee, I was told to learn as much as I could about the college and how it works, and to network with the right people. I worked in various departments and was liked by all of my supervisors. I was a member of the Phi Theta Kappa honors society and the state Parliamentarian for Delta Epsilon Chi a Marketing Club. I was also involved in the student government and the Inner Club Council. My first job at the college was as a monitor in one of the student computer labs. There I found it rewarding to help the students learn the computer skills they needed. After that I worked in the Center for Professional Development which is where the teachers come to use the computer lab. I enjoyed this very much since I had a good rapport with many of them. From there I moved over to Media Services, which is part of the Library. Almost near completing my degree, I was hired as an assistant to the Coordinator in the Enrollment Information Center. After the coordinator accepted another job, I served as Acting Coordinator of the department and was eventually offered the job full time.

Job description: The Coordinator of the College Information Center is responsible for supervising the operation of a total customer service and community outreach center. The Center serves to help PBCC students achieve their goals and to help inform the Palm Beach County community of educational programs and activities of Palm Beach Community College. It provides timely information to the public, students and/or college staff regarding programs and services of the college.

Career path: From Office Assistant to Coordinator, College Information Center

Ideal next job: Unknown at this time

Best part of your job: Helping the students and community

Worst part of your job: There is none, I love my job!

Educational background: Associate's degree in Business Administration and Management

Favorite course: Introduction to Business

Best course for your career: Introduction to Business

Recommended by Susan Thompson, Palm Beach Community College.

17

Using Technology to Manage Information

LEARNING GOALS

AFTER YOU HAVE READ AND STUDIED THIS CHAPTER, YOU SHOULD BE ABLE TO

1 Outline the changing role of business technology.

2 Compare the scope of the Internet, intranets, and extranets as tools in managing information.

3 List the steps in managing information, and identify the characteristics of useful information.

4 Review the hardware most frequently used in business, and outline the benefits of the move toward computer networks.

5 Classify the computer software most frequently used in business.

6 Evaluate the human resource, security, privacy and stability issues in management that are affected by information technology.

7 Identify the careers that are gaining or losing workers due to the growth of information technology.

Getting to Know Rina Delmonico of Ren Consulting, Inc.

Picture a 43-year-old grandmother who swing-dances in Denver nightclubs, has a passion for neon nail polish on her two-inch-long nails, and has recently learned to box. Does that sound like a candidate for the Executive of the Year Award given by the Association of Information Technology Professionals? Well, meet Rina Delmonico, formerly chief information officer (CIO) of Schwinn Bicycle Company. Today, Delmonico owns her own information services consulting firm.

Delmonico has been described as "eccentric" by her colleagues. They also call her brilliant. She makes no excuses for the now famous "Rina style" she sports. As she twirls her long, dark ponytail through her fingers, she seems more like a 20-year-old college coed than an information technology (IT) expert. Yet despite this youthful appearance and attitude, Delmonico boasts 25 years of experience in IT, during which time she has climbed the ladder at large financial and manufacturing companies such as Citicorp, Johns Manville and Schwinn. Innovation and a willingness to try new technology applications are the hallmarks of her success. For example, as vice president of corporate management information systems at First Data Corporation, Delmonico spearheaded the development of the corporate intranet that included a recruitment automation system that slashed hiring costs by 25 percent.

She decided to take on the challenge at Schwinn in 1996, just three years after the company almost fell into bankruptcy. Delmonico became a key player in the attempt to rebuild Schwinn's reputation as a leader in the cycling world. When she started work at Schwinn, the information systems (IS) department was in shambles. Relationships with company vendors were eroding and the firm's enterprise resource planning implementation was so far off the mark that orders could not be shipped. Ponytail pulled back and two-inch nails clawing, Delmonico jumped headfirst into action and provided the spark needed to rally the 30-person IT staff at Schwinn to help turn the company around. She started first by revamping Schwinn's telecommunications cost structure. By reworking contracts and wiring systems, she immediately saved the firm $500,000. Delmonico also directed the two-month launch of Schwinn's e-commerce website and helped install a personal computer and network infrastructure literally from scratch. Delmonico, however, is the first to admit that little could be accomplished without the support of her staff. Therefore, she regularly rewarded her 30 co-workers with small personalized gifts and took them out for pizza or to virtual reality clubs to kick back and relax from the rigors of the job.

Large businesses like Citicorp and relatively smaller firms like Schwinn will succeed or fail in the 21st century economy on their ability to manage and make use of information. New technologies enable managers to make more informed decisions and help with vital communications between workers and other stakeholders. Rapid growth of the Internet and technological developments make this one of the most exciting times in history. Rina Delmonico certainly agrees with that statement. And, by the way, she doesn't plan to miss a minute of it.

Sources: Polly Schneider, "Shifting Gears," *CIO*, October 1, 1999, pp. 62–70; and Meridith Levinson, "Zen and the Art of IT Governance," *CIO*, February 15, 2000, pp. 127–32.

THE ROLE OF INFORMATION TECHNOLOGY

Throughout this text, we have emphasized the need for managing information flows among businesses and their employees, businesses and their suppliers, businesses and their customers, and so on. Since businesses are in a constant state of change, those managers who try to rely on old ways of doing things will simply not be able to compete with those who have the latest in technology and know how to use it.

Business technology has often changed names and roles. In the 1970s, business technology was known as **data processing (DP).** (Although many people use the words *data* and *information* interchangeably, they are different. *Data* are raw, unanalyzed, and unorganized facts and figures. *Information* is the processed and organized data that can be used for managerial decision making.) DP was used to support an existing business; its primary purpose was to improve the flow of financial information. DP employees tended to be hidden in a back room and rarely came in contact with customers.

In the 1980s, business technology became known as **information systems (IS).** IS moved out of the back room and into the center of the business. Its role changed from *supporting* the business to *doing* business. Customers began to interact with a wide array of technological tools, from automated teller machines (ATMs) to voice mail. As business increased its use of information systems, it became more dependent on them.

Until the late 1980s, business technology was just an addition to the existing way of doing business. Keeping up-to-date was a matter of using new technology on old methods. But things started to change as the 1990s approached. Businesses shifted to using new technology on new methods. Business technology then became known as **information technology (IT),** and its role became to *change* business.

data processing (DP)
Name for business technology in the 1970s; included technology that supported an existing business and was primarily used to improve the flow of financial information.

information systems (IS)
Technology that helps companies *do* business; includes such tools as automated teller machines (ATMs) and voice mail.

information technology (IT)
Technology that helps companies *change* business by allowing them to use new methods.

How can retailers learn about the hottest fashion trends in time to get them in their stores before the trends cool? Zara links each of its stores electronically to the company's headquarters allowing sales information, and customer requests to be transmitted daily. Zara designers use this real-time information to quickly create the garments consumers seek. Zara can add new designs twice a week rather than the industry standard of six weeks.

How Information Technology Changes Business

Time and place have always been at the center of business. Customers had to go to the business during certain hours to satisfy their needs. We went to the store to buy clothes. We went to the bank to arrange for a loan. Businesses decided when and where we did business with them. Today, IT allows businesses to deliver products and services ➤ **P.25** ◄ whenever and wherever it is convenient for the customer. Thus, you can order clothes from the Home Shopping Network, arrange a home mortgage loan by phone or computer, or buy a car on the Internet at any time you choose.

Consider how IT has changed the entertainment industry. If you wanted to see a movie 35 years ago, you had to go to a movie theater. Thirty years ago you could wait for it to be on television. Twenty years ago you could wait for it to be on cable television. Fifteen years ago you could go to a video store and rent it. Now you can order video on demand by satellite or cable.

As IT breaks time and location barriers, it creates organizations and services that are independent of location. For example, NASDAQ and SOFFEX are electronic stock exchanges without trading floors. Buyers and sellers make trades by computer.

Being independent of location brings work to people instead of people to work. With IT, data and information can flow more than 8,000 miles in a second, allowing businesses to conduct work around the globe continuously. We are moving toward what we call **virtualization,** which is accessibility through technology that allows business to be conducted independent of location. For example, you can carry a virtual office in your pocket or purse. Such tools as cellular phones, pagers, laptop computers, and personal digital assistants allow you to access people and information as if you were in an actual office. Likewise, virtual communities are forming as people who would otherwise not have met communicate with each other through the virtual post office created by computer networks.[1]

Doing business drastically changes when companies increase their technological capabilities. For example, electronic communications can provide substantial time savings whether you work in an office, at home, or on the road. E-mail ends the tedious games of telephone tag and decreases the time needed to write and mail traditional paper-based correspondence. Internet and intranet communication using shared documents and other methods allow contributors to work on a common document without the time-consuming meetings. See Figure 17.1 for other examples of how information technology changes business.

Moving from Information Technology toward Knowledge Technology

In the mid-1990s, yet another change occurred in the terminology of business technology as we started moving away from information technology and toward **knowledge technology (KT).** Knowledge is information charged with enough intelligence to make it relevant and useful. KT adds a layer of intelligence to filter appropriate information and deliver it when it is needed. For example, consider the number 70. Alone, it doesn't mean much. Change it to 70 percent and it means a little more but still doesn't tell us a lot. Make it a 70 percent chance of rain and we have more meaning.

Now let's imagine that you are the first one on your block with a wristwatch featuring KT. As you walk out the door, the watch signals you that it has a message: "70 percent chance of rain in your city today." KT just gave you relevant and useful information at the moment you needed it. Now you can head for class with an umbrella under your arm, knowing that you made an informed decision.

KT changes the traditional flow of information; instead of an individual going to the database ➤ **P.15** ◄, the data comes to the individual. For example,

virtualization
Accessibility through technology that allows business to be conducted independent of location.

knowledge technology (KT)
Technology that adds a layer of intelligence to information technology, to filter appropriate information and deliver it when it is needed.

FIGURE 17.1

HOW INFORMATION TECHNOLOGY IS CHANGING BUSINESS

This table shows a few ways that information technology is changing businesses, their employees, suppliers, and customers.

Organization	Technology is breaking down corporate barriers, allowing functional departments or product groups (even factory workers) to share critical information instantly.
Operations	Technology shrinks cycle times, reduces defects, and cuts waste. Service companies use technology to streamline ordering and communication with suppliers and customers.
Staffing	Technology eliminates layers of management and cuts the number of employees. Companies use computers and telecommunication equipment to create "virtual offices" with employees in various locations.
New products	Information technology cuts development cycles by feeding customer and marketing comments to product development teams quickly so that they can revive products and target specific customers.
Customer relations	Customer service representatives can solve customers' problems instantly by using companywide databases to complete tasks from changing addresses to adjusting bills. Information gathered from customer service interactions can further stronger customer relationships.
New Markets	Since it is no longer necessary for customers to walk down the street to get to stores, online businesses can attract customers to whom they wouldn't otherwise have access.

using KT business training software, AT&T can put a new employee at a workstation and then let the system take over to do everything from laying out a checklist of the tasks required on a shift to answering questions and offering insights that once would have taken up a supervisor's time. Knowledge databases may one day replace the traditional mentors who helped workers up the corporate ladder.

KT "thinks" about the facts based on an individual's needs, reducing the time that person must spend finding and getting information. Businesspeople who use KT can focus on what's important: *deciding* about how to react to problems and opportunities.

The new economy, in which technology is the key to growth, is based on brains, not brawn.[2] The businesses that build flexible information infrastructures will have a significant competitive advantage. Constant changes in technology interact with each other to create more change. Maintaining the flexibility to successfully integrate these changes is crucial to business survival. History is filled with stories of once-mighty companies that couldn't keep up with the challenge of change: U.S. Steel, Packard Bell, and RCA once dominated their industries but failed to compete effectively and have lost market share. They had size and money, but not flexibility.[3] Knowledge sharing is at the heart of keeping pace with change.

CRITICAL THINKING

What information would you like to receive exactly when and where you need it? If you could design a system to provide this information, what might it look like and what would it do?

PROGRESS ASSESSMENT

- How has the role of information technology changed since the days when it was known as data processing?
- In what way is knowledge technology different from information technology?

THE ROAD TO KNOWLEDGE: THE INTERNET, INTRANETS, EXTRANETS, AND VIRTUAL PRIVATE NETWORKS

The importance of business knowledge is nothing new—what is new is the recognition of the need to manage it like any other asset. To manage knowledge, a company needs to learn how to share information throughout the organization and to implement systems for creating new knowledge.[4] This need is leading to new technologies that support the exchange of information among staff, suppliers, and customers. Who wins and who loses in the new economy will be decided by who harnesses the technology that provides the pipeline of two-way interaction and information flow between individuals and organizations.[5] At the heart of this technology are the Internet, intranets, extranets, and virtual private networks.

You already know that the Internet is a network of computer networks. (If you would like more detailed information about the Internet, you can refer back to the material called "Surfing the Internet" in the Getting Ready for Prime Time section at the beginning of the book.) A Nielsen survey indicated that U.S. workers now spend an average of 21 hours a week online.[6] Nearly 100 million people were online in the United States in 2000, up from just 36 million in 1996.[7] Internet users can point and click their way from site to site with complete freedom. But what if you don't want just anybody to have access to your website? You might create an intranet.

An **intranet** is a companywide network, closed to public access, that uses Internet-type technology. To prevent unauthorized outsiders (particularly the competition) from accessing their sites, companies can construct a "firewall" between themselves and the outside world to protect corporate information from unauthorized users. A firewall can be hardware, software, or both.[8]

One-half to two-thirds of all businesses are running intranets. Some companies use intranets only to publish information for employees, such as phone lists and employee policy manuals. These companies do not enjoy as high a return on their investment as other companies that create interactive intranet applications. Such applications include allowing employees to update their addresses or submit company forms such as supply requisitions, timesheets, or payroll forms online. These applications save money or generate greater revenue because they eliminate paper handling and enable decision making.[9]

Many businesses choose to open their intranets to other, selected companies through the use of extranets. As described in Chapter 8, an extranet is a semiprivate network that uses Internet technology and allows more than one company to access the same information or allows people on different servers to collaborate. One of the most common uses of extranets is to extend an intranet to outside customers. Extranets change the way we do business. No longer are the advantages of electronic data in-

intranet
A companywide network, closed to public access, that uses Internet-type technology.

As more and more people go online, the Internet will continue its informational influence on many facets of our lives. In business, intranets have that same effect on the job. Intranets are companywide networks that use Internet-type technologies, but are closed to public access. How do intranets help companies manage knowledge?

terchange (EDI) available only to the large companies that can afford such a system. Now almost all companies can use the extranets to share data and process orders, specifications, invoices, and payments.

Notice that we described an extranet as a *semiprivate* network. This means that outsiders cannot access the network easily, but since it does use public lines knowledgeable hackers (people who break into computer systems for illegal purposes such as transferring funds from someone's bank account to their own without authorization) can gain unauthorized access. Most companies want a network that is as private and secure as possible. One way to increase the probability of total privacy is to use dedicated lines (lines reserved solely for the network). There are two problems with this method: (1) it's expensive, and (2) it limits use to computers directly linked to those lines. What if your company needs to link securely with another firm or individual for just a short time? Installing dedicated lines between companies in this case would be too expensive and time-consuming. Virtual private networks are a solution.

A **virtual private network (VPN)** is a private data network that creates secure connections, or "tunnels," over regular Internet lines. The idea of the VPN is to give the company the same capabilities at much lower cost by using shared public resources rather than private ones. This means companies no longer need their own leased lines for wide-area communication but could use the public lines securely. Just as phone companies provide secure shared resources for voice messages, VPNs provide the same secure sharing of public resources for data. This allows for on-demand networking; an authorized user can join the network for any desired function at any time, for any length of time, while keeping the corporate network secure.[10]

Broadband Technology

As traffic on the Internet increases, the slower the connection becomes. New technologies unlock many of the traffic jams on the information superhighway. For example, **broadband technology** offers users a continuous connection to the Internet and allows them to send and receive mammoth files that include voice, video, and data much faster than ever before. The more bandwidth, the bigger pipe for data to flow through—and the bigger the pipe, the faster the flow. Whether the bandwidth connection is by cable modem, digital subscriber lines (DSL), satellite, or fixed wireless, the impact is much the same. Data can reach you more than 50 times as fast as with traditional 56k modems (the kind that came with most computers in the late 1990s and early 2000s).[11] You may want to refer to Figure G.4 in the Getting Ready for Prime Time section at the beginning of the book for a comparison of the various bandwidth connections.

Even with the new networks offered by broadband technology, the traffic on the information superhighway has become so intense that early Net settlers—scientists and other scholars—have found that they have been squeezed off the crowded Internet and are unable to access, transmit, and manipulate complex mathematical models, data sets, and other digital elements of their craft. Their answer? Create another Internet, reserved for research purposes only.

The new system, **Internet 2,** runs more than 22,000 times faster than a 56k modem and supports heavy-duty applications, such as videoconferencing, collaborative research, distance education, digital libraries, and full-body simulation environments known as teleimmersion.[12] A key element of Internet 2 is a network called very high speed backbone network service (vBNS), which was set up in 1995 as a way to link government supercomputer centers and a select group of universities. The power of Internet 2 makes it possible for a remote medical specialist to assist in a medical operation over the Internet without

virtual private network (VPN)
A private data network that creates secure connections, or "tunnels," over regular Internet lines.

broadband technology
Technology that delivers voice, video and data through the Internet.

Internet 2
The new Internet system that links government supercomputer centers and a select group of universities; it will run more than 22,000 times faster than today's public infrastructure and will support heavy-duty applications.

having to contend with degradation of the connection as, say, home users check sports scores.

Although Internet 2 became available to a few select organizations in late 1997, by 2000 there were 172 member universities.[13] Whereas the public Internet divides bandwidth equally among users (if there are 100 users, they each get to use 1 percent of the available bandwidth), Internet 2 is more capitalistic **➤ P.37 ◄**. Users who are willing to pay more can use more bandwidth.

Cynics say that soon Internet 2 itself will be overrun by networked undergrads engaged in swapping MP3 songs and other resource-hogging pursuits.[14] But the designers of Internet 2 are thinking ahead. Not only do they expect Internet history to repeat itself, but they are counting on it. They are planning to filter the Internet 2 technology out to the wider Internet community in such a way that there is plenty of room on the road for all of us—at a price, of course.

MANAGING INFORMATION

Even before the use of computers, managers had to sift through mountains of information to find what they needed to help them make decisions. Today, businesspeople are deluged with information from voice mail, the Internet, fax machines, e-mail, and instant messaging.[15] Businesspeople refer to this information overload as *infoglut*. Remember the classic episode of TV's *I Love Lucy* with Lucy and Ethel on the candy line? Everything was going okay until the candy started coming too fast for them. Then mayhem broke loose. That's what's happening to many managers today. Instead of candy, it is information that is passing by too quickly. Too much information can confuse issues rather than clarify them. How can managers keep from getting buried in the infoglut? Stepping back to gain perspective is the key to managing the flood of information.[16]

The first step toward gaining perspective is to identify the four or five key goals you wish to reach. Eliminating the information that is not related to those top priorities can reduce the amount of information flowing into your office by half. For example, as we were gathering information to include in this chapter, we collected over 400 journal articles. Feeling the pressure of information overload, we identified the goals we wanted the chapter to accomplish and eliminated all the articles that didn't address those goals. As we further refined our goals, the huge stack of paper gradually dropped to a manageable size.

Obviously, not all of the information that ends up on your desk will be useful. The usefulness of management information depends on four characteristics:

1. *Quality.* Quality means that the information is accurate and reliable. When the clerk at a fast-food restaurant enters your order into the cash register, it may be automatically fed to a computer, and the day's sales and profits can be calculated as soon as the store closes. The sales and expense data must be accurate, or the rest of the calculations will be

It truly is the Information Age. How can you conquer the mountain of information that continues to build every day? How can you judge the usefulness of the information you access?

wrong. This can be a real problem when, for example, a large number of calculations are based on questionable sales forecasts rather than actual sales.

2. *Completeness.* There must be enough information to allow you to make a decision but not so much as to confuse the issue. Today, as we have noted, the problem is often too much information rather than too little.

3. *Timeliness.* Information must reach managers quickly. If a customer has a complaint, that complaint should be handled instantly if possible and certainly within no more than one day. In the past, a salesperson would make a report to his or her manager; that report would go to a higher-level manager, and the problem would not be resolved for days, weeks, or months. E-mail and other developments make it possible for marketing, engineering, and production to hear about a problem with a product the same day the salesperson hears about it. Product changes can be made on the spot using computer integrated manufacturing, as discussed in Chapter 9.

4. *Relevance.* Different managers have different information needs. Again, the problem today is that information systems often make too much data available. Managers must learn which questions to ask to get the answers they need.

It doesn't matter how interesting your information is if nobody's paying attention. Sorting out useful information and getting it to the right people are the goals in solving information overload. There are Web software programs and services available that do just that—filter information so that users can get the customized information they need.[17] Such a program is known as **push technology** because it pushes information to users so they don't have to find it for themselves and pull it out. Push technology services deliver customized news to individual computers after sorting through thousands of news sources to find information that suits the user's identified needs. The major Web browsers, Netscape Navigator and Microsoft Internet Explorer, include push technology features.

The important thing to remember when facing information overload is to relax. You can never read everything that is available. Set goals for yourself, and do the best you can. Remember, just because there is a public library doesn't mean you should feel guilty about not reading every book in it. And so it is with the information superhighway: you can't make every stop along the route, so plan your trip wisely and bon voyage!

Managing Knowledge

Since knowledge gives a company not only power but also profits, competitive companies must find as many ways as possible to mine the knowledge that is stored in their employees. They certainly can't afford to let that knowledge walk out the door when their employees change jobs or retire. **Knowledge management** means sharing, organizing and disseminating information in the simplest and most relevant way possible for the users of the information.[18]

Consider this scenario: Hal is a project manager trying to determine the cost of lead pipe in Bangladesh. He's tried searching the Web, calling colleagues, writing e-mails, and sending faxes—with no luck. Sal, the assistant vice president of logistics in the same company as Hal, has been pricing pipe via an e-mail conversation with a Bangladeshi supplier. How does Hal find Sal? Too often, he doesn't. Now there's a way to make Sal aware of Hal's search. It's called e-mail. Well, actually one company calls it knowledge-mail.[19]

push technology
Web software that delivers information tailored to a previously defined user profile; it pushes the information to users so that they don't have to pull it out.

knowledge management
Sharing, organizing and disseminating information in the simplest and most relevant way possible for the users of the information.

Knowledge-mail sorts through the millions of e-mail messages churning throughout a company's system and tracks users' work. It can then alert them that others in the company are doing similar work. This allows people who are working on similar projects (like Hal and Sal) to share information and solve problems. You might be concerned that such monitoring of e-mail is an invasion of privacy. Knowledge-mail systems provide a feature that allow users to mark messages that they think should not be sorted in the system. Another safeguard is a feature that lets the source of the information (Sal) know that someone else (Hal) needs the data. Sal can choose whether or not to make the contact with Hal.

Knowledge management requires organizing information so that it's clean, accurate and consistent, and communicating it to those who need it in a hot second. Next we will discuss some of the technology that helps this happen.

THE ENABLING TECHNOLOGY: HARDWARE

We hesitate to discuss the advances that have been made in computer hardware because what is powerful as we write this may be obsolete by the time you read it. In the mid-1970s the chairman of Intel Corporation, Gordon E. Moore, predicted that the capacity of computer chips would double every year or so. This has since been called Moore's law. The million-dollar vacuum-tube computers that awed people in the 1950s couldn't keep up with a pocket calculator today. In fact, a greeting card that plays "Happy Birthday" contains more computing power than existed before 1950.

The speed of evolution in the computer industry has slowed little since Moore's remark, although in 1997, Moore did say that his prediction cannot hold good for much longer because chip makers will sooner or later run into a fundamental law of nature; that is, the finite size of atomic particles will prevent infinite miniaturization. That won't stop computer companies from improving chips in other ways than shrinking them.[20] Rapid advances make one product after another obsolete, helping create demand for newer chips. For example, a three-year-old personal computer is considered out-of-date. So rather than add potentially outdated facts to your information overload, we offer you a simple overview of the current computer technology.

Hardware includes computers, pagers, cellular phones, printers, scanners, fax machines, personal digital assistants, and so on. The mobile worker can find travel-size versions of computers, printers, and fax machines that are almost as powerful and feature-laden as their big brothers. All-in-one devices that address the entire range of your communications needs are now available. For example, there are handheld units that include a wireless phone, fax and e-mail capabilities, Web browsers, and a personal information manager (PIM). The Spotlight on Small Business box shows how useful these information appliances can be in the life of a home-based worker.

Researchers are working on a human computer interface that combines a video camera and

Personal digital assistants (PDAs) such as Handspring's Visor allow users to get rid of their paper address books, calendars, memo pads, and all those napkin scribbles. Basic PDAs help keep track of contacts, activities, to-do lists all with one pocket-sized handheld computer. Higher-end models allow users to add on wireless modems, digital cameras, and more. How could a PDA help you organize your life?

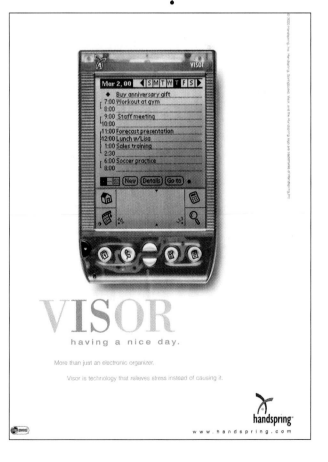

A Day in Your Life As a Wired Home-Office Worker

6:30   Get your blood moving with a jog on your Web-enabled treadmill. Log on simultaneously with a friend for a virtual race. On the nearby computer screen, you see your sprint to the finish displayed graphically. You win, of course!

7:30   As you fix your breakfast, you touch the screen of your countertop Internet appliance to see if you received that important e-mail message you are expecting. Yes! You type a quick response and press another on-screen icon for the latest news in your industry. On the way out of the kitchen you press yet another icon to select music downloaded from the Web.

8:00   Time to get to work. You still use a personal computer (PC), but the flat-panel monitor and keyboard are the only hardware parts cluttering your desk. (Of course, there's plenty of paper clutter—the promise of a paperless office has been a dream since the 1950s.) You use the PC for heavy computational tasks and graphics design, but you rely on multiple smaller devices such as your Internet phone for moment-to-moment tasks. Your Internet phone automatically checks for e-mail and alerts you with a blinking light.

11:30   Time to meet a client for lunch at that great new restaurant. Since you don't know the way, your car's in-dash computer with global positioning system (GPS) capabilities guides you with turn-by-turn directions. Speaking to you as you drive, the system warns you to switch lanes and put on your turn signals. You missed a turn; it tells you so and guides you back on track.

12:00   Between the appetizer and the entrée, you realize you forgot to turn off the stove at home. You use your smart phone to call your household computer that monitors all of your appliances and tell it which burner to turn off—and you adjust the house's temperature while you're at it.

2:30   You make it to your next appointment on time because your in-dash computer warns you of an accident and reroutes you.

6:00   Finally back home, you see the Internet phone blinking at you as you walk in the door. You respond and then call it a day. You turn to a good book to relax. You put your electronic book in its cradle and download the newest best-seller from the Web. You turn on your television and play a game of Jeopardy that's been download from your satellite dish. That answer can't be right—you open a picture-in-picture view of the Web and search for more info. But one site leads to another and, before you know it, you've found your answer, downloaded a new album, and bought half your Christmas presents.

10:00   You call it a day and make a mental note to finish that budget spreadsheet tomorrow. You'll use your PC for that, of course. You sleep comfortably, knowing that taking advantage of a wide range of technological options has made both your home and home office life better.

Sources: David Haskin, "A Day in the Post-PC Life," *Home Office Computing*, February 2000, pp. 67–71; and Harold Goldberg, "Gimme That! The Latest Gotta Have Stuff," *Entertainment Weekly*, February 9, 2001.

personal computer (PC). When you approach the PC, it recognizes you, asks you how you feel, and determines what tasks you want to complete that day. Instead of hearing a mechanical beep to remind you of your next class, you'll hear a soothing voice say, "Sam, your Introduction to Business final will begin in 30 minutes." Sorry, it won't take the test for you—some things you still have to do for yourself.

Cutting the Cord: Wireless Information Appliances

Some experts think we are entering the post-PC era; that is, that we are moving away from a PC-dominant environment toward an array of Internet appli-

REACHING BEYOND OUR BORDERS

www.tellme.com

If You Need Me Just Call Me

There's no question that broadband Internet access is the future for PCs, TVs, and other information appliances. In fact, it's hard to pick up a newspaper, watch television, or surf the Net and not be deluged with advertisements promoting superspeed Internet connections via cable modem or digital phone lines. Companies like America Online (AOL) are gearing up their products to include rich audio, video, and interactive media that take advantage of the fatter Net connections. But a challenge looms on the horizon from an unlikely competitor—the telephone.

It seems a number of companies are rolling out Internet-access services that work over both wired and wireless phones. These "narrowband" connections use a fraction of frequencies to deliver a tiny trickle of data compared to their broadband counterparts. Users, though, can customize and access useful data just by dialing a toll-free number. For example, recent start-up Tellme Networks provides its users with headlines, sports scores, traffic information, weather reports, and horoscopes. While hardly competition for a colorful Web page, the information is delivered in a pleasant digital voice you can access easily, even as you drive to your next appointment. Besides receiving free customized information, Tellme subscribers can also get movie listings and restaurant reviews—and then be connected directly to the theaters or restaurants. Users navigate the system simply by speaking commands into the phone instead of having to use cumbersome Touch-Tones.

Since narrowband connections are priced low and available almost everywhere, they could become one of the world's most popular pathways to the Internet. This is particularly important in countries like Japan, where traditional phone lines do not exist as we know them in the United States. The country is so densely populated that it would cost too much to string wire lines today. Therefore, wireless phones may be the most efficient way for many Japanese to surf the Net.

International Data Corporation, an Internet research firm, projects that by 2004, some 600 million people will be hooked up to the Net via PCs. However, the corporation also forecasts that 1.4 billion people will connect through cell phones and another 1.4 billion will get on via wired phones. Such estimates are driving an explosion of new investments in narrowband from Internet heavyweights such as Oracle, IBM, and Amazon.com. It's clear that the global battle for control of information promises to be intense throughout the 21st century. Who knows, maybe an old standby from Alexander Graham Bell will become the hot new Web tool.

Sources: Andy Reinhardt, "The Good Old Telephone Becomes a Hot New Web Tool," *Business Week*, April 24, 2000; Irene M. Kunii, "Japan's Cutting Edge," *Business Week*, May 22, 2000; and Nikki Swartz, "Say Hello to Voice Portals," *Wireless Review*, February 1, 2001.

---

ance options. Internet appliances are designed to connect people to the Internet and to e-mail.[21] They include set-top boxes and gaming devices (such as Sega Dreamcast and Sony PlayStation 2) that provide Web-surfing capabilities on standard TVs and stand-alone devices such as Netpliance's i-opener.

The biggest move away from PCs, however, is in the direction of wireless handhelds like the Palm, smart-phones, and two-way paging devices. Samsung even offers a watch-phone for wrist-top computing, and GM offers in-dash computers for cars. The point is that people are taking the Internet with them, tapping in from time to time to gather information and transact business. This will necessarily change the format in which information is delivered. Because wireless devices are by necessity small, and Web pages have been designed for display on big, high-resolution monitors, it won't work to display Web pages in the same format. Information must be delivered in small bits, using brief lines of text and tiny icons and images. Since mobile users are almost always in a hurry, they will not tolerate irrelevant content.[22] Read the Reaching Beyond Our Borders box for a discussion of "narrowband" technology, which holds promise around the world.

Computer Networks

Perhaps the most dynamic change in business technology in recent years is the move away from mainframe computers that serve as the center of information processing and toward network systems that allow many users to access information at the same time. In an older system, the mainframe performed all the tasks and sent the results to a "dumb" terminal that could not perform those tasks itself. In a **network computing system** (also called **client/server computing**), the tasks, such as searching sales records, are handled by personal computers called clients. The information needed to complete the tasks is stored in huge databases controlled by the central computer (the server). Networks connect people to people and people to data. The major benefits of networks are the following:

> *Saving time and money.* SynOptics Communications found that electronic delivery of mail and files increased the speed of project development by 25 percent.
>
> *Providing easy links across functional boundaries.* With networks, it's easy to find someone who can offer insightful solutions to a problem. The most common questions on computer bulletin boards begin, "Does anyone know . . . ?" Usually someone does.
>
> *Allowing employees to see complete information.* In traditional organizations, information is summarized so many times that it often loses its meaning. For example, a sales representative's two-page summary may be cut to a paragraph in the district manager's report and then to a few numbers on a chart in the regional manager's report. Networks, on the other hand, catch raw information.

Here's how networks helped software giant Lotus Development. Instead of waiting for the information gained from 4 million annual phone calls to be summarized by technical support people, Lotus Development now sends the information straight into a database, where it's available on demand. Rather than accept someone else's idea of what information is needed, any Lotus development employee can access the data and search according to his or her needs. The result is that many more employees than before have direct access to market information and can act accordingly.

Networks have their drawbacks as well. Maintaining a fleet of finicky desktop PCs can be expensive. Studies show that the cost of maintaining one corporate Windows desktop computer can run up to $10,000 a year.[23] The cost of the computer itself is just the down payment. Computing costs go up with productivity ➤ **P.23** ◄ losses as you upgrade and troubleshoot equipment and train employees to use it. By the time you've recouped your costs, it's time for another upgrade. A large part of PC support costs comes from adding software that causes conflicts or disables other software on the system. Doing this upgrading to two or three PCs in a small home office is annoying; doing it to dozens or hundreds of PCs in a corporation is daunting. Using networks requires so many organizational changes and incurs such high

network computing system (client/server computing)
Computer systems that allow personal computers (clients) to obtain needed information from huge databases in a central computer (the server).

For a flat monthly fee, companies such as Everdream can solve computing problems remotely. Hardware, software, and troubleshooting experts are available 24 hours a day, 365 days a year. What are the benefits of outsourcing such information technology services?

support and upgrade costs that some companies that tried networking PCs are now looking at other options.[24]

One option is a new hybrid of mainframe and network computing. In this model, applications and data reside on a server, which handles all of the processing needs for all the client machines on the networks. The client machines look similar to the PCs that most people use but lack the processing power to handle applications on their own. Called *thin-client networks,* these new networks may resemble the old ill-tempered dumb terminals of the 1980s, but the execution is much better. Users can still use the Windows applications that they had been using. In a thin-client network, software changes and upgrades need to be made only on the server, so the cost of ownership can be reduced by 20 percent.

Other options to maintaining the server onsite are to contract with a remote service provider and to lease specific software applications. When you lease software from an applications service provider (ASP), the provider maintains and upgrades the software on its servers.[25] You connect to the ASP's servers via the Internet. You are then using the most current applications without the hassles of upgrading software yourself.[26] A new company called Everdream takes it a step further: Its single-fee service includes a powerful PC, unlimited Internet access, daily data backup, e-mail, popular business software, training, and around-the-clock support that includes remote management. If you have a software or hardware question, you don't have to call a long series of phone numbers until you find someone who can help. All you need is one phone number; Everdream staff members are always there, and they won't hang up until your problem is solved.[27]

When Gloria Kellerhal changed her executive search firm to a client/server network and turned the entire systems management over to a remote service provider, she said, "That's it, I'm out of the race. I'm going to get the latest technology, do e-commerce and e-mail and join the 21st century; but I'm not going to chase the rabbit around the dog track anymore."[28] The greatest benefit of thin-client computing or ASP is that it frees up more time for your business since you'll spend less time tinkering with technological tools.

CRITICAL THINKING

What are the implications for world peace and world trade given the ability firms and government organizations now have to communicate with one another across borders? Could the cooperation needed among telecommunications firms worldwide lead to increased cooperation among other organizations on issues such as world health care and worldwide exchanges of technical information?

SOFTWARE

Computer software programs provide the instructions that enable you to tell the computer what to do. Although many people looking to buy a computer think first of the equipment, it is important to find the right software before finding the right hardware. The type of software you want dictates the kind of equipment you need.

Some software programs are easier to use than others. Some are more sophisticated and can perform more functions than others. A businessperson must decide what functions he or she wants the computer system to perform and then choose the appropriate software. That choice will help determine what brand of computer to buy, how much power it should have, and what other peripherals it needs.

shareware
Software that is copyrighted but distributed to potential customers free of charge.

public domain software (freeware)
Software that is free for the taking.

While most software is distributed commercially through suppliers like retail stores or online etailers, there is some software, called **shareware,** that is copyrighted but distributed to potential customers free of charge. The users are asked to send a specified fee to the developer if the program meets their needs and they decide to use it. The shareware concept has become very popular and has dramatically reduced the price of software. **Public domain software (freeware)** is software that is free for the taking. The quality of shareware and freeware varies greatly. To help you have an idea of the quality of such programs, find a website that rates shareware and freeware programs. For example, SoftSeek.com lists the programs downloaded most often, editors' picks, and links to downloadable programs. (See the Making Ethical Decisions box for another factor to consider in choosing software.)

Businesspeople most frequently use software for (1) writing (word processors), (2) manipulating numbers (spreadsheets), (3) filing and retrieving data (databases), (4) presenting information visually (graphics), (5) communicating (e-mail and instant messaging), and (6) accounting. Today's software can perform many functions in one kind of program known as *integrated software* or a *software suite.* Another class of software program, called *groupware,* has emerged for use on networks. Figure 17.2 describes these types of software. The *Business Week* box identifies new types of software that help businesses conduct operations online.

There's the right tool for every job. Bigger isn't always better. The first step in choosing the right information technology tool is to identify what it is you want to accomplish and then go from there. For example, there is no need to invest in a screaming, state-of-the-art computer if you only plan to use it for simple word processing.

Word processing programs	With word processors, standardized letters can be personalized quickly, documents can be updated by changing only the outdated text and leaving the rest intact, and contract forms can be revised to meet the stipulations of specific customers. The most popular word processing programs include Corel WordPerfect, Microsoft Word, and Lotus WordPro.
Desktop publishing software (DTP)	DTP combines word processing with graphics capabilities that can produce designs that once could be done only by powerful page-layout design programs. Popular DTP programs include Microsoft Publisher, Adobe PageMaker Plus, and Corel Print Office.
Spreadsheet programs	A spreadsheet program is simply the electronic equivalent of an accountant's worksheet plus such features as mathematical function libraries, statistical data analysis, and charts. Using the computer's speedy calculations, managers have their questions answered almost as fast as they can ask them. Some of the most popular spreadsheet programs are Lotus 1-2-3, Quattro Pro, and Excel.
Database programs	A database program allows users to work with information that is normally kept in lists: names and addresses, schedules, inventories, and so forth. Using database programs, you can create reports that contain exactly the information you want in the form you want it to appear in. Leading database programs include Q&A, Access, Approach, Paradox, PFS: Professional File, PC-File, R base, and FileMaker Pro for Apple computers.
Personal information managers (PIMs)	PIMs or contact managers are specialized database programs that allow users to track communication with their business contacts. Such programs keep track of everything—every person, every phone call, every e-mail message, every appointment. Popular PIMs include Goldmine, Lotus Organizer, ACT, and ECCO Pro.
Graphics and presentation programs	Computer graphics programs can use data from spreadsheets to visually summarize information by drawing bar graphs, pie charts, line charts, and more. Inserting sound clips, video clips, clip art, and animation can turn a dull presentation into an enlightening one. Some popular graphics programs are Illustrator and Freehand for Macintosh computers, Microsoft PowerPoint, Harvard Graphics, Lotus Freelance Graphics, Active Presenter, and Corel Draw.
Communications programs	Communications software enables a computer to exchange files with other computers, retrieve information from databases, and send and receive electronic mail. Such programs include Microsoft Outlook, ProComm Plus, Eudora, and Telik.
Message center software	Message center software is more powerful than traditional communications packages. This new generation of programs has teamed up with fax/voice modems to provide an efficient way of making certain that phone calls, e-mail, and faxes are received, sorted, and delivered on time, no matter where you are. Such programs include Communicate, Message Center, and WinFax Pro.
Accounting and finance programs	Accounting software helps users record financial transactions and generate financial reports. Some programs include online banking features that allow users to pay bills through the computer. Others include "financial advisers" that offer users advice on a variety of financial issues. Popular accounting and finance programs include Peachtree Complete Accounting, Simply Accounting, Quicken, and QuickBooks Pro.
Integrated programs	Integrated software packages (also called suites) offer two or more applications in one package. This allows you to share information across applications easily. Such packages include word processing, database management, spreadsheet, graphics, and communications. Suites include Microsoft Office, Lotus SmartSuite, and Corel WordPerfect Suite.
Groupware	Groupware is software that allows people to work collaboratively and share ideas. It runs on a network and allows people in different areas to work on the same project at the same time. Groupware programs include Lotus Notes, Frontier's Intranet Genie, MetaInfo Sendmail, and Radnet Web Share.

FIGURE 17.2

**TYPES OF POPULAR
COMPUTER SOFTWARE**

FROM THE PAGES OF **BusinessWeek** *www.saleslobby.com*

Getting Down to E-Business

As businesses move their operations online, a new breed of software has emerged. New types of e-business software include:

- *Content management*—helps businesses organize and manage websites.

- *E-commerce*—allows companies to manage catalogs, collect payments, and track deliveries.

- *Electronic marketing*—maps customers' interests and predicts when and what they might buy.

- *Online customer support*—responds to Web-based questions or e-mail questions about billing, delivery, and products.

- *Purchasing*—automates purchasing systems and coordinates suppliers.

- *E-marketplace*—builds online marketplaces and connects buyers with sellers.

Source: Spencer E. Ante, "The Second Coming of Software," *Business Week*, June 19, 2000, pp. 88–90; David Shook, "Software: Hard to Overlook," *Business Week*, October 26, 2000; and Jarad Wilk, "Customized Software for Smaller Outfits," *Newsday*, January 7, 2001.

PROGRESS ASSESSMENT

- What are the four characteristics of information that make it useful?
- How do computer networks change the way employees gather information?
- Can you list and describe the major types of computer software used in business?

EFFECTS OF INFORMATION TECHNOLOGY ON MANAGEMENT

The increase of information technology has already affected management ➤ **P.206** ◄ and will continue to do so. Three major issues arising out of the growing reliance on information technology are: human resource changes, security threats, and privacy concerns.

Human Resource Issues

By now, you may have little doubt that computers are increasingly capable of providing us with the information and knowledge we need to do our daily tasks. The less creative the tasks, the more likely they will be managed by computers. For example, many telemarketing workers today have their work structured by computer-driven scripts. That process can apply to the work lives of customer service representatives, stockbrokers, and even managers. Technology makes the work process more efficient as it replaces many bureaucratic functions. We talked in Chapter 8 about tall versus flat organization structures. Computers often eliminate middle management functions and thus flatten organization structures.

One of the major challenges technology creates for human resource managers is the need to recruit employees who know how to use the new technology or train those who already work in the company. Often they hire consultants instead of internal staff to address these concerns. Outsourcing ➤ **P.254** ◄ technical training allows companies to concentrate on their core businesses. Even techno-savvy companies outsource technology training. Computer companies such as 3Com, Cisco, and Microsoft often hire a technology training company called Information Management Systems to train employees to use their own systems.[29]

Perhaps the most revolutionary effect of computers and the increased use of the Internet and intranets is that of telecommuting ➤ **P.22** ◄. Mobile employees using computers linked to the company's network can transmit their work to the office, and back, from anywhere as easily as (and sometimes more easily than) they can walk into the boss's office.

Naturally, such work involves less travel time and fewer costs, and often increases productivity. Telecommuting helps companies save money by allowing them to retain valuable employees during long pregnancy leaves or to tempt experienced employees out of retirement. Companies can also enjoy savings in commercial property costs, since having fewer employees in the office means a company can get by with smaller, and therefore less expensive, offices than before. Telecommuting enables men and women to stay home with small children. It has also been a tremendous boon for disabled workers.[30]

Employees who can work after hours on their home computers rather than at the office report less stress and improved morale. Studies show that telecommuting is most successful among people who are self-starters, who don't have home distractions, and whose work doesn't require face-to-face interaction with co-workers.

Even as telecommuting has grown in popularity, however, some telecommuters report that a consistent diet of long-distance work gives them a dislocated feeling of being left out of the office loop. Some feel a loss of the increased energy people can get through social interaction.[31] In addition to the isolation issue is the intrusion that work brings into what is normally a personal setting. Often people working from home don't know when to turn the work off. Some companies are pulling away from viewing telecommuting as an either–or proposition: either at home or at the office. Such companies are using telecommuting as a part-time alternative. In fact, industry now defines telecommuting as working at home a minimum of two days a week.

Electronic communication can never replace human communication for creating enthusiasm and esprit de corps. Efficiency and productivity can become so important to a firm that people are treated like robots. In the long run, such treatment results in less efficiency and productivity. Computers are a tool, not a total replacement for managers or workers, and creativity is still a human trait. Computers should aid creativity by giving people more freedom and more time. Often they do, but unfortunately many Americans take the results of their productivity gains not in leisure (as do the Europeans), but in increased consumption, making them have to work even harder to pay for it all. Information technology allows people to work at home, on vacation, and in the car at any time of the day. Now U.S. citizens work longer hours than people in any other nation on earth.[32]

Figure 17.3 illustrates how information technology changes the way managers and workers interact. For additional information about telecommuting and home-based workers, review Chapters 6 and 11.

The search for qualified information technology specialists has taken the old complaint, "You can't find good help anymore," to a new level. Companies across the country are competing to attract the most talented employees. Have you considered a career in information technology services?

FIGURE 17.3

**WHEN INFORMATION
TECHNOLOGY ALTERS THE
WORKPLACE**

MANAGERS MUST	WORKERS MUST
• Instill commitment in subordinates rather than rule by command and control. • Become coaches, training workers in necessary job skills, making sure they have resources to accomplish goals, and explaining links between a job and what happens elsewhere in the company. • Give greater authority to workers over scheduling, priority setting, and even compensation. • Use new information technologies to measure workers' performance, possibly based on customer satisfaction or the accomplishment of specific goals.	• Become initiators, able to act without management direction. • Become financially literate so they can understand the business implications of what they do and changes they suggest. • Learn group interaction skills, including how to resolve disputes within their work group and how to work with other functions across the company. • Develop new math, technical, and analytical skills to use newly available information on their jobs.

Security Issues

One current problem with computers that is likely to persist in the future is that they are susceptible to hackers. In 1994, officials were unable to find the hackers who broke into Pentagon computers through the Internet and stole, altered, and erased numerous records. Ironically, one of the Pentagon systems to which the hackers gained access was that of computer security research. In 2000, hackers tried to blackmail an e-tailer, saying that if the company didn't pay a ransom, they would sell the credit card numbers they had retrieved from its website.[33] Cybercrimes cost businesses $266 million in 1999.[34]

Computer security is more complicated today than ever before. When information was processed in a mainframe environment, the single data center was easier to control since there was limited access to it. Today, however, computers are accessible not only in all areas within the company but also in all areas of other companies with which the firm does business. Many companies have turned to outsource companies to monitor their security needs.[35] "Security is a process, not a product" is the mantra of Counterpane, a computer security company. Software products are created by humans and are therefore flawed. It takes skilled knowledge about how to use them to keep hackers at bay. Oddly enough, the most skilled security consultants are former hackers. Members of what was once known as a "hackers think tank" formed a company called AtStake that advises the world's largest banks and hospitals about how to keep their data safe.[36]

Another security issue involves the spread of computer viruses over the Internet. A **virus** is a piece of programming code inserted into other programming to cause some unexpected and, for the victim, usually undesirable event. Viruses are spread by downloading infected programming over the Internet or by sharing an infected diskette. Often the source of the file you downloaded is unaware of the virus. The virus lies dormant until circumstances cause its code to be executed by the computer. Some viruses are playful ("Kilroy was here!"), but some can be quite harmful, erasing data or causing your hard disk to crash. There are software programs, such as Norton's AntiVirus, that "inoculate" your computer so that it doesn't catch a known

virus
A piece of programming code inserted into other programming to cause some unexpected and, for the victim, usually undesirable event.

Security. It's one of our most basic needs and yet the more we use information technology, the more we seem to put the security of our data and privacy at risk. What can you do to secure your data and your privacy while online?

virus. But because new viruses are being developed constantly, antivirus programs may have only limited success. Therefore, you should keep your antivirus protection program up-to-date and, more important, practice "safe computing" by not downloading files from unknown sources and by using your antivirus program to scan diskettes before transferring files from them.[37]

Existing laws do not address the problems of today's direct, real-time communication. As more and more people merge onto the information superhighway, the number of legal issues will likely increase. Already, copyright and pornography laws are crashing into the virtual world. Other legal questions—such as those involving intellectual property and contract disputes, online sexual and racial harassment, and the use of electronic communication to promote crooked sales schemes—are being raised as millions of people log on to the Internet.[38] Read the Legal Briefcase box for more examples of cybercrime.

Privacy Issues

The increase of technology creates major concerns about privacy. For example, e-mail is no more private than a postcard. You don't need to be the target of a criminal investigation to have your e-mail snooped. More than one-fourth of U.S. companies scan employee e-mail regularly and *legally*. Just as they can log and listen to your telephone conversations, they can track your e-mail, looking for trade secrets, non-work-related traffic, harassing messages, and conflicts of interest. Also, most e-mail travels over the Internet in unencrypted plain text. Any hacker with a desire to read your thoughts can trap and read your messages. Some e-mail systems, such as Lotus Notes, can encrypt messages so you can keep corporate messages private. If you use browser-based e-mail, you can obtain a certificate that has an encryption key from a company such as VeriSign; the cost is about $10 a year. Of course, users who want to decrypt your mail need to get an unlocking key.[39]

The Internet presents increasing threats to your privacy, as more and more personal information is stored in computers and people are able to access that data, legally or illegally. The Internet allows Web surfers to access all sorts of information about you. For example, some websites allow people to search for vehicle ownership from a license number or to find individuals'

Point and Click, Then Stick 'Em Up

The phrase "point and click, then stick 'em up" may not replace the old favorites "Freeze" or "Spread 'em" on TV crime shows, but cybercrime is becoming a common threat in the wired world of the 21st century. According to FBI crime statistics, computer crime losses total an estimated $10 billion a year.

Cybercriminals do everything from stealing intellectual property and committing fraud to spreading computer viruses. At times, Internet attacks have shaken electronic commerce worldwide. For example, "denial-of-service" attacks on February 2, 2000, shut down such popular websites as Yahoo!, Amazon.com, and eBay for hours. In the assault, attackers meticulously obtained remote control of many computers around the world. They then used the computers to bombard the targeted websites, flooding them with so much data that legitimate users were temporarily denied access or service. The victim sites lost hundreds of millions of dollars in business.

Companies are acutely aware that computer hackers know the vulnerabilities of the information superhighway. The problems promise to get worse as broadband connections increase and Web access changes from the intermittent dial-up service connection to being always on. The longer the connection, the more time hackers have to work on breaking in. The coming age of information appliances could also cause the situation to worsen. According to computer analysts, techno-savvy homes will contain Web-browsing televisions, smart refrigerators, and Web telephones that download software from the Net that could be abused by cyberattackers.

Computer networks provide ready access points for anyone from disgruntled employees to spies, thieves, sociopaths, and even bored teenagers (like the 15-year-old alleged to have made the denial-of-service attacks). Once hackers penetrate a corporate network, they can pilfer intellectual property, destroy or tamper with company data, sabotage operations, even subvert a specific deal or cripple someone's career. According to Paul Field, a reformed computer hacker who now works as a security consultant, "Any business on the Internet is a target as far as I'm concerned."

For its part, the government has committed itself to combating cybercrime and promised quick retaliation and prosecution of cybercriminals. But government alone cannot ensure Internet security. That's why companies spent $4.4 billion in 1999 on Internet security software that includes such protections as firewalls, intrusion-detection programs, digital certificates, and authentication and authorization software. By 2004, such expenditures could exceed $8.5 billion. Internet security could be the next supergrowth business in the technology revolution.

Source: Ira Sager, Steve Hamm, Neil Gross, John Carey, and Robert D. Hof, "Cyber Crime," *Business Week*, February 21, 2000, pp. 37–42; and Kevin Johnson and M. J. Zuckerman, "Teen Arrested in Attacks on E-commerce," *USA Today*, April 19, 2000, p. 1A.

real estate property records. One key question in the debate over protecting our privacy is "Isn't this personal information already public anyway?" Civil libertarians have long fought to keep certain kinds of information available to the public. If access to such data is restricted on the Internet, wouldn't we have to reevaluate our policies on public records entirely? The privacy advocates don't think so. After all, the difference is that the Net makes obtaining personal information too easy. Would your neighbors or friends even consider going to the appropriate local agency and sorting through public documents for hours to find your driving records or to see your divorce settlement? Probably not. But they might dig into your background if all it takes is a few clicks of a button.

Average PC users are concerned that websites have gotten downright nosy. In fact, many Web servers track users' movements online. Web surfers seem willing to swap personal details for free access to online information. This personal information is shared with others without your permission (regardless of the promises made in the websites' privacy policy statements). Websites often send **cookies** to your computer that stay on your hard drive. These little tidbits often simply contain your name and a password that the website recognizes the next time you visit the site so that you don't have to reenter the same information every time you visit.[40] Other cookies track your movements around the Web and then blend that information with a database so that a company can tailor the ads you receive accordingly.[41] Do you mind someone watching over your shoulder while you're on the Web? Tim Berners-Lee, the researcher who invented the World Wide Web, is working on a way to prevent you from receiving cookies without your permission. His Platform for Privacy Preferences, or P3, would allow a website to automatically send information on its privacy policies. You would be able to set up your Web browser to communicate only with those websites that meet certain criteria. You need to decide how much information about yourself you are willing to give away. Remember, we are living in an information economy, and information is a commodity—that is, an economic good with a measurable value.[42]

cookies
Pieces of information, such as registration data or user preferences, sent by a website over the Internet to a Web browser that the browser software is expected to save and send back to the server whenever the user returns to that website.

Stability Issues

While technology can provide significant increases in productivity and efficiency, instability in technology also has a significant impact on business. In fact, some industry experts estimate that computer glitches account for a remarkable $100 billion in lost productivity each year.[43] In 1999, candy maker Hershey discovered the Halloween trick was on it when the company couldn't get its treats to the stores on time. Failure of its new $115 million computer system disrupted shipment, and retailers were forced to order from other companies. Consequently, Hershey suffered a 12 percent decrease in sales that quarter. Also in 1999, hundreds of flights across the United States were delayed by a glitch at a Memphis, Tennessee, air traffic control center. And in Maryland, victims of crime were kept waiting an agonizing two to four months for money collected on their behalf; the delay in payments was attributed to computer malfunctions.[44] The list of computer glitches that have caused delays, outages, garbled data, and general snafus could go on and on.

What's to blame? Experts say it is a combination of computer error; human error; malfunctioning software; and overly complex marriage of software, hardware, and networking equipment. Some systems are launched too quickly to be bug-proof, and some executives are too naive to challenge computer specialists. Industry consultant Howard Rubin says, "This stuff is becoming more critical to big business, yet some of it is built like Lego sets and Tinker toys. It's not built for rigorous engineering, and people aren't properly trained to use it. As things get more complex, we'll be prone to more errors."[45]

TECHNOLOGY AND YOU

If you are beginning to think that being computer illiterate may be occupational suicide, you are getting the point. Mike Maternaghan, a business development manager for British Telecom remarked, "It's tempting to say that if you can't use a computer in a couple of years, it will be like not being able to read."[46] Workers in every industry come in contact with computers to some degree. Even fast-food workers read orders on computer screens. The U.S. Commerce Department estimated that, by 2006, half of all American workers will be employed in information technology positions or within industries that use information technology, products, and services intensively.[47]

The Commerce Department also warned that the United States is facing an increasing shortage of information technology workers. Such a shortage could have

FIGURE 17.4

FASTEST-GROWING OCCUPATIONS

This figure shows the projected increase from 1996 to 2006. Notice that three of the five fastest-growing occupations are in information technology fields.

Database administrators, computer-support specialists, and all other computer scientists	118%
Computer engineers	109
Systems analysts	103
Personal and home care aides	85
Physical- and corrective-therapy assistants	79

Source: Bureau of Labor Statistics.

"severe consequences," the department said, for American competitiveness, economic growth, and job creation. The shortage is increasing quickly. In 2000, there was a shortage of almost 850,000 skilled information technology (IT) workers.[48] The increase in demand for skilled IT workers is driving up pay scales. The average annual salary for a chief information officer ranges between $100,000 and $250,000 depending on the location. In fact, a Wall Street CIO with more than four years' experience can command a half-million-dollar salary—and that doesn't include perks such as stock options that can add millions more.[49] Figure 17.4 lists the fastest-growing occupations, according to the U.S. Bureau of Labor Statistics.

If you are still among those considered computer illiterate, do not feel alone. Researchers have found that 55 percent of Americans have some degree of computerphobia (fear of computers). Amazingly, half of all white-collar workers say they are afraid of trying new technologies. Gender, age, and income level don't appear to be linked to computerphobia. The key variable is exposure—that's why Nintendo-era kids take to computers so easily. Computerphobes do not do as well in school as their mouse-clicking classmates. In the workplace, they may get passed up for promotions or lose their jobs. On a psychological level, they often feel inadequate and outdated—sort of like outcasts in a technological, digitized world. Here's the good news: computerphobia is curable, and computer training (the best medicine) is readily available. You may want to start out with low-tech learning aids such as videos and computer books and then gradually move up to training classes or CD-ROMs.

As information technology eliminates old jobs while creating new ones, it is up to you to learn and maintain the skills you need to be certain you aren't left behind.[50]

PROGRESS ASSESSMENT

- How has information technology changed the way people work?
- What management issues have been affected by the growth of information technology?
- What career areas are growing as information technology expands?

SUMMARY

1. Outline the changing role of business technology.

1. Business technology is continuously changing names and changing roles.
   - *What have been the various names and roles of business technology since 1970?*
   In the 1970s, business technology was called data processing (DP) and its role was to *support* existing business. In the 1980s, its name became information systems (IS) and its role changed to *doing* business. In the 1990s, business technology became information technology (IT) and its role is now to *change* business.

• *How does information technology change business?*
Information technology has minimized the importance of time and place to business. Business that is independent of time and location can deliver products and services whenever and wherever it is convenient for the customer. See Figure 17.1 for examples of how information technology changes business.
• *What is knowledge technology?*
Knowledge technology adds a layer of intelligence to filter appropriate information and deliver it when it is needed.

2. To become knowledge-based, businesses must know how to share information and design systems for creating new knowledge.
• *What information technology is available to help business manage information?*
The heart of information technology involves the Internet, intranets, and extranets. The Internet is a massive network of thousands of smaller networks open to everyone with a computer and a modem. An intranet is a companywide network protected from unauthorized entry by outsiders. An extranet is a semiprivate network that allows more than one company to access the same information.

2. Compare the scope of the Internet, intranets, and extranets as tools in managing information.

3. Information technology multiplies the mountains of information available to businesspeople.
• *How can you deal with information overload?*
The most important step in dealing with information overload is to identify your four or five key goals. Eliminate information that will not help you meet your key goals.
• *What makes information useful?*
The usefulness of management information depends on four characteristics: quality, completeness, timeliness, and relevance.

3. List the steps in managing information, and identify the characteristics of useful information.

4. Computer hardware changes rapidly.
• *What was the most dynamic change in computer hardware in the last decade?*
Perhaps the most dynamic change was the move away from mainframe computers that serve as the center of information processing toward network systems that allow many users to access information at the same time.
• *What are the major benefits of networks?*
Networks' major benefits are (1) saving time and money, (2) providing easy links across functional boundaries, and (3) allowing employees to see complete information.

4. Review the hardware most frequently used in business, and outline the benefits of the move toward computer networks.

5. Computer software provides the instructions that enable you to tell the computer what to do.
• *What types of software programs are used by managers most frequently?*
Managers most often use word processing, electronic spreadsheet, database, graphics, e-mail and instant messaging, and accounting programs. Another class of software program, called groupware, allows people to work collaboratively and share ideas.

5. Classify the computer software most frequently used in business.

6. Information technology has a tremendous effect on the way we do business.
• *What effect has information technology had on business management?*
Computers eliminate some middle management functions and thus flatten organization structures. Computers also allow employees to work from their own homes. On the negative side, computers sometimes allow information to fall into the wrong hands. Managers must find ways to prevent

6. Evaluate the human resource, security, privacy and stability issues in management that are affected by information technology.

stealing by hackers. Concern for privacy is another issue affected by the vast store of information available on the Internet. Finding the balance between freedom to access private information and individuals' right to privacy will require continued debate.

7. Identify the careers that are gaining or losing workers due to the growth of information technology.

7. Information technology eliminates old jobs while creating new ones.
   - *Which careers are gaining workers because of the growth of information technology?*
   Database administrators, computer engineers, and systems analysts are in demand. See Figure 17.5 for other employment changes caused by the growth of information technology.

KEY TERMS

broadband
  technology   526
cookies   541
data processing
  (DP)   522
information
  systems (IS)   522
information
  technology (IT)   522

Internet 2   526
intranet   525
knowledge
  management   528
knowledge
  technology (KT)   523
network computing
  system (client/server
  computing)   532

public domain
  software
  (freeware)   534
push technology   528
shareware   534
virtual private
  network (VPN)   526
virtualization   523
virus   538

DEVELOPING WORKPLACE SKILLS

1. Imagine that you have $3,000 to buy a computer system or to upgrade a computer you already have. Research the latest in hardware and software in computer magazines and on websites such as www.zdnet.com. Then go to a computer store or to online computer sites such as Dell, Gateway, and Micron to find the best value. Make a list of what you would buy, and then write a summary explaining the reasons for your choices.

2. Interview someone who bought a computer system to use in his or her business. Ask why that person bought that specific computer and how it is used. Ask about any problems that occurred during the purchase process or in installing and using the system. What would the buyer do differently next time? What software does he or she find especially useful?

3. If you have worked with computers, you've probably experienced times when the hard drive crashed or the software wouldn't perform as it should have. Describe one computer glitch you've experienced and what you did to resolve it. Analyze and discuss the consequences of the interruption (e.g., decreased productivity, increased stress). If you haven't had a problem with a personal computer, talk with a friend or classmate who has.

4. Choose a topic that interests you and then, on the Internet, use two search engines to find information about the topic. (If you are unfamiliar with search engines, you can learn about them in the Getting Ready for Prime Time skills section at the beginning of the book.) If the initial result of your search is a list of thousands of sites, narrow your search using the tips offered by the search engine. Did both search engines find the same websites? If not, how were the sites different? Which engine found the most appropriate information?

5. Discuss how technology has changed your relationship with specific businesses or organizations such as your bank, your school, and your favorite places to shop. Has it strengthened or weakened your relationship? On a personal level, how has technology affected your relationship with your family, friends, and community? Take a sheet of paper and write down how technology has helped build your business and personal relationships on one side. On the other side of the paper, list how technology has weakened the relationships. What can you and others do to use technology more effectively to reduce any negative impact?

TAKING IT TO THE NET

Purpose

To critically evaluate information found on websites.

Exercise

Unlike most print resources, such as magazines and journals, that go through a filtering process (e.g., editing, peer review), information on the Web is mostly unfiltered. The Web has a lot to offer, but not all sources are equally valuable or reliable. Since almost anyone can publish on the Web, accepting information from the Web can be like accepting advice from strangers. It's best to look at all websites with critical eyes.

Let's look at two websites that discuss possible causes of cancer:
- A Star Compendium of Important Tobacco Facts
  (www.starscientific.com/main_pages/factsheet.htm)
- Power Lines and Cancer: Nothing to Fear
  (www.quackwatch.com/01QuackeryRelatedTopics/emf.html)

Write a one-paragraph evaluation of each site using the following criteria:

1. *Accuracy.* How reliable and free from error is the information? Are there editors and fact checkers?

2. *Authority.* What is the authority or expertise of the individual or group that created this site? How knowledgeable is the individual or group on the subject matter of the site? Is the site sponsored or co-sponsored by an individual or group that has created other websites? Is contact information for the author or producer included in the document?

3. *Objectivity.* Is the information presented with a minimum of bias? To what extent is the information trying to sway the opinion of the audience?

4. *Currency.* Is the content of the work up-to-date? When was the Web item produced? When was the website last revised? How up-to-date are the links? How reliable are the links—that is, are there blind links or references to sites that have moved?

5. *Coverage.* Are the topics included explored in depth? What is the overall value of the content? What does it contribute to the literature in its field? Given the ease of self-publishing on the Web, this is perhaps even more important in reviewing Web resources than in reviewing print resources. Is the arrangement appropriate for the topic, and does it facilitate use? Does the site include a search engine? If so, can the user define search criteria?

TAKING IT TO THE NET

Purpose

To examine how information technology changes the way we do business.

Exercise

2   Let's see how one financial institution, Bank of America, uses information technology to help small businesses simplify their business processes. Go to the site www.bankofamerica.com and click on the Business Services—Business Center button.

Bank of America says that the Business Center is "your company Intranet, support for your HR department, purchasing, accounting, marketing and more." Click on the Business Center tour button. After viewing the slide show, explain how the Business Center helps companies operate more efficiently and effectively.

PRACTICING MANAGEMENT DECISIONS

CASE

THE SUPER BOWL OF NETWORKS

Couch potatoes may think of the kickoff of the football season as the time to relax and settle in until Super Bowl Sunday, but for the NFL's information technology's networking groups it's the start of frantic work marathon that won't stop until the championship rings are engraved. Imagine keeping 31 teams connected to the NFL's New York headquarters not only during game time but also at off-site summer training camps, at the annual owners' meeting, and during draft announcements. And, of course, during the event of the year, on Super Bowl Sunday, last-minute venue changes and different networking configurations present ample opportunities to fumble.

The networking team must create quick-turn networks that are used for a limited amount of time and then quickly dismantled. In just one month in 1996, the NFL wired more than 3,000 national and international media people, installed 20 miles of telephone cable, set up 800 phone lines and 600 cell phone lines, and created a 140-node network in New Orleans. To make sure that no one drops the ball, the NFL has teamed up with Sprint to create a best-practices playbook for creating quick-turn networks. Having a game plan is definitely worth the effort since the NFL has to do this on a regular basis, according to Craig Johnson, a research analyst at CurrentAnaylsis Inc.

Every year since its creation in 1993, the Carolina Panthers team has built a network at the team's training camp at Wofford College in Spartanburg, South Carolina, connecting it to the team's headquarters in Charlotte. The network designers use encryption to ensure security. Coaches and team managers in the field can use the network to reach key databases at headquarters to access information such as player statistics or salary figures. Even though the networking team has a system for the physical setup and breakdown of the network, it must still go through planning exercises each year because of constant changes in software and networking hardware. That means the network's performance must be reevaluated every year.

The most important lesson the NFL/Sprint team learned was to be prepared. Even the best plans can change unexpectedly. For example, just five days before the NFL's highly publicized annual draft announcements, the location was moved from Detroit to Philadelphia. The networking team put a local telecommunications provider in the new locale on alert for establishing a connection in time for the broadcast. You can't plan for everything, so you have to be prepared to move quickly. It's probably safe to say that the venue for the next Super Bowl won't change. But even if it did, the NFL/Sprint networking team will make certain that couch potatoes all over the world aren't denied.

Decision Questions

1. Most businesses don't normally need to create networks quickly, but occasionally it is necessary. Give some examples of situations in which such quick-turn networks might be used.
2. Of course, the NFL doesn't allow general Internet access to its complete network, but you can check out the NFL's website (http://www.nfl.com) to get an idea of the kinds of statistics available. What additional kinds of information do you think the NFL manages? As the general manager of an NFL team, how could you use the NFL network in negotiating your players' contracts for the coming year?
3. As the NFL expands its coverage globally, will its quick turn networks be of value in locations such as London, Tokyo, and Moscow?

VIDEO CASE

METAMOR TECHNOLOGIES — TRANSFORMING THE WAY WE DO BUSINESS

In the good old days (about 10 years ago), if a business wanted each of its employees to have a copy of the company's human resource manual, it would print copies and distribute them. You can imagine the production and distribution costs if the company had thousands of employees around the world. By the time the employees received their copies, some of the information could be obsolete. If so, pages with changes would have to be printed, distributed, and inserted in the old manual by each employee.

Today companies can store such manuals on their intranets, where they can be updated easily and be available to every employee instantaneously—all without a single sheet of paper. Remember, an intranet is companywide network, closed to public access, that uses Internet-type technology. Using the same type of Web browser interface on the intranet that employees use at home on their own computers makes training much easier and less costly.

Companies such as Metamor, featured in the video, help businesses make the transition from the old to the new ways of doing business. Offering static information (that is, information that doesn't change often) on the intranet is the most basic use of the technology. Metamor views intranet applications in a hierarchy with the applications that require the highest investment offering the greatest potential returns. Such applications include: (1) static information (e.g. manuals, newsletters, job postings, press releases); (2) simple applications (e.g. phone list databases, e-mail); (3) sophisticated applications (e.g. information management systems that track time spent on specific tasks and the progress of projects that can be accessed from anywhere in the world); and (4) enterprise collaboration (e.g. threaded discussion groups, intranet teleconferencing).

Metamor helps companies make the transition from PC-based workstations to thin-client systems. As you read in the chapter, PC-based systems require that software upgrades and other changes be made to each individual computer. This maintenance can cost many times more than the original cost of the hardware. With a thin-client system, the "smarts" are place on the server rather than the individual PCs. That way upgrades only need to be done once—to the server. This drops the support costs dramatically. More importantly, intranets reduce the time needed to look for information so that employees have more time to *use* the information.

Discussion Questions

1. Brian Farrar, President of Metamor Technologies, claims in the video that companies transforming their computer technology to intranets recoup the costs of the systems in the first year. How do intranets help companies save money?
2. What are the four levels of intranet applications Metamor describes? Which offers the greatest return on the investment? Why?
3. Imagine that you and a team of classmates are assigned a group project. Several members of the team live off-campus and traveling back and forth to campus is inconvenient. What types of applications described in the video would help you complete your project without having to meet in person regularly? Describe how you would use the applications.

CHAPTER 18

Understanding Financial Information and Accounting

LEARNING GOALS

AFTER YOU HAVE READ AND STUDIED THIS CHAPTER, YOU SHOULD BE ABLE TO

1 Understand the importance of financial information and accounting.

2 Define and explain the different areas of the accounting profession.

3 Distinguish between accounting and bookkeeping, and list the steps in the accounting cycle.

4 Explain the differences between the major financial statements.

5 Describe the role of depreciation, LIFO, and FIFO in reporting financial information.

6 Detail how computers are used to record and apply accounting information in business.

7 Explain the importance of ratio analysis in reporting financial information.

Getting to Know Scott Little of Hard Rock Cafe

In the mid-1990s, the theme-dining business seemed like a path lined with gold. With regularity, celebrity stargazers, enthusiastic press from around the globe, and hungry customers gathered at the openings of theme restaurants like Planet Hollywood and Motown Cafe. Unfortunately, the situation changed. In the late 1990s, Planet Hollywood filed for bankruptcy protection and Motown Cafe closed units across the country. Consumer boredom and a saturated market were blamed.

The changing "eatertainment" market raised eyebrows at the granddaddy of theme restaurants, the Hard Rock Cafe (HRC). HRC knew its market position was shaky due to increased competition and shifting consumer attitudes. The company also felt growing financial pressures, and speculated that a change in financial management might be needed. HRC had operated with a traditional, competent accounting department that made sure the company paid its bills, had money left at the end of the day, and could state how much it was earning. The problem was that HRC lacked the ability to analyze its financial information fully and use it to improve operations. To address these concerns, the company recruited Scott Little from the ranks of Walt Disney.

Little believed that HRC had a tremendous undervalued asset—a premium global brand. He dedicated himself to protecting and expanding that asset. He knew, however, that a company can have brand loyalty but that, without revenue, it doesn't matter. He was astonished to find that HRC sold $180 million a year in merchandise (primarily its well known T-shirts) in addition to food, yet could not explain exactly how these individual items contributed to the firm's profit. Little immediately knew that HRC's accounting and financial management had to change. First, he piloted a food and beverage management system to track usage and item profitability. His system included information such as daily and seasonal buying patterns, profitability of one menu versus another, average weekly guest counts per cafe, and specific cost of sales and profit margins per item. He then shifted the responsibility of the firm's accountants. Instead of company accountants being responsible for profit-and-loss statements for a certain number of cafes, they now were responsible for one major financial category, such as cost of goods sold, for all the company's operations. The objective was to compile company-wide information for sound decision making.

Little also broke down the barriers at HRC that existed between the finance and accounting departments and operations, merchandising, and marketing. Today, financial information is shared directly with managers who can execute the recommendations at the restaurant level. Still, Little realizes the company has an ongoing challenge. Last year, 27 million people visited a Hard Rock Cafe at the company's 103 locations. Even so, competitors such as Rainforest Cafe, Dick Clark's Bandstand Cafe, and House of Blues promise to make the fight for eatertainment customers an interesting one.

Controlling costs, managing cash flows, understanding profit margins, and reporting finances accurately are keys to survival of any business, large or small. This chapter will introduce you to the accounting fundamentals and financial information that are critical to business success. The chapter also briefly explores the financial ratios that are essential in measuring business performance.

Sources: Larry Bleiberg, "Cafe Quest Has Retiree on a Roll," *Dallas Morning News*, March 15, 2000, p. 12G; Dan Healing, "Buyer Found for Hard Rock Cafe," *Edmonton Sun*, June 7, 2000, p. 43; and "Hard Rock Giving Away Beatles' Bus," *AP Online*, January 18, 2001.

THE IMPORTANCE OF FINANCIAL INFORMATION

Stories like that of Scott Little and the Hard Rock Café are repeated hundreds of times every day throughout the business community. Small and sometimes large businesses falter or even fail because they do not follow good financial procedures. Financial information is the heartbeat of competitive businesses. Accounting keeps the heartbeat stable.

Accounting is different from marketing, management, and human resource management in that most of us have limited understanding of accounting principles. As consumers, we have all had some experience with marketing. As workers or students, we have observed and come to understand most management concepts. But accounting? What is it? Is it difficult to learn? What do accountants do? Is the work interesting? Is this a career path you may wish to pursue?

You have to know something about accounting if you want to understand business. Learning some basic accounting terms is mandatory. You also have to understand the relationship of bookkeeping to accounting and how accounts are kept. It's almost impossible to run a business without being able to read, understand, and analyze accounting reports and financial statements.

Accounting reports and financial statements reveal as much about a business's health as pulse rate and blood pressure readings tell us about a person's health. The purpose of this chapter is to introduce you to the process of obtaining needed financial information using basic accounting principles. By the end of this chapter, you should have a good idea of what accounting is, how it works, and why it is important. You should also know some accounting terms and understand the purpose of accounting statements. It's important to understand how accounting statements are constructed but even more important to know what they mean to the business. A few hours invested in learning this material will pay off handsomely as you become more involved in business or investing, or simply in understanding what's going on in the world of business and finance.

accounting
The recording, classifying, summarizing, and interpreting of financial events and transactions to provide management and other interested parties the information they need to make good decisions.

WHAT IS ACCOUNTING?

FIGURE 18.1

THE ACCOUNTING SYSTEM

The inputs to an accounting system include sales documents and other documents. The data are recorded, classified, and summarized. They're then put into summary financial statements such as the income statement and balance sheet.

Financial information is primarily based on information generated from accounting. **Accounting** is the recording, classifying, summarizing, and interpreting of financial events and transactions to provide management and other interested parties the information they need to make good decisions. Financial transactions can include such specifics as buying and selling goods and services ➤ P.25 ◄, acquiring insurance, paying employees, and using supplies. Once the business's transactions have been recorded, they are usually classified into groups that have common characteristics. For example, all purchases are grouped together, as are all sales transactions. The set of methods used to record and summarize accounting data into reports is called an accounting system (see Figure 18.1).

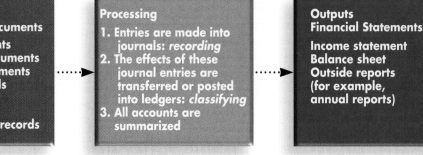

Inputs
Accounting Documents

Sales documents
Purchasing documents
Shipping documents
Payroll records
Bank records
Travel records
Entertainment records

Processing
1. Entries are made into journals: *recording*
2. The effects of these journal entries are transferred or posted into ledgers: *classifying*
3. All accounts are summarized

Outputs
Financial Statements

Income statement
Balance sheet
Outside reports
(for example, annual reports)

USERS	TYPE OF REPORT
Government taxing authorities (e.g., the Internal Revenue Service)	Tax returns
Government regulatory agencies	Required reports
People interested in the organization's income and financial position (e.g., owners, creditors, financial analysts, suppliers)	Financial statements found in annual reports (e.g., income statement, balance sheet, statement of cash flows)
Managers of the firm	Financial statements and various internally distributed financial reports

FIGURE 18.2

USERS OF ACCOUNTING INFORMATION AND THE REQUIRED REPORTS

Many types of organizations use accounting information to make business decisions. The reports needed vary according to the information each user requires. An accountant must prepare the appropriate forms.

One purpose of accounting is to help managers evaluate the financial condition and the operating performance of the firm so they may make well-informed decisions.[1] Another major purpose is to report financial information to people outside the firm such as owners, creditors, suppliers, employees, investors, and the government (for tax purposes). In basic terms, accounting is the measurement and reporting of financial information to various users (inside and outside the organization) regarding the economic activities of the firm (see Figure 18.2). Accounting work is divided into several major areas. Let's look at those areas next.

AREAS OF ACCOUNTING

Accounting has been called the language of business, which may make you think accounting is only for profit-seeking firms. Nothing could be further from the truth. It is also the language used to report financial information about nonprofit organizations such as churches, schools, hospitals, fraternities, and government agencies. The accounting profession is divided into four key working areas: managerial accounting, financial accounting, auditing, and tax accounting. All four areas present career opportunities for students who are willing to put forth the effort.

Managerial Accounting

Managerial accounting is used to provide information and analyses to managers within the organization to assist them in decision making. Managerial accounting is concerned with measuring and reporting costs of production, marketing ➤ **P.396** ◄, and other functions (cost accounting); preparing budgets (planning); checking whether or not units are staying within their budgets (controlling); and designing strategies to minimize taxes (tax accounting).

If you are a business major, it's almost certain you will be required to take a course in managerial accounting. You may even elect to pursue a career as a certified management accountant. A **certified management accountant** is a professional accountant who has met certain educational and experience requirements and been certified by the Institute of Certified Management Accountants. With growing emphasis on global competition,

managerial accounting
Accounting used to provide information and analyses to managers within the organization to assist them in decision making.

certified management accountant
A professional accountant who has met certain educational and experience requirements and been certified by the Institute of Certified Management Accountants.

At companies like J.G. Stickley's furniture plant, managerial accounting assists managers' decisions in terms of production, marketing, budgeting, even tax issues. Like most firms, Stickley is very conscious of keeping material costs at a minimum and production schedules on time. Does your college require a course in managerial accounting?

financial accounting
Accounting information and analyses prepared for people outside the organization.

annual report
A yearly statement of the financial condition and progress of an organization.

private accountants
Accountants who work for a single firm, government agency, or nonprofit organization.

public accountant
An accountant who provides his or her accounting services to individuals or businesses on a fee basis.

certified public accountant (CPA)
An accountant who passes a series of examinations established by the American Institute of Certified Public Accountants.

company rightsizing, and organizational cost cutting, managerial accounting may be one of the most important areas you study in your college career.

Financial Accounting

Financial accounting differs from managerial accounting because the information and analyses are for people outside the organization. This information goes to owners and prospective owners, creditors and lenders, employee unions, customers, suppliers, government agencies, and the general public. These external users are interested in the organization's profits, its ability to pay its bills, and other important financial information. Much of the information derived from financial accounting is contained in the company's **annual report,** a yearly statement of the financial condition and progress of an organization.

It's critical for firms to keep accurate financial information. Because of this, many organizations employ **private accountants,** who work for a single firm, government agency, or nonprofit organization. However, not all firms or nonprofit organizations want or need a full-time accountant. Therefore, thousands of accounting firms in the United States will provide the accounting services an organization needs. An accountant who provides his or her services to individuals or businesses on a fee basis is called a **public accountant.** Public accountants can provide business assistance in many ways. They may design an accounting system for a firm, help select the correct computer and software to run the system, and analyze the financial strength of an organization right from the start. Many big accounting firms now earn a sizable percentage of their revenues from consulting.[2] Arthur Andersen & Co. split off its large client-consulting business into a separate division, Accenture. The company expects its consulting division to bring in 50 percent of the $4.6 billion in revenues it generates per year.[3] The U.S. Securities and Exchange Commission regulates this fast-growing segment of the industry.[4]

It's vital for the accounting profession to assure users of financial information that the information is accurate.[5] The independent Financial Accounting Standards Board (FASB) defines the set of *generally accepted accounting principles (GAAP)* that accountants must follow. If financial reports are prepared "in accordance with GAAP," users know the information is reported according to standards agreed on by accounting professionals. The *Business Week* box highlights the importance of GAAP in reporting financial information. It's also important that the accounting profession assure firms that the accountants they employ are as professional as doctors or lawyers. Therefore, an accountant who passes a series of examinations established by the American Institute of Certified Public Accountants (AICPA) and meets the state's requirement for education and experience earns recognition as a **certified public accountant (CPA).** CPAs find careers as private accountants or public accountants, and are often sought out to fill other financial positions.[6]

FROM THE PAGES OF **BusinessWeek** www.fasb.org

Don't Mess with the GAAP

Glancing quickly at the title of this box might cause you to think we misspelled the name of the popular retail store, the GAP. Well, rest assured, we checked our spelling. GAAP refers to *generally accepted accounting principles* established by the Financial Accounting Standards Board (FASB). The FASB is an independent board formally charged with setting specific guidelines and rules in the accounting profession. If financial information is reported according to GAAP, users of the information know the firm's accounting statements are likely accurate. So while we agree it's likely few competitors in the clothing business like "messing" with the GAP, it's even more important companies not "mess" with or even "tweak" the GAAP. For those that do, such transgressions can cause big market problems.

Consider Tyco International, a widely diversified company with $22.5 billion in annual sales and over 140,000 employees. The company experienced rapid growth and was on an acquisitions spree. In just three years, Tyco spent more than $30 billion adding companies to its four basic product areas. Still, whispers in financial circles raised doubts about the company's ac-

counting practices. Finally, questions were formally raised concerning Tyco's accounting strategy of using "pumped up" earnings growth to fuel its acquisitions. While the company was not formally accused of violating GAAP, just the hint that Tyco was applying "creative" accounting brought the company stock tumbling down more than 50 percent. Similar questions concerning applications of GAAP depressed the stock prices of Waste Management and Cendant Corporation, two of the leading firms in their respective industries.

The lesson to be learned: Whether you are an entrepreneur in a start-up business, the CEO of a multinational conglomerate, or a student in an introductory accounting class, learn the GAAP and apply them as they are supposed to be applied. The cost of failing to do so could range from a grade of F in your accounting class to a loss of billions of dollars in market value.

Source: Gene Marcial, "Tyco: The Road Back," *Business Week*, April 10, 2000; Amy Barrett, Stephanie Anderson Forest, and Tom Lowry, "Henry Silverman's Long Road Back," *Business Week*, February 28, 2000, pp. 126–36.

Auditing

The job of reviewing and evaluating the records used to prepare a company's financial statements is referred to as **auditing.** Accountants within the organization often perform internal audits to ensure that proper accounting procedures and financial reporting are being carried out within the company. Public accountants also conduct independent audits of accounting and related records. Financial auditors today not only examine the financial health of an organization but also look into operational efficiencies and effectiveness. An **independent audit** is an evaluation and unbiased opinion about the accuracy of a company's financial statements.[7] A firm's annual report often includes a written opinion from an auditor.[8] An accountant who has a bachelor's degree and two years of experience in internal auditing, and who has passed an exam administered by the Institute of Internal Auditors, can earn professional standing as a **certified internal auditor.** Internal financial controls are very important for firms of any size.

Tax Accounting

Taxes are the price we pay for roads, parks, schools, police protection, and other functions provided by government. Federal, state, and local governments require submission of tax returns that must be filed at specific times and in a precise format. A **tax accountant** is trained in tax law and is responsible for preparing tax returns or developing tax strategies. Since governments often

auditing
The job of reviewing and evaluating the records used to prepare a company's financial statements.

independent audit
An evaluation and unbiased opinion about the accuracy of a company's financial statements.

certified internal auditor
An accountant who has a bachelor's degree and two years of experience in internal auditing, and who has passed an exam administered by the Institute of Internal Auditors.

tax accountant
An accountant trained in tax law and responsible for preparing tax returns or developing tax strategies.

change tax policies according to specific needs or objectives, the job of the tax accountant is certainly challenging. Also, as the burden of taxes grows in the economy, the role of the tax accountant becomes increasingly important to the organization or entrepreneur.

As you can see, managerial and financial accounting, auditing, and tax accounting each requires specific training and skill. Yet some people are confused about the difference between an accountant and a bookkeeper. We'll clarify that difference right after the Progress Assessment.

PROGRESS ASSESSMENT

- Can you explain the difference between managerial and financial accounting?
- Could you define accounting to a friend so that he or she would clearly understand what's involved?
- What's the difference between a private accountant and a public accountant?

ACCOUNTING VERSUS BOOKKEEPING

bookkeeping
The recording of business transactions.

Bookkeeping involves the recording of business transactions. Bookkeeping is an important part of accounting, but accounting goes far beyond the mere recording of financial information. Accountants classify and summarize financial data provided by bookkeepers. They interpret the data and report them to management. They also suggest strategies for improving the financial condition and progress of the firm. Accountants are especially important in financial analysis and income tax preparation.

If you were a bookkeeper, the first task you would perform is to divide all of the firm's transactions into meaningful categories such as sales documents, purchasing receipts, and shipping documents. The bookkeeper's challenge is to keep the information organized and manageable. Therefore, bookkeepers must begin by recording financial data from the original transaction documents (sales slips and so forth) into record books called journals. A **journal** is the record book or computer program where accounting data are first entered. It's interesting that the word *journal* comes from the French word *jour,* which means "day." A journal is where the day's transactions are kept.

journal
The book where accounting data are first entered.

It is quite possible when recording financial transactions that you could make a mistake. For example, you could easily write or enter $10.98 as $10.89. For that reason, bookkeepers record all their transactions in two places. They can then check one list of transactions against the other to make sure that they add up to the same amount. If they don't equal the same amount, the bookkeeper knows that he or she made a mistake. The concept of writing every transaction in two places is called **double-entry bookkeeping.** In double-entry bookkeeping, two entries in the journal and the ledgers (discussed next) are required for each company transaction.

double-entry bookkeeping
The concept of writing every transaction in two places.

To see how this system works, let's suppose a business wanted to determine how much it paid for office supplies in the first quarter of the year. Without a specific bookkeeping tool, that would be difficult even with accurate accounting journals. Therefore, bookkeepers make use of a set of books with pages labeled office supplies, cash, and so on. The entries in the journal are transferred, or posted, to these pages, making information about various accounts available quickly and easily. A **ledger,** then, is a specialized accounting book in which information from accounting journals is recorded into specific categories and posted so that managers can find all the information about a single account in one place. Today, computerized accounting programs post information from journals into ledgers daily or instanta-

ledger
A specialized accounting book in which information from accounting journals is accumulated into specific categories and posted so that managers can find all the information about one account in the same place.

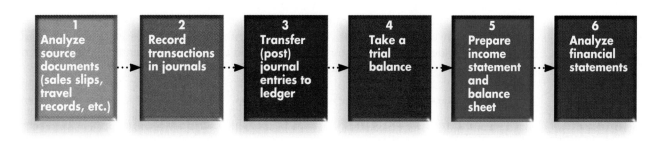

FIGURE **18.3**

STEPS IN THE
ACCOUNTING CYCLE

neously. This way the financial information is readily available whenever the organization needs it.

The Six-Step Accounting Cycle

The **accounting cycle** is a six-step procedure that results in the preparation and analysis of the two major financial statements: the balance sheet and the income statement (see Figure 18.3). The accounting cycle generally involves the work of both the bookkeeper and the accountant. The first three steps are continual: (1) analyzing and categorizing documents, (2) putting the information into journals, and (3) posting that information into ledgers. The fourth step involves preparing a trial balance. A **trial balance** is a summary of all the financial data in the account ledgers to show whether the figures are correct and balanced. If the information in the account ledgers is not accurate, it must be corrected before the firm's income statement and balance sheet are prepared. The fifth step, then, is to prepare an income statement and balance sheet. The sixth step is for the accountant to analyze the financial statements and evaluate the financial condition of the firm. After the Progress Assessment, we will look at the balance sheet and income statement, and the important information each provides.

accounting cycle
A six-step procedure that results in the preparation and analysis of the two major financial statements: the balance sheet and the income statement.

trial balance
A summary of all the data in the account ledgers to show whether the figures are correct and balanced.

• Can you explain the difference between accounting and bookkeeping?

• What's the difference between an accounting journal and a ledger?

• Why does a bookkeeper prepare a trial balance?

PROGRESS ASSESSMENT

UNDERSTANDING KEY FINANCIAL STATEMENTS

A **financial statement** is a summary of all the transactions that have occurred over a particular period. Financial statements indicate a firm's financial health and stability. That's why stockholders (the owners of the firm), banks and bondholders (people and institutions that lend money to the firm), unions, employees, and the Internal Revenue Service are interested in a firm's financial statements. Two key financial statements are

financial statement
A summary of all the transactions that have occurred over a particular period.

1. The *balance sheet*, which reports the firm's financial condition on a specific date.

2. The *income statement*, which reports revenues, cost of goods, expenses, and profits (or losses) for a specific period of time, showing the results of operations during that period.

The difference between the two statements can be summarized this way: The balance sheet is a snapshot, while the income statement is a motion picture. The former tells what the company owns and owes on a certain day; the latter, what it sells its products for and what its selling costs are over a period of time. To fully understand important financial information, you must be able to read and understand both the balance sheet and the income statement. We'll explain each statement in more detail next.

The Balance Sheet

balance sheet
The financial statement that reports a firm's financial condition at a specific time.

A **balance sheet** is the financial statement that reports a firm's financial condition at a specific time. It's composed of three major accounts: assets, liabilities, and owners' equity. It's called a *balance sheet* because it shows a balance between two figures: the company's assets on the one hand, and its liabilities plus owners' equity on the other. (These terms will be defined fully in the next sections.)

The following analogy will help explain the idea behind the balance sheet. Let's say that you want to know what your financial condition is at a given time. Maybe you want to buy a new house or car and therefore need to calculate the resources you have available. One of the best measuring sticks is your balance sheet. First, you would add up everything you own—cash, property, money owed you, and so forth (assets). Subtract from that the money you owe others—credit card debt, IOUs, current car loan, and so forth (liabilities)—and you have a figure that tells you that, as of today, you are worth so much (equity). This is fundamentally what companies are doing in preparing a balance sheet. In that preparation, they must follow clearly established accounting procedures. The fundamental accounting equation sets those procedures.

The Fundamental Accounting Equation

Imagine that you don't owe anybody money. That is, you don't have any liabilities. In this case, the assets you have (cash and so forth) are equal to what you *own* (equity). However, if you borrow some money from a friend, you have incurred a liability. The assets that you hold are now equal to what you *owe* plus what you *own*. Translated into business terms,

$$\text{Assets (\$50,000)} = \text{Liabilities (\$30,000)} + \text{Owners' equity (\$20,000)}$$

fundamental accounting equation
Assets = liabilities + owners' equity; this is the basis for the balance sheet.

This formula is called the **fundamental accounting equation** and is the basis for the balance sheet. As Figure 18.4 (a sample balance sheet for Fiber-rific, the hypothetical cereal company we introduced in Chapter 13) highlights, on the balance sheet you list assets in a separate column from liabilities and owners' (or stockholders') equity. The assets are equal to or are balanced with the liabilities and owners' (or stockholders') equity. It's that simple. The complicated part is determining what is included in the asset account and what is included in the liabilities and owners' equity accounts. It's critical that businesspeople understand the important financial information on the balance sheet. To do so, they must first understand the *accounts* of the balance sheet.

The Accounts of the Balance Sheet

assets
Economic resources owned by a firm.

Assets are economic resources owned by a firm. Assets include productive, tangible items (such as equipment, buildings, land, furniture, fixtures, and motor vehicles) that help generate income, as well as intangibles with value such as patents or copyrights.[9] Think, for example, of the value of brand names ➤ **P.400** ◄ such as Coca-Cola, McDonald's, and Intel.[10] Such intangibles as brand names can be among the firm's most valuable assets.[11] Assets are listed on the balance sheet according to their liquidity (see Figure 18.5). **Liquidity** refers to how fast an asset can be converted into cash. For example, land is difficult to turn into cash quickly because it takes much time and paperwork to sell land;

liquidity
How fast an asset can be converted into cash.

FIGURE 18.4

SAMPLE FIBERRIFIC
BALANCE SHEET

FIBERRIFIC
Balance Sheet
March 31, 2002

Assets

① Current assets

Cash	$ 15,000	
Accounts receivable	200,000	
Notes receivable	50,000	
Inventory	335,000	
Total current assets		$600,000

② Fixed assets

Land		$40,000	
Building and improvements	$200,000		
Less: Accumulated depreciation	−90,000		
		110,000	
Equipment and vehicles	$120,000		
Less: Accumulated depreciation	−80,000		
		40,000	
Furniture and fixtures	$26,000		
Less: Accumulated depreciation	−10,000		
		16,000	
Total fixed assets			206,000

③ Intangible assets

Goodwill	$20,000	
Total intangible assets		20,000
Total assets		826,000

Liabilities and Owners or Stockholders' Equity

Liabilities

④ Current liabilities

Accounts payable	$40,000	
Notes payable (due Dec. 2002)	8,000	
Accrued taxes	150,000	
Accrued salaries	90,000	
Total current liabilities		$288,000

⑤ Long-term liabilities

Notes payable (due Mar. 2004)	$35,000	
Bonds payable (due Dec. 2014)	290,000	
Total long-term liabilities		325,000
Total liabilities		$613,000

⑥ Stockholders' equity

Common stock (1,000,000 shares)	$100,000	
Retained earnings	113,000	
Total stockholders' equity		213,000
Total liabilities & stockholders' equity		$826,000

① Current assets: Items that can be converted to cash within one year.

② Fixed assets: Items such as land, buildings, and equipment that are relatively permanent.

③ Intangible assets: Items of value such as patents and copyrights that don't have a physical form.

④ Current liabilities: Payments that are due in one year or less.

⑤ Long-term liabilities: Payments not due for one year or longer.

⑥ Stockholders' equity: The value of what stockholders own in a firm (also called owner's equity.

FIGURE 18.5

CLASSIFICATIONS OF ASSETS

Assets are classified by how quickly they can be turned into cash (liquidity). The most liquid are called *current assets*. Those that are hard to sell quickly are called *fixed assets* or *property, plant, and equipment*. *Intangible assets* include patents and copyrights.

Current assets

Property, plant, and equipment

Copyright

Intangible assets

current assets
Items that can be converted into cash within one year.

fixed assets
Assets that are relatively permanent, such as land, buildings, and equipment.

intangible assets
Items of value such as patents and copyrights that have no real physical form.

liabilities
What the business owes to others.

thus, land is considered illiquid. In contrast, stock is considered highly liquid because it can be sold almost instantaneously. Assets are divided into three categories according to how quickly they can be turned into cash:

1. **Current assets** are items that can be converted into cash within one year.
2. **Fixed assets** such as land, buildings, and equipment are assets that are relatively permanent. (These assets are also referred to as property, plant, and equipment.)
3. **Intangible assets** include items of value such as patents and copyrights that have no real physical form.

Liabilities and Owners' Equity Accounts

Another important accounting term is liabilities. **Liabilities** are what the business owes to others. *Current liabilities* are payments due in one year or less; *long-term liabilities* are payments not due for one year or longer. The following are common liability accounts recorded on a balance sheet (see again Figure 18.4):

1. *Accounts payable*—money owed to others for merchandise or services purchased on credit but not yet paid. If you have a bill you haven't paid, you have an account payable.
2. *Notes payable*—short-term or long-term loans (e.g., from banks) that have a promise for future payment.
3. *Bonds payable*—money lent to the firm that must be paid back. If a firm sells someone a bond, it agrees to pay that person the money he or she lent the company plus interest. (We will discuss bonds in depth in Chapters 19 and 20.)

As shown earlier in the fundamental accounting equation, the value of things you own (assets) minus the amount of money you owe others (liabilities) is called *equity*. The value of what stockholders own in a firm (minus liabilities) is called *stockholders' equity* (or *shareholders' equity*). Because stockholders are the owners of a firm, stockholders' equity can also be called owners' equity or partnership equity.

You, Incorporated

How do you think You, Inc., stacks up financially? Let's take a little time and find out. You may be pleasantly surprised, or you may realize that you need to think hard about planning your financial future. Remember, your net worth is nothing more than the difference between what you own (assets) and what you owe (liabilities). Be honest, and do your best to give a fair evaluation of your private property's value.

ASSETS		LIABILITIES	
Cash	$_____	Installment loans and interest	$_____
Savings account	_____	Other loans and interest	_____
Checking account	_____	Credit card accounts	_____
Home	_____	Mortgage	_____
Stocks & bonds	_____	Taxes	_____
Automobile	_____	Other debts	_____
IRA or Keogh	_____		
Personal property	_____		
Other assets			
Total assets	$_____	Total liabilities	$_____

Determine your net worth:

Total assets	$_____
– Total liabilities –	_____
= Net worth	$_____

The formula for **owners' equity,** then, is assets minus liabilities. Differences can exist in the owners' equity account according to the type of organization, however. Businesses not incorporated identify the investment of the sole proprietor or partner(s) through a *capital account.* For such sole proprietors and partners, owners' equity means the value of everything owned by the business minus any liabilities of the owner(s) such as bank loans. For corporations, the owners' equity account records the owners' claims to funds they have invested in the firm (such as capital stock) plus earnings kept in the business and not paid out to stockholders (called retained earnings). Take a few moments to review Figure 18.4 and see what facts you can determine about Fiberrific from its balance sheet. Then take a few minutes and try to estimate your own personal net worth, following the directions in the Spotlight on Small Business box.

owners' equity
Assets minus liabilities.

PROGRESS ASSESSMENT

- What's the formula for the balance sheet? What do we call this formula?
- What does it mean to list various assets by liquidity?
- What goes into the account called liabilities?
- What's the formula for determining owners' equity?

The Income Statement

The financial statement that shows a firm's bottom line—that is, its profit after costs, expenses, and taxes—is the income statement (also called the profit and loss statement). The **income statement** summarizes all of the resources (called revenue) that have come into the firm from operating activities, money resources that were used up, expenses incurred in doing business, and what resources were left after all costs and expenses, including taxes, were paid. The resources left over are referred to as **net income or net loss** (see Figure 18.6). The income statement reports the results of operations over a particular period of time, usually a year, a quarter of a year, or a month. It's the financial statement that reveals whether the business is actually turning a profit. The formula used to prepare an income statement is as follows:

Revenue − Cost of goods sold = Gross margin (or gross profit)

Gross margin − Operating expenses = Net income before taxes

Net income before taxes − Taxes = Net income (or loss)

The income statement includes valuable financial information for stockholders, lenders, investors (or potential investors), and employees. Because of the importance of this financial report, let's take just a moment to look at the income statement and learn what each step means. Before we start, take a quick look at how the income statement is arranged according to generally accepted accounting principles (GAAP):

Revenue
− Cost of goods sold
_____

Gross margin (gross profit)
− Operating expenses
_____

Net income before taxes
− Taxes
_____

Net income or loss

Revenue

Revenue is the value of what is received for goods sold, services rendered, and other financial sources. Note that there is a difference between revenue and sales. Most revenue (money coming into the firm) comes from sales, but there are other sources of revenue, such as rents received, money paid to the firm for use of its patents, and interest earned. Be careful not to confuse the terms *revenue* and *sales,* or to use them as if they were synonymous. Also, a quick glance at the income statement shows that revenue is at the top of the statement and income is at the bottom: Net income is revenue minus sales returns, costs, expenses, and taxes. Net income can also be referred to as net earnings or net profit.

Cost of Goods Sold (Cost of Goods Manufactured)

The **cost of goods sold (or cost of goods manufactured)** is a measure of the cost of merchandise sold or cost of raw materials and supplies used for producing items for resale. It's simple logic to calculate how much a business earned by selling merchandise over the period evaluated, compared to how much it spent to buy the merchandise. The cost of goods sold includes the purchase price plus any freight charges paid to transport goods plus any costs associated with storing the goods. In other words, all the costs of buying and

income statement
The financial statement that shows a firm's profit after costs, expenses, and taxes; it summarizes all of the resources that have come into the firm (revenue), all the resources that have left the firm, and the resulting net income or loss.

net income or net loss
Revenue minus expenses.

revenue
The value of what is received for goods sold, services rendered, and other financial sources.

cost of goods sold (or cost of goods manufactured)
A measure of the cost of merchandise sold or cost of raw materials and supplies used for producing items for resale.

FIGURE 18.6

SAMPLE FIBERRIFIC INCOME STATEMENT

FIBERRIFIC
Income Statement
For the Year Ended December 31, 2002

Assets

① Revenues			
Cash		$ 15,000	
Gross sales		$720,000	
Less: Sales returns and allowances	$12,000		
Sales discounts	8,000	−20,000	
Net sales			$700,000
② Cost of goods sold			
Beginning inventory, Jan. 1		$200,000	
Merchandise purchases	$400,000		
Freight	40,000		
Net purchases		440,000	
Cost of goods available for sale	$640,000		
Less ending inventory, Dec. 31		−230,000	
Cost of goods sold			−410,000
③ Gross profit			$290,000
④ Operating expenses			
Selling expenses			
Salaries for salespeople	$90,000		
Advertising	18,000		
Supplies	2,000		
Total selling expenses		$110,000	
General expenses			
Office salaries	$67,000		
Depreciation	1,500		
Insurance	1,500		
Rent	28,000		
Light, heat, and power	12,000		
Miscellaneous	2,000		
		112,000	
Total operating expenses			222,000
Net income before taxes			$68,000
Less: Income tax expense			19,000
⑤ Net income after taxes			$49,000

① Revenue: Value of what's received from goods sold, services rendered, and other financial sources.

② Cost of goods sold: Cost of merchandise sold or cost of raw materials or parts used for producing items for resale.

③ Gross profit: How much the firm earned by buying or selling merchandise.

④ Operating expenses: Cost incurred in operating a business.

⑤ Net income after taxes: Profit or loss over a specific period after subtracting all costs and expenses including taxes.

keeping merchandise for sale are included in the cost of goods sold. It's critical that companies accurately report and manage this important income statement item. Remember in the chapter opening profile the problems Scott Little discovered concerning Hard Rock Café's handling of its cost of goods sold?

When you subtract the cost of goods sold from net sales, you get what is called gross margin or gross profit. **Gross margin (gross profit)** is how much a firm earned by buying (or making) and selling merchandise. In a service firm, there may be no cost of goods sold; therefore, net revenue could equal gross margin. In a manufacturing firm, however, it's necessary to estimate the cost of goods manufactured. In either case (selling goods or services), the gross margin doesn't tell you everything you need to know about the financial performance of the firm. The financial evaluation of an income statement also in-

gross margin (gross profit)
How much a firm earned by buying (or making) and selling merchandise.

cludes determining the *net* profit or loss a firm experienced. To get that, you must subtract the business's expenses.

Operating Expenses

expenses
Costs involved in operating a business, such as rent, utilities, and salaries.

To sell goods or services, a business has certain expenses. **Expenses** are the costs involved in operating a business. Obvious expenses include rent, salaries, supplies, utilities, insurance, and even depreciation of equipment. Expenses can generally be classified into two categories: selling and general expenses. Accountants are trained to help you record all applicable expenses and find other expenses you need to deduct.

After all expenses are deducted, the firm's net income before taxes is determined (see again Figure 18.6). After allocating for taxes, we get to what's called the *bottom line,* which is the net income (or perhaps net loss) the firm incurred from operations. It answers the question "How much did the business earn or lose in the reporting period?"

While you may not yet be familiar with the terms associated with the key financial statements, and may even think they are quite complex, you use accounting concepts all the time. For example, you know the importance of keeping track of costs and expenses when you prepare your own budget. If your expenses (e.g., rent and utilities) exceed your revenues (how much you earn), you are in deep trouble. If you need more money (revenue), you may need to sell some of the things you own to meet your expenses. The same is true in business. Companies need to keep track of how much money is earned and spent, how much cash they have on hand, and so on. The only difference is that companies tend to have more complex problems and more information to record than you as an individual do.

Finally, as growing numbers of firms involve themselves deeper in global markets, accurate financial reporting is equally important but even more difficult (see the Reaching Beyond Our Borders box).[12] Also, handling the flow and disbursement of cash is another problem that plagues both businesses and individuals. Keep these facts in mind as we explore accounting information a bit more in depth in the next section after the progress assessment.

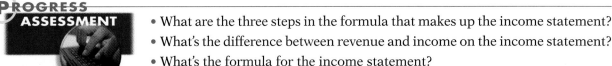

PROGRESS ASSESSMENT

- What are the three steps in the formula that makes up the income statement?
- What's the difference between revenue and income on the income statement?
- What's the formula for the income statement?

The Importance of Cash Flow Analysis

Understanding cash flow is an important part of financial reporting. If not properly managed, cash flow can cause a business much concern. Cash flow analysis is really rather simple to comprehend. Let's say you borrow $100 from a friend to buy a used bike and agree to pay him back at the end of the week. In turn, you sell the used bike for $150 to someone else, who also agrees to pay you in a week. Unfortunately, at the end of the week the person who bought the bike from you doesn't have the money and says that she will have to pay you next month. Meanwhile, your friend wants the $100 you agreed to pay him by the end of the week! What seemed like a great opportunity to make a $50 profit is a real cause for concern. Right now, you owe $100 and have no cash. What do you do when your friend shows up at the end of the week and demands to be paid? If you were a business, this might cause you to default on the loan and possibly go bankrupt, even though you had the potential for profits.

cash flow
The difference between cash coming in and cash going out of a business.

It's very possible that a business can increase sales and increase profit, and still suffer greatly from cash flow problems. **Cash flow** is simply the difference

Speaking the Universal Financial Language

The Asian financial crisis of the late 1990s reminded us that we live in a global economy. As the bad news from Asian markets grew more distressing, U.S. firms watched their stock prices edge downward due to concerns about Asian finances. Yet it was the once-mighty Japanese economy that felt the market gyrations most severely. Unfortunately, the repercussions from the crisis are not over. The Japanese government is forcing tougher accounting standards on its corporations, an act that promises to continue the economic "shock therapy" over the next several years. The government's actions are referred to in Japan as the "Accounting Big Bang." The results of the change, however, could prove disturbing for many of Japan's most established companies, including Mazda and Toyota Motors.

The purpose of the accounting changes is to provide a more precise picture of a Japanese firm's financial statements and position. Accountants in the United States and Europe have maintained that Japanese financial statements did not present a complete picture of the financial health of a Japanese firm. For example, Japanese companies that control smaller subsidiaries have often shifted laid-off employees and unwanted financial losses to the smaller firms. Such actions were not reported on the company financial statements. Practices like that will change with the new accounting rules. Japanese corporations will also have to disclose the true market value of their pension liabilities, and any pension shortfalls. Some financial analysts and accountants believe that unfunded pension liabilities in Japan could approximate $661 billion (that's right, billion).

While the accounting changes will create problems for many companies, they will not affect all Japanese firms. Twenty-four of Japan's largest companies (including Sony and Honda) already follow U.S. accounting standards and procedures. The International Accounting Standards Committee is working to achieve a global acceptance of international standards. Time will tell if this objective is achievable in the 21st century.

Sources: Brian B. Stanko "The Case for International Accounting Rules," *Business & Economic Review*, July–September 2000, pp. 21–25; John P. Mello Jr., "Accounting Standards: Relaxing Overseas Regs," *CFO*, May 2000, p. 22; Mike McNamee, "Can the SEC Make Foreign Companies Play by Its Rules?" *Business Week*, March 6, 2000, p. 46; and "EU to Move Over to International Accounting Standards by 2005?" *European Report*, February 14, 2001.

between cash coming in and cash going out of a business. Poor cash flow constitutes a major operating problem for many companies and is particularly difficult for small businesses.[13] Cash flow problems, however, are not exclusive to small businesses. Such problems can also occur in an emerging business or an established one like the Hard Rock Café. What often happens is that, in order to meet the demands of customers, the business buys more and more goods on credit (no cash is involved). Similarly, more and more goods are sold on credit (no cash is involved). This can go on until the firm uses up all the credit it has with the banks that lend it money. When the firm requests more money from the bank to pay a crucial bill, the bank refuses the loan because the credit limit has been reached. All other credit sources refuse funds as well. The company desperately needs financial resources to pay its bills, or else its creditors could force it into bankruptcy. Unfortunately, all too often, the company does go into bankruptcy simply because there was no cash available when it was most needed.

Cash flow analysis points out clearly that a businessperson's relationship with his or her banker is critical. Maintaining a working relationship with a bank is one possible solution to preventing cash flow problems that often develop. The value that accounting provides to the firm is also obvious in this area. Accountants tell the firm whether it needs cash and, if so, how much. They offer advice on how a company is managing its cash position.[14] Accounting further provides the key insights into how, when, and where finance

MAKING ETHICAL DECISIONS

Counting Cash before It's Collected

You are the only accountant employed by a small manufacturing firm. You are in charge of keeping the books for the company, which is not in good shape due to an economic downturn that shows no signs of lessening in the near future.

You know that your employer is going to ask the bank for an additional loan so that the company can continue to pay its bills. Unfortunately, the financial statements for the year will not show good results, and you know that the bank will not approve a loan increase based on those figures.

Your boss approaches you in early January before you have closed the books for the preceding year and suggests that perhaps the statements can be "improved" by treating the sales that were made at the beginning of January as if they were made in December. He also asks you to do a number of other things that will cover up the trail so that the auditors will not discover the padding of the year's sales.

You know that it is against the professional rules of the Financial Accounting Standards Board (FASB), and you argue with your boss. Your boss tells you that, if the company does not get the additional bank loan, there's a very good chance the business will close. That means you and everyone else in the firm will be out of a job. You believe your boss is probably right and you know that with the current economic downturn finding a job will be tough for you and almost impossible for others in the company. What are your alternatives? What are the likely consequences of each alternative? What will you do?

managers can get the money a firm needs. The statement of cash flows is a good barometer of measuring the cash position within a firm.

The Statement of Cash Flows

statement of cash flows
Financial statement that reports cash receipts and disbursement related to a firm's three major activities: operations, investment, and financing.

In 1988, the Financial Accounting Standards Board (FASB) required firms to replace the statement of changes in financial position with the statement of cash flows. The **statement of cash flows** reports cash receipts and disbursements related to the three major activities of a firm:

- *Operations*—cash transactions associated with running the business.
- *Investments*—cash used in or provided by the firm's investment activities.
- *Financing*—cash raised from the issuance of new debt or equity capital or cash used to pay business expenses, past debts, or company dividends.

Accountants analyze all of the cash changes that have occurred from operating, investing, and financing and determine the firm's net cash position. The cash flow statement also gives the firm some insight into how to handle cash better so that no cash flow problems occur in the future.

Figure 18.7 shows a statement of cash flows, again using the Fiberrific example. As you can see, the cash flow statement answers such questions as the following: How much cash came into the business from current operations? That is, how much cash came into the firm from buying and selling goods and services? Was cash used to buy stocks, bonds, or other investments? Were some investments sold that brought in cash? How much money came in from issuing stock? These and other financial transactions are analyzed to see their effect on the cash position of the firm. Consider these facts and then read the Making Ethical Decisions box to see how accountants can sometimes face some tough ethical challenges.

FIGURE 18.7

FIBERRIFIC STATEMENT OF CASH FLOWS

FIBERRIFIC
Statement of Cash Flows
For the Year Ended December 31, 2002

① Cash flows from operating activities

Cash received from customers	$150,000	
Cash paid to suppliers and employees	(90,000)	
Interest paid	(5,000)	
Income tax paid	(4,500)	
Interest and dividends received	1,500	
Net cash provided by operating activities		$52,000

② Cash flows from investing activities

Proceeds from sale of plant assets	$4,000	
Payments for purchase of equipment	(10,000)	
Net cash provided by investing activities		(6,000)

③ Cash flows from financing activities

Proceeds from issuance of short-term debt	$3,000	
Payment of long-term debt	(7,000)	
Payment of dividends	(15,000)	
Net cash inflow from financing activities		(19,000)
Net change in cash and equivalents		$27,000
Cash balance, December 31, 2002		(2,000)
Cash balance, December 31, 2002		$25,000

① Cash receipts from sales, commissions, fees, interest, and dividends. Cash payments for salaries, inventories, operating expenses, interest, and taxes.

② Includes cash flows that are generated through a company's purchase or sale of long-term operational assets, investments in other companies, and its lending activities.

③ Cash inflows and outflows associated with the company's own equity transactions or its borrowing activities.

APPLYING ACCOUNTING KNOWLEDGE

If accounting consisted of nothing more than the repetitive function of gathering and recording transactions and preparing financial statements, the major functions could be assigned to computers. In fact, most medium and large firms as well as growing numbers of small businesses have done just that. The Internet has even initiated a whole new way of managing a firm's finances: online accounting.[15] But the truth is that *how* you record and report financial data is also critically important.[16] Take a look at Figure 18.4 again. Note that Fiberrific lists accumulated depreciation on its property, plant, and equipment. What does accumulated depreciation mean, and how does it affect the company's financial position? Let's take a look.

Depreciation is the systematic write-off of the cost of a tangible asset over its estimated useful life. Have you ever heard the comment that a new car depreciates in market value as soon as you drive it off the dealer's lot? Well, the same holds true for equipment and other specific assets of the firm that are considered depreciable. Companies are permitted to recapture the cost of these assets over time using depreciation as a business operation expense. Subject to certain technical accounting rules, which are beyond the scope of this chapter, a firm may use one of several different techniques for calculating depreciation. Each technique could result in a different net income for the firm. Accountants are able to offer financial advice and recommend ways of legally handling questions regarding depreciation, insurance, inventory valuation, and other accounts that can clearly affect the firm's financial performance.

depreciation
The systematic write-off of the cost of a tangible asset over its estimated useful life.

Intense global competition makes the job of controlling costs paramount to business success. While the cost of holding inventory is expensive, companies such as Trek's Bike Factory must maintain adequate inventory because customers want products when they want them. How does inventory valuation affect the cost of goods sold?

The valuation of a firm's inventory presents another interesting accounting application. Inventories are a critical part of a company's financial statements and are important in determining a firm's cost of goods sold (or cost of goods manufactured). (Take a look again at Fiberrific's income statement in Figure 18.6.) When a firm sells merchandise from its inventory, it can calculate the cost of that item in different ways. In financial reporting, it doesn't matter when a particular item was actually placed in firm's inventory, but it does matter which method an accountant uses to record how much that item cost when it was sold. Sound a bit confusing? Look at the example below.

Let's say that a college bookstore's business is to buy textbooks for resale. It buys 100 copies of a particular textbook in July 2002 at a cost of $50 a copy. When classes begin in August, the bookstore sells 50 copies of the text to students for $60 each. The 50 copies not sold are placed in the bookstore's inventory. In late December the bookstore orders 50 additional copies of the same text to sell for the next term. Unfortunately, the price of the book to the bookstore has increased to $60 a copy due to inflation and other costs. The bookstore now has 100 copies of the same textbook from different purchase cycles in its inventory. Same book, but different costs to the bookstore. If the bookstore sells 50 copies of the book to students for a price of $70 in mid-January, what's the bookstore's cost of the book for accounting purposes? It depends.

first in, first out (FIFO)
Accounting method for calculating cost of inventory; it assumes that the first goods to come in are the first to go out.

last in, first out (LIFO)
Accounting method for calculating cost of inventory; it assumes that the last goods to come in are the first to go out.

If the bookstore's accountant uses a method called **first in, first out (FIFO),** the cost of goods sold (cost of 50 textbooks) recorded by the bookstore would be $50 each, because the textbook that was bought first cost $50. The bookstore's accountant, however, could have selected another method, called **last in, first out (LIFO).** Using LIFO, the bookstore's last purchase of the textbook cost $60 each. Can you see how the difference in accounting methods could affect the bookstore's bottom line? The books are the same and contain the same information. However, if the book sells for $70, FIFO would report $10 more of net income before taxes than LIFO would (see Figure 18.8).

What's important to understand is that generally accepted accounting principles (GAAP) can permit an accountant to use different methods of depreciating a firm's long-term assets and valuing a firm's inventory. That's why the American Institute of Certified Public Accountants (AICPA) insists that com-

	FIFO	LIFO
Revenue	$70	$70
Cost of goods sold	50	60
Income before taxes	20	10
Taxes of 40%	8	4
Net income	12	6

FIGURE 18.8

ACCOUNTING USING LIFO VERSUS FIFO INVENTORY VALUATION

panies provide readers of their financial statements complete information concerning their financial operations.

ACCOUNTANTS AND THE BUDGETING PROCESS

The budgeting process also relies on accuracy in financial statements. (We will discuss budgets in more depth in Chapter 19.) Put simply, a budget is a financial plan. To be a bit more specific, a **budget** sets forth management's expectations for revenues and, based on those expectations, allocates the use of specific resources throughout the firm. The key financial statements—the balance sheet, income statement, and statement of cash flows—form the basis for the budgeting process. Why is this the case? Because financial information from the firm's past is what's used as the basis to project future financial needs.

Today many companies, both large and small, use the budget process as an opportunity to plan and to improve the management of the business. Telecommunications giant MCI/Worldcom, for example, has designed its budgeting process as part of a larger organizational effort to improve forecasting and overall business planning. Other innovative companies use budgeting to determine the profitability of individual products, customers, and channels of distribution. Therefore, financial statements must be prepared according to legal and accepted accounting principles; this process cannot be compromised.[17]

budget
A financial plan that sets forth management's expectations for revenues and, based on those expectations, allocates the use of specific resources throughout the firm.

PROGRESS ASSESSMENT

- What is cash flow, and how can a small business protect against cash flow problems before they occur?
- What is the relevance of the statement of cash flows?
- What is the difference between LIFO and FIFO inventory valuation? How could the use of these methods change financial results?
- Why is the budgeting process important to a business?

THE IMPACT OF COMPUTER TECHNOLOGY ON ACCOUNTING

Financial information and transactions may be recorded by hand or by computer. Of course, today most companies have found that computers greatly simplify the task, enabling managers and other employees to get financial reports exactly when they want them. Also, as a business grows, the number of accounts a firm must keep and the reports that need to be generated expand in scope. You no doubt can recognize how computers can help in the accounting process. Even small-business owners have learned that accounting records can

A small business often lives or dies according to how effectively financial information is handled. Peachtree's complete accounting software prolongs the life of small businesses as well as offers peace of mind to small business owners. Peachtree is one of several companies that offer software packages that specifically meet small businesses needs.

be maintained and analyzed best by a computer. Many of the latest accounting packages address the specific needs of small businesses, which are often significantly different from the needs of a Fortune 500 company.

Using computers to record and analyze data and to print out financial reports allows managers to obtain up-to-the-minute financial information for the business.[18] It's now even possible, thanks to computers, to have continuous auditing, which helps managers prevent cash flow problems and other financial difficulties by allowing them to spot trouble earlier than ever before.[19] Today software programs allow even novices to do sophisticated financial analyses within days.

It's important to remember, though, that no computer yet has been programmed to make good financial decisions by itself. Granted, a computer is a wonderful tool for businesspeople to use. Yet business owners should understand exactly what computer system is best suited for their particular needs. That's one reason why we say that, before they get started in business, potential small-business owners should hire or consult with an accountant to identify the particular needs of their proposed firm.[20] Once the exact criteria are determined, it's necessary for a small business to develop a specific accounting system that works within the chosen predesigned package. Today's accounting packages offer ease of use, customization, and efficient Internet functioning.[21]

Computers can also help make accounting work less monotonous. Still, the work of an accountant requires training and very specific competencies.[22] It's interesting that beginning business students sometimes assume that opportunities in accounting are rather limited and narrow in scope. Nothing could be further from the truth. Accountants not only provide financial information to the firm; they assist in interpreting that information. One last bit of advice: Even if you know that accounting is not your career choice, you need to speak the language of accounting to succeed in business.

USING FINANCIAL RATIOS

By now, you know that accurate financial information forms the basis of the financial analysis performed by accountants and other financial specialists inside and outside the firm. Financial ratios are especially helpful to use in analyzing the actual performance of the company compared to its financial objectives and compared to other firms in its industry.[23] At first glance, ratio analysis may seem somewhat complicated, but most of you already use ratios quite often. For example, in basketball, the number of shots made from the foul line is expressed by a ratio: shots made to shots attempted. A player who shoots 85 percent from the foul line is considered an outstanding foul shooter, and suggestions are to not foul him or her in a close game.

Whether ratios measure an athlete's performance or the financial health of a business, they provide a good deal of valuable financial information. Financial ratios particularly provide key insights into how a firm compares to other firms in its industry in the important areas of liquidity (speed of changing assets into cash), debt (leverage), profitability, and business activity.[24] Understanding and interpreting business ratios is a key to sound financial analysis. Let's look briefly at four key types of ratios used to measure financial performance.

Liquidity Ratios

As explained earlier, the word *liquidity* refers to how fast an asset can be converted to cash. Liquidity ratios measure a company's ability to pay its short-term debts. These short-term debts, to be repaid within one year, are of particular importance to the firm's creditors who expect to be paid on time. Two key liquidity ratios are the current ratio and the acid-test ratio.

The *current ratio* is the ratio of a firm's current assets to its current liabilities. This information can be found on the firm's balance sheet. Look back at Figure 18.4, which details Fiberrific's balance sheet. Fiberrific has current assets of $600,000 and current liabilities of $288,000. The firm has a current ratio of 2.08, which means Fiberrific has $2.08 of current assets for every $1 of current liabilities:

$$\text{Current ratio} = \frac{\text{Current assets}}{\text{Current liabilities}} = \frac{\$600,000}{\$288,000} = 2.08$$

An obvious question to ask is "How well positioned financially is Fiberrific for the short term (less than one year)?" Usually a company with a current ratio of 2 or better is generally considered a safe risk for granting short-term credit. Such a firm appears to be performing in line with market expectations. However, before we jump to conclusions, we should compare Fiberrific's current ratio to that of competing firms in its industry. It's also important for the firm to compare its current ratio with its current ratio from the previous year to note any significant changes.

Another key liquidity ratio, called the *acid-test* or *quick ratio*, measures the cash, marketable securities (such as stocks and bonds), and receivables of a firm, compared to its current liabilities:

$$\text{Acid-test ratio} = \frac{\text{Cash} + \text{Marketable securities} + \text{Receivables}}{\text{Current liabilities}} = \frac{\$265,000}{\$288,000} = .92$$

Faucets, faucets, and more faucets. Home Depot stores stock over 36,000 items that cover over 130,000 square feet of floor space. Maintaining such an enormous inventory is no small task. That's why Home Depot depends heavily on financial ratios to make certain they are correctly managing their inventory compared to the competition.

This ratio is particularly important to firms with difficulty converting inventory into quick cash. It helps answer such questions as the following: What if sales drop off and we can't sell our inventory? Can we still pay our short-term debt? Though ratios vary among industries, an acid-test ratio of between 0.50 and 1.0 is usually considered satisfactory. However, going under 1.0 could be a hint of some cash flow problems. Generally, the higher the better. Fiberrific's acid-test ratio of .92 could raise concerns. That's important because an organization that cannot meet its short-term debt often has to go to a high-cost lender for financial assistance.

Leverage (Debt) Ratios

Leverage (debt) ratios measure the degree to which a firm relies on borrowed funds in its operations. A firm that takes on too much debt could experience problems repaying lenders or meeting promises made to stockholders. The *debt to owners' equity ratio* measures the degree to which the company is financed by borrowed funds that must be repaid. Again, we can use Figure 18.4 to measure Fiberrific's level of debt:

$$\text{Debt to owners' equity ratio} = \frac{\text{Total liabilities}}{\text{Owners' equity}} = \frac{\$613,000}{\$213,000} = 2.87\%$$

A ratio above 1 (i.e., above 100 percent) would show that a firm has more debt than equity. Fiberrific obviously has a rather high degree of debt. It's possible the firm could be perceived as quite risky to both lenders and investors. However, it's always important to compare a firm's ratios to those of other firms in the same industry because debt financing is more acceptable in some industries than in others. Comparisons with past ratios can also identify trends that may be occurring within the firm or industry.

Profitability (Performance) Ratios

Profitability (performance) ratios measure how effectively a firm is using its various resources to achieve profits. Management's performance is often accurately reflected in the firm's profitability ratios. Three of the more important ratios used are earnings per share, return on sales, and return on equity.

In 1997, a new Financial Accounting Standards Board rule went into effect that requires companies to report their quarterly earnings per share in two ways: basic and diluted. The *basic earnings per share (basic EPS) ratio* helps determine the amount of profit earned by a company for each share of outstanding common stock. The *diluted earnings per share (diluted EPS) ratio* measures the amount of profit earned by a company for each share of outstanding common stock, but also takes into consideration stock options, warrants, preferred stock, and convertible debt securities, which can be converted into common stock. For simplicity's sake, we will compute only the basic earnings per share.

As you might have guessed, this is a very important ratio for corporations ➤ **P.140** ◄, since earnings help stimulate growth in the company and pay for stockholders' dividends. Continued earnings growth

Companies like Northwest Airlines have a tremendous investment in capital equipment (like the airplanes pictured here). That's why Northwest Airlines has a bevy of accountants who assist the company in keeping track of important issues like depreciation and inventory valuation.

is well received by both investors and lenders. The basic EPS ratio is calculated for Fiberrific as follows:

$$\text{Basic earnings per share} = \frac{\text{Net income after taxes}}{\begin{array}{c}\text{Number of}\\\text{common shares}\\\text{outstanding}\end{array}} = \frac{\$49,000}{1,000,000} = \$.049 \text{ per share}$$

Another reliable indicator of performance is obtained by using a ratio that measures the return on sales. Firms use this ratio to see if they are doing as well as the companies they compete against in generating income from the sales they achieve. *Return on sales* is calculated by comparing a company's net income to its total sales: Fiberrific's return on sales is 7%, a figure that must be measured against competing firms in its industry to judge its performance.

$$\text{Return on sales} = \frac{\text{Net income}}{\text{Net sales}} = \frac{\$49,000}{\$700,000} = 7\% \text{ return on sales}$$

Risk is a market variable that concerns investors. The higher the risk involved in an industry, the higher the return investors expect on their investment. Therefore, the level of risk involved in an industry and the return on investment of competing firms is important in comparing the firm's performance. *Return on equity* measures how much was earned for each dollar invested by owners. It is calculated by comparing a company's net income to its total owners' equity. Fiberrific's return on equity looks reasonably sound:

$$\text{Return on equity} = \frac{\text{Net income after tax}}{\text{Total owners' equity}} = \frac{\$49,000}{\$213,000} = 23\% \text{ return on equity}$$

It's important to remember that profits help companies like Fiberrific grow. Therefore, these and other profitability ratios are considered vital measurements of company growth and management performance.

Activity Ratios

Converting the firm's resources to profits is a key function of management. Activity ratios measure the effectiveness of a firm's management in using the assets that are available.

The *inventory turnover ratio* measures the speed of inventory moving through the firm and its conversion into sales. Inventory sitting by idly in a business costs money. Think of the fixed cost of storing inventory in a warehouse as opposed to the variable revenue that's available when companies sell (turn over) inventory. The more efficiently a firm manages its inventory, the higher the return. The inventory turnover ratio for Fiberrific is measured as follows:

$$\text{Inventory turnover ratio} = \frac{\text{Cost of goods sold}}{\text{Average inventory}} = \frac{\$410,000}{\$215,000} = 1.9 \text{ times}$$

A lower-than-average inventory turnover ratio in an industry often indicates obsolete merchandise on hand or poor buying practices. A higher than average ratio may signal lost sales because of inadequate stock. An acceptable turnover ratio is generally determined industry by industry. Fiberrific's inventory turnover of 1.9 times would need to be measured with its main competitors to estimate maximum efficiency in handling its inventory.

Managers need to be aware of proper inventory control and expected inventory turnover to ensure proper performance. Have you ever worked as a food server in a restaurant? How many times did your employer expect you to turn over a table (keep changing customers at the table) in an evening? The more times a table turns, the higher the return to the owner.

FOR THE BALANCE SHEET			FOR THE INCOME STATEMENT			
ASSETS	**OWNERS' LIABILITIES**	**EQUITY**	**STOCKHOLDERS' COST OF REVENUES**	**COST OF GOODS SOLD**	**EXPENSES**	
Cash	Accounts payable	Capital stock	Sales revenue	Cost of buying goods	Wages	Interest
Accounts receivable	Notes payable	Retained earnings	Rental revenue	Cost of storing goods	Rent	Donations
Inventory	Bonds payable	Common stock	Commissions revenue		Repairs	Licenses
Investments	Taxes payable	Treasury stock	Royalty revenue		Travel	Fees
Equipment					Insurance	Supplies
Land					Utilities	Advertising
Buildings					Entertainment	Taxes
Motor vehicles					Storage	
Goodwill						

FIGURE 18.9

SAMPLE OF SPECIFIC ACCOUNT TITLES IN GENERAL ACCOUNT CLASSIFICATIONS

Accountants and other finance professionals use several other specific ratios, in addition to the ones we have discussed, to learn more about a firm's financial condition. The key purpose here is to acquaint you with the idea of what financial ratios are, the relationship they have with the firm's financial statements, and how businesspeople—including investors, creditors, lenders, and managers—use them. If you can't recall what kinds of information are used in ratio analysis and where it comes from, see Figure 18.9 for a quick reference. It's also important for you to note that financial analysis begins where the accounting statements end.

We hope that you can see from this chapter that there is more to accounting than meets the eye. Keep in mind that accounting is roughly a $40 billion industry. It can be fascinating and is critical to the firm's operations. It's worth saying one more time that, as the language of business, accounting is a worthwhile language to learn.

PROGRESS ASSESSMENT

• What key advantages do computers provide businesses in maintaining and compiling accounting information?

• What's the major benefit of a business performing ratio analysis based on its financial statements?

SUMMARY

1. Understand the importance of financial information and accounting.

1. Financial information is critical to the growth and development of an organization. Accounting provides the information necessary to measure a firm's financial condition.

    • *What is accounting?*

    Accounting is the recording, classifying, summarizing, and interpreting of financial events and transactions that affect an organization. The methods used to record and summarize accounting data into reports are called an accounting system.

2. The accounting profession covers four major areas: managerial accounting, financial accounting, auditing, and tax accounting.

   • *How does managerial accounting differ from financial accounting?*
   Managerial accounting provides information and analyses to managers within the firm to assist them in decision making. Financial accounting provides information and analyses to external users of data such as creditors and lenders.

   • *What is the job of an auditor?*
   Auditors review and evaluate the standards used to prepare a company's financial statements. An independent audit is conducted by a public accountant and is an evaluation and unbiased opinion about the accuracy of company financial statements.

   • *What is the difference between a private accountant and a public accountant?*
   A public accountant provides services for a fee to a variety of companies, whereas a private accountant works for a single company. Private and public accountants do essentially the same things with the exception of independent audits. Private accountants do perform internal audits, but only public accountants supply independent audits.

2. Define and explain the different areas of the accounting profession.

3. Many people confuse bookkeeping and accounting.

   • *What is the difference between bookkeeping and accounting?*
   Bookkeeping is part of accounting, and includes the mechanical part of recording data. Accounting also includes classifying, summarizing, interpreting, and reporting data to management.

   • *What are journals and ledgers?*
   Journals are original-entry accounting documents. That means they are the first place transactions are recorded. Summaries of journal entries are recorded (posted) into ledgers. Ledgers are specialized accounting books that arrange the transactions by homogeneous groups (accounts).

   • *What are the six steps of the accounting cycle?*
   The six steps of the accounting cycle are (1) analyzing documents, (2) recording information into journals, (3) posting that information into ledgers, (4) developing a trial balance, (5) preparing the income statement and balance sheet, and (6) analyzing financial statements.

3. Distinguish between accounting and bookkeeping, and list the steps in the accounting cycle.

4. Financial statements are a critical part of the firm's financial position.

   • *What is a balance sheet?*
   A balance sheet reports the financial position of a firm on a particular day. The fundamental accounting equation used to prepare the balance sheet is Assets = Liabilities + Owners' equity.

   • *What are the major accounts of the balance sheet?*
   Assets are economic resources owned by the firm, such as buildings and machinery. Liabilities are amounts owed by the firm to others (e.g., creditors, bondholders). Owners' equity is the value of the things the firm owns (assets) minus any liabilities; thus, owners' equity equals assets minus liabilities.

   • *What is an income statement?*
   An income statement reports revenues, costs, and expenses for a specific period of time (e.g., for the year ended December 31, 2002). The formula is Revenue − Cost of goods sold = Gross margin; Gross margin − Operating expenses = Net income before taxes; and Net income before taxes − Taxes = Net income (or net loss). (Note that income and profit mean the same thing.)

   • *What is a statement of cash flows?*
   Cash flow is the difference between cash receipts (money coming in) and cash disbursements (money going out). The statement of cash flows reports cash receipts and disbursements related to the firm's major activities: operations, investments, and financing.

4. Explain the differences between the major financial statements.

5. Describe the role of depreciation, LIFO, and FIFO in reporting financial information.

5. Applying accounting knowledge makes the reporting and analysis of data a challenging occupation. Depreciation is a key account that accountants evaluate. Also, two accounting techniques for valuing inventory are known as LIFO and FIFO.
    • *What is depreciation?*
    Depreciation is the systematic writing off of the value of a tangible asset over its estimated useful life. Depreciation must be noted on both the balance sheet and the income statement.
    • *What are LIFO and FIFO?*
    LIFO and FIFO are methods of valuing inventory. FIFO means first in, first out; LIFO means last in, first out. The method an accountant uses to value inventory, FIFO or LIFO, can affect its net income.
    • *What is involved in the budgeting process?*
    A budget is a financial plan that sets forth management's expectations for revenues, and based on the expectations allocates specific resources throughout the firm. Accounting information is a key to setting realistic budgets for the firm.

6. Detail how computers are used to record and apply accounting information in business.

6. Computers greatly simplify accounting tasks.
    • *How can computers help accountants?*
    Computers can record and analyze data and provide financial reports. Software is available that can continuously analyze and test accounting systems to be sure they are functioning correctly. Computers can help decision making by providing appropriate information, but they cannot make good financial decisions independently. Accounting applications and creativity are still human traits.

7. Explain the importance of ratio analysis in reporting financial information.

7. Financial ratios are a key part of analyzing financial information.
    • *What are the four key categories of ratios?*
    There are four key categories of ratios: liquidity ratios, leverage (debt) ratios, profitability (performance) ratios, and activity ratios.
    • *What is the major value of ratio analysis to the firm?*
    Ratio analysis provides the firm with financial information about its financial position in key areas compared to comparable firms in its industry and its past performance.

KEY TERMS

accounting 550
accounting cycle 555
annual report 552
assets 556
auditing 553
balance sheet 556
bookkeeping 554
budget 567
cash flow 562
certified internal auditor 553
certified management accountant 551

certified public accountant (CPA) 552
cost of goods sold (or cost of goods manufactured) 560
current assets 558
depreciation 565
double-entry bookkeeping 554
expenses 562
first in, first out (FIFO) 566
financial accounting 552

financial statement 555
fixed assets 558
fundamental accounting equation 556
gross margin (gross profit) 561
income statement 560
independent audit 553
intangible assets 558
journal 554

DEVELOPING
WORKPLACE
SKILLS

1. Visit, telephone, or e-mail a CPA from a local company in your area, or talk with a CPA in your college's business department. Ask what challenges, changes, and opportunities he or she foresees in the accounting profession in the next five years. List the forecasts on a sheet of paper and then compare them with the information in this chapter.

2. Obtain the most recent annual report for a company of your choice. (Hint: *The Wall Street Journal* has a free annual reports service. Call them at 1-800-654-2582). Look over the company's financial statements and see if they coincide with the information in this chapter. Read the opinion of the auditing firm (usually at the end of the report). Write down important conclusions the auditors have made about the company's financial statements.

3. Go to the website of the American Institute of Certified Public Accountants (www.aicpa.org), the Institute of Certified Management Accountants (www.imanet.org), and the Institute of Internal Auditors (www.theiia.org). Browse through the sites and find information concerning the requirements for becoming a certified public accountant (CPA), certified management accountant (CMA), and certified internal auditor (CIA). Compare the different requirements of the programs and choose which program is most interesting to you.

4. Place yourself in the role of a small-business consultant. One of your clients, Be Pretty Fashions, is considering opening two new stores. The problem is that the business often experiences cash flow problems due to continuous style changes that occur in its industry. Prepare a formal draft memo to Be Pretty Fashions that explains the problems a firm experiences when it encounters the cash flow problems that typically occur with such growth. Think of a couple possible business options Be Pretty Fashions could try to avoid cash flow problems.

5. This chapter describes two ways of accounting for cost of goods sold: first in, first out (FIFO) and last in, first out (LIFO). Compute the net income using FIFO and LIFO with the information listed below. Write down the factors you should consider in deciding which inventory valuation method is best for a firm to use.

Beginning inventory:	25,000 units @ $20.00
Purchases (new inventory):	25,000 units @ 25.00
Sales:	25,000 units @ 55.00
Tax rate:	33%

TAKING IT TO THE NET

Purpose

To calculate and analyze current ratios and quick (acid-test) ratios.

Exercise

Thingamajigs and Things, a small gift shop, has total assets of $45,000 (including inventory valued at $30,000) and $9,000 in liabilities. WannaBees, a specialty clothing store, has total assets of $150,000 (including inventory valued at $125,000) and $85,000 in liabilities. Both businesses have applied for loans. Use the calculators on the Bankrate.com website to answer the following questions:

1. Calculate the current ratio for each company. Comparing the ratios, which company is more likely to get the loan? Why?

2. The quick (acid-test) ratio is considered an even more reliable measure of a business's ability to repay loans than the current ratio. Because inventory is often difficult to liquidate, the value of the inventory is subtracted from the total assets. Calculate the quick ratio for each business. Do you think either business will get the loan? Why?

PRACTICING MANAGEMENT DECISIONS

CASE

APPLYING FINANCIAL INFORMATION

DaVinci Painting and Decorating was started by high school senior Keith Allen. As the business grew, Allen hired several of his friends; his business is now doing well. At first, Allen did not consider keeping records to be that important, but over time he learned this was not a good business practice. Now he is in a position to begin keeping good records. Allen has written down some of his figures, but he isn't quite sure how to interpret them or what exactly to do with them. He plans to request another loan from a local bank and has been told to prepare a balance sheet to calculate his financial position. These are his figures:

Cash on hand	$5,100
Equipment loan	1,200
Supplies	500
Bank loan	7,500
Truck	13,750
Equipment	4,520
Money owed for materials	900
Office furniture	945
Accounts receivable	2,400
Notes payable	1,900

Allen collected some other figures he felt might be important in determining the performance of his firm. These were put together fast and in no apparent order:

Income from work	$74,000
Salaries to employees	38,000
Advertising expense	1,720
Insurance	2,000
Offices costs (rent, heat, etc.)	8,040
Depreciation on truck	4,000

Allen also recently purchased some wallpapering materials for $1,800 for a job he expects to start in a week.

Decision Questions

1. What additional information, if any, would you need to construct a balance sheet? If DaVinci Painting and Decorating is a sole proprietorship, can you prepare a balance sheet for Keith Allen from the information provided? Is Allen in a strong or poor financial condition? How can you determine this?

2. Take the figures Allen provided and prepare an income statement. How much did he earn before taxes?

3. Is the bank being unreasonable by asking Allen to put together a balance sheet? What other information might interest the bank if Allen wants to get this additional loan?

**LEARNING THE
LANGUAGE OF
BUSINESS**

Games and sports are more fun to play when you know the rules and regulations. Once you begin playing, it's a challenge to see how well you can do relative to other players. Each game has its own rules and measures of success. In baseball, you can strike out two out of three times at bat yet still be considered a good player. In basketball, on the other hand, if you miss two out of three foul shots you wouldn't seem so good.

Businesses also follow rules and regulations. As in sports, there are various ways of "scoring" and measuring the effectiveness of one business against others in the same field. For example, you can compare supermarkets to other supermarkets in efficiency, return on investment, turnover of goods, and so forth.

The people who keep such records are called accountants. Their function is to act as the score and record keepers of business. Accounting is thus called the language of business because accounting terms such as assets, liabilities, revenues, expenses, and owners' equity are as important to business as "balls," "strikes," and "outs" are to baseball.

The score sheets in accounting, as you have read in this chapter, include the income state-

ment, the balance sheet, and the statement of cash flows. Such statements tell a business how it is doing internally. But how does the success of the business compare to its competitors. Lots of people would like to know that answer: potential stockholders, union negotiators, potential employees, bankers, and other lenders. Accountants calculate and prepare such comparison measures as return on investment, inventory turnover, debt ratios, price/earnings ratios, and more. In order to be considered a pro in business, you have to know the language and the importance and meaning of key ratios. Just as a professional baseball player can tell you his or her batting average, a professional businessperson can tell you his or her company's return on investment and explain its significance.

Discussion Questions

1. Which accounting terms and concepts do you need to know to prepare a balance sheet? What is the formula?
2. Which terms and concepts do you need to know to prepare an income statement?
3. Why should accountants compare the success of one business against others?
4. Can you prove that you are ready for at least the amateur ranks of business by explaining what return on equity, cash flow, and price/earnings ratio mean?

PART 6

MANAGING INFORMATION (INFORMATION SYSTEMS)

Information management is a major growth industry of the future. To understand either the past or the present conditions of a company, we must have information. The process of getting the right information and processing it efficiently is an important part of staying competitive in today's business world. In a world constantly reshaped by new technology, the field of information management plays a key role.

Changing technologies have created a large number of different job titles in this exciting area. Careers are available in: information systems management, computer programming, cost estimating, and troubleshooting, just to name a few. All future forecasts predict that career opportunities in computer-related businesses and industries will continue to grow more rapidly than the average for other occupations.

SKILLS

Anyone who chooses to work with information technology should be comfortable with change and have a willingness to keep abreast of changes. Such a person also needs to have an interest in and aptitude for data and information and have an ability to see trends and relationships. People in this area are usually involved in some way with problem solving. An aptitude for seeing possible solutions to problems is important.

CAREER PATHS

In this ever-changing field, up-to-date knowledge is the key. A formal education in computer science, for example, would be almost useless if it was obtained 10 years ago and not updated. Most employers prefer hiring people who have had recent college coursework in software applications, programming, and general business. Business knowledge is important for the employee to place his or her work in context.

Computer skills are taught at public and private vocational schools, community colleges, and universities. Many programmers and systems analysts are college graduates, and a degree is helpful in getting hired. However, vocational schools can often provide the knowledge and skill necessary to excel.

SOME POSSIBLE CAREERS IN INFORMATION SYSTEMS

JOB TITLE	SALARY	JOB DUTIES	CAREER PATH	PROSPECTS
Systems analyst	$32,470–$87,810 Median: $52,180	Advise computer programmers on problem solutions. Implement management decision on data processing issues.	Can start as a trainee, then be promoted into management.	One of the fastest growing occupations through 2008.
Computer programmer	$27,670–88,730 Median: $47,550	Work for systems analyst to write programs needed by management.	Promotions often mean greater task complexity. Start out as programmer.	Growth will be much faster than average through 2008. Great opportunity.
Cost estimator	$20,000–$30,000 (to start)	Prepare specifications using precedent, math, and computer data to predict cost requirements.	Career path varies greatly from company to company and from industry to industry.	Prospects are average through 2008. Good in construction.
Operations research analyst	$29,780–$87,720 Median: $49,070	Solve problems by the use of computerized data. Nature of problems varies.	Master's degree or Ph.D. very desirable. High level of computer skills is mandatory. Promotion into management quite possible. Bachelor's degree graduates start as research assistants.	Good for those with bachelor's degree. Very good for master's and Ph.D. degree.

Source: *Occupational Outlook Handbook,* Bureau of Labor Statistics.

HAY GROUP, INC.

Name: James J. Hoisington

Age: 30

Position/title: Reward Services Associate

Salary range: $45,000–$55,000 + annual bonus

Time in this position: Less than 1 year

Company name: Hay Group, Inc.

Company's Web address: www.haygroup.com

Company description: The Hay Group, one of the world's largest human resource consulting firms, is well suited for the challenge of putting people before strategy. For 50 years they have helped organizations around the globe achieve their goals by addressing critical people issues. Hay Group also includes an information business with the largest single database on people and pay worldwide—information can be delivered through their consulting business, through information agreements, and through their online subscription services.

Major factors in the decision to take this position: As an accountant, I enjoy working with numbers. By working within reward consulting I am able to use my accounting background and add human substance to it.

Job description: As a reward associate we work with all types of organizations in developing effective reward strategies for all types of employees.

Career path: I started my business career working for a family-owned architectural and engineering firm in Princeton, NJ. After graduating from the Wharton School with a dual concentration in accounting and management, I went into the accounting field and took a position with a big-five accounting firm. After some research I found my way into the career of reward consulting.

Ideal next job: I'm an associate now and plan to "fast track" to a consultant level within the Hay Group.

Best part of your job: In consulting you work on many different projects that vary immensely from job to job. It forces me to always seek new ways to find solutions and reformulate strategy. I am never bored!

Worst part of your job: In the consulting field you can't just keep up with the challenges of today's chaotic environment. You have to be entirely on the forefront of change, and that can be sometimes difficult and even frustrating. It is probably the best and worst part of the job. However, there is also the constant temptation to eat junk food at the street vendor directly in front of the office building.

Educational background: I graduated from the Wharton School of Business of the University of Pennsylvania in 1998. I also attended a few classes at Ocean County College of Tom's River, NJ.

Favorite course: There are two: Operations and information management systems. Also, an introduction to business class determined my business career path and I also had a great professor.

Best course for your career: Finance, accounting, statistics and as many technology classes as possible.

Recommended by Karl Kleiner, Ocean County College.

CHAPTER 19

Financial Management

LEARNING GOALS

AFTER YOU HAVE READ AND STUDIED THIS CHAPTER, YOU SHOULD BE ABLE TO

1. Explain the importance of finance.

2. Describe the responsibilities of financial managers.

3. Tell what financial planning involves and define the three key budgets of finance.

4. Recognize the financial needs that must be met with available funds.

5. Distinguish between short-term and long-term financing, and between debt capital and equity capital.

6. Identify and describe several sources of short-term financing.

7. Identify and describe several sources of long-term financing.

Getting to Know Joy Covey, Former CFO of Amazon.com

If we asked you to picture a typical chief financial officer (CFO) of a major company, you might describe the common stereotype portrayed in the movies: a slow moving, balding, middle-aged man with no sense of humor and a monotone voice spouting formulas related to return on capital. Well, meet the complete opposite. Joy Covey doesn't share any of those characteristics. In fact, she hates to stand still; she prefers to play fast and keep moving. That's one reason why she rode to her wedding on a snowmobile. It's also why she prefers to conduct business on the run through the streets of Seattle, talking to clients and associates through a headset. After the run and conversation are finished, it's off to Starbucks for a double latte. It's her full-speed-ahead business approach that has molded Covey into one of the leading pioneers in the new financial frontier of e-commerce, where the business model stresses risk and rapid change.

Covey is an ardent proponent of what's been termed the *profitless corporation*. In a profitless corporation, the mind-set is "Growth first, profits later." This philosophy runs contrary to Covey's MBA studies at Harvard (she also holds a law degree and is a CPA), where more traditional financial principles were the order of the day. She joined Internet bookseller Amazon.com in 1996 and became its CFO. "The profitless corporation is a different way of thinking," Covey says. "In my case, it means thinking about a new kind of business model that hasn't existed before." In general, leading the finance department in an Internet company means downplaying many of the traditional foundations and tools used by financial managers. "What we chose to do are the things that are most essential to the long-term leadership position of Amazon." Covey's financial philosophy is actually quite simple. Her top priorities during her tenure at Amazon.com were

to grow the business and increase its efficiencies. When asked one time by a financial analyst if there was anything Amazon would not sell over the Internet, she responded, "Cement." Her feeling was that company profits would come later.

By the time Covey became vice president of strategy at Amazon.com, the market capitalization of the company had grown to over $27 billion before the dot-coms' bubble burst. By the spring of 2001, the company's market cap plummeted to $3.5 billion—still not bad for a company that had yet to make a profit.

Covey decided in late 1999 to take a leave of absence to spend more time with her family. In April 2000, she left the company. Odds are that she will not let much grass grow under her feet.

Can Amazon.com continue its market growth without profitability? Many other dot-coms found out that they could not and are now out of business. The sudden fall of these companies indicates that profitability still counts. The ideas of risk, complexity, and uncertainty clearly define the role of financial management. This is especially true in emerging firms such as Internet companies. Add to these challenges fluctuating interest rates and enhanced expectations of investors and lenders, and the challenge of financial management is indeed accelerated. In this chapter, you'll explore the role of finance in business and the tools financial managers use to seek financial stability and future growth.

Sources: Mark Leibovich, "Child Prodigy, Online Pioneer, Amazon.com Founder Bezos Hires Great Minds: But Will It Matter?" *Washington Post*, September 3, 2000; "Discreet Departure," *CFO*, August 2000, p. 128; Chris Taylor, "What Works for Amazon?" *Time*, February 5, 2001, p. 51; Alec Appelbaum, "Amazon's Amazing Juggling Act," *Money*, March 1, 2001, p. 35.

THE ROLE OF FINANCE AND FINANCIAL MANAGERS

The purpose of this chapter is to answer two major questions: What is finance? and What do financial managers do? Before we go any further, let's review the role of an accountant and compare it with that of a financial manager. An accountant is like a skilled laboratory technician who takes blood samples and other measures of a person's health and writes the findings on a health report (in business, the equivalent of a set of financial statements). A financial manager for a business is the doctor who interprets the report and makes recommendations to the patient regarding changes that would improve health.[1] In short, **financial managers** examine the data prepared by accountants and make recommendations to top executives regarding strategies for improving the health (financial strength) of the firm.

It should be clear that financial managers are unable to make sound financial decisions without understanding accounting information. That's why we examined accounting in Chapter 18. Similarly, a good accountant needs to understand finance. Accounting and finance—the two go together like peanut butter and jelly. In large and medium-sized organizations, both the accounting and finance functions are generally under the control of a person such as Joy Covey, the former chief financial officer (CFO) at Amazon.com. Finance, however, is a critical activity in all organizations , no matter what size.

As you may remember from Chapter 6, financing a small business is a difficult but essential function if a firm expects to survive those important first five years.[2] But the need for careful financial management goes beyond the first five years and remains a challenge a business, large or small, must face throughout its existence. Even a market giant cannot afford to ignore finance; Chrysler Corporation, for example, faced extinction in the late 1970s due to severe financial problems. Had it not been for a government-backed loan of $1 billion, Chrysler might have joined the ranks of defunct auto companies such as Packard and Hudson. The following are three of the most common ways for a firm to fail financially:

1. Undercapitalization (lacking enough funds to start a business).
2. Poor control over cash flow.
3. Inadequate expense control.

The Importance of Understanding Finance

Consider the financial problems encountered by a small organization called Parsley Patch. Two friends, Elizabeth Bertani and Pat Sherwood, started the company on what can best be described as a shoestring budget. It began when Bertani prepared salt-free seasonings for her husband, who was on a no-salt diet. Her friend Sherwood thought the seasonings were good enough to sell. Bertani agreed, and Parsley Patch, Inc., was born.

The business began with an investment of $5,000, which was rapidly eaten up for a logo and a label design. Bertani and Sherwood quickly learned the importance of capital in getting a business going. Eventually, the two women personally invested more than $100,000 to keep the business from experiencing severe undercapitalization.

Everything started well, and hundreds of gourmet shops adopted the product line. But when sales failed to meet expectations, the women decided the health-food market offered more potential than gourmet shops, because salt-free seasonings were a natural for people with restricted diets. The choice was

financial managers
Managers who make recommendations to top executives regarding strategies for improving the financial strength of a firm.

a good one. Sales took off and approached $30,000 a month. Still, the company earned no profits. Bertani and Sherwood were not trained in monitoring cash flow ➤ **P.562** ◄ or in controlling expenses. In fact, they had been told not to worry about costs, and they hadn't. They eventually hired a certified public accountant (CPA) ➤ **P.552** ◄ and an experienced financial manager, who taught them how to compute the costs of the various blends they produced and how to control their expenses. The financial specialists also offered insight into how to control cash coming in and out of the company. Soon Parsley Patch earned a comfortable margin on operations that ran close to $1 million a year. Luckily, the owners were able to turn things around before they went broke.

If Bertani and Sherwood had understood finance before starting their business, they may have been able to avoid many of the problems they encountered. The key word here is *understood*. You do not have to pursue finance as a career to understand finance. Financial understanding is important to anyone who wants to start a small business, invest in stocks and bonds, or plan a retirement fund. In short, finance and accounting are two areas everyone involved in business needs to study. Let's take a closer look at what finance is all about.

WHAT IS FINANCIAL MANAGEMENT?

Finance is the function in a business that acquires funds for the firm and manages funds within the firm (e.g., preparing budgets, doing cash flow analysis, and planning for the expenditure of funds on such assets as plant, equipment, and machinery). Without a carefully calculated financial plan, the firm has little chance for survival regardless of its product or marketing effectiveness. **Financial management** is the job of managing a firm's resources so it can meet its goals and objectives. Most large and medium-sized organizations will designate a manager in charge of financial operations, generally the *chief financial officer (CFO)*.[3] However, financial management could also be in the hands of a person who serves as the company treasurer or vice president of finance. A *comptroller* is the chief accounting officer. Figure 19.1 highlights the tasks a financial manager performs. As you can see, the fundamental charge is to obtain money and then control the use of that money effectively. That includes managing cash, accounts receivable, and inventory. Where a company invests its cash may have a major impact on profits.

You are probably familiar with such finance functions as buying merchandise on credit and collecting payment from customers. Both of these functions are responsibilities of financial managers. This means that financial managers are responsible for collecting overdue payments and making sure that the company does not lose too much money to bad debts (people or firms that don't pay). While these functions are critical to all types of businesses, they are particularly critical to small and medium-sized businesses, which typically have smaller cash or credit cushions than large corporations. It's vital that financial

finance
The function in a business that acquires funds for the firm and manages funds within the firm.

financial management
The job of managing a firm's resources so it can meet its goals and objectives.

- Planning
- Budgeting
- Obtaining funds
- Controlling funds (funds management)
- Collecting funds (credit management)

- Auditing
- Managing taxes
- Advising top management on financial matters

FIGURE 19.1

WHAT FINANCIAL MANAGERS DO

All these functions depend greatly on the information provided by the accounting statements discussed in Chapter 18.

managers in any business are aware of changes or opportunities in finance that may arise and be ready to adjust to them.[4]

As Chapter 18 stated, tax payments represent an outflow of cash from the business. Therefore, they too fall under finance. Finance specialists have become increasingly involved in tax management. In keeping with changes in the law, they carefully analyze the tax implications of various managerial decisions in an attempt to minimize the taxes paid by the business. (Remember Chapter 18's discussion of tax accounting and issues such as LIFO and FIFO?) Businesses of all sizes must concern themselves with managing taxes.

Usually a member of the firm's finance department, the *internal auditor*, checks on the journals, ledgers, and financial statements prepared by the accounting department to make sure that all transactions have been treated in accordance with generally accepted accounting principles (GAAP). If there were no such audits, accounting statements would be less reliable. Therefore, it's important that internal auditors be objective and critical of any improprieties or deficiencies they might note in their evaluation. Regular internal audits offer the firm assistance in the important role of financial planning, which we'll look at next.[5]

Do you see the link between accounting and finance? They're mutually supportive functions in a firm. A firm cannot get along without accounting, but neither can it prosper without finance. The importance of finance is such that many successful finance executives go on to be company presidents and chief executive officers. What would be the advantages and disadvantages of having a president with a background in finance versus a marketing background? Do you think Joy Covey might be in line to become CEO of a major corporation in the future? Why?

FINANCIAL PLANNING

Planning has been a recurring theme of this book. We've stressed planning's importance as a managerial function and offered insights into planning your career. Financial planning involves analyzing short-term and long-term money flows to and from the firm. The overall objective of financial planning is to optimize the firm's profitability and make the best use of its money. Financial planning is one of the key responsibilities of the financial manager. It's probably safe to assume that we all could use better financial planning in our lives.[6]

Financial planning involves three steps: (1) forecasting both short-term and long-term financial needs, (2) developing budgets to meet those needs, and (3) establishing financial control to see how well the company is doing what it set out to do (see Figure 19.2). Let's look at each step's role in the financial health of an organization.

Forecasting Financial Needs

short-term forecast
Forecast that predicts revenues, costs, and expenses for a period of one year or less.

cash flow forecast
Forecast that predicts the cash inflows and outflows in future periods.

Forecasting is an important part of any firm's financial plan. A **short-term forecast** predicts revenues, costs, and expenses for a period of one year or less. This forecast is the foundation for most other financial plans, so its accuracy is critical. Part of the short-term forecast may be in the form of a **cash flow forecast,** which predicts the cash inflows and outflows in future periods, usually months or quarters. Naturally, the inflows and outflows of cash recorded in the cash flow forecast are based on expected sales revenues and on various costs and expenses incurred and when they'll come due. The company's sales forecast estimates the company's projected sales for a particular period. A firm

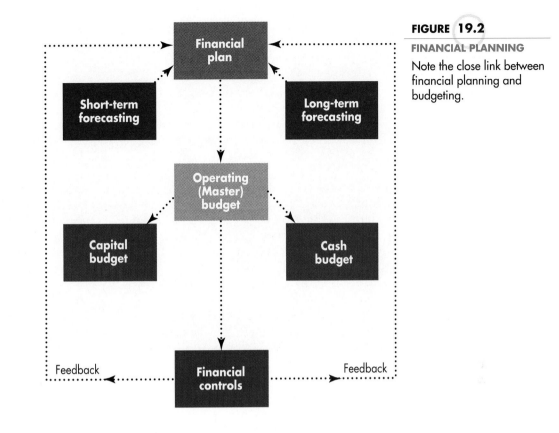

FIGURE 19.2

FINANCIAL PLANNING

Note the close link between financial planning and budgeting.

often uses its past financial statements as a basis for projecting expected sales and various costs and expenses.

A **long-term forecast** predicts revenues, costs, and expenses for a period longer than 1 year, and sometimes as far as 5 or 10 years into the future. This forecast plays a crucial part in the company's long-term strategic plan. Remember, a firm's strategic plan asks questions such as these: What business are we in? Should we be in it five years from now? How much money should we invest in technology and new plant and equipment over the next decade? Will there be cash available to meet long-term obligations? Innovations in Web-based software provide assistance to financial managers in dealing with these long-term forecasting questions.[7]

The long-term financial forecast gives top management, as well as operations managers, some sense of the income or profit potential possible with different strategic plans. Additionally, long-term projections assist financial managers with the preparation of company budgets.

long-term forecast
Forecast that predicts revenues, costs, and expenses for a period longer than 1 year, and sometimes as far as 5 or 10 years into the future.

Working with the Budget Process

Chapter 18 identified a budget as a financial plan. You may live under a carefully constructed budget of your own. A business operates in the same way. A budget becomes the primary basis and guide for the firm's financial operations and financial needs.[8]

Most firms compile yearly budgets from short-term and long-term financial forecasts. It's important that these financial forecasts be as accurate as possible. Therefore, businesses use historical cost and revenue information derived from past financial statements as the basis for forecasting company budgets. Since budgeting is clearly tied to forecasting, financial managers

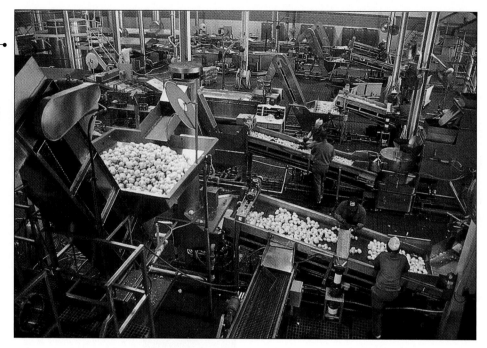

Ever wonder how the average potato becomes the tasty chips and fries we love to eat? It happens with the help of specialized processing equipment such as the type pictured here. The firm's capital budget is the financial tool that controls business spending for expensive assets such as this processing equipment. Such major assets are referred to as property, plant, and equipment.

must take forecasting responsibilities seriously. There are usually several budgets established in a firm's financial plan:

- A capital budget.
- A cash budget.
- An operating (master) budget.

capital budget
A budget that highlights a firm's spending plans for major asset purchases that often require large sums of money.

A **capital budget** highlights a firm's spending plans for major asset purchases that often require large sums of money. The capital budget primarily concerns itself with the purchase of such assets as property, buildings, and equipment.

cash budget
A budget that estimates a firm's projected cash balance at the end of a given period.

A **cash budget** estimates a firm's projected cash balance at the end of a given period (e.g., monthly, quarterly). Cash budgets are important guidelines that assist managers in anticipating borrowing, debt repayment, operating expenses, and short-term investments. Cash budgets assist the firm in planning for cash shortages or surpluses. The cash budget is often the last budget that is prepared. A sample cash budget for our continuing example company, Fiber-rific, is provided in Figure 19.3.

operating (master) budget
The budget that ties together all of a firm's other budgets; it is the projection of dollar allocations to various costs and expenses needed to run the business, given projected revenues.

The **operating (master) budget** ties together all the firm's other budgets and summarizes the businesses proposed financial activities. It can be defined more formally as the projection of dollar allocations to various costs and expenses needed to run or operate a business, given projected revenues. How much the firm will spend on supplies, travel, rent, advertising, salaries, and so forth is determined in the operating (master) budget.

Clearly, financial planning plays an important role in the operations of the firm. This planning often determines what long-term investments are made, when specific funds will be needed, and how the funds will be generated. Once a company has forecast its short-term and long-term financial needs and established budgets to show how funds will be allocated, the final step in financial planning is to establish financial controls.

FIGURE **19.3**

A SAMPLE CASH BUDGET

FIBERRIFIC
Monthly Cash Budget

	January	February	March
Sales forecast	$50,000	$45,000	$40,000
Collections			
Cash sales (20%)		$9,000	$8,000
Credit sales (80% of past month)		$40,000	$36,000
Monthly cash collection		$49,000	$44,000
Payments schedule			
Supplies and material		$11,000	$10,000
Salaries		12,000	12,000
Direct labor		9,000	9,000
Taxes		3,000	3,000
Other expenses		7,000	6,000
Monthly cash payments		$42,000	$39,000
Cash budget			
Cash flow		$7,000	$5,000
Beginning cash		−1,000	6,000
Total cash		$6,000	$11,000
Less minimum cash balance		−6,000	−6,000
Excess cash to market securities		$0	$5,000
Loans needed for minimum balance		0	0

Establishing Financial Controls

Financial control is a process in which a firm periodically compares its actual revenues, costs, and expenses with its projected ones. Most companies hold at least monthly financial reviews as a way to ensure financial control. This helps managers identify deviations and take corrective action if necessary. Such controls provide feedback to help reveal which accounts, which departments, and which people are varying from the financial plans. Finance managers can judge if such deviations may or may not be justified. In either case, managers can make some financial adjustments to the plan. Read the Making Ethical Decisions box to see a type of situation a manager can face related to financial control. After the Progress Assessment we shall explore specific reasons why firms need to have funds readily available.

financial control
A process in which a firm periodically compares its actual revenues, costs, and expenses with its projected ones.

PROGRESS ASSESSMENT

- Name three finance functions important to the firm's overall operations and performance.
- What are the three primary financial problems that often cause firms to fail?
- In what ways do short-term and long-term financial forecasts differ?
- What is the organization's purpose in preparing budgets? Can you identify at least three different types of budgets?

MAKING ETHICAL DECISIONS

No Questions Asked

You are the chairperson of the business administration department at a local community college. Like many other colleges, your campus has been affected financially by declining enrollments and increasing expenses. As the end of the college's fiscal year approaches, you review your departmental budget and note that your department has some unused travel funds available for faculty and staff development. The faculty and staff have not seemed interested in using the travel money for developmental purposes throughout the year even though it has been readily available. You fear that if the funds are not spent this year, there's a good chance the division dean will recommend cutting your travel budget for next year.

You consider telling faculty and staff that this money is now available for just about any type of travel they desire on a first-come, first-served basis, with no questions asked concerning the educational or college benefit of the travel request. It's almost certain the division dean will not contest any request you put in for travel funds, and you can certainly be a hero in the eyes of your faculty and staff. However, you could just return the unused funds to the dean's office for disbursement to the college's general fund. What will you do? What could result from your decision?

THE NEED FOR OPERATING FUNDS

In business, the need for operating funds never seems to cease. That's why sound financial management is essential to businesses. Like our personal financial needs, the capital needs of a business change over time. For example, as a small business grows, its financial requirements shift considerably. (Remember the example of Parsley Patch.) The same is true with large corporations such as AT&T, Cisco Systems, and PepsiCo. As they venture into new product areas or markets, their capital needs increase. Different firms need funds available for different reasons. However, in virtually all organizations there are certain operational needs for which funds must be available. Let's take a look at these financial needs that affect both the smallest and the largest of businesses.

Managing Daily Business Operations

If workers are to be paid on Friday, they don't want to have to wait until Monday for their paychecks. If tax payments are due on the 15th of the month, the government expects the money on time. If the interest payment on a business loan is due on the 30th, the lender doesn't mean the 1st of the next month. As you can see, funds have to be available to meet the daily operational costs of the business.

The challenge of sound financial management is to see that funds are available to meet these daily cash needs without compromising the firm's investment potential. Money has what is called a *time value*. In other words, if someone offered to give you $200 today or $200 one year from today, you would benefit by taking the $200 today. Why? It's very simple. You could start collecting interest or invest the $200 you receive today, and over a year's time your money would grow. The same thing is true in business; the interest gained on the firm's investments is important in maximizing the profit the company will gain. That's why financial managers encourage keeping a firm's cash expenditures to a minimum. By doing this, funds can be freed for investment in interest-bearing accounts. It's also not unusual for finance managers to suggest that a company pay its bills as late as possible (unless a cash discount is available) but try to collect what's owed to it as fast as possible. This way, they maximize the investment potential of the firm's funds. Efficient cash management is particularly important to small firms in conducting their daily operations.

Managing Accounts Receivable

Financial managers know that making credit available helps keep current customers happy and attracts new customers. In today's highly competitive business environment, many businesses would have trouble surviving without making credit available to customers.

The major problem with selling on credit is that as much as 25 percent or more of the business's assets could be tied up in its account receivables. This means that the firm needs to use some of its available funds to pay for the goods or services already given customers who bought on credit. This outflow of funds means financial managers must develop efficient collection procedures. For example, businesses often provide cash or quantity discounts to buyers who pay their accounts by a certain time.

Collecting accounts receivable from some customers can be time-consuming and costly. Accepting credit cards like Visa, MasterCard, or American Express simplifies transactions, guarantees payment, and provides convenience for both customers and businesses.

Also, finance managers carefully scrutinize old and new credit customers to see if they have a favorable history of meeting their credit obligations on time. In essence, the firm's credit policy reflects its financial position and its desire to expand into new markets.

One way to decrease the time, and therefore expense, involved in collecting accounts receivable is to accept bank credit cards such as MasterCard or Visa. This is convenient for both the customer and the merchant. The banks that issue such credit cards have already established the customer's creditworthiness, which reduces the business's risk. Businesses must pay a fee to accept credit cards, but the fees are not excessive compared to the benefits they provide. In fact, credit card rates are dropping as competition in the industry intensifies.[9]

Obtaining Needed Inventory

As we noted earlier in the text, effective marketing implies a clear customer orientation. This focus on the customer means that high-quality service and availability of goods are vital if a business expects to prosper in today's markets. Therefore, to satisfy customers, businesses must maintain inventories that often involve a sizable expenditure of funds. Although it's true that firms expect to recapture their investment in inventory through sales to customers, a carefully constructed inventory policy assists in managing the use of a firm's available funds and maximizing profitability. For example, Chips & Dips, a neighborhood ice cream parlor, ties up more funds in inventory (ice cream) in the summer months than in winter. It's obvious why. Demand for ice cream goes up in the summer. As you learned in Chapter 9, innovations such as just-in-time inventory are reducing the amount of funds a firm must tie up in inventory. Also, carefully evaluating its inventory turnover ratio (discussed in Chapter 18) helps a firm control its financial outlays for inventory.

It's important for a business of any size to understand that a poorly managed inventory investment plan can drain its finances dry.

Major Capital Expenditures

capital expenditures
Major investments in long-term assets such as land, buildings, equipment, or research and development.

Capital expenditures are major investments in tangible long-term assets such as land, buildings, equipment, and intangible assets such as patents ➤ **P.120** ◄, trademarks, and other forms of intellectual property.[10] In many organizations the purchase of major assets—such as land for future expansion, plants to increase production capabilities, research to develop new product ideas, and equipment to maintain or exceed current levels of output—is essential. As you can imagine, these expenditures often require a huge portion of the organization's funds. Remember from the profile at the beginning of this chapter the situation confronting Amazon.com? Such companies often must spend large sums of money to develop products that may not be commercially successful for some time.[11] Therefore, it's critical that companies weigh all the possible options before committing what may be a large portion of their available resources. For this reason, financial managers and analysts evaluate the appropriateness of such purchases or expenditures. Consider the situation in which a firm needs to expand its production capabilities due to increases in demand. One option is to buy land and build a new plant from scratch. Another option would be to purchase an existing plant or consider renting. Can you think of financial and accounting considerations that would come into play in this decision?

The need for available funds raises several questions in any firm: How does the firm obtain funds to finance operations and other business necessities? How long will specific funds be needed by the organization? How much will it cost to obtain the needed funds? Will these funds come from internal sources or external sources? These questions will be addressed in the next section, after the Progress Assessment.

PROGRESS ASSESSMENT

- Money is said to have a time value. What does this mean?
- Why are accounts receivable a financial concern to the firm?
- What's the primary reason an organization spends a good deal of its available funds on inventory and major capital expenditures?

ALTERNATIVE SOURCES OF FUNDS

Earlier in the chapter, you learned that finance is the function in a business that is responsible for acquiring and managing funds for the firm. Determining the amount of money needed for various time periods and finding out the most appropriate sources from which to obtain these funds are fundamental steps in sound financial management. Next we'll look at methods of acquiring funds from a variety of sources. Before we begin this discussion, it's important to highlight some key distinctions involved in funding a firm's operations.

short-term financing
Borrowed capital that will be repaid within one year.

long-term financing
Borrowed capital that will be repaid over a specific time period longer than one year.

debt capital
Funds raised through various forms of borrowing that must be repaid.

Organizations typically encounter both short- and long-term financing needs. **Short-term financing** refers to borrowed capital that will be repaid within one year. In contrast, **long-term financing** refers to borrowed capital for major purchases that will be repaid over a specific time period longer than one year. We shall explore sources of both short- and long-term financing fully in the next sections. It's important to know that businesses can use different methods of raising money. A firm can seek to raise needed capital through borrowing money (debt), selling ownership (equity), or earning profits (retained earnings). **Debt capital** refers to funds raised through various forms of borrowing that must be repaid. Funds borrowed could be either short-term, due to be repaid within one year, or long-term, due over a period longer than one year. **Equity capital** is money raised from within the firm or through the sale of ownership in the firm.

Obtaining Short-Term Financing

The bulk of a finance manager's job does not involve obtaining long-term funds. Instead, the nitty-gritty, day-to-day operation of the firm calls for the careful management of short-term financial needs. Firms need to borrow short-term funds for purchasing additional inventory or for meeting bills that come due unexpectedly. As we do in our personal lives, a business sometimes needs to obtain short-term funds when the firm's cash reserves are low. This is particularly true of small businesses. It's rare that a newly formed small business even attempts to find funding for long-term needs. Most are concerned more with just staying afloat until they are able to build capital and creditworthiness.[12] Firms can obtain short-term financing in several different ways. Also, suppliers of short-term financing can require that the funds provided be secured or unsecured. Let's look at the major forms of short-term financing and what's meant by *secured* and *unsecured* with regard to funds.

Trade Credit

The most widely used source of short-term funding, trade credit, is the least expensive and most convenient form of short-term financing. **Trade credit** is the practice of buying goods or services > **P.25** < now and paying for them later. For example, when a firm buys merchandise, it receives an invoice (bill) much like the one you receive when you buy something on credit.

It's common for business invoices to contain terms such as *2/10, net 30*. This means that the buyer can take a 2 percent discount for paying the invoice within 10 days. The total bill is due (net) in 30 days if the purchaser does not take advantage of the discount. Finance managers need to pay close attention to such discounts because they create opportunities to reduce the cost of financing. Think about it for a moment: if the discount offered to the customer is 2/10, net 30, the customer will pay 2 percent more for waiting an extra 20 days to pay the invoice. Some uninformed businesspeople feel that 2 percent is insignificant, so they pay their bills after the discount period. In the course of a year, however, 2 percent for 20 days adds up to a 36 percent interest rate (because there are eighteen 20-day periods in the year.) If the firm is capable of paying within 10 days, it is needlessly increasing its cost of financing by not doing so.

Promissory Notes

Some suppliers hesitate to give trade credit to organizations with a poor credit rating, no credit history, or a history of slow payment. In such cases, the supplier may insist that the customer sign a promissory

promissory note
A written contract with a
promise to pay.

note as a condition for obtaining credit. A **promissory note** is a written contract with a promise to pay.[13] Promissory notes can be sold by the supplier to a bank at a discount (the amount of the note less a fee for the bank's services).

Family and Friends

Many small firms obtain short-term funds by borrowing money from family and friends. Because such funds are needed for periods of less than a year, friends or relatives are sometimes willing to help. The loans can be dangerous, however, if the firm does not understand cash flow ➤ **P.562** ◄. As we discussed earlier, the firm may suddenly find several bills coming due at the same time and have no other sources of funds. It is better, therefore, not to borrow from friends or relatives; instead, go to a commercial bank that fully understands the risk and can help analyze your firm's future financial needs.

Entrepreneurs appear to be listening to this advice. According to the National Federation of Independent Business, entrepreneurs ➤ **P.20** ◄ today rely less on family and friends as a source of borrowed funds than they have in the past. If an entrepreneur does, however, decide to ask family or friends for financial assistance, it's important that both parties (1) agree on specific loan terms, (2) put the agreement in writing, and (3) arrange for repayment in the same way they would for a bank loan. Such actions help keep family relationships and friendships intact.

Commercial Banks and Other Financial Institutions

Banks are highly sensitive to risk and are therefore often reluctant to lend money to small businesses. Nonetheless, a promising and well-organized venture may be able to get a bank loan. If it is able to get such a loan, a small or medium-sized business should have the person in charge of the finance function keep in close touch with the bank. It's also wise to see a banker periodically (as often as once a month) and send the banker all the firm's financial statements so that the bank continues to supply funds when needed.

If you try to imagine the different types of businesspeople who go to banks for a loan, you'll get a better idea of the role of the financial manager. Picture, for example, a farmer going to the bank to borrow funds for seed, fertilizer, equipment, and other needs. The farmer may buy such supplies in the spring and pay for them after the fall harvest. Now picture a local toy store buying merchandise for Christmas sales. The store may borrow the money for such purchases in the summer and pay it back after Christmas. Restaurants may borrow funds at the beginning of the month and pay by the end of the month. Can you see that how much a business borrows and for how long depends on the kind of business it is and how quickly the merchandise purchased with a bank loan can be resold or used to generate funds?

Like you, a business sometimes finds itself in a position where many bills come due at once: utilities, insurance, payroll, new equipment, and more. Most businesses can meet such sudden cash demands. But sometimes a business gets so far into debt or so far behind in its payments that the bank refuses to lend it more funds. Suddenly the business is unable to pay its bills. In such a case, the business may either fail or file for bankruptcy, a result that's often chalked up to cash flow problems. Persimmon IT, a small software developer in North Carolina, fell victim to just such financial difficulties. As the business grew and new products were rolled out, the company ran head-on into cash problems. When Jinny Crum-Jones, the company founder, looked for sources of funding to save the company, she came up empty-handed. Unfortunately, even though it had highly respected products and great potential, the company folded.[14]

We hope you see now how important it is for specialists in the finance and accounting departments to do a cash flow forecast. By anticipating times when many bills will come due, a business can begin early to seek funds or sell other assets to prepare for the crunch. Can you also see why it is important for a businessperson to keep friendly and close relations with his or her banker? The banker may spot cash flow problems early and point out the danger. Or the banker may be more willing to lend money in a crisis if the businessperson has established a strong, friendly relationship built on openness, trust, and sound management practices. It's always important to remember that your banker wants you to succeed almost as much as you do. Bankers can be an invaluable support, especially to small but growing businesses.

Tis the season to be jolly: not to mention the season to shop, shop, shop. Did you ever wonder where large department stores get the money to buy all the treasures we splurge on at Christmastime? Department stores and other large retailers make extensive use of commercial banks and other financial institutions to borrow the capital needed to buy merchandise to stock their shelves. Ho! Ho! Ho!

Different Forms of Bank Loans

Banks and other financial institutions offer different types of loans to customers. A **secured loan** is a loan that's backed by something valuable, such as property. The item of value is called *collateral*. If the borrower fails to pay the loan, the lender may take possession of the collateral. That takes some of the risk out of the bank's lending money. Accounts receivable, for example, are assets that can be quickly converted into cash. Therefore, they are often used as security. When accounts receivable or other assets are used as collateral for a loan, the process is called **pledging.** Some percentage of the value of accounts receivables pledged is advanced to the borrowing firm. Then, as customers pay off their accounts, the funds received are forwarded to the firm's lender in repayment of the funds that were advanced. **Inventory financing** means that inventory such as a raw material (e.g., coal, steel), is used as collateral or security for a loan. Other assets that can be used as collateral include buildings, machinery, and company-owned stocks and bonds.

The most difficult kind of loan to get from a bank or other financial institution is an unsecured loan. An **unsecured loan** doesn't require a borrower to offer the lending institution any collateral to obtain the loan. It's basically a loan that's not backed by any specific assets. Normally, only highly regarded customers (e.g., long-standing customers or customers considered financially stable) of the lender receive unsecured loans.

Another advantage of developing a good relationship with a bank is that often the bank will open a line of credit for you. A **line of credit** is a given amount of unsecured short-term funds a bank will lend to a business, provided the bank has the funds readily available. In other words, a line of credit is not guaranteed to a business. The primary purpose of a line of credit is to speed the borrowing process so that a firm does not have to go through the hassle of applying for a new loan every time it needs funds.[15] The funds are generally available as long as the credit limit set by the bank is not exceeded. As businesses mature and become more financially secure, the amount of credit often is increased. Some firms will even apply for a **revolving credit agreement,** which is a line of credit that's guaranteed. However, banks usually charge a fee for guaranteeing such an agreement. Both lines of credit and revolving credit agreements are particularly good sources of funds for unexpected cash needs.

secured loan
A loan backed by something valuable, such as property.

pledging
The process of using accounts receivable or other assets as collateral for a loan.

inventory financing
The process of using inventory such as raw materials as collateral for a loan.

unsecured loan
A loan that's not backed by any specific assets.

line of credit
A given amount of unsecured short-term funds a bank will lend to a business, provided the funds are readily available.

revolving credit agreement
A line of credit that is guaranteed by the bank.

No one ever said that finding capital for your business is an easy task. Technology and the Internet, however, are helping things along a bit. At LiveCapital.com, you can submit a loan proposal to multiple lenders and get an answer back about your financing almost immediately, right at your desktop.

commercial finance companies
Organizations that make short-term loans to borrowers who offer tangible assets as collateral.

factoring
The process of selling accounts receivable for cash.

commercial paper
Unsecured promissory notes of $25,000 and up that mature (come due) in 270 days or less.

A financial manager may also obtain short-term funds from **commercial finance companies.**[16] These non-deposit-type organizations (often called nonbanks) make short-term loans to borrowers who offer tangible assets (such as property, plant, and equipment) as collateral.[17] Since commercial finance companies are willing to accept higher degrees of risk than commercial banks, they usually charge higher interest rates than banks do. General Electric Capital Corporation is the largest commercial finance company in the United States, with $345 billion in assets in its 28 diversified commercial and consumer finance businesses.[18]

Factoring

One relatively expensive source of short-term funds for a firm is **factoring,** which is the process of selling accounts receivable for cash. Factoring dates as far back as 4,000 years, during the days of ancient Babylon. Here's how it works: Let's say that a firm sells many of its products on credit to consumers and other businesses, creating a number of accounts receivable. Some of the buyers may be slow in paying their bills, causing the firm to have a large amount of money due to it. A *factor* is a market intermediary (an individual or a company) that agrees to buy the accounts receivable from the firm, at a discount, for cash.[19] The factor then collects and keeps the money that was owed the firm. How much this costs the firm depends on the discount rate the factor requires. The discount rate, in turn, depends on the age of the accounts receivable, the nature of the business, and the condition of the economy.

Even though factoring can be an expensive way of raising cash, it is popular among small businesses. It's important for you to note that factoring is not a loan; factoring is the *sale* of an asset (accounts receivable). And while it's true that discount rates charged by factors are usually higher than loan rates charged by banks or commercial finance companies, remember that many small businesses cannot qualify for a loan. Also, a company can reduce the cost of factoring if it agrees to reimburse the factor for slow-paying accounts, and it can reduce them even further if it assumes the risk of those people who don't pay at all. Factoring can be used by large firms. Macy's Department Store, for example, used factoring during its reorganization. It is also used to finance growing numbers of global trade ventures. Read the Reaching Beyond Our Borders box to see why firms are turning to export factoring as a means of financing global trade.

Commercial Paper

Sometimes a large corporation needs funds for just a few months and wants to get lower rates than those charged by banks. One strategy is to sell commercial paper. **Commercial paper** consists of unsecured promissory notes, in amounts of $25,000 and up, that mature (come due) in 270 days or less. The promissory note states a fixed amount of money the business agrees to repay to the lender (investor) on a specific date. The interest rate is stated in the note. Commercial paper is unsecured (no collateral is offered) and is sold at a public sale. How-

Factoring Your Way into Global Markets

The trading boom in global markets shows no sign of slowing down. The lure of the world's 6 billion customers is too enticing for ambitious U.S. businesses to ignore. Unfortunately, the path of would-be exporters is often blocked by such financing constraints as the complications of trading in foreign currencies and difficulty in collecting money owed from global accounts. When these financing challenges are combined with political instability, high loan defaults, and unstable currencies, the problems of doing business can accelerate. Imagine selling Fiberrific cereal to a foreign buyer who later refuses to pay the bill. What would you do to collect? What legal recourse would you have if the buyer lives in a country torn by political upheaval?

This shaky environment requires U.S. companies to use new financing methods that help protect them in global markets. International factoring is one such method. International factoring involves negotiating with intermediaries who make sure the payment for the goods gets from the foreign buyer back to the seller. There are four parties involved in a transaction: the exporter (seller), the U.S. factor (called the export factor), the foreign factor (called the import factor), and the importer (buyer). The exporter and the export factor sign a factoring agreement that transfers the exporter's accounts receivable to the U.S. factor in exchange for coverage against any credit losses that could be incurred globally. In other words, the export factor guarantees the exporter that it will receive the money it is owed (minus fees, of course). The export factor selects an import factor to act on the seller's behalf under the export factor's supervision. The import factor assists in finding local customers in global markets to whom the seller can sell its goods or services. When an exporter receives an order from a customer, the import factor collects payment from the global buyer. The import factor deducts a fee and gives the remainder to the export factor. The export factor deducts a fee and gives that remainder to the selling company (exporter). By using these agreements, U.S. exporters can do business even in risky global markets without risking significant credit losses.

Though global networks of factoring organizations are just emerging, growth prospects look promising. If these networks are developed to their fullest, exporters will be able to do business abroad as easily as if their customers were right next door.

Sources: David Schmidt, "Migrating to Export Financing," *Business Finance,* July 2000, pp. 63–67; and "The Emerging Market Crisis and Its Effects on Forfaiting and Other Trade Financial Tools," *Review of Export Financing and Forfaiting,* Issue 4, www.forfaiting.com.

ever, major firms like Ford Motor Company and American Express are exploring the possibility of offering commercial paper over the Internet.[20] Still, because it is unsecured, only financially stable firms (mainly large corporations) are able to sell commercial paper. For these companies it's a way to get short-term funds quickly and for less than the interest charged by banks. Since most commercial paper matures in 30 to 90 days, it's also an investment opportunity for buyers who can afford to put up cash for short periods to earn some interest on their money.

PROGRESS ASSESSMENT

- What does the term *3/10, net 25* mean?
- What's the difference between trade credit and a line of credit at a bank?
- What is factoring? What are some of the considerations involved in establishing a discount rate in factoring?
- How does commercial paper work, and what's the main advantage of issuing commercial paper?

OBTAINING LONG-TERM FINANCING

Forecasting helps the firm develop a financial plan. This plan specifies the amount of funding the firm will need over various time periods and the most appropriate sources of obtaining those funds. In setting long-term financing objectives, financial managers generally ask three major questions:

1. What are the organization's long-term goals and objectives?
2. What are the financial requirements needed to achieve these long-term goals and objectives?
3. What sources of long-term capital are available, and which will best fit our needs?

In business, long-term capital is used to buy fixed assets such as plant and equipment, and to finance expansion of the organization. In major corporations, decisions involving long-term financing normally involve the board of directors and top management, as well as finance and accounting managers. Take pharmaceutical producer Merck, for example. A seven-member chairman's staff at Merck makes senior policy decisions involving factors such as long-term financing at the company. Merck expends as much as $1 billion a year for researching new products.[21] The actual development of a new product can sometimes take over 10 years and cost $350 million in company funds before the product is ever introduced in the market. It's easy to see why long-term financing decisions involve high-level managers at Merck. In some instances, a company may even employ an expert like an investment banker (we will look at investment bankers in Chapter 20) to assist with important and risky financing decisions. In small and medium-sized businesses, the owners are always actively involved in analyzing long-term financing opportunities that affect their company.

Initial long-term funding usually comes from either of two major types of financing, debt capital or equity capital. Let's look at these two sources of long-term financing next.

Debt Financing

Long-term financing of a business can be achieved by securing debt capital. If a company uses debt financing, it has a *legal obligation* to repay the amount borrowed. All businesses must keep in mind this legal requirement. Debt capital may be obtained from lending institutions or from the sale of bonds.

Firms that establish and develop a rapport with a bank, insurance company, pension fund, commercial finance company, or other financial institutions often are able to secure a long-term loan. Long-term loans are usually repaid within 3 to 7 years but may extend to perhaps 15 or 20 years. For such loans, a business must sign what is called a term-loan agreement. A **term-loan agreement** is a promissory note that requires the borrower to repay the loan in specified installments (e.g., monthly or yearly). A major advantage of a business using this type of financing is that the interest paid on the long-term debt is tax deductible.

term-loan agreement
A promissory note that requires the borrower to repay the loan in specified installments.

Because they involve larger amounts of capital, long-term loans are often more expensive to the firm than short-term loans are. Also, since the repayment period could be as long as 20 years, lenders are not assured that their capital will be repaid in full. Therefore, most long-term loans require collateral, which may be in the form of real estate, machinery, equipment, stock, or other items of value. Lenders will also often require certain restrictions on a firm's operations to force it to act responsibly in its business practices. The interest

1. Federal, state, and local governments
2. Federal government agencies
3. Corporations
4. Foreign governments and corporations

Source: *The Wall Street Journal Guide to Money and Markets.*

FIGURE 19.4

WHO CAN ISSUE BONDS?

rate for long-term loans is based on the adequacy of collateral, the firm's credit rating, and the general level of market interest rates. The greater the risk a lender takes in making a loan, the higher the rate of interest it requires. This is known as the **risk/return trade-off.**

If an organization is unable to obtain its long-term financing needs from a lending institution, it may try to issue bonds. (Figure 19.4 lists what types of organizations can issue bonds.) To put it simply, a bond is like a company IOU with a promise to repay on a certain date. It is a binding contract through which the organization issuing the bond agrees to specific terms with investors in return for the money those investors lend to the company. The terms of the agreement in a bond issue are referred to as the **indenture terms.** Let's see how bonds fit into a firm's long-term financing plans.

risk/return trade-off
The principle that the greater the risk a lender takes in making a loan, the higher the interest rate required.

indenture terms
The terms of agreement in a bond issue.

Secured and Unsecured Bonds

A bond is a long-term debt obligation of a corporation ▸ **P.140** ◂ or government. You are probably somewhat familiar with bonds. For example, you may own investments like U.S. government savings bonds, or perhaps you have volunteered your time to help a local school district pass a bond issue. Maybe your community is building a new stadium or cultural center that requires selling bonds. It's fair to say that businesses compete with government for the sale of bonds. Potential investors in bonds measure the *risk* involved in purchasing a bond against the *return* (interest) the bond promises to pay.

Like other forms of long-term debt, bonds can be secured or unsecured. A **secured bond** is issued with some form of collateral, such as real estate, equipment, or other pledged assets. If the bond's indenture terms are violated, the bondholder can issue a claim on the collateral. An **unsecured bond** is a bond backed only by the reputation of the issuer. Bondholders that invest in such bonds simply have trust in the organization issuing the bond. These bonds are generally referred to as *debenture bonds.*

secured bond
A bond issued with some form of collateral.

unsecured bond
A bond backed only by the reputation of the issuer.

Bonds are a key means of long-term financing for many organizations. If bonds interest you, once again stay tuned for Chapter 20, where we discuss them in greater detail.

Equity Financing

If a firm cannot obtain a long-term loan from a lending institution, or if it is unable to sell bonds to investors, it may look for long-term financing from equity capital. Equity financing comes from the owners of the firm. Therefore, equity financing involves selling ownership in the firm in the form of stock, or using retained earnings the firm has accumulated and kept to reinvest in the business. A business can also seek equity financing through venture capitalist's investments in the firm.

Issuing stock is covered at length in Chapter 20, but a basic understanding of stock as a source of equity financing is important here. We will next take a short look at issuing stock, followed by an explanation of other equity financing

FIGURE 19.5

DIFFERENCES BETWEEN
DEBT AND EQUITY
FINANCING

CONDITIONS	TYPE OF FINANCING	
	DEBT	**EQUITY**
Management influence	There's usually none unless special conditions have been agreed on.	Common stockholders have voting rights.
Repayment	Debt has a maturity date. Principal must be repaid.	Stock has no maturity date. The company is never required to repay equity.
Yearly obligations	Payment of interest is a contractual obligation.	The firm isn't legally liable to pay dividends.
Tax benefits	Interest is tax-deductible.	Dividends are paid from aftertax income and aren't deductible.

options using retained earnings and venture capital. If you are a bit confused about exactly how debt and equity financing differ, please review Figure 19.5 for a quick comparison of the pros and cons of the two options.

Selling Stock

Regardless of whether or not a new firm can obtain debt financing, there usually comes a time when it needs additional funds. One way to obtain such funds is to sell ownership shares (called stock) in the firm to private investors. The key word to remember here is *ownership*. The purchasers of stock become owners in the organization. The number of shares of stock that will be available for purchase is generally decided by the organization's board of directors. The company's board of directors can authorize the firm to sell all or part of its stock. Shares of stock the company decides not to offer for sale are referred to as *unissued* or *treasury stock*.

Selling stock to the public as a way to obtain equity financing is by no means easy or automatic. U.S. companies can issue stock for public purchase only if they meet requirements set by the Securities and Exchange Commission (SEC) as well as various state agencies. Companies can issue different types of stock, such as preferred and common stock. Both types will also be discussed in depth in Chapter 20.

Retained Earnings

Have you ever heard a businessperson say that he or she reinvests the firm's profits right back into the business? You probably remember from Chapter 18 that the profits the company keeps and reinvests in the firm are called *retained earnings*. Retained earnings often are a major source of long-term funds. This is especially true for small businesses, which have fewer financing alternatives, such as selling bonds or stock, than large businesses do. However, large corporations also depend on retained earnings for needed long-term funding. In fact, retained earnings are usually the most favored source of meeting long-term capital needs since a company that uses them saves interest payments, dividends (payments for investing in stock), and any possible underwriting fees for issuing bonds or stock. Also, there is no dilution of ownership in the firm, as occurs with selling stock.

The major problem with relying on retained earnings as a source of funding is that many organizations do not have on hand sufficient retained earnings to finance extensive capital improvements or business expansion. If you think about it for a moment, it makes sense. What if you wanted to buy an expensive personal asset such as a new car? The ideal way to purchase the car would be to go to your personal savings account and take out the necessary cash. No hassle! No interest! Unfortunately, few people have such large amounts of cash available. Most businesses are no different. Even though they would like to finance long-term needs from operations, few have the resources on hand to accomplish this.

Venture Capital

The hardest time for a business to raise money is when it is just starting. A start-up typically has few assets and no market track record, so the chances of borrowing significant amounts of money from a bank are slim.[22]

Venture capital is money that is invested in new companies that have great profit potential. Venture capital has helped firms such as Intel, Apple Computer, Compaq, Sun Microsystems, and dozens of other fast-growth companies get started.[23] Venture capital firms are one of the sources of start-up capital for new companies. From 1995 to 2000, nearly $90 billion in venture capital was invested in U.S. firms.[24]

venture capital
Money that is invested in new companies that have great profit potential.

The venture capital industry began about 50 years ago as an alternative investment vehicle for wealthy families. The Rockefellers (a family whose vast wealth came from John D. Rockefeller's Standard Oil Company, started in the 19th century) financed Sanford McDonnell, for example, when he was operating his company from an airplane hangar. That small venture grew into McDonnell Douglas, a large aerospace and defense contractor that merged with Boeing Corporation in 1997. The venture capital industry grew significantly in the 1980s, when many new high-tech companies were being started. In the 1990s the search for venture capital intensified, especially in high-tech centers such as California's Silicon Valley, where the focus of venture capitalists increasingly concentrated on Internet-related companies.[25] Venture capitalists have recently broadened their reach into global markets, such as Japan, where growing numbers of entrepreneurs ➤ **P.20** ◄ are seeking private funding.[26] Women entrepreneurs are also increasingly gaining attention from venture capital firms.[27] Today, private investors can even buy stock in a growing number of companies such as CMGI Inc. and Safeguard Scientifics Inc., which are venture capital firms in all but name because their main assets are ownership stakes in growing Internet companies.[28]

A finance manager has to be careful when choosing a venture capital firm to help finance a new business.[29] For one thing, the venture capital firm generally wants a stake in the ownership of the business. Venture capitalists also expect a very high return on their investment, usually 20 percent or more. More important, the venture capital firm should be able to come up with and be willing to provide more financing if the firm needs it. The search for venture capital actually begins with a good business plan ➤ **P.181** ◄ (see Chapter 6).[30] This document must convince investors that the firm will be a success. Part of the business plan should be a clear financing proposal that spells out exactly how much capital the firm needs, how to raise it, and how it will be paid back.

The dangers of having the wrong venture capital firm are illustrated in the experience of Jon Birck, who started Northwest Instrument Systems with venture capital. Birck worked until 11:00 or 12:00 each night to build the company. After having dedicated three years to the company, he was asked to leave by the venture capital firm, which wanted a more experienced chief executive officer to protect its investment. Birck had left a secure job, put his marriage on the line, taken out a second mortgage on his house, and given himself a below-average salary to get Northwest on its feet; then, just when the firm was ready for rapid growth, he was asked to resign.

SPOTLIGHT ON SMALL BUSINESS

The Myths of Venture Capital

Mention venture capitalists to aspiring entrepreneurs and you will likely hear a wide variety of opinions. While one entrepreneur might describe them as angels, another might believe that *vampires* is a more appropriate word. Venture capitalists have neither wings nor fangs, and they generally agree that most entrepreneurs misunderstand them. According to venture capitalists, misperceptions about the industry are based on myths that have developed among capital-seeking entrepreneurs. According to venture capital firms, the top six myths of the industry are the following:

1. *Venture capitalists want to take control of a company.* While most venture capital firms want a fair share of a company in return for the capital invested, they don't consider taking control unless a firm's management fails.
2. *Venture capitalists load their deals with unfair terms.* Though some terms may sound unfair to an entrepreneur, the purpose is to keep the entrepreneur focused. If entrepreneurs remember that they have responsibilities to the venture capital firm, they will keep their minds on growing the business.
3. *Venture capitalists have unrealistic performance expectations.* High expectations yes, unrealistic no. Venture capital firms like to remind entrepreneurs

that their limited partners are taking on high risk in the firm and therefore expect high rewards.

4. *Venture capitalists won't invest in small deals.* Small deals can always get financed if you look in the right places and have a solid business plan.
5. *Venture capitalists are too quick to pull the plug.* It's in the best interest of the venture capital firm to keep the company afloat. Only in situations that look lost or desperate will they pull the plug.
6. *Venture capitalists are impossible to talk to.* Somewhat true. Venture capitalists would much prefer that entrepreneurs send them a business plan they can absorb on their own time. They will then make the necessary phone calls or set up a meeting.

Even though perceptions of venture capitalists differ, it's obvious they are a growing source of seed funding for aspiring businesses. In 1999, for example, over $20 billion in venture capital was invested in new business ventures. Work on the business plan and know something about the venture capital firm, and funding might just come your way.

Sources: Paul DeCeglie, "The Truth about Venture Capital," *Business Start-Ups,* February 2000, pp. 40–47; and Randall E. Stross, "Venture Capitalists Aren't Villians," *The Wall Street Journal,* July 25, 2000, p. A22.

As Jon Birck's story shows, financing a firm's long-term needs through venture capitalists clearly involves a high degree of risk. Venture capitalists concede that they expect higher-than-average returns and competent management performance for their investment. They disagree, however, with the negative assumptions often associated with their industry. The Spotlight on Small Business box discusses what venture capitalists consider to be the myths of their business.

Still, no one would argue that there are risks when firms borrow funds from venture capitalists. Knowing this, you might be inclined to ask some questions: Why do firms borrow funds at all? Why not just use the other forms of equity funding? The reason involves the use of leverage. Let's look at using leverage next.

Making Decisions on Using Financial Leverage

leverage
Raising needed funds through borrowing to increase a firm's rate of return.

Raising needed funds through borrowing to increase the firm's rate of return is referred to as **leverage.** While it's true that debt increases the risk of the firm, it also enhances the firm's ability to increase profits. Two key jobs of the finance manager or CFO are to forecast the need for borrowed funds and to plan how to manage these funds once they are obtained. (Refer back to Figure 19.5 for a comparison of debt and equity financing alternatives.)

LEVERAGE—SELLING BONDS		EQUITY—SALE OF STOCK	
Common stock	$50,000	Common stock	$500,000
Bonds (at 10% interest)	450,000		
	$500,000		$500,000
Earnings	$125,000	Earnings	$125,000
Less bond interest	45,000		
	$80,000		$125,000

$$\text{Return to stockholders} = \frac{\$80,000}{\$50,000} = 160\% \qquad \text{Return to stockholders} = \frac{\$125,000}{\$500,000} = 25\%$$

FIGURE 19.6

USING LEVERAGE VERSUS EQUITY FINANCING: FIBERRIFIC INC. NEEDS TO RAISE $500,000

If the firm's earnings are larger than the interest payments on the funds borrowed, business owners can realize a higher rate of return than if it used equity financing. Look at Figure 19.6, which describes an example involving our cereal company, Fiberrific (introduced in Chapter 13). If Fiberrific needed $500,000 in financing, it could consider selling bonds (debt) or stock (equity) to investors. Comparing the two options, you can see that Fiberrific would benefit by selling bonds since the company's earnings are greater than the interest paid on borrowed funds (bonds). However, if the firm's earnings were less than the interest paid on borrowed funds (bonds), the owners could lose money on their investment.

Normally, it's up to each individual firm to determine exactly how to balance debt and equity financing. For example, the communications giant Viacom took on billions of dollars of new debt in its acquisitions of Paramount Pictures, MTV, and CBS.[31] In contrast, consumer products maker Gillette became a major player in the battery market with its $7 billion purchase of Duracell, all in stock. Some firms, such as Wm. Wrigley Jr. Co. and Hershey Foods, have little long-term debt. Leverage ratios (which we discussed in Chapter 18) give companies a standard of the comparative leverage of firms in their industries. According to Standard & Poor's and Moody's Investor Services, the debt of a large industrial corporation typically ranges between 33 and 40 percent of its total assets. Leverage among large companies dropped in the decade from 1990 to 2000.[32] Small-business debt varies considerably. As the requirements of financial institutions become more stringent and investors more demanding, it's certain that the job of the finance manager will become more challenging.

Chapter 20 takes a closer look at bonds and stocks both as financing tools for businesses and as investment options for private investors. You will learn about bond and stock issues, the securities exchanges, how to buy and sell stock, how to choose the right investment strategy, how to read the stock and bond quotations in *The Wall Street Journal* and other financial publications, and more. Finance takes on a whole new dimension when you see how you can participate in financial markets yourself.

PROGRESS ASSESSMENT

- What are the two major forms of debt financing available to a firm?
- How does debt financing differ from equity financing?
- What are the two major forms of equity financing available to a firm?
- What is leverage, and why would firms choose to use it?

SUMMARY

1. Explain the importance of finance.

1. Sound financial management is critical to the well-being of any business.
   - *What are the most common ways firms fail financially?*
   The most common financial problems are (1) undercapitalization, (2) poor control over cash flow, and (3) inadequate expense control.

2. Describe the responsibilities of financial managers.

2. *Finance* is that function in a business responsible for acquiring funds for the firm, managing funds within the firm (e.g., preparing budgets and doing cash flow analysis), and planning for the expenditure of funds on various assets.
   - *What do financial managers do?*
   Financial managers plan, budget, control funds, obtain funds, collect funds, audit, manage taxes, and advise top management on financial matters.

3. Tell what financial planning involves and define the three key budgets of finance.

3. Financial planning involves forecasting short- and long-term needs, budgeting, and establishing financial controls.
   - *What are the three budgets of finance?*
   The *capital budget* is the spending plan for expensive assets such as property, plant, and equipment. The *cash budget* is the projected cash balance at the end of a given period. The *operating* (master) budget summarizes the information in the other three budgets; it projects dollar allocations to various costs and expenses given various revenues.

4. Recognize the financial needs that must be met with available funds.

4. During the course of a business's life, its financial needs shift considerably.
   - *What are the major financial needs for firms?*
   Businesses have financial needs in four major areas: (1) managing daily business operations, (2) managing accounts receivable, (3) obtaining needed inventory, and (4) planning major capital expenditures.

5. Distinguish between short-term and long-term financing, and between debt capital and equity capital.

5. Businesses often have needs for short-term and long-term financing and for debt capital and equity capital.
   - *What's the difference between short-term and long-term financing?*
   Short-term financing refers to funds that will be repaid in less than one year, whereas long-term financing refers to funds that will be repaid over a specific time period of more than one year.
   - *What's the difference between debt capital and equity capital?*
   Debt capital refers to funds raised by borrowing (going into debt), whereas equity capital is raised from within the firm (through retained earnings) or by selling ownership in the company by issuing stock or selling ownership to venture capitalists.

6. Identify and describe several sources of short-term financing.

6. Sources of short-term financing include trade credit, promissory notes, family and friends, commercial banks and other financial institutions, factoring, and commercial paper.
   - *Why should businesses use trade credit?*
   Trade credit is the least expensive and most convenient form of short-term financing. Businesses can buy goods today and pay for them sometime in the future.
   - *What's a line of credit?*
   It is an agreement by a bank to lend a specified amount of money to the business at any time, if the money is available. A revolving credit agreement is a line of credit that guarantees a loan will be available—for a fee.

• ***What's the difference between a secured loan and an unsecured loan?***
An unsecured loan has no collateral backing it. Secured loans have collateral backed by assets such as accounts receivable, inventory, or other property of value.
• ***Is factoring a form of secured loan?***
No, factoring means *selling* accounts receivable at a discounted rate to a factor (an intermediary that pays cash for those accounts).
• ***What's commercial paper?***
Commercial paper is a corporation's unsecured promissory note maturing in 270 days or less.

7. One of the important functions of a finance manager is to obtain long-term capital.
• ***What are the major sources of long-term financing?***
Debt financing involves the sale of bonds and long-term loans from banks and other financial institutions. Equity financing is obtained through the sale of company stock, from the firm's retained earnings, or from venture capital firms.
• ***What are the two major forms of debt financing?***
Debt capital comes from two sources: selling bonds and borrowing from individuals, banks, and other financial institutions. Bonds can be secured by some form of collateral or can be unsecured. The same is true of loans.
• ***What's leverage, and how do firms use it?***
Leverage is raising funds from borrowing. It involves the use of borrowed funds to invest in such undertakings as expansion, major asset purchases, and research and development. Firms measure the risk of borrowing (leverage) against the potential for higher profits.

7. Identify and describe several sources of long-term financing.

KEY TERMS

capital budget 588
capital expenditures 592
cash budget 588
cash flow forecast 586
commercial finance companies 596
commercial paper 596
debt capital 592
equity capital 593
factoring 596
finance 585
financial control 589
financial managers 584

financial management 585
indenture terms 599
inventory financing 595
leverage 602
line of credit 595
long-term financing 592
long-term forecast 587
operating (master) budget 588
pledging 595
promissory note 594

revolving credit agreement 595
risk/return trade-off 599
secured bond 599
secured loan 595
short-term financing 592
short-term forecast 586
term-loan agreement 598
trade credit 593
unsecured bond 599
unsecured loan 595
venture capital 601

DEVELOPING WORKPLACE SKILLS

1. Obtain the most recent annual report of a major corporation in your area. Read the information provided about the company and review its balance sheet. See how much the company has borrowed short-term and long-term. (Hint: Look under liabilities.) Does the firm appear to be "safe" in terms of its leverage? Be prepared to offer opinions as to why or why not.

2. Visit the website of a local bank. Check what the current interest rate is and what rate small businesses would pay for short-term and long-term loans.

See if blank forms that borrowers use to apply for loans are available online. Share these forms with your class and explain the types of information the bank is seeking.

3. Go to the campus library and ask the reference librarian for information from Standard & Poor's and Moody's Investors Service concerning bond ratings. Analyze the process used by these two firms in evaluating and rating corporate bonds, and report what you find to the class.

4. One small-business consultant has commented that the most difficult concept to get across to small-business owners is the need to take all the trade credit (e.g., 2/10, net 30) they can get. He simply could not convince owners that they would save over 36 percent a year by doing that. Work with a small group of classmates and build a convincing argument to small-business owners of the benefits of using this concept.

5. Team up with at least two of your classmates and seek out at least two venture capital firms in your area. Set an appointment to interview them and find out what business criteria each firm uses in making investments in emerging companies. Ask how important they feel a company's business plan is in determining if they are worthy of the firm's investment. Compare what they tell you with the information in the text, and report your conclusions in a draft memo.

TAKING IT TO THE NET

Purpose

To investigate what types of businesses are attracting venture capital financing.

Exercise

To learn more about how start-up businesses can attract venture capital financing go to www.financehub.com/vc.

1. Click on the How to Get Venture Capital button. According to the latest venture capital survey listed on the site, who's getting the funding? What fields? What regions?

2. Click on the Checklist. List at least three things to do and not do when searching for venture capital.

3. From the sites home page click on the Venture Capital Firms button. Compare three venture capital firms. What types of businesses do they invest in?

PRACTICING MANAGEMENT DECISIONS

CASE

YOUR MISSION . . . SHOULD YOU DECIDE TO ACCEPT IT

Looking for a career that's challenging, with opportunities for advancement, and large numbers of openings? Then welcome to the world of financial management in nonprofit organizations. Nonprofits are crying out for the talents of skilled financial managers who often overlook nonprofits in favor of profit-seeking firms. As the availability of public funding becomes scarcer, the demand for financing expertise has soared among nonprofits. The call for innovative and experienced financial managers has grown louder.

Don't be fooled, however, into thinking that "nonprofit" means "no money." The size and scope of the nonprofit sector often surprises even seasoned business professionals. Also, misconceptions abound about work in nonprofits. For starters, many people assume that the nonprofit sector of the economy is quite small. In reality, it is valued at approximately $625 billion per year. This makes the U.S. nonprofit sector twice as large as the U.S. construction industry. Also, the term *nonprofit* is sometimes deceiving, bringing to mind church-sponsored bingo games or bake sales. Unfortunately, people forget that the nonprofit sector contains such notables as the National Football League, the Smithsonian Institution, and the National Audubon Society, none of which sponsors bingo or bake sales. In the United States today, the nonprofit sector includes over 1 million institutions, including schools, hospitals, human service organizations, religious groups, museums, and more. Over 15 million people are employed in the nonprofit sector of the economy.

Work in nonprofits often includes important interactions with the profit-seeking sector. For example, Sandy Boutin works as the director of Great Dane Rescue in Plymouth, Michigan. Her organization is always in need of dog food but has a very small budget. Boutin decided to invite dog food manufacturers to participate in her group's fund-raising. The companies got their name exposed to a large group of prospective customers in return for donating dog food to the rescue program. Through Boutin's efforts, both groups got what they wanted. Often large nonprofits like the Smithsonian Institute actively seek corporate sponsorship programs to help fund such activities as its traveling exhibitions. One nonprofit, the Rockland Family Shelter in Rockland County, New York, even enlisted a financial specialist to start a for-profit business to help finance the work of the shelter.

Many nonprofit organizations experience problems at the top of their organizations. David LaGreca, a manager with the Volunteer Consulting Group implies sarcastically that top management positions at nonprofits are often filled with highly "trained" businesspeople such as social workers, former dancers, and musicians. These individuals have creative and artistic skills but lack the training and business expertise of executives at profit-seeking firms. Chris Perks, pres-

ident of Perks Reutter Associates, an engineering consulting firm, agrees. According to Perks, "In nonprofits you are often dealing with people whose expertise is in the mission of the organization, not necessarily in administration or management. Furthermore, many employees do not come from business backgrounds. They are often hired as staffers because they are committed to what they are doing." It's also difficult to recruit qualified individuals to serve on nonprofit boards. Many prospective board members fear that the potential of scandal or poor business practices at a nonprofit could damage their reputation or business standing.

Nonprofits are also severely lacking in another critical aspect of 21st-century business: Most are not taking advantage of the powerful technology of the Web. According to strategic management firm Peppers and Rogers, nonprofits exercise poor use of such tools as tracking software and databases. With the proper financial management and technological expertise, nonprofits could use the Internet to enhance their fund-raising capabilities. The possibilities for nonprofits are clearly there if they can attract qualified business and financial expertise.

Decision Questions

1. How is the job of a financial manager in a nonprofit organization different from that of a financial manager with a profit-seeking firm?
2. Should financial managers in nonprofit organizations be compensated equally to their counterparts in profit-seeking firms? Why or why not?
3. Do you see the job of the nonprofit financial manager as getting easier or more difficult in the future? Where might you get facts to support your conclusions?
4. How can a financial manager at a nonprofit make better use of Web capabilities to enhance the financial position of the organization?

Sources: Jacquelyn Lynn, "Hidden Resources," *Entrepreneur*, January 2000, pp. 102–8; Michael Freedman, "Charity Chic," *Forbes*, February 7, 2000, pp. 82–84; Ann Marsh, "Medicine Man," *Forbes*, January 24, 2000, pp. 84–86; and Diane Brady, "When Nonprofits Go After Profits," *Business Week*, June 26, 2000, pp. 173–78.

VIDEO CASE

THE ROLE OF THE FINANCIAL MANAGER

Financial managers play one of the most complex roles in business. These managers are responsible for forecasting financial needs, budgeting, obtaining and controlling funds, auditing, managing accounts receivable, and advising management on financial affairs. In addition, financial managers handle tax questions, manage cash, and conduct internal audits. In short, financial managers are responsible for anything having to do with obtaining, spending, and managing money.

Financial management, then, can be defined simply as assuming responsibility for acquiring the necessary funds to start a business and then to manage the cash inflow and outflow once it is established. But such a definition doesn't capture the dynamics of financial management. It may be easier to picture part of finance as a four-step process: (1) forecasting financial needs, (2) preparing budgets, (3) establishing controls to ensure the company follows its financial plans, and (4) obtaining short-term and long-term financing.

Short-term financing involves using trade credit, issuing promissory notes, borrowing from friends and family, going to commercial banks, and collecting funds from those who owe the company. Financial managers are responsible for minimizing the costs of borrowing and decreasing costs in general.

Long-term financing, on the other hand, is usually provided by retained earnings (profit not distributed in the form of dividends) or from the sale of stock or bonds. When a company sells stock, the ownership is spread among many people. A board of directors represents these owners, and the board selects the company's managers. When a company sells bonds, it obtains funds without losing any of its ownership. A bond is like a corporate IOU. The rate a company must pay depends on the economy and competition from government bonds.

Clearly, financial managers are in touch with the company's lifeblood—money. In many ways, financial management is a form of risk management. Financial managers must weigh their risks of borrowing money against the potential earnings. They must also weigh the risks of investing the firm's profits, in the stocks or bonds of other companies or in other types of investments. Additionally, financial managers play key roles in deciding which of the firm's projects to finance and which to deny or cut off. Given such responsibility, it's easy to see why a career in finance is both rewarding and challenging.

Discussion Questions

1. What are the financial conditions of the economy today, and how do those conditions affect financial managers?
2. If you were a financial manager today at a major corporation, would you try to raise investment capital through the sale of stock or bonds or through some other source? Why?
3. What is the relationship between accounting and finance? Could you be an outstanding financial manager without a good understanding of accounting?
4. Does finance seem like a good career for you? Why or why not?

CHAPTER 20

Securities Markets: Financing and Investing Opportunities

LEARNING GOALS

AFTER YOU HAVE READ AND STUDIED THIS CHAPTER, YOU SHOULD BE ABLE TO

1 Examine the functions of securities markets and investment bankers.

2 Compare the advantages and disadvantages of issuing bonds, and identify the classes and features of bonds.

3 Compare the advantages and disadvantages of issuing stock, and outline the differences between common and preferred stock.

4 Describe the various stock exchanges and how to invest in securities markets, and explain various investment objectives such as long-term growth, income, cash, and protection from inflation.

5 Analyze the opportunities bonds offer as investments.

6 Explain the opportunities stocks and mutual funds offer as investments and the advantages of diversifying investments.

7 Discuss specific high-risk investments, including junk bonds, buying stock on margin, and commodity trading.

8 Explain securities quotations listed in the financial section of a newspaper, and describe how stock market indicators like the Dow Jones Average affect the market.

Getting to Know Jonathan Hoenig of Capitalistpig

Jonathan Hoenig admits he first became "addicted to greed" while working at the coffee-shop franchise Starbucks as a teenager. He discovered that the money he earned after buying a few shares of Starbucks stock far surpassed what he made toiling behind the counter making lattes. Since that "grinding" experience, Hoenig has proudly proclaimed himself a "capitalist pig" and has personally ascribed to the philosophy that "greed is good."

During his senior year at Northwestern University, Jonathan decided that his calling in life was to spread the message of financial opportunity to his fellow members of Generation X (born between 1964 and 1976). He passionately believed that, despite the prevailing stereotype, Gen Xers were not slackers but were instead a unique group more savvy than previous generations. His mission was to share the wealth with his post-baby-boom generation by preaching the gospel of investing. As a springboard for his crusade, Hoenig developed a relationship with a local radio station. Soon he began broadcasting his own show called, appropriately, "Capitalist Pig." The radio show is now broadcast in 18 states and has attracted growing attention among his target market. He's also attracted the attention of respected investment gurus such as Michael Bloomberg and Louis Rukeyser, who have both made guest appearances on Hoenig's show. In 1999, Hoenig spread his wings again and took time to write *Greed Is Good: The Capitalist Pig Guide to Investing*. He also joined the Chicago Board of Trade to begin investing on his own.

Today, Hoenig's life continues on the fast track. He starts his day about 5:00 AM and doesn't call it quits until late evening. He serves as an adviser to financial institutions, including brokerage firms such as Charles Schwab.

He counsels them on how to market financial advice, services, and products to Gen Xers. He also writes a financial advice column for an ultra-hip magazine and runs his own asset management firm in Chicago. His website (www.capitalistpig.com) is attracting growing numbers of prospective investors every day. Still, Hoenig feels that many brokerage firms and mutual funds are not getting the message about young investors. He also admits that many young investors are ill informed and remain more attracted to high-interest credit cards than to stocks, bonds, and mutual funds. That leaves a good deal of work to accomplish on both sides of Hoenig's equation.

According to Hoenig, being a capitalist pig isn't about being materialistic. It's about knowing what you want and doing what it takes to get it. Dressed casually (with sockless feet in a pair of high-top sneakers) and sporting two-toned hair, he doesn't look the part of a Wall Street operator. He is, however, intense in his passion to spread the message that securities markets can offer financial opportunity to all.

This chapter discusses securities markets and how they assist companies as well as individual investors such as Jonathan Hoenig in achieving their financial goals and objectives. Read this chapter carefully and perhaps you will become a disciple or competitor of Hoenig in spreading the word of financial freedom through capitalism.

Source: Regina Fazio Maruca, "State of the New Economy," *Fast Company*, September 1, 2000, p. 106; Donna M. McKenna, "Unleashing the Pig," *Ticker*, August 1999, p. 18; Jonathan Hoenig, "Capitalistpig," *Business Start-Ups*, March 2000, p. 41; and Robert Frick, "Investing Taken to Xtremes," *Kiplinger.com*, March 2001.

THE FUNCTION OF SECURITIES MARKETS

Securities markets such as the New York Stock Exchange (NYSE) are financial marketplaces for stocks and bonds. These institutions serve two major functions: First, they assist businesses in finding long-term funding to finance large capital needs such as beginning operations, expanding their businesses, or buying major goods and services. Second, they provide private investors a place to buy and sell investments, such as stocks, bonds, and mutual funds, that can help them build their financial future. In this chapter, we will look at securities markets from the perspectives of both businesses and private investors.

Securities markets are divided into primary and secondary markets. Primary markets handle the sale of new securities. This is an important point to understand. Corporations make money on the sale of their securities only once—when they are first bought on the primary market. The first public offering of a corporation's stock is called an **initial public offering (IPO).** After that, the secondary market handles the trading of securities between investors, with the proceeds of a sale going to the investor selling the stock, not to the corporation whose stock is sold. For example, if you, the maker of Fiberrific cereal, offer 2 million shares of stock in your company at $15 a share, you would raise $30 million at this initial offering. However, if Shareholder Jones sells 100 shares of her Fiberrific stock to Investor Smith, you collect nothing. Smith bought the stock from Jones, not from Fiberrific. However, companies like Fiberrific can decide to offer additional shares of stock to raise additional capital.

As Chapter 19 implied, the importance of long-term funding to businesses can't be overemphasized.[1] Unfortunately, many new companies start without sufficient capital and many established firms fail to do adequate long-term planning. If given a choice, businesses normally prefer to meet long-term financial needs by using retained earnings or by borrowing from a lending institution. However, if such types of long-term funding are not available, a company may be able to raise capital by issuing corporate bonds (debt) or selling stock (ownership). Recall that issuing corporate bonds is a form of *debt* financing and selling stock in the corporation is a form of *equity* financing. These forms of debt or equity financing are not available to all companies (especially small businesses), but many firms use such financing to meet long-term financial needs.

For example, what if you needed long-term financing to expand your operations at Fiberrific? Your chief financial officer (CFO) ➤ **P.585** ◄ explains that the company doesn't have sufficient retained earnings, and it's unlikely you can secure the needed funds from a lender. The CFO suggests that you might want to issue corporate bonds or offer shares of stock to private investors to secure the financing needed. She warns, however, that being able to issue corporate bonds or shares of stock in the company is not an automatic right. Getting approval for bond or stock issues requires extensive financial dis-

initial public offering (IPO)
The first public offering of a corporation's stock.

Initial Public Offerings (IPOs) are a way for a company to finance growth. However, there's no guarantee investors will be willing to buy a company's stock. Wired Ventures, publishers of *Wired* magazine, hoped to raise millions of dollars from an IPO that unfortunately fell through when the market soured on the offering. What are the risks of investing in IPOs?

closures and detailed scrutiny by the U.S. Securities and Exchange Commission (SEC). Because of such requirements, she recommends the company turn to an investment banker for assistance. Let's see why.

The Role of Investment Bankers

Investment bankers are specialists who assist in the issue and sale of new securities. Investment banking firms such as Goldman Sachs or large financial institutions like Bank of America help companies prepare the extensive financial analyses necessary to gain SEC approval for stock or bond issues.[2]

Investment bankers also underwrite new issues of bonds or stocks. In other words, the investment banking firm buys the entire bond or stock issue a company wants to sell at an agreed-on discount (which can be quite sizable), and then sells the issue to private or institutional investors at full price. **Institutional investors** are large organizations—such as pension funds, mutual funds, insurance companies, and banks—that invest their own funds or the funds of others. Because of their vast buying power, institutional investors are a powerful force in securities markets.

Securities markets, as we have said, help companies raise needed long-term capital through debt financing by issuing bonds or equity financing by selling stock. Let's look first at issuing bonds.

DEBT FINANCING THROUGH SELLING BONDS

A **bond** is a corporate certificate indicating that a person has lent money to a firm (see Figure 20.1).[3] A company that issues bonds has a legal obligation to make regular interest payments to investors and to repay the entire bond principal amount at a prescribed time, called the maturity date. Let's explore the language of bonds a bit more carefully so you understand exactly what's involved.

investment bankers
Specialists who assist in the issue and sale of new securities.

institutional investors
Large organizations—such as pension funds, mutual funds, insurance companies, and banks—that invest their own funds or the funds of others.

bond
A corporate certificate (IOU) indicating that a person has lent money to a firm.

FIGURE 20.1

A SAMPLE BOND CERTIFICATE FROM IBM

Learning the Language of Bonds

A more specific definition of a bond than the one given above is that a bond is a contract of indebtedness issued by a corporation or government unit that promises payment of a principal amount at a specified future time.[4] Interest is paid to the holder of the bond until the principal amount is due. Thus, in this context, **interest** is the payment the issuer of the bond makes to the bondholders for use of the borrowed money. The interest rate paid on a bond may also be called the bond's *coupon rate*. This term dates back to when bonds were issued as *bearer bonds* and the holder, or bearer, was considered the owner. The company issuing the bond kept no accounts of transfers in ownership, and the interest on the bond was obtained by clipping "coupons" attached to the bond and sending them to the issuing company. Today bonds are registered to particular owners, and changes in ownership are recorded electronically. Take a look again at the bond in Figure 20.1 and see if you can tell whether it is a registered bond or a bearer bond.

The interest rate paid on a bond varies according to factors such as the state of the economy, the reputation of the company issuing the bond, and the going interest rate for government bonds or bonds of similar companies.[5] The interest rate being paid by U.S. government bonds clearly affects the interest rate a firm must agree to pay, since government bonds are considered safe investments. (Remember the risk/return trade-off defined in Chapter 19.) Bonds of all types are evaluated (rated) in terms of their risk to investors by independent rating firms such as Standard & Poor's and Moody's Investors Service.[6] Bond ratings can range from high-quality, gilt-edged bonds to bonds considered junk (which we discuss later in this chapter). Figure 20.2 describes the range of ratings these two firms attach to bond issues. Once an interest rate is set for a bond issue, it cannot be changed.

In reference to bonds, bonds are issued with a denomination. The **denomination** is the amount of debt represented by one bond. (Bonds are almost always issued in multiples of $1,000.) The **principal** is the face value of a bond. The issuing company is legally bound to repay the bond principal to the bondholder in full on the **maturity date.** For example, if Fiberrific issues a $1,000 bond with an interest rate of 9 percent and a maturity date of 2020, you are agreeing to pay a bondholder $90 in interest *each year* until a specified date in 2020, when the full $1,000 must be repaid. Maturity dates for bonds can vary. For example, firms such as Disney and Coca-Cola have issued bonds with 50-year maturity dates.

interest
The payment the issuer of the bond makes to the bondholders for use of the borrowed money.

denomination
The amount of debt represented by one bond.

principal
The face value of a bond.

maturity date
The exact date the issuer of a bond must pay the principal to the bondholder.

FIGURE 20.2

BOND RATINGS

RATING		
MOODY'S	**STANDARD & POOR'S**	**DESCRIPTIONS**
Aaa	AAA	Highest quality (lowest default risk)
Aa	AA	High Quality
A	A	Upper medium grade
Baa	BBB	Medium grade
Ba	BB	Lower medium grade
B	B	Speculative
Caa	CCC, CC	Poor (high default risk)
Ca	C	Highly speculative
C	D	Lowest grade

Advantages and Disadvantages of Issuing Bonds

Bonds offer several long-term financing advantages to an organization. The decision to issue bonds is generally based on advantages such as the following:

- Bondholders are creditors, not owners, of the firm and have no vote on corporate matters; thus, management maintains control over the firm's operations.
- Interest paid on bonds is tax deductible. Chapter 18 explained how certain interest expenses help a firm limit its tax responsibilities to the government.
- Bonds are a temporary source of funding for a firm. They're eventually repaid and the debt obligation eliminated.

But bonds also have their drawbacks:

- Bonds increase debt (liabilities) and may adversely affect the market's perception of the firm.
- Interest on bonds is a legal obligation. If interest is not paid, bondholders can take legal action to force payment.
- The face value of bonds must be repaid on the maturity date. Without careful planning, this repayment can cause cash flow problems when the bonds come due.

Different Classes of Bonds

As mentioned in Chapter 19, corporations can issue two different classes of corporate bonds. The first class is *unsecured bonds,* which are not supported by any type of collateral. These bonds are usually referred to as **debenture bonds.** Generally, only well-respected firms with excellent credit ratings can issue debenture bonds, since the only security the bondholder has is the reputation and credit history of the company.

    The second class of bonds is *secured bonds,* which are backed by some tangible asset (i.e., collateral) that is pledged to the bondholder if bond interest isn't paid or the principal isn't paid back. For example, a mortgage bond is a bond secured by company assets such as land and buildings.

    Figure 20.3 lists and describes several types of bonds that compete in securities markets with U.S. corporate bonds. In issuing bonds, a company can include different features in the various issues. Let's look at some possible special bond features.

debenture bonds
Bonds that are unsecured (i.e., not backed by any collateral such as equipment).

Special Bond Features

By now you should know that bonds are issued with an interest rate, are unsecured or secured by some type of collateral, and must be repaid at their maturity date. This repayment requirement often leads companies to establish what is called a **sinking fund** whose primary purpose is to ensure that enough money will be available to repay bondholders on the bond's maturity date. Sinking fund bond issuers regularly set aside funds in a reserve account (a sinking fund) so that enough capital will be accumulated by the maturity date to pay off the bond. Sinking funds can be attractive to firms and potential investors for several reasons:

sinking fund
Special provision of a bond that requires the issuer to retire (put in a trust fund), on a periodic basis, some part of the bond principal prior to maturity.

- They provide for an orderly retirement of a bond issue.
- They reduce the risk the bond will not be repaid.
- The market price of the bond is supported because the risk of the firm's not repaying the principal on the maturity date is reduced.

FIGURE 20.3

TYPES OF BONDS THAT COMPETE WITH CORPORATE BONDS

U.S. government bonds are considered the safest bond investments since they have the full faith and credit of the federal government behind them. There are different kinds of bonds with different risks for every kind of investor.

BOND	DESCRIPTION
U.S. government bond	Issued by the federal government; considered the safest type of bond investment
Treasury bills (T-bills)	Bonds that mature in less than a year and are issued with a minimum par value of $10,000
Treasury notes and bonds	Bonds that mature in 10 to 25 years and are sold in denominations of $1,000 and $5,000
Municipal bonds	Bonds issued by state or local governments; interest payments are exempt from federal taxes
Yankee bond	Bonds that are issued by a foreign government and are payable in U.S. dollars
Zero-coupon bond	Bonds that pay no interest prior to maturity; the return to the investor comes from the difference between the purchase price and the bond's face value

callable bond
A bond that gives the issuer the right to pay off the bond before its maturity.

Another special feature that can be included in a bond issue is a call provision. A **callable bond** permits the bond issuer to pay off the bond's principal prior to its maturity date. Call provisions must be included when a bond is issued, and bondholders should be aware of whether a bond is callable. Callable bonds give companies some discretion in their long-term forecasting. Suppose Fiberrific issued $50 million in 20-year bonds in 2002 with an interest rate of 10 percent. The yearly interest expense would be $5 million ($50 million times 10 percent). If market conditions change in 2007, and bonds issued of the same quality are only paying 7 percent, Fiberrific would be paying 3 percent, or $1.5 million, in excess interest yearly ($50 million times 3 percent). Obviously, Fiberrific could benefit if it could call in (pay off) the old bonds and reissue new bonds at the lower interest rate. If a company calls a bond before maturity, investors in the bond are often paid a price above the bond's face value.

convertible bond
A bond that can be converted into shares of common stock in the issuing company.

Another feature sometimes included in bonds is convertibility.[7] A **convertible bond** is a bond that can be converted into shares of common stock in the issuing company.[8] This feature is often an incentive for an investor to buy a bond. Why, you may ask, would bond investors want to convert their investment to stock? That's easy. If the value of the firm's common stock grows sizably over time, bondholders can compare the value of continued bond interest with the possible sizable profit they could gain by converting to a specified number of shares of common stock. When we discuss common stock in the next section, this advantage will become more evident to you.

PROGRESS ASSESSMENT

- Why are bonds considered to be a form of debt financing?
- What does it mean when a firm states that it is issuing a 9 percent debenture bond due in 2020?
- Explain the difference between an unsecured and a secured bond.
- Why do companies like to issue callable bonds? Why do investors dislike them?
- Why are convertible bonds attractive to investors?

EQUITY FINANCING THROUGH SELLING STOCK

Equity financing ▸ **P.599** ◂ is the other form of long-term funding first introduced in Chapter 19. One popular form of equity financing is obtaining funds through the sale of ownership (stock) in the corporation. As we did with bonds, let's look first at the language of stock.

Learning the Language of Stock

Stocks are shares of ownership in a company. A **stock certificate** is evidence of stock ownership that specifies the name of the company, the number of shares it represents, and the type of stock being issued (see Figure 20.4). Today stock certificates are generally held electronically for the owners of the stock. Certificates sometimes indicate a stock's **par value,** which is a dollar amount assigned to each share of stock by the corporation's charter. Some states use par value as a basis for calculating the state's incorporation charges and fees; but today, since par values do not reflect the market value of the stock, most companies issue "no-par" stock. **Dividends** are part of a firm's profits that *may* be distributed to stockholders as either cash payments or additional shares of stock.[9] Although companies that issue bonds are required to pay interest, companies that issue stock are *not* required to pay dividends.[10]

Advantages and Disadvantages of Issuing Stock

Since securities markets include the names of almost every large company in the United States, companies apparently feel that equity financing is a good way to raise long-term funds. The following are some advantages to the firm of issuing stock:

- As owners of the business, stockholders never have to be repaid.
- There's no legal obligation to pay dividends to stockholders; therefore, income (retained earnings) can be reinvested in the firm for future capital needs.
- Selling stock can improve the condition of the firm's balance sheet since the sale creates no debt and makes the company stronger financially.

Disadvantages of issuing stock include the following:

- As owners, stockholders (usually only common stockholders) have the right to vote for the company's board of directors. Typically one vote is granted for each share of stock. Hence, the direction and control of the firm can be altered by the sale of stock.
- Dividends are paid out of profit after taxes and thus are not tax deductible.
- Management's decisions can be affected by the need to keep stockholders happy.

Companies can issue two classes of stock: preferred and common. Let's see how these forms of equity financing differ.

Issuing Shares of Preferred Stock

Preferred stock gives its owners preference (hence the term *preferred*) in the payment of dividends and an earlier claim on company assets than common stock if the firm is forced out of business and its assets sold. Normally,

stocks
Shares of ownership in a company.

stock certificate
Evidence of stock ownership that specifies the name of the company, the number of shares it represents, and the type of stock being issued.

par value
A dollar amount assigned to each share of stock by the corporation's charter.

dividends
Part of a firm's profits that may be distributed to stockholders as either cash payments or additional shares of stock.

preferred stock
Stock that gives its owners preference in the payment of dividends and an earlier claim on assets than common stockholders if the company is forced out of business and its assets sold.

preferred stock does not include voting rights in the firm. Preferred stock is frequently referred to as a hybrid investment because it has characteristics of both bonds and stocks. To illustrate this, consider the treatment of preferred stock dividends.

Preferred stock dividends differ from common stock dividends in several ways. Preferred stock is generally issued with a par value that becomes the base for the dividend the firm is willing to pay. For example, if a preferred stock's par value is $100 a share with a dividend rate of 6 percent, the firm is committing to a $6 dividend for each share of preferred stock the investor owns (6 percent of $100 = $6). An owner of 100 shares of this preferred stock is promised a fixed yearly dividend of $600. The owner is also assured that this dividend *must* be paid in full before any common stock dividends can be distributed.

Preferred stock is therefore quite similar to bonds in that both have a face (or par) value and both have a *fixed* rate of return. Also, as with bonds, Standard & Poor's and Moody's Investor Service rate preferred stock according to risk. So how do bonds and preferred stock differ? Remember that companies are legally bound to pay bond interest and to repay the face value of the bond on its maturity date. In contrast, even though preferred stock dividends are generally fixed, they do not legally have to be paid, and stock never has to be repurchased. Though both bonds and stock can increase in market value, the price of stock generally increases at a higher percentage than the price of bonds. Of course, the market value of both could also go down.

Special Features of Preferred Stock

Preferred stock can have special features that do not apply to common stock. For example, like bonds, preferred stock can be callable. This means a company could require preferred stockholders to sell back their shares. Preferred stock can also be convertible to shares of common stock. An important feature of preferred stock is that it's often cumulative. That is, if one or more dividends are not paid when due, the missed dividends of **cumulative preferred stock** will be accumulated and paid later. This means that all dividends, including the back dividends, must be paid in full before any common stock dividends can be distributed.

cumulative preferred stock
Preferred stock that accumulates unpaid dividends.

Issuing Shares of Common Stock

Common stock is the most basic form of ownership in a firm. In fact, if a company issues only one type of stock, it must be common. Holders of common stock have the right (1) to vote for board directors and important issues affecting the company and (2) to share in the firm's profits through dividends, if offered by the firm's board of directors. Having voting rights in a corporation allows stockholders to influence corporate policy since the elected board chooses the firm's top management and makes major policy decisions. Also, common stockholders have what is called a **preemptive right,** which is the first right to purchase any new shares of common stock the firm decides to issue. This right allows common stockholders to maintain a proportional share of ownership in the company.

Now that we have looked at stocks and bonds from a company's perspective as a source of long-term financing, we need to look at them from an investor's perspective. Before we do that, though, it's important to discuss stock exchanges—the places where stocks and bonds are traded.

common stock
The most basic form of ownership in a firm; it confers voting rights and the right to share in the firm's profits through dividends, if offered by the firm's board of directors.

preemptive right
Common stockholders' right to purchase any new shares of common stock the firm decides to issue.

PROGRESS ASSESSMENT

- Name at least two advantages and two disadvantages of issuing stock as a form of equity financing.

- What are the major differences between preferred stock and common stock?

- In what ways is preferred stock similar to bonds? How are they different?

STOCK EXCHANGES

As its name implies, a **stock exchange** is an organization whose members can buy and sell (exchange) securities for companies and investors. Brokerage firms such as A. G. Edwards and Merrill Lynch purchase memberships, or seats, on the exchanges, but the number of seats available is limited. The New York Stock Exchange (discussed below), for example, has only 1,366 members. This limitation pushed the price of a seat on the NYSE to over $2.5 million in 1999.

Stock exchanges operate all over the world in cities such as Paris, London, Sydney, Buenos Aires, and Tokyo. Even former communist-bloc countries such as Hungary and Poland have opened stock exchanges that enable businesses and individuals to buy securities from companies almost anywhere in the world.[11] For example, if you hear of a foreign company that has great potential for growth, you may be able to obtain shares of its stock with little difficulty from U.S. brokers who have access to the foreign stock exchanges. In fact, the number of foreign firms listed on the NYSE stood at 382 in 2000.

stock exchange
An organization whose members can buy and sell (exchange) securities for companies and investors.

U.S. Exchanges

The largest stock exchange in the United States, the New York Stock Exchange (NYSE), was founded in 1792.[12] The NYSE is a floor-based exchange (trades take place on the floor of the stock exchange) that lists about 3,100 companies, mostly very large. For example, in 2000 the NYSE listed 3,025 companies, with

It's a far cry from meeting under an oak tree to trade stocks. Today, stock exchanges, like the Madrid Exchange pictured here, are located throughout the world, including former communist-bloc nations. On large exchanges like the New York Stock Exchange, over a billion shares of stock have been traded in a single day.

over-the-counter (OTC) market
Exchange that provides a means to trade stocks not listed on the national exchanges.

National Association of Securities Dealers Automated Quotations (NASDAQ)
A nationwide electronic system that communicates over-the-counter trades to brokers.

a total market value of over $16 trillion. Because of such large market capitalization, the NYSE is often referred to as the Big Board. The second largest floor-based U.S. exchange is the American Stock Exchange (AMEX).[13] These two exchanges are national exchanges because they handle stocks of companies from all over the United States. In addition to the national exchanges, there are several regional exchanges in cities such as Chicago, San Francisco, Philadelphia, Cincinnati, Spokane, and Salt Lake City. The regional exchanges deal mostly with firms in their own areas and handle the stock of many large corporations listed on the Big Board. Regional exchanges are often used by big institutional investors to trade stock since their transaction costs are less than those of large exchanges like the New York Stock Exchange.

The **over-the-counter (OTC) market** provides companies and investors with a means to trade stocks not listed on the national securities exchanges. The OTC market is a network of several thousand brokers. These brokers maintain contact with one another and buy and sell securities through a nationwide electronic system known as the **National Association of Securities Dealers Automated Quotations** (NASDAQ—pronounced *nazz-dak*). In 1998, a merger between the NASDAQ and American Stock Exchange created the NASDAQ-AMEX Market Group.

Originally, the over-the-counter market dealt mostly with small firms that could not qualify for listing on the national exchanges or did not want to bother with the procedures. Today, however, well-known firms such as Intel, Cisco, Dell and Microsoft have their stock traded on the OTC market. The over-the-counter market also handles corporate and U.S. government bonds as well as many city and state government bonds. The NASDAQ today lists approximately 5,600 stock issues, including many technology companies and emerging small companies.[14] The NASDAQ exchange expects to expand operations into Europe and other global markets.[15] Frank Zarb, the chairman and CEO of NASDAQ, confidently predicts that a new global stock exchange will emerge and that trading securities will be digital, global, and accessible 24 hours a day.[16] The NASDAQ is well on its way to accomplishing this objective.[17]

EXCHANGE	REQUIREMENTS	TYPE OF COMPANY
New York Stock Exchange (NYSE)	Pretax income of $2.5 million; 1.1 million shares outstanding at a minimum market value of $18 million	Oldest, largest, and best-known companies
American Stock Exchange (AMEX)	Pretax income of $750,000; 500,000 shares publicly held at a minimum market value of $3 million (a second AMEX listing requires only 250,000 share publicly held at a minimum market value of $2.5 million)	Midsized growth companies
NASDAQ	Pretax income of $750,000 or a total market value of all shares outstanding at $1 million; 400 shareholders; net assets of $4 million	Large, midsized, and small growth companies

Source: <www.nyse.com/public/listed/3b/3bfm.htm>.

FIGURE 20.5

REQUIREMENTS FOR REGISTERING STOCK ON THE NEW YORK, AMERICAN, AND NASDAQ EXCHANGES

Figure 20.5 lists the requirements for registering stocks on the various exchanges. Adding a company to an exchange is a highly competitive undertaking, and the battle is often outright fierce.

Securities Regulations

The Securities Act of 1933 protects investors by requiring full disclosure of financial information by firms selling new stocks or bonds. The U.S. Congress passed this act to deal with the free-for-all atmosphere that existed in the securities markets during the Roaring Twenties and the early 1930s. The Securities and Exchange Act of 1934 created the **Securities and Exchange Commission (SEC),** which has responsibility at the federal level for regulating activities in the various exchanges. Companies trading on the national exchanges must register with the SEC and provide it annual updates. The act also established specific guidelines that companies must follow when issuing stock. For example, before issuing stock for sale to the public, a company must file

Securities and Exchange Commission (SEC)
Federal agency that has responsibility for regulating the various exchanges.

Firms wanting to sell stocks or bonds must fully disclose all relevant financial information to the Securities and Exchange Commission (SEC) in a detailed registration statement. Investors receive a condensed version of the statement called a prospectus. Here, former SEC chairman, Arthur Levitt answers questions related to a firm's prospectus.

The Inside Scoop

Insider trading was a burning issue in the "greed-is-good" days of the late 1980s. Big-time dealers like Ivan Boesky and Michael Milkin became household names as reports of their alleged dishonest stock deals unfolded before investors' eyes. Insider trading is said to occur when someone buys or sells a stock based on information not available to the investing public. Still, the answer to "What exactly is insider trading?" often remains sort of cloudy. The hypothetical examples below will give you an idea of what's legal and illegal concerning insider trading. See how many you can get right. The answers are at the bottom of this box.

1. You work in research and development at a large company and have been involved in a major effort that should lead to a blockbuster new product coming to the market. News about the product is not public, and very few other workers even know about it. Can you purchase stock in the company?

2. Pertaining to the above situation, you are in a local coffee bar and mention to a friend about what's going on at the company. Another customer seated at an adjoining table overhears your discussion. Can this person buy stock in the company before the public announcement?

3. You work as an executive secretary at a major investment banking firm. You are asked to copy documents that detail a major merger about to happen that will keenly benefit the company being taken over. Can you buy stock in the company before the announcement is made public?

4. Your stockbroker recommends that you buy shares in a little-known company. The broker seems to have some inside information, but you don't ask any questions about his source. Can you buy stock in this company?

5. You work as a cleaning person at a major securities firm. At your job you come across information from the trash cans and computer printers of employees of the firm that provide detailed information about several upcoming deals the firm will be handling. Can you buy stock in the companies involved?

(Answers: 1. No; 2. Yes; 3. No; 4. Yes; 5. No.)

Sources: Lisa Gibbs, "Following the In-the-Know Crowd: Insider Trades Offer Clues to a Stock's Prospects, But Beware of False Leads," *Money*, March 1, 2000, pp. 38A–45A; Francis A. McMorris, Randall Smith, and Michael Schroeder, "Insider Case Involves a Temp at Two Brokers and Web Ring," *The Wall Street Journal*, March 15, 2000, pp. C1–C13; and Albert B. Crenshaw, "CEO Traded on Insider Tip," *The Washington Post*, January 30, 2001, p. E1.

---

prospectus
A condensed version of economic and financial information that a company must file with the SEC before issuing stock; the prospectus must be sent to potential stock purchasers.

with the SEC a registration statement with detailed economic and financial information relevant to the firm. The condensed version of that registration document—called a **prospectus**—must be sent to potential investors.

The 1934 act also established guidelines to prevent company insiders from taking advantage of privileged information they may have. Insider trading ► P.106 ◄ involves the use of knowledge or information that individuals gain through their position that allows them to benefit unfairly from fluctuations in security prices. The key words here are *benefit unfairly*. Insiders within a firm are permitted to buy and sell stock in the company they work for so long as they do not take unfair advantage of information.[18]

Originally, the Securities & Exchange Commission (SEC) defined the term *insider* rather narrowly as consisting of a company's directors, employees, and relatives. Today the term has been broadened to include just about anyone with securities information that is not available to the general public.[19] For example, say that the chief financial officer of Fiberrific tells her next-door neighbor that she is finalizing paperwork to sell the company to a major cereal producer. The neighbor buys the stock on this information. A court may well consider that insider trading. Penalties for insider trading can include fines or imprisonment. The Legal Briefcase box describes situations that could involve insider

www.nasdaq.com

MAKING ETHICAL DECISIONS

Getting Through the Dog Days

After 35 years of hard work you finally made it to the post of chief executive officer of Laddie-Come-Home, a large producer of pet foods. As part of your compensation package, you are offered bonuses based on the company's stock performance. If the stock price of Laddie-Come-Home exceeds $50 a share during the current fiscal year, you could realize a windfall of close to $3 million in bonuses. It's been brought to your attention by an investment-banking firm that a major competitor, Barking-Up-the-Wrong-Tree, has an interest in taking over your company. The investment banker hinted that Barking-Up-the-Wrong-Tree would pay upward of $55 a share for Laddie-Come-Home. You realize that the board of directors would probably follow your recommendation if you suggested selling the company, but you also know that at least half of the current employees would lose their jobs in the takeover.

You plan to retire within the next two years, and $3 million could make life easier. What are the ethical considerations in this situation? What are your alternatives? What are the consequences of each alternative? What will you do?

trading. See how well you interpret this important legal issue. After that, judge the manager's dilemma in the Making Ethical Decisions box, which also involves the question of insider actions.

When most people think of securities markets, they picture them as sources of investment opportunities for individuals rather than financing opportunities for businesses. Let's look at this side of securities markets next.

HOW TO INVEST IN SECURITIES MARKETS

Investing in bonds, stocks, or other securities is not very difficult. First, you decide what bond or stock you want to buy. After that, it's necessary to find a registered representative authorized to trade stocks and bonds that can call a member of the stock exchange to execute your order. A **stockbroker** is a registered representative who works as a market intermediary to buy and sell securities for clients. Stockbrokers place an order with a stock exchange member, who goes to the place at the exchange where the bond or stock is traded and negotiates a price.[20] After the transaction is completed, the trade is reported to your broker, who notifies you to confirm your purchase. Large brokerage firms like Merrill Lynch or A. G. Edwards have automated order systems that allow their brokers to enter your order the instant you make it. Seconds later, the order can be confirmed. Online brokers (discussed below), such as Datek Online or E*Trade, can also confirm investor trades in a matter of seconds.[21]

The same procedure is followed if you wish to *sell* stocks or bonds. Brokers historically held on to stock or bond certificates for investors for safekeeping and to allow investors to sell their securities easily and quickly. Today brokers keep most records of bond or stock ownership electronically and transactions are almost instantaneous. A broker can also be a valuable source of information about what stocks or bonds would best meet your financial objectives. It's important, however, that you learn about and follow stocks and bonds on your own, because stock analysts' advice may not always meet your specific expectations and needs. In fact, a Stockholm newspaper gave five Swedish stock analysts and a chimpanzee each the equivalent of $1,250 to make as much money as they could in the stock market. The chimp made his selections by throwing

stockbroker
A registered representative who works as a market intermediary to buy and sell securities for clients.

SPOTLIGHT ON SMALL BUSINESS

www.etrade.com

Not Going Broke with an Online Broker

The aroma of a sizzling stock market coupled with the growth of online brokerage firms has attracted growing numbers of small-business investors to the stock market. Investment analysts project the numbers should continue to skyrocket primarily because of the ease of trading and low transaction costs charged by online firms. But small-business investors, like all investors, need to ask a few questions before selecting an online broker. Here's a list of the top 10 questions to ask yourself and your potential broker before you click that mouse:

1. What kind of investor are you, and what are your objectives?
2. How much money do you have to invest?
3. What is the broker's history and background?
4. How reliable is its customer service?
5. What is the commission structure?
6. Are there additional fees or charges to think about?
7. What types of investments are available?
8. Is the broker's site easy to use?
9. What types of research tools are available?
10. What special services are offered?

After going through these 10 questions, you should make a list of five or so possible online firms that meet your objectives. Research each one of them individually before making your choice. Remember, it's your money!

Source: "Going for Brokers," *The Economist*, May 20, 2000; Carrie Lee, "Online Trading Checklist," *The Wall Street Journal*, September 8, 1999, p. R12; Emily Thornton, "Brokerages: Take That, Cyber Boy," *Business Week*, July 10, 2000, p. 58; and "SEC: Online Trading Needs Monitoring," *APOnline*, January 25, 2001.

---

darts, and won the competition. *The Wall Street Journal* also periodically compares the predictions of a panel of experts to those of "dart throwers." Make sure to look for these contests in the *Journal*. You might want to compete against the experts to test your knowledge.

Investing Online

As we have stressed throughout this book, technology has affected virtually every aspect of business, and trading in investment securities is no exception. Investors can use online trading services to buy and sell stocks and bonds, and are doing so in growing numbers. It's estimated that, in 2000, one-fifth of all stockholders had an online-brokerage account.[22] Datek Online, Ameritrade, and E*Trade are a few of the leading providers of Web-based stock trading services. The commissions charged by these trading services are far less than those of regular stockbrokers.

Trades that traditionally cost hundreds of dollars with traditional brokerage firms may cost as low as $5 each on the Web. Traditional brokerage companies, such as Merrill Lynch, have adopted their own online capabilities to serve customers who want to trade electronically.[23] Customers interested in online trading services are primarily investors who are willing to do their own research and make their own investment decisions without the assistance of a broker.[24] The leading online services, however, do provide important market information such as company financial data, price histories of a stock, and consensus analysts' reports.[25] Read the Spotlight on Small Business box for advice in selecting an online broker.

Whether you use an online trading service or a stockbroker, investing means committing your capital with the expectation of making a profit. The first step in any investment program is to analyze such factors as desired income, cash requirements, growth prospects, level of risk, and hedging against inflation. You are never too young or too old to get involved. Let's look at some alternatives and questions you should consider before investing.

Choosing the Right Investment Strategy

As you might suspect, investment objectives change over the course of a person's life. Key investment decisions often center on personal objectives such as growth and income. For example, a young person can afford more high-risk investment options (such as stocks) than a person nearing retirement. Often young investors are looking for significant growth in the value of their investments over time. If stocks slump, the younger person has time to wait for stocks to rise again. An older person, perhaps on a fixed income, doesn't have that luxury. Such an investor might be prone to invest in bonds that offer a steady return as a protection against inflation. To this investor, additional income is more important than potential growth. Inherent in this risk/return trade-off ➤ **P.599** ◄ are questions regarding such strategies as growth, income, inflation protection, or liquidity. Should you consider stocks or bonds? Do you want common or preferred stock? Do you want corporate-issued or government-issued bonds? These tough questions vary by investor. That's why it's important to consider five key criteria when selecting investment options to achieve your objectives:

1. *Investment risk*—the chance that an investment will be worth less at some future time than it's worth now.
2. *Yield*—the percentage return on an investment, such as interest or dividends, usually over a period of one year.
3. *Duration*—the length of time assets are committed.
4. *Liquidity*—how quickly you can get back invested funds when you want or need to.
5. *Tax consequences*—how the investment will affect your tax situation.

Since new investors are not generally well versed in the world of investing or in choosing proper investment strategies, an investment planner such as a chartered financial analyst (CFA) can be very helpful.[26] A short course in investments can also be very useful. Setting investment objectives such as growth, income, or cash clearly set the tone for your investment strategy.

Let's look first at the potential of bonds as an investment. Then we'll move on to stocks.

INVESTING IN BONDS

For investors who desire low risk and guaranteed income, U.S. government bonds are a secure investment because these bonds have the financial backing and full faith and credit of the federal government. Municipal bonds, also secure, are offered by local governments and often have advantages such as tax-free interest.

Two questions often bother first-time bond investors. The first question is "If I purchase a corporate bond, do I have to hold it until the maturity date?" The answer is no: You do not have to hold a bond until maturity. Bonds are bought and sold daily on major securities exchanges. However, if you decide to sell your bond to another investor before its maturity date, you are not guaranteed to get the face value of the bond (usually $1,000). For example, if your bond does not have features (high interest rate, early maturity, etc.) that make it attractive to other investors, you may be forced to sell your bond at a *discount* (a price less than the face value). But if your bond is highly valued by other investors, you may be able to sell it at a *premium* (a price above face value). Bond prices generally fluctuate with current market interest rates. As interest rates go up, bond prices fall, and vice versa. Thus, like all investments, bonds have a degree of risk.

The second question is "How can I assess the investment risk of a particular bond issue?" Standard & Poor's and Moody's Investors Service rate the level of risk of many corporate and government bonds (refer back to Figure 20.2). Naturally, the higher the market risk of one bond compared to other bonds, the higher the interest rate the issuer of the bond must offer to investors. This again refers to the risk/return trade-off discussed in Chapter 19. Investors will invest in a bond considered risky only if the potential return to them is high enough. It's important to remember that investors have many investment options besides bonds. One such option is to buy stock. After the Progress Assessment, let's look at stock as an investment.

PROGRESS ASSESSMENT

- What is the primary purpose of a stock exchange? Can you name the largest stock exchange in the United States?
- What does NASDAQ stand for? How does this exchange work?
- What role do Standard & Poor's and Moody's Investors Service play in bond markets?

INVESTING IN STOCKS AND MUTUAL FUNDS

Buying stock makes the investor an owner of the firm. Stocks provide investors an opportunity to participate in the success of emerging or expanding companies. In fact, since 1925, the average annual return on stocks has been about 12 percent, the highest return of any popular investment. As owners, however, stockholders can also lose money if a company does not do well. Again, it's up to investors to choose the investment that best fits their overall investment objectives.

According to investment analysts, the market price (and growth potential) of common stock depends heavily on the overall performance of the corporation in meeting its business objectives. If a company reaches its stated objectives, there are great opportunities for capital gains. **Capital gains** are the positive difference between the price at which you bought a stock and what you sell it for. For example, a $1,000 investment made in Microsoft when its stock was first offered to the public would be worth well over $1 million today. Stocks can be subject to a high degree of risk, however. Drops in the stock market such as the ones in 1987, 1997, and 2000–2001 (discussed later in the chapter) certainly caught investors' attention.

Stock investors are often called bulls or bears depending on their perceptions of the market. *Bulls* are investors who believe that stock prices are going to rise, so they buy stock in anticipation of the increase. When overall stock prices are rising, the market is called a bull market.[27] *Bears* are investors who expect stock prices to decline. Bears sell their stocks in anticipation of falling prices. When the prices of stocks decline steadily, the market is called a bear market.

As we discussed previously, setting investment objectives such as growth, income, inflation protection, or cash can set the tone for your investment strategy. Investors may select several different investment opportunities in stock depending on their strategy. **Growth stocks,** for example, are stocks of corporations (often Internet-related firms) whose earnings are expected to grow at a

capital gains
The positive difference between the purchase price of a stock and its sale price.

growth stocks
Stocks of companies whose earnings are expected to grow faster than other stocks or the overall economy.

rate faster than other stocks in the market. While often considered speculative (very risky), such stocks offer investors the potential for high returns. Another option is **income stocks.** These are stocks that offer investors a rather high dividend yield on their investment. Public utilities are often considered good income stocks that will generally keep pace with inflation. The stock of high-quality companies such as Coca-Cola, Boeing, and Gillette are referred to as **blue chip stocks.** These stocks pay regular dividends and generally experience consistent growth in the company's stock price. Investors can even invest in a type of stock called a penny stock. **Penny stocks** are stocks that sell for less than $2 (some analysts say less than $5).[28] Such stocks frequently represent ownership in firms, such as mining or oil exploration companies, that compete in highly speculative industries. Penny stocks are considered very risky investments. Investors can also choose to invest in the stock of foreign companies. It's important to remember that we live in a global economy and that the United States is not the only country that offers investment opportunities. The Reaching Beyond Our Borders box looks into challenging investment opportunities globally.

It's also interesting to note that investors who buy stock have more options for placing an order than investors buying and selling bonds. Stock investors, for example, can place a **market order,** which tells a broker to buy or to sell a stock immediately at the best price available. This type of order can be processed quickly, and the trade price can be given to the investor almost instantaneously. A **limit order** tells the broker to buy or to sell a particular stock at a specific price, if that price becomes available.[29] Let's say, for example, that a stock is selling for $40 a share; you believe that the price will go up eventually but that it might drop a little before it goes higher. You could place a limit order at $36. The broker will buy the stock for you at $36 if the stock drops to that price. If the stock never falls to $36, the broker will not purchase it.

Stock Splits

Companies and brokers prefer to have stock purchases conducted in **round lots,** that is, purchases of 100 shares at a time. However, investors often buy stock in **odd lots,** or purchases of less than 100 shares at a time. The problem is that many investors cannot afford to buy 100 shares of a stock in companies that may be selling for perhaps as high as $150 per share. Such high prices often induce companies to declare **stock splits;** that is, they issue two or more shares for every share of stock that's currently outstanding. For example, if Fiberrific stock were selling for $150 a share, Fiberrific could declare a two-for-one split. Investors who owned one share of Fiberrific would now own two shares; each share, however, would now be worth only $75 (one-half as much as before the split). As you can see, there is no change in the firm's ownership structure and no change in the investment's value after the stock split. Investors generally approve of stock splits because often the demand for the stock at $75 per share may be greater than the demand at $150 per share. Thus, the $75 stock price may go up in the near future.

One of the most popular means and simplest ways of investing in the market is through mutual funds. Let's see why.

Investing in Mutual Funds

A **mutual fund** buys stocks and bonds and then sells shares in those securities to the public. Mutual fund managers are experts who pick what they consider to be the best stocks and bonds available. Investors can buy shares of the mutual funds and thus take part in the ownership of many different companies they could not afford to invest in individually. Thus, for a normally

income stocks
Stocks that offer investors a high dividend.

blue chip stocks
Stocks of high-quality companies that pay regular dividends and generate consistent growth in the company's stock price.

penny stocks
Stocks that sell for less than $2 (some analysts say $5); considered risky investments.

market order
Instructions to a broker to buy or sell a stock immediately at the best price available.

limit order
Instructions to a broker to buy or sell a particular stock at a specific price, if that price becomes available.

round lots
Purchases of 100 shares of stock at a time.

odd lots
Purchases of less than 100 shares of stock at a time.

stock splits
An action by a company that gives stockholders two or more shares of stock for each one they own.

mutual fund
An organization that buys stocks and bonds and then sells shares in those securities to the public.

REACHING BEYOND OUR BORDERS

www.merrilllynch.com

Think Global, Young Investor, Think Global

Given the incredible growth of the U.S. stock market during the 1990s, it's understandable that investors might wonder whether investment opportunities in global markets are even worth considering. After all, investing is a risky business and investing in global markets clearly involves more risk than investing in the U.S. market. Still, financial analysts argue that putting some money overseas might be a good bet. Many believe that as we turn the corner into the 21st century, overseas markets are ready to perform as well as or better than the U.S. market.

If an investor is considering investments in global stocks and bonds, it's helpful to follow a few guidelines from experts, whose advice is, granted, not foolproof. Read over these tips, which may help you find that foreign treasure right in front of your eyes:

- Consider mutual funds. In 1990, 116 mutual stock funds held part of their money in multinational stocks. Today, there are over 1,700 mutual funds that invest in international stocks. Mutual funds can offer global portfolios that include U.S. stocks, ones totally international in scope, or funds that invest in individual countries or regions such as Asia or Latin America.

- Look into American depository receipts (ADRs) that can be purchased from American brokers. ADRs represent a set number of shares in a foreign company held on deposit at a foreign branch of an American bank.

- Invest in global companies listed on U.S. stock exchanges. Companies listed on U.S. securities markets must comply with U.S. accounting procedures, and rules of the Securities and Exchange Commission.

- Trade with a domestic broker (such as Merrill Lynch and Morgan Stanley Dean Witter) that has opened an office abroad. Many U.S. brokers also produce detailed research on foreign companies.

- Invest in stocks of companies in industrialized (developed) countries rather than emerging (less developed) countries. If you do invest in emerging countries, put no more than 5 percent of your portfolio into these markets.

- Invest in global companies that have a solid track record like Shell Oil, Nestlé, Sony, and Siemens.

- Be wary of investing in countries that have a history of currency problems or political instability.

As more Americans realize the potential of global markets, it's certain that global investments will grow. However, it's important to remember that markets have varying degrees of risk. Keep the risk/return trade-off in mind in considering any investments, especially global ones.

Sources: Harvey Shapiro, "Over There: The ABCs of Global Investing," *Individual Investor*, March 2000, pp. 93–98; and Peter Diplaros, "Global Investing Just Got Easier Mutual Funds," *The Toronto Star*, January 24, 2001.

---

small fee, mutual funds provide professional investment management and help investors diversify. Today, mutual funds control over $6 trillion of investors' money.[30]

Buying shares in a mutual fund is probably the best way for a small investor to get started. The funds available range from very conservative ones that invest only in government securities or secure corporate bonds to others that specialize in emerging high-tech firms, Internet companies, foreign companies, precious metals, and other investments with greater risk. Some mutual funds even invest exclusively in socially responsible companies.[31] Read the *Business Week* box to see how the Internet is affecting the mutual fund business. A stockbroker, financial planner, or banker can help you find the mutual fund that best fits your investment objectives. In addition, the newsletter *Morningstar Investor* is an excellent resource for evaluating mutual funds, as are business periodicals such as *Business Week*.

One key advantage of mutual funds is that you can buy most funds directly and save any fees or commissions. The Internet has made access in and out of

The Internet Proudly Presents . . . E-Funds

It seems like only yesterday that online stockbrokers vaulted into the world of securities trading. But each day now, E*Trade, Ameritrade, Datek, and others are attracting growing numbers of investors. Well, get ready for step two. Over the past year, e-funds (mutual funds on the Net) with clever handles such as Stockjungle, whatif, and X.com have entered the mutual fund industry. These mutual funds are exclusively for online customers.

E-funds offer tempting benefits to investors willing to trade online. One temptation is cost savings. At Stockjungle, for example, management fees are waived on its Standard & Poor's stock index fund. (Other mutual fund firms charge as much as 4 percent.) It also subsidizes a portion of its money-market and bond funds. At competitors such as whatif and X.com, there's no minimum-investment policy and no charges for keeping a low account balance. Large mutual funds such as Vanguard often charge $20 annually if the customer's balance falls below $2,500. X.com boasts that your account can fall to $2.50 without charges.

E-fund investors, however, must agree to certain account conditions and specific risks not typical at traditional mutual funds. To keep costs low, one such condition is that e-fund investors must agree to receive communications—including prospectuses and statements—electronically. At e-funds such as X.com, investors must also agree to open a bank account with the firm. E-fund investors additionally face the market reality that e-funds lack the track records of older, established mutual funds such as Vanguard, Scudder, and T. Rowe Price. Also, there's no guarantee that costs will not increase in the future.

It's safe to say that e-funds have a long way to go in challenging traditional mutual funds. To date, e-funds have attracted about $250 million from investors, a mere pittance compared to the $104 billion in Vanguard's 500 fund alone and the trillions of dollars (as in $6 trillion) spread throughout the industry. If you consider an e-fund, be prepared to rely on electronic service, untested funds, and perhaps appeals for other products you may not want. Is there a future for e-funds? Let's all stayed tuned and watch the e-volution.

Sources: Anne Tergesen, "Here Come the E-Funds," *Business Week*, January 31, 2000, p.125; and Mara De Hovanesian, "Newsletters Discover the New Economy," *Business Week*, July 10, 2000, p. 60.

mutual funds easier than ever.[32] A true *no-load fund* is one that charges no commission to either buy or sell its shares. A *load fund* would charge a commission to investors to buy shares in the fund. It's important to check the costs involved in a mutual fund, such as any fees and charges imposed in the managing of a fund, because these can differ significantly. Some funds, called *open-end funds*, will accept the investments of any interested investors. *Closed-end funds* offer a specific number of shares for investment; once a closed-end fund reaches its target number, no new investors are admitted.

The key points to remember about mutual funds is that they offer small investors a way to spread the risk of stock ownership and a way to have their investments managed by a trained specialist for a nominal fee. Most financial advisers put mutual funds high on the list of recommended investments for beginning investors.

Diversifying Investments

Diversification involves buying several different investment alternatives to spread the risk of investing. For example, an investor may put 20 percent of his or her money into growth stocks that have relatively high risk. Another 30 percent may be invested in conservative government bonds, 15 percent in income stocks,

diversification
Buying several different investment alternatives to spread the risk of investing.

Just about any investment opportunity you desire is available in a mutual fund. Investors can choose from thousands of funds offering a wide range of investment options. The Parnassus Socially Responsible Fund pictured here invests in companies with a positive social impact on business. Do you know the difference between load and no-load funds?

junk bonds
High-risk, high-interest bonds.

buying on margin
Purchasing stocks by borrowing some of the purchase cost from the brokerage firm.

20 percent in a mutual fund, and the rest placed in the bank for emergencies and possible other investment opportunities. By diversifying investments, investors decrease the chance of losing everything they have invested. This type of investment strategy is often referred to as a *portfolio strategy*.

Stockbrokers and financial planners are both trained to give advice about the portfolio that would best fit each client's financial objectives.[33] However, the more investors read and study the market on their own, the higher the potential for gain. It's also important for investors to remember the risk/return trade-off and be aware that some investments carry rather heavy risks. Let's take a look at several of these high-risk investments.

INVESTING IN HIGH-RISK INVESTMENTS

At a racetrack some bettors always pick the favorites; others like the long shots. The same thing is true in the investment market. Some investors think that high-rated corporate bonds are clearly the investment of choice; others want to take more market risk. Let's look at three relatively risky investment options: junk bonds, buying on margin, and commodities.

Investing in High-Risk (Junk) Bonds

Although bonds are generally considered relatively safe investments, some investors look for higher returns through riskier bonds called **junk bonds.** Standard & Poor's Investment Advisory Service and Moody's Investor Service consider junk bonds as non-investment-grade bonds because of their high risk and high bond default rates.[34] Junk bonds rely on the firm's ability to pay investors interest based on the company's asset valuation remaining high and its cash flow staying strong.[35] Although the interest rates are attractive, if the company can't pay off the bond, the investor is left with a bond that isn't worth more than the paper it's written on—in other words, junk.[36]

Buying Stock on Margin

Buying on margin involves purchasing stocks by borrowing some of the purchase cost from the brokerage firm. The *margin* is the amount of money an investor must invest in the stock.[37] The Board of Governors of the Federal Reserve System sets margin rates in the U.S. market. (You will read about this in more detail in Chapter 21.) Briefly, if the margin rate is 50 percent, an investor may borrow 50 percent of the stock's purchase price from a broker.[38] Margin debt reached its highest levels ever in early 2000.[39] Although buying on margin sounds like an easy way to buy stocks, the downside is that investors must repay the credit extended by the broker, plus interest. Additionally, if the investor's account goes down in market value, the broker will issue a *margin call*, requiring the investor to come up with more money to cover the losses the investor's portfolio has suffered. If the investor is unable to make the margin call, the broker can legally sell off shares of the investor's stock to reduce the broker's chance of loss. Margin calls can force the investor to repay a significant portion of his or her account's loss within days or even hours.[40]

Investing in Commodities

Commodities can be high-risk investments for most investors. Investors willing to speculate in commodities hope to profit handsomely from the rise and fall of prices of items such as coffee, wheat, pork bellies, petroleum, and other articles of commerce (commodities) that are scheduled for delivery at a given (future) date. Trading in commodities demands much expertise. Small shifts in the prices of certain items can result in significant gains and losses. It's estimated, in fact, that 75 to 80 percent of the investors who speculate in commodities lose money in the long term.

Trading in commodities, however, can also be a vehicle for protecting businesspeople, farmers, and others from wide fluctuations in commodity prices and thus can be a very conservative investment strategy. A **commodity exchange** specializes in the buying and selling of precious metals and minerals (e.g., silver, foreign currencies, gasoline) and agricultural goods (e.g., wheat, cattle, sugar). The Chicago Board of Trade (CBOT), with its 60,000-square-foot trading floor is the largest commodity exchange in terms of floor size. The CBOT is involved with a wide range of commodities, including corn, plywood, silver, gold, and U.S. Treasury bonds.

Commodity exchanges operate much like stock exchanges: members of the exchange meet on the exchange's floor to transact deals. Yet a commodities exchange looks quite different from a stock exchange, and is interesting to observe. Transactions for a specific commodity take place in a specific trading area, or "pit," that can only be described as an exciting spectacle. Trades result from the meeting of a bid and offer in an open competition among exchange members. The bids and offers are made in a seemingly impossible-to-understand blend of voices, with all participants shouting at once. Today, however, the old color and excitement of the pits are becoming somewhat obsolete. More and more traders and brokers are working electronically at computer screens where millions of contracts are zipping around on global computer networks.[41] In fact, the CBOT has relinquished its long-standing title as the largest trading futures exchange in the world to the Frankfurt, Germany–based Eurex exchange.[42]

Many companies use commodities markets to their advantage by dealing in the futures market. **Futures markets** involve the purchase and sale of goods for delivery sometime in the future. Take, for example, a farmer who has oats growing in the field. He or she is not sure what price the oats will

commodity exchange
A securities exchange that specializes in the buying and selling of precious metals and minerals (e.g., silver, foreign currencies, gasoline) and agricultural goods (e.g., wheat, cattle, sugar).

futures markets
The purchase and sale of goods for delivery sometime in the future.

Welcome to what's often referred to as organized chaos. Commodity exchanges deal with the buying and selling of agricultural goods (like oats and wheat) as well as precious metals and minerals. The scene in the pit at a commodity exchange, like the London Metal Exchange here, is often very confusing to most observers.

sell for at harvest time. To be sure of a price, the farmer could sell the oats on the commodity floor for delivery in the future. The price is now fixed, and the farmer can plan his or her budget and expenses accordingly. In contrast, as producers of Fiberrific, you are worried about the possibility of oat prices rising. If you buy the oats in the futures market, you know what you will have to pay and can plan accordingly. All of this is possible because of commodity exchanges.

- What is a stock split? Why do companies sometimes split their stock?
- What is a mutual fund? How do mutual funds benefit small investors?
- What is meant by *buying on margin?*
- Why would a restaurant chain be interested in the futures market?

UNDERSTANDING INFORMATION FROM SECURITIES MARKETS

You can find a wealth of investment information in newspapers, in magazines, on television, and on websites. Such information is useless, however, until you understand what it means. Look through *The Wall Street Journal, Barron's, Investor's Business Daily, USA Today,* and your local newspaper's business section; listen carefully to business reports on radio and TV for investment analysis and different viewpoints; and visit different sites on the Internet that provide information about companies and markets. But keep in mind that investing is an inexact science and few people are consistently right in predicting future market movements. Everytime someone sells a stock believing it will go up no higher, someone else is buying it, believing it will still go higher. By reading the following sections carefully, you will begin to understand investment information.

Understanding Bond Quotations

Bonds, remember, are issued by corporations and governments. Government issues are covered in *The Wall Street Journal* in a table called Treasury Issues. These issues are traded on the over-the-counter (OTC) market. The price of a bond is quoted as a percentage of $1,000. The interest rate is often followed by an *s* for easier pronunciation. For example, 9 percent bonds due in 2015 are called 9s of 15.

Figure 20.6 gives a sample of bond quotes for corporations. Look at the quotes and note the variation in interest rates and maturity dates. The more you know about the bond market, the better prepared you will be to talk intelligently with investment counselors and brokers. You want to be sure that their advice is consistent with your best interests and investment objectives.

Understanding Stock Quotations

If you look in the Money & Investing section of *The Wall Street Journal,* you will see stock quotations from the New York Stock Exchange, the American Stock Exchange, and the NASDAQ over-the-counter markets. Look at the top of the columns and notice the headings. To understand the headings better, look carefully at Figure 20.7. This example highlights the information on the New York and American Stock Exchanges. Stocks are quoted in 16ths of a dollar, illustrated as fractional or decimal amounts. For example, a stock

Bonds	Cur Yld	Vol	High	Low	Close		Net Chg
LaQuin 10s02	cv	4	102	102	102	−	$1\frac{1}{4}$
LearS 10s04	10.0	3	100	100	100	+	$1\frac{5}{8}$
LearS $11\frac{1}{2}$10	11.1	5	$103\frac{1}{2}$	$103\frac{1}{2}$	$103\frac{1}{2}$	−	$1\frac{1}{2}$
LearS $11\frac{1}{4}$15	10.8	2	$104\frac{1}{4}$	$104\frac{1}{4}$	$104\frac{1}{4}$	−	$\frac{3}{4}$
Leget $6\frac{1}{2}$06	cv	36	103	102	102		...
LipGp $8\frac{5}{8}$01	9.4	10	$92\frac{1}{8}$	$92\frac{1}{8}$	$92\frac{1}{8}$	−	$1\frac{7}{8}$
LincFl $8\frac{1}{2}$09	8.7	5	$97\frac{1}{2}$	$97\frac{1}{2}$	$97\frac{1}{2}$	−	$1\frac{3}{8}$
LomN 7s11	cv	4	104	104	104		...
LonSl $11\frac{1}{4}$12	11.7	5	$100\frac{3}{8}$	$100\frac{3}{8}$	$100\frac{3}{8}$	−	2
Loral $7\frac{1}{4}$10	cv	2	121	121	121	−	$\frac{1}{2}$
Lorilld $6\frac{7}{8}$05	7.6	62	$90\frac{7}{8}$	$90\frac{3}{8}$	$90\frac{3}{8}$		...
LouGs $9\frac{1}{4}$07	9.2	10	$101\frac{1}{8}$	101	101		...
Lowen $8\frac{1}{8}$10	9.4	18	90	89	90	+	7
viLykes $7\frac{1}{2}$99	...	35	$19\frac{1}{2}$	18	18	−	1
viLykes $7\frac{1}{2}$08	...	79	$20\frac{1}{2}$	$19\frac{7}{8}$	$20\frac{1}{2}$	+	$\frac{7}{8}$
viLykes 11s10	...	25	21	$20\frac{1}{2}$	$20\frac{1}{2}$	−	$\frac{1}{2}$
MACOM $9\frac{1}{4}$06	cv	30	101	$99\frac{1}{4}$	$99\frac{1}{4}$	−	$1\frac{1}{4}$

CV means convertible bond.

5 bonds were traded that day.

These Lowen bonds are due in 2010 and originally paid $8\frac{1}{8}$%. The current yield is 9.4%.

This bond sold for a high of $900 and the low for the day was $890. It ended the day at $900, up $70 from the previous day.

FIGURE 20.6

UNDERSTANDING BOND QUOTATIONS

listed at $65 9/16 is selling for $65.5625. The New York Stock Exchange officially shifted in late August 2000 from trading stocks in fractions to trading in decimals.[43] It did so by starting out slowly, with only seven stocks listed as decimals. The number grew to 100 stocks the next month, with the remainder to follow accordingly. The NASDAQ plans to begin its conversion to the decimal program in the spring of 2001.[44] Preferred stocks are identified by the letters *pf* following the abbreviated company name. Corporations can have several different preferred stock issues.

Let's look at the columns and headings more closely. Moving from left to right, the stock quote tells us the following:

- The highest and lowest price the stock has sold for over the past 52 weeks.
- The abbreviated company name and the company's stock symbol.
- The last dividend paid per share.
- The stock's dividend yield (the return expected).

Want to know what's going on in business or how to build a great stock portfolio? It starts with a commitment to learn and getting acquainted with publications like *The Wall Street Journal* and *Business Week*. These publications and others prepare you to become the next Warren Buffett (America's most successful investor).

Hi	Lo	Stock	Sym	Div	Yld %	P/E	Vol 100s	Hi	Lo	Close	Net Chg
49^{75}	28^{38}	GATX	GMT	1.20	2.5	15	1632	48^{69}	48^{19}	48^{31}	$+0^{19}$
9^{63}	6^{50}	G&L Rlty	GLR	.50	5.4	dd	8	9^{25}	9^{19}	9^{25}	$+0^{06}$
16^{88}	13^{25}	G&L Rlty	pfA	2.56	18.4	...	31	13^{94}	13^{75}	13^{94}	$+0^{19}$
16^{50}	12	G&L Rlty	pfB	2.45	18.5	...	58	13^{50}	13^{25}	13^{25}	-0^{31}
35^{75}	1^{19}	GC Cos	GCX		...	dd	904	1^{63}	1^{25}	1^{44}	-0^{31}
7^{13}	3^{06}	GP Strategs	GPX		...	dd	80	5^{19}	4^{88}	5^{06}	...
35^{75}	$23^{44}+$	GPU Inc	GPU	2.18	6.1	45	5833	36^{06}	35^{38}	36	$+0^{50}$
36^{88}	14^{94}	Gabelli A	GBL		...	15	392	28^{94}	28^{50}	28^{63}	$+0^{13}$
11	8^{94}	GabelliConv	GCV	.80a	9.1	...	53	9	8^{63}	8^{81}	$+0^{25}$
25^{56}	23^{06}	GabelliConv	pf	2.00	8.0	...	7	25	25	25	$+0^{06}$
12^{94}	10^{81}	GabelliTr	GAB	1.08a	9.7	...	1130	11^{25}	11^{13}	11^{19}	-0^{06}
24^{25}	20^{50}	GabelliTr	pf	1.81	7.6	...	117	24^{50}	23^{63}	23^{94}	-0^{31}
19^{75}	11^{13}	GabelliMlti	GGT	1.53e	14.6	...	501	10^{94}	10^{38}	10^{50}	$+0^{13}$
25^{13}	22	GabelliMlti	pf	1.98	7.9	...	16	25	24^{69}	25	...
9^{19}	7^{31}	GabelliUt	GUT	.60a	6.5	...	413	9^{38}	8^{94}	9^{19}	$+0^{25}$
29^{31}	20^{25}	GblsRsdntl	GBP	2.27	8.4	12	343	26^{94}	26^{75}	26^{88}	...
22^{13}	16^{06}	GblsRsdntl	pfA	2.08	10.0	...	41	21^{25}	20^{81}	20^{81}	-0^{38}
6^{38}	$2^{38}+$	Gainsco	GNA	.07	2.7	dd	1205	2^{63}	2^{50}	2^{56}	-0^{06}
4^{75}	$1^{63}+$	GaleyLord	GNL		...	dd	41	2^{75}	2^{56}	2^{63}	$+0^{06}$
29^{94}	$13^{44}+$	GalileoInt	GLC	.36	1.8	12	856	19^{81}	19^{56}	19^{63}	$+0^{06}$
68^{50}	23^{06}	Gallagr	AJG	.92	1.4	34	5390	67^{94}	65^{88}	66^{06}	-0^{94}
26	12^{75}	GallaherGo	GLH	1.54e	6.4	...	669	24^{31}	23^{94}	23^{94}	-0^{06}
83^{63}	$48^{38}+$	Gannett	GCI	.88	1.5	10	15320	61^{25}	58	60^{06}	$+2^{31}$
53^{75}	18^{50}	Gap Inc	GPS	.09	.4	22	36379	26^{13}	25	25^{44}	-0^{38}
20^{75}	$14^{25}+$	GardnrDenvr	GDI		...	16	109	18^{20}	17^{84}	17^{90}	-0^{35}
22^{25}	7^{15}	GartnerGp	IT		...	24	1900	7^{49}	7^{12}	7^{15}	-0^{45}
17^{63}	6^{75}	GartnerGp B	ITB		...	...	1583	7^{15}	6^{35}	6^{50}	-0^{60}
75^{19}	16^{50}	Gateway	GTW		...	11	35021	18^{05}	17^{26}	17^{68}	$+0^{08}$
31^{50}	19^{50}	GaylEnt	GET		...	3	259	22^{13}	21^{69}	21^{69}	-0^{50}

Left annotations:
- High and low price for last 52 weeks.
- Abbreviated name of company.
- Pf stands for preferred.
- 34,300 shares of this stock traded today.
- Gannett pays a dividend of $.88 per share.
- Gateway's highest price was 18.05. The lowest price was 17.26. It was up 8 cents from the previous day's close.

Right annotations:
- This stock yields a 5.4% dividend.
- Price of GPU stock is 45 times its earnings.
- Gap went down 38 cents since the previous day's close.

FIGURE 20.7

UNDERSTANDING STOCK QUOTATIONS

- The price/earnings (P/E) ratio is the price of the stock divided by the firm's per share earnings. (For example, Price of Fiberrific stock ($50) ÷ Company earnings per share ($5) = Fiberrific's P/E ratio (10).
- The number of shares traded that day in 100s.
- The stock's high, low, and closing price for the day.
- The net change in the stock's price from the previous day.

Look down the columns and find the stock that's had the biggest price change over the past 52 weeks, the stock that pays the highest dividend, and the stock that has the highest price/earnings ratio. The more you look through the figures, the more sense they begin to make. You might want to build a hypothetical portfolio of stocks and track how they perform over the next six months. (See the Developing Workplace Skills and Taking It to the Net exercises at the end of this chapter for suggested exercises.)

	Inv Obj	NAV	Offer Price	NAV Chg	YTD	Total Return 13 wks	3 yrs
AIM Funds:							
AdIGV p	BST	9.63	9.73		+0.1	+0.2	NS ..
Agrsv p	SML	24.43	25.85	−0.09	−0.1	−1.2	+25.2 A
BalB t	S & B	15.30	15.30	−0.04	−4.2	+0.3	NS ..
Chart p	G & I	8.73	9.24	−0.03	−2.7	0.0	+7.0 D
Const p	CAP	16.57	17.53	−0.16	−5.3	−2.9	+16.8 A
BalA p	S & B	15.29	16.05	−0.05	−3.9	+0.5	+12.3 A
GoScA p	BND	9.38	9.85	+0.01	−2.8k	+0.8k	+6.2k E
GrthA p	GRO	10.29	10.89	−0.09	−9.1	−5.2	+2.1 E
GrthB t	GRO	10.22	10.22	−0.09	−9.6	−5.5	NS ..
HYldA p	BHI	9.34	9.81	...	−2.0k	−0.7k	+15.4k B
HYldB t	BHI	9.33	9.33	...	−2.4k	−1.0k	NS ..
IncoA p	BND	7.49	7.86	...	−7.6k	−0.7k	+8.8k B
IntlE p	ITL	13.02	13.78	−0.07	−0.2	+2.4	NS ..
LimM p	BST	9.96	10.06	+0.01	+0.5	+0.8	+5.5 C
MunIA p	GLM	8.16	8.57	+0.02	−2.2k	+2.2k	+8.4k A
SumIt	GRO	9.14	NA	−0.08	−5.8	−2.2	+7.7 C
TeCt p	SSM	10.72	11.25	+0.03	−2.2k	+1.9k	+7.9k B
TF Int	IDM	10.65	10.76	+0.02	−1.0k	+1.6k	+7.1k B
UtIIA p	SEC	12.35	13.07	+0.01	−10.1k	−2.3k	+8.9k C
UtIIB t	SEC	12.35	12.35	+0.01	−10.4k	−2.5k	NS ..
ValuA p	GRO	20.83	22.04	−0.11	0.0	−0.5	+17.5 A
ValuB t	GRO	20.74	20.74	−0.12	−0.4	−0.8	NS ..
Weing p	GRO	16.65	17.62	−0.12	−2.9	−1.1	+4.9 E

Price to buy one share. *(points to Offer Price column)*

Investment objective of the fund. GRO means growth fund. (Other mutual fund objective categories can be found in *The Wall Street Journal*.) *(points to Inv Obj column)*

Change in NAV (net asset value) from previous day. *(points to NAV Chg column)*

Return on investment year-to-date, 13 weeks, and over 3-year periods. *(points to Total Return columns)*

NAV refers to net asset value of the fund. *(points to NAV column)*

FIGURE 20.8

UNDERSTANDING MUTUAL FUND QUOTATIONS

Understanding Mutual Fund Quotations

Buying into mutual funds is a way to get expert investment advice and diversify your investments at a minimum cost. Look up the listing of mutual funds in *The Wall Street Journal* (see Figure 20.8). You will see that many different companies offer mutual funds. The various funds offer many alternatives to meet investors' objectives. For example, the AIM mutual fund listed in Figure 20.8 highlights many different kinds of funds that may meet your investment objectives. You can learn about the specifics of the various funds by contacting a broker or contacting the fund directly by phone or through its Web page. Business publications can also guide you to free information from various mutual funds.

As you look across the columns in the mutual fund quotations, the information is rather simple to understand. The fund's name is in the first column, followed by the fund's *net asset value (NAV)*. The net asset value is the market value of the mutual fund's portfolio divided by the number of shares it has outstanding. (If the fund is a no-load fund, again meaning there is no commission to buy or sell fund shares, the NAV is the price per share of the mutual fund.) The next column lists the sale price (the net asset value plus charges and fees). The last column displays the net change in the NAV from the previous day's trading. It's simple to change your investment objectives with mutual funds.

Today, research abounds concerning bonds, stocks, and mutual funds. Much of this information can be obtained from brokerage firms such as Charles Schwab or from private research conducted on the Internet. You can learn about specific mutual funds directly from the fund by telephone or through its Web page.

Switching your money, for example, from a bond fund to a stock fund and back is generally no more difficult than calling an 800 number or clicking a mouse. Mutual funds are a great way to begin investing to meet your financial objectives.

Stock Market Indicators

When you listen to news reports, you often hear announcers say things like "The Dow Industrials are up 90 points today in active trading." Wonder what's going on? The **Dow Jones Industrial Average** (the Dow) is the average cost of 30 selected industrial stocks, used to give an indication of the direction (up or down) of the stock market over time. A man named Charles Dow began the practice of measuring stock averages in 1884, using the prices of 12 important stocks. The 12 original stocks in the Dow are illustrated in Figure 20.9. Do you recognize any of these companies?

New stocks are substituted on the Dow when it's deemed appropriate. For example, the Dow was broadened in 1982 to include 30 stocks and the list was changed in 1991 by adding Disney to reflect the increased importance of the service sector (again, see Figure 20.9). In 1997, the list was again altered with Hewlett-Packard, Johnson & Johnson, Wal-Mart, and Citigroup replacing Texaco, Woolworth, Bethlehem Steel, and Westinghouse. In 1999, the Dow added Home Depot and SBC Communications along with its first NASDAQ stocks, Intel and Microsoft. Chevron, Sears Roebuck, Union Carbide, and Goodyear were eliminated. The 30 stocks in the Dow Jones Industrial Average also include such notables as General Electric, IBM, and Coca-Cola. (See Figure 20.9).

Critics argue that if the purpose of the Dow is to give an indication of the direction of the broader market over time, the 30-company sample is too small to get a good statistical representation. Many investors and market analysts therefore prefer to follow stock indexes like the Standard & Poor's 500

Dow Jones Industrial Average
The average cost of 30 selected industrial stocks, used to give an indication of the direction (up or down) of the stock market over time.

THE ORIGINAL DOW 12	THE 30 CURRENT DOW COMPANIES	
American Cotton Oil	Exxon Mobil	Microsoft
American Sugar Refining Co.	McDonald's	Intel
American Tobacco	SBC Communications	Citigroup
Chicago Gas	J.P. Morgan	Home Depot
Distilling & Cattle Feeding Co.	DuPont	Wal-Mart Stores
General Electric Co.	General Motors	General Electric
Laclede Gas Light Co.	AT&T	International Business Machines (IBM)
National Lead	Coca-Cola	American Express
North American Co.	Minnesota Mining & Manufacturing	Hewlett-Packard
Tennessee Coal, Iron & Railroad Co.	Walt Disney	United Technologies
U.S. Leather	Caterpillar	Alcoa
U.S. Rubber Co.	Boeing	Merck
	International Paper	Procter & Gamble
	Eastman Kodak	Johnson & Johnson
	Philip Morris	Honeywell International

FIGURE 20.9

THE ORIGINAL DOW AND THE CURRENT DOW

(S&P 500), which tracks the performance of 400 industrial, 40 financial, 40 utility, and 20 transportation stocks.

Staying abreast of what's happening in the market will help you decide what investments seem most appropriate to your needs and objectives. However, it's important to remember two key investment realities: The first is that your personal financial objectives and needs change over time. The second is that markets can be volatile. Let's look at the volatility that's inherent in the market and new challenges in the 21st century that promise to present investors with new risks and opportunities.

The Market's Roller-Coaster Ride

Throughout the 1900s, the stock market had its ups and downs, spiced with several major tremors. The first "crash" occurred on Tuesday, October 28, 1929, when the stock market lost almost 13 percent of its value in a single day. That "Black Tuesday" brought home to investors the reality of market volatility, especially to those who were heavily margined. Many investors lost everything they had invested.[45] On October 19, 1987, the stock market suffered the largest one-day drop in its history: The Dow Jones Industrial Average fell 508 points and lost over 22 percent of the market's value. The loss caused $500 billion dollars to vanish before bewildered investors' eyes. The crash prompted Texas billionaire H. Ross Perot to caution, "It was God tapping us on the shoulder and warning us to get our act together before we get the big shock." On October 27, 1997, investors felt the fury of the market once again. The Dow fell 554 points, primarily because of investors' fears of an impending economic crisis in Asian markets. Luckily, the market regained its strength after a short downturn. On Friday, April 14, 2000, the Dow fell 616 points and the NASDAQ 385, points again warning investors of the market's unpredictability. The market continued to drop in 2001.

program trading
Giving instructions to computers to automatically sell if the price of a stock dips to a certain point to avoid potential losses.

What caused the market turmoil of 1929, 1987, 1997, and 2000–2001? Ask a dozen financial analysts and you will probably get a dozen different answers. In 1987, however, many analysts agreed that "program trading" was a big cause of the disastrous fall. In **program trading,** investors give their computers instructions to sell automatically if the price of their stock dips to a certain point to avoid potential losses. On October 19, 1987, the computers became trigger-happy and sell orders caused many stocks to fall to unbelievable depths.

Many market watchers believe that the 1997 market drop could have been much worse had it not been for rules adopted in the wake of the crash of 1987. The 1997 plunge was, in fact, the first real test of the stock market's new "circuit breakers." Under the new market rules, if the market falls 350 points, the circuit breakers will kick in and halt trading for half an hour to give investors a chance to assess the situation. Since the 1997 sell-off, U.S. stock exchanges have agreed to halt trading for the day if the Dow Jones Industrial average drops 20 percent. Still, market gyrations will likely persist, causing investors many headaches and sleepless nights.

Investing in the 21st-Century Market

It's obvious from the market slides discussed above that what goes up can also go down. Furthermore, it's a safe bet to presume that 21st-century markets will undergo changes that will only heighten their volatility. For example, today we live in a global market that links the economies of all countries closely together. As we saw with the Asian crisis in 1997, what affects one region economically can have a domino effect on others. Dramatic change affects the securities exchanges as well. The New York and NASDAQ exchanges are intensely competitive in the search for investors' dollars. The "battle of the boards" is no longer limited to the National Basketball Association—it's alive and well on Wall Street. Traditional brokers such as Merrill Lynch can expect enhanced challenges from online brokers like E*Trade, which are attracting more and more investors. The effect of *day traders,* investors who trade online and move rapidly into and out of stocks, can also cause markets to gyrate considerably. These changes, along with the growing influence of institutional investors, promise to make securities markets exciting but not always stable places to be in the 21st century.

The basic lessons to keep in mind are the importance of diversifying your investments and understanding the risks of investing. Taking a long-term perspective is also wise idea. The late 1990s and early 2000s saw the market reach unparalleled heights. Advertisements by brokerage firms in print and on television could make you think that investing in the market is "guaranteed money in the bank."[46] However, it's critical for you to know that there's no such thing as easy money or a sure thing. Investing is a challenging and interesting field that's always changing. If you carefully research companies and industries, keep up with the news, and make use of investment resources such as newspapers, magazines, newsletters, the Internet, and TV programs, the payoff can be highly rewarding. You may want to refer to this chapter again when you read about personal finance in Chapter 22.

PROGRESS ASSESSMENT

• What exactly does the Dow Jones Industrial Average measure? Why is it important?

• Why do the 30 companies comprising the Dow change periodically?

• Explain program trading and the problems it can create.

SUMMARY

1. Securities markets provide opportunities for businesses and investors.
   - *What opportunities are provided to businesses and individual investors by securities markets?*
   Businesses are able to raise much-needed capital to help finance major expenses of the firm. Individual investors can share in the success and growth of emerging firms by having the opportunity of investing in the firm.
   - *What role do investment bankers play in securities markets?*
   Investment bankers are specialists who assist in the issue and sale of new securities.

1. Examine the functions of securities markets and investment bankers.

2. Companies can raise capital by debt financing, which involves issuing bonds.
   - *What are the advantages and disadvantages of issuing bonds?*
   The advantages of issuing bonds include the following: (1) Management retains control since bondholders cannot vote; (2) interest paid on bonds is tax deductible; and (3) bonds are only a temporary source of finance, and after they are paid off the debt is eliminated. The disadvantages of bonds include the following: (1) Because bonds are an increased debt, they may affect the market's perception of the company adversely; (2) interest on bonds must be paid; and (3) the face value must be repaid on the maturity date.
   - *Are there different types of bonds?*
   Yes. There are unsecured (debenture) and secured bonds. Unsecured bonds are not supported by collateral, whereas secured bonds are backed by tangible assets such as mortgages, buildings, and equipment.

2. Compare the advantages and disadvantages of issuing bonds, and identify the classes and features of bonds.

3. Companies can also raise capital by equity financing, which involves selling stock.
   - *What are the advantages and disadvantages of selling stock?*
   The advantages of selling stock include the following: (1) The stock price never has to be repaid since stockholders are owners in the company; (2) there is no legal obligation to pay dividends; and (3) no debt is incurred, so the company is financially stronger. Disadvantages of selling stock include the following: (1) Stockholders become owners of the firm and can affect its management by voting for the board of directors; (2) it is more costly to pay dividends, since they are paid after taxes; and (3) managers may be tempted to make stockholders happy in the short term rather than plan for long-term needs.
   - *What are the differences between common and preferred stock?*
   Common stockholders have voting rights in the company. Preferred stockholders generally have no voting rights. In exchange for voting privileges, preferred stocks offer a fixed dividend that must be paid in full before common stockholders receive a dividend.

3. Compare the advantages and disadvantages of issuing stock, and outline the differences between common and preferred stock.

4. Stock exchanges afford investors the opportunity of investing in securities markets through the different investment options that are offered.
   - *What is a stock exchange?*
   An organization whose members are involved in buying and selling securities.
   - *What are the different exchanges?*
   There are stock exchanges all over the world. The largest U.S. exchange is the New York Stock Exchange (NYSE). It and the American Stock

4. Describe the various stock exchanges and how to invest in securities markets, and explain various investment objectives such as long-term growth, income, cash, and protection from inflation.

Exchange (AMEX) together are known as national exchanges because they handle stock of companies all over the country. In addition, there are several regional exchanges that deal primarily with companies in their own areas.
  • *What is the over-the-counter (OTC) market?*
The OTC market is a system for exchanging stocks not listed on the national exchanges. It also handles bonds issued by city and state governments.
  • *How do investors normally make purchases in securities markets?*
Investors generally purchase investments through market intermediaries called stockbrokers, who provide many different services. However, online investing is also very popular.
  • *What are the criteria for selecting investments?*
Investors should determine their overall financial objectives. Are they interested in growth, income, cash, or a hedge against inflation? Investments should be evaluated with regard to (1) risk, (2) yield, (3) duration, (4) liquidity, and (5) tax consequences.
  • *How are securities exchanges regulated?*
The Securities and Exchange Commission (SEC) is responsible for regulating securities exchanges.
  • *What is insider trading?*
Insider trading involves the use of information or knowledge that individuals gain through their position that allows them to benefit unfairly from fluctuations in security prices.

5. Analyze the opportunities bonds offer as investments.

5. Bonds present opportunities for investors.
  • *What is the difference between a bond selling at a discount and a bond selling at a premium?*
A bond selling at a premium is a bond that can be sold in securities markets at a price above its face value. A bond selling at a discount is a bond that can be sold in securities markets but at a price below its face value.

6. Explain the opportunities stocks and mutual funds offer as investments and the advantages of diversifying investments.

6. Stocks and mutual funds present opportunities for investors to enhance their financial position.
  • *What is a market order?*
A market order tells a broker to buy or to sell a security immediately at the best price available. A limit order tells the broker to buy or sell at a specific price if the stock reaches that price.
  • *What does it mean when a stock splits?*
When a stock splits, stockholders receive two or more shares for each share they own. Each share is then worth half or less of the original share. Therefore, while the number of the shares in the company increases, the total value of the stockholders' holdings stays the same. The lower price per share may increase demand for the stock.
  • *How can mutual funds help individuals diversify their investments?*
A mutual fund is an organization that buys stocks and bonds and then sells shares in those securities to the public. Individuals who buy shares in a mutual fund are able to invest in many different companies they could not afford to invest in otherwise.
  • *What is diversification?*
Diversification means buying several different types of investments (government bonds, corporate bonds, preferred stock, common stock, etc.) with different degrees of risk. The purpose is to reduce the overall risk an investor would assume by just investing in one type of security.

7. Other types of speculative investments are available for investors seeking large returns on their investments.
   - ***What is a junk bond?***
   Junk bonds are high-risk, high-interest debenture bonds that speculative investors often find attractive.
   - ***What does buying on margin mean?***
   It means that the investor borrows up to 50 percent of the cost of a stock from the broker so he or she can get more shares of stock without paying the full price.
   - ***What are commodity exchanges?***
   Commodity exchanges specialize in the buying and selling of precious metals and minerals (e.g., silver, oil) and agricultural goods (e.g., wheat, cattle, sugar).

   7. Discuss specific high-risk investments, including junk bonds, buying stock on margin, and commodity trading.

8. Security quotations and Dow Jones Averages are listed daily in newspapers.
   - ***What information do stock quotations give you?***
   The stock quotations give you all kinds of information: the highest price in the last 52 weeks; the lowest price; the dividend yield; the price/earnings ratio; the total shares traded that day; and the high, low, close, and net change in price from the previous day. Bond quotations give you information regarding trading bonds in securities markets, as do quotations concerning mutual funds.
   - ***What is the Dow Jones Industrial Average?***
   The Dow Jones Industrial Average is the average price of 30 specific stocks traded on the New York Stock Exchange.

   8. Explain securities quotations listed in the financial section of a newspaper, and describe how stock market indicators like the Dow Jones Average affect the market.

KEY TERMS

blue chip stocks 627	growth stocks 626	over-the-counter (OTC) market 620
bond 613	income stocks 627	par value 617
buying on margin 630	institutional investors 613	penny stocks 627
callable bond 616	initial public offering (IPO) 612	preemptive right 619
capital gains 626	interest 614	preferred stock 617
commodity exchange 631	investment bankers 613	principal 614
common stock 619	junk bonds 630	program trading 638
convertible bond 616	limit order 627	prospectus 622
cumulative preferred stock 619	market order 627	round lots 627
debenture bonds 615	maturity date 614	Securities and Exchange Commission (SEC) 621
denomination 614	mutual fund 627	sinking fund 615
diversification 629	National Association of Securities Dealers Automated Quotations (NASDAQ) 620	stockbroker 623
dividends 617		stock certificate 617
Dow Jones Industrial Average 636		stock exchange 619
futures markets 631	odd lots 627	stock splits 627
		stocks 617

DEVELOPING WORKPLACE SKILLS

1. Go to the websites of Charles Schwab (www.schwab.com), E*Trade (www.etrade.com), Ameritrade (www.ameritrade.com), and Datek (*www.datek.com*). Investigate each of the brokerage companies and compare what they offer to investors and how their price structures work. Evaluate each of the brokers according to specific services they offer and decide which

service you consider most appropriate to your investment objectives. Be prepared to defend your choice to the class.

2. Read *The Wall Street Journal, Investor's Business Daily,* or the business section of your local newspaper each day for two weeks and then select three stocks for your portfolio from the New York Stock Exchange and three from the NASDAQ. Track the stocks in your portfolio and use a computer to graphically display the trends of each one on a weekly basis. See how market trends and information affect your stocks and write out a brief explanation of why your stocks were affected.

3. See if anyone is interested in setting up an investment game in your class. Each student should choose one stock (100 shares) and one mutual fund (100 fund shares). Record each student's selections and the corresponding prices on a chart. In six weeks, look up and chart the prices again. Discuss with your fellow competitors the results on a percentage gain or loss situation.

4. Analyze the risk/return trade-off involved in investing in today's market. Prepare a brief written financial analysis of stocks, bonds, and mutual funds. Then imagine that a distant relative gives you $10,000 that you don't need for your education at the moment. Write down your investment objectives and plan how to invest the $10,000. Select your investments and explain why you chose them.

5. Many businesses try to raise capital by offering new stock offerings called initial public offerings (IPOs). Go to the library, obtain recent financial publications like *The Wall Street Journal* or *Investor's Business Daily,* or go to the websites listed in exercise 1 above (www.schwab.com, www.etrade.com, www.ameritrade.com, www.datek.com) to find two IPOs that have been offered during the past six months. Track the performance of each IPO from its introduction to its present price.

TAKING IT TO THE NET

Purpose

To experience investing in the stock market.

Exercise

One of the safest ways to learn about trading stocks is to invest with "virtual" money (the modern name for play money). Go to InvestSmart Stock Game (http://library.advanced.org/10326/market_simulation/index.html). Here you can buy virtual stock on the New York Stock Exchange (NYSE), NASDAQ, or the American Stock Exchange (AMEX). The stock quotes used are actual data from the exchange, delayed 20 minutes because of SEC regulations. You will start out with a virtual $100,000 in your cash account.

1. Research companies and decide which stocks you want to buy or sell. We suggest that you invest in no more than five stocks and that you choose companies in different industries. There will be a $15 to $30 commission for every transaction, depending on which brokerage firm you use.

2. You may sign up for this game more than once by entering a different user name each time. That way, you can trade different stocks in each account to test out various investing strategies. A ranking of all the players is generated daily. This ranking will show who can build up stock portfolios with the greatest value.

Purpose

To experience the excitement of the New York Stock Exchange trading floor and to explain the anatomy of a stock trade.

Exercise

Go to the New York Stock Exchange's website at www.nyse.com.

1. Click on the Trading Floor button to find panoramic views of the NYSE trading floor from a variety of perspectives. How many people work on the trading floor? What roles do the specialists play in stock exchanges?

2. Describe the anatomy of a trade from the moment an investor places an order until the investor receives confirmation that the trade has been made.

3. If you have a high-speed connection (higher than 56K), you can experience the fast pace of the trading floor for yourself by clicking About NYSE, then Education. There you will find a series of videos prepared in conjunction with Cornell University. Click on the segment Broker Technology. How has technology helped brokers keep up with the pace of the trading floor?

PRACTICING MANAGEMENT DECISIONS

CASE

KEEPING YOUR HEAD ABOVE WATER

Carlos Galendez had big dreams but very little money. He had worked more than 10 years washing dishes and then as a cook for two major restaurants. Finally, his dream to save enough money to start his own Mexican restaurant came true. Galendez opened his restaurant, Casa de Carlos, with a guaranteed loan from the Small Business Administration. His old family recipes and appealing Hispanic decor helped the business gain immediate success. He repaid his small-business loan within 14 months and immediately opened a second, and then a third, location. Casa de Carlos became one of the largest Mexican restaurant chains in the nation. Galendez decided the company needed to go public to help finance a nationwide expansion. He believed that continued growth was beneficial to the company, and that offering ownership was the way to bring in loyal investors. Nevertheless, he wanted to make certain his family maintained a controlling interest in the firm's stock. Therefore, in its initial public offering (IPO), Casa de Carlos offered to sell only 40 percent of the company's available shares to investors. The Galendez family kept control of the remaining 60 percent.

As the public's craving for Mexican food grew, so did the fortunes of Casa de Carlos, Inc. Heading into the 2000s, the company enjoyed the position of being light on debt and heavy on cash. But the firm's debt position changed dramatically when it bought out Captain Al's Seafood Restaurants and, three years later, expanded into full-service wholesale distribution of seafood products with the purchase of Ancient Mariner Wholesalers. The firm's debt increased, but the price of its stock was up and all its business operations were booming.

Then tragedy struck the firm when Carlos Galendez died suddenly from a heart attack. His oldest child, Maria, was selected to take control as chief executive officer. Maria Galendez had learned the business from her father, who had taught her to keep an eye out for opportunities that seemed fiscally responsible. Even so, the fortunes of the firm began to shift. Two major competitors were taking market share from Casa de Carlos, and the seafood venture began to flounder (pun intended). Also, consumer shifts in eating habits and a slight fear of a recession encouraged consumers to spend less, causing some severe cash problems. It was up to Maria Galendez to decide how to get the funds the firm needed for improvements and other expenses. Banks wouldn't expand the firm's credit line, so she considered the possibility of a bond or stock offering to raise capital for the business.

Decision Questions

1. What advantages do bonds offer a company such as Casa de Carlos? What disadvantages do bonds impose?

2. What would be the advantages and disadvantages of the company's offering new stock to investors?

3. Are any other options available to Maria Galendez?

4. What choice would you make and why?

VIDEO CASE

GETTING FOOLISH FINANCIAL ADVICE

Beginning investors are often confused about how to get started. There are so many terms to learn—stocks, bonds, mutual funds, and the like—and the process seems confusing and complex. That's where a company like The Motley Fool can help. Two brothers, David and Tom Gardner began the company in the mid-1990s. They got its name from the fact that the court jester (The Fool) was the only one who could tell the truth to the king without endangering his life. David and Tom thought they would tell investors the truth about stocks and bonds and other investments so that the investors could make money. Investors, in turn, would be willing to pay for the books, newsletters, and online advice David and Tom provided.

You can visit The Motley Fool website yourself at www.fool.com. There you will find all kinds of investment advice, including the "Fool's School" where you learn how to get started in investing. It doesn't take a lot of money—just a few hundred dollars—to get started.

One of the first suggestions that the Fools make is to get rid of credit card debt because it costs around 18 percent a year. College students especially are warned not to pile up too much debt. Credit card companies will offer all kinds of enticements to get students to sign up for their cards, but be careful and use your cards sparingly, is their Foolish advice.

As far as investing is concerned, their advice is to buy an index fund, like the S&P 500 index fund.

That is a fund made up of the top 500 stocks. If the U.S. Economy grows, you will make money regardless of which companies were the winners and which were the losers. An index fund is a form of mutual fund. Mutual funds are groups of stocks that professionals believe will beat the market. Often the mutual fund managers are wrong in that they don't beat the market, but when they do they can make you lots of money. You can buy mutual funds, including index funds from an online broker or from a private broker. You will find them in the phone book or in most investment magazines, such as *Money*.

What Motley Fool is better known for, however, is providing investment advice for individual stocks. They do the research for you and then provide that information at their website, on radio, and in books. In the long run, their advice has paid off handsomely. You may want to join other investors on their discussion board where people share their insights about various stocks. Overall, The Motley Fool is a good place to get started in investing.

Discussion Questions

1. What kind of investment advice would you like to get from a company like The Motley Fool?

2. Do you think it is effective for the company to be so casual as to call themselves The Motley Fool and to offer Foolish advice? To whom would such an approach appeal?

3. What other sources might you use to find out more about stocks and bonds?

CHAPTER

21

Understanding Money and Financial Institutions

Learning Goals

AFTER YOU HAVE READ AND STUDIED THIS CHAPTER, YOU SHOULD BE ABLE TO

1 Explain what money is and how its value is determined.

2 Describe how the Federal Reserve controls the money supply.

3 Trace the history of banking and the Federal Reserve System.

4 Classify the various institutions in the U.S. banking system.

5 Explain the importance of the Federal Deposit Insurance Corporation and other organizations that guarantee funds.

6 Discuss the future of the U.S. banking system.

7 Evaluate the role and importance of international banking and the role of the World Bank and the International Monetary Fund.

Getting to Know Alan Greenspan, Chairman of the Federal Reserve

Alan Greenspan, the head of the U.S. Federal Reserve System (the Fed) since 1987, is one of the most powerful individuals in the United States. An example of his influence occurred in 1996 when Greenspan suggested in a speech that stock prices may be too high. His comment triggered a global sell-off of stocks.

How did one person get to be so powerful? Greenspan went to New York University, where he earned both a BA and an MA in economics. He then began work as an economist for the Conference Board, a nonprofit research group. Later he started his own consulting firm. After that, he devoted his energies to public service and began a distinguished career in government that included service for five presidents. As one of President Richard Nixon's top economic aides, Greenspan worked on several economic task forces and served as an informal adviser. As chairman of the Council of Economic Advisers under President Gerald Ford, he became an intense inflation fighter. He also argued that government spending must be cut. That's one reason why President Ronald Reagan chose him to be Fed chairman.

In 1991, President George Bush reappointed Greenspan to another term, citing his success in fighting inflation and leading the economic recovery from the recession of 1990. President Bill Clinton retained him for much the same reason. Clinton reappointed Greenspan in 2000 to keep the economy growing without causing inflation and now he's working with George W. Bush.

Under Greenspan's leadership, the United States enjoyed the longest economic expansion in its history. As chairman of the Federal Reserve, Greenspan has control over the nation's money supply. One tool he uses is interest rates. He raised interest rates several times in 1999–2000 to slow the growth of the economy. He felt it was overheated; that is, he feared inflation. As it turned out, the economy slowed too fast and Greenspan began cutting interest rates to get the economy moving again. Those cuts proved to be too little, too late, and the stock market fell. The United States was facing a recession. People hoped that cutting taxes and lowering interest rates together would get the economy moving again.

Clearly, Greenspan is one of the most influential people in the world and someone you need to study if you want to understand what is happening in the financial sector. You will see from future economic changes whether he has lowered interest rates just about right or not enough. And you will see whether or not he will be appointed for another term at the Fed.

Sources: Lawrence Kudlow, "Risking Fed Overkill?" *Washington Times*, May 19, 2000; Joan Szabo, "Beating the Odds," *Success*, July–August 2000, pp. 28–31; Fareed Zakarin, "Greenspan's Global Problem," *Newsweek*, February 19, 2001, p. 39; and Justin Fox, "Did He Blow It?" *Fortune*, April 2, 2001, pp. 26–27.

THE IMPORTANCE OF MONEY

The U.S. economy depends heavily on money: its availability, its value relative to other currencies, and its cost. Economic growth and the creation of jobs depend on money. Money is so important to the economy that many institutions have evolved to manage money and to make it available to you when you need it. Today you can easily get cash from an automated teller machine (ATM) almost anywhere in the world, but in many places cash isn't the only means of payment you can use. Most organizations will accept a check, credit card, debit card, or smart card to pay for things you buy. Behind the scenes of this free flow of money is a complex system of banking that makes it possible for you to do all these things.

The complexity of the banking system has increased as the electronic flow of money from country to country has become as free as the flow from state to state. Each day, more than $1.5 trillion is exchanged in the world's currency markets.[1] Therefore, what happens to any major country's economy has an effect on the U.S. economy and vice versa. Clearly, there's more to money and its role in the economies of the world than meets the eye. There's no way to understand the U.S. economy without understanding global money exchanges and the various institutions involved in the creation and management of money.

We'll explore such institutions in this chapter. Let's start at the beginning by discussing exactly what people mean when they say "money" and how the supply of money affects the prices you pay for goods and services.

What Is Money?

money
Anything that people generally accept as payment for goods and services.

barter
The trading of goods and services for other goods and services directly.

Money is anything that people generally accept as payment for goods and services. In the past, objects as diverse as salt, feathers, stones, rare shells, tea, and horses have been used as money. In fact, until the 1880s, cowrie shells were one of the world's most abundant currencies.[2] **Barter** is the trading of goods and services for other goods and services directly; though barter may sound like something from the past, many people have discovered the benefits of bartering online.[3] Many people today still barter goods and services the old-fashioned way—face-to-face. For example, in Siberia two eggs have been used to buy one admission to a movie, and customers of Ukraine's Chernobyl nuclear plant have paid in sausages and milk. Much of the trade in Russia today is now barter.

The problem is that eggs and milk are difficult to carry around. People need some object that's portable, divisible, durable, and stable so that they can trade goods and services without carrying the actual goods around with them. One answer to that problem over the years was to create coins made of silver or gold. Coins met all the standards of a useful form of money:

- *Portability.* Coins are a lot easier to take to market than are pigs or other heavy products.
- *Divisibility.* Different-sized coins could be made to represent different values. For example, prior to 1963 a U.S. quarter had half as much silver content as a half dollar, and a dollar had four times the silver of a quarter. Because silver is now too expensive, today's coins are made of other metals, but the values remain.
- *Stability.* When everybody agrees on the value of coins, the value of money is relatively stable. In fact, U.S. money has become so stable that much of the world uses the U.S. dollar as the measure of value.
- *Durability.* Coins last for thousands of years, even when they've sunk to the bottom of the ocean, as you've seen when divers find old Roman

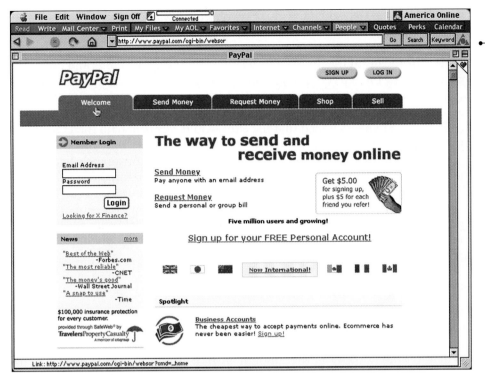

In the new Internet age, we are supposed to be sending money back and forth to each other on the Net using PayPal or some similar service. This surely is an easier way of sending money from one place to another, but do you have reservations about using such a service? What are they?

coins in sunken ships. One of the reasons the United States is producing new Sacagawea dollar coins is because they last much longer than paper money.

- *Difficult to counterfeit.* It's hard to copy elaborately designed and minted coins. But with the latest color copiers, people are able to duplicate the look of paper money relatively easily. Thus, the government has had to go to extra lengths to make sure real dollars are readily identifiable. That's why you have new paper money with the picture slightly off center and with new invisible lines that quickly show up when reviewed by banks and stores.

When coins and paper money become units of value, they make exchanges easier. Most countries have their own coins and paper money; they're all about equally portable, divisible, and durable. However, they're not always equally stable. For example, the value of money in Russia is so uncertain and so unstable that other countries won't accept Russian money (rubles) in international trade. For Russia to participate in global markets, it must develop money that's tradable.

Electronic cash (e-cash) is the latest form of money. In addition to being able to make online bill payments using software programs such as Quicken or Microsoft Money, you can e-mail e-cash to anyone using websites such as Paypal.com.[4] Recipients get an e-mail message telling them they have several choices for how they can receive the money: automatic deposit (the money will be sent to their bank), e-dollars for spending online, or a traditional check in the mail. Today the transaction is charged to the sender's credit card, but the day is coming when most such transactions will be conducted using e-cash alone.[5]

Changing the Currency in Europe

The exchange of goods and services among European countries was hindered in the past by the fact that each country had its own currency (money). For example, trading German marks for French francs was a bother at best and, on a larger scale, hindered the free flow of commerce. Recently, 12 European countries decided to create one common currency, called the euro. It exists only electronically at the time of this writing, but the actual coins and notes are expected to go into circulation in 2002. Four other European countries (Denmark, Greece, Sweden, and Britain) are waiting to see what happens to the new currency before joining the others in changing their monies.[6]

European bankers hoped that the euro would compete with the U.S. dollar as an international currency of choice, but right after it was introduced the euro fell 25 percent against the dollar.[7] That means that Europeans had to pay more for U.S. goods and European goods were cheaper for U.S. purchasers. You can check the value of the euro against the dollar yourself to see whether it has become a more viable international currency. How the euro stands up against the dollar depends greatly on the strength of the U.S. economy versus the European economy. And the strength of the U.S. economy depends partially on its money supply, as you shall see next.

What Is the Money Supply?

This chapter's opening profile says that Fed chairman Alan Greenspan is in control of the money supply. Two questions emerge from that simple statement: (1) What is the money supply? and (2) Why does it need to be controlled?

The **money supply** is the amount of money the Federal Reserve Bank makes available for us to buy goods and services. There are several ways of referring to the money supply. They're called M-1, M-2, and so on. The *M* stands for money, and the *1* and *2* stand for different definitions of the money supply. **M-1,** for example, includes coins and paper bills, money that's available by writing checks, and money that's held in traveler's checks—that is, money that can be raised quickly and easily. **M-2** includes everything in M-1 plus money in savings accounts (time deposits) and money in money market accounts, mutual funds, certificates of deposit, and the like—that is, money that may take a little more time to obtain than coins and paper bills. M-2 is the most commonly used definition of money.

Why Does the Money Supply Need to Be Controlled?

Imagine what would happen if governments (or in the case of the United States, the Federal Reserve) were to generate twice as much money as exists now. There would be twice as much money available, but there would be the same amount of goods and services ➤ **P.25** ◄. What would happen to prices in that case? Think about the answer for a minute. (Hint: Remember the laws of supply and demand ➤ **P.39** ◄ from Chapter 2.) The answer is that prices would go up because more people would try to buy goods and services with their money and would bid up the price to get what they wanted. This is called *inflation* ➤ **P.53** ◄. That is why some people define inflation as "too much money chasing too few goods."

Now think about the opposite: What would happen if the Fed took some of the money out of the economy? What would happen to prices? Prices would go down because there would be an oversupply of goods and services compared to the money available to buy them. If we take too much money out of the economy, a recession ➤ **P.53** ◄ might occur. That is, people would lose jobs and the economy would stop growing.

Now we come to a second question about the money supply: Why does the money supply need to be controlled? The money supply needs to be controlled because doing so allows us to manage the prices of goods and services somewhat. And controlling the money supply affects employment and economic growth or decline.

money supply
How much money there is to buy available goods and services.

M-1
Money that can be raised quickly and easily (coins and paper money, checks, traveler's checks, etc.).

M-2
Money included in M-1 plus money that may take a little more time to raise (savings accounts, money market accounts, mutual funds, certificates of deposit, etc.).

The Global Exchange of Money

A *falling dollar* means that the amount of goods and services you can buy with a dollar decreases. A *rising dollar* means that the amount of goods and services you can buy with a dollar goes up. Thus, in real terms, the price you pay for a German car today is lower than it was 10 years ago because the American dollar has risen relative to the euro (Germany's new unit of money).

What makes the dollar weak (falling dollar value) or strong (rising dollar value) is the position of the U.S. economy relative to other economies. When the economy is strong, people want to buy dollars and the value of the dollar rises. When the economy is perceived as weakening, however, people no longer desire dollars and the value of the dollar falls. The value of the dollar thus depends on a strong economy. Clearly, control over the money supply is important. In the following section, we'll discuss in more detail the money supply and how it's managed. Then we'll explore the U.S. banking system and how it lends money to businesses and individuals, such as you and me.

What will happen to the value of the dollar if Japanese businesspeople stop investing in the United States? What will happen to the value of the yen? Can you see that Japanese car prices will rise if the value of the dollar falls?

CONTROL OF THE MONEY SUPPLY

You already know that money plays a huge role in the American economy and in the economies of the rest of the world. Therefore, it's important to have an organization that controls the money supply to try to keep the U.S. economy from growing too fast or too slow. Theoretically, with the proper monetary policy, you can keep the economy growing without causing inflation. (See Chapter 2 to review monetary policy.) The organization in charge of monetary policy is the Federal Reserve System (the Fed). As we said in the chapter opening profile, the head of the Federal Reserve (at the moment, Alan Greenspan) is one of the most influential people not only in the country but also in the world because he or she controls the money that much of the world depends on for trade.

Basics about the Federal Reserve

The Federal Reserve System consists of five major parts: (1) the board of governors; (2) the Federal Open Market Committee (FOMC); (3) 12 Federal Reserve banks; (4) three advisory councils; and (5) the member banks of the system. Figure 21.1 shows where the 12 Federal Reserve banks are located. Member banks may be chartered by the federal government or by the state in which they're located.

The board of governors administers and supervises the 12 Federal Reserve banks. The seven members of the board are appointed by the president and confirmed by the Senate. The board's primary function is to set monetary policy. The Federal Open Market Committee (FOMC) has 12 voting members and is the policymaking body. The committee is made up of the seven-member board of governors plus the president of the New York reserve bank. Four others rotate in from the other reserve banks. The advisory councils offer suggestions to the board and to the FOMC. The councils represent the various banking districts, consumers, and member institutions, including banks, savings and loan institutions, and credit unions.

The Federal Reserve buys and sells foreign currencies, regulates various types of credit, supervises banks, and collects data on the money supply and other economic activity. As part of monetary policy, the Fed determines the

FIGURE 21.1

THE 12 FEDERAL RESERVE DISTRICT BANKS

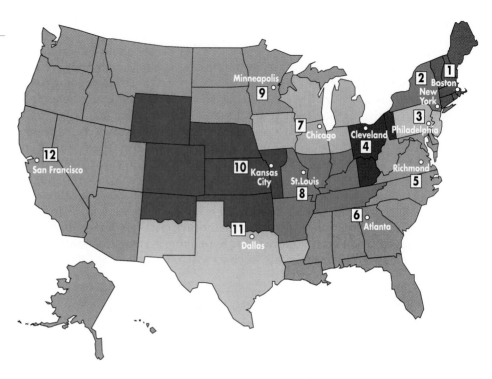

FIGURE 21.1

THE 12 FEDERAL RESERVE DISTRICT BANKS

level of reserves that must be kept at the 12 Federal Reserve banks by all financial institutions (reserve requirement). It also lends money to member banks and sets the rate for such loans (called the discount rate). Finally, it buys and sells government securities, or open-market operations. It is important to understand how the Fed controls the money supply, so we'll explore that in some depth next. As noted, the three basic tools the Fed uses to manage the money supply are reserve requirements, open-market operations, and the discount rate (see Figure 21.2).[8] Let's explore how each of these is administered.

The Reserve Requirement

reserve requirement
A percentage of commercial banks' checking and savings accounts that must be physically kept in the bank.

The **reserve requirement** is a percentage of commercial banks' checking and savings accounts that must be physically kept in the bank (e.g., as cash in the vault) or in a non-interest-bearing deposit at the local Federal Reserve district bank. The reserve requirement is the Fed's most powerful tool. When the Fed increases the reserve requirement, banks have less money for loans and thus make fewer loans. Money becomes more scarce, which in the long run tends to reduce inflation. For instance, if Omaha Security Bank holds deposits of $100 million and the reserve requirement is, say, 10 percent, then the bank must keep $10 million on reserve. If the Fed were to increase the reserve requirement to 11 percent, then the bank would have to put an additional $1 million on reserve, thus reducing the amount it could lend out. Since this increase in the reserve requirement would affect all banks, the money supply would be reduced and prices would likely fall.

A decrease of the reserve requirement, in contrast, increases the funds available to banks for loans, so banks make more loans and money becomes more readily available. An increase in the money supply stimulates the economy to achieve higher growth rates, but it can also create inflationary pressures. Because this tool is so potent and can cause such major changes in the U.S. economy, it is rarely used.

Open-Market Operations

open-market operations
The buying and selling of U.S. government securities by the Fed with the goal of regulating the money supply.

Open-market operations are a commonly used tool by the Fed. To decrease the money supply, the federal government sells U.S. government bonds to the

CONTROL METHOD	IMMEDIATE RESULT	LONG-TERM EFFECT
Reserve Requirements		
A. Increase.	Banks put more money into the Fed, *reducing* money supply; thus, there is less money available to lend to customers.	Economy slows.
B. Decrease.	Banks put less money into the Fed, *increasing* the money supply; thus, there is more money available to lend to customers.	Economy speeds up.
Open Market Operations		
A. Fed sells bonds.	Money flows from economy to the Fed.	Economy slows.
B. Fed buys bonds.	Money flows into the economy from the Fed.	Economy speeds up.
Managing the Discount Rate		
A. Rate increases.	Banks borrow less from the Fed; thus, there is less money to lend.	Economy slows.
B. Rate decreases.	Banks borrow more from the Fed; thus, there is more money to lend.	Economy speeds up.

FIGURE 21.2

HOW THE FEDERAL RESERVE CONTROLS THE MONEY SUPPLY

public. The money it gets as payment is no longer in circulation, decreasing the money supply. If the Fed wants to increase the money supply, it buys government bonds from individuals, corporations, or organizations that are willing to sell. The money paid by the Fed in return for these securities enters circulation, resulting in an increase in the money supply.

The Discount Rate

The Fed has often been called the banker's bank. One reason for this is that member banks can borrow money from the Fed and then pass it on to their customers in the form of loans. The **discount rate** is the interest rate that the Fed charges for loans to member banks. An increase in the discount rate by the Fed discourages banks from borrowing and consequently reduces the number of available loans, resulting in a decrease in the money supply. In contrast, lowering the discount rate encourages member banks to borrow money and increases the funds available for loans, which increases the money supply.

discount rate
The interest rate that the Fed charges for loans to member banks.

The Federal Reserve's Check-Clearing Role

One of the functions of the Federal Reserve System is to help process your checks. If you write a check to a local retailer, that retailer will take the check to its bank. If your account is also at that bank, it is a simple matter to reduce your account by the amount of the check and increase the amount in the retailer's account. But what happens if you write a check to a retailer in another state? That retailer will take the check to its bank. That bank will deposit the check for credit in the closest Federal Reserve bank. That bank will send the check to your local Federal Reserve bank for collection. The check will then be sent to your bank and the amount of the check will be withdrawn. Your bank will authorize the Federal Reserve bank in your area to deduct the amount of the check. That bank will pay the Federal Reserve bank that began the process in the first place. It will then credit the deposit account in the bank where the retailer has its account. That bank will then credit the account of the retailer. (See Figure 21.3 for a diagram of such an interstate transaction.) This long and involved process is a costly one; therefore, banks take many measures to lessen

FIGURE 21.3

CHECK-CLEARING PROCESS THROUGH THE FEDERAL RESERVE BANK SYSTEM

Suppose Mr. Brown, a farmer from Quince Orchard, Maryland, purchases a tractor from a dealer in Austin, Texas.

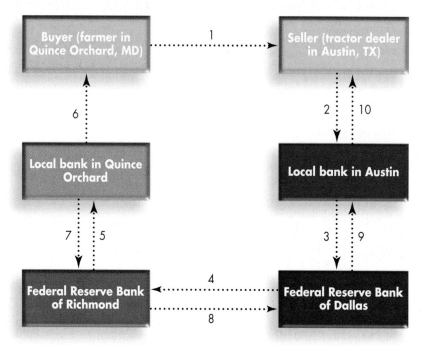

1. Mr. Brown sends his check to the tractor dealer.
2. The dealer deposits the check in his account at a local bank in Austin.
3. The Austin bank deposits the check for credit in its account at the Federal Reserve Bank of Dallas.
4. The Federal Reserve Bank of Dallas sends the check to the Federal Reserve Bank of Richmond for collection.
5. The Federal Reserve Bank of Richmond forwards the check to the local bank in Quince Orchard, where Mr. Brown opens his account.
6. The local bank in Quince Orchard deducts the check amount from Mr. Brown's account.
7. The Quince Orchard bank authorizes the Federal Reserve Bank of Richmond to deduct the check amount from its deposit account with the Federal Reserve Bank.
8. The Federal Reserve Bank of Richmond pays the Federal Reserve Bank of Dallas.
9. The Federal Reserve Bank of Dallas credits the Austin bank's deposit account.
10. The Austin bank credits the tractor dealer's account.

the use of checks. Such efforts include the use of credit cards and electronic transfers of money.

As you can see, the whole economy is affected by the Federal Reserve System's actions. In the following sections, we'll briefly discuss the history of banking to give you some background information on why the Fed came into existence. Then we'll explore what's happening in banking today.

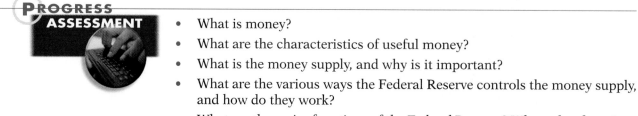

PROGRESS ASSESSMENT

- What is money?
- What are the characteristics of useful money?
- What is the money supply, and why is it important?
- What are the various ways the Federal Reserve controls the money supply, and how do they work?
- What are the major functions of the Federal Reserve? What other functions does it perform?

THE HISTORY OF BANKING AND THE NEED FOR THE FED

It will be easier for you to understand why we have a Federal Reserve System and why it is so important to the economy if we trace the history of banking in the United States. At first, there were no banks. Strict laws in Europe limited the number of coins that could be brought to the colonies in the New World. Thus, colonists were forced to barter for goods; for example, cotton and tobacco may have been traded for shoes and lumber.

The demand for money was so great that Massachusetts issued its own paper money in 1690, and other colonies soon followed suit. But continental money, the first paper money printed in the United States, became worthless after a few years because people didn't trust its value.

Land banks were established to lend money to farmers. But Great Britain, still in charge of the colonies at that point, ended land banks by 1741. The colonies rebelled against these and other restrictions on their freedom, and a new bank was formed in Pennsylvania during the American Revolution to finance the war against England.

In 1791, after the United States gained independence, Alexander Hamilton persuaded Congress to form a *central bank* (a bank where banks could keep their funds and borrow funds if needed), over the objections of Thomas Jefferson and others. This first version of a federal bank closed in 1811, only to be replaced in 1816 because state-chartered banks couldn't support the War of 1812. The battle between the Second (Central) Bank of the United States and state banks got hot in the 1830s. Several banks in Tennessee, President Andrew Jackson's home state, were hurt by pressure from the Central Bank. The fight ended when the bank was closed in 1836.

By the time of the Civil War, the banking system was a mess. Different banks issued different kinds of currencies. During the Civil War, coins were hoarded because they were worth more as gold and silver than as coins. The chaos continued long after the war ended, reaching something of a climax in 1907 when many banks failed. People got nervous about their money and went to banks to withdraw their funds. This is now known as a "run on the banks." Shortly thereafter, the cash ran out and some banks had to refuse money to depositors. This caused people to distrust the banking system in general.

It was the cash shortage problems of 1907 that led to the formation of an organization that could lend money to banks—the Federal Reserve System. It was to be a "lender of last resort" in such emergencies. Under the Federal Reserve Act of 1913, all federally chartered banks had to join the Federal Reserve. State banks could also join. The Federal Reserve became the banker's bank. If banks had excess funds, they could deposit them in the Fed; if they needed extra money, they could borrow it from the Fed. The Federal Reserve System has been intimately related to banking ever since.

The Great Depression

The Federal Reserve System was designed to prevent a repeat of the 1907 panic. Nevertheless, the stock market crash of 1929 led to bank failures in the early 1930s. When the stock market began tumbling, people ran to banks to get their money out. In spite of the Federal Reserve System, the banks ran out of money and states were forced to close banks. President Franklin D. Roosevelt extended the period of the bank closings in 1933 to gain time to come up with some solution to the problem.

In 1933 and 1935, Congress passed legislation to strengthen the banking system. The most important move was to establish federal deposit insurance, which

This sign says that the bank was taken over by the FDIC until it could find a larger bank to take over. All accounts in banks are insured up to $100,000 by the federal government. Are you more willing to put your money in a bank because of that guarantee?

you'll learn more about later in this chapter. At this point, it's important for you to know that in the 1930s, during the Great Depression, the government started an insurance program to further protect us from bank failures.

The Federal Reserve and the Banking Industry

The Federal Reserve is frequently in the news as it tries to keep the economy growing at an even pace. In the early 1990s, the Fed increased the money supply and lowered interest rates to get the economy growing. As inflation threatened in the mid-1990s and into the new century, the Fed increased short-term interest rates. That caused bond prices to fall and threatened the stock market. Alan Greenspan became the center of attention as the whole financial community waited for the Fed's next move. When the stock market began falling in the latter part of 2000 and into 2001, Greenspan cut interest rates to get the economy growing again. As of the writing of this text, we don't know the final result. What do the papers now report?

In short, the whole world has been watching and continues to watch the Federal Reserve System to see what direction the U.S. economy will take next. No group of people is more concerned than the nation's bankers. If businesses stop borrowing, then business growth slows, people are fired, and the whole economy stagnates. In fact, it's quite possible to have both slow growth and inflation. (That's called *stagflation*.) Thus, money and banking, especially the Federal Reserve Bank, are critical to business leaders. You now know about money and the money supply. The following sections explore banking and its importance to businesspeople.

THE AMERICAN BANKING SYSTEM

nonbanks
Financial organizations that accept no deposits but offer many of the services provided by regular banks (pension funds, insurance companies, commercial finance companies, consumer finance companies, and brokerage houses).

commercial bank
A profit-making organization that receives deposits from individuals and corporations in the form of checking and savings accounts and then uses some of these funds to make loans.

The American banking system consists of commercial banks, savings and loan associations, credit unions, and mutual savings banks. In addition, various organizations perform several banking functions, although they aren't true banks. These nondeposit institutions (often called **nonbanks**) include pension funds, insurance companies, commercial finance companies, consumer finance companies, and brokerage houses. In the following sections we'll discuss the activities and services provided by each of these institutions, starting with commercial banks.

Commercial Banks

A **commercial bank** is a profit-making organization that receives deposits from individuals and corporations in the form of checking and savings accounts and then uses some of these funds to make loans. Figure 21.4 lists the largest banks in the United States. Commercial banks have two types of customers: depositors and borrowers (those who take out loans). A commercial bank is equally responsible to both types of customers. Commercial banks try to make a profit by efficiently using the funds depositors give them. In essence, a commercial bank uses customer deposits as inputs (on which it pays interest) and invests that money in interest-bearing loans to other customers (mostly businesses). Commercial banks make a profit if the revenue generated by loans exceeds the interest paid to depositors plus all other operating expenses.

Services Provided by Commercial Banks

Individuals and corporations that deposit money in a checking account have the privilege of writing personal checks to pay for almost any purchase or transaction. The technical name for a checking account is a **demand deposit,** because the money is available on demand from the depositor. Typically, banks impose a service charge for check-writing privileges or demand a minimum deposit. Banks might also charge a small handling fee for each check written. For corporate depositors, the amount of the service charge depends on the average daily balance in the checking account, the number of checks written, and the firm's credit rating and credit history.

In the past, checking accounts paid no interest to depositors, but interest-bearing checking accounts have experienced phenomenal growth in recent years. Most commercial banks offer negotiable order of withdrawal (NOW) and Super NOW accounts to their depositors. A NOW account typically pays an annual interest rate but requires depositors always to maintain a certain minimum balance in the account (e.g., $500) and may restrict the number of checks that depositors can write each month.

A Super NOW account pays higher interest to attract larger deposits. However, Super NOW accounts require a larger minimum balance. They sometimes offer free, unlimited check-writing privileges. Individual banks determine the specific terms for their NOW and Super NOW accounts. The longer you keep your funds in such accounts, the more interest they pay.

In addition to these types of checking accounts, commercial banks offer a variety of savings account options. A savings account is technically called a **time deposit** because the bank can require a prior notice before withdrawal.

A **certificate of deposit (CD)** is a time-deposit (savings) account that earns interest to be delivered at the end of the certificate's maturity date. The depositor agrees not to withdraw any of the funds in the account until the end of the specified period. CDs are now available for periods of three months up to many years; interest rates vary according to the period of the certificate. The interest rates also depend on economic conditions and the prime rate at the time of the deposit. In addition to the checking and savings accounts discussed above, commercial banks offer a variety of other services to their depositors including automated teller machines and credit cards. The Making Ethical Decisions box discusses the kind of situation that led to more automated banking.

Automated teller machines (ATMs) give customers the convenience of 24-hour banking at a variety of outlets such as supermarkets, department stores, and drugstores in addition to the bank's regular branches. Depositors can now—almost anywhere in the world—transfer funds, make deposits, and get cash at their own discretion with the use of a computer-coded personalized plastic access card.

Commercial banks also offer credit cards to creditworthy customers, life insurance, inexpensive brokerage services, financial counseling, automatic payment of telephone bills, safe-deposit boxes, tax-deferred individual retirement

Bank of America
*Chase Manhattan
 Citibank
 First Union National Bank
*Morgan Guarantee Trust
 Wells Fargo Bank
 Bank One

*Proposed merger in 2001.

FIGURE 21.4

LARGEST U.S. BANKS

demand deposit
The technical name for a checking account; the money in a demand deposit can be withdrawn anytime on demand from the owner.

time deposit
The technical name for a savings account; the bank can require prior notice before the owner withdraws money from a time deposit.

certificate of deposit (CD)
A time-deposit (savings) account that earns interest to be delivered at the end of the certificate's maturity date.

MAKING ETHICAL DECISIONS

www.keepyourword.com

To Tell the Teller or Not

You have been banking at the same bank for some time, but the tellers at the bank keep changing, so it is difficult to establish a relationship with any one teller. You don't like using the automated teller machine because the bank has decided to charge for each transaction. Therefore, you are working with a teller and withdrawing $300 for some expenses you expect to incur. The teller counts out your money and says: "OK, here's your $300." Before you leave the bank, you count the money once more. You notice that the teller has given you $350 by mistake. You return to the teller and say, "I think you have made a mistake in giving me this money." She replies indignantly, "I don't think so. I counted the money in front of you."

You are upset by her quick denial of a mistake and her attitude. You have to decide whether or not to give her back the overpayment of $50. What are your alternatives? What would you do? Is that the ethical thing to do?

FIGURE 21.5

SERVICES AVAILABLE AT MOST COMMERCIAL BANKS

The number of services has expanded recently as banks seek to provide more and more assistance to consumers and businesses.

- Demand deposits (checking accounts)
- Time deposits (savings accounts)
- Loans
- Financial counseling
- Safe deposit boxes
- Certified checks
- Overdraft protection
- Insurance

- Traveler's checks
- Credit cards
- Certificates of deposit (CDs)
- NOW accounts
- Super NOW accounts
- Online banking
- Automated teller machines (ATMs)
- Brokerage services

accounts (IRAs) for qualified individuals and couples, traveler's checks, and over-draft checking account privileges. The latter means that preferred customers can automatically get loans at reasonable rates when they've written checks exceeding their account balance. Figure 21.5 lists key banking services.

Services to Borrowers

Commercial banks offer a variety of services to individuals and corporations in need of a loan. Generally, loans are given based on the recipient's creditworthiness. Banks want to manage their funds effectively and are supposed to screen loan applicants carefully to ensure that the loan plus interest will be paid back on time. Small businesses and minority businesses often search out banks that cater to their needs. The Spotlight on Small Business box discusses such banks in more depth.

Savings and Loan Associations (S&Ls)

savings and loan association (S&L)
A financial institution that accepts both savings and checking deposits and provides home mortgage loans.

A **savings and loan association (S&L)** is a financial institution that accepts both savings and checking deposits and provides home mortgage loans. S&Ls are often known as thrift institutions because their original purpose (starting in 1831) was to promote consumer thrift and home ownership. To help them encourage home ownership, thrifts were permitted for many years to offer slightly higher interest rates on savings deposits than banks. Those rates at-

SPOTLIGHT ON SMALL BUSINESS

www.nationalbankers.org

Where Can Entrepreneurs Go to Get Financing?

Susan Ernst is copresident of Royal Electric Company in Columbus, Ohio. She went to two banks, a large national bank and Commerce National Bank, a local bank that specializes in serving small businesses. Ernst says, "It was remarkable how different those two experiences were . . . With the big bank, the employees who dealt with us seemed to treat us like we were not important . . . With the local bank, we got personal attention from the beginning."

Louis E. Prezeau Sr., president and CEO of City National Bank, says that a small-business owner will have a lot more access to somebody who can make decisions in a minority-owned or small bank than in a large bank. That was true for Adetunde Dada when he sought funding for Tunde Dada House of Africa in Orange, New Jersey. He got great service from the African American–owned City National Bank of New Jersey in Newark. Other banks had not turned him down, but they were really slow in responding to his request.

The National Bankers Association (NBA) is a Washington, D.C.–based trade group that represents some 50 minority- and women-owned banks. Its members are committed to providing employment opportunities, entrepreneurial capital, and economic revitalization in neighborhoods that often have little access to financial services. A large bank may hesitate to make a small loan to a small business, but a small bank can get to know that business and that businessperson well. As a result, a small business can get not only money but financial advice and other services as well.

Minority banks usually have more experience dealing with minority borrowers and thus can help them with more than simple banking services. If you are thinking of starting a small business, to impress any banker you should first open a checking and savings account in that bank. The bank will help with the writing of a business plan and make sure you have the kind of financial backing you need to succeed in the long run. The banker is likely to visit your business to see the operation. Such close cooperation and participation makes the link between small businesses and small bankers intimate and beneficial to both.

Sources: Jill Andresky Fraser, "Entrepreneurs in Search of a Deal," *Inc.*, April 2000, pp. 116–20; and Jill Andresky Fraser, "The Money Hunt," *Inc.*, March 2001, pp. 49-63.

---

tracted a large pool of funds, which were then used to offer long-term fixed-rate mortgages at whatever the rate was at the time.

Between 1979 and 1983, about 20 percent of the nation's S&Ls failed. Faced with this situation, the federal government permitted S&Ls to offer NOW and Super NOW accounts, to allocate up to 10 percent of their funds to commercial loans, and to offer mortgage loans with adjustable interest rates based on market conditions. In addition, S&Ls were permitted to offer a variety of other banking services, such as financial counseling to small businesses and credit cards. As a result, S&Ls became much more similar to commercial banks than before.

Credit Unions

Credit unions are nonprofit, member-owned financial cooperatives that offer the full variety of banking services to their members. Today the 12,000 or so credit unions in the United States hold about 7 percent of all savings and deposits. Typically, credit unions offer their members interest-bearing checking accounts (called share draft accounts) at relatively *high* rates, short-term loans at relatively *low* rates, financial counseling, life insurance policies, and a limited number of home mortgage loans. Credit unions may be thought of as

credit unions
Nonprofit, member-owned financial cooperatives that offer the full variety of banking services to their members.

AXA Group (France)

Allianz Group (Germany)

Nippon Life (Japan)

Zenkyoren and Prefectural Insurance Federations (Japan)

Dai-ichi Mutual Life (Japan)

American International Group (U.S.)

Metropolitan Life Insurance (U.S.)

FIGURE 21.6

WORLD'S LARGEST INSURANCE FIRMS

pension funds
Amounts of money put aside by corporations, nonprofit organizations, or unions to cover part of the financial needs of members when they retire.

commercial and consumer finance companies
Organizations that offer short-term loans to businesses or individuals who either can't meet the credit requirements of regular banks or else have exceeded their credit limit and need more funds.

financial cooperatives organized by government agencies, corporations, unions, or professional associations. As nonprofit institutions, credit unions enjoy an exemption from federal income taxes. You might want to visit a local credit union and see if you are eligible to belong and then compare the rates you get to local banks.

Other Financial Institutions (Nonbanks)

As we explained earlier, *nonbanks* are financial organizations that accept no deposits but offer many of the services provided by regular banks. Nonbanks include life insurance companies, pension funds, brokerage firms, commercial finance companies, and corporate financial services. As competition between these organizations and banks has increased, the dividing line between banks and nonbanks has become less and less apparent. This is equally true in Europe, where companies from the United States such as Fidelity Investment and GE Capital Corporation compete with European banks. The diversity of financial services and investment alternatives offered by nonbanks has led banks to expand the services they offer. In fact, banks today are merging with brokerage firms to offer full-service financial assistance.

Life insurance companies provide financial protection for policyholders, who periodically pay premiums. In addition, insurers invest the funds they receive from policyholders in corporate and government bonds. In recent years, more insurance companies have begun to provide long-term financing for real estate development projects. Figure 21.6 lists the top insurance companies in the world. Note that the largest ones are not in the United States.

Pension funds are amounts of money put aside by corporations, nonprofit organizations, or unions to cover part of the financial needs of members when they retire. Contributions to pension funds are made either by employees, by employers, or by both employers and employees. A member may begin to collect a monthly draw on this fund upon reaching a certain retirement age. To generate additional income, pension funds typically invest in low-return but safe corporate stocks or in other conservative investments such as government securities and corporate bonds.

Many large pension funds such as the California Public Employees Retirement System (CalPERS) are becoming a major force in U.S. financial markets. Formidable rivals such as the Teachers Insurance and Annuity Association (TIAA) lend money directly to corporations.

Brokerage firms have traditionally offered services related to investments in the various stock exchanges in this country and abroad. However, brokerage houses have made serious inroads into regular banks' domain by offering high-yield combination savings and checking accounts. In addition, brokerage firms offer checking privileges on accounts (money market accounts). Also, investors can get loans from their broker, using their securities as collateral.

Commercial and consumer finance companies offer short-term loans to businesses or individuals who either can't meet the credit requirements of regular banks or have exceeded their credit limit and need more funds. These finance companies' interest rates are higher than those of regular banks. The primary customers of these companies are new businesses and individuals with no credit history. In fact, college students often turn to consumer finance companies for loans to pay for their education. One should be careful when borrowing from such institutions because the interest rates can be quite high.

Corporate financial systems established at major corporations such as General Electric, Sears Roebuck, General Motors, and American Express offer considerable financial services to customers. To compete with such nonbank organizations, banks have had to offer something extra—guaranteed savings.

Do you keep your savings in a bank, a S&L, a credit union, or some combination? Have you compared the benefits you could receive from each? Where would you expect to find the best loan values?

* Why did the United States need a Federal Reserve Bank?
* What's the difference between a bank, a savings and loan association, and a credit union?
* What is a nonbank?

HOW THE GOVERNMENT PROTECTS YOUR FUNDS

The American economic system learned a valuable lesson from the depression of the 1930s. To prevent investors from being completely wiped out during an economic downturn, several organizations evolved to protect your money. The three major sources of financial protection are the Federal Deposit Insurance Corporation (FDIC); the Savings Association Insurance Fund (SAIF), originally called the Federal Savings and Loan Insurance Corporation (FSLIC); and the National Credit Union Administration (NCUA). All three insure deposits in individual accounts up to $100,000.

The Federal Deposit Insurance Corporation (FDIC)

The **Federal Deposit Insurance Corporation (FDIC)** is an independent agency of the U.S. government that insures bank deposits. If a bank were to fail, the FDIC would arrange to have its accounts transferred to another bank or pay off depositors up to a certain amount ($100,000 per account.) The FDIC covers about 13,000 institutions, mostly commercial banks. What would happen if one of the top 10 banks in the United States were to fail? The FDIC has a contingency plan to nationalize the bank so that it wouldn't fail. The idea is to maintain confidence in banks so that others don't fail if one happens to falter.

Federal Deposit Insurance Corporation (FDIC)
An independent agency of the U.S. government that insures bank deposits.

The Savings Association Insurance Fund (SAIF)

The **Savings Association Insurance Fund (SAIF)** insures holders of accounts in savings and loan associations. It's now part of the FDIC. As just noted, it was originally called the Federal Savings and Loan Insurance Corporation (FSLIC) and was an independent agency. A brief history will show why the association was created.

Both the FDIC and the FSLIC were started during the Great Depression. The FDIC was begun in 1933, and the FSLIC in 1934. Some 1,700 bank and thrift institutions had failed during the previous few years, and people were losing confidence in them. The FDIC and FSLIC were designed to create more confidence in banking institutions. To get more control over the banking system in general, the government placed the FSLIC under the Federal Deposit Insurance Corporation (FDIC) and gave it a new name: the Savings Association Insurance Fund.

Savings Association Insurance Fund (SAIF)
The part of the FDIC that insures holders of accounts in savings and loan associations.

National Credit Union Administration (NCUA)

The National Credit Union Administration (NCUA) provides up to $100,000 coverage per individual depositor per institution. This coverage includes all accounts, including share draft checking, savings or money market accounts, and certificates of deposit. Additional protection can be obtained by holding accounts jointly or in trust. Individual retirement accounts (IRAs) are also separately insured. A family of four can thus have insured accounts totaling over $1 million.

THE FUTURE OF BANKING

Banking in the future is likely to change dramatically. One cause of change is the repeal of the Glass-Steagall Act of 1933, which prohibited banks from owning brokerages. The new law—the Gramm-Leach-Bliley Act of 1999—allows banks, insurers, and securities firms (brokers) to combine and sell each other's services.[9] This allows you and other consumers one-stop shopping for all your financial needs. One company can provide you with banking services, including credit cards and mortgages; insurance of all kinds, including life and car; and brokerage services, including the ability to buy stocks, bonds, and mutual funds. As companies compete for business, the total cost of banking and other financial services is likely to go down.[10] Furthermore, since all of your financial records can be kept in the same company, it may be easier for you to compute your taxes. In fact, the financial firm may do much of that work for you. Online banking is poised for future growth. We'll explore that trend next.

Electronic Banking on the Internet

Not only have banking, insurance, and brokerage services been combined in one company, but they are also available online. All of the nation's top 25 retail banks now allow customers access to their accounts online, and most have bill-paying capacity.[11] Thus, you may now be able to do all of your financial transactions from home, using your telephone or your computer. That includes banking transactions such as transferring funds from one account to another (e.g., savings to checking), paying your bills, and finding out how much is in your various accounts.[12] You can apply for a car loan or mortgage online and get a response almost immediately. The company can check your financial records and give you a reply while you wait. Buying and selling stocks and bonds is equally easy. (See the *Business Week* box for a discussion of the Internet and global banking.)

New Internet banks (e.g., NetBank) have been created that offer online banking only; they do not have physical branches. Such banks can offer better interest rates and lower fees because they do not have the costs of physical overhead that brick-and-mortar banks have. While many consumers are pleased with the savings and convenience, not all consumers are entirely happy with the service they receive with Internet banks. A recent study found that of the 9 million customers who signed up for online banking, 3 million discontinued using the service. Less than half of those who still have the service say they are completely satisfied.[13] Why are they dissatisfied? First of all, they are nervous about security. People fear

*S*1 invented Internet banking. The ad talks about its 21 offices in 11 countries. Half of the world's top 100 banks are its customers. Do such ads give you enough confidence in online banks to do most of your banking there?

FROM THE PAGES OF **BusinessWeek**   *www.ml.com/*

The Internet and Global Banking

The U.S. market for banking services is relatively mature; therefore, the growth markets of the future will be overseas. Few firms understand the potential of international banking better than Merrill Lynch, a leader in brokering and in financing corporations. Nonetheless, the company recognizes the competition from other international banks, insurance companies, mutual fund companies, financial planners, and brokers.

To expand overseas, Merrill Lynch bought the British brokerage Smith New Court; Spain's Iversiones; and stakes in brokerages in India, Thailand, South Africa, Indonesia, and Italy. It is also expanding to Latin America and recently acquired Australia's McIntosh Securities. In all, it is present in over 40 countries. As a consequence, about 30 percent of Merrill Lynch's revenues now come from overseas. Merrill Lynch is using the same concepts it developed in the United States to develop globally. In fact, it was one of the biggest losers during the Asian banking crisis.

Jeff Bahrenburg, global investment strategist at Merrill Lynch, says, "The Internet hastens the speed of financial flows and the pace at which the world is getting smaller." Andrew W. Lo, an economist at MIT, adds, "The most significant effect of the Internet on finance is that it will greatly facilitate the efficient matching of borrowers and investors in the global economy." To give you some idea of the dollar amount involved, consider this: In 1980, the world's stock of equities, bonds, and cash totaled some $11 trillion; by 2000 these financial figures were at $78 trillion.

Other leading U.S. investment firms, insurance companies, and banks are going global as well. Names like Charles Schwab and Travelers Group are becoming familiar all over the world. You can understand the potential when you learn that only 44 percent of the total value of stocks traded worldwide is traded in the United States. That means 56 percent is traded in foreign markets. That is an attractive situation for brokers and other financial institutions from all nations. It also means that there will be opportunities for tomorrow's college graduates in finance to work anywhere in the world.

Meanwhile, European banks are not standing still. Germany's Deutsche Bank is merging with Dresdner Bank to create a huge institution with $1.25 trillion in assets. The new bank will be twice the size of the U.S.'s Citigroup. The combined banks may go after Morgan Stanley Dean Witter and other American firms for investment banking deals. Thus, international banking will be a major source of competition in the future.

Sources: Christopher Farrell, "All the World's an Auction Now," *Business Week*, October 4, 1999, pp. 120–28; and Daniel Fairlamb and Stanley Reed, "Uber Bank," *Business Week*, March 20, 2000, pp. 52–53.

putting their financial information into cyberspace, where others may see it. Despite all the assurances of privacy, people are still concerned. Furthermore, some people want to be able to talk to a knowledgeable person when they have banking problems. They miss the service, the one-on-one help, and the security of local banks.

Because of these issues, the future seems to be with organizations like Wells Fargo, Citigroup, and Bank One, which are traditional banks that offer both online services and brick-and-mortar facilities.[14] Combined online and brick-and-mortar banks offer online services of all kinds, but also have automated teller machines (ATMs), places to go to deposit and get funds, and real people to talk to in person.

In the future, ATMs will be able to do much more for customers than at present. In the Dallas–Fort Worth, Texas, area, you can go to an ATM at the local 7-Eleven and cash checks and wire money. E*Trade, the online brokerage service, bought an online bank and 9,000 ATMs that bear the E*Trade name. Such ATMs link banking and brokerage accounts. In some places, you can even pick up tickets to events or download MP3 files (music) from ATMs.[15] In short, online banking will be combined with ATMs to provide whole new services to customers. Nonetheless, the traditional bank will still be there for those who want personal care and attention.[16]

Using Technology to Make Banking More Efficient

The way things have traditionally been done in banking—depositing money, writing checks, protecting against bad checks, and so on—is expensive. Imagine the cost to the bank of approving a check, processing it through the banking system, and mailing it back to you. Bankers have long looked for ways to make the system more efficient.

One step in the past was to issue credit cards. Credit cards reduce the flow of checks, but they too have their costs: There's still paper to process. The future will see much more electronic exchange of money because it is the most efficient way to transfer funds. In an **electronic funds transfer (EFT) system,** messages about a transaction are sent from one computer to another. Thus, funds can be transferred more quickly and more economically than with paper checks. EFT tools include electronic check conversion, debit cards, smart cards, direct deposits, and direct payments.

Electronic check conversion (ECC) converts a traditional paper check into an electronic transaction at the cash register (called a point-of-sale terminal) and processes it through the Federal Reserve's Automated Clearing House (ACH). ECC saves time and money while reducing the risks of bounced checks. When a customer makes payment with a check, it is run through a check reader where magnetic ink character recognition (MICR) information is captured. The check is verified against a database for acceptance. The transaction is electronically transferred through the ACH, where funds are debited directly from the customer's account and deposited automatically into the merchant's account. Since checks are electronically deposited, there are no trips to the bank, deposit slips, or risks of lost or stolen checks.

Whereas ECC *reduces* the paper-handling processes of using checks, debit cards *eliminate* them. A **debit card** serves the same function as checks: it withdraws funds from a checking account. Debit cards look like credit cards, but work very differently.[17] The difference between a debit card and a credit card is that you can spend no more than is in your account. You put the card into a slot in a point-of-sale terminal at a retailer. When the sale is recorded, an electronic signal is sent to the bank, transferring funds from your account to the store's account automatically. A record of transactions appears immediately online. One problem, however, is that people tend not to be as careful in keeping track of their debit card use as they are when they write checks. They end up withdrawing more from their checking account than they intended to do, and end up writing checks on money that isn't there. The cost for a returned check can be $30.

Smart cards are a combination of credit cards, debit cards, phone cards, drivers license cards, and more. Smart cards replace the typical magnetic strip on a credit or debit card with a microprocessor. The card can then store a variety of information including a person's bank balance. Each merchant can use this information to check the card's validity and spending limits, and the transaction can debit the amount on the card. Visa USA introduced its smart Visa card in 2000. It is embedded with a chip that transmits information online via a card reader plugged into the user's computer.[18] American Express had one of its most successful launches ever with its Blue Card, a smart card with an embedded chip that holds a "certificate of authenticity." That certificate, along

---

electronic funds transfer (EFT) system

A computerized system that electronically performs financial transactions such as making purchases, paying bills, and receiving paychecks.

electronic check conversion (ECC)

An electronic funds transfer tool that converts a traditional paper check into an electronic transaction at the cash register and processes it through the Federal Reserve's Automated Clearing House.

debit card

An electronic funds transfer tool that serves the same function as checks: it withdraws funds from a checking account.

smart card

An electronic funds transfer tool that is a combination credit card, debit card, phone card, and more.

with a personal identification number (PIN), secures information that makes Internet shopping safer and more convenient.

Some smart cards have embedded radio-frequency antennae that make it possible to access buildings and secure areas within buildings, and to buy gas and other items with a swipe of the card. A biometric function lets you use your fingerprint to boot up your computer. Students are using smart cards to open locked doors to dorms and identify themselves to retailers near campus and on the Internet. The cards also serve as ATM cards.[19]

Visa Buxx and Cobalt-card have new debit cards for teenagers. They work like this: Parents can deposit or withdraw funds from their child's account over the phone or the Internet. That amount is then added to or subtracted from the value on the card. The company then reports where the money is being spent over time. Thus, parents can monitor their children's transactions. Such cards are also made available to employees, nannies, and others.[20] The idea is to have an easy-to-use source of money that can be controlled. It is easier to use such a card than to drive to an ATM every time you need a few dollars.

For many, the ultimate convenience in banking involves automatic transactions such as direct deposit and direct payments. A *direct deposit* is a credit made directly to a checking or savings account. Because of direct deposit, some workers today receive no paycheck. Rather, their employer contacts the bank and orders it to transfer funds from the employer's account to the worker's account. Individuals can use direct deposits to transfer funds to other accounts, such as from a checking account to a savings account.

You can not only deposit funds directly into bank accounts automatically but also withdraw them automatically. A *direct payment* is a preauthorized electronic payment. Customers sign a separate authorization form for each company they would like the bank to pay automatically. This form authorizes the designated company to collect funds for the amount of the bill from the customer's checking or savings account on the specified date. The customer's financial institution provides information regarding the transaction on the monthly statement. EFT tools such as debit cards, smart cards, and automatic transactions are likely to continue taking over much of what is being done by checks today.

INTERNATIONAL BANKING AND BANKING SERVICES

Banks help companies conduct business in other countries by providing three services: letters of credit, banker's acceptances, and money exchange. If a U.S. company wants to buy a product from Germany, the company could pay a bank to issue a letter of credit. A **letter of credit** is a promise by the bank to pay the seller a given amount if certain conditions are met. For example, the German company may not be paid until the goods have arrived at the U.S. company's warehouse. A **banker's acceptance** promises that the bank will pay some specified amount at a particular time. No conditions are imposed. Finally, a company can go to a bank and exchange American dollars for euros to use in Germany; that's called currency or money exchange.

Banks are making it easier than ever before for travelers and businesspeople to buy goods and services overseas as well. Automated teller machines now provide yen, euros, and other foreign currencies through your personal Visa, MasterCard, Cirrus, Plus, or American Express card. You can usually get a better exchange rate with an ATM than you can from your hotel or corner money exchange facility.

letter of credit
A promise by the bank to pay the seller a given amount if certain conditions are met.

banker's acceptance
A promise that the bank will pay some specified amount at a particular time.

Deutsche Bank
(Germany)

UBS (Switzerland)

Bank of Tokyo—
Mitsubishi (Japan)

Bank of America (U.S.)

Fuji Bank (Japan)

ABN Amro (Netherlands)

FIGURE 21.7

WORLD'S LARGEST BANKS

World Bank
The bank primarily responsible
for financing economic
development; also known as the
International Bank for
Reconstruction and
Development.

Michael Máreg (foreground) of Pulte was unable to sell
the homes the company built in Mexico without
providing mortgage money to home buyers. Pulte bought
part of a firm in Mexico that gets most of its money from
the World Bank. Can you see the opportunities in
international finance?

Leaders in International Banking

This chapter has focused on banking within the United States. In the future, though, it's likely that many crucial financial issues will be international in scope. In today's financial environment, it's foolish to discuss the American economy apart from the world economy. If the Federal Reserve decides to lower interest rates, foreign investors can withdraw their money from the United States in minutes and put it in countries with higher rates. Of course, the Fed's increasing interest rates can draw money to the United States equally quickly.

Today's money markets form a global market system. The United States is just a part of that system. Figure 21.7 lists the world's largest banks. You can see that there are banks larger than U.S. banks all over the world. International bankers tend not to be nationalistic in their dealings. That is, they make investments in any country where they can get a maximum return for their money at a reasonable risk. That's how more than $1.5 trillion is traded daily! The net result of international banking and finance has been to link the economies of the world into one interrelated system with no regulatory control. American firms must compete for funds with firms all over the world. An efficient firm in London or Tokyo is more likely to get international financing than a less efficient firm in Detroit or Chicago.

What all this means to you is that banking is no longer a domestic issue; it's an international issue. To understand the U.S. financial system, you must learn about the global financial system. To understand America's economic condition, you'll have to learn about the economic condition of countries throughout the world. What has evolved, basically, is a world economy financed by international banks. The United States is just one player in the game. To be a winning player, America must stay financially secure and its businesses must stay competitive in world markets. The Reaching Beyond Our Borders box discusses a potential problem of globalization.

The World Bank and the International Monetary Fund (IMF)

To understand what is happening in the global banking world, you have to understand what the International Monetary Fund (IMF) is. The World Bank and the IMF are twin intergovernmental pillars that support the structure of the world's banking community:

The **World Bank** (also known as the International Bank for Reconstruction and Development) is primarily responsible for financing economic development. For example, it lent money to countries in Western Europe after World War II so they could rebuild. Today, the World Bank lends most of its money to poor nations to improve productivity and help raise the standard of living and quality of life.

Recently, the World Bank has come under considerable criticism, with major protests taking place in Seattle, Washington, and Washington, D.C. There have been a variety of protestors at such events. Environmentalists charge that the

The "Bank of Crooks and Criminals, International"

Many in the banking world feel that the now-defunct Bank of Credit and Commerce, International (BCCI) is a textbook example of what's wrong in international banking. BCCI was fined for laundering drug money in Florida and was involved in a foreign exchange scandal in Kenya. Its customers included former Panamanian strongman Manuel Noriega and Colombian drug lords. The bank was so bad, in fact, that it earned the name "Bank of Crooks and Criminals, International." Yet for almost 20 years, BCCI stayed one step ahead of the law. This financial reign of terror came to a crashing end in the early 1990s when bank regulators from the United States, Britain, and five other countries shut down BCCI. The estimated losses from BCCI's operations amounted to almost $5 billion, making it one of the world's biggest banking failures. How did all this happen, and what can be done to prevent future BCCIs from developing?

Most experts agree that the absence of any type of global regulatory agency permitted BCCI to remain untouchable. For example, the bank's registered home base was Luxembourg, but its managers worked from London. Its shareholders were wealthy Persian Gulf oil sheiks, and its assets were tangled in a branch network that included 70 different countries. Many operations were channeled through the Cayman Islands. The complexity of the bank prevented any banking authority from performing regulatory audits. Fraud, corruption, and money laundering became the order of the day. *Time* magazine called the bank the largest corporate criminal enterprise ever.

BCCI's actions have caused many industrialized nations to consider imposing tighter controls on international banks. The U.S. Senate and the Federal Reserve support global actions to control international banking activity. International banks will undergo more intensive scrutiny in the future in an attempt to prevent another BCCI-type scandal.

Meanwhile, U.S. authorities were able to convince authorities in Abu Dhabi to free BCCI files in return for dropping all criminal charges against Abu Dhabi officials. Furthermore, the Abu Dhabi government allowed the U.S. government to keep some $400 million being held in the United States.

It's been almost a decade since the BCCI scandal broke, but the court cases still go on. One BCCI official paid a $1.2 billion fine in 1999. But employees who worked in BCCI branches are having trouble finding jobs elsewhere. Who would hire someone from such a corrupt bank? Although this banking scandal goes back a long time, it is helpful to keep it in mind because it shows the legal problems that can arise in an unregulated world banking market.

Sources: Rudolph A. Pyatt Jr., "BCCI, a Tragedy without a Last Act," *Washington Post*, July 1, 1999, p. E3; "BCCI: Dead and Buried," *The Economist*, April 15, 2000; and "BCCI Creditor Ordered to Pay $1 Billion," *AP Online*, May 30, 2000.

World Bank finances projects that damage the ecosystem, such as China's Three Georges Dam. Human rights activists and unionists argue that the bank supports countries that restrict religious freedoms and tolerate sweatshops. AIDS activists complain that the bank does not do enough to get low-cost AIDS drugs to developing nations.[21] As a result of such protests, the World Bank is trying to develop strategies that focus more on the poor and do less to damage the environment.[22]

Protestors have been upset with the IMF as well. In contrast to the World Bank, the **International Monetary Fund (IMF)** was established to assist the smooth flow of money among nations. It requires members (who are voluntary) to allow their own money to be exchanged for foreign money freely, to keep the IMF informed about changes in monetary policy, and to modify those policies on the advice of the IMF to accommodate the needs of the entire membership. The IMF is not *supposed to* be a lending institution primarily, as is the World Bank. Rather, it is designed to be an overseer of member coun-

International Monetary Fund (IMF)
Organization that assists the smooth flow of money among nations.

tries' monetary and exchange rate policies. The IMF's goal is to maintain a global monetary system that works best for all nations. Members of the IMF contribute funds (rich countries pay more, poor countries pay less). Those funds are available to countries when they get into financial difficulty.

The IMF was in the news almost daily in the late 1990s and early part of this century because it was lending money (billions of dollars) to nations whose currencies had fallen dramatically and whose banks were failing (e.g., Asian countries and Russia). Many believe that the IMF bungled the Asian and Russian crises and are now calling for reform.[23] Many of the protestors in Seattle and Washington were there to protest actions taken by the World Bank and the IMF. Debt relief advocates want the World Bank and IMF to forgive the debts of poor countries because many of them cannot afford to feed their people, much less pay back huge loans. But the failure of such loans shows that the World Bank and IMF's actions have not been very successful.[24] Therefore, they are both under attack from all directions and are planning to change their policies.[25] Only time will tell what will finally emerge. There was some question about whether or not the World Bank and IMF's money was being wasted because of corrupt governments and poor economic decision making. The debate over such issues is likely to continue well into this century.

PROGRESS ASSESSMENT

- What's the difference between the FDIC and the SAIF?
- Describe an electronic funds transfer (EFT) system. What are its benefits?
- What are the limitations of online banking?
- What are the roles of the World Bank and the International Monetary Fund?

SUMMARY

1. Explain what money is and how its value is determined.

1. Money is anything that people generally accept as payment for goods and services.
   How is the value of money determined?
   The value of money depends on the money supply, that is, how much money is available to buy goods and services. Too much money in circulation causes inflation. Too little money causes recession and unemployment.

2. Describe how the Federal Reserve controls the money supply.

2. Because the value of money is so important to the domestic economy and international trade, an organization was formed to control the money supply.
   • *What's that organization and how does it work?*
   The Federal Reserve makes financial institutions keep funds in the Federal Reserve System (reserve requirement), buys and sells government securities (open-market operations), and lends money to banks (the discount rate). To increase the money supply, the Fed can cut the reserve requirement, buy government bonds, and lower the discount rate.

3. Trace the history of banking and the Federal Reserve System.

3. In the American colonies there were no banks at first and coins were limited. The colonists traded goods for goods instead of using money.
   • *How did banking evolve in the United States?*
   Massachusetts issued its own paper money in 1690; other colonies followed suit. British land banks lent money to farmers but ended such loans by

1741. After the American Revolution, there was much debate about the role of banking, and there were heated battles between the Central Bank of the United States and state banks. The banking system was a mess by the time of the Civil War, with many banks issuing different kinds of money. Eventually, a federally chartered and state-chartered system was established, but chaos continued until many banks failed in 1907. The system was revived by the Federal Reserve only to fail again during the Great Depression. The Fed, banks, and S&Ls were in the news during the 1990s because many banks and S&Ls failed and the Federal Reserve kept raising interest rates. These events greatly affected the economy.

4. Savings and loans, commercial banks, and credit unions are all part of the banking system.
   - *How do they differ from one another?*
   Before deregulation in 1980, commercial banks were unique in that they handled both deposits and checking accounts. At that time, savings and loans couldn't offer checking services; their main function was to encourage thrift and home ownership by offering high interest rates on savings accounts and providing home mortgages. Deregulation closed the gaps between banks and S&Ls so that they now offer similar services.
   - *What kinds of services do they offer?*
   Banks and thrifts offer such services as savings accounts, NOW accounts, CDs, loans, individual retirement accounts (IRAs), safe-deposit boxes, online banking, insurance, stock, and traveler's checks.
   - *What is a credit union?*
   A credit union is a member-owned cooperative that offers everything that a bank does. That is, it takes deposits, allows you to write checks, and makes loans. It also may sell life insurance and make home loans. Because credit unions are member-owned cooperatives rather than profit-seeking businesses like banks, credit union interest rates are sometimes higher than those from banks, and loan rates are often lower.
   - *What are some of the other financial institutions that make loans and do other banklike things?*
   Nonbanks include life insurance companies that lend out their funds, pension funds that invest in stocks and bonds and make loans, brokerage firms that offer investment services, and commercial finance companies.

   4. Classify the various institutions in the U.S. banking system.

5. The government has created organizations to protect depositors from losses such as those experienced during the Great Depression.
   - *What agencies ensure that the money you put into a bank, S&L, or credit union is safe?*
   Money deposited in banks is insured by an independent government agency, the Federal Deposit Insurance Corporation (FDIC). Money in S&Ls is insured by another agency connected to the FDIC, the Savings Association Insurance Fund (SAIF). Money in credit unions is insured by the National Credit Union Administration (NCUA). These organizations protect your savings up to $100,000 per account.

   5. Explain the importance of the Federal Deposit Insurance Corporation and other organizations that guarantee funds.

6. There will be many changes in the banking system in coming years.
   - *What are some major changes?*
   One important change will be more services offered by banks including insurance, securities (stocks, bonds, and mutual funds), and real estate sales. Electronic funds transfer systems will make it possible to buy goods and services with no money. Automated teller machines enable you to get foreign money whenever and wherever you want it. Online banking may change the banking process dramatically as people become more used to paying bills

   6. Discuss the future of the U.S. banking system.

and conducting other transactions online. ATMs will offer more services, including the ability to pick up tickets to events and download music.

7. Evaluate the role and importance of international banking and the role of the World Bank and the International Monetary Fund.

7. Today's money markets aren't national; they are global.
• *What do we mean by global markets?*
Global markets mean that banks don't necessarily keep their money in their own countries. They make investments where they get the maximum return.
• *What are the roles of the World Bank and the IMF?*
The World Bank (also known as the International Bank for Reconstruction and Development) is primarily responsible for financing economic development. The International Monetary Fund (IMF), in contrast, was established to assist the smooth flow of money among nations. It requires members (who join voluntarily) to allow their own money to be exchanged for foreign money freely, to keep the IMF informed about changes in monetary policy, and to modify those policies on the advice of the IMF to accommodate the needs of the entire membership.

KEY TERMS

banker's
  acceptance 665
barter 648
certificate of deposit
  (CD) 657
commercial and
  consumer finance
  companies 660
commercial
  bank 656
credit unions 659
debit card 664
demand deposit 657
discount rate 653
electronic check
  conversion
  (ECC) 664

electronic funds
  transfer (EFT)
  system 664
Federal Deposit
  Insurance
  Corporation
  (FDIC) 661
International
  Monetary Fund
  (IMF) 667
letter of credit 665
M-1 650
M-2 650
money 648
money supply 650
nonbanks 656

open-market
  operations 652
pension funds 660
reserve
  requirement 652
savings and loan
  association
  (S&L) 658
Savings Association
  Insurance Fund
  (SAIF) 661
smart card 664
time deposit 657
World Bank 666

DEVELOPING WORKPLACE SKILLS

1. Compare a local bank with a local credit union exploring interest rates given on accounts, the services available, and the loan rates. Be prepared to give a one-minute summary to the class.

2. Use the information you obtained from question 1 to compare local organizations with banking on the Internet. Do an Internet search for online banks and compare them to your local institutions. Again, be prepared to discuss your findings in class.

3. What is happening with the euro today? What is its value relative to the U.S. dollar? How is the use of the euro affecting European economies?

4. Alan Greenspan is one of the most powerful and important people in the world. Do an Internet search and find out more about him and what he does, including controlling the money supply through raising and lowering interest rates. Be prepared to discuss what new things you discovered.

5. Write a two-page paper on the role of the World Bank and the International Monetary Fund in providing loans to countries. Is it important for U.S. citizens to lend money to people in other countries through such organizations? Why or why not?

Purpose:

To learn a few fun facts about U.S. currency.

Exercise:

Your parents always told you money doesn't grow on trees. Other than that what else do you know about money?

1. Go to the Bureau of Engraving and Printing's (BEP) website at www. moneyfactory.com and answer the following questions:
   a. What is currency paper made of?
   b. How much ink does the BEP use to print money each day?
   c. How much does it cost to produce a paper currency note?
   d. Approximately how many times could you fold a piece of currency before it would tear?
   e. How long is the life span of $1 bill?
   f. What is the origin of the dollar sign ($)?
   g. Why did the BEP print paper notes in 3-, 5-, 10-, 25-, and 50-cent denominations during the Civil War?
   h. If you had 10 billion $1 notes and spent one every second of every day, how long would it take you to go broke?
   i. Who was the only woman whose portrait appeared on a paper U.S. currency note?
   j. When did "In God We Trust" become part of the U.S. currency design?

2. Whose picture is on a $100 bill? If you're still a kid at heart, you might enjoy playing the money trivia games at the Treasury Dome at www.bep.treas.gov/kids_site/tdome.html.

PRACTICING MANAGEMENT DECISIONS

CASE

LEARNING ABOUT THE FEDERAL RESERVE SYSTEM

Unlike other cases in this text, this case requires you to gather the facts and figures. Consult *The Wall Street Journal* or other business publications to see how the Federal Reserve System is strengthening the economy. This is an important exercise because few people know much about the Federal Reserve.

The Coalition for Monetary Education conducted a random survey of 2,000 people to see what they knew about the Federal Reserve and monetary policy in general. Only about 1 percent (some 20 out of 2,000) understood the monetary basics. Over 75 percent of the respondents knew that the Federal Reserve's board of governors controlled the money supply, but only 9 percent of those polled were aware that the Federal Reserve's policies influenced the inflation rate, and only 13 percent were aware that the Fed's policies affected interest rates.

Only 31 percent of the people knew that U.S. dollars aren't redeemable in gold or silver. Less than 30 percent knew that bank failures were widespread. Reacting to these findings, the coalition planned a campaign to educate the public about the effects of federal policies on banking.

Decision Questions

1. How do the Federal Reserve's policies affect interest rates and the inflation rate? Why is it important for people to know that?
2. What action, if any, has the Federal Reserve taken in the past year to control the money supply and inflation? What are the results?

(The answer to this question can be found in past issues of *The Wall Street Journal*.)

3. Go back to Chapter 2 and read about fiscal and monetary policy. Which seems to be having the greater effect on the U.S. economy today: monetary or fiscal policy? Why?

VIDEO CASE

ONLINE BANKING

Get ready to hear the word *virtual* a lot in the next century: virtual shopping, virtual malls, and virtual banking. Virtual, in more common terms, means electronic. So you could call it electronic shopping, electronic malls, and electronic banking. The bottom line is that people will be able to shop, buy stocks and bonds, pay their bills, get price quotes, and conduct all kinds of business using their phone or their computer. Chances are that most will use their computer because it is easier to do transactions when you can see what is happening.

Let's focus for a minute on online banking. Imagine the convenience of sitting at your desk and paying your bills, reviewing your bank accounts, and even buying and selling stock, insurance, and more—all via computer. It is estimated that about 18 million households will be banking online by the year 2002. Some of the advantages are:

1. *Convenience.* With online banking, you can bank from anywhere at any time: 24 hours a day, 7 days a week. It takes just a few keystrokes, so you save the time of writing checks, addressing them, stamping the envelopes, and taking them to the mailbox. Money can also be transferred from one account to the other.
2. *Fast information.* You can quickly determine what your balance is in any account.
3. *Financial planning.* You can access all kinds of information dealing with personal financial planning, such as budgeting and forecasting.
4. *Low cost.* Many banks offer free software and charge minimal amounts per month (about

$5 for writing 20 checks). Some charge less, as little as nothing.

Potential disadvantages include:

1. *Security.* Some people are worried about sending private information about money matters electronically. But bankers say that the latest encryption technology makes it as safe to bank online as to go through a teller.
2. *Computer overuse.* Many people work all day behind a computer. They may not want to come home and spend more time at a computer doing their banking. Furthermore, there is the possibility that the system may go down and they'll have to revert to the old banking methods. Some people also prefer having a paper trail to follow their transactions.
3. *Limited services.* You cannot make deposits online or get cash. If you're going to the bank anyhow, it may be easier and faster to use the ATM or the teller. Having person to person contact with a banker is comforting to some people. Some organizations won't participate in electronic banking, so you may not be able to pay all your bills that way.

Small businesses may find online banking much more advantageous because they have too many bills to pay. The cost savings and convenience are much greater than for consumers, and record keeping may be easier.

Banks are now merging with mutual funds, insurance companies, and other services to offer even more services online. Some see the end of traditional banking as banks become more complex financial institutions offering a wider variety of services, including financial counseling, online stock reports, and more. Soon you will be able to shop at a virtual mall, check the status of your accounts at the bank, make payments online, take out a loan if you need one, and invest money left over—all electronically from your home office.

Discussion Questions

1. Some people enjoy shopping at traditional malls and working with real tellers at the bank. What can banks and retailers do to encourage people to move to online banking and shopping?

2. Brainstorm the kinds of services that could be combined with banking services to make your life easier. Don't forget to include government services such as paying for your auto license and paying your taxes.

3. What are some of the dangers you see of conducting your banking, stock transactions, and insurance payments electronically? What happens when the electricity goes out? What happens if files get erased, as so often happens on your home PC? What can be done to minimize such dangers?

CHAPTER 222

Managing Personal Finances: Who Wants to Be a Millionaire?

LEARNING GOALS

AFTER YOU HAVE READ AND STUDIED THIS CHAPTER, YOU SHOULD BE ABLE TO

1. Describe the six steps one can take to generate capital.

2. Identify the best ways to preserve capital, begin investing, and buy insurance.

3. Outline a strategy for retiring with enough money to last a lifetime.

There are about 7 million people in the world with more than $1 million in financial assets. More than 5 million of these millionaires live in the United States. Would you like to be one of them? One of the best ways to learn how to become a millionaire is to do what companies do: benchmark those who are successful. That is, you should find out what all those millionaires did to make their money. For over 20 years, Thomas Stanley has been doing just that—studying wealthy people. His research is available in a book called *The Millionaire Next Door: The Surprising Secrets of America's Wealthy,* which he co-authored with William Danko. You may enjoy reading the book yourself, but in the following paragraphs we'll give you some hints you may use immediately.

Getting to Know Thomas Stanley, Expert on Millionaires

The rule for house buying is to spend no more than twice your annual income for a home. The millionaires tried not to spend much money on things that had no lasting value: clothing, eating out, dry cleaning, and the like. In short, Stanley and Danko say that becoming a millionaire has more to do with thrift than with how much you earn. Many high-wage earners spend all their money on big homes and fancy cars but have relatively little left when they retire.

Stanley's latest book, *The Millionaire Mind,* is good news for the "average" student. After surveying another 1,500 millionaires, Stanley found that their average score on the Scholastic Aptitude Test (SAT) was 1190 and that most millionaires made Bs and Cs in college. The trick, the millionaires said, is

Some millionaires work for big companies. The majority, however, are entrepreneurs who own one or more small businesses. Self-employed people are four times as likely to be millionaires as people who earn a paycheck working for others.

The average income of American millionaires is $131,000 a year. So how did they get to be millionaires? They saved their money. To become a millionaire by the time you are 50 or so, you have to save about 15 percent of your income every year—starting when you are in your 20s. If you start later, you have to save an even larger percentage. The secret is to put your money in a place where it will grow without your having to pay taxes on it.

To save that 15 percent a year, you have to spend less than you earn. That discipline must begin with your first job and stay with you all your life. To save money, the millionaires Stanley studied tended to own modest homes and to buy used cars.

to choose a career that matches your ability. They also said it was important to focus on a goal, take calculated risks, and *work harder than other people.* Finally, they said that the other keys to success are being honest and disciplined, getting along with others, and having a supportive spouse.

Do you want to be a millionaire? If so, then you need to do what millionaires have done. You need to get an education, work hard, save your money, and make purchases carefully. This chapter will give you more insight into how to manage your finances. Are you ready to do the hard work it takes to become a millionaire? To reach your goal, your final answer must be "Yes!"

Sources: Chad Roedmeier, "Most Millionaires Were So-So Students, Writer Says," *The Plain Dealer,* February 7, 2000, pp. 1A, 7A; "Who Wants to Be a Millionaire?" *Business Week,* August 28, 2000, p. 16; and Tom Fetzer, "Never Say Die," *Success,* December/January 2001, p. 60.

The Need for Personal Financial Planning

America is largely a capitalist ➤ **P.37** ◄ country. It follows, then, that the secret to success in such a country is to have capital. With capital, you can take nice vacations, raise a family, invest in stocks and bonds, buy the goods and services you want, give generously to others, and retire with enough money to see you through. Money management, however, is not easy. You have to earn the money in the first place. Then you have to learn how to save money, spend money wisely, and insure yourself against the risks of serious accidents, illness, or death. We shall discuss each of these issues in this chapter so that you can begin making financial plans for the rest of your life. With a little bit of luck, you may be one of the millionaires Thomas Stanley interviews for his next book.

Financial Planning Begins with Making Money

A major reason for studying business is that it prepares you for finding and keeping a good job. Today, that usually means learning how to communicate well, how to use a computer, and how to apply some of the skills you have learned in your college classes and in life. It also means staying out of financial trouble. When people get into financial trouble, they often make moral and ethical as well as economic mistakes. Read the Making Ethical Decisions box to review such a situation.

You already know that one of the best assets in finding a well-paying job is having a good education. Throughout history, an investment in education has paid off regardless of the state of the economy or political ups and downs. Benjamin Franklin said, "If a man empties his purse into his head, no one can take it away from him. An investment in knowledge always pays the best interest." Education has become even more important since we entered the information age. Today, a person with an undergraduate degree earns about twice as much as someone with only a high school diploma.[1]

The government is eager for you to go to college and is willing to help you by giving you various tax breaks to do so. Figure 22.1 lists some of the incen-

---

MAKING ETHICAL DECISIONS   *www.abiworld.org*

Bankruptcy

An estimated 10 percent of all U.S. households declared bankruptcy in the 1990s. In 1999 alone, over 1.3 million Americans declared personal bankruptcy. Slightly fewer declared bankruptcy in 2000.

Bankruptcy makes it possible for people to buy a big home, a new car, clothes, and luxury items of all kinds and then declare themselves bankrupt. That means the courts may relieve them of most or all of the debt. In many states, bankrupts can default on mortgage payments and still keep their homes. In one year, some $30 billion in household debt was discharged by the bankruptcy courts.

Imagine that you have piled up debts of $15,000 and want to purchase many more items, like an expensive va-

cation. You could go ahead and take that vacation knowing that you can't possibly pay for it and the government can't take it back. Then you could declare bankruptcy and ask the courts to forgive your debts. Your credit rating would plummet, but you would be able to keep some (or perhaps all) of what you have and make no further payments. What is the ethical thing to do? What conditions or circumstances would make such a decision more ethical? What would you do? What would be the consequences?

Sources: "Fewer Firms, People Bankrupt," *The Washington Times*, February 24, 2001, p. C11.

BENEFIT	ANNUAL LIMIT	EXPENSES THAT QUALIFY	CONDITIONS	MAXIMUM INCOME*
Scholarships				
Generally tax free	NA	Tuition, fees, books, supplies related to course work	Amounts designated specifically for services rendered or to cover living expenses are taxable income	None
Lifetime Learning Credit				
Tax credit	Up to $1,000 per family after second year of college	Tuition and Fees	Applies to expenses paid for school attendance after June 30, 1998	$50,000; joint returns: $100,000
Hope Credit				
Tax credit	Up to $1,500 per student for first 2 years of undergraduate study	Tuition and Fees	Must be enrolled at least part-time in a degree program	$50,000; joint returns: $100,000
Traditional and Roth IRAs				
No 10% penalty for early withdrawal	Amount of qualifying expenses	Tuition and fees, books, supplies, room and board	Must receive entire balance or begin receiving withdrawals by April 1 of year following year you reach age 70 1/2	(See Figure 22.8)
Education IRA				
Withdrawals are tax free	$500 contribution per child under 18	Tuition and fees, books, supplies, room and board	Contributions not deductible; cannot contribute to qualified state tuition program or claim an education credit; must withdraw assets by age 30	$110,000; joint returns: $160,000
Employers' Educational Assistance Program				
Employer benefits are excludable from income	$5,250	Tuition and fees, books, supplies, room and board	Cannot also claim an education credit; for undergraduate work only	None
Interest Paid on Student Loans				
Deduction from income	1999: $1,500; 2000: $2,000; 2001: $2,500	Tuition and fees, books, supplies, room and board, transportation	Applies to the first 60 months' interest; must be enrolled at least part time in a degree program	$55,000; joint returns: $75,000
Qualified State Tuition Programs				
Tax on earnings is deferred	None	Tuition and fees, books, supplies, room and board	Earnings are taxed to beneficiary when withdrawn	None
Education as a Miscellaneous Itemized Deduction				
Deduction from income	With other miscellaneous deductions, must exceed 2% of AGI	Tuition, fees, books, supplies. Some costs related to transportation, travel and research	Must be work-related and undertaken to maintain or improve job skills	None
U.S. Savings Bonds				
Interest is not taxed	Amount of qualifying expenses	Tuition, fees, payments to education IRAs and state tuition plans	Applies only to qualified series EE bonds issued after 1989 or series I bonds	$68,100; joint returns: $109,650

*Denotes top of an income range in which the benefit is first reduced then eliminated.

FIGURE 22.1

GETTING A TAX BREAK TO PAY FOR COLLEGE

The tax code provides many incentives for higher education. This chart shows the major tax benefits available to people attending college, saving for college, or paying off student loans.

tives the government provides and the conditions you must meet to get them. Many people use their education to find successful careers and to improve their earning potential, but at retirement they have little to show for their efforts. Making money is one thing; saving, investing, and spending it wisely is something else. Less than 10 percent of the U.S. population has accumulated enough money by retirement age to live comfortably. Following the six steps listed in the next section will help you become one of those with enough to retire in comfort.

Six Steps in Learning to Control Your Assets

The only way to save enough money to do all of the things you want to do later in life is to make more than you spend! We know you may find it hard to save today, but saving money isn't only possible, it's imperative if you want to accumulate enough to be financially secure. The following are six steps you can take today to get control of your finances.

Step 1: Take an Inventory of Your Financial Assets To take inventory, you need to develop a balance sheet ► **P.556** ◄ for yourself. Remember, a balance sheet starts with the fundamental accounting equation: Assets = Liabilities + Owners' equity. You can develop your own balance sheet by listing your assets (e.g., TV, VCR, DVD, computer, bicycle, car, jewelry, and clothes) on one side and liabilities (e.g., mortgage, credit card debt, and auto loans) on the other. Assets include anything you own. For our purpose, evaluate your assets based on their current value, not purchase price as required in formal accounting statements.

If the value of your liabilities exceeds the value of your assets, you aren't on the path to financial security. In fact, you may be one of those who find the Making Ethical Decisions box about bankruptcy particularly interesting. You need some discipline in your life.

Since we're talking about accounting, let's talk again about an income statement ► **P.560** ◄ . At the top of the statement is revenue (everything you take in from your job, investments, etc.). You subtract all your costs and expenses to get net income or profit. Software programs such as Quicken and websites such as www.dinky.town have a variety of tools that can easily help you with these calculations.

This may also be an excellent time to think about how much money you will need to accomplish all your goals. The more you visualize your goals, the easier it is to begin saving for them.

Step 2: Keep Track of All Your Expenses You may often find yourself running out of cash (a cash flow ► **P.562** ◄ problem). In such circumstances, the only way to trace where the money is going is to keep track of every cent you spend. Keeping records of your expenses can be a rather tedious but necessary chore if you want to learn discipline. Actually, it could turn out to be an enjoyable task because it gives you such a feeling of control. Here's what to do: Carry a notepad with you wherever you go and record what you spend as you go through the day. That notepad is your journal. At the end of the week, record your journal entries into a record book or computerized accounting program.

Develop certain categories (accounts) to make the task easier and more informative. For example, you can have a category called "food" for all food you

FIRST CHOICE COST PER MONTH	ALTERNATE CHOICE COST PER MONTH	SAVINGS PER MONTH
Starbucks caffe latte $3.00 for 20 days = $60.00	Quick Trip's Cappuccino $.60 for 20 days = $12.00	$48.00
Fast-food lunch of burger, fries, and soft drink $4.00 for 20 days = $80.00	Lunch brought from home $2 for 20 days = $40.00	40.00
Evian bottled water $1.50 for 20 days = $30.00	Generic bottled water $.50 for 20 days = $10.00	20.00
CD = $15.00	Listen to your old CDs = $0.00	15.00
Banana Republic T-shirt = $34.00	Old Navy T-shirt = $10.00	24.00
	Total savings per month	$147.00
		× 48 months
	Total savings through 4 years of college	$7,056.00
	12% compounded annually	$8,969.00

FIGURE 22.2

POSSIBLE COST-SAVING CHOICES

Budgeting your money requires making choices. The effect of the choices you make today can have a dramatic impact on your financial future. Compare the differences these few choices you can make now would mean to your future net worth. If you would make the lower-cost choices every month during your four years of college, and invest the savings in a mutual fund earning 12 percent compounded annually, you would have nearly $9,000 when you graduate.

bought from the grocery or the convenience store during the week. You might want to have a separate account for meals eaten away from home because you can dramatically cut such costs if you make your lunches at home. Other accounts could include automobile, clothing, utilities, entertainment, donations to charity, and gifts. Most people like to have a category called "miscellaneous" where they put expenditures for things like caffe latte. You won't believe how much you fritter away on miscellaneous items unless you keep a detailed record for at least a couple of months.

You can develop your accounts based on what's most important to you or where you spend the most money. Once you have recorded all of your expenses, it is relatively easy to see where you are spending too much money and what you have to do to save more money.

Step 3: Prepare a Budget Once you know your financial situation and your sources of revenue and expenses, you're prepared to make a personal budget.[2] Remember, budgets are financial plans. Items that are important in a household budget include mortgage or rent, utilities, food, life insurance, car insurance, and medical care. You'll need to make choices regarding how much to allow for such expenses as eating out, entertainment, and so on. Keep in mind that what you spend now reduces what you can save later. For example, spending $3.50 for a pack of cigarettes a day adds up to about $25 a week, $100 a month, $1,200 a year. If you saved that $1,200 each year instead, at 12 percent compounded annually you would have over $550,000 in 35 years—that's more than half of your million-dollar goal right there. Other cost-saving choices you might consider are listed in Figure 22.2.

You'll learn that running a household is similar to running a small business. It takes the same careful record keeping, the same budget processes and forecasting, the same control procedures, and often (sadly) the same need to periodically borrow funds. Suddenly, concepts such as credit and interest rates become only too real. This is where some knowledge of finance, investments,

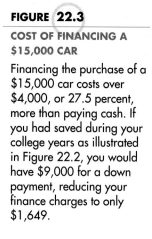

FIGURE 22.3

COST OF FINANCING A $15,000 CAR

Financing the purchase of a $15,000 car costs over $4,000, or 27.5 percent, more than paying cash. If you had saved during your college years as illustrated in Figure 22.2, you would have $9,000 for a down payment, reducing your finance charges to only $1,649.

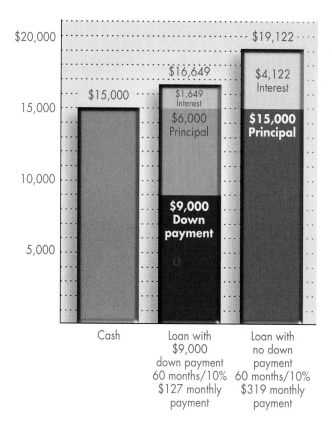

and budgeting pays off. Thus, the time you spend learning budgeting techniques will benefit you throughout your life.

Step 4: Pay Off Your Debts The first thing to do with the money remaining after you pay your monthly bills is to pay off your debts. Start with the debts that carry the highest interest rates. Credit card debt, for example, may be costing you 16 percent or more a year. Merely paying off such debts will set you on a path toward financial freedom. It's better to pay off a debt that costs 16 percent than to put the money in a bank account that earns, say, only 3 percent.

Step 5: Start a Savings Plan It's important to save some each month in a separate account for large purchases you're likely to make (such as a car). Then, when it comes time to make that purchase, you'll have the cash so you won't have to pay finance charges. You should save at least enough for a significant down payment so you can reduce the finance charges. Figure 22.3 compares the costs of financing versus paying cash for a $15,000 car.

The best way to save money is to *pay yourself first.* That is, take your paycheck, take out money for savings, and then plan what to do with the rest. You can arrange with your bank or mutual fund to deduct a certain amount every month. You will be pleasantly surprised when the money starts accumulating and earning interest over time. With some discipline, you can eventually reach your goal of becoming a millionaire. It's not as difficult as you may think. You simply have to save $6 a day and be patient. After 35 years, you'll have accumulated a million dollars. Well, not exactly. You will have saved just $76,440. But if you invest that money each year and make 12 percent compound interest, it would be worth $1 million in 35 years.[3]

SPOTLIGHT ON SMALL BUSINESS

www.countmein.com

Women Have More Trouble Getting Credit and Funding

Women-owned businesses are America's fastest-growing employers. That is good for the women and good for the community because small businesses provide both jobs and wealth to help a community grow. Yet at a White House women's economic summit, Iris Burnett and Nell Merlino found that women were having a serious problem getting access to credit. Often, their work and their family lives did not conform to the standard credit-rating scores. They found, for example, that women may be out of the workforce for years or they may get a bad credit rating because they were once married to men who had bad credit ratings. In any case, getting money from the bank or other standard sources was very difficult for some women.

Merlino is the woman who started Take Our Daughters to Work Day. She and Burnett decided that it would be a good idea to create a fund that would lend money to women who were starting or expanding a small business. The fund drive is called "Count Me In for Women's Economic Independence." They developed a website as well: www.count-me-in.org. The idea is for lots of people to donate $5 or more to create a fund. That fund would make loans of $500 to $5,000 to women. If the women repaid a $5,000 loan on time, they could get a loan of up to $10,000. The goal is to show banks that women are good risks in the hope that banks will make more such loans themselves. Meanwhile, the founders of the fund are working to rewrite the conventional credit-scoring system to reflect the realities of women's lives. "Even if women aren't in the workforce, they often have been doing volunteer work on the side, such as fundraising for a homeless shelter," Burnett says. That experience should count toward getting funds.

While women own 38 percent of the businesses in the United States, only 1.7 percent of the $12 billion in venture capital committed to new businesses went to projects owned by women in a recent year. Count Me In is raising the funds that women can use to start more businesses and help themselves and their communities. When you see facts and figures like these, you understand just a little better how important credit is and the need to build a strong credit rating.

Sources: Judy Mann, "Helping Women Become Better Capitalists," *The Washington Post*, May 5, 2000, p. C9, and Sharon Nelton, "Who's the Boss?" *Success*, June 2000, pp. 76–79.

Step 6: Borrow Money Only to Buy Assets That Have the Potential to Increase in Value Don't borrow money for ordinary expenses; you'll only get into more debt that way. If you have budgeted for emergencies, such as car repairs and health care costs, you should be able to stay financially secure. Only the most unexpected of expenses should cause you to borrow. It is hard to wait until you have enough money to buy what you want, but learning to wait is a critical part of self-discipline. If you must borrow, consider seeking alternative sources—see the Spotlight on Small Business box for a source of credit for women.

If you follow all six of these steps, you'll not only have money for investment but you'll have developed most of the financial techniques needed to become a millionaire. At first you may find it hard to live within a budget. Nonetheless, the payoff is well worth the pain.

How would your life change if you were to implement the six steps outlined above? Would it be worth the time and effort if you knew you could become a millionaire by following them? What advice would you give college students who are not sure they should follow such a program?

BUILDING YOUR CAPITAL ACCOUNT

The path to success in a capitalist system is to have capital (money) to invest, yet the trend today for young graduates is not only to be capital-poor but to be in debt. As you've read, accumulating capital takes discipline and careful planning.[4]

Living frugally is extremely difficult for the average young person. Most people are eager to spend their money on a new car, furniture, CDs, clothes, and the like. They tend to look for a fancy apartment with all the amenities. A capital-generating strategy may require forgoing most (though not all) of these purchases to accumulate investment money. The living style required is similar to the one adopted by most college students: a relatively inexpensive apartment furnished in hand-me-downs from parents, friends, and resale shops. For five or six years, you can manage with the old sound system, a used car, and a few nice clothes. The necessary living style is one of sacrifice, not luxury. It's important not to feel burdened by this plan; instead, feel happy knowing that your financial future will be more secure.

After six years of careful saving, you can accumulate a sizable nest egg. Let's assume that the starting salary of your first job after graduation is $30,000 (after taxes). If you save 15 percent of that, you would save $4,500 a year. Remember from the rule of 72 that money that earns 12 percent annually doubles in just six years! An annual investment of $4,500 for six years can grow with compounding to $41,000—a healthy start.

What do you do with the money you accumulate? The first investment might be a low-priced home. You should make this investment as early as possible. The purpose of this investment is to lock in payments for your shelter at a fixed amount. This is possible by owning a home, but not by renting. Through the years, home ownership has been a wise investment.

Crystal Hanlon started with Home Depot as a cashier several years ago. She began buying stock in the company as part of an employee ownership plan and is now worth over a million dollars. There are over a million other employees who got to be millionaires the same way. Are you getting the idea that it is a good idea to participate in such ownership programs and to put the maximum you can into such accounts?

Applying the Strategy

Some people have used the seed money from the strategy outlined above to buy a duplex home (two attached homes). They live in one part of the duplex and rent out the other. The rent covers a good part of the payments for both homes, so they can be housed very cheaply while their investment in a home appreciates. They learn that it's quite possible to live comfortably, yet inexpensively, for several years. In this way they accumulate capital. As they grow older, they see that such a strategy has put them years ahead of their peers in terms of financial security. They can eventually sell their duplex home and buy a single-family home with the profits. The money saved can also be invested in everything from stocks and bonds to precious metals, additional real estate, and higher education.

This strategy may seem too restrictive for you, but you still can apply the principles even if you choose not to

INCOME	7%	8%	9%	10%
	INTEREST RATE			
$25,000	$104,167	$ 94,516	$ 86,180	$ 79,015
50,000	208,333	189,033	172,360	158,030
75,000	312,500	283,549	258,540	237,044
100,000	416,667	378,065	344,720	316,059

Source: National Association of Home Builders.

FIGURE 22.4

HOW MUCH HOUSE CAN YOU AFFORD?

Monthly mortgage payments—including interest, principal, real estate taxes, and insurance—generally shouldn't amount to more than 28 percent of monthly income. Assuming that principal and interest equal 25 percent of household income, and taxes and insurance 3 percent, here's how much people in various income categories can afford to pay for a home if they use a 30-year mortgage and make a 10 percent down payment.

save the suggested 15 percent. The idea is to generate capital to invest. It's better to save a smaller amount than none at all. People are wise to plan their financial future with the same excitement and dedication they bring to other aspects of their lives.

Real Estate: A Relatively Secure Investment

As we noted above, historically one of the better investments a person can make is in his or her own home. Homes provide several investment benefits. First, a home is the one investment that you can live in. Second, once you buy a home, the payments are relatively fixed (though taxes and utilities go up). As your income rises, the house payments get easier and easier to make, but renters often find that rents tend to go up at least as fast as income.

Paying for a home is a good way of forcing yourself to save. Every month you must make the payments. Those payments are an investment that will prove very rewarding over time for most people. As mentioned earlier, investing in a duplex or small apartment building is also an excellent strategy. As capital accumulates and values rise, you can sell and buy an even larger apartment building. Many fortunes have been made in real estate in just such a manner. Furthermore, a home is a good asset to use when applying for a loan. Figure 22.4 will give you some idea of how expensive a house you can afford, given your income. You can find current mortgage interest rates and mortgage calculators at www.interest.com.

Once you understand the benefits of home ownership versus renting, you can decide whether those same principles apply to owning the building if you set up your own business—or owning versus renting equipment, vehicles, and the like. Furthermore, you may start thinking of real estate as a way to earn a living. You could, for example, buy older homes, fix them up, and sell them—a path many millionaires have taken to attain financial security.

Tax Deduction and Home Ownership

Buying a home is likely to be the largest and perhaps the most important investment you'll make. It's nice to know that the federal government is willing to help you with that investment. Here's how: Interest on your home mortgage payments is tax deductible. So are your real estate taxes. Since during the first few years, virtually all the mortgage payments go for interest on the loan, almost all the early payments are tax deductible—a tremendous benefit for home owners and investors. If, for example, your payments are $1,000 a month and your income is in the 28 percent tax bracket, then during the early years of your mortgage Uncle Sam will, in effect, give you credit for about $280 of your payment, lowering your real cost to $720. This makes home ownership much more competitive with renting than it may appear on the surface.

Experienced real estate investors will tell you that there are three keys to getting the optimum return on a home: location, location, and location. A home in the "best part of town," near schools, shopping, and work, is usually a sound financial investment. Often young people tend to go farther away from town, where homes are less expensive, but such homes may appreciate in value much more slowly. It's important to learn where the best place to buy is. It's better, from a financial viewpoint, to buy a small home in a great location than a large home in a not-so-great setting.

PROGRESS ASSESSMENT

- What are the six steps you can take today to control your finances?
- What steps should a person follow to build capital?
- Why is real estate a good investment?

Where to Put Your Savings

You have learned that one place to invest the money you have saved is in a home. What are some other good places to save your money? For a young person, one of the worst places to keep long-term investments is in a bank or savings and loan. It is important to have a month or two of savings in the bank for emergencies, but the bank is not the place to invest. A recent survey of high school students found that 85 percent believed that a savings account or a U.S. savings bond would offer the highest growth over the 18 years of saving for a child's education.[5] That has simply not been true historically. One of the best places to invest over time has been the stock market. The stock market does tend to go up and down, but over a longer period of time it has proved to be one of the best investments. Figure 22.5 compares the difference between depositing $100 a month for 18 years in a traditional savings account versus depositing the same amount in a stock mutual fund.

FIGURE 22.5

SAVINGS ACCOUNT VERSUS STOCK MUTUAL FUND

Interest rates fluctuate, but most banks pay very low interest rates (1–3 percent) on traditional savings accounts. In contrast, stock mutual funds have historically earned an annual average around 12 percent. This chart compares saving for a child's education with $100 a month for 18 years in a savings account with similar savings in a stock mutual fund.

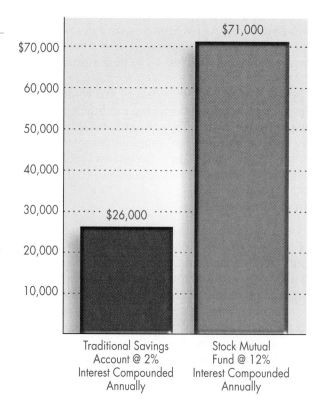

$71,000

$70,000

60,000

50,000

40,000

30,000 $26,000

20,000

10,000

Traditional Savings Account @ 2% Interest Compounded Annually

Stock Mutual Fund @ 12% Interest Compounded Annually

REACHING BEYOND OUR BORDERS

www.numeraire.com

Looking Beyond Our Borders for Investments and Jobs

One key to investment success over a longer period of time is to diversify your investments. The younger you are, the more time you have to invest and the more risky your investment choices can be. That means, for example, that you can put more money into stocks versus bonds because stocks have offered a much higher return over the long run.

Another way to diversify is to invest in international stocks. Some advisers say that young people can allocate as much as 20 percent of their portfolio (that is, the group of stocks and bonds they own) into stocks of firms in other countries. Standard & Poor's, for example, recommended stocks in companies such as BP Amoco (BPA), Vodafone Airtouch (VOD), and Taiwan Semiconductor (TSM). The three-letter symbols indicate that the stocks are listed on the New York Stock Exchange.

Other financial advisers caution against investing too much in foreign countries because currency fluctuations can amplify or erase gains in such stocks. One way to invest internationally without buying foreign stocks is to buy stocks in multinational companies such as McDonald's or Coca-Cola that make a significant part of their income overseas. Another way to invest in overseas markets is to buy international mutual funds that invest in small businesses. For example, the T. Rowe Price International Discovery Fund buys fast-growing small companies in other countries.

Of course, one way to profit from the faster growth of some countries is to actually work there yourself. The world is a big place, and over 90 percent of the people in the world live in countries outside of the United States. The job market in the United States was excellent when this text was being written (in the year 2001), but that won't always be the case. You can greatly expand your career options and lifestyle options by looking globally for at least part of your career. That includes government service as well as working for a company. Living costs in some countries are much lower than in the United States (but they may be much higher). The moral of the story is that is pays to explore the world for both careers and investments to optimize your expenditure of time and money.

Sources: Megan Mulligan, "Eurogems," *Forbes*, August 21, 2000, p. 258; Tripp Reynolds, "In Assets, It's All in the Mix," *Business Week*, July 17, 2000, p. 106; and Steve Thorley, "Very Tricky Stock Market," *Bottom Line Personal*, September 1, 2000, pp. 3–4.

Chapter 20 gave you a foundation for starting an investment program. That chapter also talked about bonds ➤ **P.613** ◄, but bonds have traditionally lagged behind stocks ➤ **P.617** ◄ as a long-term investment. Don't forget the possibility, too, of investing in international stocks; see the Reaching Beyond Our Borders box for more details.

Learning to Manage Credit

Known as *plastic* to young buyers, credit cards are no doubt familiar to you. Names like Visa, MasterCard, American Express, Discover, and Diners Club are well known to most people. In a credit card purchase, finance charges usually amount to anywhere from 12 to 20 percent annually. This means that if you finance a TV, home appliances, and other purchases with a credit card, you may end up spending much more than if you pay with cash. A good manager of personal finances, like a good businessperson, pays on time and takes advantage of savings made possible by paying early (see again Chapter 19), and see the *Business Week* box). Those people who've established a capital fund can tap that fund to make large purchases and pay the fund back (with interest if so desired) rather than pay a bank finance charges.

FROM THE PAGES OF **BusinessWeek** www.americanexpress.com

Surviving the Plastic Wars

Ever had daydreams about the impossible happening, such as your winning the lottery, becoming a movie star, or negotiating your interest rates with credit card companies? Well, don't go out and spend your lottery winnings or call Paramount Studios about your next picture; unfortunately those *are* just dreams. Perk up, though—at least one of your fantasies can come true.

More and more consumers are finding warmer, friendlier credit card issuers willing to discuss terms and conditions personally with them. Negotiating with credit card companies would have been unthinkable a few years back. Why the abrupt change? The American public is saturated with plastic; 68 percent of Americans pack credit cards. Also, even though credit card and revolving debt totaled a whopping $589 billion last year, it has shown little growth over the past few years. However, an even greater problem for credit card companies is the growing number of customers "freeloading" by paying off their credit card debt each month. If they pay off their balances, they pay no interest, and the credit card companies earn no profit. The numbers of freeloaders jumped from 29 percent in 1990 to 45 percent in 2000. David Robertson of *The Nilson Report* laments, "Demographics are completely against the credit industry. Baby boomers need less revolving credit, are paying off their balances each month, and are willing to jump fast to low-rate cards."

The industry is not giving up without a fight, however. Many card companies are refocusing their targeting efforts, and some are creating new products. Providian, a San Francisco–based card issuer, is targeting customers it traditionally shunned, particularly customers with credit blemishes on their records. The company is taking the financial risk of betting on borrowers others won't touch. Its interest rates provide steeper returns than the industry average, but its loss rates are a bit higher. American Express has taken a different tack. It now offers (by invitation only) the Centurion card, which carries a $1,000 annual fee. Centurion holders get free upgrades on Concorde seating and a personal counselor for travel needs. They also receive special privileges such as private shopping hours at Nieman Marcus and Saks Fifth Avenue. American Express has also introduced a Blue credit card, equipped with computer chips that help companies do business online.

As you can see, how well you survive the plastic wars depends on the strength of your credit history. If you have strong credit, you will triumph and be able to negotiate low interest rates and special privileges. If you have weak credit, you will suffer the pain of higher interest rates from the rare company willing to take a risk on you.

Source: Joseph Weber, "The Perils of Plastic," *Business Week,* February 14, 2000, pp. 127–28.

Credit cards are an important element in a personal financial system, even if they're rarely used. First, some merchants request credit cards as a form of identification. It may be difficult to buy certain goods or even rent a car without owning a credit card because businesses use them for identification and assured payment. Second, credit cards can be used to keep track of purchases. A gasoline credit card, for example, gives you records of purchases over time for income tax and financial planning purposes. It's sometimes easier to write one check at the end of the month for several purchases than to carry cash around. Besides, when cash is stolen or lost, it is simply gone; a stolen credit card can be canceled to protect your account.

Finally, a credit card is simply more convenient than cash or checks. If you come upon a special sale and need more money than you usually carry, paying by credit is quick and easy. You can carry less cash and don't have to worry about keeping your checkbook balanced as often.

If you do use a credit card, you should pay the balance in full during the period when no interest is charged. Not having to pay 16 percent interest is as

You are likely to get solicited by a number of credit card companies to use their cards. Be careful. Millions of students have piled up huge amounts of debt while in college using such cards. Credit cards are a real benefit as ID cards and as a quick source of funding, but don't go overboard. Do you have friends who cannot control their credit card use?

good as earning 16 percent tax free. Also, choose a card that pays you back in cash, like the Discover card, or others that offer paybacks like credits toward the purchase of a car, free long-distance minutes, or frequent flier miles. The value of these givebacks can be from 1 to 5 percent. Rather than pay 16 percent, you earn a certain percentage—quite a difference. To compare credit cards, check out www.cardratings.com or www.angelfire.com/ny/erte2001/cardinfo.html.

The danger of a credit card is the flip side of its convenience. Too often, consumers buy goods and services that they wouldn't normally buy if they had to pay cash or write a check on funds in the bank. Using credit cards, consumers often pile up debts to the point where they're unable to pay. If you aren't the type who can stick to a financial plan or household budget, *it may be better not to have a credit card at all.*

Credit cards are a helpful tool to the financially careful buyer. They're a financial disaster to people with little financial restraint and tastes beyond their income. College students take note: Of the debtors seeking help at the National Consumer Counseling Service, more than half were between 18 and 32.

Buying Life Insurance

One of the last things young people think about is the idea that they may get sick or have an accident and die. It's not a pleasant thought. Even more unpleasant, though, is the reality of young people dying every day in accidents and other unexpected ways. You have to know only one of these families to see the emotional and financial havoc such a loss causes.

Today, with so many husbands and wives both working, the loss of a spouse means a sudden drop in income. To provide protection from such risks, a couple or business should buy life insurance.

Today, the least expensive and simplest form of life insurance is **term insurance.** It is pure insurance protection for a given number of years that typically costs less the younger you buy it (see Figure 22.6). Every few years, however, you might have to renew the policy, and the premium could go higher. It's helpful to check out prices for term insurance through a Web-based service. For example, try www.quickeninsurance.com or www.insweb.com. Be sure to give them as much information as possible to get the most accurate and best rates.

term insurance
Pure insurance protection for a given number of years.

FIGURE 22.6

WHY BUY TERM INSURANCE?

INSURANCE NEEDS IN EARLY YEARS ARE HIGH.	INSURANCE NEEDS DECLINE AS YOU GROW OLDER.
1. Children are young and need money for education.	1. Children are grown.
2. Mortgage is high relative to income.	2. Mortgage is low or completely paid off.
3. Often there are auto payments and other bills to pay.	3. Debts are paid off.
4. Loss of income would be disastrous.	4. Insurance needs are few.
	5. Retirement income is needed.

whole life insurance
Life insurance that stays in effect until age 100.

variable life insurance
Whole life insurance that invests the cash value of the policy in stocks or other high-yielding securities.

annuity
A contract to make regular payments to a person for life or for a fixed period.

It is a good idea before buying to check out the insurance company through a rating service such as A. M. Best (www.ambest.com) or Moody's Investment Service (www.moodys.com). One of the newer forms of term insurance is something called multiyear level-premium insurance. It guarantees that you'll pay the same premium for the life of the policy. Recently, 40 percent of new term policies guaranteed a set rate for 20 years or more. Some companies allow you to switch your term policy for a more expensive whole or universal life policy.

Whole life insurance is another type of life insurance. It stays in effect until age 100. Some part of the money you pay goes toward pure insurance and another part goes toward savings, so you are buying both insurance and a savings plan when you buy whole life insurance. This is a good idea for those people who have trouble saving money otherwise. A universal life policy lets you choose how much of your payment should go to insurance and how much to investments. The investments traditionally were very conservative but paid a steady interest rate.

Variable life insurance is a form of whole life insurance that invests the cash value of the policy in stocks or other higher-yielding securities. Death benefits may thus vary, reflecting the performance of the investments. Some people, seeing the stock market go up for so many years, switched out of whole life policies to get the higher potential returns of variable life insurance.

Life insurance companies recognized the desire that people had for higher returns on their insurance (and for protecting themselves against running out of money before they die) and began selling annuities. An **annuity** is a contract to make regular payments to a person for life or for a fixed period. With an annuity, you are guaranteed to have an income until you die. There are two kinds of annuities: fixed and variable. *Fixed annuities* are investments that pay the policyholder a specified interest rate. They are not as popular as *variable*

David Riker is with eCoverage, a San Francisco-based company that is selling online insurance through Pacific Specialty Insurance Company. With no local agents, the company can save 10 to 20 percent on the cost of distributing its products. Users can buy a policy after just a few minutes online. Do you like the idea of buying insurance online or would you prefer to deal with an agent who can answer your questions and help you apply?

annuities, which provide investment choices identical to mutual funds. Such annuities are gaining in popularity relative to term or whole life insurance, which gained about 3–5 percent in sales over the last decade. During that same period, variable annuities went from $17.2 billion to $99.5 billion.[6] Clearly, people are choosing more risk to get greater returns when they retire. This means, however, that people must be more careful in selecting an insurance company and what investments are made with their money.

Because insurance is getting much more complex, before buying any insurance, it may be wise to consult a financial adviser who is not an insurance agent. He or she can help you make the wisest decision about insurance versus other investments.

Buying Health Insurance

Individuals need to consider protecting themselves from losses due to health problems. You may have health insurance coverage through your employer. If not, you can buy insurance from a health insurance provider (e.g., Blue Cross/Blue Shield), a health maintenance organization (HMO), or a preferred provider organization (PPO). For quick online help in picking a health insurance provider, try www.EHealthInsurance.com or www.healthaxis.com (not available in all areas).

It's dangerous financially not to have any health insurance. Hospital costs are simply too high to risk financial ruin by going uninsured. In fact, it's often a good idea to supplement health insurance policies with disability insurance that pays part of the cost of a long-term sickness or an accident. Your chances of becoming disabled at an early age are much higher than your chances of dying from an accident. Therefore, it's important to have the proper amount of disability insurance. Call an insurance agent or check the Internet for possible costs of such insurance. The cost is relatively low to protect yourself from losing your income for an extended period.

Homeowners or Renter's Insurance

As you begin to accumulate possessions, you may want to seriously consider getting insurance to cover their loss. You may be surprised to see how much it would cost to replace all the clothes, furniture, pots and pans, appliances, sporting goods, electronic equipment (e.g., computers, VCRs, and the like), and the other things you own.[7] Apartment insurance or homeowners insurance covers such losses. But you must be careful to specify that you want guaranteed replacement cost.[8] That means that the insurance company will give you whatever it costs to buy all of those things new. Such insurance costs a little bit more than a policy without guaranteed replacement, but you will get a lot more if you have a loss.

The other option is to buy insurance that covers the depreciated cost of the items. For example, a sofa you bought five years ago for $600 may only be worth $150 now. The current value is what you would get from insurance, not the $700 or more you may need to buy a brand-new sofa. The same is true for a computer you paid $1,500 for a few years ago. If it were to be stolen, you would get only a few hundred dollars for it rather than the replacement cost.

Buying Other Insurance

You should buy insurance for your car. In fact, most states require that drivers have automobile insurance. Get a large deductible of $500 or so to keep the premiums lower, and cover small damage on your own. You'll also need liability insurance to protect yourself against being sued by someone accidentally injured by you. Often you can get a discount by buying all your insurance with one company. GEICO, for example, gives discounts for safe driving, good grades, and more.

PLANNING YOUR RETIREMENT

It may seem a bit early to be planning your retirement; however, not doing so would be a big mistake. Successful financial planning means long-range planning, and retirement is a critical phase of life. What you do now could make a world of difference in your quality of life after age 65.

Social Security

Social Security
The term used to describe the Old-Age, Survivors, and Disability Insurance Program established by the Social Security Act of 1935.

Social Security is the term used to describe the Old-Age, Survivors, and Disability Insurance Program established by the Social Security Act of 1935. There's little question that by the time you retire, there will have been significant changes in the Social Security system. There is even talk today of making part of the system private. The problem is that the number of people retiring and living longer is increasing dramatically, though the number of workers paying into Social Security per retiree is declining. The results are likely to include serious cuts in benefits, a much later average retirement age, reduced cost-of-living adjustments (COLAs), and/or much higher Social Security taxes. Don't count on Social Security to provide you with ample funds for retirement.[9] Rather, plan now to save funds for your nonworking years (see Figure 22.7). Recognizing Social Security's potential downfall, the government has established incentives for you to save money now for retirement. The following section gives the specifics.

Individual Retirement Accounts (IRAs)

individual retirement account (IRA)
Traditionally, a tax-deferred investment plan that enables you (and your spouse, if you are married) to save part of your income for retirement.

Traditionally, an **individual retirement account (IRA)** has been a tax-deferred investment plan that enables you (and your spouse, if you are married) to save part of your income for retirement. A traditional IRA allows people who qualify to deduct from their reported income the money they put into an account. The contributions are tax-deferred. *Tax-deferred* means you pay no current taxes, but the earnings gained in the IRA are taxed as income when they are withdrawn from your IRA after retirement.

Let's see why a traditional IRA is a good deal for a young investor. The tremendous benefit is the fact that the invested money is not taxed. That means fast, and good, returns for you. For example, say you put $2,000 a year into an IRA. Normally, you'd pay taxes on that $2,000. But because you put the money into an IRA, you won't have to pay those taxes. If you're in the 28 percent tax bracket, that means you save $560 in taxes! Put another way, the $2,000 you save only costs $1,440—a huge bargain.

If you save $2,000 a year for 35 years and earn 12 percent a year, you'll accumulate savings of nearly $900,000. If you start when you are just out of school, you'll be a millionaire by the time you retire.

How do you plan on funding your retirement?

Conseco's annuities have tax advantages to help make the most of your money. Call 1-877-CONSECO or visit CONSECO.COM.

CONSECO.
INSURANCE INVESTMENTS LENDING ———————— Step up.™

This humorous ad for annuities discusses a serious problem—protecting yourself from running out of money when you retire. Do you think you're too young for such concerns?

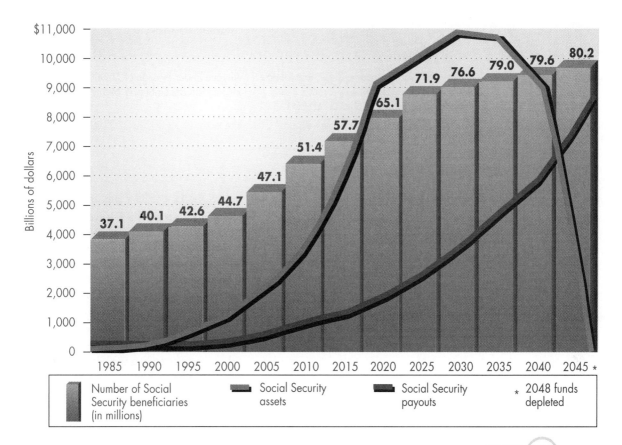

Billions of dollars

1985 1990 1995 2000 2005 2010 2015 2020 2025 2030 2035 2040 2045 *

37.1 40.1 42.6 44.7 47.1 51.4 57.7 65.1 71.9 76.6 79.0 79.6 80.2

Number of Social Security beneficiaries (in millions)

Social Security assets

Social Security payouts

* 2048 funds depleted

FIGURE 22.7

THE FATE OF YOUR SOCIAL SECURITY INVESTMENT

This chart shows that, at present rates, Social Security funds will run out in the year 2048. That is about 46 years from now. Much sooner than that, the outgo will exceed revenues. It's a good idea to begin your own retirement account to supplement Social Security. You're likely to live a long time after retirement and will need the money.

All you have to do is save $2,000 a year and earn 12 percent. The earlier you start the better. Consider this: If you were to start contributing $2,000 to an IRA earning 12 percent when you're 23 years old and do so for only five years, you'd have $13,000 by the time you're 28. Even if you *never added another penny* to the IRA, by the time you're 65 you'd have almost $900,000. If you waited until you were 30 to start saving, you would need to save $2,000 every year for 35 years to have the same nest egg. And what would you have if you started saving at 23 *and* continued nonstop every year until 65? Almost $2 million! Can you see why investment advisers often say that an IRA is the best way to invest in your retirement?

A more recent kind of IRA is called a Roth IRA. People who invest in a Roth IRA don't get up-front deductions on their taxes as they would with a traditional IRA, but the earnings grow tax-free and are also tax-free when they are withdrawn. So in sum, traditional IRAs offer tax savings when they are deposited and Roth IRAs offer tax savings when they are withdrawn. Financial planners highly recommend IRAs, but they differ as to which kind is best. Both have advantages and disadvantages, so you should check with a financial adviser to determine which would be best for you. You may decide to have both kinds of accounts. For more details about IRAs, check out the datachimp website (www.datachimp.com), run by a group of self-proclaimed amateur investors. See Figure 22.8 for a brief comparison of Roth versus traditional IRAs. In general, a Roth IRA is probably best for younger workers because their savings can compound year after year with no further taxes being paid.

One key point to remember is you can't take the money out of either type of IRA until you are 59 1/2 years old without paying a 10 percent penalty and paying taxes on the income. On the one hand, that's a benefit for you, because it can keep you from tapping into your IRA when an emergency comes up or

TERMS	ROTH IRA	TRADITIONAL IRA
Eligibility	Anyone with earned income under these limits: Single: AGI of $110,000. Married (filing jointly): AGI of $160,000.	Anyone under the age of 70 with earned income (on December 31 of this tax year).
Annual contributions (The maximum you can contribute to all of your IRA accounts combined is $2,000.)	Maximum $2,000 if you're single with an AGI of $95,000 or less; or maximum $4,000 if you're married, filing jointly, with an AGI of $150,000 or less.	The lesser of $2,000 or 100% of earned income.
Withdrawals and distributions	No mandatory withdrawal age. You cannot make withdrawals until age 59 (with some exceptions). No income tax on withdrawals after age 59. Take a lump sum or withdraw in installments.	You must begin to withdraw a required minimum distribution (RMD) amount from your account no later than April 1 of the year after the year you turn 70½. You cannot make withdrawals until age 59 (with some exceptions). Take a lump sum or withdraw in installments.
Deductions	No deductions allowed.	Your contribution is fully deductible if (1) neither you nor your spouse participated in a company-sponsored retirement plan or (2) you contributed to a company-sponsored retirement plan and are: Single and had an AGI of $30,000 or less for 1998 ($31,000 for 1999), or Married and, filing jointly, had an AGI of $50,000 or less for 1998 ($51,000 for 1999).
Taxes and limitations	You cannot make withdrawals until age 59 (with some exceptions). No income tax on withdrawals after age 59.	You cannot make withdrawals until age 59 (with some exceptions). You must start withdrawing by age 70 to avoid penalties. You pay regular income tax on withdrawals of all earnings and pretax dollars you contributed.
Conversions	Conversion from an IRA to a Roth is allowed if your AGI is $100,000 or less, filing singly or jointly. Direct rollovers from qualified retirement plans into a Roth IRA are prohibited; you must convert to an IRA first.	Direct rollovers from qualified retirement plans to IRAs are tax-free.

FIGURE 22.8

THE ROTH IRA VERSUS THE TRADITIONAL IRA

you're tempted to make a large impulse purchase. On the other hand, the money is there if a real need or emergency arises. For example, the government now allows you to take out some funds to invest in an education or a first home. But check the rules; they change over time.

A wide range of investment choices is available when you open an IRA. Your local bank, savings and loan, and credit union all have different types of IRAs. Insurance companies offer such plans as well. You may prefer to be a bit aggressive with this money to earn a higher return. In that case, you can put your IRA funds into stocks, bonds, mutual funds, or precious metals. Some mutual funds have multiple options (gold stocks, government securities, high-tech stocks, and more). You can switch from fund to fund or from investment to investment with your IRA funds. You can even open several different IRAs as long as the total amount invested doesn't exceed the government's limit; currently the limit is $2,000 a year, but an increase to $5,000 is being considered by Congress at the time of this writing. You might consider contributing to an IRA through payroll deductions to ensure that the money is invested before you're tempted to spend it. Opening an IRA may be one of the wisest investments you make.

Simple IRAs

Companies with 100 or fewer employees can provide their workers with a simple IRA. Basically, that means that employees can contribute up to $6,000 of their income annually, compared with the $2,000 limit of regular IRAs. The company matches the contribution. This new plan enables people to save much more money over time and makes for a good employee benefit for smaller companies.[10] Simple IRAs can help companies with 100 or fewer employees compete for available workers.

401(k) Plans

More than 220,000 companies now offer 401(k) retirement plans covering some 30 million workers. These plans have three benefits: (1) The money you put in reduces your present taxable income, (2) tax is deferred on the earnings, and (3) employers often match part of your deposit—50 cents or more for every dollar deposited. You should deposit at least as much as your employer matches, often up to 15 percent of your salary.[11] You normally can't withdraw funds from this account until you're 59, but often you can borrow from the account. You can usually select how the money in a 401(k) plan is invested: stocks, bonds, and, in some cases, real estate. If the policy is held until death, no income taxes will ever be due on the investment gains that have built up in the policy.

Like the simple IRA, there is a simple 401(k) plan for those firms that employ 100 or fewer employees. Employees are allowed to invest a maximum of $6,000 that is matched by the employer. This is a rather new program, but it should also prove popular among small businesses in attracting new workers.

Keogh Plans

Millions of small-business owners don't have the benefit of a corporate retirement system. Such people can contribute to an IRA, but the amount they can invest is limited. The alternative for all those doctors, lawyers, real estate agents, artists, writers, and other self-employed people is to establish their own Keogh plan. It's like an IRA for entrepreneurs ➤ **P.4** ◄. You can also check into simplified employee pension (SEP) plans, which are the best types of IRAs for sole proprietors.

The advantage of Keogh plans is that the maximum that can be invested is more than $30,000 per year. The original amount was much lower, but the government wanted to encourage self-employed people to build retirement funds.

Like traditional IRAs, Keogh funds aren't taxed until they are withdrawn, nor are the returns the funds earn. Thus, a person in the 28 percent tax bracket who invests $10,000 yearly in a Keogh saves $2,800 in taxes. That means, in essence, that the government is financing 28 percent of his or her retirement fund. As with an IRA, this is an excellent deal. If a person were to put the full $30,000 a year into a Keogh plan that earns 10 percent a year, he or she would have over $5 million in the account after 30 years.

As with an IRA, there's a 10 percent penalty for early withdrawal. Also like an IRA, funds may be withdrawn in a lump sum or spread out over the years.

Once you have accumulated some savings, you may want to seek advice from a financial adviser. He or she can point you to the proper balance among stocks, bonds, insurance, and money in the bank.

However, the key decision is the one you make now—to begin early to put funds into an IRA, a Keogh plan, or both so that the "magic" of compounding can turn that money into a sizable retirement fund.

Financial Planners

If the idea of developing a comprehensive financial plan for yourself or your business seems overwhelming, relax; help is available. The people who assist in developing a comprehensive program that covers investments, taxes, insurance, and other financial matters are called financial planners.[12] Be careful, though anybody and his brother or sister can claim to be a financial planner today. It's often best to find a person that has earned the distinction of being a certified financial planner (CFP). To earn the distinction of CFP, a person must complete a curriculum on 106 financial topics and a 10-hour examination. In the United States today there are about 36,000 planners with the CFP distinction.[13] Unfortunately, many so-called financial planners are simply life insurance salespeople or mutual fund salespeople. Businesspeople often turn to their accountants or finance department for legitimate financial planning help.

In the past few years, there has been an explosion in the number of companies offering financial services. Such companies are sometimes called one-stop financial centers or financial supermarkets because they provide a variety of financial services, ranging from banking service to mutual funds, insurance, tax assistance, stocks, bonds, and real estate. It pays to shop around for financial advice. A good source to look to is available from the Vanguard Group: "How to Select a Financial Advisor" is a brochure you can obtain by calling 800-662-7447 or visiting the Vanguard website at www.vanguard.com. You can also go to an independent financial planner or a financial service company. In either case, ask around among your friends and family. Find someone who understands your situation and is willing to spend some time with you.

Most financial planners begin with life insurance. They feel that most people should have basic term insurance coverage. They also explore your health insurance plans. They look for both medical expense and disability coverage. They may also recommend major medical protection to cover catastrophic illnesses.

Financial planning covers all aspects of investing, all the way to retirement and death. (Planning for estate taxes is important early in life.) Financial planners can advise you on the proper mix of IRAs, stocks, bonds, real estate, and so on.

As you can see, accumulating enough funds to be financially secure is a complex and difficult matter. Investing that money and protecting it from loss makes the process even more involved. It is never too early to start a saving and investment program. As you have learned, there are many, many millionaires in the United States and around the world.[14] They have taken various paths to their wealth, but the most common ones are entrepreneurship and wise money management. We hope this chapter helps you join their ranks.

PROGRESS ASSESSMENT

- What are three advantages of using a credit card?
- What kind of life insurance is recommended for most people?
- What are the advantages of investing through an IRA? A Keogh account? A 401(k) account?

SUMMARY

1. There are six steps you can take today to get control of your finances.
   - *What are the six steps to managing personal assets?*
   (1) Take an inventory of your financial assets. That means that you need to develop a balance sheet for yourself: Assets = Liabilities + Owners' equity. (2) Keep track of all your expenses. (3) Prepare a budget. (4) Pay off your debts. (5) Start a savings plan. The best way to save money is to pay yourself first. That is, take your paycheck, take out money for savings, and then plan what to do with the rest. (6) If you have to borrow money, only borrow it to buy assets that have the potential to increase in value, such as a house or business.
   - *How can a person accumulate enough capital to become financially secure?*
   First, find a job. Try to live as frugally as possible. The savings can then be used to generate even more capital. Invest the money wisely; real estate is a great start.
   - *Why is real estate a good investment?*
   Over the years real estate has grown in value. Furthermore, the government allows you to deduct interest payments on the mortgage, which allows you to buy more home for the money than you could otherwise.
   - *Where is the best place to keep savings?*
   It is not wise to keep long-term savings in a bank or savings and loan. It is best, in the long run to invest in stock. Bonds have not traditionally been as good an investment. Although stocks go up and down, in the long run they earn more than most other investments.

   1. Describe the six steps one can take to generate capital.

2. Term insurance is pure insurance protection for a given number of years.
   - *Why is term insurance preferred?*
   You can buy much more term insurance than whole life insurance for the same amount of money.
   - *Do I need other insurance?*
   It's important to have health insurance to protect against large losses. You also need car insurance (get a large deductible—$500 or so) and liability insurance in case you injure someone.

   2. Identify the best ways to preserve capital, begin investing, and buy insurance.

3. Outline a strategy for retiring with enough money to last a lifetime.

3. It may seem too early to begin planning your retirement, but not to do so would be a big mistake. Successful financial planning means long-range planning, and retirement is a critical phase of life.

• *What are some basics?*

Supplement Social Security with savings plans of your own. Everyone should have an IRA to begin with. Let the government pay for some of your retirement savings. All tax-free savings are good. That's why a Keogh plan or an IRA-SEP is wise. An IRA-SEP is a savings plan for entrepreneurs. If you work for someone else, check out the 401(k) plan. Find a financial adviser who can recommend the best IRA and help you make other investments.

KEY TERMS

annuity 688	**Social Security** 690	**whole life insurance** 688
individual retirement account (IRA) 696	**term insurance** 687	
	variable life insurance 688	

DEVELOPING WORKPLACE SKILLS

1. Few things are more surprising to a new college graduate, single or married, than the cost of living in an apartment. To prevent such surprises, research and calculate these costs now and share them with the class. Be sure to include rent, utilities, food, clothes, health care, insurance (life, auto, disability), transportation, vacation, charity, recreation, furniture, and depreciation. Then prepare a two-page paper on the concept of living on one income, given these figures. Older students in class are great for offering realistic facts and figures.

2. Talk with your parents or others you know who have invested in a family home. What appreciation have they gained on the purchase price? What other benefits has the home brought? Compose a list of the benefits and the drawbacks of owning a home and real estate in general as an investment. Be prepared to give a one-minute presentation on what you learned.

3. For one month keep a record of every expenditure you make. Based on the results, share what you learn with your class. Use a computer spreadsheet or personal finance software to establish an annual budget.

4. "The best investment one can make is in education, including education in the arts, literature, music, and dance." Talk with people in business and in various departments on campus (e.g., business and the arts) and get their reactions to this statement. Then prepare a one-page statement of your conclusions, including the value of lifetime education.

5. Check out the benefits and drawbacks of both traditional and Roth IRAs. Be prepared to make a two-minute presentation on the benefits of each and to discuss your findings in class.

Purpose:

To use online resources to make smart personal finance decisions.

Exercise:

Use the calculators on the FinanCenter website (www.financenter.com) to answer the following questions:

1

1. You need $5,000 for a trip to Europe in two years. How much would you have to deposit monthly in a savings account paying 3 percent in order to meet your goal?

2. Investing $1,000 at 6 percent for five years, what is the difference in purchasing power of your savings if inflation increases by 2 percent annually during that time? By 4 percent?

3. Starting today, how much would you need to save each month in order to become a millionaire before you retire?

4. You need a new car. What car can you afford if you have $1,500 for a down payment, can make monthly payments of $300, and get $1,000 for trading in your old clunker?

5. How much house can you afford if you earn $36,000 a year and have $10,000 savings for a down payment, a $6,000 car loan balance, and no credit card debts?

Purpose:

To evaluate credit card offers.

Exercise:

Not all credit cards are created equal. Some have low interest rates, but charge annual fees. Others have higher interest rates, but no annual fees. Some offer premiums such as rebates or frequent flyer miles. How can you compare all of the credit card offers that fill your mailbox? Go to www.creditcardfreedom.com for reviews and comparisons of a variety of credit cards. Choose one of the best cards for the following individuals and explain your choices:

2

1. A highly paid professional who pays the entire credit card balance each month.

2. A newlywed couple who only intends to use the card for big-ticket items and pay down the balance gradually.

3. A student whose parents want to provide a convenient method of paying for incidental expenses, but want to limit the amount their child can spend.

4. A person struggling to overcome a poor credit history.

CASE

BECOMING FINANCIALLY SECURE

Mike and Priscilla Thomas are a married couple with two incomes and no children. Their cars are both paid for. They've saved enough money to buy a new house without selling their old one. (Real estate is typically a sound investment.) They're renting out their town house for added income. They hope to buy more rental property to use as an income producer so that they can both retire at age 50!

Priscilla runs a company called Cost Reduction Services and Associates. It advises small firms on ways to cut overhead expenses. The couple also owned a window-washing business when they were in college. Priscilla loves being in business for herself because, she says, "when you own your own business, you can work hard and you get paid for your hard work." Mike is a pharmaceutical salesperson.

How did the Thomases get the money to start their own businesses and buy a couple of homes? They committed themselves from the beginning of their marriage to live on Mike's income and to save Priscilla's income. Furthermore, they decided to live frugally. The goal of early retirement was their incentive. They "lived like college kids" for five years, cutting out coupons and saving every cent they could. They don't often go out to eat, and they rent movies for their VCR instead of going to the movie theater. Their first investment was a town house. They used the tax deductions to help offset their income.

Mike puts the maximum amount into his company's 401(k) plan. It's invested in a very aggressive growth fund: half U.S. stocks and half international stocks. Now that the couple is financially secure, they're planning to have children.

Decision Questions

1. What steps would the average young couple have to follow to be like Mike and Priscilla and become financially secure all their lives?

2. What kind of goals could you establish to make it worthwhile to scrimp and save your money rather than spend it on today's pleasures?

3. How much money would one person have to earn to support two people living in an apartment in your area?

4. Can you see now why money management is one of the keys to both entrepreneurship and personal financial security?

VIDEO CASE

MANAGING YOUR MONEY

There are lots of books and magazines on the market that will help you plan your personal finances. *Personal Finance for Dummies*, by Eric Tyson, has some down-to-earth recommendations for overcoming common mistakes people make with their money and some tips for saving money. The five mistakes mentioned are:

1. Not planning. It is a good idea to save a little money each month. and you should start with your very first job. That allows compounding to take over to increase your life savings.
2. Overspending. Over a million people go bankrupt each year because they spend much more than they earn. The secret is to spend *less* than you earn..
3. Cut expenses. You need to keep track of where you're spending money and use that information to establish a budget that will keep spending below revenue.
4. Overpaying taxes. You need to save your money in a tax-free IRA or company 401K to minimize taxes.
5. Resist sales and advertising pitches for the latest goods and services.

What happens if you do overspend? How do you get out of debt? Tyson has several recommendations:

1. Declare bankruptcy. Your debts are sometimes forgiven when you declare bankruptcy, but for moral and ethical reasons, you should only use this as a last resort.
2. Find a lower-interest credit card. You can search the Internet for the lowest fees.
3. Cut expenses. Again, the trick is to spend less than you earn. Often this is easier said than done, but necessary anyway.

Tyson also has some ideas about ways to save money:

1. Find the best value. Look for sales at your local stores. Buy after the new year.
2. Use tax sheltered retirement accounts. For young people, that often mean a Roth IRA.
3. Cut up your credit cards. You should use your credit card for ID purposes and maybe to buy gas, but not as a substitute for cash.
4. Use a debit card. You can't spend more than the money allotted on the card.

Tyson also says to get more balance in your life. That is, spend more attention on things other than money, such as your friends and family. All work and no play is not a good idea. And too much play with no money is not good either. That's why you study personal finance.

Discussion Questions

1. Have you ever tracked your spending over a period of time, such as several months? Where would you expect that you are spending too much money? What can you do about that?
2. Do you pay off all your credit cards each month? If not, you may consider not using credit cards at all. What would be the benefits and drawbacks of doing that?
3. Have you ever established a budget to help you control spending? What would be the likely benefits and drawbacks of doing so?
4. Have you checked into the different IRA types and 401K plans? If not, you might do that right away because they are the best places to save money for retirement. Are you interested in starting a retirement account now so that the money can compound over time? Why or why not?

APPENDIX

Managing Risk

THE INCREASING CHALLENGE OF RISK MANAGEMENT

The management of risk is a major issue for businesses throughout the country. Almost every day you hear about an earthquake, flood, fire, airplane crash, riot, or car accident that destroyed property or injured someone. An accident that involves a major personality may be front-page news for weeks. Such reports are so much a part of the news that we tend to accept these events as part of everyday life. But events involving loss mean a great deal to the businesspeople involved. They must pay to restore the property and compensate those who are injured. In addition to the newsmaking stories, thousands of other incidents involve businesspeople in lawsuits. Lawsuits in recent years have covered everything from job-related accidents to product liability—for example, a woman who was burned by spilled coffee at McDonald's brought a suit against the company.

How Rapid Change Affects Risk Management

Changes are occurring so fast in the business world that it is difficult to keep up with the new risks involved. For example, who in the organization can evaluate the risks of selling products over the Internet? As companies reach global markets over the Internet, who watches for fluctuations in the world's currencies and how they may affect profits? Will global warming affect weather conditions and how will that affect our farms and our cattle raising?[1] As you can see, risk management is getting more complex and more critical for all businesses. Those who do business in other countries face increasing risk from social unrest. Given such risks, let's explore how companies go about managing risk.

MANAGING RISK

The term **risk** refers to the chance of loss, the degree of probability of loss, and the amount of possible loss. There are two different kinds of risk:

- **Speculative risk** involves a chance of either profit or loss. It includes the chance a firm takes to make extra money by buying new machinery, acquiring more inventory, and making other decisions in which the probability of loss may be relatively low and the amount of loss is known. An entrepreneur takes speculative risk on the chance of making a profit. In business, building a new plant is a speculative risk because it may result in a loss or a profit.
- **Pure risk** is the threat of loss with no chance for profit. Pure risk involves the threat of fire, accident, or loss. If such events occur, a company loses money; but if the events do not occur, the company gains nothing.

The risk that is of most concern to businesspeople is pure risk. Pure risk threatens the very existence of some firms. Once such risks are identified, firms have several options:

1. Reduce the risk.
2. Avoid the risk.
3. Self-insure against the risk.
4. Buy insurance against the risk.

We'll discuss the option of buying insurance in detail later in this appendix. In the next sections, we will discuss each of the alternatives for managing risk. These steps should be taken to lower the need for outside insurance.

I'm always in the right place **at the wrong time.**

Bob Edwards LIBERTY MUTUAL CLAIMS MANAGER

\\ Call it a gift. But when disaster strikes, I'm always around. Whether it's a hurricane, fire or any other catastrophic event, I'm there to help my customers when they need it most. That's because I get to know each business from the ground up, so I understand what it takes to keep them running when something goes wrong. I help prepare for storms. I arrange for backup production facilities when plants go down. It's all about anticipating my customers' concerns. Some might say my life is one disaster after another. But if it helps my customers, it's OK by me. //

INSURANCE *in* ACTION *Our "Severe Weather Alert System" provides our customers with warnings of incoming storms and step-by-step checklists on how to prepare for them.*

Insurance is not the only way to manage risk, but it is an important way. Your insurance agent is there to help when a disaster strikes and can get money to you very quickly. Do you have insurance covering where you live and your other possessions? If not, how are you covering the risk?

Reducing Risk

A firm can reduce risk by establishing loss-prevention programs such as fire drills, health education, safety inspections, equipment maintenance, accident prevention programs, and so on. Many retail stores, for example, use mirrors, video cameras, and other devices to prevent shoplifting. Water sprinklers and smoke detectors are used to minimize fire loss. In industry, most machines have safety devices to protect workers' fingers, eyes, and so on.

Product recalls can also reduce risk. A classic example is the highly publicized decision in the 1980s by Johnson & Johnson Company to pull its Tylenol pills off the shelves across the country when sabotaged capsules killed several people. More recently when an estimated 400 deaths in traffic accidents were

risk
The change of loss, the degree of probability of loss, and the amount of possible loss.

speculative risk
A chance of either profit or loss.

pure risk
The threat of loss with no chance for profit.

The Concorde had experienced years of service without a major accident. But this flight proved to be a disaster when the plane caught fire and crashed because of debris on the runway. What can airlines do, other than insurance, to cover the risk of such accidents?

self-insurance
The practice of setting aside money to cover routine claims and buying only "catastrophe" policies to cover big losses.

blamed on faulty tires, Firestone and Ford recalled thousands of tires before more people were killed or hurt.[2]

Employees, as well as managers, can reduce risk. For example, truck drivers can wear seat belts to minimize injuries from accidents, operators of loud machinery can wear earplugs to reduce the chance of hearing loss, and those who lift heavy objects can wear back braces. The beginning of an effective risk management strategy is a good loss-prevention program. However, high insurance rates have forced some people to go beyond merely preventing risks to the point of avoiding risks, and in extreme cases by going out of business.

Avoiding Risk

Many risks cannot be avoided. There is always the chance of fire, theft, accident, or injury. But some companies are avoiding risk by not accepting hazardous jobs and by outsourcing shipping and other functions. The threat of lawsuits has driven away some drug companies from manufacturing vaccines, and some consulting engineers refuse to work on hazardous sites. Some companies are losing outside members of their boards of directors for lack of liability coverage protecting them from legal action against the firms they represent.

Self-Insuring

Many companies and municipalities have turned to **self-insurance** because they either can't find or can't afford conventional property/casualty policies. Such firms set aside money to cover routine claims and buy only "catastrophe" policies to cover big losses. Self-insurance, then, lowers the cost of insurance by allowing companies to take out insurance only for larger losses.

Self-insurance is most appropriate when a firm has several widely distributed facilities. The risk from fire, theft, or other catastrophe is then more manageable. Firms with huge facilities, in which a major fire or earthquake could destroy the entire operation, usually turn to insurance companies to cover the risk.

One of the more risky strategies for self-insurance is for a company to "go bare," paying claims straight out of its budget. The risk here is that the whole firm could go bankrupt over one claim, if the damages are high enough. A less risky alternative is to form risk retention group-insurance pools that share similar risks. It is estimated that about one-third of the insurance market is using such alternatives.

Buying Insurance to Cover Risk

Although well-designed, consistently enforced risk-prevention programs reduce the probability of claims, accidents do happen. Insurance is the armor individuals, businesses, and nonprofit organizations use to protect themselves from various financial risks. For this protection, such organizations spend about 10 percent of GDP on insurance premiums. Some insurance protection is provided by the federal government (See Figure A.1), but most risks must be covered by individuals and businesses on their own. We will continue our discussion of insurance by identifying the types of risks that are uninsurable, followed by those that are insurable.

TYPE OF INSURANCE	WHAT IT DOES
Unemployment Compensation	Provides financial benefits, job counseling, and placement services for unemployed workers.
Social Security	Provides retirement benefits, life insurance, health insurance, and disability income insurance.
Federal Housing Administration (FHA)	Provides mortgage insurance to lenders to protect against default by home buyers.
National Flood Insurance Association	Provides compensation for damage caused by flooding and mud slides to properties located in flood-prone areas.
Federal Crime Insurance	Provides insurance to property owners in high-crime areas
Federal Crop Insurance	Provides compensation for damaged crops.
Pension Benefit Guaranty Corporation	Insures pension plans to prevent loss to employees if the company declares bankruptcy or goes out of business.

FIGURE A.1

PUBLIC INSURANCE
State or federal government agencies that provide insurance protection.

What Risks Are Uninsurable? Not all risks are insurable, even risks that once were covered by insurance. An **uninsurable risk** is one that no insurance company will cover. Examples of things that you cannot insure include market risks (e.g., losses that occur because of price changes, style changes, or new products that make your product obsolete); political risks (e.g., losses from war or government restrictions on trade); some personal risks (such as loss of a job); and some risks of operation (e.g., strikes or inefficient machinery).

uninsurable risk
A risk that no insurance company will cover.

What Risks Are Insurable? An **insurable risk** is one that the typical insurance company will cover. Generally, insurance companies use the following guidelines when evaluating whether or not a risk is insurable:

insurable risk
A risk that the typical insurance company will cover.

1. The policyholder must have an **insurable interest,** which means that the policyholder is the one at risk to suffer a loss. You cannot, for example, buy fire insurance on your neighbor's house and collect if it burns down.
2. The loss should be measurable.
3. The *chance* of loss should be measurable.
4. The loss should be accidental.
5. The risk should be dispersed; that is, spread among different geographical areas so that a flood or other natural disaster in one area would not bankrupt the company.
6. The insurance company can set standards for accepting risks.

insurable interest
The possibility of the policyholder to suffer a loss.

The Law of Large Numbers An **insurance policy** is a written contract between the insured (an individual or organization) and an insurance company that promises to pay for all or part of a loss. A **premium** is the fee charged by the insurance company or, in other words, the cost of the insurance policy to the insured.

As in all private businesses, the objective of an insurance company is to make a profit. To ensure that it makes a profit, an insurance company gathers

insurance policy
A written contract between the insured and an insurance company that promises to pay for all or part of a loss.

premium
The fee charged by an insurance company for an insurance policy.

data to determine the extent of the risk. What makes the acceptance of risk possible for insurance companies is the law of large numbers.

law of large numbers
Principle that if a large number of people are exposed to the same risk, a predictable number of losses will occur during a given period of time.

The **law of large numbers** states that if a large number of people or organizations are exposed to the same risk, a predictable number of losses will occur during a given period of time. Once the insurance company predicts the number of losses likely to occur, it can determine the appropriate premiums for each policy it issues. The premium is supposed to be high enough to cover expected losses and yet earn a profit for the firm and its stockholders. Today, many insurance companies are charging high premiums, not for past risks but for the anticipated costs associated with the increasing number of court cases and high damage awards.

rule of indemnity
Rule says that an insured person or organization cannot collect more than the actual loss from an insurable risk.

Rule of Indemnity The **rule of indemnity** says that an insured person or organization cannot collect more than the actual loss from an insurable risk. One cannot gain from risk management; one can only minimize losses. One cannot, for example, buy two insurance policies and collect from both for the same loss. If a company or person carried two policies, the two insurance companies would calculate any loss and divide the reimbursement.

stock insurance company
A type of insurance company owned by stockholders.

mutual insurance company
A type of insurance company owned by its policyholders.

Sources of Insurance There are two major types of insurance companies. **A stock insurance company** is owned by stockholders, just like any other investor-owned company. **A mutual insurance company** is owned by its policyholders. The largest life insurance company, Prudential, is a mutual insurance company. A mutual insurance company, unlike a stock company, does not earn profits for its owners. It is a nonprofit organization, and any excess funds (over losses, expenses, and growth costs) go to the policyholders/investors in the form of dividends or premium reductions.

TYPES OF INSURANCE

As we have discussed, risk management consists of reducing risk, avoiding risk, self-insuring, and buying insurance. There are many types of insurance that cover various losses: property and liability insurance, health insurance, and life insurance. Property losses result from fires, accidents, theft, or other perils. Liability losses result from property damage or injuries suffered by others for which the policyholder is held responsible. Let's begin our exploration of insurance by looking at health insurance.

Health Insurance

Businesses and nonprofit organizations may offer their employees an array of health care benefits to choose from. Everything from hospitalization to physician fees, eye exams, dental exams, and prescriptions can be covered. Often, employees may choose between options from health care providers (e.g., Blue Cross/Blue Shield); health maintenance organizations (HMOs, e.g., Kaiser Permanente); or preferred provider organizations (PPOs).

health maintenance organizations (HMOs)
Health care organizations that require members to choose from a restricted list of doctors.

Health Maintenance Organizations (HMOs) Health Maintenance Organizations (HMOs) offer a full range of health care benefits. Emphasis is on helping members stay healthy instead of on treating illnesses. Two nice features typical of HMOs are that members do not receive bills and do not have to fill out claim forms for routine service. HMOs employ or contract with doctors, hospitals, and other systems of health care, and members must use those providers. In other words, they cannot choose any doctor they wish but can select one doctor from the approved list to be their primary care physician. That doctor will then recommend specialists, if necessary. The HMO system is called managed care.

HMOs are less expensive than comprehensive health insurance providers, but members sometimes complain about not being able to choose doctors or to get the care they want or need. Some physicians also complain that they lose some freedom to do what is needed to make people well and often receive less compensation than they feel is appropriate for the services they provide. To save money, HMOs usually must approve treatment before it is given. People who prefer to have their doctor make such decisions often choose a PPO, as we shall see next.

Preferred Provider Organizations (PPOs) Preferred provider organizations (PPOs) also contract with hospitals and physicians, but unlike an HMO, a PPO does not require its members to choose only from those physicians. However, members do have to pay more if they don't use a physician on the preferred list. Also, members usually have to pay a deductible (e.g., $250) before the PPO will pay any bills. When the plan does pay, members usually have to pay part of the bill. This payment is called co-insurance. Some people feel that the added expense of PPOs over HMOs is worth the freedom to select their own physicians.

Since both HMOs and PPOs can cost as much as 80 percent less than comprehensive individual health insurance policies, most businesses and individuals choose to join one.

preferred provider organizations (PPOs)
Health care organizations similar to HMOs except that they allow members to choose their own physicians (for a fee).

Disability Insurance

Disability insurance replaces part of your income (50 to 70 percent) if you become disabled and unable to work. There usually is a period of time you must be disabled (e.g., 60 days) before you can begin collecting. Many employers provide this type of insurance, but some do not. In either case, insurance experts recommend that you get this type of insurance because the chances of becoming disabled by a disease or accident are much higher than the chance of dying. The premiums for such insurance vary depending on your age, occupation, and income.

It helps for insurance companies to spread the risk among lots of customers. Then, when a tornado like the one that hit this town comes, they can cover the costs. Can you see why insurance rates could rise if there is an increase in such natural disasters in all parts of the world?

Workers' Compensation

Workers' compensation insurance guarantees payment of wages, medical care, and rehabilitation services (e.g., retraining) for employees who are injured on the job. Employers in all 50 states are required to provide this insurance. This insurance also provides benefits to the survivors of workers who die as a result of work-related injuries. The cost of insurance varies by the company's safety record, its payroll, and the types of hazards faced by workers. For example, it costs more to insure a steelworker than an accountant.

Liability Insurance

Professional liability insurance covers people who are found liable for professional negligence. For example, if a lawyer gives advice carelessly and the client loses money, the client may then sue the lawyer for an amount

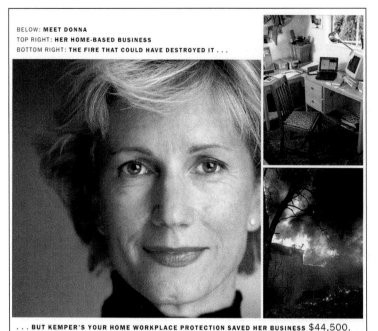

It is so easy to start a home-based business that it can be easy to forget insurance. On the other hand, fire and water damage can lead to major bills. Can you see any reason why a home-based business would not buy a workplace policy?

equal to that lost. This type of insurance is also known as malpractice insurance. While you may think of doctors and dentists when you hear that term, the fact is that many professionals, including mortgage brokers and real estate appraisers, are buying this insurance because of large lawsuits their colleagues have faced.

Product liability insurance provides coverage against liability arising out of products sold. If a person is injured by a ladder or some other household good, he or she may sue the manufacturer for damages. Insurance usually covers such losses.

Other Business Insurance

It is impossible in an introductory course like this to discuss in detail all the insurance coverage that businesses may buy. Naturally, businesses must protect themselves against property damage, and they must buy car and truck insurance and more. Figure A.2 will give you some idea of the types of insurance available.

The point to be made in this appendix is that risk management is critical in all firms. That includes the risk of investing funds and the risk of opening your own business (speculative risk). Remember from Chapter 1, though, that risk is often matched by opportunity and profits. Taking on risk is one way for an entrepreneur to prosper. Regardless of how careful we are, however, we all face the prospect of death, even entrepreneurs. To ensure that those left behind will be able to continue the business, entrepreneurs often buy life insurance that will pay partners and others what they will need to keep the business going. We'll explore that next.

Life Insurance For Businesses

We discussed life insurance in Chapter 22. There, the focus was on life insurance for you and your family. Everything said there applies to life insurance for business executives as well. The best kind of insurance to cover executives in the firm is term insurance, but dozens of new policies with interesting features have been emerging recently.

Insurance Coverage for Home-Based Businesses

Homeowner's policies usually don't have adequate protection for a home-based business.[3] For example, they may have a limit of $2,500 for business equipment. For more coverage, you may need to an endorsement (sometimes called a "rider") to your homeowner's insurance. For about $25, you can increase the coverage to $10,000. Check with your insurance agent for details. If you have clients visit your office and receive deliveries regularly, you may need

TYPES OF INSURANCE	WHAT IT DOES
Property and Liability	
Fire	Covers losses to buildings and their contents from fire.
Automobile	Covers property damage, bodily injury, collision, fire, theft, vandalism, and other related vehicle losses.
Homeowners'	Covers the home, other structures on the premises, home contents, expenses if forced from the home because of an insured peril, third-party liability, and medical payments to others.
Computer coverage	Covers loss of equipment from fire, theft, and sometimes spills, power surges, and accidents.
Professional liability	Protects from suits stemming from mistakes made or bad advice given in a professional context.
Business interruption	Provides compensation for loss due to fire, theft, or similar disasters that close a business. Covers lost income, continuing expenses, and utility expenses.
Nonperformance loss protection	Protects from failure of a contractor, supplier, or other person to fulfill an obligation.
Criminal loss protection	Protects from loss due to theft, burglary, or robbery.
Commercial credit insurance	Protects manufacturers and wholesalers from credit losses due to insolvency or default.
Public liability insurance	Provides protection for businesses and individuals against losses resulting from personal injuries or damage to the property of others for which the insured is responsible.
Extended product liability insurance	Covers potentially toxic substances in products; environmental liability; and, for corporations, directors and officer liability.
Fidelity bond	Protects employers from employee dishonesty.
Surety bond	Covers losses resulting from a second party's failure to fulfill a contract.
Title insurance	Protects buyers from losses resulting from a defect in title to property.
Health Insurance	
Basic health insurance	Covers losses due to sickness or accidents.
Major medical insurance	Protects against catastrophic losses by covering expenses beyond the limits of basic policies.
Hospitalization insurance	Pays for most hospital expenses.
Surgical and medical insurance	Pays costs of surgery and doctor's care while recuperating in a hospital.
Dental insurance	Pays a percentage of dental expenses.
Disability income insurance	Pays income while the insured is disabled as a result of accident or illness.
Life Insurance	
Group life insurance	Covers all the employees of a firm or members of a group.
Owner or key executive insurance	Enables businesses of sole proprietors or partnerships to pay bills and continue operating, saving jobs for the employees. Enables corporations to hire and train or relocate another manager with no loss to the firm.
Retirement and pension plans	Provides employees with supplemental retirement and pension plans.
Credit life insurance	Pays the amount due on a loan if the debtor dies.

FIGURE A.2

PRIVATE INSURANCE

Insurance companies not government-owned (stock companies or mutual companies).

There are many ways that a company can harm the environment. In some cases, such as the damage caused by oil drilling, the potential harm is obvious. But in other cases, such as the use of chemicals in dry cleaning plants, the damage is less obvious. Would you agree that we all should be more conscious of the environment as we go about our daily work?

home office insurance. It costs more like $150 a year, but protects you from slip-and-fall lawsuits and other risks associated with visitors. More elaborate businesses, such as custom cabinetmakers and others who do manufacturing and inventory keeping, a business owner policy may be needed. That costs $300 a year or more. Few of us are experts on insurance, so we need to consult our insurance agent about the best insurance for our home-business needs.

THE RISK OF DAMAGING THE ENVIRONMENT

The risk of environmental harm reaches international proportions in issues such as global warming. The explosion at the Chernobyl nuclear plant in the former Soviet Union caused much concern throughout the world. Due to violations of various safety standards, several U.S. nuclear power plants have been shut down. Yet since coal-fired power plants are said to cause acid rain, and other inexpensive fuel sources haven't been developed, there may be more research into nuclear plants in order to make them safer. Clearly, this will be an issue well into the next century.

Many people feel there is a need for a more careful evaluation of environmental risks than currently is done. How much risk is there in global warming and the depletion of the ozone layer? We don't yet know, but the risks may be substantial.

Clearly, risk management now goes far beyond the protection of individuals, businesses, and nonprofit organizations from known risks. It means the evaluation of worldwide risks such as global warming. It also means prioritizing these risks so that international funds can be spent where they can do the most good. No insurance company can protect humanity from such risks. These risks are the concern of international governments throughout the world, with the assistance of the international scientific community. They should also be your concern as you study risk management in all its dimensions.

KEY TERMS

health maintenance
  organizations
  (HMOs) 704
insurable interest 703
insurable risk 703
insurable policy 703
law of large
  numbers 704

mutual insurable
  company 704
preferred provider
  organizations
  (PPOs) 705
premium 703
pure risk 701
risk 701

rule of indemnity 704
self-insurance 702
speculative risk 701
stock insurance
  company 704
uninsurable risk 703

FINANCIAL MANAGEMENT (FINANCE AND ACCOUNTING)

Accounting and finance are career areas that have existed for many centuries. Records discovered in the ruins of ancient Babylon dating back to 300 B.C. show that financial records were kept by the ancients. European monarchs, particularly in the 18th and 19th centuries, relied on bankers and other professional financiers to recover from wars and to build the new industrial revolution.

Today, accountants and financial managers are as much in demand as ever. Computerization has enriched both career areas immensely. Because of changing laws and regulations, companies and their personnel in these positions must place a greater emphasis than ever on accurate reporting of financial data. This field, like so many others, is dynamic and changing.

Nearly two million people work in some area of finance or accounting, most as accountants, financial managers, banking personnel, or financial consultants. Nearly every company—whether in manufacturing, transportation, retailing, or a variety of services—employs one or more financial managers. Accountants and bookkeepers are equally in demand.

SKILLS

Anyone who enters these areas must have a mathematical aptitude, an interest in numbers, and a considerable amount of patience. As with nearly every other area, speaking and writing skills are a must, because the financial information must be communicated to people. Good ethical judgment is also essential, because areas of finance and accounting both contain more "gray areas" than many of us imagine.

CAREER PATHS

A bachelor's degree in accounting or finance is usually a prerequisite, although accountants with two-year degrees and outstanding abilities have been hired as bookkeepers and accounting assistants. In some states, tax preparers do not need formal degrees, only mastery of current tax law. In all cases, though, continuing education is becoming increasingly important because of the growing complexity of global commerce, changing federal and state laws, and the constant introduction of new, complex financial instruments.

A well-trained, experienced financial manager is a prime candidate for promotion into top management. Junior public accountants usually advance to semi-senior positions within two to five years and to senior positions within six to eight years. Although advancement can be rapid for well-prepared accountants, especially in public accounting, employees without adequate college preparation are often dead-ended in routine jobs. Also, even CPAs must constantly be reeducated in today's changing environment.

SOME POSSIBLE CAREERS IN FINANCE AND ACCOUNTING

JOB TITLE	SALARY	JOB DUTIES	CAREER PATH	PROSPECTS
Accountant	Entry level: $34,500 (bachelor's degree) Experienced: Median: $87,400	Depends on size and nature of firm as well as specific job title. Public accountants work independently on a fee basis. Private accountants handle financial records in the company where they are salaried employees. The general accountant supervises, installs, and devises systems. The cost accountant determines unit costs of products and services. The auditor examines and vouches for the accuracy of records.	Start with either an accounting degree or many courses in accounting. Certified Public Accountant must take comprehensive exam, then intern as auditor for two years. Able accountants, especially CPAs, can be promoted rapidly. By specializing in certain accounting areas, an accountant can often be promoted.	Openings in all accounting areas are expected to be average through 2008.
Financial Manager	$27,680–$118,950 Median: $55,070	As with accountants, duties depend on size and nature of firm as well as specific job title. Titles include treasurer, controller, credit manager, cash manager. Controllers direct preparation of financial reports; cash and credit managers monitor and control the flow of receipts and disbursements; risk and insurance managers work to minimize risk and cut risk costs.	Most start with a degree in finance or accounting. A Master of Business Administration degree (MBA) is becoming increasingly required by some companies. Often promoted into top management.	Average growth through 2008.
Securities and financial services sales workers	$22,660–$124,800 Once established, changes to commission only. Median: $48,090	Open accounts for new customers, execute buy and sell orders based on information from the securities exchange. Get information on company's progress from the research dept. Must be able to anticipate buying and selling trends in the markets.	Many brokerage concerns hire trainees, then place them on a probationary track of around six months. Depending on ability and ambition, promotion can be rapid. Bank employees make much less.	For the talented and ambitious person, the opportunities will remain numerous through 2008. But depends on the growth of the economy.

Source: *Occupational Outlook Handbook,* Bureau of Labor Statistics.

A.G. Edwards & Sons, Inc.

Name: Jerome R. Laughlin

Age: 50

Position/title: Financial Consultant

Time in this position: 7 years

Company Name: A.G. Edwards & Sons, Inc.

Company's Web Address: www.agedwards.com

Company Description: A.G. Edwards & Sons, Inc. is one of the nation's largest full service investment firms. Headquartered in St. Louis, Missouri, the company encompasses more than 7,000 financial consultants in 690 offices throughout 49 states, the District of Columbia, and London, England. A.G. Edwards is a member of all major stock and commodity exchanges, including the New York Stock Exchange.

Major factors in the decision to take this position: When I was only 12 years old, I purchased my first stock with profits from my newspaper route. From that time, I've always had a strong interest in investments. After graduation from college, I had many opportunities to pursue a career in investments, but never felt the timing was right until I reached my early 40s.

Job Description: I help clients set both short-term and long-term financial goals, and design detailed financial strategies to meet their needs. I then review their strategies on a regular basis to check their performance and make adjustments accordingly.

Career Path: With over 20 years in Hospital Administration, I wanted to find a career where I was in more control of my professional career. I transitioned from an avocation in investments to a career as a financial consultant. Many of my skills in strategic planning, communications, marketing, and organization were very beneficial.

Ideal Next Job: Vice President—Investments

Best Part of the Job: Every day is different. Educating clients and helping them to determine their financial needs. I take a great deal of satisfaction when I listen to clients and help them meet their needs and achieve their financial goals.

Worst Part of the Job: Most challenging is communicating with clients about the overwhelming amount of information they hear or read about in the news, keeping them focused on their financial goals, and framing realistic expectations.

Education Background: I received an undergraduate degree in business and public administration and a master's in Business Administration.

Favorite Course: Sales Management

Best course for your career: Public Speaking and Communications

Recommended by Bob Ulbrich, Parkland College

Chapter Notes

Prologue

1. Joshua Mills, "Computer Science and Engineering Majors Earn Top Dollars," *University Wire*, January 9, 2001; "The Old College Try," *The Wall Street Journal*, March 4, 1999, p. A14; and Sergio Bustos, "Hispanics in America: Education and the Work Force," *Gannett News Service*, December 20, 2000.
2. "Postsecondary Education," *Education Statistics Quarterly*, Spring 2000.
3. Sally Johnston, "Casualties of Relaxed Dressing/Wardrobe Can Spell Success or Failure," *Edmonton Sun*, February 1, 2000 and Patricia Kitchen, "The Proper Attire Will Suit You Well," *Newsday*, January 6, 2001.
4. Marjorie Brody, "Wardrobe Wisdom: Dress for Success," Special to CNBC.com, May 25, 2000 and Lesley Kennedy, "Putting 'Casual' in Black and White Terms," *Denver Rocky Mountain News*, January 7, 2001.
5. Zatni Arbi, "Some Small Things to Remember about E-Mail," *Jakarta Post*, May 8, 2000 and Karla Dougherty, *The Rules to be Cool: Etiquette and Netiquette* (Berkeley Heights, New Jersey: Enslow Publishers, 2001).
6. "Broadband Bulletin," *Cablefax Daily*, January 3, 2001; "Internet Fuels Demand for Faster Access," *Nation*, January 3, 2001; and Ephraim Schwartz, "Broadband Wireless is Getting Closer," *InfoWorld*, January 8, 2001.
7. Margaret Littman, "Good Economy, Bad Candidates," *Marketing News*, April 10, 2000, pp. 12–13; "Planning Helps Students Get Good Recommendations," *The Dallas Morning News*, January 4, 2001, p. 6C; and Maria Mallory, "In Hiring Personality Still Counts," *The Atlanta Journal and Constitution*, January 7, 2001, p. R1.
8. Bill Breen, "Full House," *Fast Company*, January 1, 2001; Jerry Useem, "For Sale Online: You," *Fortune*, July 5, 1999, pp. 67–78; and Bob Edwards, "War Over Classified Ads," *Morning Edition*, January 1, 2001.

Chapter 1

1. Walter Russell Mead, "In 2025," *Worth*, March 2000, p. 134.
2. Anne Field, "A Living or a Life," *Fast Company*, January–February 2000, pp. 256–67.
3. H. James Harrington, "Rethinking Quality," *Quality Digest*, February 2000, p. 20.
4. Joshua Hyatt, "The Death of Gut Instinct," *Inc.*, January 2001, pp. 38–44.
5. You can read about the 100 top leaders in "Powerhouses of the New Economy," *Black Enterprise*, June 2000, pp. 107–29.
6. George Gendron, "The Failure Myth," *Inc.*, January 2001, p. 13.
7. Erica Morphy, "Grease Busting," *Global Business*, January 2001, pp. 48–53.
8. Jeffrey Davis, "The Net Impact," *Business 2.0*, January 2000.
9. Kim Cross, "Who's Online," *Business 2.0*, January 2000.
10. Elizabeth Clampet, "Department of Commerce Offers E-Commerce Stats," *InternetNews.com*, March 3, 2000.
11. Jefrey Davis, "Chasing Retail's Tail," *Business 2.0*, January 2000.
12. Beth Belton, "Amazon's Jeff Bezos: 'We Sell Dollar Bills for $1.20,'" *Business Week Online*, June 30, 2000 and Clay Shirky, "The Wal-Mart Future," *Business 2.0*, January 9, 2001.
13. "New Venture Question.com Debuts—Growing Business within B2B Marketplaces," *Business Wire*, March 6, 2000; and Len Grzanka, "Moving beyond B2C to B2B," *Inter@ctive Week*, February 21, 2000

and Beth Synder Bulik, "Dot-Coms Hits and Bombs," *Business 2.0*, January 9, 2001.
14. "B2B E-Commerce: A Beginners Guide," *About.com Guide to E-Commerce*, March 4, 2000.
15. Richard Karpinski, "B-to-B Woes Play Part in Pummeling of B-to-C Stocks," *BtoB*, April 10, 2000, p. 13 and Jennifer Gilbert, "When Brands Get Burned," *Business 2.0*, January 23, 2001.
16. Carol Patton, "Analyze This: 2000 Revisited," *B to B*, January 8, 2001.
17. "Baldrige Award Winner Profile," *Quality Digest*, May 2000, pp. 45–46.
18. M. Scott Evans, "The Customer-Centric Corporation: How to Be One," *Harvard Business Review*, May–June 2000, pp. S3–S23.
19. Michael Beer and Nitin Nohria, "Cracking the Code of Change," *The Harvard Business Review*, May–June 2000, pp. 133–41.
20. "Census Bureau Projects Doubling of Nation's Population by 2100," *Regulatory Intelligence Data*, January 13, 2000.
21. Randolph E. Schmid, "Twice as Many Americans by 2100," *AP Online*, January 13, 2000.
22. Keith H. Hammonds, "Difference Is Power," *Fast Company*, July 2000, pp. 258–66.
23. Yochi J. Ddreazen, Carlos Tejada, and Patrick Barta, "Jobless Rate Declines to 30-Year Low," *The Wall Street Journal*, March 5, 2000, p. A2.

Chapter 2

1. "Taiwan and China," *The Economist*, January 6, 2001, pp. 35–38.
2. "The Church of Malthus," *The Wall Street Journal*, July 6, 1999, p. A14.
3. Stephen Moore and Philip D. Harvey, *Investor's Business Daily*, May 5, 2000, p. A28.
4. Quentin Hardy, "The Radical Philanthropist," *Forbes*, May 1, 2000, pp. 114–21.
5. Paul Krugman, "Unleashing the Millennium," *Fortune*, March 6, 2000, pp. F16–F20.
6. Thomas J. DiLorenzo, "Capitalism Is the Best Income Equalizer," *The Wall Street Journal*, May 26, 1999, p. A23.
7. Gregg Easterbrook, "Capitalism, Friend of the Earth," *The Wall Street Journal*, February 8, 2000, p. A24.
8. Cait Murphy, "The Next French Revolution," *Fortune*, June 12, 2000, pp. 157–68.
9. Figures are from the year 2000.
10. Richard Behar, "Capitalism in a Cold Climate," *Fortune*, June 12, 2000, pp. 195–216.
11. Ching-Ching Ni, "China Kick-Starting Entrepreneurs' Engines with Venture Funding," *Los Angeles Times*, May 21, 2000, pp. 1, 8, and Blaise Zerega, "What Would Mao Think?," *Red Herring*, October 2000, pp. 120–132.
12. Gary S. Becker, "Egads! The Left Is Unchaining the World's Economies," *Business Week*, May 22, 2000, p. 32.
13. Yochi J. Dreazen, Carlos Tejada, and Patrick Barta, "Jobless Rate Declines to 30-Year Low," *The Wall Street Journal*, May 8, 2000, pp. A2, A4.
14. M. E. Cohen, "Taxing Times," *Barron's*, June 21, 1999, p. 27.
15. Robert J. Samuelson, "Let Them Be Lame Ducks," *Newsweek*, February 7, 2000, p. 30.
16. J. Bradford Delong, "Estimating Growth Is a True Odyssey," *Fortune*, June 26, 2000, pp. 62–64.

17. Robert Samuelson, "Who Governs? Maybe Nobody," *Newsweek*, February 21, 2000, p. 33.

18. Donald Lambro, "The Correct Economic Medicine," *The Washington Times,* January 11, 2001, p. A13.

Chapter 3

1. Sam Register and Kate Stroup, "81,421,906 People–And Counting," *Newsweek*, January 8, 2001, p. 13.

2. Doug Struck, "Japan Gets Ready for Real Baseball," *Washington Post*, March 26, 2000, p. D-1.

3. Jeremy Laurence, "The Habit Hollywood Just Can't Stub Out," *Independent*, January 5, 2001.

4. Laura Sowinski, "Exporting American Know-How," *World Trade*, April 2000, pp. 42–48 and "IMF Cuts 2001 U.S. Growth Forecast," *AP Online*, January 12, 2001.

5. Aaron Bernstein, "Backlash: Behind the Anxiety over Globalization," *Business Week*, April 24, 2000, pp. 39–44.

6. "Starbucks to Become World's Largest Cybercafe," *United Press International*, January 9, 2001.

7. Christopher D. Lancette, "Hitting the Spot," *Entrepreneur*, April 1999, p. 40.

8. Moira Allen, "Net the World: International Web Users Want to Buy from Your Site—Make It Easy on Them," *Entrepreneur*, June 2000, p. 46.

9. "Antidumping—Remedy of Protection," *Jakarta Post*, May 19, 2000 and "EU Imposes Anti-Dumping Duties on Polish and Ukranian Ammonium Nitrate," *European Report*, January 4, 2001.

10. "Asians Set for Overkill in Mickey Mouse Rivalry," Kyodo News Service, January 1, 2000.

11. Teri Agins and Rebecca Quick, "Behind a Bitter Suit Filed by Calvin Klein Lies Grit of Licensing," *The Wall Street Journal*, June 1, 2000, pp. A1, A7.

12. "International Trade and Development: David L. Aaron," *Congressional Testimony*, June 9, 1999.

13. "Have Factory, Will Travel," *The Economist*, February 12, 2000.

14. Laurie McGinley, "Joint Venture Displays New American Export: High-Tech Medicine," *The Wall Street Journal*, February 14, 2000, pp. A1, A11.

15. Steve Hamm, "Why It's Cool Again," *Business Week*, May 8, 2000, pp. 115–24.

16. Ernest Beck, "Nestlé Feels Little Pressure to Make Big Acquisitions," *The Wall Street Journal*, June 22, 2000, p. B6.

17. Hester Abrams and Michael Shields, "Nestlé Interested in Part of Nabisco," *Rueters*, June 13, 2000.

18. Peter Grant, "Rockefeller Center Is Put Up for Sale in the Booming New York City Market," *The Wall Street Journal*, May 22, 2000, p. A6.

19. Timothy D. Shellhardt, "In a Factory Schedule, Where Does Religion Fit In?" *The Wall Street Journal*, March 3, 1999, p. B1.

20. Moni Basu, "65 Million Hindus Gather at the River," *The Atlanta Constitution*, January 11, 2001.

21. Miriam Jordan, "Debut of Rival Diet Colas in India Leaves a Bitter Taste," *The Wall Street Journal*, July 21, 1999, pp. B10–B11.

22. Raki Sayid and Suzy Jagger, "The Euro's on its Way," *The Mirror*, January 11, 2001, p.6.

23. Scott Baldauf, "Politics Is Twice as Complicated along the Border," *Christian Science Monitor*, June 14, 2000, p. 3.

24. "Nestlé Chief to Head Local Perrier Board," *The Nation*, May 24, 1999.

25. Bob Groves, "History in Your Hands and in Your Pockets," *The Record (Bergen County, N.J.)*, April 17, 2000, p. A-3 and Suzanne Lazanov, "Fair Trade: Good Services and the Barter System," *The Washington Post*, January 9, 2001, p. C4.

26. Bob Meyer, "The Original Meaning of Trade Meets the Future in Barter," *World Trade*, January 2000, pp. 46–50.

27. Mari Shaw, "Global Benefits from the National Patent Board," *World Trade*, January 2000, pp. 72–73.

28. Jess Dhaliwal, "Holier Than Thou," *CFO*, February 2000, p. 20.

29. M. Ray Perryman, "Full Access to Trade Key to Economic Success," *Arlington Morning News*, May 28, 2000, p. 11A.

30. Philip Brasher, "Clinton Inclined to Sign Cuban Bill," *AP Online*, June 29, 2000. www.associatedpress.com

31. Anita Snow, "Cuba Seeks Aid in Ending Embargo," *AP Online*, January 11, 2001.

32. Peter Landers and Phred Dvorak, "Foreign Investment in Japan Accelerates," *The Wall Street Journal*, March 28, 2000, p. A24.

33. "The Electronic Pill Box," *The Economist*, April 22, 2000.

34. Michael Williams and Peter Landers, "When Keiretsu Lose Their Wa, It's Time for a Name Change," *The Wall Street Journal*, April 27, 2000, p. A11, A12.

35. "Nissan to Revamp Ties with Parts Suppliers," *Kyodo World News*, April 18, 2000.

36. John Sorenson, "The New Rising Sun," *Business 2.0*, May 2000, p. 90.

37. Julie Schmit, "Japan Undergoes E-Makeover," *USA Today*, April 19, 2000, pp. 1B, 2B and "Late Starter in E-Commerce Plays Catch-up," *Inter Press Service English News Wire,"* January 10, 2001.

38. "China Trade Bill—Charleen Barshefsky," *Congressional Testimony*, May 25, 2000.

39. "Sweden Seeks to Boost Confidence in WTO, *European Report*, January 6, 2001.

40. Geoff Winestock, "China, EU Gain an Edge in WTO Deal," *The Wall Street Journal*, May 22, 2000, p. A30 and Naomi Koppel, "China: We're a Developing Nation," *AP Online*, January 12, 2001.

41. Ibid.

42. Juan Williams, "Analysis: China–Taiwan Relations and the Historical Background Leading Up to the Latest Bout of Tension Between Them," *Talk of the Nation* (National Public Radio), March 1, 2000.

43. Robert Evans, "EU Said Sure WTO Ruling Limits Trade Bloc Action," *Reuters*, January 13, 2000.

44. Julian M. Weiss, "Mercosur on the Road to Recovery," *World Trade*, February 2000, pp. 26–30.

45. "Argentine President Supports Single Mercosur Currency," *Reuters*, April 14, 2000.

46. Stanley A. Weiss, "Mexico after NAFTA Becomes a Home for Democracy," *International Herald Tribune*, June 28, 2000 and "Mexican Agricultural Imports from NAFTA Partners Rise," *Infolatina*, January 2, 2001.

47. Peter McKenna, "Canada's Growing Hemispheric Influence," *London Free Press*, June 3, 2000 and Peter C. Newnan, "The End of Canada?" *Maclean's*, January 8, 2001, p. 18.

48. "Leashing Multinational Key in Globalization," *Toronto Star*, May 27, 2000.

49. Ching-Ching Ni, "China Kick-Starting Entrepreneurs' Engines with Venture Funding," *Los Angeles Times*, May 21, 2000, pp. C1, C8.

50. Helene Cooper and Ian Johnson, "Congress's Vote Primes U.S. Firms to Boost Investments in China," *The Wall Street Journal*, May 25, 2000, p. A1 and "China's Trade with Top 10 Partner on the Rise," *Xinhua News Agency*, January 11, 2001.

51. Dexter Roberts, "China's Wealth Gap," *Business Week*, May 15, 2000, pp. 170–80.

52. Ian Johnson, "Foreign Profits in China May Remain Elusive," *The Wall Street Journal*, May 25, 2000, pp. A21, A22 and "Long Way Ahead for Asian Economic Integration," *Xinhua News Agency*, January 10, 2001.

Chapter 4

1. Christina Hoff Sommers, "Are We Living in a Moral Stone Age?" *USA Today Magazine*, March 1, 1999; Barbara Frank, "Knowing Yourself Is the First Step," *Toronto Sun*, April 17, 2000, p. 54; and Jack Kemp, "A Golden Age to Sustin," *The Washington Times*, January 3, 2001, p. A13.

2. Julia Levy, "Trends Show Cheating on the Rise in U.S.," *University Wire*, February 24, 2000; Lauren Wiener, "Half of College Students Have Cheated, Study Says," *University Wire*, February 23, 2000; and Hank Daniszewski, "Pulling the Plug on Cheats," *The London Free Press*, January 4, 2001, p. A3.

3. Jamie Reno, "Need Someone in Creative Accounting?" *Newsweek*, May 17, 1999.

4. Kenneth Blanchard and Norman Vincent Peale, *The Power of Ethical Management* (New York: William Morrow, 1996).

5. John McCormick, "The Sorry Side of Sears," *Newsweek*, February 22, 1999, pp. 36–39.

6. Caroline E. Mayer, "Suit Accuses Sears of Tire-Balancing Fraud," *Washington Post*, June 17, 1999, p. E3.

7. Ethics Resource Center, 2000 National Business Ethics Survey ,www.ethics.org/2000survey.html..

8. Brian Sharp, "Ethics in Workplace Hit," Gannett News Service, June 6, 2000; and Craig Savoye, "Workers Say Honesty Is Best Company Policy," *Christian Science Monitor*, June 15, 2000,p. 3.

9. "Clinton Honors Bayer's Volunteerism," www.responsibilityinc.com., June 12, 2000 and Stephen Buckley, "Volunteerism is Blossoming," *The Washington Post*, January 9, 2001, p. A1.

10. Wanda Menke-Gluckert, "Baby Benz Faces the Moose," *Europe*, February 2, 1998, pp. 40–44 and Anita Lienhart, "She Drove, He Drove Mercedes C320," *Gannett News Service*, January 9, 2001.

11. "Doing Well by Doing Good," *The Economist*, April 22, 2000 and "Happy Meal Literacy Campaign Serves Up a Different Kind of Prize," *PR News*, January 9, 2001.

12. "Eleven Sued by SEC for Alleged Insider Trading," *Reuters Business Report*, June, 23, 1999; "Money Managers Worry about Insider Trading," *Reuters Business Report*, June 14, 1999; Sharon Walsh, "25 Charged with Insider Trading in Lotus Stock," *Washington Post*, May 27, 1999, p. E1; and Edward Robinson, "The Shareholder from Hell," *Business 2.0*, January 9, 2001.

13. Janet Rae-Dupree, "Anatomy of a Shareholder Slaughter," *Business Week*, May 17, 1999, p. 44; and Adam Shell, "Investors Punish Two-Time Losers," *USA Today*, June 12, 2000, p. 1B.

14. Philip Schofield, "Good Ethics Lead to Healthy Profits," *Independent on Sunday*, May 2, 1999, p. 1; and Doug Treen, "Strategic Human Resources," *Ivey Business Journal*, January/February 2000.

15. ,www.rhino.com/about/support.html.

16. James Graff, "Business/World Economic Forum: Giving Some of It Back," *Time International*, February 15, 1999, p. 40; and "Samsung Thrives on People, Technology, Future," *Korea Times*, January 30, 2000.

17. Forest Reinhardt, "Bringing the Environment Down to Earth," *Harvard Business Review*, July 1, 1999, p. 149; and "New Standards Dog Canned-Tuna Market," *Arizona Republic*, January 5, 2000, p. G5.

18. Sandra Waddock and Neil Smith, "Corporate Responsibility Audits: Doing Well by Doing Good," *Sloan Management Review*, Winter 2000, pp. 75–83.

19. "A Global War against Bribery," *The Economist*, January 16, 1999; "Corrupt Official Sentenced to 13 Years in Jail," *Xinhua News Agency*, April 26, 2000; and "Bribery Claims to be Probed," *Africa News Service*, January 6, 2001.

20. Sir Geoffrey Chandler, "Business/Davos Special Report: Viewpoint: The New Corporate Challenge," *Time International*, February 1, 1999, p. 64.

21. J. D. Walker, "Nike Profits from World's Vulnerable," *University Wire*, April 3, 2000; Steven Greenhouse, "USA: Nike CEO Cancels Gift to University Over Monitoring," *New York Times*, April 25, 2000; "USA: Protesters Tell Nike—No More Sweatshops!" *Stop Sweatshops News*, May 3, 2000; and "Buyers Should Know Where Merchandise is Produced," *University Wire*, January 11, 2001.

22. Karen D. Lock, "Viewing Ethics through a Global Lens," *Beyond Computing*, May 2000, pp. 12–13 and "Critics Score Global Firms' Commitment to Rights," *Inter Press Service English News Wire*, January 3, 2001.

23. "Finance: Four Latin American Nations Sign Anti-Bribery Pact," *Inter Press Service English News Wire*, January 13, 2000; "OECD Calls for Early Launch of New WTO Round," *Kyodo World News Service*, June 27, 2000; John Burgess, "35 Countries Named as Unfair Tax Havens," *Washington Post*, June 27, 2000, p. E02; and "Anti-Graft Bill Still With Legal Drafters," *Africa News Service*, January 4, 2001.

Chapter 4 Appendix

1. Charles Haddad, "Why Big Tobacco Can't Be Killed," *Business Week*, April 24, 2000, p. 68 and "Tobacco Can't Kick Habit," *The Palm Beach Post*, January 12, 2001, p. 14A.

2. Michael Rubinkam, "Philadelphia Files Gun Lawsuit," AP Online, www.associated press.com, April 11, 2000 and "Gun Makers' Lawsuit

Against Atlantia HUD is Dropped," *The Atlanta Journal and Constitution*, January 6, 2001, p. C4.

3. Ed Timms, "Gun-Control Legacy of Columbine Tragedy Still Unfolding," *Dallas Morning News*, April 12, 2000, p. 1A and "Gun Toting America," *The Press*, January 2, 2001, p. 4.

4. Samuel Maull, "New York Sues Gun Manufacturers," AP Online, www.associatedpress.com, June 26, 2000.

5. U.S. Patent and Trademark Office, U.S. Patent Act (1999–2000 edition); and Elizabeth Price, "WTO Rules Ottawa Must Extend Life of Certain Patents," *The Wall Street Journal*, May 8, 2000, p. A8.

6. Pamela L. Moore, "For Sale: Great Ideas, Barely Used," *Business Week*, April 3, 2000, pp. 78–80.

7. Melinda Beck, "So Sue Me: Patent Attorneys Are a Necessary Evil," *Industry Standard*, May 8, 2000, p. 250, and "Pay Incentive Lures Patent Office Workers Into Computer Age," *The Washington Post*, January 6, 2001, p. B2.

8. Mari Shaw, "Global Benefits From the National Patent Board," *World Trade*, January 2000, pp. 72–73.

9. Philip E. Ross, "Patently Absurd," *Forbes*, May 29, 2000, pp. 180–82.

10. Timothy J. Mullaney, "Those Web Patents Aren't Advancing the Ball," *Business Week*, April 17, 2000, p. 62.

11. Ibid.

12. Barry Fox, "Connected: When Quixote Loved Lucy Technoturkey," *Daily Telegraph*, January 27, 2000.

13. Victoria Slind-Flor, "Stalking the Submarine Patent King," *IP Worldwide*, October 1999.

14. U.S. Copyright Office.

15. Michael Ferry, "Incapacitation Can Delay Onset of Statute of Limitations," *St. Louis Post Dispatch*, May 22, 2000, p. 6.

16. Michael Mandel, Dan Carney, and Andy Reinhardt, "Antitrust for the Digital Age," *Business Week*, May 15, 2000, pp. 46–49.

17. Amy Kovar, "Charged! Credit Card Outfits Face Antitrust Suits," *Fortune*, April 17, 2000, pp. 82–84 and "Microsoft Wins Cases," *The Toronto Star*, January 13, 2001.

18. Steven C. Bahls and Jane Easter Bahls, "In a Fix," *Entrepreneur*, May 2000, pp. 127–29.

19. "FTC: Major U.S. Manufacturers Agree to Settle Charges of Making Misleading 'Made in USA' Claims," *M2 Press Wire*, January 20, 2000.

20. Dominic Gates, "Still Rooting for Bill's Team," *Industry Standard*, June 12, 2000, pp. 63–65 and "U.S. Government Files Brief on Microsoft Antitrust Case," *Xinhua News Agency*, January 12, 2001.

21. James Grimaldi, "Judge Says Microsoft Broke Antitrust Law," *Washington Post*, April 4, 2000, p. A1 and James V. Grimaldi, "Microsoft's Competitors Hire Starr to Back Breakup," *The Washington Post*, January 12, 2001, p. E1.

22. Andrew J. Glass, "More to Come on Microsoft; McCain Vows Senate Hearings; Appeals Could Take Years," *Atlanta Journal*, April 4, 2000, p. A1 and D. Ian Hopper, "Feds Defend Microsoft Judge," *AP Online*, January 12, 2001.

23. Neil Munro, "Technology: Cautious Course on Internet Taxes," *National Journal*, May 20, 2000 and John Millar, "Taxing E-Commerce Thorny Issue," *The London Free Press*, January 5, 2001, p. D3.

24. Scott Hiaasen, "Bankruptcy Bill May End State's Reign as Debtor's Haven," *Palm Beach Post*, January 1, 2000, p. 1A.

25. Yochi J. Dreazen, "Bankruptcy Bills May Proceed Despite New Data," *The Wall Street Journal*, March 7, 2000, p. A4 and Hal Mattern, "Credit Troubles Predicted to Rise," *The Arizona Republic*, January 1, 2001, p. D3.

26. William March, "Tightening Law on Bankruptcy Draws Scrutiny," *Tampa Tribune*, May 21, 2000, p. 1 and Daniel Ruth, "And You Think You Have Debts!" *The Tampa Tribune*, January 10, 2001, p. 2.

27. Donald L. Barlett, James B. Steele, Laura Karmatz, and Andrew Goldstein, "Big Money & Politics: Who Gets Hurt?" *Time*, May 15, 2000, pp. 64–73.

28. Ibid.

29. Tim Reason, "Power Struggle," *CFO*, June 2000, pp. 111–116 and Matthew C. Quinn, "Utility Deregulation Faces Uncertain Future," *The Atlanta Constitution*, January 10, 2001, p. C1.

30. Kenneth Bredemeier, "Electricity Rates Fall for Maryland Customers; New Suppliers Shun Deregulation," *Washington Post*, July 1, 2000, p. E1; and Jonathan Weisman, "California Crisis Threatens to Spread Utility Deregulation," *USA Today*, January 10, 2001, p. 1A.

Chapter 5

1. Justine Ancheta, "Running a Business from Two States," *Home Office*, July 2000; and Rieva Lesonsky, "Howdy, Partner: Don't Buddy Up without a Partnership Agreement," *Entrepreneur*, February 2000.
2. Alilza Sherman, "Partners Are from Mars: Advice for Choosing a Business Partner," *Business Start-Ups*, April 2000; Kim T. Gordon, "Two's Company," *Home Office*, May 2000; and "The Start-Up Issue," *Inc.*, January 1, 2001.
3. Carlotta Roberts, "Corporate Office," *Starting a Business*, February 2000 and Robert McGarvey, "Inc. Easy," *Entrepreneur*, January 2001.
4. Rieva Lesonsky, "Putting Inc. to Paper," *Entrepreneur*, February 2000.
5. Rieva Lesonsky, "S Corporations," *Entrepreneur*, February 2000 and Laurie Asseo, "Justices Side with Shareholders," *AP Online*, January 9, 2001.
6. Conrad Ciccotello and C. Terry Grant, "LLCs and LLPs: Organizing to Deliver Professional Services," *Business Horizons*, March 19, 1999, pp. 85–92.
7. Carlotta Roberts, "LLC 101," *Starting a Business*, February 2000.
8. Peter Coy, "Running the Numbers on the Deal," *Business Week*, January 24, 2000 and David Shook, "AOL Time Warner: Analysts vs. Investors," *Business Week*, January 8, 2001.
9. Bill Vlasic and Bradley A. Stertz, "Taken for a Ride," *Business Week*, June 5, 2000 and Nancy Ferris, "Chrysler's New Boss," *Business Week*, January 10, 2001.
10. "Entrepreneur's 22nd Annual Franchise 500," *Entrepreneur*, January 2001.
11. Karen Spaeder, " Mac Is Back," *Entrepreneur*, January 2000, pp. 180–82.
12. Julie Bennett, "Inspired by America's Consumer Boom, Entrepreneurs Pursue New Markets," *The Wall Street Journal*, June 17, 1999, p. B18.
13. Dan Morse, "Fast-Food Franchise Bank Loans Fall Out of Favor with Lenders," *The Wall Street Journal Interactive*, July 11, 2000 and Paul DeCeglie, "Funny Money," *Entrepreneur*, January 2001.
14. Dan Morse, "Flaming Foils a Franchise ForumOnline, but Another Starts Up," *The Wall Street Journal*, May 16, 2000.
15. Dan Morse, "Franchisees Battle Mergers by Seeking Concessions," *The Wall Street Journal*, February 8, 2000 and Todd D. Maddocks, "Write the Wrongs," *Entrepreneur*, January 2001.
16. Michelle Prather, "Heat of the Moment: Our In-Depth Look at the Current State of Franchising," *Entrepreneur*, January 2000, pp. 157–61.
17. "Churchs Chicken Launches Year-Long Initiative to Attract Women Entrepreneurs to Franchising Industry," *PR Newswire*, May 9, 1999; Ellen Paris, "A Franchise of Her Own," *Entrepreneur*, June 2000, pp. 163–70; and Cynthia E. Griffer, "Fair Financing," *Entrepreneur*, January 2001.
18. Dan Morse, "Individual Outlet Owners Set Up E-Commerce Sites," *The Wall Street Journal*, March 28, 2000.
19. Todd D. Maddocks, "Catch the Wave: How to Harness the Power of the Internet and Find a Franchise That's Right for You," *Entrepreneur*, January 2000, pp. 169–73.

Chapter 6

1. U.S. Internal Revenue Service and "Over 40 and Still Entrepreneurial," *Independent*, January 16, 2001.
2. Stephanie Armour, "Net Firms Soar on Campus," *USA Today*, April 12, 2000, pp. 2A, 2B and Laura E. Vasilion, "Beep, Beep!" *Entrepreneur's Start-Ups*, January 2001.
3. Geoff Williams, "There Ought to Be a Law," *Entrepreneur*, February 2000, pp. 104–9 and Joyce Rosenberg, "Break Out of Entrepreneurial Isolation When You Go Solo," *The Washington Times*, January 15, 2001

4. Kirsten Haukebo, "Driven Founder Loves Running a Sizzling Business," *USA Today*, February 22, 2000.
5. Bonny L. Georgia, "Going Solo: Working for Yourself Sounds Great, but Is It Right for You?" *Home Office Computing*, April 2000, p. 92.
6. Sonya Donaldson, "Who Works at Home?" *Home Office Computing*, April 1999; and Candee Wilde, "Transforming the Enterprise: Telework Programs—High-Speed Access Technologies Like Cable Modems and DSL Give Telecommuting a Lift," *InternetWeek*, April 17, 2000.
7. Beth Cox, "Small Business Internet Use Exploding," Internetnews.com, February 2, 2000.
8. "Small Biz Heads to the Web," *PC Magazine*, February 8, 2000, p. 88.
9. "Taking the Net by Storm," *Entrepreneur*, January 2000, p. 50 and George Anders and Polly LaBarre," What's Next for the Net?" *Fast Company*, January 1, 2001.
10. Marshall Brain, "How E-Commerce Works," Howstuffworks.com, March 1, 2000.
11. Libby Copeland, "Dot's All, Folks," *The Washington Post*, June 29, 2000, p. C1 and Leslie Walker, "The Short Story of the Web's Generation Ex," *The Washington Post*, January 11, 2001.
12. John A. Byrne, "The Fall of a Dot-Com," *Business Week*, May 1, 2000, pp. 150–59; Ambre S. Brown, "Have Web Site, Will Sell? Well, Maybe," *Philadelphia Inquirer*, February 19, 2000, pp. C1, C7; Melissa Campanelli, "E-Business Busters," *Entrepreneur*, January 2000, pp. 46–50; and Robert McGarvey, "Ding!" *Entrepreneur*, January 2001.
13. Alison Eadie, "Business File: Title or No Title, You Still Put In a Full Day" Management Matters, *Daily Telegraph*, February 3, 2000.
14. John Dodge, "Rise of Incubators Challenges Old Rules of Venture Capital," *The Wall Street Journal Interactive Edition*, February 29, 2000; Luisa Kroll, "Mad Hatchery Syndrome," *Forbes*, April 17, 2000, pp. 132–40; Alex Gove, "Entrepreneurs Should Be Wary of Incubators," *Red Herring*, March 2000, p. 86; Peter D. Henig, "And Now, Econets," *Red Herring*, February 2000, pp. 96–108; Katia Hetter, "Off-Stage Experiences Help Out Entrepreneurs," *Newsday*, January 11, 2001; Amy Wilson Sheldon, "Slow Down You Move Too Fast," *Fast Company*, February 1, 2001.
15. Cleary, "Incubators Nurture Tech Revolution," *Washington Times*, April 17, 2000, pp. D12–D14.
16. Ron Weinberg, "Business: Stumping for Customers," *Telephony*, June 5, 2000; Theresa Forsman, "Struggling Amid Prosperity," *The Record (Bergen County, NJ,)* March 26, 2000; Marci McDonald, "A Start-Up of Her Own," *U.S. News & World Report*, May 15, 2000; Kevin Ferguson, "Frontier: Features: Nothing Ventured," *Business Week*, July 10, 2000; and Elizabeth Freeman, "Here's How to Beat the Office Grind in the Virtual Business World, Conference Rooms Are Out; Coffeehouses Are In," *St. Louis Post-Dispatch*, July 9, 2000.
17. Brad Reagan, "Budding Entrepreneurs Can Learn Critical Skills in Class," *The Wall Street Journal Interactive Edition*, July 28, 1999; and J. Sharon Yee, "New UCLA Center to Aid Study of Information Economy," *University Wire*, February 7, 2000.
18. Jeff Sciortino, "The Origin of the Entrepreneurial Species," *Inc.*, February 2000, pp. 105–14.
19. John Grossman, "Money Hunt," *Sky*, February 2000, pp. 28–33 and Peter Kooiman, "On the Money," *Entrepreneur's Start-Ups*, January 2001.
20. Beth Brophy, "Venture Capital: Angels Who Hope to Make a Killing," *Business Week*, June 12, 2000; Sebastian Rupley, "Start-Ups Wanted," *PC Magazine*, February 8, 2000; "Seeking Capital Seeks to Help Find Funding for Entrepreneurs," *Electronic Advertising and Marketplace Report*, January 9, 2001.
21. Jane Easter Bahls, "Cyber Cash," *Entrepreneur*, March 1999, pp. 108–13; Michael Liedtke, "Women Firms Getting Venture Capital," *AP Online*, July 18, 2000; and Jim Hopkins, "Savings, Family, and Friends Among Top Investor Sources," *USA Today*, January 10, 2001.
22. David R. Evanson, "No Hot Air," *Entrepreneur*, May 2000, pp. 72–75.
23. D. M. Osborne, "Start-ups for Start-ups," *Inc.*, February 2000, pp. 23–26.

24. Timothy Long. "The Small Business Market: E-Commerce Accelerates," *Computer Reseller News*, March 1, 1999; and "Dell Unveils a Web-Hosting Service for Businesses," *Dallas Morning News*, February 23, 2000.
25. James Daly, "Over There," *Business 2.0*, January 23, 2001.

Chapter 7

1. "Big Company, Big Change," *Fast Talk*, May 2000, p. 86.
2. Cheryl D. Krivda, "E-Supply Chain," advertisement in *Fortune*, June 26, 2000, pp. 341ff.
3. Jenny C. McCune, "Becoming a Customer-Driven Company," *Beyond Computing*, May 2000, pp. 18–24.
4. Andrew Murr, "The New Age Boss," *Newsweek*, February 1, 1999, pp. 50–51.
5. Edward Iwata, "Despite the Hype, B2B Marketplaces Struggle," *USA Today*, May 10, 2000, pp. 1–2.
6. Nicholas G. Carr, "On the Edge," *Harvard Business Review*, May–June, 2000, pp. 118–25.
7. Charles Fishman, "Team-Work," *Fast Company*, April 2000, pp. 156–61.
8. Bob Thompson, "Customer Relationship Management," advertisement in *Business Week*, July 3, 2000, pp. 67ff.
9. Claire Ansberry, "Let's Build an Online Supply Network!" *The Wall Street Journal*, April 17, 2000, pp. B1, B10.
10. Christopher Bartlett and Sumantra Ghoshal, "Going Global," *Harvard Business Review*, March–April 2000, pp. 132–42.
11. Kevin Werbach, "Syndication," *Harvard Business Review*, May–June 2000, pp. 85–93.
12. Gary Hamel, "Reinvent Your Company," *Fortune*, June 12, 2000, pp. 99–118.
13. "United States of Diversity," *Fast Company*, July 2000, p. 280.
14. Daniel Goleman, "Leadership That Gets Results," *Harvard Business Review*, March–April, 2000, pp. 78–90.
15. Suzy Wetlaufer, "Organizing for Empowerment: An Interview with AES's Roger Sant and Dennis Bakke," *Harvard Business Review*, January–February 1999, pp. 111–23.
16. Alan M. Webber, "Why Can't We Get Anything Done?" *Fast Company*, June 2000, pp. 168–80.
17. Charles Fishman, "The Greener Cleaner," *Fast Company*, July 2000, pp. 54–56.

Chapter 8

1. Robert D. Hof, "Remember the Tortoise," *Business Week E.BIZ*, January 22, 2001, p. 66.
2. J. Stewart Black and Lyman W. Porter, *Management: Meeting New Challenges* (Upper Saddle River, NJ: Prentice-Hall, 2000), pp. 44–45.
3. Mark Henricks, "Span Control," *Entrepreneur*, January 2001, p. 97.
4. Chris Nolan, "Attention KMART Shoppers," *Smart Business*, February 2001, pp. 113–119.
5. Scott Kirsner, "Faster Company," *Fast Company*, May 2000, pp. 163–72.
6. "Wake-Up Call for HP," *Technology Review*, May–June 2000, pp. 94–100.
7. Cheryl D. Krivda, "E-Supply Chain," a special advertising section in *Fortune*, June 26, 2000, pp. 341ff.
8. Suzy Girard, "Extranet: If You Build One, Will They Come?," *Success*, December/January 2001, p. 42.
9. Jeffrey E. Christian, "Leading in a Team-Based Culture," *Beyond Computing*, May 2000, p. 10.
10. Almar Latour, "Ericsson Plan to Outsource Handsets," *The Wall Street Journal*, January 29, 2001, p. B8.
11. Erika Morphy, "Best Practices Made Perfect," *Global Business*, May 2000, pp. 60–63.
12. Gary McWilliams, "Motorola Joins Technology-Outsourcing Wave," *The Wall Street Journal*, June 1, 2000, p. B6. Sheridan Prasso, "Boeing Jettisons a Plant," *Business Week*, February 5, 2001, p. 14.
13. Jim Collins, "Level 5 Leadership," *Harvard Business Review*, January 2001, pp. 67–76.

Chapter 9

1. Howard Rudnitsky, "Changing the Corporate DNA, " *Forbes*, July 17, 2000, pp. 38–40.
2. Sheridan Prasso, "Slimming Down," *Business Week*, February 5, 2001, p. 14.
3. Mary Ellen Mark, "The New Fabric of Success," *Fast Company*, June 2000, pp. 252–70.
4. Kevin Voigt, "For Extreme Telecommuters, Remote Work Means Really Remote," *The Wall Street Journal*, January 31, 2001, pp. B1 & B7.
5. Linda Sandler, "A Genesis of Sorts, in Downtown Los Angeles," *The Wall Street Journal*, July 26, 2000, p. B12.
6. William M. Bulkeley, "Clicks and Mortar," *The Wall Street Journal*, July 17, 2000, p. R4.
7. David Dorsey, "Change Factory," *Fast Company*, June 2000, pp. 209–24.
8. Scott Thurm, "…Is a Call That Will Bolster Flextronics," *The Wall Street Journal*, January 29, 2001, p. B8.
9. Steven Kaplan and Mohanbir Sawhney, "E-Hubs: The New B2B Marketplaces," *Harvard Business Review*, May –June, 2000, pp. 97–103.
10. Ahmad Diba, "The B2B Boom: What's What," *Fortune*, May 15, 2000, pp. 142–43.
11. "Baldrige Award Winner Profile," *Quality Digest*, May 2000, p. 45.
12. Scott Madison Paton, "Transitioning to ISO 9001:2000," *Quality Digest*, March 2001, p. 4.
13. Jeanne Ketola and Kathy Roberts, "Product Realization," *Quality Digest*, May 2000, pp. 39–43.
14. Judith Evans, "Executive with a First-Class Vision," *Washington Business*, August 23, 1999, pp. 13–14; and Salina Khan, "Hotels Target Generation X," *USA Today*, February 10, 2000, pp. B1, B2.
15. Doug Tsuruoka, "Marriott, Hyatt Plan Own E-Room Service," *Investor's Business Daily*, May 9, 2000, p. A8.
16. J. Bradford Delong, "Estimating Growth Is a True Odyssey, "*Fortune*, June 26, 2000, pp. 62–64.
17. Curt Suplee, "Scientists Claim to Pinpoint Cerebral Source of Human IQ," *The Washington Post*, July 21, 2000, pp. A14, A15.
18. Kathleen Seiders, Leonard Berry and Larry G. Gresham, "Attention, Retailers! Is Your Convenience Strategy?" *Sloan Management Review*, Spring 2000, pp. 79–89.
19. "Air-Traveler Abuse," *The Washington Post*, July 25, 2000, p. A22.
20. Barbara McNurlin, "Will Users of ERP Stay Satisfied?," *MIT Sloan Management Review*, Winter 2001, p. 13.
21. Jerry Bowles, "How Digital Marketplaces Are Shaping the Future of B2B Commerce," *Forbes*, July 24, 2000, pp. 215ff.
22. Darnell Little, "Old MacDonald Has a Web Site," *Business Week E.BIZ*, May 15, 2000, pp. EB83–EB88.
23. Howard Rudnitsky, "Changing the Corporate DNA," *Forbes*, July 17, 2000, pp. 38–40.

Chapter 10

1. John van Maurik, "Yes, It's Really True. People Can Enjoy Their Jobs," *Independent on Sunday*, July 11, 1999, p. 3.
2. "The Real Meaning of Empowerment," *The Economist*, March 25, 2000; Sheila M. Pool, "Happy Workers Equals Happy Guests," *Atlanta Journal and Constitution*, June 25, 2000; and Matthew Boyle, "On the Job Happiness Index," *Fortune*, February 19, 2001.
3. Steve Lopez, "What You Need Is More Vacation!" *Time*, June 12, 2000, p. 8; Geoffrey Downey, "Happy Employees Increase Profits," *Computing Canada*, July 7, 2000; and Gordon Miller, "Most Workers Call Their Bosses 'Lousy'," *Denver Rock Mountain News*, January 7, 2001, p. 2G.
4. Tony Bonardi, "Psychologist Says He Knows Secrets of Motivation," news release, University Wire, August 17, 2000; Cass R. Sunstein, "The Human Variables," *The New Republic*, August 7, 2000; Mark Haynes Daniell, "Rapid Change Calls for New Model of Strategy," *Business Times*, August 21, 2000; and David Whitford, "Best Companies: A Human Place to Work," *Fortune*, January 8, 2001, p. 108.
5. Alan Kruglak, "Management Perspective: Motivating Your Employees," *Sound & Video Contractor*, April 1, 2000, and Alfie Kohn, *Punished by Rewards*, (Boston: Houghton Mifflin CA, 2001).

6. Geoffrey Colvin, "Capitalist Century: Managing in the Info Era," *Fortune,* March 6, 2000.

7. John A. Byrne, "The 21st Century Corporation: Back to the Future: Visionary vs. Visionary," *Business Week,* August 28, 2000, p. 210.

8. Michael A. Lev, "Recession Forcing Japanese to Rethink Business Methods," *Arizona Republic,* May 5, 1999, p. E5.

9. Demelza Baer, "Speaker Visits Northwestern U., Criticizes Japanese Business Structure," news release, University Wire, May 19, 2000 and Cait Murphy, "What's Up in Japan," *Fortune,* January 8, 2001, p. 46.

10. Robert Levering, Milton Moskowitz, Feliciano Garcia, and Matthew Boyle, "The 100 Best Companies to Work for in America," *Fortune,* January 8, 2001.

11. "Organizing for Empowerment: An Interview with AES's Roger Sant and Dennis Bakke," *Harvard Business Review,* January 1, 1999, p. 110.

12. David Nadler and Edward Lawler, "Motivation—a Diagnostic Approach," in *Perspectives on Behavior in Organizations,* ed. Richard Hackman, Edward Lawler, and Lyman Porter (New York: McGraw-Hill, 1977).

13. "Organizing for Empowerment," p. 110.

14. Ibid.

15. "Internal Relations Helps Airline Fly Higher," *PR News,* January 10, 2000 and Rachel S. Garron, "Increasing In-House Feedback," *InfoWorld,* January 29, 2001.

16. "Mustang Muscle Car Makes a Comeback," *Sunday Star Times (New Zealand),* April 4, 2000, p. 10 and Dave Moore, "Mustang Gets the Bullitt, *The Press,* January 13, 2001, p. 65.

17. Laura Trujillo, "For a Few Days, Phoenix Is a Mary Kay Place," *Arizona Republic,* January 21, 2000, p. B1.

18. Sharon Williams, "Generation Xers Dedicated but Know How to Have Fun," *Evening Post (Wellington, New Zealand),* April 12, 2000, p. 3; Ann Dickerson, "Couple Probes What Makes the Generations Tick," *Atlanta Journal and Constitution,* January 27, 2000, p. J5; John Eckberg, "Weighing Future of Work Force," *Gannett News Service,* May 31, 2000; Mark Memmott, "Reich Knows High Cost of Success," *USAToday,* January 8, 2001, and Jim Miller, "Motivation, Flexibility Key to Retaining GenX Workers," *The Arlington Morning News,* January 25, 2001.

19. Maria Mallory, "Platinum Rule Rules How to Meet Challenge of Generational Conflict," *Atlanta Journal and Constitution,* March 5, 2000, p. R1; Carla D'Nan Bass, "Seeking Insight into Work Force, Sonic Study Finds Kids Are All Right," *Dallas Morning News,* June 18, 2000, p. 12L; and Vicky Uhland, "Generations at Crossroads Boomers and Xers Butt Heads over Values in the Workplace," *Denver Rocky Mountain News,* February 6, 2000, p. 1J.

Chapter 11

1. Peter Cappelli, "A Market-Driven Approach to Retaining Talent," *Harvard Business Review,* January–February 2000, pp. 103–11.

2. Howard LaFranchi, "Retailoring in a Bluejeans Border Town," *Christian Science Monitor,* June 15, 1999, p. 1; and Steven H. Lee, "E-Powerment: Laid Off by Levi Strauss, Seamstress Sells Jeans Online," *Dallas Morning News,* July 12, 2000, p. 1D.

3. Nair Chendakera, "International: Motorola to Open R&D Centers in Two India Cities," *Electronic Engineering Times,* April, 3, 2000, p. 38.

4. "Unemployment Rate Cranks Down to 30-Year Low," *Dallas Morning News,* May 6, 2000, p. 2F and "Plenty of Work But Few to Do It," *The Evening Post,* January, 24, 2001, p. 13.

5. Steve DiMeglio, "Companies Warn High-Tech Worker Shortage Could Send Jobs Overseas," *Gannett News Service,* April 10, 2000, p. ARC.

6. "The Price of Illiteracy: Marketplace Cruel for the Unlearned," *Tampa Tribune,* June 26, 2000, p. 6 and Gary Massaro, "Learning a New Love," *Denver Rocky Mountain News,* January 12, 2001, p. 28A.

7. George J. Church, "To Work We Go: New People—Immigrants, Mothers, and the Old and the Young—Are Entering the Labor Force and Keeping the U.S. Economy Humming," *Time,* May 8, 2000, p. B23.

8. Spencer Rich, "Pensions: Again, a Boon for Boomers," *National Journal,* April 29, 2000 and Stephanie Armour, "More Firms Ask Retirees to Stay," *USA Today,* January 4, 2001.

9. Mark Schlinkmann, " 'Living Wage' Proposal for City Probably Would Help Few Workers," *St. Louis Post-Dispatch,* May 7, 2000, p. C2 and "Living-Wage Law Makes Big Difference to Alexandria Workers," *The Washington Times,* January 1, 2001, p. D7.

10. Terrance Hurley, Peter Oraze, James Kliebenstein, and Dale Miller, "Work Environment, Time Off Lead Job Satisfaction List," *National Hog Farmer,* June 1, 2000.

11. Timothy Aeppel, "Young and Old See Technology Sparking Friction on Shop Floor," *The Wall Street Journal,* April 7, 2000, p. 1; Abhi Raghunathan, "Ready for a Break: Employers Use Vacations to Lure, Retain Workers," *Newsday,* July 22, 2000, p. A06; Laura Koss-Feder, "What Benefits Would Perk Up Company's Employment Policy?" *Newsday,* March 26, 2000, p. 14; and Ira Mathia and Marian Salzman, "The Future of Work," *CIO,* March 1, 2000, pp. 196–200.

12. Elizabeth Chang, "Flexibility Can Cure Problems with Sick Pay," *St. Louis Post-Dispatch,* May 11, 2000, p. C7 and Michelle Conlin, Joseph Weber, A.T. Palmer and Liz Garone, "Jobs: How Long Can Services Pick Up the Slack?" Business Week, February 19, 2001, pp. 34–35.

13. Edward Iwata, "Staff-Hungry Tech Firms Cast Exotic Lures: Pet Insurance, BMWs, Day Care Are among Perks," *USA Today,* February 1, 2000, p. 1B and Susan T. Port, "Staff Leasing Firms Help Small Businesses Compete," *The Palm Beach Post,* January 27, 2001, p. 2D.

14. Arthur A. Fletcher, "The Capitalist Century: Business and Race: Only Halfway There," *Fortune,* March 6, 2000, p. F76.

15. Amy Martinez, "Money Won't Buy Loyalty Anymore," *Palm Beach Post,* July 30, 2000, p. 1F and Scott Thurm, "No-Exit Strategies," *The Wall Street Journal,* February 6, 2001, pp. A1 & A8.

16. Edward Wakin, "Recruiting the Right People," *Beyond Computing,* May 2000, pp. 54–55.

17. Janet Moore, "Fingerhut Chairman Lansing Leaving as Part of a Corporate Reshuffling—Analyst Says His Style Didn't Fit," *Minneapolis Star Tribune,* March 24, 2000, p. 3D; and Dawne Shand, "Talent Scouts," *Computerworld,* April 10, 2000, pp. 52–54.

18. Ted Samson, "Tools of the Recruitment Trade," *InfoWorld,* July 31, 2000 and David Raths, "Driving Home Recruitment," *InfoWorld,* February 5, 2001.

19. Cora Daniels, "To Hire a Lumber Expert, Click Here," *Fortune,* April 3, 2000, pp. 267–70 and John Kador, "Re-recruitment: Keep Your People From Walking Out the Door," *InfoWorld,* January 15, 2001.

20. Carol Hymowitz, "Managers Often Miss the Promising Talent on Their Own Staffs," *The Wall Street Journal,* May 9, 2000, p. B1.

21. Joan Hamilton, "The Panic over Hiring," *Business Week,* April 3, 2000, pp. EB130–32 and Daniel Lyons, " 'A' Is for Effort," *Forbes,* March 6, 2000; Jeff Rubin, "Forget Stock Options, Referrals Are the Recruiter's Latest Weapon," *The Wall Street Journal,* August 1, 2000, p. B16; and Michelle Bearden, "Casting the Net," *The Tampa Tribune,* January 6, 2001, p. 4.

22. Alan S. Kay, "E-Business: Recruiters Embrace the Internet—Employers Tout the Lower Cost, Wider Reach, and Targeting Ability of Online Job Boards," *Information Week,* March 20, 2000, p. 72.

23. Anita Bruzzese, "Whether You Flip Hamburgers for a Living or Hold a . . .," news release, Gannett News Service, May 28, 1999, p. ARC and "Log on to the Virtual Reality of Top-Flight Job Opportunities," Birmingham Post, February 6, 2001, p. 23.

24. Stephanie Armour, "Training Takes Front Seat at Offices," *USA Today,* January 19, 1999, p. 6B.

25. George Donnelly, "Recruiting, Retention, and Returns," *CFO,* March 2000, pp. 68–76.

26. Megan Santosus, "The Visible Employee," *CIO,* January 15, 2000, p. 44.

27. Samuel Elkin, "How to Establish a Drug-Free Workplace Program," *Occupational Hazards,* March 1, 1999; Linda Wertheimer and Robert Siegel, "Analysis: Despite Federal Efforts to Encourage Workplace Drug Testing, Many Small Business Are Reluctant to Screen Prospective Employees," *All Things Considered,* (National Public Radio broadcast), February 25, 2000; and Fergal Dowling, "Just the Job: Breath Tests Could be Legal," *Birmingham Post,* January 20, 2001, p. 22.

28. Debrorah Giattina, "HR Outsourcerers," *Industry Standard,* May 8, 2000, p. 262 and Loretta W. Prencipe, "Review Temporary Workers' Status," *InfoWorld,* January 8, 2001.

29. Liese Hutchison, "Avoid the Summer Staffing Blues," *St. Louis Commerce,* July 2000, p. 16.

30. Gene Koretz, "The Temp Surge Isn't Temporary," *Business Week,* February 21, 2000, p. 25.

31. Kirstin Downey Grimsley, "Temporary Workers Exploited, Group Says," *Washington Post,* May 24, 2000, p. E1.

32. "News and Advice for Working with Temporary Employees," InfoWorld, January 8, 2001.

33. Don Mogelefsky, "Extended Reach," *Incentive,* June 2000, p. 15 and Steve Alexander, "Program Your Staff," *InfoWorld,* January 29, 2001.

34. Chern Yeh Kwok, "A New Hire's First Impression Foreshadows Tenure," *St. Louis Post-Dispatch,* July 13, 2000, p. C1.

35. Cathy Olofson, "Let Outsiders In, Turn Your Insiders Out," *Fast Company,* February–March 1999, p. 46.

36. "MCI World Com Honored by CIO Magazine as Top 50 Internet/Intranet Site,"PR Newswire, July 13, 1999; and Margie Semilof, "MCI WorldCom Mantra: We Do More Than Just Sell Pipes," *Computer Reseller News,* April 17, 2000, p. 7.

37. Monica Sambataro, "Just-in-Time Learning," *ComputerWorld,* April 3, 2000, p. 50 and Arlene Levinson, "Online Classes Serve Millions," *AP Online,* January 22, 2001.

38. Teresa L. Ebert and Mas'ud Zavarzadeh, "E-Education Is Really Job Training," *Newsday,* March 26, 2000, p. A27 and Arlene Levinson, "Online Classes Serve Millions," *AP Online,* January 22, 2001.

39. Thomas E. Weber, "The New Dress Code for Corporate Training," *The Wall Street Journal Interactive Edition,* January 31, 2000.

40. Carol Orsag Madigan, "But What Have You Done for Them Lately?" *Business Finance,* June 2000, pp. 81–86 and John W. McCurry, "Management: New Generation of Leaders Pace Textiles," *Textile World,* January 1, 2001.

41. Mary Beth Grover, "Preshrunk," *Forbes,* March 6, 2000, pp. 82–84; Rochelle Garner, "Coach Works," *CIO,* February 1, 2000, pp. 114–22; Mary Beth Ingram, "Coaching for Better Customer Support," *Customer Relationship Management,* May 2000, pp. 36–37; and Anne Fisher, "Executive Coaching," *Fortune,* February 19, 2001, p. 250.

42. Glen Creno, "More Companies Serving Up Training/Corporate 'Colleges' Take Lead from McDonald's Hamburger University," *Arizona Republic,* May 16, 1999, p. AZ4; and Carla Power, "McParadox," *Newsweek International,* July 10, 2000, p. 12.

43. Richard Pastore, "Virtual Mentor," *CIO,* January 15, 2000, pp. 99–103 and Jennifer Reingold, "Want to Grow as a Leader? Get a Mentor," *Fast Company,* January 1, 2001, p. 58.

44. Polly Schneider, "Are You a Bad Boss?" *CIO,* April 1, 2000, pp. 141–54.

45. Laura Koss-Feder, "It's Still Who You Know," *Time,* March 22, 1999.

46. Dick Kirschten, "The Workforce: Kicking Glass," *Government Executive,* February 1, 2000, p. 16 and Rana Foroohar, "Gender Politics in the Age of Dot-Coms," *Newsweek International,* January 8, 2001, p. 19.

47. "A Slice of the Pie: Corporate Diversity/Resource Guide," *Newsday,* April 8, 2000, p. J11; and Todd Datz, "Equity?" *CIO,* January 15, 2000, pp. 74–84.

48. Dean Takahashi, "Ethnic Network Helps Immigrants Succeed," *The Wall Street Journal Interactive Edition,* July 28, 1999.

49. Anita Bruzzese, "On the Job," *Gannett News Service,* February 25, 2000, p. ARC; Julie Newberg, "Cash to Cars Incentives Increasingly Innovative," *Arizona Republic,* February 29, 2000, p. W11; Geoffrey James, "Staffing Challenges Call for New Breed of IT Manager," *ComputerWorld,* March 27, 2000, p. 38; Joanne Y. Cleaver, "The Best Way to Show Appreciation to Employees Isn't Always a Raise," *Ticker,* May 2000, p. 100; Sherwood Ross, "Workers Are Rejecting Some Key 1990s Pay Plans," *St. Louis Post-Dispatch,* January 3, 2000, p. BP4; and Robert McGarvey, "What's It Worth?" *Entrepreneur,* March 2000, p. 22.

50. C. James Novak, "Proceed with Caution When Paying Teams," *HR Magazine,* April 1997, pp. 73–77.

51. Perry Pascarella, "Compensating Teams," *Across the Board,* February 1997, pp. 16–23.

52. Julie Deardorff, "To Lure Workers, Companies Offering Some Unusual Perks," *Philadelphia Inquirer,* May 15, 2000, p. D2; and Johnathan Rabinovitz, "Free Bagels and a Venture Fund," *Industry Standard,* May 15, 2000, p. 77.

53. "Taking Care of Fuzzy Friends," *CFO,* June 2000, p. 27; and Edward Iwata, "Staff-Hungry Tech Firms Cast Exotic Lures," *USA Today,* February 1, 2000, p. B1 and Robert Levering and Milton Moskowitz, "The 100 Best Companies to Work For," *Fortune,* January 8, 2001, p. 148.

54. Michael Schrage, "Cafeteria Benefits? Ha! You Deserve a Richer Banquet," *Fortune,* April 3, 2000 and Stephen Barr, "Intrepid Bush Aids Are Searching for Savings in Employee Health Program," *The Washington Post,* January 25, 2001, p. B2.

55. Marilyn Gardner, "Childless Adults Ask, 'Why Am I Minding the Kids?' " *Christian Science Monitor,* March 2, 2000, p. 21 and Matthew Boyle, "Gearing Down: How to Cut Perks Without Killing Morale," *Fortune,* February 19, 2001, p. 241.

56. Julie Hyman, "Studies of American Workplaces Show Trends in Habits," *Washington Times,* August 21, 2000, p. D6 and Elaine St. James, "More Employees Offer Flexible Work Policies," *The Washington Times,* January 30, 2001, p. E2.

57. Winston Wood, "Work Week," *The Wall Street Journal,* April 11, 2000, p. A1.

58. Donna Fenn, "Personnel Best," *Inc.,* February 2000, pp. 75–83.

59. Ellen Ullman, "Kiss a Teleworker Today," *Home Office Computing,* January 2000, pp. 107–8 and John Murawski, "Boca Might Set Example for Cutting Traffic," *The Palm Beach Post,* February 1, 2001, p. 18.

60. Nancy B. Kurland,"Telework: The Advantages and Challenges of Working Here, There, Anywhere," *Organizational Dynamics,* October 1, 1999.

61. Neil Strother, "Is Your Job Goin' Mobile?" *ZDNet AnchorDesk,* June 14, 2000.

62. "HOC's Virtual Roundtable," *Home Office Computing,* April 2000, pp. 52–55; Joanne Cleaver, "Take Your Kids to Work Day," *Home Office Computing,* February 2000, pp. 100–3 ; and Pamela Kruger, "Finding a Family-Friendly Boss," *Parenting,* February 1, 2001, p. 55.

63. "Telework: More Than Just a Perk," *Home Office Computing,* March 2000, p. 97.

64. Daniel Eisenberg, "Visions 21/Our Work, Our World: What Will Our Offices Look Like?" *Time,* May 22, 2000, p. 82.

65. Nancy B. Kurland, "Telework: The Advantages and Challenges of Working Here, There, Anywhere," *Organizational Dynamics,* October 1, 1999; and Mark Henricks, "Musical Chairs," *Entrepreneur,* April 1999, pp. 77–79.

66. Sue Shellenbarger, "An Overlooked Toll of Job Upheavals: Valuable Friendships," *The Wall Street Journal,* January 12, 2000, p. B1 and Ben W. Johnson, "Outsourcing: Big and Getting Bigger," *National Real Estate Investor,* January 1, 2001.

67. Steve Ulfelder, "Signs of Defection," *ComputerWorld,* April 3, 2000, pp. 42–43; and "Keeping Your Star Performers," *ComputerWorld,* April 3, 2000, p. 44.

68. Dave D. Buss, "Be Ready When Employees Walk out the Door," startup.wsj.com, June 30, 1999.

69. Steven C. Bahls and Jane Easter Bahls, "Playing Fair," *Entrepreneur,* April 2000, pp. 135–37.

70. "Assessing Protection for the Disabled," *The Washington Post,* January 3, 2001, p. E1.

71. Gene Koretz, "Did Maternity Leave Law Help?" *Business Week,* April 17, 2000, p. 36.

Chapter 12

1. Kathleen Melonakos, Shelia Denne, and S. Benjamin Prasad, "Time to Separate Schools and State," *Christian Science Monitor,* March 31, 2000, p. 10 and Kevin G. DeMarrais, "Unions Hold the Key to the Future of Grand Unions Workforce," *The Record,* February 4, 2001, p. B8.

2. Walter Williams, "Heavy-Handed Threats to Liberty," *Washington Times*, January 13, 2000, p. A13 and Leigh Strope, "Union Leaders Face New Challenges," *AP Online*, February 13, 2001.

3. Paul Pringle, "L.A.'s 'Bandit factories' Operate outside the Law," *Arizona Republic*, March 12, 2000, p. D1 and Mark Luce, "New Gilded Age Provides Rich Stories of Mighty Money," *The Atlanta Journal and Constitution*, January 21, 2001, p. E5.

4. Bruce Bartlett, "Economic Transformation," *Washington Times*, January 5, 2000, p. A12.

5. Richard Leiby, "Anarchy Anyone? With Protests Looming Here This Month, the Anti-Capitalist League Gets into Shape by Kicking Some Ball," *Washington Post*, April 4, 2000, p. C1.

6. Rachel Cohen, "Archives Help Finance University of Maryland Research Projects," *University Wire*, June 16, 2000.

7. See the AFL–CIO website at <www.aflcio.org>.

8. Charles Babington and Matthew Vita, "President Begins China Trade Push: Tough Fight Predicted in the House," *Washington Post*, March 9, 2000, p. A1 and "China to Enter Into WTO Soon," *Asia Info Services*, January 9, 2001.

9. "NAFTA Impact on North America Mostly a Plus," *Reuters Business Report*, April 10, 2000 and Thomas Sowell, "Economic Outages," *The Washington Times*, January 27, 2001, p. A12.

10. Donald M. Davis, "Lease Language: Arbitration of Disputes," *Shopping Center World*, May 21, 2000.

11. Shawn Young, "Verizon Feels the Pain of Change: Earnings Miss Target, Strike Adds Tension," *USA Today*, August 9, 2000, p. 3B and Silja J.A. Talvi, "Unions Take to the Web," *The Christian Science Monitor*, January 29, 2001, p. 14.

12. Mark, Boslet, "Workers of the New World Unite," *Industry Standard*, August 14, 2000, pp. 58–59.

13. Peter Elstrom, "Needed: A New Union for the New Economy," *Business Week*, September 4, 2000, p. 48.

14. Paul D. Standohar, "Labor Relations in Basketball: the Lockout of 1998–99," *Monthly Labor Review*, April 1, 1999 and Gary Haber, "Face Off," *The Tampa Tribune*, February 5, 2001, p. 8.

15. "Labor Gets Louder: CFO Forum," *Institutional Investor*, June 2000, p. 36.

16. Tom Incantalupo, "US Airways Makes Plans for Strike," *Newsday*, March 24, 2000, p. A8.

17. Joseph H. Foegen, "Temp Workers: Ready for Unions?" *Business & Economic Review*, July–September 2000, pp. 28–30 and Silja J.A. Talvi, "Labor's New Front Lines," *The Christian Science Monitor*, January 29, 2001, p. 11.

18. Richard Whitmire, "Gore, Bush Carving Out New Federal Education Roles," *Gannett News*, July 1, 2000, p. ARC.

19. Thomas B. Edsall, "Unions See Nader as Leverage on Trade," *Washington Post*, June 22, 2000, p. A6.

20. See the AFL–CIO website at <www.aflcio.com>.

21. David Welch, "Hard at Work under Saturn's Hood," *Business Week*, February 21, 2000, p. 118.

22. Peter Kafka, "Boffo Bucks," *Forbes*, March 20, 2000, pp. 196–214.

23. Joan Lublin, "Who Made the Biggest Bucks," *The Wall Street Journal*, April 6, 2000, p. R1 and Ken Wright, "Money Player," The *Washington Times*, January 27, 2001, p. C1.

24. Joann S. Lublin, "Net Envy," *Business Week*, April 6, 2000, p. B1.

25. Michael K. Ozanian, "Upward Bias," *Forbes*, May 15, 2000, pp. 210–15 and Peter Coy, "Funny Money, or Real Incentive?" *Business Week*, January 15, 2001, p. 71.

26. Rachel Emma Silverman, "Heads I Win, Tails I Win," *The Wall Street Journal*, April 6, 2000, p. R4 and Gene Kortz, "Money Can't Buy a Loyal CEO," *Business Week*, February 5, 2001. p. 30.

27. Lisa Bannon, "Mattel Proxy Says Jill Barad Received Severance Package of about $50 Million," *The Wall Street Journal*, May 1, 2000, p. B27.

28. Sharon Walsh Washington, "No Year-End Bonus for Eisner; Disney Did Not Meet Earnings Target," *Washington Post*, January 6, 2000, p. E3 and Gary Gentle, "Walt Disney Chief Receives Bonus," *AP Online*, January 12, 2001.

29. Charles Whalen, "Closing the Pay Gap," *Business Week*, August 28, 2000, p. 38 and David Moberg, "Labor is Still Under the Gun," *Newsday*, January 9, 2001, p. A35.

30. Ronald Bird, "Unions Take to the Streets: Movement of the Past Looks for a Cause," *Washington Times*, April 12, 2000, p. A21 and Lorna Duckworth, "Women Need 'Fire in Their Bellies' for Equal Pay," *Independent*, January 17, 2001, p. 10.

31. Ellen Paris, "A Woman's Wage," *Entrepreneur*, March 2000, p. 32.

32. Diana Furchtgott-Roth, "Equal or Equivalent?" *Investor's Business Daily*, May 11, 2000, p. A24 and "Wage Gap Not Just a Matter of Nickels and Dimes," *U.S. Newswire*, February 2, 2001.

33. Katia Hetter, "A White Man's World: Diversity in Management/EEOC Still on Guard/Defying Critics, Federal Watchdog Touts Success," *Newsday*, April 15, 2000, pp. A06 and "Justice Thomas Comes Out Swinging," *United Press International*, February 14, 2001.

34. Jeffrey Rosen, "Sexual Harassment: a Solution," *New Republic*, June 12, 2000 and Alessandra Rizzo," Court Rules on Sex Harassment Case," *AP Online*, January 25, 2001.

35. "Work Pays More Than Welfare," *Washington Times*, April 30, 2000, p. B5 and Marilyn Weber Serafini, "Welfare: Till Death (Or Uncle Sam) Do Us Part," *National Journal*, February 3, 2001.

36. Don Fernandez, "Day Care Center Groundbreaking Draws the Governor," *Atlanta Journal and Constitution*, April 3, 2000, p. J1.

37. See the Haemonetics Corporation's website at <www.haemonetics.com>.

38. Greg Halverson, "Coming to Terms with Long-Term Care," *Christian Science Monitor*, January 13, 2000, p. 11.

39. Ibid.

40. George Johnson, "Combination Drug Buys Time but Is Not a Cure" *St. Louis Post-Dispatch*, September 9, 1999; and John Carey, "Rethinking the Aids Arsenal," *Business Week*, July 17, 2000.

41. Joe Barton, "Members of Congress Should Take the Lead in War on Drugs," *Arlington Morning News*, May 9, 2000, p. 9A and Bill Boll, "War Isn't the Right Approach for Stopping Drug Use," St. Louis Post-Dispatch, January 6, 2001.

42. "Worker Drug Use on the Decline," *Minneapolis Star Tribune*, August 13, 2000, p. 1D and "Traffic Brings Failures of War on Drugs to a Wide Audience," *University Wire*, January 12, 2001.

43. Janie Magruder, "Violence: A Growing Occupational Hazard," *Arizona Republic*, March 1, 2000, p. E1 and "How to Spot, Deal with Potentially Dangerous Worker," *USA Today*, February 6, 2001, p. 3A.

44. Michael Arndt and Aaron Bernstein, "The Workplace: Labor: From Milestone to Millstone," *Business Week*, March 20, 2000, p. 120.

45. David Gowrie, "Sharing a Stake in Their Destiny," *The Record* (Bergen County, NJ), November 17, 1999.

Chapter 13

1. Kristina Blachere, "Satisfaction Guaranteed," *Smart Business*, March 2001, pp. 126-131.

2. Thomas H. Davenport, Jeanne G. Harris and Ajay K. Kohli, "How Do They Know Their Customers So Well," *Sloan Management Review*, Winter 2001, pp. 63–73.

3. Michael Krauss, "Filter Out Archaic, One-Size-Fits-All Strategies," *Marketing News*, March 27, 2000, p. 9.

4. Greg Jaffe, "Target Market," *The Wall Street Journal*, February 14, 2001, pp. A1 & A10.

5. Alan R. Andreasen, Rob Gould and Karen Gutierrez, "Social Marketing Has a New Champion," *Advertising Age*, February 7, 2000, p. 38.

6. Amy Kover, "Why the Cereal Business Is Soggy," *Fortune*, March 6, 2000, p. 74.

7. Charles Newman, "Online Testing Rated," *Advertising Age*, May 8, 2000, p. 64.

8. Mary Jo Hatch and Majken Schultz, "Are the Strategic Stars Aligned for Your Corporate Brand?," *Harvard Business Review*, February 2001, pp. 129–34.

9. Courtney Fingar, "Supply Chain," *Global Business*, January 2001, pp. 28–32.

10. Jonathan Kaufman, "The Omnipresent Persuaders," *The Wall Street Journal*, January 1, 2000, p. R26.

11. James Heckman, "Turning the Focus Online," *Marketing News*, February 28, 2000, p. 15.

12. Ruth L. Williams, "Four Smart Ways to Run Online Communities," *Sloan Management Review,* Summer 2000, pp. 81–91.
13. Cristina Gair, "Who Needs FedEx, Anyway?" *Home Office Computing,* May 2000, p. 20.
14. Peter Coy, "The Creative Economy," *Business Week,* August 28, 2000, pp. 76–82.
15. Shari Caudron, "Consumer Revenge," *Business Finance,* June 2000, pp. 36–40.
16. William M. Bulkeley, "Clicks and Mortar," *The Wall Street Journal,* July 17, 2000, p. R4.
17. E.S. Browning, "Stocks Rise, Then Fall on Greenspan Talk," *The Wall Street Journal,* February 14, 2001, p. C1.
18. Eleena De Lisser, "Online Retailers Slice and Dice Niches Thinner Than Julienne Fries," *The Wall Street Journal,* November 29, 1999, pp. B1 and B5.
19. Frederick F. Reichheld and Phil Shefter, "E-Loyalty," *Harvard Business Review,* July–August 2000, pp. 105–13.
20. Jerry Bowles, "How Digital Marketplaces Are Shaping the Future of B2B Commerce," *Forbes* (advertisement), July 24, 2000, pp. 215ff.
21. Mark Henricks, "More Than a Fling," *Entrepreneur,* September 2000, pp. 124–27.
22. Laurie Freeman, "Top 10 Trends for 2001 Rooted in B-to-B Reality," *B to B,* January 8, 2001, pp. 22 & 24.

Chapter 14

1. Keith Naughton, "Tired of Smile-Free Service?" *Newsweek,* March 5, 2000, pp. 44–45.
2. Stefan Thomke, "Enlightened Experimentation," *Harvard Business Review,* February 2001, pp. 67–73.
3. Aixa M. Pascual, "The Whopper Plays Catch-Up," *Business Week,* May 25, 2000, pp. 98–100.
4. Robert Frank, "Big Boy's Adventures in Thailand," *The Wall Street Journal,* April 12, 2000, pp. B1, B4.
5. "Building the New Basics of Branding," *Advertising Age,* May 15, 2000, pp. 40, 42.
6. Rebecca Gardyn, "I'll Have What He's Having," *American Demographics,* July 2000, p. 22.
7. Mercedes M. Cordona, "Trendsetting Brands Combat Knock-Offs," *Advertising Age,* August 21, 2000, pp. 20, 24.
8. Jack Neff, "New Dial CEO Baum Will Stress Marketing," *Advertising Age,* August 14, 2000, p. 8.
9. "Brands In Trouble - In Demand," *Advertising Age,* January 8, 2001, p. 4.
10. David J. Lipke, "Product by Design," *American Demographics,* February 2001, pp. 38–41.
11. Dana Blankenhorn, "How to Manage Your Online Campaign," *BtoB,* April 24, 2000, pp. 17–20.
12. "The Power of Smart Pricing," *Business Week,* April 10, 2000, pp. 160–64.
13. Mark Henricks, "On the House," *Entrepreneur,* June 2000, pp. 114–17.
14. Indrajit Sinha, "Cost Transparency: The Net's Real Threat to Prices and Brands," *Harvard Business Review,* March–April 2000, pp. 43–50.
15. Paul Nunes, Diane Wilson, and Ajit Kambil, "The All-in-One Market," *Harvard Business Review,* May–June 2000, pp. 19–20.
16. Walter Baker, Mike Marn and Craig Zawada, "Price Smarter on the Net," *Harvard Business Review,* February 2001, pp. 122–27.
17. Akshay R. Rao, Mark E. Bergen, and Scott Davis, "How to Fight a Price War," *Harvard Business Review,* March–April 2000, pp. 107–16.
18. Kristina Blachere, "Satisfaction Guaranteed," *Smart Business,* March 2001, pp. 126-131.

Chapter 15

1. Courtney Fingar,"Are you World Ready?" *Global Business,* January 2001, pp. 28-30.
2. Carol Patton, "B-to-B Marketing 2001," *BtoB,* January 8, 2001, p. 17.
3. Richard Karpinski, "E-marketplaces Come Full Circle," *BtoB,* January 8, 2001, p. 23.

4. Anthony B. Perkins, "When We're Down on the Internet, Up Pops the Evernet," *Red Herring,* January 16, 2001, pp. 19-20.
5. Charles Fishman, "But Wait, You Promised . . . ," *Fast Company,* April 2001, pp. 114–118.
6. Amy Borrus, "The Broad Backlash Against E-Tailers," *Business Week,* February 5, 2001, p. 102.
7. William M. Bulkeley, "Cut Down to Size," *The Wall Street Journal,* March 9, 2000, pp. A1, A8.
8. Gwen Moran, "Adventures in Shopping," *Entrepreneur,* January 2000, p. 38.
9. Penelope Rowlands, "Reinventing Retailing,", *Worth,* April 2001, pp. 114–18.
10. Sandra Keeley, "Setting Up an E-Commerce Site Isn't So Cheap—Or So Easy," *The Philadelphia Inquirer,* November 7, 1999, p. E3.
11. Ellen Neuborne, "It's the Service, Stupid," *Business Week e.biz,* April 3, 2000, p. EB 18.
12. Kara Swisher, "A Matchmaker for 'Bricks' and 'Clicks,' " *The Wall Street Journal,* March 13, 2000, pp. B1, B10.
13. Tobi Elkin, "Best Buy Takes Cue from Retail Shops," *Advertising Age,* March 6, 2000, p. S8.
14. Allanna Sullivan, "From a Call to a Click," *The Wall Street Journal,* July 17, 2000, p. R30.
15. Bill Fahrenwald, Dean Wise, and Diane Glynn, "Supply Chain Collaboration, *Business Week,* March 26, 20012000, pp. 265ff.
16. Rivka Tadjer, "Breaking the Chain," *Red Herring,* September 2000, pp. 424–28.
17. John Dodge, "A Customer-Service Mantra Can Rebound on E-Tailers," *The Wall Street Journal Interactive Edition,* January 18, 2000.
18. Donna De Marco, "Shoppers Trade Carts for Clicks," *The Washington Times,* March 5, 2001, pp. D10–D11.
19. "interBiz Goes Logistical," *Global Business,* February 2001, p. 18.

Chapter 16

1. Luc Hatlestad, "Branding," *Red Herring,* January 2000, pp. 172–73.
2. Kate Fitzgerald, "All Eyes Zero On Emerging T-Commerce," *Advertising Age,* January 15, 2001, p. 512.
3. Tobi Elkin, "Interacting with ITV: Marketers Are Tuning In," *Advertising Age,* January 15, 2001, pp. S2-S4.
4. Pamela Houghtaling, "Mobilizing Your Sales Force," *Beyond Computing,* April 2000, pp. 31–35.
5. Eric Fisher, "Just 3 Dot-Coms on Super Bowl," *The Washington Times,* January 24, 2001, pp. B7 & B9.
6. Jon Fine, "Cross-media Catches Fire," *Advertising Age,* October 25, 2000, pp. S2 & S4.
7. Vera Gibbons, "Smoothie Operators," *SmartMoney,* April 2000, pp. 156–58.
8. "RotoZip: You Have to See It to Believe It," *Marketing News,* March 27, 2000, p. 17.
9. Paul C. Judge, "Will Online Ads Ever Click?," *Fast Company,* March 2001, pp. 182-191.
10. Peter Schwartz, "Internet Advertising Is Going to Change. But How?" *Red Herring,* February 2000, pp. 76–78.
11. Jacqueline Emigh, "Many Hands Make Site Work," *Sm@rt Reseller,* February 16, 2000.
12. Lisa Vaas, "Earn Customers' Love," *PC Week,* February 13, 2000.
13. Dana James, "Hit the Bricks," *Marketing News,* September 13, 1999, pp. 1, 15.
14. Kelly Shermach, "As PR Changes, the More it Stays the Same," *Marketing News,* March 12, 2001, p. 4.
15. Kenneth Neil Cukier, "Crisis in PR," *Red Herring,* May 2000, pp. 207–18.
16. Stephanie Thompson, "Marketers Embrace Latest Health Claims," *Advertising Age,* February 28, 2000, p. 20.
17. Roger O. Crockett, "Penny Pinchers' Paradise," *Business Week E.BIZ,* January 22, 2001, p. EB12.
18. "Boosting Sales Through In-Store Sampling Programs," *Incentive,* August 2000, p. 85.
19. Stephanie Thompson, "Pepsi Favors Sampling over Ads for Fruit Drinks," *Advertising Age,* January 24, 2000, p. 8.

20. Steve Jurvetson, "What Exactly Is Viral Marketing?" *Red Herring*, May 2000, pp. 110–12.
21. Laurel Merlino, "Bulls Eye!," Smart Business, April 2001, pp. 130–135.
22. Don E. Schultz, "ARF's New Model Rooted in Old Ideas," *Marketing News*, September 25, 2000, p. 8.
23. John Ellis, "The Wireless Technology Gap," *Fast Company*, July 2000, pp. 302–6.

Chapter 17

1. Reg Gale, "There's a Community Spirit on the Net," *Newsday*, February 6, 2001.
2. Don Tapscott, "Minds over Matter," *Business 2.0*, March 2000, and Rache Boddy, "Farmers Slow on the IT Uptake," *Waikato Times*, January 27, 2001, p. 18.
3. Craig K. Dillon, "Be Nimble," *CIO*, April 15, 2000, p. 190; and Allan E. Alter, "Knowledge Management's 'Theory-doing Gap,' " *Computerworld*, April 10, 2000, p. 33.
4. John Storck and Patricia A. Hill, "Knowledge Diffusion through 'Strategic Communities,' " *Sloan Management Review*, Winter 2000, pp. 63–74, and Mike Heck, "K-Station Portal Brings New Life to Business Information," *Info World*, February 5, 2001.
5. Steve Mott, "Winning One Customer at a Time," *Business 2.0*, March 2000 and Ann Orubeondo and Mario Apicella, *InfoWorld TestCenter*, February 5, 2001.
6. Greg Farrell, "Online Time Soars at the Office," *USA Today*, February 18, 2000, p. 1A, and Dan Beyers, "Internet Use Slipped Late Last Year, *The Washington Post*, February 22, 2001, p. E10.
7. Jeffrey Davis, "The Net Impact," *Business 2.0*, January 2000, and Janet Kornblum, "Net Gets Picked Over TV, But Use Is Leveling Off," *USA Today*, February 6, 2001.
8. Ann Harrison, "Corporate Security Begins at Home," *Computerworld*, March 6, 2000, p. 14, and Bill Husted, "Firewalls Still Your Best Bet For Security," *The Palm Beach Post*, February 11, 2001.
9. Mark Hall, "Intranet Developers Say Systems, Security Top Priorities," *Computerworld*, March 6, 2000, p. 28, and Ian Howell, "Doing Projects Online Boosts Your Bottom Line," *Electrical Constuction and Maintenance*, January 1, 2001.
10. Frank J. Derfler Jr., "Virtual Private Networks," *PC Magazine*, January 4, 2000, pp. 146–48; Eric Greenberg, "VPNs and Windows 2000," *PC Magazine*, January 18, 2000, p. 139; Frank J. Derfler Jr. and Gary Gunnerson, "Ready, Set, Retool," *PC Magazine*, March 7, 2000, pp. 142–52; Steve Ulfelder, "Virtual Private Networks Made Easy," *Computerworld*, March 6, 2000, p. 80; Frank Derfler Jr., "Internet Infrastructure," *PC Magazine*, February 22, 2000, p. 124; and Jim Barthold, "Networking the Internet," *Telephony*, February 5, 2001.
11. Dana James, "Broadband Horizons," *Marketing News*, March 13, 2000, pp. 1, 9; Dave Johnson, "The Fastest Towns in America," *Home Office Computing*, April 2000, pp. 46–50; Alan Cohen, "High-Speed Browsing," *PC Magazine*, January 18, 2000, p. 32; David A. Harvey, "Broadband—Anywhere and Everywhere," *Home Office Computing*, January 2000, p. 22; David Haskin, "The Need for Speed," *Home Office Computing*, January 2000, p. 40; and "Broadband Bulletin," *Cablefax Daily*, January 3, 2001, and Jennifer Jones, "Cable Cuts Out a Slice of the Broadband Pie," *Info World*, January 29, 2001.
12. Yael Li-Ron, "This Will Change Everything," *Newsweek*, September 18, 2000, and Bob Low, "Twelve Months That Shook Cyberspace," *Daily Record*, January 6, 2001, pp. 38-39.
13. Josh Bozarth, "Companies Showcase Internet 2 Technologies at Oklahoma State U.," *University Wire*, March 8, 2000.
14. Sue Zeidler, "Napster Changes Tune to Overcome Network Overload," *Reuters Business Report*, March 23, 2000, and Ahron Shapiro, "Life in the Fast Lane," *Jerusalem Post*, February 9, 2001, p. 4.
15. Thomas E. Weber, "Instant Messages Aren't Just for Chat," *The Wall Street Journal Interactive Edition*, April 11, 2000, and Chad Hammond, "The Intelligent Enterprise," *Info World*, February 5, 2001.

16. Jesse Berst, "B2B? That's Like, So Last Month," *ZDNet AnchorDesk*, April 13, 2000, and Michael Vizard, "Top Ten Technology Trends for 2001," *Info World*, January 8, 2001.
17. Jane Linder and Drew Phelps, "Call to Act," *CIO*, April 1, 2000, pp. 166–74; Lester C. Thurow, "The Wealth of Knowledge," *CIO*, January 1, 2000, pp. 81–86; and Michelle Bearden, "Casting the Net," *The Tampa Tribune*, January 6, 2001, p. 4.
18. Meg Mitchell, "Law in Order," *CIO*, April 1, 2000, pp. 158–62; Carol Hildebrand, "Case Files: United Technologies," *CIO*, February 1, 2000, pp. 134–36; Carol Hildebrand, "It's a Jungle in There," *CIO*, April 15, 2000, p. 42; Rosemary Faya Prola, "Knowledge Management Nets Big Rewards," *Smith Business*, Winter 2000, pp. 6–13, and Tim Fielden, "A Knowledge Management State of Mind," *Info World Test Center*, February 5, 2001.
19. John Webster, "Getting to Know You," *CIO*, February 15, 2000, pp. 150-56; Fraser Rolff, "Down-time Vital for Sharing Knowledge," *New Zealand Infotech Weekly*, January 29, 2001, p. 5; and Victoria Murphy, 'You've Got Expertise,' *Forbes Magazine*, February 5, 2001, p. 132.
20. Peter Cochrane, "Hard Drive Powering Down to Quantum Level," *Daily Telegraph*, March 2, 2000, p. 12, and "The Intel Economy?" *Newsweek International*, January 29, 2001, p. 22.
21. Harold Goldberg, "Gimme That! The Latest Gotta Have Stuff," *Entertainment Weekly*, February 9, 2001; Brice Scheschuk, "My Pipe Dream," *Maclean's*, February 12, 2001; and Ernest Holsendolph, "Internet Growing Without PC Use," *The Atlanta Constitution*, February 21, 2001.
22. Rhonda L. Wickman, "The Always Onslaught," *Wireless Review*, January 31, 2001; Christopher Dickey, "The Cold Facts," *Newsweek International*, January 15, 2001; Tim Larimer, "Internet A La I-Mode," *Time*, March 5, 2001; and "Wireless Web History in the Making," *Wireless Today*, March 1, 2001.
23. Bill Howard, "Thin Is Back," *PC Magazine*, April 4, 2000, pp. 168–82, and Barry Kipnis, "Technology 2001: A Glimpse to the Future," *National Real Estate Investor*, January 1, 2001.
24. Peter Burrows, "Technology on Tap," *Business Week*, June 19, 2000, pp. 74–84; and Barry Nance, "Down on the (Server) Farm," *Computerworld*, April 3, 2000, pp. 68–70.
25. Robert Lau, "Flexible Infrastructure: The Key for ASPs," *Business Times*, August 16, 2000, and Ben W. Johnson, "Outsourcing: Bigger and Getting Better," *National Real Estate Investor*, January 1, 2001.
26. Wayne Walley, "Making the Right Move," *Global Telephony*, February 1, 2001 and Tyler Hamilton, "Workplace Revolution," *The Toronto Star*, February 26, 2001.
27. Jennifer Hagendorf, "Everdream Touts SMB Subscription Service," *Computer Reseller News*, February 24, 2000; Alfred Poor, "Why Own When You Can Rent?" *PC Magazine*, March 7, 2000; Jonathan Burton, "Putting Their Money Where the Future Is," *New York Times*, March 29, 2000; Bronwyn Fryer, "PC Subscription Services," *Upside Today*, March 31, 2000; and "Bulletproof PCs," *Business 2.0*, January 2000.
28. Mike Hogan, "Thin Is In," *Entrepreneur*, February 2000, pp. 50–53.
29. Sakina Spruell, "Training an IT Nation," *Black Enterprise*, February 2000, pp. 69–70 and Sheila Poole, "Innovator Cites Education's Value," *The Atlanta Journal and Constitution*, January 28, 2001.
30. "Adaptive Technology: Seeing It Their Way," *CIO*, February 1, 2000, p. 50; Joanne Cleaver, "Homeward Bound," *Home Office Computing*, March 2000, pp. 68–71; and Deborah K. Dietsch, "Universal Design is No Barrier to Style," *The Washngton Post*, February 22, 2001, p. H1.
31. Jonathan Coleman, "Is Technology Making Us Intimate Strangers?" *Newsweek*, March 27, 2000, p. 12, and Anne Meyers, "Telework Requires Extensive Preparation," *The Atlanta Journal and Constitution*, January 4, 2001, p. 3.
32. Tom Davenport, "In the Year 2525," *CIO*, January 1, 2000, pp. 44–49, and Kemba J. Dunham, "Execs Seek to Cut Back Workday," *The Arizona Republic*, January 22, 2001, p. D1.
33. Jeffrey Kluger, "Extortion on the Internet," *Time*, January 24, 2000.
34. Ann Harrison, "Survey: Cybercrime Cost Firms $266M in '99," *Computerworld*, March 27, 2000, p. 28, and "Commission Unveils

Legislative Proposal to Fight Cybercrime," *Tech Europe*, February 2, 2001.

35. Elinor Abreu, "Leave It to the Experts," *Industry Standard*, April 10, 2000, p. 120, and Jeff Smith, "Onesecure Launches New System Platform Making Protecting Computers Easier, Cheaper," *Denver Rocky Mountain News*, January 29, 2001, p. 11B.

36. Ted Bridis, "Hackers Become Security Consultants," *AP Online*, January 6, 2000.

37. Robin Marshall, "Update for Virus-Buster," *The Press*, January 11, 2001, p. 15; Doug Stanley, "Worm Digging Its Way Through E-mail," *The Tampa Tribune*, January 22, 2001, p. 3; and Robin Marshall, "Hunting for the Snow White Virus," *The Press*, February 1, 2001, p. 17.

38. Bill Machrone, "Law and Technology Collide," *PC Magazine*, April 18, 2000, p. 93; "EU Seeks to Clamp Down on Drug Trafficking on the Internet," *European Report*, February 14, 2001; "Analysts Worry Over Internet Regulations," *The St. Petersburg Times*, February 13, 2001; and "Gulf Countries Urged to Adopt E-Commerce Regulations," *Xinhug*, February 27, 2001.

39. David Crowe, "Cutting Edge Security," *Wireless Review*, January 1, 2001.

40. "Watch Your Cookies," *International Herald Tribune*, February 12, 2001.

41. Sebastian Rupley, "You, Under the Microscope," *PC Magazine*, January 18, 2000, p. 30; Elizabeth Weise, "A New Wrinkle in Surfing the Net," *USA Today*, March 21, 2000, p. 3D; Daintry Duffy, "You Know What They Did Last Night," *CIO*, April 1, 2000, p. 188; and Cass Rains, "Cookies Leave Bad Taste Behind," *University Wire*, January 16, 2001.

42. Patricia Keefe, "Privacy: Fight for It," *Computerworld*, March 27, 2000, p. 36; John Buskin, "Our Data, Ourselves," *The Wall Street Journal*, April 17, 2000, pp. R34, R36; "The Privacy Debate," *The Wall Street Journal Interactive Edition*, April 11, 2000; Mindy Blodgett, "E-Business and Privacy for All?" *CIO*, April 15, 2000, pp. 101–4; and "How to Keep Electronic 'Big Brother' At Bay," *The Toronto Star*, January 8, 2001.

43. Gary Strauss, "When Computers Fail," *USA Today*, December 7, 1999, P. A2; "Local Power Bill Doubled by Computer Glitch," *The Edmonton Sun*, February 8, 2001, p. 14.

44. Margie Hyslop, "Checks in Mail to Crime Victims, Minus Interest," *Washington Times*, January 11, 2000; "Computer Scores Students 0," *The Evening Post*, January 13, 2001, p. 8; and Joe-suk Yoo, "World Cup Ticket Sales Hit Glitch," *AP Online*, February 15, 2001.

45. Strauss, "When Computers Fail."

46. Meg Mitchell, "Children of the Revolution," *CIO*, January 1, 2000, pp. 159–68.

47. U.S. Department of Commerce, "The Emerging Digital Economy II," June 1999, and "Fed Survey Shows Slow Growth But No Recession," *Minneapolis Star Tribune*, January 18, 2001, p. 4D.

48. "Demand for Information Tech Workers to Exceed Supply," *Reuters*, April 10, 2000, and Sean McKibbon, "It Pays to Work in Hi-Tech," *The Ottawa Sun*, January 24, 2001, p. 46.

49. Bronwyn Fryer, "Payroll Busters," *Computerworld*, March 6, 2000, p. 82, and Kenneth Bredemeier, "What Slump? Forecast Still Bright for Tech," *The Washington Post*, February 5, 2001, p. E3.

50. Sharon Watson, "The Best Jobs," *Computerworld*, April 3, 2000, pp. 46–48, and Daniel McGinn and Keith Naughton, "How Safe is Your Job?" *Newsweek*, February 5, 2001, p. 36.

Chapter 18

1. Elizabeth MacDonald, "Are Those Revenues for Real?" *Forbes*, May 29, 2000, pp. 108–10, and Doug Innis, "Warning Signs," *Soybean Digest*, January 1, 2001.

2. Tom Philpott, "Accountable Accountants," *Ticker*, July 2000, p. 12, and Susan Hart, "Accounting, Consulting Firms Form HA&W Mescom," *The Atlanta Constitution*, February 23, 2001, p. F4.

3. Elizabeth MacDonald, "Arthur Andersen Sets Up Fund to Take in Web Start-Ups," *The Wall Street Journal Interactive*, January 24, 2000, and "Counting Cost of the Name Game," *Birmingham Post*, January 10, 2001, p. 8.

4. Stephen Barr, "Breaking Up the Big Five," *CFO*, May 2000, pp. 57–64, and Roger Trapp, "Anderson Courts Digital Solutions for a Competitive Edge," *Independent*, February 7, 2001, p. 4.

5. Justin Schack, "Bending the Rules," *Institutional Investor*, August 2000, p. 36, and Hope Yen, "Former Rite Aid Execs in Fraud Suit," *AP Online*, February 8, 2001.

6. Sara Rosenberg, "CPAs Turn RIAs," *Ticker*, May 2000, p. 17.

7. "Audit Methods Need Updating, " *Birmingham Post*, January 12, 2001, p. 24, 8 and Matthew Benjamin, "When Earnings Aren't: Spotting Financial Follies," *U.S. News & World Report*, February 26, 2001, p. 65.

8. "Auditors' Investing Questioned," *Tampa Tribune*, January 7, 2000, p. 1.

9. Alan M. Webber, "New Math for a New Economy," *Fast Company*, January–February 2000, pp. 214–24.

10. Larry Downes, "The Secret Balance Sheet," *Industry Standard*, June 12, 2000, pp. 297–300, and "In Brand Business, Cowboys are MVP," *The Dallas Morning News*, February 2, 2001, p. 10.

11. Webber, "New Math for a New Economy," p. 214; John Duckers, "Critics Deny That New Name Delivers the Goods," *Birmingham Post*, February 9, 2001, p. 27; and Mary Jo Hatch and Maj Ken Schultz, "Are the Strategic Stars Aligned for Your Corporate Brand?" *Harvard Business Review*, February 2001, pp. 129-134.

12. Albert S. Golbert, "Principles of International Taxation," *World Trade*, August 2000, pp. 42–45, and John Duckers, "Quarterly Reports Will Add Pressure," *Birmingham Post*, February 16, 2001, p. 24.

13. Lori Rohik Pfeiffer, "Staying Afloat," *Black Enterprise*, May 2000, p. 50.

14. Carol Holzberg, "Keep It Coming," *Home Office Computing*, May 2000, pp. 100–1, and Mark Krieger, "Bookkeeping Basics," *BE Radio*, January 1, 2001.

15. Stewart McKie, "A Balance Sheet for Online Accounting," *Business Finance*, July 2000, pp. 75-80, and Jennifer Jacobs, "Ready for Self-Service Accounting? February 21, 2001.

16. Andy Kessler, "Creative Accounting.com," *The Wall Street Journal*, July 24, 2000, p. A26.

17. Robert J. Samuelson, "A High-Tech Accounting," *Newsweek*, April 3, 2000, p. 37, and Madhavi Acharya, "Adopt U.S. GAAP," *The Toronto Star*, February 14, 2001.

18. Jeffrey Kutler, "Analysis Made Easy, Via the Web," *Institutional Investor*, June 2000, p. 30, and David Armstrong, "Moving Into the PC Age, " *The Press*, January 30, 2001, p. 14

19. Steward McKie, "Zooming In on Business Events," *Business Finance*, June 2000, pp. 75-80, and K.W. Meyers, "Accountants Platable to Restaurant Industry," *Denver Rocky Mountain News*, February 11, 2001, p. 3G.

20. Mike McNamee, "The PC vs. the CPA," *Business Week*, January 31, 2000, pp. 120–21, and Albert B. Crenshaw, "Accounting With No Loss of Goodwill," *The Washington Post*, January 29, 2001, p. E3.

21. John J. Xenakis, "Shopping Spree," *CFO*, March 2000, pp. 87–102, and Warren Marett, "Coming of Age for Replacement Software," *The Press*, February 27, 2001, p. 15.

22. Timothy J. Mullaney, "Show Me a Real Live CPA," *Business Week e.biz*, February 7, 2000, pp. 92–94, and Kate Hilpern, "Your Finger on the Pulse," *Independent*, March 4, 2001, p. 10.

23. David Pratt, "Monitor Your Financial Vital Signs," *Beef*, August 1, 2000, and Mariko Hayashibra, "Accounting Rule Unnerves Healthy Japanese Insurers," *Reuters*, February 21, 2001.

24. Gene Koretz, "Little Threat of Crushing Debt," *Business Week*, July 10, 2000, p. 34.

Chapter 19

1. Eric Krell, "Lessons from the New Economy," *Business Finance*, July 2000, pp. 27–33.

2. Jill Andresky Fraser, "Where Has All the Money Gone?" *Inc.*, April 2000, pp. 101–10, and Janin Friend, "Batten Down the Hatches," *Business Week*, February 5, 2001, p. F8.

3. Marcia Vickers, "Chief Financial Officer: Up from Bean Counter," *Business Week*, August 28, 2000, pp. 118–20.

4. Stephen Barr, "The Outlook. What Does the Next Century Hold for Corporate Finance?" *CFO*, January 2000, pp. 44–54.

5. Jeffrey Kutler, "Analysis Made Easy, Via the Web," *Institutional Investor*, June 2000, p. 30, and "KPMG Offers Cost-Effective Approach to Managing Risk," *Business Times*, February 19, 2001.

6. Jane Bryant Quinn, "Curing Dysfunctional Financial Planning," *Washington Post*, January 9, 2000, p. H2, and "Let's Hear It! Debt-Free 2003," *The Washington Post*, January 7, 2001, p. H1.

7. Tad Leahy, "The Shift to Forecasting Overdrive," *Supplement to Business Finance*, September 2000, pp. 10–12, and "WebMart: Command Data Speaks Site Language," *Concrete Products*, January 1, 2001.

8. Brian O'Connell, "Beyond Budgeting and Forecasting: New Tools, Strategies Making an Old Job Easier," *Business Finance*, July 2000, pp. S2–S8.

9. Thor Valdmanis, "Citigroup Buys No. 1 Finance Firm; $31.1 Billion in Stock Creates Consumer-Lending Behemoth," *USA Today*, September 7, 2000, p. 1B, and Christine Dugas, "Debt: Pay It Down, Switch to Lower Rates," *USA Today*, January 5, 2001, p. 3B.

10. Rivette and Kline, "Discovering New Value in Intellectual Property," *Harvard Business Review*, January–February 2000, p. 54.

11. Ron MacLean, "What Business Is Amazon.com Really In?" *Inc.*, February 2000, pp. 86–88, and "Amazon.com's New Strategy," *Book Publishing Report*, February 5, 2001.

12. D. M. Osborne, "Start-Ups for Start-Ups," *Inc.*, February 2000, pp. 23–26, and "Low Interest Rates Won't Help Troubled Firms Get Loans," *The Washington Times*, February 5, 2001, p. D13.

13. "SEC, State Regulators Target Bogus Sales of Promissory Notes," *The Wall Street Journal*, June 2, 2000, p. C15.

14. Julie Carrick Dalton, "Start-up's Epitaph: One Product Beats Three," *Inc.*, February 2000, p. 28, and Anne Tergesen, "Accounting: The Ins and Outs of Cash Flow," *Business Week*, January 22, 2001, p. 102.

15. Ilan Mochari, "Who Needs a Bank Anyway?" *Inc.*, February 2000, pp. 129–30, and Moe Russell, "Alternative Financing Makes Sense," *Soybean Digest*, January 1, 2001.

16. Cynthia E. Griffin, "GE Whiz," *Entrepreneur*, January 2000, p. 32.

17. Mochari, "Who Needs a Bank Anyway?"

18. "GE Capital Japan Business On Track," *Reuters Business Report*, February 7, 2001.

19. Joshua Harris Prager, "Small Businesses Find Cash Infusions Harder to Secure," *The Wall Street Journal*, May 23, 2000, p. B2.

20. Robert Clow, "Commercial Paper Goes Virtual," *Institutional Investor*, April 2000, p. 28.

21. "Merck Opens New Target in AIDS Drug," *USA Today*, January 27, 2000, p. D1.

22. Cynthia Griffin, "A Good Rejection," *Entrepreneur*, March 2000, p. 28, and Jim Hopkins, "Where to Find the Money to Make Your Dream a Business," *USA Today*, January 10, 2001, p. 6B.

23. "Adventurous Venture Capital," *The Economist*, May 27, 2000, and "Venture Capital Spurs Faster Growth at Startups-Study, *Reuters Business Report*, January 30, 2001.

24. Gene Koretz, "Where Venture Capital Ventures," *Business Week*, February 7, 2000, p. 30., and Nicholas Johnson, "Venture Firms Make Big Bets on Telecom," *The Washington Post*, February 28, 2001, p. G8.

25. Jim Evans, "The Content Quandary," *Industry Standard*, April 3, 2000, pp. 88–89, and Jon Schwartz, "Venture Capital Firm Follow Techies Inland," *USA Today*, February 5, 2001, p. 4B.

26. Bill Spindle, "Japan Becomes a Mecca for Venture Capitalists," *The Wall Street Journal*, February 24, 2000, p. A13, and "Equit Markets Key to Economic Growth," *The Toronto Star*, March 3, 2001.

27. Cynthia E. Griffin, "Girls Just Wanna Have Funds," *Entrepreneur*, March 2000, p. 38, and Pradnya Joshi, "Connecting Women to Venture Capital Dough, *Newsday*, February 5, 2001, p. 4B.

28. Steven Lipin, "Venture Capitalists 'R' Us," *The Wall Street Journal*, February 22, 2000, pp. C1–C18, and Caroline Hubbard, "Trickle-Down Affects Dot.com Dynamics, "*The Atlanta Constitution*, January 24, 2001, p. C7.

29. Eric J. Adams, "Surfing for Venture Capital," *World Trade*, May 2000, pp. 68–71, and "Venture Capital Search: Careful Planning Needed," *Business Times*, February 8, 2001.

30. Jacquelyn Lynn, "What's the Plan?" *Business Start-Ups*, March 2000, pp. 48–53, and Vincent Ryan, "A New Standard for IPOs," *Telephony*, January 8, 2001.

31. "Viacom Earnings Surge, but Stock Slumps," *Reuters*, February 16, 2000, and Harry Berhowitz, "Viacom Lone Bidder," *Newsday*, January 22, 2001, p. A41.

32. Gene Koretz, "Little Threat of Crushing Debt," *Business Week*, July 10, 2000, p. 34.

Chapter 20

1. Eric Krell, "Lessons from the New Economy," *Business Finance*, July 2000, pp. 28–33.

2. Paul M. Sherer and Carrick Mollenkamp, "Bank of America Aspires to Be a Big Investment Banker," *The Wall Street Journal*, February 16, 2000, p. C1, and Lucy Baker, "Goldman Triumphs In Merger Rankings Table," *Independent*, January 5, 2001, p. 17.

3. Jonathan Hoenig, "No Respect," *Business Start-Ups*, March 2000, p. 41.

4. Richard H. Gamble, "Why Bonds Aren't Boring," *Business Finance*, September 2000, pp. 57–64, and Jo-Ann Johnson, "PaineWebber Analyst Recommends Bonds," *The Tampa Tribune*, February 10, 2001, p. 1.

5. Debra Sparks, "Bonds Step into the Limelight," *Business Week*, June 26, 2000, pp. 235–36, and Chris Goodmacher, "Bonds An Option Instead of Stocks During Economic Slowdowns," *University Wire*, February 26, 2001.

6. William P. Barrett, "The Real College Scorecard," *Forbes*, February 7, 2000, p. 30, and Walter Updegrave, "Investing 101: The Ratings Game," *Money*, January 1, 2001, p. 59.

7. Joan Warner, "Bonds: Bond Investors Go to Extremes," *Business Week*, March 20, 2000, p. 142, and Mara Der Hovanesian, "Can Bond Funds Do It Again?" *Business Week*, February 5, 2001, p. 72.

8. Donald Jay Korn, "Convertible Funds Can Protect Portfolios from Market Storms," *Ticker*, March 2000, pp. 62–64, and Jonathan Stempel, "Convertible Bond Investors Balk at Newfangled Issues," *Reuters*, February 15, 2001.

9. Jonathan Hoenig, "Stock It to Me," *Business Start-Ups*, February 2000, p. 37, and "Dividend Yield a Key Component of Capital Growth," *The Toronto Star*, January 14, 2001.

10. Karen Hube, "More Dividends Go the Way of the Dinosaur," *The Wall Street Journal*, February 24, 2000, p. R6.

11. Robert J. Samuelson, "Where the Money Flows," *The Washington Post*, September 27, 2000, p. A23, and Sandor Peto, "Matav Falls Demise For Hungary Bourse," *Reuters*, February 22, 2001.

12. Maria Trombly, "SEC OKs All-Electric Stock Exchanges," *Computerworld*, March 6, 2000, p. 24, and "NYSE Trades Cheaper Than Nasdaq," *Newsday*, January 8, 2001, p. A38.

13. "MyWeb Inc.com, to Trade on the AMEX: Leading Asian Internet Portal Will Move Off of OTC Bulletin Board," *Business Wire*, March 10, 2000

14. NASDAQ website <www.nasdaq.com>, and Albert B. Crenshaw, "NYSE Edges Nasdaq on Prices," *The Washington Post*, January 9, 2001, p. E2.

15. Huw Jones, "Nasdaq Europe Set for First Quarter 2001 Launch," *Reuters Business Report*, January 14, 2000, and William Echikson, "This Beachhead Isn't Much to Land On," *Business Week International*, February 12, 2001, p. 56.

16. A. Stoley, "Nasdaq's Pan-European Platform for IPO's," *Global Technology Business*, February 2000, p. 16.

17. "NASDAQ: The World in Its Hands," *The Economist*, May 6, 2000, and Albert B. Crenshaw, "SEC Approves New Trading System For Nasdaq," *The Washington Post*, January 11, 2001, p. E1.

18. Linda Stern, "There Are Ways to Legally Win with Insider Trading," *St. Louis Post-Dispatch*, August 14, 2000, p. BP8, and Denise McNabb, "Insider Trading Query Surprises Chairman," *The Dominion*, January 31, 2001, p. 17.

19. Megan Barnett, "Net Stock Fraud, without the Net," *The Industry Standard,* March 27, 2000, p. 73, and "Four Face Civil Action on Alledger Insider Trading," *The Press,* March 5, 2001, p. 20.

20. John Carey, "Stockbrokers Still No.1 with Investors," *Business Week,* January 31, 2000, p. 8.

21. Margaret Popper, "Online Investing: Brokers: Brokers Clicks of the Trade," *Business Week,* May 22, 2000, pp. 154–58, and Huw Jones, "Days of Many Trade-Only E-Brokers Seem Numbered," *Reuters,* February 28, 2001.

22. Mark A. Mowrey, "The Habits of Ameritraders," *The Industry Standard,* March 20, 2000, p. 180, and Emily Thornton, "Why E-Brokers Are Broker and Broker," *Business Week,* January 22, 2001, p. 94.

23. Randall Smith, "Web Trading Is Going Upscale as Big Players Join the Fray," *The Wall Street Journal,* March 9, 2000, p. C22.

24. Jonathan Burton, "E-Investing," *Investment Advisor,* March 2000, pp. 125–28, and Charles Zehren, "Trading Expo's New Sentiment," *Newsday,* February 20, 2001, p. A55.

25. Jeff Schlegel, "Trading: How Much Broker Do You Really Need?" *Individual Investor,* March 2000, pp. 79–84, and Borzou Daragahi, "A Hype-Free Look At What's Next For Online Investing, Banks, And Insurance," *Money,* March 1, 2001, p. 129.

26. Daniel Fisher, "Credentialer to the World," *Forbes,* February 21, 2000, p. 94.

27. David Rynecki, "Market Madness: What the Hell Is Going On?" *Fortune,* April 3, 2000, pp. 102–18, and Carol Vinzant And Steven Pearlstein, "Bear Sightings On Wall Street; Some Analysts Foresee Lower Lows," *The Washington Post,* March 1, 2001, p. A1.

28. David Nicklaus, "It's Not Hip, but the OTC Market Serves Its Members Well," *St. Louis Post-Dispatch,* July 31, 2000, p. 10, and "Interest On Penny Stocks Rekindled," *Business Times,* March 5, 2001.

29. Michael Schroeder, "SEC Studies Brokers' Failure to Disclose Stock Limit Orders," *The Wall Street Journal,* March 17, 2000, p. C16, and Christopher H. Schmitt, "How Penny Pricing is Pounding Investors," *Business Week,* January 15, 2001, p. 74.

30. Jeffrey M. Laderman and Amy Barrett, "Mutual Funds: What's Wrong?" *Business Week,* January 24, 2000, pp. 66–72.

31. Linda Stern, "Socially Responsible Investing Jumps 82 Percent in Two Years," *St. Louis Post-Dispatch,* January 10, 2000, p. BP8, and Jeff Nash, "The Ultimate Mutual Fund Guide 2001/Ethical Funds," *Money,* February 1, 2001, p. 131.

32. Amy Debra Feldman, "Mutual Fund Leaders Explore Future Frontiers," *Ticker,* April 2000, p. 30.

33. Eli Guro, "Retooling the Schooling," *Ticker,* January 2000, pp. 16–20, and "Advisers Face New Standards," *The Toronto Star,* February 24, 2001.

34. Gary Halverson, "For Growth with Stability, the Game Is Bonds," *Christian Science Monitor,* June 26, 2000, p. 13, and Jonathan Stempel, "Junk Bond Returns Soar. So Do Junk Bond Defaults," *Reuters Business Report,* February 13, 2001.

35. Marilyn Cohen, "Junkyard Armor," *Forbes,* February 7, 2000, p. 204, and Jonathan Stempel, "Junk Bond Rally Stalls, Mutual Funds See Outflows," *Reuters Business Report,* March 2, 2001.

36. Paul M. Sherer and Gregory Zuckerman, "Fund Managers Analysts Predict Bullish Market in Junk Bonds," *The Wall Street Journal,* July 26, 2000, p. C1, and Clint Willis, "Funds: The Other Bond Funds — Junk," *Reuters Business Report,* February 1, 2001.

37. Fred Vogelstein, Paul Sloan, and Anne Kates Smith, "In Hock for Hot Stocks," *U.S. News & World Report,* April 17, 2000, p. 36, and Eric Tyson, "Weigh Risk of Buying Stocks On Margin," *The Washington Times,* February 14, 2001, p. B11.

38. Anne Tergesen, "Dealing with Risk," *Business Week,* January 17, 2000, pp. 102–4, and Eric Tyson, "Buying On Margin Often Not A Good Idea," *The Arizona Republic,* February 15, 2001, p. 4.

39. Marcia Vickers, Jeffrey M. Laderman, Geoffrey Smith, Rich Miller, and Laura Cohn, "Is the Party Over?" *Business Week,* April 17, 2000, pp. 40–49, and Brian Kelleher, "With Tech Burnout, Main Street Shuns Wall Street," *Reuters Business Report,* March 2, 2001.

40. Greg Ip and Susan Pulliam, "A Day of Margin Calls and Bargain Hunting Whipsaws the Markets," *The Wall Street Journal,* April 5,

2000, pp. A1–A8, and Stephanie N. Mehta, "Can Bernie Bounce Back?," *Fortune,* January 22, 2001, p. 84.

41. Joseph Weber, "The Pits Are Becoming a Relic," *Business Week,* March 6, 2000, p. 156, and "E-Trade Japan To Offer Online Broking Via Palm PDA," *Reuters,* February 2, 16-2001.

42. Andrew Osterland, "Wall Street Wired," *CFO,* February 2000, pp. 35–42, and Philip Thornton, "Strong UK Demand Boosts Deutsche Borse IPO," *Independent,* February 5, 2001, p. 19.

43. Guy Halverson, "Stocks Priced Down to the Decimal," *Christian Science Monitor,* September 5, 2000, p. 19, and Carol Vinzant, "Wall Street Taking Another Look At Decimals," *The Washington Post,* February 13, 2001, p. E1.

44. Sandra Sugawara, "The Debut of Decimal Trading," *Washington Post,* August 27, 2000, p. H1, and Amy Baldwin, "Nasdaq Ready For Decimals," *AP Online,* February 22, 2001.

45. Jacob Schlesinger and Nicholas Kulish, "A Century of Booms, and How They Ended," *The Wall Street Journal,* February 1, 2000, pp. B1–B14, and Andrew Leckey, "There's No Right Time And No Wrong Time To Play The Markets," *The Washington Times,* February 22, 2001, p. B9.

46. Marcia Vickers and Gary Weiss, "Wall Street's Hype Machine: It Could Spell Trouble for Investors," *Business Week,* April 3, 2000, pp. 113–26, and "SEC: Online Trading Needs Monitoring," *AP Online,* January 25, 2001.

Chapter 21

1. "Figuratively Speaking," *Endless Vacation,* May–June 2000, p. 14.

2. T. J. Stiles, "As Good as Gold?" *Smithsonian,* September 2000, pp. 106–17.

3. Richard Linnett, "More Marketers Turn to Bartering," *Advertising Age,* February 19, 2001, pp. 1, 32.

4. Robert X. Cringely, "Meet Your New Banker," *Worth,* December/January 2001, pp. 51–52.

5. Melynda Dovel Wilcox, "A Chip off the Old Card," *Kiplinger's,* June 2000, pp. 26–28.

6. Mindy Belz, "Is It Only Money?" *World,* March 3, 2001, p. 24.

7. Christopher Cooper, "Euro's Drop Is Hardest for the Smallest," *The Wall Street Journal,* October 2, 2000, p. A21.

8. James L. Rowe Jr., "What Goes On behind the Doors of the Federal Reserve," *The Washington Post,* February 10, 1999, pp. H1, H4.

9. Sara Garlick and Michelle Andrews, "What's in It for Us?" *Smart Money,* January 2000, pp. 71–72.

10. Martin Mayer, "On the Slopes of Vesuvius," *Bloomberg Personal Finance,* March 2000, pp. 33–36.

11. Heather Timmons, "Online Banks Can't Go It Alone," *Business Week,* July 31, 2000, pp. 86–87.

12. Janet Bigham Bernstel, "Convenience You Can Bank On," *Access Magazine,* January 21, 2001, pp. 8-9.

13. Sarah Rose, "The Truth about Online Banking," *Money,* April 2000, pp. 115–22.

14. Carrick Mollenkamp, "Old-Line Banks Advance in Bricks-vs.-Clicks Battle," *The Wall Street Journal,* January 21, 2000, pp. C1, C2.

15. "You Want Fries with That?" *Kiplinger's,* October 2000, pp. 27–28.

16. Jeffrey McKinney, "More Bank for the Buck," *Black Enterprise,* May 2000, pp. 130–38.

17. Albert B. Crenshaw, "Accounting for Checks' Popularity," *The Washington Post,* January 14, 2001, p. H2.

18. Alan Zeichick, "Smart Cards Explained," *Red Herring,* January 16, 2001, pp. 82-83.

19. Wilcox, "A Chip off the Old Card."

20. Patrice D. Johnson, "Kids and Money," *Money,* December 2000, p. 215.

21. Rich Miller and Laura Cohn, "Seattle without the Tear Gas?" *Business Week,* April 17, 2000, p. 55.

22. Michael M. Phillips, "World Bank Rethinks Strategy for Poor," *The Wall Street Journal,* September 13, 2000, p. A2.

23. Rich Miller, "Does Anyone Love the IMF or World Bank?" *Business Week,* April 24, 2000, pp. 46–47.

24. Allan Meltzer, "A Blueprint for IMF Reform," *The Wall Street Journal,* March 8, 2000, p. A22.

25. Robert J. Barro, "If We Can't Abolish the IMF, Let's at Least Make Big Changes," *Business Week,* April 10, 2000, p. 28.

Chapter 22

1. Jeremy Kahn, "Is Harvard Worth It?" *Fortune,* May 1, 2000, pp. 201–04.

2. Ivan Cintron, "The Art of Savvy Budgeting," *Black Enterprise,* May 2000, pp. 77–80.

3. Paul Katzeff, "Time Is Key Ingredient in Your Nest Egg," *Investor's Business Daily,* May 11, 2000, p. B1.

4. Derek T. Dingle, "Getting Started," *Black Enterprise,* January 2000, pp. 61–66.

5. Kimberly Lankford, "Insurance Made Easy," *Kiplinger's,* October 2000, pp. 82–87.

6. Howard Rudnitsky, "Showing New Life," *Bloomberg Personal Finance,* July–August 1999, pp. 59–65.

7. Janelle Erlichman, "Renter's Insurance: It Keeps You Covered," *The Washington Post,* September 14, 2000, pp. H1, H8.

8. Janet Bamford, "Changes in the Fine Print," *Bloomberg Personal Finance,* October 2000, pp. 106–9.

9. Gerda Gallop-Goodman, "Retire With Style," *American Demographics,* August 2000, pp. 12–15.

10. Niles Howard, "Build the Perfect Retirement Plan," *Inc.,* September 2000, pp. 97ff.

11. Ibid.

12. Mark Schwanhausser, "Financial Planning Widens," *Philadelophia Inquirer,* April 11, 2000, pp. C1 and C4.

13. Sandra Block, "Financial Planners Abound; Trick Is Finding Good One," *USA Today,* September 19, 2000, p. 3B.

14. Tom Fetzer, "Never Say Die," *Success,* December/January 2001, p. 60.

Glossary*

absolute advantage (p. 66) When a country has a monopoly on producing a product or is able to produce it more efficiently than all other countries.

accounting (p. 550) The recording, classifying, summarizing, and interpreting of financial events and transactions to provide management and other interested parties the information they need to make good decisions.

accounting cycle (p. 555) A six-step procedure that results in the preparation and analysis of the two major financial statements: the balance sheet and the income statement.

acquisition (p. 148) A company's purchase of the property and obligations of another company.

Active Corps of Executives (ACE) (p. 189) SBA volunteers from industry, trade associations, and education who counsel small businesses.

administered distribution system (p. 478) A distribution system in which producers manage all of the marketing functions at the retail level.

administrative agencies (p. 117) Institutions created by Congress or state legislatures with delegated power to pass rules and regulations within their mandated area of authority.

advertising (p. 491) Paid, nonpersonal communication through various media by organizations and individuals who are in some way identified in the advertising message.

affirmative action (p. 352) Employment activities designed to "right past wrongs" by increasing opportunities for minorities and women.

agency shop agreement (p. 368) Clause in a labor–management agreement that says employers may hire nonunion workers; employees are not required to join the union but must pay a union fee.

American dream *Americans' hope for a better quality of life and a higher standard of living than their parents'.*

American Federation of Labor (AFL) (p. 364) An organization of craft unions that championed fundamental labor issues; founded in 1886.

annual report (p. 552) A yearly statement of the financial condition and progress of an organization.

annuity (p. 688) A contract to make regular payments to a person for life or for a fixed period.

apprentice programs (p. 339) Training programs involving a period during which a learner works alongside an experienced employee to master the skills and procedures of a craft.

arbitration (p. 369) The agreement to bring in an impartial third party (an arbitrator) to render a binding decision in a labor dispute.

assembly process (p. 276) That part of the production process that puts together components.

assets (p. 556) Economic resources owned by a firm.

auditing (p. 553) The job of reviewing and evaluating the records used to prepare a company's financial statements.

autocratic leadership (p. 217) Leadership style that involves making managerial decisions without consulting others.

automatically fed to a computer *Standard procedure of inputting specific information into a computer on a regular basis.*

B2B *Business to business.*

B2C *Business to consumer.*

balance of payments (p. 69) The difference between money coming into a country (from exports) and money leaving the country (for imports) plus money flows from other factors such as tourism, foreign aid, military expenditures, and foreign investment.

balance of trade (p. 68) A nation's relationship of exports to imports.

balance sheet (p. 556) The financial statement that reports a firm's financial condition at a specific time.

banker's acceptance (p. 665) A promise that the bank will pay some specified amount at a particular time.

bankruptcy (p. 127) The legal process by which a person, business, or government entity unable to meet financial obligations is relieved of those obligations by having the court divide any assets among creditors, freeing the debtor to begin anew.

*Terms and definitions printed in italic are considered business slang, or jargon.

bargaining zone (p. 369) Range of options between the initial and final offer that each party will consider before negotiations dissolve or reach an impasse.

barter (p. 648) The trading of goods and services for other goods and services directly.

been there, done that *Having prior experience with a situation or task.*

benefit segmentation (p. 412) Dividing the market by determining which benefits of the product to talk about.

bit of kick *A rather strong or spicy taste added to a product or beverage.*

black mark *A negative evaluation.*

blue chip stocks (p. 627) Stocks of high-quality companies that pay regular dividends and generate con sistent growth in the company's stock price.

blue flu *Calling in sick when you're really not. The blue refers to the color of the uniform some workers wear.*

bond (p. 613) A corporate certificate (IOU) indicating that a person has lent money to a firm.

bookkeeping (p. 554) The recording of business transactions.

bossy *Telling employees what to do and not listening to their suggestions.*

bottom line *The last line in a profit and loss statement; it refers to net profit.*

bought into *To have accepted completely.*

bowing to competition *Following what competition does.*

brand (p. 436) A name, symbol, or design (or combination thereof) that identifies the goods or services of one seller or group of sellers and distinguishes them from the goods and services of competitors.

brand association (p. 438) The linking of a brand to other favorable images.

brand awareness (p. 438) How quickly or easily a given brand name comes to mind when a product category is mentioned.

brand equity (p. 437) The combination of factors such as awareness, loyalty, perceived quality, images, and emotions people associate with a given brand name.

brand loyalty (p. 437) The degree to which customers are satisfied, like the brand, and are committed to further purchase.

brand manager (p. 438) A manager who has direct responsibility for one brand or one product line.

brand name (p. 400) A word, letter, or group of words or letters that differentiates one seller's goods and services from those of competitors.

breach of contract (p. 122) When one party fails to follow the terms of a contract.

break-even analysis (p. 447) The process used to determine profitability at various levels of sales.

brick-and-mortar store *Stores with traditional physical buildings as opposed to stores on the Internet.*

broadband technology (p. 526) Technology that delivers voice, video, and data through the Internet.

brokers (p. 461) Marketing intermediaries who bring buyers and sellers together and assist in negotiating an exchange but don't take title to the goods.

budget (p. 567) A financial plan that sets forth management's expectations for revenues and, based on those expectations, allocates the use of specific resources throughout the firm.

bureaucracy (p. 236) An organization with many layers of managers who set rules and regulations and oversee all decisions.

business (p. 4) Any activity that seeks profit by providing goods and services to others.

business law (p. 116) Rules, statutes, codes, and regulations that are established to provide a legal framework within which business may be conducted and that are enforceable by court action.

business plan (p. 181) A detailed written statement that describes the nature of the business, the target market, the advantages the business will have in relation to competition, and the resources and qualifications of the owner(s).

business-to-business (B2B) market (p. 409) All the individuals and organizations that want goods and services for use in producing other goods and services or to sell, rent, or supply to others.

buying on margin (p. 630) Purchasing stocks by borrowing some of the purchase cost from the brokerage firm.

cafeteria-style fringe benefits (p. 347) Fringe benefits plan that allows employees to choose the benefits they want up to a certain dollar amount.

callable bond (p. 616) A bond that gives the issuer the right to pay off the bond before its maturity.

cannibalized business *One franchise pulls business away from another franchise.*

capital budget (p. 588) A budget that high-lights a firm's spending plans for major asset purchases that often require large sums of money.

capital expenditures (p. 592) Major investments in long-term assets such as land, buildings, equipment, or research and development.

capital gains (p. 626) The positive difference between the purchase price of a stock and its sale price.

capitalism (p. 37) An economic system in which all or most of the factors of production and distribution are privately owned and operated for profit.

cash-and-carry wholesalers (p. 469) Wholesalers that serve mostly smaller retailers with a limited assortment of products.

cash budget (p. 588) A budget that estimates a firm's projected cash balance at the end of a given period.

cash flow (p. 562) The difference between cash coming in and cash going out of a business.

cash flow forecast (p. 586) Forecast that predicts the cash inflows and outflows in future periods.

category killer stores (p. 472) Large stores that offer wide selection at competitive prices.

celebrity stargazers *Customers that attend the opening of a new business hoping to see or meet a celebrity.*

centralized authority (p. 244) An organization structure in which decision-making authority is maintained at the top level of management at the company's headquarters.

certificate of deposit (CD) (p. 657) A time-deposit (savings) account that earns interest to be delivered at the end of the certificate's maturity date.

certification (p. 365) Process of a union's becoming recognized by the National Labor Relations Board as the bargaining agent for a group of employees.

certified internal auditor (p. 553) An accountant who has a bachelor's degree and two years of experience in internal auditing, and who has passed an exam administered by the Institute of Internal Auditors.

certified management accountant (p. 551) A professional accountant who has met certain educational and experience requirements and been certified by the Institute of Certified Management Accountants.

certified public accountant (CPA) (p. 552) An accountant who passes a series of examinations established by the American Institute of Certified Public Accountants.

channel of distribution (p. 460) A whole set of marketing intermediaries, such as wholesalers and retailers, who join together to transport and store goods in their path (or channel) from producers to consumers.

chicken dance *An American dance that involves flapping arms like a bird.*

climbed the ladder *Promoted to higher level jobs.*

closed shop agreement (p. 368) Clause in a labor– management agreement that specified that workers had to be members of a union before being hired (outlawed in 1947).

closing techniques (p. 500) Ways of concluding a sale, including getting a series of small commitments and then asking for the order and showing the client where to sign.

collective bargaining (p. 365) The process whereby union and management representatives form a labor–management agreement, or contract, for workers.

command economies (p. 45) Economic systems in which the government largely decides what goods and services will be produced, who will get them, and how the economy will grow.

commercial and consumer finance companies (p. 660) Organizations that offer short-term loans to businesses or individuals who either can't meet the credit requirements of regular banks or else have exceeded their credit limit and need more funds.

commercial bank (p. 656) A profit-making organization that receives deposits from individuals and corporations in the form of checking and savings accounts and then uses some of these funds to make loans.

commercial finance companies (p. 660) Organizations that make short-term loans to borrowers who offer tangible assets as collateral.

commercialization (p. 442) Promoting a product to distributors and retailers to get wide distribution and developing strong advertising and sales campaigns to generate and maintain interest in the product among distributors and consumers.

commercial paper (p. 596) Unsecured promissory notes of $25,000 and up that mature (come due) in 270 days or less.

commodity exchange (p. 631) A securities exchange that specializes in the buying and selling of precious metals and minerals (e.g., silver, foreign currencies, gasoline) and agricultural goods (e.g., wheat, cattle, sugar).

common law (p. 117) The body of law that comes from judges' decisions; also referred to as unwritten law.

common market (p. 84) A regional group of countries that have a common external tariff, no internal tariffs, and a coordination of laws to facilitate exchange; also called a trading bloc; an example is the European Union.

common stock (p. 619) The most basic form of ownership in a firm; it confers voting rights and the right to share in the firm's profits through dividends, if offered by the firm's board of directors.

communism (p. 44) An economic and political system in which the state makes all economic decisions and owns all the major forms of production.

comparable worth (p. 377) The concept that people in jobs that require similar levels of education, training, or skills should receive equal pay.

comparative advantage theory (p. 65) Theory which asserts that a country should sell to other countries those products that it produces most efficiently.

competing in time (p. 281) Being as fast or faster than competition in responding to consumer wants and needs and getting goods and services to them.

competitive benchmarking (p. 254) Rating an organization's practices, processes, and products against the world's best.

compliance-based ethics codes (p. 101) Ethical standards that emphasize preventing unlawful behavior by increasing control and by penalizing wrongdoers.

compressed workweek (p. 348) Work schedule that allows an employee to work a full number of hours per week, but in fewer days.

computer-aided design (CAD) (p. 282) The use of computers in the design of products.

computer-aided manufacturing (CAM) (p. 282) The use of computers in the manufacturing of products.

computer-integrated manufacturing (CIM) (p. 282) The uniting of computer-aided design with computer-aided manufacturing.

concept testing (p. 441) Taking a product idea to consumers to test their reactions.

conceptual skills (p. 224) Skills that involve the ability to picture the organization as a whole and the relationship among its various parts.

conglomerate merger (p. 148) The joining of firms in completely unrelated industries.

Congress of Industrial Organizations (CIO) (p. 364) Union organization of unskilled workers; broke away from the AFL in 1935 and rejoined it in 1955.

consideration (p. 122) Something of value; consideration is one of the requirements of a legal contract.

consultative salesperson (p. 501) A salesperson who begins by analyzing customer needs and then comes up with solutions to those needs.

consumerism (p. 125) A social movement that seeks to increase and strengthen the rights and powers of buyers in relation to sellers.

consumer market (p. 409) All the individuals or households that want goods and services for personal consumption or use.

consumer price index (CPI) (p. 50) Monthly statistics that measure changes in the prices of about 400 goods and services that consumers buy.

contingency planning (p. 210) The process of preparing alternative courses of action that may be used if the primary plans do not achieve the objectives of the organization.

contingent workers (p. 337) Workers who do not have the expectation of regular, full-time employment.

continuous improvement (p. 251) Constantly improving the way the organization does things so that customer needs can be better satisfied.

continuous process (p. 276) A production process in which long production runs turn out finished goods over time.

contract (p. 122) A legally enforceable agreement between two or more parties.

contract law (p. 122) Set of laws that specify what constitutes a legally enforceable agreement.

contract manufacturing (p. 73) A foreign country's production of private-label goods to which a domestic company then attaches its brand name or trademark; also called outsourcing.

contractual distribution system (p. 477) A distribution system in which members are bound to cooperate through contractual agreements.

controlling (p. 207) A management function that involves determining whether or not an organization is progressing toward its goals and objectives, and taking corrective action if it is not.

convenience goods and services (p. 431) Products that the consumer wants to purchase frequently and with a minimum of effort.

conventional (C) corporation (p. 140) A state-chartered legal entity with authority to act and have liability separate from its owners.

convertible bond (p. 616) A bond that can be converted into shares of common stock in the issuing company.

cookies (p. 541) Pieces of information, such as registration data or user preferences, sent by a website over the Internet to a Web browser that the browser software is expected to save and send back to the server whenever the user returns to that website.

cooling-off period (p. 372) When workers in a critical industry return to their jobs while the union and management continue negotiations.

cooperative (p. 157) A business owned and controlled by the people who use it—producers, consumers, or workers with similar needs who pool their resources for mutual gain.

copyright (p. 121) Exclusive rights to materials such as books, articles, photos, and cartoons.

core competencies (p. 254) Those functions that the organization can do as well or better than any other organization in the world.

core time (p. 348) In a flextime plan, the period when all employees are expected to be at their job stations.

corporate distribution system (p. 477) A distribution system in which all of the organizations in the channel of distribution are owned by one firm.

corporate philanthropy (p. 103) Dimension of social responsibility that includes charitable donations.

corporate policy (p. 103) Dimension of social responsibility that refers to the position a firm takes on social and political issues.

corporate responsibility (p. 103) Dimension of social responsibility that includes everything from hiring minority workers to making safe products.

corporation (p. 134) A legal entity with authority to act and have liability separate from its owners.

cost of goods sold (or cost of goods manufactured) (p. 560) A measure of the cost of merchandise sold or cost of raw materials and supplies used for producing items for resale.

couch potatoes *People who sit and watch TV for hours at a time.*

countertrading (p. 79) Bartering among several countries.

counting on it *Expecting it.*

craft union (p. 363) An organization of skilled specialists in a particular craft or trade.

credit unions (p. 659) Nonprofit, member-owned financial cooperatives that offer the full variety of banking services to their members.

critical path (p. 283) The sequence of tasks that takes the longest time to complete.

cross-functional teams (p. 248) Groups of employees from different departments who work together on a semipermanent basis.

cumulative preferred stock (p. 619) Preferred stock that accumulates unpaid dividends.

current assets (p. 558) Items that can be converted into cash within one year.

customer relationship management (p. 396) Learning as much as possible about customers and doing everything you can to satisfy them or even delight them with goods and services over time.

cyber shop *To shop online.*

damages (p. 123) The monetary settlement awarded to a person who is injured by a breach of contract.

database (p. 15) Electronic storage file where information is kept.

data processing (DP) (p. 522) Name for business technology in the 1970s; included technology that supported an existing business and was primarily used to improve the flow of financial information.

dead duck *Something doomed to failure.*

a deal *A special price or some other benefit that all people don't get.*

dealer (private) brands (p. 437) Products that don't carry the manufacturer's name but carry a distributor or retailer's name instead.

debenture bonds (p. 615) Bonds that are unsecured (i.e., not backed by any collateral such as equipment).

debit card (p. 664) An electronic funds transfer tool that serves the same function as checks: It withdraws funds from a checking account.

debt capital (p. 592) Funds raised through various forms of borrowing that must be repaid.

decentralized authority (p. 244) An organization structure in which decision-making authority is delegated to lower-level managers more familiar with local conditions than headquarter's management could be.

decertification (p. 365) The process by which workers take away a union's right to represent them.

decision making (p. 211) Choosing among two or more alternatives.

deflation (p. 53) A situation where prices are actually declining.

demand (p. 39) The quantity of products that people are willing to buy at different prices at a specific time.

demand deposit (p. 657) The technical name for a checking account; the money in a demand deposit can be withdrawn anytime on demand from the owner.

demographic segmentation (p. 412) Dividing the market by age, income, and education level.

demography (p. 21) The statistical study of human population to learn its size, density, and other characteristics.

denomination (p. 614) The amount of debt represented by one bond.

departmentalization (p. 241) The dividing of organizational functions into separate units.

depreciation (p. 565) The systematic write-off of the cost of a tangible asset over its estimated useful life.

depression (p. 53) A severe recession.

deregulation (p. 129) Government withdrawal of certain laws and regulations that seem to hinder competition.

devaluation (p. 78) Lowering the value of a nation's currency relative to other currencies.

discount rate (p. 653) The interest rate that the Fed charges for loans to member banks.

disinflation (p. 53) A condition where price increases are slowing (the inflation rate is declining).

diversification (p. 629) Buying several different investment alternatives to spread the risk of investing.

diversity, multiculturalism (p. 21) Words used almost interchangeably to refer to the process of optimizing (in the workplace) the contributions of people from different cultures.

dividends (p. 617) Part of a firm's profits that may be distributed to stockholders as either cash payments or additional shares of stock.

dot-com company (p. 13) An Internet company whose Web address ends with .com.

double-entry bookkeeping (p. 554) The concept of writing every transaction in two places.

Dow Jones Industrial Average (p. 636) The average cost of 30 selected industrial stocks, used to give an indication of the direction (up or down) of the stock market over time.

downsizing (p. 236) The process of eliminating managerial and non-managerial positions.

drop shippers (p. 469) Wholesalers that solicit orders from retailers and other wholesalers and have the merchandise shipped directly from a producer to a buyer.

duck the opportunity *Avoid the opportunity.*

ducks in row *To have all one's tasks lined up and ready to be executed.*

dug down *Worked hard and diligently.*

dumping (p. 69) Selling products in a foreign country at lower prices than those charged in the producing country.

e-commerce (p. 13) Electronic commerce; the buying and selling of products and services over the Internet.

economic pie *The money available in the economy.*

economics (p. 34) The study of how society chooses to employ resources to produce goods and services and distribute them for consumption among various competing groups and individuals.

economy of scale (p. 234) The situation in which companies can produce goods more inexpensively if they can purchase raw materials in bulk; the average cost of goods goes down as production levels increase.

electronic check conversion (ECC) (p. 664) An electronic funds transfer tool that converts a traditional paper check into an electronic transaction at the cash register and processes it through the Federal Reserve's Automated Clearing House.

electronic funds transfer (EFT) system (p. 664) A computerized system that electronically performs financial transactions such as making purchases, paying bills, and receiving paychecks.

e-mail snooped *When someone other than the addresses reads e-mail messages.*

embargo (p. 82) A complete ban on the import or export of a certain product.

employee orientation (p. 338) The activity that introduces new employees to the organization; to fellow employees; to their immediate supervisors; and to the policies, practices, and objectives of the firm.

employee stock ownership plans (ESOPs) (p. 383) Programs that enable employees to buy part or total ownership of the firm.

empowerment (p. 20, 221) Giving employees the authority and responsibility to respond quickly to customer requests.

enabling (p. 221) Giving workers the education and tools they need to assume their new decision-making powers.

enterprise resource planning (ERP) (p. 276) Computer-based production and operations system that links multiple firms into one integrated production unit.

entrepreneur (p. 4) A person who risks time and money to start and manage a business.

entrepreneurial team (p. 168) A group of experienced people from different areas of business who join together to form a managerial team with the skills needed to develop, make, and market a new product.

entrepreneurship (p. 166) Accepting the risk of starting and running a business.

environmental scanning (p. 407) The process of identifying the factors that can affect marketing success.

equity capital (p. 593) Money raised from within the firm or through the sale of ownership in the firm.

equity theory (p. 313) The idea that employees try to maintain equity between inputs and outputs compared to others in similar positions.

e-tailing (p. 473) Selling goods and services to ultimate customers (e.g., you and me) over the Internet.

ethics (p. 96) Standards of moral behavior, that is, behavior that is accepted by society as right versus wrong.

everyday low pricing (EDLP) (p. 448) Setting prices lower than competitors and then not having any special sales.

exchange rate (p. 78) The value of one currency relative to the currencies of other countries.

exclusive distribution (p. 473) Distribution that sends products to only one retail outlet in a given geographic area.

expectancy theory (p. 312) Victor Vroom's theory that the amount of effort employees exert on a specific task depends on their expectations of the outcome.

expenses (p. 562) Costs involved in operating a business, such as rent, utilities, and salaries.

exporting (p. 64) Selling products to another country.

express warranties (p. 121) Specific representations by the seller regarding the goods.

external customers (p. 223) Dealers, who buy products to sell to others, and ultimate customers (or end users), who buy products for their own personal use.

extranet (p. 250) An extension of the Internet that connects suppliers, customers, and other organizations via secure websites.

extrinsic reward (p. 296) Something given to you by someone else as recognition for good work; extrinsic rewards include pay increases, praise, and promotions.

facility layout (p. 268) The physical arrangement of resources (including people) in the production process.

facility location (p. 266) The process of selecting a geographic location for a company's operations.

factoring (p. 596) The process of selling accounts receivable for cash.

factors of production (p. 9) The resources used to create wealth: land, labor, capital, entrepreneurship, and knowledge.

The fed *Refers to the Federal Reserve Bank.*

Federal Deposit Insurance Corporation (FDIC) (p. 661) An independent agency of the U.S. government that insures bank deposits.

finance (p. 585) The function in a business that acquires funds for the firm and manages funds within the firm.

financial accounting (p. 552) Accounting information and analyses prepared for people outside the organization.

financial control (p. 589) A process in which a firm periodically compares its actual revenues, costs, and expenses with its projected ones.

financial management (p. 585) The job of managing a firm's resources so it can meet its goals and objectives.

financial managers (p. 584) Managers who make recommendations to top executives regarding strategies for improving the financial strength of a firm.

financial statement (p. 555) A summary of all the transactions that have occurred over a particular period.

first in, first out (FIFO) (p. 566) Accounting method for calculating cost of inventory; it assumes that the first goods to come in are the first to go out.

fiscal policy (p. 54) Government efforts to keep the economy stable by increasing or decreasing taxes or government spending.

fixed assets (p. 558) Assets that are relatively permanent, such as land, buildings, and equipment.

flexible manufacturing (p. 280) Designing machines to do multiple tasks so that they can produce a variety of products.

flextime plan (p. 348) Work schedule that gives employees some freedom to choose when to work, as long as they work the required number of hours.

focus group (p. 404) A small group of people who meet under the direction of a discussion leader to communicate their opinions about an organization, its products, or other given issues.

foreign direct investment (p. 75) The buying of permanent property and businesses in foreign nations.

foreign subsidiary (p. 74) A company owned in a foreign country by another company (called the parent company).

form utility (p. 275) The value added by the creation of finished goods and services, such as the value added by taking silicon and making computer chips or putting services together to create a vacation package.

formal organization (p. 255) The structure that details lines of responsibility, authority, and position; that is, the structure shown on organization charts.

"fowl" *A pun or a play on words, in which the word "fowl" (a bird, such as a duck) was used in place of the similar sounding word "foul" (unpleasant, obstructed).*

franchise (p. 150) The right to use a specific business's name and sell its products or services in a given territory.

franchise agreement (p. 150) An arrangement whereby someone with a good idea for a business sells the rights to use the business name and sell a product or service to others in a given territory.

franchisee (p. 150) A person who buys a franchise.

franchisor (p. 150) A company that develops a product concept and sells others the rights to make and sell the products.

freelancers *People who work independently of a firm and offer their work to anyone who is willing to pay.*

free-market economies (p. 45) Economic systems in which decisions about what to produce and in what quantities are decided by the market, that is, by buyers and sellers negotiating prices for goods and services.

free trade (p. 65) The movement of goods and services among nations without political or economic obstruction.

freight forwarder (p. 470) An organization that puts many small shipments together to create a single large shipment that can be transported cost-effectively to the final destination.

fringe benefits (p. 346) Benefits such as sick-leave pay, vacation pay, pension plans, and health plans that represent additional compensation to employees beyond base wages.

from scratch *To make something completely new.*

fundamental accounting equation (p. 556) Assets = liabilities + owners' equity; this is the basis for the balance sheet.

futures markets (p. 631) The purchase and sale of goods for delivery sometime in the future.

Gantt chart (p. 283) Bar graph showing production managers what projects are being worked on and what stage they are in at any given time.

general partner (p. 137) An owner (partner) who has unlimited liability and is active in managing the firm.

general partnership (p. 137) A partnership in which all owners share in operating the business and in assuming liability for the business's debts.

generic goods (p. 437) Nonbranded products that usually sell at a sizable discount compared to national or private brands.

generic name (p. 437) The name for a product category (versus a brand name).

geographic segmentation (p. 411) Dividing the market by geographic area.

givebacks (p. 373) Concessions made by union members to management; gains from labor negotiations are given back to management to help employers remain competitive and thereby save jobs.

goals (p. 208) The broad, long-term accomplishments an organization wishes to attain.

goal-setting theory (p. 310) The idea that setting ambitious but attainable goals can motivate workers and improve performance if the goals are accepted, are accompanied by feedback, and are facilitated by organizational conditions.

go for the gold *To work to be the very best (figuratively winning a gold medal).*

goods (p. 24) Tangible products such as computers, food, clothing, cars, and appliances.

goof off *1. To take unauthorized time off from work. 2. Doing things at work not associated with the job, such as talking with others at the drinking fountain.*

go out with me *Go with me to dinner or to a movie or some other entertainment.*

green product (p. 419) A product whose production, use, and disposal don't damage the environment.

grievance (p. 369) A charge by employees that management is not abiding by the terms of the negotiated labor–management agreement.

gross domestic product (GDP) (p. 49) The total value of goods and services produced in a country in a given year.

gross margin (gross profit) (p. 561) How much a firm earned by buying (or making) and selling merchandise.

growth stocks (p. 626) Stocks of companies whose earnings are expected to grow faster than other stocks or the overall economy.

Hawthorne effect (p. 300) The tendency for people to behave differently when they know they are being studied.

health maintenance organizations (HMOs) (p. 704) Health care organizations that require members to choose from a restricted list of doctors.

heavy hitters *People with power and influence—and probably money.*

helped turn around *Helped reverse the downward trend.*

hierarchy (p. 236) A system in which one person is at the top of the organization and there is a ranked or sequential ordering from the top down of managers who are responsible to that person.

high gear *Going at full strength.*

high–low pricing strategy (p. 449) To set prices that are higher than EDLP stores, and to have many special sales where the prices are lower than competitors.

high tech *Anything having to do with advances in technology, such as computers, computer software, pagers, scanners, and the like.*

horizontal merger (p. 148) The joining of two firms in the same industry.

hot second *Immediately.*

human relations skills (p. 224) Skills that involve communication and motivation; they enable managers to work through and with people.

human resource management (p. 328) The process of evaluating human resource needs, finding people to fill those needs, and getting the best work from each employee by providing the right incentives and job environment, all with the goal of meeting the needs of the firm.

hygiene factors (p. 307) Job factors that can cause dissatisfaction if missing but do not necessarily motivate employees if increased.

implied warranties (p. 121) Guarantees legally imposed on the seller.

importing (p. 64) Buying products from another country.

import quota (p. 82) A limit on the number of products in certain categories that can be imported.

income statement (p. 560) The financial statement that shows a firm's profit after costs, expenses, and taxes; it summarizes all of the resources that have come into the firm (revenue), all the resources that have left the firm, and the resulting net income.

income stocks (p. 627) Stocks that offer investors a high dividend.

incubators (p. 175) Centers that offer new businesses low-cost offices with basic business services.

indenture terms (p. 599) The terms of agreement in a bond issue.

independent audit (p. 553) An evaluation and unbiased opinion about the accuracy of a company's financial statements.

individual retirement account (IRA) (p. 696) Traditionally, a tax-deferred investment plan that enables you (and your spouse, if you are married) to save part of your income for retirement.

industrial goods (p. 434) Products used in the production of other products.

industrial unions (p. 364) Labor organizations of unskilled and semiskilled workers in mass-production industries such as automobiles and mining.

inflation (p. 53) A general rise in the prices of goods and services over time.

infomercial (p. 494) A TV program devoted exclusively to promoting goods and services.

informal organization (p. 255) The system of relationships and lines of authority that develops spontaneously as employees meet and form power centers; that is, the human side of the organization that does not appear on any organization chart.

information systems (IS) (p. 522) Technology that helps companies do business; includes such tools as automated teller machines (ATMs) and voice mail.

information technology (IT) (p. 522) Technology that helps companies change business by allowing them to use new methods.

information utility (p. 467) Adding value to products by opening two-way flows of information between marketing participants.

initial public offering (IPO) (p. 612) The first public offering of a corporation's stock.

injunction (p. 373) A court order directing someone to do something or to refrain from doing something.

insider trading (p. 106) A form of investment in which insiders use private company information to further their own fortunes or those of their family and friends.

institutional investors (p. 613) Large organizations—such as pension funds, mutual funds, insurance companies, and banks—that invest their own funds or the funds of others.

insurable interest (p. 703) The possibility of a policyholder to suffer a loss.

insurable policy (p. 703) A written contract between the insured and an insurance company that promises to pay for all or part of a loss.

insurable risk (p. 703) A risk that the typical insurance company will cover.

intangible assets (p. 558) Items of value such as patents and copyrights that have no real physical form.

integrated marketing communication (IMC) (p. 490) A technique that combines all the promotional tools into one comprehensive and unified promotional strategy.

integrity-based ethics codes (p. 101) Ethical standards that define the organization's guiding values, create an environment that supports ethically sound behavior, and stress a shared accountability among employees.

intensive distribution (p. 473) Distribution that puts products into as many retail outlets as possible.

interactive marketing program (p. 510) A system in which consumers can access company information on their own and supply information about themselves in an ongoing dialogue.

interactive promotion (p. 490) Changing the promotion process from a monologue, where sellers tried to persuade buyers to buy things, to a dialogue in which buyers and sellers can work together to create mutually beneficial exchange relationships.

interest (p. 614) The payment the issuer of the bond makes to the bondholders for use of the borrowed money.

intermittent process (p. 276) A production process in which the production run is short and the machines are changed frequently to make different products.

intermodal shipping (p. 481) The use of multiple modes of transportation to complete a single long-distance movement of freight.

internal customers (p. 223) Individuals and units within the firm that receive services from other individuals or units.

International Monetary Fund (IMF) (p. 667) Organization that assists the smooth flow of money among nations.

Internet 2 (p. 526) The new Internet system that links government supercomputer centers and a select group of universities; it will run more than 22,000 times faster than today's public infrastructure and will support heavy-duty applications.

in the right hands *To the person who can give you the most help.*

intranet (p. 250, 525) *1.* A companywide network, closed to public access, that uses Internet-type technology. *2.* A set of communications links within one company that travel over the Internet but are closed to public access.

intrapreneurs (p. 174) Creative people who work as entrepreneurs within corporations.

intrinsic reward (p. 296) The good feeling you have when you have done a job well.

inventory financing (p. 595) The process of using inventory such as raw materials as collateral for a loan.

inverted organization (p. 252) An organization that has contact people at the top and the chief executive officer at the bottom of the organization chart.

investment bankers (p. 613) Specialists who assist in the issue and sale of new securities.

invisible hand (p. 36) A phrase coined by Adam Smith to describe the process that turns self-directed gain into social and economic benefits for all.

involuntary bankruptcy (p. 127) Bankruptcy procedures filed by a debtor's creditors.

IOUs *Debt; abbreviation for "I owe you."*

is the heart *The most important part of something; the central force or idea.*

ISO 9000 (p. 271) The common name given to quality management and assurance standards.

ISO 14000 (p. 272) A collection of the best practices for managing an organization's impact on the environment.

job analysis (p. 332) A study of what is done by employees who hold various job titles.

job description (p. 332) A summary of the objectives of a job, the type of work to be done, the responsibilities and duties, the working conditions, and the relationship of the job to other functions.

job enlargement (p. 310) A job enrichment strategy that involves combining a series of tasks into one challenging and interesting assignment.

job enrichment (p. 309) A motivational strategy that emphasizes motivating the worker through the job itself.

job rotation (p. 310) A job enrichment strategy that involves moving employees from one job to another.

job sharing (p. 349) An arrangement whereby two part-time employees share one full-time job.

job simplification (p. 309) The process of producing task efficiency by breaking down a job into simple steps and assigning people to each of those steps.

job simulation (p. 340) The use of equipment that duplicates job conditions and tasks so that trainees can learn skills before attempting them on the job.

job specifications (p. 332) A written summary of the minimum qualifications required of workers to do a particular job.

joint venture (p. 73) A partnership in which two or more companies (often from different countries) join to undertake a major project.

joke around *Tell jokes and generally act less than professional.*

journal (p. 554) The book where accounting data are first entered.

judiciary (p. 116) The branch of government chosen to oversee the legal system through the court system.

jump at the idea *Respond positively to a new idea.*

jumped headfirst *Began quickly and eagerly without hesitation.*

junk bonds (p. 630) High-risk, high-interest bonds.

just-in-time (JIT) inventory control (p. 279) A production process in which a minimum of inventory is kept on the premises and parts, supplies, and other needs are delivered just in time to go on the assembly line.

key player *Important participant.*

kick back and relax *To take a rest.*

Knights of Labor (p. 364) The first national labor union; formed in 1869.

knockoff brands (p. 436) Illegal copies of national brand-name goods.

knowledge management (p. 221, 528) Sharing, organizing and disseminating information in the simplest and most relevant way possible for the users of the information.

knowledge technology (KT) (p. 523) Technology that adds a layer of intelligence to information technology, to filter appropriate information and deliver it when it is needed.

knowledge walk out the door *Lose knowledge that employees have because they don't share it with others before they leave the company.*

laissez-faire (free-rein) leadership (p. 219) Leadership style that involves managers setting objectives and employees being relatively free to do whatever it takes to accomplish those objectives.

last in, first out (LIFO) (p. 566) Accounting method for calculating cost of inventory; it assumes that the last goods to come in are the first to go out.

the last laugh *This comes from the expression, "He who laughs last, laughs loudest" because he or she has been proven right.*

law of large numbers (p. 704) Principle that if a large number of people are exposed to the same risk, a predictable number of losses will occur during a given period of time.

leading (p. 207) Creating a vision for the organization and guiding, training, coaching, and motivating others to work effectively to achieve the organization's goals and objectives.

lean manufacturing (p. 280) The production of goods using less of everything compared to mass production.

ledger (p. 554) A specialized accounting book in which information from accounting journals is accumulated into specific categories and posted so that managers can find all the information about one account in the same place.

letter of credit (p. 665) A promise by the bank to pay the seller a given amount if certain conditions are met.

leverage (p. 602) Raising needed funds through borrowing to increase a firm's rate of return.

leveraged buyout (LBO) (p. 150) An attempt by employees, management, or a group of investors to purchase an organization primarily through borrowing.

liabilities (p. 558) What the business owes to others.

licensing (p. 71) An act by which a producer (the licensor) allows a foreign company (the licensee) to produce its product in exchange for a fee (a royalty).

limited liability company (LLC) (p. 146) A company similar to an S corporation but without the special eligibility requirements.

limited liability partnership (LLP) (p. 138) A partnership that limits partners' risk of losing their personal assets to only their own acts and omissions and to the acts and omissions of people under their supervision.

limited liability (p. 137) The responsibility of business's owners for losses only up to the amount they invest; limited partners and shareholders have limited liability.

limited partner (p. 137) An owner who invests money in the business but does not have any management responsibility or liability for losses beyond the investment.

limited partnership (p. 137) A partnership with one or more general partners and one or more limited partners.

limit order (p. 627) Instructions to a broker to buy or sell a particular stock at a specific price, if that price becomes available.

line of credit (p. 595) A given amount of unsecured short-term funds a bank will lend to a business, provided the funds are readily available.

line organization (p. 245) An organization that has direct two-way lines of responsibility, authority, and communication running from the top to the bottom of the organization, with all people reporting to only one supervisor.

line personnel (p. 245) Employees who perform functions that contribute directly to the primary goals of the organization.

liquidity (p. 556) How fast an asset can be converted into cash.

lockout (p. 373) An attempt by management to put pressure on unions by temporarily closing the business.

long-term financing (p. 592) Borrowed capital that will be repaid over a specific time period longer than one year.

long-term forecast (p. 587) Forecast that predicts revenues, costs, and expenses for a period longer than 1 year, and sometimes as far as 5 or 10 years into the future.

loss (p. 7) When a business's costs and expenses are more than its revenues.

M-1 (p. 650) Money that can be raised quickly and easily (coins and paper money, checks, traveler's checks, etc.).

M-2 (p. 650) Money included in M-1 plus money that may take a little more time to raise (savings accounts, money market accounts, mutual funds, certificates of deposit, etc.).

macroeconomics (p. 34) That part of economic study that looks at the operation of a nation's economy as a whole.

management (p. 206) The process used to accomplish organizational goals through planning, organizing, leading, and controlling people and other organizational resources.

management by objectives (MBO) (p. 311) A system of goal setting and implementation that involves a cycle of discussion, review, and evaluation of objectives among top and middle-level managers, supervisors, and employees.

management development (p. 340) The process of training and educating employees to become good managers and then monitoring the progress of their managerial skills over time.

managerial accounting (p. 551) Accounting used to provide information and analyses to managers within the organization to assist them in decision making.

managing diversity (p. 215) Building systems and a climate that unite different people in a common pursuit without undermining their individual strengths.

manufacturers' brand names (p. 436) The brand names of manufacturers that distribute products nationally.

market (p. 186) People with unsatisfied wants and needs who have both the resources and the willingness to buy.

marketing (p. 396) The process of determining customer wants and needs and then providing customers with goods and services that meet or exceed their expectations.

marketing concept (p. 396) A three-part business philosophy: (1) a customer orientation, (2) a service orientation, and (3) a profit orientation.

marketing intermediaries (p. 460) Organizations that assist in moving goods and services from producers to industrial and consumer users.

marketing management (p. 397) The process of planning and executing the conception, pricing, promotion, and distribution of ideas, goods, and services (products) to create mutually beneficial exchanges.

marketing mix (p. 398) The ingredients that go into a marketing program: product, price, place, and promotion.

marketing research (p. 402) The analysis of markets to determine opportunities and challenges, and to find the information needed to make good decisions.

market order (p. 627) Instructions to a broker to buy or sell a stock immediately at the best price available.

market price (p. 41) The price determined by supply and demand.

market segmentation (p. 410) The process of dividing the total market into several groups whose members have similar characteristics.

marriage of software, hardware, etc. Combination of various technologies.

Maslow's hierarchy of needs (p. 300) Theory of motivation that places different types of human needs in order of importance, from basic physiological needs to safety, social, and esteem needs to self-actualization needs.

mass customization (p. 281) Tailoring products to meet the needs of individual customers.

mass marketing (p. 413) Developing products and promotions to please large groups of people.

mass production (p. 278) The process of making a large number of a limited variety of products at very low cost.

master limited partnership (MLP) (p. 137) A partnership that looks much like a corporation in that it acts like a corporation and is traded on the stock exchanges like a corporation, but is taxed like a partnership and thus avoids the corporate income tax.

materials handling (p. 482) The movement of goods within a warehouse, factory, or store.

materials requirement planning (MRP) (p. 276) A computer-based production management system that uses sales forecasts to make sure that needed parts and materials are available at the right time and place.

matrix organization (p. 246) An organization in which specialists from different parts of the organization are brought together to work on specific projects but still remain part of a traditional line-and-staff structure.

maturity date (p. 614) The exact date the issuer of a bond must pay the principal to the bondholder.

measuring stick *Tool used to evaluate or compare something.*

mediation (p. 369) The use of a third party, called a mediator, who encourages both sides to continue negotiating and often makes suggestions for resolving the dispute.

mentor (p. 341) An experienced employee who supervises, coaches, and guides lower-level employees by introducing them to the right people and generally being their organizational sponsor.

merchant wholesalers (p. 469) Independently owned firms that take title to (own) the goods they handle.

merger (p. 148) The result of two firms forming one company.

microeconomics (p. 34) That part of economic study that looks at the behavior of people and organizations in particular markets.

micropreneur (p. 169) An entrepreneur willing to accept the risk of starting and managing the type of business that remains small, lets them do the kind of work they want to do, and offers them a balanced lifestyle.

middle management (p. 212) The level of management that includes general managers, division managers, and branch and plant managers who are responsible for tactical planning and controlling.

mine the knowledge *Make maximum use of the knowledge employees have.*

mission statement (p. 208) An outline of the fundamental purposes of an organization.

mixed economies (p. 46) Economic systems in which some allocation of resources is made by the market and some is made by the government.

monetary policy (p. 53) The management of the money supply and interest rates.

money (p. 648) Anything that people generally accept as payment for goods and services.

money laundering *When illegal money is made to appear legal by passing it through a bank or legal business.*

money supply (p. 650) How much money there is to buy available goods and services.

monopolistic competition (p. 41) The market situation in which there are a large number of sellers that produce similar products, but the products are perceived by buyers as different.

monopoly (p. 42) A market in which there is only one seller.

more than meets the eye *There's more to something than can be seen.*

motivators (p. 307) Job factors that cause employees to be productive and that give them satisfaction.

muddy the water *Make things unclear.*

multinational corporation (MNC) (p. 86) An organization that manufactures and markets products in many different countries and has multinational stock ownership and multinational management.

mutual fund (p. 627) An organization that buys stocks and bonds and then sells shares in those securities to the public.

mutual insurance company (p. 704) A type of insurance company owned by its policyholders.

National Association of Securities Dealers Automated Quotations (NASDAQ) (p. 620) A nationwide electronic system that communicates over-the-counter trades to brokers.

national debt (p. 54) The result of a series of government deficits (when the government spends more money than it collects in taxes) over time.

negligence (p. 118) Behavior that causes unintentional harm or injury.

negotiable instruments (p. 121) Forms of commercial paper (such as checks) that are transferable among businesses and individuals and represent a promise to pay a specified amount.

negotiated labor–management agreement (labor contract) (p. 366) Agreement that sets the tone and clarifies the terms under which management and labor agree to function over a period of time.

net income or net loss (p. 560) Revenue minus expenses.

network computing system (client/server computing) (p. 532) Computer systems that allow personal computers (clients) to obtain needed information from huge databases in a central computer (the server).

networking (p. 249) Using communications technology and other means to link organizations and allow them to work together on common objectives.

networking (personal) (p. 249) The process of establishing and maintaining contacts with key managers in one's own organization and other organizations and using those contacts to weave strong relationships that serve as informal development systems.

niche marketing (p. 412) The process of finding small but profitable market segments and designing custom-made products for them.

no haggle pricing *Situation where prices are fixed and cannot be negotiated with the seller.*

nonbanks (p. 656) Financial organizations that accept no deposits but offer many of the services provided by regular banks (pension funds, insurance companies, commercial finance companies, consumer finance companies, and brokerage houses).

nonprofit organization (p. 5) An organization whose goals do not include making a personal profit for its owners.

not bat an eye *To not seem to see; to not react.*

objectives (p. 208) Specific, short-term statements detailing how to achieve the goals.

odd lots (p. 627) Purchases of less than 100 shares of stock at a time.

off-the-job training (p. 339) Training that occurs away from the workplace and consists of internal or external programs to develop any of a variety of skills or to foster personal development.

oligopoly (p. 41) A form of competition in which the market is dominated by just a few sellers.

one-to-one marketing (p. 412) Developing a unique mix of goods and services for each individual customer.

online training (p. 339) Training programs in which employees "attend" classes via the Internet.

on-the-job training (p. 338) Training program in which the employee immediately begins his or her tasks and learns by doing, or watches others for a while and then imitates them, all right at the workplace.

open-market operations (p. 652) The buying and selling of U.S. government securities by the Fed with the goal of regulating the money supply.

open shop agreement (p. 368) Agreement in right-to-work states that gives workers the option to join or not join a union, if one exists in their workplace.

operating (master) budget (p. 588) The budget that ties together all of a firm's other budgets; it is the projection of dollar allocations to various costs and expenses needed to run the business, given projected revenues.

operational planning (p. 210) The process of setting work standards and schedules necessary to implement the tactical objectives.

operations management (p. 265) A specialized area in management that converts or transforms resources (including human resources) into goods and services.

organizational design (p. 236) The structuring of workers so that they can best accomplish the firm's goals.

organizational (or corporate) culture (p. 254) Widely shared values within an organization that provide coherence and cooperation to achieve common goals.

organization chart (p. 211) A visual device which shows the relationship and divides the organization's work: it shows who is accountable for the completion of specific work and who reports to whom.

organizing (p. 206) A management function that includes designing the structure of the organization and creating conditions and systems in which everyone and everything work together to achieve the organization's goals and objectives.

out of the office loop *Not included in everyday workplace communication.*

outsourcing (p. 254) Assigning various functions, such as accounting and legal work, to outside organizations.

over-the-counter (OTC) market (p. 620) Exchange that provides a means to trade stocks not listed on the national exchanges.

owners' equity (p. 559) Assets minus liabilities.

participative (democratic) leadership (p. 217) Leadership style that consists of managers and employees working together to make decisions.

partnership (p. 134) A legal form of business with two or more owners.

par value (p. 617) A dollar amount assigned to each share of stock by the corporation's charter.

patent (p. 120) A document that gives inventors exclusive rights to their inventions for 20 years.

penetration strategy (p. 448) Strategy in which a product is priced low to attract many customers and discourage competition.

penny stocks (p. 627) Stocks that sell for less than $2 (some analysts say $5); considered risky investments.

pension funds (p. 660) Amounts of money put aside by corporations, nonprofit organizations, or unions to cover part of the financial needs of members when they retire.

perfect competition (p. 41) The market situation in which there are many sellers of nearly identical products and no seller is large enough to dictate the price of the product.

performance appraisal (p. 342) An evaluation in which the performance level of employees is measured against established standards to make decisions about promotions, compensation, additional training, or firing.

perks *Short for perquisites; compensation in addition to salary, such as day care or a company car.*

personal selling (p. 498) The face-to-face presentation and promotion of products and services.

pick up the tab *Pay for something.*

piece of the action *Part of the opportunities.*

pink slip *To be fired from a job; derived from the days when employers gave workers written notices (on pink paper) that their jobs were terminated.*

pitch in *To help as needed.*

place utility (p. 467) Adding value to products by having them where people want them.

planning (p. 206) A management function that involves anticipating trends and determining the best strategies and tactics to achieve organizational goals and objectives.

played his last card *Tried the last thing he could think of.*

pledging (p. 595) The process of using accounts receivable or other assets as collateral for a loan.

pool their creative juices *To combine their talents; to work together.*

possession utility (p. 467) Doing whatever is necessary to transfer ownership from one party to another, including providing credit, delivery, installation, guarantees, and follow-up service.

precedent (p. 117) Decisions judges have made in earlier cases that guide the handling of new cases.

preemptive right (p. 619) Common stockholders' right to purchase any new shares of common stock the firm decides to issue.

preferred provider organizations (PPOs) (p. 705) Health care organizations similar to HMOs except that they allow members to choose their own physicians (for a fee).

preferred stock (p. 617) Stock that gives its owners preference in the payment of dividends and an earlier claim on assets than common stockholders if the company is forced out of business and its assets sold.

premium (p. 705) The fee charged by an insurance company for an insurance policy.

price leadership (p. 450) The procedure by which one or more dominant firms set the pricing practices that all competitors in an industry follow.

primary boycott (p. 373) When a union encourages both its members and the general public not to buy the products of a firm involved in a labor dispute.

principal (p. 614) The face value of a bond.

principle of motion economy (p. 297) Theory developed by Frank and Lillian Gilbreth that every job can be broken down into a series of elementary motions.

private accountants (p. 552) Accountants who work for a single firm, government agency, or nonprofit organization.

process manufacturing (p. 276) That part of the production process that physically or chemically changes materials.

process planning (p. 275) Choosing the best means for turning resources into useful goods and services.

producer price index (PPI) (p. 51) An index that measures prices at the wholesale level.

product (p. 400) Any physical good, service, or idea that satisfies a want or need.

product analysis (p. 440) Making cost estimates and sales forecasts to get a feeling for profitability of new product ideas.

product differentiation (p. 430) The creation of real or perceived product differences.

production (p. 264) The creation of finished goods and services using the factors of production: land, labor, capital, entrepreneurship, and knowledge.

productivity (p. 23) The total output of goods and services in a given period of time divided by work hours (output per work hour).

product liability (p. 118) Part of tort law that holds businesses liable for harm that results from the production, design, sale, or use of products they market.

product life cycle (p. 442) A theoretical model of what happens to sales and profits for a product class over time.

product line (p. 430) A group of products that are physically similar or are intended for a similar market.

product mix (p. 430) The combination of product lines offered by a manufacturer.

product screening (p. 440) A process designed to reduce the number of new-product ideas being worked on at any one time.

profit (p. 4) The amount a business earns above and beyond what it spends for salaries and other expenses.

program evaluation and review technique (PERT) (p. 282) A method for analyzing the tasks involved in completing a given project, estimating the time needed to complete each task, and identifying the minimum time needed to complete the total project.

program trading (p. 638) Giving instructions to computers to automatically sell if the price of a stock dips to a certain point to avoid potential losses.

promissory note (p. 594) A written contract with a promise to pay.

promotion (p. 402, 490) *1.* All the techniques sellers use to motivate people to buy products or services. *2.* An attempt by marketers to inform people about products and to persuade them to participate in an exchange.

promotion mix (p. 490) The combination of promotional tools an organization uses.

prospecting (p. 499) Researching potential buyers and choosing those most likely to buy.

prospects (p. 499) People with the means to buy a product, the authority to buy, and the willingness to listen to a sales message.

prospectus (p. 622) A condensed version of economic and financial information that a company must file with the SEC before issuing stock; the prospectus must be sent to potential stock purchasers.

provided the spark *Supplied the energy that motivated others.*

psychographic segmentation (p. 412) Dividing the market using the group's values, attitudes, and interests.

public accountant (p. 552) An accountant who provides his or her accounting services to individuals or businesses on a fee basis.

public domain software (freeware) (p. 534) Software that is free for the taking.

publicity (p. 503) Any information about an individual, product, or organization that's distributed to the public through the media and that's not paid for or controlled by the seller.

public relations (PR) (p. 502) The management function that evaluates public attitudes, changes policies and procedures in response to the public's requests, and executes a program of action and information to earn public understanding and acceptance.

pull strategy (p. 509) Promotional strategy in which heavy advertising and sales promotion efforts are directed toward consumers so that they'll request the products from retailers.

purchasing (p. 279) The function in a firm that searches for quality material resources, finds the best suppliers, and negotiates the best price for goods and services.

pure risk (p. 701) The threat of loss with no chance for profit.

push strategy (p. 509) Promotional strategy in which the producer uses advertising, personal selling, sales promotion, and all other promotional tools to convince wholesalers and retailers to stock and sell merchandise.

push technology (p. 528) Web software that delivers information tailored to a previously defined user profile; it pushes the information to users so that they don't have to pull it out.

qualify (p. 499) In the selling process, to make sure that people have a need for the product, the authority to buy, and the willingness to listen to a sales message.

quality control (p. 270) The measurement of products and services against set standards.

quality of life (p. 4) The general well-being of a society.

quite a stir *A situation where people are all excited about something.*

rack jobbers (p. 469) Wholesalers that furnish racks or shelves full of merchandise to retailers, display products, and sell on consignment.

real time (p. 249) The present moment or the actual time in which something takes place; data sent over the Internet to various organizational partners as they are developed or collected are said to be available in real time.

recession (p. 53) Two or more consecutive quarters of decline in the GDP.

recruitment (p. 333) The set of activities used to obtain a sufficient number of the right people at the right time; its purpose is to select those who best meet the needs of the organization.

reengineering (p. 252) The fundamental rethinking and radical redesign of organizational processes to achieve dramatic improvements in critical measures of performance.

relationship marketing (p. 413) Marketing whose goal is to keep individual customers over time by offering them products that exactly meet their requirements.

reserve requirement (p. 652) A percentage of commercial banks' checking and savings accounts that must be physically kept in the bank.

resource development (p. 35) The study of how to increase resources and to create the conditions that will make better use of those resources.

the rest is history *What happens next is well known.*

restructuring (p. 238) Redesigning an organization so that it can more effectively and efficiently serve its customers.

retailer (p. 460) An organization that sells to ultimate consumers.

retail sale (p. 469) The sale of goods and services to consumers for their own use.

Return on investment (ROI) (p. 11) The return a businessperson gets on the money he and other owners invest in the firm; for example, a business that earned $100 on a $1,000 investment would have a ROI of 10 percent: 100 divided by 1000.

revenue (p. 7, 560) 1. The total amount of money a business earns in a given period by selling goods and services. 2. The value of what is received for goods sold, services rendered.

reverse discrimination (p. 352) Discrimina-tion against whites or males in hiring or promoting.

revolving credit agreement (p. 595) A line of credit that is guaranteed by the bank.

right-to-work laws (p. 368) Legislation that gives workers the right, under an open shop, to join or not join a union if it is present.

risk (p. 7, 701) 1. The change of loss, the degree of probability of loss, and the amount of possible loss. *2.* The chance an entrepreneur takes of losing time and money on a business that may not prove profitable.

risk/return trade-off (p. 599) The principle that the greater the risk a lender takes in making a loan, the higher the interest rate required.

robot (p. 280) A computer-controlled machine capable of performing many tasks requiring the use of materials and tools.

roller coaster ride *Volatile; refers to the resemblance to the rapid change between extreme high and low points on an amusement park ride.*

rookie mistakes *A newcomer's errors; errors made by someone inexperienced.*

round lots (p. 627) Purchases of 100 shares of stock at a time.

rule of indemnity (p. 704) Rule says that an insured person or organization cannot collect more than the actual loss from an insurable risk.

run on the banks *When people are uncertain whether or not their funds are safe in banks, they may rush to take their money out before other people do and there is none left for them.*

sales promotion (p. 505) The promotional tool that stimulates consumer purchasing and dealer interest by means of short-term activities.

sampling (p. 505) A promotional tool in which a company lets consumers have a small sample of a product for no charge.

savings and loan association (S&L) (p. 658) A financial institution that accepts both savings and checking deposits and provides home mortgage loans.

Savings Association Insurance Fund (SAIF) (p. 661) The part of the FDIC that insures holders of accounts in savings and loan associations.

S corporation (p. 145) A unique government creation that looks like a corporation but is taxed like sole proprietorships and partnerships.

scab *A person who crosses a union picket line to assume the job of a striking worker.*

scientific management (p. 297) Studying workers to find the most efficient ways of doing things and then teaching people those techniques.

sea of information *Lots of information; often too much to process.*

seat-of-the-pants start-up *A new business that has very few resources.*

second thoughts *Rethinking a decision based on more information being available.*

secondary boycott (p. 373) An attempt by labor to convince others to stop doing business with a firm that is the subject of a primary boycott; prohibited by the Taft-Hartley Act.

secured bond (p. 599) A bond issued with some form of collateral.

secured loan (p. 595) A loan backed by something valuable, such as property.

Securities and Exchange Commission (SEC) (p. 621) Federal agency that has responsibility for regulating the various exchanges.

selection (p. 335) The process of gathering information and deciding who should be hired, under legal guidelines, for the best interests of the individual and the organization.

selective distribution (p. 473) Distribution that sends products to only a preferred group of retailers in an area.

self-insurance (p. 702) The practice of setting aside money to cover routine claims and buying only "catastrophe" policies to cover big losses.

Service Corps of Retired Executives (SCORE) (p. 189) An SBA service with 13,000 volunteers who provide consulting services for small businesses free of charge (except for expenses).

services (p. 25) Intangible products such as education, health care, and insurance.

service utility (p. 467) Providing fast, friendly service during and after the sale and by teaching customers how to best use products over time.

sexual harassment (p. 378) Unwelcome sexual advances, requests for sexual favors, and other conduct (verbal or physical) of a sexual nature.

shareware (p. 534) Software that is copyrighted but distributed to potential customers free of charge.

shopping goods and services (p. 432) Those products that the consumer buys only after comparing value, quality, and price from a variety of sellers.

shop stewards (p. 369) Union officials who work permanently in an organization and represent employee interests on a daily basis.

short-term financing (p. 592) Borrowed capital that will be repaid within one year.

short-term forecast (p. 586) Forecast that predicts revenues, costs, and expenses for a period of one year or less.

sift through mountains of information Sort *through large volumes of information.*

sinking fund (p. 615) Special provision of a bond that requires the issuer to retire (put in a trust fund), on a periodic basis, some part of the bond principal prior to maturity.

skimming price strategy (p. 448) Strategy in which a new product is priced high to make optimum profit while there's little competition.

small business (p. 176) A business that is independently owned and operated, is not dominant in its field of operation, and meets certain standards of size (set by the Small Business Administration) in terms of employees or annual receipts.

Small Business Investment Company (SBIC) Program (p. 185) A program through which private investment companies licensed by the Small Business Administration lend money to small businesses.

smart card (p. 664) An electronic funds transfer tool that is a combination credit card, debit card, phone card, and more.

social audit (p. 108) A systematic evaluation of an organization's progress toward implementing programs that are socially responsible and responsive.

socialism (p. 43) An ecomonic system based on the premise that most basic businesses should be owned by the government so that profits can be evenly distributed among the people.

social responsibility (p. 95) A business's concern for the welfare of society as a whole.

Social Security (p. 690) The term used to describe the Old-Age, Survivors, and Disability Insurance Program established by the Social Security Act of 1935.

sole proprietorship (p. 134) A business that is owned, and usually managed, by one person.

span of control (p. 239) The optimum number of subordinates a manager supervises or should supervise.

specialty goods and services (p. 432) Products that have a special attraction to consumers who are willing to go out of their way to obtain them.

speculative risk (p. 701) A chance of either profit or loss.

spruce up To make something look nice.

squeezing franchisees' profits Tightening or reducing profits.

staffing (p. 214) A management function that includes hiring, motivating, and retaining the best people available to accomplish the companies objectives.

staff personnel (p. 246) Employees who perform functions that assist line personnel in achieving their goals.

stakeholder marketing (p. 419) Establishing and maintaining mutually beneficial exchange relationships over time with all the stakeholders of the organization.

stakeholders (p. 19) Those people who stand to gain or lose by the policies and activities of an organization.

standard of living (p. 4) The amount of goods and services people can buy with the money they have.

start-up business A new company.

statement of cash flows (p. 564) Financial statement that reports cash receipts and disbursement related to a firm's three major activities: operations, investment, and financing.

statutory law (p. 117) State and federal constitutions, legislative enactments, treaties, and ordinances—in other words, written laws.

stockbroker (p. 623) A registered representative who works as a market intermediary to buy and sell securities for clients.

stock certificate (p. 617) Evidence of stock ownership that specifies the name of the company, the number of shares it represents, and the type of stock being issued.

stock exchange (p. 619) An organization whose members can buy and sell (exchange) securities for companies and investors.

stock insurance company (p. 704) A type of insurance company owned by stockholders.

stocks (p. 617) Shares of ownership in a company.

stock splits (p. 627) An action by a company that gives stockholders two or more shares of stock for each one they own.

strategic alliance (p. 74) A long-term partnership between two or more companies established to help each company build competitive market advantages.

strategic planning (p. 209) The process of determining the major goals of the organization and the policies and strategies for obtaining and using resources to achieve those goals.

strict product liability (p. 118) Legal responsibility for harm or injury caused by a product regardless of fault.

strike (p. 371) A union strategy in which workers refuse to go to work; the purpose is to further workers' objectives after an impasse in collective bargaining.

strikebreakers (p. 373) Workers hired to do the jobs of striking workers until the labor dispute is resolved.

supervisory management (p. 212) Man-agers who are directly responsible for supervising workers and evaluating their daily performance.

supply (p. 39) The quantity of products that manufacturers or owners are willing to sell at different prices at a specific time.

supply chain (p. 478) The sequence of linked activities that must be performed by various organizations to move goods from the sources of raw materials to ultimate consumers.

supply-chain management (p. 479) The process of managing the movement of raw materials, parts, work in progress, finished goods, and related information through all the organizations involved in the supply chain; managing the return of such goods, if necessary.

SWOT analysis (p. 208) An analysis of an organization's strengths, weaknesses, opportunities, and threats.

tactical planning (p. 210) The process of developing detailed, short-term decisions about what is to be done, who is to do it, and how it is to be done.

to take a break *To slow down and do something besides work.*

take the plunge *To finally get started.*

talking the talk *Promising things to people, but not following through with action.*

target costing (p. 446) Designing a product so that it satisfies customers and meets the profit margins desired by the firm.

target marketing (p. 411) Marketing directed toward those groups (market segments) an organization decides it can serve profitably.

tariff (p. 82) A tax imposed on imported products.

tax accountant (p. 553) An accountant trained in tax law and responsible for preparing tax returns or developing tax strategies.

taxes (p. 125) How the government (federal, state, and local) raises money.

technical skills (p. 224) Skills that involve the ability to perform tasks in a specific discipline or department.

teens *Young people between the ages of 13 and 19.*

telecom *Short for telecommunications.*

telecommute (p. 22) To work at home and keep in touch with the company through telecommunications.

telemarketing (p. 475) The sale of goods and services by telephone.

telephone tag *To leave a telephone message when you attempt to return a message left for you.*

term insurance (p. 687) Pure insurance protection for a given number of years.

term-loan agreement (p. 598) A promissory note that requires the borrower to repay the loan in specified installments.

test marketing (p. 400) The process of testing products among potential users.

thorny issue *An issue that can cause pain (as a thorn on a rose bush may).*

time deposit (p. 657) The technical name for a savings account; the bank can require prior notice before the owner withdraws money from a time deposit.

time in the trenches *Working out with the other employees and experiencing what they content with as opposed to managing from an office and relying solely on reports about what is happening in the workplace.*

time-motion studies (p. 297) Studies, begun by Frederick Taylor, of which tasks must be performed to complete a job and the time needed to do each task.

time utility (p. 466) Adding value to products by making them available when they're needed.

tip of the iceberg *There is much more to the issue than what appears on the surface.*

top management (p. 212) Highest level of management, consisting of the president and other key company executives who develop strategic plans.

tort (p. 117) A wrongful act that causes injury to another person's body, property, or reputation.

total fixed costs (p. 447) All the expenses that remain the same no matter how many products are sold.

total quality management (TQM) (p. 251) The practice of striving for customer satisfaction by ensuring quality from all departments in an organization.

trade credit (p. 593) The practice of buying goods and services now and paying for them later.

trade deficit (p. 68) An unfavorable balance of trade; occurs when the value of a country's imports exceeds that of its exports.

trademark (p. 121, 436) *1.* A brand that has been given exclusive legal protection for both the brand name and the pictorial design. *2.* A legally protected name, symbol, or design (or combination of these) that identifies the goods or services of one seller and distinguishes them from those of competitors.

trade protectionism (p. 82) The use of government regulations to limit the import of goods and services; advocates believe that it allows domestic producers to survive and grow, producing more jobs.

training and development (p. 338) All attempts to improve productivity by increasing an employee's ability to perform.

transparency (p. 249) A concept that describes a company being so open to other companies working with it that the once-solid barriers between them become "see-through" and electronic information is shared (often on extranets) as if the companies were one.

trial balance (p. 555) A summary of all the data in the account ledgers to show whether the figures are correct and balanced.

turn the work off *Stop working.*

unemployment rate (p. 49) The number of civilians at least 16 years old who are unemployed and tried to find a job within the prior four weeks.

Uniform Commercial Code (UCC) (p. 121) A comprehensive commercial law adopted by every state in the United States; it covers sales laws and other commercial laws.

uninsurable risk (p. 703) A risk that no insurance company will cover.

unions (p. 362) Employee organizations that have the main goal of representing members in employee–management bargaining over job-related issues.

union security clause (p. 367) Provision in a negotiated labor–management agreement that stipulates that employees who benefit from a union must either officially join or at least pay dues to the union.

union shop agreement (p. 368) Clause in a labor–management agreement that says workers do not have to be members of a union to be hired, but must agree to join the union within a prescribed period.

unlimited liability (p. 136) The responsibility of business owners for all of the debts of the business.

unsecured bond (p. 599) A bond backed only by the reputation of the issuer.

unsecured loan (p. 595) A loan that's not backed by any specific assets.

unsought goods and services (p. 433) Products that consumers are unaware of, haven't necessarily thought of buying, or find that they need to solve an unexpected problem.

up front *To be forthcoming, to be honest from the start.*

utility (p. 466) An economic term that refers to the value or want-satisfying ability that's added to goods or services by organizations when the products are made more useful or accessible to consumers than before.

value (p. 428) Good quality at a fair price; when consumers calculate the value of a product, they look at the benefits and then subtract the cost to see if the benefits exceed the costs.

value package (p. 428) Everything that consumers evaluate when deciding whether to buy something; also called the total product offer.

value pricing (p. 446) When marketers provide consumers with brand-name goods and services at fair prices.

variable costs (p. 447) Costs that change according to the level of production.

variable life insurance (p. 688) Whole life insurance that invests the cash value of the policy in stocks or other high-yielding securities.

venture capital (p. 601) Money that is invested in new companies that have great profit potential.

venture capitalists (p. 184) Individuals or companies that invest in new businesses in exchange for partial ownership of those businesses.

vertical merger (p. 148) The joining of two companies involved in different stages of related businesses.

vestibule training (p. 340) Training done in schools where employees are taught on equipment similar to that used on the job.

viral marketing (p. 507) The term now used to describe everything from paying people to say positive things on the Internet to setting up multilevel selling schemes whereby consumers get commissions for directing friends to specific websites.

virtual bank *A bank with no building to go to.*

virtual corporation (p. 250) A temporary, networked organization made up of replaceable firms that join the network and leave it as needed.

virtualization (p. 523) Accessibility through technology that allows business to be conducted independent of location.

virtual private network (VPN) (p. 526) A private data network that creates secure connections, or "tunnels," over regular Internet lines.

virus (p. 538) A piece of programming code inserted into other programming to cause some unexpected and, for the victim, usually undesirable event.

vision (p. 207) An explanation of why the organization exists and where it's trying to head.

volume segmentation (p. 412) Dividing the market by usage (volume of use).

walking the walk *Doing what you say you will do.*

wannabes *Individuals who want to be something.*

watching over your shoulder *Someone look-ing at everything you do.*

voluntary bankruptcy (p. 127) Legal proce-dures initiated by a debtor.

whole life insurance (p. 688) Life insurance that stays in effect until age 100.

wholesaler (p. 460) A marketing intermediary that sells to other organizations.

wholesale sale (p. 469) The sale of goods and services to businesses and institutions (e.g., hos-pitals) for use in the business or to wholesalers or retailers for resale.

word-of-mouth promotion (p. 506) A promo-tional tool that involves people telling other peo-ple about products they've purchased.

World Bank (p. 666) The bank primarily re-sponsible for financing economic development; also known as the International Bank for Reconstruction and Development.

World Trade Organization (WTO) (p. 83) The international organization that replaced the General Agreement on Tariffs and Trade, and was assigned the duty to mediate trade disputes among nations.

yellow-dog contract (p. 373) A type of con-tract that required employees to agree as a condi-tion of employment not to join a union; prohib-ited by the Norris–La Guardia Act.

you get what you pay for *If you pay a low price, you'll probably get a low-quality product.*

zero sum game *A game in which, if one side wins, the other side must lose—as opposed to a game where both sides can win, which is called a win-win game.*

Photo Credits

Frontmatter

About the Authors, p. xvii, William Nickels, Susan McHugh, James McHugh. TOC-01, p. v, Courtesy of Pierce College. Created by Sharavsky Communications, Plymouth Meeting, PA. TOC-02, p. vi, Courtesy of Accenture. TOC-03, p. vii, STR/Hulton Archive. TOC-04, p. viii, Courtesy of Ford Motor Company. TOC-05, p. ix, Michael Darter. TOC-06, p. x, Courtesy of KillerBiz. TOC-07, p. xi, Tony Stone Images/Ed Honowitz. TOC-08, p. xii, TOLES © 2000 The Buffalo News. Reprinted with permission of UNIVERSAL PRESS SYNDICATE. TOC-09, p. xiii, Courtesy of AllBusiness. TOC-10, p. xiv, Courtesy of cruelworld.com.
G-02, p. GR-03, Photo Disk. G-03, p. GR-04, J. Sohm/The Image Works. G-04, p. GR-05, John Thoeming. G-05, p. GR-07, Photo Disk. G-06, p. GR-08, Dave Bartruff/Stock Boston. G-07, p. GR-09, The Image Works/B. Mahoney. G-08, p. GR-12, Bob Thaves. G-09, p. GR-14, Rosemary Hedger. G-11, p. GR-16, Tony Stone Images/Jay Coneyl. G-10, p. GR-17, McGraw-Hill. G-13, p. GR-22, John Thoeming. G-12, p. GR-24, John Thoeming. G-14, p. GR-26, McGraw-Hill. G-15, p. GR-27, Rosemary Hedger. G-16, p. GR-29, Courtesy of Hoovers Online. G-17, p. GR-31, Travel Montana/Wyoming Business Council.

Chapter 1

1-01, p. 03, William McLeod/Business Week Magazine. 1-02, p. 05, Courtesy of ByeByeNow.com. 1-04, p. 07, Courtesy of Olajuwon Holdings. 1-05, p. 12, A. Ramey/Stock Boston. 1-07b, p. 14, Stephen Schmitt/The Journal News. 1-07a, p. 14, Courtesy of Burrston House. 1-08, p. 16, Courtesy of Business Week. 1-11, p. 19, © Frederic Brenner/Courtesy of UPS. 1-12, p. 20, Courtesy of Toyota. 1-13, p. 21, Courtesy of Pepsi-Cola Company. 1-14, p. 23, Courtesy of Burrston House. 1-15, p. 25, Mitch Kezar/Tony Stone.

Chapter 2

2-01, p. 33, Rex Rystedt. 2-02 A, p. 34, © George Chan/Photo Researchers, Inc. 2-02 B, p. 34, Yann Layma/Liaison Agency. 2-04, p. 36, The Bettmann Archive. 2-05, p. 37, Frank Siteman/Stock Boston. 2-06, p. 38, Courtesy of TechnoServe. 2-07, p. 39, Vladimir Voronov/Hulton Archive. 2-08, p. 42, John Thoeming. 2-09, p. 45, Ricky Wong/Knight-Ridder Tribune—Press Link. 2-10, p. 46, Viktor Korotayen/Hulton Archive. 2-11, p. 49, Mark Richards/Photo Edit. 2-12, p. 52, Courtesy of Boeing.

Chapter 3

3-01, p. 63, Courtesy of Mary Lou Wilson. 3-02, p. 64, AP Photo/Greg Baker. 3-03, p. 67, Courtesy of Tullycross Fine Irish Imports. 3-04, p. 67, AP/Wide World Photos. 3-05, p. 68, Courtesy of USA Today. 3-06, p. 72, Adrian Bradshaw/Hulton Archive. 3-07, p. 73, Courtesy of Domino's Pizza. 3-08, p. 74, Aimee Wiles/Democrat & Chronicle. 3-09, p. 76, Courtesy of Systems Union. 3-10, p. 82, Orion Press/Tony Stone. 3-11, p. 83, STR/Hulton Archive. 3-12, p. 85, Christian Vioujard/Liaison Agency.

Chapter 4

4-01, p. 95, Toby Seger. 4-02, p. 96, AP Photo/POOL/Patrick Boutroux. 4-03, p. 98, Steve Wilson/Hulton Archive. 4-04, p. 101, AP Photo/Tsugufumi Matsumoto. 4-05, p. 103, Denver Post/Lew Sherman/Courtesy of Xerox Corp. 4-06, p. 105, Warren Holden, eNet Media Group. 4-07, p. 107, AP Photo/Dennis Cook. 4-08, p. 109, Jeff Greenberg/Photo Edit. 4-09, p. 110, AP Photo/Alan Mothner. 4A-01, p. 117, AP Photo/Dennis Cook. 4A-02, p. 119, Courtesy of USA TODAY. 4A-03, p. 120, Courtesy of Coca-Cola. 4A-04, p. 125, AP Photo/Hillery Smith Garrison. 4A-05, p. 128, Courtesy of Burrston House. 4A-06, p. 129, Courtesy of Teligent.

Chapter 5

5-01, p. 133, Courtesy of Job Direct. 5-02, p. 135, Courtesy of Kellogg's. 5-03, p. 136, John Thoeming. 5-04, p. 138, Matthew F. Witchell. 5-05, p. 141, V. Craig Sands. 5-06, p. 149, AP Photo/Stuart Ramson. 5-07, p. 151, The Crown Plaza Hotel, Edinburgh. 5-08, p. 152, Courtesy of Burrston House. 5-10, p. 156, VCG, 1998/FPG International.

Chapter 6

6-01, p. 165, Courtesy of Boston Duck Tours. 6-02, p. 166, Kristine Dittmer. 6-03, p. 170, AP Photo/Nati Harnik. 6-04, p. 172, Philadelphia Inquirer/Jay Gorodetzer. 6-05, p. 174, Courtesy of 3M. 6-06, p. 175, © Martin Klimek. 6-07, p. 176, Peter Freed. 6-08, p. 182, Piranha Illustrations/Krzysztof Palonka. 6-09, p. 185, Philadelphia Inquirer/Vickie Valerio. 6-10, p. 188, Patrick Hood © 1999. 6-11, p. 190, James Wasserman.

Chapter 7

7-01, p. 203, AFP/Corbis. 7-02, p. 204, Sun Microsystems. 7-03, p. 207, The Image Works/Esbin Anderson. 7-05, p. 211, Courtesy of immedient.com. 7-06, p. 212, Published Image. 7-07, p. 215, Courtesy of Amerada Hess. 7-08, p. 218, Barbel Schmidt. 7-09, p. 223, Courtesy of peoplesoft.com. 7-10, p. 225, Courtesy of thingamajob.com.

Chapter 8

8-01, p. 233, Corbis Images. 8-02, p. 236, Courtesy of German Information Center, NY. 8-03, p. 237, Courtesy of DaimlerChrysler Corporation. 8-04, p. 239, Reprinted with permission from General Motors Corporation. 8-05, p. 240, AP Photo/Jack Plunkett. 8-06, p. 241, Billey E. Barnes/Stock Boston. 8-08, p. 245, Bruce Avres/Tony Stone Images. 8-09, p. 248, Janet Horton. 8-11, p. 253, Angela Wyantt/Courtesy of K2 Corp. 8-12, p. 256, © 1998 Danny Turner.

Chapter 9

9-01, p. 263, Courtesy of Demetria Giannisis. 9-02, p. 264, Knight-Ridder Tribune/Charles Osgood. 9-03, p. 265, Max Hirshfeld. 9-04, p. 267, Courtesy of 24-Hour Flower. 9-05, p. 268, AP Photo/Lenny Ignelzi. 9-06, p. 269, Courtesy of Delphi Automotive Systems. 9-07, p. 272, Courtesy of National Institute of Standards & Technology. 9-08, p. 273, Kelly J. Huff. 9-09A&B, p. 277, Courtesy of Decorators Supply. 9-11, p. 279, Courtesy of farmbid.com. 9-12, p. 281, Keith Seaman/Camer Ad Inc.

Chapter 10

10-01, p. 295, Courtesy of Southwest Airlines. 10-02, p. 296, Donna McWilliam. 10-03, p. 300, Courtesy of AT&T Corporate Archives. 10-04, p. 302, John Thoeming. 10-05, p. 304, Jason Grow/SABA. 10-07, p. 309, Bill Baptist/NBA Photos. 10-08, p. 312, James Schnepf/Liaison Agency. 10-09, p. 315, Ford Motor Corporation. 10-10, p. 317, Courtesy of Mary Kay.

Chapter 11

11-01, p. 327, Sean Dougherty/Washington Times. 11-02, p. 329, Motorola Archives. 11-03, p. 334, John Thoeming. 11-04, p. 336, John Thoeming. 11-05, p. 339, Steve Jones. 11-06, p. 340, John Thoeming. 11-08, p. 342, Bruce Ayres/Tony Stone Images. 11-09, p. 344, Dan Koeck. 11-10, p. 346, Seth Resnick/Stock Boston. 11-11, p. 347, Courtesy of Principal Financial Group. 11-12, p. 354, Bob Daemmrich/The Image Works.

Chapter 12

12-01, p. 361, AP Photo/Adam Nadel. 12-02, p. 363, Photo Researchers, Inc. 12-03, p. 364, AP Photo/Al Behrman. 12-04, p. 367, AP Photo/James Finley. 12-05, p. 370, Reproduced with permission of the American Arbitration Association. 12-06, p. 372, AP Photo/Ben Margot. 12-07, p. 377, Courtesy of Institute for Women's Policy Research. 12-08, p. 378, Courtesy of USA Today. 12-09, p. 380, Seth Resnick/Stock Boston. 12-10, p. 382, John Thoeming.

Chapter 13

13-01, p. 395, Courtesy of Black Entertainment Television/Holdings (BET). 13-02, p. 396, GTE Sprint. 13-03, p. 397, The Journal News. 13-04, p. 402, Courtesy of Federal Express Corporation. 13-05, p. 404, Spencer Grant/PhotoEdit. 13-06, p. 408, Phila. Inquirer/Ron Tarver. 13-07, p. 410, Design by Treacyfaces, Inc. 13-08, p. 412, Rosemary Hedger. 13-09, p. 413, William Steinmetz/Phila. Inquirer. 13-10, p. 415, Courtesy of AXA Advisors. 13-11, p. 419, Lee Snider/The Image Works. 13-12, p. 420, Courtesy of Patagonia.

Chapter 14

14-01, p. 427, Courtesy of McDonald's. 14-02, p. 428, Courtesy of Siemens Corp. 14-03, p. 430, Courtesy of Home Depot. 14-04, p. 431, Joe McGinn/Courtesy of Jyoti Cuisine India. 14-05, p. 435, AP/Keith Srakocic. 14-07, p. 437, Courtesy of General Motors Corporation. 14-08, p. 439, Michael J. Okoniewski/Liaison Agency. 14-10, p. 443, Tim Dillon/USA Today. 14-11, p. 447, Courtesy of the U. S. Postal Service. 14-12, p. 449, John Thoeming. 14-13, p. 450, Courtesy of DealTime.com.

Chapter 15

15-01, p. 459, Courtesy of United Stationers. 15-02, p. 460, Courtesy of Business Express. 15-03, p. 464, Used with permission from iSolve Inc. 15-04, p. 466, Knight Ridder Tribune/ENIDOI. 15-05, p. 467, Courtesy of Burrston House. 15-06, p. 469, Photo by Cesar Rubio/Courtesy of freshnex.com. 15-07, p. 471, Courtesy of AllBusiness. 15-08, p. 473, Chris Droste/Vans, Inc. 15-09, p. 475, Kaku Ku-

rita/Liaison Agency. 15-10, p. 476, Courtesy of Land's End. 15-11, p. 478, Courtesy of CNF. 15-12, p. 480, Courtesy of NYK. 15-13, p. 481, Courtesy of Harry and David.

Chapter 16

16-01, p. 489, Photo Disk. 16-02, p. 490, © 2000 Tommy Hilfiger Licensing, Inc./Liz Collins. 16-04, p. 491, Bob Riha, Jr. 16-05, p. 494, Bill Tarver. 16-06, p. 496, © ePrize, Inc. All rights reserved. 16-07, p. 498, Artwork: Saatchi & Saatchi/Photo: Oriani & Origone. 16-08, p. 499, Siebel Systems, Inc. 16-09, p. 501, Todd Lillard. 16-10, p. 502, Copyright © 1999 Factory Mutual Insurance Company. 16-11, p. 506, Courtesy of FSI Council. 16-12, p. 507, Courtesy of Lee Jeans. 16-13, p. 508, John Thoeming.

Chapter 17

17-01, p. 521, Patricia Barry Levy. 17-02, p. 522, © Jessica Wecker 2000. 17-03, p. 525, Courtesy of Sun Microsystems. 17-04, p. 527, Christoph Rehben/SI International. 17-05, p. 529, Courtesy of Handspring.com. 17-06, p. 532, Courtesy of Everdream. 17-07, p. 534, Courtesy of Veritas. 17-08, p. 537, Courtesy of Oracle Corporation. 17-09, p. 539, Vladimir Pcholkin, 1997/FPG.

Chapter 18

18-01, p. 549, Courtesy of Hardrock Café. 18-02, p. 552, B. Mahoney/The Image Works. 18-05, p. 566, Henry Horenstein/Stock Boston. 18-07, p. 568, Courtesy of Peachtree. 18-08, p. 569, Courtesy of Home Depot. 18-06, p. 570, Owen Franken/Stock Boston.

Chapter 19

19-01, p. 583, CFO magazine. 19-02, p. 588, Jeff Greenberg/Photo Edit. 19-03, p. 591, Courtesy of nextcard.com. 19-04, p. 593, Courtesy of All Business.com. 19-05, p. 595, R. Crandall/The Image Works. 19-06, p. 596, Courtesy of LiveCapital.com.

Chapter 20

20-01, p. 611, Courtesy of Capitalistpig Asset Management. 20-02, p. 612, Richard Laird/FPG International/Aaron Goodman Illus. 20-03, p. 620, Explorer/Photo Researchers, Inc. 20-04, p. 621, Steve Castillo. 20-05, p. 630, Courtesy of the Parnassus Fund. 20-06 B, p. 631, SPL/Photo Researchers, Inc. 20-07, p. 633, Courtesy of *The Wall Street Journal.* 20-08, p. 636, James Keyser.

Chapter 21

21-01, p. 647, Georges DeKeerle/Liaison Agency. 21-02, p. 649, John Thoeming. 21-03, p. 656, B. Daemmrich/The Image Works. 21-05, p. 662, Courtesy of S1.com. 21-06, p. 666, Keith Dannemiller/SABA.

Chapter 22

22-01, p. 675, Rosemary Hedger. 22-02, p. 678, Courtesy of Neuberger Berman. 22-03, p. 682, AP Photo/Ric Feld. 22-04, p. 687, Manuel Chavez. 22-05, p. 688, Fred Mertz. 22-06, p. 690, Courtesy of Conseco. 22-07, p. 694, Courtesy of A.G. Edwards & Sons. 22A-01, p. 701, Courtesy of Liberty Mutual. 22A-02, p. 702, AP Photo/Toshihiko Sato. 22A-03, p. 705, B. Daemmrich/Stock Boston. 22A-04, p. 706, Courtesy of Kemper Insurance Companies. 22A-05, p. 708, Heidi Bradner/Liaison Agency.

Name Index

Organization Index

Subject Index

E-COMMERCE AND TECHNOLOGY COVERAGE

In addition to the wealth of e-commerce and technology coverage sited below, each chapter contains numerous additional Internet examples throughout the text discussion.